THE AMERICAN JOURNEY

A History of the United States

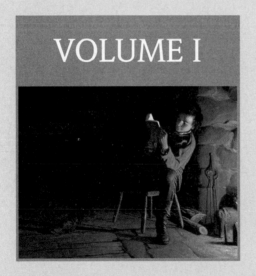

VOLUME I

THIRD EDITION

DAVID GOLDFIELD

CARL ABBOTT

VIRGINIA DEJOHN ANDERSON

JO ANN E. ARGERSINGER

PETER H. ARGERSINGER

WILLIAM L. BARNEY

ROBERT M. WEIR

PEARSON

Prentice
Hall

Upper Saddle River, New Jersey 07458

Library of Congress Cataloging-in-Publication Data
The American journey : a history of the United States / David
  Goldfield . . . [et al.]. — 3rd ed.
    p. cm
  "Combined volume."
  Includes bibliographical references and index.
  ISBN 0-13-182553-4
  1.United States—History. I.Goldfield, David R.,
E178.1.A4925 2003
973—dc21

2003040460

FOR OUR STUDENTS,
WHO HELPED US WRITE THIS BOOK.

VP, Editorial Director: Charlyce Jones Owen
Senior Acquisitions Editor: Charles Cavaliere
Editor-in-Chief, Development: Rochelle Diogenes
Senior Development Editors: Roberta Meyer and Carolyn
  Viola-John
Editorial Assistant: Adrienne Paul
AVP, Director of Production and Manufacturing:
  Barbara Kittle
Project Manager: Lee Shenkman of Victory Productions, Inc.
Liaison Editor: Jean Lapidus
Prepress and Manufacturing Manager: Nick Sklitsis
Prepress and Manufacturing Buyer: Sherry Lewis

Creative Design Director: Leslie Osher
Art Director: Nancy Wells
Interior and Cover Designer: Kenny Beck
Cover Art: University of Michigan Museum of Art, Bequest of
  Henry C. Lewis, 1895.90.
Photo Researchers: Barbara Salz and Linda Sykes
Manager of Production Services: Guy Ruggiero
Map and Art Coordinator: Maria Piper
Copy Editor: Ruth Hein
Indexer: Northwind Editorial
Image Permission Coordinator: Craig A. Jones
Text Permissions: RGA Enterprises, Inc.

This book was set in 10.5/12 New Baskerville Roman by Victory Productions
  and was printed and bound by Von Hoffman Press, Inc. The cover was
  printed by Phoenix Color Corp.

Credits and acknowledgments for materials borrowed from other sources and
reproduced with permission, in this textbook, appear on page C-1.

© 2004, 2001, 1998 by Pearson Education, Inc.
Upper Saddle River, New Jersey 07458

Printed in the United States of America
10 9 8 7 6 5 4 3 2 1

ISBN 0-13-182552-6

PEARSON EDUCATION (UK) LIMITED, *London*
PRENTICE-HALL OF AUSTRALIA PTY. LIMITED, *Sydney*
PRENTICE-HALL CANADA INC., *Toronto*
PRENTICE-HALL HISPANOAMERICANA, S.A., *Mexico*
PRENTICE-HALL OF INDIA PRIVATE LIMITED, *New Delhi*
PRENTICE-HALL OF JAPAN, INC., *Tokyo*
PEARSON EDUCATION PTE. LTD., *Singapore*
EDITORA PRENTICE-HALL DO BRASIL, LTDA., *Rio de Janeiro*

BRIEF CONTENTS

1 WORLDS APART   1

2 TRANSPLANTATION 1600–1685   35

3 THE CREATION OF NEW WORLDS   67

4 CONVERGENCE AND CONFLICT 1660s–1763   99

5 IMPERIAL BREAKDOWN 1763–1774   137

6 THE WAR FOR INDEPENDENCE 1774–1783   165

7 THE FIRST REPUBLIC 1776–1789   201

8 A NEW REPUBLIC AND THE RISE OF PARTIES 1789–1800   233

9 THE TRIUMPH AND COLLAPSE OF JEFFERSONIAN REPUBLICANISM 1800–1824   261

10 THE JACKSONIAN ERA 1824–1845   293

11 SLAVERY AND THE OLD SOUTH 1800–1860   323

12 THE MARKET REVOLUTION AND SOCIAL REFORM 1815–1850   351

13 THE WAY WEST   389

14 REFORMING ANTEBELLUM SOCIETY 1815–1850   417

15 BATTLE CRIES AND FREEDOM SONGS: THE CIVIL WAR 1861–1863   453

16 RECONSTRUCTION 1865–1877   497

CONTENTS

American Views   xi
From Then to Now   xi
Maps   xii
Figures and Tables   xiii
Overview Tables   xiv
U.S. History Documents CD-ROM   xv
Preface   xviii
About the Authors   xxiv
Student Tool Kit   xxv

1

WORLDS APART

VOICES FROM THE AMERICAN JOURNEY:
   MOCTEZUMA   1
Native American Societies before 1492   2
   Paleo-Indians and the Archaic Period   3
   The Development of Agriculture   4
   Nonfarming Societies   5
   Mesoamerican Civilizations   5
   North American Cultures   7
   The Caribbean Islanders   9
West African Societies   9
   Geographical and Political Differences   11
   Family Structure and Religion   12
   European Merchants in West Africa and the
      Slave Trade   12
Western Europe on the Eve
   of Exploration   13
   The Consolidation of Political and Military
      Authority   13
   Religious Conflict and the Protestant
      Reformation   13
Contact   16
   The Lure of Discovery   16
   Christopher Columbus and the Westward
      Route to Asia   17
   The Spanish Conquest and Colonization   19
   The Columbian Exchange   25
   Cultural Perceptions and Misperceptions   26
Competition for a Continent   27
   Early French Efforts in North America   27
   English Attempts in the New World   28
Conclusion   31
Review Questions   32
Key Terms   32
Recommended Reading   32
Additional Sources   32
Where to Learn More   33

2

TRANSPLANTATION 1600–1685

VOICES FROM THE AMERICAN JOURNEY:
   THOMAS DUDLEY   35
The French in North America   37
   The Quest for Furs and Converts   37
   The Development of New France   38
The Dutch Overseas Empire   39
   The Dutch East India Company   40
   The West India Company and
      New Netherland   40
English Settlement in the Chesapeake   42
   The Ordeal of Early Virginia   42
   The Importance of Tobacco   44
   Maryland: A Refuge for Catholics   46
   Life in the Chesapeake Colonies   47
The Founding of New England   48
   The Pilgrims and Plymouth Colony   48
   Massachusetts Bay Colony and
      Its Offshoots   49

Families, Farms, and Communities
in Early New England   52
Competition in the Caribbean   55
Sugar and Slaves   55
A Biracial Society   57
The Proprietary Colonies   57
Early Carolina: Colonial Aristocracy
and Slave Labor   57
Pennsylvania: The Dream of Toleration
and Peace   60
New Netherland Becomes New York   62
Conclusion   62
Review Questions   63
Key Terms   63
Recommended Reading   63
Additional Sources   64
Where to Learn More   64

3

THE CREATION OF NEW WORLDS

VOICES FROM THE AMERICAN JOURNEY:
OLAUDAH EQUIANO   67
Indians and Europeans   68
Indian Workers in the Spanish Borderlands   69
The Web of Trade   70
Displacing Native Americans in the
English Colonies   72
Bringing Christianity to Native Peoples   73
After the First Hundred Years: Conflict and
War   76
Africans and Europeans   80
Labor Needs and the Turn to Slavery   80
The Shock of Enslavement   81
African Slaves in the New World   82
African American Families and
Communities   88
Resistance and Rebellion   89
European Laborers in Early America   91
A Spectrum of Control   91
New European Immigrants   93
Conclusion   95
Review Questions   96
Key Terms   96
Recommended Reading   96

Additional Sources   96
Where to Learn More   97

4

CONVERGENCE AND CONFLICT
1660s–1763

VOICES FROM THE AMERICAN JOURNEY:
GEORGE WASHINGTON   99
Economic Development and Imperial Trade
in the British Colonies   101
The Regulation of Trade   101
The Colonial Export Trade and the Spirit of
Enterprise   103
The Import Trade and Ties of Credit   106
Becoming More Like England: The Growth of
Cities and Inequality   107
The Transformation of Culture   109
Goods and Houses   110
Shaping Minds and Manners   111
Colonial Religion and the Great Awakening   113
The Colonial Political World   116
The Dominion of New England and the Limits
of British Control   116
The Legacy of the Glorious Revolution   118
Diverging Politics in the Colonies and Great
Britain   119
Expanding Empires   121
British Colonists in the Backcountry   121
The Spanish in Texas and California   123
The French along the Mississippi and in
Louisiana   125
A Century of Warfare   125
Imperial Conflict and the Establishment of an
American Balance of Power, 1689–1738   126
King George's War Shifts the Balance,
1739–1754   127
The French and Indian War, 1754–1760:
A Decisive Victory   129
The Triumph of the British Empire, 1763   132
Conclusion   133
Review Questions   133
Key Terms   133
Recommended Reading   133
Additional Sources   134
Where to Learn More   134

5

IMPERIAL BREAKDOWN 1763–1774

VOICES FROM THE AMERICAN JOURNEY:
ELIZA FARMAR   137

Imperial Reorganization   139
British Problems   139
Dealing with the New Territories   141
Indian Affairs   142
Curbing the Assemblies   144
The Sugar and Stamp Acts   144

American Reactions   145
Constitutional Issues   145
Taxation and the Political Culture   146
Protesting the Taxes   147

The Aftermath of the Stamp Act Crisis   149
A Strained Relationship   149
Regulator Movements   150

The Townshend Crisis   150
Townshend's Plan   150
American Boycott   151
The Boston Massacre   152
The "Quiet Period"   152
The Boston Tea Party   153
The Intolerable Acts   154

The Road to Revolution   154
American Response to the Intolerable Acts   154
The First Continental Congress   155
The Continental Association   157
Political Divisions   157

Conclusion   160
Review Questions   161
Key Terms   161
Recommended Reading   161
Additional Sources   162
Where to Learn More   163

6

THE WAR FOR INDEPENDENCE 1774–1783

VOICES FROM THE AMERICAN JOURNEY:
JOHN LAURENS   165

The Outbreak of War and The Declaration of Independence, 1774–1776   167
Mounting Tensions   167
The Loyalists' Dilemma   167
British Coercion and Conciliation   168
The Battles of Lexington and Concord   168
The Second Continental Congress, 1775–1776   170
Commander in Chief George Washington   170
Early Fighting: Massachusetts, Virginia, the Carolinas, and Canada   171
Independence   172
Republicanism   174

The Combatants   175
Professional Soldiers   175
Women in the Contending Armies   180
African American Participation in the War   180
Native Americans and the War   181

The War in the North, 1776–1777   181
The British Army Hesitates: Battles in New York and New Jersey   181
The Year of the Hangman: Victory at Saratoga and Winter at Valley Forge   183

The War Widens, 1778–1781   184
The United States Gains an Ally   184
Fighting on the Frontier and at Sea   185
The Land War Moves South   186
American Counterattacks   188

The American Victory, 1782–1783   190
The Peace of Paris   190
The Components of Success   192

War and Society, 1775–1783   193
The Women's War   193
Effect of the War on African Americans   193
The War's Impact on Native Americans   193
Economic Disruption   193
The Price of Victory   196

Conclusion   196
Review Questions   197
Key Terms   197

Recommended Reading   197
Additional Sources   198
Where to Learn More   199

7

THE FIRST REPUBLIC 1776–1789

VOICES FROM THE AMERICAN JOURNEY:
  WILLIAM SHEPARD   201
The New Order of Republicanism   203
  Defining the People   203
  The State Constitutions   207
  The Articles of Confederation   210
Problems at Home   210
  The Fiscal Crisis   211
  Economic Depression   212
  The Economic Policies of the States   214
  Congress and the West   216
Diplomatic Weaknesses   218
  Impasse with Britain   218
  Spain and the Mississippi River   219
Toward a New Union   221
  The Road to Philadelphia   221
  The Convention at Work   222
  Overview of the Constitution   224
  The Struggle over Ratification   225
Conclusion   228
Review Questions   229
Key Terms   229
Recommended Reading   230
Additional Sources   230
Where to Learn More   230

8

A NEW REPUBLIC AND THE RISE OF PARTIES 1789–1800

VOICES FROM THE AMERICAN JOURNEY:
  WILLIAM MACLAY   233
Washington's America   235
  The Uniformity of New England   235
  The Pluralism of the Mid-Atlantic Region   237
  The Slave South and Its Backcountry   239
  The Growing West   240
Forging a New Government   240
  "Mr. President" and the Bill of Rights   241
  Departments and Courts   241
  Revenue and Trade   242
  Hamilton and the Public Credit   242
  Reaction and Opposition   244
The Emergence of Parties   245
  The French Revolution   245
  Securing the Frontier   247
  The Whiskey Rebellion   247
  Treaties with Britain and Spain   250
  The First Partisan Election   251
The Last Federalist Administration   252
  The French Crisis and the XYZ Affair   252
  Crisis at Home   253
  The End of the Federalists   254
Conclusion   257
Review Questions   258
Key Terms   258
Recommended Reading   258
Additional Sources   259
Where to Learn More   259

9

THE TRIUMPH AND COLLAPSE OF JEFFERSONIAN REPUBLICANISM 1800–1824

VOICES FROM THE AMERICAN JOURNEY:
  ROSALIE CALVERT   261
Jefferson's Presidency   263
  Reform at Home   263
  The Louisiana Purchase   266
  Florida and Western Schemes   269
  Embargo and a Crippled Presidency   268
Madison and the Coming of War   270
  The Failure of Economic Sanctions   271
  The Frontier and Indian Resistance   271
  Decision for War   272
The War of 1812   273
  Setbacks in Canada   273
  Western Victories and British Offensives   276
  The Treaty of Ghent and the Battle of New
    Orleans   278

The Era of Good Feelings 280
  Economic Nationalism 280
  Judicial Nationalism 281
  Toward a Continental Empire 282
The Breakdown of Unity 283
  The Panic of 1819 283
  The Missouri Compromise 284
  The Election of 1824 287
Conclusion 288
Key Terms 289
Review Questions 289
Recommended Reading 289
Additional Sources 290
Where to Learn More 290

10

THE JACKSONIAN ERA 1824–1845

VOICES FROM THE AMERICAN JOURNEY:
  BENJAMIN B. FRENCH 293
The Egalitarian Impulse 295
  The Extension of White Male Democracy 295
  The Popular Religious Revolt 297
  The Rise of the Jacksonians 299
Jackson's Presidency 301
  Jackson's Appeal 302
  Indian Removal 303
  The Nullification Crisis 305
  The Bank War 308
Van Buren and Hard Times 309
  The Panic of 1837 309
  The Independent Treasury 311
  Uproar over Slavery 312
The Rise of the Whig Party 312
  The Party Taking Shape 313
  Whig Persuasion 314
  The Election of 1840 315
The Whigs in Power 316
  Harrison and Tyler 316
  The Texas Issue 317
  The Election of 1844 318
Conclusion 318
Review Questions 319
Key Terms 319
Recommended Reading 319

Additional Sources 320
Where to Learn More 320

11

SLAVERY AND THE OLD SOUTH 1800–1860

VOICES FROM THE AMERICAN JOURNEY:
  HANNAH CRAFTS 323
The Lower South 325
  Cotton and Slaves 325
  The Profits of Slavery 326
The Upper South 328
  A Period of Economic Adjustment 329
  The Decline of Slavery 331
Slave Life and Culture 332
  Work Routines and Living Conditions 332
  Families and Religion 334
  Resistance 336
Free Society 337
  The Slaveholding Minority 338
  The White Majority 341
  Free Black People 342
The Proslavery Argument 344
Conclusion 347
Review Questions 348
Key Terms 348
Recommended Reading 348
Additional Sources 348
Where to Learn More 349

12

THE MARKET REVOLUTION AND SOCIAL REFORM 1815–1850

VOICES FROM THE AMERICAN JOURNEY:
  ANGELINA GRIMKÉ 351
Industrial Change and Urbanization 353
  The Transportation Revolution 353
  Cities and Immigrants 357
  The Industrial Revolution 361
  Growing Inequality and New Classes 364

Reform and Moral Order 367
  The Benevolent Empire 368
  The Temperance Movement 369
  Women's Role in Reform 370
  Backlash against Benevolence 371
Institutions and Social Improvement 371
  School Reform 372
  Prisons, Workhouses, and Asylums 373
  Utopian Alternatives 375
Abolitionism and Women's Rights 378
  Rejecting Colonization 378
  Abolitionism 379
  The Women's Rights Movement 381
  Political Antislavery 382
Conclusion 383
Review Questions 385
Key Terms 385
Recommended Reading 385
Additional Sources 386
Where to Learn More 387

13
THE WAY WEST

VOICES FROM THE AMERICAN JOURNEY:
  GEORGE CATLIN 389
The Agricultural Frontier 391
  The Crowded East 391
  The Old Northwest 393
  The Old Southwest 395
The Frontier of the Plains Indians 397
  Tribal Lands 397
  The Fur Traders 399
  The Oregon Trail 400
The Mexican Borderlands 403
  The Peoples of the Southwest 403
  The Americanization of Texas 405
  The Push into California and the Southwest 406
Politics, Expansion, and War 408
  Manifest Destiny 408
  The Mexican War 410
Conclusion 413
Review Questions 414
Key Terms 414
Recommended Reading 414

Additional Sources 414
Where to Learn More 415

14
THE POLITICS OF SECTIONALISM 1846–1861

VOICES FROM THE AMERICAN JOURNEY:
  HARRIET BEECHER STOWE 417
Slavery in the Territories 419
  The Wilmot Proviso 419
  The Election of 1848 420
  The Gold Rush 421
  The Compromise of 1850 422
  Response to the Fugitive Slave Act 423
  Uncle Tom's Cabin 425
  The Election of 1852 426
Political Realignment 427
  Young America's Foreign Misadventures 427
  Stephen Douglas's Railroad Proposal 428
  The Kansas-Nebraska Act 428
  "Bleeding Kansas" 429
  Know-Nothings and Republicans: Religion and
    Politics 430
  The Election of 1856 432
  The Dred Scott Case 432
  The Lecompton Constitution 433
  The Lincoln-Douglas Debates 434
The Road to Disunion 435
  North-South Differences 436
  John Brown's Raid 438
  The Election of 1860 440
  Secession Begins 442
  Presidential Inaction 443
  Peace Proposals 443
  Lincoln's Views on Secession 444
  Fort Sumter: The Tug Comes 444
Conclusion 448
Review Questions 450
Key Terms 450
Recommended Reading 450
Additional Sources 450
Where to Learn More 451

15

BATTLE CRIES AND FREEDOM SONGS: THE CIVIL WAR 1861–1865

VOICES FROM THE AMERICAN JOURNEY:
SULLIVAN BALLOU 453
Mobilization, North and South 455
War Fever 455
The North's Advantage in Resources 458
Leaders, Governments, and Strategies 459
The Early War, 1861–1862 461
First Bull Run 462
The War in the West 462
Reassessing the War: The Human Toll 463
The War in the East 465
Turning Points, 1862–1863 466
The Naval and the Diplomatic War 466
Antietam 467
Emancipation 468
From Fredericksburg to Gettysburg 471
Vicksburg, Chattanooga, and the West 474
The War Transforms the North 477
Wartime Legislation and Politics 477
The Northern Economy 479
Northern Women and the War 480
The Confederacy Disintegrates 481
Southern Politics 481
The Southern Economy 482
Southern Women and the War 483
The Union Prevails, 1864–1865 483
Grant's Plan to End the War 484
The Election of 1864 and Sherman's March 486
The Road to Appomattox and the Death of
Lincoln 490
Conclusion 492
Review Questions 493
Key Terms 493
Recommended Reading 494
Additional Sources 494
Where to Learn More 495

16

RECONSTRUCTION 1865–1877

VOICES FROM THE AMERICAN JOURNEY:
T. THOMAS FORTUNE 497
White Southerners and the Ghosts
of the Confederacy, 1865 499
More than Freedom: African American
Aspirations in 1865 500
Education 501
"Forty Acres and a Mule" 502
Migration to Cities 504
Faith and Freedom 505
Federal Reconstruction, 1865–1870 506
Presidential Reconstruction, 1865–1867 507
Congressional Reconstruction, 1867–1870 512
Southern Republican Governments 513
Counter-Reconstruction, 1870–1874 516
The Uses of Violence 516
The Failure of Northern Will 517
Liberal Republicans and the
Election of 1872 518
Redemption, 1874–1877 519
The Democrats' Violent Resurgence 519
The Weak Federal Response 519
The Election of 1876 and the Compromise
of 1877 520
The Memory of Reconstruction 520
The Failed Promise of Reconstruction 522
Sharecropping 523
Modest Gains and Future Victories 523
Conclusion 525
Review Questions 526
Key Terms 526
Recommended Reading 526
Additional Sources 526
Where to Learn More 527

APPENDIX   A-1
GLOSSARY   G-1
CREDITS   C-1
INDEX   I-1

AMERICAN VIEWS

CHAPTER

1 Cabeza de Vaca among the Indians (1530) 22

2 Miantonomo's Plea for Indian Unity (1642) 52

3 Mary Rowlandson Among the Indians 78

4 Boston Celebrates a New King (August 1727) 118

5 Social Status and the Enforcement of the Nonimportation Movement 158

6 A British Woman Observes an American Militia Exercise in 1775 176

7 A French Observer Describes a New Society 208

8 Little Turtle Defends the Miami Lands 248

9 Federalist Antiwar Resolutions 276

10 Memorial and Protest of the Cherokee Nation, 1836 306

11 A Letter from an Escaped Slave to His Former Master 338

12 Appeal of a Female Abolitionist 376

13 A Mexican View of the Texans in 1828 408

14 Lincoln on Slavery 446

15 A Soldier Promotes the Union Cause 473

16 Mississippi's 1865 Black Codes 508

FROM THEN TO NOW

CHAPTER

1 The Disappearance of Cod off the Grand Banks 30

3 The Legacy of Slavery 94

6 The American Revolution and the Teaching of American History 195

8 Hamilton's Legacy and the National Debt 256

9 The Lewis and Clark Expedition in Their World and Ours 286

11 The Economic Legacy of Slavery 346

12 Immigration: An Ambivalent Welcome 384

13 Manifest Destiny and American Foreign Policy 412

14 Religion and Politics 448

15 Gettysburg 491

16 African American Voting Rights in the South 524

MAPS

CHAPTER 1

1-1 North American Culture Areas, c. 1500 6
1-2 West Africa and Europe in 1492 10
1-3 European Voyages of Discovery in the Atlantic in the Fifteenth and Sixteenth Centuries 18
1-4 Spanish, English, and French Settlements in North America in the Sixteenth Century 20

CHAPTER 2

2-1 New France, c. 1650 38
2-2 English and Dutch Mainland Colonies in North America, c. 1655 42
2-3 Principal European Possessions in the Caribbean in the Seventeenth Century 54
2-4 English North American Colonies, c. 1685 58

CHAPTER 3

3-1 A,B,& C Spanish and French Missions in North America 74
3-2 African Origins of North American Slaves, 1690–1807 82
3-3 Ethnic Distribution of Settler Population in British Mainland Colonies, c. 1755 95

CHAPTER 4

4-1 Anglo-American Transatlantic Commerce 104
4-2 Expanding Settlement, c. 1750 121
4-3 The French and Indian War, 1754–1763 128
4-4 European Empires in North America, 1750–1763 132

CHAPTER 5

5-1 Colonial Settlement and the Proclamation Line of 1763 141
5-2 The Quebec Act of 1774 155

CHAPTER 6

6-1 The Battles of Lexington and Concord 169
6-2 Early Fighting, 1775–1776 171
6-3 The War in the North, 1776–1777 182
6-4 The War on the Frontier, 1778–1779 187
6-5 The War in the South, 1778–1781 188
6-6 North America after the Peace of Paris, 1783 191

CHAPTER 7

7-1 Cession of Western Lands by the States 211
7-2 Disputed Territory in the West after the Treaty of Paris 220
7-3 The Ratification Vote on the Constitution 227

CHAPTER 8

8-1 Indian Land Cessions, 1784–1800 249
8-2 The Election of 1800 257

CHAPTER 9

9-1 The Louisiana Purchase and the Lewis and Clark Expedition 268
9-2 The War of 1812 274
9-3 The Missouri Compromise of 1820 and Territorial Treaties with Britain and Spain, 1818–1819 285
9-4 The Election of 1824 288

CHAPTER 10

10-1 Methods of Electing Presidential Electors, 1800 and 1824 296
10-2 The Election of 1828 301
10-3 Indian Removals 305
10-4 The Election of 1840 316

CHAPTER 11

11-1 The Spread of Slavery: New Slave States Entering the Union 326
11-2 Cotton and Other Crops in the South, 1860 330

Chapter 12

12-1 The Transportation Revolution, 354
12-2 A, & B The Growth of Cities 358, 359

Chapter 13

13-1 A,B, & C The Westward Shift of the United States Population, 1790–1850 392
13-2 Western Overland Trails 401
13-3 Texas and Mexico after the Texas Revolt 406
13-4 The Mexican War 411

Chapter 14

14-1 The Compromise of 1850 424
14-2 The Kansas-Nebraska Act, 1854 429
14-3 Railroads in the United States, 1860 437
14-4 The Election of 1860 442
14-5 The Course of Secession 443

Chapter 15

15-1 From the First Bull Run to Antietam: The War in the East, 1861–1862 462
15-2 The War in the West, 1861–1862 463
15-3 From Fredericksburg to Gettysburg: The War in the East, December 1862–July 1863 472
15-4 The Battle of Gettysburg, July 1–3, 1863 474
15-5 Vicksburg and Chattanooga: The War in the West, 1863 476
15-6 Grant and Lee in Virginia, 1864–1865 485
15-7 The Atlanta Campaign and Sherman's March, 1864–1865 486

Chapter 16

16-1 Congressional Reconstruction, 1865–1877 512
16-2 The Election of 1876 522

FIGURES AND TABLES

Figures

1-1 Value of New World Treasure Imported into Spain, 1506–1655 24

2-1 European Populations of New France (Quebec) and English Colonies in 1650 and 1700 40

2-2 The Supply and Price of Chesapeake Tobacco, 1620–1700 46

3-1 Estimated Population of Selected Indian Peoples, 1600–1730 70

3-2 Destination of Slaves Imported from Africa to the Americas between 1451 and 1810 81

3-3 Estimated Population of Black and White Settlers in British Colonial Regions, 1650–1750 84

3-4 Ethnic Distribution of Non-Indian Inhabitants of British Mainland Colonies, c. 1770 93

4-1 Average Annual Value of Colonial Exports by Region, 1768–1772 105

4-2 Population Growth in British Mainland Colonies, 1700–1760 122

5-1 Value of American Exports to and Imports from England, 1763–1776 152

7-1 Growth of the Free Black Population between 1750 and 1800 205

7-2 American Exports to and Imports from Britain between 1783 and 1789 213

7-3 Land Ordinance of 1785 217

8-1   Ethnic Breakdown of the United States in 1790, by Region **236**

10-1   Cotton Prices and the Value of Federal Land Sales in Five Southern States, 1825–1845 **310**

10-2   Voter Turnout in Presidential Elections, 1824–1840 **316**

11-1   U.S. Cotton Production, 1800–1860 **327**

11-2   The Changing Regional Pattern of Slavery in the South, 1800–1860 **331**

11-3   Slave, Free Black, and White Population in Southern States, 1850 **343**

12-1   Immigration to the United States, 1820–1860 **361**

12-2   Growth in Wealth Inequality, 1774–1860 **364**

12-3   Mob Violence and the Abolitionists **381**

13-1   Overland Emigration to the West, 1840–1860 **401**

15-1   A Comparison of the Union and Confederate Control of Key Resources at the Outset of the Civil War **458**

TABLES

12-1   Impact of the Transportation Revolution on Traveling Time **353**

OVERVIEW TABLES

CHAPTER

1 The Columbian Exchange **25**

2 English Colonies in the Seventeenth Century **59**

3 Predominant Colonial Labor Systems, 1750 **92**

4 British Imperial Trade Regulations, 1651–1733 **102**

4 The Colonial Wars, 1689–1763 **126**

5 New Restraints and Burdens on Americans, 1759–1774 **156**

6 Important Battles of the Revolutionary War **178**

7 The Articles of Confederation and the Constitution Compared **224**

7 Federalists versus the Antifederalists **226**

8 Federalist Party versus Republican Party **244**

10 The Second Party System **313**

11 Structure of Free Society in the South, c. 1860 **340**

12 Changes Promoting Growth in the Transformed Economy **360**

12 Types of Antislavery Reform **380**

13 Westward Expansion and the Growth of the Union, 1815–1850 **396**

14 South and North Compared in 1860 **436**

14 The Emerging Sectional Crisis **445**

15 Major Battles of the Civil War, 1861–1865 **489**

16 Contrasting Views of Reconstruction: President and Congress **507**

U.S. HISTORY DOCUMENTS CD-ROM

MEETING OF THREE CULTURES

Marco Polo Recounts His Travels Through Asia (1324)

Christopher Columbus, Letter to Ferdinand and Isabella of Spain (1494)

Alvar Núñez Cabeza de Vaca, "Indians of the Rio Grande" (1528–1536)

Jacques Cartier: First Contact with the Indians (1534)

Bartolomé de Las Casas, "Of the Island of Hispaniola" (1542)

Thomas Mun, from England's Treasure by Foreign Trade (1664)

Don Juan de Oñate, Plaus: A Settlement in New Mexico (1599)

The Founding of St. Augustine, 1565

The Columbian Exchange (1590)

Thomas Harriot, The Algonquian Peoples of the Atlantic Coast (1588)

Jose de Acosta, A Spanish Priest Speculates on the Origins of the Indians (1590)

COLONIZING THE NEW WORLD

John White, The Lost Colony (1590)

Samuel de Champlain's Battle with the Iroquois, July 1609

An Act Concerning Servants and Slaves

Reasons for the Plantation in New England (1629)

John Winthrop, "A Model of Christian Charity" (1630)

The Taking of the Fort at Mystic: A Brief History of the Pequot War

The Trial of Anne Hutchinson (1638)

A Jesuit Priest Describes New Amsterdam (1642)

George Alsop, The Importance of Tobacco (1660)

The Examination and Confession of Ann Foster at Salem Village (1692)

Onandogas and Cayugas: Iroquois Chiefs Address the Governors of New York and Virginia (1684)

James Oglethorpe: The Stono Rebellion (1739)

Gottlieb Mittelberger, The Passage of Indentured Servants (1750)

COLONIAL AMERICA

Navigation Act of September13, 1660

Nathaniel Bacon's Challenge to William Berkeley and the Governor's Response (1676)

Early French Explorations of the Mississippi River (1673)

Edward Randolph Describes King Philip's War (1685)

Excerpt from Cotton Mather's "Memorable Providences, Relating to Witchcrafts and Possessions" (1689)

William Penn's Charter of Privileges (1701)

William Byrd II, Diary (1709)

Manners and Etiquette in the Eighteenth Century

"The Storm Arising in the West," George Washington Delivers a Warning to the French (1753)

The Closing of the Frontier (1763)

The Adventures of Daniel Boone (1769)

Alexander Falconbridge, The African Slave Trade (1788)

Olaudah Equiano, The Middle Passage (1788)

PRELUDE TO REVOLUTION

John Peter Zenger and the Responsibility of the Press (1734)

Declaration of the Injured Frontier Inhabitants [of Pennsylvania] (1764)

Benjamin Franklin, Testimony Against the Stamp Act (1766)

"Letters from a Farmer in Pennsylvania" (1767)

John Dickinson, from Letters from a Farmer in Pennsylvania (1768)

The Boston "Massacre" or Victims of Circumstance? (1770)

John Andrews to William Barrell, Letter Regarding the Boston Tea Party (1773)

Address of the Inhabitants of Anson County to Governor Martin (1774)

J. Hector St. John Crèvecoeur, "What Is an American?" (1782)

THE AMERICAN REVOLUTION

Benjamin Franklin, "Observations Concerning the Increase of Mankind, Peopling of Countries, &c." (1751)

James Otis, The Rights of the British Colonies Asserted and Proved (1763)

The Crisis Comes to a Head: April 19, 1775

A Freelance Writer Urges His Readers To Use Common Sense (1776)

Abigail Adams and John Adams Letters; Abigail Adams Letter to Mercy Otis Warren

Petition of "A Grate Number of Blackes of the Province" to Governor Thomas Gage and the Members of the Massachusetts General Court (1774)

Joseph Warren, "Account of the Battle of Lexington" (1775)

Thomas Jefferson, "Original Rough Draught" of the Declaration of Independence (1776)

Rights of Women in an Independent Republic

The Rise of Partisan Warfare in the South (1778)

FORGING A CONSTITUTION

Constitution of Pennsylvania (1776)

A Declaration of the Rights of the Inhabitants of the Commonwealth of Massachusetts (1780)

George Washington, The Newburgh Address (1783)

Henry Knox, Letter to George Washington (1786)

Marquis de Chastellux, Travels in North America (1786)

Shays's Rebellion: Letters of Generals William Shepard and Benjamin Lincoln to Governor James Bowdoin of Massachusetts (1787)

Divergent Reactions to Shays's Rebellion

The "Distracting Question" in Philadelphia (1787)

Patrick Henry Speaks Against Ratification of the Constitution (1788)

Benjamin Banneker, Letter to Thomas Jefferson (1791)

James Wilson, An Introductory Lecture To a Course of Law Lectures (1791)

Molly Wallace, Valedictory Oration (1792)

The Federalist Era

James Madison Defends the Constitution (1788)
[William Maclay], "For the Independent Gazetteer" (1790)
Alexander Hamilton, Final Version of "An Opinion on the Constitutionality of an Act to Establish a Bank" (1791)
Questions Concerning the Constitutionality of the National Bank (1791)
Opposing Visions for the New Nation (1791)
An African American Calls for an End to Slavery (1791)
Backcountry Turmoil Puts the New Government to the Test (1794)
George Washington, Farewell Address (1796)
The Alien and Sedition Acts (1798)
Questions of Constitutionality and the Roots of Nullification (1798)
Reverend Peter Cartwright on Cane Ridge and the "New Lights" (1801)
Marbury v. Madison(1803)

Jefferson and the Republic

Memoirs of a Monticello Slave, as Dictated to Charles Campbell by Isaac" (1847)
Thomas Jefferson, "First Inaugural Address" (1801)
Margaret Bayard Smith Meets Thomas Jefferson (1801)
Constitutionality of the Louisiana Purchase (1803)
The United States Navy and the Bombardment of Tripoli (1803)
A Matter of Honor or Vengeance? (1804)
Fisher Ames, "The Republican. No. II" (1804)
Sacagawea Interprets for Lewis and Clark (1804)
An "Uncommon Genius" Advocates Indian Unity (1809)
Indian Hostilities (1812)
The British Attack Baltimore (1814)
Report and Resolutions of the Hartford Convention (1814)
Davy Crockett, Advice to Politicians (1833)

Economic and Social Change

The Western Country, "Extracts from Letters Published in Niles' Weekly Register" (1816)
The Cherokee Treaty of 1817
The Case for the Erie Canal
John Marshall Affirms the Power of the Federal Government
Thomas Jefferson Reacts to the "Missouri Question" (1820)
The Monroe Doctrine and a Reaction (1823)
Henry Clay, "Defense of the American System" (1832)
Imminent Dangers to the Free Institutions of the United States through Foreign Immigration (1835)
The Harbinger, Female Workers of Lowell (1836)
James F. Cooper, Notions of the Americans (1840)
Resolutions of the Boston Carpenters' Strike (1845)
The Trials of a Slave Girl

Jacksonian Democracy

Joseph Smith and the Beginnings of Mormonism (1823)
A "Corrupt Bargain" or Politics as Usual? (1824)
A Disaffected Mason Speaks Out Against the Order (1826)
The " Commoner" Takes Office (1828)
Andrew Jackson, First Annual Message to Congress (1829)
"Memorial of the Cherokee Nation" (1830)
Andrew Jackson, Veto of the Bank Bill (1832)
President Andrew Jackson's Proclamation Regarding Nullification (1832)
The Force Bill (1833)
Black Hawk, "Life of Black Hawk" (1833)
A French Traveler Reports on American Society (1835)
Female Industry Association, from the New York Herald (1845)

Reforming the Nation

Joshua and Sally Wilson Letters to George Wilson (1823)
Lyman Beecher, Six Sermons on Intemperance (1828)
"Early Habits of Industry," The Mother's Magazine (1834)
Charles Finney, "What a Revival of Religion Is" (1835)
Temperance and the Washingtonians (1836)
A Lowell Mill Girl Tells Her Story (1836)
"Petition of the Catholics of New York" (1840)
Ralph Waldo Emerson, "Self-Reliance" (1841)
Ja Norcom, Letter to Mary Matilda Norcom (1846)
Declaration of Sentiments and Resolutions, Woman's Rights Convention, Seneca Falls, New York (1848)
Horace Mann on Education and National Welfare
John Humphrey Noyes and Bible Communism (1845 and 1849)
Sojourner Truth, Address to the Woman's Rights Convention, Akron, Ohio (1851)

Manifest Destiny

The Treaties of Velasco (May 14, 1836)
The Aroostook War (1839)
Across the Plains With Catherine Sager Pringle in 1844
John L. O'Sullivan, "The Great Nation of Futurity" (1845)
Thomas Corwin, Against the Mexican War (1847)
Chief Seattle, Oration (1854)

Antebellum South

State v. Boon (1801)
A Black Abolitionist Speaks Out (1829)
Nat Turner, Confession (1831)
An Abolitionist Defends the Amistad Mutineers (1839)
De Bow's Review, "The Stability of the Union," (1850)
Benjamin Drew, Narratives of Escaped Slaves (1855)
George Fitzhugh, "The Blessings of Slavery" (1857)

The Sectional Crisis

William Lloyd Garrison, from The Liberator (1831)
Harriet Beecher Stowe, from Uncle Tom's Cabin
National Convention of Colored People, Report on Abolition (1847)
A Dying Statesman Speaks out Against the Compromise of 1850
Frederick Douglass, Independence Day Speech (1852)
Kansas Begins to Bleed (1856)
A White Southerner Speaks Out Against Slavery (1857)
Dred Scott v. Sanford (1857)
Abraham Lincoln, "A House Divided" (1858)

THE CIVIL WAR

Jefferson Davis, Address to the Provisional Congress of the Confederate States of America (1861)

The "Cornerstone Speech" (1861)

Mary Boykin Chesnut, A Confederate Lady's Diary (1861)

Why They Fought (1861)

A Confederate General Assesses First Bull Run (1861)

Charles Harvey Brewster, Three Letters from the Civil War Front (1862)

Clara Barton, Medical Life at the Battlefield (1862)

James Henry Gooding, Letter to President Lincoln (1863)

Abraham Lincoln, Gettysburg Address (1863)

John Dooley, Passages from a Journal (1863)

A Firsthand Account of the New York Draft Riots (1863)

Susie King Taylor, Reminiscences of an Army Laundress (1902)

General William Tecumseh Sherman on War (1864)

RECONSTRUCTION

"Address from the Colored Citizens of Norfolk, Virginia, to the People of the United States" (1865)

Carl Schurz, Report on the Condition of the South (1865)

Clinton B. Fisk, Plain Counsels for Freedmen (1865)

Mississippi Black Code (1865)

James C. Beecher, Report on Land Reform in the South Carolina Islands (1865, 1866)

The Memphis Riot (1866)

The Fourteenth Amendment (1868)

Albion W. Tourgee, Letter on Ku Klux Klan Activities (1870)

The Nation, "The State of the South" (1872)

Susan B. Anthony and the "New Departure" for Women (1873)

James T. Rapier, Testimony Before U.S. Senate Regarding the Agricultural Labor Force in the South (1880)

A Sharecrop Contract (1882)

PREFACE

The path that led us to *The American Journey* began in the classroom with our students. Our goal is to make American history accessible to students. The key to that goal—the core of the book—is a strong clear narrative. American history is a compelling story and we seek to tell it in an engaging, forthright way. But we also provide students with an abundance of tools to help them absorb that story and put it in context. We introduce them to the concerns of the participants in America's history with primary source documents. The voices of contemporaries open each chapter, describing their own personal journeys toward fulfilling their dreams, hopes, and ambitions as part of the broader American journey. These voices provide a personal window on our nation's history, and the themes they express resonate throughout the narrative.

But if we wrote this book to appeal to our students, we also wrote it to engage their minds. We wanted to avoid academic trendiness, particularly the restricting categories that have divided the discipline of history over the last twenty years or so. We believe that the distinctions involved in the debates about multiculturalism and identity, between social and political history, between the history of the common people and the history of the elite, are unnecessarily confusing.

What we seek is integration—to combine political and social history, to fit the experience of particular groups into the broader perspective of the American past, to give voice to minor and major players alike because of their role in the story we have to tell.

APPROACH

In telling our story, we had some definite ideas about what we might include and emphasize that other texts do not—information we felt that the current and next generations of students will need to know about our past to function best in a new society.

CHRONOLOGICAL ORGANIZATION A strong chronological backbone supports the book. We have found that the jumping back and forth in time characteristic of some American history textbooks confuses students. They abhor dates but need to know the sequence of events in history. A chronological presentation is the best way to be sure they do.

GEOGRAPHICAL LITERACY We also want students to be geographically literate. We expect them not only to know what happened in American history, but where it happened as well. Physical locations and spatial relationships were often important in shaping historical events. The abundant maps in The American Journey—all numbered and called out in the text—are an integral part of our story.

REGIONAL BALANCE. *The American Journey* presents balanced coverage of all regions of the country. In keeping with this balance, the South and the West receive more coverage in this text than in comparable books.

POINT OF VIEW *The American Journey* presents a balanced overview of the American past. But "balanced" does not mean bland. We do not shy away from definite positions on controversial issues, such as the nature of early contacts between Native Americans and Europeans, why the political crisis of the 1850s ended in a bloody Civil War, and how Populism and its followers fit into the American political spectrum. If students and instructors disagree, that's great; discussion and dissent are important catalysts for understanding and learning.

RELIGION Nor do we shy away from some topics that play relatively minor roles in other texts, like religion. Historians are often uncomfortable writing about religion and tend to slight its influence. This text stresses the importance of religion in American society both as a source of strength and a reflection of some its more troubling aspects.

Historians mostly write for each other. That's too bad. We need to reach out and expand our audience. An American history text is a good place to start. Our students are not only our future historians, but more important, our future. Let their American journey begin.

FEATURES OF THE TEXT

The American Journey includes an array of features designed to make American history accessible to students. It provides more learning tools than any other U.S. history text.

- The **Student Tool Kit** that follows this preface helps students get the most out of the text and its features. It introduces students to key conventions of historical writing and it explains how to work with maps, graphs, tables, and other visuals.

- A new feature, **Voices from the American Journey**, opens each chapter. Consisting of letters, diary entries, and other first-hand accounts, these voices highlight the personal dimension of the American journey and show students the wealth and variety of experiences that make up this country's history. From Olaudah Equiano's narrative of his forced journey to Virginia as a slave, to the ultimate journey Sullivan Ballou made during the Civil War defending the Union, to Cambodian refugee Celia Noup's harrowing journey to California where she took her place as one of the thousands of new immigrants who are reshaping the face of our nation, "Voices from the American Journey" set the stage for the key themes that are explored in each chapter.

- The **American Views** box in each chapter contains a relevant primary source document. Taken from letters, diaries, newspapers, government papers, and other sources, these bring the people of the past and their concerns vividly alive. An introduction and prereading questions relate the documents to the text and direct students' attention to important issues. New "American Views" include the internment of Japanese Americans in Chapter 26 and working in the New Economy in Chapter 31.

- **America's Journey: From Then to Now**, found in more than half the chapters, relates important issues and events in each chapter to the issues and events of today, letting students see the relevance of history to their lives. Several are new to this edition. Examples include, "The Disappearance of Cod on the Grand Banks" (Chapter 1); "Medical Research on Polio and AIDS" (Chapter 28) and "Loyalty in 2001 and 1917" (Chapter 31).

- An **Outline** and **Key Topics** list give students a succinct overview of each chapter.

- **Overview Tables** in each chapter summarize complex issues.

- Chapter **Chronologies** help students build a framework of key events.

- **Third-level subheads**, new to the Third Edition, highlight key topics in the narrative and make them more accessible for study and review. In the sections on social history, for example, these headings help highlight the roles of women and minorities in the American journey.

- **Key Terms** are highlighted within each chapter and defined in an end-of-book **Glossary**. The end of each chapter now includes a list of key terms and relevant page numbers.

- Chapter **Review Questions** help students review the material in each chapter and relate it to broader themes.

- A list of **Key Readings** and **Additional Sources** at the end of each chapter directs interested students to further information about the subject of the chapter.

- **Where To Learn More** sections describe important historical sites students can visit to gain a deeper understanding of the events discussed in the chapter. Websites for the historical sites as well as other websites relevant to the chapter topics are now included.

- Abundant maps, charts, and graphs help students understand important events and trends. The topographical detail in many of the maps helps students understand the influence of geography on history.

- Illustrations and photographs—tied to the text with detailed captions—provide a visual dimension to history. Approximately ninety new photos have been added to the Third Edition.

CHANGES TO THE THIRD EDITION

ORGANIZATION

- To make the text even more accessible to students—and to better match the teaching calendars of many institutions—the number of chapters in the Third Edition has been reduced from thirty-three to thirty-one.

- The chapters on urbanization and social change and reform movements in the antebellum period have been combined into a new chapter, "The Market Revolution and Social Reform" (Chapter 12). The chapter focuses on economic changes and industrialization as well as the connections between these forces and reform movements. Chapter 11, "Slavery and the Old South," now precedes this chapter.

- The Civil War is now treated in a single chapter (Chapter 15).
- The Eighties is now examined in an entirely re-vamped Chapter 30, "The Reagan Revolution and a Changing World."
- An all-new final chapter "Complacency and Crisis," examines America at the millennium and after September 11, 2001.

Taken together, these organizational changes make *The American Journey* an even more effective textbook for both students and instructors.

OTHER CHANGES

In the Third Edition of *The American Journey,* coverage of women, minorities, and Native Americans has been expanded. The active role of Native Americans in shaping the encounters with European settlers has been emphasized. Coverage of the institution of slavery and the Holocaust has also been expanded. Additional coverage of foreign policy during the 1980s and 1990s will help students understand the dilemmas our nation faces in the post-September 11th world. The following list highlights some of these additions:

- Chapter 1. Coverage of Native American and West African societies has been expanded significantly.
- Chapter 2. The Dutch mercantile empire, trade with West Africa, and the beginnings of the slave trade with the Portuguese and Dutch receive more discussion.
- Chapter 3. Coverage of Native Americans has been consolidated and expanded; their role as actors in the encounter with Europeans is emphasized. Increased coverage of the origins of slavery and its social and economic aspects.
- Chapter 6: Expanded coverage of Native Americans' role during the War for Independence.
- Chapter 20: Expanded coverage of women in politics, especially their partisan role and involvement in the temperance movement.
- Chapter 21. A section on trans-Atlantic influences during the Progressive era has been included. Coverage of the education of Native Americans, women in the election of 1912, and the antiprostitution campaign has been expanded.
- Chapter 25. A new section on foreign policy during the New Deal, which provides a background for understanding the U.S. role in World War II, has been added.

- Chapter 26. Discussion of the rise of anti-Semitism in Nazi Germany has been added and coverage of the Holocaust has been expanded. Coverage of the economic and social history of the war effort has been reorganized, and coverage of women and minorities in the war effort has been increased.
- Chapter 27. Includes fuller discussion of the Civil Rights movement.
- Chapter 28. Coverage of cultural history has been increased, a section on "Science and Foreign Affairs" has been added, and there is expanded discussion of Vietnam and LBJ.
- Chapter 29. Now examines the period from 1965—1980 in a single unit, examining feminism, suburban life, Vietnam, and de-industrialization.
- Chapter 30. Includes detailed discussion of the new conservatism and Reaganomics, in-depth treatment of social and cultural history of the period, coverage of women and poverty, and enhanced discussion of foreign policy.
- Chapter 31. Provides in-depth treatment of the New Economy, the Clinton presidency, the attacks of September 11, 2001, and America's role as the remaining superpower in a post-September 11th world.

SUPPLEMENTARY INSTRUCTIONAL MATERIALS

The American Journey comes with an extensive package of supplementary print and multimedia materials for both instructors and students.

PRINT SUPPLEMENTS

Instructor's Resource Manual
The *Instructor's Resource Manual* contains chapter outlines, chapter overviews, activities, discussion questions, readings, and information on audio-visual resources that are useful for lectures and assignments.

Test Item File
The *Test Item File* includes over 200 multiple-choice, true-false, essay, and map questions organized by chapter.

Prentice Hall Custom Test
This commercial-quality computerized test management program, available for Windows and Macintosh environments, allows instructors to select items from the Test Item File and design their own exams.

Transparency Pack

This set of transparencies provides instructors with full-color acetates of all the maps, charts, and graphs in the text for use in the classroom.

Practice Tests (Volumes I and II)

The two-volume *Practice Tests* provides students with a brief overview of each chapter; a list of chapter objectives; study exercises; and multiple-choice, short answer, and essay questions.

Retrieving the American Past: A Customized U.S. History Reader, 2003 Edition

This collection of documents is an on-demand history database written and developed by leading historians and educators. It offers eighty compelling modules on topics in American history, such as "Women on the Frontier," "The Salem Witchcraft Scare," "The Age of Industrial Violence," and "Native American Societies, 1870–1995." Approximately thirty-five pages in length, each module includes an introduction, several primary documents and secondary sources, follow-up questions, and recommendations for further reading. Instructor-originated material, including other readings and exercises, can be incorporated. Contact your local Prentice Hall representative for more information about this exciting custom-publishing option.

American Stories: Biographies in United States History

This two-volume collection of sixty-two biographies in United States history is free when packaged with *The American Journey*. Introductions, pre-reading questions, and suggested resources enrich this new supplement.

Prentice Hall and Penguin Bundle Program

Prentice Hall is pleased to provide adopters of *The American Journey* with an opportunity to receive significant discounts when copies of the text are bundled with Penguin titles in American history. Contact your local Prentice Hall representative for details.

Reading Critically about History

This brief guide provides students with helpful strategies for reading a history textbook. It is available free to students when packaged with *The American Journey*.

Understanding and Answering Essay Questions

This helpful guide provides analytical tools for understanding different types of essay questions and for preparing well-crafted essay answers. It is available free to students when packaged with *The American Journey*.

MULTIMEDIA SUPPLEMENTS

Companion Website

Available at http://www.prenhall.com/goldfield
The American Journey Companion Website™ offers students multiple choice, true-false, essay, identification, map labeling, and document questions based on material from the text, organized by the primary subtopics in each chapter. Additionally, the *Companion Website* provides numerous interactive maps tied to the text, source documents, and other interactive modules related to the content in each chapter. The Faculty Module contains materials for instructors, including the entire instructor's manual in PDF file, and downloadable presentations with maps, charts, graphs, summary tables, and illustrations.

U.S. History Documents CD-ROM

Bound in every new copy of *The American Journey*, and organized according to the main periods in American history, the U.S. History Documents CD-ROM contains over 300 primary sources in an easily-navigable PDF file. Each document is accompanied by essay questions that allow students to read important sources in U.S. history via the CD-ROM and respond online via a dedicated website.

Exploring America CD-ROM

The new *Exloring America CD-ROM* features thirty-one interactive learning activities that drill down to explore the impact of key episodes and developments in United States history, including such topics as industrialization, immigration, the women's suffrage movement, the Harlem Renaissance, the American Indian Movement, and globalization.

Evaluating Online Sources with Research Navigator, 2003 Edition

This brief guide focuses on developing critical thinking skills necessary to evaluate and use online sources. It provides a brief introduction to navigating the Internet with comprehensive references to History web sites. It also provides an access code and instruction on using Research Navigator, a powerful research tool that provides access to three exclusive databases of reliable source material: ContentSelect Academic Journal Database, *The New York Times* Search by Subject Archive, and Link Library.

Course Management Systems

For instructors interested in distance learning, Prentice Hall offers fully customizable, online courses with enhanced content, web links, online testing, and many other course-management features using the best available course management systems available, including WebCT, Blackboard, and CourseCompass. Contact your local Prentice Hall representative or visit our special Demonstration Central Website at http://www.prenhall.com/demo for more information.

ACKNOWLEDGMENTS
We would like to thank the reviewers whose thoughtful and often detailed comments helped shape this and the previous editions of *The American Journey*:

Joseph Adams, Saint Louis Community College
David Aldstadt, Houston Community College
William Allison, Weber State University
Janet Allured, McNeese State University
Tyler Anbinder, George Washington University
Michael Batinski, Southern Illinois University
Michael Bellesiles, Emory University
Eugene Berwanger, Colorado State University
Terry Bilhartz, Sam Houston State University
Fred Blue, Youngstown State University
Eric J. Bolsteri, University of Texas at Arlington
Charles Bolton, University of Arkansas at Little Rock
James Bradford, Texas A&M University
Michael Bradley, Motlow State Community College
Henry William Brands, Texas A&M University
Neal Brooks, Essex Community College
Richard Brown, University of Connecticut
Tom Bryan, Alvin Community College
Randolph Campbell, University of North Texas
Dale Carnagey, Blinn College
E. Wayne Carp, Pacific Lutheran University
JoAnn Carpenter, Florida Community College
David Castle, Ohio University, Eastern Campus
Andrew Cayton, Miami University
Bill Cecil-Fronsman, Washburn University
John Chalberg, Normandale Community College
Myles Clowers, San Diego City College
David Conrad, Southern Illinois University
William Corbett, Northeastern State University
Robert Cray, Montclair State College
Richard Crepeau, University of Central Florida
Samuel Crompton, Holyoke Community College
Gilbert Cruz, Glendale Community College
Light T. Cummins, Austin College
Paul K. Davis, University of Texas at San Antonio
Eugene Demody, Cerritos College
Joseph Devine, Stephen F. Austin State University
Donald Dewey, California State University
Leonard Dinnerstein, University of Arizona
Dean Dunlap, Rose State College
Marvin Dulaney, University of Texas at Arlington
Jonathan Earle, University of Kansas
Leflett Easley, Campbell University
Iris Engstrand, University of San Diego
Robin Fabel, Auburn University

Jay Fell, University of Colorado
Nancy Gabin, Purdue University
Scott Garrett, Paducah Community College
Marilyn Geiger, Washburn University
George Gerdow, Northeastern Illinois University
Gerald Ghelfi, Rancho Santiago College
Louis Gimelli, Eastern Michigan University
James Goode, Grand Valley State University
Gregory Goodwin, Bakersfield College
Ralph Goodwin, East Texas State University
Robert Greene, Morgan State University
Mark Grimsley, Ohio State University
Ira Gruber, U.S. Military Academy
Harland Hagler, University of North Texas
Steve Haley, Shelby State Community College
Gwendolyn Hall, Rutgers University
Timothy D. Hall, Central Michigan University
David Hamilton, University of Kentucky
Joe Hapak, Moraine Valley Community College
Ronald Hatzenbuchler, Idaho State University
David G. Hogan, Heidelberg College
Alfred Hunt, SUNY Purchase
John Ingham, University of Toronto
Priscilla Jackson-Evans, Longview Community College
Donald Jacobs, Northeastern University
Frederick Jaher, University of Illinois
John Johnson, University of Northern Iowa
Wilbur Johnson, Rock Valley College
Yvonne Johnson, Central Missouri State University
Yasuhide Kawashima, University of Texas at El Paso
Joseph E. King, Texas Tech University
Gene Kirkpatrick, Tyler Junior College
Lawrence Kohl, University of Alabama at Tuscaloosa
Michael Krenn, University of Miami
Michael Krutz, Southeastern Louisiana University
Robert LaPorte, North Texas University
Armand LaPotin, SUNY Oneonta
John LaSaine, University of Georgia
Bryan LeBeau, Creighton University
J. Edward Lee, Winthrop University
Mark Leff, University of Illinois, Urbana-Champaign
Richard Lowe, University of North Texas
Ed Lukes, Hillsborough Community College
Leo Lyman, Victor Valley College
Scott Martin, Bowling Green State University
Ronald McArthur, Atlantic Community College
Donald McCoy, University of Kansas
David McFadden, Fairfield University
Gerald MacFarland, University of Massachusetts
Thomas McLuen, Spokane Falls Community College
Peter C. Mancell, University of Kansas
Norman Markowitz, Rutgers University
Frank Marmolejo, Irvine Valley College
James Matray, New Mexico State University
Karen Miller, Oakland University
Otis Miller, Belleville Area College
Nancy Smith Midgette, Elon College
Worth Robert Miller, Southwest Missouri State University

Timothy Morgan, Christopher Newport University
Christopher Moss, University of Texas at Arlington
Harmon Mothershead, Northwest Missouri State University
Benjamin Newcomb, Texas Technological University
Elizabeth Nybakken, Mississippi State University
Colleen O'Connor, San Diego Mesa College
Chris Padgett, Weber State University
David Parker, Kennesaw State College
Peggy Pascoe, University of Utah
Christopher Phillips, Emporia State University
Thomas L. Powers, University of South Carolina, Sumter
Kay Pulley, Trinity Valley Community College
Norman Raiford, Greenville Technical College
John Rector, Western Oregon State University
Thomas C. Reeves, University of Wisconsin, Parkside
Gary Reichard, Florida Atlantic University
Joseph Reidy, Howard University
Ronald Reitvald, California State University, Fullerton
Howard Rock, Florida International University
Hal Rothman, University of Nevada, Las Vegas
Richard Sadler, Weber State University
Henry Sage, Northern Virginia Community College, Alexandria
Bufford Satcher, University of Arkansas at Pine Bluff
Sandra Schackel, Boise State University
Michael Schaller, University of Arizona
Dale Schmitt, East Tennessee State University
Ronald Schultz, University of Wyoming
Nancy Shoemaker, University of Connecticut
Rebecca Shoemaker, Indiana State University
Frank Siltman, U.S. Military Academy
David Sloan, University of Arkansas
J.B. Smallwood, University of North Texas
Sherry Smith, University of Texas at El Paso
Kenneth Stevens, Texas Christian University
William Stockton, Johnson County Community College
Mark Summers, University of Kentucky
William Tanner, Humbolt State University
Quintard Taylor, University of Oregon
Emily Teipe, Fullerton College
Frank Towers, Clarion University
Paula Trekel, Allegheny College
Stanley Underal, San Jose University
Andrew Wallace, Northern Arizona University
Harry Ward, University of Richmond
Ken Weatherbie, Del Mar College
Stephen Webre, Louisiana Tech University
Edward Weller, San Jacinto College, South
Michael Welsh, University of Northern Colorado
James Whittenberg, College of William and Mary
Brian Wills, Clinch Valley Community College
John Wiseman, Frostburg State University
James Woods, Georgia Southern University
Mark Wyman, Illinois State University
Neil York, Brigham Young University
William Young, Johnson County Community College
Nancy Zen, Central Oregon Community College

All of us are grateful to our families, friends, and colleagues for their support and encouragement. Jo Ann and Peter Argersinger would like in particular to thank Anna Champe, Linda Hatmaker, and John Willits; William Barney thanks Pamela Fesmire and Rosalie Radcliffe; Virginia Anderson thanks Fred Anderson, Kim Gruenwald, Ruth Helm, Eric Hinderaker, and Chidiebere Nwaubani; and David Goldfield thanks Frances Glenn and Jason Moscato. Jim Miller, Sylvia Mallory, and Sally Constable played key roles in the book's inception and initial development.

Finally, we would like to acknowledge the members of our Prentice Hall family. They are not only highly competent professionals but also pleasant people. We regard them with affection and appreciation. None of us would hesitate to work with this fine group again. We would especially like to thank our editorial team: Charles Cavaliere, senior acquisitions editor, Roberta Meyer, senior development editor, and Carolyn Viola-John for their creativity and skill in crafting the plan for the third edition, and for helping us to execute it. Charlyce Jones Owen, vice president and editorial director for the Humanities, who organized her team flawlessly; Heather Shelstad, executive marketing manager, and Beth Meija, marketing director, whose creative and informed marketing strategies demonstrated a unique insight into the textbook market; Kenny Beck and Nancy Wells, art directors, and Leslie Osher, creative design director; Jan Stephan and Jean Lapidus for keeping the production on schedule; Maria Piper, line art formatter; Barbara Salz and Linda Sykes for their photo research; Rochelle Diogenes, editor in chief for development, for ensuring that the book had the developmental resources it needed; Nick Sklitsis, manufacturing manager, Sherry Lewis, manufacturing buyer, and Yolanda deRooy, president of Prentice Hall's Humanities and Social Sciences division, who had the good sense to let her staff run with this book.

DG
CA
VDJA
JEA
PHA
WLB
RMW

ABOUT THE AUTHORS

David Goldfield received his Ph.D. in history from the University of Maryland. Since 1982 he has been Robert Lee Bailey Professor of History at the University of North Carolina in Charlotte. He is the author or editor of thirteen books on various aspects of southern and urban history. Two of his works—*Cotton Fields and Skyscrapers: Southern City and Region, 1607-1980* (1982) and *Black, White, and Southern: Race Relations and Southern Culture, 1940 to the Present* (1990)—received the Mayflower Award for non-fiction and were nominated for the Pulitzer Prize in history. His most recent book is *Still Fighting the Civil War: The American South and Southern History* (2002). When he is not writing history, Goldfield applies his historical craft to history museum exhibits, voting rights cases, and local planning and policy issues.

Carl Abbott is a professor of Urban Studies and planning at Portland State University. He taught previously in the history departments at the University of Denver and Old Dominion University, and held visiting appointments at Mesa College in Colorado and George Washington University. He holds degrees in history from Swarthmore College and the University of Chicago. He specializes in the history of cities and the American West and serves as co-editor of the *Pacific Historical Review.* His books include *The New Urban America: Growth and Politics in Sunbelt Cities* (1981, 1987), *The Metropolitan Frontier: Cities in the Modern American West* (1993), *Planning a New West: The Columbia River Gorge National Scenic Area* (1997), and *Political Terrain: Washington, D.C. from Tidewater Town to Global Metropolis* (1999). He is currently working on a comprehensive history of the role of urbanization and urban culture in the history of western North America

Virginia DeJohn Anderson is Associate Professor of History at the University of Colorado at Boulder. She received her B.A. from the University of Connecticut. As the recipient of a Marshall Scholarship, she earned an M.A. degree at the University of East Anglia in Norwich, England. Returning to the United States, she received her A.M. and Ph.D. degrees from Harvard University. She is the author of *New England's Generation: The Great Migration and the Formation of Society and Culture in the Seventeenth Century* (1991) and several articles on colonial history, which have appeared in such journals as the *William and Mary Quarterly* and the *New England Quarterly.* She is currently finishing a book entitled *Creatures of Empire: People and Animals in Early America.*

Jo Ann E. Argersinger received her Ph.D. from George Washington University and is Professor of History at Southern Illinois University. A recipient of fellowships from the Rockefeller Foundation and the National Endowment for the Humanities, she is a historian of social, labor, and business policy. Her publications include *Toward a New Deal in Baltimore: People and Government in the Great Depression* (1988) and *Making the Amalgamated: Gender, Ethnicity, and Class in the Baltimore Clothing Industry* (1999).

Peter H. Argersinger received his Ph.D. from the University of Wisconsin and is Professor of History at Southern Illinois University. He has won several fellowships as well as the Binkley-Stephenson Award from the Organization of American Historians. Among his books on American political and rural history are *Populism and Politics* (1974), *Structure, Process, and Party* (1992), and *The Limits of Agrarian Radicalism* (1995). His current research focuses on the political crisis of the 1890s.

William L. Barney is Professor of History at the University of North Carolina at Chapel Hill. A native of Pennsylvania, he received his B.A. from Cornell University and his M.A. and Ph.D. from Columbia University. He has published extensively on nineteenth century U.S. history and has a particular interest in the Old South and the coming of the Civil War. Among his publications are *The Road to Secession* (1972), *The Secessionist Impulse* (1974), *Flawed Victory* (1975), *The Passage of the Republic* (1987), and *Battleground for the Union* (1989). He is currently finishing an edited collection of essays on nineteenth-century America and a book on the Civil War. Most recently, he has edited *A Companion to 19th-Century America* (2001) and finished *The Civil War and Reconstruction: A Student Companion* (2001).

Robert M. Weir is Distinguished Professor of History Emeritus at the University of South Carolina. He received his B.A. from Pennsylvania State University and his Ph.D. from Case Western Reserve University. He has taught at the University of Houston and, as a visiting professor, at the University of Southampton in the United Kingdom. His articles have won prizes from the Southeastern Society for the Study of the Eighteenth Century and the *William and Mary Quarterly.* Among his publications are *Colonial South Carolina: A History,* "*The Last of American Freemen*": *Studies in the Political Culture of the Colonial and Revolutionary South,* and, most recently, a chapter on the Carolinas in the new *Oxford History of the British Empire* (1998).

STUDENT TOOL KIT

When writing history, historians use maps, tables, graphs, and visuals to help their readers understand the past. What follows is an explanation of how to use the historian's tools that are contained in this book.

TEXT

Whether it is a biography of George Washington, an article on the Civil War, or a survey of American history such as this one, the text is the historian's basic tool for discussing the past. Historians write about the past using narration and analysis. Narration is the story line of history. It describes what happened in the past, who did it, and where and when it occurred. Narration is also used to describe how people in the past lived, how they passed their daily lives and even, when the historical evidence makes it possible for us to know, what they thought, felt, feared, or desired. Using analysis, historians explain why they think events in the past happened the way they did and offer an explanation for the story of history. In this book, narration and analysis are interwoven in each chapter.

STUDY AIDS

A number of features in this book are designed to aid in the study of history. Each chapter begins with Key Topics, a short list of the most important issues that will be covered in the chapter. The narrative is organized into three levels of subtopics, that carefully structure information (see example below). A Conclusion at the end of each chapter puts the subject of the chapter in the broader perspective of U.S. history. All of these study aids can be used to review important concepts.

HOLDING THE LINE

When Japan was considering war with the United States and Great Britain in 1940, Admiral Isoroku Yamamoto, the chief of Japan's Combined Fleet, weighed the chances of victory: "If I am told to fight regardless of the consequences, I shall run wild for the first six months or a year, but I have utterly no confidence for the second or third year." The admiral was right. Japan's armies quickly conquered most of Southeast Asia; its navy forced the United States on the defensive in the central Pacific. As it turned out, Japan's conquests reached their limit after six months, but, in early 1942, it was far from clear that such would be the case. At the same time, in Europe, Allied fortunes went from bad to worse. Again, no one knew that German and Italian gains would peak at midyear. Decisive turning points did not come until November 1942, a year after the United States had entered the war, and not until the middle of 1943 could the **Allies**–the United States, Britain, the Soviet Union, China, and other nations at war with Germany, Japan and Italy–begin with confidence to plan for victory.

STOPPING GERMANY

In December 1941, the United States plunged into a truly global war that was being fought on six distinct fronts (see Map 26–2). In North Africa, the British battled Italian and German armies that were trying to seize the Suez Canal, a critical transportation link to Asia. Along the 1,000 miles of the vast **Eastern Front**, Soviet armies held defensive positions against an

The Eastern Front and the Battle of Stalingrad. The strategy recognized that the Eastern Front held the key to Allied hopes. In 1941, Germany had seized control of 45 percent of the Soviet population, 47 percent of its grain production, and more than 60 percent of its coal, steel, and aluminum industries. Hitler next sought to destroy the Soviet capacity to wage war. "Our aim," said the Führer Directive No. 41, "is to wipe out the entire defense potential remaining to the Soviets, and to cut them off. . . . from their most important centers of war industry." Hitler targeted southern Russia, an area rich in grain and oil. [T]he thrust in 1942 was also designed to eliminate [the British] from the Middle East.

The scheme was easier to [plan] than to carry out in the fields of Russia. [The] offensive opened with stunning su[ccess. The army's] advance, however, stretched supply lines. Tanks ran out of fuel and spare parts. The horses that pulled German supply wagons died for lack of food.

The turning point of the war in Europe came at Stalingrad (present-day Volgograd), an industrial center on the western bank of the Volga River. After initially aiming at the city, German armies had turned south toward Russian oil fields, leaving a dangerous strongpoint on their flank that the German command decided to capture. In September and October, 1942, German, Italian, and Romanian soldiers fought their way house by house into the city. At night, the Soviets ferried their wounded across the Volga and brought [in] ammuni[tion. For] both Hit[ler an]d Stalin, th[e]

> Three levels
> of subtopics

MAPS

Maps are important historical tools. They show how geography has affected history and concisely summarize complex relationships and events. Knowing how to read and interpret a map is important to understanding history. Map 5-1 from Chapter 5 shows the British colonies on the eastern seaboard of North America in 1763, about twelve years before the American Revolution. It has three features to help you read it: a caption, a legend, and a scale. The caption explains the historical significance of the map. Here the caption tells us that in 1763 the British government sought to restrict colonial settlement west of the Appalachian Mountains to prevent conflict between colonists and Indians. Colonial frustration with this policy contributed to the outbreak of the American Revolution.

The legend and the scale appear in the lower right corner of the map. The legend provides a key to what the symbols on the map mean. The solid line stretching along the Appalachian Mountains from Maine to Georgia represents the Proclamation Line of 1763—the line meant to restrict colonial settlement. Cities are marked with a dot, capitals with a star, and forts by a black square. Spanish territory west of the Mississippi River is represented in yellow-brown; territory settled by Europeans is represented in green. The scale tells us that 7/8ths of an inch on the map represents 300 miles (about 480 kilometers) on the ground. With this information, estimates of the distance between points on the map are easily made.

The map also shows the topography of the region—its mountains, rivers, and lakes. This helps us understand how geography influenced history in this case. For example, the Appalachian Mountains divide the eastern seaboard from the rest of the continent. The mountains obstructed colonial migration to the west for a long time. By running the Proclamation Line along the Appalachians, the British hoped to use this natural barrier to separate Indians and colonists. Note how small the green areas are, that is, the areas of European settlement, relative to the immense size of North America. Note also how the map shows that the Europeans tended to settle near the coasts and along rivers and across plains.

MAP EXPLORATIONS

Many of the maps in each chapter are provided in a useful interactive version on the text's Companion Website. These maps are easily identified by a bar along the top that reads "Map Explorations." An interactive version of Colonial Settlements and the Proclamation Line of 1763 can be found at www.prenhall.com/goldfield/map5.1. The interactive version of this particular map provides an opportunity to pan over an enlarged version of the territory in question. Cities, forts, settlements, and terrain are shown in detail. By moving the cursor north, south, east, or west one can gain a bird's-eye view of the entire region.

MAP EXPLORATION To explore an interactive version of this map, go to http://www.prenhall.com/goldfield/map5.1

MAP 5-1 **Colonial Settlement and the Proclamation Line of 1763**
This map depicts the regions claimed and settled by the major groups competing for territory in eastern North America. With the Proclamation Line of 1763, positioned along the crest of the Appalachian Mountains, the British government tried to stop the westward migration of settlers under its jurisdiction and thereby limit conflict with the Indians. The result, however, was frustration and anger on the part of land-hungry settlers.

GRAPHS

Historians use graphs to make comparisons and summarize trends. Comparisons can be between groups of people, regions of the country, products, time periods—whatever focuses the reader's attention on an important historical development. Various types of graphs are used in this book, including line graphs, pie charts, and bar graphs. The names denote the way the graphs are drawn to make comparisons. All graphs show the numbers of some significant factor—like people, goods, or prices—at a given time or how they fluctu- ated over a given period. Figure 18-2 is a line graph that shows the dramatic rise in immigration to the United States from eastern and southern Europe in the late nineteenth and early twentieth centuries. Figure 3-4, for example, is a pie chart—so called because it looks like a pie cut into slices. It shows the ethnic origins of the non-Indian population of the thirteen colonies at the start of the American Revolution. Figure 4-2 is a bar graph that compares the growth in population of the four major colonial regions.

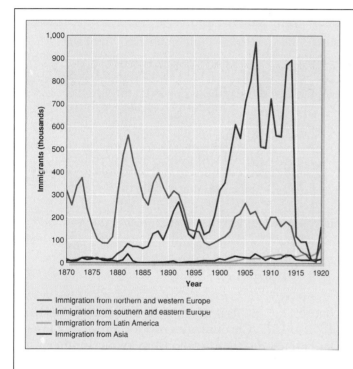

FIGURE 18-2   Immigration to the United States, 1870–1915
The graph illustrates the dramatic change in immigration to the United States during the late nineteenth and early twentieth centuries. As immigration from northern and western Europe slackened, the numbers of newcomers from southern and eastern Europe swelled. Latin American and Asian immigration also increased during this period.

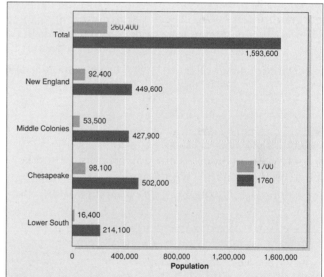

FIGURE 4-2   Population Growth in British Mainland Colonies, 1700–1760
Both natural increase and immigration contributed to a staggering rate of population growth in British North America. Some colonists predicted that Americans would soon outnumber Britain's inhabitants—a possibility that greatly concerned British officials.
Data Source: John J. McCusker and Russell R. Menard, *The Economy of British America, 1607–1789*, rev. ed. (1991). University of North Carolina Press.

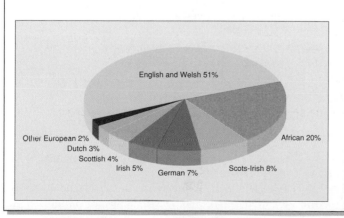

FIGURE 3-4   Ethnic Distribution of Non-Indian Inhabitants of British Mainland Colonies, c. 1770
By the third quarter of the eighteenth century, the colonial population was astonishingly diverse. Only two out of three settlers claimed British ancestry (from England, Wales, Scotland, or northern Ireland), while one out of five was African in origin.
Data Source: Thomas L. Purvis, "The European Ancestry of the United States Population, 1790," *William and Mary Quarterly*, 3d series, 41 (1984), p. 98.

OVERVIEW TABLES

The Overview tables in this text are a special feature designed to highlight and summarize important topics within a chapter. The Overview table shown here, for example, summarizes the purpose and significance of the major laws and constitutional amendments passed during the Reconstruction era following the Civil War.

Overview

Constitutional Amendments and Federal Legislation of the Reconstruction Era

Amendment or Legislation	Purpose	Significance
Thirteenth Amendment (passed and ratified in 1865)	Prevented southern states from reestablishing slavery after the war	Final step toward full emancipation of slaves
Freedmen's Bureau Act (1865)	Oversight of resettlement, relief, education, and labor for former slaves	Involved the federal government directly in assisting the transition from slavery to freedom; worked fitfully to achieve this objective during its seven-year career
Southern Homestead Act (1866)	Provided black people preferential access to public lands in five southern states	Lack of capital and poor quality of federal land thwarted the purpose of the act
Civil Rights Act of 1866	Defined rights of national ~~citizenship~~	Marked an important change in federal–state relatio~~ns, tilting balance of power to national~~

CHRONOLOGIES

Each chapter includes a Chronology, a list of the key events discussed in the chapter arranged in chronological order. The chronology for Chapter 16 lists the dates of key events during the Reconstruction era from 1865 to 1877. Chronologies provide a review of important events and their relationship to one another.

Chronology

1863 Lincoln proposes his Ten Percent Plan.

1864 Congress proposes the Wade-Davis Bill.

1865 Sherman issues Field Order No. 15.

Freedmen's Bureau is established.

Andrew Johnson succeeds to the presidency, unveils his Reconstruction plan.

Massachusetts desegregates all public facilities.

Black citizens in several southern cities organize Union Leagues.

Former Confederate states begin to pass black codes.

1866 Congress passes Southern Homestead Act, Civil Rights Act of 1866.

Republican regimes topple in North Carolina and Georgia.

1871 Congress passes Ku Klux Klan Act.

1872 Freedmen's Bureau closes down.

Liberal Republicans emerge as a separate party.

Ulysses S. Grant is reelected.

1873 Severe depression begins.

Colfax Massacre occurs.

U.S. Supreme Court's decision in the Slaughterhouse cases weakens the intent of the Fourteenth Amendment.

Texas falls to the Democrats in the fall elections.

1874 White Leaguers attempt a coup against the Re-

PRIMARY SOURCE DOCUMENTS

Historians find most of their information in written records, original documents that have survived from the past. These include government publications, letters, diaries, newspapers—whatever people wrote or printed, including many private documents never intended for publication. Each chapter in the book contains a feature called American Views—a selection from a primary source document. The example shown here is a letter from a Union soldier fighting during the Civil War. Each American Views feature begins with a brief introduction followed by several questions—for discussion or written response—on what the document reveals about key issues and events.

AMERICAN VIEWS

A Soldier Promotes the Union Cause

Introduction

Soldiers wrote their thoughts down in diaries, in letters to their families, and, as in the case of the infantryman here, D. Beardsley, from Tompkins County, New York, to newspapers. Morale faltered in both the civilian and military ranks on both sides during the Civil War as this excerpt indicates. At the same time, Beardsley is buoyed by the elevated sense of mission in Union ranks, brought about by Abraham Lincoln's Emancipation Proclamation, which took effect one month prior to this letter.

Questions

● How to balance civil liberties with the necessity of carrying on a war is a dilemma of all armed conflicts involving democratic societies. What does this soldier think about where the balance ought to occur?

● The writer refers to "desertion" in the ranks indicating a morale problem in the

In addition, each chapter begins with Voices from the American Journey, a brief firsthand account from an individual that powerfully recounts the personal journey he or she took in their lives. Each of these "voices" relates to the themes that follow in the chapter. The example here, from Chapter 18, is an excerpt from a letter written by Mary Antin, a Russian-Jewish immigrant who came to America at the turn of the last century.

We are forced to pick out our clothes from among all the others, with the steam blinding us; we choke, cough, entreat the women to give us time; they persist, "Quick! Quick!—or you'll miss the train!"—Oh, so we really won't be murdered! They are only making us ready for the continuing of our journey, cleaning us of all suspicions of dangerous sickness. Thank God! . . .

Oh, what solemn thoughts I had! How deeply I felt the greatness, the power of the scene! The immeasurable distance from horizon to horizon; . . . the absence of any object besides the one ship; . . . I was conscious only of sea and sky and something I did not understand. And as I listened to its solemn voice, I felt as if I had found a friend, and knew that I loved the ocean.

Mary Antin

Mary Antin, *The Promised Land* (Boston: Houghton Mifflin Company, 1912), chapter VIII.

UNITED STATES HISTORY DOCUMENT CD-ROM

Bound into every new copy of this textbook is a free U.S. History Document CD-ROM. This is a powerful resource for research and additional reading that contains more than 300 primary source documents central to U.S. History. Each document provides essay questions that are linked directly to a website where short-essay answers can be submitted online or printed out. A complete list of documents on the CD-Rom is found just before the Preface.

FROM THEN TO NOW

The feature called From Then to Now connects events and trends in the past to issues that confront Americans today, illustrating the value a historical perspective can contribute to our understanding of the world we live in. The example here, from Chapter 28, compares the fight against AIDS today with the search for a polio vaccine in the middle of the twentieth century.

FROM THEN TO NOW

Medical Research on Polio and AIDS

When Dr. Jonas Salk announced an effective vaccine for polio on April 12, 1955, the United States gained a new hero. In the confident mid-1950s, the polio vaccine seemed another proof of American ability to improve the world.

Poliomyelitis, or infantile paralysis, attacks the nervous system; it can paralyze the legs or kill by short-circuiting muscles in the throat and chest. Before 1900, infants had often encountered the polio virus in their first months and developed lifelong immunity. In the twentieth century, cleaner houses and streets delayed contact with polio until the preschool years or later, when the disease could be devastating. The virus sometimes struck adults; it cost Franklin Roosevelt the use of his legs when he was in his thirties, but most victims were children.

Fear of polio haunted American families after World War II. The disease killed fewer people than heart disease or cancer, but it seemed grossly unfair. Most Americans knew at least one child who hobbled through life on crutches and metal leg braces. Hospitals filled with new cases every summer—58,000 in 1952 alone. Many children clung to life inside iron lungs, metal cylinders that pumped air in and out of a hole in the throat.

Polio season peaked in July and August. Worried parents kept their children out of movie theaters and swimming pools, but the disease struck even the most careful families. One woman who grew up in the 1950s remembered: "Polio? That was the big fear when I was young. . . . I remember going to Dallas and seeing television for the first time. . . . Every day they would report 'another so many polio cases today.'"

Salk's announcement was welcome news. A generation later, President Ronald Reagan would list the polio vaccine with the steam engine and silicon chip as one of the great modern discoveries. By 2002, the number of new polio cases around the world had fallen to fewer than 1,000 in only ten countries—not including the United States.

However, medical research in the new century was vastly different than in the 1950s. Salk's work was financed largely by private contributions—many made by individuals and families to the March of Dimes. Fifty years later, the federal government is by far the largest supporter of medical research, spending to the

ANALYZING VISUALS

Like graphs and tables, visual images can provide as much insight into our nation's history as the written word. Within photographs and pieces of fine art lies emotional and historical meaning. Captions also provide valuable information, such as in the example below. When studying the image, consider questions such as: "Who are these people?"; "How were they feeling?"; "What event motivated this photograph or painting?"; and "What can be learned from the backdrop surrounding the focal point?" Such analysis allows for a fuller understanding of the people who lived the American journey.

Noted urban photographer Lewis Hine captures the cramped working conditions and child labor in this late nineteenth-century canning factory. Women and children provided a cheap and efficient work force for labor-intensive industries.

RECOMMENDED READINGS, ADDITIONAL SOURCES, AND WHERE TO LEARN MORE

At the end of each chapter are two lists of books—Recommended Readings and Additional Sources—that provide greater information about the topics discussed in the chapter. The section called Where to Learn More lists important historical sites and museums and related Websites that provide first-hand exposure to historical artifacts and settings.

GLOSSARY

Significant historical terms are called out in heavy type throughout the text and listed at the end of each chapter with appropriate page numbers. These are listed alphabetically and defined in a glossary at the end of the book.

Steele, Ian K. *Warpaths: Invasions of North America* (1994).

Washburn, Wilcomb E. *The Governor and the Rebel: A History of Bacon's Rebellion in Virginia* (1957).

White, Richard. *The Middle Ground: Indians, Empires, and Republics in the Great Lakes Region, 1650–1815* (1991).

Africans in America

Blackburn, Robin. *The Making of New World Slavery: From the Baroque to the Modern 1492–1800* (1997).

Breen, T. H., and Stephen Innes. *"Myne Owne Ground": Race and Freed___ ___ Virginia's ___ ___ Shore,*

WHERE TO LEARN MORE

- **Ste. Marie among the Hurons, near Midland, Ontario, Canada.** This site contains a reconstructed Jesuit mission from the seventeenth century. There is a museum with information about seventeenth-century France as well as life among the Huron Indians. Further information may be found at www.saintemarieamongthehurons.on.ca.

- **Taos Pueblo, Taos, New Mexico.** Still a residence for Pueblo Indians, portions of this multistoried

➤ An unknown artist depicted the fateful first encounter between Moctezuma and Hernán Cortés on November 8, 1519. Forewarned of the Spaniards' arrival by a series of ominous portents, the Aztec ruler greeted Cortés with a mixture of majesty and apprehension. Less than a year later, Moctezuma was dead and by 1521 the Aztec empire had fallen to the Spanish.

WORLDS APART

After a difficult journey of over two hundred miles, the ex-hausted man arrived at the royal palace in the grand city of Tenochtitlán. He had hurried all the way from the Gulf Coast with important news for the Aztec leader, Moctezuma.

Our lord and king, forgive my boldness. I am from Mictlancuauhtla. When I went to the shores of the great sea, there was a mountain range or small mountain float-ing in the midst of the water, and moving here and there without touching the shore. My lord, we have never seen the like of this, although we guard the coast and are always on watch.

[When Moctezuma sent some officials to check on the messenger's story, they confirmed his report.]

Our lord and king, it is true that strange people have come to the shores of the great sea. They were fishing from a small boat, some with rods and others with a net. They fished until late and then they went back to their two great towers and climbed up into them. . . . They have very light skin, much lighter than ours. They all have long beards, and their hair comes only to their ears.

Miguel Leon–Portilla, *The Broken Spears: The Aztec Account of the Conquest of Mexico* (Boston, 1962).

CHAPTER OUTLINE

Native American Societies before 1492

Paleo-Indians and the Archaic Period
The Development of Agriculture
Nonfarming Societies
Mesoamerican Civilizations
North American Cultures
The Caribbean Islanders

West African Societies

Geographical and Political Differences
Family Structure and Religion
European Merchants in West Africa and the Slave Trade

Western Europe on the Eve of Exploration

The Consolidation of Political and Military Authority
Religious Conflict and the Protestant Reformation

Contact

The Lure of Discovery
Christopher Columbus and the Westward Route to Asia
The Spanish Conquest and Colonization
The Columbian Exchange
Cultural Perceptions and Misperceptions

Competition for a Continent

Early French Efforts in North America
English Attempts in the New World

Conclusion

Moctezuma received news, like the messenger's initial report, filled with foreboding. Aztec religion placed great emphasis on omens and prophecies, which were thought to foreshadow coming events. Several unusual omens had recently occurred—blazing lights in the sky, one temple struck by lightning and another that spontaneously burst into flames, monstrous beings that appeared and then vanished. Now light-skinned strangers suddenly appeared offshore. Magicians regarded all these signs as unfavorable and warned that trouble lay ahead.

The messenger's journey to Tenochtitlán occurred in 1519. The "mountains" he saw were in fact the sails of European ships, and the strange men were Spanish soldiers under the command of Hernán Cortés. Like Columbus's voyage to the Caribbean in 1492, Cortés's arrival in Mexico is often considered a key episode in the European discovery of the "New World." But we might just as accurately view the messenger's entry into the Aztec capital as announcing the native Mexicans' discovery of a New World to the east, from which the strangers must have come. Neither the Aztecs nor the Spaniards could have foreseen the far-reaching consequences of these twin discoveries. Before long, a variety of peoples—Native Americans, Africans, and Europeans—who had previously lived worlds apart would come together to create a world that was new to all of them.

This new world reflected the diverse experiences of the many peoples who built it. Improving economic conditions in the fifteenth and early sixteenth centuries propelled Europeans overseas to seek new opportunities for trade and settlement. Spain, Portugal, France, and England competed for political, economic, and religious domination within Europe, and their conflict carried over into the Americas. Native Americans drew upon their familiarity with the land and its resources, their patterns of political and religious authority, and their systems of trade and warfare to deal with the European newcomers. Africans did not come voluntarily to the Americas but were brought by the Europeans to work as slaves. They too would draw on their cultural heritage to cope with both a new land and a new, harsh condition of life.

KEY TOPICS

- Native American, West African, and European societies on the eve of contact
- The reasons for Europe's impulse to global exploration
- The Spanish, French, and English experiences in America in the sixteenth century
- Consequences of contact between the Old and New Worlds

NATIVE AMERICAN SOCIETIES BEFORE 1492

In 1492, the year Columbus landed on a tiny island in the Caribbean, perhaps 70 million people—nearly equal to the population of Europe at that time—lived on the continents of North and South America, most of them south of what is now the border between the United States and Mexico. They belonged to hundreds of groups, each with its own language or dialect, history, and way of life. In their own languages, many native groups called themselves "the original people" or "the true men." Europeans came to call them "Indians," following Columbus's mistaken first impression that he had arrived in the East Indies when his ships reached an island in the Bahamas.

From the start, the original inhabitants of the Americas were peoples in motion. The first migrants may have arrived over forty thousand years ago, traveling from central Siberia and slowly making their way to southern South America. These people, and subsequent migrants from Eurasia, probably traveled across a land bridge that emerged across what is now the Bering Strait. During the last Ice Age, much of the earth's water was frozen in huge glaciers. This process lowered ocean levels, exposing a 600-mile-wide land bridge between Asia and America. Recent research examining genetic and linguistic similarities between Asian and Native American populations suggests that there may have been later migrations as well. Asian seafarers may have crossed the Pacific to settle portions of western North and South America, while as recently as eight thousand years ago, a final

Chronology

c. 40,000–8,000 B.C.	Ancestors of Native Americans cross Bering land bridge.		**1494**	Treaty of Tordesillas.
c. 10,000–9000 B.C.	Paleo-Indians expand through the Americas.		**1497**	John Cabot visits Nova Scotia and Newfoundland.
c. 9000 B.C.	Extinction of large land mammals in North America.		**1497–1499**	Vasco da Gama sails around Africa to reach India.
c. 8000–1500 B.C.	Archaic Indian era.		**1517**	Protestant Reformation begins in Germany.
c. 3000 B.C.	Beginnings of agriculture in Mesoamerica.		**1519–1521**	Hernán Cortés conquers the Aztec empire.
c. 1500 B.C.	Earliest mound-building culture begins.		**1532–1533**	Francisco Pizarro conquers the Inca empire.
c. 500 B.C.–A.D. 400	Adena-Hopewell mound-building culture.		**1534–1542**	Jacques Cartier explores eastern Canada for France.
c. A.D. 700–1600	Rise of West African empires.		**1540–1542**	Coronado explores southwestern North America.
c. 900	First mounds built at Cahokia. Ancestral Puebloan expansion.		**1542–1543**	Roberval's failed colony in Canada.
c. 1000	Spread of Islam in West Africa.		**1558**	Elizabeth I becomes queen of England.
c. 1000–1500	Last mound-building culture, the Mississippian.		**1565**	Spanish establish outpost at St. Augustine in Florida.
c. 1290s	Ancestral Puebloan dispersal into smaller villages.		**1560s–1580s**	English renew attempts to conquer Ireland.
1400–1600	Renaissance in Europe.		**1587**	Founding of "Lost Colony" of Roanoke.
1430s	Beginnings of Portuguese slave trade in West Africa.		**1598**	Spanish found colony at New Mexico.
1492	End of *reconquista* in Spain. Columbus's first voyage.			

migration may have brought Siberians to what is now Alaska and northern Canada.

PALEO-INDIANS AND THE ARCHAIC PERIOD

The earliest Americans, whom archaeologists call *Paleo-Indians*, traveled in small bands, tracking and killing mammoths, bison, and other large game. These animals were often easy prey, for they had never before encountered human hunters. Archaeologists working near present-day Clovis, New Mexico, have found numerous carefully crafted spear points—some of which may be over thirteen thousand years old— that testify to Paleo-Indians' expertise. Such efficient tools possibly contributed to overhunting, for by about 9000 B.C., mammoths, mastodons, and other large game had become extinct in the Americas. Climatic change also hastened the animals' disappearance. Around twelve thousand years ago, the world's climate began to grow warmer, turning grasslands

into deserts and reducing the animals' food supply. This meant that humans too had to find other food sources.

Between roughly 8000 B.C. and 1500 B.C. —what archaeologists call the Archaic period—Native Americans adapted to regional environments, learning to use local resources efficiently. Gradually, populations grew and people began living in larger communities. In these villages, men and women began to assume more specialized roles. Men did most of the hunting and fishing, activities that required travel. Women remained closer to home, gathering and preparing wild plant foods and caring for children. Each group made the tools it used, with men carving fishhooks and arrowheads and women making such items as bone needles and baskets.

Archaic Indians also collected local nonfood resources, such as minerals, rare shells, and bones, some of which were thought to have special spiritual significance. Native peoples traded these materials,

Women were the principal farmers in most Native American societies, growing corn, beans, and other crops that made up most of their food supply. This sixteenth-century French engraving shows Indian men preparing the soil for cultivation and Indian women sowing seeds in neat rows.

often over vast distances. At Indian Knoll, in western Kentucky, archaeologists have found copper from the Great Lakes area and shells from as far away as the Gulf of Mexico. Competition for control of lands where desirable materials could be found may have sparked conflict. Three bodies buried around 5000 B.C. in northwestern Alabama had stone arrowheads embedded in their backbones or ribcages, clear evidence of violent death.

Ideas as well as goods circulated among Archaic Indian peoples. Across the continent, human burials became more elaborate, suggesting that ideas about death and the afterlife passed between groups. Bodies might be wrapped in woven mats or cloths and the deceased's personal possessions placed in the grave. Certain valuable trade goods, such as exotic shell beads and animal figurines, accompanied some individuals to the grave, lending the deceased their spiritual power.

THE DEVELOPMENT OF AGRICULTURE

In the latter half of the Archaic period, some Native Americans made a momentous social and economic adaptation when they began farming. Agriculture in the Americas began around 3000 B.C., when the people of central Mexico started raising an ancient type of maize, or corn. Farming had already appeared independently in other parts of the world. People in the Middle East turned to agriculture around 9000 B.C.; a few thousand years later, farming appeared in South-

east Asia, China, and India. Archaeologists speculate that agriculture first developed in areas where population growth threatened to outrun the wild food supply. Women, with their knowledge of wild plants, probably discovered how to save seeds and cultivate them, becoming the world's first farmers.

At first, farming in the Americas supplemented a diet still largely dependent on hunting and gathering. But agriculture gradually became more widespread. In addition to maize, the main crop in both South and North America, farmers in Mexico, Central America, and the Peruvian Andes learned to cultivate peppers, beans, pumpkins, squash, avocados, sweet and white potatoes (native to the Peruvian highlands), and tomatoes. Mexican farmers also grew cotton. Maize and bean cultivation spread from Mexico in a wide arc to the north and east. Peoples in what is now the southwestern United States began farming between 1500 and 500 B.C., and by A.D. 200, farmers tilled the soil in present-day Georgia and Florida.

Wherever agriculture took hold, important social changes followed. Populations grew, because farming produced a more secure food supply than did hunting and gathering. Permanent villages appeared as farmers settled near their fields. In central Mexico, agriculture eventually sustained the populations of large cities. Trade in agricultural surpluses flowed through networks of exchange. In many Indian societies, women's status improved because of their role as the principal farmers. Specialized craft workers produced sophisticated pottery and baskets to store harvested grains. Even religious beliefs and practices reflected the centrality of farming. In describing the origins of their people, Pueblo Indians of the Southwest compared their emergence from the underworld to a maize plant sprouting from the earth.

The development of agriculture contributed to the diversity of Native American peoples. Even so, certain generalizations can be made about societies that developed within broad regions, or culture areas (see Map 1–1). Within each area, inhabitants shared basic patterns of subsistence and social organization, largely reflecting the natural environment to which they had adapted.

NONFARMING SOCIETIES

Throughout the North and West, Indians prospered without adopting agriculture. In the challenging environment of the Arctic and Subarctic, small nomadic bands moved seasonally to fish, follow game, and in the brief summers, gather wild berries. Far to the north, Eskimos and Aleuts hunted whales, seals, and other sea mammals. Farther inland, the Crees and other peoples followed migrating herds of caribou and moose. Northern peoples fashioned tools and weapons of bone and ivory, clothing and boats from animal skins, and houses of whalebones and hides or blocks of sod or snow. Many of their rituals and songs celebrated the hunt and the spiritual connection between humans and the animals on which they depended.

Along the Northwest Coast and Columbia River Plateau, abundant resources supported one of the most densely populated areas of North America. With rivers teeming with salmon and other fish, and forests full of game and edible plants, people prospered without resorting to farming. Among such groups as the Kwakiutls and Chinooks, extended families lived in large communal houses located in villages of up to several hundred residents. Local rulers displayed their prominence most conspicuously during potlatches, or ceremonies in which they gave away or destroyed food and other possessions. Artisans used the region's plentiful wood supply to make many items, including distinctive religious masks and memorial poles carved with images of supernatural beings.

Farther south, in present-day California, hunter-gatherers lived in smaller villages, several of which might be led by the same chief. These settlements usually adjoined oak groves, where Indians gathered acorns. Preparing the nuts was time-consuming, for they had to be ground into meal, leached with water to remove bitter acid, and then cooked. To protect their access to this important food, chiefs and villagers vigorously defended their territorial claims to the oak groves. Elsewhere, in the foothills of the Sierras, Indians periodically set fire to thick underbrush to hasten the growth of new shoots that would attract deer and other game.

Small nomadic bands in the Great Basin, where the climate was warm and dry, lived in caves and rock shelters, surviving on the region's limited resources. Shoshone hunters captured antelope in corrals and trapped small game, such as squirrels and rabbits. In what is now Utah and western Colorado, Utes hunted elk, bison, and mountain sheep and fished in mountain streams. Women gathered pinyon nuts, seeds, and wild berries. In hard times, people ate rattlesnakes, horned toads, and insects. They celebrated whenever food was plentiful and urged religious leaders to seek supernatural help when starvation loomed.

MESOAMERICAN CIVILIZATIONS

Mesoamerica, the birthplace of agriculture in North America, extends from central Mexico into Central America. A series of complex, literate, urban cultures emerged in this region beginning around 1200 B.C. Among the earliest was that of the Olmecs, who flourished on Mexico's Gulf Coast from about 1200 to 400 B.C. The Olmecs and other early Mesoamerican peoples built cities featuring large pyramids, developed religious practices that included human sacrifice, and devised calendars and writing systems. Two of the most prominent Mesoamerican civilizations to follow the Olmecs were that of the Mayans in the Yucatán and Guatemala and that of Teotihuacán in central Mexico.

The Mayans. Mayan civilization reached its greatest glory between about A.D. 150 and 900 in the southern Yucatán, creating Mesoamerica's most advanced writing and calendrical systems and developing a sophisticated mathematics that included the concept of zero. The Mayans of the southern Yucatán suffered a decline after 900, but there were still many thriving Mayan centers in the northern Yucatán when Europeans arrived in the Americas. The great city of Teotihuacán dominated central Mexico from the first century to the eighth century A.D. and influenced much of the rest of Mesoamerica through trade and conquest.

The Aztecs. Some two hundred years after the fall of Teotihuacán, the Toltecs, a warrior people, rose to prominence, dominating central Mexico from about 900 to 1100. In the wake of the Toltec collapse, the

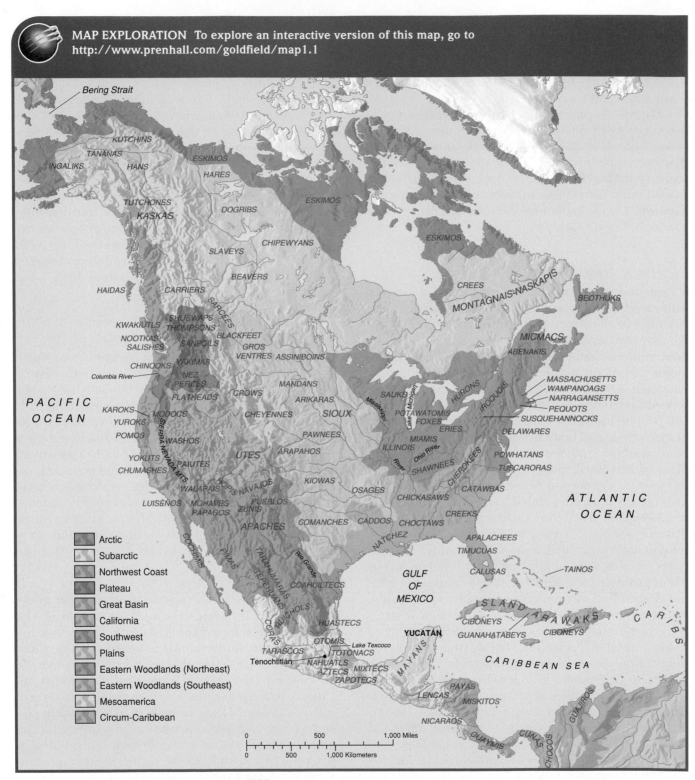

MAP 1-1   North American Culture Areas, c. 1500

Over the course of centuries, Indian peoples in North America developed distinctive cultures suited to the environments in which they lived. Inhabitants of each culture area shared basic patterns of subsistence, craft work, and social organization. Most, but not all, Indian peoples combined farming with hunting and gathering.

Aztecs, another warrior people, migrated from the north into the Valley of Mexico and built a great empire that soon controlled much of Mesoamerica. The magnificent Aztec capital, Tenochtitlán, was a city of great plazas, broad avenues, magnificent temples and palaces, ball courts, and busy marketplaces. Built on islands in the middle of Lake Texcoco, it was connected to the mainland by four broad causeways. In 1492, Tenochtitlán was home to some 200,000 people, making it one of the largest cities in the world at the time.

The great pyramid in Tenochtitlán's principal temple complex was the center of Aztec religious life. Here Aztec priests sacrificed human victims—by cutting open their chests and removing their still-beating hearts—to offer to the gods. Human sacrifice had been part of Mesoamerican religion since the time of the Olmecs. People believed that such ceremonies pleased the gods and prevented them from destroying the earth. The Aztecs, however, practiced sacrifice on a much larger scale than ever before. Hundreds, even thousands, of victims died in ceremonies that sometimes lasted for days.

Aztec culture expanded through continuous military conquest, driven by a quest for sacrificial victims and for wealth in the form of tribute payments of gold, food, and handcrafted goods. But as the empire grew, it became increasingly vulnerable to internal division. Neighboring peoples hated the Aztecs and submitted to them out of fear. With a powerful ally to lead them, they would readily turn on their overlords and bring the empire down.

NORTH AMERICAN CULTURES

North of Mexico, the introduction of a drought-resistant type of maize around 400 B.C. enabled a series of cultures sharing certain characteristics with Mesoamerica to develop. Beginning about 300 B.C., the Hohokams settled in southern Arizona, eventually building villages of several hundred people. Harvests of beans, corn, and squash (sometimes two a year), watered by a complex system of canals, fed Hohokam villagers. In large communities, inhabitants built ball courts similar to those found in Mexico. Artisans wove cotton cloth and made goods reflecting Mesoamerican artistic styles out of shell, turquoise, and clay. Extensive trade networks linked the Hohokams to people living as far away as California and Mexico. Their culture endured for over a thousand years but had disappeared by 1450.

Ancestral Puebloans. Beginning about A.D. 1, Ancestral Puebloan peoples (sometimes called Anasazis) settled where the borders of present-day Colorado, Utah, Arizona, and New Mexico meet. They gradually adopted agriculture, first adding maize to a diet of wild foods and later beans and squash. Scarce rainfall, routed through dams and hillside terraces, watered the crops. Networks of roads carried people and goods between villages. Artisans crafted intricate baskets and distinctive black-on-white pottery for use and trade.

Ancestral Puebloans originally lived in villages built on mesas and canyon floors. These settlements

Acoma Pueblo has perched atop this 300-foot-tall mesa since the twelfth century. Now used mainly for ceremonial purposes, Acoma was once a thriving Ancestral Puebloan village.

included special rooms, or *kivas*, for religious ceremonies. The largest communal dwelling, Pueblo Bonito in New Mexico's Chaco Canyon, covered 3 acres and contained 650 to 800 rooms that housed about 1,200 people. Pueblo Bonito may have been the political and ceremonial center of Puebloan society from about A.D. 900 to 1100. After about 1200, villagers began carving multistoried stone houses into steep canyon walls. These spectacular dwellings were not easy places in which to live. They could be reached only by difficult climbs up steep cliffs and along narrow ledges, and water, food, and other goods had to be carried to them. Archaeologists now think that warfare and climate change worked together to force the Puebloans into these precarious homes. Around 1200, the climate of the Southwest grew colder, making it more difficult to grow enough to feed the large population. Food scarcity, in turn, may have set village against village and encouraged attacks by outsiders. Villagers probably resorted to cliff dwellings for defensive purposes as violence spread in the region. By 1300, survivors abandoned the cliff dwellings and dispersed into much smaller villages along the Rio Grande.

Their descendants include the Hopis and Zunis, as well as other Puebloan peoples in the desert Southwest. In 1492, many lived in large communal dwellings in permanent villages (*pueblo* is the Spanish word for "village"). Men did most of the farming—in contrast to the predominant pattern of women farmers elsewhere in Native America—and tilled irrigated fields of corn, beans, squash, and sunflowers. In their religious rituals, Pueblos directed prayers to the gods for enough rain for the all-important harvest.

Plains Indians. The Great Plains of the continent's interior were much less densely settled than the desert Southwest. Scattered villages of Mandans, Pawnees, and other groups clung to tree-lined rivers. Women raised corn, squash, beans, and sunflowers and gathered wild plants for food and medicine. Men hunted bison, whose skin and bones were used for clothing, shelter, and tools. Plains Indians moved frequently, seeking more fertile land or better hunting. Wherever they went, they traded skins, food, and obsidian (a volcanic glass used for tools and weapons) with other native peoples.

Mound-building cultures. The gradual spread of agriculture transformed native societies in the Eastern Woodlands, a vast territory extending from the Mississippi Valley to the Atlantic seaboard. Although the process began around 2500 B.C., farming was not firmly established until about A.D. 700. As agriculture

spread, several "mound-building" societies—named for the large earthworks their members constructed—developed in the Ohio and Mississippi Valleys. The oldest flourished in Louisiana between 1500 and 700 B.C. The members of the Adena-Hopewell culture, which appeared in the Ohio Valley between 500 B.C. and A.D. 400, lived in small villages spread over a wide area. They built hundreds of mounds, often in the shapes of humans, birds, and serpents. Most were grave sites, where people were buried with valuable goods. Many burial objects were made from materials obtained through long-distance trade, including Wyoming obsidian, Lake Superior copper, and Florida conch shells.

The last mound-building culture, the Mississippian, emerged between 1000 and 1500 in the Mississippi Valley. Mississippian farmers raised enough maize, squash, and beans to support sizable populations and major urban centers. One of the largest of these was **Cahokia**, located near present-day St. Louis. By 1250, Cahokia had perhaps thirty thousand residents, making it about the same size as medieval London and the largest American city north of Mexico. Its central feature was a 100-foot-high mound, the world's largest earthwork.

Cahokia dominated the Mississippi Valley, but numerous other towns, some with hundreds or thousands of residents, lay scattered across the Woodlands region, linked by extensive trade networks. In major towns, religious leaders conducted ceremonies in large temples built atop platform mounds. Powerful chiefs, thought to be related to the sun, ruled these communities. When a chief died, his wives and servants were killed in order to accompany him to the afterlife.

Mississippian culture began to decline in the thirteenth century. Food shortages (probably caused by a cooling climate) and warfare drove people from the great cities into the countryside. Yet elements of the culture survived among dispersed Woodlands Indians. Most people continued to subsist through maize and bean agriculture, living part of the year in villages where women tilled lands that men had cleared. Twice a year, after crops were planted and again after the harvest, villagers separated into family groups and dispersed into the forest. Men went off to hunt, while women and children foraged for wild plants. Although the large cities of the Mississippian era had disappeared, Woodlands Indians maintained long-distance trade links throughout the region, with such precious goods as copper, shell beads, and pearls passing among groups.

Woodlands villages generally contained 500 to 2000 people, led by chiefs who inherited their posi-

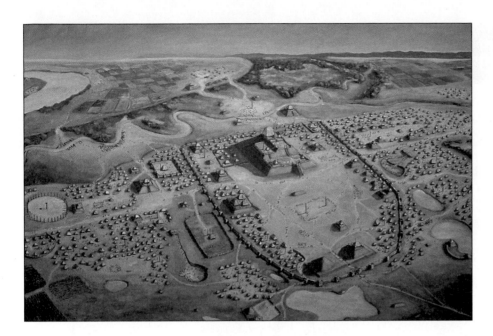

This artist's rendering, based on archaeological evidence, suggests the size and magnificence of the Mississippian city of Cahokia. By the thirteenth century, it was as populous as medieval London, and served as a center of trade for the vast interior of North America.

tions but ruled with the advice of groups of elders. In the North, Iroquois peoples took advantage of the demise of Cahokia to refocus trade and power in their own region, forming a confederation around 1450. The southern Woodlands region was more densely populated than the northern, largely because the warmer southern climate provided a longer growing season and more abundant wild foods. Patterns of settlement in the southern region, however, were more decentralized than in the north, with villages occasionally joining in loose regional confederacies.

THE CARIBBEAN ISLANDERS

The Caribbean islanders whom Columbus first encountered likewise descended from ancient cultures. Around 5000 B.C., mainland peoples began moving to the islands. Ancestors of the Tainos probably came from what is now Venezuela. The Guanahatabeys of western Cuba originated in Florida, and the Caribs of the easternmost islands moved from Brazil's Orinoco Valley. Surviving at first by hunting and gathering, island peoples began farming perhaps in the first century A.D. They raised manioc, sweet potatoes, maize, squash, beans, peppers, peanuts, and pineapple on clearings made in the tropical forests. Canoes carried trade goods throughout the Caribbean, as well as to Mesoamerica and coastal South America.

By 1492, as many as 4 million people may have inhabited the Caribbean islands. Powerful chiefs ruled over villages, conducted war and diplomacy, and controlled the distribution of food and other goods obtained as tribute from villagers. Island societies were divided into several ranks. An elite group aided the chief and supplied religious leaders. Below them were a large class of ordinary farmers and fishermen and a lower class of servants who worked for the elites. Elite islanders were easily recognized by their fine clothing, bright feather headdresses, and golden ear and nose ornaments—items that eventually attracted the attention of European visitors.

The histories of America's native peoples have largely been preserved in oral traditions and archaeological evidence, not written records, and for that reason may seem less distinct than the histories of Europeans and their descendants. But the New World, no less than the Old, had witnessed centuries of dynamic change. People adapted to many different environments, learning how to use local foods and resources not just to survive but to prosper. Empires rose and fell, and new ones took their place. Large cities flourished and disappeared. Periods of warfare occasionally disrupted the lives of thousands of individuals. At other times, military alliances sealed friendships, and networks of trade linked peoples across vast expanses of territory. Native Americans were thoroughly accustomed to dealing with new and challenging circumstances.

WEST AFRICAN SOCIETIES

In the three centuries after 1492, fully six out of seven people who crossed the Atlantic to the Americas were

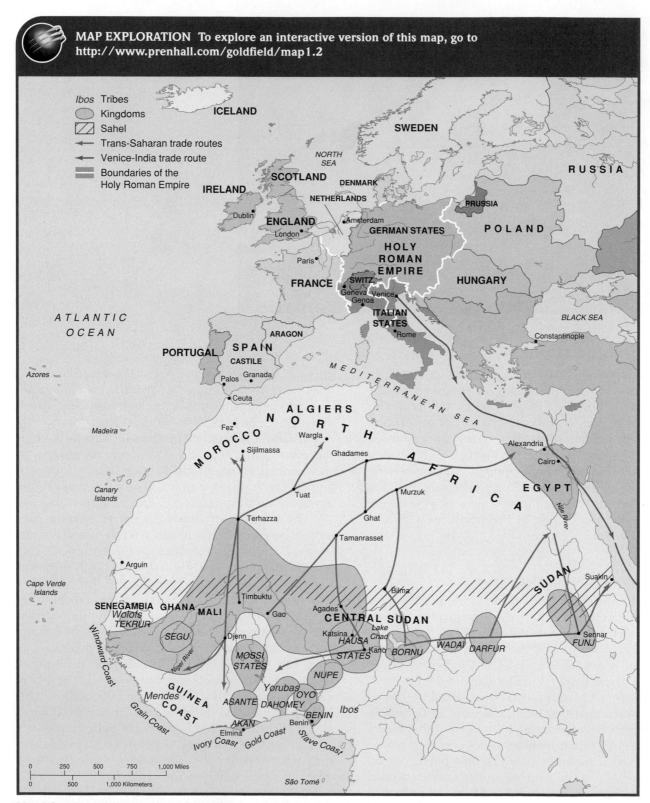

MAP EXPLORATION To explore an interactive version of this map, go to
http://www.prenhall.com/goldfield/map1.2

MAP 1-2   West Africa and Europe in 1492
*Before Columbus's voyage, Europeans knew little about the world beyond the Mediterranean
basin and the coast of West Africa. Muslim merchants from North Africa largely controlled
European traders' access to African gold and other materials.*

not Europeans but Africans. They came from the world's second largest continent and the one with the longest record of human habitation, where ancestors of modern humans (*homo sapiens*) appeared 130,000 or more years ago. Like the Americas, Africa had witnessed the rise of many ancient and diverse cultures (see Map 1-2). They ranged from the sophisticated Egyptian civilization that developed in the Nile Valley over 5000 years ago to the powerful twelfth-century chiefdoms of Zimbabwe to the West African empires that flourished in the time of Columbus and Cortés. The vast majority of Africans who came to the Americas after 1492 arrived as slaves, transported by Europeans eager to exploit their labor. Although they were involuntary immigrants, Africans could draw upon their ancient cultural heritages to help shape the New World in which they found themselves.

GEOGRAPHICAL AND POLITICAL DIFFERENCES

Most African immigrants to the Americas came from the continent's western regions. The West African city of Timbuktu was one of the continent's greatest cities in 1492. Located on the Niger River, the metropolis of perhaps seventy thousand people was the seat of the powerful Songhai empire, ruled by Sunni Ali with the support of a strong army and efficient bureaucrats. Timbuktu was a center of trade as well as government. A visitor in 1526 described its busy streets lined with "shops of artificers and merchants, and especially of such as weave linen and cotton cloth," and reported—with some exaggeration—that the inhabitants "are exceeding rich."

The Songhai empire was only the latest in a series of powerful states to develop in western Sudan, the vast plain lying south of the arid Sahara. One of the earliest, Ghana, rose to prominence in the eighth century and dominated West Africa for nearly three hundred years. Its successor, Mali, emerged around 1200 and lasted another three centuries. Songhai, the largest and wealthiest state, dominated the Sudan from around 1450 until it fell to a Moroccan invasion in 1591. Equivalently large empires did not appear in coastal West Africa, although the Asante, Dahomey, Oyo, and Bini kingdoms there grew to be quite powerful. Other coastal peoples, such as the Mendes and Igbos, were decentralized, living in autonomous villages where all adult males participated in making decisions.

Geographical as well as political differences marked the inland and coastal regions. In the vast grasslands of the Sudan, people raised cattle and cultivated millet and sorghum. In the 1500s, European visitors introduced varieties of Asian rice, which soon

Craftsmen from the West African kingdom of Benin were renowned for their remarkable bronze sculptures. This intricate bronze plaque depicts four African warriors in full military dress. The two tiny figures in the background may be Portuguese soldiers, who first arrived in Benin in the late fifteenth century.

Benin bronze plaque. National Museum of African Art, Smithsonian Institution, Washington, DC, U.S.A.

became another important crop. On the coast—where rain falls nearly every day—people grew yams, bananas, and various kinds of beans and peas in forest clearings. They also kept sheep, goats, and poultry.

Artisans and merchants. West Africans were skilled artisans and particularly fine metalworkers. Smiths in Benin produced intricate bronze sculptures, and Asante craftsmen designed distinctive miniature gold weights. West African smiths also used their skills to forge weapons, attesting to the frequent warfare between West African states.

Complex trade networks linked inland and coastal states, and long-distance commercial connections tied West Africa to southern Europe and the Middle East. For centuries, mines in the area of present-day Guinea and Mali produced tons of gold each year. West African merchants exchanged gold with traders from North Africa for salt, a commodity so rare in West Africa that it was sometimes literally worth its weight in gold. In addition to gold, North African merchants bought pepper, leather, and ivory. The wealth generated by this trans-Saharan trade contributed to the rise of the Songhai and earlier empires.

Farming and gender roles. Most West Africans, however, were farmers, not merchants. A daily round of work, family duties, and worship defined their lives. West African men and women shared agricultural tasks. Men prepared fields for planting, while women cultivated the crops, harvested them, and dried grain for storage. Men also hunted and, in the grassland regions, herded cattle. Women in the coastal areas owned and cared for other livestock, including goats and sheep. West African women regularly traded goods, including the crops they grew, in local markets. In 1495, a Muslim African leader commented disapprovingly on the "free mixing of men and women in the markets and streets" in Timbuktu and other cities, but women merchants were essential to the vitality of local economies.

FAMILY STRUCTURE AND RELIGION

Family connections were exceedingly important to West Africans, helping to define each person's place in society. Children were especially cherished; one Yoruba proverb stated that "Without children you are naked." High rates of infant and child mortality made offspring all the more precious, for parents depended on their children for labor and for support in old age. In some regions, men who could afford to do so had more than one wife, thus increasing their chances of having surviving offspring. While ties between parents and children were of central importance, West Africans also emphasized their links with aunts, uncles, cousins, and grandparents. Groups of families formed clans that further extended an individual's kin ties. Most clans were patrilineal—tracing descent through the father's line—but some, for instance among the Akans and Igbos, were matrilineal. These links enmeshed West Africans in a web of family ties.

Religious beliefs magnified the powerful influence of family on African life. Africans believed that their ancestors acted as mediators between the worlds of the living and the dead. Families held elaborate funerals for deceased members to insure their passage into the realm of the spirits. Such rituals helped keep the memory of ancestors alive for younger generations.

West Africans worshiped a supreme being and several subordinate deities, believing that the gods often sent spirits to speak to people. Like Native Americans,

they performed ceremonies to insure the goodwill of the spiritual forces that suffused the natural world. West African medicine men and women used rituals to protect people from evil spirits and sorcerers. Religious ceremonies were held in sacred places—often near water—but not in buildings that Europeans recognized as churches. And like the Indians, West Africans preserved their faith through oral traditions.

Islam began to take root in West Africa around the eleventh century, probably introduced by Muslim traders from North Africa. By the fifteenth century, the cities of Timbuktu and Djenné had become centers of Islamic learning, attracting students from as far away as southern Europe. Some African rulers began keeping records in Arabic and enforcing Islamic law, but most West Africans probably retained traditional religious beliefs and practices.

EUROPEAN MERCHANTS IN WEST AFRICA AND THE SLAVE TRADE

Before the fifteenth century, Europeans knew little about Africa beyond its Mediterranean coast, which had been part of the Islamic world since the eighth century. Spain, much of which had been subject to Islamic rule before 1492, had stronger ties to North Africa than did most of Europe. But Christian merchants from other European lands had also traded for centuries with Muslims in the North African ports. When stories of West African gold reached the ears of European traders, they tried to move deeper into the continent. But they encountered powerful Muslim merchants intent on monopolizing the gold trade.

In the early fifteenth century, the kingdom of Portugal sought to circumvent this Muslim monopoly. Portuguese forces conquered Ceuta in Morocco and gained a foothold on the continent in 1415. Portuguese mariners gradually explored the West African coast, establishing trading posts along the way. Portuguese merchants exchanged horses, clothing, wine, lead, iron, and steel for African gold, grain, animal skins, cotton, pepper, and camels.

By the 1430s, the Portuguese had discovered perhaps the greatest source of wealth they could extract from Africa—slaves. People became slaves in various ways. Some Africans lost their freedom as punishment for crime, but the majority of slaves were captured in war. Slave raids into neighboring territories were a regular feature of African life. Slavery had long been a part of West African society. African law made land available to anyone willing to cultivate it—provided that no one else was using the same plot—and the possession of a large labor force to work the land became the principal means to wealth.

Slaves enriched their masters in a number of ways. Masters sold some slaves directly, tapping into a well-developed internal trade. Merchants from the Sahara frequently trekked to West Africa to exchange horses for slaves, and West Africans traded laborers among themselves. Most slaves worked at a variety of tasks for their owners. Many labored more or less independently as farmers, producing surplus crops for their masters. Some rulers acquired female slaves to serve as wives or concubines but also as workers. One Italian visitor to the small state of Warri reported in 1656 that its ruler had many slave wives who wove cloth for sale. Powerful Sudanese rulers employed large numbers of slaves as bureaucrats and soldiers, rewarding them for loyal service with good treatment and, occasionally, freedom.

Europeans who observed African slaves' relative freedom and variety of employment often concluded that slaves in Africa were "slaves in name only." Slavery in Africa was not necessarily a permanent status and did not automatically apply to the slaves' children. European purchasers of African slaves generally treated them much more harshly. Slavery for the unwilling African immigrants ensnared in it became even more oppressive as it developed in the Americas.

Western Europe on the Eve of Exploration

When Columbus sailed from Spain in 1492, he left a continent recovering from the devastating warfare and disease of the fourteenth century and about to embark on the devastating religious conflicts of the sixteenth. Between 1337 and 1453, England and France had exhausted each other in a series of conflicts known as the Hundred Years' War. And between 1347 and 1351, an epidemic known as the Black Death (bubonic plague) wreaked havoc on a European population already suffering from persistent malnutrition. Perhaps a third of all Europeans died, with results that were felt for more than a century.

The plague left Europe with far fewer workers. To help the economy recover, the survivors learned to be more efficient and rely on technological improvements. Farmers selected the most fertile land to till, and artisans adopted labor-saving techniques to increase productivity. Metalworkers built larger furnaces with huge bellows driven by water power. Shipbuilders redesigned vessels with steering mechanisms that could be managed by smaller crews. Innovations in banking, accounting, and insurance also fostered economic recovery. Prosperity was distributed unevenly among social classes, however. In parts of England, France, Sweden, and the German states, peasants and workers protested rising rents and taxes that threatened to absorb most of their wages. Yet on the whole, Europe had a stronger, more productive economy in 1500 than ever before.

In much of western Europe, economic improvement encouraged an extraordinary cultural movement known as the Renaissance, a "rebirth" of interest in the classical civilizations of ancient Greece and Rome. The Renaissance originated in the city-states of Italy, where a prosperous and educated urban class promoted learning and artistic expression. Wealthy townspeople joined princes in becoming patrons of the arts, offering financial support to painters, sculptors, architects, writers, and musicians.

The daily lives of most Europeans, however, remained untouched by intellectual and artistic developments. Most Europeans were peasants, engaged in an annual round of agricultural labor. Within peasant families, men did most of the heavy field work, while women helped at planting and harvest time and cared for children, livestock, and the household. The economic recovery after the Black Death helped some families, but the lives of many remained hard. Crop failures and disease often brought great suffering to villages and towns.

European states were hierarchical, with their populations divided into fairly rigid classes. Monarchs stood at the top of society. Just below were the aristocrats, who, along with the royal family, dominated government and owned most of the land, receiving rents and labor services from peasants and rural artisans. Next, in descending order, came prosperous gentry families, independent landowners, and, at the bottom, landless peasants and laborers.

European society was also patriarchal, with men dominating political and economic life. Europe's rulers were, with few exceptions, men, and men controlled the Catholic Church. Inheritance was patrilineal, and only men could own property. According to an ideal not always upheld, Europeans thought that even the poorest man should be "as a king in his own house," ruling over his wife, children, and servants.

The Consolidation of Political and Military Authority

By the end of the fifteenth century, after more than a hundred years of incessant conflict, a measure of stability returned to the countries about to embark on overseas expansion. Ferdinand and Isabella of Spain, Louis XI of France, and Henry VII of England successfully asserted royal authority over their previously fragmented realms, creating strong state bureaucracies to control political rivals. They gave special trading privileges to merchants to gain their support, creating links that would later prove important in financing overseas expeditions. At the same time, Spain and Portugal negotiated an end to a long-running dispute about the succession to the throne of Castile, one of Spain's largest kingdoms.

The consolidation of military power went hand in hand with the strengthening of political authority. Portugal developed a strong navy to defend its seaborne merchants. Louis XI of France commanded a standing army, and Ferdinand of Spain created a palace guard to use against potential opponents. Before overseas expansion began, European monarchs exerted military force to extend their authority closer to home. Louis XI and his successors used warfare and intermarriage with ruling families of nearby provinces to expand French influence. In the early sixteenth century, England's Henry VIII sent soldiers to conquer Ireland. And the Spain of 1492 was forged from the successful conclusion of the *reconquista* ("reconquest") of territory from Muslim control.

Muslim invaders from North Africa first entered Spain in 711 and ruled much of the Iberian peninsula (which includes Spain and Portugal) for centuries. Beginning in the mid-eleventh century, Christian armies embarked on a long effort to reclaim the region. By 1450, only the southern tip of Spain remained under Muslim control. After the marriage of Ferdinand of Aragon and Isabella of Castile in 1469 united Spain's two principal kingdoms, their combined forces completed the *reconquista*. Granada, the last Muslim stronghold, fell in 1492, shortly before Columbus set out on his first voyage.

RELIGIOUS CONFLICT AND THE PROTESTANT REFORMATION

Even as these rulers sought to unify their realms, religious conflicts began to tear Europe apart. For more than a thousand years, Catholic Christianity had united western Europeans in one faith. All Christians believed that God sent his only son, Jesus Christ, to suffer crucifixion, die, and rise from the dead in order to redeem humans from sin and give them eternal life. The Catholic Church built on this faith included an elaborate hierarchy of clergy, ranging upward from parish priests to bishops, archbishops, and cardinals, culminating in Christ's representative on earth, the pope. It also supported monastic orders whose members often lived and prayed apart from society.

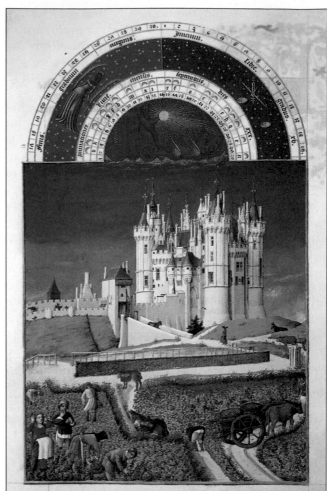

This illustration from a fifteenth-century French manuscript shows the sharp social divisions of late medieval Europe. In the forefront, a peasant family gathers in the grape harvest. The enormous fortified castle in the background was the home of an aristocratic family whose wealth derived in good part from the labor of peasants.

By the sixteenth century, the Catholic Church had accumulated enormous wealth and power. The pope wielded influence not only as a spiritual leader but also as the political ruler of parts of Italy. The church owned considerable property throughout Europe. Many Christians, especially in northern Europe, began to criticize the worldliness of the popes and the church itself for corruption, abuse of power, and betrayal of the legacy of Christ.

In 1517, a German monk, Martin Luther, invited open debate on a set of propositions critical of church practices and doctrines. Luther believed that the church had become too insistent on the performance of good works, such as charitable donations or other actions intended to please God. He called for a return to what he understood to be the purer practices and beliefs of the early church, emphasizing that salvation came not by good deeds but only by faith in God. With the help of the newly invented printing press, his ideas spread widely, inspiring a challenge to the Catholic Church that became known as the **Reformation**.

When the Catholic church refused to compromise, Luther and other critics withdrew to form their own religious organizations. Luther emphasized the direct, personal relationship of God to the individual believer. He urged people to take responsibility for their own spiritual growth by reading the Bible, which he translated for the first time into German. What started as a religious movement, however, quickly acquired an important political dimension.

Sixteenth-century Germany was a fragmented region of small kingdoms and principalities jealous of their independence. They were officially part of the Holy Roman Empire, but only loosely so, and many German princes resisted efforts by the Catholic empire to assert its authority. Realizing that religious protest reinforced their claims to independence, many princes supported Luther for both spiritual and secular reasons. When the Holy Roman Empire under Charles V (who was also king of Spain) tried to silence them, the reformist princes protested. From that point on, these princes—and all Europeans who supported religious reform—became known as **Protestants**.

The Protestant movement took a more radical turn under the influence of the French reformer John Calvin, who emphasized the doctrine of **predestination**. Calvin maintained that an all-powerful and all-knowing God chose at the moment of creation which humans would be saved and which would be damned. Each person's fate is thus foreordained, or predestined, by God, although we cannot know our fate during our lifetimes. Good Calvinists struggled to behave as God's chosen, continually searching their souls for evidence of divine grace.

Calvin founded a religious community consistent with his principles at Geneva, a Swiss city-state near the French border. Men who claimed to be "saints," or God's chosen people, led the city's government. They drove out nonbelievers, subjected all citizens to a rigid discipline, and made Geneva the center of Protestant reform in Europe. But neither Lutherans nor Calvinists could contain the powerful Protestant impulse. In succeeding years, other groups formed, split, and split again, increasing Europe's religious fragmentation.

From Germany and Geneva the Protestant Reformation spread to France, the Netherlands, Eng-

This 1568 woodcut of a European printshop shows workers setting type in the background, while the men in front print pages for a book. The invention of the printing press revolutionized European society, making information accessible to anyone who could read. During the Reformation, both Protestants and Catholics used the press to spread their views and attack their opponents.

land, and Hungary. The new religious ideas particularly interested literate city-dwellers, such as merchants and skilled artisans, who were attracted to Protestant writings as well as the sermons of Protestant preachers. Peasants adopted the new ideas more slowly, although German peasants, claiming Luther as inspiration, staged an unsuccessful revolt against their masters in 1524. Luther disavowed them, however, and supported the German princes in their brutal suppression of the revolt.

The Reformation addressed spiritual needs that the Catholic Church had left unfulfilled, but it also fractured the religious unity of western Europe and spawned a century of warfare unprecedented in its bloody destructiveness. Protestants fought Catholics in France and the German states. Popes initiated a "Counter-Reformation" to strengthen the Catholic Church—in part by internal reform and in part by persecuting its opponents and reimposing religious conformity. Europe thus fragmented into warring camps just at the moment when Europeans were coming to terms with their discovery of America and seeking ways to exploit its wealth.

CONTACT

Religious fervor, political ambition, and the desire for wealth propelled European nations into overseas expansion as well as conflict at home. Portugal, Spain, France, and England competed to establish footholds on other continents in an intense scramble for riches and dominance. The success of these early endeavors was a reflection of Europe's prosperity and a series of technological breakthroughs that enabled its mariners to navigate beyond familiar waters.

By 1600, Spain had emerged as the apparent winner among the European competitors for New World dominance. Its astonishingly wealthy empire included vast territories in Central and South America. The conquerors of this empire attributed their success to their military superiority and God's approval of their imperial ambitions. In reality, it was the result

Advances in ship design, including the development of the caravel pictured in this fifteenth-century woodcut, made transoceanic voyages possible. The arrangement of sails allowed the caravel to catch the trade winds and move more quickly across the high seas.

of a complex set of interactions with native peoples as well as an unanticipated demographic catastrophe.

THE LURE OF DISCOVERY

The potential rewards of overseas exploration captured the imaginations of a small but powerful segment of European society. Most people, busy making a living, cared little about distant lands. But certain princes and merchants anticipated spiritual and material benefits from voyages of discovery. The spiritual advantages included making new Christian converts and blocking Islam's expansion—a Christian goal that dated back to the eleventh-century Crusades against the Muslims in the Middle East and continued with the *reconquista*. On the material side, the voyages would contribute to Europe's prosperity by increasing trade.

Merchants especially sought access to Asian spices like pepper, cinnamon, ginger, and nutmeg that added interest to an otherwise monotonous diet and helped preserve certain foods. Wealthy Europeans paid handsomely for small quantities of spices, making it worthwhile to transport them great distances. But the overland spice trade—and the trade in other luxury goods such as silk and furs—spanned thousands of miles, involved many middlemen, and was controlled at key points by Muslim merchants. One critical center was Constantinople, the bastion of Christianity in the eastern Mediterranean. When it fell to the Ottomans—the Muslim rulers of Turkey—in 1453, Europeans feared that caravan routes to Asia would be disrupted. This encouraged merchants to turn westward and seek alternate routes.

The reorientation of European trade benefited western Italian cities such as Genoa as well as Portugal and Spain, whose ports gave access to the Mediterranean and the Atlantic Ocean. Mariners ventured farther into ocean waters, seeking direct access to the African gold trade and, eventually, a sea route around Africa to Asia. Had it not been for a set of technological developments that reduced the risks of ocean sailing, such lengthy voyages into unexplored areas would have been impossible.

Advances in navigation and shipbuilding. Ocean voyages required sturdier ships than those that plied the Mediterranean. Because oceangoing mariners traveled beyond sight of coastal features, they also needed reliable navigational tools. In the early fifteenth century, Prince Henry of Portugal, excited by the idea of overseas discovery, sponsored the efforts of shipbuilders, mapmakers, and other workers to solve these practical problems.

By 1500, enterprising artisans had made several important advances. Iberian shipbuilders perfected the caravel, a ship whose narrow shape and steering rudder suited it for ocean travel. Ship designers combined square sails (good for speed) with triangular lateen sails, which increased maneuverability. Two Arab inventions—the magnetic compass and the astrolabe (which allowed mariners to determine their position in relation to a star's known location in the sky)—gained popularity among European navigators. As sailors acquired practical experience on the high seas, mapmakers recorded their observations of landfalls, wind patterns, and ocean currents.

After Portugal's conquest of the Moroccan city of Ceuta in 1415, its mariners slowly worked their way along Africa's western coast, establishing trading posts where they exchanged European goods for gold, ivory, and slaves (see Map 1–3). Bartolomeu Días reached the southern tip of Africa in 1488. Eleven years later, Vasco da Gama brought a Portuguese fleet around Africa to India, opening a sea route to Asia. These initiatives gave Portugal a virtual monopoly on Far Eastern trade for some time.

The Atlantic islands and the slave trade. The new trade routes gave strategic importance to the islands that lie in the Atlantic off the west coast of Africa and Europe. Spain and Portugal vied for control of the Canary Islands, located 800 miles southwest of the Iberian peninsula. Spain eventually prevailed in 1496 by defeating the islands' inhabitants. Portugal acquired Madeira and the Cape Verde Islands, along with a set of tiny islands off Africa's Guinea Coast.

Sugar, like Asian spices, commanded high prices in Europe, so the conquerors of the Atlantic islands began to cultivate sugar cane on them, on large plantations worked by slave labor. In the Canaries, the Spanish first enslaved the native inhabitants. When disease and exhaustion reduced their numbers, the Spanish brought in African slaves, often purchased from Portuguese traders. On uninhabited islands, the Europeans imported African slaves from the start. São Tomé and the other small islands off the Guinea Coast eventually became important way stations in the transatlantic slave trade.

These island societies, in which a small European master class dominated a much larger population of native peoples or imported African slaves, were to provide a model for Spain's and Portugal's later exploitation of their American colonies. In 1494, two years after his first voyage to the New World, Christopher Columbus wrote to Ferdinand and Isabella of Spain to suggest that Caribbean islanders could be sold as slaves in order to cover the

costs of exploration. He found the inhabitants to be "a people very savage and suitable for the purpose, and well made and of very good intelligence." They "will be better than any other slaves," he went on, "and their inhumanity they will immediately lose when they are out of their own land."

CHRISTOPHER COLUMBUS AND THE WESTWARD ROUTE TO ASIA

Columbus's proposal revealed him to be very much a man of his time. Born in Genoa in 1451, he later lived in Portugal and Spain and as a young man visited Africa's Guinea Coast and Madeira. He was thus thoroughly familiar with slavery and regarded the enslavement of Caribbean islanders as an extension of established practice.

Columbus was also not the first European to believe that he could reach Asia by sailing westward. The idea developed logically during the fifteenth century as mariners gained knowledge and experience from their exploits in the Atlantic and around Africa. Columbus himself may have gained valuable experience on a voyage to Iceland. He also read widely in geographical treatises and paid close attention to the stories and rumors that circulated among mariners.

Most Europeans knew that the world was round, but most also scoffed at the idea of a westward voyage to Asia, believing that it would take so long that no ship could carry enough supplies. Columbus's confidence that he could make the voyage grew from a mathematical error. He mistakenly calculated the earth's circumference as 18,000 (rather than 24,000) miles and so concluded that Asia lay just 3,500 miles west of the Canary Islands. Columbus first sought financial support from the king of Portugal, whose advisers disputed his calculations and warned him that he would starve at sea before reaching Asia. Undaunted, he turned to Portugal's rival, Spain.

Columbus tried to convince Ferdinand and Isabella that his plan suited Spain's national goals. If he succeeded, Spain could grow rich from Asian trade, send Christian missionaries to Asia (a goal in keeping with the religious ideals of the *reconquista*), and perhaps enlist the Great Khan of China as an ally in the long struggle with Islam. If he failed, the "enterprise of the Indies" would cost little. The Spanish monarchs nonetheless kept Columbus waiting nearly seven years—until 1492, when the last Muslim stronghold at Granada fell to Spanish forces—before they gave him their support.

After thirty-three days at sea, Columbus and his men reached the Bahamas, probably landing on what is now called Watling Island. They spent four

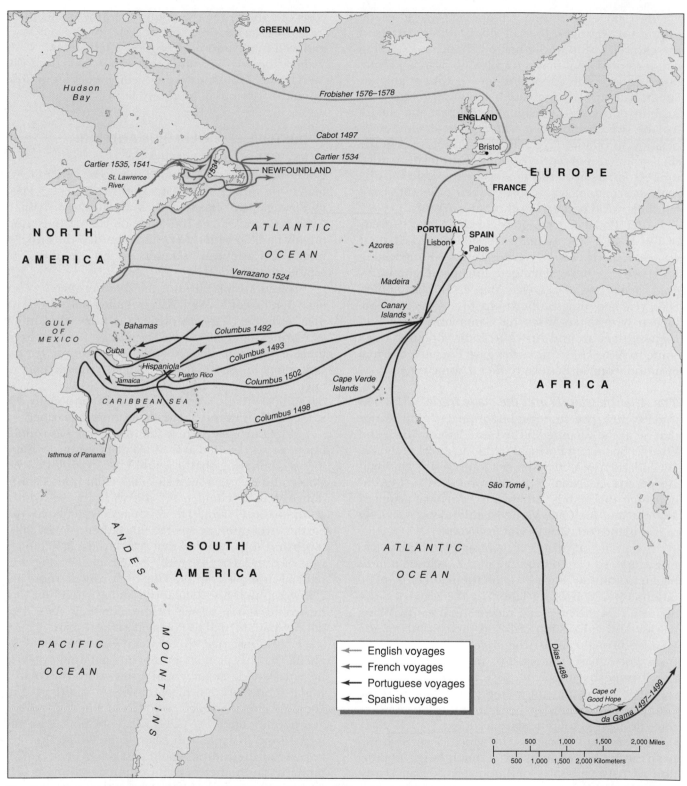

MAP 1-3   European Voyages of Discovery in the Atlantic in the Fifteenth and Sixteenth Centuries
During the fifteenth and sixteenth centuries, Europeans embarked on voyages of discovery that carried them to both Asia and the Americas. Portugal dominated the ocean trade with Asia for most of this period. In the New World, reports of Spain's acquisition of vast wealth soon led France and England to attempt to establish their own territorial claims.

A decidedly European view of Columbus's landing on Guana-hani appears in this late sixteenth-century print. Columbus and his men, armed with guns and swords, are resplendent in European attire, while nearly naked Indians offer them gifts. To the left, Spaniards erect a cross to claim the land for Christianity. In the upper right, frightened natives flee into the woods.

months exploring the Caribbean and visiting several islands, including Hispaniola (now the site of Haiti and the Dominican Republic) and Cuba. Although puzzled not to find the fabled cities of China or Japan, Columbus believed that he had reached Asia. Three more voyages, between 1493 and 1504, however, failed to yield clear evidence of an Asian landfall or samples of Asian riches. Columbus reported that the islands he encountered contained "great mines of gold and other metals" and spices in abundance, yet all he brought back to Isabella and Ferdinand were strange plants and animals, some gold ornaments, and several kidnapped Taino Indians.

Obsessed with the wealth he had promised himself and others, Columbus and his men turned vio-lent, sacking the villages of Tainos and Caribs and demanding tribute in gold. But Caribbean gold reserves, found mainly on Hispaniola, Puerto Rico, and Cuba, were not extensive. The Spanish forced native gangs to pan rivers for the precious nuggets. Dissatisfied with the meager results, Columbus sought other sources of wealth. His plan to enslave islanders was a desperate attempt to show that the Indies could yield a profit. It earned him a sharp rebuke from Queen Isabella, who, at least initially, opposed enslaving people she considered to be new Spanish subjects. This royal fastidiousness was short-lived, however. Within thirty years of Columbus's first voyage, Spanish exploitation of native labor had brought the native populations of many Caribbean islands close to extinction.

Columbus died in Spain in 1506, still convinced he had found Asia. What he had done was to set in motion a process that would transform both sides of the Atlantic. It would eventually bring wealth to many Europeans and immense suffering to Native Americans and Africans.

THE SPANISH CONQUEST AND COLONIZATION

Of all European nations, Spain was best suited to take advantage of Columbus's discovery. Its experience with the *reconquista* gave it both a religious justification for conquest (bringing Christianity to nonbelievers) and an army of seasoned soldiers—*conquistadores*—eager to seek their fortunes in America now that the last Muslims had been expelled from Spain. In addition, during the *reconquista* and the conquest of the Canary Islands, Spain's rulers had developed efficient techniques for controlling newly conquered lands that could be applied to New World colonies.

The Spanish first consolidated their control of the Caribbean, establishing outposts on Cuba, Puerto Rico, and Jamaica (see Map 1–4). The *conquistadores*

First published in 1535, this woodcut shows Taino Indians panning for gold. Columbus and his men, desperate for riches to bring back to Spain but unaware that gold reserves on most Caribbean islands were quite small, compelled the Indians to search for the precious metal. After only a few decades of forced labor and harsh treatment, the native populations of the islands had all but disappeared.

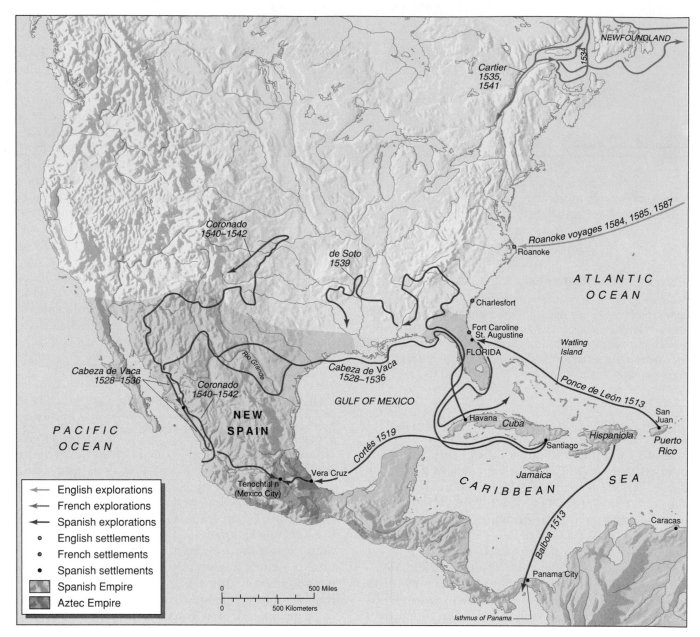

MAP 1-4   Spanish, English, and French Settlements in North America in the Sixteenth Century
By the end of the sixteenth century, only Spain had established permanent settlements in North America. French outposts in Canada and at Fort Caroline, as well as the English settlement at Roanoke, failed to thrive. European rivalries for North America, however, would intensify after 1600.

were more interested in finding gold and slaves than in creating permanent settlements. Leaving a trail of destruction, they attacked native villages and killed or captured the inhabitants. By 1524, the Tainos had all but died out; the Caribs survived on more isolated islands until the eighteenth century. Spanish soldiers then ventured to the mainland. Juan Ponce de León led an expedition to Florida in 1513. In that same

year, Vasco Núñez de Balboa arrived in Central America, crossing the isthmus of Panama to the Pacific Ocean.

The end of the Aztec Empire.   In 1519, Hernán Cortés and six hundred soldiers—the light-skinned strangers who inspired the Indian messenger to rush to Moctezuma—landed on the coast of Mexico. Their subsequent actions more than fulfilled the Aztec king's belief that the Spaniards' arrival was an evil omen. "I and my companions," Cortés announced, "suffer from a disease of the heart which can be cured only with gold." By 1521, Cortés and his men had conquered the powerful Aztec empire. The Spanish soldiers also discovered riches beyond their wildest dreams. They "picked up the gold and fingered it like monkeys," reported one Aztec witness. They were "transported by joy, as if their hearts were illumined and made new."

The swift, decisive Spanish victory depended on several factors. In part, the Spanish enjoyed certain technological advantages. Their guns and horses often enabled them to overwhelm larger groups of Aztec foot soldiers armed with spears and wooden swords edged with obsidian. But technology alone cannot account for the conquest of a vastly more numerous enemy, capable of absorbing far higher losses in combat.

Cortés benefited from two other factors. First, he exploited divisions within the Aztec empire. The Spanish acquired indispensable allies among subject Indians who resented Aztec domination, tribute demands, and seizure of captives for religious sacrifice. Cortés led only six hundred Spanish soldiers but eventually gained 200,000 Indian allies eager to throw off Aztec rule.

A second and more important factor was disease. One of Cortés's men was infected with smallpox, which soon devastated the native population. European diseases had been unknown in the Americas, and Indians lacked resistance to them. Historians estimate that nearly 40 percent of the inhabitants of central Mexico died of smallpox within a year. Other diseases followed, including typhus, measles, and influenza. By 1600, the population of Mexico may have declined from over 15 million to less than a million people.

In this illustration from a Spanish monk's history of the Aztecs, Moctezuma observes a comet plummeting toward the earth, an omen that he believed presaged disaster for his people. The appearance of the comet coincided with the first reports of white-skinned strangers arriving on the coast of Mexico.

AMERICAN VIEWS

Cabeza de Vaca among the Indians (1530)

Álvar Núñez Cabeza de Vaca came to the New World in 1527 in search of riches, not suffering. But the Spanish expedition of which he was a member met disaster shortly after it arrived in Florida on a mission to conquer the region north of the Gulf of Mexico. Of an original group of three hundred soldiers, only Cabeza de Vaca and three other men (including one African slave) survived. They did so by walking thousands of miles overland from the Gulf Coast to northern Mexico, an eight-year-long ordeal that tested the men's wits and physical endurance. Instead of entering Indian villages as proud conquistadors, Cabeza de Vaca and his companions encountered native peoples from a position of weakness. In order to survive, they had to adapt to the ways of the peoples across whose land they passed. After Cabeza de Vaca made it back to Mexico City, he described his experiences in an official report to the King of Spain. This remarkable document offers vivid descriptions of the territory extending from northern Florida to northern Mexico and the many peoples who inhabited it. It is equally interesting, as this extract suggests, for what it reveals about Cabeza de Vaca himself and the changes he made in the interest of survival.

- While living among the Capoques, what sort of work did Cabeza de Vaca have to do, and why?
- Why did Cabeza de Vaca decide to become a merchant? What advantages did this way of life offer him?
- Why did the Indians welcome Cabeza de Vaca into their communities, even though he was a stranger?

Aztec society and culture collapsed in the face of appalling mortality. "The illness was so dreadful," one survivor recalled, "that no one could walk or move. The sick were so utterly helpless that they could only lie on their beds like corpses, unable to move their limbs or even their heads. . . . If they did move their bodies, they screamed with pain." The epidemic ravaged families, wiped out whole villages, and destroyed traditional political authority. Early in their bid to gain control of the Aztec empire, the Spanish seized Moctezuma, and eventually put him to death. They did not have to kill his successor, however, for he died of disease less than three months after gaining the throne.

The fall of the Inca Empire.   In 1532, Francisco Pizarro and 180 men, following rumors of even greater riches than those of Mexico, discovered the Inca empire high in the Peruvian Andes. It was the largest empire in the Americas, stretching more than two thousand miles from what is now Ecuador to Chile. An excellent network of roads and bridges linked this extensive territory to the imperial capital of Cuzco. Economically prosperous from trade and agricultural production based on complex irrigation systems, the empire was also prone to political division. The Spaniards arrived at a moment of weakness for the empire. A few years before, the Inca ruler had died, probably from smallpox, and civil war had broken out between two of his sons. The victor, Atahualpa, was on his way from the empire's northern provinces to claim his throne in Cuzco when Pizarro intercepted him. Pizarro took Atahualpa hostage and despite receiving a colossal ransom—a roomful of gold and silver—had him killed. The Spaniards then captured Cuzco, eventually extended control over the whole empire, and established a new capital at Lima.

I had to stay with the Capoques more than a year. Because of the hard work they put me to, and their harsh treatment, I resolved to flee to the people of Charruco in the forests of the main.... My life had become unbearable. In addition to much other work, I had to grub roots in the water or from underground in the canebrakes. My fingers got so raw that if a straw touched them they would bleed. The broken canes often slashed my flesh; I had to work amidst them without benefit of clothes.

So I set to contriving how I might transfer to the forest-dwellers, who looked more propitious. My solution was to turn to trade.

[Escaping to Charruco about February 1530,] I did my best to devise ways of making my traffic profitable so I could get food and good treatment. The various Indians would beg me to go from one quarter to another for things they needed; their incessant hostilities made it impossible for them to travel cross-country or make many exchanges.

But as a neutral merchant I went into the interior as far as I pleased.... My principal wares were cones and other pieces of sea-snail, conchs used for cutting, sea-beads, and a fruit like a bean [from mesquite trees] which the Indians value very highly, using it for a medicine and for a ritual beverage in their dances and festivities. This is the sort of thing I carried inland. By barter I got and brought back to the coast skins, red ochre which they rub on their faces, hard canes for arrows, flint for arrowheads, with sinews and cement to attach them, and tassels of deer hair which they dye red.

This occupation suited me; I could travel where I wished, was not obliged to work, and was not a slave. Wherever I went, the Indians treated me honorably and gave me food, because they liked my commodities. They were glad to see me when I came and delighted to be brought what they wanted. I became well known; those who did not know me personally knew me by reputation and sought my acquaintance. This served my main purpose, which all the while was to determine an eventual road out.

Source: Cyclone Covey, ed., *Cabeza de Vaca's Adventures in the Unknown Interior of America*, pp. 66–67. Reprinted by permission of Scribner, a Division of Simon & Schuster. © 1961 by Macmillan Publishing Company.

By 1550, Spain's New World empire extended from the Caribbean through Mexico to Peru. It was administered from Spain by the Council of the Indies, which enacted laws for the empire and supervised an elaborate bureaucracy charged with their enforcement. The council aimed to project royal authority into every village in New Spain in order to maintain political control and extract as much wealth as possible from the land and its people.

For more than a century, Spanish ships crossed the Atlantic carrying seemingly limitless amounts of silver, gold, and jewels from the colonies. To extract this wealth, the colonial rulers subjected the native inhabitants of New Spain to compulsory tribute payments and forced labor. Tens of thousands of Indians toiled in silver mines in Peru and Bolivia and on sugar plantations in the Caribbean. When necessary, Spaniards imported African slaves to supplement a native labor force ravaged by disease and exhaustion.

Spanish incursions to the north. The desire for gold eventually lured Spaniards farther into North America. In 1528, an expedition to Florida ended in disaster when the Spanish intruders provoked an attack by Apalachee Indians. Most of the Spanish survivors eventually perished, but Álvar Núñez Cabeza de Vaca and three other men (including an African slave) escaped from their captors and managed to reach Mexico after a grueling eight-year journey. In a published account of his ordeal, Cabeza de Vaca insisted that the interior of North America contained a fabulously wealthy empire (see "American Views: Cabeza de Vaca among the Indians").

This report inspired other Spaniards to seek the treasures that had eluded its author. In 1539, Hernán de Soto—who tried unsuccessfully to get Cabeza de Vaca to serve as a guide—led an expedition from Florida to the Mississippi River. Along the way, the Spaniards harassed the native peoples, demanding provisions, burning villages, and capturing women to be servants and concubines. De Soto, who reportedly enjoyed "the sport of hunting Indians on horseback," ordered natives who resisted him to be mutilated, thrown to dogs, or burned alive. He and his men also exposed the Indians to deadly European diseases. Although weakened by native resistance, the expedition kept up its rampage for three years, turning toward Mexico only after de Soto died in 1542. In these same years, Francisco Vásquez de Coronado led three hundred troops on an equally destructive expedition through present-day Arizona, New Mexico, and Colorado on a futile search for the mythical Seven Cities of Cíbola, rumored to contain hoards of gold and precious stones.

The failure to find gold and silver halted the Spanish attempt to extend their empire to the north. By the end of the sixteenth century, they maintained just two precarious footholds north of Mexico. One was at St. Augustine, on Florida's Atlantic coast. Founded in 1565, this fortified outpost served as a naval base to defend Spanish treasure fleets from raids by English and French privateers. The other settlement was located far to the west in what is now New Mexico. Juan de Oñate, on a futile search for silver mines, claimed the region for Spain in 1598. He and his men proceeded to antagonize the area's inhabitants. In one surprise attack, the Spaniards destroyed the ancient town of Acoma, killing or enslaving most of the residents. Having earned the enmity of the Pueblo people—astonishing even his own superiors with his brutality—Oñate barely managed to keep his tiny colony together.

Almost from the start of the conquest, the bloody tactics of men such as Oñate aroused protest back in Spain. The Indians' most eloquent advocate was Bartolomé de Las Casas, a Dominican priest shamed by his own role (as a layman) in the conquest of Hispaniola. In 1516, the Spanish king appointed him to the newly created office of Protector of the Indians, but his efforts had little effect. To publicize the horrors he saw, Las Casas wrote *In Defense of the Indians*, including graphic descriptions of native sufferings. Instead of eliciting Spanish reforms, however, his work inspired Protestant Europeans to create the "Black Legend," an exaggerated story according to which a fanatical Catholic Spain sought to spread its control at any cost.

The seeds of economic decline.

Meanwhile, the vast riches of Central and South America glutted Spain's treasury. Between 1500 and 1650, an estimated 181 tons of gold and 16,000 tons of silver were shipped from the New World to Spain, making it the richest and most powerful state in Europe (see Figure 1–1). But this influx of American treasure had unforeseen consequences that would soon undermine Spanish predominance.

In 1492, the Spanish crown, determined to impose religious conformity after the *reconquista*, expelled from Spain all Jews who refused to become Christians. The refugees included many leading merchants who had contributed significantly to Spain's economy. The remaining Christian merchants, now awash in American riches, saw no reason

FIGURE 1-1 **Value of New World Treasure Imported into Spain, 1506–1655**
During the sixteenth and early seventeenth centuries, Spain was the only European power to reap great wealth from North America. The influx of New World treasure, however, slowed the development of Spain's economy in the long run. [Note: A ducat was a gold coin.]

Data Source: J.H. Elliott, *Imperial Spain, 1469–1716* (1964), p. 175.

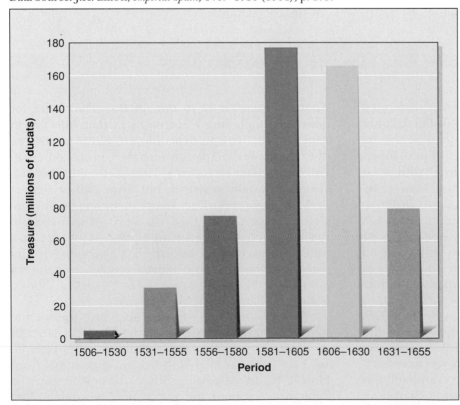

Overview

The Columbian Exchange

	From Old World to New World	From New World to Old World
Diseases	Smallpox, measles, plague, typhus, influenza, yellow fever, diphtheria, scarlet fever	Syphilis
Animals	Horses, cattle, pigs, sheep, goats, donkeys, mules, black rats, honeybees, cockroaches	Turkeys
Plants	Wheat, sugar, barley, coffee, rice, dandelion and other weeds	Maize, beans, peanut, potato, sweet potato, manioc, squash, papaya, guava, tomato, avocado, pineapple, chili pepper, cocoa

to invest in new trade or productive enterprises that might have sustained the economy once the flow of New World treasure diminished. As a result, Spain's economy eventually stagnated.

Compounding the problem, the flood of American gold and silver inflated prices throughout Europe, hurting both workers, whose wages failed to rise as fast, and aristocrats, who were dependent on fixed rents from their estates. Most damaging of all, Spain's monarchs wasted their American wealth fighting expensive wars against their European enemies that ultimately only weakened the nation. By 1600, some disillusioned Spaniards were arguing that the conquest had brought more problems than benefits to their country.

THE COLUMBIAN EXCHANGE

Spain's long-term economic decline was just one of many consequences of the conquest of the New World. The arrival of Europeans in America set in motion a whole series of changes. In the long run, the biological consequences of contact—what one historian has called the **Columbian Exchange**—proved to be the most momentous (see the Overview table, "The Columbian Exchange").

The most catastrophic result of the exchange was the exposure of Native Americans to Old World diseases. Europeans and Africans, long exposed to these diseases, had developed some immunity to them. Native Americans, lacking such contact, had not. The Black Death of 1347–1351, Europe's worst epidemic, killed perhaps a third of its population. Epidemics of smallpox, measles, typhus, and influenza struck Native Americans with far greater force, killing half, and sometimes as much as 90 percent, of the people in communities exposed to them. The only American disease to infect the Old World was syphilis, a serious but far less catastrophic malady, which appeared in Spain just after Columbus returned from his first voyage.

Another important aspect of the Columbian exchange was the introduction of Old World livestock to the New World, which began when Columbus brought horses, sheep, cattle, pigs, and goats with him on his second voyage in 1493. Native Americans had few domesticated animals (mainly dogs, and, in the Peruvian Andes, llamas and alpacas). The large European beasts created problems as well as opportunities for native peoples. With few natural predators to limit their numbers, livestock populations boomed in the New World, competing with native mammals for grazing. At least at first, the Indians' unfamiliarity with the use of horses in warfare often gave mounted European soldiers a decisive military advantage. But some native groups adopted these animals for their own purposes. Yaquis, Pueblos, and other peoples in the Southwest began to raise cattle and sheep. By the eighteenth century, Plains Indians had reoriented their culture around the use of horses, which had become essential for travel, hunting buffalo, and carrying burdens. Horses also became a primary object for trading and raiding among Plains peoples.

European ships carried unintentional passengers as well. The black rat, a carrier of disease, arrived on the first voyages. So did insects, including honeybees, previously unknown in the New World. Ships also brought weeds such as thistles and dandelions, whose seeds were often embedded in hay for animal fodder.

Europeans brought a variety of seeds and plants in order to grow familiar foods. Columbus's men planted wheat, chickpeas, melons, onions, and fruit trees on Caribbean islands. Although they optimistically reported that crops "sprouted in three days and were ready to eat by the twenty-fifth day," they—and later colonists—often found that European plants

Smallpox wreaked havoc among Native Americans who lacked biological resistance to European diseases. This drawing by Aztec illustrators shows Aztec victims of a smallpox epidemic that struck Tenochtitlán in 1520. Historians estimate that up to 40 percent of the population of central Mexico died within a year. This catastrophic decline weakened the Aztecs' ability to resist the Spanish conquest of their land.

did not always grow quite so easily. As a result, Europeans learned to cultivate native foods, such as corn, tomatoes, squash, beans, and potatoes, as well as non-food plants such as tobacco and cotton. They carried many of these plants back to Europe, enriching Old World diets with new foods. By the late seventeenth century, potatoes had become the mainstay of the Irish diet. Throughout Europe, new foods contributed to a sharp rise in population—thus, in time, swelling the numbers of Europeans eager to leave their overcrowded communities for the New World.

CULTURAL PERCEPTIONS AND MISPERCEPTIONS

For thousands of years, Indian and European societies developed in isolation from one another. When members of these societies met for the first time, confusion inevitably resulted. Even simple transactions produced unexpected results. When Columbus showed swords to Caribbean islanders, for example, "they took them by the edge and through ignorance cut themselves" because they had never touched metal weapons. The first Indians whom Cortés allowed aboard a Spanish ship fainted at the sound of a large cannon being fired. French explorers were similarly taken by surprise when they choked while smoking

Iroquois tobacco, which they thought tasted like "powdered pepper." These were relatively minor mishaps and were soon overshadowed by more substantial interactions which seemed to exaggerate the differences between Indians and Europeans.

Religion was extremely important to both Native Americans and Europeans, but differences in forms and practices encouraged misunderstandings. Most Indians believed that the universe contained friendly and hostile spiritual forces in human and other-than-human forms (such as plants, animals, and stars). People interacted with the spirit world through ceremonies that often involved exchanging gifts and performing certain rituals. North of Mexico, Indians passed on religious beliefs through oral traditions, not in writing. To Europeans accustomed to worshiping one God in an organized church and preserving their beliefs in a written Bible, Indian traditions were incomprehensible. When Columbus noted that the Tainos on the Caribbean island of Guanahani had no churches, he concluded that "I do not detect in them any religion." Some Europeans, including Cortés, went further, assuming that Indians worshiped the Devil. Indians, in turn, often found Christianity confusing and at first rejected European pressure to convert. As some Iroquois explained to colonists, "We do not know that God, we have never seen him, we know not who he is."

Different understandings of the roles of men and women provided another source of confusion. Europeans assumed that men were naturally superior to women and should dominate them and rule society. They disapproved of the less rigid gender divisions among Native American peoples. Wampanoags and Powhatans sometimes accepted female leaders, for instance, and Huron women helped to select male chiefs. Many Indian societies, including the Pueblos, Hurons, and Iroquois, were matrilineal, tracing descent through the mother's family instead of the father's, as Europeans did. In matrilineal societies, married couples lived with the wife's family, children inherited property from their mother's brother, and rulers succeeded to their positions through their mother's family line. Europeans, accustomed to societies in which men did most agri-cultural work, also objected to Indian women's dom-inant role in farming and assumed that men's hunting was more for recreation than subsistence. They often concluded that Indian women lived "a most slavish life." Indians, in turn, sometimes thought that European men failed to make good use of their wives. In Massachusetts, some native men ridiculed colonists "for spoiling good working crea-tures" by not making their women work in the fields.

These were some of the many cultural differ-ences that separated Indian and European societies. In order for natives and newcomers to get along peaceably with each other, each side would have to adapt to the new circumstances under which both groups now lived. At first, such harmony seemed possible. Columbus initially reported that the Taino Indians "became so much our friends that it was a marvel." But it soon became clear that Europeans intended to dominate the lands they discovered. Only three days after he arrived in America, Colum-bus announced his intention "not to pass by any is-land of which I did not take possession" and soon speculated on the possibility of enslaving Indians. Such claims to dominance sparked vigorous resis-tance from native peoples everywhere who strove to maintain their autonomy in a changed world.

COMPETITION FOR A CONTINENT

Spain's New World bonanza attracted the attention of other European states eager to share in the wealth. Portugal soon acquired its own profitable piece of South America. In 1494, the pope resolved the conflicting claims of Portugal and Spain with the **Treaty of Tordesillas**. The treaty drew a north–south line approximately 1,100 miles west of the Cape Verde Islands. Spain received all lands west of the line, while Portugal held sway to the east. This lim-ited Portugal's New World empire to Brazil, where settlers followed the precedent of the Atlantic island colonies and established sugar plantations worked by slave labor. But the treaty also protected Portugal's claims in Africa and Asia, which lay east of the line.

France and England, of course, rejected the papal grant of the Western Hemisphere to Spain and Portugal. Their initial challenges to Spanish domi-nance in the New World, however, proved quite fee-ble. Domestic troubles—largely sparked by the Protestant Reformation—distracted the two coun-tries from the pursuit of empire. By the close of the sixteenth century, both France and England insisted on their rights to New World lands, but neither had created a permanent settlement to support its claim.

EARLY FRENCH EFFORTS IN NORTH AMERICA

France was a relative latecomer to New World explo-ration. In 1494, French troops invaded Italy, begin-ning a long and ultimately unsuccessful war with the Holy Roman Empire. Preoccupied with European af-fairs, France's rulers paid little attention to America. But when news of Cortés's exploits in Mexico arrived in the 1520s, King Francis I wanted his own New World empire to enrich France and block further Spanish expansion.

In 1524, Francis sponsored a voyage by Giovanni da Verrazano, an Italian navigator, who mapped the North American coast from present-day South Car-olina to Maine. During the 1530s and 1540s, the French mariner Jacques Cartier made three voyages in search of rich mines to rival those of Mexico and Peru. He explored the St. Lawrence River up to what is now Montreal, hoping to discover a water route through the continent to Asia (what came to be called the Northwest Passage). His second voyage, in 1535, nearly ended in disaster. Unaware of the harsh-ness of Canadian winters, he and his crew almost froze to death and suffered from scurvy, a disease caused by a lack of vitamin C. Many men died, and the rest survived only because the Iroquois showed them how to make a vitamin-rich concoction of boiled white cedar needles and bark.

On his third voyage, in 1541, Cartier was to serve under the command of a nobleman, Jean-François de la Rocque, Sieur de Roberval, who was commis-sioned by the king to establish a permanent settle-ment in Canada. Troubles in recruiting colonists delayed Roberval, who—when he finally set sail in 1542—ended up taking convicts as his settlers. Cartier sailed ahead, gathered samples of what he thought were gold and diamonds, and returned to France without Roberval's permission.

This first attempt to found a permanent French colony failed miserably. Roberval's expedition was poorly organized, and his cruel treatment of the con-victs provoked several uprisings. The Iroquois, suspi-cious of repeated French intrusions on their lands, saw no reason to help them. A year after they arrived in Canada, Roberval and the surviving colonists were back in France. Their return coincided with news that the gold brought back by Cartier was iron pyrite ("fool's gold") and the diamonds were worthless quartz crystals.

Disappointed with their Canadian expeditions, the French made a few brief forays to the south, establishing outposts in what is now South Carolina in 1562 and Florida in 1564. They soon abandoned the Carolina colony (though not before the starving settlers resorted to cannibalism), and Spanish forces captured the Florida fort. Then, back in France, a prolonged civil war broke out between Catholics and Protestants. Renewed interest in colonization would have to await the return of peace at home.

ENGLISH ATTEMPTS IN THE NEW WORLD

The English were quicker than the French to stake a claim to the New World but no more successful at colonization. In 1497, King Henry VII sent John Cabot, an Italian mariner, to explore eastern Canada on England's behalf. But neither Henry nor any of his wealthy subjects would invest the funds necessary to follow up on Cabot's discoveries. For nearly half a century, English contact with America was limited to the seasonal voyages of fishermen who lived each summer in Newfoundland, fished offshore, and returned in autumn with ships full of cod.

The lapse in English activity in the New World stemmed from religious troubles at home. Between 1534 and 1558, England changed its official religion several times. King Henry VIII, who had once defended the Catholic Church against its critics, took up the Protestant cause when the pope refused to annul his marriage to Catherine of Aragon. In 1534, Henry declared himself the head of a separate Church of England and seized the Catholic Church's English property. Because many English people sympathized with the Protestant cause, there was relatively little opposition to Henry's actions. But in 1553, Mary—daughter of the spurned Catherine of Aragon—became queen and tried to bring England back to Catholicism. She had nearly three hundred Protestants burned at the stake for their beliefs (earning her the nickname "Bloody Mary"), and many others went into exile in Europe.

After Mary's brief but destructive reign, which ended with her death in 1558, her half-sister Elizabeth, a committed Protestant, became queen. Elizabeth ruled for forty-five years (1558–1603), restoring Protestantism as the state religion, bringing stability to the nation, and renewing England's interest in the New World. She and her subjects saw colonization not only as a way to gain wealth and political advantage but also as a Protestant crusade against Catholic domination.

The Colonization of Ireland.
England's first target for colonization, however, was not America but Ireland. Located less than 60 miles west of England and populated by Catholics, Ireland threatened to be-

come a base from which Spain or another Catholic power might invade England. Henry VIII had tried, with limited success, to bring the island under English control in the 1530s and 1540s. Elizabeth renewed the attempt in the 1560s with a series of brutal expeditions that destroyed Irish villages and slaughtered the inhabitants. Several veterans of these campaigns later took part in New World colonization and drew on their Irish experience for guidance.

Two aspects of that experience were particularly important. First, the English transferred their assumptions about Irish "savages" to Native Americans. Englishmen in America frequently observed similarities between Indians and the Irish. "When they [the Indians] have their apparel on they look like Irish," noted one Englishman. "The natives of New England," he added, "are accustomed to build their houses much like the wild Irish." Because the English held the "wild Irish" in contempt, these observations encouraged them to scorn the Indians. When Indians resisted their attempts at conquest, the English recalled the Irish example, claiming that native "savagery" required brutal suppression.

Second, the Irish experience influenced English ideas about colonial settlement. English conquerors set up "plantations" surrounded by palisades on seized Irish lands. These plantations were meant to be civilized outposts in a savage land. Their aristocratic owners imported Protestant tenants from England and Scotland to farm the land. Native Irish people, considered too wild to join proper Christian communities, were excluded. English colonists in America followed this precedent when they established plantations that separated English and native peoples.

Expeditions to the New World.
Sir Humphrey Gilbert, a notoriously cruel veteran of the Irish campaigns, became fascinated with the idea of New World colonization. He composed a treatise to convince Queen Elizabeth to support such an endeavor. The queen, who counted Gilbert among her favorite courtiers, authorized several exploratory voyages, including Martin Frobisher's three trips in 1576–1578 in search of the Northwest Passage to Asia. Frobisher failed to find the elusive passage and sent back shiploads of glittering ore that proved to be fool's gold. Elizabeth had better luck in allowing privateers, such as John Hawkins and Francis Drake, to raid Spanish ships and New World ports for gold and silver. The plunder taken during these raids enriched both the sailors and their investors—one of whom was the queen herself.

Meanwhile, Gilbert continued to promote New World settlement, arguing that it would increase

England's trade and provide a place for the nation's unemployed people. Like many of his contemporaries, Gilbert believed that England's "surplus" population threatened social order. The population was indeed growing, and economic changes often made it difficult for people to support themselves. Many landlords, for instance, had been converting farmland into sheep pastures. They profited from the wool trade, but their decision threw tenant families off the land. Gilbert suggested offering free land in America to English families willing to emigrate.

In 1578, Gilbert received permission to set up a colony along the North American coast. It took him five years to organize an expedition to Newfoundland, which he claimed for England. After sailing southward seeking a more favorable site for a colony, Gilbert headed home, only to be lost at sea during an Atlantic storm. The impetus for English colonization did not die with him, however, for his half-brother, Sir Walter Raleigh (another veteran of the Irish wars), immediately took up the cause.

The towne of Pomeiock and true forme of their howses, couered and encloſed ſome wᵗʰ matts, and ſome wᵗʰ barcks of trees. All compaſſed abowt wᵗʰ ſmale poles ſtuck thick together in ſtedd of a wall.

John White's picture of the village of Pomeiooc offers a rare glimpse of a sixteenth-century Eastern Woodlands Indian community. The village is surrounded by a palisade with two entrances; evidence suggests that White exaggerated the spacing of the poles in order to depict the houses inside. Eighteen dwellings constructed of poles and mats are clustered around the village circumference; inside some of them raised sleeping platforms can be seen. Many of the villagers are clustered around a central fire, while others are working or conversing.

The Roanoke Colony. In 1584, Raleigh sent an expedition to find a suitable location for a colony. Learning that the Carolina coast seemed promising, Raleigh sent men in 1585 to build a settlement on Roanoke Island. Most colonists were soldiers fresh from Ireland who refused to grow their own food, insisting that the Roanoke Indians should feed them. When the local chief, Wingina, organized native resistance, they killed him. Eventually, the colonists, disappointed not to have found gold or precious stones and exhausted by a harsh winter, returned to England in 1586.

Two members of these early expeditions, however, left a more positive legacy. Thomas Hariot studied the Roanoke and Croatoan Indians and identified plants and animals in the area, hoping that some might prove to be profitable commodities. John White drew maps and painted a series of watercolors depicting the natives and the coastal landscape. When Raleigh tried once more, in 1587, to found a colony, he chose White to be its leader.

This attempt also failed. The ship captain dumped the settlers—who, for the first time, included women and children—on Roanoke Island so that he could pursue Spanish treasure ships. White waited until his granddaughter, Virginia Dare (the first English child born in America), was safely born and then sailed to England for supplies. But the outbreak of war with Spain delayed his return for three years. Spain had gathered an immense fleet to invade England, and all English ships were needed for defense. Although England defeated the Armada in

FROM THEN TO NOW

The Disappearance of Cod off the Grand Banks

Not long after John Cabot returned from his voyage to America in 1497, rumors began to swirl in port towns and European capitals alike. The Italian mariner who had sailed on behalf of England, it was said, had discovered astonishingly rich fishing grounds. One envious diplomat reported to the duke of Milan that Cabot and his men had caught enormous numbers of cod simply by dropping weighted baskets into the sea. As it happened, Basque fishermen sailing from ports in northern Spain and southwestern France already knew about these fishing grounds. But Cabot's discovery spread the news and soon fishermen from all over western Europe scrambled to capture some of the bounty for themselves. By the 1550s, over a hundred ships a year traveled from French ports alone to fish in the waters of the Grand Banks off the coasts of Newfoundland and Labrador.

In 1994, on the eve of the five-hundredth anniversary of Cabot's historic voyage, Brian Tobin, a Canadian fisheries minister, reported that cod had become so scarce in the Grand Banks that fishing was no longer commercially viable. He announced that a moratorium on At-

lantic cod fishing, first declared in 1992, would have to be extended. This measure was the latest in a series of efforts to address the decline in the cod population. In 1977, Canada's government had prohibited foreign fishing vessels from working within 200 miles of the Canadian coast. Nine years later, foreign boats fishing just beyond the 200-mile limit were no longer allowed to visit the city of St. John's in Newfoundland for repairs and supplies. Although these measures were designed mainly to protect Canadian fisheries from competition rather than to address issues of conservation, they clearly recognized that a valuable resource was in grave danger.

How had such abundant codfish stocks declined so dramatically? Ecological and historical factors combined to produce this result. Cod prefer to swim near the ocean floor in shallow waters, and migrate to even shallower places rich in plankton and krill—such as the Grand Banks—when they are ready to spawn. These locations are particularly vulnerable to climatic change, and that in turn affects the cod. Ten years after Canada de-

1588, White could not obtain a relief ship for Roanoke until 1590.

White found the colony deserted. Digging through the ruins of the village, he found "my books torn from the covers, the frames of some of my pictures and Maps rotten and spoiled with rain." He also saw the word CROATOAN carved on a post and assumed that the colonists had moved to nearby Croatoan Island. But bad weather prevented him from searching there. For years, English and Spanish mariners reported seeing white people along the coast of Chesapeake Bay. But no Roanoke colonists were ever found. They may have moved to the mainland and intermarried with local Indians. One historian has speculated that they survived until 1607 when Powhatan Indians, angered by the appearance of more English settlers,

killed them. The actual fate of the "Lost Colony" at Roanoke will probably never be known.

At this point, Raleigh gave up on North America and turned his attention to his Irish plantations. But England's interest in colonization did not wane. In 1584, Richard Hakluyt had aroused enthusiasm for America by writing the *Discourse on the Western Planting* for the queen and her advisers. He argued that England would prosper from the expansion of trade and the sale of New World commodities. Once the Indians were civilized, Hakluyt added, they would eagerly purchase English goods. Equally important, England could plant "sincere religion" (that is, Protestant Christianity) in the New World and prevent the power of "the Spanish king from flowing over all the face . . . of America."

clared the moratorium on fishing, cod populations on the Grand Banks have yet to rebound. Some scientists speculate that the depletion of the Earth's ozone layer may be allowing ultraviolet rays to penetrate shallower ocean waters, killing off young cod at a high rate.

Centuries of fishing have also taken their toll. Cabot's voyage sparked tremendous interest in the Grand Banks fisheries. By the middle of the sixteenth century, 60 percent of all the fish eaten in Europe was cod, and most of it came from the Grand Banks region. English and French fishing enterprises found particularly lucrative markets in Mediterranean countries, whose primarily Catholic populations had to abstain from eating meat on Fridays and during the six weeks of Lent because of religious restrictions. By the eighteenth century, New England colonists, plying the waters off their own coast as well as near the Grand Banks, had initiated a thriving trade with the West Indies, where planters purchased relatively cheap salted cod to feed their slaves. After the Revolution, victorious Americans insisted that Great Britain recognize their "right to take fish of every kind on the Grand Bank." This provision became part of the 1783 Treaty of Paris, testify-

ing to the continued significance of the fishing industry.

Economic competition also encouraged technological developments. By the early nineteenth century, most fishermen had switched from using handlines—single baited hooks fastened to a weight and dropped in the water—to longlines, consisting of ropes anywhere from half a mile to four or more miles long, with baited hooks attached every three feet or so. Gill nets, positioned just above the ocean floor to catch "ground feeders" like cod, eventually made enormous catches possible. These changes, combined with the transition from sailing vessels to boats using first steam power and then diesel fuel, spelled doom for the once-plentiful supplies of cod on the Grand Banks.

Experts differ on whether cod populations can recover. In addition to the possible effects of climatic change, cod continue to be threatened by overfishing. In February of 2002, Canadian officials investigated reports of foreign boats ignoring the moratorium on cod and infringing on the 200-mile limit. The long-term legacy of John Cabot's voyage may well be the disappearance of the resource that drew him and so many early European adventurers to North America in the first place.

Hakluyt's arguments fired the imaginations of many people, and the defeat of the Spanish Armada only emboldened England to challenge Spain's New World dominance. The experience of Roanoke should have tempered that enthusiasm, illustrating the problems as well as benefits of colonization. The colony's fate underscored the need for adequate funding, the unsuitability of soldiers as colonists, and the need to maintain good relations with the Indians. But the English were slow to learn these lessons; when they resumed colonization efforts in 1607, they repeated Roanoke's mistakes, with disastrous results for the people involved. As it was, the sixteenth century ended with no permanent English settlement in the New World.

CONCLUSION

Dramatic changes occurred in North America during the century after Moctezuma's messenger spotted the Spanish ships. Europeans, eager for wealth and power, set out to claim a continent that just a hundred years earlier they had not dreamed existed. African slaves were brought to the Caribbean, Mexico, and Brazil, and forced to labor under extremely harsh conditions for white masters in unfamiliar lands. The Aztec and Incan empires collapsed in the wake of the Spanish conquest. In the Caribbean and parts of Mexico and Peru, untold numbers of native peoples succumbed to European diseases they had never before encountered.

And yet conditions in 1600 bore clearer witness to the past than to the future. Despite all that had happened, North America was still Indian country. Only Spain had established North American colonies, and even its soldiers struggled to expand north of Mexico. Spain's outposts in Florida and New Mexico staked claims to territory that it did not really control. Except in Mexico and the Caribbean, Europeans had merely touched the continent's shores—often only briefly. In 1600, despite the virulent epidemics, native peoples (even in Mexico) still greatly outnumbered European and African immigrants. The next century, however, brought many powerful challenges both to native control and to the Spanish monopoly of settlement.

REVIEW QUESTIONS

1. How did the Aztecs who first glimpsed Spanish ships off the coast of Mexico describe to Moctezuma what they had seen? What details most captured their attention?
2. Compare men's and women's roles in Native American, West African, and European societies. What were the similarities and differences? How did differences between European and Native American gender roles lead to misunderstandings?
3. Many of the first European colonizers in North America were military veterans. What impact did this have on their relations with Indian peoples?
4. Why did Spain so quickly become the dominant colonial power in North America? What advantages did it enjoy over France and England?
5. What role did religion play in early European efforts at overseas colonization? Did religious factors always encourage colonization, or did they occasionally interfere with European expansion?

KEY TERMS

Aztecs (p. 7)

Cahokia (p. 8)

Columbian Exchange (p. 25)

Predestination (p. 15)

Protestants (p. 15)

Reconquista (p. 14)

Reformation (p. 15)

Tordesillas, Treaty of (p. 27)

RECOMMENDED READING

Covey, Cyclone, ed. *Cabeza de Vaca's Adventures in the Unknown Interior of America* (1998). A remarkable account of the Spanish explorer's harrowing eight-year-long journey from Florida to Mexico.

Hassig, Ross. *Mexico and the Spanish Conquest* (1994). A brief account of Cortés's expedition, focusing on the military aspects of the Spanish conquest.

Josephy, Alvin M., Jr. *America in 1492: The World of the Indian Peoples before the Arrival of Columbus* (1991). A collection of essays describing the wide variety of Indian cultures in North America prior to contact with Europeans.

Leon-Portillo, Miguel. *The Broken Spears: The Aztec Account of the Conquest of Mexico* (1962). Reprints of translated Indian chronicles, providing a moving account of the Aztec experience of the Spanish conquest.

Phillips, William D., Jr., and Carla Rahn Phillips. *The Worlds of Christopher Columbus* (1992). A judicious biography of Columbus that places him firmly in the context of fifteenth-century European culture.

Thornton, John. *Africa and Africans in the Making of the Atlantic World, 1400–1680*, 2nd ed. (1998). A thorough examination of the causes and consequences of the movement of Africans throughout the Atlantic world and the rise of the slave trade.

ADDITIONAL SOURCES
Native American Cultures

Bragdon, Kathleen J. *Native People of Southern New England, 1500–1650* (1996).

Clendinnen, Inga. *Aztecs: An Interpretation* (1991).

Fagan, Brian M. *Ancient North America: The Archaeology of a Continent*, 3rd ed. (2000).

Fiedel, Stuart J. *Prehistory of the Americas*, 2nd ed. (1992).

Jennings, Francis. *The Founders of America: How Indians Discovered the Land, Pioneered in It, and Created Great Classical Civilizations . . .* (1993).

Milner, George. *The Cahokia Chiefdom: The Archaeology of a Mississippian Society* (1998).

Rouse, Irving. *The Tainos: Rise and Decline of the People Who Greeted Columbus* (1992).

West African Society

Bohannan, Paul, and Curtin, Philip. *Africa and Africans*, 3rd ed. (1988).

Fage, J. D. *A History of West Africa: An Introductory Survey*, 4th ed. (1969).

Olaniyan, Richard, ed. *African History and Culture* (1982).

Reader, John. *Africa: A Biography of the Continent* (1998).

Europe in the Age of Discovery

Bainton, Roland H. *Here I Stand: A Life of Martin Luther* (1955).

Braudel, Fernand. *The Mediterranean and the Mediterranean World in the Age of Philip II*, 2nd ed. (1966; English trans., 1972).

Canny, Nicholas. *Making Ireland British, 1580–1650* (2000).

Cantor, Norman F. *In the Wake of the Plague: The Black Death and the World It Made* (2001).

Cipolla, Carlo M. *Guns, Sails, and Empire: Technological Innovation and the Early Phases of European Expansion, 1400–1700* (1965).

Elliott, J. H. *Imperial Spain, 1469–1716* (1964).

Lewis, Bernard. *Cultures in Conflict: Christians, Muslims, and Jews in the Age of Discovery* (1995).

Morison, Samuel Eliot. *The European Discovery of America: The Northern Voyages, A.D. 500–1600* (1971).

Morison, Samuel Eliot. *The European Discovery of America: The Southern Voyages, A.D. 1492–1616* (1974).

Scammell, G. V. *The First Imperial Age: European Overseas Expansion, c. 1400–1715* (1989).

Conquest and Colonization

Andrews, Kenneth R. *Trade, Plunder, and Settlement: Maritime Enterprise and the Genesis of the British Empire, 1480–1630* (1984).

Crosby, Alfred W., Jr. *Ecological Imperialism: The Biological Expansion of Europe, 900-1900* (1986).

De Las Casas, Bartolomé. *Short Account of the Destruction of the Indies* (several editions).

Eccles, W. J. *France in America*, rev. ed. (1990).

Elliott, J. H. *The Old World and the New, 1492–1650* (1970).

Hudson, Charles. *Knights of Spain, Warriors of the Sun: Hernando de Soto and the South's Ancient Chiefdoms* (1997).

Kupperman, Karen Ordahl. *Roanoke: The Abandoned Colony* (1984).

Meinig, D. W. *The Shaping of America*, Vol. 1: *Atlantic America, 1492–1800* (1986).

Seed, Patricia. *Ceremonies of Possession in Europe's Conquest of the New World 1492–1640* (1995).

Todorov, Tzvetan. *The Conquest of America* (1984).

Weber, David J. *The Spanish Frontier in North America* (1992).

WHERE TO LEARN MORE

- **Cahokia Mounds State Historic Site, Collinsville, Illinois.** This site, occupied from A.D. 600-1500, was the largest Mississippian community in eastern North America. It now includes numerous exhibits, and archaeological excavations continue in the vicinity. The website, www.siue.edu/CAHOKIAMOUNDS, contains information and photos of archaeological excavations, as well as a link to a virtual tour.

- **Mashantucket Pequot Museum, Mashantucket, Connecticut.** This tribally owned and operated complex offers a view of eastern Woodlands Indian life, focusing on the Pequots of eastern Connecticut. Exhibits include dioramas, films, interactive programs, and a reconstructed sixteenth-century Pequot village. The homepage for the Mashantucket Pequot Museum and Research Center is www.mashantucket.com.

- **Mesa Verde National Park, Colorado.** Occupied by Ancestral Puebloan peoples as early as A.D. 550, the area contains a variety of sites, from early pithouses to spectacular cliff dwellings. The official National Park webpage for Mesa Verde is www.nps.gov/meve. Information on individual houses and sites within the park, plus travel and lodging information can be found at www.mesa.verde.national-park.com.

- **St. Augustine, Florida.** Founded in 1565, St. Augustine is the site of the first permanent Spanish settlement in North America. Today the restored community resembles a Spanish colonial town, with narrow, winding streets and seventeenth- and eighteenth-century buildings. The site also contains the restored Castillo de San Marcos, now a national park. The official website for Historic St. Augustine, www.oldcity.com/his2.html, provides considerable information about the origins and development of the Spanish settlement.

 Please refer to the document CD-ROM for primary sources related to this chapter.

➜ *The unknown artist who painted this portrait of Elizabeth Freake and her daughter Mary (c.1671) captured the quiet elegance of prosperous second-generation New Englanders. The wife of a successful merchant, Mrs. Freake wears a pearl necklace and a skirt edged with gold embroidery. Her collar, and her baby's bonnet and sleeves, are edged with fine Dutch lace.*

Oil on canvas, 42 1/2 x 36 3/4 in. (108 x 93.4 cm). Worcester Art Museum. Worcester, Massachusetts.

TRANSPLANTATION 1600–1685

CHAPTER OUTLINE

The French in North America
The Quest for Furs and Converts
The Development of New France

The Dutch Overseas Empire
The Dutch East India Company
The West India Company and New Netherland

English Settlement in the Chesapeake
The Ordeal of Early Virginia
The Importance of Tobacco
Maryland: A Refuge for Catholics
Life in the Chesapeake Colonies

The Founding of New England
The Pilgrims and Plymouth Colony
Massachusetts Bay Colony and Its Offshoots
Families, Farms, and Communities in Early New England

Competition in the Caribbean
Sugar and Slaves
A Biracial Society

The Proprietary Colonies
Early Carolina: Colonial Aristocracy and Slave Labor
Pennsylvania: The Dream of Toleration and Peace
New Netherland Becomes New York

Conclusion

Boston in New England
March 28, 1631

To the Right Honorable my very good lady, the Lady Bridget, Countess of Lincoln,
Madam:

I have . . . thought fit to commit to memory our present condition and what hath befallen us since our arrival here . . . . [I] must do [so] rudely, having yet no table nor other room to write in than by the fireside upon my knee in this sharp winter. . . .

[In] April 1630 we set sail from old England with four good ships. And in May following, eight more followed, two having gone before in February and March and two more following in June and August, besides another set out by a private merchant. These seventeen ships arrived all safe in New England for the increase of the plantation here this year 1630, but made a long, a troublesome and costly voyage, being all windbound long in England and hindered with contrary winds after they set sail, and so scattered with mists and tempests that few of them arrived together. . . .

[Once we disembarked in mid-June, after more than nine weeks at sea] we began to consult of the place of our sitting down, for Salem, where we landed, pleased us not. And to that purpose some were sent to the Bay to search up the rivers for a convenient place. . . . [We] found a place . . . three leagues up Charles river, and thereupon unshipped our goods into other vessels and with much cost and labor brought them in July to Charlestowne, but there receiving advertisements by some of the late arrived ships from London and Amsterdam of some French preparations against us . . . we were forced to change counsel and for our present shelter to plant dispersedly. . . . This dispersion troubled some of us, but help it we could not. . . . The best counsel we could find out was to build a fort to retire to, in some convenient place, if an enemy pressed thereunto, after we should have fortified ourselves against the injuries of wet and cold.

Everett Emerson, ed., *Letters from New England: The Massachusetts Bay Colony, 1629–1638* (Amherst, 1976).

Thomas Dudley, the man who wrote this letter, was 54 years old when he decided to move with his family to New England. He had reached an age when most men avoided making such major changes in their lives. Married for 27 years, Thomas and his wife Dorothy had six children ranging in age from 9 to 25 years old. Dudley had prospered in England by working as a steward for local aristocrats, including the Countess of Lincoln to whom he addressed his letter. A man of talent and education, he had been chosen to serve as deputy governor of the new colony of Massachusetts. Eager as he was to see the colony succeed, Dudley worried that it might not survive its first months.

The Countess of Lincoln, reading this letter in the warmth of her grand home, could not help but sense the contrast between her comfortable situation and the hardships Dudley endured. Neither could she miss the deputy governor's preoccupation with the French, who had established a colony in Canada. Remote as they were from England and Europe, the English colonists worried more about Old World enemies than about hostile reactions from the Indians whose lands they now occupied.

Rumors of a French attack sparked concern that Massachusetts would make an easy target if all settlers clustered in a single community. So Dudley and his companions planted "dispersedly" in seven towns around Boston Harbor and agreed to seek shelter in the hastily-constructed fort should French ships appear over the horizon.

The Dudleys ended up in Newtown (now Cambridge) and not only survived but prospered. Thomas Dudley went on to serve four terms as governor and accumulate a large estate to bequeath to his seven surviving children. He died in July 1653 at the age of 76, an unusually long life span for the seventeenth century. But Dudley could not have predicted such a happy outcome in the first difficult months following his voyage to America. His journey took place at a time of increased rivalry among European nations for New World territory. England's greatest adversaries were France and the Netherlands. Each nation scrambled to claim pieces of the North American mainland and islands in the Caribbean, hoping to match Spain's earlier success. As Thomas Dudley's letter suggests, this international race for overseas possessions was never far from colonists' minds.

KEY TOPICS

- Development of New France
- The Dutch Empire and New Netherland
- Diversity of English colonies in the seventeenth century
- Growth of staple crop economies in the southern and Caribbean colonies
- Role of religion in the founding of colonies
- Creation of biracial slave societies in the West Indies and Carolina

Chronology

1603–1625	James I reigns as king of England.
1607	Founding of English colonies at Jamestown and Sagadahoc.
1608	Establishment of French colony at Quebec.
1619	First Africans arrive in Jamestown.
	Virginia's House of Burgesses meets for the first time.
1620	Founding of Plymouth Colony in New England.
	Mayflower Compact signed.
1620s	Tobacco boom in Virginia.
1624	Dutch found colony of New Netherland.
1625	Virginia becomes a royal colony.
	Fort Amsterdam founded.
1625–1649	Charles I reigns as king of England.
1627	English colony at Barbados founded.
1630	Massachusetts Bay Colony founded.
1630–1642	Great Migration to New England.
1634	Lord Baltimore (Cecilius Calvert) founds proprietary colony of Maryland.
1635–1636	Roger Williams banished from Massachusetts, founds Providence, Rhode Island.
1637	Anne Hutchinson banished from Massachusetts.
	Pequot War.
1638	New Haven colony founded.
1640s	Sugar cultivation and slavery established in West Indies.
1642–1660	English Civil War and Interregnum.
1649	Maryland's Act for Religious Toleration.
1660	Charles II restored to English throne; reigns until 1685.
1663	Founding of Carolina colony.
1664	New Netherland conquered by the English, becomes New York.
	New Jersey established.
1673	French explorers reach the Mississippi River.
1681	Founding of Pennsylvania.

THE FRENCH IN NORTH AMERICA

In the mid-sixteenth century, religious warfare between Catholics and Protestants at home had interrupted France's efforts to establish a foothold in North America. So long as this conflict divided the nation, the only French subjects who maintained regular contact with the New World were fishermen making seasonal voyages to the bountiful waters of the Grand Banks off the coast of Newfoundland. But in the early seventeenth century, once King Henry IV restored civil order in France, the situation changed dramatically. With the creation of permanent settlements first along the St. Lawrence River and later in the continent's interior, France staked its claim to an expansive and profitable New World empire.

THE QUEST FOR FURS AND CONVERTS

French fishermen who set up frames on the Newfoundland shore to dry their catch frequently encountered Indians interested in trading beaver pelts for European goods. There was a ready market for these furs in Europe, where broad-brimmed beaver hats had become highly fashionable. Thus furs joined fish as a source of wealth, and a reason for French explorers and entrepreneurs to establish the colony of New France.

In 1608, Samuel de Champlain led an expedition more than 130 miles up the St. Lawrence River to found a permanent settlement at Quebec. This village was eventually joined by two others—Trois-Rivières (founded 1634) and Montreal (1642)—located farther up the river (see Map 2–1). For several decades, the colony was managed by the Company of New France, a private corporation working on its own behalf as well as in France's imperial interests. At first New France grew slowly; by the 1660s, there were only 3,200 colonists clustered in and around the three main villages.

The fur trade supporting the colony's development functioned as a partnership between Indians and Europeans. Indians performed most of the work–trapping beavers, preparing skins, carrying pelts from the interior to trading posts along the St. Lawrence–in return for axes, knives, metal pots, and glass beads. At first, some colonists anticipated that economic ties between the two peoples would be supplemented by marital ones, as French traders

MAP 2-1   New France, c. 1650

By 1650, New France contained a number of thinly populated settlements along the St. Lawrence River Valley and the eastern shore of Lake Huron. Most colonists lived in Quebec and Montreal; other sites served mainly as fur-trading posts and Jesuit missions to the Huron Indians.

took Indian wives. Intermarriage, however, was never widespread, occurring mainly among ***coureurs de bois*** ("woods runners"), independent fur traders who ventured into the forests to live and trade among native peoples. Much to the consternation of colonial officials, these traders often seemed to abandon their French ways for Indian ones.

Indian peoples such as the Montagnais and Hurons welcomed the French not only as trading partners, but also as military allies, making sure that the newcomers understood that the two roles had to be linked. As a result, the fur trade entangled the French in rivalries among Indian groups that long predated European contact. Champlain's alliance with the Hurons and other St. Lawrence Valley Indians drew the French into conflict with their Iroquois enemies, forcing colonial authorities for more than a century thereafter to engage in delicate diplomatic maneuvers to ensure New France's security.

For some French colonists, saving Indian souls was even more important than profiting from furs. Beginning in the 1630s, Jesuit missionaries—members of a Catholic religious order founded during the Counter-Reformation—tried to convince Indians to come to the French settlements to hear Christian preaching and learn European ways. When that tactic failed, Jesuits traveled to native villages and learned native languages, bringing Christianity directly to Indian populations.

At times, this strategy aroused Indian suspicions. Jesuits who baptized dying victims of epidemics raised fears that the priests themselves might have caused the outbreak of disease. By the 1650s, however, the Jesuits claimed to have produced thousands of genuine converts, some of whom formed separate native Christian communities. They also publicized extraordinary examples of Indian piety, particularly the story of Kateri Tekakwitha. An orphaned Mohawk girl who joined the Christian Indian village of Kahnawake, Tekakwitha sparked a religious revival among other female converts and went on to become the first Native American candidate for sainthood.

THE DEVELOPMENT OF NEW FRANCE

After 1663, New France underwent several important changes. Keen on asserting his royal authority, King Louis XIV disbanded the Company of New France and assumed direct control of the colony, entrusting one of his key ministers, Jean-Baptiste Colbert, with its administration. Political reorganization followed. New France was henceforth ruled by two royal appointees: a governor charged with military and diplomatic affairs, and an *intendant* who oversaw colonial finances and the judicial system. The French government also vastly improved Canada's military defenses, investing money in the construction of forts and sending several companies of professional soldiers. This was a greater investment in defense than English kings would provide for their colonies until the middle of the eighteenth century.

The king and Colbert launched a massive campaign to increase French migration to the colony. Colbert arranged to send over 700 women—called *filles du roi,* or king's daughters—to provide wives in a colony where there were six men of marriageable age for every unmarried French woman. Many male immigrants were *engagés,* or **indentured servants** who agreed to work for three years in return for food, lodging, a small salary, and a return passage to France.

Despite these efforts, only about 250 French immigrants arrived each year. Several factors contributed to this reluctance to emigrate, not least of which was Canada's reputation as a distant and inhospitable place. "Canada has always been regarded as a country at the end of the world," admitted one official. Rumors

Because Indians expected their trading partners also to be military allies, Europeans were often drawn into native conflicts. This illustration, from Samuel de Champlain's 1613 description of the founding of New France, shows him joining his Huron allies in an attack on the Iroquois.

about frigid winters and surprise Indian attacks dissuaded many potential colonists. In addition, the government required settlers to be Catholic (although Protestants often resided in Canada temporarily), reducing the pool from which colonists could be recruited. In the end, nearly three out of four immigrants who went to Canada returned home.

By 1700, the population had increased to about 15,000 (less than 7 percent of the English population in the mainland colonies that year; see Figure 2-1), mostly clustered in the three major towns along the St. Lawrence. This growth testified to a remarkable level of natural increase. Because land for farms was readily available, couples faced few obstacles in supporting themselves. Since *engagés* could not marry until their labor contracts had expired, men tended to wed around the age of 28. Intense competition for marriageable women drove the average age for brides before 1660 down to as young as 16. It was not unknown for some women to bear ten or even fifteen children. As late as 1666, only one out of three French settlers were women, and very few women failed to find husbands. Some who remained single chose to do so, preferring a religious vocation with the Ursulines or one of the other orders of nuns, devoting their energies to teaching or administering care to the sick and indigent.

Many families established farms along the St. Lawrence river, producing wheat and other provisions mostly for local consumption. Often the land was technically owned by a gentleman, or *seigneur*, who received a rent payment. *Seigneurs* claimed other privileges, including rights to fishing and timber, and collected other fines and taxes. Though powerful, these gentlemen never enjoyed anything comparable to the status of aristocrats with vast estates back in France.

French officials sought to restrict settlement to the St. Lawrence Valley, fearing that further expansion would render the empire impossible to defend. The impetus to move inland however, could not be restrained. By the 1670s, French traders and missionaries had reached the Mississippi river. In 1681–82, Robert, Sieur de La Salle, followed the Mississippi to the Gulf of Mexico, claiming the entire valley (which he named Louisiana in honor of the king) for France. When officials tried to restrict the direct trade between Indians and the *coureurs de bois*, many of these Frenchmen simply drifted off to settle in what eventually became known as the *pays des Illinois* along the Mississippi. This expansion of French influence alarmed the English, who had founded colonies along the Atlantic seaboard and feared a growing French presence in the west.

Prosperous and expansive, if not completely manageable from Paris, Canada provided France with a secure foothold on the North American mainland. Its successful establishment contributed to an escalating European competition for land and trade in the New World. It would not be long before new rivals entered onto the scene.

THE DUTCH OVERSEAS EMPIRE

Small but densely populated, the Dutch Republic joined the scramble for empire in the early seventeenth century. The Northern Provinces, sometimes known as Holland, had declared their independence from Spain (whose kings ruled the region as leaders of the Holy Roman Empire) in 1581, although sporadic fighting continued for another half-century. The new republic, dominated by Protestants, was intent on challenging Catholic Spain's power for religious as well as

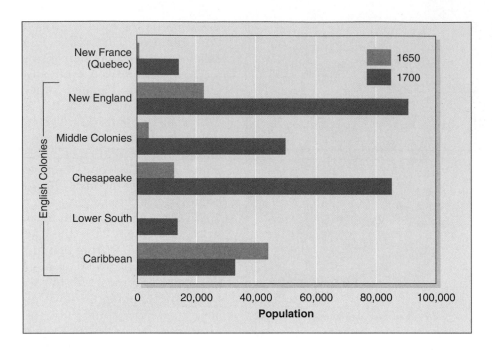

FIGURE 2-1   European Populations of New France (Quebec) and English Colonies in 1650 and 1700

Although New France's population grew rapidly between 1650 and 1700, it remained only a tiny fraction of the population of England's North American colonies. By 1700, English colonists on the mainland outnumbered New France's inhabitants by a factor of about 16 to 1.

Data Source: From John J. McCusker and Russell R. Menard, *The Economy of British America, 1607–1789* (1985). The University of North Carolina Press.

political reasons in the New World as well as the Old. More than any other factor, however, the desire for profit drove the Dutch quest for colonies.

THE DUTCH EAST INDIA COMPANY

By 1600, the Dutch had become the leading economic power in Europe. Skilled craftsmen specialized in the production of fine textiles, jewelry, glass, and colored tiles, making the Republic the dominant manufacturing center on the Continent. Amsterdam emerged as a key financial capital, particularly after the Bank of Amsterdam was founded in 1609. The centerpiece of Dutch prosperity, however, was commerce, which expanded dramatically in the first decades of the seventeenth century.

The Dutch Republic served as a major center of world trade. Bulk goods such as grain, salt, lumber, and fish arrived from the Baltic countries. Merchants established an equally lucrative trade in luxury items, including sugar, dyestuffs, wine, and other Mediterranean products. By 1590, the Dutch had supplanted the English as primary traders with Russia for timber and furs. Before long, thousands of Dutch ships plied the world's oceans and the Republic's earnings from foreign trade may have surpassed those of the rest of Europe combined. This commercial vitality provided the context for overseas expansion.

The instrument of colonial dominance was the Dutch East India Company, founded in 1602. Eager to reap profits from spices and other exotic goods,

the Company challenged what had until then been a virtual Portuguese monopoly of Asian trade. Its first success was the capture of the Spice Islands (now Indonesia and East Timor), followed by the takeover of Batavia (Jakarta), Ceylon (Sri Lanka), and Sumatra. The Company established trading posts on the Gold Coast of West Africa, where it competed with the Portuguese in the slave trade, and at the Cape of Good Hope on Africa's southern tip. Its far-flung commercial net eventually encompassed parts of India and Formosa (Taiwan). These possessions sealed Dutch trading predominance for decades to come.

THE WEST INDIA COMPANY AND NEW NETHERLAND

The Dutch next set their sights on the Americas, creating the West India Company in 1621. After taking control of West African slave-trading posts and temporarily occupying part of Brazil, the West India Company moved into the Caribbean (acquiring four islands by the 1640s) and North America. Its claim to the Connecticut, Hudson, and Delaware valleys stemmed from the 1609 voyage of Henry Hudson, an Englishman sailing for the Dutch, who discovered the river that bears his name.

The first permanent Dutch settlers on mainland North America arrived in 1624 to set up a fur-trading post at Fort Orange (now Albany). Two years later, Peter Minuit and a company of Protestant refugees established New Amsterdam on Manhattan Island, which Minuit had purchased from the Indians. The

Cornelius de Zeeuw depicted a prosperous Dutch merchant family in this sixteenth-century painting. The arrangement of figures indicates the hierarchies of gender and age that prevailed in Dutch society, while the family members' serious expressions suggest their strict Calvinist beliefs.

Hudson River corridor between these two settlements became the heart of the New Netherland colony. Like New France, its economic focus was the fur trade. Dutch merchants forged ties with the Iroquois, who brought furs to exchange for European tools and weapons.

In the 1630s, to help supply colonial traders, the West India Company offered large landed estates (called patroonships) to wealthy Dutchmen who would be responsible for populating them with tenant farmers. The plan never really worked, in part because most would-be patroons disliked company-imposed limits on their rights, and in part because few Dutch people wanted to emigrate only to live as peasants. At its peak, New Netherland's colonists only numbered about ten thousand.

What they lacked in numbers the colonists made up for in divisiveness. New Netherland became a magnet for religious refugees from Europe, as well as a destination for Africans acquired through the slave trade. (In 1638, about 100 Africans—free and slave—lived in New Amsterdam, constituting nearly a third of that city's population.) Ethnic differences hindered a sense of community. In 1643, a French Jesuit visitor reported hearing at least eighteen languages spoken on the streets of New Amsterdam. Among the colony's Dutch, German, French, English, Swedish, Portuguese, and African settlers were Calvinists, Lutherans, Quakers, Catholics, Jews, and Muslims.

The West India Company, more interested in making money than keeping order, dispatched sev-

eral inept but aggressive governors who made an unstable situation worse by provoking conflict with Indians. Although colonists generally maintained good relations with their Iroquois trading partners on the upper Hudson River, they had far less friendly dealings with Algonquian peoples around New Amsterdam. In one particularly gruesome incident in 1645, Governor Willem Kieft ordered a massacre at an encampment of Indian refugees who

This engraving depicts New Amsterdam in 1643 as a bustling port. The figures of African laborers in the background attest to the importance of slavery in the Dutch colonial city, where perhaps a quarter of the residents had been born in Africa.

had refused to pay tribute. A horrified Dutch witness described Indian children being "thrown into the river, and when the fathers and mothers endeavored to save them, the soldiers would not let them come on land, but made both parents and children drown." He saw victims "with their hands, some with their legs cut off, and some holding their entrails in their arms." Ten years later, Governor Peter Stuyvesant antagonized Susquehannock Indians along the Delaware River by seizing a small Swedish colony where the Susquehannocks had traded.

Such actions provoked retaliatory raids by the Indians, further weakening the colony. Though profitable, the fur trade did not generate the riches to be found in other parts of the Dutch empire. By the 1650s and 1660s, New Netherland increasingly looked like a poor investment to company officials back in Europe.

ENGLISH SETTLEMENT IN THE CHESAPEAKE

Following the Roanoke colony's disappearance after 1587 (see Chapter 1), twenty years passed before the English again attempted to settle in America. When they did, in 1607, it was in the lower Chesapeake Bay region. The new settlement, Jamestown, at first seemed likely to share Roanoke's dismal fate. But it endured, eventually developing into the prosperous colony of Virginia. The reason for Virginia's success was an American plant—tobacco—that commanded good prices from European consumers. Tobacco also underlay the economy of a neighboring colony, Maryland, founded by English settlers on the northern and eastern shores of Chesapeake Bay, and had a profound influence on the development of Chesapeake society.

THE ORDEAL OF EARLY VIRGINIA

In 1606, several English merchants, convinced that they could succeed where others had failed, petitioned King James I for a charter incorporating two companies to attempt New World settlement. One, the London, or Virginia, Company, included merchants from the city of London; the other, the Plymouth Company, included merchants from England's western ports. James I issued a charter granting the companies two tracts of land along the mid-Atlantic coast but refrained from investing any money himself in such a risky enterprise. These **joint-stock compa-**

nies sold shares to investors (who expected a profit in return) to raise money for colonization.

The Jamestown colony. Three small ships carried 104 settlers, all men, to the mouth of Chesapeake Bay in May 1607 (see Map 2–2). On a peninsula about fifty miles up a river they named the James in honor of their king, the colonists built a fortified settlement they called Jamestown. Hoping to earn quick profits for Virginia Company investors, they immediately began hunting for gold and exploring the James in search of the Northwest Passage to Asia. But Jamestown was no Mexico. All they found was disappointment and suffering. The swampy region was a perfect breeding area for malarial mosquitoes and parasites carrying other diseases. Spending all their time in search of riches, the settlers neglected to plant crops, and their food sup-

MAP 2-2 **English and Dutch Mainland Colonies in North America, c. 1655**
Early English colonies clustered in two areas of the Atlantic seaboard—New England and the Chesapeake Bay. Between them lay Dutch New Netherland, with settlements stretching up the Hudson River. The Dutch also acquired territory at the mouth of the Delaware River in 1655 when they seized a short-lived Swedish colony located there.

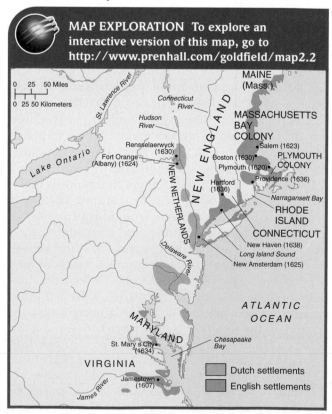

MAP EXPLORATION To explore an interactive version of this map, go to http://www.prenhall.com/goldfield/map2.2

plies dwindled. By January 1608, only thirty-eight colonists were still alive.

After the disastrous first year, the colony's governing council turned to Captain John Smith for leadership. Just 28 years old, Smith was a seasoned adventurer who had fought against Spain in the Netherlands and the Ottoman Turks in Hungary. He imposed military discipline on Jamestown, organizing settlers into work gangs and decreeing that "he that will not worke shall not eate." His high-handed methods revived the colony but antagonized certain settlers who believed that their social status exempted them from manual labor and who bristled at taking orders from a man of lower social rank. When a gunpowder explosion wounded Smith in 1609 and forced him to return to England, his enemies had him replaced as leader.

Once again, the colony nearly disintegrated. Shiploads of new settlers arrived, only to starve or die of disease. Of the five hundred people in Jamestown in the autumn of 1609, just sixty remained alive by the spring of 1610—some of whom survived only by eating their dead companions. Facing financial ruin, company officials back in England tried to conceal the state of the colony. They reorganized the company twice and sent more settlers, including glassmakers, winegrowers, and silkmakers, in a desperate effort to find a marketable colonial product. They experimented with harsh military discipline, instructing governors to enforce a legal code—the *Lawes Divine, Morall and Martiall*—that prescribed the death penalty for offenses as trivial as swearing or killing a chicken. When it became clear that such severity discouraged immigration, the company tried more positive inducements.

The first settlers had been expected to work together in return for food and other necessities; only Company stockholders were to share in the colony's profits. But surviving settlers wanted land, so governors began assigning small plots to those who finished their terms of service to the company. In 1616, the company instituted the **headright system**, giving 50 acres to anyone who paid his own way to Virginia and an additional 50 for each person (or "head") he brought with him.

In 1619, three other important developments occurred. That year, the company began transporting women to become wives for planters and induce them to stay in the colony. It was also the year in which the first Africans arrived in Virginia. In addition, the company created the first legislative body in English America, the **House of Burgesses**, setting a precedent for the establishment of self-government in other English colonies. Landowners elected repre-

sentatives to the House of Burgesses, which, subject to the approval of the company, made laws for Virginia. In 1621 the *Lawes Divine, Morall and Martiall* gave way to a code based on English common law.

Despite these changes, the settlers were still unable to earn the company a profit, and life in the colony barely improved. To make things worse, the headright system expanded English settlement beyond Jamestown. This strained the already tense relations between the English and the Indians onto whose lands they had intruded.

The Powhatan Confederacy and the colonists.
When the English arrived in 1607, they planted their settlement in the heart of territory ruled by the Indian leader Powhatan, who was then at the peak of his power. Chief of a confederacy of about thirty tribes with some fourteen thousand people, including 3,200 warriors, Powhatan had little to fear at first from the struggling English outpost. After an initial skirmish with English soldiers, he sent gifts of food, assuming that by accepting the gifts, the colonists acknowledged their dependence on him. Further action against the settlers seemed unnecessary, because they seemed fully capable of destroying themselves.

This conclusion was premature. Armed colonists began seizing corn from Indian villages whenever the natives refused to supply it voluntarily. During one raid in 1609, John Smith held a pistol to the chest of Opechancanough, Powhatan's younger brother, until the Indians ransomed him with corn. Protesting that the English came "to invade my people and possesse my Country," Powhatan besieged Jamestown and tried to starve the colony to extinction. The colony was saved by the arrival of reinforcements from England, but war with the Indians continued until 1614.

The marriage of the colonist John Rolfe to Pocahontas, Powhatan's daughter, helped seal the peace in 1614. Pocahontas had briefly been held captive by the English during the war and had been instructed in English manners and religion by Rolfe. Sent to negotiate with Powhatan in the spring of 1614, Rolfe asked the chief for his daughter's hand. Powhatan gave his consent, and Pocahontas—baptized in the Church of England and renamed Rebecca—became Rolfe's wife.

Powhatan died in 1618, and Opechancanough succeeded him as chief. Still harboring intense resentment against the English, the new chief made plans for retaliation. Pocahontas had died on a trip to England in 1617, severing the tie between her family and the English. With new settlers arriving each year and the ranks of his warriors depleted by

This illustration shows John Smith seizing the scalplock of Opechancanough, Chief Powhatan's brother, during an English raid on an Indian village. Smith released his prisoner only after Indians ransomed him with corn. Thirteen years later, Opechancanough led a surprise attack against the colonists.

the ravages of European diseases, Opechancanough could not wait long to act. Early in the morning on March 22, 1622, hundreds of Indian men traveled to the scattered English settlements, as if they meant to visit or trade. Instead, they attacked the unsuspecting colonists, killing 347 by the end of the day—more than one-fourth of the English population.

Opechancanough assumed that the survivors would recognize his authority and confine themselves to trading posts in Jamestown. Instead, they plotted revenge. Believing that "now we have just cause to destroy them by all meanes possible," English forces struck at native villages, killing the inhabitants and burning cornfields. At peace talks held in April 1623, the English served poisoned wine to their enemies, killing two hundred more. During the ensuing nine years of war, the English treated the In-

dians with a ferocity that recalled their earlier subjugation of the Irish.

Although Opechancanough's attack failed to restrain the colonists, it destroyed the Virginia Company. Economic activity ceased as settlers retreated to fortified garrisons. The company went bankrupt, and a royal commission investigating the 1622 attack was shocked to discover that nearly ten times more colonists had died from starvation and disease than at the hands of Indians. King James had little choice but to dissolve the company in 1624, and Virginia became a royal colony the following year. The settlers continued to enjoy a measure of self-government through the House of Burgesses, but now the king chose the colony's governor and council, and royal advisers monitored its affairs.

THE IMPORTANCE OF TOBACCO

Ironically, the demise of the Virginia Company helped the colony succeed. In their search for a marketable product, settlers had begun growing tobacco after 1610. Europeans had acquired a taste for tobacco in the late sixteenth century when the Spanish brought samples from the West Indies and Florida. Initially expensive, it became popular among wealthy consumers. The high price appealed to Virginians, but they found that native Virginia leaf was of poor quality. John Rolfe began experimenting with seeds from Trinidad, which did much better. The first cargo of Virginia-grown tobacco arrived in England in 1617 and sold at a highly profitable 3 shillings per pound.

Settlers immediately planted tobacco everywhere—even in the streets of Jamestown. Company officials, unwilling to base the colony's economy on a single crop, tried to restrict annual production to 100 pounds per person. Colonists, busy "rooting in the ground about Tobacco like Swine" as one observer reported, ignored these restrictions. But it was only after company rule ended that tobacco planting really surged.

Between 1627 and 1669, annual tobacco exports climbed from 250,000 pounds to more than 15 million pounds. As the supply grew, the price per pound plunged from 13 pence in 1624 to a mere penny in the late 1660s, where it remained for the next half century. What had once been a luxury product thus became affordable for Europeans of average means. Now thoroughly dependent on tobacco for their livelihood, the only way colonists could compensate for falling prices was to grow even more, pushing exports to England to more than 20 million pounds per year by the late 1670s (see Figure 2-2).

Virginia-grown tobacco found a ready market among European consumers such as this contemplative smoker. As tobacco prices declined during the seventeenth century due to increased production, even people of modest means could take up the habit of smoking.

Tobacco shaped nearly every aspect of Virginia society, from patterns of settlement to the recruitment of colonists. Planters scrambled to claim lands near navigable rivers so that ships could easily reach their plantations and carry their crops to market. As a result, the colonists dispersed into plantations located along waterways—wherever, one governor wrote, "a choice veine of rich ground invited them, and further from neighbours the better." Colonists competed to produce the biggest and best crop and get it to market the fastest, hoping to enjoy even a small price advantage over everyone else.

The key to success was to control a large labor force. Tobacco kept workers busy nine months of the year. Planters sowed seeds in the early spring, transplanted seedlings a few weeks later, and spent the summer pinching off the tops of the plants (to produce larger leaves) and removing worms. After the harvest, the leaves were "cured"—dried in ventilated sheds—and packed in large barrels. During the winter, planters cleared and fenced more land and made barrels for next year's crop. Working on his own, one planter could tend two thousand plants, which yielded about 500 pounds of cured tobacco. Early on, when the price was high, this supplied a comfortable income. But as the price plummeted, planters could keep up only by producing more tobacco, and to do that they needed help.

The planters turned to England, importing thousands of indentured servants, or contract workers, who agreed to a fixed term of labor, usually four to seven years, in exchange for free passage to Virginia. The master provided food, shelter, clothing, and, at the end of the term of service, "freedom dues" paid in corn and clothing. Between 1625 and 1640, an estimated one thousand or more indentured servants arrived each year. Some were orphans; others were condemned criminals given a choice between execution and transportation to Virginia. The vast majority, however, came from the ranks of England's unemployed, who emigrated in hopes of "bettering their condition in a Growing Country."

Most found such hopes quickly dashed. Servants died in alarming numbers from disease, and those who survived faced years of backbreaking labor. Masters squeezed as much work out of them as possible with long hours and harsh discipline. Some servants died from mistreatment. Richard Price beat his servant, Endymion Inleherne, for "being a common runaway and one that did use to feign himself sick," so severely that the young man died. A jury refused to charge Price with murder, reasoning that Inleherne deserved punishment and Price had not intended to kill him. Few masters matched Price's cruelty, but because the courts (administered by masters) favored masters' authority over servants' rights, those who did generally escaped prosecution.

New obstacles faced servants who managed to survive their terms of indenture. For every ex-servant who became a landholder, dozens died in poverty. To prevent freed servants from becoming economic rivals, established planters avoided selling them good land, particularly after tobacco prices hit bottom in the 1660s. Many ex-servants found land only in places less suitable for tobacco cultivation and more vulnerable to Indian attack. Forced to choose between eking a "poor living with hard labor out of the ground in a terrible Wilderness" or giving up all hope for ownership and either becoming ten-

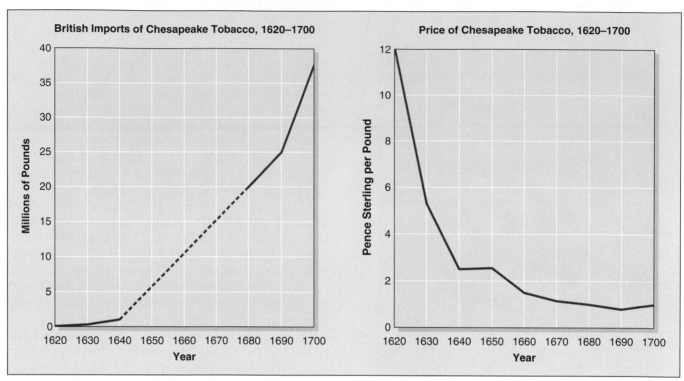

FIGURE 2-2   The Supply and Price of Chesapeake Tobacco, 1620–1700
Tobacco cultivation dominated the economy of the Chesapeake region throughout the seventeenth century. As planters brought more and more land under cultivation, the amount of tobacco exported to Britain shot up and the price plummeted. (As the dashed line indicates, no data on tobacco imports are available for the years 1640–1680.)

Data Source: From Russell R. Menard, "The Tobacco Industry in the Chesapeake Colonies, 1617–1730: An Interpretation," *Research in Economic History,* 5 (1980), app. Jai Press, Inc.

ants or laborers, ex-servants were a discontented group. In 1675, their discontent would flare into rebellion (discussed in Chapter 3).

MARYLAND: A REFUGE FOR CATHOLICS

The success of tobacco in Virginia encouraged further English colonization in the Chesapeake Bay region. In 1632, King Charles I granted 10 million acres of land north of the bay to the nobleman George Calvert, Lord Baltimore. Unlike Virginia, which was founded by a joint-stock company, Maryland was a **proprietary colony**—the sole possession of Calvert and his heirs. They owned all the land, which they could divide up as they pleased, and had the right to set up the colony's government.

Calvert, who was Catholic, intended Maryland to be a refuge for others of his faith. When Queen Elizabeth's accession made England a Protestant nation, Catholics became a disadvantaged minority. They paid double taxes and could not worship in public, hold political office, or send their children to univer-

sities. In Maryland, Calvert wanted Catholic colonists to enjoy economic and political power. He intended to divide the land into manors—large private estates like those of medieval England—and distribute them to wealthy Catholic friends. These manor lords would live on rents collected from tenant farmers, hold the most important governmental offices, and run their own law courts.

Calvert died before settlement began, and it was the sad fate of his son, Cecilius, to see his father's plans unravel. The majority of colonists, who began arriving in 1634, were Protestants who despised Catholics. Refusing to live as tenants on Catholic estates, they claimed land of their own—a process that accelerated after 1640, when Maryland adopted a headright system like Virginia's as a way to recruit settlers.

Maryland's problems intensified when civil war broke out in England in 1642. For years, political and religious disputes had divided the nation. Charles I, who became king in 1625, clashed with **Puritans** who called for further reform of the Church of England. He also antagonized many government leaders by dissolving Parliament in 1629 and ruling on his own for eleven years. Needing funds to suppress a rebellion in Scotland in 1640, however, Charles was forced to recall Parliament. Its leaders, sympathetic to the Puritan cause, quickly turned against him. Both king and Parliament recruited armies and went to war in 1642. Parliamentary forces triumphed, and in 1649, they executed Charles. For the next decade, England was governed as a protectorate, not a monarchy. Oliver Cromwell, a Puritan general, ruled until his death in 1658. His son, Richard, proved an inept successor, however, and in 1660 a group of army officers invited Charles's exiled son to accept the throne.

During the 1640s and 1650s, Maryland Protestants took advantage of the upheaval in England to contest the Calverts' control of the colony. To pacify them, Cecilius Calvert established a legislature, assuming that Protestants would dominate the elective lower house while he could appoint Catholics to the upper house. In 1649, Calvert also approved the **Act for Religious Toleration**, the first law in America to call for freedom of worship for all Christians, but even this brought no peace. The Protestant majority, supported during the 1650s by Cromwell and Parliament, continued to resist Catholic political influence, at one point passing a law that prohibited Catholics from voting.

Instead of the peaceful Catholic refuge Calvert intended, Maryland soon resembled neighboring Virginia. Its settlers raised tobacco and imported as many indentured servants as possible. Because Maryland initially provided freed servants with 50 acres of land, more became landholders than in Virginia. As in Virginia, however, economic opportunity diminished after 1660 when the price of tobacco dropped. Maryland's settlers enjoyed more peaceful relations with the Indians than Virginians had, but they fought intensely among themselves. Throughout the seventeenth century, Protestants kept up their opposition to the proprietor's control of land and political power and resisted all attempts by Catholics to govern the colony that was supposed to have been theirs.

LIFE IN THE CHESAPEAKE COLONIES

Few people could have predicted how much life in the Chesapeake colonies would differ from England. Many of those differences stemmed from the region's distinctive population. Because of their labor needs, masters preferred to recruit young men in their teens and twenties as indentured servants, importing three or four times as many of them as women. As a result, the populations of Virginia and Maryland were overwhelmingly young and male. Even as late as 1700, Virginia had three English men for every two women.

As a consequence of this gender imbalance, many male ex-servants found that marriage was as remote a possibility as landownership. Very few chose Indian wives: John Rolfe's union with Pocahontas was one of only three English-Indian marriages in seventeenth-century Virginia. One planter suggested that, in contrast to Englishmen's experience, the Chesapeake was a "paradise for women" because their scarcity made them the object of men's competition. While few unmarried women failed to find husbands, and widows usually remarried soon after their spouses' deaths, their lives were hardly easy.

Malaria and other diseases inflicted hardship on nearly everyone. Few colonists lived past 50, and women's susceptibility to disease during pregnancy meant that many of them barely made it to 40. Such high mortality, combined with late marriages (because servants could not wed until their terms were up), limited the size of families and thus slowed population growth from natural increase. As many as one out of four children died in their first year, and more than half failed to reach the age of 20.

Under such conditions, the only way the populations of the Chesapeake colonies could grow during most of the seventeenth century was through continued heavy importation of servants. The number of English settlers rose from about 8,000 in 1640 to 24,000 in 1660. Still mostly young and mostly male, the immigrants helped the region's distinctive demographic patterns persist until the end of the century.

These conditions hindered colonists from reproducing customary patterns of family life. The frequency of early death produced unusual households, containing various combinations of stepparents and children from different marriages living under the same roof. There were so many orphans in Maryland that the colony created special courts to protect whatever property they might have inherited. Many women would be widows at some point in their lives, which gave them temporary control over the family property. Husbands often arranged for their widows to manage their estates, until such time as the eldest son reached age 21. Few women ever received land outright, and if widows remarried, their new spouses usually took control of the estates left by their first husbands. As in England itself, the Chesapeake colonies accorded women little formal authority within society.

The precariousness of life encouraged settlers to invest every penny of profit in land and labor, postponing investment in goods that would bring a more comfortable existence. Early houses were often no larger than 16 by 20 feet, with one or two rooms. Poor settlers slept on the floor on straw mattresses and had few other furnishings—often not even a chair or bench to sit on. Rich planters owned more goods, but often of poor quality. In 1655, for instance, William Brocas, a prominent colonial official, owned several curtains "very thin and much worn," seven chairs "most of them unusefull," and seven guns "most unfixt." Nearly everyone subsisted on a rude diet of pork and corn. Servants and poor colonists had no choice but to accept crude living conditions. Their more fortunate neighbors tolerated discomfort in order to invest in family estates where their descendants might live in greater luxury.

Rough as these conditions were, they far surpassed the circumstances of most native peoples in the Chesapeake. The English population may have been growing slowly, but it still overwhelmed the Indian population which increasingly suffered high mortality from European diseases. Opechancanough led the Powhatans on another raid against the colonists in 1644, killing nearly 500 of them, but this had a far less devastating effect than his attack of 1622 because the colonists now outnumbered the Indians. By 1685, there were more than ten colonists for every Indian living in eastern Virginia. By that point, many Native Americans in the Chesapeake had retreated to their own towns, keeping their distance from the colonists in hopes of preserving control over dwindling lands and maintaining a measure of independence from English domination.

THE FOUNDING OF NEW ENGLAND

The first English attempt to settle the northeastern coast of North America, what would soon be called New England, was a miserable failure. In 1607, the same year that the Virginia Company founded Jamestown, the Plymouth Company sent two ships with 120 Englishmen (and one Indian captive from an earlier raid) to found a colony at the mouth of the Sagadahoc River in present-day Maine. The colonists alienated the Abenaki Indians who lived there (and who consequently refused to trade with the belligerent newcomers), suffered through a harsh winter, and abandoned their settlement the next summer. But explorers and fishermen continued to visit the area, and it was not long before the English renewed their efforts to settle New England.

Six colonies appeared in the region between 1620 and 1640, settled by thousands of people troubled by religious, political, and economic upheavals in England. Even before the colonists established permanent settlements, New England's native population felt the effects of European contact. Between 1616 and 1618, a terrible epidemic swept through coastal New England, killing up to 90 percent of the Indians living there. The devastated survivors were struggling to cope with the consequences of this disaster just as colonists began to arrive.

THE PILGRIMS AND PLYMOUTH COLONY

Plymouth Colony, the first of the New England settlements, was founded in 1620. Its origins lay in religious disputes that had plagued England since the late sixteenth century. Most of Queen Elizabeth's subjects approved of her efforts to keep England a Protestant nation, but some reformers believed that she had not rid the Church of England of all Catholic practices. The enemies of these reformers, ridiculing them for wanting to purify the Church of England (or **Anglican** Church) of all corruption, called them Puritans.

Following the doctrine of predestination taught by John Calvin and other Protestant reformers, English Puritans believed in an all-powerful God who, at the moment of Creation, determined which humans would be saved and which would be damned. They held that salvation came through faith alone, not good works, and urged believers to seek a direct, personal relationship with God. The centerpiece of their spiritual life was conversion: the transforming experience that occurred when individuals felt the stirrings of grace in their souls and began to hope that they were among the saved. Those who experienced conversion were considered saints and acquired new strength to live godly lives.

Puritans believed that certain Anglican practices interfered with conversion and the believer's relationship with God. They rejected the Book of Common Prayer, which regulated Anglican worship, insisting that ministers should pray from the heart and preach from the Bible. They objected when Anglican clergy wore rich vestments that set them apart from ordinary Christians. And they objected to any church organization above the level of individual congregations, seeing no need for bishops and archbishops. But what they hated most about the Anglican Church was that anyone could be a member. Puritans believed that everyone should attend church services, but they wanted church membership, which conferred the right to partake in the Lord's Supper, or communion, to be limited to saints who had experienced conversion.

Puritans thus insisted on further reform. Elizabeth and the rulers who followed her—who as monarchs were the "supreme heads" of the Church of England—disagreed and tried to silence them. James I viewed the Puritans' demands as a challenge to his authority and threatened to "harry them out of the land." Some Puritans, known as **separatists**, were convinced that the Church of England would never change and left it to form their own congregations. One such group, mainly artisans and middling farmers from the village of Scrooby, in Nottinghamshire, became the core of Plymouth Colony.

The Scrooby separatists, seeking refuge from persecution, left England in 1607–1608 for Holland, where they stayed for more than a decade. Although they could worship in peace there, many struggled to make a living and feared that their children were being tempted by the worldly pleasures of Dutch city life. Some Scrooby separatists contemplated moving to America and contacted the Plymouth Company, which was eager to make another colonization attempt after the Sagadahoc failure. Called **Pilgrims** because they thought of themselves as spiritual wanderers, they were joined by other separatists and by nonseparatist "strangers" hired to help get the colony started. In all, 102 men, women, and children set sail on the *Mayflower* in September 1620.

After a long and miserable voyage, they landed near Massachusetts Bay. Because this was about 200 miles north of the land their charter permitted them to settle, some of the "strangers" claimed that they were no longer legally bound to obey the expedition's separatist leaders. To prevent the colony from disintegrating into factions before their ship had even landed, the leaders drafted the Mayflower Compact, a document that bound all signers to abide by the decisions of the majority.

The Pilgrims settled at Plymouth, the site of a Wampanoag village recently depopulated by disease. William Bradford, a Pilgrim leader and Plymouth's governor for many years, described finding abandoned cornfields, a clearing "where lately a house had been," Indian graves, and baskets of corn buried underground. Although it helped feed them for a while, this corn was not enough to prevent the Pilgrims from suffering their first winter through a terrible "starving time" that left nearly half of them dead.

When two natives, Squanto and Samoset, emerged from the woods the next spring and began speaking English, the surviving Pilgrims marveled at them as "special instruments sent of God." Samoset had learned English from traders, and Squanto had learned it in England, where he lived for a time after being kidnapped by a sea captain. Upon his return to New England, Squanto found that he was the sole survivor of the Patuxets, who had succumbed to disease while he had been away. The two native men approached the Pilgrims on behalf of Massasoit, the Wampanoag leader. Although suspicious of the newcomers, the Wampanoags thought the Pilgrims might be useful allies against Wampanoag enemies, such as the Narragansetts, who had escaped the recent epidemics.

In 1621, the Wampanoags and the Pilgrims signed a treaty of alliance, although each side (working through translators) understood its terms differently. The Pilgrims assumed that Massasoit had submitted to the superior authority of King James, whereas Massasoit assumed that he and the English king were equal partners. Until his death in 1622, Squanto offered advice to each side, hoping to achieve honor and influence as a mediator.

Economic ties strengthened the alliance. The Indians taught the English how to plant corn and traded corn with them for manufactured goods. The Pilgrims also exchanged corn with other Indians to the north for furs, which they shipped back to England to help pay off their debts to English investors. In the autumn of 1621, Indians and Pilgrims gathered for a feast celebrating the settlers' first harvest—an event Americans still commemorate as the first Thanksgiving.

Plymouth remained small, poor, and weak, never exceeding about seven thousand settlers. Although its families achieved a modest prosperity, the colony as a whole never produced more than small shipments of furs, fish, and timber to sell in England. It took the Pilgrims more than twenty years to repay their English creditors. After 1630, the first New England colony was overshadowed by a new and more powerful neighbor, Massachusetts Bay.

MASSACHUSETTS BAY COLONY AND ITS OFFSHOOTS

Not long after his arrival in New England, Thomas Dudley became a member of a Puritan church. Dudley, like the other Puritans who founded Massachusetts, shared many beliefs with the Pilgrims of Plymouth Colony—with one important exception. They insisted that the Anglican Church could be reformed and so were not separatists. When they went to New England, it was to create godly churches to serve as models for English reform. And England, they believed, was in more desperate need of reformation than ever.

Charles I, who became king in 1625, opposed Puritans more forcefully than his father had and supported changes in Anglican worship that recalled Catholic practices. England at the time also suffered from economic troubles—including crop failures and a depression in the wool industry—that many Puritans saw as signs of God's displeasure with their country, encouraging them to move to the New World.

In 1629, a group of Puritan merchants and gentlemen received a royal charter for a joint-stock enterprise, the Massachusetts Bay Company, to set up a colony north of Plymouth. Its founding members included Thomas Dudley and John Winthrop, a prosperous lawyer chosen to lead the new colony. In the spring of 1630, a fleet of eleven ships carried the Winthrops, Dudleys, and about a thousand other men, women and children across the Atlantic.

Before Winthrop's ship landed, he preached a lay sermon, called "A Model of Christian Charity," to his fellow passengers, describing his vision of the society they were about to create. The governor reminded them of their goal "to do more service to the Lord." They should "love one another with a pure heart" and place the good of all above private ambitions. Winthrop argued that the Lord had made them his chosen people and that as a result, "we shall be as a city upon a hill, the eyes of all people are upon us." If they failed to live up to God's expectations, he would punish them, and the spectacle of their failure would allow their enemies "to speak evil of the ways of God." With this mingled encouragement and threat ringing in their ears, the emigrants set about establishing their colony. Within a few months of their landing, they founded Boston and six adjoining towns.

Stability, conformity, and intolerance.

Winthrop described the settlers' mission in New England as a **covenant**, or contract, with God, binding them to meet their religious obligations in return for God's favor. The settlers also created covenants to define their duties to one another. When they founded towns, colonists signed covenants agreeing to live together in peace. The settlers of Dedham, for example, agreed to "walk in a peaceable conversation," seeking "the good of each other." Worshipers in each town's church likewise wrote covenants binding themselves to live in harmony.

The desire for peace and purity could breed intolerance. Settlers scrutinized their neighbors for signs of unacceptable behavior. Standards for church membership were strict; only those who could prove they were saints by describing their conversion expe-

John Winthrop (1588–1649) served as the Massachusetts Bay Colony's governor for most of its first two decades. Throughout his life, Winthrop—like many fellow Puritans—struggled to live a godly life in a corrupt world.

Courtesy, American Antiquarian Society.

riences were admitted. But the insistence on covenants and conformity also created a remarkably stable society, far more peaceable than Virginia's.

That stability was enhanced by the development of representative government. Colony leaders in effect translated the charter of the Massachusetts Bay Company into a plan of government, a process completed by 1634. The General Court, which initially included only the shareholders of the joint-stock company, was transformed into a two-house legislature. Freemen—adult males who held property and were church members—had the right to elect representatives to the lower house, as well as eighteen members (called "assistants") to the upper house. They also chose a governor and a deputy governor.

The Connecticut Valley and the Pequot War.

At least thirteen thousand settlers came to New England and established dozens of towns between 1630 and 1642, when the outbreak of the English Civil War halted emigration. The progress of settlement was generally untroubled in coastal Massachusetts, but when colonists moved into the Connecticut River Valley, tensions with Indians grew rapidly. These erupted in 1637 in the brief, tragic conflict called the **Pequot War**.

English settlers from Massachusetts first arrived in the Connecticut Valley in the mid-1630s. The migration accelerated in 1636 when the Reverend Thomas Hooker led part of his congregation from Cambridge, Massachusetts, to what became Hartford. The new arrivals found themselves in a dangerous situation. For several years, the Pequot Indians had used their partnership with Dutch traders in the region to monopolize the trade in European goods and exert dominance over their native neighbors. This political and economic strategy was endangered in 1633 when the Dutch built an outpost near the site of Hartford and invited the Pequots' rivals—including the Narragansetts and Mohegans—to trade. The Pequots, suffering terribly from a recent smallpox epidemic, resented losing their special trading rights and approached Massachusetts Bay as an ally against the Dutch. But when English settlers poured into Connecticut and demanded Pequot submission to English authority as the price of an alliance, the Pequots turned against them too in a struggle to retain control over the land and trade of eastern Connecticut.

The English settlers allied with the Pequots' enemies, the Narragansetts and Mohegans. Together they overwhelmed the Pequots in an astonishingly bloody war. In May 1637, English forces surrounded a Pequot village inhabited mainly by women and children, located on the Mystic River. They set it ablaze and shot anyone who tried to escape. Between three hundred and seven hundred Pequots died, a toll that shocked the settlers' Indian allies, who protested that English-style warfare was "too furious, and slays too many men" (see "American Views: Miantonomo's Plea for Indian Unity").

The English, for their part, thanked God for giving them "so speedy a victory over so proud and insulting an enemy." After the surviving Pequots had fled or been sold into slavery, many more settlers moved to Connecticut, which soon declared itself a separate colony. In 1639, the settlers adopted the Fundamental Orders, creating a government similar to that of Massachusetts, and the English government granted them a royal charter in 1662.

Roger Williams and the founding of Rhode Island.
Massachusetts spun off other colonies as its population expanded in the 1630s and dissenters ran afoul of its intolerant government. Puritan leaders tried to suppress unorthodox religious opinions whenever they emerged, for fear that God would interpret their failure to do so as a breach of their covenant with Him. Some dissenting colonists, however, refused to conform. Roger Williams, who founded Rhode Island, was one such irrepressible dissenter. Williams was a separatist minister who declared that because Massachusetts churches had not rejected the Church of England, they shared its corruption. He opposed government interference in religious affairs—such as laws requiring settlers to attend worship services—and argued for the separation of church and state. Williams even attacked the Massachusetts charter, insisting that the king had no right to grant Indian lands to English settlers.

Despite his fiery opinions, Williams was an immensely likable man; even Governor Winthrop remained on friendly terms with him and tried to persuade him to change his views. When Williams refused to be silenced, the General Court sentenced him to banishment, intending to ship him back to England. But in the winter of 1635, Williams slipped away and followed Winthrop's advice to "steer my course to Narragansett Bay." There he and a few followers found refuge among the Narragansett Indians, from whom he purchased land for the village of Providence, founded in 1636. More towns soon sprang up nearby when a new religious crisis, provoked by a woman named Anne Hutchinson, sent additional refugees to Rhode Island from Massachusetts.

Anne Hutchinson's challenge to the Bay Colony.
Anne Hutchinson arrived in Boston from England with her husband and seven children in 1634. Welcomed by the town's women for her talents as a midwife, she also began to hold religious meetings in her house. During these meetings, she denounced several ministers, who had taught worshipers that there were certain spiritual exercises they could perform that might prepare them for sainthood. Hutchinson insisted that there was nothing humans could do to encourage God to make them saints. She implied that any minister who taught otherwise could not be a saint himself, in which case he had no authority over the true saints in his church.

Many people, including prominent Boston merchants, flocked to Hutchinson's meetings. But her critics believed her to be a dangerous antinomian (someone who claimed to be free from obedience to moral law), because she seemed to maintain that saints were accountable only to God and not to any worldly authority. Her opponents also objected to her teaching of mixed groups of men and women. Governor Winthrop complained that such behavior was neither "comely in the sight of God nor fitting for your sex." This comment suggests that Hutchinson's breach of normal gender roles, which placed

AMERICAN VIEWS

Miantonomo's Plea for Indian Unity (1642)

Until European colonization began to force a change in outlook, the native inhabitants of North America never thought of themselves as one people, any more than Europe's residents considered themselves "Europeans." Miantonomo, a Narragansett living in Rhode Island, was one of the first native leaders to call for a unified response to English intrusion. With the gruesome lessons of the Pequot War fresh in his mind, he urged the Montauks of Long Island to put aside their differences with the Narragansetts and join them in opposing the settlers. His appeal, recorded by Lion Gardiner, an English officer during the Pequot War, was uttered in vain. Captured by the English and tried and convicted of the murder of an Indian, Miantonomo was turned over to a Mohegan rival for execution.

- How did Miantonomo describe Indian life before the arrival of the English?
- What changes occurred as a result of their settlement?

Brothers, we must be as one as the English are, or we shall all be destroyed. You know our fathers had plenty of deer and skins and our plains were full of game and turkeys, and our coves and rivers were full of fish.

But, brothers, since these Englishmen have seized our country, they have cut down the grass with scythes, and the trees with axes. Their cows and horses eat up the grass, and their hogs spoil our bed of clams; and finally we shall all starve to death; therefore, stand not in your own light, I ask you, but resolve to act like men. All the sachems both to the east and the west have joined with us, and we are resolved to fall upon them at a day appointed, and therefore I come secretly to you, [be]cause you can persuade your Indians to do what you will.

Source: Steven Mintz, ed., *Native American Voices: A History and Anthology* (1995), pp. 84–85. Reprinted with permission of Brandywine Press.

---

women subordinate to men, upset him as much as her religious views did. Colony magistrates arrested her and tried her for sedition—that is, for advocating the overthrow of the government.

During her trial, Hutchinson mounted a lively defense. When asked to explain her views, she reminded her opponents of their objections to her teaching and asked them, "Why do you call me to teach the court?" In the end, however, the court found her guilty and banished her from the colony. With many of her followers, she moved to Rhode Island, where Roger Williams had proclaimed a policy of religious toleration. Other followers returned to England or moved north to what became in 1679 the separate colony of New Hampshire.

At the height of the Hutchinson controversy, a group of zealous Puritan emigrants led by the Reverend John Davenport arrived in Boston. Appalled by the religious turmoil, they departed for the coast of Long Island Sound, where they founded New Haven in 1638. Davenport's efforts to impose perfect Puritan conformity in his colony made Massachusetts seem easygoing in comparison. But New Haven failed to thrive, and in 1662, the poor, intolerant, and isolated colony was absorbed into Connecticut.

FAMILIES, FARMS, AND COMMUNITIES IN EARLY NEW ENGLAND

"This plantation and that of Virginia went not forth upon the same reasons," declared one of Massachusetts's founders. Virginians came "for profit," whereas New Englanders emigrated to bear witness to their Puritan faith. They too hoped for economic prosperity but believed that it would come only if God blessed their efforts to create a godly society. Most New Eng-

Most New Englanders came in family groups, bringing many children with them. The lace and ribbons on the clothing of the Mason children, depicted in this 1670 portrait, suggest that they came from a well-to-do family. Like many seventeenth-century portraits, this one is rich in symbolism. The cane in David Mason's hand indicates his status as the male heir, while the rose held by his sister Abigail was a symbol of childhood innocence.

land settlers arrived in the brief span between the founding of Massachusetts in 1630 and 1642, when the outbreak of the English Civil War convinced many Puritans to stay at home and fight on Parliament's behalf against the king. Unlike the unmarried young men who moved in great numbers to Virginia, most New Englanders settled with their families. This had important implications for the development of New England society.

Even though emigration from England slowed to a trickle after 1642, New England's population continued to grow. By 1660, the number of colonists exceeded 33,000. This demographic expansion stemmed from the initial emigration of families. With a more balanced sex ratio (about three men to two women) than there was in the early Chesapeake, marriage and childbearing were more common. Emigrant families that already had children produced more of them, and newly married couples soon added to the population. Families frequently had seven or eight children, compared to the two or three offspring common to Chesapeake families.

Settling in a region with a healthier climate, New Englanders were also largely spared early deaths from malaria and other diseases that ravaged Chesapeake settlers and devastated Indian populations.

Most children survived to reach adulthood and form families of their own. Many New Englanders enjoyed unusually long lives (for the seventeenth century), reaching their seventies and even eighties. Unlike most Chesapeake children, young New Englanders got to know their grandparents.

Long-lived parents exercised considerable control over their children's lives. This was especially true for sons, who could not marry until their fathers provided them with sufficient land to support a family. Because fathers depended on their sons for labor, they often postponed granting them the means to economic independence until they were 26 or 27. Daughters, too, contributed their labor to the household economy, but generally married between the ages of 21 and 23. They also depended on the willingness of their fathers to supply them with a dowry (usually livestock and household goods) to bring to their new homes.

Women in early New England.   In New England, as in other colonies and England itself, women were assumed to be legally and economically dependent on the men in their families. Since fewer New England marriages were shortened by the early death of a spouse, fewer New England women experienced widowhood, the one time in their lives when they might enjoy legal independence and exercise control over property. During the seventeenth century, widows occasionally exercised more extensive property rights than the law dictated. By law, they had "dower rights" to possess one-third the value of the husband's personal estate and to use one-third of the land for the remainder of their lives. Many husbands, however, gave their widows control over greater amounts of property, perhaps to recognize their important contributions to building the family estate.

Women's economic contributions were indeed central to the family's success. In addition to raising the children, women performed essential domestic tasks, including cooking, sewing, gardening, and cleaning. Many also engaged in household production and traded the fruits of their labor with other families. They cared for poultry and sold eggs, made butter and cheese, brewed beer, and spun yarn. Wives of shopkeepers and craftsmen occasionally managed their husbands' businesses when the men had to travel or became ill.

Community and economic life.   New Englanders' lives were shaped not only by their families, but by their towns. Unlike Chesapeake colonists, who tended to disperse into separate plantations, New Englanders clustered into more populous communities that eventually contained between fifty and a

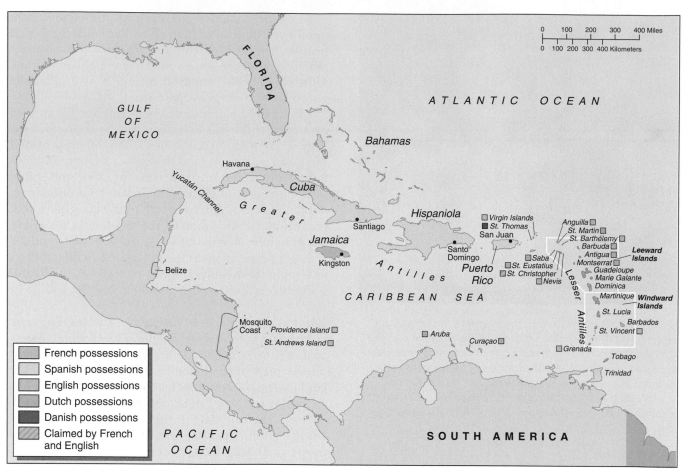

MAP 2-3   Principal European Possessions in the Caribbean in the Seventeenth Century
Europeans scrambled for control of Caribbean islands, where they raised sugar cane with slave labor. On many islands, Africans soon formed the majority of the population. In some cases, colonists from one European country settled on lands claimed by a rival power. For instance, English settlers established bases in Belize and on the Mosquito Coast, both of which were claimed by Spain.

hundred or so families. The Massachusetts government strongly encouraged town formation by granting tracts of land to groups of families who promised to settle together. Once they received a grant, the families in a group divided it among themselves, allotting each family a farm of sufficient size to support its members. Social distinctions were maintained: people who had higher standing in England received larger farms than those of lower status. Land that the original families could not yet use was held "in common" to be distributed to their children as they grew up. Once they found a town they liked, families tended to stay in place. Grown children, inheriting parental estates and finding spouses nearby, often settled in the same community as their parents.

At the center of each town stood the meetinghouse, used both for religious and secular purposes. Every Sunday, townspeople gathered there to listen to the minister preach God's word. The importance

Puritans placed on worship with fellow Christians helped promote community feeling. At other times, the meetinghouse served as a town hall, where men assembled to discuss matters ranging from local taxes to making sure everyone's fences were mended. Massachusetts law required towns with at least fifty families to support a school (so children could learn to read the Bible) and men often wrangled at town meetings over the choice of a schoolmaster and what salary to pay him. Townsmen tried to reach decisions by consensus, although that was not always possible. To oversee day-to-day local affairs, they chose five to seven trusted neighbors to serve as selectmen. Each town could also elect two men to represent it in the colony legislature. Many towns neglected to do so, either because their citizens could not afford to pay the representative's expenses or because they lacked sufficient interest in outside political affairs.

Economic life likewise centered on the family and the town. New England's stony soil and short growing season offered few ways to get rich, but most people achieved a modest prosperity mainly by farming. They grew corn and other foods and raised livestock to feed their families, selling or trading what they could not use. Their goal was to achieve what they called competency—the possession of enough property to ensure the family's economic independence. Without the income generated by a staple crop like tobacco, New England farmers lacked adequate resources to hire large numbers of indentured servants and so relied on family members. Even children as young as five or six contributed their labor to the household economy, perhaps by caring for younger siblings or fetching water and wood.

No family could produce all that it needed, so New Englanders regularly traded goods and services with their neighbors. A skilled carpenter might erect a house—usually larger and sturdier than the ramshackle dwellings of Chesapeake settlers—in return for barrels of salted beef. Men with several sons sent them to help neighbors whose children were too young to work. Midwives delivered babies in return for cheese or eggs. Women nursed sick neighbors, whom they might one day call on for similar help. These sorts of transactions allowed most New Englanders to enjoy a fairly comfortable life, one that many Virginians might have envied.

Lacking a single staple crop like tobacco, New England prospered by exploiting a variety of resources, developing a diversified economy that was less vulnerable to depression than Virginia's. Farmers sent livestock and meat to merchants to be marketed abroad. Fishermen caught thousands of pounds of cod, haddock, and other fish to be sold in Europe. Some of the region's timber found its way abroad, but most of it ended up in shipyards. New Englanders became such skilled shipbuilders and seafaring merchants that by the 1670s, London merchants were complaining about competition from them. England itself had little use for the dried fish, livestock, salted meat, and wood products that New England vessels carried, but enterprising merchants found exactly the market they needed in the West Indies.

COMPETITION IN THE CARIBBEAN

The Spanish claimed all Caribbean islands by right of Columbus's discovery, but during the seventeenth century, French, Dutch, and English adventurers boldly defied them. Spain retained the largest and most lucrative islands—Cuba, Hispaniola, Puerto Rico, Trinidad—but others were seized, one by one, by rival European powers. The French eventually obtained Guadaloupe, Martinique, St. Lucia, St. Vincent, and smaller outposts in the Leeward and Windward Islands. Aruba, Curaçao, St. Martin, Saba, and St. Eustatius became Dutch possessions. Even the Danes took control of St. Thomas in the Virgin Islands. England's share of the West Indies included Antigua, Barbados, Montserrat, Nevis, and St. Christopher; in 1655, the English wrested Jamaica from Spain (see Map 2–3). Although a few English efforts, including an attempt to found a Puritan colony on Providence Island off Nicaragua's coast, failed, the West Indies soon became the jewel of England's empire in the Americas.

Europeans competed for these islands at first in the hope that they would yield precious metals and also provide bases for privateering expeditions. It eventually became clear that the islands would produce treasure of another sort—sugar, which was in great demand in Europe. In order to reap the enormous profits that sugar could bring, Caribbean planters of all nationalities imported enormous numbers of African people to work as slaves under the harshest conditions to be found in the New World.

SUGAR AND SLAVES

The Spanish and Portuguese first experimented with sugar production on Atlantic islands such as São Tomé and the Canaries in the fifteenth century, importing their workers from Africa. Europeans prized sugar as a sweetener, preservative, decoration—even a medicine—and paid high prices for it. Columbus accordingly brought sugar canes to the New World on his second voyage, in 1493. Soon after the Spanish began growing sugar on Santo Domingo, they began importing African slaves as workers because Indian slaves were dying in great numbers. The Spanish brought sugar to the South American mainland as well, as did the Portuguese, who turned Brazil into one of the world's major producers. And everywhere that sugar flourished, first Indian slaves and then enslaved African workers could be found. It seemed as if Europeans could not imagine growing sugar any other way. For the Portuguese and Dutch, who dominated the African slave trade, sugar and slaves provided twin sources of profit. In the early seventeenth century, Portugal alone shipped 10,000 to 20,000 Africans to the New World every year.

The English in the Caribbean eventually made the same decisions, after a false start. Like the early Virginians, the first English colonists who came to

*In this seventeenth-century drawing, African slaves are shown toiling in a Brazilian sugar mill.
Similar scenes prevailed on Barbados and other Caribbean colonies dominated by sugar production.*

the West Indies in the 1620s and 1630s raised tobacco and imported indentured servants to work their fields. By that time, however, tobacco prices were dropping. Moreover, the disease environment of the West Indies proved even harsher than that of the Chesapeake and settlers died in great numbers. That thousands came anyway testified more to their hopes for prosperity than their actual chances of success. Until the 1660s the islands actually attracted more emigrants than the mainland colonies did.

By the 1640s, a Barbados planter boasted of "a great change on this island of late from the worse to the better, praised be God." That change was a shift from tobacco to sugar cane. Dutch merchants helped finance this transition. The Dutch, who had briefly taken control of Brazil, were being driven out by the Portuguese, and looked to the English islands as a new market for the Dutch slave trade. They taught the English how to grow sugar, supplied them with slaves, and dominated the marketing of the English crop. Before long, many English sugar planters grew astonishingly wealthy. In 1646, a 500-acre plantation on Barbados sold for £16,000—more than the whole island had been worth just a few years before. On average, the estate of a Caribbean sugar planter was worth four times as much as a prosperous Chesapeake plantation.

Sugar rapidly transformed the West Indies. Planters deforested whole islands to raise sugar cane. They stopped planting food crops and raising livestock—thereby creating a demand for lumber and provisions that boosted New England's economy. In 1647, John Winthrop noted that Barbadians "had rather buy food at very dear rates than produce it by labor, so infinite is the profit of sugar works."

For some years after the transition to sugar, English planters continued to import white indentured servants, including some kidnapped English and Irish youths, and supplemented the labor force with African slaves. They eventually grew dissatisfied with this labor force. Due to the islands' unhealthy environment and extremely harsh working conditions, servants died in great numbers. England could barely meet the demand for workers, and English workers, if they survived, often proved rebellious. Given the example of prosperous Spanish and Portuguese plantations using slave labor, and the willingness of the Dutch to supply them with slaves, the English too switched to African laborers whom they considered better suited to agricultural work in a tropical climate. The planters' choice has been called an "unthinking decision," but it had an enormous impact on English colonial life, first in the islands and then on the mainland, where slavery would develop later in the seventeenth century (see Chapter 3).

A BIRACIAL SOCIETY

As happened on virtually all Caribbean islands, the English West Indies developed a biracial plantation society—the first in the English colonial world. By 1700, more than 250,000 slaves had been brought to the English islands, and they soon constituted a majority of the population. In Barbados, black slaves increased from 50 percent to more than 70 percent of the population between 1660 and 1700. Slaves lived in wretched conditions, underfed, poorly dressed, and housed in rough huts. They labored six days a week from sunrise to sunset—except at harvest time, when they toiled seven days a week in round-the-clock shifts. Masters considered them property, often branding them like livestock and hunting them with bloodhounds when they ran away.

Laws, sometimes called **slave codes**, declared slavery to be a lifelong condition that passed from slave parents to their children. Slaves had no legal rights and were under the complete control of their masters. Only rarely would masters who killed slaves face prosecution, and those who did and were found guilty were subject only to fines. Slaves, in contrast, faced appalling punishments even for minor offenses. They could be whipped, branded, or maimed for stealing food or harboring a runaway compatriot. Serious crimes such as murder or arson brought execution without trial. Slaves who rebelled were burned to death.

Astonishingly, slaves managed to preserve some elements of normal life even under these brutal conditions. When masters began to import African women as well as men—hoping to create a self-reproducing labor force—slaves formed families and preserved at least some African traditions. They gave their children African names (although masters often gave them English names as well). They celebrated with African music and worked to the rhythm of familiar songs. And they drew on their West African heritage to perform elaborate funeral rituals, often burying their dead with food and other goods to accompany them on the journey to what they believed to be a much happier afterlife.

Some planters, profiting handsomely from their slaves' toil, lived better than many English gentlemen. They indulged in large houses, fine furnishings, and expensive clothing. Even so, many hated the hot, humid West Indian climate and feared the constant threat of disease. After making their fortunes, planters often fled to England, leaving their estates under the care of hired overseers.

But sugar made relatively few white colonists wealthy. Its production required a heavy investment in land, slaves, mills, and equipment. As great planters took vast amounts of land for themselves, freed servants and small farmers struggled to survive. After 1650, many of these poor men, looking for other places to live, headed for the mainland. They were joined by planters looking for a place to expand their operations once most of the good land on the islands had been brought under cultivation.

THE PROPRIETARY COLONIES

The initial burst of English colonization ended in 1640 when England tottered on the brink of civil war. With the accession of Charles II to the throne in 1660, however, interest in North America revived. Charles II needed to reward the supporters who had remained loyal to him during his long exile in France. One of the easiest ways for him to do so was with huge grants of American land. During his reign (1660–1685), four new colonies—Carolina, Pennsylvania, New Jersey, and New York—resulted from such grants (see Map 2-4). All were proprietary colonies, essentially the private property of the people to whom they had been given. Two of them—Carolina and Pennsylvania—like the earlier proprietary colony of Maryland, provided their owners the chance to test idealistic social visions. The origins of New York and New Jersey as English colonies, by contrast, lay not in proprietary visions of social harmony but in the stern reality of military conquest (see the Overview table, "English Colonies in the Seventeenth Century").

EARLY CAROLINA: COLONIAL ARISTOCRACY AND SLAVE LABOR

In 1663, Charles II granted a group of supporters an enormous tract of land stretching from southern Virginia to northern Florida. The proprietors, who included several Barbados planters, called their colony Carolina, after *Carolus*, the Latin form of the king's name. They envisioned it growing from the few English outposts already in the region, established by settlers from New England and the West Indies, into a prosperous, orderly society.

One of the proprietors, Anthony Ashley Cooper, working closely with his secretary, John Locke, devised the **Fundamental Constitutions of Carolina**, a plan to ensure the colony's stability by balancing property ownership and political rights. It called for the creation of a colonial aristocracy, who would own two-fifths of the land and wield extensive political power. Below them, a large class of freeholders would own small farms and elect representatives to

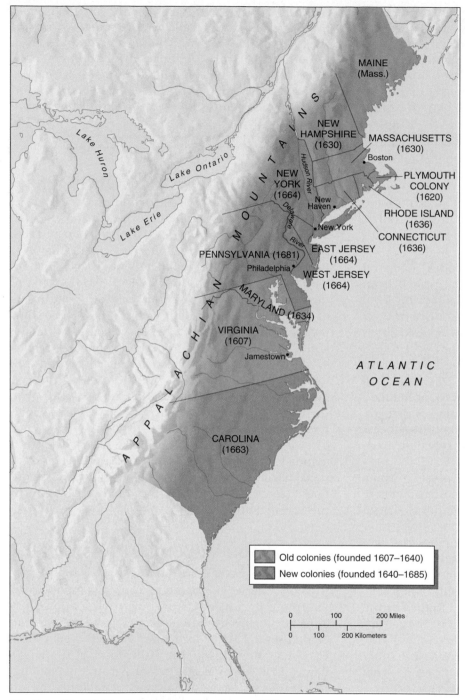

MAP 2-4   English North American Colonies, c. 1685
After the restoration of Charles II in 1660, several large proprietary colonies joined earlier English settlements in New England and the Chesapeake. By 1685, a growing number of English settlers solidified England's claim to the Atlantic coast from Maine (then part of Massachusetts Bay Colony) to the southern edge of Carolina.

where they pleased. They even voted in the assembly to reject the Fundamental Constitutions. They antagonized the Indians in the region, who numbered perhaps fifteen thousand when settlers first arrived. When English traders first appeared, eager to buy deerskins, many Indians had welcomed them. But they grew hostile when traders began selling guns to some tribes in exchange for captives from rival tribes. The captives were later sold as slaves to the West Indies. Native resentments deepened as settlers moved onto their lands. The result was a deadly cycle of violence.

The colonists at first raised livestock to be sold to the West Indies. But the introduction of rice in Carolina in the 1690s transformed the settlers' economy, making it, as one planter noted, "as much their staple Commodity, as Sugar is to Barbados and Jamaica, or Tobacco to Virginia and Maryland." The English had never grown rice, but West Africans had raised it since the 1500s. Rice cultivation in Carolina coincided with an increase in the number of African slaves there, who probably introduced the crop. Ironically, the profits earned from rice persuaded Carolina planters to invest even more heavily in slave labor.

Carolina society soon resembled the sugar islands from which many of its founders had come. By 1708, there were more black slaves than white settlers in the colony, and two decades after that, black people outnumbered white people by two to one. Rice farming required a substantial investment

an assembly. At the bottom of the social order would be slaves.

This plan never went into effect. People moved in from Virginia and the West Indies and settled

in land, labor, and equipment, including dikes and dams for flooding fields. Those who could afford such an investment set themselves up as planters in Carolina's coastal rice district, acquiring large es-

Overview

English Colonies in the Seventeenth Century

Colony	Date of Founding	Established Religion	Economy	Government
Virginia	1607	Anglican	Tobacco	Royal (after 1625)
Plymouth	1620	Puritan	Mixed farming	Corporate
St. Christopher	1624	Anglican	Sugar	Royal
Barbados	1627	Anglican	Sugar	Royal
Nevis	1628	Anglican	Sugar	Royal
Massachusetts (including present-day Maine)	1630	Puritan	Mixed farming, fishing, shipbuilding	Corporate
New Hampshire	1630 (first settlement, annexed to Mass. 1643–1679; royal colony after 1679)	Puritan	Mixed farming	Corporate (royal after 1679)
Antigua	1632	Anglican	Sugar	Royal
Montserrat	1632	Anglican	Sugar	Royal
Maryland	1634	None (Anglican after 1692)	Tobacco	Proprietary
Rhode Island	1636	None	Mixed farming	Corporate
Connecticut	1636	Puritan	Mixed farming	Corporate
New Haven	1638	Puritan	Mixed farming	Corporate
Jamaica	1655 (captured from Spanish)	Anglican	Sugar	Royal
Carolina	1663	Anglican	Rice	Proprietary
New York	1664 (captured from Dutch)	None	Mixed farming, furs	Proprietary (royal after 1685)
New Jersey	1664	None	Mixed farming	Proprietary
Pennsylvania	1681	None	Wheat, mixed farming	Proprietary

tates and forcing poorer settlers to move elsewhere.

Some of these dislocated settlers went to the northern part of Carolina, where the land and climate were unsuited to rice. There they raised tobacco and livestock, and produced pitch, tar, and timber products from the region's pine forests. So different were the two regions that the colony formally split into two provinces—North and South Carolina—in 1729.

South Carolina rice planters became some of the wealthiest colonists on the mainland. But their luxurious style of life came at a price. As Carolina began to look "more like a negro country than like a country settled by white people," planters dreaded the prospect of slave rebellion. To avert this nightmare, they enacted slave codes as harsh as those of the sugar islands.

Although John Locke went on to become one of England's most important philosophers, the visionary

Thomas Coram's oil painting (c. 1770) shows the main residence and slave quarters on the Mulberry Plantation near Charleston, South Carolina. The distinctive steep-roofed design of the slave cabins on the left probably reflects African building styles. Slave quarters may not have been located quite as close to the main house as this picture suggests.

plan he and Cooper had devised for Carolina disintegrated on contact with American conditions. Carolina would not be a harmonious colony that balanced wealth and power; it evolved instead into a racially divided society founded on the oppression of a black majority and permeated by fear.

PENNSYLVANIA: THE DREAM OF TOLERATION AND PEACE

Even as early Carolina diverged from the plans of its founders, another Englishman dreamed of creating a colonial utopia. William Penn put his plans into action in 1681, when Charles II granted him a huge tract of land north of Maryland as payment for a royal debt owed to Penn's father. Penn intended his colony to be a model of justice and peace, as well as a refuge for members of the Society of Friends, or **Quakers**, a persecuted religious sect to which Penn himself belonged.

The Society of Friends was one of many radical religious groups that emerged in England during the civil war. Like the separatists, Quakers abandoned the Church of England as hopelessly corrupt. But they went even further in their beliefs. Rejecting predestination, they maintained that every soul had a spark of grace and that salvation was possible for all who heeded that "Inner Light." They rejected trained clergy and elaborate church rituals as unnecessary to salvation. Instead of formal religious services, Quakers held meetings at which silence reigned until someone, inspired by the Inner Light, rose to speak.

Quaker beliefs had disturbing social and political implications. Although they did not advocate complete equality of the sexes, Quakers granted women spiritual equality with men, allowing them to preach, hold separate prayer meetings, and exercise authority over "women's matters." Arguing that social distinctions were not the work of God, Quakers refused to defer to their betters. People of lower social rank were expected to remove their hats in the presence of superiors, but Quakers would not do so. And instead of the formal *you,*

Quakers addressed superiors with the informal *thee* and *thou*. Because their faith required them to renounce the use of force, Quakers also refused to perform military service, which their enemies considered tantamount to treason.

When English authorities began harassing Quakers, William Penn, who was himself jailed briefly, conceived his plan for a New World refuge. He aimed to launch a "holy experiment," a harmonious society governed by brotherly love. Knowing that Quakers were unwelcome in the existing colonies—Massachusetts had hanged four of them—Penn looked elsewhere. His aristocratic background gave him advantages that other Quakers, who were mainly of humble origins, lacked. Using his father's connection with the king, he acquired the land that became Pennsylvania ("Penn's Woods") and recruited settlers from among Europe's oppressed peoples and persecuted religious sects. By 1700, eighteen thousand emigrants had left England, Wales, Scotland, Ireland, and various German provinces for the new colony.

Many came in families and settled in an area occupied by the Delaware Indians, whose numbers, though still substantial, had recently been reduced by disease and warfare. The "holy experiment" required colonists to live "as Neighbours and friends" with the Indians as well as with one another. Penn aimed to accomplish this by paying Indians for land and regulating trade. As long as Penn controlled his colony, relations between the settlers and the Indians were generally peaceful—so much so that refugee Indians from nearby colonies moved into Pennsylvania. Relations between Penn and the settlers, however, were less cordial.

In the **Frame of Government**, his constitution for Pennsylvania, Penn remained true to his Quaker principles with a provision allowing for religious freedom. But true to his aristocratic origins, he designed a legislature with limited powers and reserved considerable authority for himself. When Penn returned to England after a brief stay in the colony (1682–1684), the settlers immediately began squabbling among themselves. The governor and council, both appointed by Penn, fought with elected members of the assembly. Penn's opponents—many of whom were fellow Quakers—objected to his proprietary privileges, including his control of foreign trade and his collection of fees from landholders. Settlers on the lower Delaware River, which the crown had added to Penn's colony to give its port city, Philadelphia, access to the sea, gained autonomy for themselves with their own legislature, in ef-

No colonial proprietor was more idealistic than William Penn, shown here in a portrait made in about 1698 by Francis Place. Penn wanted Pennsylvania to be a place of peace, prosperity, and religious toleration—especially for his fellow Quakers. The colony eventually became an economic success but failed to achieve the social harmony that Penn had wanted.

fect creating an unofficial colony that later became Delaware.

A disappointed Penn lamented that the settlers had become "so brutish." He spent his fortune on his beloved colony, only to die in debt with his hopes for a harmonious society dashed. Settlers continued to fight among themselves, and with Penn's heirs, after his death. A flood of increasingly aggressive immigrants undermined peaceful relations with the Indians, forcing many natives to abandon their homelands and move west.

By 1720, Pennsylvania's ethnically and religiously diverse colonists numbered more than thirty thousand. The colony had some of the richest farmland along the Atlantic coast and was widely known as the "best poor man's country in the world." Growing wheat and other crops, the settlers lived mostly on scattered farms rather than in towns. From the busy port of Philadelphia, ships carried much of the harvest to markets in the West Indies and southern Europe. Penn's "holy experiment" in social harmony may have failed, but, as a thriving colony, Pennsylvania succeeded handsomely.

NEW NETHERLAND BECOMES NEW YORK

The proprietary colonies of New York and New Jersey were carved out of the Dutch colony of New Netherland. Competition between the English and the Dutch had intensified in the mid-seventeenth century as the two peoples struggled for trade supremacy on the high seas. Their antagonism generated two Anglo-Dutch wars, first in 1652–1654, and again in 1665–1667. In the New World, tensions were heightened by the presence of numerous English colonists on Long Island, which the Dutch claimed for themselves. The governors of New Netherland at first welcomed the *Yankees* (a Dutch word for "land pirates") in the expectation that crops raised on their prosperous farms would enrich Dutch trade. At the same time, Dutch leaders worried about the English settlers' loyalty.

In 1664, Charles II brought matters to a head by claiming that since the site of New Netherland lay within the bounds of the original charter of Virginia, the land belonged to England. He granted the territory to his brother James, Duke of York, who sent ships to Long Island to back up England's claim. Their arrival provoked a rebellion by the island's English colonists, leading the Dutch governor, Peter Stuyvesant—who commanded just 150 soldiers—to surrender without firing a shot.

The Duke of York became proprietor of this new English possession, which was renamed New York. James immediately created another colony, New Jersey, when he granted some of the land to a group of his supporters. New Jersey's proprietors struggled to control the diverse people already living there and fighting among themselves. At one point the colony split in two parts, East and West Jersey, which reunited to become a single royal colony in 1702 when the frustrated proprietors surrendered their rights to the king.

New York, which James retained for himself, was the most valuable part of the former Dutch colony. It included the port of New York City (the former New Amsterdam) and the Hudson Valley with its fur trade. James, who succeeded his brother to the English throne in 1685, encouraged Dutch colonists to remain on rather generous terms and promoted immigration from England to strengthen the colony and gain income from land sales. By 1700, the settlers numbered twenty thousand.

For nearly twenty years after its takeover by the English, New York lacked something all other English colonies had—a representative assembly. The Dutch had never created one, and James saw no reason to change that policy, despite the friction it created with his colonists. Particularly after neighboring New Jersey and Pennsylvania created their own assemblies, however, New Yorkers pressed their proprietor to follow suit. Only in 1683, when it became clear that New York might lose population to Pennsylvania, did James relent and create the assembly that brought New York into line with other English colonies.

CONCLUSION

During the seventeenth century, France, the Netherlands, and England competed for land and trade in North America, with France and England gaining colonies on the mainland and all three joining Spain in the Caribbean. New France's small and scattered settlements clung to the St. Lawrence River Valley. The profits from the fur trade encouraged the French to maintain friendly relations with their Indian allies and ensured that French kings would monitor the colony's affairs and invest in its defense. English colonization, by contrast, was a more haphazard process. English kings granted charters—sometimes to joint-stock companies (Virginia, Plymouth, Massachusetts), sometimes to proprietors (Maryland, Carolina, New York, New Jersey, Pennsylvania)—and let the colonies develop more or less on their own. England had no equivalent in the seventeenth century of the imperial bureaucracies Spain and France created to manage their New World holdings.

The result was a highly diverse set of English colonies stretching from the Maine coast to the Caribbean. Settlers adjusted to different environments, developed different economies and labor systems, and worshiped in different churches. In South Carolina, New York, Pennsylvania, the West Indies, the majority of settlers were not even of English origin. What held these colonies together—besides their establishment under English charters and their enmity toward the Spanish and French—was an overlay of common English institutions of government. By the mid-1680s, all the colonies had legislatures that provided for self-government and laws and judicial institutions based on English models.

The planting of French, Dutch, and English colonies not only ended Spain's monopoly of settlement in North America but also challenged the Indians' hold on the continent. Forced to deal with a rising tide of settlers and often to choose sides between European antagonists, native peoples had to adapt to rapidly changing circumstances. Transplanted Europeans adapted too, not only in their dealings with native peoples but also in finding and controlling the supply of laborers they needed to make their colonies prosper. For English colonists this meant the widespread adoption of slavery, an institution that did not exist in England itself. For millions of Africans, the result was forced migration to the New World.

REVIEW QUESTIONS

1. According to Thomas Dudley's letter to the Countess of Lincoln, why did the first Massachusetts colonists worry about their safety? What preparations did they think were necessary to insure the survival of their colony?

2. Comparing French, Dutch, and English colonies, which ones attracted the most settlers, and which the fewest? In what colonies were women scarce? What impact did these differences in emigration have on the various colonies' development?

3. Which English settlements were proprietary colonies? Did they share any common characteristics? What plans did the various proprietors have for their colonies, and to what extent were those plans put into effect?

4. When Virginia's settlers first arrived, they encountered a numerous and powerful confederation of Powhatan Indians. New England's colonists, in contrast, began settlement after epidemics had drastically reduced the local native population. In what ways did the presence or absence of substantial Indian populations affect each region's early history?

5. In both Massachusetts and Pennsylvania, religion figured prominently as a motive for settlement. What were the religious beliefs of the settlers in each colony, and how did those beliefs help shape each colony's development?

6. Three colonial regions—the Chesapeake, the West Indies, and Carolina—developed economies dependent on staple crops. What were those crops? In what ways did staple crop agriculture shape society in each region?

KEY TERMS

Act for Religious Toleration (p. 46)
Anglican (p. 48)
Coureur de bois (p. 37)
Covenant (p. 49)
Frame of Government (p. 61)
Fundamental Constitutions of Carolina (p. 57)
Headright system (p. 42)
House of Burgesses (p. 42)
Indentured servants (p. 38)
Joint-stock company (p. 41)
Pequot War (p. 50)
Pilgrims (p. 48)
Proprietary colony (p. 46)
Puritans (p. 46)
Quakers (p. 60)
Separatists (p. 48)
Slave codes (p. 57)

RECOMMENDED READING

Anderson, Virginia DeJohn. *New England's Generation: The Great Migration and the Formation of Society and Culture in the Seventeenth Century* (1991). Examines the experiences of nearly seven hundred emigrants to New England and explores the ways in which the composition of the settler population shaped New England society.

Dunn, Richard S. *Sugar and Slaves: The Rise of the Planter Class in the English West Indies, 1624–1713* (1972). The authoritative account of British settlement in the West Indies and the development of the slave labor system.

Greer, Allan. *The People of New France* (1997). A brief and readable overview of the origins and development of New France.

Morgan, Edmund S. *American Slavery, American Freedom: The Ordeal of Colonial Virginia* (1975). A vividly written account of the founding of Virginia and the development of an unfree labor system that remains the best study of an early American colony.

Wood, Peter H. *Black Majority: Negroes in Colonial South Carolina from 1670 through the Stono Rebellion* (1974). A study of the founding of South Carolina that emphasizes the contributions of the black slaves who eventually comprised a majority of the colony's settlers.

ADDITIONAL SOURCES

New France

Choquette, Leslie. *Frenchmen into Peasants: Modernity and Tradition in the Peopling of French Canada* (1997).

Eccles, W. J. *Essays on New France* (1987).

Moogk, Peter. *La Nouvelle France: The Making of French Canada—A Cultural History* (2000).

New Netherland

Israel, Jonathan. *The Dutch Republic: Its Rise, Greatness, and Fall, 1477–1806* (1995).

Price, J. L. *The Dutch Republic in the Seventeenth Century* (1998).

Rink, Oliver. *Holland on the Hudson: An Economic and Social History of Dutch New York* (1986).

Chesapeake Society

Carr, Lois Green, Russell R. Menard, and Lorena S. Walsh. *Robert Cole's World: Agriculture and Society in Early Maryland* (1991).

Horn, James. *Adapting to a New World: English Society in the Seventeenth-Century Chesapeake* (1994).

Rutman, Darrett, and Anita Rutman. *A Place in Time: Middlesex County, Virginia, 1650–1750* (1984).

New England

Cave, Alfred. *The Pequot War* (1996).

Hall, David D. *Worlds of Wonder, Days of Judgment: Popular Religious Belief in Early New England* (1989).

Main, Gloria. *Peoples of a Spacious Land: Families and Cultures in Colonial New England* (2001).

Morgan, Edmund S. *Puritan Dilemma: The Story of John Winthrop* (1958).

Ulrich, Laurel Thatcher. *Good Wives: Image and Reality in the Lives of Women in Northern New England, 1650–1750* (1982).

The West Indies

Beckles, Hilary. *White Servitude and Black Slavery in Barbados, 1627–1715* (1989).

Bridenbaugh, Carl and Roberta Bridenbaugh. *No Peace Beyond the Line: The English in the Caribbean, 1624–1690* (1972).

Mintz, Sidney. *Sweetness and Power: The Place of Sugar in Modern History* (1985).

The Proprietary Colonies

Dunn, Richard S., and Mary Maples Dunn, eds. *The World of William Penn* (1986).

Goodfriend, Joyce D. *Before the Melting Pot: Society and Culture in Colonial New York City, 1664–1730* (1992).

Illick, Joseph. *Colonial Pennsylvania: A History* (1976).

Levy, Barry. *Quakers and the American Family: British Settlement in the Delaware Valley* (1988).

Ritchie, Robert. *The Duke's Province: A Study of New York Politics and Society, 1664–1691* (1977).

Weir, Robert. *Colonial South Carolina: A History* (1983).

WHERE TO LEARN MORE

- Jamestown Settlement, near Williamsburg, Virginia. Site includes replicas of first English passenger ships to Virginia, a reconstructed Powhatan Village, the recreated James Fort, and galleries with Indian and English artifacts. Visitors can also see archaeological excavations of site of the actual James Fort, as well as sample artifacts recovered from the area.

  For updated information about archaeological excavations at Jamestown, see **www.apva.org**. At **http:jeffersonvillage.virginia.edu**, you can take a virtual tour of the Jamestown settlement.

- St. Mary's City, Maryland. Visitors to this site of the first permanent settlement under the Calvert family may tour the area and view exhibits and living history programs that describe life in early Maryland. The website **www.somd.com** contains information about the historic site of St. Mary's City and has links to a virtual tour of the area.

- Plimoth Plantation, Plymouth, Massachusetts. A living history museum, Plimoth Plantation recreates colony life in the year 1627. There are reproductions of the English village and a Wampanoag settlement. Visitors may also see a replica of the Mayflower. For a virtual tour, go to **pilgrims.net/plimothplantation/vtour**. Information on Pilgrims and early years of the colony can be found at **pilgrims.net/plymouth/history**.

- Pennsbury Manor, Morrisville, Pennsylvania. A reconstruction of William Penn's seventeenth-century plantation, this site includes furnished buildings and restored gardens. There are also guided tours and demonstrations of colonial crafts. Both www.bucksnet.com/pennsbury and www.pennsburymanor.org provide information about William Penn, the historic site, and various activities at the manor.

Please refer to the document CD-ROM for primary sources related to this chapter.

➤ As the top portion of this eighteenth-century French engraving suggests, the horrors of slavery
began as soon as Africans were torn from their families and marched to ships anchored off the
coast. The bottom part of the picture shows how tightly slaves were packed below the decks of
these vessels, evidence that merchants' thirst for profit overrode concerns for the slaves' health
or welfare.

THE CREATION OF NEW WORLDS

3

One day [in 1756], when all our people were gone out to their work as usual, and only I and my sister were left to mind the house, two men and a woman got over our walls, and in a moment seized us both; and without giving us time to cry out, or to make any resistance, they stopped our mouths and ran off with us into the nearest wood. Here they tied our hands, and continued to carry us as far as they could. . . . Thus I continued to travel, both by land and by water, through different countries and various nations, till at the end of six or seven months after I had been kidnapped, I arrived at the sea coast. . . .

The first object that saluted my eyes when I arrived on the coast was the sea, and a slave ship, which was then riding at anchor, and waiting for its cargo. These filled me with astonishment, that was soon converted into terror, which I am yet at a loss to describe. . . . I was immediately handled and tossed up to see if I was sound, by some of the crew; and I was now persuaded that I had got into a world of bad spirits, and that they were going to kill me. Their complexions too, differing so much from ours, their long hair, and the language they spoke, which was very different from any I had ever heard, united to confirm me in this belief. . . . I asked . . . if we were not to be eaten by those white men with horrible looks, red faces, and long hair. . . .

In a little time after, amongst the poor chained men, I found some of my own nation. . . . They gave me to

CHAPTER OUTLINE

Indians and Europeans
Indian Workers in the Spanish Borderlands
The Web of Trade
Displacing Native Americans in the English Colonies
Bringing Christianity to Native Peoples
After the First Hundred Years: Conflict and War

Africans and Europeans
Labor Needs and the Turn to Slavery
The Shock of Enslavement
African Slaves in the New World
African American Families and Communities
Resistance and Rebellion

European Laborers in Early America
A Spectrum of Control
New European Immigrants

Conclusion

understand we were to be carried to these white people's country to work for them. . . . [Many weeks later] we were landed up a river a good way from the sea, about Virginia county, where we saw few of our native Africans, and not one soul who could talk to me.

Olaudah Equiano, *The Interesting Narrative of the Life of Olaudah Equiano, or Gustavus Vassa, The African.*

Olaudah Equiano, born in 1745 in the African kingdom of Benin, was only a boy when his terrifying journey to America began. The son of an Igbo chief, he was caught in the web of an expanding transatlantic slave trade that reached from the African interior to nearly every port town in the Americas and the Caribbean. From modest beginnings in the sixteenth century, the slave trade had expanded dramatically, transforming all societies it touched. Equiano's Virginia scarcely resembled that of John Smith. Tobacco still reigned supreme, but by the mid-eighteenth century, more black workers than white ones bent their backs to the hoe. Slavery had spread from England's Caribbean colonies to dominate the Chesapeake settlements as well.

At the same time, in Virginia and elsewhere in North America, Indian peoples faced new challenges as they endeavored to maintain their independence despite a flood of immigrants from Europe and Africa. Depending on the circumstances, Indians employed different tactics—adaptation, coexistence, diplomacy, resistance—to assert their claims to land and their right to participate in the events and deliberations that affected their lives as much as those of colonists. The America to which Olaudah Equiano had been forcibly transported remained a place where Indian voices had to be heeded.

Equiano's journey did not end in Virginia. Over the next quarter-century, he visited nearly every part of England's empire and beyond—traveling to other mainland colonies, the West Indies, England, Turkey, Portugal, and Spain. He worked as the servant of a naval officer, a barber, a laborer, an overseer, saving money until he could purchase his own freedom. Such an extraordinary career testified to Equiano's versatility, resilience, and determination. It also bore witness to the emergence of an international market for laborers, which—like slavery and Indian relations—shaped the development of North America. Thousands of people from England, Scotland, Ireland, and Germany attempted to take advantage of that market and seek their fortunes in America, increasing the white population and expanding onto new lands. The interactions of Indians, Africans, and Europeans created not one but many New Worlds.

KEY TOPICS

- Patterns of contact between Native Americans and Spanish, French, and English colonists

- The development of slavery and other labor systems in early America

- The formation of African American communities

- Causes and consequences of European immigration to America

INDIANS AND EUROPEANS

Although, by 1750, European colonists and African slaves together outnumbered Indians north of the Rio Grande, Native Americans continued to dominate much of the continent. The colonists remained clustered along the coasts and had yet to make significant movement into the interior. Some native peoples had scarcely seen any colonists. Indians living along the northern Pacific coast, for instance, met their first white men—Russian fur traders—only in the 1740s. By this time, the Pueblos of the Southwest, the Hurons of Canada, and the Algonquians of the Atlantic seaboard had more than a century's experience dealing with Europeans and their American-born descendants.

The character of the relationship between Indians and Europeans depended on more than relative population size and the length of time they had been in contact. It was also shaped by the intentions of the newcomers—whether they came to extract resources, to trade, to settle, or to gain converts—and

Chronology

1440s	Portuguese enter slave trade in West Africa.
c. 1450	Iroquois form Great League of Peace and Power.
1610–1614	First war between English settlers and Powhatan Indians.
1619	First Africans arrive in Virginia.
1622–1632	Second war between English settlers and Powhatan Indians.
1637	Pequot War in New England.
1640s	Slave labor begins to dominate in the West Indies.
	First phase of the Beaver Wars.
1651	First "praying town" established at Natick, Massachusetts.
1661	Maryland law defines slavery as lifelong, inheritable status.
1670	Virginia law defines status of slaves.
1675–1676	King Philip's War in New England.
1676	Bacon's Rebellion in Virginia.
1680	Pueblo Revolt in New Mexico.
1680s	Second phase of Beaver Wars begins.
1690s	Shift from white indentured servants to black slaves as principal labor force in the Chesapeake.
1701	Iroquois adopt policy of neutrality toward French and English.
1711–1713	Tuscarora War in Carolina.
1713	Beginnings of substantial Scottish, Scots-Irish, and German immigration to colonies.
1715–1716	Yamasee War in Carolina.
1720s	Black population begins to increase naturally in English mainland colonies.
1732	Georgia established.
1739	Stono Rebellion in South Carolina.
1741	Slave conspiracy discovered in New York City.
1750	Slavery legalized in Georgia.
1760–1775	Peak of European and African immigration to English colonies.

the responses of particular Native American groups intent on preserving their cultures. The result was a variety of regionally distinctive New World communities. Many of the strategies Native Americans developed as they adapted to new conditions and tried to counter the intrusions of settlers would persist into the twentieth century.

INDIAN WORKERS IN THE SPANISH BORDERLANDS

More than any other European colonists, the Spanish sought direct control over Indians who labored in their mines or in their fields. Their ability to marshal Indian workers for Spanish gain depended on two factors: the existence of sizable Indian communities and Spanish military force. In North America outside of Mexico itself, these conditions could be found in New Mexico, and to a lesser extent in Florida. Native villages provided plenty of workers as well as existing structures of government that the Spanish could convert to their own uses. At the same time, Spanish soldiers insured that the Indians obeyed orders even though they greatly outnumbered the colonists.

One of the Spaniards' most important methods of labor control was the *encomienda*. Encomiendas, granted to influential Spaniards in New Mexico, gave these colonists the right to collect tribute from the native peoples living on a specific piece of land. That tribute usually took the form of corn, blankets, and animal hides, which the Spanish could either use themselves or sell. It was not supposed to include forced labor, but often it did.

The *repartimiento* was another Spanish technique for exploiting Native American labor. This was a mandatory draft of Indian labor for public projects, such as building forts, bridges, and roads. Laws stated that native workers should be paid and limited the length of their service, but the Spanish often ignored these provisions and sometimes compelled Indians to work on private estates.

Spaniards also acquired laborers by ransoming captives that Indian groups seized from one another. This practice was called *rescate*, and it obliged rescued Indians to work for those who had paid their ransom. These "freed" Native Americans usually became servants in Spanish households, often for years. Some colonial families welcomed them as

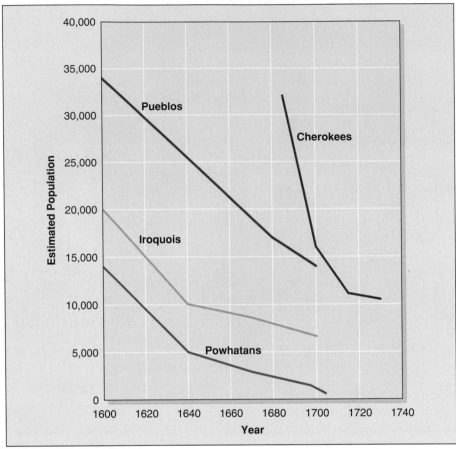

FIGURE 3-1   Estimated Populations of Selected Indian Peoples, 1600–1730
Indian populations shrank dramatically due to diseases brought by Europeans from the Old World. By about 1750, native peoples had become a minority of the inhabitants of America north of the Rio Grande.

Data Sources: Daniel Richter, *The Ordeal of the Longhouse* (1992); Helen Rountree, *Pocahontas's People* (1990); David Weber, *The Spanish Frontier in North America* (1992); Peter Wood, et al., eds., *Powhatan's Mantle* (1989).

foster members, but others mistreated them and even sold them into slavery.

Together these Spanish strategies for controlling Indian labor aroused considerable resentment on the part of native peoples. Spanish demands for labor and tribute remained constant, even when Indian populations declined from disease or crops failed in bad weather. Workers who resisted were severely punished by their masters or by soldiers. Resentments simmered beneath a surface of cooperation until late in the seventeenth century, when longstanding native anger burst forth in rebellion.

THE WEB OF TRADE

Not all economic exchanges between Indians and Europeans were as directly coercive as the *encomiendas* imposed by the Spanish. In many other instances,

Indians used trade relations to exert considerable influence over Europeans. They made colonists understand that Native Americans thought of trade not simply as an economic activity but rather as one aspect of a broader alliance between peoples. If Europeans wished to trade with Indians, they would have to prove their friendship by offering gifts such as wampum (shell beads used as a kind of currency) and military aid as well as manufactured goods. The names that native peoples bestowed on their European neighbors and allies often indicated the kinds of goods they provided. The Narragansetts in New England, for instance, called the English "coat-men" or "knife-men."

The French were among the most successful in adapting to the Native American understanding of trade, for they knew that good relations were essential to keeping New France's fur trade operating smoothly. The fur trade benefited Indians too. "The Beaver does everything perfectly well," noted one native leader; "it makes kettles, hatchets, swords, knives, bread; and, in short, it makes everything." Initially, Indians used European goods as raw materials to be reshaped as they saw fit. Thus copper kettles might be cut into pieces and hammered into ornaments instead of used for cooking. As such goods became more readily available, Indians replaced traditional objects with them: metal kettles for ceramic pots, wool blankets for skins and furs, metal knives for stone ones, glass beads for carved shells.

The benefits of trade were immediate and obvious, but most of the problems were slower to appear. The one exception was the problem of disease, which followed almost immediately from Indians' contacts with European traders (see Figure 3–1). The Huron population declined by half in just six years between 1634 and 1640. Indians trading with the Dutch in New Netherland in the 1650s insisted that they had once been "ten times as numerous as

This eighteenth-century engraving illustrates, in idealized form, the way Indian peoples traded furs for European goods. The barrel may have contained kettles or other metalware packed in sawdust, while the bale to the left probably held cloth.

they now are," but "their population had been melted down" by smallpox.

Although Indian hunters enjoyed considerable autonomy in their work, French merchants began to use economic pressure to exert greater control over them. By supplying Indians with trade goods in advance, merchants obligated them to bring in furs as payment. One year's hunting, in short, paid the previous year's debts. If hunters tried to avoid payment, merchants refused to give them any more of the trade goods they needed. Extending credit in this way allowed the French to control native workers without having to subjugate them.

The French could control the Indians through credit because native peoples had grown increasingly dependent on European manufactures. In many communities, Indians had abandoned native crafts and instead relied on imported goods. As a result, they had no alternative but to increase their hunting in order to have enough furs to trade for what they needed. "The Cloaths we wear, we cannot make ourselves," a Carolina Cherokee observed in 1753. "We cannot make our Guns. . . . Every necessary Thing in Life we must have from the white People." One consequence of this predicament was overhunting; as early as the 1640s, beaver could no longer be found in much of New England, New York, and Pennsylvania.

Trade with Europeans eventually encouraged violence and warfare. Indians had certainly fought one another before European colonization. But these wars were generally limited in scope and destructiveness. In much of eastern North America, "mourning wars" predominated. Warriors conducted raids mainly to seize captives rather than to kill large numbers of their enemies. The captives would either be ritually killed to avenge the deaths of individuals lost in earlier conflicts or adopted into the captors' group to replace the dead. After Europeans arrived, Indians adapted the mourning war tradition to deal with new circumstances. Warriors raided their enemies to replace family members lost to disease and fought to avenge losses resulting from the increasingly fierce competition for a diminishing supply of fur-bearing animals. The proliferation of firearms made the conflicts deadlier, and more casualties led to further mourning wars.

The **Beaver Wars,** a long struggle between the Hurons and the Iroquois that began in the 1640s, illustrated the ferocity of such contests. The Hurons were trading partners and allies with the French, and the Iroquois had forged ties with Dutch merchants in the Hudson River Valley. The Iroquois belonged to a league composed of five separate nations: the Mohawks, Oneidas, Onondagas, Cayugas, and Senecas. The **Great League of Peace and Power** had formed c. 1450, initially as a religious organization designed to eliminate mourning wars among the five nations and strengthen them in their conflicts with Indians outside the league.

To satisfy the European demand for furs, the Hurons and Iroquois both hunted beaver at an unsustainable rate. By the 1630s, they had killed nearly all the beavers on their own lands and began to look elsewhere for furs. The Hurons started to raise more corn, intending to trade the surplus for furs with Indians living north of the Great Lakes, where beavers were still abundant. The Iroquois, however, began to raid Huron trading parties and then to attack Huron villages.

The Iroquois triumphed in this struggle largely because the Dutch supplied them with guns while the French were reluctant to arm the Hurons. In the end, the Hurons were destroyed. Thousands were killed or captured, and many others fled westward. A French traveler reported seeing no Hurons in "districts which, not ten years ago, I reckoned to contain eight or ten thousand men. . . . A little farther on, were but the shells of cabins abandoned to the fury of the enemy—those who had dwelt in them having fled into the forest."

The cycle of warfare did not end with the Hurons' destruction. To maintain control over the fur supply, the victorious Iroquois went on to challenge Indian nations near the Great Lakes and in the Ohio Valley. Although trade brought improvements to native life, cemented alliances with Europeans, and strengthened the economic and diplomatic positions of such successful participants as the Iroquois, over the long run its disadvantages—especially Indians' eventual dependence on Europeans and the escalation of violence—threatened to overshadow its benefits.

DISPLACING NATIVE AMERICANS IN THE ENGLISH COLONIES

In New France and New Netherland, where the fur trade took precedence over farming, Indians always outnumbered Europeans. This numerical superiority and their key role as suppliers of furs to the Europeans allowed native peoples to negotiate with settlers from a position of strength and to retain control of much of their land. The situation was much different in the English colonies, whose settlers came to farm and thus competed directly with Indians for land. It did not help matters that, as Indian populations declined as the result of onslaughts of European diseases, colonial populations burgeoned through immigration and natural increase. As early as 1650,

colonists outnumbered Native Americans in coastal Massachusetts and eastern Virginia.

English settlers at first assumed that there was enough land for everyone. Colonists thrilled at the sight of what they considered vast unoccupied territory. "The Indians are not able to make use of the one fourth part of the Land," declared one New England settler. Another insisted that the natives "do but run over the grass, as do also the foxes and wild beasts" and that therefore the "spacious and void" land was free for the taking.

Land use and property rights. But the settlers misunderstood how Indians used their territory. Eastern Algonquian peoples moved frequently to take advantage of the land's diversity. They cleared areas for villages and planting fields, which native women farmed until the soil grew less fertile. Then they moved to a new location, allowing the former village site to return to forest. In ten to twenty years, they or their descendants might return to that site to clear and farm it again. Indians often built villages near the seacoast or rivers so that they could fish and use reeds and grasses for weaving. In the winter, village communities broke up into small bands to hunt in the forest for deer and other animals.

Thus what the colonists considered "vacant" lands were in fact either being used for nonfarming activities or recovering from human occupation in order to be farmed in years to come. Settlers who built towns on abandoned native village sites deprived the Indians of these future planting fields. Indians tolerated such intrusions for a while, but competition from the rapidly increasing settlers threatened their survival.

Disputes between Europeans and Indians frequently arose from misunderstandings about the definition of land ownership and property rights. Indian villages claimed sovereignty over a certain territory, which their members collectively used for farming, fishing, hunting, and gathering. No Indian claimed individual ownership of a specific tract of land. Europeans, of course, did, and for them ownership conferred on an individual the exclusive right to use or sell a piece of land.

These differences created problems whenever Indians transferred land to settlers. The settlers assumed that they had obtained complete rights to the land, whereas the Indians assumed that they had given the settlers not the land itself but only the right to use it. The Indians soon learned what the English meant by a land sale, however, because it was the English understanding that prevailed, enforced in the settlers' courts under the settlers' laws.

Many of the settlers' agricultural practices also strained relations with the Indians. Cutting down forests destroyed Indian hunting lands. When colonists dammed rivers, they disturbed Indian fishing. When they surrounded their fields with log fences and stone walls, they made trespassers of natives who crossed them. Colonial laws prohibited Indians from burning parts of the forest—something they had regularly done to destroy underbrush and make the woods suitable for hunting and travel—because settlers feared that fires might spread to their property. Yet the colonists felt free to let their cattle and pigs loose to graze in the woods and meadows, where they could wander into unfenced Indian cornfields and damage the crops.

Colonial land acquisition. As their numbers grew, the colonists displaced Indian inhabitants, acquiring their lands in various ways. Some colonial leaders, such as Roger Williams in Rhode Island and William Penn of Pennsylvania, insisted on buying land. But even purchasers who tried to be fair encountered difficulties. Because Indians owned land collectively, only their leaders had the authority to negotiate sales. Settlers, however, sometimes bought land from individual Indians, who had no right to sell it. Because land transfers were usually arranged through interpreters and recorded in English, Indians were not always fully informed of the terms of sale. And even Indians who willingly sold land to begin with grew resentful as colonists approached them for more. Finally, native peoples could be forced to sell land to settle debts they had run up with English creditors.

Settlers occasionally obtained land by fraud. In 1734, for instance, James Logan of Pennsylvania produced what he insisted was a copy of a deed from 1686 by which the Delaware Indians had supposedly transferred a large tract of land to William Penn. Although Logan did not have the original deed and there was no reference to it in the colony's land records, the Delawares eventually had to give up the territory. By the eighteenth century, some colonists moved farther inland, simply settled on Indian lands without any legal pretense at all, and appealed to colonial governments for help when the Indians objected. Land speculators amplified this kind of unrest on the edges of settlement as they sought to acquire land as cheaply as possible and sell it for as much as they could.

Finally, colonists often seized Indian lands in the aftermath of war, as befell, among many others, the Pequots in 1637 in Connecticut and, in Carolina, the Tuscaroras in 1713 and the Yamasees in 1715. In each case, settlers moved onto land left vacant as native peoples were killed, captured, and dispersed by colonial forces. Sometimes colonial leaders contrived for some Indian groups to help them displace others. During the Pequot War, Narragansetts aided Connecticut settlers' efforts to oust the Pequots. Carolina colonists enlisted the help of the Yamasees against the Tuscaroras and then turned to the Cherokees to help them against the Yamasees.

Some Indians who survived warfare and disease staved off the worst effects of English encroachments by regrouping to form new native communities just beyond the edges of colonial settlements. The Catawba Nation in the Carolina Piedmont employed this strategy to preserve their independence and, as a nineteenth-century visitor observed, "be Indians still." Although English colonists continued to covet Catawba lands, the Carolina government realized the advantages of having friendly native allies in a volatile frontier region and tried to discourage settlers' incursions.

Such small victories helped to sustain Indian autonomy in various parts of the English colonies. But the general trend was hardly encouraging. The colonists' insatiable hunger for land generated relentless pressure on native peoples, who were viewed more as impediments to English expansion than as trading partners or potential neighbors. Once the pattern of mutual suspicion and territorial competition had been established, it would be difficult to alter.

BRINGING CHRISTIANITY TO NATIVE PEOPLES

In addition to trade and settlement, religion played a powerful role in shaping relations between Native Americans and Europeans in colonial North America. The three major New World empires of Spain, France, and England competed for Indians' souls as well as their lands and riches.

Catholic missionaries in Spanish colonies. Franciscan priests were the driving force behind Spain's efforts to control its colonies of New Mexico and Florida (see Map 3–1). Spain valued both regions for strategic reasons. Its bases in Florida helped protect Spanish ships bearing treasure from the mines of Mexico and Peru and discouraged the southward spread of English settlement. New Mexico similarly served as a buffer between the silver mines of northern Mexico and roaming Plains Indians. Neither colony attracted many settlers, however, because neither offered much opportunity for wealth. When Franciscan missionaries proposed to move in, Spanish officials, who were eager to back up their claims

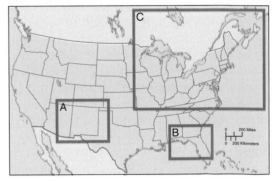

MAP 3-1 Spanish and French Missions in Seventeenth-Century North America
*Spanish Franciscans in New Mexico (A) and Florida (B) and French Jesuits in New France
(C) devoted considerable effort to converting native peoples to Catholic Christianity.*

with a more visible Spanish presence, agreed and even provided financial support.

Franciscans settled near native villages in New Mexico and Florida in order to convert their inhabitants to Christianity. The priests wore their finest vestments and displayed religious paintings and statues, trying to impress the Indians with European goods and Catholic ceremonies. They gave away bells, knives, cloth, and food. According to one Franciscan in New Mexico, these gifts functioned as bait,

bringing Indians to the missions "like fish to the fish hook." The natives believed that accepting these gifts obliged them to listen to the priests' Christian message and help the Franciscans build houses and churches.

After brief religious instruction, the missionaries convinced many Indians to accept baptism into the Catholic Church and with it, the promise of salvation and a heavenly afterlife. Although many of these conversions were doubtless genuine, they also had practical motivations. They often followed epidemics that devastated native villages but spared the Spanish, leading many Indians to wonder if the Christian God might indeed be more powerful than their own gods. In New Mexico, the Spanish offered Pueblo converts protection against Apache raids and access to Franciscan storehouses in times of famine. Ironically, the corn in the storehouses often came from the Indians' own fields, collected by the Spanish as tribute.

The Franciscans insisted that converts abandon their former ways of life and adopt Spanish food, clothing, gender relations, and work routines along with Catholicism. Their efforts met with mixed success. Many Indians, particularly in the densely settled communities of New Mexico, preferred to supplement native beliefs and practices with the new teachings. They added Jesus, Mary, and the Catholic saints to the list of Indian supernatural beings and considered missionaries as counterparts of, rather than replacements for, native religious leaders. Because missionaries reacted to this spiritual mixture with horror, inflicting severe punishments that sometimes led to victims' deaths, native peoples often practiced their own rituals in secret. Some groups, such as the Zuni and Hopi peoples, responded to the missionaries' intolerance by rejecting Christianity altogether. By the mid-seventeenth century, Spanish missionaries claimed to have made thousands of converts, many of whom were mestizos—people of mixed Spanish and Indian ancestry—occupying a difficult position between two cultures. Christianity had been securely planted in the Spanish borderlands, but not quite as deeply as the missionaries assumed.

French Jesuits in Canada.

To a certain extent, French Jesuits in Canada followed a similar strategy, moving to native villages and seeking to awe Indians with European technology and Catholic rituals. Priests exhibited the "magical" powers of clocks and magnets before Indian audiences and impressed native peoples by predicting eclipses. Missionaries demonstrated their ability to read and write, which fascinated Indian peoples who had no experience with written language. "All this serves to gain their affections, and to render them more docile when we introduce the admirable and incomprehensible mysteries of our Faith," explained one priest, who assumed that suitably impressed Indians would then "accept without reply what we say to them."

When Indians failed to relinquish their religious beliefs quite so easily, French missionaries resorted to economic pressure. They convinced merchants to sell guns only to converted Indians and to offer them other trade goods at a discount. Such tactics doubtless brought some success but, as in New Mexico, the crises engendered by epidemics more often than not sparked an upsurge in conversions. Converts in New France also preferred to meld Catholic teachings with native beliefs. Missionaries hardly condoned this response; one Jesuit complained that Indians "cannot suffer any opposition to their ceremonies." Vastly outnumbered by the Indians and intent on achieving their ultimate goal of winning souls for the Christian God, Jesuits resigned themselves at least in the short run to a gradual approach. "One must be careful before condemning a thousand things among their customs," warned one priest, because to do so would "greatly offend minds brought up and nourished in another world." Although the Jesuits were just as convinced of their own cultural superiority as any other Europeans, they reduced the potential for confrontation with the Indians by accepting small changes in converts at first in hopes of a wholesale transformation to follow.

Missionaries in English colonies.

The Protestant English were less successful at attracting Native

This Jesuit missionary, wearing his distinctive Catholic vestments, is baptizing an Indian in New France. French Jesuits proved to be more tolerant than most European missionaries in allowing Indian converts to retain at least some of their own customs.

This ball-headed war club, carved of maple wood, is thought to have been owned by King Philip, who led a confederation of Wampanoags and other New England Indians in a war against the colonists in 1675–1676. It is inlaid on both sides with pieces of white and purple wampum, which supposedly represented the number of English and Indian enemies killed.

American converts. Puritans frowned on the rituals and religious objects that drew Indians to Catholicism, but Protestant practices, including lengthy sermons and an emphasis on Bible study, held little allure for Indians accustomed to a more ritualistic spiritual life. Even so, Protestant missionaries achieved some success, principally in New England. Beginning in the 1650s and 1660s, Puritan ministers such as John Eliot and Thomas Mayhew, Jr. attracted converts. Eliot helped to establish several "praying towns," where Indians received instruction in Protestant Christianity and English ways. By 1674, about 2,300 Indians resided in these towns.

Elsewhere in the English colonies, missionaries enjoyed little success. Anglican missionaries in the southern colonies did not even begin conversion work until the eighteenth century and then often directed their efforts toward settlers who seemed to need religious instruction more urgently than the Indians. In the 1730s and 1740s, German Moravians, a Protestant group that stressed personal piety, managed to convert some Indians in western Pennsylvania. Although individual ministers showed genuine interest in conversion, and Anglican officials in England devoted some resources to missionary activities by the eighteenth century, the Protestant English never matched the efforts of Spanish or French Catholics. Rapidly growing English colonial populations were more interested in acquiring Indian lands than in converting Indian peoples.

AFTER THE FIRST HUNDRED YEARS: CONFLICT AND WAR

After nearly a century of European settlement, violence between colonists and Indians erupted in all three North American empires. Each deadly encounter—**King Philip's War** in New England, **Bacon's Rebellion** in Virginia, the **Pueblo Revolt** in New Mexico, and the resumption of the Beaver Wars in New

France—reflected distinctive features of English, Spanish, and French patterns of colonization.

King Philip's War. The growing frustration of the Wampanoags, who had befriended the Pilgrims more than a half-century earlier, with the land-hungry settlers whose towns now surrounded them sparked King's Philip's War, which broke out in 1675. Massasoit's younger son, Metacom—called King Philip by the English—led the Wampanoags and struggled to preserve their independence against the incursions of the colonists, who now numbered more than fifty thousand. He had little reason to trust the colonists. His older brother had died mysteriously while being questioned by colonial officials about rumors of an Indian conspiracy. Philip himself had been accused of plotting against the settlers and then forced to sign a treaty submitting to English authority.

In the spring of 1675, a colonial court found three Wampanoags guilty of murdering a Christian Indian who had warned the English of Wampanoag preparations for war. Despite Philip's protest that the evidence against the men was tainted, the court sentenced them to be hanged. This act convinced the Wampanoags that they had to strike back against the English before it was too late. Only "a small part of the dominion of my ancestors remains," declared Philip. "I am determined not to live until I have no country." The final blow occurred in June 1675, when colonists killed an Indian they found looting an abandoned house and then ignored the Indians' outrage at the murder.

Native warriors attacked outlying villages in Plymouth Colony, moved into the Connecticut River Valley, and then turned eastward again to strike towns within 20 miles of Boston. As the Narragansetts and other groups joined the uprising, Philip successfully eluded the combined forces of Massachusetts, Connecticut, and Plymouth for months (see "American Views: Mary Rowlandson

Among the Indians" on page 78). By the summer of 1676, however, the Indians were exhausted, weakened by disease and food shortages. Philip moved into western New England, where his men clashed with the powerful Mohawks, long-standing enemies of the Wampanoags and allies of English fur traders in New York. Philip died in an ambush in August 1676, and the war ended soon after.

At least a thousand colonists and perhaps three thousand Indians died in King Philip's War. One out of every sixteen male colonists of military age was killed, making this the deadliest conflict in American history in terms of the proportion of casualties to total population. The Indians succeeded in forcing back the line of settlement—it would be forty years before colonists again occupied land they had first claimed before the war—but lost what remained of their independence in New England. The victorious English sold many native survivors, including Philip's wife and young son, into slavery in the West Indies. Others they employed in marginal jobs or confined in one of the few remaining praying towns. Philip's head, impaled on a stake, was left for decades just outside Plymouth as a grisly warning of the price to be paid for resisting colonial expansion.

Bacon's Rebellion. As King Philip's War raged in New England, a bloody conflict erupted in Virginia that had a similarly devastating effect on that colony's native population. Frustrated by shrinking economic opportunities in eastern Virginia, where established planters controlled all the good land, many settlers, including new arrivals and recently freed indentured servants, moved to Virginia's western frontier. There they came into conflict with the region's resident Indians. In the summer of 1675, a group of frontier settlers attacked the Susquehannocks in order to seize their lands. The Indians struck back, prompting Nathaniel Bacon, a young, wealthy planter who had only recently arrived in Virginia, to lead the settlers in a violent campaign against all Indians, even those at peace with the colonial government. Governor William Berkeley ordered Bacon and his men to stop their attacks. They defied him and marched on Jamestown, turning a war between settlers and Indians into a rebellion of settlers against the colonial authorities.

The rebels believed that Berkeley and the colonial government represented the interests of established tobacco planters who wanted to keep men like themselves from emerging as potential competitors. Desperate because of the low price of tobacco, they demanded lower taxes and easier access to land—meaning, in effect, the right to take land from the Indians. Berkeley offered to build forts along the frontier to protect the settlers from the Indians, but the rebels were not interested in protection. What they wanted was help in exterminating the Indians. They captured and burned the colonial capital at Jamestown, forcing Berkeley to flee. Free to direct their aggression against Indians once more, they burned Indian villages and massacred the inhabitants. Trying to appease the rebels, the House of Burgesses passed measures allowing them to seize lands belonging to Indians who had left their villages without permission—even though many had fled to escape the rebels. The assembly also legalized the enslavement of Indians.

By the time troops arrived from England to put down the rebellion, Bacon had died of a fever and most of his men had drifted home. Berkeley arrested and hanged twenty-three rebels, but the real victims of the rebellion were Virginia's Indians. The remnants of the once-powerful Powhatans lost their remaining lands and either moved west or lived in poverty on the edges of English settlement. In the wake of the rebellion, hatred of Indians became a permanent feature of frontier life in Virginia, and government officials appeared more eager to spend money "for extirpating all Indians" than for maintaining peaceful relations.

The Pueblo Revolt. In 1680, the Pueblo Revolt against the Spanish in New Mexico had a very different outcome than did the rebellion in Virginia or the war in New England. Nearly 20,000 Pueblo Indians had grown increasingly restless under the harsh rule of only 2,500 Spaniards. Incessant Spanish demands for tribute under the *encomienda* system fed native discontent. A prolonged drought that began in the 1660s only increased their distress. Corn harvests dwindled, and many people starved. The Apaches, who had once traded with the Pueblos for corn, now raided their storehouses instead, and Spanish soldiers could not stop them.

The spark that ignited the revolt, however, was an act of religious persecution. Spanish officials unwisely chose this troubled time to stamp out all remaining traces of Pueblo religion. In 1675, the governor arrested forty-seven native religious leaders on charges of sorcery. The court ordered most of them to be publicly whipped and released but sentenced four of them to death.

Led by Popé, one of the freed leaders, the outraged Pueblos organized for revenge. A growing network of rebels emerged as Spanish soldiers marched into Pueblo villages and destroyed kivas, the chambers that Indians used for religious ceremonies. Working from the village of Taos in northern New

AMERICAN VIEWS

Mary Rowlandson Among the Indians

In February 1676, in the midst of King Philip's War, Indian warriors attacked the town of Lancaster, Massachusetts. They killed many inhabitants and took 23 colonists captive, including Mary Rowlandson and three of her children. Rowlandson spent the next three months traveling with various groups of Nipmucs, Narragansetts, and Wampanoags. She suffered physically and emotionally, watching her youngest daughter die in her arms and worrying about her other two children, from whom she was frequently separated. During her captivity, Rowlandson survived by accepting her fate and adapting to the Indians' way of life. Finally, with an English victory imminent, Rowlandson was ransomed and rejoined her husband (who had been away at the time of the attack) and family. In 1682, she published an account of her captivity in which she explored the meaning of her experience. Rowlandson's narrative proved so popular that three editions were printed in the first year.

- How did Rowlandson describe the Indians? How did she characterize her encounter with King Philip?
- In what ways did Rowlandson accommodate herself to the Indians' way of life? How did she employ her skills to fit in? Did her gender make a difference in her experience of captivity?
- How did Rowlandson's Puritan faith shape her narrative?

We travelled on till night; and in the morning, we must go over the River to Philip's crew. When I was in the Cannoo, I could not but be amazed at the numerous crew of Pagans that were on the Bank on the

---

Mexico, by the summer of 1680, Popé commanded an enormous force of rebels drawn from twenty Pueblo villages. On August 10, they attacked the Spanish settlements. Popé urged them to "break up and burn the images of the holy Christ, the Virgin Mary and the other saints, the crosses, and everything pertaining to Christianity" and ordered Indian converts to "plunge into the rivers and wash themselves" to remove the taint of baptism. Within a few weeks, the rebels had destroyed or damaged every Spanish building and killed more than four hundred Spaniards, including twenty-one of the colony's thirty-three missionaries. By October, all Spaniards had fled New Mexico.

They did not return for thirteen years. By then, internal rivalries had split the victorious Pueblo coalition, and Popé had been overthrown as leader. Few Pueblo villages offered much resistance to the new Spanish intrusion. Even so, the Spanish now understood the folly of pushing the Indians too far. Fearful of inciting another rebellion, officials reduced demands for tribute, and ended the *encomienda* system. The Franciscans eased their attacks on Pueblo religion. New Spanish governors, backed by military force, were responsible for keeping peace as best they could in a place where Indians still outnumbered Europeans.

The Iroquois adopt neutrality. The Iroquois experience in the last phase of the Beaver Wars threatened to parallel that of the Indians of New England and Virginia rather than that of the Pueblos in New Mexico. What began as a struggle between the Iroquois and western native peoples for control of the fur trade blossomed into a larger conflict as it was absorbed into the imperial rivalry between England and other side. When I came ashore, they gathered all about me, I sitting alone in the midst: I observed they asked one another questions, and laughed, and rejoyced over their Gains and Victories. Then my heart began to fail: and I fell a weeping which was the first time to my remembrance, that I wept before them. Although I had met with so much Affliction, and my heart was many times ready to break, yet could I not shed one tear in their sight: but rather had been all this while in a maze, and like one astonished: but now I may say as, Psal. 137.1 *By the rivers of Babylon, there we sat down: yea, we wept when we remembered Zion.* There one of them asked me, why I wept, I could hardly tell what to say: yet I answered, they would kill me: No, said he, none will hurt you. Then came one of them and gave me two spoon-fulls of Meal to comfort me. . . .Then I went to see King Philip, he bade me come in and sit down, and asked me whether I would smoke (a usual Complement now adayes amongst Saints and Sinners) but this no way suited me. For though I had formerly used Tobacco, yet I had left it ever since I was first taken, *It seems to be a bait, the devil lays to make men loose their precious time.* . . .

During my abode in this place, Philip spake to me to make a shirt for his boy, which I did, for which he gave me a shilling: I offered the money to my master, but he bade me keep it: and with it I bought a piece of Horse flesh. Afterwards he asked me to make a Cap for his boy, for which he invited me to Dinner. I went, and he gave me a Pancake, about as big as two fingers; it was made of parched wheat, beaten, and fryed in Bears grease, but I thought I never tasted pleasanter meat in my life. There was a Squaw who spake to me to make a shirt for her *Sannup* [husband], for which she gave me a piece of Bear. Another asked me to knit a pair of Stockins, for which she gave me a quart of Pease. . . . Hearing that my son was come to this place, I went to see him, and found him lying flat upon the ground: I asked him how he could sleep so? He answered me, *That he was not asleep, but at Prayer;* and lay so, that they might not observe what he was doing. I pray God he may remember these things now he is returned in safety.

Source: Neal Salisbury, ed., *The Sovereignty and Goodness of God, Together with the Faithfulness of His Promises Displayed. . . .* (Boston, 1997), pp. 82–83.

France. Although the Iroquois suffered devastating losses similar to those inflicted on the Indians in the English colonies, they did not similarly suffer a loss of independence. The key to Iroquois survival in the war's aftermath was the adoption of a position of neutrality between the European powers.

Looking for new trading partners to replace the Hurons, the French turned in the 1680s to the Ottawas, Wyandots, and other Indian peoples living near the Great Lakes. But the Iroquois had begun to raid these same peoples for furs and captives, much as they had attacked the Hurons in the first phase of the Beaver Wars in the 1640s. They exchanged the furs for European goods with English traders, who had replaced the Dutch as their partners after the conquest of New Netherland. Many of the captives were adopted into Iroquois families, replacing victims of warfare and disease. When the French

moved into the Great Lakes territory, the Iroquois objected to their attempt to "have all the Bevers" for themselves.

The French attacked the Iroquois to prevent them and their English allies from extending their influence in the west. In June 1687, a combined force of French and Christian Indian soldiers invaded the lands of the Senecas, the westernmost of the five nations of the Iroquois League. The Iroquois retaliated by besieging a French garrison at Niagara, where nearly two hundred soldiers starved to death, and killing hundreds of colonists in attacks on French villages along the St. Lawrence River.

The French participated much more directly and suffered greater losses in this renewal of the Beaver Wars than they had in the fighting of the 1640s. In 1689, France and England went to war in Europe, and the struggle between them and their

Indian allies for control of the fur trade in North America became part of a larger imperial contest between the two countries. The European powers made peace in 1697, but calm did not immediately return to the Great Lakes region.

The conflict was even more devastating for the Iroquois. The English, still solidifying their control over their new colony of New York, provided minimal military assistance, and the Iroquois suffered heavy casualties. Perhaps a quarter of their population died from disease and warfare by 1689. The devastation encouraged Iroquois diplomats to find a way to extricate themselves from future English–French conflicts. The result, in 1701, was a pair of treaties, negotiated separately with Albany and Montreal, that recognized Iroquois neutrality and, at least for several decades, prevented either the English or the French from dominating the western lands.

Each of these conflicts grew from a distinctive pattern of contact between different groups of colonists and native peoples. English settlers fought with Wampanoags, Powhatans, and Susquehannocks for control of land, and the losers were the outnumbered Indians. Spanish colonists clashed with Pueblos over religion, and the more numerous natives won a temporary victory and accommodation in the long run with the Spanish Catholic minority. French soldiers battled with the Iroquois over control of the fur trade until both sides agreed to an uneasy truce. In each case, nearly a century of contact culminated in a struggle that revealed the fragility of Indian autonomy as European populations continued to grow and to seek domination.

AFRICANS AND EUROPEANS

The movement of Africans to the Americas was one of the largest forced migrations in world history. By the time New World slavery finally ended, with its abolition in Brazil in 1888, over twelve million Africans had arrived on American shores. From a relatively small stream in the sixteenth century, African migration ac-

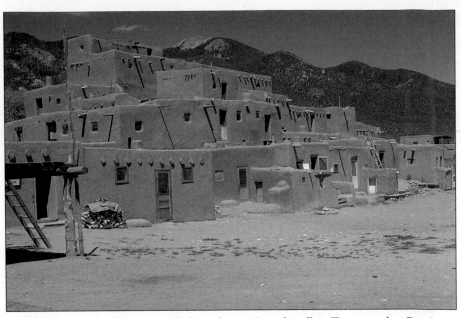

One of the many pueblos scattered along the Rio Grande valley, Taos served as Popé's headquarters at the start of the Pueblo Revolt in August 1680. Within a few weeks, the Indians drove the Spanish from New Mexico and destroyed most of their settlements. The Spanish did not return until 1693.

celerated to a great flood by the 1700s. Over 350,000 Africans crossed the Atlantic before 1600. More than five times as many, nearly 1.8 million Africans, arrived in the Americas in the seventeenth century. In the eighteenth century, another 6.1 million African migrants reached American destinations.

Virtually all Africans arrived as slaves, making the history of African experience in the Americas inseparable from the history of slavery and the slave trade. As one eighteenth-century English observer noted, Africans became "the strength and sinews of this western world," performing much of the labor of colonization. The vast majority of African slaves ended up in Brazil, the West Indies, or New Spain. Only 1 out of 20 Africans came to the British mainland colonies, but this still amounted to well over 300,000 individuals (see Figure 3–2). Their presence transformed English colonial societies everywhere, but particularly in the South. At the same time, Africans were themselves transformed. Out of their diverse African ethnic backgrounds and the experience of slavery itself they gradually forged new identities as African American peoples.

LABOR NEEDS AND THE TURN TO SLAVERY

Europeans in the New World were thrilled to find that land was abundant and quite cheap by European standards. They were perplexed, however, by

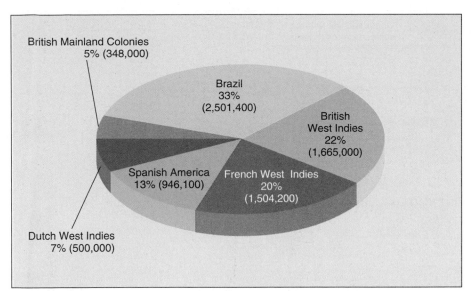

FIGURE 3-2   Destination of Slaves Imported from Africa to the Americas between 1451 and 1810

Approximately 7.5 million Africans were brought as slaves to the Americas before 1810. The vast majority went to the Caribbean, Mexico, and South America, where they toiled in mines and on sugar plantations.

Data Source: Philip Curtin, *The Atlantic Slave Trade: A Census* (1969), p. 268.

the unexpectedly high cost of labor. In Europe, the reverse had been true. There land was expensive but labor cheap, because competition for jobs among large numbers of workers pushed wages down. Colonial workers commanded high wages because there were so few of them compared to the supply of land waiting to be developed. Making matters worse, few settlers wanted to work for others when they could get farms of their own. The scarcity and high cost of labor created a major problem for colonial employers, leading some to turn to enslaved Africans as a solution.

The development of slavery in the colonies was not inevitable. Europeans had owned slaves (both white and black) long before the beginning of American colonization, but slaves formed a small—and shrinking—minority of European laborers. By the fifteenth century, slavery had all but disappeared in northern Europe except as punishment for serious crimes. English laws in particular protected the personal freedom of the king's subjects.

Slavery persisted longer in southern Europe and the Middle East. In both regions, religion influenced the choice of who was enslaved. Because neither Christians nor Muslims would hold as slaves members of their own faiths, Arab traders turned to sub-Saharan Africa to find slaves who did not belong to either religion. Eventually the Arabic word for slave—'*abd*—became a synonym for "black man." By the fifteenth century, a durable link between slave status and black skin had been forged in European minds.

Europeans in the New World, however, first attempted to force Indians into slavery as a way of addressing the labor shortage. Columbus's enslavement of Caribbean islanders marked only the beginning. Spaniards held Indian slaves in all their New World colonies, as did the Portuguese in Brazil. French Canadians enslaved Pawnee Indians captured in wars in the North American interior. English colonists condemned Indian enemies they captured in wartime to slavery as punishment for their opposition to English rule. And in early Carolina, English traders saw an opportunity to profit by enslaving Indians without any judicial niceties. They encouraged Indians "to make War amongst themselves to get Slaves" whom the traders could buy and then resell to West Indian and local planters.

Native American slaves, however, could not fill the colonists' labor needs. Everywhere disease and harsh working conditions reduced their numbers. English colonists also discovered practical reasons not to enslave Indians. When traders incited Indian wars to gain slaves, bloodshed often spread to English settlements. Moreover, enslaved Indian men refused to perform agricultural labor, which they considered women's work. Because they knew the land so well, Indians could easily escape and make their way back to their own people. As a result, although the Indian slave trade persisted in the English colonies through the eighteenth century (and there were still Indian slaves in the nineteenth century), by 1700 it had given way to a much larger traffic in Africans. Virtually all European colonizers had, by that point, made the same decision to rely principally on African laborers.

THE SHOCK OF ENSLAVEMENT

European traders did not themselves enslave Africans. Instead, they relied on other Africans to capture slaves for them, tapping into a preexisting African slave trade and helping to expand it beyond previous bounds. With the permission of local rulers, Europeans built forts and trading posts (called factories) on the West African coast and bought slaves from African traders (see Map 3–2). African rulers occasionally enslaved and sold their own people as punishment for crimes, but most slaves were seized by one group from another. Attracted by European cloth, iron, liquor, guns, and other goods, West Africans fought increasingly among themselves to secure captives and began kidnapping individuals from the interior.

People of all social ranks ended up on the slave ships. Some had been slaves in Africa; others had been village leaders or, like Olaudah Equiano, members of chiefs' families and the educated elite. In 1730, for example, Mandingo tribesmen captured Job ben Solomon, an accomplished Arabic scholar of the Fula tribe of Senegal, and sold him to English traders. In the end, slavery reduced all Africans, regardless of their social origins, to the same degraded status.

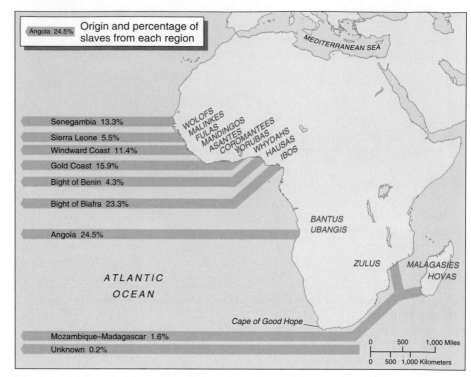

MAP 3-2   African Origins of North American Slaves, 1690–1807
Nearly all slaves in English North America were West Africans. Most had been captured or purchased by African slave traders, who then sold them to European merchants.

Once captured, slaves marched in chains to the coast, to be confined in cages called *barracoons* until there were enough to fill a ship. Captains examined them to insure their fitness and branded them like cattle with a hot iron. The slaves then boarded canoes to be ferried to the ships. Desperation overwhelmed some of them, who, according to an English captain, jumped "out of the canoes. . . . and kept under water till they were drowned, to avoid being taken up and saved." Slaves brought aboard ships waiting to leave for America sometimes mutinied. These rebellions, fought against great odds, rarely succeeded.

Slaves who could not escape while still in Africa suffered through a horrendous six- to eight-week-long ocean voyage known as the **Middle Passage**. Captains wedged men below decks into spaces about 6 feet long, 16 inches wide, and 30 inches high. Women and children were packed even more tightly. Except for brief excursions on deck for forced exercise, slaves remained below decks, where the air grew foul from the vomit, blood, and excrement in which the terrified victims lay. "The shrieks of the women, and the groans of the dying," recalled Olaudah Equiano, "rendered it a scene of horror almost in-

conceivable." Some slaves went insane. Others tried to commit suicide by jumping overboard or starving themselves. Captains force-fed those who refused to eat, prying their mouths open and pouring food in through a funnel. On many voyages, between 5 and 20 percent of the slaves perished from disease, but captains had usually packed the ships tightly enough to make a profit from selling the rest.

Those who survived the dreadful voyage endured the fear and humiliation of sale. Sometimes buyers rushed aboard ship in a scramble to choose slaves. Planters generally preferred males and often sought slaves from particular African ethnic groups, in the belief that some Africans would work harder than others. Ship captains also sold slaves at public auctions, where purchasers poked them, looking for signs of disease. Many terrified Africans, like Equiano, thought they were going to be eaten.

AFRICAN SLAVES IN THE NEW WORLD

The Spanish and Portuguese first brought Africans to the Americas, using them to replace or supplement the dwindling numbers of Indian slaves toiling in silver mines and on sugar plantations. The Dutch, who scrambled for a share of the lucrative slave trade, quickly followed suit. English colonists, less familiar with slavery, adopted it more slowly. West Indian planters were the first Englishmen to do so on a large scale in the 1640s, buying thousands of slaves from Portuguese and Dutch traders to work on sugar plantations. In most other English colonies, however, different economic conditions either postponed or prevented slavery's widespread adoption.

Slavery in the southern colonies.

Black slaves first arrived in Virginia in 1619, but they did not form a significant portion of the colony's population until the end of that century (see Figure 3–3). For decades, tobacco planters saw no reason to switch from white indentured servants to slaves. Servants (because they worked for masters only for a period of years rather than for life) cost less than slaves, were more readily available, and were familiar. For most of the seventeenth century, by contrast, slaves were expensive, difficult to obtain, and exotic. By the 1680s, however, planters in the Chesapeake colonies of Virginia and Maryland began to shift from servants to slaves.

Two related developments caused this change. First, white indentured servants became harder to

The freed slave Olaudah Equiano appears in this 1780 portrait by an unknown artist. After purchasing his freedom, Equiano wrote a vivid account of his capture in Africa and his life in slavery. One of the first such accounts to be published (in 1789), this narrative testified to slavery's injustice and Equiano's own fortitude and talents.

find. Fewer English men and women chose to emigrate as servants after 1660 because an improving economy in England provided jobs for them at home. At the same time, Virginia's white population tripled between 1650 and 1700, rapidly increasing the number of planters now competing for a shrinking supply of laborers. Planters also faced competition from newer colonies. Pennsylvania and New Jersey, with generous land policies, attracted immigrant laborers away from the longer-settled Chesapeake colonies.

Second, even as white servants grew scarcer, African slaves became more available, largely because of changes in the slave trade. Before the 1660s, Dutch and Portuguese merchants who dominated the trade mainly supplied their own colonies and the profitable West Indian market. But beginning in 1674, England's Royal African Company began shipping slaves to English buyers in the Caribbean and on the mainland. The supply of slaves surged after 1698, when the Royal African Company lost its special trading rights and many English merchants and New Englanders entered the fiercely competitive trade.

Chesapeake planters eventually found reasons besides availability to prefer slaves to servants. Although more expensive than servants, slaves were a better long-term investment. Because slave status passed from slave mothers to their children, buying both men and women gave planters a self-reproducing labor force. Runaway black slaves were more easily recaptured than were escaped servants, who blended into the white population. And unlike indentured servants, slaves were slaves for life. They would never compete as planters with their former masters or, like Nathaniel Bacon's followers, pose a threat to order if they failed to prosper.

Chesapeake planters had already come to see white servants as possessions, people whose labor could be bought and sold like any other commodity. This attitude doubtless eased the transition in the 1680s and 1690s to the much harsher system of slavery. In Carolina, of course, the introduction of slavery was not gradual at all. Slaves arrived there right from the start, brought in the 1670s by colony founders accustomed to slavery in Barbados. By 1720, slavery was firmly embedded in all the southern colonies except sparsely settled North Carolina. In that year, one-third of Virginia's settler population, and nearly three-quarters of South Carolina's, were black.

Slavery grew rapidly in the southern colonies because it answered the labor needs of planters engaged in the commercial production of tobacco and rice. The demand for slaves became so powerful that it

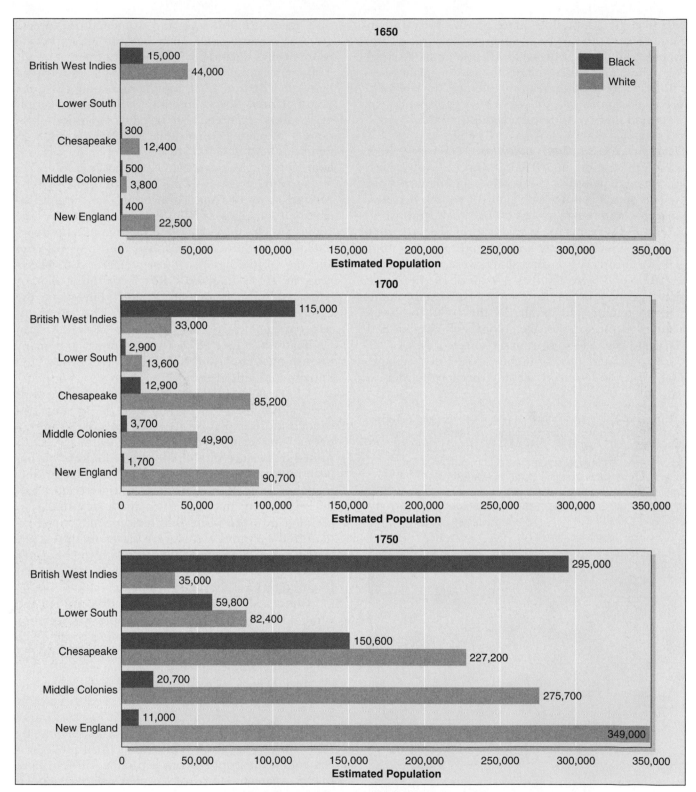

FIGURE 3-3 Estimated Population of Black and White Settlers in British Colonial Regions, 1650–1750

Settler populations increased rapidly in all colonial regions, but the racial composition varied. By 1750, black people overwhelmingly predominated in the West Indies and were quite numerous in the southern colonies; north of Maryland, however, their numbers remained small.

Data Source: John J. McCusker and Russell Menard, *The Economy of British America, 1607–1789* (1985).

Although this watercolor of a slave ship bound for Brazil dates from the nineteenth century, it depicts a scene common on slavers in the 1700s. The artist's attention to detail suggests both the misery of the slaves' surroundings and the dignity of the individuals forced to live under such conditions.

destroyed James Oglethorpe's plan to keep them out of the new colony of Georgia, founded in 1732. Oglethorpe intended Georgia to be a refuge for English debtors, who normally were jailed until they could repay their creditors. His idea was to send debtors to Georgia to produce such exotic goods as silk and wine, benefiting both themselves and the English economy. Only rice turned a profit in Georgia, however, and colonists insisted that they needed slaves to keep up with South Carolina's planters. By 1750, Georgia's founders reluctantly legalized slavery; by 1770, slaves made up nearly half of the colony's population.

Slavery in the northern colonies. Far fewer slaves lived north of the Chesapeake, although they were present in every British colony. They were too

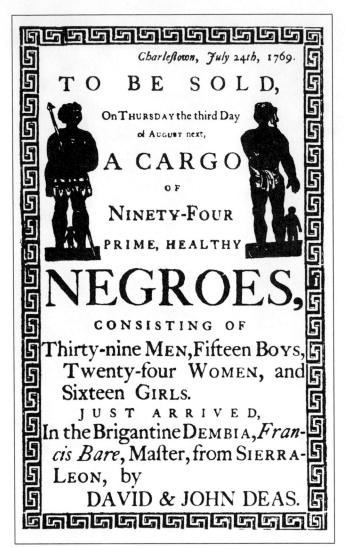

This 1769 broadside advertised the arrival of a cargo of West African slaves in Charleston, South Carolina. By that date, slaves made up over two-thirds of the colony's settlers. Note that nearly equal numbers of men and women have been imported. This practice would eventually contribute to the formation of slave families and communities.

expensive for most northern farmers—who mainly produced food for their families, not staple crops for an international market—to use profitably. This was not true, however, for farmers with larger properties in parts of Long Island, the Hudson Valley, Rhode Island, northern New Jersey, and southeast Pennsylvania, where commercial wheat farming and livestock raising prevailed. Especially in the eighteenth century, these landowners acquired significant numbers of slaves. By the 1760s, for instance, one-fifth of the farmers in Chester County, Pennsylvania, owned slaves. Some rural slaves also worked in local indus-

tries, such as tanneries and iron foundries, often alongside white servants and hired laborers.

Northern slaves could often be found in cities, especially busy ports such as Newport, Rhode Island, where newly arrived Africans landed. At the start of the eighteenth century, one out of six Philadelphia residents was a slave; by 1740, slaves made up 15 percent of the city's workingmen. In mid-eighteenth-century New York City, slaves comprised between 12 and 14 percent of the population. Urban slaves worked at a variety of occupations, including seafaring and maritime trades such as rope and sail making. Many were domestic servants in the homes of rich merchants, gentlemen, and professionals. Substantial numbers found employment as artisans, to such an extent that white workers occasionally protested that they were being left behind. In 1737, for instance, New York City's white coopers complained about "the pernicious custom of breeding slaves to trades whereby the honest and industrious tradesmen [are] reduced to poverty for want of employ."

Changing race relations in the colonies. Race relations in the mainland colonies were less rigid in the seventeenth century than they would later become. Before 1700, slaves did not form a majority of the population in any colony, a situation that may have made them seem less threatening to white people. Most seventeenth-century Chesapeake planters did not own slaves. Those who did often held only a few slaves along with white servants. In these households, white and black people lived and worked in close contact. Black slaves and white servants ran away together and cooperated during Bacon's Rebellion. In some areas, free black people—often slaves who had bought their own freedom—prospered in an atmosphere of racial tolerance that would be unthinkable by the eighteenth century.

The career of an ambitious black Virginian named Anthony Johnson, for example, resembled that of many white settlers—a remarkable achievement, given that he arrived in the colony in 1621 as a slave known only as "Antonio a Negro." Johnson's master allowed him to marry and start a family while he was still a slave and may even have allowed Anthony to earn the money to purchase his and his family's liberty. Once free, the Johnsons settled near their former master in eastern Virginia. By 1651, Johnson owned a 250-acre plantation, and his sons eventually acquired even larger estates. Like white settlers, Johnson occasionally took his neighbors to court and even successfully sued them. He and his sons also owned slaves. When his plantation burned to the ground in 1653, local authorities granted

Johnson relief from taxes in recognition of his family's "hard labor and known services" in supporting themselves.

Anthony Johnson belonged to the first or what one historian has called the "charter" generation of American slaves, and his experience reveals how much slavery changed over time. This generation of slaves mainly came from African port towns, where Europeans and Africans had mingled for generations, or by way of the West Indies or New Netherland. Familiar with European ways, often fluent in European languages, they acquired skills and knowledge that enabled them to bargain with their masters in ways their descendants would not be able to replicate. They came in small groups, cultivated their masters as patrons, negotiated for property of their own, and often gained their freedom. They enjoyed such advantages because they came to colonies where slavery had not yet become firmly embedded, where the meaning of bondage was still being worked out.

As this nineteenth-century engraving indicates, slaves were often subjected to humiliating physical inspections so that potential buyers could be convinced of their good health and strength.

Repressive laws and slave codes.

But Johnson's descendants, and the generations of slaves and free black people who came after them, encountered much harsher conditions. Once slavery became the dominant labor system in the Chesapeake, tobacco planters no longer welcomed free black people, fearing that they might encourage slaves to escape. In 1691, Virginia's legislature prohibited individual masters from freeing their slaves. Eight years later, lawmakers passed another measure requiring newly freed black people to leave the colony altogether. Black people like the Johnsons, who were already free, suffered under an increasing burden of legal discrimination. Laws prohibited them from employing white servants, holding office, bearing arms, and voting. Free black people paid extra taxes and suffered more severe punishments than white people did for the same crimes. Interracial marriages, never common, were prohibited as "shameful Matches."

Bad as the situation of free black people had grown, the condition of slaves was far worse. Slave codes, laws governing slavery, essentially reduced an entire class of human beings to property. In Virginia, from the middle of the seventeenth century on, a series of new laws added to slaves' oppression. A 1662 measure defined slavery as a lifelong and inherited status that passed from slave mothers to their children—even children with white fathers. Masters who might have felt uneasy about holding fellow Christians as slaves were relieved in 1667 when another law stated that baptism would not release slaves from bondage. Two years later, the House of Burgesses gave masters the power of life and death over their slaves, decreeing that masters would not be charged with felony if their slaves died during punishment. These and other measures were gathered into a comprehensive slave code in Virginia in 1705. Additional restrictions prohibited slaves from testifying in court against white colonists, required them to carry passes whenever they left their masters' estates, and forbade them to gather in groups of more than four people.

Slave codes appeared virtually everywhere, North and South, but were particularly harsh in the southern colonies. White colonists in the Tidewater Chesapeake and South Carolina feared the consequences of a growing black population. One South Carolina planter predicted in 1720 that slaves would soon rise up against their masters because black people were "too numerous in proportion to the White Men there."

The changing composition of the slave labor force also created tensions. Unlike the charter generation, slaves who arrived in the eighteenth century usually came from the African interior and had had less contact with European customs and language. Worried planters commented on the strange appearance and behavior of these people, with whom they could barely communicate. Their uneasiness, of course, scarcely compared to the Africans' harrowing experience of being torn away from the only world they knew and thrust into the harsh and unfamiliar condition of slavery.

AFRICAN AMERICAN FAMILIES AND COMMUNITIES

The harshness of slaves' condition could be relieved somewhat by the formation of close ties with others who shared their circumstances. For those ties to be created, however, several developments had to occur. Slaves had to become sufficiently numerous in specific localities so that black people could have regular contact with one another. Ethnic and language barriers carried over from Africa had to erode so that slaves could communicate with one another. And for family ties to be formed, there had to be adequate numbers of slave women as well as men. Because these conditions were slow to develop, occurring at different rates in different colonies, the formation of African American families and communities was delayed until well into the eighteenth century.

The situation was perhaps most difficult for slaves in the northern colonies. Many slaves there lived alone or in pairs with their master's family, with few opportunities to associate with fellow slaves. Only in cities and on substantial commercial farms were slaves numerous enough to create their own communities. The formation of families, however, was slowed by a relative scarcity of women. When slave families did appear, husbands and wives often lived in different households as the property of different masters.

The rise of the creole slave population.
Slaves were far more numerous in the southern colonies, and it is there that African American families and communities emerged with greater success. This fact was especially true in South Carolina and parts of the Tidewater Chesapeake, where in certain localities slaves formed a majority of the population. Even more significant, these regions witnessed the rise of a creole, or American-born, slave population by about the 1750s. This development distinguished slavery in the mainland British colonies from that in the West Indies, where disease and overwork killed so many slaves that the black population grew only because of the constant importation of Africans.

The rise of a creole slave population in the Chesapeake and in Carolina set off a chain of related events that fostered family and community life. Creoles lived longer than African immigrants, and creole women usually bore twice as many children as African-born mothers. This circumstance allowed the slave population to grow by natural increase and more closely resemble a normal population of men and women, children and elders. Greater equality between the numbers of men and women helped in the creation of families. At the same time, creole slaves grew up without personal memories of Africa, and thus African ethnic differences receded in importance. Most creoles knew some English and spoke dialects, such as Gullah in parts of South Carolina, that mixed English and African words and speech patterns, so that they were able to communicate with other slaves and form African American communities.

Work and family life.
Most of a slave's life was structured by work. The vast majority of southern slaves were field hands. On tobacco plantations, they toiled in gangs supervised by overseers. In Carolina, rice planters allowed their workers more flexibility, assigning them tasks in the morning and permitting them free time after they finished. On large plantations, masters selected some slave men to be trained as shoemakers, weavers, or tailors and chose others as drivers or leaders of work gangs. With the exception of nurses and cooks, few slave women avoided the drudgery of field labor. If they had families, the end of the day's work in the fields only marked the start of domestic duties back in the slave quarters. But no matter how onerous, work did not absorb every minute of the slaves' lives, and in the intervals around their assigned duties many slaves nurtured ties of family and community. Combining aspects of their African heritage and American experience, they created a new identity for themselves.

By the late eighteenth century, more than half of Chesapeake and Carolina slaves lived in family groups. These were fragile units, subject to the whims of masters who did not recognize slave marriages as legal, who broke up families by sale, and who could take slave women as sexual partners at will. Many slave husbands and wives resided on different plantations, although on larger Carolina estates two-parent slave households grew increasingly common. Over time, dense kinship networks formed, linking slaves across greater distances. To a certain extent, kinship structures reflected West African influences. Slaves placed great emphasis on kin connections, even using familiar terms such as "aunt" and "uncle" to address friends. Some slave husbands, like West African men, took more than one wife. In naming their children, slaves mingled old and new practices, sometimes giving them the African names of distant kin and sometimes using English names.

Community life and religion. Community life forged ties between slave families and single slaves on the plantations and offered further opportunities to preserve elements of African heritage. Traces of African religious practices endured in America. Magical charms and amulets have been found buried in slave quarters, indicating that certain spiritual ceremonies may have been conducted out of sight of white masters. Slave conjurors told fortunes, concocted herbal potions, and placed curses on their clients' enemies. Reflecting their West African background, slaves placed great emphasis on funerals, in the belief that relatives remained members of kin communities even after death. Funerals were sometimes divided into two distinct ceremonies. First, the deceased received a somber burial, often with beads or other ceremonial objects placed in the grave; some weeks later, slaves played music and danced at livelier funeral rites.

Christianity offered little competition to African religious practices during most of the colonial period. Few masters showed much interest in converting their slaves. Evangelical ministers, who began to preach to slave audiences around the middle of the eighteenth century, did gain some converts, but the widespread adoption of Christianity by slaves did not occur until after the Revolution.

African influences shaped aspects of slaves' recreational activity and material life. Slave musicians used African-style instruments, including drums and banjos, to accompany traditional songs and dances. In parts of South Carolina, slaves enjoyed *papaw*, an African game with dice. Storytellers entertained audiences with folk tales that may have had African roots. Where slaves were allowed to build their own houses, they often incorporated African elements into the designs—for instance, by using mud walls and roofs thatched with palmetto leaves. Their gardens frequently contained African foods such as millet, yams, peppers, and sesame seeds along with European and Native American crops.

Family and community ties gave a sense of belonging and dignity to people whose masters treated them as outcasts. Working and living together, slaves preserved at least some elements of African culture despite the harrowing conditions of their forced migration. Out of their African past and their American experience, they created new identities as African Americans as they coped with the oppressiveness of slavery.

RESISTANCE AND REBELLION

Even as family ties made a life in bondage more tolerable, they made it more difficult for slaves to attempt escape or contemplate rebellion. Slaves who resisted their oppression ran the risk of endangering families and friends as well as themselves. But the powerful desire for freedom and the spirit of resistance were not easily suppressed, and slaves found numerous ways to defy the dehumanization that slavery entailed.

Running away from a master was a desperate act, but thousands of slaves did just that. Few runaways shared the mistaken impression of some new arrivals in eighteenth-century Virginia who thought they could "find the Way back to their own Country." But deciding where else to go posed a problem. Escape out of the South did not bring freedom because slavery was legal in every colony. After 1733, some runaways went to Florida, where Spanish officials promised them freedom. Others tried to survive on their own in the woods or join the Indians—a choice that carried the risk of capture or death. South Carolina planters paid Indians to catch escaped slaves, largely to sow seeds of distrust between the two peoples and prevent them from joining forces against white colonists. For slaves with families, running away carried the high emotional cost of separation from loved ones as well as physical danger. Perilous as it was, escape proved irresistible to some slaves, especially young males. In a few isolated areas on the South Carolina frontier, runaways formed "maroon" settlements, always on the lookout for the white soldiers sent to attack them.

Many slaves chose less perilous ways to resist their bondage. Landon Carter, one of Virginia's wealthiest tobacco planters, once complained that his slaves "seem to be quite dead hearted and either cannot or will not work." He did not seem to realize that he had become the target of forms of resistance more subtle, but every bit as real, as running away. Slaves worked slowly, broke tools, and pretended to be ill in order to conserve strength and exert some control over their working lives. When provoked, they also took more direct action, damaging crops, stealing goods, and setting fire to their masters' barns, houses, and fields. Slaves with knowledge of poisonous plants occasionally tried to kill their white owners, although the penalty for being caught was to be burned to death.

The most serious, as well as the rarest, form of resistance was organized rebellion. South Carolinians and coastal Virginians, who lived in regions where

This eighteenth-century painting from South Carolina records the preservation of certain African traditions in American slave communities. The dance may be Yoruba in origin, while the stringed instrument and drum were probably modeled on African instruments.

black people outnumbered white people, had a particular dread of slave revolt. But because rebellions required complete secrecy, careful planning, and access to weapons, they were extremely hard to organize. No slave rebellion succeeded in the British colonies. Rumors usually leaked out before any action had been taken, prompting severe reprisals against the alleged conspirators. In Charleston, South Carolina, rumors of a planned uprising in 1740 led to the torture and execution of fifty black suspects. The following year, thirty-five alleged rebels (including four white people) were executed in New York City.

Two slave revolts did occur in the colonial period, however, and instilled lasting fear in the white colonists. In 1712 in New York City, where black people made up perhaps 20 percent of the population, about twenty slaves set a building on fire and killed nine white men who came to put it out. The revolt was quickly suppressed. The court tried forty-three rebels and sentenced twenty-four to death. Their punishments revealed the extent of white terror: thirteen were hanged, three burned at the stake, one

starved to death, and one broken on the wheel. Six committed suicide before execution.

The **Stono Rebellion**, colonial America's largest slave uprising, occurred in South Carolina in 1739. It began when about twenty slaves—including several recently arrived Angolans—broke into a store and armed themselves with stolen guns. As the rebels marched southward along the Stono River, their ranks grew to perhaps a hundred. Heading for freedom in Spanish Florida, they attacked white settlements along the way. White troops (with Indian help) defeated the rebels within a week, but tensions remained high for months. The death toll, in the end, was about two dozen white people and perhaps twice as many black rebels. Planters boasted that they "did not torture one Negroe, but only put them to an easy death," although one settler claimed that white soldiers "Cutt off their heads and set them up at every Mile Post they came to."

In the wake of the Stono Rebellion, South Carolina's assembly passed a law requiring stricter supervision of slave activities. Other measures encouraged more white immigration to offset the colony's black majority. But the colony continued to rely on the labor system that generated so much fear and brutality. In South Carolina, as in the rest of the southern colonies, planters considered slavery indispensable to their economic survival and would not willingly give it up. Their slaves, in turn, obeyed when necessary, resisted when possible, and kept alive the hope that freedom would one day be theirs.

EUROPEAN LABORERS IN EARLY AMERICA

Slavery was one of several responses to the scarcity of labor in the New World. It took hold mainly in areas where the profits from growing export crops such as sugar, rice, and tobacco offset the high purchase price of slaves and where a warm climate permitted year-round work. Elsewhere European masters and employers found various ways to acquire and manage European laborers. Indentured servitude, forced labor, tenancy, and the extension of credit, all aimed at limiting the freedom of some people in order to make them work for others.

A SPECTRUM OF CONTROL

In the English colonies, slavery was merely the most oppressive extreme in a spectrum of practices designed to exert control over workers and relieve the problems caused by the easy availability of land and the high cost of labor. Most colonial laborers were, in some measure, unfree (see the Overview table, "Predominant Colonial Labor Systems, 1750").

One-half to two-thirds of all white immigrants to the English colonies arrived as indentured servants, bound by contract to serve masters for a period of years. Tens of thousands of people accepted temporary servitude in return for passage across the Atlantic and the chance for a more prosperous future in America. But indentured servants, though less costly than slaves, carried too high a price for farmers who raised crops mainly for subsistence rather than for sale. Thus, although servants could be found in every colony, they were most common in the Chesapeake and, to a lesser extent, in Pennsylvania, where they produced export crops valuable enough to enable their masters to feed, clothe, and shelter them—and still make a profit.

Slaves replaced white indentured servants in Chesapeake tobacco fields during the eighteenth century. Masters continued to import servants for a while to fill skilled jobs but in time trained the more plentiful slaves to fill those positions. Thus, by the middle of the eighteenth century, white servitude, although it still existed in the Chesapeake region as well as in Pennsylvania and New York, was in decline as a dominant labor system.

Eighteenth-century Chesapeake planters also availed themselves of another unfree labor source: transported English convicts. Lawmakers in England saw transportation as a way of getting rid of large numbers of criminals who might otherwise be executed. Between 1718 and 1775, nearly fifty thousand convicts were sent to the colonies, 80 percent of whom ended up in the Chesapeake. Most were young, lower-class males forced by economic hardship to turn to lives of crime. Although some colonists objected to England's policy of sending its undesirables to America, labor-hungry planters eagerly bought them for seven-year terms at relatively low prices and exploited them ruthlessly. A few convicts eventually prospered in America, but most faced lives as miserable as those they had known in England.

An arrangement similar to indentured servitude—the **redemptioner** system—brought many families, especially from German provinces, to the colonies in the eighteenth century. Instead of negotiating contracts for service before leaving Europe, as indentured servants did, redemptioners promised to redeem, or pay, the costs of passage on arrival in America. They often paid part of the fare themselves before sailing. If they could not raise the rest of it soon after landing, the ship captain who brought them sold them into servitude. The length of their service depended on how much they still owed. Most Germans went to Pennsylvania, where they hoped to find friends or relatives willing to help them pay off their debt quickly

Purchasing slaves, servants, or convicts did not make sense for everyone. Colonists who owned undeveloped land faced many tasks—cutting trees, clearing fields, building fences and barns—that brought no immediate profit. Rather than buy expensive laborers to accomplish these ends, landowners rented undeveloped tracts to families without property. Both tenants and landlords benefited from this arrangement. Tenants enjoyed greater independence than servants and could save toward the purchase of their own farms. The landlord secured the labor necessary to transform his property into a working farm, thus increasing the land's value. He also received an annual rent payment, usually a portion of the tenant's crop, and eventually profited from selling the land, often to the tenant family who had rented it. Tenancy worked best in Pennsylvania, New Jersey, and the Hudson and Connecticut River Valleys, where farmers raised wheat and other grains for the market.

Overview

Predominant Colonial Labor Systems, 1750

	Colony	Labor System
New England	Massachusetts	Family farms
	Connecticut	Family farms
	New Hampshire	Family farms
	Rhode Island	Family farms
Middle Colonies	New York	Family farms, tenancy
	Pennsylvania and Delaware	Indentured servitude, tenancy, family farms
	New Jersey	Family farms, tenancy
South	Maryland	Slavery
	Virginia	Slavery
	North Carolina	Family farms, slavery
	South Carolina	Slavery

Merchants eager to develop New England's fisheries devised other means to fill their labor needs. Because it was fairly easy to get a farm, few New Englanders cared to take on the difficult and risky job of fishing. Moreover, few could afford the necessary equipment, including boats, sails, provisions, and salt (used for preserving fish). Merchants learned to recruit fishermen by advancing credit to coastal villagers so that they could outfit their own boats. To pay off the debt, the fishermen were legally bound to bring their catch to the merchant, who then sold it to Europe and the West Indies. Many fishermen ran up such large debts that they were obliged to continue supplying fish to their creditors, whether they wanted to or not. Toward the end of the seventeenth century, as the rising population of coastal villages lowered the cost of labor, merchants abandoned the credit system and paid wages to fishermen instead.

In the northern colonies, the same conditions that made men reluctant to become fishermen deterred them from becoming farm laborers, except perhaps for high wages. Paying high wages, however, or the high purchase cost of servants or slaves was difficult, if not impossible, for New Englanders with farms that produced no export crops and could not be worked during cold winter months. So northern farmers turned to the cheapest and most dependable workers they could find—their children.

Children as young as 5 or 6 years old began with simple tasks and moved on to more complex work as they grew older. By the time they were in their late teens, girls knew how to run households, and boys knew how to farm. Instead of contracts or outright coercion, fathers used their ownership of property to prolong the time their sons worked for them. Young men could not marry until they could set up their own households and relied on their fathers to provide them with land to do so. Fathers often waited until their sons were in their mid-twenties, compelling them until then to invest their labor in the paternal estate.

Thus New England's labor shortage produced strong ties of dependency between generations. Fathers kept their sons working for them as long as possible; sons accepted this arrangement because they had no other way to become independent farmers. They would eventually employ their own children in the same way. As New England's population increased in the eighteenth century, and vacant land grew scarcer, the price of labor came down. Some fathers could then afford to hire occasional helpers and loosen their hold on their sons, allowing them to marry earlier.

Property owners in all the English colonies found different ways to control the laborers they so desperately needed. But where property owners saw problems—high wages (often twice what workers in England received) and abundant land (which deterred colonists from working for others when they could have their own farms)—others saw opportunities. For tens of thousands of Europeans, the chance to own or rent a farm or to find steady employment made North America an irresistible magnet, promising a prosperity that was beyond their reach at home.

NEW EUROPEAN IMMIGRANTS

European immigrants flooded into America in the seventeenth and eighteenth centuries (see Figure 3-4). Nearly 250,000 Scots-Irish people—descendants of Protestant Scots who had settled in northern Ireland in the sixteenth and seventeenth centuries—came to the colonies after 1718, when their landlords raised rents to intolerable levels. Tens of thousands of immigrants arrived from Scotland during the same period, some seeking economic improvement and some sent as punishment for rebellions against the king in 1715 and 1745. Thousands of Irish Catholics arrived as servants, redemptioners, and convicts. By 1773, the tremendous outflow of Britons to America sparked debate in England over whether emigration should be prohibited lest the British Isles themselves be left empty.

Continental Europe contributed another stream of emigrants. Perhaps 100,000 German Protestants left the Rhine Valley, where war, economic hardship, and religious persecution had brought misery. French Protestants (known as Huguenots) began emigrating after 1685, when their faith was made illegal in France, and continued to arrive for decades. Swiss Protestants likewise fled religious persecution. Even a few Poles, Greeks, Italians, and Jews reached the colonies in the eighteenth century.

Many emigrants responded to pamphlets and newspaper articles that exaggerated the bright prospects of life in America. Others studied more realistic accounts from friends and relatives who had already emigrated. One Scot who had moved to North Carolina warned his countrymen that at first "poor people will meet with many Difficulties" but they should "take courage and Come to this Country [for] it will be of Benefitt" to their families. Landowners eager for workers sent agents to port towns to recruit new arrivals to become tenants, often on generous terms. One happy immigrant wrote to his wife, who remained behind in England, that he had signed a lease for a farm in New York that exempted him from paying rent for the first 5 years and charged him only 7 pence an acre after that.

Streams of emigrants flowed to places where land was cheap and labor most in demand (see Map 3-3). Few went to New England, where descendants of the first settlers already occupied the best land. They also avoided areas where slavery predominated—the Chesapeake Tidewater and lowland South Carolina—in favor of the foothills of the Appalachian Mountains, from western Pennsylvania to the Carolinas. There, one emigrant declared, a "poor man that will incline to work may have the value of his labour."

This observation, though partly true, did not tell the whole story. Any person who came as a servant, redemptioner, or tenant learned that his master or landlord received much of "the value of his labour."

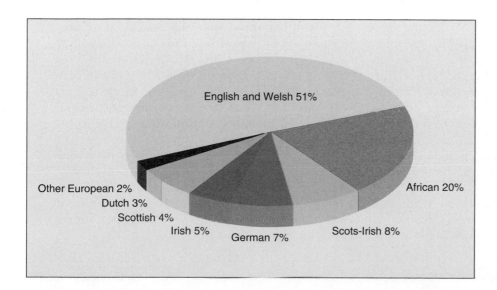

FIGURE 3-4 Ethnic Distribution of Non-Indian Inhabitants of British Mainland Colonies, c. 1770
By the third quarter of the eighteenth century, the colonial population was astonishingly diverse. Only two out of three settlers claimed British ancestry (from England, Wales, Scotland, or northern Ireland), while one out of five was African in origin.

Data Source: Thomas L. Purvis, "The European Ancestry of the United States Population, 1790," *William and Mary Quarterly*, 3d series, 41 (1984), p. 98.

FROM THEN TO NOW

The Legacy of Slavery

As the twenty-first century begins, Americans continue to grapple with the social, economic, and political consequences of the nation's past involvement in the enslavement of Africans. Slavery's roots extend deeply into American history, reaching back before nationhood itself. White colonists, facing a New World labor shortage in the seventeenth century, chose to fill their need for workers by purchasing slaves from Africa. Seeking to produce as much tobacco, rice, or sugar as they could for as little cost as possible, they left a painful legacy that has shaped America's history for centuries.

By the early eighteenth century, slavery was a fixture in every colony, and white colonists had come to associate slave status with black skin. The Revolution, with its rhetoric of freedom, challenged slavery but did not end it. It took another, far bloodier, war in the following century to accomplish that end. But the constitutional amendments outlawing slavery and guaranteeing black people's civil rights that passed after the Civil War—important milestones though they were—still could not eradicate the racism that had become deeply ingrained in American life.

Even today, well over a century after the Civil War ended, problems persist. Many black Americans have joined the middle class, but many others continue to suffer from discrimination and poverty. Black Americans' average incomes lag behind those of white people, fewer black people attend college, more of them live in impoverished neighborhoods in decaying urban centers. Black victims occasionally become targets of hate crimes merely because of the color of their skin. To a considerable extent, these economic and social dislocations, and the racial attitudes that help to shape them, can be traced to the lingering effects of slavery.

Recent public and private efforts to address the condition of African Americans have sought to highlight that longstanding connection. In 1997, for instance, President Bill Clinton appointed a commission to study the persistent problem of race in America. That he chose an historian, John Hope Franklin, to head the group suggested that Clinton recognized the link between America's past involvement with slavery and the nation's current racial divisions. But when some of his supporters subsequently urged Clinton to issue a formal apology for slavery, he refused to take what would have been a highly controversial step.

The reluctance of political leaders to take on such a sensitive issue may explain the recent search for private remedies. Among the most prominent of these efforts was a federal lawsuit filed in March 2002 against the Aetna Insurance Company, the FleetBoston Financial Corporation, and the CSX Corporation. A group of black plaintiffs charged that these companies profited from slavery in the past, and ought to make restitution. In the 1850s the Aetna Insurance Company, for example, made money insuring the lives of slaves. Deandria Farmer-Paellmann, the lead plaintiff in the lawsuit and a descendant of slaves, discovered the connection as she researched the slave reparations issue for a law-school class. These companies, she suggested, "should be held responsible, and later on down the road there will be more companies."

Whether these suits will be any more successful than the push for a presidential apology remains to be seen. How reparations, if granted, would be used to ameliorate the condition of black Americans is also unclear. This lawsuit joins a host of earlier strategies, including constitutional amendments and civil rights legislation, in seeking to reverse the legacy of slavery and to make equality and justice a reality for all Americans. Even in the first decade of the twenty-first century, the nation is still contending with the consequences of decisions made by some of the earliest colonists almost four hundred years ago.

MAP EXPLORATION To explore an interactive version of this map, go to http://www.prenhall.com/goldfield/map3.3

MAP 3-3   **Ethnic Distribution of Settler Population in British Mainland Colonies, c. 1755**
Settlers of different ethnic backgrounds tended to concentrate in certain areas. Only New Englanders were predominantly English, while Africans dominated in the Chesapeake Tidewater and South Carolina. German, Scottish, and Scots-Irish immigrants often settled in the backcountry.

Not all emigrants realized their dreams of becoming independent landowners. The scarcity of labor in the colonies led as easily to the exploitation of white workers as of slaves and Indians. Even so, for many people facing bleak prospects in Europe, the chance that emigration might bring prosperity was too tempting to ignore.

CONCLUSION

Eighteenth-century America offered a strikingly diverse mosaic of peoples and communities. Along the St. Lawrence River lay Kahnawake, a village of Mohawks and Abenakis who had adopted Catholicism and French ways under Jesuit instruction. In Andover, Massachusetts, New Englanders tilled fields that their Puritan grandparents had cleared. German immigrants seeking spiritual perfection populated the isolated Pennsylvania settlement of Ephrata. The hundred or so slaves on Robert Carter's Virginia plantation at Nomini Hall gathered on Sunday evenings to nurture ties of community with songs and dances, while the master cultivated his very different sense of community with the neighboring planters whom he invited to the great house to sip fine wine. In North Carolina, Swiss settlers rebuilt the coastal town of New Bern, destroyed during the Tuscarora War, while 100 miles farther west, Scottish emigrants cleared land for farms near present-day Fayetteville. Catawba Indians formed new villages in the South Carolina foothills to distance themselves from white settlers. In Mose, Florida, near St. Augustine, runaway slaves farmed and gathered shellfish under the protection of Spanish soldiers. Far to the west, the Spanish, mestizo, and Pueblo residents of Santa Fe warily reestablished ties broken during the Pueblo Revolt.

In these and many other communities, peoples from three continents adapted to one another and to American conditions. Indians struggled with the consequences of disease, trade, religious conversion, settlement, and warfare resulting from European immigration. Some native peoples managed to preserve their autonomy, others did not. Millions of African slaves suffered under the most repressive labor regime but fought its grip whenever possible. Slave communities testified to African Americans' assertion of their humanity in the face of a system that sought to deny it. English settlers became landowners in unprecedented numbers and adopted new ways to control laborers, reinventing slavery, unknown in England for centuries. For many European immigrants, the colonies offered the chance for economic improvement. Impoverished servants, transported convicts, and slaves, however, found America to be no land of opportunity

As the eighteenth century wore on, the North American colonies attracted more attention from their home countries. Spain, France, and England all recognized the colonies' growing economic power and strove to harness it to block the expansion of their rivals. Everywhere the effort to strengthen imperial ties created ambivalence among colonists.

Because the English settlers were by far the most numerous, their responses were the most pronounced. As they saw more clearly the differences between themselves and England itself, some colonists began to defend their distinctive habits, while others tried more insistently than ever to imitate English ways. The tension between new and old had, of course, characterized colonial development from the start. What made the eighteenth century distinctive were the many ways in which those tensions worked themselves out.

REVIEW QUESTIONS

1. The first phase of Olaudah Equiano's journey into slavery took him from Africa's interior to the coast. What part of this journey most frightened him? Why?

2. English colonists experienced more frequent, and more violent, conflicts with Indians than the settlers of New France did. Why was this so? What factors affected Indian–European relations in the two colonial regions?

3. Why were Catholic missionaries more successful than Protestants in converting Indians to Christianity in early America?

4. When did Chesapeake planters switch from servants to slaves? What factors contributed to their decision to make this change?

5. By about 1750, more slaves in the mainland British colonies were creoles (American-born) than African-born. What effects did this have on the formation of African American communities in America?

6. Different labor systems predominated in various regions of British America. How did the economy of each region help determine its labor system?

7. Tens of thousands of European immigrants came to America in the eighteenth century, but they tended to settle only in certain colonial regions. What destinations did they favor and why?

KEY TERMS

Bacon's Rebellion (p. 76)

Beaver Wars (p. 71)

Encomienda (p. 69)

Great League of Peace and Power (p. 71)

King Philip's War (p. 76)

Middle Passage (p. 82)

Pueblo Revolt (p. 76)

Redemptioner (p. 91)

Repartimiento (p. 69)

Rescate (p. 69)

Stono Rebellion (p. 90)

RECOMMENDED READING

Berlin, Ira. *Many Thousands Gone: The First Two Centuries of Slavery in North America* (1998). A magisterial synthesis of the evolution of slavery from its beginnings in America through the Revolution.

Equiano, Olaudah. *The Interesting Narrative of the Life of Olaudah Equiano, or Gustavus Vassa, the African* (numerous editions). A vivid and moving story of an extraordinary individual's passage from Africa to New World slavery and, ultimately, to freedom.

Moore, Brian. *Black Robe* (1985). A powerful novel that explores the experiences of a Jesuit missionary among the Indians in seventeenth-century New France.

Richter, Daniel. *Facing East from Indian Country: A Native History of Early America* (2001). A brilliant synthesis of early American history viewed from the perspective of native peoples.

Vickers, Daniel. *Farmers and Fishermen: Two Centuries of Work in Essex County, Massachusetts, 1630–1830* (1994). A beautifully written and sophisticated analysis that explores the way in which settlers adapted their English experiences to deal with the shortages of labor and capital in New England.

ADDITIONAL SOURCES
Indians and Europeans

Axtell, James. *The Indians' New South: Cultural Change in the Colonial Southeast* (1997).

Calloway, Colin. *New Worlds for All: Indians, Europeans, and the Remaking of Early America* (1997).

Cronon, William. *Changes in the Land: Indians, Colonists, and the Ecology of New England* (1983).

Delage, Denys. *Bitter Feast: Amerindians and Europeans in Northeastern North America, 1600–64* (English ed., 1993).

Drake, James. *King Philip's War: Civil War in New England, 1675–1676* (2000).

Gutierrez, Ramon. *When Jesus Came, the Corn Mothers Went Away: Marriage, Sexuality, and Power in New Mexico, 1500–1846* (1991).

Hinderaker, Eric. *Elusive Empires: Constructing Colonialism in the Ohio Valley, 1673–1800* (1997).

Knaut, Andrew L. *The Pueblo Revolt of 1680: Conquest and Resistance in Seventeenth-Century New Mexico* (1995).

Merrell, James H. *Into the American Woods: Negotiators on the Pennsylvania Frontier* (1999).

Rountree, Helen. *Pocahontas's People: The Powhatan Indians of Virginia through Four Centuries* (1990).

Steele, Ian K. *Warpaths: Invasions of North America* (1994).

Washburn, Wilcomb E. *The Governor and the Rebel: A History of Bacon's Rebellion in Virginia* (1957).

White, Richard. *The Middle Ground: Indians, Empires, and Republics in the Great Lakes Region, 1650–1815* (1991).

Africans in America

Blackburn, Robin. *The Making of New World Slavery: From the Baroque to the Modern 1492–1800* (1997).

Breen, T. H., and Stephen Innes. *"Myne Owne Ground": Race and Freedom on Virginia's Eastern Shore, 1640–1676* (1980).

Curtin, Philip. *The Atlantic Slave Trade: A Census* (1969).

Davis, David Brion. *The Problem of Slavery in Western Culture* (1966).

Jordan, Winthrop. *White over Black: American Attitudes toward the Negro, 1550–1812* (1968).

Littlefield, Daniel. *Rice and Slaves: Ethnicity and the Slave Trade in Colonial South Carolina* (1981).

Morgan, Philip. *Slave Counterpoint: Black Culture in the Eighteenth-Century Chesapeake & Lowcountry* (1998).

Morris, Thomas. *Southern Slavery and the Law 1619–1860* (1996).

Mullin, Michael. *Africa in America: Slave Acculturation and Resistance in the American South and the British Caribbean 1736–1831* (1994).

Piersen, William. *Black Yankees: The Development of an Afro-American Subculture in Eighteenth-Century New England* (1988).

Wood, Betty. *The Origins of American Slavery: Freedom and Bondage in the English Colonies* (1997).

Labor Systems and European Immigration

Bailyn, Bernard. *The Peopling of British North America: An Introduction* (1986).

Bailyn, Bernard. *Voyagers to the West: A Passage in the Peopling of America on the Eve of the Revolution* (1986).

Bascler, Marilyn. *"Asylum for Mankind": America 1607–1800* (1998).

DeWolfe, Barbara, ed. *Discoveries of America: Personal Accounts of British Emigrants to America in the Revolutionary Era* (1997).

Ekirch, A. Roger. *Bound for America: The Transportation of British Convicts to the Colonies, 1718–1775* (1987).

Griffin, Patrick. *The People With No Name: Ireland's Ulster Scots, America's Scots Irish, and the Creation of a British Atlantic World, 1689–1764* (2001).

Innes, Stephen, ed. *Work and Labor in Early America* (1988).

Roeber, A. G. *Palatines, Liberty, and Property: German Lutherans in Colonial British America* (1993).

Salinger, Sharon V. *"To Serve Well and Faithfully": Labor and Indentured Servants in Pennsylvania, 1682–1800* (1987).

Wokeck, Marianne. *Trade in Strangers: The Beginnings of Mass Migration to North America* (1999).

WHERE TO LEARN MORE

- **Ste. Marie among the Hurons, near Midland, Ontario, Canada.** This site contains a reconstructed Jesuit mission from the seventeenth century. There is a museum with information about seventeenth-century France as well as life among the Huron Indians. Further information may be found at www.saintemarieamongthehurons.on.ca.

- **Taos Pueblo, Taos, New Mexico.** Still a residence for Pueblo Indians, portions of this multistoried pueblo date from the fifteenth century. This was the site from which Popé directed the beginnings of the Pueblo Revolt in 1680. Pictures and other information are available at www.cr.nps.gov/worldheritage/taos.htm.

- **Ephrata Cloister, Ephrata, Pennsylvania.** Founded by German immigrants in the eighteenth century, the Ephrata community attracted religious pietists. The site now contains a museum, buildings that reflect medieval German architectural styles, and a collection of decorative art objects. The website www.cob-net.org/cloister.htm includes a biography of Ephrata's founder, Johann Conrad Beissel.

- **Carter's Grove Slave Quarter, near Williamsburg, Virginia.** Site includes reconstructed eighteenth-century slave quarters on original site where slave cabins once stood. Costumed African American interpreters show visitors around and tell stories about actual slaves who lived on the plantation. Information about the house and plantation can be found at www.williamsburg.com/plant/carter.html. Pictures of the plantation may also be seen at www.wise.virginia.edu.

 Please refer to the document CD-ROM for primary sources related to this chapter.

→ *This painting hung over the fireplace in the home of eighteenth-century Massachusetts merchant Moses Marcy. The ledger book and the trading ship symbolize the central figure's commercial career. The fine wineglass in his hand, the elegant punch bowl on the table, and the gracious home in the background represent the prosperity that trade could bring.*

Old Sturbridge Village Photo by Henry E. Peach. 20.19.1

CONVERGENCE AND CONFLICT
1660s–1763

4

Virginia 26th April 1763

Mr. Lawrence

Be pleased to send me a genteel sute of Cloaths made of superfine broad Cloth handsomely chosen; I shou|l|d have Inclosed |for| you my measure but in a general way they are so badly taken here that I am convinced it wou|l|d be of very little service; I wou|l|d have you therefore take measure of a Gentleman who wears well made Cloaths of the following size—to wit—Six feet high & proportionably made; if any thing rather Slender than thick for a Person of that highth with pretty long arms & thighs—You will take care to make the Breeches longer than those you sent me last, & I wou|l|d have you keep the measure of the Cloaths you now make by you and if any alteration is required, in my next |letter| it shall be pointed out. Mr Cary will pay your Bill—& I am Sir Yr Very H|um|ble Serv|an|t . . .

George Washington

W.W. Abbot and Dorothy Twohig, eds., *The Papers Of George Washington*, Colonial Series, vol. 7 (Charlottesville, 1990).

CHAPTER OUTLINE

Economic Development and Imperial Trade in the British Colonies

The Regulation of Trade
The Colonial Export Trade and the Spirit of Enterprise
The Import Trade and Ties of Credit
Becoming More Like England: The Growth of Cities and Inequality

The Transformation of Culture

Goods and Houses
Shaping Minds and Manners
Colonial Religion and the Great Awakening

The Colonial Political World

The Dominion of New England and the Limits of British Control
The Legacy of the Glorious Revolution
Diverging Politics in the Colonies and Great Britain

Expanding Empires

British Colonists in the Backcountry
The Spanish in Texas and California
The French along the Mississippi and in Louisiana

A Century of Warfare

Imperial Conflict and the Establishment of an American Balance of Power, 1689–1738
King George's War Shifts the Balance, 1739–1754
The French and Indian War, 1754–1760: A Decisive Victory
The Triumph of the British Empire, 1763

Conclusion

George Washington, along with a few dozen other privileged Virginians, had traveled to Williamsburg for a visit that mixed politics, business, and pleasure. Like Washington, these men had come to the capital to represent their respective counties in the House of Burgesses. When not engaged in government business, they attended to private affairs. They arranged to ship tobacco from their plantations to England, to pay outstanding debts, or to seek credit until the harvest was in. Washington was surely not the only one to take the opportunity to write to his London tailor and order the fashionable clothing that advertised his status as a gentleman. He and his fellow burgesses donned their best coats and breeches to attend evening dinner parties and theater performances that enlivened days otherwise devoted to debating politics and rendering accounts.

April 1763 marked the fourth time Washington had gone to Williamsburg to take his seat in the legislature. Each journey carried him further away from a youth spent as a surveyor and soldier toward his future as a respected planter and public servant. Just 31 years old in 1763, he had recently married Martha Custis, a wealthy widow, and inherited his older brother's plantation at Mount Vernon. He had served his king in battle during the Seven Years' War; now he was eager to exchange his military uniform for the "genteel" broadcloth suits appropriate to his new station. Washington already owned vastly more land than most English gentlemen. With land and wealth to support his ambitions, he wanted to live, look, and behave like an English country gentleman, not merely like a Virginia planter.

But Washington could not be sure what an English gentleman wore. While some of his fellow Virginia planters, like William Byrd, had been sent to England to obtain education and social graces to smooth over the rough edges of their provincial origins, Washington had never been to England and trusted neither his own judgment nor Williamsburg tailors to know how a proper English gentleman should dress. So, while he instructed Mr. Lawrence about measurements and fabric quality, Washington said nothing about the color or style of his new suit. He had to trust his tailor to make him clothing as suitable for the drawing rooms of London as for the parlors of Williamsburg.

Throughout British America, colonists who had achieved wealth and power tried, like Washington, to imitate the habits and manners of the English gentry. Their aspirations testified to important developments in the eighteenth century. Prosperity and the demand of a growing population for English products tied the colonies ever more tightly into a trade network centered on the imperial metropolis, London. The flow of goods and information between England and America fueled the desires of Washington and other successful colonists for acceptance as transatlantic members of the English elite. No longer a collection of rough outposts clinging to the Atlantic seaboard, British America was growing in size and sophistication.

These developments in Britain's American colonies brought them to the attention of European statesmen, who increasingly factored North America into their economic, political, diplomatic, and military calculations. Parliament devised legislation that would channel tobacco and other colonial goods into England and away from its European competitors. Spain and France viewed the economic growth and geographic expansion of British North America as a threat to their own colonial possessions, and they responded aggressively by augmenting their territorial claims. With expansion came conflict, and with conflict, war: a series of four imperial wars, which themselves became powerful engines of change in the New World.

KEY TOPICS

- Development of closer connections between Britain and the colonies
- Rising aspirations of the colonial elite
- Eighteenth-century religious life
- Political developments in England and the colonies
- Renewed competition among Britain, France, and Spain in North America
- Impact of imperial warfare in North America

Chronology

1651–1733	Parliament passes series of Navigation Acts to regulate imperial trade.
1660	Charles II becomes king of England.
1662	Halfway Covenant adopted by Massachusetts clergy.
1685	James II becomes king of England.
1686–1689	Dominion of New England.
1688	Glorious Revolution in England; James II loses the throne.
1689	William and Mary become English monarchs; Leisler's Rebellion begins in New York.
1689–1697	King William's War in America.
1691–1692	Witchcraft trials in Salem, Massachusetts.
1698	First French settlements near mouth of Mississippi River.
1701	Iroquois adopt policy of neutrality toward France and Britain.
1702–1713	Queen Anne's War in America.
1718	Establishment of San Antonio, Texas; New Orleans founded.
1734–1735	Jonathan Edwards leads religious revival in Northampton, Massachusetts.
1739	Great Awakening begins in Middle Colonies with George Whitefield's arrival.
1744–1748	King George's War in America.
1754–1763	Seven Years' War in America.
1760s	Spanish begin establishing missions in California.

ECONOMIC DEVELOPMENT AND IMPERIAL TRADE IN THE BRITISH COLONIES

The greatest assets that Great Britain could call on in its competition with other European nations were a dynamic economy and a sophisticated financial system that put commerce at the service of the state. In the century after 1690, England became the most advanced economic power in Europe. England's leaders came to see colonies as indispensable to the nation's economic welfare. Colonies supplied raw materials unavailable in the mother country, and colonists and Indians provided a healthy market for English manufactured goods.

As the eighteenth century progressed, colonial economies grew in tandem with England's. Parliament knitted the colonies into an empire with commercial legislation, while British merchants traded with and extended credit to growing numbers of colonial merchants and planters. Over time, these developments made colonial societies resemble England more closely than ever before and integrated the economies of the colonies with that of the metropolis in a vast transatlantic system.

THE REGULATION OF TRADE

England, Holland, and France competed vigorously in transatlantic trade. To capture a greater share of commerce, England pursued a policy of national self-sufficiency in which its American colonies played a key role (see the Overview table, "British Imperial Trade Regulations, 1651–1733"). Between 1651 and 1733, Parliament passed laws that regulated trade to insure that more wealth flowed into England's treasury than out of it. This governmental intervention in the economy for the purpose of increasing national wealth—called **mercantilism**—aimed to draw the colonies into a mutually beneficial relationship with England.

Parliament enacted four types of mercantilist regulations. The first aimed at ending Dutch dominance in England's overseas trade. Beginning with the Navigation Act of 1651, all trade in the empire had to be conducted in English or colonial ships, with crews of which at least half were Englishmen or colonists. The act stimulated rapid growth in both England's merchant marine and New England's shipping industry. Shipbuilding and earnings from what was called the carrying trade soon became the most profitable sector of New England's economy.

The second type of legislation channeled most colonial trade through England, giving it control over raw materials it would otherwise have to buy from rival nations. Certain colonial goods, called **enumerated products**, could be shipped only to England or to another English colony. These goods initially included tobacco, sugar, indigo, and cotton; other products, such as rice, were added later.

Overview

British Imperial Trade Regulations, 1651–1733

Name of Act	Key Features
Navigation Act of 1651	Aimed to eliminate Dutch competition in overseas trade
	Required most goods to be carried in English or colonial ships
	Required crews to be at least half English
Navigation Act of 1660	Required all colonial trade to be carried in English ships
	Required master and three-quarters of crew to be English
	Created list of enumerated goods, such as tobacco and sugar, that could be shipped only to England or another English colony
Staple Act of 1663	Required products from Europe, Asia, and Africa to be landed in England before being shipped to the colonies
Plantation Duty Act of 1673	Attempted to reduce smuggling
	Required captains of colonial ships to post bond that they would deliver enumerated goods to England or pay the "plantation duty" that would be owed in England
Navigation Act of 1696	Plugged loopholes in earlier laws
	Created vice-admiralty courts in colonies to enforce trade regulations
Woolens Act of 1699	Forbade export of woolen cloth made in the colonies, to prevent competition with English producers
Hat Act of 1732	Prohibited export of colonial-made hats
Molasses Act of 1733	Placed high tax on French West Indian and other foreign molasses imported into colonies to encourage importation of British West Indian molasses

These laws also required European goods to pass through England before they could be shipped to the colonies. When these goods entered English ports, they were taxed, making them more expensive and encouraging colonists to buy English-made items.

The third and fourth sorts of regulation further enhanced the advantage of English manufacturers who produced for the colonial market. Parliament subsidized certain goods, including linen, gunpowder, and silks, to allow manufacturers to undersell European competitors in the colonies. Other laws protected English manufacturers from colonial competition by prohibiting colonists from manufacturing wool, felt hats, and iron on a large scale.

England's commercial goals were largely achieved. The Dutch eventually lost their preeminence in the Atlantic trade. Colonial trade helped the English economy to grow and contributed to London's emergence as western Europe's largest city. Although some tobacco and rice planters complained about restraints on their freedom to seek markets on their own, the colonies as a whole prospered. Between 1650 and 1770, the colonial economy expanded twice as fast as England's did. Colonists enjoyed protected markets for their staple crops and low prices on English imports. Because colonial merchants operated on equal terms with English traders, they could take full advantage of commercial opportunities within the empire.

Occasionally, merchants evaded these laws by smuggling. Customs officials, sent over from England beginning in the 1670s, were hard-pressed to stop them. Although they derived much of their income from fines collected from smugglers, officials generally found it easier to accept bribes and look

Scenes like this were common in the dockyards at Deptford and other parts of eighteenth-century London. Boxes and barrels of English goods were loaded aboard sailing ships that returned months later with sugar, tobacco, rice, and other products from every part of England's worldwide empire.

the other way when a suspicious ship arrived in port with, say, an illicit cargo of French West Indian sugar. Most colonial trade, however, followed the proper routes. By not pushing for perfect compliance, British officials did not put too much pressure on a system that in fact worked remarkably well.

THE COLONIAL EXPORT TRADE AND THE SPIRIT OF ENTERPRISE

By the mid-eighteenth century, the Atlantic had become a busy thoroughfare of international commerce (see Map 4–1). Between 1700 and 1770, the number of British merchant ships nearly tripled,

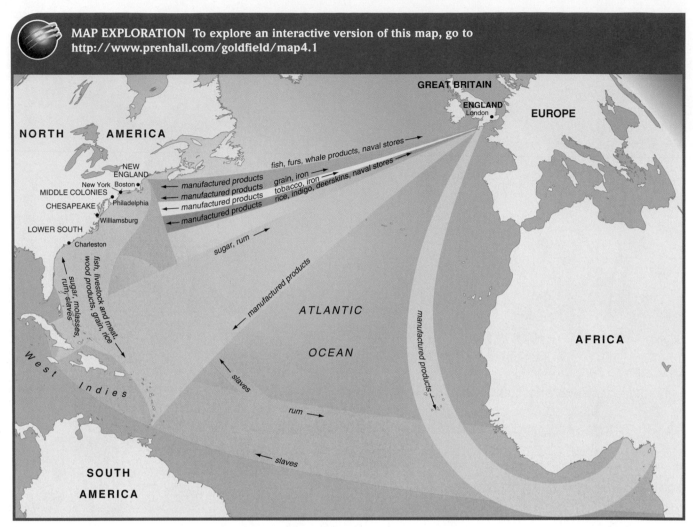

MAP EXPLORATION To explore an interactive version of this map, go to http://www.prenhall.com/goldfield/map4.1

MAP 4-1 **Anglo-American Transatlantic Commerce**
By the eighteenth century, Great Britain and its colonies were enmeshed in a complex web of trade. Britain exchanged manufactured goods for colonial raw materials, while Africa provided the enslaved laborers who produced the most valuable colonial crops.

from 3,300 to 9,400. They, along with colonial vessels, carried goods and people from Great Britain, continental Europe, and West Africa to the British colonies and returned tons of raw materials to the Old World. At the heart of Anglo-American trade lay the highly profitable commerce in staple crops, most of which were produced by slave labor.

West Indian sugar far surpassed all other colonial products in importance (see Figure 4–1). By the late 1760s, the value of sugar and sugar by-product exports reached almost £4 million per year—nearly 50 percent more than the total value of exports from all the other British American colonies combined. Prominent West Indian planters joined with the English merchants who marketed their sugar to lobby Parliament for favorable treatment. Because

these planters and merchants—known as the sugar interest—wielded so much economic power, politicians listened. It was at their insistence that Parliament in 1733 passed the Molasses Act, which taxed sugar products from foreign sources, especially the French West Indies. Parliament also removed sugar from the list of enumerated items in 1739, allowing merchants to ship it directly from the islands to southern Europe.

Tobacco from the Chesapeake colonies was the second most valuable staple crop. Exports worth about £750,000 arrived each year in England during the late 1760s. Nearly 90 percent of the crop was later reexported to continental Europe. Persistent low prices, however, led many tobacco planters to sow some of their land with wheat after about 1750. This

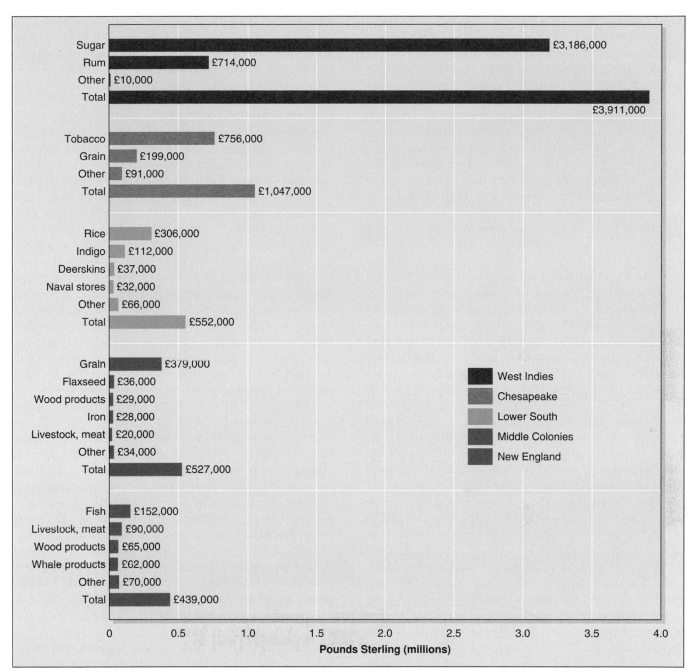

FIGURE 4-1 Average Annual Value of Colonial Exports by Region, 1768–1772
*Staple crops—especially sugar—produced by slave labor were the most valuable items exported
from Britain's North American colonies.*

Data Source: John J. McCusker and Russell R. Menard, *The Economy of British America, 1607–1789*,
rev. ed. (1991). University of North Carolina Press.

change lessened their dependence on tobacco and allowed them to take advantage of the high demand for flour in southern Europe and the West Indies.

Exports of rice and indigo (a plant that produced an expensive blue dye used in textile manufacture), helped make South Carolina planters some of the richest mainland colonists. Most of the rice went to England and the West Indies, although, after 1731, Parliament permitted direct shipments to southern Europe. Parliament encouraged indigo production by granting subsidies to growers and placing stiff taxes on foreign indigo. It also subsidized colonial production of naval stores—such as tar, pitch, and turpentine—to reduce England's dependence on Swedish suppliers. The export of these items made up a small but important part of the North and South Carolina economies.

Wheat exports from the Middle Colonies boomed after 1750, when a combination of poor harvests and warfare in Europe created strong overseas demand. West Indian planters (though not their slaves) also ate bread made from Pennsylvania flour. Since farmers in England grew enough wheat to supply the domestic market, there was little demand there for colonial flour. Ships traveling from Philadelphia or New York to English ports instead carried a variety of other goods, including unrefined iron, potash (used in making soap and glass), salted meats, and wood products.

New England had no staple crop and produced little for export except whale products, such as oil used in lamps. The region's merchants nevertheless developed a thriving transatlantic trade by grasping whatever opportunities came their way. Realizing that profits could be made from carrying other colonies' goods to market, New Englanders built thousands of vessels and eventually dominated shipping within the empire. Captains sailed from port to port, assembling mixed cargoes of goods from different regions and carrying them to England to exchange for manufactured items. By 1770, New England's earnings from shipping fees, freight charges, and insurance exceeded the total value of its own exports.

New England merchants also strengthened trade links to the West Indies that had first been forged in the 1650s. By the mid-eighteenth century, more than half of all New England exports went to the islands: salted meat for planters' dinners, salted fish for slaves, wood for sugar barrels, and other equipment. Merchants accepted molasses and other sugar by-products in payment, bringing them back to New England to be distilled into cheap rum. Enterprising traders then carried rum to Africa to exchange for slaves. Although English merchants dominated the African slave trade, New Englanders also profited. Less than 10 percent of New England's population were slaves, but because New Englanders trafficked in human cargo and provisioned the West Indies, their commercial economy depended on the institution of slavery.

THE IMPORT TRADE AND TIES OF CREDIT

By the late 1760s, over £4 million worth of English manufactured goods flowed into the colonies. This import trade satisfied a demand for items that could not be produced—at least not cheaply—in North America. Bales of English cloth and leather, crates of glassware and pottery, casks of nails and lead shot piled onto the wharves of Philadelphia and New York. Dockworkers emptied ships' holds of wrought iron, brass, and copper, barrels of refined sugar, and bundles of beaverskin hats. Some of these goods—ironware, sugar, hats—were made of materials that had come from the colonies in the first place.

A small but not insignificant number of imported items made their way into Indian villages. These goods included weapons, woolen cloth, linen garments, knives, hatchets, and jewelry. Indians were discerning customers and rejected goods not made to their liking. Native consumers, for instance, preferred textiles dyed dark blue, dark red, or gray, and wanted kettles lighter in weight than those made for English purchasers. As in the seventeenth century, Indians continued to use such items after their own fashion. An Indian woman might wear a linen shift with an English blanket worn as a mantle, fastened with a beaded belt. Native leaders sometimes acquired goods, not to use themselves, but to exchange with allies in formal ceremonies. By this period, Indians had become adept at comparing prices for furs and European goods in order to calculate how many pelts they needed to bring in so they could buy the items they desired.

The colonists' even heavier consumption of manufactured goods was vital to British overseas commerce. In terms of value, colonists imported more goods than they exported. This imbalance, however, was remedied in good part by colonial earnings from shipping fees as well as by payments from the British government for colonial military expenses. The colonial economy ran an annual deficit of £40,000 by the late 1760s, but that was only about 1 percent of a transatlantic trade worth over £4 million a year.

British merchants extended credit to colonists on generous terms, making it easy for them to buy British products. Great tobacco planters, of whom Washington was typical, virtually lived on the easy credit that British merchants provided. These merchants marketed the planters' tobacco and supplied them with English goods, charging the costs of purchase and transportation against the profits they expected the next year's crop to bring.

Easy credit let planters indulge themselves, and many ordered English goods without stopping to worry about how they would pay for them. Gradually they sank into debt. A Virginian noted that in the 1740s, no planter would have dared run up a debt of £1,000 but that by the 1760s, "Ten times that sum is . . . spoke of with Indifference." When trade was brisk and tobacco prices high, neither the planters nor their

During the eighteenth century, quantities of imported English manufactures began to appear in many colonial houses. This elegant mahogany clothespress, made in England in the 1740s, may have graced the Boston home of Charles Apthorp, once called "the greatest and most noble merchant" in America.

British creditors worried. But when tobacco prices dropped or an international crisis made overseas trading risky, creditors called in the debts owed to them. At such times, colonial debtors realized how much they (like Indians involved in European trade) depended on goods and credit supplied by distant merchants.

BECOMING MORE LIKE ENGLAND: THE GROWTH OF CITIES AND INEQUALITY

As colonial commerce grew, so did colonial cities—the connecting points in the economic network tying the colonies to London. Boston, New York, Philadelphia, and Charleston were as large as many British provincial towns. By 1770, Philadelphia's population had reached 30,000, New York's 25,000, Boston's 16,000, and Charleston's 12,000. A fifth city, Baltimore, was rapidly developing at the best harbor on Chesapeake Bay. Only about 5 percent of all mainland colonists lived in cities, but the influence of urban centers far outweighed their size.

European visitors marveled at America's bustling cities and remarked on their resemblance to England's. One Englishman declared in 1759 that Philadelphia "must certainly be the object of every one's wonder and admiration." Less than 80 years old, it already boasted three thousand houses, impressive public buildings, "handsomely built" streets, two libraries, eight or ten churches, and a college (chartered as the College of Philadelphia in 1755, now the University of Pennsylvania). This same visitor judged Boston to be a "most flourishing" place with "much the air of some of our best country towns in England."

All colonial cities (like England's major ones) were seaports, and Europeans took note of the appearance and activity of their dockyards. Oceangoing ships sailed "right up to the town" of Philadelphia on the Delaware River, according to one observer. Boston had "a very fine wharf, at least half a mile long, undertaken at the expense of a number of private gentlemen" to facilitate shipping. New York, then as now, had one of the world's finest harbors, from which it conducted "a more extensive commerce than any town in the English North American provinces."

Indeed, in their bustle and cosmopolitan atmosphere, colonial cities resembled English provincial cities more than they did the farming villages of the American countryside. Cities provided all sorts of amenities, including inns, taverns, coffeehouses, theaters, and social clubs. Their populations were much more diverse in ethnic origin and religion. Dr. Alexander Hamilton, a Scottish immigrant, recalled dining at a Philadelphia tavern with "Scots, English, Dutch, Germans, and Irish" and "Roman Catholics, Church [of England] men, Presbyterians, Quakers, Newlightmen, Methodists, Seventh day men, Moravians, Anabaptists, and one Jew." In addition, the African American population in the northern colonies tended to live in cities. By 1750, slaves made up 20 percent of New York City's population, about 10 percent of Philadelphia's, and nearly 9 percent of Boston's.

Artisans in colonial cities. Colonial cities had higher proportions of artisans than did rural villages. Perhaps two out of three adult white males living in cities worked at a craft. Many of them—shipbuilders, ropemakers, sailmakers—labored at trades directly related to overseas commerce. Others produced pottery, furniture, paper, glassware, iron tools, and various household items. Colonial products tended to be somewhat cruder and cheaper than British-made goods. Yet talented colonists such as the Boston silversmith Paul Revere and the Philadelphia furniture maker John Folwell fashioned goods that would have been prized possessions in any English gentleman's home.

Colonial manufacturing took place not in factories but in workshops often attached to artisans' houses. Artisans managed a workforce consisting of their wives and children, along with journeymen or apprentices. Usually teenage boys, apprentices contracted to work for a master for 4 to 7 years in order to learn the "mysteries" of his craft. Like indentured servants, they received no wages but worked for food, clothing, shelter, and a small payment at the end of their service. Once an apprentice finished his training, he became a journeyman, working for a master but now earning wages and saving until he could afford to set up his own shop. Like farmers, colonial artisans valued household independence and aimed to limit the time during which they worked for others.

Many artisans flourished in colonial cities. Adino Paddock, for example, moved from the countryside to Boston in 1736 to learn how to make the light carriages known as chaises. By 1758, he had his own shop, and as his business prospered, Bostonians elected him to important local offices. As a gesture of public spirit, Paddock arranged for the transplanting of elm trees on Boston Common, to beautify the city where he had made his fortune, which by 1775 amounted to more than £3,000.

Paddock's rise was more spectacular than that of most craftsmen, since prosperity for urban artisans was by no means guaranteed. In Philadelphia, artisans typically accumulated property worth £50 to £200, enough for a modest subsistence. Workers at less skilled crafts often earned only a bare living, and ordinary laborers faced seasonal unemployment. The irregular delivery of raw materials idled even the most industrious artisans. Silversmiths, tailors, and furniture makers, relying on overseas suppliers of metal, cloth, and exotic woods, suffered when supply ships sank or wars hindered ocean traffic. Makers of luxury goods also feared downturns in the economy, for such trends discouraged nervous customers from purchasing their wares.

Cities like Philadelphia, New York, and Charleston provided an important setting for some women to support themselves with craft work. Mary Wallace and Clementia Ferguson, for instance, stitched fashionable hats and dresses for New York customers. Nonetheless, even in cities, women's options were limited. Most employed women were widows striving to maintain a family business until sons grew old enough to take over. This was true for printers such as Elizabeth Timothy, who ran the *South Carolina Gazette* after her husband's death in 1739, and Anne Catherine Green, who managed the *Maryland Gazette* for nine years. Other widows toiled at less prestigious—and less remunerative—jobs as nurses, laundresses, and boardinghouse keepers.

The growing gap between rich and poor.

Wherever colonists engaged heavily in commerce—in cities or on plantations—the gap between rich and poor widened during the eighteenth century. In 1687, the richest 10 percent of Boston residents owned 46 percent of the taxable property in the town; by 1771, the top tenth held 63 percent of taxable wealth. Similar changes occurred in Philadelphia. In South Carolina and the Chesapeake, many planters added to the already substantial estates they had inher-

This view of the Philadelphia waterfront dates from 1720. It shows how the city had developed into one of British America's principal ports just forty years after its founding.

Peter Cooper "The Southeast Prospect of the City of Philadelphia" ca. 1720. The Library Company of Philadelphia.

John Singleton Copley's portrait of the silversmith Paul Revere, painted about 1769, depicts one of Boston's most prominent artisans. As colonists grew wealthier, some commissioned portraits for their homes to serve as emblems of their rising social aspirations. Even so, Copley despaired that America would ever provide a suitable market for his artistic talents and he eventually moved to England.

ited. This elite group controlled vast amounts of land and of slaves. It became increasingly difficult for newcomers to enter their ranks. At the same time, the colonies' growing reliance on slave labor—especially in the South—created a sizeable class of impoverished people denied the chance to better their condition. By 1770, slaves, for whom America was anything but a land of opportunity, constituted one out of five British colonists.

To address the growing problem of poverty among white colonists, cities built workhouses, and towns collected funds for poor relief in greater amounts than ever before. Many poor people were aged or ill, without families to help them. Able-bodied workers forced to accept public relief usually owed their misfortune to temporary downturns in the economy, more often than not the result of wartime dislocations. Such was the case in

1757, for example, when Boston's leaders complained about rising poor relief expenses. England was then at war with France, and the British commander in chief had halted Boston's overseas trade, a military expedient that hurt the city's economy.

Even in the worst of times, no more than one out of ten white colonists (mainly city dwellers) depended on public assistance. For free black people who were unemployed and denied public relief, conditions were far worse. A Pennsylvania law went so far as to allow them to be enslaved. This was a threat no impoverished white colonist faced. And, bad as it was, the problem of poverty among white colonists had not reached anything like the levels seen in England. As much as one-third of England's population regularly received relief, and the numbers swelled during hard times. Eighteenth-century white colonists, on average, enjoyed a higher standard of living than most English or other Europeans. So long as land was available—even if one had to move to the edges of settlement to get it—colonists could at least eke out a bare subsistence, and many did much better.

No one would have mistaken Philadelphia for London or Virginia planters for British lords. Even so, colonial society resembled Great Britain more than ever before. The growth of cities mirrored British urban development. The widening gap between rich and poor convinced many colonists that their society had at last matured from its crude beginnings. Eighteenth-century Britons on both sides of the Atlantic believed that societies ought to be organized hierarchically, that God intended for people to be arranged in ranks from rich to poor. The more America resembled Britain, many colonists assumed, the more stable and prosperous it would be.

THE TRANSFORMATION OF CULTURE

Despite the convergence of English and colonial society, many influential settlers worried that America remained culturally inferior to Great Britain. Just as Washington trusted a London tailor to make him a fashionable suit—assuming that Virginia tailors could not do the job—other colonial gentlemen tended to see American architecture, fashion, manners, and intellectual life as at best poor imitations of superior British models. During the eighteenth century, newly prosperous colonists strove to overcome this provincial sense of inferiority. They built grand houses and filled them with imported goods, cultivated what they took to be the manners of the British gentry, and followed English and European intellectual developments. Some colonial gentlemen even reshaped their religious beliefs to reflect European notions that God played only an indirect role in human affairs.

These elite aspirations, however, were not shared by most settlers. The majority of colonists, although they might purchase a few imported goods, had little interest in copying the manners of the English elite, and very few of them altered their spiritual beliefs to fit European patterns. Indeed, familiar religious practices flourished in eighteenth-century America, and when a tremendous revival swept through the colonies beginning in the 1730s, religion occupied center stage in American life.

As second- and third-generation Chesapeake planters achieved greater prosperity, they often remodeled their homes to make larger and more imposing structures. This watercolor depicts Green Spring Mansion as it looked in 1770, significantly modified from the smaller brick dwelling where Governor William Berkeley lived a century earlier.

GOODS AND HOUSES

Eighteenth-century Americans imported more manufactured products from England with every passing year. This practice did not simply reflect the growth of the colonial population, for the rate at which Americans bought British goods exceeded the rate of population increase. Colonists owned more goods, often of better quality, than their parents and grandparents had possessed.

In the less secure economic climate of the seventeenth century, colonists had limited their purchases of goods, investing instead in land to pass on to their children. But by the eighteenth century, prosperous colonists felt secure enough to buy goods to make their lives more comfortable. Chairs replaced benches, and carpets covered wooden floors. Colonists hung mirrors and perhaps a portrait or two on their walls. At mealtimes, the table might be covered with a damask cloth and set with individual porcelain plates instead of a common wooden dish. Wealthier colonists ate with forks and knives, not just spoons.

Benjamin Franklin described such changes in his own household. Accustomed to eating his breakfast of bread and milk with a pewter spoon from an earthenware bowl, he found it one morning "in a China Bowl with a Spoon of Silver" that had cost "the enormous Sum of three and twenty Shillings." His wife, Deborah, justified the purchase by declaring "that she thought her Husband deserved a Silver Spoon & China Bowl as well as any of his Neighbors." Deborah Franklin knew that silver and china, although they served the same

function as pewter and earthenware, signified her family's prosperity and good taste. Many colonists likewise acquired such goods to advertise their refined style of life.

By the 1760s, nearly every item that George Washington ordered from his London agent could have been purchased in Philadelphia. But Washington wanted the latest English styles and even worried that his agent might take advantage of him by sending goods that were no longer in fashion in England. He once complained that "instead of getting things good and fashionable . . . we often have Articles sent Us that cou[l]d only have been us[e]d by our Forefathers in the days of yore." Washington's desires were hardly unique. One visitor to Maryland, astonished at the speed with which colonists adopted English styles, declared that he was "almost inclined to believe that a new fashion is adopted earlier by the polished and affluent American than by many opulent persons" in London. Colonial shopkeepers regularly assured the "ladies and gentlemen" among their customers that their wares reflected the latest English styles.

Prosperous colonists built grand houses where they lived in greater comfort than ever before. In the seventeenth century, Virginia's governor lived in the finest house in the colony—a four-room dwelling. His eighteenth-century counterpart, however, resided in Williamsburg in the Governor's Palace, an elegant two-storied mansion designed after British architectural styles. By the 1730s, numerous southern planters had built "great houses" with expensive paneling and marble fireplaces. Others transformed older houses into more stylish residences. Washington extensively remodeled Mount Vernon, adding a second story and extra wings on each side to create a home fit for a gentleman. In the northern colonies, merchants built the most impressive houses, often following architectural pattern books imported from England.

These houses were not only larger but also different in design from the homes of less affluent colonists. Most settlers lived in one- or two-room dwellings and thus cooked, ate, and slept in the same chamber. Under such conditions, privacy was virtually unknown. But the owners of great houses could devote rooms to specialized uses. Cooking and other domestic work took place in back or in separate outbuildings. Private bedrooms were located upstairs, allowing first-floor rooms to be used for public activities. The most distinctive feature of these grand homes was the parlor, an elaborately decorated room used for receiving guests and entertaining them with music, dancing, and card games. Parlor doors often opened onto lawns and formal gardens where guests could stroll and engage in polite conversation.

Prosperous colonists did not build such homes merely to advertise their wealth. They wanted to create the proper setting for a refined way of life, emulating the English gentry in their country estates and London townhouses. But they knew that the true measure of their gentility lay not just in where they lived and what they owned but in how they behaved.

SHAPING MINDS AND MANNERS

Colonists knew that the manners of English gentlefolk set them apart from ordinary people. Many Americans therefore imported "courtesy books," which contained the rules of polite behavior. In previous centuries, such books had prepared princes for life at court and for their future duties as kings. Eighteenth-century versions advised would-be gentlemen on how to show regard for social rank, practice personal cleanliness, and respect other people's feelings.

The young George Washington studied such books carefully. At the age of 13, he copied 110 rules from *Youth's Behaviour, or Decency in Conversation among Men,* including such advice as "In the Presence of Others Sing not to yourself with a humming Noise, nor Drum with your Fingers or Feet" and "In Company of those of Higher Quality than yourself Speak not till you are ask'd a Ques-

tion then Stand upright put of[f] your Hat and Answer in few words." Many colonists subscribed to English journals such as *The Tatler* and *The Spectator* that printed articles describing good manners.

Women, too, cultivated genteel manners. In Charleston, South Carolina, and other colonial cities, dozens of girls' boarding schools advertised instruction in "the different branches of Polite Education." Female pupils received only the rudiments of intellectual training in reading, writing, and arithmetic, for it was assumed that women had little need of such accomplishments. Only rarely did young women receive a more rigorous education, for few parents thought it appropriate to their gender. The private schools' curriculum instead focused on French, music, dancing, and fancy needlework. These were skills that advertised girls' genteel status and prepared them for married lives as mistresses of great houses, mothers of future gentlemen and ladies, and hostesses of grand entertainments.

Such entertainments proliferated in the eighteenth century. Invitations to balls, musical performances, and fancy dinners circulated among well-bred neighbors. Women who could afford to do so invited their neighbors to tea parties, where they could display good manners and fine silver and china at the same time. Robert Carter, one of Virginia's wealthiest gentlemen, once hosted an "elegant" dinner that lasted for nearly eight hours. Between half past four and seven o'clock, Carter's guests enjoyed a sumptuous meal. Then they turned to dancing and card playing, and only at midnight did they begin to return to their homes. Such occasions excluded ordinary settlers and reinforced elite colonists' sense of themselves as a separate—and better—class of people.

Some people expressed their gentility through more intellectual pursuits, taking advantage of the relatively high literacy rates among white colonists. In New England, where settlers placed great emphasis on Bible study, about 70 percent of men and 45 percent of women could read and write. Only a third of men in the southern colonies, and even fewer women, could read and write, but even these literacy rates were higher than among England's general population. Eighteenth-century colonists enjoyed greater access to printed material than ever before. In 1704, the *Boston News-Letter* became the first continuously published newspaper in British America. By the 1760s nearly every colony had a regularly published newspaper, printers were publishing almanacs,

Robert Feke (1707–1752), Portrait of Benjamin Franklin (1706–1790), c. 1746. Oil on canvas, 127 x 102 cm. Courtesy of the Harvard University Portrait Collection. Bequest of Dr. John Collins Warren, 1856

Painted at about the time Franklin retired from his printing business, this portrait depicts the one-time craftsman as an aspiring gentleman. Wearing a wig and a shirt with ruffled cuffs, Franklin would no longer work with his hands but would pursue his scientific experiments and other studies.

and booksellers opened shops in several cities. Prominent colonists, intent on developing America's intellectual life, began to participate in a transatlantic world of ideas.

These colonists, however, were consumers of British and European ideas rather than producers of an American intellectual tradition. They imported thousands of books, subscribed to British journals, and established libraries in cities such as Philadelphia, Charleston, and New York where borrowing privileges could be purchased for a modest fee. Libraries and private collections contained sermons and other religious writings, classical Greek and Roman texts, political and philosophical works by prominent European thinkers, and mainly British examples of poetry, drama, essays, and novels. Colonists with literary aspirations emulated their favorite writers. Students at Harvard in Cambridge (founded in 1636) modeled their college newspaper on an English periodical, *The Spectator.* In Virginia, William Byrd II, whose father got his

start as an Indian trader and tobacco farmer, advertised his own genteel pretensions by composing verse in the style of contemporary English poets. The young Thomas Jefferson copied out passages from the English novel *Tristram Shandy.* Benjamin Franklin honed his writing skills by rewriting essays from *The Spectator* and comparing his versions to the originals.

Educated colonists were especially interested in the new ideas that characterized what has been called the **Age of Enlightenment**. The European thinkers of the Enlightenment drew inspiration from recent advances in science—such as the English scientist Isaac Newton's explanation of the laws of gravity—that suggested that the universe operated according to natural laws that human reason could discover. They also drew on the work of the English philosopher John Locke, who maintained that God did not dictate human knowledge but rather gave us the power to acquire knowledge through experience and understanding. The hallmark of Enlightenment thought was a belief in the power of human reason to improve the human condition.

This optimistic worldview marked a profound intellectual shift. Enlightenment thinkers rejected earlier ideas about God's unknowable will and continued intervention in human and natural events. They instead assigned God a less active role as the creator of the universe, who had set the world running according to predictable laws, and then let nature—and human beings—shape events. Such ideas inspired a growing international community of scholars to try to discover the laws of nature and to work toward human progress.

Colonial intellectuals sought membership in this scholarly community. A few of them—the Reverend Cotton Mather of Massachusetts, William Byrd, Benjamin Franklin—gained election to the Royal Society of London, the most prestigious learned society in England. Most of their scholarly contributions were unimpressive. Byrd, for instance, sent the Royal Society a rather superficial manuscript titled "An Account of a Negro Boy That Is Dappled in Several Places of His Body with White Spots."

Benjamin Franklin, by contrast, achieved genuine intellectual prominence. Even as a youth, Franklin hungered after learning and demonstrated a particular gift for science. His experiments with a kite proved that lightning was electricity (a natural force whose properties were poorly understood at the time) and gained him an international reputation. He also found practical uses for his scientific knowledge. Franklin invented the lightning rod (which prevented fires in wooden buildings by channeling the electrical charge of a lightning bolt into the ground), bifocal spectacles, the iron "Franklin stove" (in which wood burned more efficiently than in fireplaces), and the glass harmonica, an instrument that made him famous among European musicians and composers.

If Franklin's career embodied the Enlightenment ideal of the rational exploration of nature's laws, it also revealed the limited impact of Enlightenment thought in colonial America. Only a few prosperous and educated colonists could afford such intellectual pursuits. Franklin came from humble origins—his father was a maker of candles and soap—but his success as a printer eventually allowed him to retire from business at the age of 42. Only then did he purchase the equipment for his electrical discoveries and begin his scientific work, devoting the "leisure during the rest of my life for philosophical studies and amusements." Franklin's equipment—and leisure—were as much badges of gentlemanly status as George Washington's London-made suit.

Most colonists remained ignorant of scientific advances and Enlightenment ideas. Unlike aspiring gentlemen and ladies, they had little leisure to devote to literature and polite conversation. When they found time to read, they picked up not a courtesy book or *The Spectator* but the Bible, which was the best-selling book of the colonial era. Religion principally shaped the way in which they viewed the world and explained human and natural events.

COLONIAL RELIGION AND THE GREAT AWAKENING

Church steeples dominated the skylines of colonial cities. By the 1750s, Boston and New York each had eighteen churches, and Philadelphia boasted twenty. Churches and meetinghouses likewise dominated country towns, though more sparsely in the scattered settlements of the South than in the northern colonies. Often the largest and finest buildings in town, they bore witness to the diverse and thriving condition of religion in America.

In all New England colonies except Rhode Island, the Puritan (or Congregationalist) faith was the established religion. The many Congregational churches in the region, headed by ministers trained at Harvard College and Yale (founded in 1701), served the majority of its colonists and received financial support from their taxes. Though proud of the Puritan tradition that had inspired New England's origins, ministers and believers nonetheless had to adapt to changing social and religious conditions.

The principal adaptation consisted of a move away from strict requirements for church membership. In order to keep their churches pure, New England's founders had required prospective members to give convincing evidence that they had experienced a spiritual conversion. Once admitted, members could receive communion and have their children baptized. By the 1660s, however, fewer colonists sought admission under such strict standards, which left them and their unbaptized children outside the church. To address this problem, the clergy in 1662 adopted the **Halfway Covenant**, which allowed adults who had been baptized (because their parents were church members), but who had not themselves experienced conversion, to have their own children baptized. The Halfway Covenant slowly gained acceptance in subsequent decades. By the 1680s, some ministers made church admission even easier, requiring members only to demonstrate knowledge of the Christian faith and to live godly lives.

The Congregational Church also had to accept a measure of religious toleration in New England. In 1691, Massachusetts received a royal charter granting "liberty of Conscience" to all Protestants, bringing the colony into line with England's religious policy. Anglicans and Baptists eventually won exemptions from paying taxes to support the Congregational Church. At the same time, some Congregationalist preachers began emphasizing personal piety and good works in their sermons, ideas usually associated with Anglicanism. These changes indicated a shift away from the Puritan exclusiveness of New England's early years.

In the South, the established Church of England consolidated its authority in the early eighteenth century but never succeeded in exerting effective control over spiritual life. The bishop of London began appointing agents to oversee church matters, and the Society for the Propagation of the Gospel in Foreign Parts, founded in 1701, attempted to provide ministers for colonial parishes. Even so, these parishes often lacked trained clergy, and those who did emigrate encountered unexpected obstacles.

Many a parson in England could easily ride from one side of his parish to the other in an hour, but Anglican clergymen in the southern colonies served parishes that were vast and sparsely settled.

One South Carolina parish contained 10,400 square miles—and only seven hundred white residents. Ministers also found that influential planters, who had grown used to running parishes when preachers were unavailable, resisted their efforts to take control of churches. Aware that the planters' taxes paid their salaries, many ministers found it easiest simply to preach and behave in ways that offered the least offense. Frontier regions often lacked Anglican churches and clergymen altogether. In such places, dissenting religious groups, such as Presbyterians, Quakers, and Baptists, gained followers among people neglected by the Anglican establishment.

No established church dominated in the Middle Colonies of New York, New Jersey, and Pennsylvania. The region's ethnically diverse population and William Penn's policy of religious toleration guaranteed that a multitude of groups would compete for followers. One observer, accustomed to an established church, characterized these conditions as a "soul-destroying whirlpool." Yet religion flourished in the Middle Colonies. By the middle of the eighteenth century, the region had more congregations per capita than even New England.

Groups such as the Quakers and the Mennonites, who did not believe in having specially trained ministers, easily formed new congregations in response to local demand. Lutheran and German Reformed churches, however, required European-educated clergy, who were always scarce. Pious laymen held worship services in their homes even as they sent urgent letters overseas begging for ordained ministers. When more Lutheran and Reformed clergy arrived in the 1740s and 1750s, they sometimes discovered, as Anglican preachers did in the South, that laymen balked at relinquishing control of the churches. Lutheran and Reformed ministers also learned that their professional training alone could not command respect; their congregations demanded that they be powerful preachers. Because so many other religious alternatives were available, these ministers had to compete for their parishioners' allegiance.

Bewildering spiritual diversity, relentless religious competition, and a comparatively weak Anglican Church, all distinguished the colonies from England. Yet in one important way, religious developments during the middle third of the eighteenth century drew the colonies closer to England. A great transatlantic religious revival, originating in Scotland and England, first touched the Middle Colonies in the 1730s. In 1740–1745, it struck the northern colonies with the force of a hurricane, and in the 1760s, the

George Whitefield (who, contemporaries noted, was cross-eyed) enjoyed a remarkable career as a powerful preacher on both sides of the Atlantic. This portrait shows him preaching indoors to a rapt audience. During his tour of the colonies, Whitefield reportedly had a similar effect on crowds of thousands who gathered outdoors to hear his sermons.

last phase of the revival spread through the South. America had never seen anything like this immense revival, which came to be called the **Great Awakening**.

By 1730, Presbyterians in Pennsylvania had split into factions over such issues as the disciplining of church members and the requirement that licensed ministers have university degrees. One group, led by an immigrant Scottish evangelist, William Tennent, Sr., and his four sons, denounced their opponents as men more interested in regulations than conversion. In the 1730s, Tennent set up the Log College in Neshaminy, Pennsylvania, to train his sons and other young men to be evangelical ministers. What began as a dispute among clergymen eventually blossomed into a broader challenge to religious authority. That challenge gained momentum in late 1739, when one of the most charismatic evangelists of the century, George Whitefield, arrived in the colonies from England.

Whitefield, an Anglican priest, had experienced an uncommonly intense religious conversion while he was still a university student. Already famous in Britain as a preacher of great emotional fervor, he embarked on a tour of the colonies in the winter of 1739–1740. As soon as Whitefield landed in Delaware, his admirers whipped up local enthusiasm, insuring that he would preach to huge crowds in Pennsylvania and New Jersey. Whitefield's powerful preaching on the experience of conversion lent support to the Presbyterian faction led by the Tennents and sparked local revivals. Whitefield then moved on to New England, where some communities had already experienced small, local awakenings. In 1734–1735, for instance, the Congregationalist minister Jonathan Edwards had led a revival in Northampton, Massachusetts, urging his parishioners to recognize their sinfulness and describing hell in such a terrifying way that many despaired of their salvation.

Whitefield's tour through the colonies knitted these scattered local revivals into the Great Awakening. Crowds gathered in city squares and open fields to listen to his sermons. Whitefield exhorted his audiences to examine their souls for evidence of the "indwelling of Christ" that would indicate that they were saved. He criticized most ministers for emphasizing good works and "head-knowledge" instead of the emotional side of religion.

Whitefield's open-air sermons scarcely resembled the colonists' accustomed form of worship. Settlers normally gathered with family and neighbors in church for formal, structured services. They sat in pews assigned on the basis of social status, with wealthier members in front and poorer folk in the back. Such worship services reinforced standards of order and community hierarchy. But Whitefield's sermons were highly dramatic performances. He preached for hours in a booming voice, accompanying his words with spirited gestures and even occasionally dissolving in tears. Thousands of strangers, jostling in crowds that often outnumbered the populations of several villages put together, wept along with him. When the sermon ended, his listeners dispersed, many never to see each other again.

In the wake of Whitefield's visits, Benjamin Franklin noted, "it seem'd as if all the World were growing Religious." Revivals and mass conversions often followed his appearances, to the happy astonishment of local clergy. But their approval evaporated when more extreme revivalists appeared. Gilbert Tennent, William's son, followed Whitefield to Boston and derided the town's ministers as unconverted "dead Drones." James Davenport—a preacher so erratic that many thought him mad—claimed that God gave him the knowledge of other ministers' spir-

itual state and routinely denounced by name those he "knew" to be damned. Once, in the midst of a sermon urging his audience to rid itself of worldly finery, Davenport set an example by tearing off his velvet breeches and throwing them into a bonfire. Officials who valued civic order soon tried to silence such extremists by passing laws that prohibited them from preaching in a town without the local minister's permission.

Disputes between individuals converted in the revivals—called **New Lights**—and those who were not (Old Lights) split churches. New Lights insisted, as the separatist founders of Plymouth once had, that they could not remain in churches with sinful members and unconverted ministers and so left to form new churches. "Formerly the People could bear with each other in Charity when they differ'd in Opinion," lamented one colonist, "but they now break Fellowship and Communion with one another on that Account."

The Awakening came late to the southern colonies, but it was there, in the 1760s, that it produced perhaps its greatest controversy. Many southern converts became Baptists, combining their religious criticism of the Anglicans with a condemnation of the wealthy planters' way of life. Plainly dressed Baptists criticized the rich clothes, drinking, gambling, and pride of Virginia's gentry. Planters, in turn, viewed Baptists as dangerous people who could not "meet a man upon the road, but they must ram a text of Scripture down his throat." Most of all, they hated the Baptists for their willingness to preach to slaves. More than once, irate gentlemen burst in on Baptist services and beat the preacher senseless.

Although the revivals themselves gradually waned, the Great Awakening had a lasting impact on colonial society. It forged new links between Great Britain and the colonies. Evangelical ministers on both sides of the Atlantic exchanged correspondence. Periodicals such as *The Christian History*—over which Whitefield exercised considerable control—informed British and American subscribers of advances in true religion throughout the empire.

In the colonies, the Awakening brought numerous changes. It led to the founding of new colleges to serve members of different religious denominations. Middle Colony evangelicals founded the College of New Jersey (now Princeton University) in 1746. In the 1760s, New England Baptists established the College of Rhode Island (now Brown University). An evangelical wing of the Dutch Reformed Church founded Queens College (now Rutgers University) in 1766. These colleges drew their exclusively male students from all colonies, not just the local area.

The revivals also brought newcomers into Christian congregations. Chesapeake slaves responded to the evangelists' message and—often contrary to the intent of white preachers—drew lessons from sermons about the equality of humankind. A few black preachers circulated among slave quarters, spreading the message of salvation and freedom. The impact of revivalism on Indians was less dramatic, but still significant. Evangelicals enjoyed their greatest success in small Native American communities, whose inhabitants were attracted to a less formal style of preaching, particularly in New England. Native converts often urged fellow Indians to heed the Christian message of self-discipline, not to emulate English colonists, but to revitalize villages beset by alcoholism and other problems linked to European domination. Samson Occom, a Mohegan convert and the best-known native preacher, worked as a missionary among the Montauks on Long Island. His experience of poor pay and white prejudice, however, discouraged other converts from following his example.

The Awakening did not greatly increase women's church membership, since women already constituted majorities in many congregations. But by emphasizing the emotional power of Christianity, revivals accorded greater legitimacy to what were thought to be women's more sensitive temperaments. And some women, such as Bathsheba Kingsley, were inspired by the power of their conversions to become traveling preachers. More often, female evangelicals stayed within the bounds of social convention and limited their activities to conducting prayer meetings for other women.

Everywhere, the New Light challenge to established ministers and churches undermined habits of deference to authority. Revivalists urged colonists to think for themselves in choosing which church to join and which minister to follow, not just to conform to what the rest of the community did. As their churches fractured, colonists—particularly New Englanders—faced more choices than ever before in their religious lives.

The exercise of religious choice also influenced political behavior. Voters noticed whether candidates for office were New or Old Lights and cast their ballots for men on their own side. Tactics first used to mobilize religious groups—such as organizing committees and writing petitions and letters—proved useful for political activities as well. Though hardly the intent of Whitefield or other revivalists, the Awakening thus fostered greater political awareness and participation among colonists.

THE COLONIAL POLITICAL WORLD

The political legacy of the Great Awakening—particularly the emphasis on individual choice and resistance to authority—corresponded to developments in the colonial political world. For most of the seventeenth century, ties within the empire developed from trade rather than governance. But as America grew in wealth and population, king and Parliament sought to manage colonial affairs more directly than before.

In the late seventeenth century, upheavals on both sides of the Atlantic seemed to confirm for both colonists and Englishmen a common interest in protecting the rights and liberties they derived from their shared heritage. The English overthrew King James II, and the people of New England successfully resisted the king's attempt to impose autocratic government in the colonies. But even as colonists and Englishmen asserted their common political culture at the dawn of the eighteenth century, differences in their political practices and ideas began to emerge.

THE DOMINION OF NEW ENGLAND AND THE LIMITS OF BRITISH CONTROL

Before 1650, England made little attempt to exert centralized control in North America. Each colony more or less governed itself, and most political activity occurred at the town or county level. Local officials kept the peace, resolved disputes, hired schoolmasters, arranged for the construction of roads and bridges, and collected taxes. Busy with the routines of daily life, most colonists devoted little time, and even less interest, to politics.

When Charles II became king in 1660, he initially showed little interest in the colonies except as sources of land and government offices with which he could reward his supporters. The grandest prizes, of course, were the great proprietorships, such as Pennsylvania and Carolina, but the creation of a rudimentary imperial bureaucracy also yielded rewards for the king to distribute. With the passage of mercantilist regulations governing colonial trade, for example, Parliament required customs officers to administer the imperial trading system and thus created a certain number of jobs.

Charles's brother James, the Duke of York, envisioned a more tightly controlled empire. He encouraged Charles to appoint military officers with strong ties of loyalty to him, as royal governors in

America. In 1675, James convinced Charles to create the Lords of Trade, a committee of the Privy Council (the group of nobles who served as royal advisers), to oversee colonial affairs.

When James became king in 1685, the whole character of the empire abruptly changed. Seeking to transform it into something much grander and more susceptible to England's control, James set out to reorganize it along the lines of Spain's empire, combining the colonies into three or four large provinces. He appointed powerful governors to carry out policies that he himself would formulate.

James began in the north, creating the **Dominion of New England** out of eight previously separate colonies stretching from Maine (then part of Massachusetts) to New Jersey. He chose Sir Edmund Andros, a former army officer, to govern the vast region with an appointive council but no elective assembly. Andros moved to Boston and initially gained some support from merchants excluded from politics by Massachusetts's insistence that only church members could vote. But he eventually antagonized them and other New Englanders by rigidly enforcing the Navigation Acts, limiting towns to just one annual meeting, remodeling the law courts, challenging property titles, and levying taxes without the colonists' consent. He even compelled Boston Puritans to share a meetinghouse with Anglicans.

Events in England ultimately sealed the fate of the Dominion. For years, English Protestants had worried about James's absolutist governing style and his conversion to Catholicism. Their fears increased in 1688, when the queen bore a son to carry on a Catholic line of succession. Parliament's leaders invited James's Protestant daughter, Mary, and her husband, William of Orange, the Stadtholder of the Netherlands, to take over the throne. In November 1688, William landed in England and gained the support of most of the English army. In December, James fled to France, ending a bloodless coup known as the **Glorious Revolution**.

Bostonians overthrew Andros the following April, even before they knew for sure that William was king, and later they had him shipped back to England. Massachusetts colonists hoped that their original charter of 1629 would be reinstated, but a new one was issued in 1691. It made several important changes. Massachusetts now included within its borders what had formerly been Plymouth Colony as well as Maine. Its colonists no longer elected their governor, who would instead be appointed by the monarch. Voters no longer had to be church members, and religious toleration was extended to all Protestants.

The new charter ended exclusive Puritan control in Massachusetts but also restored political stability. During the three years between Andros's overthrow and the arrival of a royal governor in 1692, the colony lacked a legally established government. In this atmosphere of uncertainty, an outbreak of accusations of witchcraft in Salem grew to unprecedented proportions. Colonists, like most Europeans of the time, believed in the existence of witches—humans who acted as Satan's agents and used supernatural powers to hurt their enemies. Over the years, New Englanders had executed a dozen or so accused witches, usually older women. But in the winter of 1691–1692, when several young girls of Salem experienced fits and other strange behavior, hundreds of settlers were accused of witchcraft, and nineteen were hanged. Salem's crisis occurred against a backdrop of local economic change, but it gathered momentum because the Dominion crisis had generated uncertainty about political and legal authority. Special courts had to be created to deal with the witchcraft outbreak. The judges' unusual methods, including the acceptance of "spectral evidence," or accusers' uncorroborated testimony that they had seen apparitions, later aroused considerable criticism.

The impact of the Glorious Revolution in other colonies likewise reflected local conditions. In New York, after Andros's deputy left, Jacob Leisler, a rich merchant and militia captain, gained power and ruled in a dictatorial fashion, persecuting men against whom he held personal grievances. Too slow in relinquishing command to the newly arrived royal governor in 1691, Leisler was arrested for treason and executed. In Maryland, Protestants used the occasion of William and Mary's accession to the throne to lobby for the end of the Catholic proprietorship. They were partly successful. The Calvert family lost its governing powers but retained rights to vast quantities of land. The Anglican Church became the established faith, and Catholics were barred from public office.

The colonists rejected James, not English authority in general. Their motives (especially in New England) largely reflected powerful anti-Catholic sentiment. William's firm Protestantism reassured them, and most colonists assumed that

AMERICAN VIEWS

Boston Celebrates a New King (August 1727)

The first colonial newspaper, the *Boston News-Letter,* appeared in that city in 1704. By the 1720s, Bostonians could choose from three newspapers, and New York and Philadelphia each had one. Published weekly, these papers mainly reported on English and European affairs and often reprinted essays by prominent English political writers. Their pages carried little local news, on the assumption that colonists could learn of this by word of mouth. But when truly extraordinary events occurred, such as the accession of a new British monarch, colonial newspapers reported on the local response. The following extract describes Bostonians' reaction to news that George II had become Britain's new king.

- How did Bostonians commemorate the new king's accession?
- What does this reveal about their attitudes toward George II and British government in general?
- Who was invited to the "splendid Entertainment," and what does this reveal about the structure of Boston society?

On Wednesday Morning by order of His Honour William Dummer, Esq., our Lieut. Governour & Commander in chief[,] three Regiments of the Militia and five Troops of horse were under arms in the great street before the State-house, making a very fine appearance. The number of Spectators exceeded the Men in Arms, covering the houses on every side. As soon as the Herauld had said his Amen to God Save the King, the loud and joyful Huzza's of so great a multitude rent the skies, the Regiments made a tripple discharge, the Castle Forts & Ships fir'd their cannon; and a splendid Entertainment follow'd for the Lieut. Governour and his Majesty's Council, Officers, Justices, and the Rev[eren]d Ministers present; with suitable provisions for the Regiments and Troops. The bells rung all the day, and in the Evening the

Rejoycing was continued with Fireworks and Bonfires, and the whole Town illuminated in an extraordinary manner, the Windows of each story of the Houses in the principal streets having three or four rows of candles in them. The streets were fill'd all the Evening with the Gentry of both Sexes, who appear'd with much decency and gravity, and with gayety and chearfulness. At nine of the clock a welcome rain, after a time of much heat and drought, put an end to the Ceremony. . . . We pray God, by whom Kings reign, that the royal smiles of His Majesty King George the Second, and the happy influences of his wise and just Government, may ever be falling on all his Majesty's Dominions, and on this loyal and dutiful Province in particular.

Source: *New England Weekly Journal* (August 21, 1727).

life would return to normal. But the Glorious Revolution in England and the demise of the Dominion had long-lasting effects that shaped political life in England and America for years to come.

THE LEGACY OF THE GLORIOUS REVOLUTION

In England, the Glorious Revolution signaled a return to political stability after years of upheaval. English people celebrated the preservation of their rights from the threat of a tyrannical king. In 1689, Parliament passed the Bill of Rights, which justified James's ouster and bound future monarchs to abide by the rule of law. They could not suspend parliamentary laws, collect taxes, or engage in foreign wars without Parliament's consent, or maintain a standing army in peacetime. Parliamentary elections and meetings would follow a regular schedule, without royal interference. In sum, Parliament claimed to be the crown's equal partner in governing England.

Colonists, too, celebrated the vindication of their rights as Englishmen. They believed that their successful resistance to Andros confirmed that their membership in the empire was founded on voluntary allegiance and not on forced submission to the mother country. Observing the similarity between Parliament and the colonial assemblies, they concluded that their own legislatures had a critical role in governance and in the protection of their rights and liberties. On both sides of the Atlantic, representative government had triumphed.

In fact, Parliament claimed full authority over the colonies and did not recognize their assemblies as its equal. For more than a half-century, however, it did not vigorously assert that authority. At the same time, William and his immediate successors lacked James's compulsion to control the colonies. William did make a few changes to imperial administration. In 1696, he replaced the Lords of Trade with a new committee, the Board of Trade. This advisory body gathered information from the colonies and recommended policy changes but itself had no executive role. William also approved the Navigation Act of 1696, which closed loopholes in earlier laws and created vice-admiralty courts in the colonies similar to those of England. Admiralty judges settled maritime disputes and smuggling cases without using juries.

During the early eighteenth century, Parliament and royal ministers confined their attention to matters of trade and military defense and otherwise left the colonies on their own. This mild imperial rule, later called the era of "salutary neglect," allowed the colonies to grow in wealth, population, and self-government. It also encouraged colonial self-confidence, leading colonists to assume equality with the English as members of the empire.

DIVERGING POLITICS IN THE COLONIES AND GREAT BRITAIN

English people on both sides of the Atlantic believed that politics ought to reflect social organiza-tion. They often compared the state to a family. Just as fathers naturally headed families, adult men led societies. In particular, adult male property holders, who enjoyed economic independence, claimed the right to vote and hold office. Women (who generally could not own property), property-less men, and slaves had no political role because they, like children, were subordinate to the authority of others. Their dependence on husbands, fathers, masters, or employers—who could influence their political decisions—rendered them incapable of exercising freedom of choice.

States, like families, worked best when all members fulfilled their responsibilities. Rulers ought to govern with the same fairness and benevolence that fathers presumably exercised within their families. When George II became king in 1727, he reassured Parliament of his "constant care" to "secure to All My subjects, the full Enjoyment of their religious and civil Rights." In return for protection, the people owed their rulers the same obedience that children accorded their parents. The House of Commons responded to George II's assurance of goodwill with its own promise of "Duty, Zeal and Affection to Your Majesty's Person and Government." Such phrases often disguised actual struggles between rulers and people but nevertheless expressed firmly held ideals.

Eighteenth-century people also believed that government should reflect society's hierarchical organization. In England, this idea was embodied in the institutions of monarchy and Parliament. The crown, of course, represented the interests of the royal family. Parliament represented society's two main divisions: the aristocracy in the House of Lords and the common people in the House of Commons. Americans shared the view that government should mirror social hierarchies but found it much more difficult to put the idea into practice.

American society grew closer to the British model during the eighteenth century but was never identical to it. Thus its political structure would never fully mirror that of England. One obvious difference was that America lacked an aristocracy. In England, the members of this tiny privileged minority were easily recognizable by their great wealth, prestigious family lines, leisured lives, and official titles of nobility. British America had elites but no titled aristocracy. Elite colonists were often just two or three generations removed from humble beginnings. Hence the acute anxiety that inspired George Washington and other colonial gentlemen to seek refinement, to gain the automatic recognition that England's more secure elites enjoyed.

In both England and America, land ownership was the prerequisite for political participation, on the grounds that it freed people from dependence on others and gave them a stake in society. In England, this requirement sharply limited participation. By the mid-eighteenth century, only one-tenth of all English heads of households owned all the country's land, and thus only a correspondingly tiny proportion of men could vote. Landholding in America, however, was much more widespread. By late in life, a large majority of white male farmers owned the land they tilled. The expansion of landholding swelled the ranks of voters. In most colonies, 50 to 75 percent of white men were eligible to vote, although not all exercised this right at election time.

Distinctive social conditions in England and America also gave rise to different notions of political representation. Electoral districts for Parliament came in a confusing mixture of shapes, reflecting their status in past centuries. Once-important towns sent representatives on the basis of their former prominence. Dunwich even retained its right to elect a parliamentary representative long after the city itself had washed into the North Sea. At the same time, rapidly growing cities, such as Manchester, lacked any representative at all. Some English radicals protested this inequity during the eighteenth century. Most of their countrymen, however, accepted the idea of **virtual representation**, which held that representatives served the interests of the nation as a whole, not just the locality from which they came. They assumed that since the colonists held interests in common with English people at home, they were virtually represented in Parliament, just like Manchester's residents.

Since the founding of their colonies, however, Americans had experienced **actual representation** and believed that elected representatives should be directly responsive to local interests. They were accustomed to sending written instructions to their legislators, informing them how to vote on important issues. Colonial representatives, unlike members of Parliament, resided in their districts. The Americans' experience with actual representation made them extremely skeptical of Parliament's claims to virtual representation. For the first half of the eighteenth century, however, Parliament did not press this claim, and the tensions between the two ideas remained latent.

The most direct political confrontations between England and the colonies instead focused on the role of colonial governors. In every colony except Connecticut and Rhode Island (where voters chose the executive), either the king or proprietors appointed the governors. Their interests thus lay with their English patrons and not the colonies. More important, governors exercised greater powers over the colonial assemblies than the king (after the Glorious Revolution) did over Parliament. Governors could veto laws enacted by the assemblies and initiate legislation in consultation with councilors, whom they appointed. They could delay legislative sessions and dissolve the assemblies at will. Governors could also nominate and dismiss colonial judges as they wished.

In practice, several conditions hampered governors' efforts to exercise their legal authority. Many arrived with detailed instructions on how to govern, a condition that limited their ability to negotiate with colonists over sensitive issues. Governors controlled few offices or other prizes with which to buy the allegiance of their opponents. They struggled to dominate assemblies that grew in size as the colonial population expanded. And in several colonies, including Massachusetts and New York, governors relied on the assemblies to appropriate the money for their salaries—a financial dependence that restrained even the most autocratic executive.

In response to the perceived, if not always realized, threat of powerful governors, colonial assemblies asserted themselves as never before. They sent agents (including such prominent figures as Benjamin Franklin) to England to lobby on behalf of colonial interests. Local factions fought for election to the increasingly important legislature, leading to some of the most contentious politics in the British Empire. Governors often stood on the sidelines, either frustrated with their inability to govern or, at times, enlisted on the side of one faction or another.

Decades of struggles with governors led colonists to exalt the assemblies' role as the guarantors of their liberties. In 1738, one Pennsylvanian went so far as to declare that the "necessity of reducing the form of this government to the British mode" by strengthening the executive was a "wicked" design. Most colonists, however, accepted the loose and sometimes contradictory political ties of empire. They assumed that their connections to Britain were voluntary, based on common identity and rights. So long as Parliament treated the Americans as partners in empire and refrained from ruling by coercion, colonists could celebrate British government as "the most perfect combination of human powers in society . . . for the preservation of liberty and the production of happiness."

By the middle of the eighteenth century, the blessings of British government extended to more colonists than ever before. The population of

British America grew rapidly and spread out over vast amounts of land. The expansion of British settlement, in turn, alarmed other European powers with American colonies. Both Spain and France launched new settlements as the competition for the continent entered a new and volatile phase.

EXPANDING EMPIRES

During the first half of the eighteenth century, England, Spain, and France all enlarged their North American holdings according to patterns established during the previous century. England's empire expanded in tandem with the unrelenting growth of its colonial population. Spain and France still relied on missionaries, soldiers, and traders to stake their claims to American territory. In the eighteenth century, as in the seventeenth, English settlement displaced native peoples. Newly established Spanish and French colonies, however, contained small numbers of Europeans amid much larger populations of Indians. Over time, these empires came into closer contact with one another, intensifying the competition for land, trade, resources, and Indian allies (see Map 4–2).

BRITISH COLONISTS IN THE BACKCOUNTRY

Population growth in British North America during the eighteenth century was truly astonishing. The non-Indian population in the mainland

MAP 4-2   Expanding Settlement, c. 1750
Imperial rivalries drove Spain, France, and England to expand their North American empires in the mid-eighteenth century. Once again, this sparked conflict with native peoples as well as with European competitors.

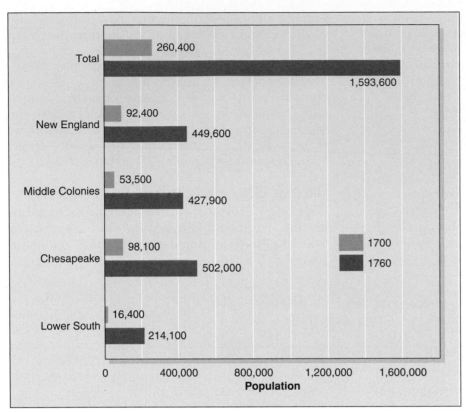

FIGURE 4-2 **Population Growth in British Mainland Colonies, 1700–1760**
Both natural increase and immigration contributed to a staggering rate of population growth in British North America. Some colonists predicted that Americans would soon outnumber Britain's inhabitants—a possibility that greatly concerned British officials.
Data Source: John J. McCusker and Russell R. Menard, *The Economy of British America, 1607–1789*, rev. ed. (1991). University of North Carolina Press.

colonies numbered about 260,000 in 1700; by 1760, it had increased to over 1.5 million (see Figure 4–2). In 1750, Benjamin Franklin predicted that if the colonial population continued to grow at this rate, within two hundred years "the greatest Number of Englishmen will be on this Side" of the Atlantic Ocean.

Much of this growth stemmed from natural increase. Many white families, particularly in the northern colonies, had between five and ten children, most of whom survived to produce more offspring. The descendants of a single couple could, after three or four generations, people small towns. When 80-year-old Judith Coffin, the matriarch of an unusually large Massachusetts family, died in 1705, she had a total of 177 children and grandchildren. By the mid-eighteenth century, even the slave population, first in the Chesapeake and later in the Lower South, began to reproduce itself, although more slowly than the white population.

Immigration also boosted the population, making some regions grow faster than others. Thou-

sands of Scots-Irish and German settlers, in addition to thousands of African slaves, helped the population of the Lower South increase at nearly twice the rate of New England, which attracted few immigrants (and therefore remained the most thoroughly English of all colonial regions). Pennsylvania absorbed a continuous stream of immigrants. By 1770, it had 240,000 settlers, ten times the number it had in 1710. Indeed, extensive German immigration worried Pennsylvania leaders. Like Benjamin Franklin, they feared that the newcomers would "never adopt our Language or Customs" and would soon "be so numerous as to Germanize us."

Most of the coast from Maine to Georgia was settled by 1760, forcing new immigrants to move inland. Descendants of earlier settlers often joined them, seeking farms that could no longer be had in the more crowded towns of their birth. New Englanders pushed up the Connecticut River Valley and into the hills of western Massachusetts. Settlement in New York followed the Hudson, Mohawk, and Schoharie Rivers deep into the interior. But the most dramatic expansion occurred in the foothills and valleys of the Appalachian Mountains from Pennsylvania to Georgia, a region known as the backcountry.

Between 1730 and 1770, nearly a quarter of a million German, Scots-Irish, and English colonists entered the backcountry. For the most part, they raised crops and livestock for subsistence on small, isolated farms. Community life developed slowly, in part because many backcountry settlers moved frequently. In addition, a surplus of men among the first settlers delayed the formation of families.

Contemporary observers derided the crudeness of frontier life. William Byrd scornfully described one backcountry house as a "castle containing of one dirty room with a dragging door to it that will neither open or shut." Charles Woodmason, an English-born Anglican missionary, was appalled by the sight of western Carolina settlers

This log house, built in Pennsylvania in the early eighteenth century, suggests the sort of dwellings that dotted the backcountry. Most such houses would have been smaller than this two-story example. Scandinavian colonists, who settled on the lower Delaware River in the early seventeenth century, introduced log construction to America.

who "Live in Logg Cabbins like Hogs." Most of them, he reported, were "very loose, dissolute, Idle People—Without either Religion or Goodness." Genteel observers offered what they considered the most damaging insult by referring to such settlers as "white Indians."

These comments reflect emerging tensions between backcountry settlements and older seacoast communities. George Washington, William Byrd, and other coastal planters acquired vast tracts of western land with the intent of selling it to these "crude" settlers. During the 1740s and 1750s, scores of Virginia planters, northern merchants, and London investors formed companies whose purpose was to profit from this kind of land speculation. Their interests collided with those of many backcountry settlers, including squatters who occupied the land without acquiring legal title in the hope that their labor in clearing farms would establish their property rights.

Backcountry settlers often complained that rich eastern planters, who dominated the colonial legislatures, ignored western demands for adequate representation. Many argued that the crudeness of frontier life was only temporary. Perhaps the best measure of their desire to resemble eastern planters was the spread of slaveholding among prosperous backcountry farmers. In one western Virginia county in 1750, only one-fifth of the household heads owned slaves. Just nineteen years later, more than half of them did.

Tensions grew throughout the backcountry as English settlers encroached on Indian lands. Colonists who moved to Pennsylvania's fertile Susquehanna Valley displaced Delawares, Shawnees, and other native peoples who had sought refuge there from earlier white migrations. In South Carolina, the Catawbas moved to ever more remote sites to keep their distance from white settlers. Indians moving to avoid friction with whites, however, frequently encroached on lands claimed by other tribes—particularly those of the Iroquois Confederacy—leading to conflict among native peoples.

Even where British settlers had not yet appeared, English and Scottish traders could often be found, aggressively pursuing trade with the Indians. Spanish and French observers feared this commercial expansion even more than they did the movement of settlers. Knowing that the Indians viewed trade as a counterpart to military alliance, they worried that the English, with cheaper and better trade goods, would lure away their native allies. In response, the Spanish and French expanded their own territorial claims and tried to strengthen relations with Indian peoples.

THE SPANISH IN TEXAS AND CALIFORNIA

Spain worried that its existing North American colonies would be overwhelmed by its enemies. Florida had become the target of English raiders from South Carolina, who attacked Spanish missions with the help of local Indians. Years of religious persecution and forced labor encouraged Florida's Indians to oppose the Spanish, but the natives also wanted English trade goods, such as guns, which Spanish traders were officially prohibited from selling. Spain maintained a precarious hold on coastal bases at St. Augustine, San Marcos de Apalachee, and Pensacola. By the mid-eighteenth century, however, control of Florida's interior effectively passed to Indian bands allied with English (and in the west, French) traders.

In 1700, New Mexico still suffered from the effects of the Pueblo Revolt. Spanish farmers and ranchers slowly moved back up the Rio Grande Valley. Franciscans returned to build fewer missions than before. Fearful of sparking another revolt, the priests eased their labor demands and avoided outright religious persecution, allowing the Pueblos to retain many of their customs and religious practices. New Mexican officials worried about news brought by Apache hunters that Frenchmen had been seen on the plains. French traders did not reach Santa Fe until 1739, but persistent rumors of

This panel of an eighteenth-century painting by an unknown Mexican artist is representative of a genre of portraits illustrating the categories Spanish colonists developed to designate the offspring of various kinds of mixed marriage. This one, labeled Español, con India, Mestizo, *depicts a Spanish father, an Indian mother, and their mestizo child. The scarcity of European women made mixed marriage common in Spanish colonies. Such unions were exceedingly rare in the English colonies, where cultural preferences and the relative abundance of European women discouraged intermarriage.*

their approach fueled Spanish fears that New Mexico would fall into French hands.

To create a buffer zone around their existing colonies, the Spanish moved into Texas and California. Franciscan priests led the way into east Texas, establishing several missions between 1690 and 1720. San Antonio was founded in 1718 as a way station between the Rio Grande and east Texas missions; its fortified chapel, San Antonio de Valero, later became famous as the Alamo. The Spanish advance into Texas, however, met with resistance from the French (who also had outposts on the Gulf Coast) and from the Caddos and other Indians armed with French guns. Efforts to fill east Texas with settlers from Spain, Cuba, and the Canary Islands, all failed when Spanish officials could not guarantee their safety. With only 1,800 settlers there as late as 1742, Spain exerted a weak hold on Texas.

Sixteenth-century Spaniards had considered building outposts in California to supply ships traveling between Mexico and the Philippines but were deterred by the region's remoteness. Spanish interest revived in the 1760s, when it seemed that Russia, which had built fur-trading posts in Alaska, might occupy California. Largely through the efforts of two men—José de Gálvez, a royal official, and Junípero Serra, a Franciscan priest—the Spanish constructed a string of forts and missions from San Diego north to San Francisco between 1769 and 1776.

They initially encountered little opposition from California's Indians, who lived in small, scattered villages and lacked experience with organized warfare. With no European rivals nearby to compete with them, the Spanish erected an extensive mission system designed to convert and educate Indians and set them to work. Thousands of native laborers farmed irrigated fields and tended horses, sheep, and cattle. They did so under extremely harsh conditions.

According to one observer, Indians who became Christians and settled at the missions endured a fate "worse than that of slaves." The Spanish worked them hard and maintained them in overcrowded, unsanitary dwellings. Native women suffered from sexual exploitation by Spanish soldiers. Epidemics of European diseases swept through the Indian population, reducing it from 300,000 in 1769 to about 200,000 fifty years later. Signs of native resistance met with quick and cruel punishment—including whipping, burning, and execution—so that the Indians would not (as one official later wrote) "come to know their power" over the vastly outnumbered Spanish. (As late as 1790, California had only 990 Spanish residents.) Despite the gruesome consequences, Indians staged several revolts during the eighteenth century, but Spanish soldiers usually suppressed them quickly.

Spain's empire grew, even as it weakened, during the eighteenth century. Its scattered holdings north of the Rio Grande functioned as colonies of another colony—Mexico—shielding it from foreign incursion. The scarcity of Spanish settlers, especially women, encouraged racial intermixture in the borderlands and insured that racial distinctions would never be drawn as sharply there as in the English colonies. From the beginning, Spain's vision of empire had rested not on extensive settlement but on expansive territorial claims backed up by soldiers and missionaries who subjugated native peoples in order to control their labor for Spanish profit. After 1700, however, the limitations of this coercive approach to empire, which had served Spain well for nearly two centuries, became apparent. As their experiences in Florida and Texas vividly demonstrated, the Spanish simply could not compete with the vigorous commercial empires of France and England.

THE FRENCH ALONG THE MISSISSIPPI AND IN LOUISIANA

French expansion followed major waterways of the St. Lawrence River, the Great Lakes, and the Mississippi into the heart of North America. Explorers reached the Mississippi Valley in the 1670s. Within twenty years, French outposts appeared along the Gulf Coast. New Orleans, the capital and main port of French Louisiana, was founded in 1718. Soon forts, trading posts, and villages sprang up in the continent's interior and formed a chain of way stations between Canada and the Gulf of Mexico, with military garrisons strategically located on lakes and rivers. Concerned about defending scattered settlements, French officials forbade colonists to move into the interior. But colonists went anyway, building six villages along the Mississippi in a place they called the pays des Illinois.

The first Illinois settlers were independent fur traders (*coureurs de bois,* or "woods runners") unwilling to return to Canada after the French government tried to prohibit their direct trade with Indians. Many found Christian Indian wives and began farming the rich lands along the river. Several hundred emigrants from Canada eventually joined them. The settlers, using the labor of their families and of black and Indian slaves, produced profitable surpluses of wheat, corn, and livestock to feed the growing population of New Orleans and the lower Mississippi Valley.

French Louisiana contained a remarkably diverse population of Indian peoples, French soldiers and settlers, and German immigrants, as well as African slaves who, by the 1730s, outnumbered European colonists. Settlers and slaves raised some tobacco and indigo as cash crops, but Louisiana's economy depended mainly on food crops, herding, fishing, and the deerskin trade. Discouraged by the lack of profits, French officials and merchants neglected Louisiana, and even Catholic missionaries failed to establish a strong presence. Significant European emigration to Louisiana essentially ceased after the 1720s.

But the French approach to empire in Louisiana as in Canada had always depended more on

Indian alliances than on settlement. Louisiana's principal allies were the Choctaws, whom one military official called "the bulwark of the colony." The Choctaws and other native allies offered trade and military assistance in return for guns, trade goods, French help in fighting English raiders seeking Indian slaves, and occasional French mediation of Indian disputes.

French expansion along the Mississippi Valley drove a wedge between Florida and Spain's other mainland colonies; it also blocked the westward movement of English settlers. But France's enlarged empire was only as strong as the Indian alliances on which it rested. Preserving good relations was expensive, however, requiring the constant exchange of diplomatic gifts and trade goods. When France ordered Louisiana officials to limit expenses and reduce Indian gifts in 1745, the officials objected that the Choctaws "would ask for nothing better than to have such pretexts in order to resort to the English."

The fear of losing Indian favor preoccupied officials in 1745 because at that moment France's empire in America consisted of two disconnected pieces: New France, centered in the St. Lawrence Valley and the Great Lakes basin, and Louisiana, stretching from New Orleans to the pays des Illinois. Between them lay a thousand miles of wilderness, through which only one thoroughfare passed—the Ohio River. For decades, communication between the two parts of France's North American empire posed no problem because Indians in the Ohio Valley allowed the French free passage through their lands. If that policy ended, however, France's New World empire would be dangerously divided.

A CENTURY OF WARFARE

The expansion of empires in North America reflected the policies of European states locked in a relentless competition for power and wealth. From the time of the Glorious Revolution, English foreign policy aimed at limiting the expansion of French influence. This, in turn, resulted in a series of four wars. As the eighteenth century wore on, the conflicts between the two countries increasingly involved their American colonies as well as Spain and its colonies. The outcome of each of the wars in America depended no less on the participation of colonists and Indians than on the policies and strategies of the European powers. The conclusion of the final conflict signaled a dramatic

Overview

The Colonial Wars, 1689–1763

Name in the Colonies	European Name and Dates	Dates in America	Results for Britain
King William's War	War of the League of Augsburg, 1688–1697	1689–1697	Reestablished balance of power between England and France
Queen Anne's War	War of Spanish Succession, 1702–1714	1702–1713	Britain acquired Nova Scotia
King George's War	War of Austrian Succession, 1739–1748	1744–1748	Britain returned Louisbourg to France British settlers began moving westward Weakening of Iroquois neutrality
French and Indian War	Seven Years' War, 1756–1763	1754–1763	Britain acquired Canada and all French territory east of Mississippi Britain gained Florida from Spain

shift in North American history (see the Overview table, "The Colonial Wars, 1689–1763").

IMPERIAL CONFLICT AND THE ESTABLISHMENT OF AN AMERICAN BALANCE OF POWER, 1689–1738

When he became king of England in 1688, the Dutch Protestant William of Orange was already fighting the War of the League of Augsburg against France's Catholic king, Louis XIV. Almost immediately, William brought England into the conflict. The war lasted until 1697 and ended, as most European wars of this period did, in a negotiated peace that reestablished the balance of power. Little territory changed hands, either in this war or in the War of the Spanish Succession (1702–1713), which followed it

In America, these two imperial wars—known to British colonists as **King William's War** and **Queen Anne's War**, after the monarchs on the throne at the time—ended with equal indecisiveness. New France's Indian allies attacked New England's north-

ern frontier with devastating success, destroying the Massachusetts town of Deerfield in 1704. New Englanders struck back at the exposed settlements of Acadia, which ultimately entered the British Empire as Nova Scotia, and tried unsuccessfully to seize Quebec. Neither war caused more than marginal changes for the colonies in North America. Both had profound effects, however, on the English state and the Iroquois League.

All European states of the eighteenth century financed their wars by borrowing. But the English were the first to realize that wartime debts did not necessarily have to be repaid during the following peace. The government instead created a funded debt. Having borrowed heavily from large joint-stock corporations, the government agreed to use tax revenues to pay interest on those loans, but it did not agree to pay off the loans themselves. The corporations agreed because the interest payments amounted to a steady form of income that over the long run could amount to more than the original loans. In this way, England became the first European country to harness its national economy efficiently to military ends.

As the debt grew larger, more and more taxes were necessary to pay interest on it. Taxes also rose to pay for a powerful navy and a standing army. When the treasury created a larger and more efficient bureaucracy to collect taxes, many Englishmen grew nervous. Their anxiety emerged as a strain of thought known as **Country**, or **"Real Whig," ideology**. Country ideology stressed the threats that a standing army and a powerful state posed to personal liberty. It also emphasized the dangers of taxation to property rights and the need for property holders to retain their right to consent to taxation. Real Whig politicians publicized their fears but could not stop the growth of the state. In every successive war, the claims of national interest and patriotism—and the prospect of profit for parties rich enough to lend money to the government—overrode the objections of those who feared the expansion of state power.

In America, the first two imperial wars transformed the role of the Iroquois League. After the English took over New Netherland in 1664, the Five Nations cultivated trading connections with them and later allied with England during King William's War. But the English offered little help when the French and their Indian allies attacked the Iroquois during that conflict. By 1700, the Iroquois League had suffered such horrendous losses—perhaps a quarter of the population had died from causes related to the war—that its leaders sought an alternative to direct alliance with the British.

With the so-called **Grand Settlement of 1701**, the Iroquois adopted a policy of neutrality with regard to the French and British Empires. Their goal was to refrain from alliances with either European power—which were likely to fight each other again—and instead maneuver between them. The Iroquois's strategic location between New France and the English colonies allowed them to serve as a geographical and diplomatic buffer between the two. Neutral Iroquois diplomats could play the English against the French, gaining favors from one side in return for promises not to ally with the other. This neutralist policy insured that for nearly fifty years neither England nor France could gain ascendancy in North America.

Iroquois neutrality offered benefits to the Europeans as well as the Indians. The English, for instance, began to negotiate with them for land. The

This cartoon, the first to appear in a colonial American newspaper, was printed in the Pennsylvania Gazette in the spring of 1754. It refers to the plan for a colonial union that was put forward at the Albany Congress. The image alludes to the folk belief that a severed snake could revive if its parts were rejoined before sundown.

Iroquois claimed sovereignty over much of the country west of the Middle and Chesapeake colonies. To smooth relations with the English, the Iroquois sold them land formerly occupied by Delawares and Susquehannocks. This transaction simultaneously helped to satisfy the colonists' land hunger and to enrich the Iroquois League.

Meanwhile a neutral Iroquois League claiming control over the Ohio Valley and blocking English access across the Appalachian Mountains helped the French protect the strategic corridor of the Ohio and Mississippi Valleys that linked Canada and Louisiana. If the English ever established a permanent presence in the Ohio Valley, however, the Iroquois would cease to be of use to the French. The Iroquois remained reasonably effective at keeping the British out of the Valley until the late 1740s. The next European war, however, altered these circumstances, increasing French anxiety about their empire and compelling British strategists to incorporate their colonies into war plans more fully than ever before.

KING GEORGE'S WAR SHIFTS THE BALANCE, 1739–1754

The third confrontation between Britain and France in Europe, the War of the Austrian Succession—**King George's War** to the British colonists—began as a small war between Britain and Spain in 1739. Its immediate cause was British attempts to poach on trade

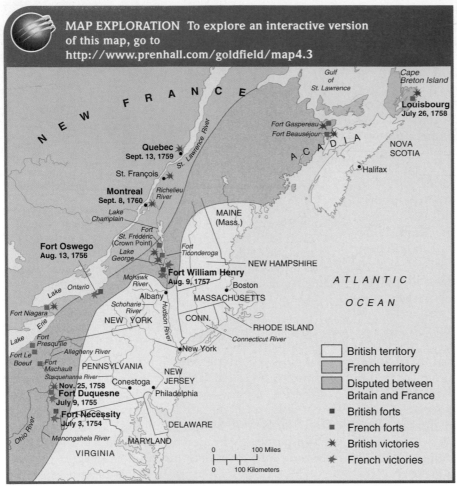

MAP EXPLORATION To explore an interactive version of this map, go to http://www.prenhall.com/goldfield/map4.3

MAP 4-3   The French and Indian War, 1754–1763
Most of the battles of the French and Indian War occurred in the frontier regions of northern and western New York and the Ohio Valley. The influx of settlers into these areas created tensions that eventually developed into war.

to Spain's Caribbean colonies. But in 1744, France joined in the war against Britain. An Anglo-French conflict once again erupted in North America.

New Englanders saw yet another chance to attack Canada. This time, their target was the great fortress of Louisbourg on Cape Breton Island, a naval base that dominated the Gulf of St. Lawrence. An expedition from Massachusetts and Connecticut, supported by a squadron of Royal Navy warships, captured Louisbourg in 1745. This success cut Canada off from French reinforcement and resupply. English forces should now have been able to conquer New France.

Instead, politically influential merchants in Albany, New York, chose to continue their profitable trade with the enemy over Lake Champlain, enabling Canada to hold out until the end of the war.

When the peace treaty was signed in 1748, Britain, which had fared badly in the European fighting, returned Louisbourg to France. This diplomatic adjustment, routine by European standards, shocked New Englanders. At the same time, New York's illegal trade with the enemy appalled British administrators. They began thinking of ways to prevent such independent behavior in any future war.

King George's War furnished an equal share of shocks for New France, which had suffered more than in any previous conflict. Even before the war's end, aggressive English traders from Pennsylvania began moving west to buy furs from Indians who had once traded with the French. The movements of these traders, along with the appearance of Virginians in the Ohio Valley after 1748, gravely concerned the French.

In 1749, the governor general of New France set out to assert direct control over the region by building a set of forts from Lake Erie to the Forks of the Ohio (where the Monongahela and Allegheny Rivers meet to form the Ohio River). This decision signaled the end of France's commitment to Iroquois neutrality. Instead of enjoying their old position as neutral mediators, the chiefs of the Iroquois League now found themselves trapped between empires edging closer to confrontation in the Ohio Valley.

The Iroquois, in fact, had never exerted direct power in the Ohio Country. Their control instead depended on their ability to dominate the peoples who actually lived there—western Senecas, as well as the Delawares and Shawnees, both in theory Iroquois dependents. The appearance of English traders in the valley offering goods on better terms than the French or the Iroquois had ever provided undermined Iroquois dominance.

The Ohio Valley Indians increasingly ignored Iroquois claims of control and pursued their own independent course. One spur to their disaffection from the Iroquois was the 1744 **Treaty of Lancaster**, by which Iroquois chiefs had sold the rights to trade at the Forks of the Ohio to a group of Virginia land speculators. The Virginians assumed that these trading rights included the right to acquire land for eventual sale to settlers. The Ohio Valley Indians found this situation intolerable, as did the French. When, in 1754, the government of Virginia sent out a small body of soldiers under Lieutenant Colonel George Washington to protect Virginia's claims to the Forks of the Ohio, the French struck decisively to stop them.

THE FRENCH AND INDIAN WAR, 1754–1760: A DECISIVE VICTORY

In April 1754, French soldiers overwhelmed a group of Virginians who had been building a small fort at the Forks of the Ohio. They then erected a much larger fort of their own, Fort Duquesne, on the spot. The French intended to follow up by similarly ousting Washington's weak, untrained troops, who had encamped further up the Monongahela River. However, at the end of May, Washington's men killed or captured all but one of the members of a small French reconnaissance party. The French decided to teach the Virginians a lesson. On July 3, they attacked Washington at his encampment, Fort Necessity. The following day, with a quarter of his troops killed or wounded, Washington surrendered.

Even before news of these engagements reached Britain, imperial officials worried that the Iroquois might ally with the French. Britain ordered New York's governor to convene an intercolonial meeting in Albany—known as the Albany Congress—to discuss matters with the Iroquois. Several prominent colonists, including Governor William Shirley of Massachusetts and Benjamin Franklin, took advantage of the occasion to put forward the **Albany Plan of Union**, which called for an intercolonial union to coordinate colonial defense, levy taxes, and regulate Indian affairs. But the colonies, too suspicious of one another to see their common interests, rejected the Albany Plan. Meanwhile, events in the west took a turn for the worse.

The French expulsion of the Virginians left the Indians of the region, Delawares and Shawnees, with no choice but to ally with the French in what came to be called the French and Indian War (see Map 4–3). Soon French and Indian attacks fell like hammer blows on backcountry settlements from

This, *the earliest known portrait of George Washington, was painted by Charles Willson Peale in 1772. It depicts him in his military uniform from the French and Indian War. Military service helped to strengthen Washington's ties with the British Empire.*

Washington/Custis/Lee Collection, Washington and Lee University, Lexington, VA.

Pennsylvania to the Carolinas. The Iroquois tried to remain neutral, but their neutrality no longer mattered. Europeans were at last contending directly for control of the Ohio Country.

The **French and Indian War** blazed in America for two years before it erupted as a fourth Anglo-French war in Europe in 1756. Known in Europe as the Seven Years' War (1756–1763), it involved fighting in the Caribbean, Africa, India, and the Philippine Islands as well as in Europe and North America. It was unlike any other eighteenth-century conflict, not only in its immense scope and expense but also in its decisive outcome.

The war had two phases in North America—one from 1754 to 1758 and the other from 1758 through 1760—that corresponded to shifts in European involvement. During the first phase, the French enjoyed a string of successes as they followed what had been a proven strategy in previous conflicts—guerrilla war. Relying on Indian allies acting with Canadian soldiers, the French raided

English frontier settlements, killing and capturing hundreds of civilians and forcing tens of thousands more to flee. Then they attacked fortified outposts whenever the opportunity appeared. This style of warfare allowed the Canadians' Indian allies—who came from all over the Northeast and the upper Midwest—to act independently in choosing targets and tactics.

The first full campaign of the war, in 1755, saw not only the British colonial frontiers collapsing in terror but also a notable defeat inflicted on the troops Britain had dispatched to attack Fort Duquesne. The British commander in chief, Major General Edward Braddock, with immense self-confidence and no real knowledge of the countryside or his enemy, marched to within 10 miles of Fort Duquesne, only to have his 1,450-man force surrounded and destroyed by Indians and Canadian militiamen. Braddock's defeat set the tone for virtually every military engagement of the next three years and opened a period of demoralization and internal conflict in the British colonies.

Britain responded to Braddock's defeat by sending a new commander in chief with more trained British soldiers. The new commander, Lord Loudoun, tried to set colonial military affairs on a professional footing. He insisted on managing every aspect of the war effort, not only directing the campaigns but also dictating the amount of support, in men and money, that each colony would provide. The colonists, who had plenty of experience with war, had never experienced anything like Loudoun's high-handed style and grew increasingly stubborn in response to it. Colonial soldiers, who had volunteered to serve under their own officers, objected to Loudoun's command. By the end of 1757, a year of disastrous military campaigns, colonial assemblies were also refusing to cooperate.

Britain's aim had been to "rationalize" the war by making it conform to European professional military standards. This approach required soldiers to advance in formation in the face of massed musket fire without breaking rank. It needed iron discipline, which was enforced—as in the British army—by savage punishments, including hundreds of lashes at the whipping post. Few colonial volunteers met professional standards, and few colonists thought them necessary, especially when British soldiers suffered defeat after defeat at the hands of French and Indian guerrillas. British officers assumed that colonial soldiers were simply lazy cowards. But colonial volunteers, appalled to see men lashed "till the blood came out at the knee" of their breeches, saw British officers as brutal task-masters.

They resisted all efforts to impose such discipline on their own units, even to the point of desertion and mutiny.

Despite the astonishing success of their guerrilla tactics, the French, too, began moving toward a more European style of warfare. In the process, they destroyed their strategic and tactical advantages. In 1756, the Marquis de Montcalm, a strong proponent of European professional standards of military conduct, assumed command of French forces. In his first battle, the successful siege of Fort Oswego, New York, Montcalm was horrified by the behavior of his Indian allies, which included killing wounded prisoners, taking personal captives, and collecting scalps as trophies. He came to regard the Indians—so essential to the defense of New France—as mere savages.

Following his next victory, the capture of Fort William Henry, New York, Montcalm conformed to European practice by allowing the defeated garrison to go home in return for the promise not to fight again. Montcalm's Indian allies, a thousand or more strong, were not to take prisoners, trophies, or plunder. The tragic result came to be known as the Massacre of Fort William Henry. Feeling betrayed by their French allies, the Indians took captives and trophies anyway, killing as many as 185 defenders and capturing about 300 people. This action not only outraged the New England colonies (most of the victims were New Englanders) but also alienated the Indians on whom the defense of Canada depended. Ironically, Montcalm's efforts to limit the war's violence—to impose European standards of conduct—prepared the way for the British army and its colonial auxiliaries to win an unlimited victory.

For at the same time that the Europeanization of the war was weakening the French, the British moderated their policies and reached accommodation with the colonists. A remarkable politician came to power in London as England's chief war minister. William Pitt, who as secretary of state directed the British war effort from late 1757 through 1761, realized that friction between the colonists and the commander in chief arose from the colonists' sense that they were bearing all the financial burdens of the war without having any say in how the war was fought. Pitt's ingenious solutions were to promise reimbursements to the colonies in proportion to their contribution to the war effort, to deemphasize the power of the commander in chief, and to replace the arrogant Loudoun with a less objectionable officer.

Pitt's money and measures restored colonial morale. He sent thousands of British soldiers to America to fight alongside colonial troops. As the Anglo-American forces grew stronger, they operated more successfully, seizing Louisbourg again in 1758. Once more, Canada experienced crippling shortages of supplies, weapons, and trade goods. But this time, unlike the situation in 1745, the Anglo-Americans were united and able to take advantage of the situation. British emissaries persuaded the Delawares and Shawnees to abandon their French alliance, and late in 1758, an Anglo-American force again marched on Fort Duquesne. In command of its lead battalion was Colonel George Washington. The French defenders, abandoned by their native allies and confronted by overwhelming force, blew up the fort and retreated to the Great Lakes.

From this point on, the Anglo-Americans suffered no setbacks, and the French won no victories.

The war became a contest in which the larger, better-supplied army would triumph. Montcalm, forced back to Quebec, decided to risk everything in a European-style, open-field battle against a British force led by General James Wolfe. At the Battle of Quebec (September 13, 1759), Montcalm lost the gamble—and his life (as did the victorious General Wolfe).

But the French had not yet lost the war. If they could revive their Indian alliances, with weapons and trade goods sent from France, the French still had a chance to recover. What finally decided the outcome of the war in America was not the Battle of Quebec but two other developments: the Battle of Quiberon Bay in France (November 20, 1759) and the Iroquois' decision to join the Anglo-American side in 1760. The sea battle cost the French navy its ability to operate on the Atlantic, preventing it from carrying the reinforcements and

In his most famous painting, American artist Benjamin West depicted the death of the British general James Wolfe at the Battle of Quebec. He portrays Wolfe as a glorious martyr to the cause of British victory. In the left foreground, West added the figure of an Indian, a "noble savage" who contemplates the meaning of Wolfe's selfless sacrifice of his life.

MAP 4-4 European Empires in North America, 1750–1763
Great Britain's victory in the French and Indian War transformed the map of North America. France lost its mainland colonies, England claimed all lands east of the Mississippi, and Spain gained nominal control over the Trans-Mississippi West.

supplies Canada needed to survive. Montcalm's successor could not rebuild the Indian alliances he so desperately needed. At the same time, the Iroquois decision to enter the war on the side of the Anglo-Americans tipped the balance irrevocably against the French. The last ragged, hungry defenders of Canada, surrounded at Montreal by a vastly superior Anglo-American-Iroquoian force, surrendered on September 8, 1760.

THE TRIUMPH OF THE BRITISH EMPIRE, 1763

The war pitting Britain against France and Spain (which had entered the fighting as a French ally in 1762), concluded with an uninterrupted series of British victories. In the Caribbean, where every valuable sugar island the French owned came under British control, the culminating event was the surrender of Havana on August 13, 1762. Even more spectacular was Britain's capture of the Philippine capital of Manila on October 5—a victory that liter-

ally carried British power around the world.

These conquests created the unshakable conviction that British arms were invincible. An immense surge of British patriotism spread throughout the American colonies. When news of the conquest of Havana reached Massachusetts, bells rang, cannons fired salutes, and bonfires blazed. General John Winslow of Plymouth, a portly man, rejoiced by becoming "so intoxicated as to jump on the table, and break a great number of bowls."

Hostilities ended formally on February 10, 1763, with the conclusion of the **Treaty of Paris**. France regained its West Indian sugar islands—its most valuable colonial possessions—but lost the rest of its North American empire. France ceded to Britain all its claims to lands east of the Mississippi River (except the city of New Orleans) and compensated Spain for the losses it had sustained as an ally by handing over all claims to the Trans-Mississippi West and the port of New Orleans (see Map 4–4). Britain returned Cuba and the Philippines to

Spain and in compensation received Florida. Now Great Britain owned everything east of the Mississippi, from the Gulf of Mexico to Hudson's Bay. With France and Spain both humbled and on the verge of financial collapse, Britain seemed preeminent in Europe and ready to dominate in the New World. Never before had Americans felt more pride in being British, members of the greatest empire on earth.

CONCLUSION

The George Washington who ordered a suit from England in 1763 longed to be part of the elite of the great British Empire. If he feared any threat to his position in that elite, it was not Parliament and the king but the uncomfortably large debts he owed to his London agents for the goods he wanted or perhaps the unruly Baptists who challenged the superiority of the great planters. But those worries, though real, were merely small, nagging doubts, shared by most of his fellow planters.

What was more real to Washington was the great victory that the British empire had just gained over France, a victory that he had helped to achieve. With the French eliminated as an imperial power in North America, Washington could look forward to increasing his fortune by speculating in the western lands he knew so well. For Washington, as for virtually all other colonial leaders, 1763 was a moment of great promise and patriotic devotion to the British Empire. It was a time to rejoice in the fundamental British identity and liberty and rights that seemed to ensure that life in the colonies would be better and more prosperous than ever.

REVIEW QUESTIONS

1. Why did George Washington prefer to order a suit from London rather than trust a Virginia tailor to make him one? How does his decision reflect elite colonists' attitudes about American society and culture in the eighteenth century?

2. In what ways did economic ties between Britain and the colonies grow closer in the century after 1660?

3. What was the Great Awakening, and what impact did it have? How did it affect different groups in colonial society?

4. In what ways were colonial and British political ideas and practices similar? In what ways were they different?

5. Why did England, Spain, and France renew their competition for North America in the eighteenth century?

6. What role did warfare play in North America in the eighteenth century? What role did the Iroquois play?

KEY TERMS

Actual representation (p. 120)
Age of Enlightenment (p. 112)
Albany Plan of Union (p. 129)
Country, or "Real Whig" ideology (p. 127)

Dominion of New England (p. 117)
Enumerated products (p. 102)
French and Indian War (p. 129)
Glorious Revolution (p. 117)
Grand Settlement of 1701 (p. 127)
Great Awakening (p. 114)
Halfway Covenant (p. 113)
King George's War (p. 127)
King William's War (p. 126)
Mercantilism (p. 102)
New Lights (p. 115)
Queen Anne's War (p. 126)
Treaty of Lancaster (p. 129)
Treaty of Paris (p. 132)
Virtual representation (p. 120)

RECOMMENDED READING

Anderson, Fred. *Crucible of War: The Seven Years' War and the Fate of Empire in British North America, 1754–1766* (2000). A vivid narrative of the last great imperial war.

Bushman, Richard L. *The Refinement of America: Persons, Houses, Cities* (1992). A sophisticated exploration of the quest for gentility in early America.

Franklin, Benjamin. *Autobiography* (numerous editions). The classic account of Franklin's rise from poor beginnings to prominence in colonial Philadelphia.

McCusker, John J., and Russell R. Menard. *The Economy of British America, 1607–1789,* rev. ed. (1991). The most comprehensive study of the economies of each colonial region.

Stout, Harry S. *The Divine Dramatist: George Whitefield and the Rise of Modern Evangelicalism* (1991). A clear and thorough account of Whitefield's career and the religious context in which it occurred.

ADDITIONAL SOURCES
Colonial Economic Development

Marshall, Peter, and Glyn, Williams, eds. *The British Atlantic Empire before the American Revolution* (1980).

Steele, Ian K. *The English Atlantic, 1675–1740: An Exploration of Communication and Community* (1986).

Walton, Gary M., and James F. Shepherd. *The Economic Rise of Early America* (1979).

Waterhouse, Richard. *A New World Gentry: The Making of a Merchant and Planter Class in South Carolina, 1670–1770* (1989).

Religion, Society, and Culture in Early America

Bonomi, Patricia. *Under the Cope of Heaven: Religion, Society, and Politics in Colonial America* (1986).

Boyer, Paul, and Stephen Nissenbaum. *Salem Possessed: The Social Origins of Witchcraft* (1974).

Breen, Timothy H. *Tobacco Culture: The Mentality of the Great Tidewater Planters on the Eve of Revolution* (1985).

Brown, Richard D. *Knowledge Is Power: The Diffusion of Information in Early America, 1700–1865* (1991).

Bushman, Richard L. *From Puritan to Yankee: Character and the Social Order in Connecticut, 1690–1765* (1967).

Butler, Jon. *Becoming America: The Revolution before 1776* (2000).

Dayton, Cornelia Hughes. *Women Before the Bar: Gender, Law, & Society in Connecticut, 1639–1789* (1995).

Demos, John. *Entertaining Satan: Witchcraft and the Culture of Early New England* (1982).

Hall, Gwendolyn Midlo. *Africans in Colonial Louisiana: The Development of Afro-Creole Culture in the Eighteenth Century* (1992).

Isaac, Rhys. *The Transformation of Virginia, 1740–1790* (1982).

Karlsen, Carol. *The Devil in the Shape of a Woman: Witchcraft in Colonial New England* (1987).

May, Henry. *The Enlightenment in America* (1976).

Colonial and Imperial Politics

Bailyn, Bernard. *The Origins of American Politics* (1968).

Bliss, Robert. *Revolution and Empire: English Politics and the American Colonies in the Seventeenth Century* (1990).

Brewer, John. *The Sinews of Power: War, Money, and the English State, 1688–1783* (1989).

Bushman, Richard. *King and People in Provincial Massachusetts* (1985).

Johnson, Richard. *Adjustment to Empire: The New England Colonies, 1675–1715* (1981).

Jones, J. R. *Country and Court: England, 1658–1714* (1978).

Lovejoy, David S. *The Glorious Revolution in America, 1660–1692* (1972).

Morgan, Edmund S. *Inventing the People: The Rise of Popular Sovereignty in England and America* (1988).

Nash, Gary B. *The Urban Crucible: The Northern Seaports and the Origins of the American Revolution,* abr. ed. (1986).

Shannon, Timothy. *Indians and Colonists at the Crossroads of Empire: The Albany Congress of 1754* (1999).

Speck, W. A. *Stability and Strife: England, 1714–1760* (1977).

The Expansion of Empires

Chipman, Donald E. *Spanish Texas, 1519–1821* (1992).

Hinderaker, Eric. *Elusive Empires: Constructing Colonialism in the Ohio Valley 1673–1800* (1997).

Mancall, Peter. *Valley of Opportunity: Economic Culture along the Upper Susquehanna, 1700–1800* (1991).

Richter, Daniel. *Ordeal of the Longhouse: The Peoples of the Iroquois League in the Era of European Colonization* (1992).

Usner, Daniel H., Jr. *Indians, Settlers, and Slaves in a Frontier Exchange Economy: The Lower Mississippi Valley before 1783* (1992).

Weber, David J. *The Spanish Frontier in North America* (1992).

Imperial Warfare

Black, Jeremy. *Britain as a Military Power, 1688–1815* (1999).

Jennings, Francis. *Empire of Fortune: Crowns, Colonies, and Tribes in the Seven Years' War in America* (1988).

Selesky, Harold. *War and Society in Colonial Connecticut* (1990).

Steele, Ian K. *Betrayals: Fort William Henry and the "Massacre"* (1990).

Titus, James. *The Old Dominion at War: Society, Politics, and Warfare in Late Colonial Virginia* (1991).

WHERE TO LEARN MORE
- **Mission Parkway, San Antonio, Texas.** Three Spanish missions (Mission Nuestra Señora de la Purisma Concepción, Mission San Francisco de la Espada, Mission San Juan Capistrano) founded in the early eighteenth century are located along this road. Their architecture indicates that they were intended to be fortifications as well as

churches. The website http://hotx.com/missions/ has links to each mission, offering pictures, descriptions, and historical background.

- **Ste. Genevieve Historic District, Ste. Genevieve, Missouri.** This restored site of an early eighteenth-century French settlement in the pays des Illinois contains many historic buildings open for tours. A general description of the site is at the website http://rosecity.net/rhr/stegenevieve.html. Descriptions and pictures of historic houses can be found at http://www.ste-genevieve.com/histsite.htm.

- **Colonial Williamsburg, Williamsburg, Virginia.** A reconstruction of the capital of eighteenth-century Virginia, this site covers 173 acres and contains many restored and rebuilt structures, including houses, churches, the House of Burgesses, and the Governor's Palace. Many educational and cultural programs are available. Historical interpreters, dressed in period costume, provide information about eighteenth-century Chesapeake life. The website www.colonialwilliamsburg.com/history/index.cfm has a variety of links that include biographical information on eighteenth-century residents of Williamsburg, aspects of colonial life, and material culture. The link to "Electronic Field Trips" has information on how to arrange for an interactive television program and special Internet activities.

- **Mount Vernon, Virginia.** Site of George Washington's much refurbished home. There is also a reconstructed gristmill and barn, as well as various outbuildings. Exhibits include information on Washington's agricultural experiments. The website www.mountvernon.org offers virtual tours of the house and grounds, as well as information on "George Washington, Pioneer Farmer."

- **Johnson Hall, Johnstown, New York.** Eighteenth-century home of William Johnson, who served as Superintendent of Indian Affairs and directed much of Britain's diplomacy with the Iroquois. Biographical information and pictures can be found at the website www.johnstown.com/city/johnson.html.

- **Berkeley and Westover Plantations, Charles City, Virginia.** These two eighteenth-century James River plantations suggest the elegance of elite planters' lives. The house and grounds at Berkeley are open to the public, the grounds only at Westover, the home of William Byrd. Pictures, descriptions of the sites, and background on their owners can be found at www.jamesriverplantations.org, which has links to each plantation.

 Please refer to the document CD-ROM for primary sources related to this chapter.

→ *Having apparently originated in a May Day-like celebration of the repeal of the Stamp Act in the spring of 1766, liberty poles were particularly characteristic of New York City, where citizens of all social classes supported their erection (as in the picture). However, British soldiers repeatedly destroyed them, thereby prompting serious rioting. Elsewhere, liberty trees served similar symbolic functions. John C. McRae of New York published this print in 1875.*

IMPERIAL BREAKDOWN
1763–1774

Philadelphia, January 1774

My Dear Jack,

Your Uncle wrote the 27 Dec. by Capt. Ayres who brought the Tea. His ship came within four miles of this City on Sunday the 26th where she was stopped, not being suffered to come any farther…. The inhabitants sent a Supply of fresh provisions & a Pilot on board [who put them on course for England]. I believe they were glad they came off so well, for at Boston they threw it all into the River, and it would have gone near to have shared the same fate here, but the Capt. had more prudence than to endeavour to force a landing by which means he prevented a great deal of Mischief & Confusion, for they were all determined to oppose it. They think now that the India Company will get the Act which imposes a duty of 3d per pound repealed and then send more over.

Kensington, September 19, 1774

Dear Jack,

The Congress [The First Continental Congress] are now Setting here & have been a fortnight but nothing Transpires. All is kept a profound Secret. There was a [false] report the other day of the Town of Boston being Bombarded by the Men of War lying off the Town…which Occasioned a general consternation along the Continent,

CHAPTER OUTLINE

Imperial Reorganization
British Problems
Dealing with the New Territories
Indian Affairs
Curbing the Assemblies
The Sugar and Stamp Acts

American Reactions
Constitutional Issues
Taxation and the Political Culture
Protesting the Taxes

The Aftermath of the Stamp Act Crisis
A Strained Relationship
Regulator Movements

The Townshend Crisis
Townshend's Plan
American Boycott
The Boston Massacre
The "Quiet Period"
The Boston Tea Party
The Intolerable Acts

The Road to Revolution
American Response to the Intolerable Acts
The First Continental Congress
The Continental Association
Political Divisions

Conclusion

and in some parts of the Country they Armed and Marched to the Number of 15,000 & more were getting ready.... In Short the Provinces are determined one and all to stand by each other. What the Consequences will be we don't know. To be sure thy [they] may send Men of War and destroy the Towns on the sea shore but its Impossible to take the Country, and the damage they do in destroying the Towns will fall on the English in the end.

Kensington Nov 1, 1774

My Dear Jack,

Our Congress are broke up and are come to a great Spirited Resolves ... together with a petition to his Majestie.... It is to be published and they have bound themselves to abide by those resolves ... and if Necessitated to repel force with force. All Importation ceases after the first of December next.

April 28, 1775

Dear Jackey,

The Provinces are all Arming themselves, and the men are almost all for inlisting as fast as they take them so am afraid we shall have Troublesome times. I heartily wish the Authors of all this Mischief may be brought to Justice.

Kensington June 28, 1775

My Dear Jack,

All the Provinces [are] arming and Training in the same Manner, for they are all determined to die or be Free. It is not the low Idle Fellows that fight only for pay but Men of great property are Common Soldiers who say they are fighting for themselves and Posterity..... The People are getting in Manufactures of different sorts, particularly Salt Peter and Gunpowder. The Smiths are almost all turnd Gunsmiths and cannot work fast enough. God knows how it will end but I fear it will be very bad on both sides, and if your drivalish minestry and parliament dont make some concessions and Repeal the Acts, England will lose America for as I said before they are determined to be free.

Eliza Farmar

Pennsylvania Magazine of History and Biography, vol. 40 (1916): 199-207.

Eliza Farmar and her family had recently moved to Kensington, a suburb of Philadelphia, when she wrote these letters, and her ties to relatives in England remained strong. Jack, the recipient of these letters, was her nephew and a clerk in the London office of the East India Company, whose shipment of tea precipitated the Boston Tea Party. Although she hoped that he might come to America, she minced no words in emphasizing the determination of Americans to resist British measures that appeared to infringe upon their freedoms. These letters accordingly chronicle a psychological counterpart to her move to Kensington. She began both journeys as an English subject; she ended them as an American citizen. Her initial reports of political developments, though sympathetic to the colonial point of view, were fairly objective, but by the eve of the Revolution she had disowned the British government by referring to "your ministry and parliament" as "drivalish," a slip of the pen that covered ineffective and devilish.

Like most colonists, she started out proud to be a British subject and part of Britain's increasingly powerful empire. Americans had fought the king's enemies as well as their own in a series of imperial wars and had gloried in British successes. But over the course of the eighteenth century, they had also developed a sense of their identity as Americans. Largely governing themselves through their own legislatures, they believed that they enjoyed all the rights of British subjects anywhere.

But in the wake of the French and Indian War, British authorities found themselves with a burdensome debt and vastly increased territory to administer. In response, they attempted to change the way they governed the colonies and, for the first time, imposed direct taxes on the colonists. Most Americans saw these measures as violations of their rights and opposed them, although they disagreed over how far to carry their resistance.

KEY TOPICS

- British problems and policies in North America after the French and Indian War
- Native Americans' conflicts with the colonists
- The American reaction to British attempts to tax the colonies
- Social tensions and the Regulator movements in the Carolinas
- Intercolonial union and resistance to British measures

IMPERIAL REORGANIZATION

At the close of the French and Indian War, British officials adopted a new and ultimately disastrous course in dealing with America. Lacking experience and led by the young and somewhat naive new monarch, George III, they panicked at the magnitude of the problems confronting them. Trying to fix a relationship between England and the colonies that most Americans would have said was not broken, they took measures that worked mostly to the disadvantage of the colonies. As one contemporary critic observed, "A great Empire and little minds go ill together."

BRITISH PROBLEMS

Britain's empire in 1763 was, in fact, immense, and the problems its rulers faced were correspondingly large. Its territories in North America stretched from Hudson's Bay in the north to the Caribbean Sea in the south and from the Atlantic Ocean west to the Mississippi River. Britain also had possessions in the Mediterranean region, Africa, and India. It still faced threats, if diminished ones, from its traditional European enemies. French territory on the North American mainland had been reduced to two tiny islands in the Gulf of St. Lawrence. But France would be eager for revenge, and French inhabitants in the recently acquired territories might prove disloyal to their new rulers in any future war between the two countries.

Spain was less powerful militarily than France but a more significant presence on the North American mainland. In the territorial settlement at the end of the French and Indian War, it surrendered East and West Florida to Britain but got back its possessions in Cuba and the Philippines that the British had captured. Spain acquired Louisiana from its French ally as compensation for the loss of the Floridas. Shocked by their inability to defend Cuba and the Philippines, Spanish officials stepped up the pace of reforms that they had begun making earlier in the century. Following the efficient French model of colonial government, they appointed *intendants*—generally Spaniards rather than colonials—to insure better tax collection. Spain also expelled the Jesuit order from its dominions, because Jesuit priests were too independent of royal control to suit Spanish officials. And Spain strengthened its military forces in much of the empire, including Mexico, which then encompassed Texas, New Mexico, and California as well as present-day Mexico.

Spain began to establish settlements in California in 1769 (see Chapter 4), but these were too weak and too far from the British colonies on the eastern seaboard to worry officials in London. British authorities were similarly little concerned about Louisiana, though it was closer and more populated. As for Florida, under British control after 1763, the Spanish authorities evacuated it completely, taking with them not only the free black population of Mose (a settlement of former slaves who had escaped from Georgia and South Carolina) but even the bones of one of the late royal governors.

Protecting and controlling the old and new territories in North America as inexpensively as possible presented British officials with difficult questions. How should they administer the new territories? How should they deal with Indians likely to resist further encroachments on their lands? And perhaps most vexing, how could they rein in the seemingly out-of-control colonists in the old territories?

Permitting most of the new areas to have their own assemblies appeared inadvisable but unavoidable if these areas were to attract settlers. Believing that the increasing power of the legislatures had long since "unhinged" the government of the older colonies, British authorities hoped to avoid similar unruliness in the new territories. In fact, they had long wanted to roll back the power of the old colonial assemblies. But Britain had needed the cooperation of these assemblies during the years of war with France. Now, with France vanquished, imperial officials felt that they could crack down on the local governments. Some British statesmen, however, recognized that this new approach was risky. With France gone from the continent, Americans would be less dependent on Britain for protection and therefore more inclined to resist unpopular restrictions.

Resentment against American conduct during the war also colored British thinking. Some of the colonies had failed to enlist their quota of recruits, and for this the British blamed the local assemblies. Worse yet, some Americans continued to smuggle goods to and from the enemy in the French West Indies during the war. Illicit trade was so common in New England that it cost Britain more to operate the customs service in America than it collected in duties.

England emerged from the war with what was then an immense national debt of approximately £146 million, nearly double the amount at the beginning of the conflict. Interest payments alone

Chronology

1759–1761	Cherokee War takes place.
1760	George III becomes king.
1761–1762	Writs of Assistance case in Massachusetts.
1763	Peace of Paris ends French and Indian War.
	Spanish accelerate imperial reforms.
	British troops remain in America.
	Proclamation Line of 1763 limits western expansion of colonial settlement.
	Pontiac's Rebellion begins.
	Paxton Boys murder peaceful Indians.
	Virginia Court decides Parson's Cause.
1764	Sugar Act passed.
	Currency Act passed.
1765	Quartering Act passed.
	Stamp Act passed.
	Stamp Act Congress meets in New York.
1766	Stamp Act repealed; Declaratory Act passed.
	New York Assembly refuses to comply with the Quartering Act.
1767	Townshend duties imposed.
	Regulator movements begin in North and South Carolina.
1770	Boston Massacre takes place.
	Tea duty retained, other Townshend duties repealed.
1771	North Carolina Regulator movement defeated.
1772	*Gaspee* burned.
	Committees of Correspondence formed.
1773	Boston Tea Party takes place.
1774	Coercive Acts passed.
	Quebec Act passed.
	First Continental Congress meets and agrees to boycott British imports.

accounted for half the government's annual expenditures after the war. Alarmed by the unprecedented debt, many Britons concluded that Americans should bear more of the financial burden of running the empire. The colonists certainly appeared prosperous to British soldiers who had served in America. But compared to the English, who paid on average perhaps a third of their income in taxes, many Americans normally rendered no more than 5 percent. An economic recession—triggered by the reduction in spending that followed the war—put further pressure on British officials to reduce taxes in England.

DEALING WITH THE NEW TERRITORIES

In 1763, the British government took several important steps to deal with the new territories, protect the old colonies, and maintain peace with the Indians. One was to keep a substantial body of troops—10,000 were initially planned—stationed in America even in peacetime. Another, announced in the royal **Proclamation of 1763**, was to establish civilian governments in East and West Florida (Canada remained under military rule). A third, in the same proclamation, was to temporarily forbid white settlement west of the Appalachian Mountains. The purpose of the **Proclamation Line** restricting white settlement was presumably twofold: to keep white settlers and Indians apart, preventing fighting between them, and to hold the colonists closer to the coast where they would be easier to control (see Map 5–1). Permanent arrangements for the Mississippi Valley could come later, after British officials had time to ponder matters.

Neither the Proclamation Line nor the stationing of troops in America was particularly wise. The

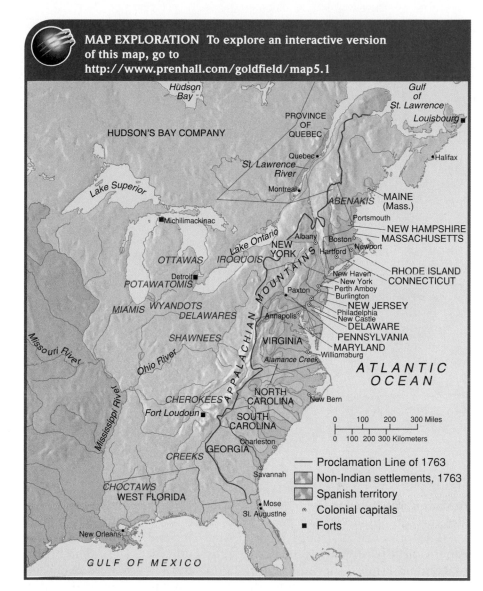

MAP EXPLORATION To explore an interactive version of this map, go to http://www.prenhall.com/goldfield/map5.1

MAP 5-1   Colonial Settlement and the Proclamation Line of 1763
This map depicts the regions claimed and settled by the major groups competing for territory in eastern North America. With the Proclamation Line of 1763, positioned along the crest of the Appalachian Mountains, the British government tried to stop the westward migration of settlers under its jurisdiction and thereby limit conflict with the Indians. The result, however, was frustration and anger on the part of land-hungry settlers.

Proclamation Line provoked resentment because it threatened to deprive settlers and speculators in the rapidly developing colonies of the land they coveted. Some who had moved into the Ohio area were forcefully removed. Other Americans merely ignored the restriction. Moreover, someone had to pay for the troops, forcing the British government to take additional measures that further provoked American resentment. These measures included the imposition of direct taxes and the passage of **Quartering Acts**

IN THE BLUE RIDGE.

This clearing and cabin in the Blue Ridge Mountains of the southern Appalachian chain typifies the hope and homes of many small farmers who resented the British Proclamation Line of 1763, which barred white settlement west of the eastern continental divide.

that required colonial assemblies to provide barracks and certain supplies for the soldiers.

The presence of troops in peacetime alarmed Americans. Sharing the traditional English distrust of standing armies, they wondered whether the soldiers were there to coerce rather than protect them. And the military presence may, in fact, have made imperial authorities less cautious in dealing with the colonies. Given their wariness, Americans would doubtless have objected to the troops and to the taxes necessary to support them even if the troops had done an exemplary job of protecting the frontiers. But conflicts with Indians cast doubt on their ability to do even that.

INDIAN AFFAIRS

If Britain confronted complex problems in North America, Native Americans would have said those problems were nothing compared to their own troubles in dealing with the British. Colonial settlers and their livestock were displacing Indians from their ancient lands. Free-flowing rum and rampant cheating among traders were making the fur and deer-

skin trades increasingly violent. Each of the colonies tried to regulate its Indian traders, but lack of coordination made most of these efforts ineffective.

The British victory over the French and the westward expansion of British territory undermined the Indians' traditional strategies and alignments. British officials no longer found Native American neutrality or military help as important as they once had. Increasingly superfluous as allies and unable to play the European powers off against each other, Native Americans lost much of their former ability to protect themselves by any means short of military resistance. The British took advantage of this increasing vulnerability: Traders exploited the Indians, and settlers encroached on their lands.

Two major Indian wars—one breaking out in the late 1750s, during the closing years of the French and Indian War, and the other erupting in its aftermath in the early 1760s—tested British policy toward Native Americans. The first conflict, the **Cherokee War**, took place in the southern Appalachian highlands. Though increasingly alarmed at the abuses and encroachments of their white neighbors, the Cherokees had long remained allies of the British. But in 1759,

The legend on this scrimshaw powder horn, "New Map of Carolina and Likewise a plan of Ye Cherokee Nation Conqurd by the arme Commandt by Lieutt Col Jas Grant," and the date, 1762, suggest that the soldier who engraved it was, like his commander, British and that he finished his elaborate depiction of the campaign shortly after the Cherokee War.

Cherokee warriors (who were returning home from a campaign with the British against the French and their Indian allies in western Pennsylvania) may have stolen horses belonging to Virginia colonists. The colonists attacked the Cherokees, killing some of them. The Cherokees retaliated with attacks on western settlements in all of the southern colonies. In 1760, they captured Fort Loudoun in eastern Tennessee, stuffing the commander's mouth full of dirt and telling him, "Dog, since you are so hungry for land, eat your fill." Three expeditions, manned by British as well as colonial troops, eventually forced the Cherokees to agree, in a 1761 treaty, to surrender land in the Carolinas and Virginia to the colonists.

The second major conflict, **Pontiac's Rebellion**, broke out in 1763 among Indians in the Great Lakes and Ohio Valley regions formerly claimed by France. Many Native American groups feared that the British planned to exterminate them and take their lands now that the French could no longer help them. They also resented the increased stinginess of British traders and officials, who were no longer forced to compete commercially with the French to secure Indian allegiance. These concerns helped to inspire a united effort to resist the British and revitalize Indian cultures. Neolin, also known as the Delaware Prophet, urged Native Americans to reject European goods and ways. Pontiac, an Ottawa chief, joined other chiefs in leading at least eight major groups of Native Americans in attacking British forces and American settlers from the Great Lakes to Virginia in 1763.

Pontiac's Rebellion raged until 1766. During intermittent negotiations, Pontiac insisted that British possession of the old French forts in western Pennsylvania and Ohio did not give Great Britain title to the area. The French, he maintained, had been there merely as tenants of the Indians, not owners of the land. But the British eventually forced the Indians to give up portions of their territory in return for compensation and guarantees that traditional hunting grounds in the Ohio Valley would remain theirs.

At one point during the war, a British commander used germ warfare against the Indians, sending them blankets that smallpox victims had used. Settlers in Paxton township (near modern Harrisburg, Pennsylvania) were equally unrestrained. Angered by the Pennsylvania Assembly's lack of aggressive action against the Indians, the settlers lashed out at convenient targets, massacring their peaceful neighbors, the Conestogas. Facing arrest and trial for this outrage, the so-called Paxton Boys marched toward Philadelphia, threatening the Pennsylvania Assembly. Benjamin Franklin convinced them to disperse. Despite the government's efforts, the Paxton Boys were never effectively prosecuted for their acts.

Pontiac's Rebellion and the Cherokee War were costly for both sides, claiming the lives of hundreds of Indians and white settlers. Hoping to prevent such outbreaks, British officials began experimenting with centralized control of Indian affairs during the 1760s. Following the recommendations of the

Albany Congress in 1754 (see Chapter 4), they had already created two districts, northern and southern, for the administration of Indian affairs, each with its own superintendent. The Proclamation of 1763, and the line it established restricting further white settlement, gave these officials increased responsibility for protecting the Indians against the encroachments of settlers. But land-hungry Americans objected to efforts to keep them off Indian lands, and white traders resented restrictions on their activities. Centralized control of the fur and deerskin trades also proved to be expensive for the British government. British authorities therefore permitted several adjustments in the Indian boundary line and in 1768 returned supervision of the Indian traders to the individual colonies. But such tacit recognition of local autonomy conflicted with imperial authorities' plans to restrict the powers of the colonial assemblies.

CURBING THE ASSEMBLIES

As early as the 1750s, in an episode known as the **Parson's Cause**, British authorities took advantage of opportunities to curb the American legislatures. Anglican ministers in Virginia drew tax-supported salaries computed in pounds of tobacco. As a result, when a drought in the mid-1750s caused a sharp rise in tobacco prices, they expected a windfall. The Virginia House of Burgesses, however, restricted their payment to two pennies a pound, below the market value of the tobacco that backed their salaries. Lobbying by the clergy convinced the king to disallow the Two Penny Act, and some Virginia clergymen sued for the unpaid portion of their salaries.

In the most famous of these cases, the Virginia government was defended by Patrick Henry, a previously obscure young lawyer who looked like "a Presbyterian clergyman, used to haranguing the people." Henry gained instant notoriety when he declared that a king who vetoed beneficial acts became a tyrant and thereby forfeited "all right to his subjects' obedience." Given Henry's eloquence, and its own sense of fair play, the jury found in favor of the suing minister but awarded him only one penny in damages. This pittance reflected the hostility many Virginians of all denominations felt toward the pretensions of the Anglican clergy.

Meanwhile, still in response to the Two Penny Act, the crown further dismayed Virginians by instructing the colony's governor not to sign any new law that modified existing laws unless it contained a suspending clause making it inoperative until the king approved it. This restriction severely hampered the assembly's ability to respond to emergencies such as the drought. As one Virginian observed, it "put us under the despotic Power of a French or Turkish Government; for what is the real Difference between a French Edict and an English Instruction if they are both equally absolute?" The legislators of the colony, Virginians maintained, had the "Right to enact ANY Law they shall think necessary for their INTERNAL Government."

British authorities also sought to restrict the power of colonial legislatures to issue legal tender currency, paper notes that could be used to settle debts. These notes frequently depreciated to only a fraction of their face value in British money. Not surprisingly, British merchants who had to accept them felt cheated and complained. Parliament had responded in 1751 by forbidding further issues of legal tender paper money in New England. In the **Currency Act** of 1764, Parliament extended this restriction to the rest of the colonies, prohibiting all of them from printing their own legal tender paper money. Because the new restrictions came when most colonies were in an economic recession, Americans considered this step an especially burdensome attempt to curtail the assemblies' powers. To deprive them of their paper money was, in the words of one American, "downright Robbery." Worse, however, was yet to come.

THE SUGAR AND STAMP ACTS

In 1764, the British Parliament, under Prime Minister George Grenville, passed the American Revenue Act, commonly known as the **Sugar Act**. The main purpose of this act, as stated in its preamble, was "for improving the revenue of this kingdom." To generate funds, the Sugar Act and its accompanying legislation combined new and revised duties on colonial imports with strict provisions for collecting these impositions. The act lowered the duty on molasses from the French West Indies from 6 pence a gallon to 3 pence a gallon. Smugglers had long evaded the earlier duty with bribes to customs officials. By lowering the duty and improving its collection, Grenville hoped to capture for the crown what customs officials had been siphoning off for themselves without excessively increasing the shippers' cost of business.

The Sugar Act legislation also lengthened the list of enumerated products—goods that could be sent only to England or within the empire—and required that ships carry elaborate new documents certifying the legality of their cargoes. The purpose of the new paperwork was to prevent illegal trade with other countries. A ship's captain, however, could have his entire cargo seized if any of the complicated documents were out of order.

To enforce these cumbersome regulations, the British government continued to use the Royal Navy to seize smugglers' ships, a practice authorized by the Revenue Act of 1762 during the French and Indian War. It also ordered colonial customs collectors to discharge their duties personally. Previously, the collectors had often lived in England, leaving the work of collection in the colonies to poorly paid deputies, who were susceptible to bribes. Finally, Parliament gave responsibility for trying violations of the laws to a new vice-admiralty court in Halifax, Nova Scotia. Vice-admiralty courts had jurisdiction over maritime affairs. Unlike other courts, they normally operated without a jury and were therefore more likely to enforce trade restrictions. For this reason, and because of the remote location of the Halifax court—getting to it would be a hardship—Americans immediately opposed this provision of the Sugar Act. In response, Parliament created three more-conveniently located vice-admiralty courts in Boston, Philadelphia, and Charleston, a decision that was not exactly what the colonists had had in mind.

In the spring of 1765, Parliament enacted another tax on Americans, the **Stamp Act**. This legislation required all valid legal documents, as well as newspapers, playing cards, and various other papers, to bear a government-issued stamp, for which there was a charge. The Sugar Act, though intended to raise revenue, appeared to fall within Britain's accepted authority to regulate commerce; the Stamp Act, by contrast, was the first internal tax (as opposed to an external trade duty) that Parliament had imposed on the colonies. Grenville, a lawyer, realized that it raised a constitutional issue: Did Parliament have the right to impose direct taxes on Americans when Americans had no elected representatives in Parliament? Following the principle of virtual representation—that members of Parliament served the interests of the nation as a whole, not just the locality from which they came—Grenville maintained that it did. Americans, he would find, vigorously disagreed, and so did some members of Parliament. One, Colonel Isaac Barré, who had served in the colonies, opposed the Stamp Act and referred to Americans as "Sons of Liberty"—a label Americans would soon adopt for themselves.

AMERICAN REACTIONS

The measures Britain took to solve its financial and administrative problems first puzzled, then shocked, and eventually outraged Americans. The colonists

had emerged from the French and Indian War believing that they had done their fair share and more toward making Great Britain ruler of the greatest empire the world had yet seen. They expected to be rewarded for their efforts and treated with the respect that they assumed they deserved. They were certain that as British Americans they shared in the glory and enjoyed all the rights of Englishmen in England. The new restrictions and taxes accordingly hit them like a slap in the face, made worse by a postwar economic recession in many of the colonies.

CONSTITUTIONAL ISSUES

To Americans, it was self-evident that the British measures were unfair. It was difficult to contend, however, that the British authorities had no right

The last issue of the Pennsylvania Journal *on the day before the Stamp Act was to go into effect. Note the caricature of a stamp in the lower right corner. William Bradford, who printed this paper, was one of the organizers of the Sons of Liberty in Philadelphia.*

to impose them. The king and Parliament were considered the sovereign, or highest, authority in the empire. Then as now, the **British Constitution** was not a single written document. It consisted, rather, of the accumulated body of English law and custom, including acts of Parliament. How, then, could the colonists claim that an act of Parliament was unconstitutional?

Constitutional conflict surfaced early in Massachusetts over the issue of **writs of assistance**. These general search warrants, which gave customs officials in America the power to inspect virtually any building suspected of holding smuggled goods, had to be formally renewed at the accession of a new monarch. When George III became king in 1760, Massachusetts merchants—perhaps out of a fondness for smuggling as well as for liberty—sought to block the reissuance of the writs. Their attorney, James Otis, Jr., arguing before the Massachusetts superior court, called the writs "instruments of slavery." Parliament, he maintained, lacked the authority to empower colonial courts to issue them. Otis lost, but "then and there," a future president of the United States, John Adams, would later write, "the child independence was born."

TAXATION AND THE POLITICAL CULTURE

The constitutional issue that most strained the bond between the colonies and the empire was taxation. British measures on other issues annoyed and disturbed Americans, and their cumulative effect helped to alienate the colonists from England. But it was outrage over taxation—the most fundamental issue—that would be the midwife of American independence. Because Parliament had customarily refrained from taxing them, Americans assumed that it could not, and because their own assemblies had taxed them, they believed that those legislatures were in fact their parliaments.

Most Americans, including many who would later side with the British, believed that to deprive them of the right to be taxed only by their own elected representatives was to deny them one of the most basic rights of Englishmen. If taxes were imposed "without our having a legal Representation where they are laid," one American asked, "are we not reduced from the Character of free Subjects to the miserable State of tributary Slaves?"

British subjects everywhere believed that Parliament's exclusive authority to impose taxes on its constituents made Britain the freest country in the world. British officials, who believed in parliamentary sovereignty, counted the colonists among those constituents. Americans, who understood that their

interests might conflict with those of England, thought otherwise. Given the selfishness of human nature, they believed that to have governing officials who could do unto them without doing the same to themselves was to risk disaster.

American views on taxation and the role of government reflected the influence of country ideology. As mentioned in Chapter 4, this opposition political philosophy emerged in England in the late seventeenth and early eighteenth centuries partly in response to the development of Britain's powerful standing army and navy. It viewed these forces, and the financial measures needed to support them, as threats to personal liberty. Country ideology proceeded from two basic assumptions: that human beings are selfish and that they need governments to protect them from one another. But country ideology also held that government power, no matter how necessary or to whom entrusted, is inherently aggressive and expansive. According to the English political philosopher John Locke, rulers have the authority to enforce law "only for the public good." When government exceeds this proper function, the people have the right to change it. Only in the last resort does this right justify revolution; the preferable alternative is a system with less-disruptive ways of protecting the freedom of the people.

Country ideology stressed that in the English system of government, it was the duty of Parliament, in particular the House of Commons (which represented the people as a whole), to check the executive power of the crown. The House of Commons's control of taxation enabled it to curb tyrannical rulers. When the crown did its job properly, the Commons appropriated the necessary funds; when rulers infringed on the liberty of the people, the Commons restrained them by withholding taxes.

Such important responsibilities required the people's representatives to be men of sufficient property and judgment to make independent decisions. A representative should be "virtuous" (meaning public-spirited), and he should avoid political partisanship, because divisions within the House of Commons could undermine its ability to resist or curb the executive. A representative of the appropriate social status who exhibited the proper behavior deserved the deference of his constituents. They should assume, in other words, that he was more qualified to understand and manage public affairs than they were, and they should accordingly follow his lead. But if he did not measure up, the people should be able to vote him out.

Country ideology appealed to Americans for a number of reasons. In part, colonists were drawn to it as they were to other English ideas and trends. The works of Alexander Pope, the most widely read English poet of the eighteenth century and a proponent of a version of country ideology, appeared in many colonial libraries. So also did the works of two readable and prolific country ideology publicists, John Trenchard and Thomas Gordon, who collaborated in writing *Cato's Letters* (1720–1724) and the *Independent Whig* (1721). More important, country ideology's suspicion of those in power suited American politics on the local level, where rivalries and factionalism fostered distrust between those with and without power. And it emboldened the many Americans who feared they had no voice in the decisions of the government in London on matters of vital importance to them. Finally, with its insistence on the important political role of the propertied elite, country ideology appealed to America's local gentry. It suggested that it was their duty, as elected political officials, to safeguard the freedom of their constituents.

These ideas have had an enduring influence on American politics, surfacing even today in the suspicion of Washington and "big government." During the eighteenth century, they predisposed Americans to value local control and to expect the worst from remote governments. In so doing, they helped inspire the American Revolution. Many Americans were ready to attribute any new imperial regulations or taxes to a conspiracy of corrupt British officials to tyrannize them.

PROTESTING THE TAXES

Given this ideological background, the initial American response to the Sugar Act was surprisingly mild. This was because the new taxes it imposed took the form of duties on trade and thus appeared consistent with the earlier Navigation Acts. The actual reaction varied from colony to colony in ways that reflected regional self-interest. The speaker of the legislature in one southern colony commented that it was "much divided" over the effects of the act and would probably not petition against it. In New England, by contrast, the Sugar Act threatened to cut into the profits of the lucrative smuggling trade with the French West Indies. As a result, people there and in other northern colonies were quicker to recognize the act's implications. The legislative body that imposed it—Parliament—and whose constituents in England stood to gain from it was not accountable to the people on whom it was imposed, the colonists. As one alarmed colonist noted, if his fellow Americans

submitted to any tax imposed by Parliament, they were dumb and docile donkeys; "more Sacks, more Sacks," or burdens, were coming.

The size of the burden was less important than the principle involved. To Americans steeped in country ideology, direct taxation by London threatened to undercut the elected representatives' power of the purse and thereby remove the traditional first line of defense against a tyrannical executive. Thus all the assemblies eventually passed resolutions flatly maintaining that any parliamentary tax on America, including the Sugar Act, was unconstitutional. Colonists in New York, their assembly stated, claimed to be exempt from taxation by anyone but their own representatives not "as a Privilege" but "as their Right." By the end of 1764, New York merchants had joined the artisans and merchants of Boston in a **nonimportation movement**, an organized boycott of British manufactured goods. The goal was to cut into the profits of British employers, inducing them and the workers laid off as a result to bring pressure on the government to back down.

Unlike the Sugar Act, the Stamp Act had an equal impact throughout the colonies, and the response to it was swift and vociferous. Newspapers and pamphlets were filled with denunciations of the supposedly unconstitutional measure, and in taverns everywhere outraged patrons roundly condemned it. "The minds of the freeholders," wrote one observer, "were inflamed . . . by many a hearty damn of the Stamp Act over bottles, bowls and glasses." Parliament, Americans were convinced, did not represent them. Its members did not share their economic interests and would not pay the taxes that they imposed on Americans. Parliament therefore could not legitimately tax Americans.

The colonial legislatures were also quick to condemn the new measure. Virginia's lower house was the first to act, approving Patrick Henry's strong resolutions against the Stamp Act. These were then reprinted in newspapers throughout the colonies, and other legislatures passed similar formal objections.

Popular protest also expressed widespread outrage at the Stamp Act. Crowds had long gathered in the colonies for public purposes, such as closing houses of prostitution or rolling back exorbitant price increases. With a postwar economic slump in some of the colonies, many people now turned to direct action. The **Sons of Liberty**, a collection of loosely organized protest groups, put pressure on stamp distributors and British authorities. In August 1765, a Boston crowd led by Ebenezer MacIntosh, a volunteer fireman with engine company number nine and a shoemaker, demolished property belonging to a revenue agent, and another mob sacked Lieutenant Governor Thomas Hutchinson's house. About a month later, other rioters roamed the streets of New York, smashing windows and telling the governor, "[Y]ou'll die a Martyr to your own villany . . . and every man, that assists you, shall be, surely, put to Death." The Sons of Liberty organized similar demonstrations in other cities but kept most of them more peaceful with tighter discipline.

Members of the Sons of Liberty included people from all ranks of society. The leaders, however, came mostly from the middle and upper classes. Often pushed by more radical common people, some of the elite doubtless joined in the hope of protecting their own positions and interests. Indeed, in Charleston, slaves paraded through the streets crying, "Liberty!" much to the dismay of their masters and the rest of the city's white population.

Movement leaders were also concerned that violence could discredit the American cause. Even the fiery Samuel Adams, one of the leading organizers of the protest in Boston, would later claim, "I am no friend to Riots." Still, he added, "when the People are oppressed," they will be "discontented, and they are not to be blamed."

Partly as a result of the growing unrest, leaders throughout the colonies determined to meet and agree on a unified response to Britain. As Christopher Gadsden of South Carolina, an ardent advocate of American rights and opponent of taxation, observed at the time, "There ought to be no New England men, no New Yorker, etc. known on the Continent, but all of us Americans." Nine colonies eventually sent delegates, including Gadsden, to the **Stamp Act Congress**, which met in New York City in October 1765. A humorist in the Carolina legislature, who had opposed sending anyone, observed that the gathering would produce a most unpalatable combination: New England would throw in fish and onions; the middle provinces, flaxseed and flour; Virginia and Maryland, tobacco; North Carolina, pitch, turpentine, and tar; South Carolina, indigo and rice—and Georgia would sprinkle the whole with sawdust. "Such an absurd jumble will you make if you attempt to form [a] union among such discordant materials as the thirteen British provinces," he concluded. A quick-witted member of the assembly shot back that he would not choose his colleague for a cook, but that the congress would prepare a dish fit for any king.

It did indeed. The congress adopted the **Declaration of Rights and Grievances**, which denied Parliament's right to tax the colonies, and petitioned both king and Parliament to repeal the Stamp and Sugar acts. Parliament, unwilling to acknowledge this challenge to its authority, refused to receive the colonial petitions.

As protests spread, the stamp distributors got the message and resigned "for the welfare of the people." In some areas, Americans went about their business as usual without using stamped paper. In other places, they avoided activities that required taxed items. They also stepped up the boycott of British goods that had begun in response to the Sugar Act. British merchants, hurt by this economic pressure, petitioned Parliament for repeal of the Stamp Act, and a new ministry obliged them by rescinding it in March 1766. Modifications in the provisions of the Sugar Act came later in the year.

Samuel Adams, the leader of the Boston radicals, as he appeared to John Singleton Copley in the early 1770s. In this famous picture, thought to have been commissioned by another revolutionary leader, John Hancock, Adams points to legal documents guaranteeing American rights.

A satirical British engraving from 1766 showing English politicians burying the Stamp Act, "born 1765 died 1766." The warehouses in the background symbolize the revival of trade with America.

THE AFTERMATH OF THE STAMP ACT CRISIS

During the Stamp Act crisis, Benjamin Franklin appeared before Parliament to present American objections to the Stamp and Sugar acts. Some members apparently concluded from his remarks that the colonists would accept port duties but would oppose direct taxes. They were wrong. At this point, Americans were in no mood to accept any tax imposed by Parliament.

Americans in turn misunderstood the **Declaratory Act** that accompanied the repeal of the Stamp Act. Intended to make Parliament's retreat more acceptable to its members, this act stated that Parliament had the right to "legislate for the colonies in all cases whatsoever." Did *legislate* mean *tax*? Not necessarily, for taxes were traditionally deemed to be a voluntary gift to the king from the people acting through their own representatives. (This is why money bills, as distinct from other acts, had to originate in the House of Commons.) Americans therefore tended to consider the Declaratory Act a mere face-saving gesture. Unfortunately, it was more than that. As one colonist later observed, it created a "platform for the Invincible Reasoning from the

Mouths of four and twenty pounders [cannons]."

A STRAINED RELATIONSHIP

Most members of Parliament continued to believe that they represented everyone in the empire and that they could therefore tax people in the colonies as well as in England. Americans believed just as strongly that "in taxing ourselves and making Laws for our own internal government . . . we can by no means allow our Provincial legislatures to be subordinate to any legislative power on earth."

Relations were never quite the same between England and America after the Stamp Act crisis. Each side became ever more suspicious of the other. Americans were convinced that they had forced British authorities to back down and that, if need be, they could do it again. Or so they told themselves every March 18, the anniversary of the repeal of the Stamp Act. This date became an occasion for celebration, giving Americans a national holiday before they had a nation.

An exchange between British merchants and their American correspondents in the wake of the Stamp Act's repeal illustrates how far apart Englishmen and Americans had become. The British merchants lectured the Americans, enjoining them "to express filial duty and gratitude to your parent country." To which one Virginia planter tartly replied, "We rarely see anything from your side of the water free from the authoritative style of a master to a schoolboy." This, he observed, was more than "a little ridiculous."

Events likewise testified to continuing tensions between the two sides. When British authorities required Massachusetts to compensate those who had suffered damage in the Stamp Act rioting, the legislature complied but pardoned the rioters. In 1767, an irritated Parliament then passed an act suspending the New York legislature because it had not complied with the Quartering Act of 1765. This law required colonial assemblies to provide facilities and certain supplies for royal troops. The New York legislature finally obeyed before the suspending act went into effect, and it remained in business. But such incidents boded ill for the hopes of some colonists that a British government that had repealed the Stamp Act would prove cooperative in other ways.

REGULATOR MOVEMENTS

In 1766, a committee of the South Carolina legislature appointed to consider "the State of the Province" recommended that it establish courts in the rapidly growing backcountry and petition Parliament for repeal of the Currency Act. These suggestions were prompted by mounting unrest in the southern backcountry. Vigilante groups calling themselves **Regulators** had emerged in North Carolina in response to official corruption and in South Carolina in response to lawlessness. High taxes and high court costs in North Carolina oppressed the colony's western farmers. Because the Currency Act reduced the amount of money in circulation, it compounded their problems, leaving them "crouched beneath their sufferings" and unable to pay their debts and taxes. In South Carolina, the devastation and disruptions of the Cherokee War left a legacy of violence. Outlaws roamed the backcountry, stealing livestock and raiding isolated houses. In both colonies, because representation in the assemblies failed to reflect the rapidly growing backcountry populations, legislatures were slow to respond to their needs. As a result, the Regulators did by extralegal action what they could not do through legal channels. In North Carolina, they closed courts and intimidated tax officials. In South Carolina, they pursued outlaws and whipped people suspected of harboring them.

These activities brought the Regulators into conflict with the local elites of both North and South Carolina. British officials, however, only made matters worse. Instead of encouraging the assemblies to increase western representation, the crown did exactly the opposite. As part of its effort to limit the power of colonial legislatures, it forbade them from increasing their size. Americans termed this instruction "perhaps [as] peculiar as any that have been given on the continent." As for the shortage of currency, Lord Hillsborough, the secretary of state for the colonies, callously informed North Carolinians that "no Consideration of a possible local inconvenience" would prompt Britain to modify the "sound Principles" of the Currency Act. And instead of approving legislation in South Carolina that would have established courts in the backcountry, British officials disallowed it because it specified that judges would hold their positions contingent on good behavior rather than at the pleasure of the crown.

Thanks to such help from London as well as to their own mistakes, a crisis confronted local authorities by 1767. In South Carolina, the assembly belatedly reapportioned itself, giving the backcountry some representation, and permitted the crown to dictate the terms of judicial appointments. These and other concessions to western residents narrowly averted bloodshed. But in North Carolina, fighting broke out in 1771. Governor William Tryon led the local militia against the Regulators who had gathered near Alamance Creek. There, he ordered the Regulators to disperse or his men would fire. "Fire and be damned," someone replied, and gunfire erupted, killing 29 men and wounding more than 150 on both sides. During the next several weeks, seven Regulators were hanged and six thousand pardoned.

The confrontation in North Carolina was the most serious of its kind, but similar social tensions were apparent in other colonies. To deal with them, colonial leaders had to understand local conditions and be able to act on their knowledge. But British attempts to reform colonial governments threatened to hamstring them.

THE TOWNSHEND CRISIS

British authorities had not given up the idea of taxing the colonies with the repeal of the Stamp Act in 1766. Little over a year later, Parliament passed a new collection of taxes, the Townshend duties. Another crisis ensued, lasting until an American boycott of British goods forced repeal of most of the new duties. The relatively quiet period that followed ended when Britain made a serious attempt to enforce compliance with the one Townshend duty still on the books, the duty on tea.

TOWNSHEND'S PLAN

Charles Townshend became the leading figure in Britain's government in 1767. A former member of the Board of Trade, he thought he understood the colonies, and he knew that many members of Parliament still wanted to tax Americans. The legislation that bears his name, the **Townshend Duty Act,**

Mr. and Mrs. Thomas Mifflin of Philadelphia. A prominent merchant and radical opponent of British policy toward the colonies, Mifflin and his wife were visiting Boston in 1773, when John Singleton Copley painted them. Working at a small loom, Sarah Morris Mifflin weaves a decorative fringe. She no doubt did the same during the nonimportation movement against the Townshend duties, thereby helping to make importation of such goods from England unnecessary.

was intended to help pay the cost of government in America. It imposed new duties, or external taxes, which Townshend believed the colonists were willing to accept, but no direct, or internal, taxes like the Stamp Tax. The duties covered a number of items the colonists regularly imported—tea, paper, paint, lead, and glass. To make sure that the duties were collected, British authorities added a new board of customs commissioners for America and located its headquarters in Boston, the presumed home of many smugglers.

Coming on top of the threatened suspension of the New York legislature, the Townshend Duty Act seemed to foreshadow greater British interference in colonial affairs. And the new customs officials were, in fact, far more diligent than their predecessors. One of them, taking advantage of

technicalities in the law, entrapped Henry Laurens, a prominent merchant in South Carolina. Other officials harassed the wealthy Boston merchant John Hancock, perhaps because he was openly contemptuous of them. Seizing his appropriately named vessel *Liberty,* they accused him of smuggling. Hancock may indeed have violated the acts of trade at times, but in this case the accusations were apparently false. The incident sparked a riot in Boston during which a crowd on the waterfront roughed up members of the customs service. British authorities responded in 1768 by sending troops to Boston. The soldiers would remain there amid mounting hostility for the next year and a half.

AMERICAN BOYCOTT

The Townshend duties, like the stamp tax, provoked resistance throughout the colonies. Rejecting the argument that duties were somehow different from taxes, John Dickinson, a wealthy lawyer who wrote under the pen name A Farmer in Pennsylvania, asserted that a tax was a tax, whatever its form. The purpose of the taxes—to help pay the costs of government in the colonies, including the salaries of governors and judges—also seemed dangerous. Americans believed it was the role of their own assemblies to raise revenues for these costs. By bypassing the assemblies, the Townshend Act threatened to undermine their authority.

There was no equivalent to the Stamp Act Congress in response to the Townshend Act, because British officials (acting through the colonial governors) barred the assemblies from sending delegates to such a meeting. Even so, Americans gradually organized an effective nonimportation movement. When, for example, the governor of Virginia dissolved the House of Burgesses for resolutions opposing British measures, the members met on their own in the Raleigh Tavern at Williamsburg and adopted a nonimportation agreement. Once again, vigilant laborers and artisans threatened violators of the general boycott with physical violence, but few disturbances occurred. Many Americans signed subscription lists binding themselves, with the other signers, to buy only goods made in the colonies and nothing made in Great Britain. Handbills, like one urging "the Sons and Daughters of LIBERTY" to shun a particular Boston merchant, brought pressure to bear on uncooperative importers. To avoid imported English textiles, American women spun more thread and wove more cloth at home. Wearing homespun became a moral virtue, a sign of self-reliance, personal

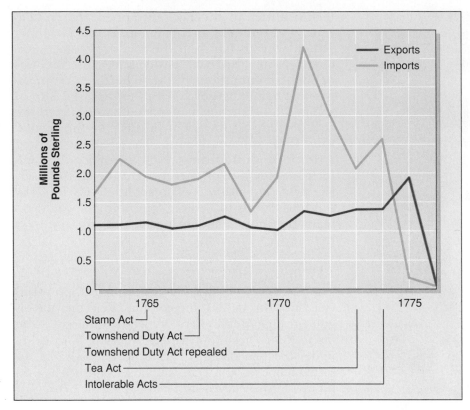

FIGURE 5-1 Value of American Exports to and Imports from England, 1763–1776
This figure depicts the value of American exports to and imports from England. The decrease of imports in 1765–1766 and the even sharper drop in 1769 illustrate the effect of American boycotts in response to the Stamp Act and Townshend duties.

Data Source: U.S. Bureau of the Census, *Historical Statistics of the United States, Colonial Times to 1970, Bicentennial Edition, Part 1* (1975).

independence, and the rejection of "corrupting" English luxuries (see "American Views: Social Status and the Enforcement of the Nonimportation Movement" page 158).

The nonimportation movement forged a sense of common purpose among all who participated in it—men and women, southern planters and northern artisans alike—giving them the sense of belonging to a larger community of fellow Americans. Although it was at this point more an imagined community than a political community, it was real enough and large enough to reduce imports from Britain by 40 percent after only one year.

Because Britain had increased its exports to Europe since the Stamp Act crisis, it took longer than before for the nonimportation movement to produce a reaction in London (see Figure 5–1). Still, the troubles in America contributed to the king's decision to appoint a new prime minister, Lord North. Thinking—and even looking—remarkably alike, George III and North complemented each other. At

the king's insistence, North would remain prime minister until 1782. In 1770, he was prepared to concede that the Townshend duties had been counterproductive because they interfered with British trade. But when Parliament repealed most of them, it left the duty on tea. This symbolic equivalent of the Declaratory Act served to assert Parliament's continuing right to tax the colonies.

THE BOSTON MASSACRE

Ironically, on the same day that North proposed that Parliament rescind most of the Townshend duties—March 5, 1770—British troops fired on American civilians in Boston. This incident, which came to be known to Americans everywhere as the **Boston Massacre**, resulted from months of increasing friction between townspeople and the British troops stationed in the city. The townspeople complained that the soldiers insulted them, leered at women, and competed for scarce jobs. Samuel Adams recounted these real and imagined misdeeds in a column called "A Journal of the Times" that he circulated to other American cities. The hostility was so great, complained a British officer, that "twenty" soldiers could be "knocked down in the Streets" and nothing be heard of it, but if a soldier merely kicked a resident, "the Town is immediately in an Alarm."

The Boston Massacre occurred when angry and frightened British soldiers fired on a crowd that was pelting them with sticks and stones. Five men died, including Crispus Attucks—subsequently described as "that half Indian, half negro and altogether rowdy"— who has since become the most celebrated casualty of the incident. To preserve order, the troops withdrew from the city. Later two prominent local lawyers successfully defended the soldiers accused of murder.

THE "QUIET PERIOD"

In the so-called Quiet Period that followed, no general grievance united all Americans. But in almost

The Boston Massacre, March 5, 1770, in an engraving by Paul Revere. Copied from an earlier print, Revere's widely circulated version shows—somewhat inaccurately—well-organized soldiers firing on helpless civilians; the names of the dead, including Crispus Attucks, appear below.

every colony, issues continued to simmer. In Massachusetts and South Carolina, for example, the royal governors temporarily moved the meeting places of the legislatures to small towns miles away from the capital, "for the sole Purpose," as the Declaration of Independence would later charge, "of fatiguing them into compliance" with British measures.

Local circumstances produced a more spectacular confrontation in Rhode Island. The crew of a British revenue schooner, the *Gaspee*, had been patrolling Narragansett Bay, seizing smugglers and, it was said, stealing livestock and cutting down farmers' fruit trees for firewood. When the *Gaspee* ran aground while chasing some American ships, Rhode Islanders got even. Led by John Brown, a local merchant, they boarded the vessel, shot its captain in the buttocks, and putting him and his crew ashore, burned the ship. The British government appointed a commission of inquiry with instructions to arrest the culprits and send them to England for trial. Despite its offer of a reward for information about the incident, the commission learned nothing. The British attempt to stamp out

smuggling in the colonies was so heavy-handed that it offended the innocent more than it frightened the guilty.

Such incidents, and in particular the British threat to send Americans to England for trial, led American leaders to resolve to keep one another informed about British actions. Twelve colonies established **committees of correspondence** for this purpose. Leaders in Boston established similar committees in Massachusetts. There would soon be plenty for these organizations to do, for Boston was about to become the scene of a showdown between imperial authority and colonial resistance.

THE BOSTON TEA PARTY

During the Quiet Period, Americans drank smuggled (and therefore untaxed) Dutch tea. Partly as a result, the British East India Company, which had the exclusive right to distribute tea in the British Empire, nearly went bankrupt. Lord North tried to rescue it with the **Tea Act of 1773.** The act permitted the company to ship tea from its warehouses in Britain without paying the duty normally collected there. Because its tea would therefore be cheaper, British authorities assumed that Americans would buy it and simultaneously pay the old Townshend duty. The company selected a few merchants to act as its exclusive agents in the colonies. These merchants stood to reap substantial profits from their position.

This plan angered Americans. Some may have been jealous at being excluded from the tea trade. Most, however, were outraged at the attempt to trick them into paying the tax on tea. Thousands decided not to touch the stuff. Newspapers discussed its dangers to the body as well as to the body politic and offered recipes for substitutes. "To their great honor," according to the newspapers, many women rejected the tea and put pressure on others to do likewise, while schoolboys collected and burned tea leaves.

Thomas Hutchinson, who had been lieutenant governor of Massachusetts during the Stamp Act riots, was now the colony's royal governor. Two of his sons were among those chosen to be the East India Company's agents. In most other cities, threats from the Sons of Liberty convinced the captains of the tea ships to return to England without landing their cargo. Hutchinson, however, was determined to have the tea unloaded in Boston, and he barred the tea ships there from leaving. As a result, violence once again erupted in the city.

When the Sons of Liberty realized that they could not force the ships to leave, they decided on dramatic

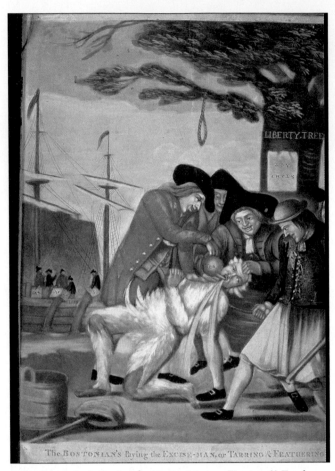

"The Bostonian's Paying the Excise-Man or Tarring & Feathering." This print, published in London in 1774, satirizes American resistance to British tax measures. Four men representing a broad range of social classes pour tea down the throat of a tax collector while the Boston Tea Party takes place in the background.

action. On December 16, 1773, Samuel Adams reportedly told a large gathering at Old South Meeting House that it "could do nothing more to preserve the liberties of America." This remark was apparently a prearranged signal for what came to be known as the **Boston Tea Party**. War whoops immediately answered him from the street outside, and a well-organized band of men disguised as Indians raced aboard the *Dartmouth* and two other tea ships, broke open 342 chests of tea, and heaved the contents into the harbor. In a similar action in 1774, residents of Annapolis, Maryland, forced some merchants to burn their own ship when it arrived with dutied tea.

THE INTOLERABLE ACTS

The destruction of property in the Boston Tea Party shocked many Americans. Surprised and angry, British officials reacted even more strongly. Parlia-

ment passed a series of repressive measures known as the **Coercive Acts**. The first of these, effective June 1, 1774, was the Boston Port Act, which closed the port of Boston to all incoming and outgoing traffic until the East India Company and the crown received payment for the destroyed tea and lost duties. The Administration of Justice Act, which followed, declared that an official who, while performing his duties, killed a colonist could be tried in England (where he would almost certainly receive sympathetic treatment) rather than in Massachusetts. The third measure, the Massachusetts Government Act, drastically modified that colony's charter of 1691. Under the old document, the legislature had elected members to the governor's council; henceforth, the crown would appoint them. And appointed, rather than elected, sheriffs would now name juries. In addition, the Massachusetts Government Act limited the number of town meetings that could be held without the governor's prior approval. In another measure, the British government made its commander in chief in America, General Thomas Gage, the governor of Massachusetts and, in the Quartering Act of 1774, declared that the troops under his command could be lodged in virtually any uninhabited building.

On the same day that Parliament enacted these measures, it also passed the **Quebec Act**. This statute enlarged the boundaries of Quebec south to the Ohio River and stipulated that it be governed by an appointed governor and council but no elected assembly (see Map 5–2). The act also provided for the trial of civil cases without a jury and gave the Catholic Church the same privileges that it had enjoyed under the French. The colonists linked the Quebec Act with the Coercive Acts and labeled them the **Intolerable Acts**.

THE ROAD TO REVOLUTION

Americans throughout the colonies considered the Intolerable Acts so threatening that they organized another gathering, the **First Continental Congress**, to respond to them. Congress renewed the nonimportation movement and took measures to enforce it strictly. These measures widened the gap between those who supported British authorities and those who opposed them.

AMERICAN RESPONSE TO THE INTOLERABLE ACTS

Americans found the territorial, administrative, and religious provisions of the Quebec Act deeply disturbing. As one royal governor observed, "The securing of lands for the rising Generation is a matter of great importance to a poor and provident Man with a large family." The Quebec Act, however, gave Canada jurisdiction over lands in the area north of the Ohio River claimed by Connecticut, Pennsylvania, and Virginia. This deprived settlers of their hoped-for homesteads and land speculators of their hoped-for profits, angering both. The administrative provisions of the act—appointed government, no assemblies, no jury for civil cases—also suggested to Americans what Britain might have in store for them.

Americans had similar fears about the religious provisions of the Quebec Act. During the 1760s, some Anglican clergymen had sought to have a bishop appointed for America. But most Americans, including Anglicans, opposed this proposal. They were convinced that the creation of such an office would strengthen the Anglican Church at the expense of other denominations, weaken local control of religious affairs, and require the payment of additional taxes. Many Americans believed that British authorities had scrapped the idea. The Quebec Act's concessions to Canadian Catholics, however, seemed to resurrect it in more ominous form. As one Virginian had observed, the hierarchical organization of the Anglican Church was "a Relick of the Papal Incroachments" on English law. The Quebec Act accordingly "gave a General Alarm to all Protestants," whose ministers throughout the continent warned their congregations that they might be "bound by Popish chains."

American reaction to the religious provisions of the Quebec Act may have been exaggerated, but some features of the Coercive Acts were cause for real concern. The Boston Port Act arbitrarily punished innocent and guilty Bostonians alike. The Administration of Justice Act—which some with vivid imaginations dubbed the Murder Act—seemed to declare an open season on colonists, allowing crown officials to kill them without fear of punishment. The Massachusetts Government Act raised the more realistic fear that no colonial charter was safe. A Parliament that had stripped the Massachusetts legislature of an important power might equally decide to abolish the lower houses of all the colonies.

Nightmarish scenarios filled the colonial newspapers. One clergyman observed that the terms of the Coercive Acts were such that if someone were to "make water" on the door of the royal customs house, an entire colonial city "might be laid in Ashes." He undoubtedly knew that he exaggerated, but his words embodied real fear and anger, and many other Americans shared his feelings. Trying to

MAP EXPLORATION To explore an interactive version of this map, go to http://www.prenhall.com/goldfield/map5.2

MAP 5-2   The Quebec Act of 1774
The Quebec Act enlarged the boundaries of the Canadian province southward to the Ohio River and westward to the Mississippi, thereby depriving several colonies of claims to the area granted to them by their original charters.

make an example of Boston, British authorities had taken steps that united Americans as nothing had ever done before (see the Overview table, "New Restraints and Burdens on Americans, 1759–1774").

THE FIRST CONTINENTAL CONGRESS

Massachusetts wanted to respond to the Intolerable Acts with an immediate renewal of the nonimportation movement. Leaders in other colonies wanted to organize a more coordinated response and called for another meeting like the Stamp Act Congress. The colonies accordingly agreed to send delegates to a

Overview

New Restraints and Burdens on Americans, 1759–1774

	Limits on Legislative Action	Curbs on Territorial Expansion	Burdens on Colonial Trade	Imposition of New Taxes
1759	Royal instructions restrict the ability of the Virginia assembly to pass timely legislation.			
1762			Writs of assistance issued. Revenue Act authorizes Navy to help enforce customs regulation.	
1763		Proclamation Line keeps white settlement east of the Appalachians.	Peacetime use of the navy and new customs officials to enforce Navigation Acts.	
1764	Currency Act limits the colonial legislatures' ability to issue paper money.		Vice-admiralty courts strengthened for Sugar Act.	Sugar Act imposes taxes for revenue (modified 1766).
1765				Quartering Act requires assemblies to provide facilities for royal troops. Stamp Act imposes internal taxes on various items (repealed 1766).
	Declaratory Act proclaims Parliament's right to legislate for colonies in all cases whatsoever.			
1767	Royal instructions limit the size of colonial assemblies.		Vice-admiralty courts strengthened for Townshend duties. American Customs Service established in Boston.	Townshend duties imposed on some imported goods in order to pay colonial officials. (All but tax on tea repealed, 1770.)
1773				Tea Act reduces duty and prompts Boston Tea Party.
1774 (Intolerable Acts)	Massachusetts Government Act limits town meetings, changes legislature, and violates Massachusetts charter.	Quebec Act enlarges Quebec at expense of colonies with claims in the Ohio River Valley.	Boston Port Act closes harbor until East India Company's tea is paid for.	Quartering Act of 1774 declares that troops could be lodged in virtually any uninhabited building in Boston.

meeting in Philadelphia that came to be called the First Continental Congress. Because royal governors attempted to prevent the meeting by barring the legislatures from naming delegates, the colonies called extralegal public meetings for the purpose. In the end, all the colonies except Georgia were represented.

The First Continental Congress met at Carpenter's Hall in Philadelphia from September 5 to October 26, 1774, with fifty-five delegates present at one time or another. All were leading figures in their home colonies, but only a few knew members from elsewhere. Each colony had one vote, irrespective of the size of its delegation. Some of the more conservative participants favored a compromise with Britain. The speaker of the Pennsylvania Assembly, Joseph Galloway, introduced a measure reminiscent of the Albany Plan of Union. It called for creation of an American "grand council" that would have veto power over parliamentary legislation dealing with America. His plan failed in the Congress by one vote. Instead, those who favored stronger measures—such as Samuel Adams and his cousin John, Patrick Henry, and Christopher Gadsden—prevailed. They persuaded most of their colleagues to endorse the **Suffolk Resolves**, which had been passed at a meeting held in Suffolk County (the site of Boston). These strongly worded resolves denounced the Coercive Acts as unconstitutional, advised the people to arm, and called for general economic sanctions against Britain. Learning of them, one British official told an American, "If these Resolves of your people are to be depended on, they have declared War against us."

THE CONTINENTAL ASSOCIATION

The Congress created the **Continental Association** to organize and enforce sanctions against the British. As a first step, the Association pledged Americans to cut off imports from Britain after December 1, 1774. If the dispute with Britain was not resolved by September 1775, the Association called for barring most exports to Britain and the West Indies. Voters in every district throughout the colonies were to choose committeemen to enforce the terms of the Association. All who violated them were to be considered "enemies of American liberty." Their names were to be published, and associators (people agreeing to the Association) would "break off all dealings" with them.

Congress also issued a declaration of rights and grievances summarizing its position. This declaration condemned most of the steps taken by British authorities since 1763, but "cheerfully" consented to trade regulations for the good of the whole empire. In addition, the Congress sent addresses to the people of America, to the inhabitants of Great Britain, and to the king. The address to the king asked him to use his "royal authority and interposition" to protect his loyal subjects in America. The words were significant, for protection and allegiance were considered the reciprocal duties of a sovereign and his people. After agreeing to convene again on May 10, 1775, if its grievances had not been redressed by then, the First Continental Congress adjourned.

The proceedings of the First Continental Congress revealed division as well as agreement among its delegates. All the delegates believed that the Coercive Acts were unconstitutional, but they differed on methods to resist them. Only a minority was prepared to take up arms against Britain. Most representatives tried to protect the interests of their own colonies. Those from Virginia and Maryland, for example, insisted that the embargo on exports not begin until planters had finished shipping the current tobacco crop. Even more alarming, some South Carolina delegates, in an early example of the sectional stubbornness that would culminate nearly a century later in the United States Civil War, threatened to walk out of the meeting unless the nonexportation agreement omitted rice, most of which went to northern Europe by way of Britain. To placate the Carolinians, northerners agreed to the exemption. Gadsden, the most radical of the South Carolina delegates, was disgusted with his self-serving South Carolina colleagues. Their actions, he felt, betrayed the spirit of united purpose Patrick Henry had spoken of so stirringly earlier in the Congress: "The distinctions between Virginians, Pennsylvanians, New Yorkers and New Englanders are no more. I am not a Virginian, but an American."

POLITICAL DIVISIONS

In the wake of the First Continental Congress, Americans were forced to take sides for and against the Continental Association. At this point, not even such well-known radicals as Samuel Adams and Gadsden were advocating independence. Throughout the pre-Revolutionary period, most colonists hoped and expected that imperial authorities would change their policy toward America. English history, Americans believed, was full of instances in which the resolute opposition of a free people forced oppressive ministries and tyrannical kings to back down. They were confident that it could happen again.

AMERICAN VIEWS

Social Status and the Enforcement of the Nonimportation Movement

Many Americans enthusiastically supported the nonimportation movement called in response to the Townshend Duty Act crisis of the late 1760s. A few, however, openly opposed it. Among these was the aristocratic William Henry Drayton of South Carolina, who objected to the composition of the committee that had been chosen to enforce the nonimportation agreement in his region. The committee included artisans and shopkeepers, men who Drayton claimed, should have no role in public affairs. Their education prepared them only "to cut up a beast in the market to the best advantage, to cobble an old shoe in the neatest manner, or to build a necessary house [outhouse]," not to make public policy. As the following document makes clear, deference had its limits, and the committeemen emphatically disagreed with him. Drayton was later to reverse himself and actively support the Continental Association's ban on importing British goods in 1775. "The people" wanted it, he would later explain, and "it was our duty, to satisfy our constituents; as we were only servants of the public [at large]."

- Who makes policy in the United States today?
- What qualifications do you think they should have?
- How do your answers to these questions differ from Drayton's? From the "Mechanicks's"?
- How would you explain Drayton's later switch?

The Mechanicks of the General Committee to William Henry Drayton

The gracious Giver of all good things, has been pleased to bestow a certain principle on mankind, which properly may be called common sense: But, though every man hath a natural right to a determined portion of this ineffable ray of the Divinity, yet, to the misfortune of society, many persons fall short of this most necessary gift of God; the want of which cannot be compensated by all the learning of the schools.

The Mechanicks pretend to nothing more, than having a claim from nature, to their share in this inestimable favour, in common with Emperors and Kings, and, were it safe to carry the comparison still higher, they would say with William-Henry Drayton himself; who, in his great condescention, has been pleased to allow us a place amongst human beings: But whether it might have happened from an ill construc-

What Americans were divided over was the extent of Parliament's authority over them and the degree to which they could legitimately challenge its power. As British officials failed, with the passing of time, to accommodate American views of their rights, Americans began in increasing numbers to challenge London's control over them. The experience of James Wilson, a Pennsylvania lawyer, illustrates this shift. In *Considerations on the Nature and Extent of the Legislative Authority of the British Parliament* tion of his sensory, or his upper works being damaged by some rough treatment of the person who conducted his birth, we know not; however so it is, that, to us, he seems highly defective in this point, whatever exalted notions he may entertain of his own abilities.

By attending to the dictates of common sense, the Mechanicks have been able to distinguish between RIGHT and WRONG; in doing which indeed no great merit is claimed, because every man's own feelings will direct him thereto, unless he obstinately, or from a pertinacious opinion of his own superior knowledge, shuts his eyes, and stoically submits to all the illegal encroachments that may be made on his property, by an ill-designing and badly-informed ministry.

Mr. Drayton may value himself as much as he pleases, on his having had a liberal education bestowed on him, tho' the good fruits thereof have not hitherto been conspicuous either in his public or private life: He ought however to know, that this is not so absolutely necessary to these, who move in the low sphere of mechanical employments. But still, though he pretends to view them with so contemptuous and oblique an eye, these men hope, that they are in some degree useful to society, without presuming to make any comparisons between themselves and him, except with regard to love for their country; for he has amply shewn, that an attachment of this sort is not one of his ruling passions. Nor does he appear in the least to have regarded the peace and good order of that community of which he is a member; otherwise he would not wilfully, and without any cause, have knocked his head against ninety-nine out of every hundred of the people, not only in this province, but of all North-America,

not one of whom bore him any malice, nor yet do, though they may entertain what opinions they please, with respect to his want of patriotism, from his having proved a Felo de se [murderer of himself] in this point.

After an avowal of principles, incompatible with the essential rights of freemen under the English constitution, surely, no parish in this province, will ever think it prudent, to trust their interests in such hands, for the time to come? Besides, who can say he ever shewed any capacity for business, when he was honoured with a seat in the House of Assembly? . . .

Mr. Drayton may be assured, that so far from being ashamed of our trades, we are in the highest degree thankful to our friends, who put us in the way of being instructed in them; and that we bless God for giving us strength and judgment to pursue them, in order to maintain our families, with a decency suitable to their stations in life. Every man is not so lucky as to have a fortune ready provided to his hand, either by his own or his wife's parents, as has been his lot; nor ought it to be so with all men; and Providence accordingly hath wisely ordained otherwise, by appointing the greatest part of mankind, to provide for their support by manual labour; and we will be bold to say, that such are the most useful people in a community. . . .

We are, Yours, &c.
MECHANICKS of the COMMITTEE.
October 3d, 1769.

Source: *South Carolina Gazette,* October 5, 1769; reprinted in *The Letters of Freeman, etc.: Essays on the Nonimportation Movement in South Carolina* by William Henry Drayton, ed. Robert M. Weir (1977), University of South Carolina Press, pp. 111–114.

(published in 1774), Wilson wrote that he set out to find a reasonable dividing line between those areas in which Parliament had legitimate authority over the colonies and those in which it did not. But the more he thought, the more he became convinced

"that such a line does not exist" and that there can be "no medium between acknowledging and denying that power in all cases." Wilson therefore concluded that Parliament had no authority at all over the colonies, that the colonies' only legal governing bodies were their own assemblies, and that their only link to the British Empire was through the king, to whom colonists owed allegiance. British authorities and their American supporters strongly disagreed, insisting that Parliament had complete authority over the colonies.

During 1774 and early 1775, as the British–American confrontation grew more heated, lively debates raged in newspapers and pamphlets, and the colonists became increasingly polarized. In the last months before the outbreak of the American Revolution, the advocates of colonial rights began to call themselves **Whigs** and condemned their opponents as **Tories**. These traditional English party labels dated from the late seventeenth century, when the Tories had supported the accession of the Catholic King James II; the Whigs had opposed it. By calling themselves Whigs and their opponents Tories (loyalist was a more accurate label), the advocates of colonial rights cast themselves as champions of liberty and their enemies as defenders of religious intolerance and royal absolutism.

CONCLUSION

All Americans, Whigs and loyalists alike, had considered themselves good British subjects. But Americans were a more diverse and more democratic people than the English. A considerably larger percentage of them could participate in government, and for all practical purposes, they had been governing themselves for a long time.

British officials recognized the different character of American society and feared it might lead Americans to reject British control. But the steps they took to prevent this outcome had the opposite effect.

From Britain's perspective, the measures it took in the wake of the French and Indian War were a reasonable response to its administrative and financial problems in the colonies. Taken one by one from the colonists' perspective, however, they were a rain of blows that finally impelled them to rebel.

No wonder that Americans, whose political ideology had already made them wary of governmental power, believed that they were the victims of a con-

spiracy in London to deprive them of their liberty. That Parliament should be a party to this presumed conspiracy particularly shocked and offended them. Because it was the representative body in the government, Americans had long considered it their "friend," though they were certain that it was not composed of their representatives.

Yet Americans probably should not have been surprised at Parliament's role. After the Glorious Revolution, virtually the only institutional limitation on Parliament was Parliament itself. That the most powerful part of the British government should concern itself with the empire after 1763 seemed only natural in Britain; that its American counterparts should defend their own rights seemed only reasonable in America. The American assemblies, after all, had modeled themselves on Parliament. Indeed, both Parliament and the colonial assemblies were doing what similar bodies throughout Europe were also doing at roughly the same time—asserting their powers and defending their liberties against encroachments from above and below.

The attempts to protect their accustomed autonomy first brought the colonial assemblies into conflict with Parliament. Asserting their rights led the individual colonies to greater cooperatation among themselves. This development, in turn, led to increasingly widespread resistance, then to rebellion, and finally to revolution. Moving imperceptibly from one stage to the next, Americans grew conscious of their common interests and their differences from the English. They became aware, as Benjamin Franklin would later write, of the need to break "through the bounds, in which a dependent people had been accustomed to think, and act" so that they might "properly comprehend the character they had assumed."

That working men and members of the elite dressed as Indians had joined in the dangerous act of defiance known as the Boston Tea Party also foreshadowed coming developments. No one now knows for certain why they adopted that particular disguise, but Indians were a traditional symbol of the new world. And those who were making a new political world were risking much—even, it would shortly turn out, life itself.

REVIEW QUESTIONS

1. What do Eliza Farmer's letters tell us about the crisis over dutied tea in 1773 and 1774? What does she think has caused the crisis and who was at fault? What makes her increasingly sympathetic to the colonial position? How widespread is the American claim of rights in her estimation? What makes her think the colonists have any chance of success in resisting British impositions?

2. How did the British victory and French withdrawal from North America after the French and Indian War affect the relations between Native Americans and white settlers? Between British authorities and Americans?

3. What was the relationship between the French and Indian War and changes in British policy toward America? What problems were British officials trying to solve in 1763? What difficulties confronted Americans in 1763? How did the expectations of American and British authorities differ in 1763? Why were the new policies offensive to Americans?

4. How was stationing British troops in America related to British taxation of the colonists? Why did the colonists consider taxation by Parliament an especially serious threat to their freedom as well as to their pocketbooks?

5. How did Americans oppose the new measures? Who participated in the various forms of resistance? How effective were the different kinds of resistance? What were the effects of American resistance to British measures on their own sense of identity as Americans? What were the effects on their own internal politics?

6. What led to the meeting of the First Continental Congress? What steps did the Congress take? What did it expect to achieve? What were the differences between Whigs and Tories?

KEY TERMS

Boston Massacre (p. 152)
Boston Tea Party (p. 154)
British Constitution (p. 146)
Cherokee War (p. 142)
Coercive Acts (p. 154)
Committees of correspondence (p. 153)
Continental Association (p. 157)
Currency Act (p. 144)
Declaration of Rights and Grievances (p. 148)
Declaratory Act (p. 149)
First Continental Congress (p. 154)
Intolerable Acts (p. 154)
Nonimportation movement (p. 147)
Parson's Cause (p. 144)
Pontiac's Rebellion (p. 143)
Proclamation Line (p. 141)
Proclamation of 1763 (p. 141)
Quartering Acts (p. 141)
Quebec Act (p. 154)
Regulators (p. 150)
Sons of Liberty (p. 147)
Stamp Act (p. 145)
Stamp Act Congress (p. 148)
Sugar Act (p. 144)
Suffolk Resolves (p. 157)
Tea Act of 1773 (p. 153)
Tories (p. 160)
Townshend Duty Act (p. 150)
Whigs (p. 160)
Writs of assistance (p. 146)

RECOMMENDED READING

Bailyn, Bernard. *The Ideological Origins of the American Revolution,* 2nd ed. (1992). A clear and illuminating account of how the colonists' ideas about politics prepared them to resist British measures.

Countryman, Edward. *The American Revolution* (1985). A brief, readable general history of the Revolutionary period that focuses on the involvement of the common people.

Morison, Samuel Eliot, ed. *Sources and Documents Illustrating the American Revolution, 1764–1788, and the Formation of the Federal Constitution* (1965). The most readily available and conveniently used collection of documents (mostly official) from the era of the American Revolution.

Raphael, Ray. *A People's History of the American Revolution: How Common People Shaped the Fight for Independence* (2001). A readable, popular synthesis of much recent scholarship.

ADDITIONAL SOURCES
Imperial Reorganization

Alden, John R. *John Stuart and the Southern Colonial Frontier: A Study of Indian Relations, War, Trade, and Land Problems in the Southern Wilderness, 1754–1775* (1944, 1966).

Anderson, Fred. *Crucible of War: The Seven Years' War and the Fate of Empire in British North America, 1754-1766* (2000).

Barrow, Thomas C. *Trade and Empire: The British Customs Service in Colonial America, 1660–1775* (1967).

Bonwick, Colin. *The American Revolution* (1991).

Brooke, John. *King George III* (1972).

Cashin, Edward J. *William Bartram and the American Revolution on the Southern Frontier* (2000).

Dowd, Gregory. *A Spirited Resistance: The North American Indian Struggle for Unity, 1745–1815* (1992).

Hatley, Tom. *The Dividing Paths: Cherokees and South Carolinians through the Era of Revolution* (1993).

Langford, Paul. *A Polite and Commercial People: England, 1727–1783* (1989).

Peckham, Howard H. *Pontiac and the Indian Uprising* (1947).

Richter, Daniel. *Facing East from Indian Country: A Native History of Early America* (2001).

Shy, John. *Toward Lexington: The Role of the British Army in the Coming of the American Revolution* (1965).

Snapp, J. Russell. *John Stuart and the Struggle for Empire on the Southern Frontier* (1996).

Sosin, Jack M. *Whitehall and the Wilderness: The Middle West in British Colonial Policy, 1760–1775* (1961).

Weber, David J. *The Spanish Frontier in North America* (1992).

White, Richard. *The Middle Ground: Indians, Empires, and Republics in the Great Lakes Region, 1650–1815* (1991).

American Reactions

Breen, Timothy H. "Ideology and Nationalism on the Eve of the American Revolution: Revisions Once More in Need of Revising," *Journal of American History* (1998), 13-39.

Brown, Richard D. *Revolutionary Politics in Massachusetts: The Boston Committee of Correspondence and the Towns, 1772–1774* (1970).

Brown, Richard M. *The South Carolina Regulators* (1963).

Calhoon, Robert M. *Dominion and Liberty: Ideology in the Anglo-American World, 1660–1801* (1994).

Colbourn, H. Trevor. *The Lamp of Experience: Whig History and the Intellectual Origins of the American Revolution* (1965).

Countryman, Edward. *A People in Revolution: The American Revolution and Political Society in New York, 1760–1790* (1981).

Egnal, Marc. *A Mighty Empire: The Origins of the American Revolution* (1988).

Ekirch, Robert A. *"Poor Carolina": Politics and Society in Colonial North Carolina, 1729–1776* (1981).

Greene, Jack P. *Negotiated Authorities: Essays in Colonial Political and Constitutional History* (1994).

Greene, Jack P., *Understanding the American Revolution: Issues and Actors* (1995).

Hoerder, Dirk. *Crowd Action in Revolutionary Massachusetts, 1765–1780* (1977).

Jensen, Merrill. *The Founding of a Nation: A History of the American Revolution, 1763–1776* (1968).

Klein, Rachel N. *Unification of a Slave State: The Rise of the Planter Class in the South Carolina Backcountry, 1760–1808* (1990).

Knollenberg, Bernhard. *Origin of the American Revolution, 1759–1766* (1960).

Krawczynski, Keith. *William Henry Drayton: South Carolina Revolutionary Patriot* (2001).

Kurtz, Stephen G. and James H. Hutson, eds., *Essays on the American Revolution* (1973).

Labaree, Benjamin W. *The Boston Tea Party* (1964).

Maier, Pauline. *From Resistance to Revolution: Colonial Radicals and the Development of American Opposition to Britain, 1765–1776* (1972).

Maier, Pauline., *The Old Revolutionaries: Political Lives in the Age of Samuel Adams* (1980).

Morgan, Edmund S. *The Birth of the Republic, 1763–1789, 3rd ed.* (1992).

Morgan, Edmund S., and Helen M. Morgan, *The Stamp Act Crisis: Prologue to Revolution* (1963, 1995).

Nash, Gary B. *The Urban Crucible: The Northern Seaports and the Origins of the American Revolution* (1986).

Pole, J. R., and Jack P. Greene, eds., *A Companion to the American Revolution* (2000).

Reid, John P. *Constitutional History of the American Revolution: The Power to Tax* (1987).

Ryerson, Richard A. *"The Revolution Is Now Begun": The Radical Committees of Philadelphia, 1765–1776* (1978).

Thomas, Peter D. G. *The Townshend Duties Crisis: The Second Phase of the American Revolution, 1767–1773* (1987).

Ubbelohde, Carl. *The Vice-Admiralty Courts and the American Revolution* (1960).

Whittenburg, James P. "Planters, Merchants, and Lawyers: Social Change and the Origins of the North Carolina Regulation," *William and Mary Quarterly*, 34 (1977), 214–238.

Zobel, Hiller B. *The Boston Massacre* (1970).

The Road to Revolution

Ammerman, David. *In the Common Cause: American Response to the Coercive Acts of 1774* (1974).

Brown, Wallace. *The Good Americans: The Loyalists in the American Revolution* (1969).

Calhoon, Robert M. *The Loyalists in Revolutionary America, 1760–1781* (1973).

Clark, J. C. D. *The Language of Liberty, 1660–1832: Political Discourse and Social Dynamics in the Anglo-American World* (1994).

Doll, Peter. *Revolution, Religion, and National Identity: Imperial Nationalism in British North America, 1745–1795* (2000).

Holton, Woody. *Forced Founders: Indians, Debtors, Slaves, and the Making of the American Revolution in Virginia* (1999).

McCullough, David. *John Adams* (2001).

Nelson, William H. *The American Tory* (1961).

Rakove, Jack N. *The Beginnings of National Politics: An Interpretive History of the Continental Congress* (1979).

Young, Alfred F. *The Shoemaker and the Tea Party: Memory and the American Revolution* (1999).

WHERE TO LEARN MORE

- **Charleston, South Carolina.** Many buildings date from the eighteenth century. Officials stored tea in one of them—the Exchange—to prevent a local version of the Boston Tea Party. The website for Historic Charleston, http://www.cr.nps.gov/nr/travel/charleston, provides a map, a list of buildings, and information about them.

- **Philadelphia, Pennsylvania.** Numerous buildings and sites date from the eighteenth century. Independence National Historical Park, between Second and Sixth streets on Walnut and Chestnut streets, contains Carpenter's Hall, where the First Continental Congress met, and the Pennsylvania State House (now known as Independence Hall), where the Declaration of Independence was adopted. Philadelphia's Historic Mile, http://www.ushistory.org/tour/index.html, provides a virtual tour of the great landmarks of the city, including Independence Hall.

- **Boston, Massachusetts.** Many important buildings and sites in this area date from the seventeenth and eighteenth centuries. They include Faneuil Hall (Dock Square), where many public meetings took place prior to the Revolution, and the Old State House (Washington and State streets), which overlooks the site of the Boston Massacre. The Freedom Trail, http://www.thefreedomtrail.org/virtual_tour.html, provides a well illustrated virtual tour of the historic sites.

- **Fort Michilimackinac National Historic Landmark, Mackinaw City, Michigan.** Near the south end of the Mackinac Bridge, the present structure is a modern restoration of the fort as it was when Pontiac's Rebellion took a heavy toll of its garrison. The Mackinac State Historic Parks website, http://www.mackinacparks.com/michilimackinac/html, provides a brief description and photographs of the reconstructed colonial village and fort.

Please refer to the document CD-ROM for primary sources related to this chapter.

→ *George Washington's Tent. Plunkett Fleeson, a well-known Philadelphia upholsterer, made a set of three tents for Washington in 1776. One was for sleeping, one for dining, and one for baggage. This one, which measures 18 by 28 feet, could have served multiple purposes.*

Smithsonian Museum.

THE WAR FOR INDEPENDENCE
1774–1783

6

Headquarters, Valley Forge

January 14, 1778

I barely hinted to you my dearest Father my desire to augment the Continental Forces from an untried Source . . . . I would solicit you to cede me a number of your able bodied men Slaves, instead of leaving me a fortune. I would bring about a twofold good, first I would advance those who are unjustly deprived of the Rights of Mankind to a State which would be a proper Gradation between abject Slavery and perfect Liberty and besides I would reinforce the Defenders of Liberty with a number of gallant Soldiers . . . . If I could obtain authority for the purpose I would have a Corps of such men trained, uniformly clad, equip'd and ready in every respect to act at the opening of the next Campaign.

Headquarters, Valley Forge

February 2, 1778

My dear Father,

The more I reflect upon the difficulties and delays which are likely to attend the completing our Continental Regiments, the more anxiously is my mind bent upon the Scheme which I lately communicated to you . . . . I was aware of having that monster popular Prejudice open-mouthed against me . . . [and] of being obliged to combat the arguments and perhaps the intrigues of interested

CHAPTER OUTLINE

The Outbreak of War and The Declaration of Independence, 1774–1776
Mounting Tensions
The Loyalists' Dilemma
British Coercion and Conciliation
The Battles of Lexington and Concord
The Second Continental Congress, 1775–1776
Commander in Chief George Washington
Early Fighting: Massachusetts, Virginia, the Carolinas, and Canada
Independence
Republicanism

The Combatants
Professional Soldiers
Women in the Contending Armies
African American Participation in the War
Native Americans and the War

The War in the North, 1776–1777
The British Army Hesitates: Battles in New York and New Jersey
The Year of the Hangman: Victory at Saratoga and Winter at Valley Forge

The War Widens, 1778–1781
The United States Gains an Ally
Fighting on the Frontier and at Sea
The Land War Moves South
American Counterattacks

The American Victory, 1782–1783
The Peace of Paris
The Components of Success

The War and Society, 1775–1783
The Women's War
Effect of the War on African Americans
The War's Impact on Native Americans
Economic Disruption/The Price of Victory

Conclusion

persons. But zeal for the public Service and an ardent desire to assert the rights of humanity determined me to engage in this arduous business. . . .

You seem to think my dear Father, that men reconciled by long habit to the miseries of their Condition would prefer their ignominious bonds to the untasted Sweets of Liberty, especially when offer'd upon the terms which I propose. I confess indeed the minds of this unhappy species must be debased by a Servitude from which they can hope for no Relief but Death and that every motive to action but Fear must be also nearly extinguished in them. But do you think they are so perfectly moulded to their State as to be insensible that a better exists? Will the galling comparison between themselves and their masters leave them unenlightened in this respect? Can their Self-Love be so totally annihilated as not frequently to induce ardent wishes for a change? . . . I am tempted to believe that this trampled people have so much human left in them, as to be capable of aspiring to the rights of men by noble exertions, if some friend to mankind would point the Road, and give them prospect of Success.

I have long deplored the wretched State of these men and considered in their history, the bloody wars excited in Africa to furnish America with Slaves. The Groans of despairing multitudes toiling for the Luxuries of Merciless Tyrants. I have had the pleasure of conversing with you sometimes upon the means of restoring them to their rights. When can it be better done than when their enfranchisement may be made conducive to the Public Good.

John Laurens

Henry Laurens Papers, vol 12, pp. 305, 390-392.

John Laurens wrote these letters to his father, Henry, at one of the low points of the American Revolution, when victory seemed most remote. The letters reveal much, not only about the course of the war but also about the aspirations and limitations of the Revolutionary generation. Henry, a wealthy slaveholder from South Carolina, was president of the Continental Congress; his son John was an aide to General Washington while the Continental Army occupied winter quarters at Valley Forge.

John, then 23 years old, had been born in South Carolina but educated for the most part in Geneva and London, where he had been exposed to some of the most progressive currents of the Enlightenment. Among these were compassion for the oppressed and the conviction that slavery should be abolished. As the controversy between Britain and its colonies grew from a family quarrel into a war for independence, John became increasingly impatient to enlist in a cause that appealed deeply to him. The American version of republicanism combined a New Whig distrust of central authority with a belief in a government rooted in the public spirit of a virtuous citizenry. Clinging fervently to this ideology, Americans at first expected to defeat the British Army with a zealous citizens' militia. But as the war intensified, they learned that they could prevail only by developing an equally professional fighting force of their own. With vital French assistance, the new American army eventually overcame the enemy, but the Continental Army was often critically short of soldiers. During the summer of 1776, for example, Britain had 30,000 troops in New York City; at Valley Forge in 1777-1778, Washington had 8,200 men fit for duty.

Aware of this discrepancy in manpower, Laurens saw an opportunity to solve two problems at once when he returned to America in 1777. Enlisting slaves in the Army would provide blacks with a stepping stone to freedom and American forces with desperately needed troops. His father, however, was a conditional emancipationist—though he detested slavery—and conditions were never quite right for him. John, however, tried and failed repeatedly to convince legislatures in the deep south to enroll black troops in exchange for their freedom.

John's journey from South Carolina to Europe and back in his idealistic quest for social justice ended on the banks of the Combahee River in South Carolina, where he died in one of the last skirmishes of the war. "Where liberty is," he once wrote, "there is my country." Americans won their independence, but eight long years of warfare strained and in some ways profoundly altered the fabric of American society, though not as much as Laurens had wished.

KEY TOPICS

- Mounting tensions with Britain
- Declaring independence
- The contending forces
- The major campaigns of the Revolution
- The alliance with France
- The peace settlement
- The social effects of the war

THE OUTBREAK OF WAR AND THE DECLARATION OF INDEPENDENCE, 1774–1776

After the Boston Tea Party, both the British and the Americans knew that they were approaching a crisis. A British officer in Massachusetts commented in late 1774 that "it is thought by every body here" that British forces would soon have "to take the field." "The people in general are very enraged," he explained, and some would "defend what they call their Liberties," to the death. Many Americans also expected a military confrontation but continued to hope that the king would not "reason with us only by the roar of his Cannon."

MOUNTING TENSIONS

In May 1774, General Thomas Gage, the commander in chief of the British army in America, replaced Thomas Hutchinson as governor of Massachusetts. After Gage dissolved the Massachusetts legislature, the General Court, it defied him by assembling anyway. Calling itself the Provincial Congress, the legislature in October 1774 appointed an emergency executive body, the **Committee of Safety**, headed by John Hancock, which began stockpiling weapons and organizing militia volunteers. Some localities had already provided for the formation of special companies of **Minute Men**, who were to be ready at "a minute's warning in Case of an alarm."

Enforcing the Continental Association's boycott of British goods, local committees sometimes assaulted suspected loyalists and destroyed their property. The increasingly polarized atmosphere, combined with the drift toward military confrontation, drove a growing wedge between American loyalists and the patriot anti-British American Whigs.

THE LOYALISTS' DILEMMA

Loyalists and Whigs began to part company in earnest during the fall and winter of 1774–1775 as the threat of war mounted. Much like other Americans, loyalists came from all walks of life and all social classes. Most were farmers, though officeholders and professionals were more numerous among them than in the population at large. Many recent immigrants to the colonies, as well as some locally unpopular minorities (Scots in the South, Anglicans in New England), also remained loyal because they felt that the crown offered them some protection against more established Americans. Most loyalists believed, in short, that they had something to lose—including their honor—if America broke with Britain. During the War for Independence, about 19,000 American men would join British provincial units and fight to restore royal authority. (This compares with the perhaps 200,000 who served in some military capacity on the rebel side.) Including those who did not actually fight, the loyalists numbered close to half a million men and women— some 20 percent of the colonies' free population. Of

Chronology

1775	April 19: Battles of Lexington and Concord.
	May 10: Second Continental Congress meets.
	June 17: Battle of Bunker Hill.
	December 31: American attack on Quebec.
1776	January 9: Thomas Paine's *Common Sense*.
	July 4: Declaration of Independence.
	September 15: British take New York City.
	December 26: Battle of Trenton.
1777	January 3: Battle of Princeton.
	September 11: Battle of Brandywine Creek.
	October 17: American victory at Saratoga.
	Runaway inflation begins.
	Continental Army winters at Valley Forge.
1778	February 6: France and the United States sign an alliance.
	June 17: Congress refuses to negotiate with British peace commissioners.
	July 4: George Rogers Clark captures British

post in the Mississippi Valley.
December 29: British capture Savannah.

1779 June 21: Spain declares war on Britain.
Americans devastate the Iroquois country.
September 23: John Paul Jones captures the British ship *Serapis*.

1780 May 12: Fall of Charleston, South Carolina.
October 7: Americans win Battle of Kings Mountain.
Nathanael Greene takes command in the South.

1781 January 17: Americans defeat British at Battle of Cowpens.
March 15: Battle of Guilford Court House.
October 19: Cornwallis surrenders at Yorktown.

1783 March 15: Washington quells the Newburgh "Conspiracy."
September 3: Peace of Paris signed.
November 21: British begin evacuating New York.

these, up to 100,000 would leave with the British forces at the end of the war.

BRITISH COERCION AND CONCILIATION

Britain held parliamentary elections in the fall of 1774, but if Americans hoped that the outcome would change the government's policy toward them, they were disappointed. Few British voters paid much attention to colonial affairs or to opposition criticism of Prime Minister Lord North's handling of them. As one member of Parliament later noted, a robbery near London "would make more conversation than all the disturbances of America." North's supporters won easily. Angry and alarmed at the colonists' challenge to Parliament's sovereignty, they took a hard line. Under North's direction, in February 1774, Parliament resolved that Massachusetts was in rebellion and prohibited the New England colonies from trading outside the British Empire or sending their ships to the North Atlantic fishing grounds. Similar restrictions on most of the other colonies soon followed.

Meanwhile, in a gesture of appeasement, Parliament endorsed Lord North's **Conciliatory Proposition** that pledged not to tax the colonies if they would voluntarily contribute to the defense of the empire. British authorities, however, would decide what was a sufficient contribution. Parliament, as a

result, would remain sovereign and the colonial legislatures strictly subordinate to it.

Had the Conciliatory Proposition specified a maximum colonial contribution and had it been offered ten years earlier, the colonists might have found it acceptable. Now it was too late. North's government, in any case, had already sent orders to General Gage to take decisive action against the Massachusetts rebels. These orders triggered the first clash between British and American forces.

THE BATTLES OF LEXINGTON AND CONCORD

Gage received his orders on April 14, 1775. On the night of April 18, he assembled seven hundred men on the Boston Common and marched them toward the little towns of Lexington and Concord, some 20 miles away (see Map 6-1). Their mission was to arrest rebel leaders Samuel Adams and John Hancock (then staying in Lexington) and to destroy the military supplies the Committee of Safety had assembled at Concord. Patriots in Boston got wind of the troop movements and sent out riders—one of them the silversmith Paul Revere—to warn their fellows. Adams and Hancock escaped.

When the British soldiers reached Lexington at dawn, they found about seventy armed militiamen drawn up in formation on the village green. Their

MAP 6-1   The Battles of Lexington and Concord
This map shows the area around Boston, Massachusetts, where in April 1775 British and American forces fought the first military engagements of the Revolution.

precise intentions are not clear. Outnumbered ten to one, they probably did not plan to begin a fight. More likely, they were there in a show of defiance, to demonstrate that Americans would not run at the sight of a superior British force.

Months of mounting tension exploded on the Lexington green. A British major ordered the militia to disperse. They were starting to obey when a shot cracked through the dawn stillness. No one now knows who fired. The British responded with a volley that killed or wounded eighteen Americans.

The British troops pressed on to Concord and burned what few supplies the Americans had not been able to hide. When their rear guard came under patriot fire at Concord's North Bridge, the British panicked. As they retreated to Boston, patriot Minute Men and other militia harried them from both sides of the road. By the time the column reached safety, 273 British soldiers were dead, wounded, or missing. The four thousand Americans who had shot at them along the way suffered nearly a hundred dead, wounded, and missing.

News of the fighting at the **Battles of Lexington and Concord** spread quickly. Patriots in Providence, Rhode Island, knew of it by evening of the Wednesday on which it occurred. Rumors of the fighting had already reached New York by the time an express rider confirmed the stories at noon the following Sunday. The Philadelphia newspaper *Pennsylvania Packet* carried the story the next Monday. Williamsburg's *Virginia Gazette* printed an account on May 4, only two weeks after the event. South Carolinians knew by May 9, and Georgians probably soon after. The speed with which distant colonies heard

This dramatic engraving of the first battle of the American Revolution at Lexington, Massachusetts, on April 19, 1775, is not the photographic work of an eyewitness to events but a close approximation to it. Ralph Earl, a painter, and Amos Doolittle, an engraver, walked over the battlefields at Lexington and Concord a few days after the engagement, interviewed spectators and participants, and collaborated in producing four large engravings that depicted the events with considerable accuracy. This scene from the first plate shows British troops firing on the American militia at Lexington.

This fine portrait of George Washington appears in multiple versions depicting the victorious general against different backgrounds, including the battles of Princeton and Yorktown. The painter, Charles Willson Peale, served under Washington at Princeton, and the French commander at Yorktown, the Count de Rochambeau, took an appropriate version home with him in 1783.

about the outbreak of fighting suggests both the importance Americans attached to it and the extraordinary efforts patriots made to spread word of it. Everywhere, news of Lexington and Concord spurred Whigs into action.

The shots fired that April morning would, in the words of the nineteenth-century Concord philosopher and poet Ralph Waldo Emerson, be "heard round the world." They signaled the start of the American Revolution. And that revolution helped inspire the French Revolution in 1789 and other revolutions in Europe and Latin America.

THE SECOND CONTINENTAL CONGRESS, 1775–1776

By the time the **Second Continental Congress** convened in Philadelphia on May 10, 1775, it had a war on its hands. After Gage's troops had limped back into Boston from Lexington and Concord, patriot militia surrounded the city and laid siege to it. On the

first day the Congress met, militia forces from Vermont under Ethan Allen and from Massachusetts under Benedict Arnold overwhelmed the British garrison at Fort Ticonderoga at the southern end of Lake Champlain. Rebel forces elsewhere seized arms and ammunition from royal storehouses.

Assuming leadership of the rebellion, the Congress in the succeeding months became, in effect, a national government. It called for the patchwork of local forces to be organized into the **Continental Army**, authorized the formation of a navy, established a post office, and authorized the printing of paper continental dollars to meet its expenses. Denying Parliament's claim to govern the colonies but not yet ready to declare themselves independent, the delegates sought to preserve their ties to Britain by expressing loyalty to the crown. In the **Olive Branch Petition**, addressed to George III on July 5, they asked the king to protect his American subjects from the military actions ordered by Parliament. The following day, Congress approved the **Declaration of the Causes and Necessity of Taking Up Arms**, asserting the resolve of American patriots "to die freemen, rather than to live slaves." And at the end of the month, it formally rejected North's Conciliatory Proposition.

COMMANDER IN CHIEF GEORGE WASHINGTON

To take command of the patriot forces around Boston—the newly named Continental Army—Congress turned to George Washington. John Adams, a Whig leader from Massachusetts, first nominated Washington. Selecting the Virginian, Adams realized, would help transform a local quarrel in New England into a continental conflict involving all of British North America. Adams and his fellow delegates also expected Washington's leadership to help attract recruits from Virginia, which was then the most populous colony. Despite (or perhaps because of) his experience in the French and Indian War, Washington claimed to feel inadequate to the task, but by attending the Congress in military uniform, he seemed to be volunteering for it.

He was the ideal person for the job. Some of his contemporaries had quicker minds and broader educations; Washington, however, was blessed with good judgment, a profound understanding of both the uses and the limitations of power, and a quiet air of authority. In short, he had the gift of command. He soon also realized that the fate of the patriot cause depended on the survival of the army. Early in the war, he almost suffered catastrophic military defeat at least twice, but he learned from his mistakes and thereafter did not risk lives unnecessarily. The troops in turn revered him. In a crisis, wrote a man who served under him, "his likeness was worth more . . . than the British would have given for his person"—presumably a great deal.

EARLY FIGHTING: MASSACHUSETTS, VIRGINIA, THE CAROLINAS, AND CANADA

General Gage, finding himself besieged in Boston after the fighting at Lexington and Concord, decided to seize and fortify territory south of Boston, where his cannons could command the harbor. But the Americans seized high ground first, entrenching themselves on Breeds Hill north of town. On June 17, 1775, Gage sent 2,200 well-trained soldiers to drive the 1,700 patriot men and boys from their new position. The British succeeded, but at great cost. In three assaults, they suffered more than a thousand casualties. The Americans, who retreated when they ran short of gunpowder, lost just under four hundred dead or wounded. One glum British officer observed afterward that another such victory "would have ruined us." Misnamed for another hill nearby, this encounter has gone down in history as the Battle of Bunker Hill (see Map 6-2).

Washington, who arrived in Boston after the battle, took command of the American forces there in early July. Months of standoff followed, with neither side able to dislodge the other. During the winter of 1775–1776, however, the Americans dragged some sixty cannons—the largest weighing as much as a ton—300 miles through snow and over mountains from Fort Ticonderoga to Boston. In March 1776, Washington mounted the newly arrived guns to overlook Boston harbor, putting the British in an indefensible position. The British then evacuated Boston—which really had no strategic value for them—and moved

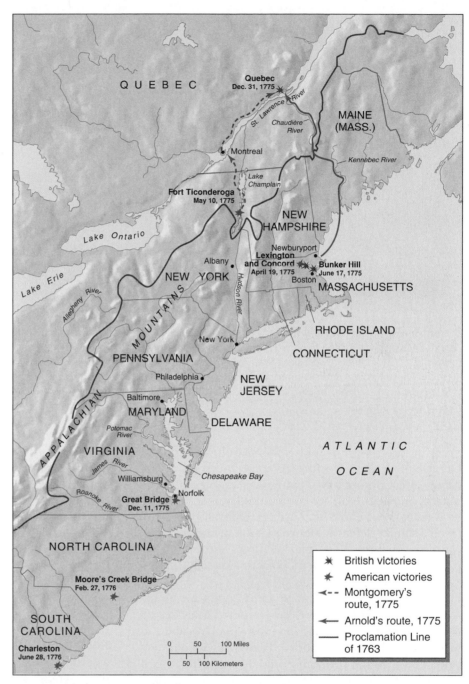

MAP 6-2   Early Fighting, 1775–1776
As this map clearly reveals, even the earliest fighting occurred in widely scattered areas, thereby complicating Britain's efforts to subdue the Americans.

their troops to Halifax, Nova Scotia. New England was for the moment secure for the patriots.

Fighting in the South also went well for the patriots. Virginia's last royal governor, Lord Dunmore, fled the capital, Williamsburg, and set up a base in nearby Norfolk. Promising freedom to slaves who joined him, he succeeded in raising a small force of black and white loyalists. On December 9, 1775, he sent these men, with some British marines, to attack a much larger force of

In this painting of The Battle of Bunker Hill, the artist John Trumbull highlighted the death of Major General Joseph Warren of the Massachusetts militia. Like Trumbull, historians have traditionally emphasized prominent historical figures. More recently, however, they have focused on the common people, such as the militiamen, black and white, who appear at the margins of this picture but who composed the majority of the American forces fighting that day.

nine hundred Virginia and North Carolina patriots at Great Bridge, near Norfolk. As it advanced up a long causeway, Dunmore's little band was slaughtered. Their march, one British officer commented, was an "extravagant Folly." On February 27, a force of loyalist Scots suffered a similar defeat at Moore's Creek Bridge in North Carolina. In June 1776, patriot forces successfully repulsed a large British expedition sent to attack Charleston, South Carolina.

In contrast, an attempt to win Canada to the patriot side met with disaster. Two American armies attacked Canada in late 1775. One quickly captured Montreal. The other, under Benedict Arnold, approached through the Maine wilderness in the face of great hardships. The two forces linked up outside heavily fortified Quebec. On December 31, their hasty attack failed, and most of the Americans who participated in it were captured. The Siege of Quebec dragged on into the spring, when a British fleet relieved the city and fresh troops forced the Americans back to Lake Champlain. Canada remained a British province.

INDEPENDENCE

The stunning American successes in New England and the South in late 1775 and early 1776 bolstered the patriots' confidence as attempts to promote an Anglo-American reconciliation failed.

In August 1775, King George III rejected the Congress's Olive Branch Petition. Instead, he issued a proclamation declaring the colonies in rebellion and denying them his protection. In December, Parliament barred all exports from the American colonies. These aggressive actions, especially the king's, persuaded many colonists to abandon their loyalty to the crown. More and more, Whigs began to think seriously of declaring full independence from Britain.

At this critical moment, a ne'er-do-well Englishman, recently arrived on American soil, gave the cause of independence a powerful boost. Thomas Paine was by trade a corsetmaker—and twice a fired tax collector. He was also a man of radical ideas—which he expressed forcefully in the everyday English of ordinary people—and he became a powerful polemicist for the American cause. Benjamin Franklin, in London as a lobbyist for the colonies, recognized Paine's talent and gave him letters of introduction when he sailed for America in 1774. In his pamphlet *Common Sense*, published in Philadelphia in January 1776, Paine denounced King George and made the case for independence. He ridiculed the absurdity of "supposing a continent to be perpetually governed by an island." America, he maintained, would be better off on every count if it were independent. The king, Paine said bluntly, was "the Royal Brute" whose tyranny should be thrown off. This assertion, which not long before would have shocked even Whigs, seemed self-evident now in light of the king's rejection of the Olive Branch Petition. Simple common sense, Paine concluded, dictated that " 'TIS TIME TO PART."

Common Sense, which promptly sold more than 100,000 copies throughout the colonies, helped predispose Americans toward independence. Tactical considerations also led patriot leaders toward a formal separation from Great Britain. Such a move would make it easier for America to gain desperately needed aid from foreign countries, especially from England's ancient enemy, France. Declaring independence would also give the local political elites leading the re-

Thomas Jefferson, author of the Declaration of Independence and future president of the United States. Mather Brown, an American artist living in England, painted this picture of Jefferson for John Adams while the two men were in London on diplomatic missions in 1786. A companion portrait of Adams that Jefferson ordered for himself also survives. Brown's sensitive portrait of a thoughtful Jefferson is the earliest known likeness of him.

sistance to British rule a solid legal basis for their newly claimed authority. Accordingly, most of the American states (as the rebellious colonies now called themselves) either instructed or permitted their delegates in the Congress to vote for independence.

On June 7, 1776, Virginian Richard Henry Lee introduced in the Congress a resolution stating that the united colonies "are, and of right ought to be, free and independent States." Postponing a vote on the issue, the Congress appointed a committee to draw up a declaration of independence. The committee turned to a young Virginian named Thomas Jefferson to compose the first draft. "You can write ten times better than I," John Adams supposedly told Jefferson. On June 28, after making revisions in Jefferson's proposed text, the committee presented the document to Congress. In the debate that followed, the South Carolina, Pennsylvania, and New York delegations initially opposed independence. As it became clear that

the majority favored it, the Pennsylvania and South Carolina delegations switched sides, and the New York delegation decided to abstain. A few delegates—including the notable patriot leaders John Dickinson and Robert Morris of Pennsylvania—clung to the hope of maintaining loyal ties to the crown. But when the Congress voted on the resolution for independence on July 2, 1776, all voting delegations approved it. After further tinkering with the wording, the Congress officially adopted the **Declaration of Independence** on July 4, 1776.

Congress intended the declaration to be a justification for America's secession from the British Empire. Jefferson later maintained that he did not write any more than what everyone was thinking. The political theory that lies behind the declaration is known as the **contract theory of government**. Developed by the late-seventeenth-century English philosopher John Locke and others, the contract theory maintains that legitimate government rests on an agreement between the people and their rulers. The people are bound to obey their rulers only so long as the rulers offer them protection. Jefferson's prose, however, transformed what might have been a bland, legalistic rehash of the contract theory into one of history's great statements of human rights.

The Declaration of Independence consists of a magnificently stated opening assumption, two premises, and a powerful conclusion. The opening assumption is that all men are created equal, that they therefore have equal rights, and that they can neither give up these rights nor allow them to be taken away. The first premise—that people establish governments to protect their fundamental rights to life, liberty, and property—is a restatement of contract theory. (With a wonderful flourish reflecting the Enlightenment's optimism about human potential, Jefferson changed "property" to "the pursuit of happiness.") The second premise is a long list of charges meant to prove that George III had failed to defend his American subjects' rights. This indictment, the heart of the declaration, justified the Americans' rejection of their hitherto legitimate ruler. Then followed the dramatic conclusion: that Americans could rightfully overthrow King George's rule and replace it with something more satisfactory to them.

Historians have spilled oceans of ink debating Jefferson's use of the expression "all men." Almost certainly he was thinking in the abstract and meant "humanity in general." In practice, of course, many people were excluded from full participation in eighteenth-century American society. Women had no formal political rights and limited legal rights.

This British engraving published in 1783 depicts one of the many public readings of the Declaration of Independence that occurred throughout the United States during the weeks following its adoption by the Second Continental Congress on July 4, 1776.

Propertyless white and free black men had similarly restricted rights, and slaves enjoyed no rights at all. (Although himself a slaveowner, Jefferson was deeply troubled by American slavery. He had wanted to include a denunciation of the slave trade among the charges against George III in the Declaration of Independence, but the Congress took it out, believing that to blame the king for this inhumane business would appear hypocritical.) But if the words "all men are created equal" had limited practical meaning in 1776, they have ever since confronted Americans with a moral challenge to make good on them.

REPUBLICANISM

Americans reacted to news of the Declaration of Independence with mixed emotions. There was rejoicing

as orators read the declaration to great crowds. Soldiers fired noisy salutes, and candles lit up the windows of public buildings at night. But even many who favored independence worried about how Americans would govern themselves. Most Whigs, animated by the political ideology known as **republicanism**, thought a republican government was best suited to American society.

John Adams once complained that republicanism was too shadowy a concept to define, and indeed it was a complex, changing body of ideas, values, and assumptions. Closely related to country (New Whig) ideology, republicanism was derived from the political ideas of classical antiquity, Renaissance Europe, and early modern England. It held that self-government—either directly by the citizens of a country or indirectly by their elected representatives—provided a more reliable foundation for the good society and individual freedom than did rule by kings. Thus drawing on contract theory, as in the Declaration of Independence, republicanism called for government by consent of the governed. Drawing on country ideology, it was suspicious of excessively centralized government and insistent on the need for a virtuous, public-spirited citizenry. The benefits of monarchy depended on the variable abilities of monarchs; the character of republican government depended on the virtue of the people. Republicanism therefore helped to give the American Revolution a moral dimension.

But other than a state that was not ruled by a hereditary king, what was a republic? And what were the chances that one would survive? Every educated person knew, of course, that ancient Rome and Athens had been republics. Classical political theory, beginning with the ancient Greek thinkers Plato and Aristotle, had insisted that republics could endure only as long as their citizens remained virtuous and self-sacrificing. Once individual citizens, greedy for wealth and power, began fighting among themselves, a republic would certainly collapse. A failed republic would give way to the despotism of one-man rule or to oligarchy—rule by a narrow clique of rich men—or, worst of all, to the "mob rule" of ignorant and violent common people. Europe's three surviving republics in the eighteenth century—the Netherlands, Switzerland, and Venice—seemed to bear out this dismal picture: All were rather corrupt and uninspiring societies, and none of them was at all democratic.

But Americans had at hand a more recent example of a republic than ancient Athens or Rome, one more closely linked to their own history than the republics of eighteenth-century Europe. During the

English Civil War of the mid-seventeenth century, English Puritans had for a time replaced the monarchy with a republican "Commonwealth," dedicated to advancing the "common weal," or common good. Most eighteenth-century Americans thought of the Puritan Commonwealth as a misguided product of fanaticism that had ended in a military dictatorship. However, some New Englanders, spiritual descendants of the Puritans, considered the Commonwealth to have been a noble experiment. To them, the American Revolution offered another chance to establish a republic of the godly.

"When the mere Politician weighs the Danger or Safety of his Country," warned one clergyman, "he computes them in Proportion to its Fortresses, Arms, Money, Provisions, Numbers of Fighting Men, and its Enemies." But, the clergyman continued, the "Christian Patriot" calculates them "by its Numbers of Sinful or praying People, and its Degrees of Holiness or Vice." Such language recalled the Great Awakening; it reached beyond the upper classes who had been directing resistance to the British and mobilized ordinary people for what their ministers repeatedly assured them was a just war against sin and despotism. Out of this fusion of republican theory (with which only the educated were familiar) and the religious heritage that all Americans understood, a common belief developed that Americans must have "resolution enough to forgo Self gratification" and be willing to stake their all "upon the prospect of Securing freedom and happiness to future Generations."

THE COMBATANTS

At the outset of the American Revolution, republican fervor produced a spontaneous eruption of patriotism that to skeptical foreign observers looked like religious fanaticism. The experience of Lancaster, Pennsylvania, where more men responded to a call for volunteers than were then needed, leaving disappointed men behind, was shared elsewhere. But this enthusiastic flocking to the colors eventually waned, and in any case, its results were often unsatisfactory.

Republican theory mistrusted professional armies as the instruments of tyrants. A free people, republicans insisted, relied for defense on their own patriotism. When individual or community rights were in danger, free men should grab their muskets from over the fireplace, assemble as the local militia, take care of the problem, and go home (see "American Views: A British Woman Observes an American Militia Exercise in 1775"). But militiamen, as one American general observed, had trouble coping with "the shocking scenes of war" because they were not "steeled by habit or fortified by military pride." In real battles, they often proved unreliable. Americans therefore faced a hard choice: Develop a professional army or lose the war. In the end, they did what they had to do. While state militias continued to offer support, it was the disciplined forces of the Continental Army that won the crucial battles. To be sure, when the war was over, Americans tried to forget about their professional troops; in American mythology, it was the "embattled farmers"—Minute Men at Lexington and Concord, swamp fighters in the South—who had won independence. But long before the struggle was over, toughened Continental soldiers knew better.

PROFESSIONAL SOLDIERS

Drawing on their colonial experience and on republican theory, the new state governments first tried to meet their military needs by relying on the militia and by creating new units based on short-term enlistments. Officers, particularly in the North, were often elected, and their positions depended on personal popularity. As a result, their orders sometimes sounded more like requests than commands, and rules were lax. Discipline became a major problem in both the militia and the new state units, and often volunteers had barely received basic training before their term of duty ended and they returned home.

Washington tightened things up in the new Continental Army. Eventually, he prevailed on Congress to adopt stricter regulations and to require enlistments for three years or the duration of the war. Although he used militia effectively, his consistent aim was to turn the Continental Army into a disciplined force that could defeat the British in the large engagements of massed troops characteristic of eighteenth-century European warfare. Guerrilla fighters shooting from behind trees like "savages" had their place in the American war effort, but they could never win a decisive, formal battle. And only such a "civilized" victory would impress the other European powers and establish the legitimacy of the United States.

Many soldiers of fortune, as well as a few idealists, offered their services to American representatives in Europe. So many came to the United States that both Washington and Congress soon regarded most of them as nuisances. But several proved especially valuable in helping Washington forge a professional army. France's 19-year-old Marquis de Lafayette was one of the youngest, wealthiest, and most idealistic. Two Poles, Tadeusz Kosciuszko, an

AMERICAN VIEWS

A British Woman Observes an American Militia Exercise in 1775

The following description of North Carolinians preparing for war in 1775 comes from the travel journal of Janet Schaw, a Scotswoman visiting her brother Robert in America. Robert Schaw, although he was appointed a colonel in the North Carolina militia, disapproved of the American cause and eventually refused to take the oath of allegiance to the new state government. His wife, by contrast, according to Janet Schaw, was "so rooted an American, that she detests every thing that is European." Early in June 1775 Janet Schaw saw the militia train outside of Wilmington under their commander, Robert Howe, who later became a major general in the Continental Army. She returned to Scotland in late 1775.

- What does this passage suggest about Janet Schaw's own views of the American cause?
- How accurately do you think it reflects the effectiveness of milita forces?
- What does it suggest about the relationship between patriots and loyalists?

We came down in the morning in time for the review, which the heat made as terrible to the spectators as to the soldiers, or what you please to call them. They had certainly fainted under it, had not the constant draughts of grog supported them. Their exercise was that of bush-fighting, but it appeared so confused and so perfectly different from any thing I ever saw, I cannot say whether they performed it well or not; but this I know that they were heated with rum till capable of committing the most shocking outrages. We stood in the balcony of Doctor Cobham's [a future loyalist] house and they were reviewed on a field mostly covered with what are called here scrubby oaks which are only a little better than brushwood. They at last however assembled on the plain field, and I must really laugh while I recollect their figures: 2000 men in their shirts and trousers, preceded by a very ill beat-drum and a fiddler, who was also in his shirt with a long sword and a cue at his hair, who played with all his might. They made indeed a most unmartial appearance. But the worst figure there can shoot from behind a bush and kill even a General Wolfe.

Before the review was over, I hear a cry of tar and feather. I was ready to faint at the idea of this dreadful operation. I would have gladly quitted the balcony, but was so much afraid the Victim was one of my friends, that I was not able to move; and he indeed proved to be one, tho' in a humble station. For it was Mr. Neilson's [a loyalist] poor English groom. You can hardly conceive what I felt when I saw him dragged forward, poor devil, frighted out of his wits. However at the request of some of the officers, who had been Neilson's friends, his punishment was changed into that of mounting on a table and begging pardon for having smiled at the regt. He was then drummed and fiddled out of the town, with a strict prohibition of ever being seen in it again.

Source: [Janet Schaw], *Journal of a Lady of Quality; Being the Narrative of a Journey from Scotland to the West Indies, North Carolina, and Portugal, in the Years 1774 to 1776,* ed. Evangeline Walker Andrews in Collaboration with Charles McLean Andrews (1923). Yale University Press.

engineer, and Kazimierz Pulaski, a cavalry commander who would be mortally wounded at the Battle of Savannah in 1779, also rendered good service. Johann Kalb, a bogus baron from Germany, became a general and died heroically at Camden, South Carolina, in 1780. Most useful of all, probably, was Baron von Steuben. His title, too, was new, but he had experience in the Prussian army, continental Europe's best. He also knew how to get along with American soldiers by explaining the reasons for his orders. He became the Continental Army's drillmaster, and thanks partly to him, Washington's troops increasingly came to resemble their disciplined European counterparts.

The enemy British troopers—and the nearly thirty thousand German mercenaries (Americans called them "Hessians") whom the British government also employed—offered Americans the clearest model of a professional army. British regulars were not (as Americans, then and later, assumed) the "dregs of society." Most enlisted men did come from the lower classes and from economically depressed areas, but many also had skills. British officers usually came from wealthy families or had simply purchased their commissions. Only in rare cases did a man rise from the enlisted ranks to commissioned officer status.

Most British troops carried the "Brown Bess" musket. With bayonet attached, it was almost 6 feet long and weighed over 16 pounds. It fired a lead ball slightly more than 1/2 inch in diameter, which might hit its target at up to 100 yards. Skilled troops could get off more than two rounds per minute under combat conditions. In battle, soldiers usually stood close together in lines three deep. They were expected to withstand bombardment without flinching, fire on command in volleys, charge with the bayonet, and use their heavy musket stock (the wooden end) to crush the skulls of any wounded enemy they strode over.

Military life was tough. On the march, seasoned troops carrying 60-pound packs normally covered about 15 miles a day but could go 30 miles in a "forced" march. In most weather conditions, they wore heavy woolen uniforms dyed bright red for visibility on smoke-filled battlefields (hence their nickname "Redcoats"). In their barracks, British soldiers doubled up in a bed slightly over 4 feet wide; in the field, they were often wet, crawling with lice, and hungry. Under the best conditions, they ate mainly beef or salt pork and bread. They were frequently undernourished, however, and many more died of disease than of injury in battle. Medical care was, by modern standards, primitive. Treatments for illness

included bleeding and purging (induced vomiting and diarrhea). Serious arm or leg wounds usually meant amputation, without antiseptics or anesthetics. But unless a man was extraordinarily lucky, a body wound or amputation usually proved fatal. If loss of blood or infection did not kill him immediately, tetanus probably would do so later.

Severe discipline held soldiers in line. Striking an officer or deserting could bring death; lesser offenses usually incurred a beating. Several hundred lashes, "well laid on" with the notorious cat-o'-nine-tails (a whip with multiple cords, each ending in a nasty little knot or a metal ball), were not uncommon.

Soldiers amused themselves with gambling (despite regulations against it) and drinking. As one foreign officer serving with the British lamented, America was a terrible country where one drank "to get warm, or to get cool, or . . . because you get no letters." Perhaps two-thirds of the Redcoats were illiterate, and all suffered from loneliness and boredom. Camaraderie and a legendary loyalty to their regiments sustained them.

After the winter of 1777–1778, conditions in the Continental Army came to resemble those of the British army. Like British regulars, American recruits tended to be low on the social scale. They included young men without land, indentured servants, some criminals and vagrants—in short, men who lacked better prospects. The chances for talented enlisted men to win an officer's commission were greater in the Continental Army than in the British army. As a German prisoner of war observed, American troops tended to be taller than their British counterparts. And despite their ragged uniforms, they carried themselves like soldiers. Indeed, Continental soldiers frequently had little more than "their ragged shirt flaps to cover their nakedness," and more than once their bare marching feet left bloody tracks in the snow.

Both British and American authorities had trouble supplying their troops. Both sides suffered from bureaucratic inefficiencies, but the fundamental problems of each were different. The British had plenty of hard-coin money with a stable value, which many American merchants and farmers were happy to take in payment for supplies. But the British had to rely mostly on supplies shipped to them from the British Isles. The Continental Army, by contrast, had to pay for supplies in paper money, both Continental dollars and state-issued currency, whose value sank steadily as the war progressed. After 1780, the burden of provisioning the Continental Army fell on the states, which did little better than Congress had done. Unable to obtain sufficient supplies, the army

Overview

Important Battles of the Revolutionary War

	Battle	Date	Outcome
Early Fighting	Lexington and Concord, Massachusetts	April 19, 1775	Contested
	Fort Ticonderoga, New York	May 10, 1775	American victory
	Breeds Hill ("Bunker Hill"), Boston, Massachusetts	June 17, 1775	Contested
	Great Bridge, Virginia	Dec. 9, 1775	American victory
	Quebec, Canada	Dec. 31, 1775	British repulse American assault
	Moore's Creek Bridge, North Carolina	Feb. 27, 1776	American victory
The War in the North	Brooklyn Heights, New York	Aug. 27, 1776	British victory
	White Plains, New York	Oct. 28, 1776	British victory
	Trenton, New Jersey	Dec. 26, 1776	American victory
	Princeton, New Jersey	Jan. 3, 1777	American victory
	Brandywine Creek, Pennsylvania	Sept. 11, 1777	British victory (opened way for British to take Philadelphia)
	Saratoga, New York	Sept. 19 and Oct. 17, 1777	American victory (helped persuade France to form an alliance with United States)
	Monmouth Court House, N. J.	June 28, 1778	Contested
The War on the Frontier	Wyoming Valley, Pennsylvania	June and July 1778	British victory
	Kaskaskia and Cahokia, Illinois; Vincennes, Indiana	July 4, 1778– Feb. 23, 1779	American victories strengthen claims to Mississippi Valley
	Cherry Valley, New York	Nov. 11, 1778	British victory
The War in the South	Savannah, Georgia	Dec. 29, 1778	British victory (took control of Georgia)
	Kettle Creek, Georgia	Feb. 14, 1779	American victory
	Savannah, Georgia	Sept. 3– Oct. 28, 1779	British victory (opened way for British to take Charleston)
	Charleston, South Carolina	Feb. 11– May 12, 1780	British victory
	Camden, South Carolina	Aug. 16, 1780	British victory
	Kings Mountain, South Carolina	Oct. 7, 1780	American victory
	Cowpens, South Carolina	Jan. 17, 1781	American victory
	Guilford Court House, North Carolina	March 15, 1781	Contested
	Yorktown, Virginia	Aug. 30– Oct. 19, 1781	American victory (persuaded Britain to end the war)

Mezzotint, 1780–1800. Size: H. 73 x 8 in., W. 93 x 4 in. Courtesy, Winterthur Museum.

Ye Foil'd, Ye Baffled Brittons This Behold   To fave their Country and Promote its Weal
Nor longer urge your Pardons,Threats or Gold; · Difdaining Bribes to wound a righteous Caufe
See in each virtuous face Patr'otic Zeal   While ANDRE falls a victim to the Laws .

This print, Ye Foil'd, Ye Baffled Brittons, *shows the capture of Major John André, the British agent who acted as the go-between for British authorities and the American General Benedict Arnold, who planned to turn over the American fortress at West Point to them. The three militiamen who captured André, who was later hanged as a spy, reportedly refused a bribe for his release. The strange facial expressions of all the participants were probably the artist's crude attempt to indicate surprise.*

sometimes provoked resentment by threatening to seize them by force. This, in turn, increased the public's republican distrust of its own professional army.

Feeling themselves outcasts from an uncaring society, the professional soldiers of the Continental Army developed a community of their own. The soldiers were "as strict a band of brotherhood as Masons," one later wrote, and their spirit kept them together in the face of misery. They groused, to be sure—sometimes alarmingly. In May 1780, Connecticut troops at Washington's camp in Morristown, New Jersey, staged a brief mutiny. A more serious mutiny erupted on January 1, 1781, when armed units from Pennsylvania stationed in New Jersey marched to Philadelphia demanding their arrears in pay. The Pennsylvania Executive Council met part of the soldiers' demands, but some of the men left the service. Washington ordered subsequent mutinies by New Jersey and Pennsylvania troops suppressed by force.

Occasionally, American officers let their disgruntlement get out of hand. The most notorious such case was that of Benedict Arnold, a general who compiled a distinguished record during the first three years of the war but then came to feel himself shabbily treated by Congress and his superiors. Seeking better rewards for his abilities, he offered to surrender the strategic fort at West Point (which he commanded) to the enemy. Before he could act, however, his plot was discovered, and he fled to the British, serving with them until the end of the war. Among Americans, his name became a synonym for traitor.

What was perhaps the most serious expression of army discontent—one that threatened the future of republican institutions and civilian government in the United Sates—occurred in March 1783, after the fighting was over. At the time, Washington's troops were stationed near Newburgh, New York, waiting to disband and for the Congress to decide how to settle up with them. During the war, the Congress had promised officers a pension of half-pay for life (the custom in Great Britain), but now many veterans demanded instead full pay for six years. When the Congress failed to grant real assurances that any pay would be forthcoming, hotheaded young officers called a meeting that could have led to an armed uprising and military coup. General Washington, who had scrupulously deferred to civilian authority throughout the war, asked permission to address the gathering and, in a dramatic speech, subtly warned the men of all that they might lose by insubordination. A military coup would "open the flood Gates of Civil discord" and "deluge" the nation in blood; loyalty now, he said, would be "one more distinguished proof" of their patriotism. With the fate of the Revolution and the honor of the army hanging in the balance, the movement collapsed. Officers and politicians behind the "conspiracy" were probably only bluffing, using the threat of a discontented army to frighten the states into granting the Congress the power (which it then lacked) to levy taxes so that it would have the funds to pay the army. If so, they may not have realized the potential harm they threatened. In any case, the Continental Army thereafter disbanded without further serious incidents.

WOMEN IN THE CONTENDING ARMIES

Women accompanied many units on both sides, as was common in eighteenth-century warfare. A few were prostitutes. Some were officers' wives or mistresses, but most were the married or common-law consorts of ordinary soldiers. These "camp followers" cooked and washed for the troops, occasionally helped load artillery, and provided most of the nursing care. A certain number in a company were subject to military orders and were authorized to draw rations and pay.

The role of these women found its way into American folklore in the legend of Molly Pitcher (perhaps Mary Ludwig Hays, the wife of a Continental artillery sergeant), who heroically carried water to gunners to cool them and their overheated guns at the Battle of Monmouth Court House in 1778. Numberless, nameless other women accompanying the troops also found themselves under fire. A British officer fighting in New York, for example, reported discovering three American bodies, one a woman with cartridges in her hands. A few women even managed to serve in the Continental Army's ranks. One was discharged only when she was hospitalized for illness and her sex was discovered.

AFRICAN AMERICAN PARTICIPATION IN THE WAR

Early in the war, some royal officials sought to recruit black slaves into the loyalist forces with a promise of freedom. Such was the case with Lord Dunmore, for example, whose black and white troops met disaster at Great Bridge in some of the earliest fighting of the war. Unfortunately for the British, these offers proved counterproductive, frightening and enraging potentially loyalist slaveowners and driving them to the Whig side. Thus it was not until June 30, 1779, that the British commander in chief, Sir Henry Clinton, promised to allow slaves who fled from rebel owners to join the royal troops to "follow . . . any Occupation" they wished. Hedged as this promise of freedom was, news of it spread quickly among the slave communities, and late in the war, enough black people flocked to the British army in South Carolina and Georgia to make feeding and housing them a serious problem.

The British shared the racial prejudices of many Americans, however, and, despite their efforts to recruit African Americans, were reluctant to arm them. Instead, the British put most of the ex-slaves to work as agricultural or construction workers (many of the free and enslaved blacks accompanying American troops were similarly employed). A few relatively

John Laurens, who hoped to raise black troops in South Carolina as a prelude to the general abolition of slavery, was the only member of George Washington's staff to be killed in battle. This commemorative portrait by Charles Willson Peale bears the Latin inscription "sweet and proper it is to die for one's country."

well equipped black British dragoons (mounted troops), however, saw some combat in South Carolina, much to the horror of local Whigs. Some of these troops later formed the nucleus of the postwar First and Second British West India Regiments.

Approximately five thousand African Americans fought against the British and for American independence, hundreds of them in the Continental Army. Many were freemen from Massachusetts and Rhode Island. Several free black men served among the defenders at Bunker Hill, and at least one distinguished himself sufficiently for his commander to commend him as "an experienced officer as well as an excellent soldier."

But farther south, as we have seen, John Laurens, a young Carolina patriot, repeatedly but vainly tried to convince the South Carolina assembly to raise and arm black troops. (On the contrary, the legislature eventually voted to give slaves confiscated from loyalists to white volunteers as a reward for their service in the state regiments.) It is therefore scarcely surprising that, as one Whig put it, many black people were "a little Toryfied," especially in the South.

NATIVE AMERICANS AND THE WAR

At first, most of the approximately 200,000 Native Americans east of the Mississippi River would probably have preferred to remain neutral. Like some Oneidas who were explicit on the subject, other Indian peoples generally hoped to stay out of the white man's conflict. Knowing that Indian allies would cost money and might be unpredictable, the British and Americans initially took them at their word. But Indians' skills and manpower were valuable, and by 1776 both sides sought their assistance. Forced to choose, many Native Americans favored the British, hoping thereby to safeguard their lands. "Remember," one Cherokee chief once told Virginians, the crucial "difference is about our land." Their prewar experience made them believe that British officials would protect them against white settlers whereas an American victory would sweep away all restraints on these incursions. The British were also in a better position to provide trade goods and arms. Accordingly, many Indian peoples, including the Cherokees, Creeks, Choctaws, and Chickasaws in the South, decided that it was in their interest to back the British. Cherokee warriors therefore raided the southern frontier starting in 1776. Virginians, North and South Carolinians, and ultimately Tennesseans countered with expeditions that repeatedly devastated Cherokee towns. But when older chiefs sought peace, Dragging Canoe (Tsi'yugunsi'ny) and the more militant younger men established new communities on the Chickamauga River in northern Georgia and continued to fight.

Pushed and pulled by the British and the Americans, other Indian groups also split. Among these were the members of the powerful Iroquois Confederation in upstate New York. Under the leadership of Thayendanegea—known to whites as Joseph Brant— the Mohawks and some of the other Iroquois nations supported the British, while most of the Oneidas and Tuscaroras joined the Americans. Thus some Iroquois attacked the northern frontiers of New York and Pennsylvania in 1777 and 1778; another Iroquois guided the American expedition that retaliated in 1779. Brother, sometimes quite literally, killed brother.

In other cases, though, the war promoted greater unity among Native Americans. Despite factionalism, the Shawnees, Delawares, Miamis, Wyandots, and others in the Ohio Valley eventually forged an alliance to preserve their control of the area with British support. And a few Native American nations even aided the Americans with relative unanimity. Most of these were small groups, like the Catawbas of South Carolina, who lived in the midst of white settlements.

In sum, the British had more Indian allies, but they seldom made unrestricted use of them. Because Native Americans pursued their own purposes, British control of them was frequently tenuous, and the result could sometimes be counterproductive. In one such incident an Indian attack in the Hudson River Valley resulted in the mistaken scalping of Jane McCrae, the fiancee of a British officer. Whig propagandists exploited this tragedy to the fullest. Neither side, however, had a monopoly on atrocities; both the Americans and the British committed more than their share.

THE WAR IN THE NORTH, 1776–1777

The Revolutionary War can be divided into three phases. In the first, from the outbreak of fighting in 1775 to 1778, most of the important battles took place in New England, New York, New Jersey, and Pennsylvania. During these years, the Americans faced the British alone. But in 1778, France entered the war on the American side, opening the second phase of the war. Fighting in the second phase would rage from 1778 to 1781 mainly in the South, at sea, and on the western frontier. The third phase of the war, from late 1781 to 1783, saw little actual fighting. With American victory assured, attention shifted to the diplomatic maneuvering leading up to the Peace of Paris (1783), which ended the war and recognized American independence.

THE BRITISH ARMY HESITATES: BATTLES IN NEW YORK AND NEW JERSEY

During the first phase of the war, the British concentrated on subduing New England, the hotbed of what they saw as "rebellious principles." Replacing General Gage, the government appointed Sir William Howe as commander in chief of British forces and his brother, Richard Howe, as admiral of the naval forces in North American waters. New York City had been the headquarters of the British army during the late colonial period, and the Howes decided to make it their base of operations. To counter this move, Washington moved his forces to New York

MAP 6-3 The War in the North, 1776–1777
Most of the fighting between the British and Americans during the first part of the war occurred in the North, partly because British authorities assumed that the New England colonies were the most rebellious.

in the spring of 1776. In August 1776, the Howes landed troops on Long Island and, in the Battle of Brooklyn Heights, quickly drove the American forces deployed there from Brooklyn Heights and back to Manhattan Island (see Map 6-3).

Following instructions to negotiate peace as well as wage war, Richard Howe then met with three envoys from Congress on Staten Island on September 11, 1776. The British commanders were prepared to offer fairly generous terms but could not grant independence. The Americans would accept nothing less. So, despite a fine meal of cold meat and wine, the meeting produced no substantive negotiations.

In the ensuing weeks, British forces overwhelmed Washington's forces, driving them out of Manhattan and then, moving north, clearing them from the area around the city at the Battle of White Plains. But the Howes were hesitant to deal a crushing blow, and the Americans were able to retreat across New Jersey into Pennsylvania. The American cause seemed lost, however; the Congress fled from Philadelphia to Baltimore, and the Continental Army almost melted away. The enlistments for most of his troops expired on January 1, and Washington realized that without a success, he would soon have no army left.

On Christmas night, he led his forces back across the icy Delaware from Pennsylvania and, in the Battle of Trenton, launched an unorthodox surprise attack on a garrison of Hessian mercenaries at Trenton, New Jersey, on the morning of December 26. Still in the midst of their Christmas celebrations, the Hessians quickly surrendered. A week later, in the Battle of Princeton, Washington overwhelmed a British force at Princeton, New Jersey. Thereafter, Washington withdrew to winter quarters in Morristown, New Jersey, and the Howes made no further effort to pursue him. Both sides suspended operations until the spring.

"These are the times that try men's souls." So wrote Tom Paine—briefly a volunteer in the Continental Army—of these difficult months. "The summer soldier and the sunshine patriot will, in this crisis, shrink from the service of his country; but he that stands it NOW, deserves the love and thanks of man and woman."

The victories at Trenton and Princeton boosted morale and saved the American cause. But why did the Howes not annihilate the Continental Army while they had the chance? Perhaps, as a favorite Whig ditty had it, it was because Sir William Howe was "snug" abed with his mistress in New York. More significantly, the Howe brothers themselves were not entirely in favor of the war. Seeking to restore peace as well as end the rebellion, they wanted to regain loyal subjects, not alienate them. But if they had inflicted a crushing defeat on the Americans, they would have risked making them permanent enemies of British rule. In short, the British had sound political reasons for not beating the Americans too thoroughly. By the time it later became apparent that this cautious strategy was not working and the Howe brothers had been replaced with more aggressive commanders, the British had lost their best chance to win the war.

THE YEAR OF THE HANGMAN: VICTORY AT SARATOGA AND WINTER AT VALLEY FORGE

Contemporaries called 1777 the Year of the Hangman because the triple sevens suggested a row of gallows. Living up to its ominous name, it was indeed a crucial year for the American cause.

The British began the year by mounting a major effort to end the rebellion. Their strategy was to send a force south from Canada down the Hudson River to link up with the Howes in New York City, separate New England from the rest of the states, and then crush the rebellion in that most recalcitrant region. Unfortunately, there was no effort to coordinate strategy between the forces advancing from Canada and the forces under the command of the Howes in New York. Thus in the end, poorly planned, poorly executed, and unsupported from the South, the campaign ended in disaster for the British.

Some five thousand Redcoats and three thousand German mercenaries assembled in Canada during the winter of 1776–1777. Ravaged by disease, the troops were unable to bury their dead until the frozen ground thawed in the spring. (To amuse himself, the officer in charge of the morgue arranged the dead around a room in lifelike poses, a morbid joke that did nothing to calm the nerves of survivors.) Under the command of the jaunty, high-living, and popular "Gentleman Johnny" Burgoyne, the army finally set off in June with 1,500 horses hauling its heavy artillery and ponderous supply train. A second, smaller column, supported by an Indian force under Thayendanegea (Joseph Brant) set out to the west to capture an American fort near Oriskany, New York, and then join up with Burgoyne's main force.

Crossing Lake Champlain, Burgoyne's army made a splendid spectacle. Indians in lightly bobbing canoes led the way, followed by row after row of boats filled with uniformed regulars resplendent in the bright sunshine. On July 5, Burgoyne's army recaptured Fort Ticonderoga, but success eluded him after that.

Trouble began as the troops started moving overland through the woods at the southern end of the lake. Forced to clear away huge trees in its path felled by American axmen, the army crawled along at only 2 or 3 miles a day. Early in August, the column under Colonel Barry St. Leger that had been sent west from the Montreal area failed to capture the American fort near Oriskany and turned back to Canada. Burgoyne's Indian allies under Joseph Brant likewise went home. Promised reinforcements never arrived. Ten days later, a Whig militia force wiped out a force of eight hundred men that

Burgoyne had sent into Vermont to round up badly needed horses.

By October 1777, Burgoyne's army was down to less than six thousand men and facing disaster. A force of nearly three thousand Continentals and nine thousand militia, commanded by General Horatio Gates, had now assembled to confront the British. The Americans exerted relentless pressure on the harassed and dispirited invaders. Unable to break through the American lines, Burgoyne surrendered to Gates following the Battle of Saratoga on October 17, 1777.

Burgoyne's defeat was a stunning reversal for the British. It also gave the American cause a significant boost in the eyes of foreign observers. It would prove an important factor in convincing the French, in particular, eager for a way to strike back at their old enemy, the British, to recognize America as an ally and join the fighting on the American side.

While Burgoyne was making his way to disaster, General William Howe, rather than moving north to support him, was making plans to destroy Washington's army and capture Philadelphia. In July 1777, Howe's troops sailed from New York to Chesapeake Bay and from there marched on Philadelphia from the south. They met Washington's army on the banks of Brandywine Creek, near the Pennsylvania–Delaware border. An American teenager who fought for the first time that day recalled that some men stiffened their courage by drinking a concoction of liquor and gunpowder. The young man himself could not stomach it, but it may have worked for some of his companions. They put up a good fight before giving way with a loss of 1,200 killed or captured (twice as many as the British).

Howe occupied Philadelphia, and his men settled down in comfortable winter quarters. The Congress fled to York, Pennsylvania, and the Continental Army established its own winter camp outside Philadelphia, at Valley Forge. Here Washington was joined by his wife, Martha, in a small stone farmhouse, surrounded by the log huts that his men built for themselves.

The Continental Army's miserable winter at **Valley Forge** has become legendary in American history. Suffering from cold, disease, and starvation, as many as 2,500 soldiers died. Meanwhile, some congressmen and a few unhappy officers intrigued unsuccessfully to replace Washington with Gates as commander in chief. Yet despite the suffering of the troops, the Continental Army managed, over the course of the winter, to transform itself into a disciplined professional army. Under the watchful eye of General von Steuben, the soldiers drilled endlessly.

Just before the encampment broke up in the spring, they put on an impressive demonstration of their new skills, including a precisely timed wave of massed musket volleys. Pleased observers felt that Washington at last had an army capable of meeting the British on equal terms. With the coming of spring, American prospects improved dramatically.

THE WAR WIDENS, 1778–1781

Since late 1776, Benjamin Franklin and a team of American diplomats had been in Paris negotiating French support for the patriot cause. In the winter of 1777–1778, aware that a Franco-American alliance was close, Parliament belatedly tried to end the rebellion by giving the Americans everything they wanted except independence itself. A peace commission sailed to America with authorization to grant the former colonies full autonomy, including the exclusive right to tax themselves, in return for a resumption of allegiance to the crown. But France and the United States concluded an alliance on February 6, 1778, and news of it reached America before the British commission arrived. Seeing independence within reach, Congress refused to negotiate.

Foreign intervention would transform the American Revolution into a virtual world war, engaging British forces in heavy fighting not only in North America but also in the West Indies and India. In the end, had it not been for French assistance, the American side probably would not have won the clear-cut victory it did.

THE UNITED STATES GAINS AN ALLY

If the American victory at Saratoga had persuaded the French that the United States had a viable future, Washington's defeat at Brandywine Creek suggested it was a fragile one. Hoping to get even with their old enemy, Britain, the French had already been secretly supplying some aid to the United States. They now became convinced that they needed to act quickly lest further reverses force the Americans to agree to a reconciliation with Britain. The agreements they signed with the United States included both a commercial treaty and a military alliance. Both sides promised to fight together until Britain recognized the independence of the United States, and France pledged not to seek the return of lands in North America.

French entry into the war was the first step in the consolidation of a formidable alliance of European powers eager to see Britain humbled and to gain trading rights in the former British colonies. In turn, France persuaded Spain to declare war on Britain in June 1779. Unlike France, Spain never recognized the independence of the United States and would give it only minimal financial aid. Spain did, however, contribute important logistical support. Much of the salt used to preserve American soldiers' provisions came from Spanish possessions. American agents also purchased other supplies in Spanish New Orleans, and American privateers used New Orleans as a base. More important, the Spanish fleet augmented the naval power of the countries arrayed against Great Britain.

Meanwhile, Catherine the Great of Russia suggested that European powers form a League of Armed Neutrality to protect their trade with the United States and other warring countries against British interference. Denmark and Sweden soon joined; Austria, the Netherlands, Portugal, Prussia, and Sicily eventually followed. Britain, however, quickly went to war with Holland, ostensibly over another issue (to avoid war with the League), but really to cut off Dutch trade with the United States.

Great Britain thus found itself nearly completely isolated and even, briefly, threatened with invasion. In the spring of 1779, a joint Franco-Spanish fleet tried to ferry thousands of French troops across the English Channel but abandoned the effort after weeks at sea. These threats did not frighten the British leaders into suing for peace. On the contrary, they inspired a wave of patriotism that swelled enlistments in the armed forces. But facing challenges on a worldwide scale, British officials were forced to make several important changes in policy and strategy.

Accordingly, early in the spring of 1778, the British replaced the Howes with a tough new commander, Sir Henry Clinton, instructing him to detach some of his troops to attack the French West Indies. To replace them, Clinton sought closer cooperation with Britain's Indian and loyalist allies. Knowing that he now faced a serious French threat, Clinton also began consolidating his forces. He evacuated Philadelphia and pulled his troops slowly back across New Jersey to New York.

On June 28, 1778, Washington caught up with the British and engaged them at the Battle of Monmouth Court House. The day was hot and the battle hard-fought. For a while, it looked as if the now well-trained Americans might win, but a mix-up in orders cost Washington the victory. This inconclusive battle proved to be the last major engagement in the North for the rest of the war. Clinton withdrew to New York, and Continental troops occupied the hills along the Hudson Valley north of the city. The war shifted to other fronts.

FIGHTING ON THE FRONTIER AND AT SEA

Native Americans called Kentucky "a dark and bloody ground," a designation that took on added meaning when Indians began raiding the territory in 1777 on British instructions. The nerve center for coordinating these attacks was the British post of Detroit, and the Americans accordingly made plans to capture it. Two expeditions from Pittsburgh in 1778 failed completely. A third, under Virginian George Rogers Clark, although it never reached Detroit, was more successful (see Map 6-4). In July 1778 Clark's force of 175 frontiersmen captured three key British settlements in the Mississippi Valley: Kaskaskia, Cahokia, and Vincennes. These successes may have strengthened American claims to the West at the end of the war.

Blood also ran on the Pennsylvania and upstate New York frontiers. In the summer of 1778, a British force of one hundred loyalists and five hundred Indians struck settlers in north-central Pennsylvania's Wyoming Valley. After the Americans' Forty Fort surrendered on July 4, raiders killed the wounded and fleeing defenders. A similar mix of attackers in November 1778 burned farmsteads and slaughtered civilians at Cherry Valley, New York. Both raids became the stuff of legends and stimulated equally savage reprisals against the Indians. Congress authorized an expedition against the Iroquois, and in the late summer of 1779, more than four thousand Continental soldiers and state militia swept through the Finger Lakes region of New York, destroying forty-one Indian villages and the crops that supported them. Among the Seneca, not enough food remained to keep even "a child one day from perishing with hunger." As a result, some five thousand Iroquois sought refuge with the British at Fort Niagara.

Anglo-American clashes at sea had begun in 1775, shortly after the Battles of Lexington and Concord, and would continue until the end of the war as Americans struggled to break the British navy's blockade. Great Britain was the preeminent sea power of the age, and the United States never came close to matching it, in either the number or the size of its ships. But Congress did its best to challenge the British at sea. In 1775, it authorized the construction of thirteen frigates—medium-sized, relatively fast ships, mounting thirty-two guns—as well as the purchase of several merchant vessels for conversion to warships. By contrast, the Royal Navy in 1779 had

"Paul Jones Shooting a Sailor." Color engraving from the Olds Collection #366, no negative number. Collection of The New York Historical Society.

This engraving, published in London in 1779, shows an apocryphal incident during the battle in which John Paul Jones's ship Bon Homme Richard *defeated the British* Serapis. *During the fighting, Jones supposedly shot an American sailor who attempted to lower the ship's flag as a sign of surrender; actually Jones only knocked him down with a pistol. Legend (and the artist) may have confused this incident with another earlier one—while Jones was still a Scotsman (note the bonnet)—in which Jones did kill a mutineer.*

more than a hundred large and heavily armed "ships of the line." The Americans therefore engaged in what was essentially a guerrilla war at sea. Their naval flag, appropriately, pictured a rattlesnake and bore the motto, "Don't Tread on Me."

The country's first naval hero, Scottish-born John Paul Jones, was primarily a hit-and-run raider. Originally named only John Paul, he had gone to sea at age 12. He took the name Jones as an alias after he killed a fellow sailor during a mutiny. In the colonies by chance when the war broke out, this adventurer offered his services to the Congress. As commander of the new frigate *Ranger*, it was Jones who brought news of the American victory at Saratoga to France in early 1777. After delivering the news—an announcement that helped Franklin clinch the alliance with France—Jones raided the British coast, inspiring local panic.

Franklin helped secure Jones an old French merchant ship, which he outfitted for war and renamed the *Bon Homme Richard* in honor of Franklin's famous *Poor Richard's Almanac*. After capturing seventeen enemy vessels, he encountered the formidable *H.M.S. Serapis* in the North Sea on September 23, 1779. Completely outgunned, Jones brought his ship close enough to make his small-arms fire more effective. Asked by the British if he were surrendering, Jones gave the legendary reply, "I have not yet begun to fight." Lashing the two ships together, Jones and his men battled the crew of the *Serapis* for more than four hours, much of it by moonlight. Finally, the *Serapis* surrendered. Jones's crew took possession of the British vessel and left the crippled *Bon Homme Richard* to sink.

The Congress and the individual states supplemented America's naval forces by commissioning individual sea captains to outfit their merchant vessels with guns and act as privateers. In effect legalized pirates, these privateers preyed on British shipping. They sold the goods they seized and divided the proceeds among their crews according to rank. The crews of captured vessels became prisoners of war. Successful privateering could bring wealth but required stealth and speed. One particularly fast vessel cruised off New York towing a buoy to make itself look like a lumbering merchantman under full sail. Once within range of a potential prize, the crew cut away the buoy and took the cannons out from under wraps. Such tactics paid off. Some two thousand American privateers captured more than six hundred British ships and forced the British Navy to spread itself thin doing convoy duty.

THE LAND WAR MOVES SOUTH

During the first three years of the war, the British had made little effort to mobilize what they believed to be considerable loyalist strength in the South. In 1778, however, facing a threat from France and with their forces in the North concentrated and inactive, they gave Southern loyalists a key role in a new strategy for subduing the rebellion. After first sending Redcoats sweeping through a large area, they would leave behind a Tory militia to reestablish loyalty to the crown and suppress local Whigs. The British hoped by this strategy to recapture everything from Georgia to Virginia; they would deal with New England later.

The British southern strategy began to unfold in November 1778, when General Clinton dispatched 3,500 troops to take control of Georgia (see Map 6-5). Meeting only light resistance, they quickly seized

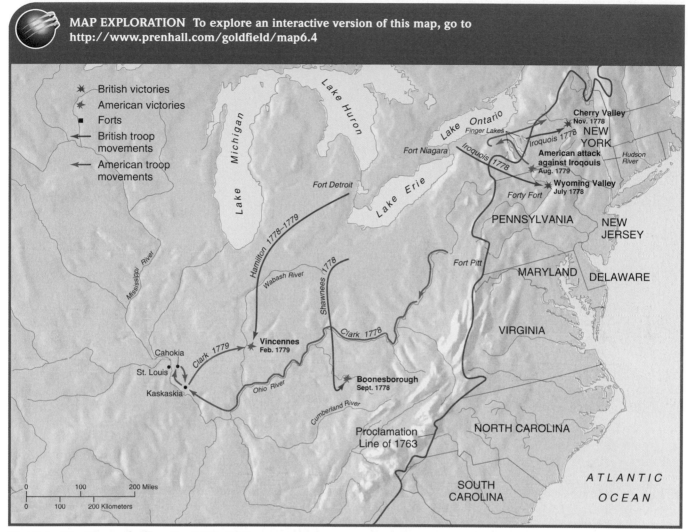

MAP EXPLORATION To explore an interactive version of this map, go to http://www.prenhall.com/goldfield/map6.4

MAP 6-4   **The War on the Frontier, 1778–1779**
Significant battles in the Mississippi Valley and the frontiers of the seaboard states added to the ferocity of the fighting and strengthened some American claims to western lands.

Savannah and Augusta. Indeed, enough inhabitants seemed happy to have the British back for the old colonial government to be restored under civilian control. After their initial success, however, the British suffered some serious setbacks. The Spanish entered the war and seized British outposts on the Mississippi and Mobile rivers. And in February 1779, at the Battle of Kettle Creek, South Carolina's Whig militia decimated a loyalist militia contingent that was trying to fight its way from the North Carolina back-country to Georgia to join up with British troops.

But the Americans could not beat the British army. In late September and early October 1779, a combined force of 5,500 American and French troops, supported by French warships, laid siege to Savannah. Moving too slowly to encircle the city, they allowed British reinforcements to get through.

Then, impatient to get their ships away from the hurricane-prone coast, the French forced the Americans to launch a premature assault on the city on October 9. The assault failed, and the French sailed off.

The way was now open for the British to attack Charleston, the military key to the Lower South. In December 1779, Clinton sailed through storm-battered seas from New York to the Carolina coast with about nine thousand troops. In the Battle of Charleston, he encircled the city, trapping the patriot forces inside. On May 12, 1780, more than five thousand Continentals and militia laid down their arms—the worst American defeat of the war and the largest single loss of United States troops to a foreign army until the surrender of American forces in the Philippines to Japan in 1942. Not everyone—even in Charleston—gave up. One woman there attacked a loyalist quartered in her house with an ax.

MAP 6-5   The War in the South, 1778–1781
During the latter part of the war, most of the major engagements occurred in the South. British forces won most of the early ones but could not control the immense territory involved and eventually surrendered at Yorktown.

But the British were now poised to sweep all the South before them. Most local Whigs, thinking the Revolution over, at first offered little resistance to

Redcoats striking into the Carolina backcountry. At the South Carolina–North Carolina border, British troops under Colonel Banastre Tarleton overwhelmed a detachment of 350 Virginia Continentals trying to retreat homeward after coming too late to Charleston's aid. When the Continentals offered to surrender, Tarleton slaughtered most of them. So complete did the British success seem that Clinton tried to force the American troops whom he had taken prisoner to resume their duties as British subjects and join the loyalist militia. Thinking that matters were now well in hand, Clinton sailed back to New York, leaving the southern troops under the command of Lord Cornwallis.

Clinton's confidence that the South had returned securely to the loyalist camp was premature. Atrocities like Tarleton's slaughter of the Virginians inflamed anti-British feelings. And Clinton's decision to force former rebels into the loyalist militia backfired, infuriating real loyalists—who saw their enemies getting off lightly—as well as Whigs. Atrocities and reprisals mounted on both sides as Whigs continued to defy British authority. "Tarleton's Quarter" and "a Georgia parole" (a bullet in the back) became Whig euphemisms for "take no prisoners."

AMERICAN COUNTERATTACKS

In the summer of 1780, Congress dispatched a substantial Continental force to the South under General Horatio Gates, the hero of Saratoga. Local patriots flocked to join him. But Gates was reckless. Pushing through North Carolina, his men tried to subsist on green corn. Weakened by diarrhea, they blundered into Cornwallis's British army near Camden, South

Carolina, on August 16, and suffered a complete rout. More than one thousand Americans were killed or wounded and many captured. Gates—transformed from the hero of Saratoga into the goat of Camden—fled to Hillsborough, North Carolina.

American morale revived on October 7, 1780, when "over mountain men" (militia) from Virginia, western North and South Carolina, and what is today eastern Tennessee inflicted a defeat on the British at Kings Mountain, South Carolina. And in December 1780, Nathanael Greene replaced the discredited Gates, bringing competent leadership to the Continentals in the South.

The daring and resourceful Greene realized that he would need an unorthodox strategy to defeat Cornwallis's larger army of seasoned professional troops. He divided his forces, keeping roughly half with him in northeastern South Carolina and sending the other half westward under General Daniel Morgan. Cornwallis ordered Tarleton to pursue Morgan's troops, who retreated northward until they reached an open area in South Carolina called Hannah's Cowpens. There Morgan rallied his men, reportedly inspiring them with the sight of his scarred back; he had been flogged by order of a British court martial during the French and Indian War. At the Battle of Cowpens on January 17, 1781, Morgan cleverly posted his least reliable troops, the militia, in the front line, telling them to run after firing two volleys. When Tarleton attacked, the militia fired and withdrew. Thinking that the American ranks had broken, the Redcoats charged—straight into devastating fire from Morgan's Continentals. Tarleton escaped, but his reputation for invincibility had been destroyed.

Cornwallis now badly needed a battlefield victory. Burning his army's excess baggage, he set off in hot pursuit of Greene and Morgan, who had rejoined forces. The Continentals had the advantage of knowing the country, which was laced with rain-swollen rivers. Greene's officers often arranged to have boats waiting at the deeper crossings. Finally, on February 13, 1781, Greene's tired men crossed the Dan River into Virginia, and Cornwallis gave up the chase, marching his equally exhausted Redcoats southward. To his surprise, Cornwallis now found himself pursued—though cautiously, to be sure—by Greene. On March 15, the opposing forces met at Guilford Court House (near present-day Greensboro, North Carolina) in one of the war's bloodiest battles. At one point, with the two sides tangled in hand-to-hand combat, the Americans drove the British back. To blunt the onslaught, Cornwallis fired cannon directly into the melee, mowing down friend and foe alike. Thanks

to such tactics, the British still held the field at the end of the day. But, as one Englishman observed, "another such victory would destroy the British Army." Cornwallis had to retreat to the coastal town of Wilmington, North Carolina, to rest and regroup. Abandoning his most seriously wounded men, he carried the rest back in wagons, their broken bones poking through their wounds as they bounced along rutted roads.

By the late summer of 1781, British fortunes were waning in the Lower South. The Redcoats held only the larger towns and the immediately surrounding countryside. With their superior staying power, they won most major engagements, but these victories brought them no lasting gain. As General Greene observed of the Americans, "We fight, get beat, and rise and fight again." When the enemy pressed him too hard, Greene retreated out of reach, advancing again as the British withdrew.

Patriot guerrilla forces, led by such colorful figures as "Gamecock" Thomas Sumter, and "Swamp Fox" Francis Marion, disrupted British communications between their Charleston headquarters and outlying garrisons. The loyalist militias that the British had hoped would pacify the countryside proved unequal to the task. Whig militiamen had often driven out any loyalists before a British sweep. And those who did welcome the British found themselves the targets of Whig retaliation once the Redcoats had left. Thus, although Greene never defeated the Redcoats outright, his campaign was a strategic success. The British could not hold what they had taken; the Americans had time on their side.

Disappointed and frustrated, Cornwallis decided to conquer Virginia to cut off Greene's line of supply and to destroy Whig resolve. British forces, including units commanded by turncoat Benedict Arnold, had already been raiding the state. Cornwallis marched north to join them, reaching Yorktown, Virginia, during the summer of 1781.

The final military showdown of the war was at hand. By now, five thousand French soldiers were in America ready to fight alongside the Continentals, and a large French fleet in the West Indies had orders to support an attack on the British in North America. Faking preparations for an assault on British-occupied New York, the Continentals (commanded by Washington) and the French headed for the Chesapeake. Cornwallis and his six thousand Redcoats soon found themselves besieged behind their fortifications at Yorktown by 8,800 Americans and 7,800 French. A French naval victory gave the allies temporary command of the waters around Yorktown. Cornwallis had nowhere to go, and Clinton—still in New York—could not reinforce him quickly enough. On October 19, 1781, the British army surrendered. The defeated men filed between rows of American and French troops to lay down their arms while a British band mournfully played a tune reputedly called "The World Turned Upside Down." When he learned the news in London, the British prime minister, Lord North, took it like "a ball in his breast." "It is all over," he groaned.

THE AMERICAN VICTORY, 1782–1783

The British surrender at Yorktown marked the end of major fighting in North America, though skirmishes continued for another year. In April 1782, the Royal Navy defeated the French fleet in the Caribbean, strengthening the British bargaining position. George III had insisted on continuing the war for so long because he feared that conceding American independence would threaten British rule in Canada and the West Indies. But the majority in Parliament now felt

that enough men and money had been wasted trying to keep the Americans within the empire. In March 1782, the king accepted Lord North's resignation and appointed Lord Rockingham as prime minister, with a mandate to make peace.

THE PEACE OF PARIS

The peace negotiations, which took place in Paris, were lengthy. The Americans demanded independence, handsome territorial concessions—Franklin, the senior American negotiator, asked for all of Canada—and access to the rich British-controlled fishing grounds in the North Atlantic. The new British prime minister, Lord Shelburne (Rockingham had died in 1782), was inclined to be conciliatory. By making concessions, he hoped to help British merchants recover their lost colonial trade. The French had achieved their objective—to weaken the British—and now wanted out of an increasingly costly worldwide war. Spain had not won its most important goal, the recovery of British-held Gibraltar, and thus gave the Americans no support at all.

The American negotiators, Franklin, John Adams, and John Jay, masterfully threaded their way among these conflicting interests. With good reason, they feared that the French and Spanish would strike a bargain with the British at the expense of the United States—one that might, for example, confine the new country to a narrow coastal strip or allow Britain to retain areas such as New York City and Charleston, which its troops still occupied. As a result, the Americans disregarded Congress's instructions to avoid making peace unilaterally. Instead, they secretly worked out their own arrangements with the British that would meet Shelburne's objective of restoring Anglo-American commercial ties. On November 30, 1782, the negotiators signed a preliminary Anglo-American treaty of peace. Its terms were embodied in the final **Peace of Paris**, signed by all the belligerents on September 3, 1783.

The Peace of Paris gave the United States nearly everything it sought except Canada (which

The surrender of Lord Cornwallis at Yorktown on October 19, 1781, led to the British decision to withdraw from the war. Cornwallis, who claimed to be ill, absented himself from the ceremony and is not in the picture. Washington, who is astride the horse under the American flag, designated General Benjamin Lincoln (on the white horse in the center) as the one to accept the submission of a subordinate British officer. John Trumbull, who painted The Battle of Bunker Hill *and some three hundred other scenes from the Revolutionary War, finished this painting while he was in London about fifteen years after the events depicted. A large copy of the work now hangs in the rotunda of the United States Capitol in Washington, D.C.*

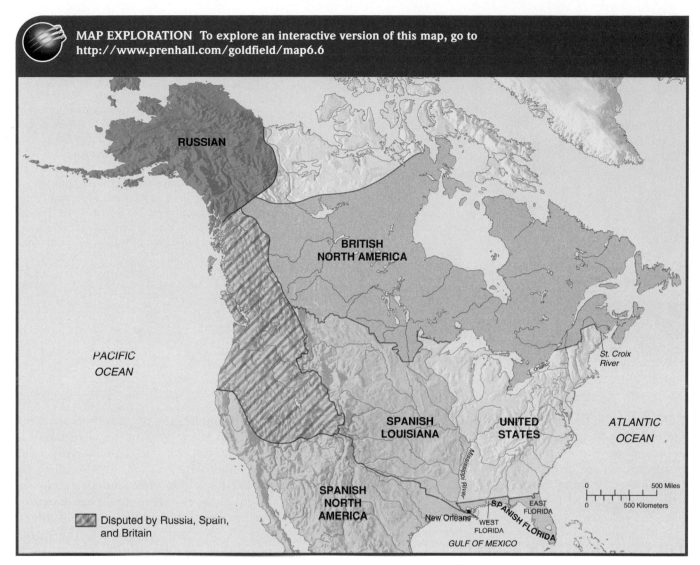

MAP EXPLORATION To explore an interactive version of this map, go to
http://www.prenhall.com/goldfield/map6.6

Disputed by Russia, Spain, and Britain

MAP 6-6　North America after the Peace of Paris, 1783
The results of the American Revolution redrew the map of North America, confining Britain to Canada and giving the United States most of the area east of the Mississippi River, though Spain controlled its mouth for most of the next twenty years.

was never really a serious issue). Great Britain acknowledged that the United States was "free, sovereign and independent." The northern boundary of the new nation extended west from the St. Croix River (which separated Maine from Nova Scotia) past the Great Lakes to what were thought to be the headwaters of the Mississippi River (see Map 6-6). The Mississippi itself—down to just north of New Orleans—formed the western border. Spain acquired the provinces of East and West Florida from Britain. This territory included a substantial chunk of present-day Louisiana, Mississippi, Alabama, and Geor-

gia. The treaty did not, however, provide the United States with access to the Gulf of Mexico, a situation that would be a source of diplomatic friction for years.

Several provisions of the treaty addressed important economic issues. Adams, on behalf of his fellow New Englanders, insisted on a provision granting American fishermen access to the waters off eastern Canada. The treaty also required that British forces, on quitting American soil, were to leave behind all American-owned property, including slaves. Another provision declared existing debts between citizens of

Benjamin West's painting of the American commissioners who negotiated the Peace of Paris includes, from left to right, John Jay, John Adams, Benjamin Franklin, and Franklin's grandson, who served as the commissioners' secretary. A fourth American commissioner who arrived only at the end of the negotiations, Henry Laurens, stands in the background. The British commissioners, who would have occupied the blank space on the right, did not sit for their portraits. Chagrin at the outcome of the war probably contributed to their absence, but an apocryphal story attributed it to the reluctance of Richard Oswald, who was blind in one eye, to have his portrait painted.

Britain and the United States still valid, giving British merchants hope of collecting on their American accounts. Congress was to "recommend" that the states restore rights and property taken from loyalists during the war. Nothing was said about the slave trade, which Jay had hoped to ban.

THE COMPONENTS OF SUCCESS

The War for Independence was over. In December 1783, the last British transports put to sea with troops evacuated from New York. Despite the provisions of the peace treaty and the objections of southern planters, about three thousand African Americans went with them. General Guy Carleton, who had replaced Clinton as commander in chief after Yorktown, agreed to keep a list of these people, but he refused to renege on British promises of freedom for slaves who fled rebel owners. (Carleton's list survived and has recently been published.)

Washington's Continental Army had already disbanded in the summer of 1783 (but not, as we have seen, before a dispute over pay came close to provoking a military coup). On December 4, the American commander said an emotional farewell to his officers at New York City's Fraunces Tavern, and on December 23, at Annapolis, Maryland, he resigned his commission to the Congress. Like the legendary citizen-soldier Cincinnatus, who after defending the ancient Roman Republic gave up his power and went back to plowing his land, Washington went home to Mount Vernon. By now he had won the respect of friend and foe alike. "You are," one British aristocrat would write to him, "the only human being for whom I ever felt an awful reverence." Only a natural genius, other Britons said, could have accomplished what he did. How else could one explain the victory of ragtag provincials over the world's greatest military and naval power?

Washington's leadership was just one of the reasons why the Americans won the Revolutionary War. French assistance played a crucial role. Some historians contend that without the massive infusion of French men and money in 1781, the Revolution would have failed. The British also contributed heavily to their own downfall. Their fatal mistakes included bureaucratic inefficiency, hesitant command, and, worst of all, overconfidence. British authorities consistently underestimated the enormous difficulty of waging war 3,000 miles from home in an era of slow and uncertain communications. The people they sought to conquer were sparsely distributed over an area that stretched more than 1,500 miles from Maine to Georgia. There was no natural center whose capture would severely cripple the rest of the country. British forces occupied, at one time or another, most of the important seaports and state capitals—Boston, New York, Philadelphia,

Charleston, and Savannah—but patriot forces driven from these centers could simply regroup in another location. Finally, Great Britain had tried to solve a political problem by military means. An occupying army is far more likely to alienate people than to secure their goodwill.

Yet it took 175,000 to 200,000 soldiers—Continentals and militia troops—to prevent Great Britain from recovering the colonies. Of these, some seven thousand died in battle. Perhaps ten thousand more succumbed to disease while on active duty, another 8,500 died while prisoners of war, and nearly 1,500 were reported missing in action. More than eight thousand were wounded and survived. Those who served in the Continental Army, probably more than half of all who fought, served the longest and saw the most action. Their casualty rate—30 to 40 percent—may have been the highest of any war in which the United States has been engaged. In proportion to the population, these losses would be the equivalent of more than two million people in the United States today.

WAR AND SOCIETY, 1775–1783

Regular combatants were not the only ones to suffer during the struggle for independence. Eight years of warfare also produced profound dislocations throughout American society. Military service wrenched families apart, sporadic raids by each side brought the war home to vast numbers of people, and everyone endured economic disruptions. As a forge of nationhood, the Revolution tested all Americans, whatever their standing as citizens.

THE WOMEN'S WAR

Everywhere women had to see their husbands, sons, brothers, and fiancés go off to fight and die. Like Mary Silliman in Connecticut, they waited, trying to stay calm until they knew "what tidings God" had for them. At first, with spirits still running high, Mary's letters to her husband, Selleck, reveal an affectionate lightheartedness. "These cold nights make me shudder for you," she wrote, adding "Oh, King George, what hardships does thy tyranny put thy late subjects to!" Selleck responded with similarly suggestive banter. Later, the couple's letters grew less playful. Then her husband was captured. The daily round of domestic duties helped to keep her going, but his extended absence increased her burdens and enlarged her responsibilities.

Such circumstances elevated women's domestic status. Couples began referring to "our"—not "my" or "your"—property. Wives frequently grew more knowledgeable about a family's financial condition than long-absent husbands. "What shall I do my Dearest? I wish I had Your Advice," wrote Selleck Silliman to his wife after he had been released from captivity.

Women also assumed new public roles during the conflict. Some nursed the wounded. More wove cloth for uniforms. The Ladies' Association of Philadelphia was established in 1780 to demonstrate women's patriotism and raise money to buy shirts for the army. Though women might not be able to march "to glory by the same path as the Men," wrote the association's founder, "we should at least equal and sometimes surpass them in our love for the public good." Similar associations formed in other states.

Despite their increasing private responsibilities and new public activities, it did not occur to most women to encroach very far on traditional male prerogatives. When John Adams's wife, Abigail, urged him and the Second Continental Congress to "Remember the Ladies," she was not expecting equal political rights. What she wanted, rather, was some legal protections for women and recognition of their value and need for autonomy in the domestic sphere. "Remember," she cautioned, "all Men would be Tyrants if they could." Why not, then, make it impossible for "the vicious and lawless" to abuse women with impunity? "I will never consent to have our sex considered in an inferior point of light," she wrote.

Republican ideology, responding to the changing status of women, assigned them a role that was at once exalted and subordinate. It was their job to nurture wise, virtuous, and public-spirited men. It was this view of women that would prevail in the post-Revolutionary era.

EFFECT OF THE WAR ON AFRICAN AMERICANS

In the northern states, where slavery was already economically marginal and where black men were welcome as volunteers in the Continental Army, the Revolutionary War helped to bring an end to slavery, although it remained legal there for some time (see Chapter 7). In the South, however, slavery was integral to the economy, and white planters viewed it as crucial to their postwar recovery. Thus, although British efforts to recruit black soldiers brought freedom to thousands and temporarily undermined slavery in the South, the war ultimately strengthened the institution, especially in

American soldiers at Yorktown in 1781 as drawn by a young officer in the French army, Jean-Baptiste-Antoine de Verger. The African American on the left is an infantryman of the First Rhode Island Regiment; the next, a musketeer; the third, with the fringed jacket, a rifleman. The man on the right is a Continental artilleryman, holding a lighted match used to fire cannons.

the Carolinas and Georgia. Of the African Americans who left with the British at the end of the war, many, both slave and free, went to the West Indies. Others settled in Canada, and some eventually went back to Africa, where Britain established the colony of Sierra Leone for them.

THE WAR'S IMPACT ON NATIVE AMERICANS

Survivors among the approximately thirteen thousand Native Americans who fought for the British did not have the option of leaving with them at the end of the war. How many died during the war is not known, but certainly many did. Not only the Iroquois but other groups lost much. The Americans repeatedly invaded the Cherokees' homeland in the southern Appalachian Mountains. "There was no withstanding them," recalled a Cherokee chief of the many frontiersmen who assaulted his people. "They dyed their hands in the blood of many of our Women and children, burnt seventeen towns, destroyed all our provisions," and spread famine across the land. Americans also attacked the Shawnees of Ohio. In one notorious incident, militiamen even massacred peaceful Christian Indians at Gnadenhutten, Ohio.

With the peace treaty of 1783, Britain surrendered its territory east of the Mississippi, shocking and infuriating the Native Americans living there. They had not surrendered, and none of them had been at the negotiations in Paris. The Iroquois told a British commander that if the English really "had basely betrayed them by pretending to give up their Country to the Americans without their Consent, or Consulting them, it was an Act of Cruelty and injustice that Christians only were capable of doing." With the Americans now claiming their country by conquest, the Revolutionary War was for most Native Americans a disaster that opened the floodgates to a torrent of white settlers. During 1779 and 1780 alone, approximately 20,000 settlers streamed into Kentucky. Five years later, there were reportedly 2,200 squatter families in parts of Ohio where the United States government forbade settlement.

ECONOMIC DISRUPTION

The British and American armies both needed enormous quantities of supplies. This heavy demand disrupted the normal distribution of goods and drove up real prices seven- or eightfold. The widespread use of depreciating paper money by the American side amplified this rise in prices and triggered severe inflation.

When the British did not simply seize what they needed, they paid for it in hard currency—gold and silver. American commanders, by contrast, had to rely on paper money because the Congress and the states had almost no hard currency at their disposal. The Continental dollar, however, steadily declined in value, and by March 1780, the Congress was forced to admit officially that it was worthless. (The popular expression, "not worth a Continental" suggests that the public had long since reached this conclusion.) Thus, not surprisingly, American farmers and merchants, whatever their political opinions, sometimes sold food to the British while their own forces went hungry.

Necessity, not folly, drove Congress and the states to rely on the printing press. Rather than alienate citizens by immediately raising taxes to pay for the war, the states printed paper money supposedly redeemable through future tax revenues. Because the quantity of this paper money rose faster than the supply of goods and services, prices skyrocketed, and the value of the money plunged. By April 1779, as

FROM THEN TO NOW

The American Revolution and the Teaching of American History

In October 1994, TV viewers saw politically conservative talk show host Rush Limbaugh hold up a history book and begin ripping out pages. "Here's Paul Revere. He's gone," he exclaimed, and out went a page. "Here's George Washington. . . . He's gone. . . ." More pages bit the dust. "This is what we're doing to American history with this stupid new book, folks." The volume that prompted his outburst was the National History Standards—"the standards from hell" according to conservative critics. In response to such outbursts, Gary Nash, a leading author of the standards and an expert in early American history, repeatedly went on television to defend them, appearing in one twenty-four hour period on ABC, NBC, and PBS.

The furor arose out of a bipartisan attempt to improve education in the nation's schools. In 1989, President George H. W. Bush and the nation's governors announced that it was time "to establish clear national performance goals, goals that will make us internationally competitive . . . in the twenty-first century." The plan called for knowledgeable professionals to establish voluntary guidelines governing what schools should expect students to know about several core subjects, including history. The development of the history standards, which involved thousands of historians and history teachers, took more than two and a half years.

The heated reaction to the standards caught many by surprise, but it probably should not have. History, Nash has pointed out, is "unceasingly controversial because it provides so much of the substance for the way a society defines itself." This is certainly true of the history of the American Revolution—the focus of much of the ire of the standard's critics—because it is from the Revolution that the founding propositions of the nation emerged.

The authors of the standards wanted students to learn the results of recent research that has given voice to African Americans, Native Americans, women, and ordinary people and documented their active role in history. But critics complained that including this material would unduly diminish coverage of prominent figures like Revere and Washington. They also worried that calling attention, say, to African American life under slavery or to such incidents as the Paxton Boys' assault on their Indian neighbors would darken the narrative of American history.

How should one tell the story of the United States? A state legislature once resolved that school textbooks should emphasize "the history of hearts and souls inspired by wonderful American principles and traditions." Those who wrote the National History Standards believed that the "governing narrative" should be "the struggle to fulfill the American ideals of liberty, equal justice, and equality" as "various groups [sought] to elbow their way under the canopy of the nation's founding promises."

Compromise eventually quieted the controversy. After the Senate rejected the history standards, blue-ribbon panels of experts reviewed them, recommended some changes, and predicted that the revised version would make an important contribution toward "developing a responsible and productive citizenry." And indeed, teachers and school administrators throughout the country now regularly consult the revised standards to help them design an appropriate history curriculum.

But such controversies—or "memory wars"— have long been, and doubtless will remain, a recurring part of American history as competing segments of society seek to sanction their aspirations and achievement with differing versions of the common past.

Washington commented, "a wagon load of money will scarcely purchase a wagon load of provisions." Savvy people tried to spend money before its value could drop further, whereas those who had salable commodities such as grain tended to hoard them in the hope that the price would go even higher. Prices also climbed much faster than wages, leaving many working people impoverished. As always happens in times of severe inflation, people resorted to bartering and demanded price-fixing laws. But often there was nothing to barter, and price controls never worked for long.

The rampant inflation was demoralizing and divisive. Lucky speculators and unscrupulous profiteers grew rich, while ordinary and patriotic people suffered. These conditions sparked more than thirty protest demonstrations. In October 1779, frustrated Philadelphia militiamen marched on the house of a local Whig leader, demanding better enforcement of price controls. The confrontation left six people dead but otherwise achieved little. Freebooters—rovers in search of plunder—sailed Long Island Sound in boats with such names as *Retrieve My Losses*, ostensibly to harry the British but all too often to trade with them. As usual, war and its deprivations brought out both the best and the worst in human nature.

Nevertheless, the successful outcome of the war and the stable peace that followed suggest that most Americans somehow managed to cope. But during the last years of the conflict, their economic and psychological reserves ran low. The total real wealth of private individuals declined by an average of 0.5 percent annually from 1774 to 1805, even with the returning prosperity of the 1790s. Such statistics suggest the true economic cost of the War for Independence. And the atrocities committed on both sides provide nearly as accurate an indicator of the conflict's psychological cost.

THE PRICE OF VICTORY

Most American and British commanders tried to keep hostilities "civilized"—if such a characterization can ever be applied to a war—but discipline sometimes broke down among regular troops. Controlling militias or civilians acting on their own was even more difficult, demonstrating once again that civil wars and guerrilla struggles often rank among the worst of human conflicts. Residents of contested areas near British-occupied cities, such as New York and Charleston, lived in almost constant danger. Their plight emerges starkly from an incident in New Jersey in 1779, when a roving Tory band

knocked on the door of a Whig militiaman. Entering his house, they announced that he was a dead man. Drinking his liquor and terrorizing his wife, they argued about how to execute him until one of the intruders abruptly resolved the dispute by shooting him. Whigs could be equally brutal. Late in the war, British sympathizers in the Lower South compiled a list of more than three hundred loyalists who had been massacred by Whigs—some, the survivors claimed, while they slept.

Although the British were probably the worse offenders, both sides burned, plundered, and murdered. One can see the results in a returning refugee's description of the area around Beaufort, South Carolina, in the early 1780s: "All was desolation. . . . Robberies and murders are often committed on the public roads. The people that remain have been peeled, pillaged, and plundered. Poverty, want, and hardship appear in almost every countenance . . . , and the morals of the people are almost entirely extirpated."

CONCLUSION

Despite the devastation and divisiveness of the war, many people in Europe and the United States were convinced that it represented something momentous. *The Annual Register*, an influential British magazine reflecting respectable opinion, commented accurately in 1783 that the American Revolution "has already overturned those favourite systems of policy and commerce, both in the old and in the new world, which the wisdom of the ages, and the power of the greatest nations, had in vain endeavored to render permanent; and it seems to have laid the seeds of still greater revolutions in the history and mutual relations of mankind."

Americans, indeed, had fired a shot heard round the world. Thanks in part to its heavy investment in the American Revolution, France suffered a grave financial crisis in the late 1780s. This, in turn, ushered in the political crisis that culminated in the French Revolution of 1789. The American Revolution helped to inspire among French people (including soldiers returning from service in America) an intense yearning for an end to arbitrary government and undeserved social inequalities. Liberty also proved infectious to thousands of German troops who had come to America as mercenaries but elected to stay as free citizens after the war was over. Once prosperous but distant provinces of a far-flung empire, the North American states had become an independent confederation, a grand experiment in republicanism whose fate mattered to enlightened men and women throughout the Western world. In his written farewell to the rank and file of his troops at the end of October 1783, Washington maintained that "the enlarged prospects of happiness, opened by the confirmation of our independence and sovereignty, almost exceed the power of description."

He urged those who had fought with him to maintain their "strong attachments to the union" and "prove themselves not less virtuous and useful as citizens, than they have been persevering and victorious as soldiers." The work of securing the promise of the American Revolution, Washington knew, would now shift from the battlefield to the political arena.

REVIEW QUESTIONS

1. Who were the loyalists, and how many of them were there? What attempts did the British and Americans make in 1775 to avert war? Why did these steps fail?

2. What actions did the Second Continental Congress take in 1775 and 1776? Why did it choose George Washington as the commander of its army? Why was he a good choice?

3. Why did Congress declare independence in July 1776? How did Americans justify their claim to independence?

4. What was republicanism, and why was the enthusiasm that it inspired insufficient to win the war?

5. What were the chief characteristics of the British and American armies?

6. Why were most of the early battles fought in the northern states? Why did the British not crush the Americans immediately? Why did France decide to enter the war as an ally of the United States? What effect did French entry into the war have on British strategy?

7. Why did the initial British victories in the South not win the war for them? Why did the United States ultimately win? What did it obtain by winning?

8. What were the effects of the war on American society? What impact did it have on the status of women? On the lives of African Americans? What did John Laurens intend for African Americans? Why did he think ex-slaves would make good soldiers? Why did his plan fail? How did the war affect Native Americans? What was the price of victory—for the victors and for the vanquished? What were the immediate results of the American victory?

KEY TERMS

Battles of Lexington and Concord (p. 168–169)

Committee of Safety (p. 167)

Conciliatory Proposition (p. 168)

Continental Army (p. 170)

Contract theory of government (p. 173)

Declaration of Independence (p. 173)

Declaration of the Causes and Necessity of Taking Up Arms (p. 170)

Minute Men (p. 167)

Olive Branch Petition (p. 170)

Peace of Paris (p. 190)

Republicanism (p. 174)

Second Continental Congress (p. 170)

Valley Forge (p. 184)

RECOMMENDED READING

Buel, Joy D., and Richard Buel, Jr. *The Way of Duty: A Woman and Her Family in Revolutionary America* (1984). A readable and unusually full biography of Mary Fish of Connecticut, who lived from 1736 to 1818. Her experiences during the Revolutionary War while her husband, Selleck Silliman, was a prisoner of the British have become the subject of a good movie, "Mary Silliman's War" (1993).

Conway, Stephen. *The War of American Independence, 1775–1783* (1995). A short, accessible account that emphasizes the degree to which the American Revolution was the first modern war.

Dann, John C. ed. *The Revolution Remembered: Eyewitness Accounts of the War for Independence* (1980). A collection of seventy-nine narratives by veterans seeking pensions for their Revolutionary War service; sometimes poignant and frequently illuminating.

Gross, Robert A. *The Minutemen and Their World* (1976). An example of "history from the bottom up" that provides a close look at the Minute Men of Concord from the late colonial period through the Revolution.

Maier, Pauline. *American Scripture: Making the Declaration of Independence* (1997). A readable account of the adoption of the Declaration of Independence and its later reputation.

Shy, John. *A People Numerous and Armed: Reflections on the Military Struggle for American Independence* (1990). A collection of essays on various aspects of the American Revolution by a perceptive military historian; full of interesting ideas.

Weigley, Russell F. *The Partisan War: The South Carolina Campaign of 1780–1782* (1970). A short, stimulating account of the American recovery of the Lower South that takes "the perspective of our recent insights into unconventional war" and communist successes in Vietnam.

ADDITIONAL SOURCES

The Outbreak of War and the Declaration of Independence

Adams, Willi Paul et al, "Interpreting the Declaration of Independence by Translation: A Round Table," *Journal of American History* (1999), pp. 1280–1458.

Calhoon, Robert M. *The Loyalists in Revolutionary America, 1760–1781* (1973).

Ellis, Joseph. *American Sphinx: The Character of Thomas Jefferson* (1996).

Fischer, David H. *Paul Revere's Ride* (1994).

Flexner, James T. *Washington: The Indispensable Man* (1984).

Foner, Eric. *Tom Paine and Revolutionary America* (1976).

Hamowy, Ronald. "Jefferson and the Scottish Enlightenment: A Critique of Garry Wills's Inventing America," *William and Mary Quarterly* (1979), pp. 503–523.

Higginbotham, Don. *The War of American Independence: Military Attitudes, Policies, and Practice, 1763–1789* (1971).

Middlekauff, Robert. *The Glorious Cause: The American Revolution, 1763–1789* (1982).

The Combatants

Billias, George A. ed. *George Washington's Generals* (1964).

Billias, George A. ed. *George Washington's Opponents: British Generals and Admirals in the American Revolution* (1969).

Frey, Sylvia R. *The British Soldier in America: A Social History of Military Life in the Revolutionary Period* (1981).

Gardiner, Robert. *Navies and the American Revolution, 1775–1783* (1996).

Mayer, Holly A. *Belonging to the Army: Camp Followers and Community during the American Revolution* (1996).

Neimeyer, Charles P. *America Goes to War: A Social History of the Continental Army* (1996).

Royster, Charles. *A Revolutionary People at War: The Continental Army and American Character, 1775–1783* (1979).

Wright, Robert K. *The Continental Army* (1984).

The War in the North

Gruber, Ira D. *The Howe Brothers and the American Revolution* (1972).

Kennett, Lee B. *The French Forces in America, 1780–1783* (1977).

Kwasny, Mark V. *Washington's Partisan War, 1775–1783* (1996).

Martin, James Kirby. *Benedict Arnold, Revolutionary Hero: An American Warrior Reconsidered* (1997).

Rosswurm, Steven. *Arms, Country, and Class: The Philadelphia Militia and "Lower Sort" during the American Revolution, 1775–1783* (1987).

Stinchcombe, William C. *The American Revolution and the French Alliance* (1969).

The War Widens

Frey, Sylvia R. *Water from the Rock: Black Resistance in a Revolutionary Age* (1991).

Graymont, Barbara. *The Iroquois in the American Revolution* (1972).

Hoffman, Ronald, Thad W. Tate, and Peter J. Albert, eds. *An Uncivil War: The Southern Backcountry during the American Revolution* (1985).

Mintz, Max. *Seeds of Empire: The American Revolutionary Conquest of the Iroquois* (1999).

O'Donnell, James H. *Southern Indians in the American Revolution* (1973).

Smith, Paul H. *Loyalists and Redcoats: A Study in British Revolutionary Policy* (1964).

Thayer, Theodore. *Nathanael Greene: Strategist of the American Revolution* (1960).

Wickwire, Franklin, and Mary Wickwire. *Cornwallis: The American Adventure* (1970).

The American Victory

Dull, Jonathan R. *A Diplomatic History of the American Revolution* (1985).

Mackesy, Piers. *The War for America, 1775–1783* (1964).

Martin, James K., and Mark E. Lender. *A Respectable Army: The Military Origins of the Republic, 1763–1789* (1982).

Morris, Richard B. *The Peacemakers: The Great Powers and American Independence* (1965).

Peckham, Howard H. *The Toll of Independence: Engagements and Battle Casualties of the American Revolution* (1974).

The War and Society

Brown, Wallace. *The Good Americans: The Loyalists in the American Revolution* (1969).

Buel, Richard Jr. *Dear Liberty: Connecticut's Mobilization for the Revolutionary War* (1980).

Calloway, Colin G. *The American Revolution in Indian Country: Crisis and Diversity in Native American Communities* (1995).

Hodges, Graham Russell, ed. *The Black Loyalist Directory: African Americans in Exile after the American Revolution* (1996).

Hoffman, Ronald, and Peter J. Albert, eds. *The Transforming Hand of Revolution: Reconsidering the American Revolution as a Social Movement* (1995).

Hoffman, Ronald, and Peter J. Albert. *Women in the Age of the American Revolution* (1989).

Kerber, Linda. *Women of the Republic: Intellect and Ideology in Revolutionary America* (1980).

Leiby, Adrian C. *The Revolutionary War in the Hackensack Valley: The Jersey Dutch and the Neutral Ground, 1775–1783* (1962).

Massey, Gregory. *John Laurens and the American Revolution* (2000).

Norton, Mary Beth. *Liberty's Daughters: The Revolutionary Experience of American Women, 1750–1800* (1980).

Ward, Harry M. *The War for Independence and the Transformation of American Society* (1999).

Young, Alfred F., ed. *The American Revolution: Explorations in the History of American Radicalism* (1976).

WHERE TO LEARN MORE

- **Gnadenhutten Monument and Schoenbrunn Village near New Philadelphia, Ohio.** Reconstructed buildings mark the Moravian Indian settlement whose inhabitants were massacred in 1782. The website for the museum and park, http://www.geocities.com/tusc_hat/gnaden.html, gives a brief history of the village and Revolutionary War massacre.

- **Independence National Historical Park, Philadelphia, Pennsylvania.** Independence Hall, where Congress adopted the Declaration of Independence, is the most historic building in Philadelphia. The informative website can be accessed through Links to the Past: National Park Service Cultural Resources' comprehensive listing of historic sites in the National Park system, http://www.cr.nps.gov.

- **Kings Mountain National Military Park and Cowpens National Battlefield, South Carolina.**

Situated approximately 20 miles apart, these were the sites of two battles in October 1780 and January 1781 that turned the tide of the war in the South. Both have museums and exhibits. The official site is accessible through Links to the Past: National Park Service Cultural Resources, http://www.cr.nps.gov. But see also Battles of the American Revolutionary War, http://www.ilt.columbia.edu/k12/history/aha/battles.html, for a brief description of the battles and their contexts.

- **Minute Man National Historical Park, Lexington and Concord, Massachusetts.** There are visitors' centers at both Lexington and Concord with explanatory displays. Visitors may also follow the self-guided Battle Road Automobile Tour. The official website is accessible through Links to the Past: National Park Service Cultural Resources, http://www.cr.nps.gov.

- **Saratoga National Historical Park, New York.** The park preserves and commemorates the American victory that led to French entry into the war. There is a museum with artifacts from the battlefield. Both the explanatory displays and the topography of the area make this an especially illuminating site. The official website is accessible through Links to the Past: National Park Service Cultural Resources, http://www.cr.nps.gov.

- **Valley Forge National Historical Park, Valley Forge, Pennsylvania.** Reconstructed huts convey a sense of life in the Continental Army camp at Valley Forge during the hard winter of 1777–1778. The official website is accessible through Links to the Past: National Park Service Cultural Resources, http://www.cr.nps.gov.

- **Yorktown Battlefield, Colonial National Historical Park, Yorktown, Virginia.** The park commemorates the great American victory here. Innovative exhibits enable visitors to follow the course of the war from a multicultural perspective. The official website is accessible through Links to the Past: National Park Service Cultural Resources, http://www.cr.nps.gov.

 Please refer to the document CD-ROM for primary sources related to this chapter.

→ *The federal ship* Hamilton *was the center of attention in the grand procession staged by supporters of the Constitution in New York City in 1788.*

7

THE FIRST REPUBLIC
1776–1789

Springfield Jan. 26, 1787

Sir,

The unhappy time is come in which we have been obliged to shed blood. Shays, who was at the head of about twelve hundred men, marched yesterday afternoon about four o'Clock, towards the public buildings in battle array. He marched his men in an open column by plattoons. I sent several times [through aides] to him to know what he was after, or what he wanted. His reply was, he wanted barracks, and barracks he would have and stores. The answer returned was he must purchase them dear, if he had them. He still proceeded on his march until he approached within two hundred and fifty yards of the arsenal. He then made a halt. I immediately sent Major Lyman, one of my aides, and Capt Buffington to inform him not to march his troops any nearer to Arsenal on his peril, as I was stationed here by order of your Excellency and the Secretary at War, for the defence of the public property, in case he did I should surely fire on him and his men. [After rebuffing Lyman and Buffington,] Shays immediately put his troops in motion, and marched on rapidly near one hundred yards. I then ordered Major Stephens, who commanded the Artillery, to fire upon them. He accordingly did. The two first shott he endeavored to overshoot them, in hopes they would have taken warning without firing among them, but it had no effect on them. Major Stevens

CHAPTER OUTLINE

The New Order of Republicanism
Defining the People
The State Constitutions
The Articles of Confederation

Problems at Home
The Fiscal Crisis
Economic Depression
The Economic Policies of the States
Congress and the West

Diplomatic Weaknesses
Impasse with Britain
Spain and the Mississippi River

Toward a New Union
The Road to Philadelphia
The Convention at Work
Overview of the Constitution
The Struggle over Ratification

Conclusion

then directed his shott thro' the center of his column. The fourth or fifth shot put their whole column into the utmost confusion. Shays made an attempt to display [spread out] the column, but in vain. We had one howitz which was loaded with grape shot, which when fired, gave them great uneasiness. Had I been disposed to destroy them, I might have charged upon their rear and flanks with my Infantry and the two field pieces, and could have killed the greater part of his whole army within twenty five minutes. There was not a single musket fired on either side. I found three men dead on the spot, and one wounded, who is since dead. ...

I am, Sir, with great respect, <u>Your</u> Excellency's most

Obedient hble Servt

W. Shepard

General Shepard to Governor Bowdoin, Jan. 26, 1787, in *American Historical Review*, Vol. 2: July 1897, p. 694.

William Shepard, the commander of the Hampshire County militia, informed Massachusets Governor James Bowdoin that the armed insurgents led by Daniel Shays had been routed the previous day in their attempt to seize the federal arsenal at Springfield. Shays was a hitherto obscure Revolutionary war captain. Born in 1747 in eastern Massachusetts, he had escaped rural poverty by acquiring his own farm before the outbreak of the Revolution. He enlisted in 1775 and served the patriot cause for five years before returning to his farm in Pelham, a village of small-scale farmers with a tradition of resisting outside authorities. Like many of his fellow farmers in western Massachusetts, Shays faced hard times in the 1780s. A combination of falling farm prices, a shortage of money, heavy taxes, and mounting debts produced an economic crisis that threatened more and more farmers with imprisonment for debt and, worse yet, the loss of their farms, the basis of their independence. Faced with an unresponsive state legislature controlled by eastern merchants and creditors, angry farmers reacted much as they had during the revolutionary agitation against the British a decade earlier: they organized, protested, and shut down the county courts. By 1786 Shays had emerged as one of their key leaders, and the ragtag army of farmers that he marched against the Springfield arsenal now aimed at nothing less than the overthrow of the state government.

State leaders and eastern merchants were horrified by this armed challenge to their authority. In quickly mobilizing forces to suppress the rebellion, they acted on their belief that the Revolution had been fought to forge a society founded on the rule of law and contract, in which the established order would be upheld. Liberty for them was equated with the right of the individual to pursue wealth and amass property. By contrast, the struggling farmers and artisans supportive of the cause of the rebels defined the liberty won in the Revolution more strongly in terms of the right of communities to defend their interests against the threat of moneyed and aristocratic elites.

Driven out of Massachusetts when his army quickly collapsed in 1787, Shays once again became an obscure figure. Few noticed when he died impoverished in upstate New York in 1825. Still, the movement that bears his name, more than any other domestic disturbance in the 1780s, dramatized the fragile nature and conflicting values of America's first republic under the Articles of Confederation. Providing for little more than a loose union of the states, the Articles were ratified in 1781. The years that followed were a period of trial and error marked by a running debate over the meaning of liberty and the extent of power to be entrusted to a national government. Americans favoring a stronger, more centralized government repeatedly cited Shays's Rebellion as an example of the impending chaos that would destroy the republic unless fundamental changes were made. Those changes came with the writing and ratification of the Constitution of the United States in 1788.

KEY TOPICS

- Republicanism and the political philosophy of the new state constitutions

- Internal problems in the United States under the Articles of Confederation

- Efforts of Britain and Spain to exploit the weaknesses of the United States after the Revolution

- The movement for a stronger national government

- The drafting and ratification of the United States Constitution

THE NEW ORDER OF REPUBLICANISM

As royal authority collapsed during the Revolution, various provincial congresses and committees assumed power in each of the former colonies. The Continental Congress, seeking to build support for the war effort, was concerned that these new institutions should have a firm legal and popular foundation. In May 1776, the Congress called on the colonies to form new state governments "under the authority of the people."

This call reflected the political philosophy of republicanism that animated the Revolution (see Chapter 6). To Americans, republicanism meant, first and foremost, that legitimate political authority derives from the people. It is they who are sovereign, not the king or the aristocracy. The people should elect the officials who govern them, and those officials should represent the interests of the people who elected them. Another key aspect of republicanism was the revolutionary idea that the people could define and limit governmental power through written constitutions.

Thus for many Americans, the Congress's call reflected the root purpose of the Revolution—to banish aristocratic tyranny and reconstruct government in the states on republican principles. But if those principles included the idea that legitimate government flowed from the people, it was not always clear just who was included in "the people."

DEFINING THE PEOPLE

When news of the peace treaty with Britain reached New Bern, North Carolina, in June 1783, the citizens held a grand celebration. As reported by Francisco de Miranda, a visiting Spanish officer, "There was a barbecue [a roast pig] and a barrel of rum, from which the leading officials and citizens of the region promiscuously drank with the meanest and lowest kind of people, holding hands and drinking from the same cup. It is impossible to imagine, without seeing it, a more purely democratic gathering."

For Miranda, this boisterous mingling of all citizens as seeming equals confirmed the central tenet of republicanism, the belief that the people were sovereign. But republicanism also taught that political rights should be limited to those who owned private property, because the independent will required for informed political judgment required economic self-sufficiency. This, in effect, restricted political participation to propertied white men. Virtually everyone else—propertyless white men, servants legally bound to others, women, slaves and most free black people—were denied political rights. As for Native Americans, they were outside the U.S. body politic and exercised political rights within their own nations.

Because the ownership of property was relatively widespread among white men, some 60 to 85 percent of adult white men could participate in politics—a far higher proportion than elsewhere in the world of the eighteenth century. The greatest concentration of the remaining 25 percent or so shut out of the political process were unskilled laborers and mariners living in port cities. The city's working poor still included indentured servants, bound by contract to give personal service for a fixed time. The walking poor—vagrants and transients—might be jailed by local authorities, confined to workhouses, or hired out in public auctions for fixed terms of labor. Those who incurred debts they were unable to pay faced imprisonment.

Women and the Revolution. The Revolution did little to change the traditional patriarchal assumption that politics and public life should be the exclusive domain of men. Women, according to republican beliefs, were part of the dependent class and belonged under the control of propertied men—their husbands and fathers. Under common law (the custom-

Chronology

1776 States begin writing the first constitutions.

1777 Articles of Confederation proposed.

1781 Articles ratified.

1783 Americans celebrate independence and the peace treaty with Britain.

1784 Onset of the postwar depression.
Spain closes the Mississippi.
Separatist plots in the West.
Treaty of Fort Stanwix.

1785 Land Ordinance of 1785.

States begin to issue more paper money.
Treaty of Fort McIntosh.

1786 Shays's Rebellion breaks out.
Jay-Gardoqui Treaty defeated.
Annapolis Convention.

1787 Constitutional Convention at Philadelphia.
Northwest Ordinance.

1788 Constitution ratified and goes into effect.
Publication of *The Federalist*.

---

ary, largely unwritten, law that Americans had inherited from Britain), women surrendered their property rights at marriage unless they made special arrangements to the contrary. Legally and economically, husbands had complete control over their wives. As a result, argued Theophilus Parsons of Massachusetts in 1778, women were, as a matter of course, "so situated as to have no wills of their own."

To be sure, some women saw in the political and social enthusiasm of the Revolution an opportunity to protest the most oppressive features of their subordination. "I won't have it thought that because we are

With the exception of New Jersey, where women meeting the property qualifications were eligible to vote, the state constitutions of the Revolutionary era prohibited women from voting.

the weaker sex as to bodily strength we are capable of nothing more than domestic concerns," wrote Eliza Wilkinson of South Carolina. Men, she lamented, "won't even allow us liberty of thought and that is all I want." Such protests, however, had little enduring effect. Most women were socialized to accept that their proper place was in the home with their families.

Gender-specific language—including such terms as "men," "Freemen," "white male inhabitants," and "free white men"—explicitly barred women from voting in almost all state constitutions of the 1770s. Only the New Jersey constitution of 1776 defined **suffrage**—the right to vote—in gender-free terms, extending it to all adults "worth fifty pounds." As a result, until 1807, when the state legislature changed the constitution, propertied women, including widows and single women, enjoyed the right to vote in New Jersey.

The Revolution otherwise did bring women a few limited gains. They benefited from slightly less restrictive divorce laws and gained somewhat greater access to educational and business opportunities, changes that reflected the relative autonomy of many women during the war when their men were off fighting. The perception of women's moral status also rose. As the Philadelphia physician Benjamin Rush argued in his *Thoughts upon Female Education* (1787), educated

Phillis Wheatley was an acclaimed African American poet. Kidnapped into slavery as a child in Africa, she was a domestic slave to the Wheatley family of Boston when her first poems were published in 1773.

and morally informed women were needed to instruct "their sons in the principles of liberty and government." Often called republican motherhood, this more positive view of women's influence entrusted mothers with the responsibility of passing on republican virtues from one generation to the next.

The Revolution and African Americans in the South.

The Revolution had a more immediate impact on the lives of many African Americans, triggering the growth of free black communities and the development of an African American culture. Changes begun by the Revolution were the main factor in the tremendous increase of free blacks from a

few thousand at midcentury to more than 100,000 by 1800 (see Figure 7–1). One key to this increase was a shift in the religious and intellectual climate. Revolutionary principles of liberty and equality and evangelical notions of human fellowship convinced many whites for the first time to challenge black slavery. In 1784, Virginia Methodists condemned slavery as "contrary to the Golden Law of God on which hang all the Laws and Prophets, and the unalienable Rights of Mankind, as well as every Principle of Revolution." As many whites grew more hostile to slavery, blacks began to seize opportunities for freedom that emerged from the disruptions of the war and the needs of both sides for military manpower.

Upwards of fifty thousand slaves, or one in ten of those in bondage, gained their freedom as a result of the war. One route was through military service, which generally carried a promise of freedom. When the British began raising black troops, the Americans followed suit. All the states except Georgia and South Carolina recruited black regiments. Some five thousand blacks served in the Continental armies, and they, like their counterparts in British units, were mostly slaves. Most slaves who gained freedom during the war, however, were those who fled their owners and made their way to the port cities of the North.

By making slave property generally less secure, the Revolution encouraged many masters to free their slaves. Once freed, blacks tried to break all the bonds of their former servitude. "Negro Soloman," his former owner griped, "now free, prefers to mould bricks rather than serve me." A Delaware mistress felt rejected when a slave she had freed spurned her offer of employment with a friend and found her own job. "I cannot help think," she noted sourly, that "it is too generally the case with all those of colour to be ungrateful." As the number of free blacks increased, those still enslaved grew bolder in their efforts to gain freedom. "Henny," warned a Maryland slaveowner in 1783, "will try to pass for a free woman as several have lately been set free in this neighbourhood."

Northern blacks and the Revolution.

If the control mechanisms of slavery experienced some strain in the South during the Revolution, in the North, where slaves were only a small percentage of the population, they crumbled. Most northern states ended slavery between 1777 and 1784. New York

FIGURE 7-1   Growth of the Free Black Population between 1750 and 1800
Gradual emancipation in the North, the freeing of many slaves by their owners in the South, and the opportunities for freedom offered by the Revolution, all contributed to an explosive growth in the free population of African Americans in the second half of the eighteenth century.
Source: *A Century of Population Growth in the United States, 1790–1900* (1909). p. 80. Data for 1750 estimated.

BETHEL AFRICAN METHODIST EPISCOPAL CHURCH, PHILAD?

The Mother Bethel Church in Philadelphia, dedicated in 1794, was home to the first independent black congregation in America and the founding establishment of the African Methodist Episcopal denomination. Churches were central to the community life of black Northerners and provided leadership in the struggle for racial justice.

followed in 1799 and New Jersey in 1804. Nonetheless, although a majority of northern whites now agreed that slavery was incompatible with the Revolution's commitment to **natural rights** (the inherent human rights to life and liberty) and human freedom, they refused to sanction a sudden emancipation. The laws ending slavery in most of the northern states called for only the children of slaves to be freed, and only when they reached adulthood.

Northern blacks had to struggle to overcome white prejudice. Although black males were allowed to vote if they met the property qualifications, most were poor and held little property. Facing discrimination in jobs and housing, barred from juries, and denied a fair share of funds for schools, urban blacks had to rely on their own resources. With the help of the small class of property holders among them, they began establishing their own churches and self-help associations.

The Revolution's Impact on Native Americans.

Most Indian peoples had stayed neutral during the war or fought for the British (see Chapter 6). Just as the Americans sought to shake off British control, so the Indians, especially the western tribes and most of the Iroquois Confederation, sought to free themselves from American dominance. The British defeat was

thus a double blow, depriving the Indians of a valuable ally and exposing them to the wrath of the victorious patriots. Late in the war a British officer observed of the pro-British southern Indians, "The minds of these people appear as much agitated as those of the unhappy Loyalists, they have very seriously proposed to abandon their country and accompany us [in an evacuation], having made all the world their enemies by their attachment to us."

The state governments, as well as the Confederation Congress, now treated Indian lands after the Revolution as a prize of war to be distributed to white settlers. Territorial demands on the Indians escalated, and even the few tribes that had furnished troops for the American side struggled to maintain control over most of their homelands. As they did so, it was clear that white Americans did not consider Native Americans to be part of their republican society. With the exception of Massachusetts, the states denied voting and legal rights to the Indians within their borders.

Still, it must be stressed that most Native Americans did not want or expect equal rights within the new American republic. They viewed themselves as belonging to their own nations, composed of distinct villages and settlements, with a common culture and interests. What they wanted were political rights and control over land within their nations. Above all, they were fiercely independent. As George Rogers Clark wrote in 1783 of the Indians he had fought during the Revolution, "They have no notion of being dependent on Either the brittish or americans, But would make war on both if Equally Insulted."

In seeking to defend their independence against the growing pressure of white Americans on their lands, Native Americans forged new confederacies in the 1780s that temporarily united them against a common enemy. They were encouraged in these efforts by the imperial powers of England and Spain, both of whom sought to curb the westward expansion of the United States. Thus, the immediate impact of the Revolution on Native Americans was a mixed one. On the one hand, the Revolution had created a new expansionist power in the United States that was intent on settling lands already occupied by Indians. On the other hand, American victory in the Revolution had broken the British monopoly of power in the region west of the Appalachian Mountains. Before the United States could consolidate its claim over the region, new imperial rivalries sprang up that allowed Native Americans to stake out a political middle ground between the competing powers. Throughout the 1780s, Native Americans continued to act as independent political agents in playing off outside powers against each other.

THE STATE CONSTITUTIONS

"Oppose everything that leans to aristocracy, of power in the hands of the rich and chief men exercised to the oppression of the poor." So the voters of Mecklenburg County, North Carolina, instructed their delegates to the state's constitutional convention in 1776. These instructions reflect a basic premise embodied in the new state constitutions of the Revolutionary period: Power had to be checked to insure individual liberty and safeguard against tyranny.

Ten new state constitutions were in place by the end of 1777. In Connecticut and Rhode Island, the new constitutions simply amended the existing colonial charters, which already provided for extensive self-rule, by dropping all references to royal authority. Massachusetts, the only state to hold elections for a special constitutional convention, ratified its constitution in 1780.

All these constitutions were written documents, a striking departure from the English practice of treating a constitution as a collection of customary rights and practices that had evolved over time. In the American view, a constitution was a formal expression of the people's sovereignty, a codification of the powers of government and the rights of citizenship that functioned as a fundamental law to which all public authority was held accountable.

Because Americans had come to associate tyranny with the privileges of royal governors, all the new state constitutions cut back sharply on executive power. Annual elections were now the norm for governors, who were also made subject to impeachment—charges of misconduct, resolved at a public trial—and limited in the number of terms they could serve. Most important, for it struck at what patriots felt was the main source of executive domination and corruption, governors lost control over patronage, the power to appoint executive and judicial officials.

As the new constitutions curbed the power of governors, they increased that of the legislatures, making them the focal point of government. Colonial assemblies had been in the forefront of popular opposition to British authority, and the state legislatures that succeeded them were now seen as the most trustworthy defenders of individual liberty. The new constitutions expanded the power of the legislatures to appoint officials and to oversee military and financial matters. To make the legislatures more expressive of the popular will, the new constitutions included provisions that lowered property requirements for voting and officeholding, mandated annual elections, increased the number of seats in the legislatures, and made representation more proportional to the geographical distribution of population. Upper houses were made independent of the executive office and opened to popular election, as opposed to the colonial practice of having their members appointed by the governor.

Americans knew that legislatures, too, could act tyrannically, as they believed Britain's Parliament had done. So in a final check on arbitrary power, each state constitution eventually included some form of a **bill of rights** that set explicit limits on the power of government to interfere in the lives of citizens. The Virginia Declaration of Rights, written by the planter George Mason and adopted in June 1776, set the precedent for this notable republican feature. By 1784, the constitutions of all thirteen states had provisions guaranteeing religious liberty, freedom of the press, and a citizen's right to such fair legal practices as trial by jury.

Toward religious pluralism. The new constitutions weakened but did not always sever the traditional tie between church and state for the support of religion. Many Americans held, as the Massachusetts Constitution of 1780 put it, that "the happiness of a people, and the good order and preservation of civil government, essentially depend upon piety, religion, and morality." Reflecting this belief, many states, notably in New England, levied taxes for the support of religion. The states of New England also continued to maintain Congregationalism as the established, or state-supported, religion, while allowing dissenting Baptists and Methodists to use funds from the compulsory religious taxes to support their ministers. The "common people," explained the Baptist leader Isaac Backus, insisted that they had "as good a right to judge and act for themselves in matter of religion as civil rulers or the learned clergy."

The mid-Atlantic states lacked the religious uniformity of New England. The region supported several prominent denominations—Quaker, Episcopalian, Presbyterian, Dutch Reformed, and Lutheran—and none was able to dominate the others. This pluralism checked legislative efforts to impose

AMERICAN VIEWS

A French Observer Describes a New Society

In 1782, J. Hector St. John Crèvecoeur, a Frenchman who had lived and traveled in British North America, published his impressions of America. The following selection from his *Letters from an American Farmer* captures the striking optimism and sense of newness that he found. More so than any other literary work, the *Letters* stamped the new American republic, especially in the minds of Europeans, as the home of the world's freest and most equal people.

- What is Crèvecoeur's image of America? Do you believe it was overly optimistic?
- Why does Crèvecoeur put such emphasis on the absence of titles and great disparities of wealth?
- Just what was so new about America to Crèvecoeur?
- Why did Crèvecoeur ignore African slaves in his definition of the American? What happened to Native Americans in his account of the making of the American?

I wish I could be acquainted with the feelings and thoughts which must agitate the heart and present themselves to the mind of an enlightened Englishman when he first lands on this continent. . . . He is arrived on a new continent; a modern society offers itself to his contemplation, different from what he had hitherto seen. It is not composed, as in Europe, of great lords who possess everything and of a herd of people who have nothing. Here are no aristocratical families, no courts, no kings, no bishops, no ecclesiastical dominion, no invisible power giving to a few a very visible one, no great manufactures employing thousands, no great refinements of luxury. The rich and the poor are not so far removed

religious taxes or designate any denomination as the established church. In the South, where many Anglican (or Episcopalian) clergymen had been Tories, the Anglican Church lost its former established status. Thomas Jefferson, in Virginia's religious freedom law of 1786, went so far as to assert that "our civil rights have no dependence on our religious opinions any more than on opinions in physics or geometry."

Radical and conservative visions of republicanism.
Although in general the executive lost power and the legislature gained power under the new state constitutions, the actual structure of each state government reflected the outcome of political struggles between those holding a radical vision of republicanism and those holding a conservative vision. The democratically inclined radicals wanted to open government to

all male citizens. The conservatives, fearing "mob rule," wanted to limit government to an educated elite of substantial property holders. Although they agreed that government had to be derived from the people, most conservatives, like Jeremy Belknap of New Hampshire, thought that the people had to be "taught . . . that they are not able to govern themselves."

In South Carolina, where conservative planters gained the upper hand, the constitution mandated property qualifications that barred 90 percent of the state's white males from holding elective public office. By contrast, Pennsylvania had the most democratic and controversial constitution. Many of Pennsylvania's conservatives had discredited themselves during the Revolution by remaining neutral or loyal to the crown. The Scots-Irish farmers and Philadelfrom each other as they are in Europe. Some few towns excepted, we are all tillers of the earth, from Nova Scotia to West Florida. We are a people of cultivators scattered over an immense territory, communicating with each other by means of good roads and navigable rivers, united by the silken bands of mild government, all respecting the laws without dreading their power, because they are equitable. We are all animated with the spirit of an industry which is unfettered and unrestrained, because each person works for himself . . . . A pleasing uniformity of decent competence appears throughout our habitations. The meanest of our log-houses is a dry and comfortable habitation. Lawyer and merchant are the fairest titles our towns afford; that of a farmer is the only appellation of the rural inhabitants of our country. It must take some time ere he can reconcile himself to our dictionary, which is but short in words of dignity and names of honour . . . . We have no princes for whom we toil, starve, and bleed; we are the most perfect society now existing in the world. Here man is free as he ought to be, nor is this pleasing equality so transitory as many others are. Many ages will not see the shores of our great lakes replenished with inland nations, nor the unknown bounds of North America entirely peopled. . . .

The next wish of this traveller will be to know whence came all these people. They are a mixture of English, Scotch, Irish, French, Dutch, Germans, and Swedes. From this promiscuous breed, that race now called Americans have arisen. . . .

What, then, is the American, this new man? He is either an European or the descendant of an European; hence that strange mixture of blood, which you will find in no other country . . . . He is an American, who, leaving behind him all his ancient prejudices and manners, receives new ones from the new mode of life he has embraced, the new government he obeys, and the new rank he holds. He becomes an American by being received in the broad lap of our Alma Mater. Here individuals of all nations are melted into a new race of men, whose labours and posterity will one day cause great changes in the world.

Source: J. Hector St. John Crèvecoeur, *Letters from an American Farmer and Sketches of Eighteenth-Century America*, ed. Albert E. Stone (1986), pp. 66–70.

---

phia artisans who stepped into the resulting political vacuum held an egalitarian view of republicanism. The constitution they pushed through in 1776 gave the vote to all free males who paid taxes, regardless of wealth, and eliminated property qualifications for officeholding. In addition, the constitution concentrated power in a unicameral (single-house) legislature, eliminating both the office of governor and the more elite upper legislative house. To prevent the formation of an entrenched class of officeholders, the constitution's framers also required legislators to stand for election annually and barred them from serving more than four years out of seven.

The constitutions of the other states, although not as bold in their democratic reforms as Pennsylvania's, typically enhanced the political influence of ordinary citizens more than the constitution of South Carolina did. Unlike the colonial assemblies, the new bicameral (two-house) legislatures included substantially more artisans and small farmers and were not controlled by men of wealth. The proportion of legislators who came from a common background—those with property valued under £200—more than tripled to 62 percent in the North and more than doubled in the South from the 1770s to the 1780s.

This growing political equality was accompanied by demands that those in government be more responsive to the people. Summing up the prevailing view among Americans about the proper basis for government, William Hooper of North Carolina wrote in 1776, "Rulers must be conceived as the creatures of the people, made for their use, accountable to them, and subject to removal as soon as they act inconsistent with the purposes for which they were formed."

THE ARTICLES OF CONFEDERATION

Once the Continental Congress decided on independence in 1776, it needed to create a legal basis for a permanent union of the states. John Dickinson of Pennsylvania, a reluctant supporter of independence, presented a draft plan for such a union as early as the summer of 1776. Dickinson favored a strong central government to prevent the collapse of the social order that he feared might follow the overthrow of imperial rule. The Congress, however, fundamentally altered Dickinson's original plan to recognize the sovereign power of the individual states. According to the key provision of the **Articles of Confederation** that the Congress finally submitted to the states more than a year later, in November 1777, "Each State retains its sovereignty, freedom and independence, and every power, jurisdiction and right, which is not by this confederation expressly delegated to the United States, in Congress assembled." The effect was to create a loose confederation of autonomous states.

The powers the Articles of Confederation delegated to the central government were extremely limited, in effect little more than those already exercised by the Continental Congress. There were no provisions for a national judiciary or a separate executive branch of government. The Articles made Congress the sole instrument of national authority but restricted it with a series of constitutional safeguards that virtually eliminated any possibility that it could ever threaten the interests of the states. Each state had only one vote in Congress, making each politically equal regardless of its size or population. State legislatures were to choose their congressional delegations in annual elections, and delegates could serve only three years out of six. Delegates were expected to follow the instructions of their state legislatures and could be recalled at any time. Important measures, such as those dealing with finances or war and peace, required approval from a majority of nine state delegations voting in the Congress. Amendments to the Articles of Confederation, including the levying of national taxes, required the unanimous consent of the states.

The Congress had authority primarily in the areas of foreign policy and national defense. It could declare war, make peace, conduct foreign affairs, negotiate with Native Americans, and settle disputes between the states. It had no authority, however, to raise troops or impose taxes on its own; it could only ask the states to supply troops and money and hope that they would comply.

The central principle behind the Articles was the fear of oppressive, centralized power encroaching on the freedoms for which the Revolution was fought. In the end, as Edward Rutledge, a delegate from South Carolina to the Continental Congress, put it, the new Confederation Congress was vested "with no more Power than is absolutely necessary." "It is freedom, Gentlemen, it is freedom, & not a choice of the forms of servitude for which we contend," resolved the residents of West Springfield, Massachusetts, in instructions to their congressional representatives in 1778.

Most states quickly ratified the Articles of Confederation, but Maryland stubbornly held out until March 1781. Because they needed the approval of all thirteen states, it was not until then that the Articles officially took effect. Surprisingly, given the prevailing deep suspicion of central power, what caused the delay was the demand of some states to give Congress a power not included in the Articles submitted for ratification in 1777.

The issue here concerned the unsettled lands in the West between the Appalachian Mountains and the Mississippi River (see Map 7–1). Some states claimed these lands by virtue of their colonial charter rights, and led by Virginia and Massachusetts, they insisted on maintaining control over these territories. The so-called landless states—those with no claim to the West—insisted that it be set aside as a national domain, a reserve of public land controlled by Congress for the benefit of all the states. Land speculators who had purchased huge blocs of land from the Indians before the Revolution sided with the landless states. Many of them leading politicians, they expected that the Congress would be more likely to honor their land titles than would the individual states.

The British threat to the Chesapeake area in early 1781 finally broke the impasse that had delayed final approval of the Articles. Though retaining control of Kentucky, Virginia gave up its claim in the west to a vast area extending north of the Ohio River. In turn, Maryland, the last holdout among the landless states and now desperate for military aid from the Congress, agreed to ratify the Articles. After more than three years of debate and the airing of jealousies among the states, the final cementing of the original Union was decidedly anticlimactic.

PROBLEMS AT HOME

Neither prosperity nor political stability accompanied the return of peace in 1783. The national government struggled to avoid bankruptcy, and in 1784, an economic depression struck the country. As fiscal problems deepened over the next few years, creditor and debtor groups clashed angrily in state legislatures. When legislatures passed measures that provided relief to debtors at the expense of creditors, the

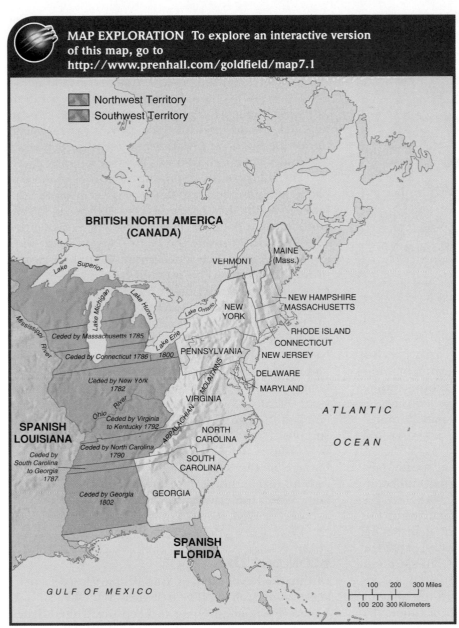

MAP EXPLORATION To explore an interactive version of this map, go to http://www.prenhall.com/goldfield/map7.1

Northwest Territory
Southwest Territory

BRITISH NORTH AMERICA
(CANADA)

Lake Superior

Lake Michigan
Lake Huron

Mississippi River

Ceded by Massachusetts 1785

Ceded by Connecticut 1786   1800

Ceded by New York
1782

Ohio River

Ceded by Virginia
to Kentucky 1792

SPANISH
LOUISIANA

Ceded by
South Carolina
to Georgia
1787

Ceded by North Carolina
1790

Ceded by Georgia
1802

VERMONT

MAINE
(Mass.)

Lake Ontario

NEW
YORK

NEW HAMPSHIRE
MASSACHUSETTS

Lake Erie

RHODE ISLAND
CONNECTICUT

PENNSYLVANIA

NEW JERSEY

DELAWARE

MARYLAND

VIRGINIA

NORTH
CAROLINA

SOUTH
CAROLINA

GEORGIA

SPANISH
FLORIDA

APPALACHIAN MOUNTAINS

ATLANTIC

OCEAN

GULF OF MEXICO

0   100   200   300 Miles
0   100 200 300 Kilometers

MAP 7-1   **Cession of Western Lands by the States**
Eight states had claims to lands in the West after the Revolution, and their willingness to cede them to the national government was an essential step in the creation of a public domain administered by Congress.

creditors decried what they saw as the interference of ignorant majorities with the rights of private property. Raising the cry of "legislative despotism," the abuse of power by tyrannical lawmakers, the creditors joined their voices to those who early on had wanted the power of the states curbed by a stronger central government. The only solid accomplishment of the Confederation Congress during this troubled period was to formulate an orderly and democratic plan for the settlement of the West under national controls.

The Fiscal Crisis. The Continental Congress and the states had incurred heavy debts to finance the Revolutionary War. Unable to impose and collect sufficient taxes to cover the debts and without reserves of gold or silver, they had little choice but to borrow funds and issue certificates or bonds pledging repayment. The Congress had the largest responsibility for meeting the war's costs, and to do so, it printed close to $250 million in paper notes backed only by its good faith. By the end of the war in 1781, these Continental dollars were nearly worthless, and the national debt—primarily certificates issued by the Continental Loan Office—stood at $11 million. As Congress issued new securities to settle claims by soldiers and civilians, this sum rose to $28 million within just a few years.

The Congress never did put its tottering finances on a sound footing, and its fiscal problems ultimately discredited the Articles of Confederation in the eyes of the **nationalists,** a loose bloc of congressmen, army officers, and public creditors who wanted to strengthen the Confederation at the expense of the states. The nationalists first began to organize in the dark days of 1780 and 1781, when inflation was rampant, the army was going unpaid, the Congress had ceased paying interest on the public debt, and the war effort itself seemed in danger of collapsing. Galvanized by this crisis, the nationalists rallied behind Robert Morris, a Philadelphia merchant appointed as superintendent of finance for the Confederation government.

Morris sought to enhance national authority through a bold program of financial and political reform. He began by securing a charter from Congress in 1781 for the Bank of North America, the nation's first commercial bank. Located in Philadelphia and partly owned by private investors, the bank had close

Issued in 1777, this Georgia four-dollar banknote was an example of the type of paper money used to finance the Revolutionary War.

connections to the Confederation government. Morris wanted it to serve as a national institution, and he used it to hold government funds, make loans to the government, and issue bank notes—paper money that could be used to settle debts and pay taxes owed to the United States.

Morris was able to resume some specie payments, and he temporarily brought order and economy to the nation's finances. As a result of his reforms, he came to be called the Financier of the Revolution. Nonetheless, he was blocked in his efforts to gain the taxing power that was essential for restoring the shattered credit of the Confederation government.

Morris's larger objective, central to the aims of the nationalists, was to create a "bond of union" by having the Congress assume payment of the entire national debt. Settling this debt would lead the propertied classes—the people who had financed the war and held the debt—to identify their economic self-interest with the effective exercise of power by the national government.

But to achieve this political goal, Morris had to gain for the Congress what it had always lacked: the power to tax. In 1781, he proposed a national impost, or tariff, of 5 percent on imported goods. Because this was a national tax, it required an amendment to the Articles of Confederation and the consent of all thirteen states. Twelve of the states quickly ratified the impost amendment, but Rhode Island—critically dependent on its own import duties to finance its war debt—rejected it, sending it

down to defeat. When a revised impost plan was considered two years later, New York blocked its passage.

These failures doomed Morris's financial reforms. He left office in 1784, and in the same year, the Bank of North America severed its ties to the national government and became a private corporation in Pennsylvania. Morris remained committed to the nationalist cause and would see his ideas resurface under the financial programs of Treasury Secretary Alexander Hamilton in the 1790s (see Chapter 8).

The failure of the impost tax was one of many setbacks that put the nationalists temporarily on the defensive. With the conclusion of peace in 1783, confidence in state government returned, taking the edge off calls to invest the central government with greater authority. The states continued to balk at supplying the money requisitioned from them by Congress and denied the Congress even limited authority to regulate foreign commerce. Most ominously for the nationalist cause, the states began to assume responsibility for part of the national debt. By 1786, New Jersey, Pennsylvania, Maryland, and New York had absorbed one-third of the debt by issuing state bonds to their citizens in exchange for national securities. As Morris had warned in 1781, such a policy entailed "a principle of disunion . . . which must be ruinous."

Without the power to tax, the Congress was a hostage to the sovereignty of the individual states with no real authority over the nation's economic affairs. When the economy plunged into a severe depression in 1784, it could only look on helplessly.

ECONOMIC DEPRESSION

During the Revolutionary War, Britain closed its markets to American goods. After the war, the British continued this policy, hoping to keep the United States weak and dependent. In the summer of 1783, they excluded Americans from the lucrative trade with the British West Indies. Before the Revolution, this trade in foodstuffs and timber with the sugar islands had been the primary means by which the colonists had built up the credits they needed to offset their imports from Britain.

Meanwhile, British merchants were happy to satisfy America's pent-up demand for consumer goods after the war. A flood of cheap British imports inundated the American market, and coastal merchants made them available to inland traders and shopkeepers by extending easy credit terms. In turn, these local businessmen sold the goods to farmers and artisans in the interior. Ultimately, however, the British merchants required payment in hard currency, gold and silver coins. Without access to its former export markets, America's only source of hard currency was foreign loans obtained by Congress and what money the French army had spent during the war. This was soon exhausted as America's trade deficit with Britain—the excess of imports over exports—ballooned in the early 1780s to £5 million (see Figure 7–2).

The result was an immense bubble of credit that finally burst in 1784, triggering a depression that would linger for the balance of the decade. As merchants began to press debtors for immediate payment, prices collapsed (they fell more than 25 percent between 1784 and 1786), and debtors were unable to pay. The best most could hope for was to avoid bankruptcy.

Small farmers everywhere had trouble paying their taxes. In 1786, James Swan of Massachusetts wrote of farmers in his state: "There is no family that does not want some money for some purposes, and the little which the farmer carries home from market, must be applied to other uses, besides paying off the [tax] collector's bills." Rural shopkeepers often could not move goods unless they agreed to barter them for farm produce. Abigail Dwight, who ran a small store in western Massachusetts, reported in 1785 that "most of these People sell on credit for To-Morrow at large—for very little Cash stirring this way—to be pay'd for in old Horses—cows—some Boards—cabbages—turnips—Potatoes etc."

In the cities, wages fell 25 percent between 1785 and 1789, and workers began to organize. They called for tariffs to protect them from cheap British imports and for legislative measures to promote American manufacturers. In the countryside, farm-

ers faced a wave of lawsuits for the collection of debts and the dread possibility of losing their land. "To be tenants to landlords, we know not who," protested the farmers of Conway, Massachusetts, "and pay rent for lands, purchased with our money, and converted from howling wilderness, into fruitful fields, by the sweat of our brows, seems. . . truly shocking."

With insufficient money in circulation to raise prices and reverse the downturn, the depression fed on itself. Congress was powerless to raise cash and was unable to pay off its old debts, including what it owed to the Revolutionary soldiers. Many state governments made things worse by imposing heavy taxes payable in the paper money they had issued during the Revolution. The result was to further reduce the amount of money in circulation, thus increasing deflationary pressures and forcing prices still lower.

Britain's trade policies caused particular suffering among New England merchants. No longer protected under the old Navigation Acts as British vessels, American ships were now barred from most ports in the British Empire. Incoming cargoes from the West Indies to New England fell off sharply, and the market for whale oil and fish, two of New England's major exports, dried up. The economy of the mid-Atlantic region held up somewhat better, but even there the loss of the provisioning trade to the British West Indies in grains, livestock, and dairy products cut into the income of merchants and farmers and forced layoffs among artisans who serviced the shipping trade.

In the southern states, British policies compounded the problem of recovering from the physical

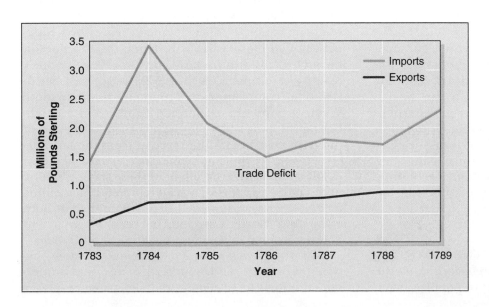

FIGURE 7-2   American Exports to and Imports from Britain between 1783 and 1789

During the 1780s, the United States imported far more from Britain than it exported there. The resulting huge trade deficit drained the country of gold and silver and was a major factor in the credit crisis that triggered an economic depression in the middle of the decade.

Source: *U.S. Bureau of the Census, Historical Statistics of the United States: Colonial Times to 1970, Part 2. (1975)* p. 1176.

damage and labor disruptions inflicted by the war. Some 10 percent of the region's slaves had fled during the war, and production levels on plantations fell in the 1780s. Chesapeake planters needed a full decade to restore the prewar output of tobacco, and a collapse in tobacco prices in 1785 left most of them in the same chronic state of indebtedness that had plagued them on the eve of the Revolution.

Farther south, in the Carolina lowcountry, the plantation economy was crippled throughout the 1780s. War damage had been extensive, and planters piled up debts to purchase additional slaves and repair their plantations and dikes. In spite of these investments, rice production was slow to recover. Burdened by new British duties on American rice, planters saw their rice exports fall by 50 percent. Small farmers in the pine barrens of North Carolina likewise had to adjust to the loss of their formerly protected British market for naval stores—tar, pitch, and turpentine.

By the late 1780s, the worst of the depression was over and an upturn was under way in the mid-Atlantic states. Food exports to continental Europe were on the rise, and American merchants were developing new trading ties with India and China. Commercial treaties with the Dutch, Swedes, and Prussians also opened up markets that had been closed to the colonists. Nonetheless, a full recovery had to await the 1790s.

The depression of the 1780s was the culmination of a decade of painful adjustment that followed the wrenching of the American economy from its traditional moorings within the British trading empire. A stagnant economy and burdensome debt combined with a growing population (there were 50 percent more Americans in 1787 than there had been in 1775) to reduce living standards. With more losers than winners, economic conflict dominated the politics of the states during the Confederation period.

THE ECONOMIC POLICIES OF THE STATES

The depression had political repercussions in all the states. Britain was an obvious target of popular anger,

Courtesy of The Historical Society of Pennsylvania.

Depicted here in a folding fan, the Empress of China *was the first American ship to undertake an extensive trading voyage to China. Sailing out of New York in February 1784, the* Empress of China *returned on May 11, 1785, and netted a profit of $37,000 for the investors who had financed the voyage. Building trading contracts to new markets in Asia and Europe helped the United States break its economic dependence on England.*

and merchants poorly positioned to adjust to the postwar dislocations of trade led a campaign to slap retaliatory duties on British ships and special taxes on the goods they carried. Likewise artisans and workers, especially in the North, pushed for tariff barriers against cheap British goods as a way to encourage domestic manufacturing and protect their jobs and wages. Most northern states imposed anti-British measures, but these varied from state to state, limiting their impact and producing squabbles when goods imported in one state were shipped to another.

State legislatures in the North responded to the protests of artisans by passing tariffs, but the lack of a uniform, national policy doomed their efforts. Shippers evaded high tariffs by bringing their cargoes in through states with no tariffs or less restrictive ones. States without ports, such as New Jersey and North Carolina, complained of economic discrimination. When they purchased foreign goods from a neighboring shipping state, they were forced to pay part of the tariff cost, but all the revenue from the tariff accrued only to the importing state. James Madison neatly summarized the plight of these states when he noted that "New Jersey, placed between Philadelphia and New York, was likened to a cask tapped at both ends; And North Carolina, between Virginia and South Carolina, to a patient bleeding at both Arms."

Tariff policies also fed sectional tensions between northern and southern states that undermined efforts to confer on the Congress the power to regulate commerce. The agrarian states of the South, which had little in the way of manufacturing to protect, had interests that differed from those of the states of the North. With the exception of Virginia, they favored free trade policies that encouraged British imports. Southern planters were also happy to take advantage of the low rates charged by British ships for transporting their crops to Europe; by doing so, they put pressure on northern shippers to reduce their rates.

The most bitter divisions exposed by the depression of the 1780s, however, were not between states but between debtors and creditors within states. As the value of debt securities the states had issued to raise money dropped during the Revolutionary War, speculators bought them up for a fraction of their face value and then put pressure on the states to raise taxes and repay the debts in full in hard currency. Wealthy landowners and merchants likewise supported higher taxes and the rapid repayment of debts in hard currency. Arrayed against these creditor groups by the mid 1780s was a broad coalition of debtors composed of middling farmers, small shop-

This clash between Shays's rebels and government troops at the Springfield arsenal marked the violent climax of the agrarian protests of the 1780s.

keepers, artisans, laborers, and people who had overextended themselves speculating in western land. The debtors wanted the states to issue paper money that they could use instead of hard money—gold and silver—to pay their debts. The paper money would have an inflationary effect, raising wages and the prices of farm commodities and reducing the value of debts contracted in hard currency. The townspeople of Atkinson, New Hampshire, expressing the feelings of many hard-pressed rural areas, put the issue this way: "For want of a suitable medium of trade the Citizens of this State are altogether unable to pay their public taxes, or private debts, or even to support the train of needless and expensive lawsuits, which alone would be an insupportable burden."

This was the economic context in which **Shays's Rebellion** exploded in the fall of 1786. Farm foreclosures and imprisonments for failure to pay debts had skyrocketed in western Massachusetts. Facing a collapse in farm prices and an impoverishing burden of debt, farmers petitioned the state legislators for economic relief. They complained of heavy taxes and the shortage of money and demanded legislation that would temporarily prohibit creditors from seizing farms and processing suits for debt. When the creditor and seaboard interests in the legislature refused to pass any relief measures, some two thousand farmers took up arms against the state government in Shays's Rebellion.

Outside of western Massachusetts, discontented debtors generally stopped short of armed resistance. Whereas the Shaysite rebels had felt betrayed by a state government that had rejected their demands, debtor interests elsewhere were often successful in changing the monetary policy of their states. In 1785 and 1786, seven states enacted laws for new paper money issues. In most cases, the result was a qualified success. Controls on the supply of the new money kept it from depreciating rapidly, so that its inflationary effect was mild. It was used chiefly to provide loans to farmers so that they could meet their tax or mortgage payments. Combined with laws that prevented or delayed creditors from seizing property from debtors to satisfy debts, the currency issues helped keep a lid on popular discontent.

The most notorious exception to this pattern of fiscal responsibility was in Rhode Island, already nicknamed "Rogue's Island" for the sharp trading practices of its merchants. A rural party that gained control of the Rhode Island legislature in 1786 pushed through a currency law that flooded the state with paper money that could be used to pay all debts. Creditors who balked at accepting the new money at face value were subject to heavy penalties. Shocked, they went into hiding or left the state entirely, and merchants denounced the law as outright fraud.

The actions of the debtor party in Rhode Island alarmed conservatives everywhere, confirming their fears that legislative bodies dominated by common farmers and artisans rather than, as before the Revolution, by men of wealth and social distinction, were dangerous. One South Carolina conservative declared that he could see nothing but an "open and outrageous . . . violation of every principle of justice" in paper money and debt relief laws. Conservatives, creditors, and nationalists alike now spoke of a democratic tyranny that would have to be checked if the republic were to survive and protect its property holders.

CONGRESS AND THE WEST

The Peace of Paris and the surrender of charter claims by the states gave the Congress control of a magnificent expanse of land between the Appalachian Mountains and the Mississippi River. This was the first American West. In what would prove the most enduring accomplishment of the Confederation government, the Congress set forth a series of effective provisions for its settlement, governance, and eventual absorption into the Union.

The Congress took several steps to establish its jurisdiction in the West. Asserting for the national government the right to formulate Indian policy, the Congress negotiated a series of treaties with the Indians beginning in 1784 for the abandonment of their land claims in the West. By threatening to use military force, congressional commissioners in 1784 coerced the Iroquois Confederation of New York to cede half of its territory to the United States in the Treaty of Fort Stanwix. Similar tactics in 1785 resulted in the Treaty of Fort McIntosh in which the Wyandots, Chippewas, Delawares, and Ottawas ceded much of their land in Ohio. Against the opposition of states intent on grabbing Indian lands for themselves, Congress resolved in 1787 that its treaties were binding on all the states. And anxious for revenue, Congress insisted on payment from squatters who had filtered into the West before provisions had been made for land sales.

The most pressing political challenge was to secure the loyalty of the West to the new and fragile Union. To satisfy the demands of settlers for self-government, the Congress resolved as early as 1779 that new states would be carved out of the western domain with all the rights of the original states. An early plan for organizing the territories, the Ordinance of 1784, was largely the work of Thomas Jefferson. In it, he proposed to create ten districts, or territories, each of which could apply for admission as a state when its population equaled that of the free inhabitants in the least populous of the existing states. Jefferson also proposed that settlers be permitted to choose their own officials, and he called for the prohibition of slavery in the West after 1800. Shorn of its no-slavery features, the ordinance passed Congress but was never put into practice.

As settlers and speculators began pouring into the West in 1784, however, the Congress was forced to move quickly to formulate a policy for conveying its public land into private hands. If it could not regulate land sales and pass on clear titles, Congress would, in effect, have surrendered its claim to govern. One way or another, settlers were going to get their land, but a pell-mell process of private acquisitions in widely scattered settlements threatened to touch off costly Indian wars, deprive the national government of vitally needed revenue, and encourage separatist movements. The members of Congress had to act on national land policy, warned a western Pennsylvanian, or else "lose the only opportunity they ever will have of extending their power and influence over this new region."

The Congress responded with the **Land Ordinance of 1785**. The crucial feature of this seminal legislation was its stipulation that public lands be surveyed in a rectangular grid pattern before being offered for sale (see Figure 7-3). By requiring that land first be plotted into townships of thirty-six uniform sections of 640 acres each, the ordinance adopted the New England system of land settlement, an approach that promoted compact settlements and produced undisputed land titles. In sharp contrast was the typical southern pattern, whereby settlers picked out a piece of land in a large tract ahead of a precise survey and then fought each other in the courts to secure legal title. In an effort to avoid endless litigation, Congress opted for a policy geared to order and regularity.

Congress also attempted to attract a certain type of settler to the West by offering the plots of 640 acres at the then hefty sum of no less than $640, or $1 per acre, payable in hard currency or its equivalent. The goal here was to keep out the shiftless poor and reserve the West for enterprising and presumably law-abiding farm families who could afford the entry cost. Concerned about westerners' reputation for lawlessness and afraid that the primitive living conditions might cause them to lapse into savagery, Congress also set aside the income from the sale of the sixteenth section in each township for the sup-

GRAPHIC EXPLORATION To explore an interactive version of this graph, go to
http://www.prenhall.com/goldfield/fig7.3

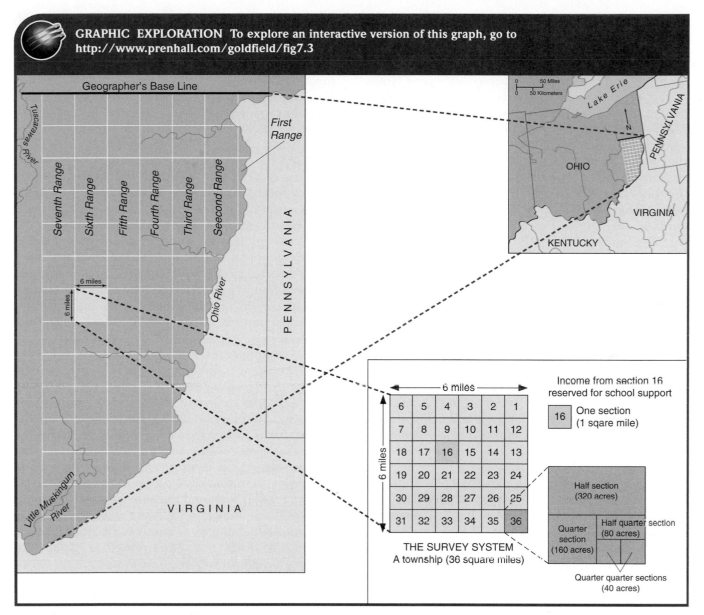

FIGURE 7-3   Land Ordinance of 1785
*The precise uniformity of the surveying system initiated in the Land Ordinance of 1785 created
a rectangular grid pattern that was the model for all future land surveyed in the public domain.*

port of public schools. Support for education, as a congressional report of 1783 put it, would help provide for "security against the increase of feeble, disorderly and dispersed settlements in those remote and extended territories [and] against the depravity of manners which they have a tendency to produce."

Before any land sales occurred under the Ordinance of 1785, impatient settlers continued to push north of the Ohio River and claim homesteads as squatters. They clashed both with local Indian tribes and with the troops sent by the Congress to evict

them. Impatient itself with the slow process of surveying, the Congress sold off 1.5 million acres to a group of New England speculators organized as the Ohio Company. The speculators bought the land with greatly depreciated loan-office certificates that had been issued to Revolutionary War veterans, and their cost per acre averaged less than 10 cents in hard money. They now pressed their allies in Congress to establish a governmental structure for the West that would protect their investment by bringing the unruly elements in the West under control.

Both the Congress and speculators wanted political stability and economic development in the West and a degree of supervision for settlers commonly viewed in the East as "but little less savage than the Indians." What was needed, wrote James Monroe of Virginia, were temporary controls—made acceptable by the promise of eventual statehood—that "in effect" would place the western territories under "a colonial government similar to that which prevail'd in these States previous to the revolution." The **Northwest Ordinance of 1787,** the most significant legislative act of the Confederation Congress, filled this need, creating a political structure for the territories and a phased process for achieving statehood that neatly blended public and private interests.

According to the ordinance, controls on a new territory were to be strictest in the early stage of settlement, when Congress would appoint a territorial government consisting of a governor, a secretary, and three judges. When a territory reached a population of five thousand adult males, those with 50 acres of land or more could elect a legislature. The actions of the legislature, however, were subject to an absolute veto by the governor. Once a territory had a population of sixty thousand, the settlers could draft a constitution and apply for statehood "on an equal footing with the original states in all respects whatsoever."

Unlike Jefferson's Ordinance of 1784, which called for ten states, the Northwest Ordinance of 1787 stipulated that only three to five states were to be formed out of the Northwest. This change was because the admission of new states would weaken the control over Congress that the original thirteen states wanted to maintain for themselves as long as possible. Although less democratic in many respects than Jefferson's plan in mandating a period of outside control by Congress, the 1787 ordinance did provide greater protection for property rights as well as a bill of rights guaranteeing individual freedoms. Most significant, it prohibited slavery.

Southern congressmen agreed to the slavery ban, in part because they feared that planters in the new states would compete with them in the production of slave-produced staples such as tobacco. More importantly, however, they expected slavery to be permitted in the region south of the Ohio River that was still under the administrative authority of Virginia, North Carolina, and Georgia in the 1780s. Indeed, slavery was allowed in this region when the **Southwest Ordinance of 1790** brought it under national control, a decision that would have grave consequences in the future sectionalization of the United States.

Although the Northwest Ordinance applied only to the national domain north of the Ohio River, it provided the organizational blueprint by which all future territory was brought into the Union. It went into effect immediately and set the original Union on a course of dynamic expansion through the addition of new states.

DIPLOMATIC WEAKNESSES

In the international arena of the 1780s, the United States was a weak and often ridiculed nation. Under the Articles of Confederation, the Congress had the authority to negotiate foreign treaties but no economic or military power to enforce their terms. Unable to regulate commerce or set tariffs, Congress had no leverage with which to pry open the restricted trading empires of France, Spain, and most important, Britain.

France and the United States, allies during the Revolutionary War, remained on friendly terms after it. The United States even had a favorable trade balance with France, selling more there than it bought. Britain, however, treated its former colonies with contempt, and Spain was also openly antagonistic to the new nation. Both Britain and Spain sought to block American expansion into the trans-Appalachian West. And a dispute with Spain over the West produced the most serious diplomatic crisis of the period, one that spilled over into domestic politics, increasing sectional tensions between northern and southern states and leading many to question the country's chances of survival. As this crisis unfolded, the British remained poised to exploit any additional signs of American weakness.

IMPASSE WITH BRITAIN

The Confederation Congress was unable to resolve any of the major issues that poisoned Anglo-American relations in the 1780s. Key among those issues were provisions in the peace treaty of 1783 that concerned prewar American debts to the British and the treatment of Loyalists by the patriots. Britain used what it claimed to be America's failure to satisfy those provisions to justify its own violations of the treaty. The result was a diplomatic deadlock that hurt American interests in the West and in foreign trade.

Article 4 of the peace treaty called for the payment of all prewar debts at their "full value in sterling money"—that is, in gold or silver coin. Among the most numerous of those with outstanding debts to British creditors were tobacco planters in the Chesapeake region of Virginia and Maryland. During the Revolution, the British army had carried off and freed many of the region's slaves without compensating the planters. Still angry, the planters were in no mood to repay their debts. Working out a scheme with their respective legislatures, they agreed only to pay the face value of their debts to their state treasuries in state or Continental paper money. Since this money was practically worthless, the planters in effect repudiated their debts.

During the Revolution, all the states had passed anti-Loyalist legislation, and many state governments had seized Loyalists' lands and goods, selling them to raise revenue for the war effort. Upwards of 100,000 Loyalists fled to Canada and England, and their property losses ran into millions of dollars. Articles 5 and 6 of the peace treaty pledged the Congress to "recommend" to the states that they stop persecuting Loyalists and restore confiscated Loyalist property. But wartime animosities remained high, ebbing only gradually as the 1780s wore on. Despite the pleadings of John Jay, the secretary for foreign affairs in the Confederation government, the states were slow to rescind their punitive legislation or allow the recovery of confiscated property.

Combined with the matter of the unpaid debts, the continued failure of the states to make restitution to the Loyalists gave the British a convenient pretext to hold on to the forts in the West that they had promised to relinquish in the Treaty of Paris. Their refusal to abandon the forts, which extended from Lake Champlain in upstate New York westward along the Great Lakes, was part of an overall strategy to keep the United States weak, divided, and small. The continued British presence in the region effectively shut Americans out of the fur trade with the Indians. It also insulted the sovereignty of the United States and threatened the security of its northern frontier. In 1784, exasperated New Yorkers warned the Congress that unless the British were forced to leave, New York would "be compelled to consider herself as left to pursue her own Councils, destitute of the Protection of the United States." Elsewhere, the British, spurred on by Canadian officials, encouraged secessionist movements in the Northwest and sought out Indian allies to fight for a possible buffer state south of the Great Lakes that would keep Americans hemmed in along the Atlantic seaboard.

Throughout the 1780s, the British also explored the possibility of entering into an economic alliance with Vermont. Created in 1777 out of land claimed by both New York and New Hampshire, Vermont proclaimed itself an independent republic, free from the control of the British Parliament and the American Congress. Ethan Allen and his brothers Ira and Levi held the power in Vermont politics, and their ambitious schemes for profiting from the sale of such raw materials as lumber and naval stores depended on a favorable treaty with Britain. The Allen brothers initiated a series of negotiations with the British in the 1780s in which they offered a treaty of friendship in exchange for recognition of Vermont's independence and trading privileges within the British Empire. The British were tempted but held back for fear of unduly antagonizing the United States. (Most Vermonters were strongly pro-American in their loyalties, and in 1791, after settlement of the disputed land claims, Vermont joined the Union as the fourteenth state.)

Although concerned by British provocations in the West and fears that the British would convert Vermont into a client state, American officials viewed Britain's retaliatory trade policies as the gravest threat to American security and prosperity. John Adams, the American minister to London, sought in vain to counter Britain's anti-American economic policies. "I may reason till I die to no purpose," Adams reported to Jay in June 1785, and he complained that he was treated as a complete "cypher."

Adams soon concluded that the British would never lift their trading and shipping restrictions until forced to do so by a uniform American system of discriminatory duties on British goods. The problem was that a uniform policy was impossible to achieve under the Articles of Confederation. Retaliatory navigation acts by individual states did little good because they left the British free to play one state off another. Adams could denounce Parliament as a "parcel of sots" for restricting American trade, but only with a strong, centralized government could Americans fashion a navigation system that would command Britain's respect.

SPAIN AND THE MISSISSIPPI RIVER

At the close of the Revolutionary War, Spain reimposed barriers on American commerce within its empire. Anxious to maintain as large a buffer zone as possible between its Louisiana and Florida possessions and the restless Americans, Spain also refused to recognize the southern and western boundaries of the United States as specified in the treaty with Britain in 1783, holding out instead for a more northerly border (see Map 7–2). And of greatest consequence, it denied the claim of the United States to free navigation of the entire length of the Mississippi River.

The Mississippi question was explosive because on its resolution hinged American settlement and control of the entire western region south of the

MAP 7-2 **Disputed Territory in the West after the Treaty of Paris**
Throughout the 1780s, Spain asserted title to a large area in the West south of the Ohio River.

Ohio River. Southerners were rapidly moving into this area, and the slave South expected to gain new support for an alliance against the commercial North as new slave states were created south of the Ohio. Free navigation of the Mississippi was essential to the realization of these expectations. Only with access to the Mississippi and the commercial right of deposit at New Orleans—that is, the right to transfer cargoes to oceangoing vessels—could the region's farmers, then mostly in what would become Tennessee and Kentucky, profitably reach national and international markets.

In the wake of the Revolution, the settlers of Kentucky, which was still part of Virginia, and Tennessee, which was still part of North Carolina, flirted with the idea of secession. According to a 1785 report, settlers in Kentucky felt that they did "not at present enjoy a greater portion of liberty [under Virginia] than an American colony might have done a few years ago had she been allowed a Representation in the British Parliament." Impatient to secure both political independence and the economic benefits that would come with access to the Mississippi, the

separatists were not particular about whom they dealt with. They became entangled in a web of diplomatic intrigue that included the Spanish, the Indians, and American authorities east of the mountains.

Spain sought to trade on the divided loyalties of American speculators and frontier settlers to its advantage, employing some of them as spies and informers. Led by General James Wilkinson in Kentucky, these agents encouraged separatist plots and talk of a western confederation under Spanish protection. Spain likewise sought to exploit divisions among Indian groups. In a bewildering variety of treaties negotiated by the Congress, individual Southern states, and land speculators, white Americans laid claim to much of the ancestral land of the major Indian nations in the Southeast—the Cherokee, Chickasaw, Choctaw, and Creek. Fraud was rampant, and many Native Americans believed, with good reason, that they had never been consulted in the dispossession of their land. The Spanish responded by recruiting disaffected Indians into an alliance system of their own. Their staunchest allies came from a faction of the Creeks led by Alexander McGillivray, the son of a trader father and a half-French, half-Creek mother. Supplied with arms from the Spanish, these Creeks succeeded in forcing white settlers off their tribal land in Georgia.

Spain stepped up pressure on the West in the summer of 1784, when it closed the Mississippi River within Spanish territory to American trade. Hoping now to benefit from American weakness, Spain also opened negotiations for a long-term settlement with the United States. The Spanish negotiator, Don Diego de Gardoqui, offered a deal that cleverly played the interests of the North against those of the South and West. In exchange for an American agreement to surrender claims to navigate the Mississippi for thirty years, Gardoqui proposed to grant the United States significant trading concessions in the Spanish Empire that would open new markets and new sources of hard money to the financially pressed merchants of the northeastern states. John Jay, his American negotiating partner, reluctantly accepted the offer.

When Jay released the terms of the proposed treaty with Spain in 1786, Congress erupted in angry debate. Southerners, who had taken the lead in the settlement of the West, accused Jay of selling out their interests. The treaty threatened the agrarian alliance they hoped to forge with the West, increasing the odds that the West would break from the East and go its own way. Vowing that they would not surrender the West, southern congressmen united to

This portrait, sketched in about 1790 by John Trumbull, is the only known likeness of Alexander McGillivray, a Creek leader who effectively played off Spanish and American interests in the Southeast to gain a measure of independence for the Creeks in the 1780s.

TOWARD A NEW UNION

In June 1786, a worried John Jay wrote to General George Washington that he was "uneasy and apprehensive; more so than during the war. Then we had a fixed object. . . . The case is now altered; we are going and doing wrong, and therefore I look forward to evils and calamities, but without being able to guess at the instrument, nature, or measure of them." Other nationalists fully shared Jay's forebodings. Everywhere they saw unsolved problems and portents of disaster: unpaid debts, social unrest, squabbling states, sectional hostilities, the uncertain status of the West, blocked channels of trade, foreign intrigues, and a paralyzing lack of centralized authority and purpose. They feared that the republic's very survival was now at stake.

In September 1786, delegates from several states met at the **Annapolis Convention,** in Annapolis, Maryland, seeking to devise a uniform system of commercial regulation for the country. While there, a group of nationalist leaders called on all the states to send delegates to a convention at Philadelphia "to devise such further provisions as shall appear to them necessary to render the constitution of the Federal Government adequate to the exigencies of the Union." The leaders who met at the **Constitutional Convention** in Philadelphia forged an entirely new framework of governance, the **Constitution of the United States,** that called for a federal republic with a powerful and effective national government. In 1788, after a close struggle in state ratifying conventions, the Constitution was adopted.

THE ROAD TO PHILADELPHIA

The road to Philadelphia began at Mount Vernon, George Washington's estate in Virginia. Commissioners from Maryland and Virginia met there in March 1785 to resolve jurisdictional and navigational disputes over the Potomac River and Chesapeake Bay, waters shared by the two states. Washington had a personal stake in hosting the conference, for he was president of the Potomac Company, a newly formed group of investors hoping to build a series of canals linking the Potomac River with the Shenandoah and Ohio Valleys. The meeting went so well that the participants invited representatives from Delaware and Pennsylvania to join them at a conference in Annapolis the following year to formulate policies for interstate commerce on the waterways that linked the Chesapeake region and the Ohio Valley. James Madison then broadened the scope of the Annapolis Conference to include representatives from all thirteen states for a general discussion of how best to promote and regulate interstate trade.

defeat the treaty. Nine states' votes were required for ratification under the Articles, and Jay's treaty could gain only seven—all in the North.

The regional antagonisms exposed by the Jay-Gardoqui talks heightened the alarm over the future of the republic provoked by Shays's Rebellion earlier in 1786. The Union had never appeared more fragile or the Congress under the Articles of Confederation so powerless to resolve its differences. Southerners openly calculated the value of remaining in a Union seemingly dominated by the commercial North, and Westerners warned that unless they were upheld on the Mississippi issue, they would consider themselves "relieved from all Federal Obligations and fully at Liberty to exact alliances & Connections wherever they find them." As the sense of crisis deepened in 1786, the nationalists grew in influence and numbers. Led by Alexander Hamilton of New York and James Madison of Virginia, they now argued that only a radical political change could preserve the republic and fulfill the promise of its greatness.

Only nine states decided to send delegates to the Annapolis Convention, and only those from five states had actually arrived when the nationalists, at the prompting of Madison and Hamilton, abruptly adjourned the meeting. They then called on the states and the Congress to approve a full-scale constitutional convention for Philadelphia in May 1787.

The timing of the call for the Philadelphia Convention could not have been better. During the fall and winter of 1786, the agrarian protests unleashed by Shays's Rebellion in Massachusetts spilled over into other states. Coupled with talk of a dismemberment of the Union in the wake of the Jay-Gardoqui negotiations, the agrarian unrest strengthened the case of the nationalists for more centralized authority.

All the states except Rhode Island, which wanted to retain exclusive control over its own trade, sent delegates to Philadelphia. The fifty-five men who attended the convention represented an extraordinary array of talent and experience. Chiefly lawyers by training or profession, most of them had served in the Confederation Congress, and more than one-third had fought in the Revolution. Extremely well educated by the standards of the day, the delegates were members of the intellectual as well as the political and economic elite. As a group, they were far wealthier than the average American. Most had investments in land and the public securities of the United States. At least nineteen owned slaves. Their greatest asset as a working body was their common commitment to a nationalist solution to the crisis of confidence they saw gripping the republic. Most of the strong supporters of the Articles of Confederation refused to attend, perhaps because, as Patrick Henry of Virginia remarked, they "smelt a rat."

THE CONVENTION AT WORK

When it agreed to the Philadelphia Convention, Congress authorized only a revision of the Articles of Confederation. Almost from the start, however, the delegates set about replacing the Articles altogether. Their first action was to elect George Washington unanimously as the convention's presiding officer, gaining credibility for their deliberations from his prestige. The most ardent nationalists then immediately seized the initiative by presenting the **Virginia Plan**. Drafted by James Madison, this plan replaced the Confederation Congress with a truly national government, organized like most state governments, with a bicameral legislature, an executive, and a judiciary.

Two features of the Virginia Plan stood out. First, it granted the national Congress power to legislate "in all cases in which the separate states are incompetent" and to nullify any state laws that in its judgment were contrary to the "articles of Union." Second, it made representation in both houses of the Congress proportional to population. This meant that the most populous states would have more votes in Congress than the less populous states, giving them effective control of the government. In short, Madison sought to all but eliminate the independent authority of the states while also forcing the smaller states to defer to the more populous ones in national affairs.

Delegates from the small states countered with the **New Jersey Plan**, introduced on June 15 by William Paterson. This plan kept intact the basic structure of the Confederation Congress—one state, one vote—but otherwise amended the Articles by giving the national government the explicit power to tax and to regulate domestic and foreign commerce. In addition, it gave acts of Congress precedence over state legislation, making them "the supreme law of the respective states."

The Great Compromise.   The New Jersey Plan was quickly voted down, and the convention remained deadlocked for another month over how to apportion state representation in the national government. The issue was finally resolved on July 16 with the so-called **Great Compromise**. Based on a proposal by Roger Sherman of Connecticut, the compromise split the differences between the small and large states. Small states were given equal footing with large states in the Senate, or upper house, where each would have two votes. In the lower house, the House of Representatives, the number of seats was made proportional to population, giving larger states the advantage. The Great Compromise also settled a sectional dispute over representation between the free (or about to be free) states and slave states. The southern states wanted slaves counted for apportioning representation in the House but excluded from direct tax assessments. The northern states wanted slaves counted for tax assessments but excluded for apportioning representation. To settle the issue, the Great Compromise settled on an expedient, if morally troubling, formula: Free residents were to be counted precisely; to that count would be added three-fifths "of all other persons," excluding Indians not taxed. Thus the slave states gained additional political representation while the states in the North received assurances that the owners of nonvoting slaves would have to bear part of the cost of any direct taxes levied by the new government.

Washington presides over the Constitutional Convention.

The Great Compromise ended the first phase of the convention, which had focused on the general framework of a stronger national government. In its next phase, the convention debated the specific powers to be delegated to the new government. It was at this point that the sectional cleavage between North and South over slavery and other issues came most prominently to the fore. As Madison had warned in late June, "the great division of interests" in the United States would arise from the effect of states "having or not having slaves."

Regulation of commerce and the issue of slavery.
The sectional clash first erupted over the power of Congress to regulate commerce. At issue was whether Congress could regulate trade and set tariffs by a simple majority vote. Southerners worried that a northern majority would pass navigation acts favoring northern shippers and drive up the cost of sending southern commodities to Europe. To counter this threat, delegates from the Lower South demanded that a two-thirds majority be required to enact trade legislation. Suddenly, the central plank

in the nationalists' program—the unified power to force trading concessions from Britain—was endangered. A frustrated Madison urged his fellow southerners to remember that "as we are laying the foundation of a great empire, we ought to take a permanent view of the subject."

In the end, Madison had his way; the delegates agreed that enacting trade legislation would require only a simple majority. In return, however, southerners exacted concessions on the slavery issue. When planters from South Carolina and Georgia made it clear that they would agree to join a new Union only if they could continue to import slaves, the convention abandoned a proposal to ban the foreign slave trade. Instead, following the lead of Roger Sherman of Connecticut, who argued that emancipation sentiment would eventually lead to abolition of slavery anyway, antislavery New Englanders reached a compromise with the delegates from the Lower South: Congress would be barred from acting against the slave trade for twenty years. In addition, bowing to the fears of planters that Congress could use its taxing power to undermine slavery, the convention denied Congress the right to tax exports from any state. And to alleviate southern concerns that slaves might escape to freedom in the North, the new Constitution included an explicit provision calling on any state to return "persons held to Service or Labour" in another.

After settling the slavery question in late August, the convention had one last significant hurdle to clear: the question of the national executive. For months the delegates had gone around in circles debating how presidents should be elected, how long they should serve, and what their powers should be. But in early September, eager to wrap matters up and close to exhaustion after working through a long, hot summer, they moved quickly to resolve these issues.

The office of the chief executive.
In large part because of their confidence in General Washington, whom nearly everyone expected to be the first president, the delegates fashioned a chief executive office with broad discretionary powers. The prerogatives of the president included the rank of commander in chief of the armed forces, the authority to conduct foreign affairs and negotiate treaties, the right to appoint diplomatic and judicial officers, and the power to veto congressional legislation. The president's term of office was set at four years, with no limits on how often an individual could be reelected.

Determining how to elect the president proved a thorny problem. The delegates envisioned a forceful, energetic, and independent executive, insulated from the whims of an uninformed public and the intrigues of the legislature. As a result, they rejected both popular election and election by Congress. The solution they hit upon was the convoluted system of an "electoral college." Each state was left free to determine how it would choose presidential electors equal to the number of its representatives and senators. These electors would then cast votes to select a president. If no candidate received a majority of the electoral votes, the election would be turned over to the House of Representatives, where each state would have one vote.

After a style committee polished the wording in the final draft of the Constitution, thirty-nine of the forty-two delegates still in attendance signed the document on September 17. The Preamble, which originally began with a list of the states, was reworded at the last minute to begin simply: "We the people of the United States, in order to form a more perfect Union . . ." This subtle change had significant implications. By identifying the people, and not a collection of states, as the source of authority, it emphasized the national vision of the framers and their desire to create a government quite different from a confederation of states.

OVERVIEW OF THE CONSTITUTION

Although not as strong as the most committed nationalists would have liked, the central government outlined in the Constitution was to have far more powers than those entrusted to Congress under the Articles of Confederation (see the Overview table, "The Articles of Confederation and the Constitution Compared.") The Constitution's provision for a strong, single-person executive had no precedent in the Articles. Nor did the provision for a Supreme Court. The Constitution vested this court, as well as the lower courts that Congress was empowered to establish, with the judicial power of the United States. In addition, the Constitution specifically delegated to Congress the powers to tax, borrow and coin money, regulate commerce, and raise armed forces that the Confederation government had lacked.

Most of the economic powers of Congress came at the expense of the states, which were prohibited from passing tariffs, issuing money, or—in an obvi-

Overview

The Articles of Confederation and the Constitution Compared

	Articles	Constitution
Sovereign power of the central government	No power to tax or raise armies	Power granted on taxes and armed forces
Source of power	Individual states	Shared through federalism between states and the national government
Representation in Congress	Equal representation of states in a unicameral Congress	A bicameral legislature with equal representation of the states in the Senate and proportional representation in the House
Amendment process	Unanimous consent of the states	Consent of three-fourths of the states
Executive	None provided for	Office of the president
National judiciary	None provided for	The Supreme Court

ous reference to the debtor relief legislation of the 1780s—enacting any law that infringed on the contractual rights of creditors to collect money from debtors. Further curbing the sovereignty of the states was a clause stipulating that the Constitution and all national legislation and treaties were to be "the supreme law of the land." This clause has subsequently been interpreted as giving the central government the power to declare state laws unconstitutional

A no-nonsense realism, as well as a nationalist outlook, infused the Constitution. Its underlying political philosophy was that, in Madison's wonderful phrase, "ambition must be made to counter ambition." Madison and the other members of the national elite who met at Philadelphia were convinced that self-interest, not disinterested virtue, motivated political behavior. As proof, they cited what to them was the sorry record of the state governments in protecting property rights and promoting social order. In their view, these governments were failures because they had been captured by unrestrained majorities corrupted by the selfishness of competing interest groups. Accepting interest group politics as inevitable and seeking to prevent a tyrannical majority from forming at the national level, the architects of the Constitution designed a central government in which competing blocs of power counterbalanced one another.

The Constitution placed both internal and external restraints on the powers granted to the central government. The functional division of the government into executive, legislative, and judicial branches, each with ways to keep the others from exercising excessive power, created an internal system of checks and balances. For example, the Senate's authority to approve or reject presidential appointments and to ratify or reject treaties was a curb on the powers of the executive. The president commanded the armed forces, but only Congress could declare war. The president could veto congressional legislation, but Congress could override that veto with a two-thirds vote. To pass in the first place, legislation had to be approved by both the House of Representatives, which, with its membership proportional to population, represented the interests of the people at large, and the Senate, which represented the interests of the states. And as an ultimate check against executive abuse of power, Congress could indict, convict, and remove from office a president who tried to set himself above the law.

Although the Constitution did not explicitly grant it, the Supreme Court soon claimed the right to invalidate acts of Congress and the president that it found to be unconstitutional. This power of **judicial review** provided another check against legislative and executive authority. To guard against an arbitrary federal judiciary, the Constitution empowered Congress to determine the size of the Supreme Court and to indict and remove federal judges appointed by the president.

The external restraints on the central government were to be found in the nature of its relationship to the state governments. This relationship was based on **federalism**, the division of power between local and central authorities. By listing specific powers for Congress, the Constitution implied that all other powers were to be retained by the states. Thus, while strengthening the national government, the Constitution did not obliterate the sovereign rights of the states, leaving them free to curb the potential power of the national government in the ambiguous areas between national and state sovereignty.

This ambiguity in the federalism of the Constitution was both its greatest strength and its greatest weakness. It allowed both nationalists and advocates of states' rights to support the Constitution. But the issue of slavery, left unresolved in the gray area between state and national sovereignty, would continue to fester, sparking sectional conflict over the extent of national sovereignty that would plunge the republic into civil war three-quarters of a century later.

THE STRUGGLE OVER RATIFICATION

The realism the Philadelphia delegates displayed in the drafting of the Constitution extended to the procedure they devised for implementing it. Knowing full well that they had exceeded their instructions by proposing an entirely new government, not an amended version of the Articles, and aware that the Articles' requirement of unanimous consent by the state legislatures to any amendment would result in certain defeat, they boldly bypassed both Congress and the state legislatures.

The last article of the Constitution stipulated that it would go into effect when it had been ratified by at least nine of the states acting through specially elected popular conventions. Influenced by the nationalist sentiments of many of its members, one-third of whom had attended the Philadelphia Convention, and perhaps weary of its own impotence, the Congress accepted this drastic and not clearly legal procedure, submitting the Constitution to the states in late September 1787.

The delegates in Philadelphia had excluded the public from their proceedings. The publication of the text of the Constitution lifted this veil of secrecy and touched off a great political debate. Although those who favored the Constitution could most accurately have been defined as nationalists, they referred to themselves as **Federalists**, a term that helped deflect charges that they favored an excessive centralization of political authority. By default, the opponents of the Constitution were known as **Antifederalists**, a negative-sounding label that obscured their support of the state-centered sovereignty that most Americans associated with federalism. Initially outmaneuvered in this way, the Antifederalists never did mount an effective campaign to counter the Federalists' output of pamphlets, speeches, and newspaper editorials (see the Overview table, "Federalists versus the Antifederalists").

The Antifederalists did attract some men of wealth and social standing. Three of them—Elbridge Gerry of Massachusetts and George Mason and Edmund Randolph of Virginia—had been delegates at

Philadelphia but refused to sign the Constitution. They feared that the new national government would swallow up the state governments.

Most Antifederalists, however, were backcountry farmers, men with mud on their boots who lived far from centers of communication and market outlets for their produce. They distrusted the social and commercial elite, and many Antifederalists saw in the Constitution a sinister plot by this elite "to lord it over the rest of their fellow citizens, to trample the poorer part of the people under their feet that they may be rendered their servants and slaves." The Antifederalists clung to the belief that only a small republic, one composed of relatively homogeneous social interests, could secure the voluntary attachment of the people necessary for a free government. They argued that a large republic, such as the one framed by the Constitution, would inevitably become tyrannical because it was too distant and removed from the interests of common citizen-farmers.

However much the Antifederalists attacked the Constitution as a danger to the individual liberties

Overview

Federalists versus the Antifederalists

	Federalists	Antifederalists
Position on the Constitution	Favored the Constitution	Opposed the Constitution
Position on the Articles of Confederation	Felt the Articles had to be abandoned	Felt the Articles needed only to be amended
Position on the power of the states	Sought to curb the power of the states with a new central government	Felt the power of the states should be paramount
Position on the need for a bill of rights	Initially saw no need for a bill of rights in the Constitution	Saw the absence of a bill of rights in the proposed Constitution as a threat to individual liberties
Position on the optimum size of the republic	Believed a large republic could best safeguard personal freedoms	Believed only a small republic formed on common interests could protect individual rights
Source of support	Commercial farmers, merchants, shippers, artisans, holders of the national debt	State-centered politicians, most backcountry farmers

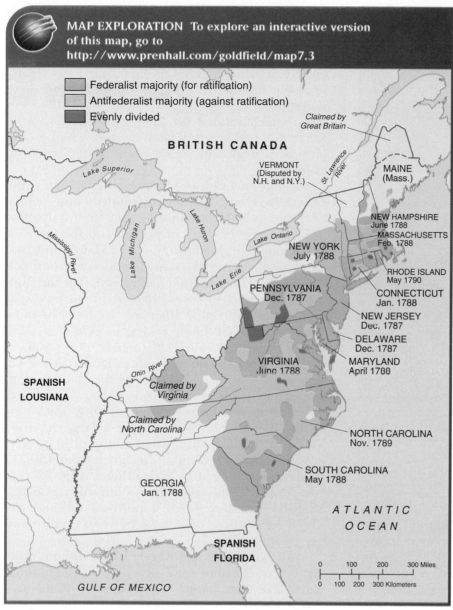

MAP EXPLORATION To explore an interactive version of this map, go to http://www.prenhall.com/goldfield/map7.3

Federalist majority (for ratification)
Antifederalist majority (against ratification)
Evenly divided

Claimed by Great Britain

BRITISH CANADA

Lake Superior

VERMONT (Disputed by N.H. and N.Y.)

St. Lawrence River

MAINE (Mass.)

Lake Michigan

Lake Huron

Lake Ontario

NEW HAMPSHIRE June 1788

MASSACHUSETTS Feb. 1788

Mississippi River

Lake Erie

NEW YORK July 1788

RHODE ISLAND May 1790

PENNSYLVANIA Dec. 1787

CONNECTICUT Jan. 1788

NEW JERSEY Dec. 1787

DELAWARE Dec. 1787

Ohio River

VIRGINIA June 1788

MARYLAND April 1788

SPANISH LOUSIANA

Claimed by Virginia

Claimed by North Carolina

NORTH CAROLINA Nov. 1789

SOUTH CAROLINA May 1788

GEORGIA Jan. 1788

ATLANTIC OCEAN

SPANISH FLORIDA

0   100   200   300 Miles
0   100   200   300 Kilometers

GULF OF MEXICO

MAP 7-3 **The Ratification Vote on the Constitution**
Aside from some frontier districts exposed to possible foreign attack, the strongest support for the Constitution came from coastal and interior areas tied into a developing commercial economy.

cities and commercial farming areas along the coast.

With talent, intellect, and political savvy on their side, the Federalists skillfully built on the momentum for change that had developed out of the crisis atmosphere of 1786. They successfully portrayed the Constitution as the best opportunity to erect a governing structure capable of preserving and extending the gains of the Revolution.

Conservatives shaken by Shays's Rebellion lined up behind the Constitution. So, too, did groups—creditors, merchants, manufacturers, urban artisans, commercial farmers—whose interests would be promoted by economic development. The enhanced powers of the national government held out the promise of protecting the home market from British imports, enlarging foreign markets for American exports, promoting a stable and uniform currency, and raising revenues to pay off the Revolutionary War debt.

In the early stages, the Federalists scored a string of easy victories (see Map 7–3). Delaware ratified the Constitution on December 7, 1787, and within a month, so, too, had Pennsylvania, New Jersey, Georgia, and Connecticut. Except for Pennsylvania, these were small, sparsely populated states that stood to benefit economically or militarily from a stronger central government. The Constitution carried in the larger state of Pennsylvania because of the Federalists' strength in the commercial center of Philadelphia.

The Federalists faced their toughest challenge in the large states that had generally been more successful in going it alone during the 1780s. One of the most telling arguments of the Antifederalists in these and other states was the absence of a

and local independence that they believed the Revolution had been fought to safeguard, they were no political match for the Federalists. They lacked the social connections, access to newspapers, and self-confidence of the more cosmopolitan and better-educated Federalists. In addition, the Federalists could more easily mobilize their supporters, who were concentrated in the port

Although physically frail, James Madison, shown here in a portrait made in about 1815, was a formidable thinker whose essays in The Federalist *endure as a lasting contribution to political theory.*

bill of rights in the Constitution. The framers had felt it unnecessary to include such an explicit protection of individual rights in a document intended to specify the powers of a national government and had barely discussed a bill of rights in Philadelphia. Realizing the importance of the issue, and citing Article 5 of the Constitution, which provided for an amendment process, the Federalists promised to recommend amending the Constitution with a bill of rights once it was ratified. By doing so, they split the ranks of the Antifederalists in Massachusetts. After the Federalists gained the support of two venerable heroes of the Revolution, John Hancock and Sam Adams, the Massachusetts convention approved the Constitution by a close vote in February 1788. To win over Hancock, the Federalists had played on his vanity, suggesting that they would back him for a top national post. Adams was convinced to back the Federalists by demonstrations of Boston artisans in favor of national tariff protection.

The major hurdles remaining for the Federalists were Virginia, the most populous state, and the strategically located New York. Technically, the Constitution could have gone into effect without them once Maryland, South Carolina, and New Hampshire had ratified it, bringing the total number of states to ratify to the required nine. But without Virginia, which ratified on June 25, and New York, which followed a month later, the new Union would have been weak and the Federalist victory far from assured.

To eke out victory in these crucial states, the Federalists drew on their pragmatism and persuasiveness. As in Massachusetts, they were helped by their promise of a bill of rights. And for the New York campaign, Madison, Jay, and Hamilton wrote an eloquent series of eighty-five essays known collectively as *The Federalist* to allay fears that the Constitution would so consolidate national power as to menace individual liberties. In the two most original and brilliant essays in *The Federalist,* essays 10 and 51, Madison turned traditional republican doctrine on its head. A large, diverse republic like the one envisaged by the Constitution, he reasoned, not a small and homogeneous one, offered the best hope for safeguarding the rights of all citizens. This was because a large republic would include a multitude of contending interest groups, making it difficult for any combination of them to coalesce into a tyrannical majority that could oppress minority rights. With this argument, Madison had developed a political rationale by which Americans could have both an empire and personal freedom.

North Carolina and Rhode Island did not ratify until after the new government was functioning. North Carolina joined the Union in 1789 once Congress submitted the amendments that constituted the Bill of Rights. The obstinate Rhode Islanders stayed out until 1790, when Congress forced them in with a threat of commercial reprisal.

CONCLUSION

In freeing themselves from British rule, Americans embarked on an unprecedented wave of constitution-making that sought to put into practice abstract principles of republicanism that held that political power should derive from the people. Between 1776 and 1780, Americans developed a unique system of constitutionalism. They proclaimed the supremacy of constitutions over ordinary legislation; detailed the powers of government in a written document; provided protection for individual freedoms in bills of rights; and fashioned a process for framing governments through the election of delegates to a special constitutional convention and the popular ratification of the work of that convention. In all of these areas, Americans were pioneers in demonstrating to the rest of the world how common citizens could create their own governments.

The curbs on centralized power that characterized the state constitutions also applied to what amounted to the first national constitution, the Articles of Confederation. Indeed, the inability of the Confederation Congress to exercise effective power in the areas of taxation and foreign trade was a crippling flaw that thoroughly discredited the Articles in the eyes of the nationalist-minded leaders who had emerged during the Revolution. These leaders overthrew the Articles at the Constitutional Convention in 1787 and en-

gineered a peaceful revolution in securing the ratification of the Constitution. Their victory in creating a new central government with real national powers was built on the foundation of constitutional concepts and mechanisms that Americans had laid down in their state constitutions. The new Contitution did rest on the consent of the governed, and it endured because it could be amended to reflect shifts in popular will and to widen the circle of Americans granted the rights of political citizenship.

Accepting as a given that self-interest drove political action, the framers of the Constitution designed the new national government to turn ambition against itself. They created rival centers of power that forced selfish factions to compete in a constant struggle to form a workable majority. That struggle occurred both within the national government and between that government and the states in the American system of federalism. The Constitution thus set the stage for an entirely new kind of national politics.

REVIEW QUESTIONS

1. How would you assess the decisions made by Shepard and Shays that resulted in the clash at the Springfield arsenal? Can you imagine any way in which the crisis could have been resolved short of violence?

2. How would you define republicanism? Do you believe that Americans today still believe in the basic tenets of republicanism?

3. What was so unprecedented about the new state constitutions, and what principles of government did they embody?

4. What were the problems of the economy in the 1780s, and why did clashes between debtors and creditors become so divisive? Do you think that an economic recovery could have been achieved under the Articles of Confederation?

5. Do you feel that the diplomatic weaknesses of the United States under the Articles were as serious as its internal problems? What were the sources of those weaknesses, and what threat did they pose for national unity?

6. What sorts of men drafted the Constitution in 1787, and how representative were they of all Americans? What explains the differences between the Federalists and Antifederalists? Do you think they shared the same vision of what they wanted America to become? How widespread was the popular backing for the Constitution, and what accounts for its ratification?

KEY TERMS

Annapolis Convention (p. 221)

Antifederalists (p. 226)

Articles of Confederation (p. 210)

Bill of rights (p. 207)

Constitutional Convention (p. 221)

Constitution of the United States (p. 221)

Federalism (p. 225)

Federalists (p. 226)

Great Compromise (p. 222)

Judicial review (p. 225)

Land Ordinance of 1785 (p. 216)

Nationalists (p. 211)

Natural rights (p. 205)

New Jersey Plan (p. 222)

Northwest Ordinance of 1787 (p. 218)

Shays's Rebellion (p. 215)

Southwest Ordinance of 1790 (p. 218)

Suffrage (p. 204)

Virginia Plan (p. 222)

RECOMMENDED READINGS

Beeman, Richard, Stephen Botein, and Edward C. Carter, III, eds., *Beyond Confederation: Origins of the Constitution and American National Identity* (1987). These twelve essays offer a fine overview of the competing ideologies and issues that shaped the history of the 1780s and pushed the republic toward a new frameowrk of government in the Constitution.

Crèvecoeur, J. Hector St. John. *Letters from an American Farmer and Sketches of Eighteenth-Century America*, ed. Albert E. Stone (1986). This modern reprint of Crèvecoeur's work provides an accessible account of Americans and their living conditions in the late eighteenth century.

Jensen, Merrill. *The New Nation: A History of the United States during the Confederation, 1781–1787* (1948). This work makes the strongest case for the Articles as a tentative success that was overturned in a conservative reaction that exaggerated threats to social order.

Morris, Richard B. *The Forging of the Union, 1781–1789* (1987). The best-balanced synthesis of the 1780s, this book documents the creative statesmanship of the leaders of the Constitutional Convention.

Wood, Gordon. *The Creation of the American Republic, 1776–1787* (1969). This masterful study is indispensable for understanding the transformation in American republicanism between the winning of independence and the ratification of the Constitution.

ADDITIONAL SOURCES
The New Order of Republicanism

Block, Ruth H. *Visionary Republic: Millennial Themes in American Thought, 1756–1800* (1985).

Frey, Sylvia R. *Water from the Rock: Black Resistance in a Revolutionary Age* (1991).

Kerber, Linda. *Women of the Republic* (1980).

Pole, J. R. *Political Representation in England and the Origins of the American Republic* (1966).

Wood, Gordon. *The Radicalism of the American Revolution* (1992).

Problems at Home

Davis, Joseph L. *Sectionalism in American Politics, 1774–1787* (1977).

Hoffman, Ronald L. and Peter Albert, eds., *Sovereign States in an Age of Uncertainty* (1981).

Main, Jackson Turner. *Political Parties before the Constitution* (1973).

Onuf, Peter S. *The Origins of the Federal Republic* (1983).

Richards, Leonard L. *Shays's Rebellion: The American Revolution's Final Battle* (2002)

Diplomatic Weaknesses

Hoxie, Frederick E. Ronald Hoffman, and Peter J. Albert, eds. *Native Americans and the Early Republic* (1999).

Ritcheson, Charles T. *Aftermath of Revolution: British Policy toward the United States, 1783–1795* (1969).

Van Alstyne Richard W. *The Rising American Empire* (1980).

Toward a New Nation

Beard, Charles. *An Economic Interpretation of the Constitution* (1913).

Brown, Roger H. *Redeeming the Republic: Federalists, Taxation, and the Origins of the Constitution* (1993).

Cornell, Saul. *The Other Founders: Anti-Federalism and the Dissenting Tradition in America, 1788-1828* (1999).

Duncan, Christopher M. *The Anti-Federalists and Early American Political Thought* (1995).

Gillespie, Michael Allen, and Michael Lienesch, eds. *Ratifying the Constitution* (1989).

McDonald, Forrest. *Novus Ordo Seclorum: The Intellectual Origins of the Constitution* (1985).

Morris, Richard B. *Witness at the Creation* (1985).

WHERE TO LEARN MORE
● **South Street Seaport Museum, New York City, New York.** Maritime commerce was the lifeblood of the postrevolutionary economy. The artifacts

and the exhibits here offer a fine introduction to the seafaring world of the port city that became the nation's first capital in the new federal Union. See www.southstseaport.org for more on the impact of trade on the development of New York and information on preservation projects underway in the city.

● **Independence National Historical Park, Philadelphia, Pennsylvania.** Walks and guided tours through this historic district enable one to grasp much of the physical setting in which the delegates to the Constitutional Convention met. The website www.nps.gov/inde/home.htm includes a virtual tour of many of the collections at the park, a portrait gallery of leading figures in the Revolution, and a look at the archaeological projects underway in the park

● **Northern Indiana Center for History, South Bend, Indiana.** The permanent exhibition on the St. Joseph River valley of northern Indiana and southern Michigan explains the material world of this region and how it changed as first Europeans and then Americans mingled and clashed with the Native American population. At www.centerforhistory.org/ one can learn more about the center and the variety of programs that it offers.

 Please refer to the document CD-ROM for primary sources related to this chapter.

→ *This engraving shows respectful crowds greeting Washington as he passes through Trenton on the way to New York City for his inauguration as president.*

A NEW REPUBLIC AND THE RISE OF PARTIES
1789–1800

8

April 30, 1789

New York City

This is the great important day. Goddess of Etiquette assist me while I describe it. . . . The President was conducted out of the middle window into the Gallery [of Federal Hall] and the Oath administered by the Chancellor [Robert R. Livingston, Chancellor of New York]. Notice that the Business was done, was communicated to the Croud by Proclamation. . . . who gave three Cheers. . . . As the Company returned into the Senate Chamber, the president took the Chair, and the Senate and representatives their Seats. He rose & all arose also and [he] addressed them [in his inaugural address]. This great Man was agitated and embarrassed more than ever he was by the levelled Cannon or pointed Musket. He trembled and several times could scarce make out to read, tho it must be supposed he had often read it before. He put part of the fingers of his left hand, into the side, of what I think the Taylors call the fall, of his Breetches. Changing the paper into his left hand, after some time, he then did the same with some of the fingers of his right hand. When he came to the Words *all the World*, he made a flourish with his right hand, which left rather an ungainly impression . . . . He was dressed in deep brown, with Metal buttons,

CHAPTER OUTLINE

Washington's America
The Uniformity of New England
The Pluralism of the Mid-Atlantic Region
The Slave South and Its Backcountry
The Growing West

Forging a New Government
"Mr. President" and the Bill of Rights
Departments and Courts
Revenue and Trade
Hamilton and the Public Credit
Reaction and Opposition

The Emergence of Parties
The French Revolution
Securing the Frontier
The Whiskey Rebellion
Treaties with Britain and Spain
The First Partisan Election

The Last Federalist Administration
The French Crisis and the XYZ Affair
Crisis at Home
The End of the Federalists

Conclusion

with an Eagle on them, White Stockings a Bag and Sword—from the Hall there was a grand Procession to St. Pauls Church where prayers were said by the Bishop. The Procession was well conducted and without accident, as far as I have heard. The Militias were all under Arms. [They] lined the Street near the Church, made a good figure and behaved well. The Senate returned to their Chamber after Service, formed & took up the Address . . . . In the Evening there were grand fire Works . . . . and after this the People went to bed.

[William Maclay]

Kenneth R. Bowling and Helen E. Veit, eds., *The Diary of William Maclay and Other Notes on Senate Debates*, March 4, 1789 – March 3, 1791 (Baltimore: The Johns Hopkins University Press, 1988), pp. 11–13.

Senator William Maclay of Pennsylvania wrote this account in his personal journal of the inauguration of George Washington as the first president of the United States at Federal Hall in New York City on April 30, 1789. Born in Pennsylvania in 1737 of Scotch-Irish parents, Maclay had amassed sizeable wealth as a surveyor and lawyer by the eve of the Revolution. He held a number of popularly elected offices in the 1780s before his selection by the Pennsylvania legislature in September 1788 as one of the state's first two U.S. senators. A Presbyterian with a strong sense of rectitude that often made him overly critical of others, he quickly broke with the Washington administration over its fiscal and diplomatic policies. Before his death in 1804, he switched his political allegiance to an opposition party led by Thomas Jefferson.

Washington's shakiness at his inaugural that so obviously pained Maclay reflected the shaky start of the country's new government. Two states, North Carolina and Rhode Island, had not yet ratified the Constitution and were still outside the federal Union. The newly elected members of Congress felt no urgency to assume their duties. They had been scheduled to meet in New York on March 4, 1789, to count the ballots of the electoral college and officially confirm Washington's election, but only one-quarter of them had arrived by then. A month would go by before the minimum needed to count the ballots could be mustered. Washington, his dignity ruffled by this show of congressional disinterest, dallied at Mount Vernon until formally notified of his election.

He had every reason to dread taking on the burden of the presidency. As head of the new national government, he would put at risk the legendary status he had achieved during the Revolution. Most Americans intensely feared centralized authority, which is why the framers deliberately left the word *national* out of the Constitution. Washington somehow had to establish loyalty to a new government whose main virtue in the eyes of many was the very vagueness of its defined powers.

The Constitution had created the framework for a national government, but pressing problems demanded the fleshing out of that framework. The government urgently needed revenue to begin paying off the immense debt incurred during the Revolution. It also had to address unstable conditions in the West. Remote from the seat of power and wooed by the British north of the Ohio River and by the Spanish in the lower Mississippi Valley, western settlers wavered in their loyalties. Ultimately, the key to solving these and other problems was to establish the new republic's legitimacy. Washington and his supporters had to inspire popular backing for the government's right to exercise authority.

The realities of governing would soon shatter the nonpartisan ideal that had prevailed when the Constitution was ratified. By the end of Washington's first term, two political parties had begun to form. The Federalist party (the name came from that used by the original backers of the Constitution), which included Washington and his successor, John Adams, favored a strong central government. The opposition party, the Jeffersonian Republicans, took shape as a result of differences over financial policy and the American response to the French Revolution. Led by Thomas Jefferson, the Republicans were distrustful of excessive central power.

The Federalists, who governed through 1800, succeeded in showing a doubting world ruled by kings and queens that the American experiment in republican government could work. But as inheritors of a political tradition that equated parties with factions—temporary coalitions of selfish private interests—the Federalists doubted the loyalty of the Republicans. When the Federalists under President Adams attempted to suppress the Republicans, the stage was set for the critical election of 1800. Jefferson's victory in that election ended both Federalist rule and the republic's first major internal crisis.

KEY TOPICS

● Regional diversity of the United States in 1789

● Laying the foundations of American government during Washington's first term

● Hamilton's financial policies

● The emergence of parties during Washington's second term

● The Adams administration and the election of 1800

WASHINGTON'S AMERICA

Who were the Americans whom Washington was called on to lead when he became president? There is no easy answer. In 1789, as now, Americans identified and grouped themselves according to many factors, including race, sex, class, ethnicity, religion, and degree of personal freedom. Geographical factors, including climate and access to markets, further divided them into regions and sections. The resulting hodgepodge sorely tested the assumption—and it was never more than an assumption in 1789—that a single national government could govern Americans as a whole (see Figure 8–1).

THE UNIFORMITY OF NEW ENGLAND

The national census of 1790 counted nearly 4 million Americans, one in four of whom lived in New England. Although often viewed as the most typically "American" part of the young nation, New England in fact was rather atypical. It alone of the nation's formative regions had largely shut itself off from outsiders. Puritan notions of religious liberty that prevailed in the region extended only to those who subscribed to the Calvinist orthodoxy of the dominant Congregationalist church. Geography conspired with this religious exclusiveness to limit population diversity. New England's poor soils and long, cold winters made it an impractical place to cultivate cash crops like the tobacco and rice of the South. As a result, New England farmers had little need of imported white indentured servants or black slaves. Family members, helped by neighbors and the occasional hired hand, provided the labor on New England farms.

Puritan values and a harsh environment thus combined to make New England the most religiously and ethnically uniform region in the United States. Most of the people living there were descended from English immigrants who had arrived in the seventeenth century. Small pockets of Quakers, Baptists, and Catholics had gained the legal right of worship by the 1720s, but Congregationalism remained the official, state-supported religion in Connecticut and Massachusetts. Blacks and Indians together barely constituted 3 percent of New England's population. The few remaining Indians lived on reservations of inferior land, which they usually left only to find work as servants or day laborers.

New Englanders found slavery incompatible with the natural rights philosophy that had emerged during the Revolution and gradually began to abolish it in the 1780s. Slavery had, in any case, always been marginal in New England's economy. Owning slaves as domestic servants or artisans had been a status symbol for wealthy urban whites in Boston, Portsmouth, and Newport. As a result, about 20 percent of New England's small African American population lived in cities, in contrast to the white population, 90 percent of which lived in the countryside. Freed slaves and their descendants tended to remain in the cities, where jobs were easier for them to find than in rural areas.

Women outnumbered men in parts of New England in 1789. This pattern—not found in other parts of the country—was the result of the pressure of an expanding population and the practice of dividing family farms among male heirs. As farms in the older, more densely settled parts of New England were divided into ever smaller lots, many young men migrated west in search of cheap, arable land. They first pushed into the hilly regions of northern New England and then, by the 1790s, through the Mohawk River Valley into New York. Thus by 1789, women formed a slight majority in Connecticut, Massachusetts, and Rhode Island.

Despite their superior numbers, women in New England, as elsewhere, remained subordinate to men. Even so, the general testing of traditional authority that accompanied the Revolution led some New England women to question male power. The Massachusetts poet Judith Sargeant Murray, for example, published essays asserting that women were the intellectual equals of men. Murray was the first woman to argue publicly in favor of equal educational opportunities for young women, and she boldly asserted that women should learn how to become economically independent.

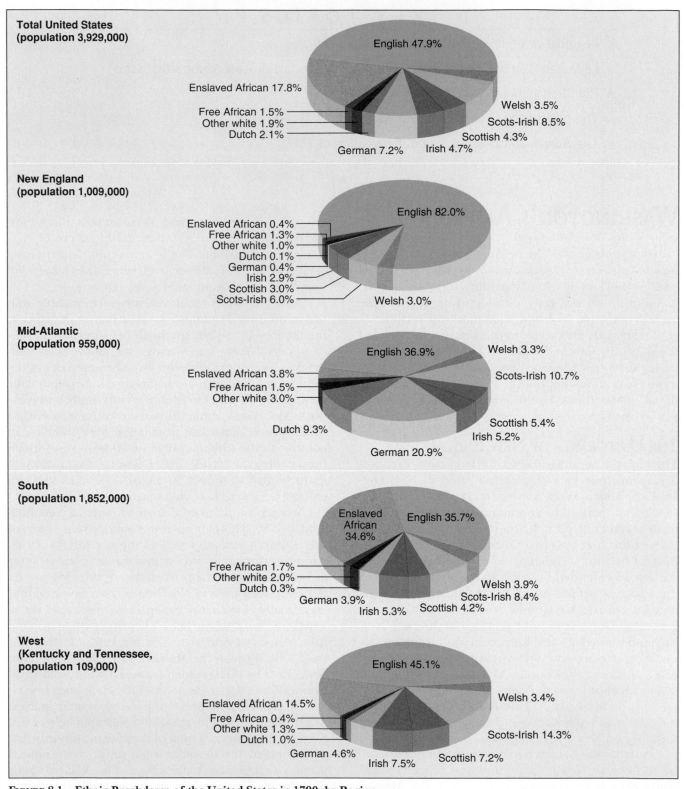

Total United States
(population 3,929,000)

English 47.9%
Enslaved African 17.8%
Free African 1.5%
Other white 1.9%
Dutch 2.1%
German 7.2%
Irish 4.7%
Scottish 4.3%
Scots-Irish 8.5%
Welsh 3.5%

New England
(population 1,009,000)

English 82.0%
Enslaved African 0.4%
Free African 1.3%
Other white 1.0%
Dutch 0.1%
German 0.4%
Irish 2.9%
Scottish 3.0%
Scots-Irish 6.0%
Welsh 3.0%

Mid-Atlantic
(population 959,000)

English 36.9%
Welsh 3.3%
Scots-Irish 10.7%
Enslaved African 3.8%
Free African 1.5%
Other white 3.0%
Dutch 9.3%
German 20.9%
Scottish 5.4%
Irish 5.2%

South
(population 1,852,000)

Enslaved African 34.6%
English 35.7%
Free African 1.7%
Other white 2.0%
Dutch 0.3%
German 3.9%
Irish 5.3%
Scottish 4.2%
Scots-Irish 8.4%
Welsh 3.9%

West
(Kentucky and Tennessee,
population 109,000)

English 45.1%
Welsh 3.4%
Enslaved African 14.5%
Free African 0.4%
Other white 1.3%
Dutch 1.0%
German 4.6%
Irish 7.5%
Scottish 7.2%
Scots-Irish 14.3%

FIGURE 8-1   **Ethnic Breakdown of the United States in 1790, by Region.**
Unique racial and ethnic patterns shaped each of the nation's four major regions in 1790.
New England was most atypical in its lack of racial or ethnic diversity.

Source: "The Statistics of the Population of the United States," comp. Francis A. Walker
(1872), pp. 3–7; Thomas L. Purvis, "The European Ancestry of the United States
Population, 1790," *William and Mary Quarterly,* 41 (1984), p. 98.

This painting of a young woman reading—General Schu-macker's Daughter, by Jacob Maentel—reflects women's in-creasing access to education in the early years of the nation. Nearly four hundred female academies and seminaries were established between 1790 and 1830.

Republican ideology, emphasizing the need of women to be intellectually prepared to raise virtuous, public-spirited children, also led reformers in New England to seek equal access for women to education. In 1789, Massachusetts became the first state to allo-cate funds specifically for girls' elementary education. And beginning in the 1780s, wealthy residents of east-ern cities set up private academies for women that would later provide the foundation for women's higher education. Liberalized divorce laws in New England also allowed a woman to seek legal separation from an abusive or unfaithful spouse.

In other respects, political and social life in New England remained rooted in the Puritan past. Age, property, and reputation determined one's standing in a culture that valued a clearly defined social order. The moral code that governed town life promoted curbs on individual behavior for the benefit of the community as a whole. With their notions of collective liberty, New Englanders subscribed to a version of republicanism that favored strong government, setting themselves apart from most other Americans, who embraced a more individualistic idea of liberty and a republicanism suspicious of government power. New Englanders per-ceived government as a divine institution with a moral responsibility to intervene in people's lives. Acting through town meetings, they taxed themselves for pub-lic services at rates two to four times higher than in the rest of the country. Their courts were also far more likely than those elsewhere to punish individuals for crimes against public order (like failing to observe the Sabbath properly) and sexual misconduct.

THE PLURALISM OF THE MID-ATLANTIC REGION

The states of the mid-Atlantic region—New York, New Jersey, and Pennsylvania—were the most ethnically and religiously diverse in the nation. People of Eng-lish descent constituted somewhat less than 40 per-cent of the population. Other major ethnic groups included the Dutch and Scots-Irish in New York and Germans and Scots-Irish in New Jersey and Pennsylva-nia. With ethnic diversity came religious diversity. Transplanted New Englanders, who brought their Congregationalism and Yankee twang with them when they settled Long Island and northern New Jer-sey, made up about 40 percent of New York's ethnic English population. Among others of English descent, Anglicans predominated in New York, and Quakers in New Jersey and Pennsylvania. The Dutch, concen-trated in the lower Hudson Valley, had their own Dutch Reformed Church, and most Germans were ei-ther Lutherans or **pietists** such as Mennonites and Moravians, who stressed personal piety over theologi-cal doctrine. The Presbyterian Scots-Irish settled heav-ily in the backcountry.

This mosaiclike pattern of ethnic and religious groupings was no accident. In contrast to Puritan New England, the Middle Colonies had offered free-dom of worship to attract settlers. In addition, eco-nomic opportunities for newcomers were much greater than in New England. The soil was better, the climate was milder, and market outlets for agricul-tural products were more abundant. These condi-tions made the mid-Atlantic region the nation's first breadbasket. It produced surpluses of wheat, flour, and corn that were shipped out of New York and Philadelphia, the two largest cities in North America by 1790. Commercial agriculture fed urban growth and created a greater demand for labor in both rural and urban areas than in New England. The influx of

Chronology

1789	Inauguration of Washington.
	Congress establishes the first federal departments.
	French Revolution begins.
1790	Hamilton submits the first of his financial reports to Congress.
1791	Bill of Rights ratified.
	Congress charters the Bank of the United States.
1792	St. Clair's defeat along the Wabash.
	Reelection of Washington.
1793	France goes to war against Britain, Spain, and Holland.
	Genêt Mission.
	Washington issues Proclamation of Neutrality.
1794	Ohio is opened with the victory of General Anthony Wayne at the Battle of Fallen Timbers.

	Suppression of the Whiskey Rebellion in western Pennsylvania.
1795	Jay's Treaty with Britain ratified.
	Treaty of Greenville with Ohio Indians.
1796	Pinckney's Treaty with Spain ratified.
	Washington's Farewell Address.
	John Adams elected president.
1797	Beginning of the Quasi-War with France.
1798	XYZ Affair.
	Alien and Sedition Acts.
	Provisional army and direct tax.
	Virginia and Kentucky Resolutions.
1799	Fries's Rebellion in Pennsylvania.
1800	Franco-American Accord.
	Thomas Jefferson elected president.

Germans and Scots-Irish into the region in the eighteenth century occurred in response to this demand.

The demand for labor had also been met by importing African slaves. Blacks, both free and enslaved, made up 5 percent of the mid-Atlantic population in 1790, and as in New England, they were more likely than whites to live in the maritime cities. New York had more slaveholders in 1790 than any other American city except Charleston, South Carolina. About 40 percent of white families in the city's nearby rural outposts of Queens, Brooklyn, and Staten Island owned slaves, a rate as high as in Maryland and South Carolina.

Despite its considerable strength in the port cities and adjacent rural areas, slavery was never an economically vital institution in most of the mid-Atlantic region. The region's major cash crop, wheat, required seasonal labor, which did not warrant tying up capital in slaves. Commercial agriculture did not rest on a slave base, nor did it produce a politically powerful class of planters. As a result, slavery in the mid-Atlantic region gave way to the demands for emancipation inspired by the natural rights philosophy of the Revolution.

Pennsylvania in 1780, New York in 1799, and New Jersey in 1804, each passed laws of gradual emancipation. These laws did not free adult slaves but provided that children born of a slave mother were to be freed at ages ranging between 18 and 28. Soon after the laws were passed, however, adult slaves began hastening their own freedom. They ran away,

set fires, and pressured their owners to accept cash payments in return for a short, fixed term of labor service. But even as they gained their freedom, African Americans had to confront enduring white racism. The comments of one white New Yorker suggest what they were up against. "We may sincerely advocate the freedom of black men," he wrote, "and yet assert their moral and physical inferiority."

The diversity of the mid-Atlantic region created a complex political environment. Competing cultural and economic interests prevented the kind of broad consensus on the meaning of republicanism that had emerged in New England. Some mid-Atlantic groups favored a strong central government to foster economic development and maintain traditional authority. Others wanted to keep government weak so as to foster a republican equality that would promote individual freedom.

Those who supported strong government included mercantile and financial leaders in the cities and commercial farmers in the countryside. These people tended to be Anglicans, Quakers, and Congregationalists of English descent. Those opposing them and favoring a more egalitarian republicanism tended to come from the middle and lower classes. They included subsistence farmers in the backcountry and artisans and day laborers in the cities. Most were Scots-Irish Presbyterians, but those in opposition also included Dutch Calvinists and German Lutherans. Fiercely independent and proud of their liberties, they resented the claims of the wealthy to political authority. They resisted government aid to business as a form of political corruption that unfairly enriched those who were already economically powerful.

THE SLAVE SOUTH AND ITS BACKCOUNTRY

In the South—the region from Maryland and Delaware to Georgia—climate and soil conditions favored the production of cash staples for world markets. Cultivating these crops required backbreaking labor that white immigrants preferred to avoid. As Thomas Jefferson put it, "In a warm climate no man will work for himself, who can make another labor for him." Southern planters relied on the coerced labor of African slaves, whose numbers made the South the most populous region in the country.

Just under 40 percent of all Southerners were slaves, but their concentration varied within the region. They were a majority in the Chesapeake Tidewater region, where slave ownership was widely distributed among white tobacco planters, including small and middling growers as well as the few great plantation owners. Farther south, in the tidal swamps of the South Carolina and Georgia lowcountry, where draining and clearing the land required huge inputs of labor, blacks outnumbered whites five to one. Slave ownership there was more concentrated than in the Tidewater. Large planters, the richest men in the country, worked hundreds of slaves in the production of rice, indigo, and sea-island cotton. Because yellow fever and malaria plagued the Carolina lowcountry, whites avoided the area, and the death rate among slaves was very high.

Slaves were less numerous in the Piedmont, or foothill, region of the South that lies between the coastal plain and the Appalachian highlands. Although sons of Tidewater planters had expanded tobacco production with slave labor into the Piedmont of Virginia and South Carolina, this was predominantly an area of nonslaveholding farmers. They relied on family labor to raise livestock, corn, and wheat. In the southern mountains, sloping to the southwest from the Blue Ridge in Virginia, the general absence of marketable crops diminished the demand for slave labor.

The free black population in the South had grown rapidly during the 1780s. Thousands of slaves fled behind British lines to win their freedom, and patriots freed others as a reward for enlisting in their forces. The Revolutionary values of liberty and equality also led many slave owners to question the morality of slavery. Legislatures in the Upper South passed laws making it financially easier than before for masters to manumit (free) their slaves. In Virginia alone, ten thousand slaves were manumitted in the 1780s. Slavery remained the foundation of the southern economy, however, and whites feared competition from freed blacks. As a result,

A frontier log cabin, such as this, was a squalid, rough-hewn structure that could be built in a day with the help of neighbors.

no southern state embarked on a general program of emancipation, and slavery in the region survived the turbulence of the Revolutionary era.

Economic conditions in the South, where the raw poverty of the backcountry offset the great wealth of the lowcountry, stamped the region's politics and culture. Tidewater planters were predominantly Anglican and of English descent. Piedmont farmers were more likely to be Scots-Irish Presbyterians and Baptists. More evangelical in their religion, and with simpler habits and tastes, the backcountry Baptists denounced the lowcountry planters for their luxury and arrogance. The planters retaliated by trying unsuccessfully to suppress the backcountry evangelicals.

The planters were indeed proud, domineering, and given to ostentatious displays of their wealth. An English traveler observed that Virginia planters "are haughty and jealous of their liberties, impatient of restraint, and can scarcely bear the thought of being controlled by any superior power." Planters understood liberty to mean the power of white males, unchecked by any outside authority, to rule over others. The only acknowledged check on this power was the planter's sense of duty, his obligation to adhere to an idealized code of conduct befitting a gentleman and a man of honor.

Backcountry farmers also jealously guarded their liberties. "They are," noted a late-eighteenth-century traveler, "extremely tenacious of the rights and liberties of republicanism. They consider themselves on an equal footing with the best educated people of the country, and upon the principles of equality they intrude themselves into every company." Backcountry farmers shared with the planters a disdain for government and restraints on the individual. But they opposed the planters' belief in a social hierarchy based on wealth and birth that left both poor whites and black slaves in a subordinate position.

THE GROWING WEST

Between the Appalachian Mountains and the Mississippi River stretched the most rapidly growing region of the new nation, the West. Land-hungry settlers poured across the mountains once the British recognized the American claim to the region in the Treaty of Paris. During the 1780s, the white population of the West exploded from less than 10,000 to 200,000. The region's Native American population was, by contrast, about 150,000.

Indians strongly resisted white claims on their lands. A confederation of tribes in the Ohio Valley, led by the Miamis and supplied with firearms by the British in exchange for furs, kept whites out of the Old Northwest territory, the area north of the Ohio River. South of the Ohio, white settlements were largely limited to Kentucky and Tennessee. In what is today Alabama and Mississippi, the Creeks and their allies blocked American expansion.

Most white migrants in Kentucky and Tennessee were the young, rural poor from the seaboard slave states. The West offered them the opportunity to claim their own farms and gain economic independence, free from the dominance of planters and the economic competition of slave labor. But planters also saw the West as a land of opportunity. The planters of Tidewater Virginia were especially likely to speculate in vast tracts of western land. And many planters' sons migrated to the West with a share of the family's slaves to become planters in their own right. This process laid the foundation for the extension of slavery into new regions. As early as 1790, slaves made up more than 10 percent of the population of Tennessee and Kentucky.

Life in the western settlements was harsh and often cruel. Mortality was high, especially among infants. Travelers from the East described settlers living in crudely built log cabins with squalid, filthy interiors infested with fleas and lice. Easterners also found an appallingly casual acceptance of violence in the West. Men commonly settled disputes in knife-slashing, eye-gouging brawls.

Isolation and uncertainty haunted frontier life. The Appalachians posed a formidable barrier to social and economic intercourse with the East. Few settlers had the labor resources, which chiefly meant slaves, to produce an agricultural surplus for shipment to market down the Ohio and Mississippi Rivers. Most farmers lived at a semisubsistence level. Many of them, mostly Scots-Irish, did not own the land they cultivated. These squatters, as they were called, occupied the land hoping someday to obtain clear title to it.

In Kentucky, squatters, aligned with a small class of middling landowners, spearheaded the movement for political separation from Virginia that gained statehood for the territory in 1792. (In similar fashion, white settlers in Vermont established their independence from New York and New Hampshire and gained statehood in 1791.) The settlers wanted to break the control that Tidewater planters had gained over most of the land and lucrative government offices in Kentucky. In their minds, planters, officeholders, land speculators, and gentlemen of leisure were all part of an aristocracy tied to the distant government in Richmond and intent on robbing them of their liberty. As one proponent of statehood proudly announced, "I never was a frend to larned men for I see it is those sort of fokes who always no how to butter thare own bred and care not for others."

Despite the movement in Kentucky for statehood, the ultimate political allegiance of the West was uncertain in 1790. Westerners wanted the freedom to control their own affairs and outlets for their crops. Apparently, they were willing to strike a deal with any outside power offering to meet these needs. The British, contrary to the terms of the Treaty of Paris, had not abandoned their military posts in the Old Northwest. Using their military position and close ties with the Indians as leverage, the British encouraged separatist movements north of the Ohio River.

Spain posed a more serious threat. It rejected the American claim to the 31st parallel as the southern boundary of the United States and asserted that most of the area south of the Ohio and east of the Mississippi was Spanish territory. Most important, Spain controlled New Orleans and hence the main outlet on the Mississippi River for western produce. Washington had warned in 1784 that the political loyalties of the West wavered "on a pivot," and the future of the region loomed as a major test for his administration.

FORGING A NEW GOVERNMENT

The Congress that assembled in New York (a temporary capital) from 1789 to 1791 faced a challenge scarcely less daunting than that of the Constitutional Convention of 1787. It had to give form and substance to the framework of the new national government outlined in the Constitution. Executive departments had to be established, a federal judiciary organized, sources of revenue found, terms of international trade and foreign policy worked out, and a commitment to add a bill of rights to the Constitution honored.

Staunch supporters of the new government had easily carried the first national elections in 1788 and enjoyed large majorities in both houses of Congress. These people brought superb administrative talents to the task of governing. Many, however, were clumsy politicians and unsympathetic to the egalitarian sensibilities of the electorate. By 1792, they faced growing political opposition.

"MR. PRESIDENT" AND THE BILL OF RIGHTS

The first problem for Washington and Congress was to decide just how the chief executive of the new republic should be addressed. Vice President John Adams of Massachusetts and his like-minded colleagues in the Senate wanted a title with dignity, something that imparted proper respect both for the office and for national political authority. They preferred "His Highness." In a debate that tied up Congress for a month, the more democratically inclined members of the House argued that such a title smacked of a longing for monarchical rule. Adams and the others grudgingly agreed to accept "Mr. President."

Whatever his title, Washington was intent on surrounding the presidency with an aura of respectability. Dismayed by the hordes of visitors and officeseekers who immediately invaded his rented mansion in New York, he set down strict rules for his interactions with the public. He met with visitors twice a week for an hour and bowed with republican deference to the people but refused to shake hands. He traveled outside New York in a luxurious coach pulled by six horses, and at all times he carried himself with stern reserve. After a dinner with the president, one senator remarked that "as usual the company was as grave as at a funeral."

While Washington was laying down guidelines for presidential etiquette, Congress got down to business. James Madison, now a representative from Virginia, early emerged as the most forceful leader in the House. He pushed for speedy action on the bill of rights, which the Federalists had promised to add to the Constitution during the ratification debate. To allay the fears of Antifederalists that the Constitution granted too much power to the national government, the Federalists had promised to consider amendments that protected both individual rights and liberties and the rights of states. But Madison, concerned not to have the new government immediately hobbled by concessions to states, astutely kept the focus of the amendments on personal liberties. He submitted nineteen amendments, and

Congress soon settled on twelve. Ten of these amendments, known collectively as the **Bill of Rights**, were ratified by the states and became part of the Constitution as of December 15, 1791.

The Bill of Rights has been one of the most enduring legacies of the first Congress. Most of the first eight amendments are concerned with individual rights. They guarantee religious freedom, freedom of expression, and the safeguarding of individuals and their property against arbitrary legal proceedings. Only three amendments speak of state interests. Citing the necessity of a "well regulated Militia" for "the security of a free State," the Second Amendment guarantees "the right of the people to keep and bear Arms." This assured the states that they could rely on their militias for protection against federal tyranny. The Ninth and Tenth Amendments stipulate that the powers not granted to the national government in the Constitution are retained by the people and the states.

The Bill of Rights broadened the government's base of popular support. Once Congress submitted the amendments to the states for ratification, North Carolina (1789) and Rhode Island (1790) overcame their lingering objections and joined the Union. The Bill of Rights also assured Americans that the central government would not try to impose on them a uniform national culture.

DEPARTMENTS AND COURTS

In the summer of 1789, Congress authorized the first executive departments: the State Department for foreign affairs, the Treasury for finances, and the War Department for the nation's defense. These departments already existed under the Articles of Confederation, and the only debate about them concerned the extent of presidential control over the officials who would head them. The Constitution gave the president the right to nominate public officials but required the consent of the Senate to confirm their appointments. The Constitution was silent, however, on whether or not the president could dismiss an official without the Senate's consent. Congress decided that the president could do so, setting an important precedent that bolstered presidential power. Department heads would now be closely bound to the president. As a group, they would evolve into the cabinet, the president's chief advisory body.

Greater controversy attended the creation of the federal judiciary. The Constitution called for "one Supreme Court" but left it up to Congress to authorize lower federal courts. The framers were deliberately vague about the federal judiciary because Antifederalists and proponents of states' rights did not want national courts enforcing a uniform judicial system. National courts, they argued, would be far removed from the people and would act as engines of oppression.

The **Judiciary Act of 1789** represented an artful compromise that balanced the concerns of the Antifederalists and states' rights advocates with the concerns of nationalists who strongly opposed leaving matters of national law up to state courts. It created a hierarchical national judiciary based on thirteen federal district courts, one for each state. Appeals from these courts were to be heard in one of three circuit courts, and the Supreme Court was to have the final say in contested cases. In a major concession to the Antifederalists, however, the act limited jurisdiction in federal courts to legal issues stemming from the Constitution and the laws and treaties of the national government. The distinctive legal systems and customs of the states remained intact. State courts would continue to hear and rule on the vast majority of civil and criminal cases.

REVENUE AND TRADE

The government's most pressing need was for revenue. Aware that Congress under the Articles of Confederation had been crippled by its inability to secure a reliable source of income, Madison acted to put the finances of the new federal government on a firm footing. Nearly everyone agreed that the government's chief source of income should be a tariff on imported goods and tonnage duties (fees based on cargo capacity) on ships entering American ports. The United States imported most of its manufactured goods, as well as many raw materials, and foreign-owned ships accounted for nearly half of entering tonnage.

The **Tariff Act of 1789** was designed primarily to raise revenue, not to protect American manufacturers by keeping out foreign goods with high duties. It did, however, seek to protect a few industries thought vital to the economic health of the nation. Thus it levied a duty of 5 percent on most imported goods but imposed tariffs as high as 50 percent on a limited number of items such as steel, salt, cloth, and tobacco. The debate on the Tariff Act provoked some sectional sparring. In general, manufacturers, who were concentrated in the North, wanted high tariffs for protection against foreign competition. In contrast, farmers and southern planters wanted low tariffs to keep down the cost of the manufactured goods they purchased.

Madison originally hoped to use tonnage duties not only to raise revenue but also to strike at foreign nations that had not signed a commercial treaty with the United States. He had in mind specifically Great Britain. Since the Revolution, Britain had kept its trading empire closed to American merchants while at the same time exploiting the United States as a market for its manufactured goods. In contrast, France, America's ally during the Revolution, had a commercial treaty with the United States that recognized the American position on equal trading relations and the rights of neutral shippers during war.

Madison wanted to punish the British with a duty of 60 cents per ton on British ships entering American ports, twice the proposed duty on French ships. He hoped to dislodge the British from their dominant position in American markets and to open up overseas trade for American and French shippers.

Madison's duties were, in effect, a declaration of economic warfare against Britain, but they failed to pass Congress, defeated by an unlikely coalition of sectional interests. Southerners voted against them because they feared their result would be to give New England merchants a monopoly on the carrying trade and raise the cost of shipping tobacco to Europe. But northern merchants, presumably the beneficiaries of the duties, also opposed them. They were leery of disrupting their profitable trade with Britain, especially with the economic slump of the 1780s abating. The **Tonnage Act of 1789**, as finally passed, treated all foreign ships equally. Foreign-owned and foreign-built ships were to pay a duty of 50 cents a ton; foreign-owned but American-built ships were to pay a duty of 30 cents a ton. The duty for American ships was only 6 cents a ton.

HAMILTON AND THE PUBLIC CREDIT

The Treasury was the largest and most important new department. To its head, Alexander Hamilton of New York, fell the task of bringing order to the nation's ramshackle finances. The basic problem was the huge debt left over from the Revolution. With interest going unpaid, the debt was growing, and by 1789, it had reached $52 million. Most of this—about $40 million—was held by Americans in the form of securities and certificates issued during the Revolution. Foreigners, mostly French and Dutch, held another $12 million. In addition, state governments had debts totaling close to $25 million. Until the government set up and honored a regular schedule for paying interest, the nation's public credit would be worthless. Unable to borrow, the government would collapse.

More than any other individual, Hamilton imparted energy and purpose to the Washington administration. He was ambitious, egotistical, and overbearing. When he spoke of the people, he usually did so with a sneer. But he also had a brilliant financial mind and a sweeping vision of national greatness. He was convinced that the economic self-interests of the wealthy and well-born offered the only sound foundation for the success of the new government.

This painting of about 1797 captures the bustle of commercial activity in New York at the end of the eighteenth century. The large building to the left is the Tontine Coffee House, the site of insurance offices and the Stock Exchange.

Born illegitimate in the West Indies in 1755 and orphaned at the age of 13, Hamilton craved power and social connections. Friends impressed with his potential sent him as a teenager to New York City for an education at Kings College (now Columbia University). An eager patriot, he served as Washington's personal aide during the Revolution. Washington's backing enabled him to marry into a wealthy New York family. He now had an entry into the world of the social and economic elite, and he parlayed it into a flourishing legal practice and a rising political career. With no ancestral loyalties to any individual state, he brought an unabashed nationalism to Washington's cabinet. And with a conviction, born of his own rise, that wealth and power were synonymous, he made no apologies for trying to link the interests of the government with those of the wealthy.

At the request of Congress, Hamilton prepared a series of reports on the nation's finances and economic condition. In the first, issued in January 1790, Hamilton proposed a bold plan to address the Revolutionary War debt. The federal government, he maintained, should fund the national debt at full face value. To do this, he proposed exchanging the old debt, including accrued interest, for new government bonds bearing interest at about 4 percent. In addition, Hamilton maintained that the federal government should assume the remaining war debt of the state governments. The intent of this plan was to give the nation's creditors an economic stake in the stability of the new nation and to subordinate state financial interests to those of the central government.

In his second report, issued in December 1790, Hamilton called for an excise tax (a tax on the production, sale, or consumption of a commodity) on distilled whiskey produced within the United States. The purpose of the tax was to raise additional revenue for interest payments on the national debt. It would also establish the government's authority to levy internal taxes on its citizens.

The third report, which followed quickly after the second, recommended the chartering of a national bank, the Bank of the United States. Hamilton patterned his proposed bank after the Bank of England and intended it to meet a variety of needs. Jointly owned by the federal government and private investors, it would serve as the fiscal (financial) and depository agent of the government and make loans to businesses. Through a provision that permitted up to three-fourths of the value of bank stock to be purchased with government bonds, the bank would create a market for public securities and hence raise their value. Most important, the bank would provide the nation with a stable currency. At the time, the country had only three private banks, and specie—hard currency in the form of gold and silver coins—was scarce. The government needed a reliable source of money, as did the economy as a whole. Hamilton proposed to allow the Bank of the United States to issue money in the form of paper banknotes that would be backed by a small reserve of specie and the security of government bonds. His goal was both to strengthen the economy and to consolidate the power of the national government.

Hamilton's final report, issued in December 1791, recommended government actions to promote industry. Looking, as always, to the British model of economic development, he argued that the United States would never become a great power until it diversified its largely agrarian economy. As long as the nation imported most of its manufactured goods, Hamilton warned, it would be no more than a second-rate power. Moreover, American manufacturers, saddled with both high labor costs and primitive technology, would

OVERVIEW

Federalist Party versus Republican Party

Federalists	Republicans
Favored strong central government	Wanted to limit the role of the national government
Supported Hamilton's economic program	Opposed Hamilton's economic program
Opposed the French Revolution	Generally supported the French Revolution
Supported Jay's Treaty and closer ties to Britain	Opposed Jay's Treaty and favored closer ties to France
In response to the threat of war with France, proposed and passed the Direct Tax of 1798, the Alien and Sedition Acts, and legislation to enlarge the size of the army	Opposed the Alien and Sedition Acts and the enlarged army as threats to individual liberties
Drew strongest support from New England; lost support in the mid-Atlantic region after 1798	Drew strongest support from the South and West

remain at a severe competitive disadvantage unless they received government assistance. Hamilton advocated aid in the form of protective tariffs (high tariffs meant to make imported goods more expensive than domestic goods) for such industries as iron, steel, and shoemaking—which had already begun to establish themselves—and direct subsidies to assist with start-up costs for other industries. Hamilton believed that such "patronage," as he called it, would ultimately foster interregional economic dependence. An industrializing Northeast, for example, would depend on the South and West for foodstuffs for its workers and raw materials for its factories. In turn, farmers and planters would buy manufactured goods from the Northeast. Thus, in Hamilton's vision, manufacturing, like a national currency, would be a great national unifier.

REACTION AND OPPOSITION

The breadth and boldness of Hamilton's program invited opposition. For many people, it reflected a vision of the nation that challenged their deeply held beliefs about the purpose and meaning of the American Revolution. Opposition began to emerge with the first report on the public credit and quickly solidified along economic, ideological, and sectional lines.

About half the members of Congress owned some of the nation's debt, and nearly all of them agreed with Hamilton that it should be paid off. Some opponents, however, were concerned that Hamilton's plan was unfair. Hard times had forced most of the original holders of the debt—by and large, ordinary citizens—to sell their certificates to speculators at a fraction of their face value. Should the government, asked Madison, reward speculators with a windfall profit when the debt was paid back in full and forget about the true patriots who had sustained the Revolution in its darkest hours?

Others objected, on republican grounds, that Hamilton had no intention of actually eliminating the government's debt. He envisioned instead a permanent debt, with the government making regular interest payments as they came due. The debt, in the form of government securities, would serve as a vital prop for the support of moneyed groups. One congressman saw this as a violation of "that great principle which alone was the cause of the war with Great Britain . . . that taxation and representation should go hand in hand." Future generations, he argued, would be unfairly taxed for a debt incurred by the present generation.

Opposition to Hamilton's proposal to have the federal government assume state debts reflected sectional differences. With the exception of South Carolina, the southern states had already paid back a good share of their war debts. Thus Hamilton's plan stood to benefit the northern states disproportionately. Because Hamilton had linked the funding of the national debt with the assumption of state debts, southern opposition to assumption threatened funding as well. Tensions mounted as the deadlock continued into the summer of 1790. Frustrated over southern intransigence, New Englanders muttered about seceding. Southerners responded in kind. A Virginia senator charged that disunion would be a small price to pay to escape "the rule of a fixed insolent northern majority."

Tempers cooled when a compromise was reached in July. Southerners agreed to accept funding in its original form because, as Hamilton correctly noted, it would be impractical, if not impossible, to distinguish between the original and current holders of the national debt. Assumption passed after Hamilton cut a deal with Virginians James Madison and Thomas Jefferson. In exchange for southern support of assumption, Hamilton agreed to line up northern votes for locating the nation's permanent capital on the banks of the Potomac River, where it would be surrounded by the slave states of Maryland and Virginia. The package was sweetened by extra grants of federal money to states with small debts.

Hamilton's alliance with Madison and Jefferson proved short-lived, dissolving when Madison led the congressional opposition to Hamilton's proposed bank. Madison and most other Southerners viewed the bank as evidence of a willingness to sacrifice the interests of the agrarian South in favor of the financial and industrial interests of the North. They feared that the bank, with its power to dispense economic favors, would re-create in the United States the kind of government corruption and privilege they associated with Great Britain. They argued that the Constitution did not explicitly authorize Congress to charter a bank or any other corporation.

The bank bill passed Congress on a vote that divided along sectional lines. Madison's objections, however, left Washington concerned that the bank might not be constitutional. He sought the cabinet's opinion, provoking the first great debate over how the Constitution should be interpreted. Thomas Jefferson, the secretary of state, sided with Madison and for the first time openly clashed with Hamilton. Taking a strict constructionist position, he argued that all powers the Constitution had not expressly delegated to the national government were reserved to the states under the Tenth Amendment. Hamilton, in a brilliant rejoinder, argued that Article 1, Section 8, of the Constitution, which declares that Congress has the right to "to make all laws which shall be necessary and proper" to exercise its powers and those of the federal government, gives Congress implicit authority beyond its explicitly enumerated powers. With this broad constructionist position, he won Washington to his side.

With Washington's signature on the bill, Hamilton's bank was chartered for twenty years. Congress also passed a hefty 25 percent excise tax on distilled liquor. Little, however, of Hamilton's plan to promote manufacturing survived the scrutiny of the agrarian opposition. Tariff duties were raised moderately in 1792, but no funds were forthcoming to accelerate industrial development.

THE EMERGENCE OF PARTIES

By the end of Washington's first term, Americans were dividing into two camps. On one side stood those who still called themselves **Federalists.** These were the supporters of Hamilton's program—speculators, creditors, merchants, manufacturers, and commercial farmers. They were the Americans most fully integrated into the market economy and in control of it. Concentrated in the North, they included New England Congregationalists and mid-Atlantic Episcopalians (former Anglicans), members of the more socially prestigious churches. In both economic and cultural terms, the Federalists were drawn from the more privileged segments of society.

Jefferson and Madison shrewdly gave the name **Republican** to the party that formed in opposition to the Federalists, thus identifying it with individual liberties and the heritage of the Revolution. The Republicans accused Hamilton and the Federalists of attempting to impose a British system of economic privilege and social exploitation. The initial core of the party consisted of southern planters and backcountry Scots-Irish farmers. These were Americans outside the market economy or skeptical of its benefits. They feared that the commercial groups favored by Hamilton would corrupt politics in their pursuit of power and foster commerce and manufacturing at the expense of agriculture. The Republicans were committed to an agrarian America in which power remained in the hands of farmers and planters.

In 1792, parties were still in a formative stage. The political divisions that had appeared first in Congress and then spread to Washington's cabinet did not yet extend very deeply into the electorate. Washington remained aloof from the political infighting and was still seen as a great unifier. Unopposed, he was reelected in 1792. However, a series of crises in his second term deepened and broadened the incipient party divisions. By 1796, rival parties were contesting the presidency and vying for the support of an increasingly politically organized electorate.

THE FRENCH REVOLUTION

The French Revolution began in 1789, and in its early phase, most Americans applauded it. France had been an ally of the United States during the Revolutionary War and now seemed to be following the example of its American friends in shaking off monarchical rule. By 1792, however, the French Revolution had turned violent and radical. Its supporters confiscated the property of aristocrats and the church, slaughtered suspected enemies, and executed the king, Louis XVI. In early 1793, republican France was at war against Britain and the European powers.

The excesses of the French Revolution and the European war that erupted in its wake touched off a bitter debate in America. Federalists drew back in horror from France's new regime. They insisted that the terror unleashed by the French was far removed from the reasoned republicanism of the American Revolution. As the *Federalist Gazette* of the United States argued: "The American Revolution, it ought to be repeated, was not accomplished as the French has been, by massacres, assassinations, or proscriptions." For the Republicans, the French remained the standard-bearers of the cause of liberty for common people everywhere. Jefferson admitted that the French Revolution was tarnished by the loss of innocent lives, "but rather than it should have failed, I would have seen half the earth desolated." He was convinced that "the liberty of the whole earth was depending on the issue in the contest."

Franco-American relations.

When the new French ambassador, Edmond Genêt arrived in the United States in April 1793—just as the debate in America over the French Revolution was heating up—Franco-American relations reached a turning point. The two countries were still bound to one another by the Franco-American Alliance of 1778. The alliance required the United States to assist France in the defense of its West Indian colonies and to open American ports to French privateers if France were attacked. Genêt, it soon became clear, hoped to embroil the United States in the French war against the British. He commissioned American privateers to attack British shipping and tried to enlist an army of frontiersmen to attack Spanish possessions in Louisiana and Florida.

Genêt's actions, as well as the enthusiastic receptions that greeted him as he traveled from Charleston to Philadelphia (chosen in 1790 as the temporary national capital), forced Washington to call a special cabinet meeting. The president feared that Genêt would stampede Americans into the European war, with disastrous results for the nation's finances. The bulk of America's foreign trade was with the British, and tariff duties on British imports were the main source of revenue to pay for Hamilton's assumption and funding programs. Hamilton urged Washington to declare American neutrality in the European war, maintaining that the president could commit the nation to neutrality on his own authority when Congress, as was then the case, was not in session. Hamilton also wanted to suspend the military and commercial

treaties of 1778 with France and refuse diplomatic recognition of Genêt. Jefferson, although he too wanted to avoid war, opposed Hamilton on these issues. Disputing Washington's power to act on his own, Jefferson maintained that the warmaking powers of Congress reserved for it alone the right to issue a declaration of neutrality.

Washington steered a middle course. He granted Genêt a formal (but cold) reception and took no action to suspend the Franco-American treaties. But he accepted Hamilton's argument on his authority to declare neutrality and issued a proclamation on April 22, 1793, stating that the United States would be "friendly and impartial toward the belligerent powers."

Despite this proclamation, Genêt continued to meddle. He finally exceeded Washington's patience in the summer of 1793, when he grandly announced that he would take his case directly to the American people and force a cowardly administration to stand up for French rights. Washington was on the verge of forcing Genêt's recall to France in August when news arrived that a new and more radical French government had decided to bring Genêt back as a political prisoner. The president graciously permitted Genêt to remain in America as a private citizen. Had he returned to France, he would have faced almost certain execution.

The growth of Democratic-Republican societies.

Genêt quickly faded from public view, but American politics became more open and aggressive in the wake of his visit. Pro-French enthusiasm lived on in a host of grass-roots political organizations known as the Democratic-Republican societies. Nearly forty of these societies formed in 1793 and 1794. As their name suggests, these societies reflected a belief that democracy and republicanism were one and the same. This was a new concept in American politics. Democracy had traditionally been equated with anarchy and mob rule. The members of the new societies argued to the contrary that only democracy—meaning popular participation in politics and direct appeals by politicians to the people—could maintain the revolutionary spirit of 1776 because the people were the only true guardians of that spirit. As a letter writer to the *Newark Gazette* put it: "It must be the mechanics and farmers, or the poorer class of people (as they are generally called), that must support the freedom which they and their fathers purchased with their blood—the nobility will never do it—they will be always striving to get the reins of government into their own hands, and then they can ride the people at pleasure."

The Democratic-Republican societies attacked the Washington administration for failing to assist France, and they expressed the popular feeling that Hamilton's program favored the rich over the poor.

Source: Painting: P & S—1914 0001; "The Treaty of Fort Greenville, Ohio;" 1795. Artist unknown, member of Gen. Anthony Wayre's staff.

This painting by an officer on General Wayne's staff shows Little Turtle, a Miami chief, speaking through an interpreter to General Wayne (with one hand behind his back) during the negotiations that led to the Treaty of Greenville.

For the first time, Washington himself was personally assailed in the press.

The core members of the societies were urban artisans whose egalitarian views shocked the Federalists, who expected deference, not criticism and political activism, from the people. In their view, the Democratic-Republicans were rabble-rousers trying to dictate policy to the nation's natural leaders. The Federalists harshly condemned the emergence of organized political dissent from below, but in so doing they only enhanced the popular appeal of the growing Republican opposition.

SECURING THE FRONTIER

Control of the West remained an elusive goal throughout Washington's first term. Indian resistance in the Northwest Territory initially prevented whites from pushing north of the Ohio River. The powerful Miami Confederacy, led by Little Turtle, routed two ill-trained American armies in 1790 and 1791. The 1791 encounter, which took place on the banks of the Wabash River in western Ohio, was the worst defeat an American army ever suffered in frontier fighting. More than nine hundred soldiers were killed or wounded, and the commander, General Arthur St. Clair, was lucky to survive. The southern frontier was quieter, but the Spanish continued to use the Creeks and Cherokees as a buffer against American penetration south of the Tennessee River.

By 1793, many western settlers felt abandoned by the national government. They believed that the government had broken a promise to protect them against Indians and foreigners. Much of the popularity of the Democratic-Republican societies in the West fed off these frustrations. Westerners saw the French, who were at war with Britain and Spain, as allies against the foreign threat on the frontier, and they forwarded resolutions to Congress embracing the French cause. These resolutions also demanded free and open navigation on the Mississippi River. This, in the minds of Westerners, was their natural right. Without it, they would be forever impoverished. "If the interest of Eastern America requires that we should be kept in poverty," argued the Mingo Creek society of western Pennsylvania, "it is unreasonable from such poverty to exact contributions. The first, if we cannot emerge from, we must learn to bear, but the latter, we never can be taught to submit to."

Submission to national authority, however, was precisely what the Federalists wanted from both the Indians and the western settlers. St. Clair's humiliating defeat in 1791 prompted a reorganization of the War Department. By the summer of 1794, Washington's administration felt prepared to move against the Indians. This time, it sent into the Ohio region not the usual ragtag crew of militia and unemployed city dwellers but a force built around veterans from the professional army. The commander, General Anthony Wayne, was a savvy, battle-hardened war hero.

Wayne's victory on August 4, 1794, at the Battle of Fallen Timbers, near present-day Toledo, broke the back of Indian military resistance in Ohio. In the resulting **Treaty of Greenville**, signed in August 1795, twelve tribes ceded most of the present state of Ohio to the U.S. government in return for an annual payment of $9,500. The Ohio country was now open to white settlement (see Map 8–1 and American Views).

THE WHISKEY REBELLION

Within a few months of Wayne's victory at Fallen Timbers, another American army was on the move. The target this time were the so-called whiskey rebels of

AMERICAN VIEWS

Little Turtle Defends the Miami Lands

The climax of what had become a thirty-year war between Native Americans and white settlers for control of the Ohio country came in 1794 with the American victory at the Battle of Fallen Timbers. The most innovative and successful of the Indian leaders who had emerged in the conflict was the Miami war chief Mishiki-nakwa, or Little Turtle as he was known by whites. The following is from one of Little Turtle's speeches during the peace negotiations with the victorious Americans at Greenville, Ohio, in July, 1795.

- How would you characterize Little Turtle's stance during the negotiations and his attitude toward Wayne?
- On what basis did Little Turtle justify the land claims of the Miamis in the Ohio country? How would this differ from the way in which whites staked their claim to the land?
- How did Little Turtle explain his leadership of the Miamis and how did this differ from white notions of leadership?
- What might account for the divisions among the Indians that were cited by Little Turtle?

"General Wayne: I hope you will pay attention to what I now say to you. I wish to inform you where your younger brothers, the Miamies, live, and, also, the Pottawatamies of St. Joseph's, together with the Wabash Indians. You have pointed out to us the boundary line between the Indians and the United States, but I now take the liberty to inform you, that the line cuts off from the Indians a large portion of country, which has been enjoyed by my forefathers time immemorial, without molestation or dispute. The print of my ancestors' houses are every where to be seen in this portion . . . . It is well known by all my brothers present, that my forefathers kindled the first fire at Detroit; from thence, he extended his lines to the head waters of Scioto; from thence, down the Ohio, to the mouth of the Wabash, and from thence to Chicago, on Lake Michigan . . . . I have now informed you of the boundaries of the Miami nation, where the Great Spirit placed my forefathers a long time ago, and charged him not to sell or part with his lands, but to preserve them for his posterity. This charge has been handed down to me . . . . I was much surprised to find that my other brothers differed so much from me on this subject: for their conduct would lead one to suppose, that the Great Spirit, and their forefathers, had not given them the same charge that was give[n] to me, but, on the contrary, had directed them to sell their lands to any white man who wore a hat, as soon as he should ask it of them. Now, elder brother, your younger brothers, the Miamies, have pointed out to you their country, and also to our brothers present. When I hear your remarks and proposals on this subject [of Miami lands], I will be ready to give you an answer; I came with an expectation of hearing you say good things, but I have not heard what I have expected."

Source: "Documents, Legislative and Executive, of the Congress of the United States, From the First Session of the First to the Third Session of the Thirteenth Congress, Inclusive: commencing March 3, 1789, and ending March 3, 1815. Vol. IV" (Washington: Gales and Seaton, 1832), pp. 570–571.

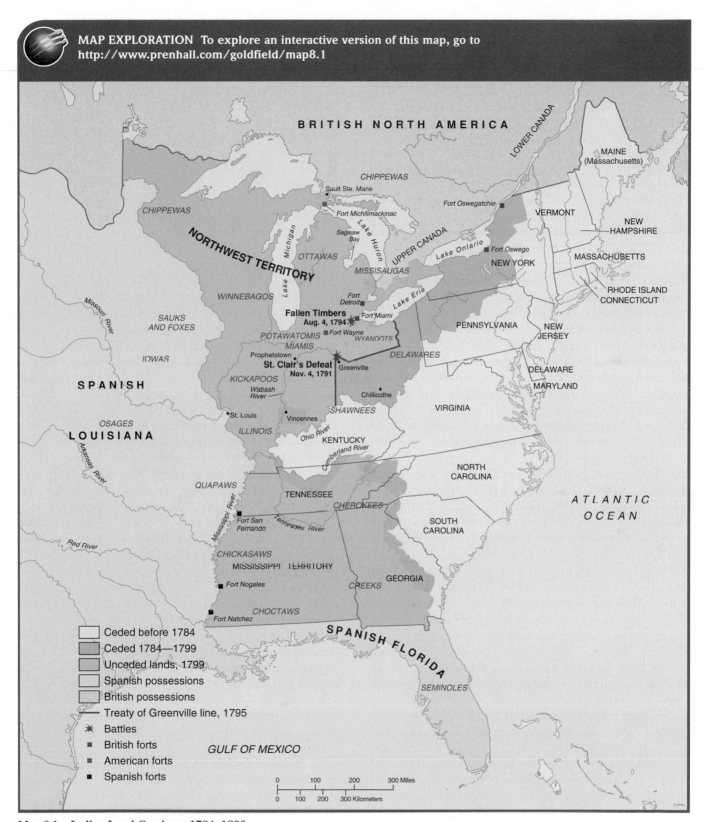

MAP 8-1   **Indian Land Cessions, 1784–1800**
*The persistent pressure of white settlers and the military forces of the new national government
forced Native Americans to cede huge tracts of their western lands.*

western Pennsylvania, who were openly resisting Hamilton's excise tax on whiskey. This tax had always been unpopular among western farmers. The high cost of transport across the mountains made it unprofitable for them to sell their grain in the east. But by distilling corn or rye into whiskey, they reduced it enough in bulk to lower transportation costs and earn a profit. Hamilton's excise tax wiped out these profits.

Hamilton was determined to enforce the tax and assert the supremacy of national laws. Although resistance to the tax was widespread, he singled out the Pennsylvania rebels. It was easier to send an army into the Pittsburgh area than into the Carolina mountains. Washington, moreover, was convinced that the Democratic-Republican societies of western Pennsylvania were behind the defiance of federal authority there. He welcomed the opportunity to chastise these organizations, which he identified with the dangerous doctrines of the French Revolution.

Washington called on the governors of the mid-Atlantic states to supply militia forces to crush the **Whiskey Rebellion**. The 13,000-man army that assembled at Harrisburg and marched into western Pennsylvania in October 1794 was larger than any Washington had commanded during the Revolution. But the rebellion, as Jefferson sardonically noted, "could never be found." The army met no resistance and expended considerable effort rounding up twenty prisoners. Two men were found guilty of treason, but Washington pardoned both. Still, at Hamilton's insistence, the Federalists had made their point: When its authority was openly challenged, this national government was prepared to use military force to compel obedience.

The Whiskey Rebellion starkly revealed the conflicting visions of local liberty and national order that divided Americans of the early republic. The non-English majority on the Pennsylvania frontier—Irish, Scots-Irish, German, and Welsh—justified resistance to the whiskey tax with the same republican ideology that had fueled the American Revolution. Mostly poor farmers, artisans, and laborers, they appealed to notions of liberty, equality, and freedom from oppressive taxation that were deeply rooted in backcountry settlements from Maine to Georgia. In putting down the Pennsylvania rebels, Washington and Hamilton acted on behalf of more English and cosmopolitan groups in the East who valued central power as a check on any local resistance movement that might begin unraveling the still fragile republic.

TREATIES WITH BRITAIN AND SPAIN

Much of the unrest in the West stemmed from the menacing presence of the British and Spanish on the nation's borders. Washington's government had the resources to suppress Indians and frontier dissidents but lacked sufficient armed might to push Spain and especially Britain out of the West.

The British, embroiled in what they saw as a life-or-death struggle against revolutionary France, clamped a naval blockade on France and its colonies in the Caribbean in the fall of 1793. They also supported an uprising of slaves on the French island of Saint-Domingue (present-day Haiti), enraging southern planters fearful that slave rebellions might spread to the United States. The French countered by opening their colonial trade, which had been closed to outsiders during peacetime, to neutral shippers. American merchants stepped in and reaped profits by supplying France. The British retaliated by seizing American ships involved in the French trade. They further claimed the right to search American ships and impress, or forcibly remove, sailors they suspected of having deserted from the British navy. News of these provocations reached America in early 1794 and touched off a major war scare. Desperate to avert a war, Washington sent John Jay, the chief justice of the United States, to London to negotiate an accord.

Jay brought a weak hand to the negotiating table. Britain had enormous military resources, the United States only a small army and navy. What is more, tariffs on British trade were the main source of revenue for the United States government. But the British, too, benefited from their trade with the United States, and they wanted to keep the United States neutral.

From the American point of view, the resulting agreement, known as **Jay's Treaty**, was flawed but acceptable. Jay had to abandon the American insistence on the right of neutrals to ship goods to nations at war without interference (meaning in this case the right of the United States to continue trading with France without British harassment). He also had to grant Britain "most favored nation" status, giving up the American right to discriminate against British shipping and merchandise. And he had to reconfirm the American commitment to assure that pre-Revolutionary debts owed by Americans to the British would be repaid in full. In return for these major concessions, Britain pledged to compensate American merchants for the ships and cargoes it had seized in 1793 and 1794, to abandon the six forts it still held in the American Northwest, and to grant the United States limited trading rights in India and the British West Indies.

Signed in November 1794, Jay's Treaty caused an uproar in the United States when its terms became known in March 1795. Southerners saw in it another sellout of their interests. It required them to pay their prewar debts to British merchants but was silent about the slaves Britain had carried off during the Revolution. And the concessions Britain did make seemed to favor the North, especially New England merchants and shippers. Republicans, joined now by urban artisans, were infuriated that Jay had stripped them of their chief weapon—economic retaliation—for breaking free of British commercial dominance. The Senate ratified the treaty in June 1795, but only because Washington backed it.

Jay's Treaty, combined with a string of French victories in Europe in 1795, convinced Spain to adopt a more conciliatory attitude toward the United States. With France apparently gaining the upper hand in the war, Spain was anxious to shift its allegiance from Britain to France. But it saw the Jay treaty as the beginning of an Anglo-American alliance and decided to reach an agreement with the United States before it changed sides, lest the United States and Britain combine forces to challenge Spain's American possessions. In the **Treaty of San Lorenzo** (also known as Pinckney's Treaty) of 1795, Spain accepted the American position on the 31st parallel as the northern boundary of Spanish Florida and granted American farmers the right of free transit through the port of New Orleans.

THE FIRST PARTISAN ELECTION

Partisanship—open identification with one of the two parties—steadily rose in the 1790s, fueled in large measure by a new print culture. The first opposition newspaper, the *National Gazette,* appeared in 1791, and the number of newspapers more than doubled within the decade. Circulated and discussed in taverns and coffeehouses, newspapers helped draw ordinary Americans into the political process. Ongoing involvement in the raucous, celebratory political culture that Americans fashioned also politicized them. Through festivals on July 4 honoring the nation's independence, street parades and demonstrations favoring or opposing such events as the French Revolution or Jay's Treaty, and an endless stream of toasts, speeches, banquets, and broadsides, various groups publicly proclaimed and acted out their version of what it meant to be an American. No single version held sway. National self-identity varied by class, race, sex, and region, but as newspaper reports of local activities were copied and disseminated across the country, Americans could feel that they were joined in a collective effort to define what the nation meant to them. As a national identity was being forged and contested, lines of partisanship were marked and deepened. Depending upon the group staging the celebration, Republican or Federalist doctrines were on display. Each of the parties competed with the other to lay claim to the Revolutionary heritage of freedom and independence.

Women also participated in this public arena of political activism. Although denied formal political rights, they wrote and attended plays with explicit political messages, joined in patriotic rituals, and organized their own demonstrations. To show their support for the French Revolution, women in Menetomy, Massachusetts, wore liberty caps and cockades, the symbols of the French cause. Two widows in Charleston, South Carolina—one American, the other French—went further in July 1793, when they staged a clever form of street theater in front of a large crowd. As reported by a Charleston newspaper, "after having repudiated their husbands on account of their ill-treatment, [they] conceived the design of living together in the strictest union and friendship in order to give a pledge of their fidelity [and] requested that their striped gowns should be penned together, that their children should be looked upon as one family, while their mothers showed them an equal affection." Here was a double-edged message. Just as a union of the French and the Americans could dispense with the need for Britain, so, it appeared, two women could enjoy domestic bliss without the need for husbands. Shocked by such pro-French sympathies and declarations of women's independence, the Federalists moved quickly to find a safe outlet for women's political activism. They invited women to join Federalist-sponsored events that denounced the French Revolution as a threat to all civilized order. By the late 1790s, both parties were seeking to broaden their popular appeal by including women in their partisan rallies.

As partisanship spread, no symbol of traditional authority, Washington included, was safe from challenge. Washington complained bitterly to friends that his political opponents had maligned him "in such exaggerated and indecent terms as could scarcely be applied to a . . . notorious defaulter, or a even a common pickpocket." He announced his decision to retire from public life in his Farewell Address of September 1796. Devoting most of this address to a denunciation of partisanship, he invoked the republican ideal of disinterested, independent statesmanship as the only sure and virtuous guide for the nation. He warned against any permanent foreign alliances and cautioned that the Union itself would be endangered if parties continued to be characterized "by geographical discriminations—*Northern* and *Southern, Atlantic* and *Western*—whence designing men may endeavor to excite a belief that there is a real difference of local interests and views."

Confirming Washington's fears, the election of 1796 was the first openly partisan election in American history. John Adams was the Federalist candidate and

Thomas Jefferson the Republican candidate. Each was selected by a party caucus, a meeting of party leaders. As a result of disunity in the Federalist ranks, the election produced the anomaly of a Federalist president (Adams) and a Republican vice president (Jefferson). Written with no thought of organized partisan competition for the presidency, the Constitution simply stated that the presidential candidate with the second highest number of electoral votes would become vice president. In this case, that candidate was Jefferson, and the result was a new administration badly divided from the start.

Despite the election's confused outcome, the sectional pattern in the voting was unmistakable. Only the solid support of regional elites in New England and the mid-Atlantic states enabled the Federalists to retain the presidency. Adams received all the northern electoral votes, with the exception of Pennsylvania's. Jefferson was the overwhelming favorite in the South.

With the horrors of the French Revolution forming a backdrop, this cartoon depicts France as a five-headed monster demanding a bribe from the three Americans sent by Adams. The Federalists hoped that such anti-French sentiments would lead to an open war.

THE LAST FEDERALIST ADMINISTRATION

The Adams administration got off to a rocky start from which it never recovered. The vice president was the leader of the opposition party; key members of the cabinet, which Adams had inherited from Washington, owed their primary loyalty to Hamilton; and the French, who saw Adams as a dupe of the British, instigated a major crisis that left the threat of war hanging over the entire Adams presidency. Adams had been a lawyer before the Revolution; he was a veteran of both Continental Congresses, had been a diplomat in Europe for a decade, and had served as Washington's vice president for eight years. But despite this extraordinarily rich background in public affairs, he was politically naive. Scrupulously honest but quick to take offense, he lacked the politician's touch for inspiring personal loyalty and crafting compromises based on a realistic recognition of mutual self-interest. But putting the interests of the country before those of his party, he almost single-handedly prevented a nearly certain war with France and a possible civil war at home. The price he paid was a badly split Federalist

party that refused to unite behind him when he sought reelection in 1800.

THE FRENCH CRISIS AND THE XYZ AFFAIR

An aggressive coalition known as the Directory gained control of revolutionary France in 1795 and denounced the Jay treaty as evidence of an Anglo-American alliance against France. When Jefferson and the pro-French Republicans lost the election of 1796, the Directory turned openly hostile. In short order, the French annulled the commercial treaty of 1778 with the United States, ordered the seizure of American ships carrying goods to the British, and declared that any American sailors found on British ships, including those forcibly pressed into service, would be summarily executed. By the time Adams had been in office barely three months, the French had already confiscated more than three hundred American ships.

In the fall of 1797, Adams sent three commissioners to Paris in an effort to avoid war. The French treated the three with contempt. Having just conquered the Netherlands and detached Spain from its British alliance, France was in no mood to compromise. Through three intermediaries—identified by Adams only as X, Y, and Z when he informed Congress of the negotiations—the French foreign minister demanded a large bribe to initiate talks and an American loan of $12 million.

In April 1798, the Senate published a full account of the insulting behavior of the French in what came to be called the **XYZ Affair**. The public was indignant, and war fever swept the country. The Federalists, who had always warned against the French, enjoyed greater popularity than they ever had or ever would again. Congress acted to upgrade the navy, which had languished since the Revolutionary War. Funds were provided to build and arm forty new ships. Responsibility for naval affairs, formerly divided between the Treasury and War Departments, was consolidated in a new Department of the Navy. By the fall of 1798, American ships were waging an undeclared war against the French in Caribbean waters, a conflict that came to be known as the **Quasi-War**.

The Federalists in Congress, dismissing Republican objections, also voted to create a vastly expanded army. They tripled the size of the regular army to ten thousand men and authorized a special provi-

Congressional Pugilists, caricature 1798. Neg. #33995. Collection of The New-York Historical Society

This contemporary cartoon shows Republican Matthew Lyon, in the center with the fire tongs, fighting against Roger Griswold, a Connecticut Federalist. This brawl in Congress on February 15, 1798, revealed the depth of the feeling that now divided the Republicans and Federalists.

sional army of fifty thousand. Congress put the provisional army under Washington's command, but he declined to come out of retirement except for a national emergency. In the meantime, he insisted that Hamilton be appointed second in command and given charge of the provisional army's field operations. To pay for both the expanded army and the naval rearmament, the Federalists pushed through the Direct Tax of 1798, a levy on the value of land, slaves, and dwellings.

CRISIS AT HOME

The thought of Hamilton in charge of a huge army convinced many Republicans that their worst nightmares were about to materialize. One congressman shuddered that "the monarchy-loving Hamilton is now so fixed, as to be able, with one-step, to fill the place of our present commander in chief." Adams shared such fears. He was furious that Hamilton had been forced on him as commander of the provisional army. Years later, he wrote that "the British faction was determined to have a war with France, and Alexander Hamilton at the head of the army and then Pres. of U.S. Peace with France was therefore treason against their fundamental maxims and reasons of State." As the Republicans immediately sensed and Adams came to realize, Hamilton's supporters, known as the High Federalists, saw the war scare with France as an opportunity to stamp out dissent, cement an alliance with the British, and strengthen and consolidate the powers of the national government.

The Federalists passed four laws in the summer of 1798, known collectively as the **Alien and Sedition Acts** that confirmed the Republicans' fears. Three of these acts were aimed at immigrants, especially French and Irish refugees who voted for the Republicans. The acts convinced hundreds of immigrants to flee the country to avoid possible arrest. The Alien Enemies Act empowered the president to deport foreigners who came from countries at war with the United States. The more sweeping Alien Friends Act authorized the president to expel any alien resident he suspected of subversive activities. The Naturalization Act extended the residency requirement for American citizenship (and hence the right to vote) from five to fourteen years.

The most dangerous of the four acts in the minds of Republicans was the Sedition Act, a measure that made it a federal crime to engage in any combination or conspiracy against the government or to utter or print anything "false, scandalous and malicious" against the government. Federalist judges were blatantly partisan in their enforcement of the Sedition Act. Twenty-five individuals, mostly Republican editors, were indicted under the act, and ten were convicted. The most celebrated case involved Matthew Lyon, a Republican congressman from Vermont. Indicted for publishing a letter criticizing President Adams, he was reelected to Congress in December 1798 while still in jail.

Facing a Congress and a Supreme Court dominated by the Federalists, Jefferson and Madison turned to the safely Republican legislatures of Kentucky and Virginia for a forum from which to attack the constitutionality of the Alien and Sedition Acts. Taking care to keep their authorship secret, they each drafted a set of resolutions—Jefferson for the Kentucky legislature and Madison for the Virginia legislature—that challenged the entire centralizing program of the Federalists. In doing so, they produced the first significant articulation of the southern stand on **states' rights**.

The resolutions—adopted in the fall of 1798—proposed a compact theory of the Constitution. They asserted that the states had delegated specific powers to the national government for their common benefit. It followed that the states reserved the right to rule whether the national government had unconstitutionally assumed a power not granted to it. If a state decided that the national government had exceeded its powers, it could "interpose" its authority to shield its citizens from a tyrannical law. In a second set of resolutions, the Kentucky legislature introduced the doctrine of **nullification**, the right of a state to render null and void a national law it deemed unconstitutional.

Jefferson and Madison hoped that these resolutions would rally voters to the Republican party as the defender of threatened American liberties. Yet not a single additional state seconded them. In the end, what aroused popular rage against the Federalists was not legislation directed against aliens and subversives but the high cost of Federalist taxes.

The Direct Tax of 1798 fell on all owners of land, dwellings, or slaves and provoked widespread resentment. Enforcing it required an army of bureaucrats—more than five hundred for the state of Pennsylvania alone. In February 1799, in the heavily German southeastern counties of Pennsylvania, a group of men led by an auctioneer named John Fries released tax evaders from prison in Bethlehem. President Adams responded to Fries's Rebellion with a show of force, but the fiercest resistance the soldiers he sent to Pennsylvania encountered was from irate farm wives, who doused them with hot water. Fries and two other men were arrested, convicted of treason, and sentenced to be executed. (Adams later pardoned them.) But the Federalists had now lost much of their support in Pennsylvania.

THE END OF THE FEDERALISTS

The events in Pennsylvania reflected an air of menace that gripped the country as the campaign of 1800 approached. The army was chasing private citizens whose only crime in the eyes of many was that they were honoring their Revolutionary heritage by resisting hateful taxes. Federal soldiers also roughed up Republican voters at polling places. No wonder Adams later wrote that

Short and pudgy, Adams had little of Hamilton's physical presence as a natural leader. But he had a first-rate mind and the political courage to place the nation's needs above those of his Federalist party when he peacefully ended the Quasi-War with France.

"the army was as unpopular as if it had been a ferocious wild beast let loose upon the nation to devour it." Southern Republicans talked in private of the possible need to resist Federalist tyranny by force and, failing in that, to secede from the Union. Hamilton and the High Federalists saw in the Kentucky and Virginia resolutions "a regular conspiracy to overturn the government." Reports that Virginia intended to strengthen its militia heightened their anxieties, and they proposed to meet force with force. Speaking of Virginia, Hamilton said that "the government must not merely defend itself, it must attack and arraign its enemies."

No one did more to defuse this charged atmosphere than President Adams. The Federalists depended for their popular support on the expectation of a war with France, which as late as 1798 had swept them to victory in the congressional elections. Still, Adams refrained from asking for a declaration of war. The United States had been successful in the Quasi-War against France. By early 1799, French ships had been forced out of the Caribbean and American coastal waters. And in Europe, the tide of war had turned against the French. As a result, Adams believed that the French would now be more open to conciliation. Of greater importance, Adams recognized that war with France could trigger a civil war at home. Hamilton and the High Federalists, he realized, would use war as an excuse to crush the Republican opposition in Virginia. Fearful of Hamilton's intentions and unwilling to run the risk of militarizing the government and saddling it with a huge war debt, Adams broke with his party and decided to reopen negotiations with France in February 1799.

The **Franco-American Accord of 1800** that resulted from Adams's initiative released the United States from its 1778 alliance with France. It also obligated the United States to surrender all claims against the French for damages done to American shipping during the Quasi-War. The negotiations in Paris dragged on through the election of 1800, but for the Hamiltonian Federalists, the political damage had already been done. The prospect of peace with France deprived them of their trump card in the election. The Republicans could no longer be branded as the traitorous friends of an enemy state. The enlarged army, with no foe to fight, became a political embarrassment, and the Federalists dismantled it. Although rumors of possible violence continued to circulate, the Republicans grew increasingly confident that they could peacefully gain control of the government.

The Federalists nonetheless ran a very competitive race in 1800. Adams's peace policy bolstered his popularity. And because American merchants had profited from supplying both sides in the European war, the country was enjoying a period of prosperity that benefited the president and his party. The Federalists put on a show of unity when they nominated Adams and Charles C. Pinckney of South Carolina as their presidential candidates at their party caucus. But the wounds opened by Adams's decision to broker a peace with France continued to fester. Hamilton and his friends felt that Adams had betrayed them, and Hamilton wrote a scathing attack on the president in a letter that fell into the hands of Aaron Burr, a crafty politician from New York whom the Republicans had teamed up with Jefferson for the presidential election. Burr published the letter, airing the Federalists' squabblings in public.

The Federalists, hampered by party disunity, could not counter the Republicans' aggressive orga-

By associating their Federalist opponents with the hated Tories of the American Revolution, the Republicans appealed to the voters as the true defenders of American liberation.

nizational tactics. They found it distasteful to appeal to common people. One party member lamented that the Republicans sent spokesmen "to every class of men, and even to every individual man, that can be gained. Every threshing floor, every husting, every party at work on a house-frame or raising a building, the very funerals are infected with bawlers or whisperers against government."

Wherever they organized, the Republicans attacked the Federalists as monarchists plotting to undo the gains of the Revolution. The Federalists responded with emotional appeals that depicted Jefferson as a godless revolutionary whose election would usher in a reign of terror. "The effect," intoned the Reverend William Linn, "would be to destroy religion, introduce immorality, and loosen all bonds of society."

Attacks like Linn's reflected the fears of Calvinist preachers that a tide of disbelief was about to submerge Christianity in the United States. Church attendance had declined in the 1790s, particularly among men, and perhaps no more than one in twenty Americans was a member of any church. **Deism**, an Enlightenment religious philosophy popular among the leaders of the Revolutionary era, was making inroads among common citizens as well. Deists viewed God as a kind of master clockmaker who created the laws by which the universe runs but otherwise leaves it alone. They rejected revelation for reason, maintaining that the workings of nature alone reveal God's design. In 1794, the famed pamphleteer Thomas Paine, in *The Age of Reason*, denounced churches as "human

FROM THEN TO NOW

Hamilton's Legacy and the National Debt

The debate over the national debt that figured so prominently in the rise of party politics in the 1790s has continued to echo throughout American history. The tripling of the debt in the 1980s, combined with a recession that hit during the presidency of George Bush, sharpened these debates and made the debt a major issue in the election of 1992.

Well into the twentieth century, a Jeffersonian bias against a large public debt dominated the fiscal policy of the federal government. Until 1930, government revenues usually exceeded expenditures, and the surplus was used to reduce the debt. Even so, except for a brief time in the mid-1830s during Andrew Jackson's presidency, the debt was never actually extinguished. This was because economic depressions periodically reduced government income, and wars periodically forced huge increases in expenditures, keeping the government perpetually in debt.

By 1860, the national debt was smaller than it had been when Alexander Hamilton took office as the first secretary of the treasury. To pay for the unprecedented expenses of the Civil War, however, the government borrowed funds, and by 1866, the debt had skyrocketed. The government then committed itself to lowering the debt, and, by the 1890s, when a depression ended twenty-eight consecutive years of budget surplus, it had declined by two-thirds. World War I began a similar cycle—a runup of the debt followed by a gradual reduction—until the onset of the Great Depression of the 1930s began a dramatic change in government policy toward the debt.

Under President Franklin Roosevelt's New Deal, the federal government responded to the length and severity of the depression with new relief programs that drove up outlays while revenues plunged. In what was highly unusual for peacetime, budget deficits piled up, and the national debt rose. It was the cost of World War II, however, that sent the debt soaring. By 1946 it stood at $271 billion, more than the entire economic output of the country. This time, after the war, the creation of surpluses to reduce the debt did not top the government agenda. On the contrary, the onset of the Cold War began an extended period of massive defense spending. At the same time, the government built on the New Deal with new spending on domestic welfare.

Many economists argue that the government's deficit spending since World War II has kept the economy healthy and helped to avert a new depression. In any case the size of the debt relative to the economy as a whole has declined since World War II—even after the runup of the 1980s—because the economy has grown faster than the debt.

Why, then, were the debt and federal deficits such potent political issues in 1992? One reason was surely that the country was just then emerging from a recession. All aspects of the economy were under intense scrutiny, as voters fearful for their jobs struggled with their own debt loads. Renewed economic growth and budgetary restraint allayed those fears by the late 1990s, when the budget was in surplus and the government was paying down some of the national debt. In the presidency of George W. Bush, however, another economic recession and the costs associated with the war on terrorism quickly converted projections of federal budgetary surpluses for the first decade of the twenty-first century into warnings of a new series of deficits. Whether this will revive concerns about the national debt that Jeffersonians first voiced in the 1790s remains to be seen.

---

inventions set up to terrify and enslave mankind, and monopolize power and profit."

These developments convinced Calvinist ministers, nearly all of them Federalists, that the atheism of the French Revolution was infecting American republicanism. They lashed out at the Republicans, the friends of the French Revolution, as perverters of religious and social order. Jefferson, a deist known for his free thinking in religion, bore the brunt of their attack in 1800.

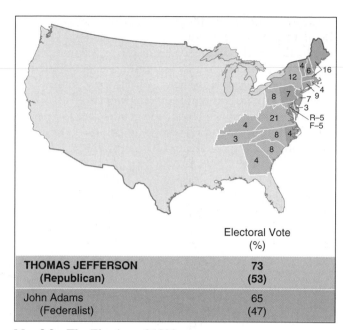

	Electoral Vote (%)
THOMAS JEFFERSON (Republican)	**73** (53)
John Adams (Federalist)	65 (47)

MAP 8-2   **The Election of 1800**
The sharp erosion of Federalist strength in New York and Pennsylvania after 1798 swung the election of 1800 to the Republicans.

The Republicans won the election by mobilizing voters through strong party organizations. Voter turnout in 1800 was twice what it had been in the early 1790s, and most of the new voters were Republicans. The Direct Tax of 1798 cost the Federalists the support of commercial farmers in the mid-Atlantic states. Artisans in port cities had already switched to the Republicans in protest over Jay's Treaty, which they feared left them exposed to a flood of cheap British imports. Adams carried New England and had a smattering of support elsewhere. With New York added to their solid base in the South and the backcountry, the Jeffersonians gained an electoral majority (see Map 8–2).

Party unity among Republican electors was so strong that Jefferson and Burr each received seventy-three electoral votes. Consequently the election was thrown into the House of Representatives, which, until the newly elected Congress was seated, was still dominated by Federalists. Hoping to deny Jefferson the presidency, the Federalists in the House backed Burr. They believed that he was untainted by the Revolutionary virus that made Jefferson seem so dangerous, even though Hamilton, who faced Burr as a political rival in New York, sought to convince them otherwise. The result was a deadlock that persisted into the early months of 1801. Pennsylvania and Virginia mobilized their state militias, a clear message that the Republicans were prepared to use force against what Jefferson termed any "legislative usurpation" of the people's will as expressed in the election.

On February 16, 1801, the Federalists yielded. Informed through intermediaries that Jefferson would not dismantle Hamilton's fiscal system, enough Federalists cast blank ballots to give Jefferson the majority he needed for election. The Twelfth Amendment to the Constitution, ratified in 1804, prevented a similar impasse from arising again by requiring electors to cast separate ballots for president and vice president.

CONCLUSION

In 1789, the American republic was little more than an experiment in self-government. The Federalists provided a firm foundation for that experiment. Hamilton's financial program, neutrality in the wars of the French Revolution, and the diplomatic settlement with Britain in Jay's Treaty bequeathed the young nation a decade of peace and prosperity.

Federalist policies, however, provoked strong opposition rooted in conflicting economic interests and contrasting regional views over the meaning of liberty and government in the new republic. Federalist leadership initially depended on a coalition of regional elites in New England, the mid-Atlantic region, and the slave districts of the South. Each of these elites favored the establishment of effective national power, though often for different reasons. Merchants in Congregationalist New England were concerned mainly with reviving their British trading connections and reversing what they saw as the social and moral decline of the 1780s. Quaker and Episcopal businessmen and commercial farmers in the mid-Atlantic states wanted a central government to promote economic development at home and expand markets abroad. Southern slaveholders, hoping to expand into the West, needed a national government strong enough to secure the trans-Appalachian region.

The Federalist coalition split during Washington's second term when southern planters joined urban artisans and backcountry Scots-Irish farmers in opposing Jay's Treaty and the commercially oriented program of the Federalists. During John Adams' administration, Quaker and German farmers in the mid-Atlantic states defected from the Federalists over the tax legislation of 1798, and three of the four regions of the country lined up behind the Republicans. The new Republican majority was united by their belief that the actions of the New England Federalists—the expansion of the army, the imposition of new taxes, and the passage of the Alien and Sedition Acts—threatened individual liberty and regional autonomy. Non-English groups and farmers south of New England turned to the Republicans as the upholders of these threatened freedoms.

The openly partisan politics of the 1790s surprised the country's founders, who equated parties with the evils of factionalism. They had not foreseen that parties would forge a necessary link between the rulers and the ruled and create a mechanism by which group values and regional interests could be given a political voice. Party formation climaxed in the election of 1800, when the Republicans ended the Federalists' rule. The Republicans won by embracing the popular demand for a more egalitarian social and political order.

To the credit of the Federalists, they relinquished control of the national government peacefully. The importance of this precedent can scarcely be exaggerated. It marked the first time in modern political history that a party in power handed over the government to its opposition. It now remained to be seen what the Republicans would do with their newfound power.

REVIEW QUESTIONS

1. What role did the "people" play in Washington's inaguration in 1789? What was the purpose of the grand procession and why were the militia present?

2. What was distinctive about the four regions of the United States in 1790? What were the common values and goals that brought white Americans together?

3. What were the major problems confronting the Washington administration, and how effectively were they resolved?

4. Who were the Federalists and the Republicans, and how did they differ over the meaning of liberty and the power of the national government? What were the major steps in the formation of two distinct parties in the early United States?

5. Why did regional differences tend to pit the North against the South by the late 1790s?

6. How did the XYZ Affair lead to a political crisis in the United States? Why did the Federalists believe that they would benefit from a war against France?

7. Jefferson called his election in 1800 the "revolution of 1800." What do you think he meant? Would you agree with him?

KEY TERMS

Alien and Sedition Acts (p. 253)

Bill of Rights (p. 241)

Deism (p. 255)

Federalists (p. 245)

Franco-American Accord of 1800 (p. 255)

Jay's Treaty (p. 250)

Judiciary Act of 1789 (p. 242)

Nullification (p. 254)

Pietists (p. 237)

Quasi-War (p. 253)

Republican (Jeffersonian) (p. 245)

States' rights (p. 254)

Tariff Act of 1789 (p. 242)

Tonnage Act of 1789 (p. 242)

Treaty of Greenville (p. 247)

Treaty of San Lorenzo (p. 251)

Whiskey Rebellion (p. 250)

XYZ Affair (p. 252)

RECOMMENDED READING

Elkins, Stanley, and Eric McKitrick. *The Age of Federalism* (1993). A magisterial work of narrative history that includes brilliant sketches of the major political actors in the 1790s.

Flexner, James T. *George Washington and the New Nation, 1783–1793* (1969) and *George Washington: Anguish and Farewell, 1793–1799* (1972). These two volumes stand out for their readable and informative account of Washington's political career after the Revolution.

Freeman, Joanne B. *Affairs of Honor: National Politics in the New Republic* (2001). By showing how politicians in the early republic based their behavior on codes of male honor, this study offers a fresh way of understanding the often bitter political divisions of the 1790s.

Hofstadter, Richard. *The Idea of a Party System, 1780–1840* (1969). This book combines political and intellectual history in a graceful account of how Americans gradually came to accept political parties as a legitimate expression of the popular will.

Lipset, Seymour. *The First New Nation: The United States in Historical and Comparative Perspective* (1963). This work draws on insights from political sociology to show what was unique and enduring in America's pioneering role as a new nation with a written constitution.

Miller, John C. *The Federalist Era, 1789–1801* (1960). This older work is still of great value for its relatively brief and well-balanced overview of the Washington and Adams administrations.

Waldstreicher, David. *In the Midst of Perpetual Fetes: The Making of American Nationalism, 1776–1820* (1997). An imaginatively conceived work that reveals how Americans in the early republic created their own sense of nationalism through popular festivals, street parades, and other forms of political celebration at the local level.

ADDITIONAL SOURCES

Washington's America

Horseman, Reginald. *The Frontier in the Formative Years, 1783–1815* (1970).

McColley, Robert. *Slavery and Jeffersonian Virginia* (1964).

Nash, Gary B. *Forging Freedom: The Formation of Philadelphia's Black Community, 1720–1840* (1988).

Newman, Simon P. *Parades and the Politics of the American Street* (1997).

Smith, Billy G. The *"Lower Sort": Philadelphia's Laboring People, 1750–1800* (1990).

Ulrich, Laurel Thatcher. *A Midwife's Tale: The Life of Martha Ballard, Based on Her Diary, 1785–1812* (1990).

Wallace, Anthony F. C. *The Death and Rebirth of the Seneca* (1970).

Wood, Betty. *Women's Work, Men's Work: The Informal Slave Economies of Lowcountry Georgia* (1995).

Forging a New Government

Cunliffe, Marcus. *George Washington: Man and Monument* (1958).

Ketcham, Ralph. *Presidents above Party: The First American Presidency, 1789–1829* (1984).

Kohn, Richard H. *Eagle and Sword: The Federalists and the Creation of the Military Establishment in America, 1783–1802* (1975).

Phelps, Glenn A. *George Washington and American Constitutionalism* (1993).

Stourzh, Gerald. *Alexander Hamilton and the Idea of Republican Government* (1970).

Ellis, Joseph J. *Founding Brothers: The Revolutionary Generation* (2000)

The Emergence of Parties

Appleby, Joyce. *Capitalism and a New Social Order: The Republican Vision of the 1790s* (1984).

Buel. Richard Jr., *Securing the Revolution: Ideology in American Politics, 1789–1815* (1972).

Branson, Susan. *Those Fiery Frenchified Dames: Women and Political Culture in Early National Philadelphia* (2001)

Cunningham, Noble E. Jr., *The Jeffersonian Republicans: The Formation of Party Organization, 1789–1801* (1957).

De Conde, Alexander. *Entangling Alliance: Politics and Diplomacy under George Washington* (1958).

Slaughter, Thomas P. *The Whiskey Rebellion: Frontier Epilogue to the American Revolution* (1986).

Young, Alfred F. *The Democratic Republicans of New York: The Origins, 1763–1797* (1967).

The Last Federalist Administration

Dauer, Manning *The Adams Federalists* (1953).

Kurtz, Stephen G. *The Presidency of John Adams: The Collapse of Federalism, 1795–1800* (1957).

Sharp, Roger. *American Politics in the Early Republic: The New Nation in Crisis* (1993).

Sisson, Daniel. *The American Revolution of 1800* (1974).

Smith, James M. *Freedom's Fetters: The Alien and Sedition Laws and American Civil Liberties,* rev. ed. (1966).

Stinchcombe, William. *The XYZ Affair* (1980).

WHERE TO LEARN MORE

- **Cincinnati Historical Society, Cincinnati, Ohio.** Collections include written and visual materials on the history of the Old Northwest Territory. Visit its website www.cincymuseum.org/ for information on its programs and the accessibility of its printed and audiovisual collections.

- **Federal Hall National Memorial, New York, New York.** This museum and historic site holds artifacts relating to President Washington's inauguration. Its website www.nps.gov/feha/ includes a printable travel guide to various sites in Manhattan administered by the National Parks Service.

- **Hamilton Grange National Memorial, New York, New York.** The home of Alexander Hamilton contains materials on his life. A brief history of the home and Hamilton's life can be found at its website www.nps/gov/hagr/.

- **Adams National Historic Site, Quincy, Massachusetts.** This site preserves buildings and manuscripts associated with four generations of the Adams family. See its website www.nps.gov/adam/ for information on guided tours and the various homes that are part of the site.

Please refer to the document CD-ROM for primary sources related to this chapter.

→ *The low point in what many Americans viewed as A Second War of Independence—the War of 1812—came when British troops seized and burned Washington, D.C., on August 24, 1814.*

THE TRIUMPH AND COLLAPSE OF JEFFERSONIAN REPUBLICANISM 1800–1824

9

Riversdale, 30 August 1814

My dear Sister,

Since I started this letter [on Aug. 9] we have been in a state of continual alarm, and now I have time to write only two or three lines to ask you to tell Papa that we are alive, in good health, and I hope safe from danger. I am sure that you have heard the news of the battle of Bladensburg where the English defeated the American troops with Madison 'not at their head, but at their rear.'

From there they went to Washington where they burned the Capitol, the President's House, all the public offices, etc. During the battle I saw several cannonballs with my own eyes, and I will write all the details to your husband. At the moment the English ships are at Alexandria which is also in their possession.

I don't know how all this will end, but I fear very badly for us. It is probable that it will also bring about a dissolution of the union of the states, and in that case, farewell to the public debt. You know I have predicted this outcome for a long time. Wouldn't it be wise to send your husband here without delay, in order to plan with me the best course to pursue for Papa's interests as well as yours?

This letter will go, I think, by a Dutch ship. If I have time with the confusion we are in, I will write again in a

CHAPTER OUTLINE

Jefferson's Presidency
Reform at Home
The Louisiana Purchase
Florida and Western Schemes
Embargo and a Crippled Presidency

Madison and the Coming of War
The Failure of Economic Sanctions
The Frontier and Indian Resistance
Decision for War

The War of 1812
Setbacks in Canada
Western Victories and British Offensives
The Treaty of Ghent and the Battle of New Orleans

The Era of Good Feelings
Economic Nationalism
Judicial Nationalism
Toward a Continental Empire

The Breakdown of Unity
The Panic of 1819
The Missouri Compromise
The Election of 1824

Conclusion

few days, perhaps by the same vessel. At present my house is full of people every day and at night my bedroom is full of rifles, pistols, sabers, etc. Many thanks to your husband for the information in his letter of 27 April, and tell him that I invested all his money in the May loan [of the U.S. Treasury]. Please give many greetings to my dear Father and to Charles [her brother]. Embrace your children for me and believe me,

Your affectionate sister,
Rosalie E. Calvert

Margaret Law Callcott, ed., *Mistress of Riversdale: The Plantation Letters of Rosalie Stier Calvert, 1795–1821* (Baltimore: The Johns Hopkins University Press, 1991), pp. 271–272.

Rosalie Calvert, from her plantation home in nearby Bladensburg, Maryland, wrote to her sister in Europe with news of the British attack on Washington, D.C. in August 1814, the low point of the American cause in the War of 1812. The youngest of three children in a wealthy Belgian family that had fled the advancing armies of revolutionary France, Rosalie was sixteen when her family arrived in Philadelphia in the summer of 1794. Her father, Henri J. Stier, had planned in advance for his family's departure and brought with him a sizeable fortune in gold, U.S. currency, and paintings. The family lived off the income from Henri's investments in U.S. securities and, unsurprisingly, was strongly Federalist in its political leanings. After resettling in Annapolis, most of the Stiers returned to Europe in 1803 when political conditions had stabilized. Left behind was Rosalie, entrusted with the management of the family's financial holdings. In 1799, Rosalie had married George Calvert, a descendent of the proprietors of the Maryland colony and a kinsman of the Washingtons.

The Calverts lived at Riversdale, a home built by her father, and shared in the responsibilities of managing three plantations worked by slave labor. Rosalie's wealth and elite social standing deepened her political conservatism. Moreover, the coming to power of the Jeffersonian Republicans in 1801 triggered bitter memories of the revolutionary turmoil she had experienced as a young woman in Belgium. In her eyes, Jefferson and his followers were demagogues who catered to the poor and threatened to infect America with the political radicalism of the French Revolution. She blamed the coming of the War of 1812 on ignorant, ill-conceived Republican policies and feared that the war would unleash massive unrest within the United States. Particularly alarming was the news that a mob in Baltimore had brutally beaten twelve prominent Federalists for their antiwar stand. Thus the sense of "continual alarm" that runs through her letter in August 1814, at a time when the war had spilled over into her home.

Her fears were overblown. The United States did weather the War of 1812 and the Calverts were spared any property damage at their Riversdale estate. Rosalie, however, survived the war by only six years. Her great wealth could not shield her from the duties of a wife, most notably frequent childbearing. The strain of having nine children and suffering one miscarriage in twenty-one years of marriage is likely to have contributed to her death at the age of 43 from congestive heart failure.

Despite her denunciations of the Republicans, Jefferson and his Republican successors, James Madison and James Monroe, succeeded in promoting the growth and independence of the United States in the first quarter of the nineteenth century. Expansionist policies to the south and west more than doubled the size of the republic and fueled the westward spread of slavery. The war against Britain from 1812 to 1815, if less than a military triumph, nonetheless freed Americans to look inward for economic development.

At the height of Republican success during the Era of Good Feelings just after the War of 1812, the Federalist party collapsed. Without an organized opposition to enforce party discipline among themselves, the Republicans soon followed the Federalists into political oblivion. The nation's expansion produced two crises—a financial panic and a battle over slavery in Missouri—that shattered the façade of republican unity. By the mid-1820s, a new party system was emerging.

KEY TOPICS

- The domination of the Republicans and the collapse of the Federalist party
- The territorial expansion of the United States to the west and the south
- The growth of nationalism and of sectional rivalry
- The first national crisis over slavery
- The collapse of the Republican party

JEFFERSON'S PRESIDENCY

Thomas Jefferson believed that a true revolution had occurred in 1800, a peaceful overthrow of the Federalist party and its hated principles of government consolidation and military force. In his eyes, the defeat of the monarchical Federalists reconfirmed the true political legacy of the Revolution by restoring the republican majority to its rightful control of the government.

Unlike the Hamiltonian Federalists, whose commercial vision of America accepted social and economic inequalities as inevitable, the Jeffersonians wanted a predominantly agrarian republic based on widespread economic equality for white yeomen families. Without such equality, Jefferson was convinced, the privileged few would threaten the people's liberties. Contemporary political thought held that all societies went through stages of economic development that ended in the consolidation of power and suppression of liberties by a wealthy minority. Jefferson hoped to break that cycle through territorial expansion that would add enough land to maintain self-reliant farmers as the guardians of republican freedoms.

Jefferson's first administration was a solid success. A unified Republican party reduced the size and scope of the federal government, allowed the Alien and Sedition Acts to lapse, and celebrated the Louisiana Purchase. An enfeebled Federalist party weakly opposed Jefferson's reelection in 1804. His second term, however, was a bitter disappointment, marked by the massive unpopularity of Jefferson's embargo on American foreign trade. The embargo, designed to compel warring Britain and France to recognize American rights as a neutral shipper, failed at home and abroad. As a result, Jefferson left his successor, James Madison, a divided party, a revived Federalism, and an unresolved crisis in foreign affairs.

REFORM AT HOME

Jefferson set the style and tone of his administration from the beginning. He was the first president to be inaugurated in Washington, D.C., and his inauguration was as unpretentious as the raw and primitive capital city itself. Then little more than a scraggly collection of huts, a few boardinghouses, and unfinished public buildings, Washington lacked, one senator ruefully noted, "only houses, wine cellars, learned men, amiable women, and other trifles to make our city perfect." Jefferson walked from his lodgings to the Capitol building to be sworn in. His dress was neat but shorn of such gentlemanly refinements as a wig. He emphasized in his inaugural address the overwhelming commitment of Americans to the "republican form" of government and affirmed his own support of civil liberties as an American principle.

Believing that the Federalists had promoted aristocratic pretensions and courtly intrigue through such practices as weekly levees (formal receptions) for presidential guests, Jefferson replaced the levees with small, men-only dinners, where he aired his political views. This effort to achieve republican purity in governance, one that denied women any political role, created a void in the capital's social life that was filled by the wives of cabinet members and women drawn from the social elite. It was their dinner parties and receptions that enabled politically minded women and men to come together, lobby on behalf of friends and relatives, and build the networks that influenced how political offices and favors were distributed. These occasions provided a setting in which politicking could occur in a capital where the formal institutions of power—the executive, legislative, and judicial branches of government—were cut off from each other, not only by the distance between their physical locations, but also by the constitutional doctrine of separation of powers. Influential Washington hostesses soon wielded a good deal of informal political power as they helped make possible a national political culture.

The cornerstone of Republican domestic policy was retrenchment, a return to the frugal, simple federal

Chronology

1801 Thomas Jefferson is inaugurated, the first Republican president John Marshall becomes chief justice.

1802 Congress repeals the Judiciary Act of 1801.

1803 *Marbury v. Madison* sets the precedent of judicial review by the Supreme Court.

Louisiana Purchase.

Lewis and Clark expedition begins.

1804 Vice President Aaron Burr kills Alexander Hamilton in a duel.

Judges John Pickering and Samuel Chase impeached by Republicans.

Jefferson is reelected.

1806 Britain and France issue orders restricting neutral shipping.

Betrayal of the Burr conspiracy.

1807 Chesapeake affair.

Congress passes the Embargo Act.

Congress prohibits the African slave trade.

1808 James Madison elected president.

1809 Repeal of the Embargo Act.

Passage of the Nonintercourse Act.

1810 Macon's Bill No. 2 reopens trade with Britain and France.

United States annexes part of West Florida.

Georgia state law invalidated by the Supreme Court in *Fletcher v. Peck*.

1811 Battle of Tippecanoe and defeat of the Indian confederation.

Charter of the Bank of the United States expires.

1812 Congress declares war on Britain.

American loss of Detroit.

Madison reelected.

1813 Perry's victory at Battle of Put-in-Bay.

Battle of the Thames and death of Tecumseh.

1814 Jackson crushes the Creeks at the Battle of Horseshoe Bend.

British burn Washington, D.C., and attack Baltimore.

Macdonough's naval victory on Lake Champlain turns back a British invasion.

Hartford Convention meets.

Treaty of Ghent signed.

1815 Jackson routs British at the Battle of New Orleans.

1816 Congress charters the Second Bank of the United States and passes a protective tariff.

James Monroe elected president.

1817 Rush–Bagot Treaty demilitarizes the Great Lakes.

1818 Anglo–American Accords on trade and boundaries.

Jackson's border campaign in Spanish East Florida.

1819 Trans-Continental Treaty between United States and Spain.

Beginning of the Missouri controversy.

Financial panic sends economy into a depression.

Dartmouth College v. Woodward upholds the charter rights of corporations.

McCulloch v. Maryland upholds constitutionality of the Bank of the United States.

1820 Missouri Compromise on slavery in the Louisiana Purchase.

Monroe reelected.

1823 Monroe Doctrine proclaims western hemisphere closed to further European colonization.

1825 John Quincy Adams elected president by the House of Representatives

---

establishment the Jeffersonians believed to be the original intent of the Constitution. Determined to root out what they viewed as the corruption and patronage of a government bloated by the power-grasping Federalists, the Republicans began with fiscal policy. Jefferson's secretary of the treasury was Albert Gallatin, a native of Switzerland who emerged in the 1790s as the best financial mind in the Republican party. He convinced Jefferson that the Bank of the United States was essential for financial stability and blocked efforts to dismantle it. Unlike Hamilton, however, Gallatin thought that a large public debt was a curse, a drag on productive capital, and an unfair burden on future generations. He succeeded in reducing the national debt from $83 million in 1800 to $57 million by 1809.

Gallatin's conservative fiscal policies shrank both the spending and taxes of the national government. The Republicans eliminated all internal taxes, including the despised tax on whiskey. Slashes in the military budget kept government expenditures below the level of 1800. The army was cut back to three thousand men, and the navy was nearly eliminated. Jefferson's

Jane Braddick Petticolas: (1791-1852) "View of the West Front of Monticello and Garden" 1825, watercolor on paper, 13 5/8 x 18 1/18 inches. Edward Owen/Monticello/Thomas Jefferson Foundation, Inc.

The classical design and bucolic setting of Monticello, Jefferson's home outside Charlottesville, Virginia, visually expressed both his aristocratic tastes and his vision of a harmonious agrarian republic.

defense strategy called for gunboats and coastal fortifications. If the country were invaded, he would rely on the militia—citizen soldiers commanded by professional officers, to be trained at the newly established (1802) military academy at West Point. The cuts in military spending, combined with soaring revenues from customs collections, left Gallatin with a surplus in the budget that he could devote to debt repayment.

Jeffersonian reform targeted the political character, as well as the size, of the national government. Of the six hundred officeholders appointed by Washington and Adams, Jefferson estimated that only six were Republicans. He moved to break the Federalist stranglehold on federal offices and appoint officials with sound Republican principles. Arch-Federalists, those Jefferson deemed guilty of misusing their offices for openly political reasons, were immediately replaced, and Republicans filled other posts opened up by attrition. By the time Jefferson left the presidency in 1809, Republicans held nearly all the appointive offices.

Jefferson moved most aggressively against the Federalists in the judiciary. Just days before they relinquished power, the Federalists passed the Judiciary Act of 1801. This act created sixteen new circuit courts; added nearly two hundred federal marshals, attorneys, and clerks; and reduced the size of the Supreme Court from six justices to five by stipulating that the next vacancy was not to be filled. The Jeffersonians were enraged. The Federalists already monopolized all federal judgeships, and this last-minute legislation both enlarged the judiciary and packed it with more Federalists appointed by Adams, the outgoing president. To add insult to injury, the Federalists had even tried to insure that Jefferson would be unable to appoint a Republican to the Supreme Court when the next opening occurred.

The Republicans fought back. Now dominant in Congress, they quickly repealed the Judiciary Act of 1801, replacing it with a measure that eliminated the new judgeships and restored the size of the Supreme Court to six members, each with responsibility for one

Dolley Madison, the engaging young wife of James Madison, Jefferson's secretary of state, served as the unofficial social hostess in the White House during the administration of Jefferson, a widower.

of the circuit courts. Frustrated Federalists now turned to John Marshall, a staunch Federalist appointed chief justice of the United States by President Adams in 1801, hoping that he would rule that Congress had acted unconstitutionally in removing the recently appointed federal judges. Marshall moved carefully to avoid an open confrontation. He was aware that the Republicans contended that Congress and the president had at least a coequal right with the Supreme Court to decide constitutional questions.

The issue came to a head in the case of ***Marbury v. Madison*** (1803), which centered on Secretary of State James Madison's refusal to deliver a commission to William Marbury, one of Adams's "midnight appointments" as a justice of the peace for the District of Columbia. Marshall held that although Marbury had a legal right to his commission, the Court had no jurisdiction in the case. The Court ruled that the section of the Judiciary Act of 1789 granting it the power to order the delivery of Marbury's commission was unconstitutional because it conferred on the Court a power not specified in Article 3 of the Constitution on cases of original jurisdiction. Stating that it was "emphatically the province and duty of the judicial department to say what the law is," Marshall created the precedent of judicial review, the power of the Supreme Court to rule on the constitutionality of federal law. Although not invoked again until the Dred Scott decision of 1857, this doctrine was of pivotal importance for the future of the Court. Marshall had brilliantly turned a threatening situation into a success for the judiciary.

Marshall's assertion of the Court's power deepened Republican suspicions of judicial tyranny. Demanding popular election for all judges, radical Republicans rejected the entire notion of an appointed judiciary. Jefferson did not want to go that far, but he felt strongly that judges should be accountable to the popular will.

At the urging of the radicals, congressional Republicans brought formal charges against two notorious Federalist judges. One of them, John Pickering, a district judge from New Hampshire and a mentally unstable alcoholic, was convicted and removed from office. The other was bigger game: Justice Samuel Chase of the Supreme Court, the most obnoxious Federalist still in a position of national power. For all his blatant partisanship, however, Chase was clearly sane, and he escaped conviction in the Senate in early 1805, when the Republicans failed to show that he was guilty of "high crimes and misdemeanors," the constitutionally defined grounds for removal from office. His acquittal ended the Republican offensive against the judiciary.

THE LOUISIANA PURCHASE

In foreign affairs, fortune smiled on Jefferson during his first term. The European war that had almost sucked in the United States in the 1790s subsided. Britain and France agreed on a truce in 1802. Meanwhile, Jefferson, despite his distaste for a strong navy, ordered a show of force in the Mediterranean to punish the Barbary pirates who were preying on American shipping and taking American sailors hostage.

For years, the North African states of Morocco, Algeria, Tunis, and Tripoli had demanded cash tribute from foreigners trading in the Mediterranean. Jefferson stopped the payments in 1801, and when attacks on American shipping resumed, he retaliated by sending warships and marines to the Mediterranean. The tribute system continued until 1815, but thanks to the success of U.S. forces in Tripoli, Jefferson got much better terms.

The Anglo-French peace was a mixed blessing for the United States. Although it removed any im-

William Clark sketched a Columbia River salmon on this page of his journal.

mediate threat of war, the return of peace also allowed Spain and France to reclaim their colonial trade in the Western Hemisphere. American shippers were thus deprived of the windfall profits they had earned while dominating that trade during the European war. Of greater long-range concern, the new military ruler of France, Napoleon Bonaparte, was now free to develop his plans for reviving the French empire in America. In a secret treaty with Spain in 1800, Napoleon reacquired for France the Louisiana Territory, a vast, vaguely defined area stretching between the Mississippi River and the Rocky Mountains.

Sketchy, unconfirmed reports of the treaty reached Jefferson in the spring of 1801, and he was immediately alarmed. He had long believed that Spain, proud but militarily impotent, would be powerless to stem the spread of the expanding American population into its territories in western North America. Indeed, Spanish military officials in Louisiana had repeatedly called in vain for mili-

tary reinforcements to block the Americans, this "new and vigorous people . . . advancing and multiplying in the silence of peace." France, by contrast, was a formidable opponent. French control of the Mississippi Valley, combined with the British presence in Canada, threatened to hem in the United States and deprive Jefferson's farmers of their empire for liberty.

Jefferson was prepared to reverse the traditional foreign policy of his party in order to eliminate this threat. He opened exploratory talks with the British on an Anglo-American alliance to drive the French out of Louisiana. Looking toward the possibility of war, he also strengthened American forces in the Mississippi Valley and secured congressional approval for the Lewis and Clark expedition through upper Louisiana. Although best known for its scientific discoveries, this expedition was designed initially as a military mission. Jefferson applied diplomatic and military pressure to induce Napoleon to sell New Orleans and a small slice of coastal territory to its east to the United States. This was his main objective: to possess New Orleans and control the mouth of the Mississippi River, outlet to world markets. To his surprise, Napoleon suddenly decided in early 1803 to sell all of the immense Louisiana Territory to the Americans (see Map 9–1).

Napoleon's failure to reconquer Saint-Domingue (modern-day Haiti) was instrumental in his about-face on plans for a revived French empire in America. He had envisioned this rich sugar island as the jewel of his new empire and intended to use the Louisiana Territory as a granary to supply the island. During the upheavals of the French Revolution, the slaves on the island, led by Touissant L'Ouverture, rebelled in a bloody and successful bid for independence. Napoleon sent a large army to reassert French control, but it succumbed to the islanders' fierce resistance.

Without firm French control of Saint-Domingue, Louisiana was of little use to Napoleon. And when the U.S. Congress passed resolutions threatening an American attack on New Orleans, he realized that he was likely to have to fight to keep it. With a renewed war against Britain looming, he had better use for his troops in Europe and wanted to keep Americans neutral. For $15 million (including about $4 million in French debts owed to American citizens), he offered to part with the whole of Louisiana. The cost to the United States was about 3.5 cents per acre.

Jefferson, the strict constructionist, now turned pragmatist. Despite the lack of any specific authorization in the Constitution for the acquisition of foreign territory or the incorporation as American citizens of the fifty thousand French and Spanish descendants then living in Louisiana, he accepted

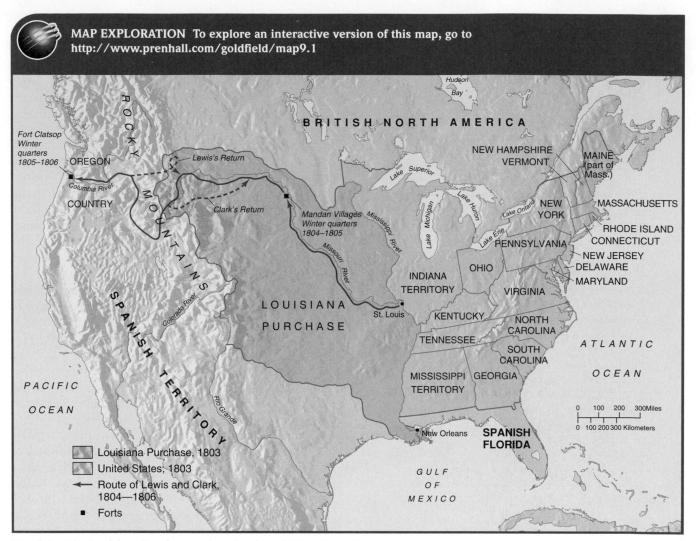

MAP EXPLORATION To explore an interactive version of this map, go to http://www.prenhall.com/goldfield/map9.1

MAP 9-1   The Louisiana Purchase and the Lewis and Clark Expedition
The vast expanse of the Louisiana Purchase was virtually unknown territory to Americans before the Lewis and Clark expedition gathered a mass of scientific information about it.

Napoleon's deal. (The Louisiana Purchase doubled the size of the United States and offered seemingly endless space to be settled by yeoman farmers.

Jefferson was willing, as the Federalists had been when they were in power, to stretch the Constitution to support his definition of the national good. Conversely, it was now the Federalists, fearful of a further decline in their political power, who relied on a narrow reading of the Constitution in a futile attempt to block the Louisiana acquisition.

FLORIDA AND WESTERN SCHEMES

The magnificent prize of Louisiana did not satisfy Republican territorial ambitions. Still to be gained were river outlets on the Gulf Coast essential for the development of plantation agriculture in Alabama

and Mississippi. As Secretary of State Madison later bluntly explained, "The free navigation of these rivers was inseparable from the very existence of the United States." The boundaries of the Louisiana Purchase were so vague that Jefferson felt justified in claiming Spanish-held Texas and the Gulf Coast eastward from New Orleans to Mobile Bay, including the Spanish province of West Florida. Against stiff Spanish opposition, he pushed ahead with his plans to acquire West Florida. This provoked the first challenge to his leadership of the party.

Once it was clear that Spain did not want to sell West Florida to the United States, Jefferson accepted Napoleon's offer to act as a middleman in the acquisition. Napoleon's price was $2 million. He soon lost interest in the project, however, and Jefferson lost prestige in 1806, when he pushed an

The caption on this 1807 illustration of a deserted pier in Portland, Maine— "And the grass literally grew upon the wharves."—reflects the hardship Jefferson's embargo caused as it choked off the American export trade.

"And the grass literally grew upon the wharves."

appropriations bill through Congress to pay for Napoleon's services. Former Republican stalwarts in Congress denounced the bill as bribe money and staged a party revolt against the president's devious tactics.

Jefferson's failed bid for West Florida emboldened Westerners to demand that Americans seize the territory by force. In 1805 and 1806, Aaron Burr, Jefferson's first vice president, apparently became entangled in an attempt at just such a land grab.

Republicans had been suspicious of Burr since his dalliance with the Federalists in their bid to make him, rather than Jefferson, president in 1800. He further alienated the party when he involved himself with the efforts of a minority of die-hard Federalists known as the Essex Junto. The members of this group feared that incorporation of the vast Louisiana Purchase into the United States would leave New England powerless in national affairs. Picking up on states' rights themes first used by Jefferson in the Kentucky Resolutions, they concocted a plan for a northern confederacy. New York was central to their scheme. Rebuffed by Hamilton, they turned to Burr and backed him in the New York gubernatorial race of 1804. Burr lost, largely because Hamilton denounced him. The enmity between the two men reached a tragic climax in July 1804, when Burr killed Hamilton in a duel at Weehawken, New Jersey. Facing murder charges in New Jersey and New York, Burr fled to the West and lined up followers for a separatist plot.

The Burr conspiracy remains mysterious. Burr was undoubtedly eager to pry land loose from the Spanish and Indians, and he may have been thinking of carving out a separate western confederacy in the lower Mississippi Valley. Whatever he had in mind, he blundered in relying on General James Wilkinson as a co-conspirator. Wilkinson, the military governor of the Louisiana Territory and also a double agent for Spain, betrayed Burr. He was tried for treason in 1807, and Jefferson made extraordinary efforts to secure his conviction. He was saved by the insistence of Chief Justice Marshall that the Constitution defined treason only as the waging of war against the United States or the rendering of aid to its enemies. The law also required the direct testimony of two witnesses to an "overt act" of treason for conviction. Lacking such witnesses, the government failed to prove its case, and Burr was acquitted.

EMBARGO AND A CRIPPLED PRESIDENCY

Concern about a possible war against Britain in 1807 soon quieted the uproar over Burr's trial. After Britain and France had resumed their war in 1803, the United States became enmeshed in the same quarrels over neutral rights, blockades, ship seizures, and impressments of American sailors that had almost dragged the country into war in the 1790s. Britain proclaimed a blockade of the European continent, which was controlled by Napoleon, and confiscated the cargoes of ships attempting to run the blockade. Napoleon retaliated with seizures of ships that adhered to the blockade by submitting to British searches and accepting the British-imposed licensing system for trading with Europe. Caught in the middle, but eager to supply both sides, was the American merchant marine, the world's largest carrier of neutral goods.

American merchants and shippers had taken full advantage of the opportunities opened by the European war. During the flush years from 1793 to 1807, American ship tonnage tripled, and the value of exports soared fivefold. Despite French and British restrictions, American merchants traded with anyone they pleased. They dominated commerce, not only between Britain and the United States, but also between the European continent and the French and Spanish colonies in the West Indies. Profits were so great that merchants made money even when only one-third of their ships evaded the blockades.

In June 1807, however, a confrontation known as the ***Chesapeake* Incident** nearly triggered an Anglo-American war. A British ship, the *Leopard,* ordered a U.S. frigate, the *Chesapeake,* to submit to a search in coastal waters off Norfolk. When the commander of the *Chesapeake* refused, the *Leopard* opened fire. Three Americans were killed, eighteen were wounded, and four others (one of whom was subsequently hanged) were impressed as alleged deserters from the Royal Navy. Although Federalists worried that "our rogue of a President will glory in a war with England," Jefferson resisted the popular outcry for revenge. Instead, he barred American ports to British warships and called both for monetary compensation and for an end to impressment.

Britain offered in response only a belated apology and a promise of reparations. Still, Jefferson desperately wanted to avoid conflict. The country was woefully unprepared for war, and he passionately believed that international law should resolve international disputes. In a resort to the Republican idealism that had animated the Revolution, Jefferson called for a trade embargo as a substitute for war. The **Embargo Act of 1807**, an expression of Jefferson's policy of "peaceable coercion," prohibited American ships from clearing port to any nation until Britain and France repealed their trading restrictions on neutral shippers.

The premise of the embargo was that Europe was so dependent on American foods and raw materials that it would do America's bidding if faced with a cutoff. This premise was not so much wrong as unrealistic. The embargo did hurt Europe, but the people who first felt the pain were British textile workers and slaves in the colonies, hardly those who wielded the levers of power. Meanwhile, politically influential landlords and manufacturers benefited from short-term shortages by jacking up prices.

The American export trade and its profits dried up with Jefferson's self-imposed blockade. Except for manufacturers, who now had the American market to themselves, nearly all economic groups suffered under the embargo. Especially hard hit were New England shippers and merchants, and they accused the Republicans of near-criminal irresponsibility for forcing a depression on the country. Jefferson responded to these criticisms and to widespread violations of the embargo with a series of enforcement acts. These acts put real teeth into the embargo and consolidated executive powers far beyond what the Federalists themselves had been able to achieve while in power.

As the embargo tightened and the 1808 presidential election approached, the Federalist party revived. The Federalist presidential candidate, Charles C. Pinckney—running against Secretary of State James Madison, Jefferson's handpicked successor—polled three times as many votes as he had in 1804. Madison won only because he carried the South and the West, the Republican heartland.

Before Madison took office, the Republicans abandoned Jefferson's embargo. Britain and France had remained defiant, and at home the embargo had become an intolerable political burden. The embargo ended on March 3, 1809, and was immediately replaced by the Nonintercourse Act, a measure that prohibited American trade only with Britain and France. At the president's discretion, trade could be reopened with either nation once it lifted its restrictions on American shipping.

MADISON AND THE COMING OF WAR

Frail-looking and short, Madison struck most contemporaries as an indecisive and weaker version of Jefferson. He never did succeed in escaping from his predecessor's shadow. Nor did he succeed, as president, in keeping America at peace. Yet in intellectual toughness and resourcefulness he was at least Jefferson's equal. He failed because of an inherited foreign policy that was partly of his own making as Jefferson's secretary of state. The Republicans' idealistic stand on neutral rights was ultimately untenable unless backed up by military and political force. Madison concluded as much when he decided on war against Britain in the spring of 1812.

A war against America's old enemy also promised to restore unity to a Republican party increasingly divided over Madison's peaceful diplomacy. What was at stake for Madison was not just the defense of America's economic independence but also the legacy of republicanism itself, now under attack by monarchists in Britain and their presumed American friends in the resurgent Federalist party. Thus did Madison and his fellow Republicans push for a war they were eager but unprepared to fight.

THE FAILURE OF ECONOMIC SANCTIONS

Early in his administration, Madison convinced himself that the impasse in Anglo–American relations was about to be broken. Britain benefited from the Nonintercourse Act at the expense of France. Unlike the embargo, which had kept American vessels at home, nonintercourse permitted ship clearances. Once at sea, American ships were kept away from France and steered to England by the strong British navy. Perhaps in recognition of this unintended consequence of the new American policy, the British began to relax their restrictions on neutral shipping, known as the Orders in Council, in favor of U.S. commerce. At the same time, the British minister in Washington, David Erskine, reached an agreement with Madison that called for completely rescinding the Orders in Council as they applied to the United States. In return, Madison pledged to terminate nonintercourse against Britain while maintaining it against France.

Madison set June 10, 1809, as the date for the resumption of Anglo–American trade. Unfortunately, Erskine had exceeded his instructions, and the Madison–Erskine agreement was disavowed as soon as news of it reached London. Although Madison reimposed sanctions on Britain in August, he was left looking the fool.

With Madison floundering, Congress stepped in with its own policy in 1810. Macon's Bill No. 2, named after congressman Nathaniel Macon, threw open American trade to everyone but stipulated that if either France or England lifted its restrictions, the president would resume trading sanctions against the other. A concession to mercantile interests in New England and the mid-Atlantic states, Macon's bill also bought Madison time before he had to decide between war or submission to the British Orders in Council. Thanks to Napoleon's duplicity, however, that time was short.

Napoleon made an offer in August 1810 that Madison felt he had to accept. The French emperor promised to withdraw his decrees against American

shipping on the condition that if Britain did not follow suit, Madison would force the British to respect American rights. Madison took the bait. He was under no illusion as to Napoleon's honesty, but he was desperate to apply pressure on the British to match the apparent French concessions. To Madison's chagrin, Napoleon's offer was an utter fraud. French seizures of American ships continued. By the time his duplicity became clear, Napoleon had already succeeded in worsening Anglo–American tensions. In November 1810, Madison reimposed nonintercourse against Britain, putting the two nations on a collision course.

THE FRONTIER AND INDIAN RESISTANCE

Mounting frustrations in the South and West also pushed Madison toward a war against Britain. Nearly one million Americans lived west of the Appalachian Mountains in 1810, a tripling of the western population in just a decade. Cheap, fertile land and markets for crops down the Ohio and Mississippi River systems drew farm families from the East. Farm prices, including those for the southern staples of cotton and tobacco, plunged when Jefferson's embargo shut off exports, and they stayed low after the embargo was lifted. Blame for the persistent agricultural depression focused on the British and their stranglehold on overseas trade after 1808. As a glut of American goods piled up in English ports, prices remained depressed.

Western settlers also accused the British of inciting Indian resistance. After the *Chesapeake* incident, the British did seek alliances with Indians in the Old Northwest, reviving the strategy of using them as a buffer against any American move on Canada. However, it was the unceasing demand of Americans for ever more Indian land, not any British incitements, that triggered the **pan-Indian resistance movement** that so frightened western settlers on the eve of the War of 1812.

In the Treaty of Greenville (1795) (see Chapter 8), the American government had promised that any future acquisitions of Indian land would have to be approved by all native peoples in the region. Nonetheless, government agents continued to play one group against another and divide groups from within by lavishing money and goods on the more accommodationist Christianized Indians. By such means, William Henry Harrison, the governor of the Indiana Territory, procured most of southern Indiana in the Treaty of Vincennes of 1804. Two extraordinary leaders, the Shawnee chief Tecumseh and his brother, the Prophet Tenkswatawa, channeled Indian outrage over this treaty into a movement to unify tribes throughout the West for a stand against the white invaders.

The Prophet Tenkswatawa was the spiritual leader of the pan-Indian movement that sought to revitalize native culture and block the spread of white settlement in the Old Northwest.

The message of pan-Indianism was unwavering: White encroachments had to be stopped and tribal and clan divisions submerged in a return to native rituals and belief systems. As preached by Tecumseh and the Prophet, Indian land could be saved and self-respect regained only through tribal cooperation and a spiritual rebirth. Tenkswatawa had undergone such a rebirth when he saved himself from alcoholism, and much of the passion he brought to preaching reflected his own sense of redemption. With the assistance of Tecumseh, Tenkswatawa established the Prophet's Town in 1808. At the confluence of the Wabash and Tippecanoe Rivers in north-central Indiana, this encampment became headquarters of an intertribal confederation. As he tried to explain to the worried Governor Harrison, his goals were peaceful. He admonished his followers, "[Do] not take up the tomahawk, should it be offered by the British, or by the long knives: do not meddle with any thing that does not belong to you, but mind your own business, and cultivate the ground, that your women and your children have enough to live on."

That ground, of course, was the very reason the Indians could not live in peace and dignity. White settlers wanted it and would do anything to get it. In November 1811, Harrison marched an army to Prophet's Town and provoked the Battle of Tippecanoe. The Indian encampment was on land claimed by the U.S. government in the Treaty of Fort Wayne (1809). Tecumseh was absent, off on a recruiting mission among the southern tribes, and without his restraining influence, impetuous young braves attacked Harrison's army. Losses were heavy on both sides, but Harrison regrouped his forces, drove the surviving Indians away, and burned the abandoned town. Harrison's victory came at a high cost: Tecumseh now joined forces with the British, leaving the frontier more unsettled than ever.

While Harrison's aggressiveness was converting fears of a British–Indian alliance into a self-fulfilling prophecy, expansionist-minded southerners struck at Britain through Spain, now its ally against Napoleon. With the covert support of President Madison, American adventurers staged a bloodless revolt in Spanish West Florida between Louisiana and the Pearl River. They raised the American flag and declared their independence. This "republic" was quickly recognized by the U.S. government and annexed as part of Louisiana in 1811. Spanish possession of the rest of Florida still galled southern planters anxious to remove the territory as a sanctuary for fugitive slaves.

Hatred of Native Americans, expansionist pressures, the lingering agricultural depression, and impatience with the administration's policy of economic coercion, all pointed in the same direction—a war against Britain coupled with an American takeover of British Canada and Spanish Florida. This was the rallying cry of the **War Hawks**, the forty or so prowar congressmen swept into office in 1810. Generally younger men from the South and West, the War Hawks were led by Henry Clay of Kentucky. Along with other outspoken nationalists, such as John C. Calhoun of South Carolina, Clay played a key role in building congressional support for Madison's growing aggressiveness on the British issue.

DECISION FOR WAR

In July 1811, Madison issued a Proclamation calling Congress into an early session on November 4. By the time of the announcement, Madison had probably accepted the inevitability of war against Britain. Deceived by Napoleon and dismissed by the British as the head of a second-rate power, Madison had run out of diplomatic options and was losing control of his party.

When Congress met, Madison tried to lay the groundwork for war. Although he did not rule out a peaceful settlement, he called for military preparations and stressed his "deep sense of the crisis." In

January 1812, the authorized size of the army was increased from 10,000 to 35,000 men. Still, fewer than 7,000 men were actually under arms throughout the spring, and Congress refused to enlarge the navy. The Republican-controlled Congress also balked at raising taxes to pay for a war that seemed ever more likely. In opposing Madison, many Republicans cited their party's traditional view of high taxes and a strong military as the tools of despots.

Madison secretly asked Congress on April 1 for a sixty-day embargo, a move designed to give American merchant ships time to return safely to their home ports. On June 1, he sent a war message to Congress in which he laid out the stark alternative of submission or resistance to British control of American commerce. Madison was now convinced that British commercial restrictions were not just a defensive measure aimed at France but an aggressive attempt to reduce the United States to the permanent status of colonial dependent.

For Madison and most other Republicans, the impending conflict was a second war for independence. Free and open access to world markets was certainly at stake, but so was national pride. The arrogant British policy of impressment was a humiliating affront to American honor and headed the list of grievances in Madison's war message.

A divided Congress declared war on Britain. The vote in the House on June 4 was seventy-nine in favor and forty-nine opposed; on June 17, the Senate concurred, nineteen to thirteen. The vote split along regional, economic, and party lines. Support for the war was strongest in regions whose economies had been damaged the most by the British blockades and control of Atlantic commerce. Thus the South and the West, trapped in an agricultural depression and anxious to eliminate foreign threats at their frontiers, favored war. Conversely, mercantile New England—a region that had, ironically, prospered as a result of British interference with ocean commerce—opposed the war.

The votes that carried the war declaration came from northern Republicans, who saw the impending struggle as a defense of America's experiment in self-government. Nine-tenths of the congressional Republicans voted for war, but not a single Federalist did so. For the Federalists, the real enemy was France, which had actually seized more American ships than had the British. From their strongholds in coastal New England, the Federalists condemned the war as a French-inspired plot and predicted that it would end in financial ruin.

The Federalists' anger increased when they learned that the British had been prepared to yield on one of the most prominent issues in the coming of war. On June 23, the British government revoked for one year its Orders in Council against the United States. A poor harvest and the ongoing economic pressure exerted by Madison had finally caused hard times in England and produced a policy reversal intended to placate the Americans. This concession, however, did not address impressment or monetary compensation, and news of it did not reach America until August. For Madison, it was too little too late, and he remained committed to war.

THE WAR OF 1812

The Republicans led the nation into a war it was unprepared to fight (see Map 9–2). Still, the apparent vulnerability of Canada to invasion made it possible to envision an American victory. Canada was thinly populated, poorly defended, and exposed to a potentially huge American army of militiamen. Yet bungled American invasions verged on tragicomedy, and British-Canadian forces and their Indian allies stymied American advances. For much of the war, Britain was preoccupied with Napoleon in Europe. When free to concentrate on the American sideshow in 1814, the British failed to secure naval control of the Great Lakes, their minimal strategic objective, and their counterinvasions of the United States bogged down. By the fall of 1814, both sides were eager for an end to the military stalemate.

Internal dissent endangered the Union as much as did British troops. The war exacerbated Federalist disenchantment with southern dominance of national affairs. Nearly all Federalists believed that pro-French fanatics and slaveholding agrarians in the Republican party had consistently sacrificed the commercial interests of New England. A minority of Federalists were convinced that New England could never regain its rightful place in shaping national policy and was prepared to lead a secession movement. Although blocked by party moderates at the Hartford Convention in 1814, the secessionists tarred Federalism with the brush of treason. Consequently, the Republicans, the party that brought the country to the brink of a military disaster, emerged from the war more powerful than ever.

SETBACKS IN CANADA

The outbreak of the **War of 1812** unleashed deep emotions that often divided along religious lines. From their strongholds in the Congregationalist churches in New England, the Federalists preached

MAP 9-2   The War of 1812
Most of the battles of the War of 1812 were fought along the Canadian–American border, where American armies repeatedly tried to invade Canada. Despite the effectiveness of the British naval blockade, the American navy was successful in denying the British strategic control of the Great Lakes. Andrew Jackson's smashing victory at the Battle of New Orleans convinced Americans that they had won the war.

that all true Christians opposed a war "against the nation from which we are descended, and which for many generations has been the bulwark of the religion we profess." Such antiwar sentiments, however, outraged the Baptists and Methodists, the largest and most popularly rooted denominations. They believed, as resolved by the Georgia Baptist Association in 1813, that the British government was "corrupt, arbitrary, and despotic" and that the war was "just, necessary, and indispensable."

Fiercely loyal to Madison, who had championed religious freedom in Virginia, these Methodists and Baptists harbored old grudges against the established churches of both Britain and New England for suppressing their religious rights. Especially for the Baptists, the war became something of a crusade to secure civil and religious liberties against their traditional enemies. For Spencer Houghton Cone, a lieutenant in a company of sharpshooters and a future president of the National Baptist Convention, service in the war seemed "as much the duty of the Christian as the honor of the soldier."

Madison hoped to channel this Christian, anti-British patriotism into the conquest of Canada. Two out of three Canadians were native-born Americans who, it was assumed, would welcome the United States Army with open arms. Only five thousand British troops were initially stationed in Canada, and Canadian militia were outnumbered nine to one by their American counterparts. No wonder Madison and his advisers felt that Canada was ripe for the taking—"a mere matter of marching," as Jefferson put it.

Canada was also the only area where the United States could strike directly against British forces. Although officially a war to defend America's neutrality on the high seas, the War of 1812 was largely a land war. The United States simply did not have enough ships to do more than harass the powerful British navy. Against sixteen ships in the U.S. Navy, only seven of which were top-of-the-line frigates (warships), the British could deploy more than two hundred vessels.

By seizing Canada, Madison also hoped to weaken Britain's navy and undercut its navigation system. Madison had been convinced that withholding American foodstuffs and provisions from the British West Indies would quickly force the British to yield to American economic pressure. But the British turned to Canada as an alternative source of supplies. Madison hoped to close off that source. And if, as Madison expected, Napoleon denied the British access to the naval stores of the Baltic region in Europe, an American monopoly on Canadian lumber would cripple British naval power. Facing such a threat, the British would have to end the war on American terms.

Madison's strategic vision was clear, but its execution was pathetic. Three offensives against Canada in 1812 were embarrassing failures. In the first, in July, General William Hull crossed into Canada from Detroit and invited Canadians to join the American cause. He found few takers. Meanwhile, Fort Michilimackinac fell, and Tecumseh's warriors cut Hull's communications. Hull hurried back to Detroit, only to surrender his army on August 16 to the smaller British-Indian force.

The loss of Detroit, preceded a day earlier by the abandonment of Fort Dearborn (present-day Chicago) and the massacre of its inhabitants, exposed western settlements to the full fury of frontier warfare. Americans in the Indiana Territory fled outlying areas for the safety of forts in the interior. The acting territorial governor scarcely exaggerated when he proclaimed, "Our former frontiers are now wilds and our inner Settlements have become frontiers." By the end of the year, the British controlled half of the Old Northwest.

Farther east, the Americans botched two offensives in 1812. In October, an American thrust across the Niagara River was defeated when a New York state militia refused to cross the river to join the regular army troops on the Canadian side. This left the isolated forces under General Stephen Van Rensselaer easy prey for the British at the Battle of Queenston Heights. Then the long-delayed third offensive, north from Lake Champlain, turned into a bloodless fiasco. It was aimed at Montreal, the center of British

POLICE.

WHEREAS authentic intelligence has been received that the Government of the United States of America did, on the 18th instant, declare War against the United Kingdom of Great Britain and Ireland and its dependencies, Notice is hereby given, that all Subjects or Citizens of the said United States, and all persons claiming American Citizenship, are ordered to quit the City of Quebec, on or before TWELVE o'clock at Noon, on WEDNESDAY next, and the District of Quebec on or before 12 o'clock at noon on FRIDAY next, on pain of arrest.   **ROSS CUTHBERT,**
C. Q. S. & Inspector of Police.

The Constables of the City of Quebec are ordered to assemble in the Police Office at 10 o'clock to-morrow morning, to receive instructions.

Quebec, 29th June, 1812.

Fearful of an American invasion, Canadian authorities ordered American residents expelled at the beginning of the War of 1812.

operations in Canada. General Henry Dearborn, the leader of the expedition, turned back in late November when he discovered, as Van Rensselaer had, that his militias would not leave their states.

Republican expectations of victory in Canada had been wishful thinking. Most Canadians fought against, not with, the Americans. Reliance on state militias proved disastrous. Poorly trained and equipped, the militias, when they did show up for battle, could not match the discipline of British soldiers or the fighting skills of their Native American allies. Nor was American generalship on a par with that of the British. Primitive land communications made the movement and coordination of troops a nightmare. New England, the obvious base for operations against the strategically critical St. Lawrence River Valley—the entry point for all British supplies and reinforcements—withheld many of its state

AMERICAN VIEWS

Federalist Antiwar Resolutions

As the policies of the Madison administration in the spring of 1812 increasingly pointed toward war against Great Britain, New England Federalists mounted protest meetings in an effort to preserve peace. Passed at a meeting in Providence, Rhode Island, on April 7, 1812, the following resolutions make the Federalist case for the disastrous consequences of a war against Britain and reveal the depths of the party divisions over foreign policy.

- On what grounds did the Federalists accuse the Republicans of an anti-British bias?
- What did the Federalists argue would be the results of a war against Britain?
- How could the Federalists now depict France, America's ally during the Revolutionary War, as a greater threat to American freedoms than Britain?

Voted and Resolved unanimously,

That, in our opinion, the peace, prosperity and happiness of these United States, are in great jeopardy; inasmuch as, we have the strongest reasons to believe, the general government have determined to make war on Great-Britain . . . .

We are further confirmed in our apprehensions . . . by the evident partiality [the Republicans] have for a long time manifested towards one of the belligerents; and their deep-rooted enmity towards the other. The decrees of both nations equally violate our neutral rights; but France by her Berlin Decree, was the first aggressor; and still persists in capturing and burning our vessels on the high seas; and in robbing, imprisoning, and insulting our citizens; yet all these atrocities have been either palliated, or excused; while every effort has been made to excite the prejudices and animosities of our people against Great Britain. British vessels are excluded from our harbors; and our citizens are forbidden to import goods of the growth and manufacture of Britain and her dependen-

---

forces from national service. Consequently, the invasions were piecemeal ineffective forays launched from western areas where anti-British and anti-Indian sentiment ran high.

All the Republicans had to show for the first year of the war were morale-boosting but otherwise insignificant naval victories. In individual combat between ships, the small American navy acquitted itself superbly. Early in the war, American privateers harassed British merchant vessels, but the easy pickings were soon gone. British squadron ships redeployed to protect shipping, and other warships kept up a blockade that stifled American commerce.

Military setbacks and antiwar feelings in much of the Northeast hurt the Republicans in the election of 1812. Madison won only narrowly. Federalists and other disaffected Northerners rallied behind DeWitt Clinton, an antiadministration Republican from New York. The now familiar regional pattern in voting repeated itself. Madison swept the electoral vote of the South and West. He ran poorly in the Northeast and won only because his party held on to Pennsylvania.

WESTERN VICTORIES AND BRITISH OFFENSIVES

American forces fared better in 1813. Motivation remained high because, as Major Isaac Roach of an artillery regiment noted, many Americans believed that "it had become a jest and byword in England that this country could not be kicked into war." In September, the navy won a major engagement on Lake Erie that opened up a supply line in the western theater. Comcies; at the same time that French privateers are suffered to refit in American ports; and French goods are received, and protected, by our government . . . . All this, too, is done, when our trade to France, is of little value; and that to England, and her dependence is, of more importance to the United States, than with all the world besides.

Resolved, That . . . believing as we most sincerely do, that a war with England, at this time, is neither necessary, nor expedient, we deem it a duty which we owe to our families, and to our country, to use our utmost efforts to avert so great a calamity; and . . . we are of opinion that this expression ought to be given in the approaching elections. If we choose Democratic [Republican] State Rulers, we choose war; if we choose Federal State Rulers, we choose peace . . . .

But should we, forgetful of our duties, elect democratic rulers, and thereby let loose this wild spirit of war, what calamities, and horrors must spread themselves over those devoted States! All the taxes proposed must fall upon us; our foreign and coasting commerce be cut off; our fisheries be destroyed; our agriculture neglected . . . . The destruction of our navigation would interrupt, and we fear, ruin our numerous, and flourishing manufactories; for, when the enemies['] ships cover our coasts, we can

neither obtain the necessary materials, nor export the manufactured goods.

But these evils are only the beginning of sorrows. When war arrives, what will give protections to our harbours and maritime towns? [The enemy] will . . . make a war of frequent, and sudden descent on our long, and defenceless sea-coast. Ships manned, and now moored on the other side of the Atlantic Ocean, can, in forty days, be riding on the waters of our bay and river. What could then save our sea-port towns, together with all the vessels in our harbours from conflagration, pillage, and military exaction?

Dreadful are these consequences of war: but more dreadful will await us. A war with England will bring us into alliance with France. This alliance would make the last page of our history as a nation. All the horrors of war might be endured; but who can endure to become a Slave?—If we are allied to that putrid pestilence of tyranny; our laws, freedom, independence, national name and glory, are blotted out from the memory of man—If Bonaparte sends to this country, ships, and French soldiers, and French generals, we shall soon be like Holland, and Italy, and Switzerland, and every other country where this scourge of nations has been permitted to set his foot.

modore Oliver Hazard Perry attacked the British fleet in the **Battle of Put-in-Bay**, on the southwestern shore of the lake, and forced the surrender of all six British ships. The victory signaled General William Henry Harrison to launch an offensive in the West.

With the loss of Lake Erie, the British were forced to abandon Detroit. Harrison caught up with the British garrison and their Indian allies on the banks of the Thames River in southern Ontario. Demonstrating bold leadership and relying on battle-tested western militias, Harrison won a decisive victory. Tecumseh, the most visionary of the Indian warriors, was killed, and the backbone of the Indian resistance was broken. The Old Northwest was again safe for American settlement.

The Battle of the Thames ended British plans for an Indian buffer state. But by 1814, Britain had big-

ger goals in mind. A coalition of European powers forced Napoleon to abdicate in April 1814, thus freeing Britain to focus on the American war. It now seemed poised to break the military stalemate with a clear-cut victory.

British strategy in 1814 called for two major offensives—an invasion south from Montreal down Lake Champlain in upstate New York and an attack on Louisiana aimed at seizing New Orleans with a task force out of Jamaica. Meanwhile, diversionary raids along the mid-Atlantic coast were to pin down American forces and undermine morale. The overall objective was nothing less than a reversal of America's post-1783 expansion. If the invasions succeeded, the British would have been in a strong position to force a southward adjustment of the Canadian–American boundary and to claim the Louisiana Purchase territory.

The British attacks could hardly have come at a worse time for the Madison administration. The Treasury was nearly bankrupt. Against the wishes of Treasury Secretary Gallatin, Congress had refused to preserve the Bank of the United States when its charter expired in 1811. Lacking both a centralized means of directing wartime finances and any significant increase in taxes, the Treasury was forced to rely on makeshift loans. These loans were poorly subscribed, largely because the cash-rich New England banks refused to buy them. Inflation also became a problem when state banks, no longer restrained by the controls of a national bank, overissued paper money in the form of bank notes.

As the country's finances tottered toward collapse, political dissent in New England was reaching a climax. In 1814, the British extended their blockade of American commerce northward to include New England. Federalist merchants and shippers, who had earlier profited from their illegal trade with the British, now felt the economic pinch of the war. Cries for resistance against "Mr. Madison's war" culminated in a call issued by the Massachusetts legislature for a convention to consider "a radical reform of the national compact." The convention was scheduled for December in Hartford, Connecticut.

The darkest hour came in August 1814. A British amphibious force occupied and torched Washington, D.C., in retaliation for an American raid on York (now Toronto), the capital of Upper Canada. The defense of Washington was slipshod at best, and a local inhabitant can be excused for scribbling on a wall: "The capital and the Union lost by cowardice." Still, the British actions stiffened American resistance, and the failure of a follow-up attack on Baltimore deprived the British of any strategic gain. Baltimore's defenses held, stirring Francis Scott Key, a young lawyer who viewed the bombardment from a British prisoner-of-war ship, to write "The Star-Spangled Banner." Fittingly in this strange war, the future national anthem was set to the tune of a British drinking song.

The Chesapeake campaign was designed to divert American attention from the major offensive General George Prevost was leading down the shores of Lake Champlain. Prevost commanded the largest and best-equipped army the British had yet assembled. His opponent was Commodore Thomas Macdonough, one of several young, talented regional commanders Madison appointed late in the war. On September 11, at the **Battle of Plattsburgh**, Macdonough smashed a British fleet on Lake Champlain.

Having counted on that fleet to protect his supply lines, Prevost retreated to Canada.

The tide had turned. When news of the setbacks at Baltimore, and especially at Plattsburgh, reached England, the foreign office scaled back the demands it had been making on American negotiators at peace talks in the city of Ghent, in present-day Belgium. The British were ready for peace, but one of their trump cards had yet to be played—the southern offensive against New Orleans. The outcome of that campaign could still upset whatever was decided at Ghent.

THE TREATY OF GHENT AND THE BATTLE OF NEW ORLEANS

By the fall of 1814, the British were eager to get on with redrawing the map of post-Napoleonic Europe, restoring profitable relations with America, and reducing their huge war debt. The British negotiators at Ghent agreed to a peace treaty on terms the Americans were delighted to accept. The **Treaty of Ghent**, signed on Christmas Eve, 1814, simply restored relations to their status at the start of the war. No territory changed hands, and nothing was said about impressment or the rights of neutrals.

The ink had barely dried on the Treaty of Ghent when the British government sent reinforcements to General Edward Pakenham, the commander of the Louisiana invasionary force. By this action, the British indicated that they were not irrevocably committed to the peace settlement, which, though signed, could not be formally ratified until weeks had passed while it was sent across the Atlantic. The British had always held that the Louisiana Purchase was fraudulent (they insisted that Louisiana was never Napoleon's to sell), and they were prepared to install a new government in Louisiana if Pakenham succeeded. Far from being an anticlimax to a war that was already over, the showdown between British and American forces at the Battle of New Orleans in January 1815 had immense strategic significance for the United States.

The hero of New Orleans, in song and legend, was Andrew Jackson. A planter-politician from Tennessee, Jackson rose to prominence during the war as a ferocious Indian fighter. The Creeks of Alabama and Georgia, much like the Shawnees farther north, had undergone a religious revival that culminated in a military effort to drive American settlers out of their tribal homelands. As a general in the Tennessee militia, Jackson crushed Indian resistance in the Old Southwest at the Battle of Horseshoe Bend

The seizure and burning of Washington, D.C., by British troops on August 24, 1814, marked the republic's most humiliating defeat in the War of 1812.

in March 1814. He then forced the vanquished Creeks to cede two-thirds of their territory to the United States.

After his Indian conquests, Jackson was promoted to general in the regular army and given command of the defense of the Gulf Coast. In November 1814, he seized Pensacola in Spanish Florida to deny the British its use as a supply depot and then hurried to defend New Orleans. The overconfident British frontally attacked Jackson's lines on January 8, 1815. The result was a massacre. Artillery fire laid down by French-speaking cannoneers from New Orleans accounted for most of the carnage. More than two thousand British soldiers were killed or wounded. American casualties totaled twenty-one.

Strategically, Jackson's smashing victory at New Orleans ended any possibility of a British sphere of influence in Louisiana. Politically, it was a deathblow to Federalism. At the Hartford Convention in December, party moderates had forestalled talk of secession with a series of proposed constitutional amendments designed to limit southern power in national affairs. At the top of their list was a demand for eliminating the three-fifths clause by which slaves were counted for purposes of congressional representation. They also wanted to require a two-thirds majority in Congress for the admission of new states, declarations of war, and the imposition of embargoes. These demands became public as Americans were rejoicing over the Treaty of Ghent and Jack-

Creek war leader Red Eagle surrenders to Andrew Jackson after the Battle of Horseshoe Bend in 1814.

son's routing of the British. Set against the revived nationalism that marked the end of the war, the Federalists now seemed to be parochial sulkers who put regional interests above the national good. Worse yet, they struck many Americans as quasi-traitors who had been prepared to desert the country in the face of the enemy. As a significant political force, Federalism was dead.

THE ERA OF GOOD FEELINGS

In 1817, on the occasion of a presidential visit by James Monroe, a Boston newspaper proclaimed the **Era of Good Feelings**, an expression that nicely captured the spirit of political harmony and sectional unity that washed over the republic in the immediate postwar years. National pride surged with the humbling of the British at New Orleans, the demise of the Federalists lessened political tensions, and the economy boomed. The Republicans had been vindicated, and for a short time they enjoyed de facto status as the only governing party.

At the end of Madison's presidency, and in the first administration of his successor, James Monroe of Virginia, the Republicans embarked on a program of economic nationalism that would have pleased Alexander Hamilton. In foreign policy, they moved aggressively to stake out American leadership in the Western Hemi-

sphere. A series of decisions handed down by the Supreme Court also reinforced the postwar nationalism. In 1819, however, an economic depression and a bitter controversy over slavery shattered the harmony. The nationalist tide set in motion by the end of the war had run its course, and the Republicans divided on sectional and economic issues.

ECONOMIC NATIONALISM

The War of 1812 had taught the Republicans to appreciate old Federalist doctrines on centralized national power. In his annual message of December 1815, Madison outlined a program of economic nationalism that was pushed through Congress by Henry Clay and John C. Calhoun, the most prominent of the new generation of young, nationalist-minded Republicans.

The first order of business was to create a new national bank. Reliance on state banks for wartime financing had proved a major mistake. The banks lacked sufficient capital reserves or, as occurred in New England, held them back. Demand for credit was met by a flood of state bank notes that fell in value because there was insufficient gold and silver to back them. Many banks suspended specie payments for their notes, and inflation was a persistent problem. After the British burned Washington, the Treasury was temporarily bankrupt, and throughout the war it could borrow only at high interest rates. Fiscal stability required the monetary coordination and restraint that only a new Bank of the United States could provide.

Introduced by Calhoun, the bank bill passed Congress in 1816. Modeled after Hamilton's original bank and also headquartered in Philadelphia, the **Second Bank of the United States** was capitalized at $35 million, making it by far the nation's largest bank. Its size and official status as the depository and dispenser of the government's funds gave the bank tremendous economic power. It also enjoyed the exclusive privilege of being able to establish branches in any state.

After moving to repair the fiscal damage of the war, the Republicans then acted to protect what the war had fostered. Embargoes followed by three years of war forced American businessmen to manufacture goods they previously had imported. This was especially the case with iron and textile goods long supplied by the British. In 1815 and again in 1816, the British inundated the American market with cheap imports to strangle American industry in its infancy. Responding to this challenge to the nation's economic independence, the Republicans passed the Tariff of 1816, the first protective tariff in American history. The act levied duties of 20 to 25 percent on imported goods that could be produced in the United States.

Responding to pressure from the War Department and western states, Congress earmarked revenue from the tariff and $1.5 million from the Bank of the United States (a cash payment in return for its charter) for transportation projects. The lack of a road system in the trans-Appalachian region had severely hampered troop movements during the war. Also, as settlers after the war moved onto lands seized from the pro-British Indians, western congressmen demanded improved outlets to eastern markets.

In early 1817, an internal improvements bill passed Congress. Despite the soaring rhetoric of John C. Calhoun, the bill's sponsor, seeking to "bind the republic together with a perfect system of roads and canals," President Madison remained unmoved. Though in agreement with the bill's objectives, he was convinced that the Constitution did not permit federal financing of primarily local projects. He vetoed the bill just before he left office.

Congressional passage of Calhoun's internal improvements bill marked the pinnacle of the Republicans' economic nationalism. Frightened by the sectional disunity of the war years, a new generation of Republicans jettisoned many of the ideological trappings of Jefferson's original agrarian party. Their program was a call for economic, and therefore political, unity. Such unity was to be achieved through a generous program of national subsidies consisting of tariffs for manufacturers in the Northeast and transportation funds for planters and farmers in the South and West. The new national bank would provide a uniform currency and credit facilities for the internal exchange of raw materials and manufactured goods.

Support for this program was strongest in the mid-Atlantic and western states, the regions that stood to gain the most economically. Opposition centered in the Southeast, notably among die-hard proponents of states' rights in the old tobacco belt of Virginia and North Carolina and in New England, a region not only well served already by banks and a road network but also anxious not to be politically overshadowed by the rising West. This opposition took on an increasingly hard edge in the South as the Supreme Court outlined an ever more nationalist interpretation of the Constitution.

JUDICIAL NATIONALISM

Under Chief Justice John Marshall, the Supreme Court had long supported the nationalist perspective Republicans began to champion after the war. A Virginia Federalist whose nationalism was forged during his service in the Revolutionary War, Marshall dominated the Court throughout his tenure (1801–1835) by his forceful personality and the logical power of his nationalist convictions. Two principles defined Marshall's jurisprudence: the primacy of the Supreme

This 1830 painting shows Chief Justice John Marshall in the full robes of his office. Marshall's leadership molded the Supreme Court into an effective instrument of the national government.

Court in all matters of constitutional interpretation and the sanctity of contractual property rights. In **Fletcher v. Peck,** (1810), for example, the Court ruled that a Georgia law voiding a land grant made by an earlier legislature—on the grounds that it had involved massive fraud—violated the constitutional provision barring any state from "impairing the obligation of contracts." Marshall held that despite the fraud, the original land grant constituted an unbreakable legal contract.

Out of the political limelight since the Burr trial in 1807, the Court was thrust back into it by two controversial decisions in 1819. The first involved Dartmouth College and the attempt by the New Hampshire legislature to amend its charter in the direction of greater public control over this private institution. In **Dartmouth College v. Woodward,** the Court ruled that Dartmouth's original royal charter of 1769 was a contract protected by the Constitution. Hence the state of New Hampshire could not alter that charter without the prior consent of the college. By so sanctifying charters or acts of incorporation as contracts, the Court prohibited states from interfering with the rights and privileges they had bestowed on private corporations.

The second important decision in 1819, *McCulloch v. Maryland,* rested on a positive assertion of national power over the states. The case involved the Bank of the United States. Many state bankers were jealous of the privileges of the national bank, and this resentment was shared by legislators who viewed the bank's branches as an infringement on the states' economic sovereignty. In 1818, the Maryland legislature placed a heavy tax on the branch of the Bank of the United States established in Baltimore (and on all other banks in the state established without legislative authority). James McCulloch, the cashier of the Baltimore branch, refused to pay the tax. This set up a test case that involved two fundamental legal issues: Was the bank itself constitutional? And could a state tax federal property within its borders?

A unanimous Court, in language similar to but even more sweeping than that used by Alexander Hamilton in the 1790s, upheld the constitutional authority of Congress to charter a national bank and thereby regulate the nation's currency and finances. As long as the end was legitimate "within the scope of the Constitution," Congress had full power to use any means not expressly forbidden by the Constitution to achieve that end. As for Maryland's claim of a constitutional right to tax a federal agency, Marshall stressed that "the power to tax involves the

power to destroy." Surely, he reasoned, when the people of the United States ratified the Constitution, they did not intend the federal government to be controlled by the states or rendered powerless by state action. Here was the boldest statement to date of the loose or "implied powers" interpretation of the Constitution and a ringing rebuke to the compact theory of the Union outlined by Southerners in the Virginia and Kentucky Resolutions and picked up by disgruntled Federalists in New England.

TOWARD A CONTINENTAL EMPIRE

Marshall's legal nationalism paralleled the diplomatic nationalism of John Quincy Adams, secretary of state from 1817 to 1825. A former Federalist and the son of the second president, Adams broke with the party over its refusal to support an expansionist policy and held several diplomatic posts under the Madison administration. Adams made few friends as a negotiator. A British statesman once described him as "doggedly and systematically repulsive." Still, he was an effective diplomat. Convinced in his Puritan soul that God and nature had ordained that America stretch from the Atlantic to the Pacific as a beacon of liberty to the world, Adams used whatever tactics were necessary to realize that vision.

Adams shrewdly exploited Britain's desire for friendly and profitable relations after the War of 1812. The British wanted access to American cotton and foodstuffs in exchange for manufactured goods and investment capital. The United States wanted more trading opportunities in the British Empire and a free hand to deal with Spain's disintegrating empire in the Americas.

The **Rush–Bagot Agreement** of 1817 signaled the new pattern of Anglo–American cooperation. The agreement strictly limited naval armaments on the Great Lakes, thus effectively demilitarizing the border with Canada. The **Anglo–American Accords** of the following year resolved several issues left hanging after the war. Of great importance to New England, the British once again recognized American fishing rights off Labrador and Newfoundland. The boundary of the Louisiana Territory abutting Canada was set at the 49th parallel, and both nations agreed to the joint occupation of Oregon, the territory in the Pacific Northwest that lay west of the Rocky Mountains.

Having secured the northern flank of the United States, Adams was now free to deal with the South and West. Adams wanted all of Florida and an undisputed American window on the Pacific. The adversary here was Spain. Much weaker than it had been in the eighteenth century and struggling to suppress independence movements in its South American possessions, Spain resorted to delaying tactics in trying to hold off the tenacious Adams. Negotiations remained deadlocked until Andrew Jackson gave Adams the leverage he needed.

In March 1818, Jackson led his troops across the border into Spanish Florida. He destroyed encampments of the Seminole Indians, seized two Spanish forts, and executed two British subjects on the grounds that they were dealing arms to the Seminoles for raids on the Alabama–Georgia frontier. Despite later protestations to the contrary, Jackson had probably exceeded his orders. He might well have been censured by the Monroe administration had not Adams supported him, telling Spain that Jackson was defending American interests and warning that he might be unleashed again.

Spain yielded to the American threat in the **Trans-Continental Treaty of 1819.** The United States annexed East Florida, and Spain recognized the prior American seizures of West Florida in 1810 and 1813. Adams secured an American hold on the Pacific Coast by drawing a boundary between the Louisiana Purchase and the Spanish Southwest that ran stepwise up the Sabine, Red, and Arkansas Rivers to the Continental Divide and then due west along the 42nd parallel to the Pacific (see Map 9-3). Spain renounced any claim to the Pacific Northwest; the United States in turn renounced its shaky claim to Texas under the Louisiana Purchase and assumed $5 million in Spanish debts to American citizens.

Adams's success in the Spanish negotiations turned on the British refusal to threaten war or assist Spain in the wake of Jackson's highhanded actions in Florida. Spanish possessions and the lives of two British subjects were worth little when weighed against the economic advantages of retaining close trading ties with the United States. Moreover, Britain, like the United States, had a vested interest in developing trade with newly independent Latin American countries now free of Spain's former imperial monopoly. Recognizing this common interest, George Canning, the British foreign minister, proposed in August 1823 that the United States and Britain issue a joint declaration opposing any European attempt to recolonize South America or to assist Spain in regaining its colonies.

President Monroe rejected the British overture, but only at the insistence of Adams. Canning's offer had a string attached to it: a mutual pledge by the British and Americans not to annex former Spanish territory. But Adams was confident that within a gen-

eration, the United States would acquire California, Texas, and perhaps Cuba as well. He wanted to maintain the maximum freedom of action for future U.S. policy and avoid any impression that America was beholden to Britain. Thus originated the most famous diplomatic statement in early American history, the **Monroe Doctrine**.

In his annual message to Congress in December 1823, Monroe declared that the Americas "are henceforth not to be considered as subjects for future colonization by any European power." In turn, Monroe pledged that the United States would not interfere in the internal affairs of European states. With its continental empire rapidly taking shape and new Latin American republics to be courted, the United States was more than willing to proclaim a special position for itself as the guardian of New World liberties.

THE BREAKDOWN OF UNITY

For all the intensity with which he pursued his continental vision, John Quincy Adams worried in early 1819 that "the greatest danger of this union was in the overgrown extent of its territory, combining with the slavery question." His words were prophetic. A sectional crisis flared in 1819 over slavery and its expansion when the territory of Missouri sought admission to the Union as a slave state. Simultaneously, a financial panic ended postwar prosperity and crystallized regional discontent over banking and tariff policies. Party unity cracked under these pressures, and each region backed its own presidential candidate in the wide-open election of 1824.

THE PANIC OF 1819

From 1815 to 1818, Americans enjoyed a wave of postwar prosperity. European markets were starved for American goods after a generation of war and trade restrictions, and farmers and planters met that demand by expanding production and bringing new land into cultivation. The availability of public land in the West on easy terms of credit sparked a speculative frenzy, and land sales soared. State banks and, worse yet, the Bank of the United States fed the speculation by making loans in the form of bank notes far in excess of their hard-currency reserves. Before the bubble burst, cotton prices doubled to 30 cents a pound, real-estate values became wildly inflated, and the money Westerners owed the federal government for the purchase of public lands rose to $21 million, an amount greater than the value of all western farm goods.

European markets for American cotton and food supplies returned to normal by late 1818. In January 1819, cotton prices sank in England, and the Panic of 1819 was on. Cotton was the most valuable American export, and expected returns from the staple were the basis for an intricate credit network anchored in Britain. The fall in cotton prices triggered a credit contraction that soon engulfed the overextended American economy. Commodity prices fell across the board, and real-estate values collapsed, especially in and around western cities.

A sudden shift in policy by the Bank of the United States virtually guaranteed that the economic downturn would settle into a depression. The Bank stopped all loans, called in all debts, and refused to honor drafts drawn on its branches in the South and West. Hardest hit by these policies were farmers and businessmen in the West, a region that had piled up debt in the expectation that the income generated by postwar prosperity would return a tidy profit. Bankruptcies mushroomed as creditors forced the liquidation of farms and real estate. For westerners, the Bank of the United States now became "the Monster," a ruthless institution controlled by eastern aristocrats, who callously destroyed the hopes of farmers.

Southern resentment over the hard times brought on by low cotton prices focused on the tariff. Planters charged that the Tariff of 1816 unfairly raised their costs and amounted to an unconstitutional tax levied for the sole benefit of northern manufacturers. Unreconstructed Jeffersonians, now known as the Old Republicans, spearheaded a sharp reaction against the South's flirtation with nationalist policies in the postwar period. Taking their cue from John Taylor, a Virginia planter and agrarian philosopher, they demanded a return to strict states' rights doctrines. If Northerners, they asked, could stretch the Constitution to incorporate a bank or impose a protective tariff, what could prevent them from emancipating the slaves?

THE MISSOURI COMPROMISE

Until 1819, slavery had not been a major divisive issue in American politics. The Northwest Ordinance of 1787, which banned slavery in federal territories north of the Ohio River, and the Southwest Ordinance of 1790, which permitted slavery south of the Ohio, represented a compromise that had allowed slavery in areas where climate and soil conditions favored slave-based agriculture. What was unforeseen in the 1780s, however, was the explosive demand for slave-produced cotton generated by the

English textile industry in the early nineteenth century. At the republic's founding in 1787, slavery was identified with the declining tobacco economy of the South Atlantic states, and many Americans felt, perhaps wishfully, that the institution would gradually wither away.

Despite the prohibition of the African slave trade in 1807 (under the sectional compromise of 1787 this was the first year in which Congress could exercise this power), all hopes for the natural death of slavery were gone by 1819. Kentucky, Tennessee, Louisiana, Mississippi, and Alabama had all been added to the Union as slave states since 1787. Florida had just been annexed and surely would be another slave state. A thriving cotton market was underwriting slavery's expansion across the South, and even Missouri, a portion of the Louisiana Purchase that Northerners initially assumed would be inhospitable to slavery, had fallen under the political control of slaveholders.

The Missouri issue increased long-simmering northern resentment over the spread of slavery and the southern dominance of national affairs under the Virginia presidents. In February 1819, James Tallmadge, a Republican congressman from New York, introduced an amendment in the House mandating a ban on future slave imports and a program of gradual emancipation as preconditions for the admission of Missouri as a state. Missourians, as well as Southerners in general, rejected the Tallmadge Amendment. The states, they argued, had absolute sovereignty in the drafting of their constitutions, and any attempt by Congress to set conditions for statehood was unconstitutional. Nonetheless, a solid phalanx of northern congressmen supported the amendment.

Without a two-party system in which each of the parties had to compromise to protect its intersectional interests, voting followed sectional lines. The northern-controlled House passed the amendment, but it was repeatedly blocked in the Senate, which was evenly divided between free and slave states. The debates were heated, and Southerners spoke openly of secession if Missouri were denied admission as a slave state.

The stalemate over Missouri persisted into the next session of Congress. Finally, Speaker of the House Henry Clay engineered a compromise in March 1820. Congress put no restrictions on slavery in Missouri, and the admission of Missouri as a slave state was balanced by the admission of Maine (formerly part of Massachusetts) as a free state. In return for their concession on Missouri, northern

MAP EXPLORATION To explore an interactive version of this map, go to
http://www.prenhall.com/goldfield/map9.3

MAP 9-3   **The Missouri Compromise of 1820 and Territorial Treaties with Britain and Spain, 1818–1819**
Treaties with Britain and Spain in 1818 and 1819 clarified and expanded the nation's boundaries. Britain accepted the 49th parallel as the boundary between Canada and the United States in the Trans-Mississippi West to the Oregon Country; Spain ceded Florida to the United States and agreed to a boundary stretching to the Pacific between the Louisiana Purchase territory and Spanish possessions in the Southwest. Sectional disputes over slavery led to the drawing of the Missouri Compromise line of 1820 that prohibited slavery in the Louisiana Territory north of 36°30'.

congressmen demanded a prohibition on slavery in the remainder of the Louisiana Purchase north of the 36° 30' parallel, the southern boundary of Missouri (see Map 9–3). With the **Missouri Compromise**, the Louisiana Purchase was closed to slavery in the future, except for the Arkansas Territory and what would become the Indian Territory of

Oklahoma. The compromise almost unraveled when Missouri submitted a constitution the following November that required the state legislature to bar the entry of free black people. This mandate violated the guarantee in the U.S. Constitution that "the citizens of each State shall be entitled to all privileges and immunities of citizens in the several

FROM THEN TO NOW

The Lewis and Clark Expedition in Their World and Ours

In its day the Lewis and Clark expedition was as daring a venture as space exploration is today. The expedition, which began in 1803, ended in 1806, and lasted 863 days, brought Americans their first knowledge of the vast territory they had secured in the Louisiana Purchase. Traveling more than seven thousand miles by foot, boat, and horseback from St. Louis to the Pacific Coast and back, the explorers compiled a detailed record of their experiences and observations. In these journals they have bequeathed to us a vivid picture of the natural environment of the trans-Mississippi West before white settlement.

The West described by Lewis and Clark was a land of change, diversity, and abundance. The Missouri River that their party of forty-five followed to the north and west up to central Montana was wild and unpredictable. Its currents were ceaselessly eroding its banks, forming and displacing sandbars, and cutting new channels as they deposited soil eroded from the Rocky Mountains onto its immense floodplain. Today, a series of dams has tamed the river, controlling floods, generating electricity, and diverting water for irrigation. But the dams have had unforeseen consequences. The fertile sediments the Missouri once deposited on its floodplain, replenishing the soil in the farm states of the midwest, now flow into the Gulf of Mexico. As Midwesterners learned in the summer of 1993, the levees and retaining walls that confine the river can sometimes result in floods far more disastrous than ever occurred under natural conditions.

Lewis and Clark passed through regions of incredible biological diversity and abundance. They catalogued 122 animals and 178 plants that were new to American science. Traveling through present-day South Dakota in September,

States." Missouri's restrictionist policy obviously denied African American citizens this constitutional right to move from one state to any other state. Southerners were quick to point out, however, that free states as well as slave states already restricted the rights of free black people to vote or to serve in the militia.

The nearly universal acceptance by white Americans of second-class citizenship for free black Americans permitted Clay to dodge the issue. Missouri's constitution was accepted with the proviso that it "shall never be construed" to discriminate against citizens in other states. In short, with meaningless words that begged the issue of Missouri's defiance of the federal Constitution, the Missouri Compromise was salvaged. With this sacrifice of the claims of free black citizens for equal treatment, the Union survived its first great sectional crisis over slavery.

The Missouri crisis made white southerners aware that they were now a political minority within the Union. More rapid population growth in the North had reduced southern representation in the House to just over 40 percent. Of greater concern was the crystallization in Congress of a northern majority arraigned against the expansion of slavery. Southern threats of secession died out in the aftermath of the Missouri Compromise, but it was an open question whether the sectional settlement really solved the intertwined issues of slavery and expansion or merely sidestepped them for a day of final reckoning.

1804, Lewis observed "Vast herds of Buffaloe deer elk and Antilopes . . . feeding in every direction as far as the eye of the observer could reach." Upon seeing the salmon in the Columbia River in 1805, Clark wrote that their numbers were "almost inconceivable."

Before the end of the nineteenth century, the great herds of grazing animals in the West and the carnivores that stalked them had nearly been wiped out by government-sponsored extermination programs. The industrialization of the Pacific Northwest in the twentieth century reduced the natural habitat essential for the spawning and rearing of salmon, and their numbers fell sharply. Even more striking, most of the vast prairie landscape that Lewis and Clark crossed from the Mississippi Valley to the Rocky Mountains has disappeared, replaced by uniform fields of row-to-row crops. The prairie grasslands were once the largest ecosystem in North America, a patchwork of native grasses and herbs that supported a wide diversity of habitats.

Lewis and Clark were hardly romantic sentimentalists. Their West was dangerous and threatening, and their supplies included the latest in scientific equipment. They fully shared American notions of progress, and they carefully noted locations that were favorably situated for settlement. Still, the West they saw often left them with a sense of awe. For Lewis, the White Cliffs of the Missouri River in Montana were a spectacle "of visionary enchantment." He described the Great Falls of the Missouri as "the grandest sight I ever beheld."

The journals of Lewis and Clark provide a baseline from which to gauge how much the West has changed, putting Americans in a better position to preserve what is left and even restore some of what has been lost.

In commemoration of their epic expedition, President George W. Bush designated 2003 through 2006 as the Lewis and Clark Bicentennial. Beginning at Monticello in January 2003, a series of bicentennial events will highlight key dates and stages in the expedition and allow the public to gain a sense of how their journey unfolded. For information on these events, access the website listed in Web Resources.

THE ELECTION OF 1824

The election of 1820 made Monroe, like both his Republican predecessors, a two-term president. Monroe was the uncontested choice of his party, and the Federalists were too weak to run a candidate. Although Monroe won all but one of the electoral votes, Republican unity was more apparent than real. Voters had no choice in 1820, and without two-party competition, no outlets existed for expressing popular dissatisfaction with the Republicans. Instead, the Republicans split into factions as they began jockeying almost immediately for the election of 1824 (see Map 9–4).

The politics of personality dominated Monroe's second administration. Monroe had no obvious successor, and five candidates competed to replace him. All of them were nominal Republicans, and three were members of his cabinet. Secretary of War John C. Calhoun soon dropped out. He preferred to accept a nomination as vice president, confident that his turn would come in 1828. The other candidates—Secretary of the Treasury William Crawford from Georgia, Secretary of State John Quincy Adams from Massachusetts, Henry Clay from Kentucky, and Andrew Jackson from Tennessee—each had a strong regional following. As the Republican party fragmented, sectional loyalties were replacing partisan allegiances.

The early favorite was Crawford. He was the "official" party nominee in the sense that he had received the support of the congressional caucus, but most Republicans had boycotted the caucus, by now a

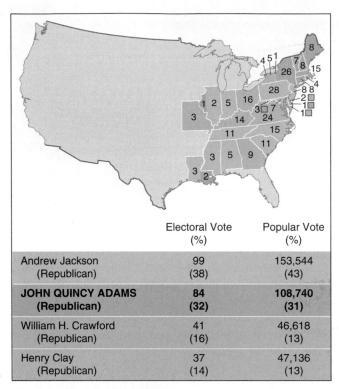

	Electoral Vote (%)	Popular Vote (%)
Andrew Jackson (Republican)	99 (38)	153,544 (43)
JOHN QUINCY ADAMS (Republican)	**84 (32)**	**108,740 (31)**
William H. Crawford (Republican)	41 (16)	46,618 (13)
Henry Clay (Republican)	37 (14)	47,136 (13)

MAP 9-4   The Election of 1824
The regional appeal of each of the four presidential candidates in the election of 1824 prevented any candidate from receiving a majority of the electoral vote. Consequently, and as set forth in the Constitution, the House of Representatives now had to choose the president from the three leading candidates. Its choice was John Quincy Adams.

useless relic of past party unity. Clay, Jackson, and Adams were nominated by their state legislatures. None of the candidates ran on a platform, but Crawford was identified with states' rights and Clay and Adams with centralized government. Clay in particular was associated with the national bank, protective tariffs, and federally funded internal improvements, a package of federal subsidies he called the **American System**. Jackson took no stand on any of the issues.

Jackson's noncommittal stance turned out to be a great asset. It helped him to project the image of a military hero, fresh from the people, who was unsullied by any connection with Washington politicians, whom the public associated with hard times and sectional controversies. He was the highest vote-getter (43 percent of the popular vote), but none of the four candidates had a majority in the electoral college.

As in 1800, the election was thrown into the House of Representatives. Each state had one vote,

and the choice was from among the top three in the electoral college. Clay, who had received the fewest electoral votes, was eliminated. Crawford had suffered a debilitating stroke and was no longer a viable candidate. Thus it came down to Adams or Jackson. Anxious to undercut Jackson, his chief rival in the West, Clay used his influence as speaker of the House to line up support for Adams, a fellow advocate of a strong centralized government.

Adams won the election, and he immediately named Clay as his secretary of state, the office traditionally viewed as a stepping-stone to the presidency. Jackson and his followers were outraged. They smelled a "corrupt bargain" in which Clay had bargained away the presidency to the highest bidder. Vowing revenge, they began building a new party that would usher in a more democratic era of mass-based politics.

CONCLUSION

In 1800, the Republicans were an untested party whose coming to power frightened many Federalists into predicting the end of the Union and constitutional government. The Federalists were correct in sensing that their days of power had passed, but they underestimated the ideological flexibility the Republicans would reveal once in office and the imaginative ways in which Jefferson and his successors would wield executive power to expand the size of the original Union. Far from being anarchists and demagogues, the Republicans were shrewd empire builders astute enough to add to their base of political support in the South and West. They also paved the way for the nation to evolve as a democratic republic rather than the more aristocratic republic preferred by the Federalists.

Most Federalists never did learn the art of popular electioneering, and they were too elitist to have any desire to do so. Although foreign-policy issues arising out of Jefferson's and Madison's attempts to assert American neutral rights during the Anglo-French war kept the Federalists alive and even briefly revived the party, the British posed the greatest test to Republican leadership. The Republicans chose war rather than surrendering their claims of American rights. Jackson's victory at the Battle of New Orleans ended the war in an American burst of glory, and the Federalists were swept aside by the postwar surge of nationalism.

By the mid-1820s, the Republicans were about to join the Federalists as political dinosaurs. The Republican era ended when the party became a victim of its own success. With no Federalist threat to enforce party discipline, the Republicans lost their organizational strength. Embracing economic nationalism after the war made the party's original focus on states' rights all but meaningless. Ideologically and organizationally adrift, the party split into regional coalitions in the wake of the Missouri controversy and the panic of 1819. But before it dissolved, the party left as its most enduring legacy the foundations of a continental empire.

REVIEW QUESTIONS

1. What changes did the Republicans bring to the federal government? How did their policies differ from those of their Federalist predecessors?

2. Why were the Republicans so intent on expanding the boundaries of the United States, and why did the Federalists oppose an expansionist program?

3. What factors accounted for the Federalists' inability to regain national power after they lost the election of 1800?

4. What external and internal factors drew the United States into war against Britain? Could this war have been avoided?

5. What accounted for the difficulties of the United States in waging the War of 1812, and why was the war widely viewed as a great American victory? How did the war lead to an increasing pattern of diplomatic cooperation between the United States and Britain?

6. Why was Rosalie Calvert so critical of the Republican Party and U.S. entry into the War of 1812? To what extent would New England Federalists have shared her views?

7. What explains the upsurge of nationalism that underlay the Era of Good Feelings? Why were the Republicans unable to maintain their party unity after 1819?

KEY TERMS

American System (p. 288)

Anglo-American Accords (p. 282)

Chesapeake Incident (p. 270)

Dartmouth College v. Woodward (p. 282)

Embargo Act of 1807 (p. 270)

Era of Good Feelings (p. 280)

Fletcher v. Peck (p. 282)

Ghent, Treaty of (p. 278)

Marbury v. Madison (p. 266)

Missouri Compromise (p. 285)

Monroe Doctrine (p. 283)

New Orleans, Battle of (p. 271)

Pan-Indian resistance movement (p. 271)

Plattsburgh, Battle of (p. 278)

Put-in-Bay, Battle of (p. 277)

Rush-Bagot Agreement (p. 282)

Second Bank of the United States (p. 280)

Trans-Continental Treaty of 1819 (p. 283)

War Hawks (p. 272)

War of 1812 (p. 273)

RECOMMENDED READING

Allgor, Catherine. *Parlor Politics: In Which the Ladies of Washington Help Build a City and a Government* (1999). A witty and engagingly written work that describes how women exercised political power in the early republic.

Hickey, Donald R. *The War of 1812: A Forgotten Conflict* (1989). Breaks no new ground, but presents a complete and very readable account of all aspects of the war.

McCoy, Drew R. *The Elusive Republic: Political Economy in Jeffersonian America* (1980). A gracefully written study that examines how attitudes on economic development influenced Jeffersonian notions of republicanism and were central to the Republicans' stand on free trade.

Onuf, Peter S., ed. *Jeffersonian Legacies* (1993). A collection of essays that presents the latest thinking on the extraordinary range of Jefferson's activities.

Smelser, Marshall. *The Democratic Republic, 1801–1815* (1968). Gives a sound overview of the Jefferson and Madison administrations. Smelser portrays Jefferson as a political moderate adept at wielding power and offers a spirited defense of Madison's record as a war president.

Vidal, Gore. *Burr* (1973). A superbly entertaining novel that satirically brings to life the leading personalities of Jefferson's America.

Weeks, William Earl. *John Quincy Adams and American Global Empire* (1992). Presents Adams as a cynical, tough-minded negotiator utterly driven by his vision of an American continental empire. Though questioning his tactics, Weeks confirms Adams's reputation as America's greatest secretary of state.

ADDITIONAL SOURCES

Jefferson's Presidency

Ambrose, Stephen. *Undaunted Courage: Meriwether Lewis, Thomas Jefferson, and the Opening of the American West* (1996).

Banning, Lance. *The Jeffersonian Persuasion: Evolution of a Party Ideology* (1978).

Ben-Atar, Doron S. *The Origins of Jeffersonian Commercial Policy and Diplomacy* (1993).

Cunningham, Jr. Noble E. *The Jeffersonian Republicans in Power: Party Operations, 1801–1809* (1963).

De Conde, Alexander. *This Affair of Louisiana* (1976).

Kennon, Donald R. ed., *A Republic for the Ages: The United States Capitol and the Political Culture of the Early Republic* (1999)

Fischer, David Hackett. *The Revolution of American Conservation: The Federalist Party in the Era of Jeffersonian Democracy* (1965).

McDonald, Forrest. *The Presidency of Thomas Jefferson* (1976).

Young, James Sterling. *The Washington Community, 1800–1828* (1966).

Madison and the Coming of War

Brown, Roger H. *The Republic in Peril* (1964).

Dowd, Gregory Evans. *A Spirited Resistance: The North American Indian Struggle for Unity, 1745–1815* (1992).

Edmunds, R. David. *The Shawnee Prophet* (1983) and Tecumseh and the Quest for Indian Leadership (1984).

Owsley, Jr. Frank Lawrence. and Smith Gene H. *Filibusters and Expansionists: Jeffersonian Manifest Destiny* (1997).

Perkins, Bradford. *Prologue to War: England and the United States, 1805–1812* (1961).

Rutland, Robert A. *Madison's Alternatives: The Jeffersonian Republicans and the Coming of War* (1975).

The War of 1812

Banner, James M. *To the Hartford Convention: The Federalists and the Origins of Party Politics in the Early Republic, 1789–1815* (1967).

Edmunds, R. David. *Tecumseh and the Quest for Indian Leadership* (1984).

Gribbin, William. *The Churches Militant: The War of 1812 and American Religion* (1973).

Horsman, Reginald. *The War of 1812* (1969).

Stagg, J. C. A. *Mr. Madison's War: Politics, Diplomacy, and Warfare in the Early Republic, 1783–1830* (1983).

Watts, Steven. *The Republic Reborn: War and the Making of Liberal America* (1987).

The Era of Good Feelings

Bemis, Samuel Flagg. *John Quincy Adams and the Foundations of American Foreign Policy* (1949).

Cunningham, Noble E. Jr. *The Presidency of James Monroe* (1996).

Livermore, Shaw. *The Twilight of Federalism: The Disintegration of the Federalist Party, 1815–1830* (1962).

May, Ernest R. *The Making of the Monroe Doctrine* (1975).

White, G. Edward. *The Marshall Court and Cultural Change, 1815–1835* (1991).

The Breakdown of Unity

Moore, Glover. *The Missouri Compromise, 1819–1821* (1953).

Rothbard, Murray N. *The Panic of 1819: Reactions and Policies* (1962).

WHERE TO LEARN MORE

- **Fort McHenry National Monument, Baltimore, Maryland.** This historic site preserves the fort that was the focal point of the British attack on Baltimore and contains a museum with materials on the battle and the writing of "The Star-Spangled Banner." For the military history of the fort and the archeological work at the site, see www.nps.gov/fomc/archeology/overview.html.

- **Tippecanoe Battlefield Museum, Battle Ground, Indiana.** This museum includes artifacts from the Indian and white settlement of Indiana and visual materials on the Battle of Tippecanoe of 1811. The museum's website at www.tcha.mus.in.us/battlefield.htm includes an account of the battle and its aftermath.

- **Monticello, Charlottesville, Virginia.** The architecturally unique home of Thomas Jefferson and the headquarters for his plantation serves as a museum that provides insights into Jefferson's varied interests. Information on educational programs and upcoming events at Monticello, as well as the new Jefferson Library in Charlottesville, can be found at www.monticello.org/.

- **Montpelier, Montpelier Station, Virginia.** The museum here was the home of James Madison, and it includes material on his life as a politician and planter. Its website at www.montpelier.org/ provides information on tours and programs and a look at the archeological findings at Montpelier.

- **Perry's Victory and International Peace Memorial, Put-in-Bay, Ohio.** At the site of Perry's decisive victory on Lake Erie in 1813 now stands a museum that depicts the role of the Old Northwest in the War of 1812. For a printable travel guide and information on the new visitor center, see www.nps.gov/pevi/.

- **Lewis and Clark Expedition.** This site provides a wealth of information and resources including photo essays, interactive maps, web resources, a list of planned events, the journals of the expedition, and a bibliography of recent works. http://www.time.com/time/2002/lewis_clark

 Please refer to the document CD-ROM for primary sources related to this chapter.

➜ *This early nineteenth-century painting of a polling place in Philadelphia illustrates the growing involvement of common Americans in politics. As suffrage broadened and more Americans came out to vote, elections became more heated and emotional.*

John L. Krimmel, Painting, (1786-1821), Oil on Canvas, H. 16 3/8" x W. 25 5/8". (AN: 59.131) Courtesy, Winterthur Museum, "Election Day in Philadelphia" (1815) - DETAIL.

THE JACKSONIAN ERA
1824–1845

10

Newport, New Hampshire
September, 1828

Wherever a person may chance to be in company, he will hear nothing but politicks discussed. In the ballroom, or at the dinner table, in the Stagecoach & in the tavern; even the social chitchat of the tea table must yield up to the everlasting subject.

How many friendships are broken up! With what rancor the political war is carried on between the editorial corps! To what meanness[,] vulgarity & abuse is that champion of liberty, in proper hands, the press prostituted! With what lies and scandal does the columns of almost every political paper abound! I blush for my country when I see such things, & I often tremble with apprehension that our Constitution will not long withstand the current which threatens to overwhelm it. Our government is so based that an honest difference between American citizens must always exist. But the rancorous excitement which now threatens our civil liberties and a dissolution of this Union does not emanate from an honest difference of opinion, but from a determination of an unholy league to trample down an Administration, be it ever so pure, & be its acts ever so just. It must not be. There is a kind Providence that overlooks the destinies of this Nation and will not suffer it to be overthrown by a party of aspiring office seekers & political demagogues.

Benjamin B. French

Donald B. Cole and John J. McDonough, eds., *Witness to the Young Republic: A Yankee's Journal*, 1828–1870 (Hanover, N.H.: University Press of New England, 1989), pp. 15–16.

CHAPTER OUTLINE

The Egalitarian Impulse
The Extension of White Male Democracy
The Popular Religious Revolt
The Rise of the Jacksonians

Jackson's Presidency
Jackson's Appeal
Indian Removal
The Nullification Crisis
The Bank War

Van Buren and Hard Times
The Panic of 1837
The Independent Treasury
Uproar over Slavery

The Rise of the Whig Party
The Party Taking Shape
Whig Persuasion
The Election of 1840

The Whigs in Power
Harrison and Tyler
The Texas Issue
The Election of 1844

Conclusion

Benjamin Brown French, a young editor and county clerk in Newport, New Hampshire, penned these words in his journal in September 1828. Like most other Americans, he was amazed—indeed, shocked—by the intense, seemingly all-pervasive partisanship stirred up in the presidential election of 1828 between Andrew Jackson and John Quincy Adams. Whether measured by the vulgar personal attacks launched by a partisan press, the amount of whiskey and beef consumed at political barbecues, or the huge increase in voter turnout, this election marked the entrance of ordinary Americans onto the political stage.

The sense of shock soon wore off for French. The son of a wealthy Federalist lawyer with whom he was always at odds, French broke with his father when, at the age of twenty-five, he married without his permission. With no income, job, or family support, he now began to make a business out of law, politics, and journalism. In so doing he was part of the first generation of professional politicians, young men who compensated for their lack of social connections and family wealth by turning to politics as a means of earning an income and building a career. The partisanship that French found so disturbing in 1828 quickly became the basis of his livelihood. After rejecting his father's politics by joining the Democrats in 1831, he spent most of his subsequent years as a political officeholder in Washington, holding a variety of appointive jobs. His own fortunes initially depended on the political success of his Democratic party. Then, after breaking with the Democrats in the 1850s over the slavery issue, he succeeded in finding government employment in Republican administrations until his death in 1870.

What had made possible French's career was an ongoing democratization of American politics that gathered momentum in the early decades of the nineteenth century. The number and potential power of the voters expanded, and professional politicians realized that party success now depended on reaching and organizing this enlarged electorate. Men like French, working for the party, could help them do this. The "Jacksonian Democrats," named for their leader, Andrew Jackson, were the first party to learn this fundamental lesson. Trumpeting Andrew Jackson as the friend of the common man and the foe of aristocratic privilege, they won a landslide victory in 1828 and held national power through the 1830s. The Jacksonians promised to protect farmers and workers from the monied elite, whom they portrayed as the enemies of equality and the corruptors of public morality.

By the mid-1830s, the Whig party had formed in opposition to the Jacksonians. The Whigs offered an ordered vision of American progress and liberty, anchored in the use of governmental power to expand economic opportunities and promote morality. By embracing electoral techniques of popular appeal first used by the Democrats, the Whigs captured the presidency in 1840. Their triumph heralded a new party system, one based on massive voter turnouts and two-party competition in every state.

The luckless Whigs failed to capitalize on their victory in 1840. Their newly elected president, William Henry Harrison, died shortly after entering office, and Vice President John Tyler, his successor, blocked the Whigs' economic program. Spurned by the Whigs as a traitor, Tyler then reopened the explosive question of slavery and territorial expansion by pushing to annex the independent republic of Texas, where slavery was legal.

The Democrats regained power in 1844 by skillfully exploiting the Texas issue, but they set an ominous precedent. Debates over the expansion of slavery became embedded in the political system, and the greatest strength of the mass-based parties—their ability to tap and unleash popular emotions—now became their greatest weakness. The slavery issue began to take on a life of its own beyond the control of party leaders. The seeds of the Civil War were being sown.

KEY TOPICS

- The rise of new political parties: Jacksonian Democrats and Whigs
- The disfranchisement of free black people and women
- Birth of the Whig party
- The Second Great Awakening
- The Bank War
- The growing conflict over slavery

THE EGALITARIAN IMPULSE

Political democracy, defined as the majority rule of white males, was far from complete in early nineteenth-century America. Acting on the belief that only property owners with a stake in society should have a voice in governing it, the landed and commercial elites of the Revolutionary era erected legal barriers against the full expression of majority sentiments. These barriers—property requirements for voting and officeholding, the prevalence of appointed over elected offices, and the overrepresentation of older and wealthier regions in state legislatures—came under increasing attack after 1800 and were all but eliminated by the 1820s.

As politics opened to mass participation, a democratization movement in American religion also gathered momentum. Popular styles of religious leadership and worship emerged in a broad reaction to the formalism and elitism of the dominant Protestant churches. The same egalitarian impulse drove these twin democratic revolutions, and both movements represented an empowerment of the common man. Popular movements now spoke his language and appealed to his quest for republican equality. (Women would have to wait longer.) John Quincy Adams and his followers never understood the more democratic America of the 1820s. As a result, they were easily routed in the election of 1828 by those who did—the **Jacksonian Democrats**.

THE EXTENSION OF WHITE MALE DEMOCRACY

In 1789, Congress set the pay of representatives and senators at $6 a day plus travel expenses. By 1816, inflation had so eroded this salary that many government clerks earned more than members of Congress. Thus Congress thought itself prudent and justified when it voted itself a hefty raise to $1,500 a year. The public thought otherwise. In a resolution typical of the popular response, the citizens of Saratoga, New York, accused Congress of "wanton extravagance" and "a daring and profligate trespass against . . . the *morals* of the *Republic.*" The outcry stunned the politicians, who found themselves deluged with protests decrying their greed.

So sharp was the reaction against the Salary Act of 1816 that 70 percent of the members of Congress were turned out of office at the next election. Congress quickly repealed the salary increase, but not before John C. Calhoun spoke for many in Congress when he plaintively asked, "Are we bound in all cases to do what is popular?" The answer was apparently yes. As Richard M. Johnson of Kentucky noted, "The presumption is, that the people are always right."

The people had spoken in 1816, and the politicians got the message. The uproar over the Salary Act marked a turning point in the transition from the deferential politics of the Federalist-Republican period to the egalitarianism of the coming Jacksonian era. Since the War of 1812, demands for a greater popular voice in government had noticeably quickened the pace of democratization. The public would no longer passively accept decisions handed down by local elites or established national figures.

Individual states, not the federal government, defined who could vote. Six states—Indiana, Mississippi, Illinois, Alabama, Missouri, and Maine—entered the Union between 1816 and 1821, and none of them required voters to own property. Meanwhile, proponents for suffrage liberalization won major victories in the older eastern states. Constitutional conventions in Connecticut in 1818 and Massachusetts and New York in 1821 eliminated property requirements for voting. By the end of the 1820s, universal white male suffrage was the norm everywhere except Rhode Island, Virginia, and Louisiana.

Extending the suffrage and democratic reform.
Broadening the suffrage was part of a general democratization of political structures and procedures in the state governments. Representation in most state legislatures was made more equal by giving more seats to newer, rapidly growing regions in the backcountry. States removed or reduced property qualifications for officeholding. The selection of local officials and, in many cases, judges, was taken out of the hands of governors and executive councils and given to the voters in popular elections. With the end of oral or "stand-up" voting, the act of casting a ballot became more private and freer from the intimidation of influential neighbors. Written ballots were the norm by the 1820s. Most significant for national politics, voters acquired the power to choose presidential electors. In 1800, only two states had provided for a statewide popular vote in presidential elections. By 1824, most did so, and by 1832 only South Carolina still clung to the practice of having the state legislature choose the electors (see Map 10–1).

Several currents swelled the movement for democratic reform. Limiting voting rights to those who owned landed property seemed increasingly elitist when economic changes were producing new classes—workers, clerks, and small tradesmen—whose livelihoods were not tied directly to the land. At the same time, the middling and lower ranks of society demanded the ballot and access to offices to protect

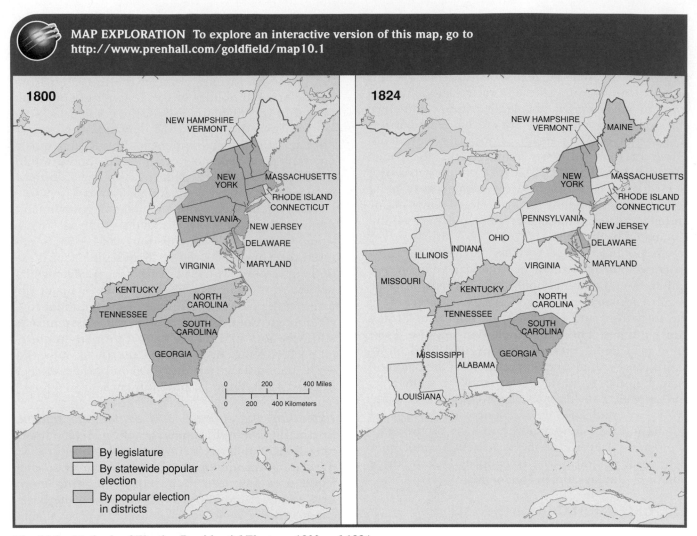

MAP EXPLORATION To explore an interactive version of this map, go to http://www.prenhall.com/goldfield/map10.1

MAP 10-1   **Methods of Electing Presidential Electors, 1800 and 1824**
The Constitution permits each state legislature to choose the method of electing presidential electors for its state. In 1800 the legislatures in most states appointed the electors. By 1824 most states had adopted more democratic systems in which electors pledged to specific presidential candidates were selected by popular vote in statewide elections.
Data Source: U.S. Bureau of the Census, *Historical Statistics of the United States, Colonial Times to 1957 (1960)*, p. 681.

themselves from the commercial and manufacturing interests, who benefited most from economic change. Propertyless laborers in Richmond argued in an 1829 petition that "virtue [and] intelligence are not among the products of the soil. Attachment to property, often a sordid sentiment, is not to be confounded with the sacred flame of patriotism."

Of greatest importance, however, was the incessant demand that all white men be treated equally. Seth Luther, an advocate for workers' rights, insisted that "we wish nothing, but those equal rights, which were designed for us all." The logical extension of the ideology of the American Revolution, with its leveling attacks against kings and aristocrats, this demand for equality made republicanism by the 1820s synonymous with simple majority rule. If any white male was the equal of any other, regardless of wealth or property holdings, then only the will of the majority could be the measure of a republican government.

The disfranchisement of free blacks and women.
As political opportunities expanded for white males, they shrank for women and free black people. In the state constitutions of the Revolutionary era, free black males who met the minimum property requirements usually had the same voting rights as white males. New Jersey's constitution of 1776 was exceptional in also granting the suffrage to single women

Chronology

1826	Disappearance of William Morgan.
1827	Emergence of the Anti-Masons, the first third party.
1828	Andrew Jackson elected president.
	John C. Calhoun writes *The South Carolina Exposition and Protest.*
1830	Congress passes the Indian Removal Act.
1831	William Lloyd Garrison starts publication of *The Liberator.*
	Nat Turner leads a slave uprising in Virginia.
1832	Jackson vetoes bill for rechartering the Second Bank of the United States; Bank War begins.
	South Carolina nullifies the Tariffs of 1828 and 1832.
	Jackson reelected.
1833	Congress passes the Force Act and the Compromise Tariff.
	American Anti-Slavery Society established.

1834	Whig party begins to organize.
1836	Texas War of Independence and establishment of the Republic of Texas.
	Congress passes first gag rule on abolitionist petitions.
	Van Buren elected president.
1837	Panic of 1837 sets off a depression.
1840	Independent Treasury Act passes.
	William Henry Harrison elected as first Whig president.
1841	John Tyler succeeds to presidency on death of Harrison.
1842	United States and Britain sign the Webster-Ashburton Treaty.
1844	James K. Polk elected president.
	Gag rule repealed.
1845	Texas admitted to the Union.

and widows who owned property. By the early 1800s, race and gender began to replace wealth and status as the basis for defining the limits of political participation. Thus, when New Jersey's new constitution in 1807 broadened suffrage by requiring only a simple taxpaying qualification to vote, it specifically denied the ballot to women and free black men. In state after state, the same constitutional conventions that embraced universal suffrage for white men deprived black men of the vote or burdened them with special property qualifications. Moreover, none of the ten states that entered the Union from 1821 to 1861 allowed black suffrage. African Americans protested in vain. "Foreigners and aliens to the government and laws," complained black New Yorkers in 1837, "strangers to our institutions, are permitted to flock to this land and in a few years are endowed with all the privileges of citizens; but we native born Americans . . . are most of us shut out." By the 1850s, black males could vote only in certain New England states.

The linkage of democracy with white manhood was not accidental. Advocates of greater democratization explicitly argued that only white males had the intelligence and love of liberty to be entrusted with political rights. Women, they said, were too weak and emotional, black people too lazy and lascivious. In denouncing distinctions drawn on property as artificial and demeaning, the white egalitarians simultaneously erected new distinctions based on race

and sex that were supposedly natural and hence immutable. Thus personal liberties were now to be guarded, not by propertied gentlemen but by all white men, whose equality ultimately rested on assumptions of their shared natural superiority over women and nonwhite people.

THE POPULAR RELIGIOUS REVOLT

In religion as well as politics, ordinary Americans demanded a greater voice in the early nineteenth century. Insurgent religious movements rejected the formalism and traditional Calvinism of the Congregational and Presbyterian churches, the dominant Protestant denominations in Washington's America. In a blaze of fervor known as the **Second Great Awakening** (recalling the Great Awakening of colonial America), evangelical sects led by the Methodists and Baptists radically transformed the religious landscape between 1800 and 1840. A more popularly rooted Christianity moved outward and downward as it spread across frontier areas and converted marginalized and common folk. By 1850, one in three Americans was a regular churchgoer, a dramatic increase since 1800.

The Baptists and Methodists, both spinning off numerous splinter groups, grew spectacularly and were the largest religious denominations by the 1820s. The key to their success was their ability to give

"Camp Meeting," color lithograph by Kennedy and Lucas after painting by A. Rider, c. 1835, negative number 26275. © collection of the New York Historical Society, NYC.

The Second Great Awakening originated on the frontier. Preachers were adept at arousing emotional fervor, and women in particular responded to the evangelical message of spiritual equality open to all who would accept Christ into their lives.

religious expression to the same popular impulse behind democratic reform. Especially in the backcountry of the South and West, where the first revivals occurred, itinerant preachers reshaped religion to fit the needs and values of ordinary Americans.

Evangelical Christianity emphasized personal, heartfelt experience that would produce a spiritual rebirth. Preaching became a form of theater in which scenes of damnation and salvation were acted out by both preacher and audience. The emotional force unleashed at the mass revivals known as camp meetings astounded observers. "The scene that then presented itself to my mind was indescribable," recalled James Finley of the camp meeting at Cane Ridge, Kentucky, in 1801. "At one time I saw at least five hundred swept down in a moment, as if a battery of a thousand guns had bccn opcncd upon them, and then immediately followed shrieks and shouts that rent the very heavens."

The evangelical religion of the traveling preachers was democratic in its populist rejection of traditional religious canons and its encouragement of

organizational forms that gave a voice to popular culture. Salvation was no longer simply bestowed by an implacable God as taught by the Calvinist doctrine of individual predestination (see Chapter 1). Ordinary people could now actively choose salvation, and this possibility was exhilarating. "Why, then, I can be saved!" exclaimed Jesse Lee upon hearing a Methodist preacher in Massachusetts. "I have been taught that only a part of the race could be saved, but if this man's singing be true, all may be saved." Evangelical churches bound the faithful into tightly knit communities that expressed and enforced local values and standards of conduct. Their hymns borrowed melodies from popular music and were accompanied by fiddles and other folk instruments.

Evangelicalism was a religion of the common people, and it appealed especially to women and African Americans. The revivals converted about twice as many women as men. Excluded from most areas of public life, women found strength and comfort in the evangelical message of Christian love and equality. As the wife of a Connecticut minister explained, church membership offered them a welcome release from "being treated like beasts of burden [and] drudges of domineering masters." In the first flush of evangelical excitement, female itinerant preachers spread the gospel up and down the East Coast. By thus defying social convention, these women offered a model of independent action. Other women organized their own institutions within denominations still formally controlled by men. Women activists founded and largely directed hundreds of church-affiliated charitable societies and missionary associations.

Evangelicalism also empowered black Americans. African American Christianity experienced its first sustained growth in the generation after the Revolutionary War. As a result of their uncompromising commitment to convert slaves, the Baptists and Methodists led the way. They welcomed slaves at their revivals, encouraged black preachers, and above all else, advocated secular and spiritual equality. Many of the early Baptist and Methodist preachers directly challenged slavery. In converting to Methodism, one slave stated that "from the sermon I heard, I felt that God had made all men free and equal, and that I ought not be a slave." Perceiving in it the promise of liberty and deliverance, the slaves received the evangelical gospel in loud, joyous, and highly emotional revivals. They made it part of their own culture, fusing Christianity with folk beliefs from their African heritage.

But for all its liberating appeal to women and African Americans, evangelicalism was eventually limited by race and gender in much the same way as the democratic reform movement. Denied positions of authority in white-dominated churches and resentful of white opposition to integrated worship, free black northerners founded their own independent churches.

As increasing numbers of planters embraced evangelicalism after the 1820s, southern evangelicals first muted their attacks on slavery and then developed a full-blown religious defense of it based on the biblical sanctioning of human bondage. They similarly cited the Old Testament patriarchs to defend the unquestioned authority of fathers over their households, the masters of slaves, women, and children. Many popular religious sects in the North also used a particular reading of the Bible to exalt the independence of white males at the expense of the dependence of everyone else.

In religion as well as politics, white men retained the power in Jacksonian America. Still, the Second Great Awakening removed a major intellectual barrier to political democracy. Traditional Protestant theology—whether Calvinist, Anglican, or Lutheran —viewed the mass of humanity as sinners predestined to damnation and hence was loath to accept the idea that those same sinners, by majority vote, should make crucial political decisions. In rejecting this theology, ordinary Americans made a fundamental intellectual breakthrough. "Salvation open to all" powerfully reinforced the legitimacy of "one man, one vote."

THE RISE OF THE JACKSONIANS

The Jacksonian Democrats were the first party to mold and organize the democratizing impulse in popular culture. At the core of the Jacksonian appeal was the same rejection of established authority that was the hallmark of the secular and religious populists. Much like the revivalists and the democratic reformers, the Jacksonians also fashioned techniques of communication that tapped into the hopes and fears of ordinary Americans. In so doing, they built the first mass-based party in American history.

In Andrew Jackson the new **Democratic Party** that formed between 1824 and 1828 had the perfect candidate for the increasingly democratic temperament of the 1820s. Born of Scots-Irish ancestry on the Carolina frontier in 1767, Jackson was a self-made product of the southern backcountry. Lacking any formal education, family connections, or inherited wealth to ease his way, he relied on his own wits and raw courage to carve out a career as a frontier lawyer and planter in Tennessee. He won fame as the military savior of the republic with his victory at the Battle of New Orleans. Conqueror of the British, the Spanish, and the Indians, all of whom had blocked frontier expansion, he achieved incredible popularity in his native South. His strengths and prejudices were those most valued by the restless, mobile Americans to whom he became a folk hero.

As a presidential candidate, Jackson's image was that of the antielitist champion of the people. "Take for your President a man from your own body, untainted by the corruption of a court and uninitiated in Cabinet secrets," urged a New Jersey Jackson convention in 1824. Jackson lost the election of 1824, but his defeat turned out to be a blessing in disguise. The wheeling and dealing in Congress that gave the presidency to John Quincy Adams enveloped that administration in a cloud of suspicion from the start. It also enhanced Jackson's appeal as the honest tribune of the people whose rightful claim to the presidency had been spurned by intriguing politicians in Washington. His supporters now claimed that the people, as well as Jackson, had been swindled by the "corrupt bargain" between Adams and Clay (see page 287). Moreover, the ill-fated Adams presidency virtually destroyed itself. Though the same age as Jackson, Adams seemed

To the opponents of the Jacksonians, elections had become a degrading spectacle in which conniving Democratic politicians, such as the one shown below handing a voting ticket to the stereotypical Irishman in the light coat, were corrupting the republic's political culture.

frozen in an eighteenth-century past, in which aloof gentlemanly statesmen disdainfully refused to turn to the people for support. Uncomfortable with the give-and-take of politics or the very idea of building a coalition to support himself, Adams was out of touch with the political realities of the 1820s.

Just how out of touch was revealed when Adams delivered his first annual message to Congress in 1825. He presented a bold vision of an activist federal government promoting economic growth, social advancement, and scientific progress. Such a vision might have received a fair hearing in 1815, when postwar nationalism was in full stride. In 1825, it amounted to political suicide. Postwar nationalism had dissolved into sectional bickering and burning resentments against banks, tariffs, and the political establishment, which were blamed for the hard times after the Panic of 1819. The Jacksonians charged that an administration born in corruption now wanted to waste the people's money by promoting more corruption and greed. And when Adams urged Americans not "to proclaim to the world that we are palsied by the will of our constituents," the Jacksonians attacked him as an arrogant aristocrat contemptuous of the common man.

Little of Adams's program passed Congress, and his nationalist vision drove his opponents into the

Jackson camp. Southern planters jumped onto the Jackson bandwagon out of fear that Adams might use federal power against slavery; more Westerners joined because Adams revived their suspicions of the East. The most important addition came from New York, where Martin Van Buren had built the **Albany Regency**, a tightly disciplined state political machine.

Van Buren was a new breed of politician, a professional who made a business out of politics. The son of a tavern keeper, he quickly grasped, as a young lawyer, how politics could open up career opportunities. The discipline and regularity of strict party organization gave him and others from the middling ranks a winning edge in competition against their social betters. In battling against the system of family-centered wealth and prestige on which politics had previously been based, Van Buren redefined parties as something good in and of themselves. Indeed, he and his followers argued that parties were indispensable instruments for the successful expression of the popular will against the dominance of elites.

State leaders such as Van Buren organized the first national campaign that relied extensively on new techniques of mass mobilization. In rallying support for Jackson against Adams in 1828, these state leaders put together chains of party-subsidized newspapers and coordinated a frantic schedule of meetings and rallies. Grassroots Jackson committees reached out to the voters by knocking on their doors, pressing party literature into their hands, dispensing mass-produced medals and buttons with a likeness of Jackson, and lavishly entertaining all who would give them a hearing. Politics became a folk spectacle as torchlight parades awakened sleepy towns and political barbecues doled out whiskey and food to farmers from the surrounding countryside.

The election of 1828 centered on personalities, not issues. This in itself was a victory for Jackson's campaign managers, who proved far more skillful in the new presidential game of image making than did their Adams counterparts, now known as the National Republicans. Although both sides tried to depict the other's candidate as morally unfit, the

Jackson men were more in tune with a public sentiment that identified Adams's call for a strong government with special privileges for the favored few. Thus for many voters, Adams personified a discredited elite and Jackson the voice of the people.

Jackson carried every state south and west of Pennsylvania in 1828 and polled 56 percent of the popular vote (see Map 10–2). Voter turnout shot up to 55 percent from the apathetic 25 percent of 1824. Adams ran well only in New England and in commercialized areas producing goods for outside markets. Aside from the South, where he was virtually untouchable, Jackson's appeal was strongest among ordinary Americans who valued their local independence and felt threatened by outside centers of power beyond their control. He rolled up heavy majorities from Scots-Irish farmers in the Baptist-Methodist evangelical belt of the backcountry and from unskilled workers with an Irish Catholic background. To these voters, Jackson was a double hero, for he had defeated their hated British enemy and promised to do the same to the Yankee capitalists of the Northeast and all the elitist politicians. Democracy, they were convinced, had at last come to presidential politics.

JACKSON'S PRESIDENCY

Once in office, Jackson proved to be the most forceful and energetic president since Jefferson. Like a military chieftain tolerating no interference from his subordinates, Jackson dominated his presidency with the sheer force of his personality. At one time or another, his administration angered southern planters, frightened eastern bankers and commercial interests, and outraged New England reformers. Nonetheless, Jackson remained popular because he portrayed himself as the embodiment of the people's will.

The Jacksonians had no particular program in 1828, and Jackson shrewdly had avoided taking a stand on divisive issues. Apart from removing Indians to areas west of the Mississippi River, Jackson's first term was notable primarily for its political infighting. Two political struggles that came to a head in 1832–1833—the **Bank War** and the **nullification crisis**—

This 1845 painting captures the heroic, forceful side of Andrew Jackson that made him so appealing to many voters.

MAP 10-2   The Election of 1828
Andrew Jackson won a decisive victory in 1828 by sweeping the South and West and making major inroads in the Northeast.

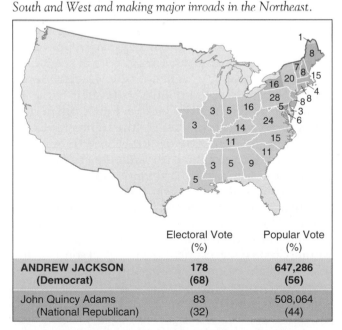

	Electoral Vote (%)	Popular Vote (%)
ANDREW JACKSON (Democrat)	**178** **(68)**	**647,286** **(56)**
John Quincy Adams (National Republican)	83 (32)	508,064 (44)

stamped the Jacksonians with a lasting party identity. By destroying the Second Bank of the United States and rejecting the attempt of South Carolina to nullify (or annul) a national tariff, Jackson firmly established the Democrats as the enemy of special privilege, the friend of the common man, and the defender of the Union. Consequently, even when Jackson stepped down in 1837, the Democrats were so identified with the interests of the people that they were able to elect Martin Van Buren, who had none of Jackson's personal magnetism or broad appeal.

JACKSON'S APPEAL

Jackson's inauguration struck many conservatives as ushering in a vulgar new order in national affairs. A vast crowd poured into Washington to applaud the people's hero. They cheered loudly when Jackson took his oath of office and then rushed to the White House for a postinauguration reception. Any semblance of order broke down as they pressed in on waiters trying to serve them refreshments. Bowls of liquor-laced punch went flying, and glass and china crashed to the floor as a seeming mob surged through the White House. "But it was the People's day," reported one conservative onlooker, "and the People's President and the People would rule. God grant that one day or other, the People do not put down all rule and rulers."

Ordinary Americans identified with Jackson as with no earlier president, and he convinced them that he was using his office as the instrument of their will. Although led by wealthy planters and entrepreneurs who were hardly average Americans, the Jacksonians skillfully depicted themselves as the champions of the common man against the aristocratic interests, who had enriched themselves through special privileges granted by the government. Jackson proclaimed his task as one of restoring the federal government to the ideal of Jeffersonian republicanism, in which farmers and artisans could pursue their individual liberty free of any government intervention that favored the rich and powerful.

Jackson began his assault on special privilege by proclaiming a reform of the appointment process for federal officeholders. Accusing his predecessors, especially Adams, of having created a social elite of self-serving bureaucrats, he vowed to make government service more responsive to the popular will. He insisted that federal jobs required no special expertise or training and proposed to rotate honest, hardworking citizens in and out of the civil service.

Jackson's reform of the federal bureaucracy had more style than substance. He removed only about one-fifth of the officeholders he inherited, and most of his appointees came from the same relatively high-status groups as the Adams people. But by providing a democratic rationale for government ser-

THE GREAT CHEESE LEVEE.

The first president to be openly embraced by the people as one of their own, Jackson received many gifts while president. One of the gifts was a 1,400-pound cheese, which he offered to well-wishers at a public reception.

Culver Pictures, Inc.

vice, he opened the way for future presidents to move more aggressively against incumbents. Thus emerged the **spoils system**, in which the victorious party gave government jobs to its supporters and removed the appointees of the defeated party. This parceling out of jobs was a powerful technique for building party strength, because it tied party loyalty to the reward of a federal appointment.

When Jackson railed against economic privilege, he most often had in mind Henry Clay's American System (see Chapter 9). Clay's program called for a protective tariff, a national bank, and federal subsidies for internal improvements; his goal was to bind Americans together in an integrated national market. To the Democrats, Clay's system represented government favoritism at its worst, a set of costly benefits at the public's expense for special-interest groups, who corrupted politicians in their quest for economic power. In 1830, Jackson found the perfect opportunity to strike a blow for the Democratic conception of the limited federal role in economic development. He vetoed the Maysville Road Bill, which would have provided federal money for a road to be built entirely within Kentucky. The bill was unconstitutional, he claimed, because it benefited only the citizens of Kentucky and not the American people as a whole. Moreover, since the Maysville project was within Clay's congressional district, Jackson had the added delight of embarrassing his most prominent political enemy.

On the issue of internal improvements, as well as bureaucratic reform, the Democrats placed party needs ahead of ideology. Jackson's Maysville veto did not rule out congressional appropriations for projects deemed beneficial to the general public. This pragmatic loophole gave Democrats all the room they needed to pass more internal-improvement projects during Jackson's presidency than during all of the previous administrations together. Having built a mass party, the Democrats soon discovered that they had to funnel federal funds to their constituents back home.

Any support Jackson might have lost among market-minded entrepreneurs and farmers in the West by his Maysville veto was more than made up by the popularity of his Indian removal policy. Jackson's strongest base of support was in the West and South, and by driving Native Americans from these regions, he more than lived up to his billing as the friend of the common (white) man.

INDIAN REMOVAL

Some 125,000 Indians lived east of the Mississippi when Jackson became president. The largest concen-

Sequoyah, a Cherokee scholar, developed a written table of syllables for the Cherokee language that enabled his people to publish a tribal newspaper in both Cherokee and English.

SE-QUO-YAH

tration was in the South, where five Indian nations—the Cherokees, Creeks, Choctaws, Chickasaws, and Seminoles—controlled millions of acres of land in what soon would become the great cotton frontiers of southwestern Georgia and central Alabama and Mississippi. That, of course, was the problem: Native Americans held land that white farmers coveted for their own economic gain.

Pressure from the states to remove the Indians had been building since the end of the War of 1812. It was most intense in Georgia. In early 1825, Georgia authorities finalized a fraudulent treaty that ceded most of the Creek Indians' land to the state. When Adams tried to obtain fairer terms for the Creeks in a new treaty, he was brazenly denounced in Georgia, which based its case for grabbing Indian territory on the inviolability of states' rights. Georgia dared Adams to do something about it; not willing to risk an armed confrontation between federal and state authorities, Adams backed down.

In 1828, Georgia moved against the Cherokees, the best-organized and most advanced (by white standards) of the Indian nations. By now a prosperous society of small farmers with their own newspaper and schools for their children, the Cherokees wanted to avoid the fate of their Creek neighbors. In 1827, they adopted a constitution declaring themselves an independent nation with complete sovereignty over their land. The Georgia legislature reacted by placing the Cherokees directly under state law, annulling Cherokee laws and even the right of the Cherokees to make laws, and legally defining the Cherokees as tenants on land belonging to the state of Georgia. By also prohibiting Indian testimony in cases against white people, the legislature stripped the Cherokees of any legal rights. They were now easy prey for white settlers, who scrambled onto Cherokee land after gold was discovered in northern Georgia in 1829. Alabama and Mississippi followed Georgia's lead in denying Indians legal rights.

Thus the stage was set for what Jackson always considered the most important measure of the early days of his administration, the **Indian Removal Act**. Jackson had no qualms about allowing state officials to override federal protection of Native Americans. He had long considered the federal policy of negotiating with the Indians as sovereign entities a farce. But it was awkward politically for the president to declare that he had no intention of enforcing treaty obligations of the U.S. government. The way out of this dilemma was to remove Native Americans from the center of the dispute. In his first annual message, Jackson sided with state authorities in the South and advised the Indians "to emigrate beyond the Mississippi or submit to the laws of those States." This advice enabled Jackson to pose as the friend of the Indians, the

For the Cherokees, the Trail of Tears stretched 1,200 miles from the homeland in the East to what became the Indian Territory in Oklahoma.

wise father who would lead them out of harm's way and save them from rapacious white people.

Congress acted on Jackson's recommendation in the Indian Removal Act of 1830. The act appropriated $500,000 for the negotiation of new treaties under which the southern Indians would surrender their territory and be removed to land in the trans-Mississippi area (primarily present-day Oklahoma). Although force was not authorized and Jackson stressed that removal should be voluntary, no federal protection was provided for Indians harassed into leaving by land-hungry settlers. Ultimately, Jackson did deploy the U.S. Army, but only to round up and push out Indians who refused to comply with the new removal treaties.

And so most of the Indians left the eastern United States—the Choctaws in 1830, the Creeks and Chickasaws in 1832, and the Cherokees in 1838 (see Map 10–3). The government was ill-prepared to supervise the removal. The private groups who won the federal contracts for transporting and provisioning the Indians were those who had entered the low-

est bids; they were a shady lot, interested only in a quick profit. Thousands of Indians, perhaps as many as one-fourth of those who started the trek, died on the way to Oklahoma, the victims of cold, hunger, disease, and the general callousness of the white people they met along the way. "It is impossible to conceive the frightful sufferings that attend these forced migrations," noted a Frenchman who observed the Choctaw removal. It was indeed, as recalled in the collective memory of the Cherokees, a **Trail of Tears**.

Tribes that resisted removal were attacked by white armies. Federal troops joined local militias in 1832 in suppressing the Sauk and Fox Indians of Illinois and Wisconsin in what was called **Black Hawk's War**. More a frantic attempt by the Indians to reach safety on the west bank of the Mississippi than an actual war, this affair ended in the slaughter of five hundred Indian men, women, and children by white troops and their Sioux allies. The Seminoles held out in the swamps of Florida for seven years between 1835 and 1842 in what became the longest Indian war in American history. Their resistance continued even after their leader, Osceola, was captured while negotiating under a flag of truce.

Jackson forged ahead with his removal policy despite the opposition of eastern reformers and Protestant missionaries. Aligned with conservatives concerned by Jackson's cavalier disregard of federal treaty obligations, they came within three votes of defeating the removal bill in the House of Representatives. Jackson ignored their protests (see "American Views: Memorial and Protest of the Cherokee Nation, 1836" page 306) as well as the legal rulings of the Supreme Court. In *Cherokee Nation v. Georgia* (1831) and *Worcester v. Georgia* (1832), the Court ruled that Georgia had violated the U.S. Constitution in extending its jurisdiction over the Cherokees. Chief Justice John Marshall defined Indian tribes as "dependent domestic nations" subject only to the authority of the federal government. Marshall may have won the legal argument, but he was powerless to enforce his decisions without Jackson's cooperation. Aware that southerners and westerners were on his side, Jackson ignored the Supreme Court rulings and pushed Indian removal to its tragic conclusion.

MAP 10-3 Indian Removals
The fixed policy of the Jackson administration and pressure from the states forced Native Americans in the 1830s to migrate from their eastern homelands to a special Indian reserve west of the Mississippi River

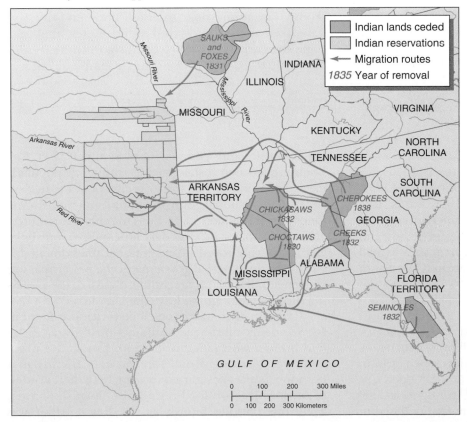

THE NULLIFICATION CRISIS

Jackson's stand on Indian removal confirmed the impression of many of his followers that when state and national power conflicted, he could be trusted to side with the states. But when states' rights forces in South Carolina, known as the nullifiers, directly challenged Jackson in the early 1830s over tariff policy—the most sensitive issue involving the power of the national government—they precipitated the nullification crisis, the most serious sectional crisis since the Missouri debates of 1819–1820. And Jackson, for all his talk of states' rights when it came to Indian policy, revealed himself to be an ardent nationalist on the issue of majority rule in the Union. He won the showdown with South Carolina and established the nationalist credentials of his Democratic party. In reaction to his strong stand, however, the solid front of Democratic power in the South began to crack.

After the first protective tariff in 1816, rates increased further in 1824 and then jumped to 50 percent in 1828 in what was denounced as the "Tariff of Abominations." Southerners were especially angry over the last tariff, because it had been contrived by northern Democrats to win additional northern support for Jackson in his presidential campaign. The outcry was loudest in South Carolina, an old cotton state losing population to the West in the 1820s as cotton prices remained low after the Panic of 1819. What fueled antitariff sentiment was not just the economic argument that high tariffs worsened the agricultural depression in the state by raising the cost of manufactured goods purchased by farmers and planters and lowering the foreign demand for agricultural exports. Protective tariffs were also denounced as an unconstitutional extension of national power over the states; many southern planters feared that they were only a prelude to forced emancipation of the slaves.

South Carolina was the only state where African Americans made up the majority of the population. Slaves were heavily concentrated in the marshes and tidal flats south of Charleston, the lowcountry district of huge rice

AMERICAN VIEWS

Memorial and Protest of the Cherokee Nation, 1836

Of the major tribes in the Southeast, the Cherokees fought longest and hardest against the Jacksonian policy of Indian removal. Led by their principal chief, John Ross, the son of a Scot and a mixed-blood Cherokee woman, they submitted the following protest to Congress against the fraudulent 1835 Treaty of New Echota forced on them by the state of Georgia. Although clearly opposed by an overwhelming majority of the Cherokees, this treaty provided the legal basis for the forced removal of the Cherokee people from Georgia to the Indian Territory.

- On what legal grounds did the Cherokees base their protest? What pledges had been made to them by the U.S. government?

- What did the Cherokees mean when they said they had been "taught to think and feel as the American citizen"? If the Cherokees had become "civilized" by white standards, why did most whites still insist on their removal?

- Why would President Jackson have allowed white intruders to remain on land reserved by treaties for the Cherokees?

- Do you feel that the Cherokees were justified in believing that they had been betrayed by the American government?

The undersigned representatives of the Cherokee nation, east of the river Mississippi, impelled by duty, would respectfully submit . . . the following statement of facts: It will be seen, from the numerous treaties between the Cherokee nation and the United States, that from the earliest existence of this government, the United States, in Congress assembled, re-

---

plantations. Here black people outnumbered white people ten to one in the summer months. Nat Turner's Rebellion, a bloody slave uprising in Virginia in 1831, and earlier aborted rebellions in the 1820s (see Chapter 11) left fearful planters convinced that growing antislavery agitation in the North and in England was feeding slave unrest. The disturbances so far would be "nothing to what we shall see," warned the South Carolina planter James Hamilton, Jr., "if we do not stand manfully at the Safety Valve of Nullification."

Led by the lowcountry planters, the antitariff forces in South Carolina controlled state politics by 1832. They called themselves the nullifiers, a name derived from the constitutional theory developed by John C. Calhoun in an anonymous tract of 1828 titled *The South Carolina Exposition and Protest.* Pushing to its logical extreme the states' rights doctrine first outlined in the Kentucky and Virginia Resolutions of 1798, Calhoun argued that a state, acting through a popularly elected convention, had the sovereign power to declare an act of the national government null and inoperative. Once a state nullified a law, it was to remain unenforceable within that state's borders unless three-fourths of all the states approved a constitutional amendment delegating to the national government the power that was challenged. If such an amendment passed, the nullifying state had the right to leave the Union.

Calhoun, who had been elected vice president in 1828, openly embraced nullification only after he had broken with Jackson in 1830. Just as the president was learning from Van Buren's friends that Calhoun, while secretary of war in 1818, had wanted to censure Jackson for his raid into Spanish Florida, a curious episode known as the Eaton Affair was ceived the Cherokees and their nation into favor and protection; and that the chiefs and warriors, for themselves and all parts of the Cherokee nation, acknowledged themselves and the said Cherokee nation to be under the protection of the United States of America, and of no other sovereign whatsoever: they also stipulated, that the said Cherokee nation will not hold any treaty with any foreign power, individual State, or with individuals of any State: that for, and in consideration of, valuable concessions made by the Cherokee nation, the United States solemnly guaranteed to said nation all their lands not ceded, and pledged the faith of the government, that "all white people who have intruded, or may hereafter intrude, on the lands reserved for the Cherokees, shall be removed by the United States, and proceeded against, according to the provisions of the act, passed 30th March, 1802," entitled "An act to regulate trade and intercourse with the Indian tribes, and to preserve peace on the frontiers." It would be useless to recapitulate the numerous provisions for the security and protection of the rights of the Cherokees, to be found in the various treaties between their nation and the United States. The Cherokees were happy and prosperous under a scrupulous observance of treaty stipulations by the government of the United States, and from the fostering hand extended over them, they made rapid advances in civilization, morals, and in the arts and sciences. Little did they anticipate, that when taught to think and feel as the American citizen, and to have with him a common interest, they were to be despoiled by their guardian, to become strangers and wanderers in the land of their fathers, forced to return to the savage life, and to seek a new home in the wilds of the far west, and that without their consent. An instrument purporting to be a treaty with the Cherokee people, has recently been made public by the President of the United States, that will have such an operation, if carried into effect. This instrument, the delegation aver before the civilized world, and in the presence of Almighty God, is fraudulent, false upon its face, made by unauthorized individuals, without the sanction, and against the wishes, of the great body of the Cherokee people. Upwards of fifteen thousand of those people have protested against it, solemnly declaring they will never acquiesce.

Source: U.S. Congress, *Executive Documents* (1836)

reaching a climax. When the wives of Jackson's cabinet members, led by Floride Calhoun, pointedly snubbed Peggy Eaton, the wife of Jackson's secretary of war, on the grounds that she was a "loose woman" who had driven her first husband to suicide, Jackson was convinced that Calhoun was plotting to discredit his administration.

The political consequences of the Eaton affair included not only Calhoun's fall from Jackson's favor but also the resignation of the entire cabinet. Much of the rancor stemmed from the belief of elite Washington women that Peggy Eaton had violated the rules of women's political behavior. Rather than exerting influence indirectly by using social gatherings to lobby on behalf of male friends, as Washington women had done since the 1790s, she seemingly sought power in her own right by appealing directly to Jackson for his support. Moreover, as the daughter of a tavernkeeper, she was overstepping her bounds by claiming political influence that Washington society felt belonged only to women of the social elite.

In addition to losing out at the national level, Calhoun also faced the danger of losing control of his political base in South Carolina. Unless he publicly identified himself with nullification, his leadership of the state would be threatened. With Calhoun's approval, a South Carolina convention in November 1832 nullified the tariffs of 1828 and 1832 (a compromise tariff that did not reduce rates to a low enough level to satisfy the nullifiers). The convention decreed that customs duties were not to be collected in South Carolina after February 1, 1833.

Calhoun always insisted that nullification was not secession. He further defended his doctrine as a constitutional means of protecting minority rights within a Union dominated by a tyrannical national majority. Jackson rejected such reasoning as the talk of a scheming disunionist. He considered nullification a dangerous and nonsensical perversion of the Constitution, and he vowed to crush any attempt to block the enforcement of federal laws. He told a congressman from South Carolina that "if a single drop of blood shall be shed there in opposition to the laws of the United States, I will hang the first man I can lay my hand on engaged in such treasonable conduct, upon the first tree I can reach."

In January 1833, Jackson, in the Force Bill, asked for and received from Congress full authorization to put down nullification by military force. Simultaneously, he worked to defuse nullification by supporting a new tariff that would cut duties by half within two years. Because Jackson's opponents in Congress did not want him to get political credit for brokering a compromise, they pushed through their own tariff measure. The Compromise Tariff of 1833 lowered duties to 20 percent but extended the reductions over a ten-year period. Up against this combination of the carrot and the stick, the nullifiers backed down.

Jackson reacted swiftly and decisively when challenged by the nullifiers. His stand established the principle of national supremacy grounded in the will of the majority. Despite his victory, however, states'-rights doctrines remained popular both in the South and among many northern Democrats. South Carolina had been isolated in its stand on nullification, but many southerners, and especially slaveholders, agreed that the powers of the national government had to be strictly limited. Their quarrel with the nullifiers was one of tactics, not of objectives. Moreover, by dramatically affirming his right to use force against a state in defense of the Union, Jackson drove many planters out of the Democratic party. In the shock waves set off by the nullification crisis, a new anti-Jackson coalition began to form in the South.

THE BANK WAR

What amounted to a war against the Bank of the United States became the centerpiece of Jackson's presidency and a defining event for the Democratic party. The Bank War erupted in 1832, when Jackson was presented with draft legislation for the early rechartering of the national bank. His thunderous veto kept banking and currency issues in the forefront of national politics for the remainder of the decade.

Like most Westerners, Jackson distrusted banks. Because gold and silver coins were scarce and the national government did not issue or regulate paper currency, money consisted primarily of notes issued as loans by private and state banks. These bank notes fluctuated in value in accordance with the reputation and creditworthiness of the issuing banks. In the credit-starved West, banks were particularly unreliable. Many were "wildcat" operations that made a quick profit by issuing notes without the gold or silver reserves to redeem them and then skipping town when they were on the verge of being found out. Even when issued by honest bankers, notes often could not be redeemed at face value because of market conditions. All of this struck many Americans, and especially farmers and workers, as inherently dishonest. They wanted to be paid in "real" money, gold or silver coin, and they viewed bankers as parasites who did nothing but fatten their own pockets by manipulating paper money.

The largest and most powerful bank was the Bank of the United States, and citizens who were wiped out or forced to retrench drastically by the Panic of 1819 never forgave the Bank for saving itself at the expense of its debtors. Still, under the astute leadership of a new president, Nicholas Biddle of Philadelphia, the Bank performed well in the 1820s. Prosperous times had returned, and the Bank underwrote the economic expansion with its healthy credit reserves and stable banknotes. By 1832, the Bank was as popular as it ever would be.

Beginning with his first annual message, Jackson had been making noise about not rechartering the Bank, at least in its present form. Searching for an issue to use against Jackson in the presidential campaign of 1832, Clay then forced Jackson's hand. Clay convinced Biddle to apply to Congress for a new charter, even though the current charter would not expire until 1836. Confident of congressional approval, Clay reasoned that he had Jackson trapped. If Jackson went along with the new charter, Clay could take credit for the measure. If he vetoed it, Clay could attack Jackson as the enemy of a sound banking system.

Clay's clever strategy backfired. Jackson turned on him and the Bank with a vengeance. As he told his heir apparent, "The bank, Mr. Van Buren, is trying to kill me, but *I will kill it!*" Jackson and his advisers realized that the Bank was vulnerable as a symbol of privileged monopoly, a monstrous institution that deprived common Americans of their right to compete equally for economic advantage. Moreover, many of these advisers were also state bankers and local developers, who backed Jackson precisely because they wanted to be free of federal restraints on their business activities. On July 10, 1832, Jackson vetoed the rechartering bill for the Bank in a message that appealed both to state bankers and to foes of all banks. He took a ringing "stand against all new grants of monopolies and exclusive privileges,

This Democratic cartoon portrays Jackson as the champion of the people attacking the Bank of the United States, a many-headed monster whose tentacles of corruption spread throughout the states.

"pet banks," state banks controlled by loyal Democrats.

Jackson won the Bank War, but he left the impression that the Democrats had played fast and loose with the nation's credit system. The economy overheated in his second term. High commodity prices and abundant credit, both at home and abroad, propelled a buying frenzy of western lands. Prices soared, and inevitably the speculative bubble had to burst. When it did, the Democrats would be open to the charge of having squandered the people's money by shifting deposits to reckless state bankers who were part of a corrupt new alliance between the government and private economic interests. Jackson was out of office when the Panic of 1837 hit; Van Buren, his successor, paid the political price for Jackson's economic policies.

against any prostitution of our Government to the advancement of the few at the expense of the many."

The business community and eastern elites lashed out at Jackson's veto as the demagogic ravings of an economic fool. For Biddle, the veto message had "all the fury of a chained panther, biting the bars of his cage." In rejecting Jackson's claims that the Bank had fostered speculative and corrupt financial practices, the pro-Bank forces had the better of the economic argument. But Jackson won the political battle, and he went to the people in the election of 1832 as their champion against the banking aristocracy. Although his support was no stronger than it had been in 1828, he easily defeated Clay, the candidate of the short-lived National Republican party that had also backed Adams in 1828.

Having blocked the rechartering of the Bank when Congress failed to override his veto, Jackson then set out to destroy it, claiming his reelection in 1832 as a mandate to do so. In Roger B. Taney he finally found a secretary of the treasury (his first two choices refused) who agreed to sign the order removing federal deposits from the Bank in 1833. Drained of its lifeblood, the deposits, the Bank was reduced by 1836 to seeking a charter as a private corporation in the state of Pennsylvania. In the meantime, the government's monies were deposited in

VAN BUREN AND HARD TIMES

Like John Adams and James Madison, Martin Van Buren followed a forceful president who commanded a strong popular following. Fairly or not, he would come out, as they did, second best compared to his predecessor. Where Jackson forged ahead regardless of consequences, Van Buren tended to hang back, carefully calculating all the political angles. This trait served him poorly as president.

Facing a sharp economic downturn, Van Buren appeared indecisive and unwilling to advance a bold program. When the rise of a radical **abolitionist movement** in the North revived sectional tensions over slavery, he awkwardly straddled the divisive issue. Van Buren's difficult position was made worse by his cautious political style. In the end, he undermined himself by failing to offer a compelling vision of his presidency.

THE PANIC OF 1837

Van Buren was barely settled into the White House when the nation was rocked by a financial panic. For over a decade, the economy had benefited from a favorable business cycle. Easy credit and the availability of territories opened up by Jackson's Indian removal policy generated a stampede to buy land in the West. Government land sales ballooned from under 4 million acres in 1833 to 20 million acres by 1836. As in 1817 and 1818, Americans piled up debt on the assumption that the good times would never end. A banking crisis in 1837 painfully reintroduced economic reality.

Even as it expanded, the American economy had remained vulnerable to disruptions in the supply of foreign capital and the sale of agricultural exports that underpinned prosperity. The key foreign nation was Britain, a major source of credit and demand for exports. In late 1836, the Bank of England tightened its credit policies. Concerned with the large outflow of specie to the United States, it raised interest rates and reduced the credit lines of British merchants heavily involved in the American trade. Consequently, the British demand for cotton fell and with it the price of cotton (see Figure 10–1). Because cotton, as the leading export, was the main security for most loans issued by American banks and mercantile firms, its drop in value set off a chain reaction of contracting credit and falling prices. When panic-stricken investors rushed to the banks to redeem their notes in specie, the hard-pressed banks suspended specie payments.

The shock waves hit New Orleans in March 1837 and spread to the major New York banks by May. What began as a bank panic soon dragged down the entire economy. Bankruptcies multiplied, investment capital dried up, and business stagnated. State governments, which had borrowed lavishly in the heady optimism of the boom years to finance canals and other internal improvements, slashed their budgets and halted all construction projects. Nine states in the South and West defaulted (stopped making payments) on their bonds. Workers in the shoe, textile, mining, and construction indus-

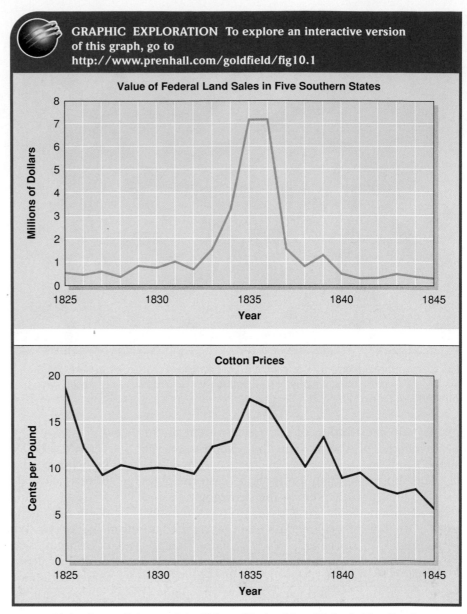

GRAPHIC EXPLORATION To explore an interactive version of this graph, go to http://www.prenhall.com/goldfield/fig10.1

FIGURE 10-1 **Cotton Prices and the Value of Federal Land Sales in Five Southern States, 1825–1845**

Because the U.S. economy was heavily dependent on cotton exports as a source of credit, the collapse of cotton prices—and a corresponding plunge in the sale of federal land after a speculative runup in the newer cotton regions of the South—triggered a financial panic in the late 1830s.

Data Source: Douglas C. North, *The Economic Growth of the United States, 1790–1860* (1966), tab. A-X, p. 257.

tries suddenly found themselves without jobs. As unemployment mounted and workers mobilized mass protest meetings in eastern cities, conservatives feared the worst. "Workmen thrown out of employ by the hundred daily," nervously noted a wealthy merchant in New York City in May 1837. He half expected that "we shall have a revolution here."

After a brief recovery in 1838, another round of credit contraction drove the economy into a depression that did not bottom out until 1843. In the manufacturing and commercial centers of the Northeast, unemployment reached an unheard-of 20 percent. The persistence of depressed agricultural prices meant that farmers and planters who had incurred debts in the 1830s faced the constant threat of losing their land or their slaves. Many fled west to avoid their creditors.

THE INDEPENDENT TREASURY

Although the Democrats bore no direct responsibility for the economic downturn, they could not avoid being blamed for it. Their political opponents, now coalescing as the **Whig party**, pointed to Jackson's destruction of the Bank of the United States, an act that, they claimed, had undermined business confidence. In their view, Jackson had then compounded his error by trying to force a hard-money policy on the state banks that had received federal deposits. The "pet banks" were required to replace small-denomination bank notes with coins or hard money. This measure, it was hoped, would protect the farmers and workers from being paid in depreciated bank notes.

Jackson had taken his boldest step against paper money when he issued the **Specie Circular** of 1836, which stipulated that large tracts of public land could be bought only with specie. Aimed at breaking the speculative spiral in land purchases, the Specie Circular is likely to have contributed to the Panic of 1837 by requiring the transfer of specie to the West for land transactions just when eastern banks were strapped for specie reserves to meet demands on their own bank notes. Bankers and speculators denounced Jackson for unwarranted government interference with the natural workings of the economy and blundering into a monetary disaster.

Conservative charges of Democratic irresponsibility were overblown, but the Democrats were caught on the horns of a dilemma. By dramatically politicizing the banking issue and removing federal monies from the national bank, the Democrats had in effect assumed the burden of protecting the people from the paper aristocrats in the banking and business commu-

Broken families and demoralized workers were among the litany of evils blamed on the Panic of 1837.

nity. Once they shifted treasury receipts to selected state banks, they had to try to regulate these banks. Otherwise they would be accused of creating a series of little "monsters" and feeding the paper speculation they so decried. But any regulatory policy contradicted the Democratic commitment to limiting governmental power. A restrictive policy, especially one aimed at replacing bank notes with specie, was bound to upset business interests and drive them out of the Democratic party. Worse yet, even the "pet banks" joined in the general suspension of specie payments when the Panic of 1837 hit. Thus the banks favored by the Democrats proved themselves unworthy of the people's trust.

The only way out of the dilemma was to make a clean break between the government and banking. Van Buren reestablished the Democrats' tarnished image as the party of limited government when he came out for the **Independent Treasury System**. Under this plan, the government would dispense with banks entirely. The Treasury would conduct its business only in gold and silver coin and would store its specie in regional vaults or subtreasuries. First proposed in 1837, the Independent Treasury System finally passed Congress in 1840 on the heels of a second wave of bank failures.

The Independent Treasury System made more political than economic sense. It restored the ideological purity of the Democrats as the friends of honest money, but it prolonged the depression. Specie locked up in government vaults was unavailable for loans in the private banking system that could have expanded the credit needed to revive the economy. The end result was to reduce the money supply and further depress prices.

UPROAR OVER SLAVERY

In 1831, William Lloyd Garrison of Boston inaugurated a radical new phase in northern attacks on slavery with the publication of his abolitionist paper *The Liberator*. The abolitionists embraced the doctrine of immediatism, an immediate moral commitment to begin the work of emancipation. Inspired by the wave of religious revivals sweeping the North in the late 1820s, they seized on slavery as the greatest sin of all. With the righteous wrath of evangelical ministers, they called on all Americans to recognize their Christian duty to end a system of human bondage that deprived the enslaved of their God-given right to be free moral beings. (For more on the abolitionists, see Chapter 11.)

The abolitionists touched off a political uproar when they launched a propaganda offensive in 1835. Taking advantage of technological improvements in the printing industry, they produced over a million pieces of antislavery literature, much of which was sent to the South through the U.S. mails. Alarmed white Southerners vilified the abolitionists as fanatics intent on enticing the slaves to revolt. Abolitionist tracts were burned, and, with the open approval of Jackson, southern postmasters violated federal law by censoring the mails to keep out antislavery materials.

Unable to receive an open hearing in the South, the abolitionists now focused on Congress. Beginning in 1836 and continuing through Van Buren's presidency, hundreds of thousands of antislavery petitions, some of them with thousands of signatures, flooded into Congress. Most of them called for the abolition of slavery in the District of Columbia. Southern congressmen responded by demanding that free speech be repressed in the name of southern white security. The enemy, they were convinced, was fanaticism, and nearly all agreed with Francis Pickens of South Carolina that they must "meet it and strangle it in its infancy." The strangling took the form of the **gag rule**, a procedural device whereby antislavery petitions were automatically tabled with no discussion.

The gag rule first passed in 1836 and was renewed in a series of raucous debates through 1844. Only the votes of some three-fourths of the northern Democrats enabled the southern minority to have its way. With Van Buren's reluctant support, the gag rule became a Democratic party measure, and it identified the Democrats as a prosouthern party in the minds of many Northerners. Ironically, while Van Buren was attacked in the North as a lackey of the slave interests, he was damned in the South, if only because he was a nonslaveholder from the North, as being unsafe on the slavery issue. In short, tensions over slavery and the economy seemingly doomed Van Buren to be cast as a vacillating president fully trusted by neither section.

THE RISE OF THE WHIG PARTY

The early opponents of the Democrats were known as the National Republicans, a label that captured the nationalist vision of former Jeffersonian Republicans who adhered to the economic program of Henry Clay and John Quincy Adams. The Bank War and Jackson's reaction to nullification shook loose pro-Bank Democrats and many southern states' righters from the original Jacksonian coalition, and these groups joined the opposition to Jackson. By 1834, the anti-Jacksonians started to call themselves Whigs, a name associated with the eighteenth-century American and

British opponents of monarchical tyranny. The name stuck because of the party's constant depiction of Jackson as King Andrew, an executive tyrant who ran roughshod over congressional prerogatives and constitutional liberties.

By 1840, the Whigs had mastered the techniques of political organization and mobilization pioneered by the Democrats in the late 1820s. They ran William Henry Harrison, their own version of a military hero, and swept to victory. The **second party system** of intense national competition between Whigs and Democrats was now in place (see the Overview table, "The Second Party System"). It would dominate politics until the rise of the antislavery Republican party in the 1850s.

THE PARTY TAKING SHAPE

The Whig party was born in the congressional reaction to Jackson's Bank veto and his subsequent attacks on the national bank. Led by the unlikely trio of Henry Clay and Daniel Webster, nationalists from the West and New England, and John C. Calhoun, a states' righter from the South, the congressional opposition accused Jackson of demagogic appeals to the poor against the rich. What upset them, apart from the specific content of Jackson's policies, was how he enforced his will. Jackson wielded his executive power like a bludgeon. Whereas all earlier presidents together had used the veto only ten times, Jackson did so a dozen times. He openly defied the Supreme Court and Congress, be it on Indian or banking policy, and unlike any of his predecessors, he took each case directly to the people. It seemed to his opponents that Jackson was threatening to undermine the constitutional system of checks and balances and bypass the established leadership of public-spirited gentlemen who had hitherto ruled on behalf of the people.

Local and state coalitions of the Whigs sent an anti-Jackson majority to the House of Representatives in 1835. The most powerful of these coalitions was in New York, where a third party, the **Anti-Masons**, joined the Whigs. The party had originated in western New York in the late 1820s as a grassroots response to the sudden disappearance and presumed murder of William Morgan, an itinerant artisan who threatened to expose the secrets of the Order of Freemasons. An all-male order steeped in ritual and ceremony, the Masons united urban and small-town elites into a tightly knit brotherhood through personal contacts and mutual aid. When efforts to investigate Morgan's disappearance ran into a legal dead end, rumors spread that the Masons constituted a vast conspiracy that conferred special privileges and legal protection on its exclusive members. To combat this "monster," farmers and townspeople flocked to the new Anti-Masonic party. They sought, in the words of an 1831 Anti-Masonic address, "equal rights and equal privileges among the freemen of the country."

Western New York, an area of religious fervor and rapid economic change after the opening of the Erie Canal in 1825, provided fertile ground for the growth of the new party. With close ties to rural landlords and town creditors, the Masons were vulnerable to the charge of economic favoritism. In addition, evangelicals accused the Masons of desecrating the Christian faith with their secret rituals. The Anti-Masons were thus the first party to combine demands for equal opportunity with calls for the moral reform of a sinful society.

Overview

The Second Party System

	Democrats	Whigs
Ideology	Favor limited role of federal government in economic affairs and in matters of individual conscience; support territorial expansion	Favor government support for economic development and controls over individual morality; opposed to expansion
Voter support	Mainly subsistence farmers, unskilled workers, and Catholic immigrants	Mainly manufacturers, commercial farmers, skilled workers, and northern evangelicals
Regional strength	South and West	New England and Upper Midwest

Although it spread into New England and the neighboring mid-Atlantic states, the Anti-Mason party was unable to sustain itself. Its presidential candidate in 1832, William Wirt of Maryland, won only Vermont. Recognizing that the opponents of the Anti-Masons were usually the entrenched local interests of the Democratic party, shrewd politicians, led by Thurlow Weed and William Seward of New York, took up the movement and absorbed most of it into the anti-Jackson coalition. They thus broadened the Whigs' mass base and added an egalitarian message to their appeal.

By 1836, the Whigs were strong enough to mount a serious challenge for the presidency. However, they still lacked an effective national organization that could unite their regional coalitions behind one candidate. They ran three candidates—Daniel Webster of Massachusetts, William Henry Harrison of Ohio, and Hugh Lawson White of Tennessee—and some Whigs hoped that the regional popularity of these candidates would siphon off enough votes from Van Buren to throw the election into the House of Representatives. The strategy, if such it can be called, failed. Van Buren won an electoral majority by holding on to the populous mid-Atlantic states and improving on Jackson's showing in New England. Still, the Whigs were encouraged by the results. Compared to Jackson, Van Buren did poorly in what had been the overwhelmingly Democratic South. He lost Tennessee and Georgia and barely carried the popular vote elsewhere. The South was now open to further Whig inroads.

WHIG PERSUASION

The Whigs, like the Democrats, based their mass appeal on the claim that they could best defend the republican liberties of the people. Whereas the Democrats attributed the threat to those liberties to privileged monopolies of government-granted power, the Whigs found it in the expansive powers of the presidency as wielded by Jackson and in the party organization that put Jackson and Van Buren into office. In 1836, the Whigs called for the election of "a president of the nation, not a president of party." Underlying this call was the persistent Whig belief that parties undermined individual liberties and the public good by fostering and rewarding the selfish interests of the party faithful. Although the Whigs dropped much of this ideology when they themselves matured as a party, they never lost their fear of the presidency as an office of unchecked, demagogic power. They always insisted that Congress should be the locus of power in the federal system.

If the Whigs were more reluctant than the Democrats to accept political change in the form of mass-based parties, they were quicker to embrace economic change in the form of banks and manufacturing corporations. Most Whigs viewed governmental power as a positive force to promote economic development. They favored encouraging the spread of banking and paper money, chartering corporations, passing protective tariffs to support American manufacturers, and opening up new markets for farmers through government-subsidized transportation projects. Such policies, they held, would widen economic opportunities for more and more Americans and provide positive incentives for material self-improvement.

The Whigs' economic program appealed mostly to Americans who were benefiting from economic change or expecting to do so. They drew heavily from commercial and planting interests in the South. They were also the party of bankers, manufacturers, small-town entrepreneurs, farmers prospering from the market outlets of canals and railroads, and skilled workers who valued a high tariff as protection from the competition of goods produced by cheap foreign labor. These Whig groups also tended to be native-born Protestants of New England or Yankee ancestry, particularly those caught up in the religious revivals of the 1820s and 1830s. The strongest Whig constituencies comprised an arc of Yankee settlements stretching from rural New England through central New York and around the southern shores of the Great Lakes.

Whether as economic promoters or evangelical reformers, Whigs believed in promoting social progress and harmony through an interventionist government. The Whigs favored such social reforms as prohibiting the consumption of alcohol; preserving the sanctity of the Protestant Sabbath through bans on business activities on Sundays; caring for orphans, the physically handicapped, and the mentally ill in state-run asylums and hospitals; and teaching virtuous behavior and basic knowledge through a centralized system of public education. Whig ideology blended economic, social, and spiritual reform into a unified message of uplift. An activist government would provide the economic opportunities and moral guidance for a harmonious, progressive society of freely competing individuals whose behavior would be shaped by the evangelical norms of thrift, sobriety, and self-discipline.

Much of the Whigs' reform impulse was directed against non-English and Catholic immigrants, those Americans whom the Whigs believed most needed to be taught the virtues of self-control and disciplined work habits. Not coincidentally, these groups—the Scots-Irish in the backcountry, the Reformed Dutch,

This cotton banner used by the Whigs in the campaign of 1840 celebrated their ticket as the friends of common Americans who had been raised in a log cabin.

and Irish and German Catholics—were the most loyal Democrats. They resented the aggressive moralism of the Whigs and the legislative attempts to interfere with their drinking habits and Sunday amusements. These Democrats were typically subsistence farmers on the periphery of market change and unskilled workers forced by industrial change to abandon their hopes of ever opening their own shops. They equated an activist government with special privileges for the economically and culturally powerful and identified with the Democrats' demand for keeping the government out of the economy and individual religious practices.

THE ELECTION OF 1840

One of the signs of the Whigs' maturing as a party was their decision in 1840 to place victory above principle. Because of the lingering economic depression, Democratic rule had been discredited for many voters. Aside from the Independent Treasury Act and legislation establishing a ten-hour workday for federal employees, the Van Buren administration had no program to combat the Whig charge of helplessness in the face of economic adversity. Henry Clay, who promised that his American System would revive the economy with government aid, appeared the most

likely Whig candidate for president against Van Buren in 1840. Yet the power brokers in the party dumped Clay, who represented the ideological heart of the party, for their version of a popular military hero, William Henry Harrison of Ohio.

Harrison had run surprisingly well as one of the Whigs' regional candidates in 1836 and had revealed a common touch with the voters that the Whigs generally lacked. Unlike Clay, he was untainted by any association with the Bank of the United States, the Masonic Order, or slaveholding. As the victor at the Battle of Tippecanoe and a military hero in the War of 1812, he enabled Whig image makers to cast him, like Jackson, as the honest, patriotic soldier worthy of the people's trust. In a decision that came back to haunt them, the Whigs geographically balanced their ticket by selecting John Tyler, a planter from Virginia, as Harrison's running mate. Tyler was an advocate of states' rights and a former Democrat who had broken with Jackson over the Force Bill.

The Democrats inadvertently gave the Whig campaign a tremendous boost. A Democratic editor wisecracked that "Old Granny" Harrison (he was 67) was such a simpleton that he would like nothing better than to retire to a log cabin with a government pension and a barrel of hard cider. Pouncing on this sneer, the Whigs created a Harrison who never was— a yeoman farmer of humble origins and homespun tastes, whose rise to prominence was a democratic model of success for other Americans to follow. Thus Harrison, who was descended from the Virginia slaveholding aristocracy, became a symbol of the common man, and the Whigs were finally able to shed their aristocratic image. Indeed, they pinned the label of the dandified and elitist aristocrat on Van Buren. "Martin Van Ruin," as effectively portrayed by the Whigs, squandered public revenue on effete luxuries and was concerned only with the spoils of office.

The Whigs beat the Democrats at their own game of mass politics in 1840. They reversed the roles and symbolism of the Jackson–Adams election of 1828 and seized the high ground as the party of the people. In a further adaptation of earlier Democratic initiatives, the Whigs put together a frolicking campaign of slogans, parades, and pageantry. Politics became a carnival in which voters were shamelessly wooed with food, drink, and music in huge rallies complete with live animals and gigantic buckskin balls that were triumphantly rolled from one rally to another. Clay muttered with some disgust that he regretted the need "of appealing to the feelings and passions of our Countrymen, rather than to their reasons and their judgments." Nonetheless, such hoopla was now essential for electoral victory.

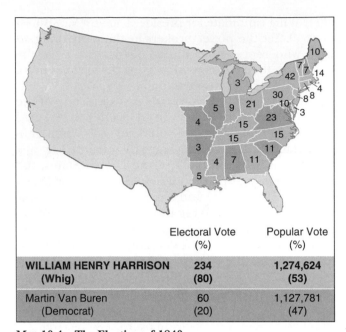

	Electoral Vote (%)	Popular Vote (%)
WILLIAM HENRY HARRISON (Whig)	**234 (80)**	**1,274,624 (53)**
Martin Van Buren (Democrat)	60 (20)	1,127,781 (47)

MAP 10-4   The Election of 1840
Building upon their strength in the commercializing North, the Whigs attracted enough rural voters in the South and West to win the election of 1840.

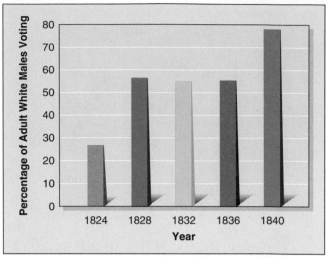

FIGURE 10-2   Voter Turnout in Presidential Elections, 1824–1840
The creation of mass-based political parties dramatically increased voter turnout in presidential elections. Voting surged in 1828 with the emergence of the Jacksonian Democratic Party and again in 1840 when the Whig Party learned to appeal to the mass electorate.

Data Source: Richard P. McCormick, "New Perspectives on Jacksonian Politics" in *The Nature of Jacksonian America*, ed. Douglas T. Miller (1972), p. 103.

The Whigs gained control of both Congress and the presidency in 1840. Harrison won 53 percent of the popular vote, and for the first time the Whigs carried the South (see Map 10–4). With the arrival of politics as mass spectacle, the turnout surged to an unprecedented 78 percent of eligible voters, a whopping increase over the average of 55 percent in the three preceding presidential elections (see Figure 10–2). The Whigs claimed most of the new voters and were now fully competitive with the Democrats in all parts of the nation. As the new majority party, they finally had the opportunity, or so they thought, to implement their economic program.

THE WHIGS IN POWER

Although the Whigs had been noncommittal on their plans during the campaign of 1840, it was common knowledge that Clay would move quickly on Whig economic policies by marshaling his forces in Congress and trying to dominate a pliant Harrison. But Harrison died from pneumonia in April 1841, barely a month after his inauguration, ruining Clay's plans. Tyler, Harrison's successor, was a particularly rigid states'-rights ideologue, who betrayed party expectations by blocking key pieces of Clay's program. The Whigs reacted by reading Tyler out of the party.

In 1843, Tyler latched on to the annexation of the slaveholding Republic of Texas as an issue that might get him back into the good graces of the Democratic party and establish his own successful record as president. At the end of his administration, Tyler did succeed in securing the annexation of Texas, but his main accomplishment was to shift the focus of national politics from economic issues to sectional ones of territorial expansion. Running on an expansionist platform, the Democrats regained the presidency in 1844.

HARRISON AND TYLER

Perhaps the Democrats had been right that Harrison was too old for the demands of the presidency. He fumed that "I am bothered almost to death with visitors. I have not time to attend to my person, not even to change my shirt, much less to attend to the public business." Still, for all his grumblings, he was the type of president the Whigs wanted. He had pledged to follow the dictates of party leaders in Congress and defer to the judgment of his cabinet. Bowing to Clay's demands, he agreed to call Congress into special session to act on Whig party measures. Thus his death was a real blow to Whig hopes of establishing the credibility of their party as an effective agent for positive change.

Just how serious that blow was soon became apparent when Tyler became president, the first vice president to succeed on the death of a president. Tyler was cut from quite different cloth from Harrison. This stiff, unbending planter subscribed to a states'-rights agrarian philosophy that put him at odds with the urban and commercial elements of the Whig party even in his home state of Virginia. Clay's economic nationalism struck him as a program of rank corruption that surrendered the constitutional rights of the South to power-hungry politicians and manufacturers in the North. Clay refused to cultivate Tyler's prickly pride with soothing gestures, and he forged ahead with the party agenda—the repeal of the Independent Treasury System and its replacement by a new national bank, a protective tariff, and the distribution of the proceeds of the government's public land sales to the states as funds for internal improvements.

A Democratic observer predicted in mid-May 1841 that "the Whigs will be very much disappointed by the course which the President will feel himself constitutionally bound to pursue." Tyler used the negative power of presidential vetoes to stymie the Whig program. He twice vetoed bills to reestablish a national bank. The second veto led to the resignation of the cabinet he had inherited from Harrison, save for Secretary of State Daniel Webster, who was in the midst of negotiations with the British. Enraged congressional Whigs then expelled Tyler from the party.

A now desperate Clay sought to salvage what was left of his American System. He lined up southern votes for the distribution of federal funds to the states by agreeing to a ceiling of 20 percent on tariff rates. Westerners were won over by Clay's support for the Preemption Act of 1841, a measure that allowed squatters to purchase up to 160 acres of public land at the minimum government price of $1.25 per acre. This act was popular in the West because squatters no longer had to match the bids of speculators at government land sales.

Clay's legislative wizardry got him nowhere. When the Whigs passed a higher tariff in 1842 with a provision for distribution, Tyler vetoed it and forced them to settle for a protective tariff with no distribution. In the end, Clay had no national bank, no funds for internal improvements, and only a slightly higher tariff. Although Clay's leadership of the Whigs was strengthened, Tyler had deprived that leadership of meaning by denying the Whigs the legislative fruits of their victory in 1840.

THE TEXAS ISSUE

Constrained by his states'-rights view to a largely negative role in domestic policy, Tyler was a much more forceful president in foreign policy, an area in which the Constitution gives the chief executive considerable latitude. In 1842, Tyler's secretary of state, Daniel Webster, wrapped up his negotiations with the British over a long-standing boundary dispute. The **Webster–Ashburton Treaty** of that year established the boundary between British Canada and Maine and parts of the Upper Midwest. An agreement was also reached to cooperate in suppressing the African slave trade. Webster now resigned from the cabinet to join his fellow Whigs, allowing Tyler to follow a pro-southern policy of expansion that he hoped would gain him the Democratic nomination for the presidency in 1844. His goal was the annexation of Texas.

Texas had been a slaveholding republic since 1836, when rebellious Americans, joined by some tejanos (Texans of Mexican descent), declared their independence from Mexico. Jackson extended diplomatic recognition before leaving office, but he refused the new nation's request to be annexed to the United States out of fear of provoking a war with Mexico, which did not recognize Texan independence. But he was also aware that the addition of Texas, a potentially huge area for the expansion of plantation slavery, would inflame sectional tensions and endanger Van Buren's chances in the upcoming presidential election. In private, however, he urged Texans to seize harbors on the Pacific Coast from Mexican control and thus make annexation more attractive to the commercial interests of the Northeast.

For the sake of sectional harmony, party leaders sidestepped the Texas issue after 1836. Spurned by the Whigs and anxious to return to the Democrats, Tyler renewed the issue in 1843 to curry favor among southern and western Democrats. He replaced Webster as secretary of state with a proannexationist Virginian, Abel P. Upshur, and secretly opened negotiations with the Texans. After Upshur's death in an accidental explosion on the battleship *Princeton,* John C. Calhoun, his successor, completed the negotiations and dramatically politicized the slavery issue. In the spring of 1844, Calhoun and Tyler submitted to the Senate a secretly drawn up treaty annexing Texas to the United States. Calhoun also made public his correspondence with Richard Pakenham, the British minister in Washington. In his letter, Calhoun accused the British of seeking to force emancipation on Texas in return for economic aid and a British-brokered Mexican recognition of Texan independence. These British efforts, warned Calhoun, were just the opening wedge in a master plan to block American expansion and destroy slavery in the South. After pointedly defending slavery as a benign institution, Calhoun concluded that the security and preservation of the Union demanded the annexation of Texas.

The Pakenham letter hit the Senate like a bombshell, convincing antislavery Northerners that the annexation of Texas was a slaveholders' conspiracy to extend slavery and swell the political power of the South. In June 1844, the Senate rejected Calhoun's treaty of annexation by a two-to-one margin. All but one Whig senator voted against it. Still, the issue was hardly dead. Thanks to Tyler and Calhoun, Texas dominated the election of 1844.

THE ELECTION OF 1844

The Whig and Democratic National Conventions met in the spring of 1844 in the midst of the uproar over Texas. Both Clay, who had the Whig nomination locked up, and Van Buren, who was the strong favorite for the Democratic one, came out against immediate annexation. Clay's stand was consistent with Whig fears that territorial expansion would disrupt the party's plans for ordered economic development. But Van Buren's anti-Texas stand cost him his party's nomination. In a carefully devised strategy, western and southern Democrats united to deny him the necessary two-thirds vote of convention delegates. A deadlocked convention turned to James K. Polk of Tennessee, a confirmed expansionist who had the blessing of Jackson, the party's patriarch.

To counter the charge that they were a pro-southern party, the Democrats ran in 1844 on a platform that linked Oregon to Texas as territorial objectives. Oregon had first attracted public attention during the Tyler presidency. Glowing reports from Protestant missionaries of the boundless fertility of Oregon's Willamette Valley triggered a migration to the new promised land on the shores of the Pacific by midwestern farm families still reeling from the Panic of 1837. At the same time, the report of a naval expedition sent to explore the Pacific aroused the interest of New England merchants in using Oregon as a jumping-off point for expanded trade with China.

Some six thousand Americans were in Oregon by the mid-1840s, and demands mounted, especially from northern Democrats, that the United States abandon its 1818 agreement of joint occupation with the British and lay exclusive claim to Oregon as far north as the 54°40' parallel, the border with Russian-owned Alaska. These were bold, even reckless, demands, because the actual area of American settlement in Oregon was south of the Columbia River, itself well south of even the 49th parallel. Nonetheless, the Polk Democrats seemed to endorse them when they asserted an American claim "to the whole of the Territory of Oregon."

Polk's expansionist program united the Democrats and enabled them to campaign with much more enthusiasm than in 1840. Acquiring Texas and Oregon not only held out the economic hope of cheap, abundant land to debt-burdened farmers in the North and planters in the South but also played on the anti-British sentiments of many voters. In contrast, the Whig campaign was out of focus. Clay sensed that his opposition to the immediate annexation of Texas was hurting him in the South, and he started to hedge by saying that he would accept Texas if the conditions were right. This wavering, however, failed to stem the defection of proslavery southern Whigs to the Democrats and cut into his support among antislavery Whigs in the North. Clay lost to Polk by less than 2 percent of the popular vote.

Tyler claimed Polk's victory as a mandate for the immediate annexation of Texas. He knew that it would still be impossible to gain the two-thirds majority in the Senate necessary for the approval of a treaty. Thus he resorted to the constitutionally unprecedented expedient of a joint resolution in Congress inviting Texas to join the Union. By the narrow margin of twenty-seven to twenty-five, the Senate concurred with the House in favor of annexation. Tyler signed the joint resolution on March 1, 1845.

Although Tyler had failed to secure the Democratic nomination in 1844, he had gained Texas. He also had the satisfaction of getting revenge against the Whigs, the party that had disowned him. Texas, more than any other issue, defeated Clay and the Whigs in 1844.

CONCLUSION

The Jacksonian era ushered in a revolution in American political life. Responding to a surge of democratization that was in full swing by the 1820s, politicians learned how to appeal to a mass electorate and to build disciplined parties that channeled popular desires into distinctive party positions. In the two decades after 1824, voter participation in national elections tripled, and Democrats and Whigs competed on nearly equal terms in every region.

Although the origins of a national political culture can be traced back to the Federalists and Jeffersonian Republicans, politics did not fully enter the mainstream of American life until the rise of the second party system of Democrats and Whigs. The election of 1824 revived interest in presidential politics, and Jackson's forceful style of leadership highlighted the presidency as the focal point of American politics. Professional politicians soon mastered the art of tailoring issues and images to reach the widest popular audience. Voters in favor of government aid for economic development and a social order based on Protestant moral controls turned to the Whigs' program of economic and moral activism. Conversely, those who saw an activist government as a threat to their economic and cultural equality turned to the Democrats.

The national issues around which the Democrats and Whigs organized and battled down to 1844 were primarily economic. As long as this was the case, party competition tended to diffuse sectional tensions and strengthen a national political culture. Slavery, in the form of the Texas question, replaced the economy as the decisive issue in the election of 1844. With this shift, party appeals began to focus on the place of slavery in American society, creating an escalating politics of sectionalism. Within a decade, the slavery issue would rip apart the second party system.

REVIEW QUESTIONS

1. Explain the democratic movements of the early nineteenth century. What role did race and gender play in these movements?

2. What distinguished Jackson's presidency from those of his predecessors? How did he redefine the role of the president?

3. How was the Bank War central to the development of the Democratic and Whig parties? Why did the political debates of the 1830s focus on financial issues?

4. In terms of ideology and voter appeal, how did the Democrats and Whigs differ? How did each party represent a distinctive response to economic and social change?

5. How would you describe the changes in American politics between 1824 and 1840? What accounted for these changes?

6. How did the annexation of Texas emerge as a political issue in the early 1840s? Why were the Democrats more in favor of territorial expansion than the Whigs?

7. What do you think accounted for the sense of shock, even outrage, with which Benjamin Brown French reacted to the partisanship of the election of 1828?

KEY TERMS

Abolitionist movement (p. 309)

Albany Regency (p. 300)

Anti-Masons (p. 313)

Bank War (p. 301)

Black Hawk's War (p. 304)

Democratic Party (p. 299)

Gag rule (p. 312)

Independent Treasury System (p. 312)

Indian Removal Act (p. 303)

Jacksonian Democrats (p. 295)

Nullification crisis (p. 301)

Second Great Awakening (p. 297)

Second party system (p. 313)

Specie Circular (p. 311)

Spoils system (p. 302)

Trail of Tears (p. 304)

Webster-Ashburton Treaty (p. 317)

Whig party (p. 311)

RECOMMENDED READING

Altschuler, Glenn C., and Stuart M. Blumin. *Rude Republic: Americans and their Politics in the Nineteenth Century* (2000). A recent work that argues that historians have exaggerated the extent of popular involvement in the party politics of the nineteenth century.

Cole, Donald B. *The Presidency of Andrew Jackson* (1993). A revisionist look at Jackson's presidency that argues that he was an uncertain leader who failed in his efforts to resist the spread of the market revolution that was transforming America.

Feller, Daniel. *The Jacksonian Promise: America, 1815–1840* (1995). An up-to-date survey that emphasizes the optimism and innovation of the Jacksonian era.

Meyers, Marvin. *The Jacksonian Persuasion* (1960). A gracefully written work that explores the beliefs of the Jacksonians and concludes that their agrarian values made them fearful of economic change.

Pessen, Edward. *Jacksonian America* (1985). A revisionist work that argues that Democrats and Whigs, for all their talk of democratic change, were driven primarily by the goal of acquiring office as an end in itself.

Remini, Robert V. *The Life of Andrew Jackson* (1988). A lively account of Jackson's career, written by his most noted biographer.

Schlesinger, Arthur Jr. *The Age of Jackson* (1945). Remains the enduring statement of the democratic impulse behind the Jackson movement.

Sellers, Charles. *The Market Revolution: Jacksonian America, 1815–1846* (1991). A boldly conceived work that places responses to market change at the center of the era's political development.

de Tocqueville, Alexis. *Democracy in America*, ed. Phillips Bradley, 2 vols. (1945). An often quoted classic, still popular for its firsthand depiction of Jacksonian society and institutions.

Varon, Elizabeth R. *We Mean To Be Counted: White Women and Politics in Antebellum Virginia* (1998). A recent work that reveals the surprising extent to which elite white women in Virginia engaged in partisan politics.

Watson, Harry. *Liberty and Power: The Politics of Jacksonian America* (1990). A very readable and concise synthesis of Jacksonian politics.

ADDITIONAL SOURCES
The Egalitarian Impulse
Butler, Jon. *Awash in a Sea of Faith: Christianizing the American People* (1990).

Hargreaves, Mary W. M. *The Presidency of John Quincy Adams* (1985).

Hatch, Nathan O. *The Democratization of American Christianity* (1989).

Peterson, Merrill D., ed. *Democracy, Liberty, and Property: The State Constitutional Conventions of the 1820s* (1966).

Williamson, Chilton. *American Suffrage from Property to Democracy, 1760–1860* (1960).

Jackson's Presidency
Debo, Angie. *And Still the Waters Run: The Betrayal of the Five Civilized Tribes* (1940; reprint, 1972).

Ellis, Richard E. *The Union at Risk: Jacksonian Democracy, States' Rights, and the Nullification Crisis* (1987).

Freehling, William W. *Prelude to Civil War: The Nullification Controversy in South Carolina, 1816–1836* (1966).

Remini, Robert V. *Andrew Jackson and the Bank War* (1967).

Rogin, Michael Paul. *Fathers and Children: Andrew Jackson and the Subjugation of the American Indian* (1975).

Ward, John William. *Andrew Jackson: Symbol for an Age* (1955).

Van Buren and Hard Times
McFaul, John M. *The Politics of Jacksonian Finance* (1972).

McGrane, Reginald Charles. *The Panic of 1837* (1924).

Sharp, Roger. *The Jacksonians versus the Banks: Politics in the States after the Panic of 1837* (1970).

Temin, Peter. *The Jacksonian Economy* (1969).

Wilson, Major L. *The Presidency of Martin Van Buren* (1984).

The Rise of the Whig Party
Ashworth, John. *"Agrarians" and "Aristocrats": Party Political Ideology in the United States, 1837–1846* (1983).

Howe, Daniel Walker. *The Political Culture of the American Whigs* (1979).

Kohl, Lawrence Frederick. *The Politics of Individualism: Parties and the American Character in the Jacksonian Era* (1989).

McCormick, Richard P. *The Second American Party System* (1966).

Peterson, Merrill. *The Great Triumvirate: Webster, Clay, and Calhoun* (1987).

The Whigs in Power
Brock, William R. *Parties and Political Conscience* (1979).

Holt, Michael F. *The Rise and Fall of the American Whig Party* (1999).

Merk, Frederick. *Slavery and the Annexation of Texas* (1972).

Peterson, Norma Louis. *The Presidencies of William Henry Harrison and John Tyler* (1990).

Remini, Robert V. *Henry Clay: Statesman for the Union* (1991).

WHERE TO LEARN MORE
- Rice Museum, Georgetown, South Carolina. Rice planters were the leaders of the nullification movement, and the interpretive materials here on the history of rice cultivation help one understand how slave labor was employed to produce their great wealth. Maps to the museum and news of special events can be found at www.ricemuseum.com/.

- The Hermitage, Hermitage, Tennessee. This site, the plantation home of Andrew Jackson, includes a museum with artifacts of Jackson's life. Its website www.thehermitage.com/ lists events and programs and examines the archeological projects undertaken at the Hermitage.

- Martin Van Buren National Historic Site, Kinderhook, New York. The site preserves Lindenwald, Van Buren's home after he left the presidency, and includes a library with materials on Van Buren and his political era. Its recently expanded website www.nps.gov/mava/home.htm discusses the history of Lindenwald and includes a virtual tour of its art collection.

 Please refer to the document CD-ROM for primary sources related to this chapter.

➔ *The spectacle of the slave market was commonplace in the cities of the antebellum South. The above scene is of a slave auction in Richmond, Virginia.*

SLAVERY AND THE OLD SOUTH
1800–1860

11

CHAPTER OUTLINE

The Lower South
Cotton and Slaves
The Profits of Slavery

The Upper South
A Period of Economic Adjustment
The Decline of Slavery

Slave Life and Culture
Work Routines and Living Conditions
Families and Religion
Resistance

Free Society
The Slaveholding Minority
The White Majority
Free Black People

The Proslavery Argument

Conclusion

Had Mrs Wheeler condemned me to the severest corporal punishment, or exposed me to be sold in the public slave market in Wilmington[N.C.]I should probably have resigned myself with apparent composure to her cruel behests. But when she sought to force me into a compulsory union with a man whom I could only hate and despise it seemed that rebellion would be a virtue, that duty to myself and my God actually required it, and that whatever accidents or misfortunes might attend my flight nothing could be worse than what threatened my stay.

Marriage like many other blessings I considered to be especially designed for the free, and something that all the victims of slavery should avoid as tending essentially to perpetuate that system. Hence to all overtures of that kind from whatever quarter they might come I had invariably turned a deaf ear. I had spurned domestic ties not because my heart was hard, but because it was my unalterable resolution never to entail slavery on any human being. And now when I had voluntarily renounced the society of those I might have learned to love should I be compelled to accept one, whose person, and speech, and manner could not fail to be ever regarded by me with loathing and disgust. Then to be driven in to the fields beneath the eye and lash of the brutal overseer, and those miserable huts, with their promiscuous crowds of dirty, obscene and degraded objects, for my home I could not, I would not bear it.

Hannah Crafts

Henry Louis Gates, Jr., ed., *The Bondwoman's Narrative* (New York: Warner Books, 2002), pp. 206–207.

Hannah Crafts was the name adopted by an African American woman after escaping from slavery in the late 1850s. This passage is from *The Bondwoman's Narrative,* a recently discovered manuscript that stands as the only known novel written by a female black slave. Although the precise identity of Crafts remains uncertain, the evidence strongly suggests that she was a house slave of John Hill Wheeler of North Carolina who fled north in the spring of 1857, married a Methodist clergyman, and merged into the black middle class of southern New Jersey. As a fugitive slave in the North, Crafts risked recapture at any time prior to the outbreak of the Civil War. Her decision not to publish her autobiographical slave narrative might well have been based on the fear that the intimate details she included on the Wheeler family would reveal her whereabouts to an owner intent on reclaiming her. Among the other details in the novel are the searingly candid observations on the brutalized living conditions that field slaves were forced to endure.

Knowing from firsthand experience that masters frequently violated the sanctity of slave marriages and, under the law, could keep any resulting children as slaves, she believed that all slaves should remain celibate: "plain, practical common sense must teach every observer that any situation involving such responsibilities as marriage can only be filled with profit, and honor, and advantage by the free." Triggering her decision to flee was Mrs. Wheeler's demand that she "marry" the field hand Bill—that is, submit to being raped by a man she despised and to living in the squalor of the huts in the slave quarter.

The system of slavery that Crafts described with revulsion increasingly defined the South as a distinctive region in the antebellum United States. Indeed, only the widespread presence of slaves makes it possible to speak of the South as a single region despite its geographical and cultural diversity. It was black slavery that created a bond among white Southerners and cast them in a common mold.

Not only did slavery make the South distinctive, it was also the source of the region's immense agricultural wealth, the foundation on which planters built their fortunes, the basis for white upward mobility, and the means by which white people controlled a large black minority. Slavery also frightened white Southerners with a vision of what might happen to them should they not protect their own personal liberties, including, paradoxically, the liberty to enslave African Americans. Southern white men were thus quick to take offense at any challenge to their honor or independence. A code of honor for planters demanded an apology or vindication in a duel for any insult, whether real or perceived. Precisely because slavery was so deeply embedded in southern life and customs, white leadership reacted to mounting attacks on slavery after 1830 with an ever more defiant defense of the institution. That defense, in turn, reinforced a growing sense of sectionalism among white Southerners, the belief that their values divided them from their fellow citizens in the Union.

Economically and intellectually, the Old South developed in stages. The South of 1860 was geographically much larger and more diverse than it had been in 1800, but it was also more uniformly committed to a single cash crop, cotton. Demand for cotton had exploded as the industrial revolution made the mass production of textiles possible. New England mill owners were now as dependent on slavery as southern planters were. Cotton became king, as contemporaries put it, and it provided the economic basis for southern sectionalism. During the reign of King Cotton, however, regional differences emerged between the Lower South, where the linkage between cotton and slavery was strong, and the Upper South, where slavery was relatively less important and the economy was more diversified.

KEY TOPICS

- How the increasing demand for cotton made slavery highly profitable in the Lower South
- The decline of slavery after 1800 in the increasingly diversified economy of the Upper South
- Slave culture and slave resistance
- The divisions of free white society
- The southern defense of slavery in response to increasing attacks from northern abolitionists

Chronology

1790s	Large-scale conversions of slaves to Christianity begin.
1793	Eli Whitney patents the cotton gin.
1800	Gabriel Prosser leads a rebellion in Richmond, Virginia.
1808	Congress prohibits the African slave trade.
1811	Slaves rebel in Louisiana.
1816–1819	First cotton boom in the South.
1822	Denmark Vesey's Conspiracy fails in Charleston, South Carolina.
1831	Nat Turner leads a rebellion in Southampton County, Virginia.

1831–1832	Virginia legislature debates and rejects gradual emancipation.
1832	Thomas R. Dew publishes the first full-scale defense of slavery.
1837–1845	Slavery issue divides Presbyterians, Methodists, and Baptists into separate sectional churches.
1845	Florida and Texas, the last two slave states, are admitted to the Union.
1850s	Cotton production doubles.
1857	Hinton R. Helper publishes *The Impending Crisis of the South.*

THE LOWER SOUTH

South and west of South Carolina in 1800 stretched some of the best cotton land in the world. A long growing season, adequate rainfall, navigable rivers, and untapped fertility gave the Lower South—consisting, in 1850, of South Carolina, Georgia, Florida, Alabama, Mississippi, Louisiana, and Texas—incomparable natural advantages for growing cotton. Ambitious white Southerners exploited these advantages by extending slavery after 1800 to the newer cotton lands that opened up in the Lower South (see Map 11–1). Cotton production and slavery thus went hand in hand.

COTTON AND SLAVES

Before 1800, slavery was associated with the cash crops of tobacco, rice, and Sea Island (or long-staple) cotton. Tobacco, the mainstay of the colonial Chesapeake economy, severely depleted the soil. Its production had stagnated after the Revolutionary War, when it lost its formerly protected markets in Britain.

Rice and long-staple cotton—named for its long, silky fibers—were profitable but geographically limited to the humid sea islands and tidal flats off the coast of South Carolina and Georgia. Like sugar cane, introduced into Louisiana in the 1790s, they required a huge capital investment in special machinery, dikes, and labor.

Upland, or short-staple, cotton faced none of these constraints, once the cotton gin removed the technical barrier to its commercial production. It could be planted far inland, and small farmers could grow it profitably because it required no additional costs for machinery or drainage systems.

As a result, after the 1790s, the production of short-staple cotton boomed. Moreover, like the South's other cash crops, upland cotton was well suited for slave labor because it required fairly continuous tending throughout most of the year. Once the harvest was in—a time when northern agricultural workers were laid off—the slaves cleared land, cut wood, and made repairs. The long work year maximized the return on capital invested in slave labor.

Despite the care required, the cultivation of cotton left plenty of time for slaves to grow food. The major grain in the southern diet was corn, which nicely complemented the labor cycle of cotton. Corn needed little attention while cotton was being harvested and could be planted earlier or later than cotton during the long growing season. Surplus corn could be fed to hogs and converted into pork. Because almost all cotton farms and plantations also raised corn and hogs, the South virtually fed itself.

The linkage of cotton and slaves was at the heart of the plantation system that spread westward after the War of 1812. From its original base in South Carolina and Georgia, the cotton kingdom moved into the Old Southwest and then into Texas and Arkansas. As wasteful agricultural practices exhausted new lands, planters moved to the next cotton frontier farther west. Cotton output exploded from 73,000 bales (each bale weighed close to 500 pounds) in 1800 to more than 2 million bales by midcentury, thanks to the fertility of virgin land and technological changes, such as improved seed varieties and steam-powered cotton gins (see Figure 11-1). Slave labor accounted for more than 90 percent of cotton production.

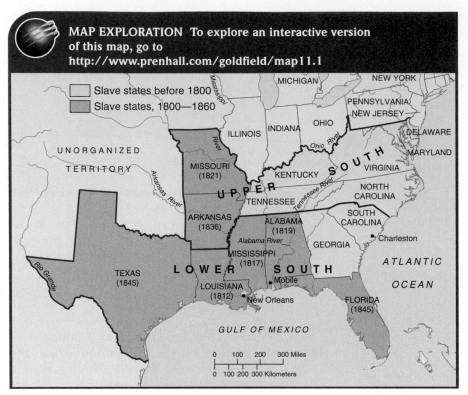

MAP EXPLORATION To explore an interactive version of this map, go to http://www.prenhall.com/goldfield/map11.1

MAP 11-1 The Spread of Slavery: New Slave States Entering the Union, 1800-1850. *Seven slave states entered the Union after 1800 as cotton production shifted westward.*

Plantations, large productive units specializing in a cash crop and employing at least twenty slaves, were the leading economic institution in the Lower South. Planters were the most prestigious social group, and, though less than 5 percent of white families were in the planter class, they controlled more than 40 percent of the slaves, cotton output, and total agricultural wealth. Most had inherited or married into their wealth, but they could stay at the top of the South's class structure only by continuing to profit from slave labor.

Plantations were generally more efficient producers of cotton than were small farms. Planters had the best land because only they commanded the labor resources to exploit the wet bottomlands, drain the swamps, or clear the raw jungle in the Mississippi Delta. They were also more likely than farmers to belong to agricultural reform societies that made them aware of superior varieties of seed and the most progressive techniques of cultivation. Most important, the ownership of twenty or more slaves enabled planters to use gangs to do both routine and specialized agricultural work. This **gang system**, a cruder version of the division of labor that was being introduced in northern factories, permitted a regimented pace of work that would have been impossible to impose on free agricultural workers. Teams of field hands, made up of women as well as men, had to work at a steady pace or else feel the lash. They were supervised by white overseers and black drivers, slaves selected for their management skills and agricultural knowledge.

By 1850, the plantations of the Lower South were larger and more specialized than was the case elsewhere in the South, and the wealth of their owners was more ostentatiously displayed. More clusters of slave cabins, overseers' quarters, and cotton gins dotted the countryside. The few towns were little more than a haphazard collection of plain wooden houses scattered around a tavern, country store, and blacksmith's shop. "During two days' sail on the Alabama River from Mobile to Montgomery," noted a traveler in 1860, "I did not see so many houses standing together in any one spot as could be dignified with the appellation of village."

The plantation districts of the Lower South stifled the growth of towns and the economic enterprise they fostered. Planters, as well as ordinary farmers, strove to be self-sufficient. The most significant economic exchange—exporting cotton—took place in international markets and was handled by specialized commission merchants in Charleston, Mobile, and New Orleans. The Lower South had amassed great wealth, but most outsiders saw no signs of progress there.

THE PROFITS OF SLAVERY

Slavery was profitable on an individual basis. Most modern studies indicate that the average rate of return on capital invested in a slave was about 10 percent a year, a rate that at least equaled what was available in alternative investments in the South or the North. Not surprisingly, the newer regions of the cotton kingdom in the Lower South, with the most productive land and the greatest commitment to plantation agriculture, consistently led the nation in per capita income.

The profitability of slavery ultimately rested on the enormous demand for cotton outside the South. This demand grew at about 5 percent a year during

The domestic slave trade brought buyers and sellers of slaves together. Slaves flowed from the older areas of the Upper South to the newer plantation districts in the Lower South. Indeed, when Congress ended the African slave trade in 1807 and it became difficult to smuggle in significant numbers of African slaves, planters in the Deep South had to depend on the internal trade for the bulk of their labor supply. This trade was extensive: more than 800,000 slaves were moved between regions in the South from 1790 to 1860, and professional slave traders transported at least 60 percent of them. Drawing on lines of credit from banks, the traders paid cash for slaves, most of whom they bought from plantations in the Upper South. By selling these slaves in regional markets where demand had driven up the price, they turned a tidy profit.

The sheer size of the internal slave trade indicates just how profit-driven slave owners were. Few of them hesitated to break up slave families for sale when market conditions were right. About half of all slave sales separated family members. Slave children born in the Upper South after 1820 stood a one-in-three chance of being sold during their lifetime. Most of the profits from slave labor and sales went into buying more land and slaves. As long as slaves employed in growing cash staples returned 10 percent a year, slave owners had little economic incentive to shift their capital resources into manufacturing or urban development. The predictable result was that industrialization and urbanization fell far behind the levels in the free states, creating what outsiders came to decry as southern "backwardness." The South had one-third of the nation's population in 1860 but produced by value only 10 percent of the nation's manufacturing output. Fewer than one in ten Southerners lived in a city, compared to more than one in three northeasterners and one in seven midwesterners.

Nowhere was the indifference of planters to economic diversification more evident than in the Lower South, which had the smallest urban population and the fewest factories. Planters here were not opposed to economic innovations that promised greater profits, but they feared social changes that might undermine the stability of slavery. Urbanization and industrialization both entailed such risks.

Most planters suspected that the urban environment weakened slavery. An editorial in the *New Orleans Crescent* charged that slaves in the city were "demoralized to a deplorable extent, all owing to the indiscriminate license and indulgence extended to them by masters, mistresses, and guardians, and to the practice of forging passes, which has now be-

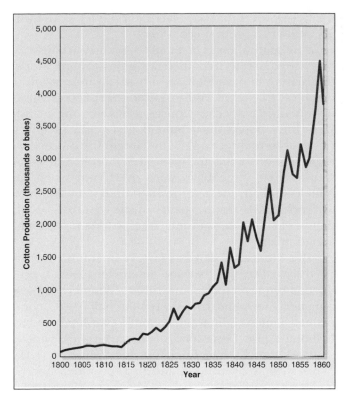

FIGURE 11-1   U.S. Cotton Production, 1800–1860
Cotton production spiraled upward after 1800, and the South became the world's leading supplier.

Data Source: U.S. Bureau of the Census, *Historical Statistics of the United States* (1960).

the first half of the nineteenth century. Although cotton prices fluctuated like those of any other commodity in an unregulated market, demand was so strong that prices held steady at around 10 cents a pound in the 1850s, even as southern production of cotton doubled. Textile mills in Britain were always the largest market, but demand in continental Europe and the United States grew even faster after 1840.

Southern law defined slaves as chattel, the personal property of their owners, and their market value increased along with the profitability of slavery. Prices for a male field hand rose from $250 in 1815 to $900 by 1860. Prices at any given time varied according to the age, sex, and skills of the slave, as well as overall market conditions, but the steady appreciation of prices for slaves meant that slave owners could sell their human chattel and realize a profit over and above what they had already earned from the slaves' labor. This was especially the case with slave mothers; the children they bore increased the capital assets of their owners. Slave women of childbearing age were therefore valued nearly as much as male field hands.

African American field hands return from a South Carolina cotton field in the 1860s. The economy of the prewar South was based on the production of cotton by a large enslaved labor force.

come a regular business in New Orleans." For a white person, a "demoralized" slave was one who behaved as if free. Urban slaves, though scarcely free, enjoyed a degree of personal and economic independence that blurred the line between freedom and servitude.

Urban slavery. Urban slaves were artisans, semi-skilled laborers, and domestics, and, unlike their rural counterparts, they usually lived apart from their owners. They had much more freedom than field hands to move around, interact with white people and other black people, and experiment with various social roles. Many of them, especially if they had a marketable skill, such as carpentry or tailoring, could hire out their labor and retain some wages for themselves after reimbursing their owners. In short, the direct authority of the slave owner was less clear-cut in the town than in the country.

Urban slavery declined from 1820 to 1860 as slaves decreased from 22 percent to 10 percent of the urban population. This decline reflected both doubts about the stability of slavery in an urban setting and

the large profits that slave labor earned for slave owners in the rural cotton economy.

The ambivalence of planters toward urban slavery also characterized their attitudes toward industrial slavery and, indeed, to industrialization itself. If based on free labor, industrialization risked promoting an antislavery class consciousness among manufacturing laborers that would challenge the property rights of slave owners. William Gregg, the owner of a large cotton mill in upcountry South Carolina, showed that these fears were overblown when he built a company town in the 1840s that kept his white workers under tight, paternalistic controls. Still, many planters considered free workers potential abolitionists.

But the use of slaves as factory operatives threatened slave discipline because an efficient level of production required special incentives. "Whenever a slave is made a mechanic, he is more than half freed," complained James Hammond, a South Carolina planter. Elaborating on Hammond's fears, a Virginian noted of slaves that he had hired out for industrial work, "They were worked hard, and had too much liberty, and were acquiring bad habits. They earned money by overwork, and spent it for whisky, and got a habit of roaming about and *taking care of themselves*; because, when they were not at work in the furnace, nobody looked out for them."

The anxieties of planters over industrialization and their refusal to shift capital from plantation agriculture to finance it insured that manufacturing played only a minor economic role in the Lower South. Planters supported industrialization only as an adjunct, not an alternative, to the plantation economy. Thus planters did invest in railroads and factories, but their holdings remained concentrated in land and slaves. They augmented their income by renting slaves to manufacturers and railroad contractors but were quick to recall these slaves to work on the plantations when they were needed.

No more than 5 percent of the slaves in the Lower South ever worked in manufacturing, and most of these were in rural enterprises serving local markets too small to interest northern manufacturers. Ever concerned to preserve slavery, planters would not risk slave discipline or the profits of cotton agriculture by embracing the unpredictable changes that industrialization was sure to bring.

THE UPPER SOUTH

Climate and geography distinguished the Upper South from the Lower South. The eight slave states

The internal slave trade was the primary means by which the slaves of the Upper South were brought into the plantation markets of the Old Southwest. This illustration shows professional slave traders driving a chained group of slaves, known as a coffle, to perspective buyers in the Lower South.

of the Upper South lay north of the best growing zones for cotton. The northernmost of these states —Delaware, Maryland, Kentucky, and Missouri— bordered on free states and were known as the Border South. The four states south of them —Virginia, North Carolina, Tennessee, and Arkansas—constituted a middle zone. Slavery was entrenched in all these states, but it was less dominant than in the cotton South.

The key difference, from which others followed, was the suitability of the Lower South for growing cotton with gangs of slave laborers. Except for prime cotton districts in middle Tennessee, eastern Arkansas, and parts of North Carolina, the Upper South lacked the fertile soil and long growing season necessary for the commercial production of cotton, rice, or sugar (see Map 11–2). Consequently, the demand for slaves was less than it was in the Lower South. Two-thirds of white southerners lived in the Upper South in 1860, but they held only 45 percent of all slaves. Percentages of slave ownership and of slaves in the overall population were roughly half those in the cotton South. While the Lower South was undergoing a cotton boom after the War of 1812, the Upper South was mired in a long economic slump, from which it did not emerge until the 1850s. The improved economy of the Upper South in the late antebellum period increasingly relied on free labor, a development that many cotton planters feared would diminish southern unity in defense of slavery.

A PERIOD OF ECONOMIC ADJUSTMENT

To inhabitants and visitors alike, vast stretches of the Upper South presented a dreary spectacle of exhausted fields and depopulation in the 1820s and 1830s. The soil was most depleted where tobacco had been cultivated extensively. Even where the land was still fertile, farmers could not compete against the agricultural commodities that the fresher lands of the Old Southwest produced. Land values fell as farmers dumped their property and headed west. "Emigration is here raging with all the strength of fanaticism," wrote a Virginian in 1837, "and nothing else can be talked of but selling estates, at a great sacrifice, and '*packing off*' for the '*far west.*'"

Agricultural reform emerged in the 1830s as one proposed solution to this economic crisis. Its leading advocate was Edmund Ruffin, a Virginia planter who tirelessly promoted the use of marl (shell deposits) to neutralize the overly acidic and worn-out soils of the Upper South. He also called for deeper plowing, systematic rotation of crops, and upgrading the breeding stock for animal husbandry.

Ruffin's efforts, and those of the agricultural societies and fairs spawned by the reform movement, met with some success, especially in the 1840s, when

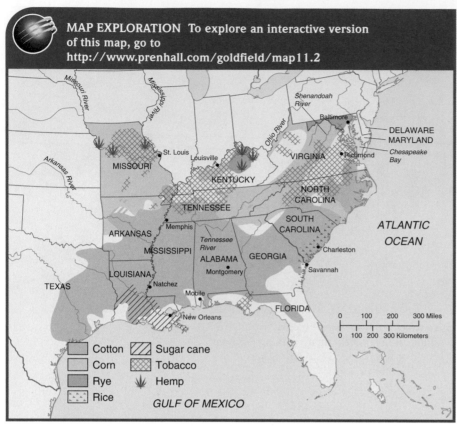

MAP EXPLORATION To explore an interactive version of this map, go to http://www.prenhall.com/goldfield/map11.2

MAP 11-2 Cotton and Other Crops in the South, 1860
Most of the Upper South was outside the cotton belt where the demand for slave labor was greatest.

the prices of all cash staples fell. Still, only a minority of farmers ever embraced reform. These were generally the well-educated planters who read the agricultural press and could afford to change their farming practices. The landscape of Ruffin's beloved Virginia Tidewater still provoked travelers to remark, as one did in the early 1850s, "I've heard 'em say out West that old Virginny was the mother of statesmen—reckon she must be about done, eh? This 'ere's about the barrenest look for a mother ever I see."

Although soil exhaustion and wasteful farming persisted, agriculture in the Upper South had revived by the 1850s. A rebound in the tobacco market accounted for part of this revival, but the growing profitability of general farming was responsible for most of it.

Particularly in the Border South, the trend was toward agricultural diversification. Farmers and planters lessened their dependence on slave labor or on a single cash crop and practiced a thrifty, efficient agriculture geared to producing grain and livestock for urban markets. Western Maryland and the Shenandoah Valley and northern sections of Virginia grew wheat, and in the former tobacco districts of the Virginia and North Carolina Tidewater, wheat, corn, and garden vegetables became major cash crops.

Expanding urban markets and a network of internal improvements facilitated this transition to general farming. Both these developments were outgrowths of the movement for industrial diversification launched in the 1820s in response to the heavy outflow of population from the Upper South.

Growing urbanization. Although not far advanced by northern standards, urbanization and industrialization in the Upper South were considerably greater than in the Lower South. The region had twice the percentage of urban residents of the cotton South, and it contained the leading manufacturing cities in the slave states—St. Louis, Baltimore, and Louisville. By 1860, the Upper South accounted for three-fourths of the South's manufacturing capital and output and nearly all of its heavy industry. Canals and railroads linked cities and countryside in a denser transportation grid than in the Lower South.

With an economy more balanced among agriculture, manufacturing, and trade than a generation earlier, the Upper South at midcentury was gradually becoming less tied to plantation agriculture and slave labor. The rural majority increasingly prospered by growing foodstuffs for city-dwellers and factory workers. The labor market for railroad construction and manufacturing work was strong enough to attract northern immigrants and help reduce the loss of the native-born population that had migrated to other states.

The economic adjustment in the Upper South converted the labor surplus of the 1820s into a labor scarcity by the 1850s. "It is a fact," noted Edmund Ruffin in 1859, "that labor is greatly deficient in all Virginia, and especially in the rich western counties, which, for want of labor, scarcely yet yield in the proportion of one tenth of their capacity." Ruffin's commitment to agricultural reform was exceeded only by his devotion to slavery. Like many planters in the cotton states, he feared that free labor was about to replace scarce and expensive slave labor in Virginia and much of the Upper South.

THE DECLINE OF SLAVERY

Slave owners tended to exaggerate all threats to slavery, and Ruffin was no exception. But slavery was clearly growing weaker in the Upper South by the 1850s (see Figure 11-2). The decline was most evident along the northern tier of the Upper South, where the proportion of slaves to the overall population fell steadily after 1830. By 1860, slaves in the Border South had dropped to 2 percent of the population in Delaware, 13 percent in Maryland, 19 percent in Kentucky, and 10 percent in Missouri. In Virginia, from 1830 to 1860, slaves fell from 39 to 31 percent of the population.

Elsewhere in the Upper South, slavery was more or less holding its own by the 1850s. Tobacco and cotton planters in North Carolina and Tennessee continued to rely heavily on slave labor, but most small farmers were indifferent, if not opposed, to the institution. Only in Arkansas, whose alluvial lands along the Mississippi River offered a new frontier for plantation agriculture, was slavery growing rapidly. Slaves, however, still made up only 25 percent of the population of Arkansas in 1860 and were confined mainly to the southeastern corner of the state. Geographically dominated by the Ozark Highlands, Arkansas was best suited to general farming.

The region's role as a slave exporter to the Lower South hastened the decline of slavery in the Upper South. In every decade after 1820, the internal slave trade drained off about 10 percent of the slaves in the Upper South—virtually the entire natural increase. Slave traders initially made most of their purchases in Virginia and Maryland, but by the 1850s, they were also active in the Carolinas, Kentucky, and Missouri. New Orleans, Memphis, and Natchez, Mississippi, were the major western distribution points for the slaves, who were sent west both by sea and by land.

Selling slaves to the Lower South reinforced the Upper South's economic stake in slavery at a time when the institution was otherwise barely profitable there. The sale of surplus slaves was a windfall for planters whose slaves had become an economic burden. This same windfall gave planters the capital to embark on agricultural reform and shift out of tobacco production. Investment capital in the Upper South was not flowing into slave property but into economic diversification that expanded urban manufacturing. Both of these structural changes increas-

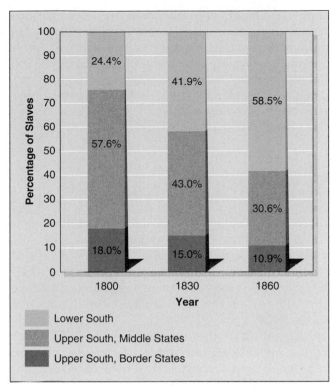

FIGURE 11-2   The Changing Regional Pattern of Slavery in the South, 1800–1860
As the nineteenth century progressed, slavery increasingly became identified with the cotton-growing Lower South.

ingly put slavery at a competitive disadvantage against free labor.

The wheat, small grains, and fodder crops that replaced tobacco in much of the Upper South did not require the nearly continuous attention of a work force. Unlike tobacco, wheat needed intensive labor only at planting and during the short harvest. Thus, as planters abandoned tobacco, they kept fewer slaves and relied on seasonal and cheap agricultural workers to meet peak labor demand.

The cheapness and flexibility of free labor made it better suited than slave labor for general farming. Urban manufacturers likewise wanted workers who could be hired and fired at a moment's notice. Despite the successful use of slaves in tobacco manufacturing and at the large Tredegar Iron Works in Richmond, immigrant workers displaced slaves in most of the factories in the Border South. By 1860, slaves made up just 1 percent of the population in St. Louis and Baltimore, the South's major industrial cities.

Slavery was in economic retreat across the Upper South after 1830. There were still plantation districts with large concentrations of slaves, and slave owners retained enough political power to defeat all challenges to their property interests. Nevertheless, the gradual turn to free labor was unmistakable. As Alfred Iveson, a Georgia planter, noted with alarm in 1860, "Those border States can get along without slavery. Their soil and climate are appropriate to white labor; they can live and flourish without African slavery; but the cotton States cannot."

SLAVE LIFE AND CULTURE

Nearly 4 million slaves lived in the South by 1860, a more than fivefold increase since the ratification of the Constitution. This population gain was overwhelmingly due to an excess of births over deaths, although as many as fifty thousand Africans may have been smuggled into the country until about 1860, despite the ban on the African slave trade that took effect in 1808.

Almost all southern slaves were thus native-born by the mid-nineteenth century. They were not Africans but African Americans, and they shared the common fate of bondage. By resisting an enslavement they could not prevent, they shaped a culture of their own that eased their pain and raised their hopes of someday being free. They managed to retain their dignity despite the humiliations to which they were subjected. In their family life and religious beliefs, slaves found the strength to sustain themselves under nearly intolerable circumstances.

WORK ROUTINES AND LIVING CONDITIONS

Being treated as a piece of property to be worked for profit and bought and sold when financially advantageous to one's owners—this was the legal and economic reality that all slaves confronted. Each southern state had its own **slave codes**, laws defining the status of slaves and the rights of masters; the codes gave slave owners near-absolute power over their human property.

"The right of personal liberty in the slave is utterly inconsistent with the idea of slavery," wrote Thomas R. R. Cobb of Georgia in a legal treatise on slavery. The slave codes, accordingly, severely restricted the lives of slaves. Slaves could not own property, make contracts, possess guns or alcohol, legally marry (except in Louisiana), leave plantations without the owner's written permission, or testify against their masters or any other white person in a court of law. Many states also prohibited teaching a slave to read or write. The law assumed that the economic self-interest of masters in their slave property gave slaves adequate legal protection against injuries inflicted by others. The murder of a slave by a master was illegal, but in practice, the law and community standards looked the other way if a disobedient slave was killed while being disciplined.

The slave codes penalized any challenge to a master's authority or any infraction of plantation rules. Whippings were the most common authorized punishment: twenty lashes on the bare back for leaving a plantation without a pass, one hundred lashes for writing a pass for another slave, and so on. Striking a master, committing arson, or conspiring to rebel were punishable by death.

The owner, as expressed in the Alabama Slave Code of 1852, had "the right to the time, labor and services of the slave." This, of course, was the whole purpose of owning a slave. Most masters recognized that it made good business sense to feed, clothe, and house their slaves well enough to insure productive labor and to encourage a family life that would enable the slave population to reproduce itself. Thus planters' self-interest probably improved the living standards for slaves in the first half of the nineteenth century, and the slave population grew at a rate only slightly below that of white Southerners.

However, planters rarely provided more than the bare necessities. The slaves lived mainly on rations of

Five generations are represented in this photograph of an African American family on a South Carolina plantation. The photograph was taken in 1862, soon after the family gained its freedom during the Civil War.

cornmeal and salt pork, supplemented with vegetables they grew on the small garden plots that many planters permitted and with occasional catches of game and fish. This diet provided ample calories but often insufficient vitamins and nutrients to protect slaves (as well as the many poor whites who ate the same diet) against such diseases as beriberi and pellagra. Intestinal disorders were chronic, and dysentery and cholera were common. About 20 percent of the slaves on a typical plantation were sick at any given time. Infant mortality was twice as high among slaves as among white southerners in 1850; so was mortality among slave children up to age 14. According to one study, the life expectancy for slaves at birth was 21 to 22 years—roughly half the white life expectancy.

Planters furnished slaves with two sets of coarse clothing, one for summer and one for winter. Their housing, typically a 15-by-15-foot one-room cabin for five or six occupants, provided little more than basic shelter against the elements. "They were built of logs," a traveler noted of slave cabins in South Carolina, "with no windows—no opening at all, except the doorway, with a chimney of sticks and mud; with no trees about them, no porches, or shades, of any kind. Except for the chimney . . . I should have conjectured that it had been built for a powder-house, or perhaps an ice-house—never for an animal to sleep in."

Small and unadorned, slave cabins emphasized, not only the planters' desire to minimize housing costs, but also their determination to treat slaves as a regimented, collective population. Large planters placed these cabins in a row—an arrangement that projected precision and undifferentiated order. Slaves expressed their own individuality by furnishing their cabins with handmade beds and benches and by pushing for the right to put in gardens.

The diet and housing of most slaves may have been no worse than that of the poorest whites in both the North and the South, but their workload was undoubtedly heavier. Just over half of the slave population at midcentury was concentrated on plantation units with twenty or more slaves, and most of these slaves worked as field hands in gang labor. Overseers freely admitted that they relied on whippings to make slaves work in these gangs.

Most plantation slaves toiled at hard physical labor from sunup to sundown. The work was more intense and sustained than that of white farmers or white factory hands. The fear of the whip on a bare back set the pace. At daybreak, recalled Solomon Northrup of his enslavement on a Louisiana plantation, "the fears and labors of another day begin; and until its close there is no such thing as rest. [The

Especially on large plantations, slave nursemaids cared for the young children in the white planter's family.

slave] fears he will be caught lagging through the day; he fears to approach the gin-house with his basketload of cotton at night; he fears, when he lies down, that he will oversleep himself in the morning."

Some 15 to 20 percent of plantation slaves were house servants or skilled artisans who had lighter and less regimented workloads than field hands. Some planters used the prospect of transfer to these relatively privileged positions as an incentive to field hands to work harder. Extra rations, time off on weekends, passes to visit a spouse on a nearby plantation, and the right to have a garden plot were among the other incentives planters used to keep labor productivity high. However, what a planter viewed as privileges, benevolently bestowed, slaves quickly came to see as customary rights. Despite the power of the whip, if planters failed to respect these "rights," slave morale would decline, and the work routine would be interrupted.

Nearly three-fourths of the slaves worked on plantations and medium-sized farms. Most of the remainder—those in units with fewer than ten slaves—worked on small farms in close contact with the master's family. Their workloads were more varied and sometimes less taxing than those of plantation hands, but these slaves were also more directly exposed to the whims of their owners and were less likely to live in complete family units. Slave couples in small holdings were more likely to live on separate farms. The owners of only a few slaves were also more vulnerable than were planters to market downturns that could force them to sell slaves and further divide families.

Of all slaves, 10 percent were not attached to the land, laboring instead at jobs that most white workers shunned. Every southern industry—but most particularly extractive industries such as mining and lumbering—relied heavily on slaves. The Tredegar Iron Company in Richmond, the largest iron foundry in the South, used slaves as its main workforce after 1847, partly to curb strikes by its white workers. Racial tensions often flared in southern industry, and when the races worked together, skilled white laborers typically insisted on being placed in supervisory positions.

Digging coal as miners or shoveling it as stokers for boilers on steamboats, laying down iron for the railroads or shaping hot slabs of it in a foundry, industrial slaves worked at least as hard as field hands. Compared to plantation slaves, however, they had more independence off the job and greater opportunities to earn money of their own. Because many of them had to house and feed themselves, they could also enjoy more time free from direct white scrutiny. By undertaking extra factory work, known as "overwork," industrial slaves could earn $50 or more a month, money they could use to buy goods for their families or, in rare cases, to purchase their freedom.

FAMILIES AND RELIGION

The core institution of slave life was the family. Except in Louisiana, southern law did not recognize slave marriages, but masters permitted, even encouraged, marital unions in order to raise the morale of their labor force and increase its value by having it produce marketable children. Slaves embraced their families as a source of loving warmth and strength in a system that treated them as commodities.

Despite all the obstacles arrayed against them, many slave marriages produced enduring commitments and a supportive moral code for family members. Most slave unions remained intact until the death or, frequently, the sale of one spouse. Close to one-third of slave marriages were broken up by sales or forced removals. A slave bitterly recalled that "the separation of slaves in this way is little thought of. A few masters regard their union as sacred, but where one does, a hundred care nothing about it."

Both parents were present in about two-thirds of slave families—the same ratio as in contemporary peasant families in western Europe. Although the father's role as protector of and provider for his wife and children had no standing under slavery, most slave fathers struggled to help feed their families by hunting and fishing, and they risked beating and death to defend their wives from sexual abuse by the overseer or master. Besides their field labors, slave mothers had all the burdens of pregnancy, child care, laundry, and cooking. After escaping from slavery, Sojourner Truth told how she placed her babies in a basket hanging from a tree while she worked in the field and had older children care for them.

No anguish under slavery was more heartrending than that of a mother whose child was sold away from her. "Oh, my heart was too full!" recalled Charity Bowery on being told that her boy Richard was sold. "[My mistress] had sent me away on an errand, because she didn't want to be troubled with our cries. I hadn't any chance to see my poor boy. I shall never see my poor boy. I shall never see him again in this world. My heart felt as if it was under a great load."

Charity Bowery's experience was hardly unique. Slave parents had to suppress the rage they felt at their powerlessness to protect their children from the cruelties of slavery. Slave accounts are full of stories of children running in vain to their parents to save them from a whipping. Most parents could only teach their children the skills of survival in a world in which white people had a legal monopoly on violence. The most valuable of these skills was the art of hiding one's true feelings from white people and telling them what they wanted to hear. As a perceptive traveler noted: "When therefore a white man approaches [the slaves] with inquiries concerning their condition, they are at once put upon their guard, and either make indefinite and vague replies, or directly contradict their real sentiments."

Extensive kinship ties provided a support network for the vulnerable slave family. Thickest on the older and larger plantations, these networks included both blood relatives and other significant people. Children were taught to address elders as "Aunt" and "Uncle" and fellow slaves as "sister" and "brother." Parents thus helped prepare their children for the day when the family might be divided. If separated from a parent, a child could turn to relatives or the larger slave community for care and assistance.

Slaves followed West African customs by prohibiting marriage between cousins and by often naming their children after departed grandparents. They also drew on an African heritage kept alive through folk-

Satirically entitled "Virginian Luxuries," this antislavery painting sought to expose how the unchecked power of slaveowners resulted in the physical beating and sexual abuse of their slaves.

lore and oral histories to create a religion that fit their needs. The ancestors of nineteenth-century slaves brought no common religion with them when they were taken to the New World. However, beliefs common to a variety of African religions survived. Once slaves began to embrace Christianity in the late eighteenth century, they blended these beliefs into an African Christianity.

In keeping with African traditions, the religion of the slaves fused the natural and spiritual worlds, accepted the power of ghosts over the living, and relied on an expressive form of worship in which the participants shouted and swayed in rhythm with the beat of drums and other instruments. Associated with reverence for ancestors, dance was sacred in Africa. Spirituals, the religious songs of the slaves, were sung in a dance known in America as the ring shout. Moving counterclockwise and stamping their feet to establish a beat, slaves blended dance and song in a religious ceremony that helped them to endure oppression and sustain their self-confidence.

By most estimates, no more than 20 percent of slaves ever converted to Christianity. Those who did found in Christianity a message of deliverance rooted in the liberation of Moses's people from bondage in Egypt. The Jesus of the New Testament spoke to them as a compassionate God who had shared their burden of suffering, so that all peoples could hope to find the Promised Land of love and justice. By blending biblical imagery into their spirituals, the slaves expressed their yearning for freedom: "Didn't my Lord deliver Daniel/Then why not every man?"

The initial exposure of slaves to Christianity usually came from evangelical revivalists, and slaves always favored the Baptists and Methodists over other denominations. The evangelical message of universal spiritual equality confirmed the slaves' sense of personal worth. Less formal in both their doctrines and organization than the Presbyterians and Episcopalians, the evangelical sects allowed the slaves more leeway to choose their own preachers and engage in their physical call-and-response pattern of worship. Perhaps because they baptized by total immersion, which evoked the purifying power of water so common in African religions, the Baptists gained the most slave converts.

Most planters were pragmatic about encouraging Christianity among their slaves. Like every other aspect of the slaves' lives, they favored it only if they could control it. Thus, while many planters allowed black preachers at religious services on their plantations, they usually insisted that white observers be present. Worried that abolitionist propaganda might attract the slaves to Christianity as a religion of secular liberation, some planters in the late antebellum period tried to convert their slaves to their own version of Christianity. They invited white ministers to their plantations to preach a gospel of passivity and obedience, centered on Paul's call for servants to "obey in all things your Masters."

Although most slaves viewed the religion of their owners as hypocritical and the sermons of white ministers as propaganda, they feigned acceptance of the religious wishes of their masters. They attended the special slave chapels some masters built and sat in segregated galleries in white churches on Sunday mornings. But in the evening, out of sight of the master or overseer, they held their own services in the woods and listened to their own preachers. As much as they could, the slaves hid their religious life from white people. Many slaves experienced religion as a spiritual rebirth that gave them the inner strength to endure their bondage. As one recalled, "I was born a slave and lived through some hard times. If it had not been for my God, I don't know what I would have done."

RESISTANCE

Open resistance to slavery was futile. The persistently disobedient slave would be sold "down river" to a harsher master or, in extreme cases, killed. The fate of Richard, Charity Bowery's son who was sold away from her, typified that of the openly defiant slave. He resisted the efforts of his new owner in Alabama to break his will. When the owner threatened to shoot him if he did not consent to being whipped, Richard replied, "Shoot away, I won't come to be flogged." The master shot and killed him.

Although the odds of succeeding were infinitesimal, slaves as desperate as Richard did plot rebellions. Four major uprisings occurred in the nineteenth century. The first, **Gabriel Prosser's Rebellion** in 1800, involved about fifty armed slaves around Richmond, though perhaps as many as one thousand slaves knew about Prosser's plans. The failure to seize a key road to Richmond and a warning to white authorities by a slave informer doomed the rebellion before it got under way. State authorities executed Prosser and twenty-five of his followers.

A decade later, in what seems to have been a spontaneous bid for freedom, several hundred slaves in the river parishes (counties) above New Orleans marched on the city. Poorly armed, they were no match for the U.S. Army troops and militiamen who stopped them. More than sixty slaves died, and the heads of the leading rebels were posted on poles along the Mississippi River to warn others of the fate that awaited rebellious slaves.

The most carefully planned slave revolt, **Denmark Vesey's Conspiracy**, like Prosser's, failed before it got started. Vesey, a literate carpenter and lay preacher in Charleston who had purchased his freedom with the money he had won in a lottery, planned the revolt in the summer of 1822. Vesey drew on biblical passages, antislavery sentiments in Congress he had gleaned from newspaper reports on the Missouri Compromise debates, and the successful revolt of slaves in Haiti to inspire his followers. He tried to steel the courage of his coconspirators by telling them that his chief lieutenant, Gullah Jack, a conjurer, or voodoo doctor, would cast spells on their enemies. He assigned teams of rebels specific targets, such as the municipal guardhouse and arsenal. Once Charleston was secured, the rebels apparently planned to flee to Haiti. The plot collapsed when two domestic servants betrayed it. White authorities responded swiftly and savagely. They hanged thirty-five conspirators, including Vesey,

After eluding his white pursuers for two months, Nat Turner, the leader of the South's most famous slave revolt, was captured on October 30, 1831.

and banished thirty-seven others. After destroying the African Methodist Episcopal Church where Vesey had preached and the conspirators had met, they tried to seal off the city from subversive outsiders by passing the Negro Seamen's Act, which mandated the imprisonment of black sailors while their ships were berthed in Charleston.

One slave revolt, **Nat Turner's Rebellion**, in Southampton County, Virginia, did erupt before it could be suppressed. Turner was a literate field hand driven by prophetic visions of black vengeance against white oppressors. Like Vesey, he was well versed in the Bible. Convinced by what he called "signs in heaven" that he should "arise and prepare myself and slay my enemies with their own weapons," he led a small band of followers on a murderous rampage in late August 1831. The first white man to be killed was Joseph Travis, Turner's owner, known for his lenient treatment of slaves. In the next two days, sixty other white people were also killed. An enraged posse, aided by slaves, captured or killed most of Turner's party. Turner hid for two months before being apprehended. He and more than thirty other slaves were executed, and panicky white people killed more than a hundred other slaves.

Slaves well understood that the odds against a successful rebellion were insurmountable. They could see who had all the guns. White people were also more numerous. In contrast to the large black majorities in the slave societies of the West Indies

After fleeing from slavery in Maryland in 1849, Harriet "Moses" Tubman, standing on the left, risked reenslavement by returning to the South on several occasions to assist other slaves in escaping. She is photographed here with some of those she helped free.

and Brazil—majorities made possible only by the continuous, heavy importation of Africans—slaves made up only one-third of the population of the antebellum American South. They lacked the numbers to overwhelm the white population and could not escape to mountain hideaways or large tracts of jungle. Surveillance by mounted white patrols—part of the police apparatus of slavery—limited organized rebellion by slaves to small, local affairs that were quickly suppressed.

Nor could many slaves escape to freedom. Few runaways made it to Canada or to a free state. White people could stop black people and demand to see papers documenting their freedom or right to travel without a master. The **Underground Railroad**, a secret network of stations and safe houses organized by Quakers and other black and white antislavery activists, provided some assistance. However, fellow slaves or free black people, especially in the cities of the Border South, provided the only help most runaways could count on. Out of more than 3 million slaves in the 1850s, only about a thousand a year permanently escaped. (See "American Views: A Letter from an Escaped Slave to His Former Master.")

The few who made it to the North did so by running at night and hiding during the day. The most ingenious resorted to clever stratagems. Henry "Box" Brown arranged to have himself shipped in a box from Richmond to Philadelphia. Ellen Craft, a light-skinned slave who could pass as white, disguised herself as a male slaveholder accompanied by his dark-skinned servant (her husband, William). What could have

been a fatal flaw in their plan as they traveled from Savannah to Philadelphia—their inability to write and hence sign their names or document their assumed identities—was overcome by having Ellen pose as a sickly, rheumatic master whose right hand had to be kept bandaged.

Running away was common, but most runaways fled no farther than to nearby swamps and woods. Most voluntarily returned or were tracked down by bloodhounds within a week. Aside from protesting a special grievance or trying to avoid punishment, these slaves usually wanted to visit a spouse or loved one. Occasionally, runaways could bargain for lenient treatment in return for faithful service in the future. Most were severely punished. Such temporary flights from the master's control siphoned off some of the anger that might otherwise have erupted in violent, self-destructive attacks on slave owners. All planters had heard about the field hand who took an ax to an overseer, the cook who poisoned her master's family, or the house servant who killed a sleeping master or mistress.

Slaves resisted complete domination by their masters in less overt ways. They mocked white people in folktales like those about Brer Rabbit, for example, in which weak but wily animals cunningly outsmart their stronger enemies. Slave owners routinely complained of slaves malingering at work, abusing farm animals, losing tools, stealing food, and committing arson. These subversive acts of protest never challenged the system of slavery itself, but they did help slaves to maintain a sense of dignity and self-respect.

FREE SOCIETY

The abolitionists and the antislavery Republican Party of the 1850s portrayed the social order of the slave South as little more than haughty planters lording it over shiftless poor white people. The reality was considerably more complex. Planters, who set the social tone for the South as a whole, did act superior, but they were a tiny minority and had to contend with an ambitious middle class of small slaveholders and a majority of nonslaveholding farmers. Some landless white people on the margin of rural society

AMERICAN VIEWS

A Letter from an Escaped Slave to His Former Master

In 1859, Jackson Whitney was one of six thousand fugitive slaves living in Canada, a sanctuary of freedom beyond the reach of the Fugitive Slave Act of 1850. Like most fugitives, he was male, and he had been forced to leave his family behind in Kentucky. His letter, as well as other direct testimony by African Americans about their experiences and feelings while enslaved, gives us information about slavery that only the slaves could provide.

- How would you characterize the tone of Whitney's letter? How did he express his joy at being a free man?
- How did Whitney feel that Riley, his former owner, had betrayed him?
- What did Whitney mean by the phrase "a slave talking to 'massa' "? How did he indicate that he had been hiding his true feelings as a slave?
- How did Whitney contrast his religious beliefs and those of Riley? How did he expect Riley to be punished?
- What pained Whitney about his freedom in Canada, and what did he ask of Riley?

March 18, 1859
Mr. Wm. Riley, Springfield, Ky. —Sir:

I take this opportunity to dictate a few lines to you, supposing you might be curious to know my whereabouts. I am happy to inform you that I am in Canada, in good health, and have been here several days. Perhaps, by this time, you have concluded that robbing a woman of her husband, and children of their father does not pay, at least in your case; and I thought, while lying in jail by your direction, that if you had no remorse or conscience that would make you feel for a poor, broken-hearted man, and his worse-than-murdered wife and child, . . . and could

---

fit the stereotype of "poor whites," but they were easily outnumbered by self-reliant farmers who worked their own land. Southern cities, though small by northern standards, provided jobs for a growing class of free workers who increasingly clashed with planters over the use of slave labor.

These same cities, notably in the Upper South, were also home to the nation's largest concentration of free black people. Their freedom, though restricted, contradicted the racial justification of slavery. They competed with white workers for jobs, and by the 1850s pressure was mounting on them to leave the South or be enslaved. The free society in the South was surely more diverse than its antislavery critics charged, but overriding racism bonded most white people together to defend the prerogatives of white supremacy.

THE SLAVEHOLDING MINORITY

The white-columned plantation estate approached from a stately avenue of shade trees and framed by luxuriant gardens remains the most popular image of the slave South. In fact, such manorial estates were utterly unrepresentative of the lifestyle of the typical slaveholder. Only the wealthiest planters could live in such splendor, and they constituted less than 1 percent of southern white families in 1860. Yet displayed not by any entreaty or permission be induced to do as you promised you would, which was to let me go with my family for $800—but contended for $1,000, when you had promised to take the same you gave for me (which was $660.) at the time you bought me, and let me go with my dear wife and children! but instead would render me miserable, and lie to me, and to your neighbors . . . and when you was at Louisville trying to sell me! then I thought it was time for me to make my feet feel for Canada, and let your conscience feel in your pocket. —Now you cannot say but that I did all that was honorable and right while I was with you, although I was a slave. I pretended all the time that I thought you, or some one else had a better right to me than I had to myself, which you know is rather hard thinking.

—You know, too, that you proved a traitor to me in the time of need, and when in the most bitter distress that the human soul is capable of experiencing; and could you have carried out your purposes there would have been no relief. But I rejoice to say that an unseen, kind spirit appeared for the oppressed, and bade me take up my bed and walk—the result of which is that I am victorious and you are defeated. I am comfortably situated in Canada, working for George Harris [another fugitive slave from Kentucky who had bought a farm in Canada] . . . .

There is only one thing to prevent me being entirely happy here, and that is the want of my dear wife and children, and you to see us enjoying ourselves together here. I wish you could realize the contrast between Freedom and slavery; but it is not likely that we shall ever meet again on this earth.

But if you want to go to the next world and meet a God of love, mercy, and justice, in peace; who says, "Inasmuch as you did it to the least of them my little ones, you did it unto me"—making the professions that you do, pretending to be a follower of Christ, and tormenting me and my little ones as you have done—[you] had better repair the breaches you have made among us in this world, by sending my wife and children to me; thus preparing to meet your God in peace; for, if God don't punish you for inflicting such distress on the poorest of His poor, then there is no use of having any God, or talking about one . . . .

I hope you will consider candidly, and see if the case does not justify every word I have said, and ten times as much. You must not consider that it is a slave talking to 'massa' now, but one as free as yourself.

I subscribe myself one of the abused of America, but one of the justified and honored of Canada.

Jackson Whitney

Source: John W. Blassingame, ed., *Slave Testimony: Two Centuries of Letters, Speeches, Interviews, and Autobiographies* (Louisiana State University Press, 1977).

in their homes and grounds, their wealth and status were so imposing that they created an idealized image of grace and grandeur that has obscured the cruder realities of the slave regime.

Only in the rice districts of the South Carolina lowcountry and in the rich sugar parishes and cotton counties of the Mississippi Delta were large planters more than a small minority of the slaveholding class, let alone the general white population. Families of the planter class—those who held a minimum of twenty slaves—constituted only around 3 percent of all southern families in 1860. Fewer than one out of five planter families—less than 1 percent of all families—owned more than fifty slaves. Far from conspicuously exhibiting their wealth, most planters lived in drab log cabins. "The planter's home is generally a rude ungainly structure, made of logs, rough hewn from the forest; rail fences and rickety gates guard its enclosures," complained a speaker to the Alabama horticultural society in 1851. "We murder our soil with wasteful culture because there is plenty of fresh land West—and we live in tents and huts when we might live in rural palaces." Most planters wanted to acquire wealth, not display it. They were restlessly eager to move on and abandon their homes when the allure of profits from a new cotton frontier

Overview

Structure of Free Society in the South, c. 1860

Group	Size	Characteristics
Large planters	Less than 1 percent of white families	Owned fifty or more slaves and plantations in excess of one thousand acres; the wealthiest class in America
Planters	About 3 percent of white families	Owned twenty to forty-nine slaves and plantations in excess of one hundred acres; controlled bulk of southern wealth and provided most of the political leaders
Small slaveholders	About 20 percent of white families	Owned fewer than twenty slaves and most often fewer than five; primarily farmers, though some were part of a small middle class in towns and cities
Nonslaveholding whites	About 75 percent of white families	Mostly yeomen farmers who owned their own land and stressed production for family use; one in five owned neither slaves nor land and squatted on least desirable land where they planted some corn and grazed some livestock; in cities they worked as artisans or, more typically, day laborers
Free blacks	About 3 percent of all free families	Concentrated in the Upper South; hemmed in by legal and social restrictions; mostly tenants or farm laborers; about one-third lived in cities and generally were limited to lowest-paying jobs

promised to relieve them of the debts they had incurred to purchase their slaves.

Most planters expected their wives to help supervise the slaves and run the plantation. Besides raising her own children, the plantation mistress managed the household staff, oversaw the cooking and cleaning, gardened, dispensed medicine and clothing to the slaves, and often assisted in their religious instruction. When guests or relatives came for an extended visit, the wife had to make all the special arrangements that this occasion entailed. When the master was called off on a business or political trip, she kept the plantation accounts. In many respects, she worked harder than her husband.

Planters' wives often complained in their journals and letters of their isolation from other white women and the physical and mental toil of managing slaves. Still, they enjoyed a wealth and status unknown to most southern women and only rarely questioned the institution of slavery. Their deepest anger stemmed from their humiliation by husbands who kept slave mistresses or sexually abused slave women. Bound by their duties as wives not to express this anger publicly, and unwilling to renounce the in-

stitution that both victimized and benefited them, white women tended to vent their frustrations on black women whose alleged promiscuity they blamed for the sexual transgressions of white males. "Sometimes white mistresses will surmise that there is an intimacy between a slave woman & the master," recalled a former slave, "and perhaps she will make a great fuss & have her whipped, & perhaps there will be no peace until she is sold."

Despite the tensions and sexual jealousies that it aroused, the ownership of slaves was the surest means of social and economic advancement for most white families. Most slave owners, however, never attained planter status. Nine in ten slave owners in 1860 owned fewer than twenty slaves, and fully half of them had fewer than five. Many white people also rented a few slaves on a seasonal basis.

Generally younger than the planters, small slaveholders were a diverse lot. About 10 percent were women, and another 20 percent or so were merchants, businessmen, artisans, and urban professionals. Most were farmers trying to acquire enough land and slaves to enter the ranks of planters. To keep costs down, they often began by purchasing children, the cheapest slaves available, or a young slave family, so that they could add to their slaveholdings as the slave mother bore more children.

Other slaveholding farmers had inherited their slaves and were trying to regain their fathers' planter status. Partible inheritance—the equal division of property among children—was the norm in the nineteenth-century South. Except among the richest planter families, this division reduced the sons to modest slaveholders who had to struggle to build their own plantations.

Small slaveholders had scant economic security. A deadly outbreak of disease among their slaves or a single bad crop could destroy their credit and force them to sell their slaves to clear their debts. Owners of fewer than ten slaves stood a fifty-fifty chance

Colonel James A. Whiteside and his family were among the small elite of white Southerners who enjoyed the wealth and ease of life on a large plantation. Reflecting the ideal of patriarchy, this portrait, c. 1858, projects the colonel as a figure of power and authority.

James Cameron (1817–1882), "Colonel and Mrs. James A. Whiteside, son Charles and servants." Oil on canvas; c. 1858–1859. Hunter Museum of Art, Chattanooga, Tennessee, Gift of Mr. and Mrs. Thomas Whiteside.

within a decade of dropping out of the slaveholding class. Nor could small holders hope to compete directly with the planters. In any given area suitable for plantations, they were gradually pushed out as planters bought up land to raise livestock or more crops. In general, only slave owners who had established themselves in business or the professions had the capital reserves to rise into the planter elite.

Especially in the Lower South, owning slaves was a necessary precondition for upward mobility, but it was hardly a sufficient one. Slaveholders who failed to advance had nonetheless acquired a badge of social respectability. As a Baptist opponent of slavery put it, "Without slaves a man's children stand but poor chance to marry in reputation." Aside from conferring status, owning a few slaves could relieve a white household of much hard domestic labor. "I wish to God every head of a family in the United States had one [slave] to take the drudgery and menial service off his family," proclaimed Andrew Johnson of Tennessee in the U.S. Senate. (Johnson replaced Abraham Lincoln as president in 1865.)

THE WHITE MAJORITY

Three-fourths of southern white families owned no slaves in 1860. Although most numerous in the Upper South, nonslaveholders predominated wherever the soil and climate were not suitable for plantation agriculture. Most were yeoman farmers who worked their own land with family labor.

These farmers were quick to move when times were bad and their land was used up, but once settled in an area, they formed intensely localized societies in which fathers and husbands held sway over their families. The community extended 5 to 10 miles around the nearest country store or county courthouse. Networks of kin and friends provided labor services when needed, fellowship in evangelical churches, and staple goods that an individual farm could not produce. Social travel and international markets, so central to the lives of planters, had little relevance in the farmers' community-centered existence. The yeomanry aimed to be self-sufficient and limited market involvement to the sale of livestock and an occasional cotton crop that could bring in needed cash.

Yeoman farmers jealously guarded their independence, and in their tight little worlds of face-to-face relationships, they demanded that planters treat them as social equals. Ever fearful of being reduced to dependence, they avoided debt and sought to limit government authority. Rather than risk financial ruin by buying slaves on credit to grow cotton, they grew food crops and depended on their sons and, when needed, their wives and daughters to work the fields. Far longer than most northern farmers, and in part because poor transportation raised the cost of manufactured goods, they continued to make their own clothes, shoes, soap, and other consumer items.

Nonslaveholding farmers from the mountains and planters on the bottomlands rarely mixed, and their societies developed in isolation from each other. In areas where there were both small farms and scattered plantations, the interests of the yeomen and the planters were often complementary. Planters provided local markets for the surplus grain and livestock of nonslaveholders and, for a small fee, access to grist mills and gins for grinding corn and cleaning cotton. They lent small sums to poorer neighbors in emergencies or to pay taxes. The yeomen staffed the slave patrols and became overseers on the plantations. Both groups sought to protect property rights from outside interference and to maintain a system of racial control in which white liberties rested on black degradation.

When yeomen and planters did clash, it was usually over economic issues. Large slaveholders needing better credit and marketing facilities gravitated toward the Whig Party, which called for banks and internal improvements. Nonslaveholding farmers, especially in the Lower South, tended to be Democrats who opposed banks and state-funded economic projects. They considered bankers grasping outsiders who wanted to rob them of their economic independence, and they suspected that state involvement in the economy led only to higher taxes and increased the public debt. These partisan battles, however, rarely involved a debate about the merits of slavery. As long as planters deferred to the egalitarian sensibilities of the yeomen by courting them at election time and promising to safeguard their liberties, the planters were able to maintain broad support for slavery across class lines.

Around 15 percent of rural white families owned neither land nor slaves. These were the so-called "poor whites," stigmatized by both abolitionists and planters as lazy and shiftless. The abolitionists considered them a kind of underclass who proved that slavery so degraded the dignity of labor that it led people to shun work and lapse into wretched poverty. To the planters, they were a constant nuisance and a threat to slave discipline. Planters habitually complained that poor whites demoralized their slaves by showing that a person could survive without steady labor. Planters also accused them of trading guns and alcohol with slaves for stolen plantation property. Despite the efforts of slaveowners to crack down on this illicit trade, poor whites and slaves continued to swap goods and socially intermingle on the fringes of the plantations.

Some landless white people did live down to their negative stereotype. Still, the "poor white trash" label with which they were stigmatized is misleading. Most were resourceful and enterprising enough to supply themselves with all the material comforts they wanted. Back in the swamps and pine barrens shunned by planters and yeomen alike, they squatted on a few acres of land, put up crude cabins for shelter, planted some corn, and grazed livestock in the surrounding woods. Aided by the mild southern climate, they had all the corn and pork they could eat. Not having to do steady work for survival, they hunted, fished, and took orders from no one. Although poor by most standards, they were also defiantly self-reliant.

Nonslaveholders were a growing majority in southern cities, especially among the working classes. These urban workers shared no agricultural interests or ties with the planters. Nor were most of them, especially in the unskilled ranks, southern-born. Northerners and immigrants dominated the urban work force.

Free workers, especially Irish and German immigrants, increasingly replaced slaves in urban labor markets. These white workers bitterly resented competition from black slaves, and their demands to exclude slaves from the urban workplace reinforced planters' belief that cities bred abolitionism. When urban laborers protested against slave competition in the 1850s, planters singled them out as the nonslaveholders most likely to attack slavery.

FREE BLACK PEOPLE

A few southern black people—6 percent of the total in 1860—were "free persons of color" and constituted 3 percent of the free population in the South (see Figure 11–2). These free black people occupied a precarious and vulnerable position between degraded enslavement and meaningful freedom. White intimidation and special legal provisions known as **black codes** (found throughout the North as well) denied them nearly all the rights of citizenship. Because of the legal presumption in the South that all black people were slaves, they had to carry freedom papers, official certificates of their freedom. They were shut out of the political process and could not testify against white people in court. Many occupations, especially those involved in the communication of ideas, such as the printing trades, were closed to them.

Every slave state forbade the entry of free black people, and every municipality had its own rules and regulations that forced them to live as an inferior caste. In Charleston, for example, a free black person could not smoke a cigar or carry a cane in public. Any sign of upward mobility or intimation of equal standing was ruthlessly suppressed. White people had the right of way, and a free black person who bumped into a white person on the street was likely to be flogged.

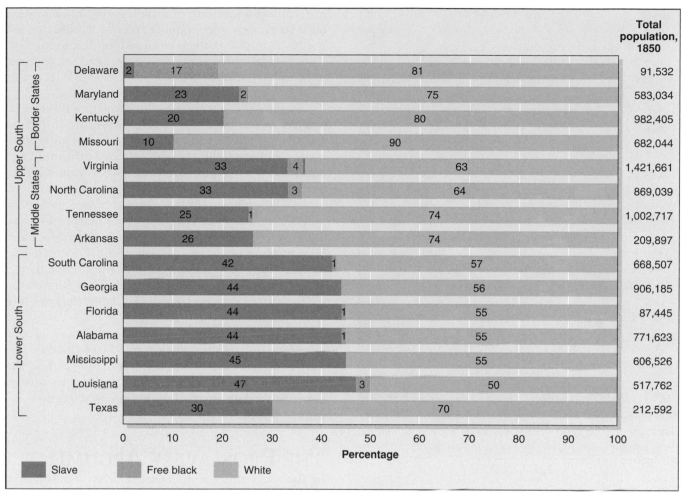

FIGURE 11-3   Slave, Free Black, and White Population in Southern States, 1850
Except for Texas, slaves by 1850 comprised over 40 percent of the population in every state of the Lower South. The small population of free black people was concentrated in the Upper South.

More than four-fifths of the southern free black population lived in the Upper South. Most were the offspring of slaves freed by private manumissions between 1780 and 1800, when slavery temporarily loosened in the Chesapeake region in the wake of the Revolutionary War. Manumissions dropped sharply after 1810, the result of heightened white anxieties over slave security after Prosser's Rebellion and the rising demand for slaves in the Lower South. From 1810 to 1860, only 13 percent of black people in the Upper South were free.

As in the North, legal barriers and white prejudice generally confined free black people to the poorest-paying and most menial work. In rural areas, a handful became independent farmers, but most worked as farm laborers or tenants. The best economic opportunities were in the cities, where some found factory jobs and positions in the skilled trades. Because the South had a general shortage of skilled labor, free black artisans—carpenters, barbers, shoemakers, tailors, and plasterers—could earn a respectable income. Indeed, the percentage of black people in the skilled trades was generally higher in the South than in the North. Talented artisans, such as Thomas Day, widely recognized as the finest cabinetmaker in North Carolina, could command a premium in wages from white employers.

One-third of free black people in the Upper South lived in cities, a much higher proportion than among white people. Cities offered black people, not only jobs, but also enough social space to found their own churches and mutual-aid associations. Especially after 1840, urban African American churches proliferated to become the center of black community life. Church Sunday schools and day schools provided black people practically their only access to education, which they persisted in pursuing despite white opposition. A "good education," declared a black schoolmaster in Baltimore,"is the *sine qua non* as regards the elevation of our people.

The Granger Collection, New York.

Barbering was one of the skilled trades open to black men during the antebellum years. Several wealthy African Americans began their careers as barbers.

Less than 2 percent of the black people in the Lower South were free in 1860. Given the greater profitability of slavery there, manumissions were rare. Most of the Lower South's free black population descended from black emigrants who fled the revolutionary unrest in Haiti in the 1790s. These refugees were artisans, shopkeepers, and farmers who settled primarily in Charleston and New Orleans. Able to secure a solid economic footing, they left their descendants wealthier than any other free black people in the United States. Free black people in the Lower South were more likely than those in the Upper South to have a marketable skill, and two-thirds of them lived in cities.

A light skin also enhanced the social standing of free black people among color-conscious whites in the Lower South. Nearly 70 percent of free black people in 1860 were mulattoes, and from their ranks came nearly all of the very small number of black planters. Mulattoes could count on greater white patronage, and they monopolized the best jobs available to free black people. A mulatto elite emerged in Charleston, Mobile, and New Orleans that carefully distanced itself from most black people, slave or free. In New Or-

leans, where a tradition of racially mixed unions dated back to French and Spanish rule, mulattoes put on lavish "octoroon balls," attended by freewomen of color and by white men. Even here, however, the mulatto elite remained suspended between black and white worlds, never fully accepted by either.

Despite the emergence of a three-tiered racial hierarchy in the port cities of the Lower South, white authorities insisted on making a white and black racial dichotomy the overriding social division in the South. As the racial defense of slavery intensified in the 1850s, more calls were made for laws to banish or enslave free black people. Arkansas passed such a law in 1859, and similar bills were proposed in Florida, Tennessee, Mississippi, and Missouri. Even Maryland held a referendum in 1859 on whether to reenslave its free black population, among the largest in the South. Only the opposition of nonslaveholders heavily dependent on cheap free black labor defeated the referendum.

Despised and feared by white people as a subversive element in a slave society, free black Southerners were daily reminded that their freedom rested on the whims of the white majority. As white attitudes turned uglier in the late antebellum period, that freedom became ever less secure.

THE PROSLAVERY ARGUMENT

In the early nineteenth century, white Southerners made no particular effort to defend slavery because the institution was not under heavy outside attack. If pressed, most white people would have called slavery a necessary evil, an unfortunate legacy from earlier generations that was needed to maintain racial peace.

The 1830s marked a turning point. After the twin shocks of Nat Turner's Rebellion and the onset of the abolitionist crusade (for more on this crusade, see Chapter 12), white mobs emerged to stifle any open criticism of slavery in the Lower South. White Southerners also began to develop a defense of slavery. By the 1850s, politicians, intellectuals, and evangelical ministers were arguing that it was a positive good, an institution ordained by God as the foundation of southern prosperity, white democracy, and Christian instruction for heathen Africans. Slavery, they insisted, was a mild, paternalistic, and even caring institution.

This defense obviously portrayed slavery as the defenders imagined it, not as it was. However comforting it may have been to individual slaveholders, the argument failed to convince abolitionists or southern dissenters who condemned slavery on moral and economic grounds.

Evangelical Protestantism dominated southern religious expression by the 1830s, and its ministers took the lead in combating abolitionist charges that slavery was a moral and religious abomination. Except for a radical minority of antislavery evangelicals in the Upper South, a group largely silenced or driven out by the conservative reaction following Nat Turner's uprising, the southern churches had always supported slavery. This support grew more pronounced and articulate once the abolitionists stepped up their attacks on slavery in the mid-1830s.

Southern evangelicals accepted the Bible as God's literal word, and through selective reading they found abundant evidence in it to proclaim slavery fully in accord with His

As this 1841 cartoon reflects, a staple of proslavery propaganda was to contrast the allegedly contented and healthy lot of slaves with that of starving factory workers exploited by the system of wage labor.

moral dictates. They pointed out, for example, that the patriarchs of Israel owned slaves. Slavery was practiced throughout the Roman world at the time of Christ, they noted, and the apostles urged obedience to all secular laws, including those governing slavery.

Southern evangelicals also turned to the Bible to support their argument that patriarchal authority—the unquestioned power of the father—was the basis of all Christian communities. Part of that authority extended over slaves, and slavery thus became a matter of family governance, a domestic institution in which Christian masters of slaves, unlike capitalist masters of free "wage slaves" in the North, accepted responsibility for caring for their workers in sickness and old age. Far from being a moral curse, slavery was part of God's plan to Christianize an inferior race and teach its people how to produce raw materials that benefited the world's masses.

The growing commitment of southern evangelicals to slavery as a positive good clashed with the antislavery position and the generally more liberal theology of northern evangelicals. In 1837, the Presbyterians split along sectional lines in part because of differences over slavery. In 1844, and as a direct result of the slavery issue, the Methodist Episcopal Church, the nation's largest, divided into northern and southern churches. The Baptists did the same a year later. These religious schisms foreshadowed the sectionalized political divisions of the 1850s; they also severed

one of the main emotional bonds between whites in the North and the South.

The religious defense of slavery was central to the slaveholding ethic of paternalism that developed after 1830. By the 1850s, planters commonly described slaves as members of an extended family who were treated better than free workers in the North. This language often reflected the psychological need of planters to feel appreciated, even loved, as caring parents by their slave dependents. Some evangelical masters tried to act as moral stewards to their slaves and to curb the worst features of their bondage. Led by Charles Colcock Jones, a minister and planter in the Georgia lowcountry, they founded religious missions to the slaves and sought reforms, such as legal measures, that would prevent the separation of slave families. Such slaveholders, however, were a minority, and efforts to reform slavery failed largely because masters would accept no limits on their power to control and work their slaves as they saw fit.

The crusade to sanctify slavery won few converts outside the South. Most northern churches did not endorse abolitionism but did have moral qualms about slavery. In a particularly stinging rebuke to southern church leaders in the 1850s, black abolitionists succeeded in having slaveholders barred from international religious conventions.

More common than the biblical defense of slavery was the racial argument that black people were unfit for freedom among white people. Drawing in part on

FROM THEN TO NOW

The Economic Legacy of Slavery

The South today enjoys one of the highest rates of economic growth in the nation and plays host to business conglomerates, bank mergers, and Olympic games. Yet as late as the 1930s, the South was so impoverished that it was labeled the nation's number-one economic problem. The key to this remarkable transformation was the way in which the South finally overcame the economic legacy of slavery.

Because slavery persisted in the South and was abolished in the North, the Northern and Southern economies developed separately before the Civil War. The key difference was the markedly lower level of Southern investment in manufacturing and transportation compared to the levels in the North. Slaveowners had invested two-thirds of their wealth in slaves and were reluctant to promote changes that would diversify their economy along northern lines through the introduction of manufacturing based on low-wage labor. On the contrary, they had every incentive to keep wages high to protect the value of their investment in human labor.

The end of slavery reversed the basic dynamic shaping the southern economy. Planters now had to derive their wealth primarily from their land, not their slaves. As a result, they encouraged low-wage policies that transformed many former slaves and poor white farmers into impoverished tenant farmers and sharecroppers. When cotton prices began a steady decline in the 1870s, Southern investors turned to manufacturing in an effort to generate economic growth, but the abundance of cheap agricultural labor kept industrial wage rates well below the national level. Consequently, the South attracted little in the way of outside labor. And with investment opportunities more attractive elsewhere, it attracted little capital for modernizing its factories. Education in the South likewise remained behind, because the white southern elite was leery of reforms that would increase workers' skills and encourage them to leave the region in search of better wages. Thus, although southern industry grew, it remained labor-intensive and failed to keep pace with the region's rising population. By the 1930s, when the Great Depression hit, the South was mired in poverty and backwardness.

Sweeping new federal policies initiated in the wake of the Depression began fundamentally to change the Southern economy, raising wages and bringing them more in line with the national average. Farm subsidies encouraged planters to take land out of production, forcing poor tenants and sharecroppers to leave the land and migrate out of the region. Abundant, well-paying jobs in Northern factories during World War II accelerated the outflow of the South's low-skill workers. Meanwhile, federal money poured into the South for new defense plants and war-related projects.

By the 1950s, the formerly insulated, low-wage southern economy had turned the corner. Southern politicians dropped the region's corporate taxes to the lowest in the nation and became adept at attracting new sources of capital and large federal subsidies. After initially opposing the black-led civil rights revolution of the 1950s and 1960s, most of the white business elite backed the formal end of racial segregation in an attempt to improve the South's image. Today, well over a century after slavery had placed it on a separate path of economic development, the Southern economy has lost nearly all traces of its distinctiveness and can boast of being in the forefront of national economic trends.

the scientific wisdom of the day, the racial defense alleged that black people were naturally lazy and inherently inferior to white people. If freed, so went the argument, they would turn to crime and sexually assault white women. Only the controls of slavery enabled the races to coexist in the South. Slavery as necessary racial control was a central theme in Thomas R. Dew's *Review of the Debates in the Virginia Legislature of 1831 and 1832*, the first major justification of slavery by a Southerner. Dew, a Tidewater planter, was responding to a proposal for gradual emancipation that had been introduced into the Virginia legislature. Although the plan was defeated (largely because the eastern plantation counties were overrepresented in the legislature), upper-class conservatives such as Dew were alarmed by the potentially dangerous class division it had revealed between slaveholders and nonslaveholders. He tried to unite white people on the issue of race.

The racial argument resonated powerfully among white people because nearly all of them, including those otherwise opposed to slavery, dreaded emancipation. The attitude of a Tennessee farmer, as recorded by a northern traveler in the 1850s, was typical: "He said he'd always wished there hadn't been any niggers here . . . , but he wouldn't like to have them free." Unable to conceive of living in a society with many free black people, most white people could see no middle ground between slavery and the presumed social chaos of emancipation.

The existence of *black* slavery also had egalitarian implications for the nonslaveholding majority of whites. Slavery supposedly spared white Southerners from the menial, degrading labor that white northerners had to perform. Moreover, because slaves lacked political rights, champions of slavery argued that black bondage buttressed the political liberties of all white males by removing from politics the leveling demands of the poor and propertyless for a redistribution of wealth.

Despite its apparent success in forging white solidarity, the racial argument could be turned on its head and used to weaken slavery. Most white Northerners were about as racist as their southern counterparts, but they were increasingly willing to end slavery on the grounds that the stronger white race should help black people improve themselves as free persons. In short, nothing in the internal logic of racist doctrines required enslaving black people. That same logic also encouraged some white Southerners to challenge the economic prerogatives of slaveholders. Why, for example, should any white people, as members of the master race, be forced into economic competition against skilled slave artisans? Why should not all nonagricultural jobs be legally reserved for white people? Doctrines of black inferiority could not prevent white unity from cracking when the economic interests of nonslaveholders clashed with those of planters.

CONCLUSION

Slavery and a biracial social order defined the South as a distinctive region. The spread of plantation agriculture across the Lower South after 1830 deepened the involvement of white Southerners in cotton and slavery. At the same time, an abolitionist movement in the North attacked slavery on moral grounds and demanded that it be abolished. As southern interests became more enmeshed in an institution that outsiders condemned, religious and intellectual leaders portrayed slavery as a Christian institution and a positive good necessary for white democracy and harmonious race relations. Proslavery ideologues stridently insisted that the South was separate from and superior to the rest of the nation.

The proslavery argument depicted a nearly ideal society blessed by class and racial harmony. In reality, social conditions in the slave South were contradictory and conflict-ridden. Slaves were not content in their bondage. They dreamed of freedom and sustained that dream through their own forms of Christianity and the support of family and kin. Relations between masters and their slaves were antagonistic, not affectionate, and wherever the system of control slackened, slaves resisted their owners.

Nor did all white southerners, who confronted increasing economic inequality after 1830, accept racial slavery as in their best interests. It divided as well as united them. The publication in 1857 of Hinton Rowan Helper's *The Impending Crisis of the South*, a scathing indictment by a white North Carolinian of slavery's harmful effect on economic opportunities for average white people, vividly showed that not all were convinced by the proslavery argument.

During the 1850s, the size of the slaveholding class fell from 31 percent of Southern white families to 25 percent. Slaveowners were a shrinking minority, and slavery was in decline throughout the Upper South. In the Border South, free labor was replacing slavery as the dominant means of organizing economic production. In these states, slavery was a vulnerable institution. Planters were not fooled by the public rhetoric of white unity. They knew that slavery was increasingly confined to the Lower South and that elsewhere in the South white support for it was gradually eroding. Planters feared the double-edged challenge to their privileged positions of outside interference with slavery and internal white disloyalty. By the 1850s, many of them were concluding that the only way to resolve their dilemma was to make the South a separate nation.

REVIEW QUESTIONS

1. What factors accounted for the tremendous expansion of cotton production in the South? How was this expansion linked to slavery and westward movement?

2. What differentiated the Upper South from the Lower South? What role did slavery play in each region after 1815?

3. How would you characterize the life of a plantation slave? What insights does Hannah Crafts's opening account provide into the special vulnerability of slave women? Why were religion and family such key features of the world that slaves built for themselves? What evidence is there of resistance and rebellion among the slaves?

4. How did most nonslaveholding white Southerners live? What values did they prize most highly? Why did most nonslaveholders accept slavery or at least not attack it directly?

5. What was the position of free black Southerners in southern society? How were their freedoms restricted?

6. How did white Southerners attempt to defend slavery and reconcile it with Christianity?

KEY TERMS

Black codes (p. 342)

Denmark Vesey's Conspiracy (p. 336)

Gabriel Prosser's Rebellion (p. 336)

Gang system (p. 326)

Nat Turner's Rebellion (p. 336)

Slave codes (p. 332)

Underground Railroad (p. 337)

RECOMMENDED READING

Bowman, Shearer. *Masters and Lords: Mid-19th Century U.S. Planters and Prussian Junkers* (1993). A fascinating study in comparative history that portrays southern planters as agrarian capitalists.

Freehling, William W. *The Road to Disunion: Secessionists at Bay, 1776-1854* (1990). A fine introduction to the social diversity of the Old South, especially strong in exploring the tensions over slavery between the Upper South and the Lower South.

Gates, Henry Louis, Jr., ed. *The Bondwoman's Narrative* (2002). A superb introduction by the editor helps the reader appreciate just how unique is this autobiographical novel by a self-educated house slave.

Genovese, Eugene D. *Roll, Jordan, Roll: The World the Slaveholders Made* (1974). A richly textured study of slavery that is an excellent source for the interaction between masters and slaves. Genovese argues that paternalistic relations of dependent rights and obligations characterized slavery.

Johnson, Walter. *Soul by Soul: Life Inside the Antebellum Slave Market* (1999). An innovative study that takes the reader inside the daily life of the slave market and lays bare its multiple meanings for slave, slave trader, and slaveholder.

Morris, Cristopher. *Becoming Southern: The Evolution of a Way of Life, Warren County and Vicksburg, Mississippi, 1770–1860* (1995). A well-crafted study that reveals how central slavery was to the evolving self-consciousness of rural white southerners.

Oakes, James. *The Ruling Race* (1982). A relatively short but provocative history of the slave-owning class that stresses the restless, acquisitive nature of the small slave owners, the most typical holders of slaves.

Stampp, Kenneth M. *The Peculiar Institution* (1956). A work that has aged well and is still the best one-volume history of southern slavery; it leaves no doubt that slavery was both brutal and profitable.

Wyatt-Brown, Bertram. *Southern Honor: Ethics and Behavior in the Old South* (1982). Valuable for its insights into the culture of the planter class and the notions of honor that structured social relations among all white people.

ADDITIONAL SOURCES

The Lower South

Fogel, Robert W., and Stanley Engerman. *Time on the Cross: The Economics of American Negro Slavery* (1974).

Ford, Lacy K., Jr. *Origins of Southern Radicalism: The South Carolina Upcountry, 1800–1860* (1988).

Lockley, Timothy J. *Lines in the Sand: Race and Class in Lowcountry Georgia, 1750-1860* (2001).

McCurry, Stephanie. *Masters of Small Worlds* (1995).

Thornton, J. Mills, III. *Politics and Power in a Slave Society* (1978).

Vlach, John Michael. *The Planter's Prospect: Privilege and Slaves in Plantation Paintings* (2002).

Wright, Gavin. *The Political Economy of the Cotton South* (1978).

The Upper South

Allmendinger, David F. *Ruffin: Family and Reform in the Old South* (1990).

Bailey, Fred Arthur. *Class and Tennessee's Confederate Generation* (1987).

Crofts, David W. *Old Southampton: Politics and Society in a Virginia County, 1834–1869* (1992).

Fields, Barbara J. *Slavery and Freedom on the Middle Ground: Maryland during the Nineteenth Century* (1985).

McKenzie, Robert Tracey. *One South or Many? Plantation Belt and Upcounty in Civil War Era Tennessee* (1994).

Tadman, Michael. *Speculators and Slaves: Masters, Traders, and Slaves in the Old South* (1989).

Slave Life and Culture

Blassingame, John W. *The Slave Community: Plantation Life in the Antebellum South* (1972).

Dew, Charles B. *Bond of Iron: Master and Slave at Buffalo Forge* (1994).

Gutman, Herbert G. *The Black Family in Slavery and Freedom, 1750–1925* (1974).

Kolchin, Peter. *Unfree Labor: American Slavery and Russian Serfdom* (1987).

McDonald, Roderick A. *The Economy and Material Culture of Slaves* (1993).

Starobin, Robert. *Industrial Slavery in the Old South* (1970).

Wade, Richard C. *Slavery in the Cities* (1964).

Free Society

Berlin, Ira. *Slaves without Masters: The Free Negro in the Antebellum South* (1974).

Bolton, Charles C. *Poor Whites of the Antebellum South* (1994).

Bynum, Victoria E. *Unruly Women: The Politics of Social and Sexual Control in the Old South* (1992).

Cecil-Fronsman, Bill. *Common Whites: Class and Culture in Antebellum North Carolina* (1992).

Fox-Genovese, Elizabeth. *Within the Plantation Household: Black and White Women of the Old South* (1988).

Harris, J. William. *Plain Folk and Gentry in a Slave Society* (1985).

Owsley, Frank. *Plain Folk in the South* (1949).

The Proslavery Argument

Bailey, David L. *Shadow on the Church: Southwestern Evangelical Religion and the Issue of Slavery, 1783–1860* (1985).

Fredrickson, George M. *The Black Image in the White Mind* (1971).

Genovese, Eugene D. *The Slaveholders' Dilemma: Freedom and Progress in Southern Conservative Thought, 1820-1860* (1992).

Jenkins, W. S. *Pro-Slavery Thought in the Old South* (1935).

Mathews, Donald G. *Religion in the Old South* (1977).

McKivigan, John R., and Mitchell Snay, eds. *Religion and the Antebellum Debate over Slavery* (1998).

Snay, Mitchell. *Gospel of Disunion: Religion and Separatism in the Antebellum South* (1993).

WHERE TO LEARN MORE

- **The Anacostia Museum Center for African American History.** This museum of the Smithsonian Institution explores American history and cultures from an African American perspective. Go to www.si.edu/anacostia/ for information on its exhibits and a calendar of events.

- **Appalachian Museum of Berea College, Berea, Kentucky.** This museum is an excellent source for understanding the lifestyles and material culture of the nonslaveholding farmers in the Appalachian highlands. For an overview of its exhibits, see www.museum.appstate.edu/exhibits/exhibits.shtml.

- **Cottonlandia Museum, Greenwood, Mississippi.** The library and museum depict the history of cotton in the Mississippi Delta. Special collections include some Native American artifacts. Information on its displays can be found at www.gcvg.com/CL.html.

- **Jarrell Plantation, Juliette, Georgia.** This state historic site consists of a fifteen-building farm complex that conveys a good sense of the physical dimensions of a nineteenth-century Georgia plantation. For a visual tour of the plantation, go to www.mylink.net/~jarrell/.

- **Meadow Farm Museum, Richmond, Virginia.** The archives and museum are especially strong on southern farm life in the mid-nineteenth century. A description of the museum is at www.co.henrico.va.us/rec/kmfarm.html.

 Please refer to the document CD-ROM for primary sources related to this chapter.

→ *Whether at home or on the road, the contributions of women were indispensable to the success of antebellum reform movements.*

THE MARKET REVOLUTION AND SOCIAL REFORM

1815–1850

12

East Boylston, Mass. 10th mo. 2d, 1837

Dear Friend: . . .

The investigation of the rights of the slave has led me to a better understanding of my own. I have found the Anti-Slavery cause to be the high school of morals in our land — the school in which *human rights* are more fully investigated, and better understood and taught, than in any other. Here a great fundamental principle is uplifted and illuminated, and from this central light, rays innumerable stream all around. Human beings have *rights*, because they are *moral* beings: the rights of *all* men grow out of their moral nature; and as all men have the same moral nature, they have essentially the same rights. These rights may be wrested from the slave, but they cannot be alienated: his title to himself is as perfect *now*, as is that of Lyman Beecher [a prominent minister]: it is stamped on his moral being, and is, like it, imperishable. Now if rights are founded on the nature of our moral being, then the *mere circumstance of sex* does not give to man higher rights and responsibilities, than to woman. To suppose that it does, would be to deny the self-evident truth, that the "physical constitution is the mere instrument of the moral nature." To suppose that it does, would be to break up utterly the relations, of the two natures, and to reverse their functions, exalting the animal nature into a monarch, and humbling the moral into a slave; making the former a pro-

CHAPTER OUTLINE

Industrial Change and Urbanization
The Transportation Revolution
Cities and Immigrants
The Industrial Revolution
Growing Inequality and New Classes

Reform and Moral Order
The Benevolent Empire
The Temperance Movement
Women's Role in Reform
Backlash against Benevolence

Institutions and Social Improvement
School Reform
Prisons, Workhouses, and Asylums
Utopian Alternatives

Abolitionism and Women's Rights
Rejecting Colonization
Abolitionism
The Women's Rights Movement
Political Antislavery

Conclusion

prietor, and the latter its property. When human beings are regarded as *moral* beings, *sex*, instead of being enthroned upon the summit, . . . sinks into insignificance and nothingness. My doctrine then is, that whatever it is morally right for man to do, it is morally right for woman to do. Our duties originate, not from difference of sex, but from the diversity of our relations in life, the various gifts and talents committed to our care, and the different eras in which we live.

Angelina Emily Grimké

Aileen S. Kraditor, ed., *Up From the Pedestal: Selected Writings in the History of American Feminism* (New York: Quadrangle, 1968), pp. 62–63.

Angelina Grimké wrote the above as part of a public letter to Catherine Beecher, a pioneer in women's education and the daughter of the evangelical preacher Lyman Beecher mentioned in the letter. In 1837, on an abolitionist lecture tour in New England with her sister Sarah, Angelina had become the first American woman to defy the social taboo against women speaking in public to a mixed audience of men and women. Catherine Beecher was among the many critics of the Grimké sisters, and Angelina publicly responded to her attacks.

Born in 1805 to a wealthy slaveholding family in Charleston, Angelina was the daughter of a prominent jurist. Despite all the social and economic benefits that membership in the planter class conferred upon her, she passionately rejected slavery when she became a young adult. As was also true for her sister, this rejection was part of a religious conversion to Quakerism. Angelina left her home in Charleston in 1829 and joined Sarah in Philadelphia. The sisters joined the abolitionist movement in 1835, and within two years had become the crusade's most celebrated (and notorious) platform lecturers. As Angelina made clear in her letter to Beecher, her commitment to women's rights flowed out of her exposure to abolitionism.

Soon after her marriage in 1838 to the abolitionist Theodore Weld, Angelina compiled much of the first-hand documentation on slavery that contributed to the popular success of Weld's *American Slavery As It Is,* an antislavery tract that appeared in 1839. For reasons that still remain mysterious, her marriage also coincided with her withdrawal from public life for a dozen years. Although she resumed her reform activities in the 1850s and worked for the emancipation of the slaves during the Civil War, she only rarely spoke in public. Before her death in 1879, Angelina learned that her brother Henry, who had become the family patriarch after the death of her father in 1819, had fathered three slave children, whom he retained as slaves. Her worst fears of the corrupting influence of slavery had been confirmed.

Although Angelina, in her commitment to radical reform, was hardly typical of antebellum American women, let alone women of the planter class, her journey from a privileged life in Charleston to one of social activism in the North speaks to the radicalizing potential of the reform impulse that swept over the nation after the War of 1812.

This reform impulse was strongest in the North, where traditional social and economic relations were undergoing wrenching changes as a market revolution accelerated the spread of cities, factories, and commercialized farms. Cities grew at the fastest relative rate in American history. Urbanization also brought new production patterns and increasingly separated one's home from one's place of work. New middle and working classes evolved in response to such changes, which were the most pronounced in the Northeast. The North was also the area where the emotional fires of evangelical revivals burned the hottest.

The religious message of the Second Great Awakening that began in the early 1800s provided a framework for responding to the changes that accompanied the market revolution. New within mainstream Protestantism was the belief that anyone who sought salvation could attain it, not just those whom God had predestined to be saved. Evangelicalism taught that in both the spiritual and secular realms, individuals were accountable for their own actions. Through Christian activism, individuals could strive toward moral perfectibility. Social evils, and the sinful consequences of economic and social changes, could be cleansed if only good Christians would help others find the path of righteousness.

The first wave of reform after the War of 1812 focused on individual behavior, targeting drinking, gambling, sexual misconduct, and Sabbath-breaking. By the 1830s, a second phase of reform turned to institutional solutions for crime, poverty, and social delinquency, largely untouched by voluntary moral suasion. The third phase of the reform cycle rejected the social beliefs and practices that prescribed fixed and subordinate positions to certain Americans based on race and also on sex. This radical phase culminated in the abolitionist and women's right's movement.

KEY TOPICS

- The increasing industrialization of the U.S. economy between 1815 and 1850

- The growth of cities and the emergence of both a new middle-class society and a lower class of working poor

- New wealth and the increasing inequalities among the rich, the middle class, and the working classes

- The rise of the reform movement after the War of 1812

- The growth of abolitionist agitation and sentiment in the North

- Women's crucial role in the reform movements and the rise of an organized women's rights movement

INDUSTRIAL CHANGE AND URBANIZATION

In 1820, four in five of the free labor force worked in agriculture, and manufacturing played a minor role in overall economic activity. Over the next three decades, however, the United States joined England as a world leader in industrialization. By 1850, manufacturing accounted for one-third of total commodity output, and nonfarm employment had more than doubled to 45 percent of the labor force.

The most direct cause of this rapid and sustained surge in manufacturing was the increasing consumption within the United States of the goods the country was producing. The **transportation revolution** dramatically reduced transportation costs and shipping times, opened up new markets for farmers and manufacturers alike, and provided an ongoing incentive for expanding production (see Table 12–1). As agricultural and manufactured goods were exchanged more efficiently, a growing home market continually stimulated the development of American manufacturing.

THE TRANSPORTATION REVOLUTION

Aside from some 4,000 miles of toll roads in the Northeast, the nation had nothing approaching a system of transportation in 1815. The cost of moving goods by land transportation was prohibitively high. It cost just as much to haul heavy goods by horse-drawn wagons 30 miles into the interior as to ship them 3,000 miles across the Atlantic Ocean. Water transportation was much cheaper, but it was limited to the coast or navigable rivers. Thus, only farmers located near a city or a river could grow surplus crops for sale in an outside market. Western farm surpluses followed the southerly flow of the Ohio and Mississippi river systems to market outlets in New Orleans.

Steamboats and canals. Steamboats provided the first transportation breakthrough. In 1807, Robert Fulton demonstrated their commercial practicality when he sent the *Clermont* 150 miles up the Hudson River from New York City to Albany. By the 1820s, steamboats had reduced the cost and the time of up-river shipments by 90 percent. As steamboats spread to western waters, more and more farmers could now reap the economic benefits of exporting corn, pork, and other regional foodstuffs.

Western trade did not start to flow eastward until the completion of the Erie Canal in 1825, the first and most successful of the artificial waterways designed to link eastern seaboard cities with western markets (see Map 12–1). Funded by the

TABLE 12.1			
Impact of the Transportation Revolution on Traveling Time			
Route	**1800**	**1830**	**1860**
New York to Philadelphia	2 days	1 day	Less than 1 day
New York to Charleston	More than 1 week	5 days	2 days
New York to Chicago	6 weeks	3 weeks	2 days
New York to New Orleans	4 weeks	2 weeks	6 days

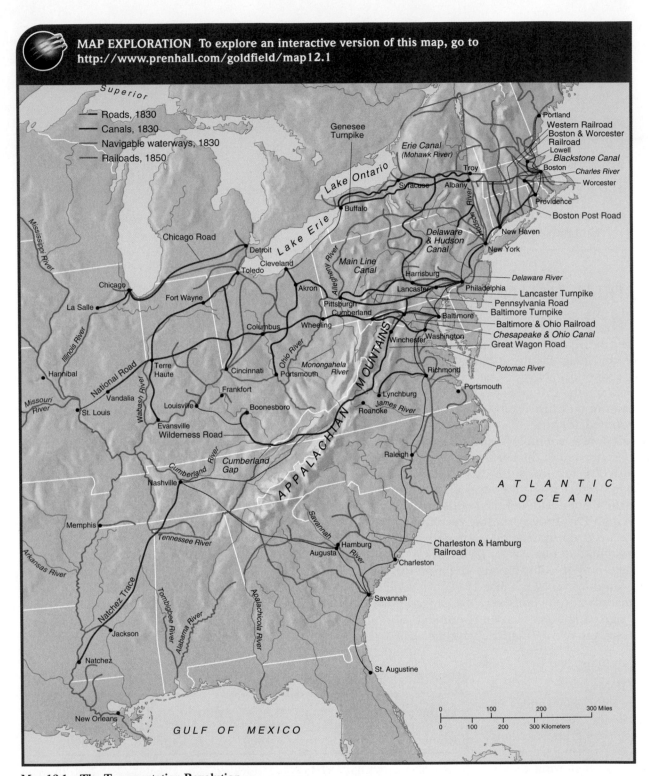

MAP EXPLORATION To explore an interactive version of this map, go to http://www.prenhall.com/goldfield/map12.1

MAP 12-1 The Transportation Revolution

By 1830, a network of roads, canals, and navigable rivers was spurring economic growth in the first phase of the Transportation Revolution. By 1850, railroads, the key development in the second phase of the Transportation Revolution, were opening up additional areas to commercial activity.

Chronology

1790	Samuel Slater opens the first permanent cotton mill in Rhode Island.
1793	Eli Whitney patents the first cotton gin.
1807	Robert Fulton's steamboat, the *Clermont*, makes its pioneering voyage up the Hudson River.
1814	The Boston Associates opens its Waltham mill, the first textile factory to mechanize all phases of production.
1817	Construction on the Erie Canal begins.
	American Colonization Society is founded.
1819–1823	Economic depression.
1824	In *Gibbons v. Ogden*, the Supreme Court strikes down a state monopoly over steamboat navigation.
1825	Erie Canal is completed.
1826	American Temperance Society launches its crusade.
1828	The Baltimore and the Ohio, the most important of the early railroads, is chartered.
1829	David Walker publishes *Appeal to the Colored Citizens of the World*.
1830	Joseph Smith founds the Church of Jesus Christ of Latter-day Saints.
1830–1831	Evangelical revivals are held in northern cities.
1831	William Lloyd Garrison begins publishing *The Liberator*.
1833	Slaves in the British Empire are emancipated.
	American Anti-Slavery Society is organized.
1834	New York Female Reform Society is founded.
	Female workers at the Lowell Mills stage their first strike.
1836	Congress passes gag rule.
1837	Horace Mann begins campaign for school reform in Massachusetts.
	Antiabolitionist mob kills Elijah P. Lovejoy.
	In *Charles River Bridge v. Warren Bridge*, the Supreme Court encourages economic competition by ruling that presumed rights of monopolistic privileges could not be used to block new economic enterprises.
1839–1843	Economic depression.
1840	Abolitionists split into Garrisonian and anti-Garrisonian societies.
	Political abolitionists launch the Liberty party.
1841	Brook Farm is established.
	Dorothea Dix begins her work to improve conditions for the mentally ill.
1842	Massachusetts Supreme Court in *Commonwealth v. Hunt* strengthens the legal right of workers to organize trade unions.
1845	Potato famine in Ireland sets off a mass migration of Irish to the United States.
1846–1848	Mormons migrate to the West.
1847	John Humphrey Noyes establishes the Oneida Community.
1848	Seneca Falls Convention outlines a program for women's rights.

New York legislature, the Erie Canal stretched 364 miles from Albany to Buffalo, a small port on Lake Erie. Begun at a time when the United States had barely 100 miles of canals, its construction by Irish immigrants was the greatest engineering feat of its era. An immediate success, the Erie reduced the cost of sending freight from Buffalo to New York City by more than 90 percent, and by the 1840s, it was pulling in more western trade than was being sent to New Orleans on the Mississippi River.

Anxious to match the Erie's success, other states launched plans for competing canals to the West. More than 3,000 miles of canal were in place by 1840, but no other canal could overcome the tremendous advantage of the Erie's head start in fixing trading patterns along its route. Before the Panic of 1837

abruptly ended the canal boom by drying up financing, three broad networks of canals had been built. One set linked seaboard cities on the Atlantic with their agricultural hinterlands, another connected the Mid-Atlantic states with the Ohio River Valley, and a third funneled western grain to ports on the Great Lakes.

Railroads. Railroads were the last and ultimately the most important link in the transportation improvements that spurred economic development in Jacksonian America. Moving at 15 to 20 miles per hour—four times as fast as a canal boat and twice the speed of a stagecoach—the railroads of the 1830s struck Americans as a radically new technology that overturned traditional notions of time and space. "I

Canal boats below a lock at the Junction of the Erie with the Northern (Champlain) Canals. Aquatint by John Hill.

(c)John Hill. Junction of Erie and Northern (Champlain) Canals. Aquatint, Number 34684. Courtesy of The New York Historical Society.

cannot describe the strange sensation produced on seeing the train of cars come up. And when I started in them . . . it seemed like a dream," exclaimed Christopher Columbus Baldwin of Massachusetts when he saw his first railroad car in 1835.

In 1825, the same year the Erie Canal was completed, the world's first general-purpose railroad, the Stockton and Darlington, opened in England. The construction of the first American railroads began in the late 1820s, and they all pushed outward from seaboard cities eager to connect to the western market. One of the first, the Baltimore and Ohio, was to cross the Appalachians and connect Baltimore with Wheeling, Virginia, on the Ohio River. The Boston and Worcester linked New England and the eastern terminus of the Erie at Albany. By 1840, U.S. rail mileage had drawn even with that of the canals and was twice as extensive as the total for all of Europe. The rails now became the most dynamic booster of interregional trade. Whereas the canal network stopped expanding after 1840, the railroads tripled their mileage in the 1840s. Revenues from freight traffic exceeded those from passenger travel for the first time in 1849. By then, trunk lines built westward from Atlantic Coast cities had reached the Great Lakes and the Ohio Valley and were about to enter the Mississippi Valley.

The rail network in place by mid-century was already altering the North-South sectional balance. The bulk of western trade no longer went downriver to New Orleans but was shipped to the East. Moving in the opposite direction to the West were northern-born settlers, manufactured goods, and cultural values that increas-ingly unified the free states east of the Mississippi into a common economic and cultural unit. As their distinctions blurred, the Northeast and the Old Northwest were becoming just the North. Significantly, no direct rail connection linked the North and the South.

Government and the transportation revolution.

Both national and state government played an active role in promoting the transportation revolution. Given high construction costs and the uncertainty of future profits, private investors were leery of risking their scarce capital in long-term transportation projects. State legislatures stepped in and furnished some 70 percent of the funding for canals and about half of all railroad capital. By the 1830s, the states were also making it easier for private businesses, and especially those in transportation, to receive the legal privileges of incorporation. Paramount among these privileges was the protection of limited liability—that is, the limiting of an investor's liability to one's direct financial stake in the company—and the power of eminent domain—the legal right to purchase whatever land was needed for rights-of-way. The federal government provided engineers for railroad surveys, lowered tariff duties on iron used in rail construction, and granted subsidies to the railroads in the form of public land. Most important, however, were two decisions of the Supreme Court that helped open up the economy to competition. In **Gibbons v. Ogden** (1824), the Court overturned a New York law that had given Aaron Ogden a monopoly on steamboat service between New York and New Jersey. Thomas Gibbons, Ogden's competitor, had a federal license for the coastal trade. The right to compete under the national license, the Court ruled, took legal precedence over Ogden's monopoly. The decision affirmed the supremacy of the national government to regulate interstate commerce.

A new Court, presided over by Roger B. Taney, who became chief justice when John Marshall died in 1835, struck a bolder blow against monopoly in the landmark case of **Charles River Bridge v. Warren Bridge** in 1837. Taney ruled in favor of the Warren Bridge Company by deciding that the older Charles River Bridge Company had not received a monopoly from Massachusetts to collect tolls across the Charles River. Any uncertainties in the charter rights of corpo-

New York City's busy harbor was the entry to the largest metropolitan center that emerged in the nineteenth-century U.S.

rations, reasoned Taney, should be resolved in favor of the broader community interests that would be served by free and open competition.

CITIES AND IMMIGRANTS

Barely one in twenty Americans in the 1790s lived in an urban area (defined by the federal census as a place with a population of 2,500 or more) and Philadelphia, with a population just over 40,000, was the nation's largest city. By 1850, more than one in seven Americans was a city-dweller, and the nation had ten cities whose population exceeded fifty thousand (see Map 12–2). The transportation revolution triggered this surge in urban growth. The cities that prospered and grew were those with access to the expanding network of cheap transport on steamboats, canals, and railroads. This network opened up the rural interior for the purchase of farm commodities by city merchants and the sale of finished goods by urban importers and manufacturers. A huge influx of immigrants after the mid-1840s and simultaneous advances in steam engines provided the cheap labor and sources of power that increasingly made cities focal points of manufacturing production.

The port cities. America's largest cities in the early nineteenth century were its Atlantic ports: New York, Philadelphia, Baltimore, and Boston. As late as the 1820s, these four cities held more than half the total urban population and packed together merchants, artisans, and laborers near the waterfronts that were their economic lifeblood. All these cities grew as a result of transportation improvements, but only New York experienced phenomenal growth. By 1810, New

York had become the largest American city, and its population exceeded 800,000 by the 1850s. One-third of the nation's exports and more than three-fifths of its imports passed through New York between 1820 and 1860. No wonder poet Walt Whitman trumpeted this metropolis as "the great place of the Western Continent, the heart, the brain, the focus, the main spring, the pinnacle, the extremity, the no more beyond of the new world."

New York's harbor gave oceangoing ships direct, protected access to Manhattan Island, and from there, the Hudson River provided a navigable highway flowing 150 miles north to Albany, deep in the state's agricultural interior. No other port was so ideally situated for trade. And no other had the advantage of access to the Erie Canal. New York City benefited, not only from the increased volume of western foodstuffs sent east across the Erie and then down the Hudson River for export to Europe, but also from the swelling flow of finished goods shipped out of New York for sale in the West to farmers increasingly specializing in the production of cash crops. New Yorkers plowed the profits of this commerce into local real estate—which soared in value fifty-fold between 1823 and 1836— and into financial institutions such as the New York Stock Exchange, founded in 1817. The city's banks brought together the capital that made New York the country's chief financial center.

As they grew, the Atlantic ports pioneered new forms of city transportation. Omnibuses—horse-drawn coaches carrying up to twenty passengers—and steam ferries were in common use by the 1820s. The first commuter railroad, the Boston and Worcester,

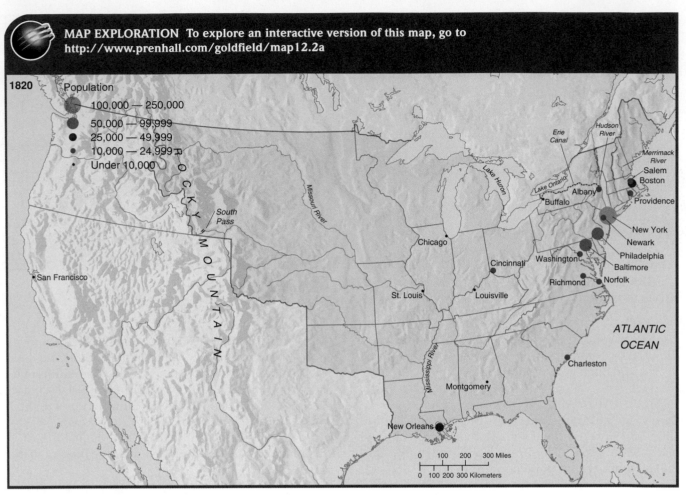

MAP EXPLORATION To explore an interactive version of this map, go to
http://www.prenhall.com/goldfield/map12.2a

MAP 12-2 **The Growth of Cities, 1820-1860**

*In 1820, most cities were clustered along the Atlantic seaboard. By 1860, new transportation
outlets—canals and railroads—had fostered the rapid growth of cities in the interior, especially
at trading locations with access to navigable rivers or to the Great Lakes. Much of this growth
occurred in the 1850s.*

Data Source: *Statistical Abstract of the United States.*

began service in 1838. At mid-century, horse-drawn street railway lines moved at speeds of about 6 miles an hour, overcoming some of the limitations of the "walking cities" of the early nineteenth century.

Accompanying this growth were the first slums, the most notorious of which was the Five Points district of New York City. In 1842, the English novelist Charles Dickens described this area of tenement houses, brothels, and saloons as "these narrow ways, diverging to the right and left, and reeking everywhere with dirt and filth." Small, flimsy wooden structures, often crammed into a back alley, housed the working poor in cramped, fetid conditions. Backyard privies, supplemented by chamber pots, were the standard means of disposing of human wastes. These outhouses overflowed in heavy rain and often contaminated private wells, the source of drinking water. Garbage and animal wastes simply accumulated on streets, scavenged by roving packs of hogs.

Inland cities. Largely because of their newness, the cities in the interior escaped the worst of these slum conditions. It was here, away from the seaboard, that the rate of urban growth was the highest. Among the fastest-growing cities was Rochester, New York, a village that the opening of the Erie Canal transformed into a major flour-milling center. Pittsburgh, at the head of the Ohio River, was the first western city to develop a manufacturing sector to complement its exchange function. With access to the extensive coalfields of western Pennsylvania, Pittsburgh had a cheap fuel that provided the high heat needed to manufacture

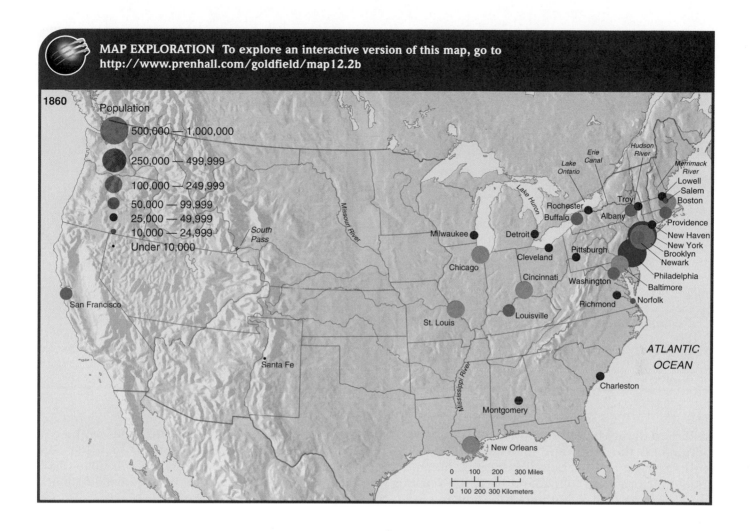

MAP EXPLORATION To explore an interactive version of this map, go to
http://www.prenhall.com/goldfield/map12.2b

1860

Population

500,000 — 1,000,000
250,000 — 499,999
100,000 — 249,999
50,000 — 99,999
25,000 — 49,999
10,000 — 24,999
Under 10,000

iron and glass. It emerged as America's best-known and most polluted manufacturing city. Cincinnati, downstream on the Ohio, soon became famous for its hogs. "Porkopolis," as it was called, was the West's first meatpacking center. St. Louis, just below the merger of the Missouri and the Mississippi Rivers, prospered by servicing American trade with the trans-Mississippi West.

By the 1840s, the Great Lake ports of Cleveland, Detroit, Milwaukee, and Chicago were the dynamic centers of western urbanization. Their combined population increased twenty-five-fold between 1830 and 1850. The Great Lakes served as an extension of the Erie Canal, and cities on the lakes where incoming and outgoing goods had to be unloaded for transshipment benefited enormously. They attracted settlers and soon evolved into regional economic centers serving the surrounding agricultural communities. They also aggressively promoted themselves into major rail hubs and thus reaped the economic advantages of being at the juncture of both water and rail transport.

New industrial cities.   The only other cities growing as fast as the Great Lakes ports were the new industrial towns. The densest cluster of these was in rural New England along the fall line of rivers, where the rapidly falling water provided cheap power to drive the industrial machinery of factories and machine shops. Each town was tied to a transportation network that brought in raw cotton for the textile mills from the mercantile centers of Boston and Providence and shipped out the finished goods.

Lowell, Massachusetts, was America's first large-scale planned manufacturing city. Founded in 1822 by Boston businessmen, Lowell was built around the falls of the Merrimack River. Within a decade, rural fields had been transformed into a city of eighteen thousand people. Multistoried brick factories surrounded by detached housing for the supervisory

Overview

Changes Promoting Growth in the Transformed Economy

Sector	1815	1850
Travel and transportation	By foot and horse-drawn wagon	Cheaper and faster with canals, steamboats, and railroads opening up new markets
Population	Overwhelmingly native-born, rural, and concentrated east of the Appalachian Mountains	Four times larger as a result of natural increase and surge of immigration after 1840; settlement of West and growth of cities
Wage labor	Native-born, primarily women and children in manufacturing	Expanding as rural poor and immigrants enter the manufacturing work force
Power	Water-driven mills	Steam-driven engines
Farming	Subsistence-oriented; surplus sold in localized markets	Commercialized agriculture spreading in response to improvements in transportation
Manufacturing	Small-scale production in household units and artisan shops	Large-scale production in eastern cities and factories

staff and large boardinghouses for the workers dominated the landscape and defined the city's industrial functions. Lowell's success became a model for others to follow, and by 1840, New England led the North in both urbanization and industrialization.

Immigration. Swelling the size of nearly all the cities was a surge of immigrants after the 1830s. From 1840 to 1860 the number of immigrants, 4.2 million, increased tenfold over the number that had come in the two preceding decades. At mid-century, most of the population in New York was foreign-born, and in all the port cities of the Northeast, immigrants dominated the manufacturing work force. Most of these immigrants were Irish and German (see Figure 12–1).

In the 1840s, economic and political upheavals in Europe spurred mass migration, mostly to the United States. Catholic peasants of Ireland, dominated by their Protestant English land-

lords, eked out a subsistence as tenants on tiny plots of land. A potato blight wiped out the crop in 1845 and 1846, and in the next five years about 1 million Irish died of malnutrition and disease. Another 1.5 million fled, many to the United States.

Lowell was the nation's leading textile center and the second-largest city in Massachusetts by 1850. The building with the cupola and the structure with dormers and chimneys were part of the mill complex. The two detached buildings were boardinghouses for the young women who worked in the mills.

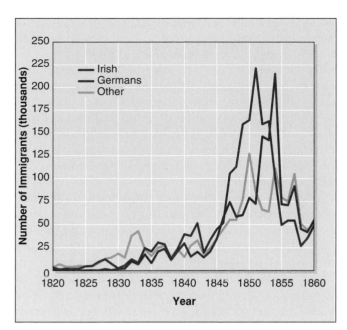

FIGURE 12-1   Immigration to the United States, 1820-1860
The potato famine in Ireland and economic and political unrest on the Continent led to a surge in immigration in the 1840s. The pace slackened in the mid-1850s, when economic conditions in Europe improved.

Data Source: U.S. Bureau of the Census, *Historical Statistics of the United States, Colonial Times to 1957* (1960), p. 57.

The Irish had no money to buy land or move west unless they joined construction gangs for canals and railroads. Without marketable skills, they had to take the worst and lowest-paying jobs: ragpickers, porters, day laborers, and unskilled factory hands. Wives and daughters became laundresses and maids for the urban middle class. Packed into dark cellars, unventilated attics, and rank tenements, the Irish suffered from very high mortality rates. Still, cash wages and access to food made the American city enviable, compared to the prospect of starvation in Ireland. Urging her parents to join her, Margaret McCarthy, an Irish domestic servant, wrote in 1850 that New York was a place "where no man or woman ever Hungered or ever will and where you will not be Seen Naked . . . where you would never want or be at a loss for a good Breakfast and Dinner."

German immigrants were second in number only to the Irish by the 1850s. They came to America to escape poor harvests and political turmoil. Far more Germans than Irish had owned property as farmers, artisans, and shopkeepers and had the capital to purchase land in the West and the skills to join the ranks of small businessmen in the cities. They were also more likely than the Irish to have entered the country through Baltimore or New Orleans, southern ports engaged in the tobacco and cotton trade with continental Europe. From there they fanned out into the Mississippi and Ohio Valleys. More so than the Irish, German immigrants settled in rural areas, but they also gravitated to cities, and by the 1850s they were close to a majority in some of the large cities of the Midwest and Northeast. With their diversified skills, they found ample economic opportunities in the fast-growing cities of the West and a setting in which to build neighborhoods of German-speaking shops, churches, schools, and benevolent societies. These tightly knit communities published their own newspapers and met most of the immigrant's cultural and economic needs.

About four in five of all the immigrants arriving after 1840 settled in the New England and mid-Atlantic states. Their sheer numbers transformed the size and ethnic composition of the working class, especially in the cities of the Northeast. And their cheap labor provided the final ingredient in the expansion of industrialization that began after the War of 1812.

THE INDUSTRIAL REVOLUTION

The Northeast led America's industrial revolution. In 1815, this region had the largest cities, the most developed capital markets, the readiest access to the technological skills of artisans, and the greatest supply of available labor. The first large-scale factories, the textile mills, were erected in New England in the 1820s. For the next thirty years, the United States had the most rapidly developing industrial economy in the world.

The household and the small workshop were the sites of manufacturing in Jefferson's America. Wider markets for household manufactures began to develop in the late eighteenth century with the coming of the **putting-out system**. Local merchants furnished ("put out") raw materials to rural households and paid at a piece rate for the labor that converted those raw materials into manufactured products. The supplying merchant then marketed and sold these goods.

In the cities and larger towns, most manufacturing was done by artisans, skilled craftsmen who were also known as mechanics. Working in their own shops and with their own tools, they produced small batches of finished goods. Artisans and their families fed, clothed, and housed the urban population and constituted close to half the population in the seaport cities. Each artisan had a specific skill that set him above common laborers. These skills came from hands-on experience and craft traditions that were handed down from one generation to the next.

The "mysteries of the craft" were taught by master craftsmen to the journeymen and apprentices who lived with them and worked in their shops. Journeymen had learned the skills of their craft but lacked the

John Neagle (American, 1796–1865). "Pat Lyon at the Forge," 1826–27. Oil on canvas, 93 3/4 x 68 in. (238.1 x 172.7 cm). Henry H. and Zoe Oliver Sherman Fund, 1975.806. Courtesy, Museum of Fine Arts, Boston. Reproduced with permission. (c)2000 Museum of Fine Arts.

As revealed in this portrait of the blacksmith Pat Lyon, the self-image of the artisans was closely related to the pride and dignity they derived from their craft work.

capital to open their own shops. Before establishing their own businesses, they saved their earnings and honed their skills while working for a wage under a master. Apprentices were adolescent boys legally sent by their fathers to live with and obey a master craftsman in return for being taught a trade. By the terms of the contract, known as an indenture, the master also provided for the apprentice's schooling and moral upbringing. An apprentice could reasonably expect to be promoted to journeyman in his late teens and begin advancement toward his competency, a secure income from an independent trade that would enable him to support a family.

The factory system of production that would undercut both household and artisanal manufacturing after 1815 had several advantages. First, the factories could produce goods far more quickly and cheaply per worker than could artisans or rural households. Factories subdivided the specialized skills of the artisan into a series of semiskilled tasks, a process foreshadowed by the putting-out system. Second, factories put workers under systematic controls. And in the final stage of industrialization, they boosted workers' productivity through the use of power-driven machinery.

Britain pioneered the technological advances that drove early industrialization. The secrets of this technology, especially the designs for the machines that mechanized textile production, were closely guarded by the British government. Despite attempts to prohibit the emigration of artisans who knew how the machinery worked, some British mechanics made it to the United States. Samuel Slater was one of them, and he took over the operation of a fledging mill in Providence, Rhode Island. With his knowledge of how to build the water-powered spinning machinery, he converted the mill into the nation's first permanent cotton factory in 1790.

Slater's factory, and those modeled after it, manufactured yarn that was put out to rural housewives to be woven into cloth. The first factory to mechanize the operations of spinning and weaving and turn out finished cloth was incorporated in Waltham, Massachusetts, in 1813 by the Boston Associates, a group of wealthy merchants. The Waltham factory was heavily capitalized, relied on the latest technology, and recruited its work force from rural farm families.

The first real spurt of factory building came with the closing off of British imports during the Embargo and the War of 1812. Hundreds of new cotton and woolen mills were established from 1808 to 1815. But the great test of American manufacturing came after 1815, when peace with Britain brought a flood of cheap British manufactured goods. If factories were to continue to grow, American manufacturers had to reach more consumers in their home market and overcome the British advantage of lower labor costs.

Sources of labor. Industrial labor was more expensive in America than in England, where the high cost of land forced the rural poor into the cities to find work. By contrast, land was cheap and plentiful in the United States, and Americans preferred the independence of farm work to the dependence of factory labor. Consequently, the first mill workers were predominately children. For example, the mills that advertised in the *Massachusetts Spy* in the 1820s called for families "of five or six children each." The owners set up the father on a plot of company-owned land, provided piecework for the mother, and put the children to work in the mills.

Although this so-called **Rhode Island system** of family employment sufficed for small mills, it was inadequate for the larger, more mechanized factories that were built in New England after the War of 1812. These mill owners recruited single, adolescent daughters of farmers from across New England as their laborers in the **Waltham system**. Jemima Sanborn, one of these young farm daughters, explained that she had left home for the mills because of "the hard times to get a living off the farm for so large a family." Although

Shown here working at power looms under the supervision of a male overseer, young single women constituted the bulk of the labor force in the first textile factories of New England.

fewer young women were available for factory work, immigrants were an important source of manufacturing workers as early as the 1820s. They played an especially crucial role in urban manufacturing. The port cities lacked usable water power, but by drawing on a growing pool of cheap, immigrant labor, manufacturers could expand production while driving down the cost. Particularly in finished consumer goods, such as the clothing and leather industries, where low-paid workers could stitch cloth or sole a shoe, urban manufacturing became labor-intensive, depending more heavily on workers than on investment in machines and other capital.

factory wages were low (a little over a dollar per week, after deductions for room and board), they were more than these young women could earn doing piecework in the home or as domestics. The wages also brought a liberating degree of financial independence. "When they felt the jingle of silver in their pockets," recalled Harriet Hanson Robinson of her fellow workers at Lowell in the 1830s, "there for the first time, their heads became erect and they walked as if on air."

To overcome parental fears that their daughters might be exposed to the same morally corrupting conditions associated with mill work in Britain, New England manufacturers set up paternalistic moral controls. Single female workers had to live in boardinghouses owned by the company. Curfews were imposed, visitors were screened, and church attendance was mandatory. Still, the mill women had to work six days a week from dawn to dusk for low wages. They tended clattering, fast-moving machinery in a work environment kept humid to minimize the snapping of threads in the machines. There were limits to what these women would endure, and in 1834 and 1836 the female hands at Lowell "turned out" to protest wage reductions in demonstrations that were the largest strikes in American history up to that time.

After the economic downturn of the late 1830s, conditions in the mills grew worse. By the mid-1840s, however, the Irish, desperate for work, sent their children into the mills at an earlier age than Yankee families had. These workers did not leave after two or three years of building up a small dowry for marriage, as many New Englanders did. By the early 1850s, more than half the textile operatives were Irish women.

In the mid-Atlantic region, where the farm population was more prosperous than in New England and

Except in New England textile factories and the smaller factories and shops in the seaboard cities, native-born males were the largest group of early manufacturing workers. They came from poor rural families that lacked enough land to pass on to male heirs. As late as 1840, women, including those working at home, made up about half of the manufacturing work force and one-quarter of the factory hands. Regardless of their sex, few of these workers brought any specific skills to their jobs, and hence they had little bargaining power. Economic necessity forced them to accept low wages and harsh working conditions. The sheer increase in their numbers, as opposed to any productivity gains from technological innovations, accounted by 1850 for two-thirds of the gains in manufacturing output.

Technological gains. After 1815, American manufacturers began to close the technological gap with Britain. They did so by drawing on the versatile, practical skills of American mechanics. The Dominy family of Easthampton, Long Island, for example, worked with wood and iron, built grist mills, and made clocks and watches. Mechanics experimented with new designs, improved old ones, and patented inventions that found industrial applications outside their own crafts.

The most famous early American invention was the cotton gin. Eli Whitney, a Massachusetts Yankee who, as a teenager, had turned out knives and blades at a forge on his father's farm, built the first prototype of the gin in 1793 while working as a tutor on a Georgia plantation. By cheaply and quickly removing the seeds from cotton fibers, the cotton gin spurred the cultivation of cotton across the South.

Whitney also pushed the idea of basing production on interchangeable parts. After receiving a federal contract to manufacture muskets, he designed new milling machines and turret lathes that transformed the technology of machine tool production. The federal arsenal at Harpers Ferry, Virginia, developed machine tools that could manufacture standardized, interchangeable parts. The new techniques were first applied in 1815 to the manufacture of wooden clocks and by the 1840s to sewing machines, farm machinery, and watch parts. The **American system of manufacturing**—low-cost, standardized mass production, built around interchangeable parts stamped out by machines—was America's unique contribution to the industrial revolution.

As the pace of technological innovation accelerated after 1840, so did the growth of manufacturing. Indeed, the 1840s registered the highest rate of expansion in the manufacturing sector of the economy in the nineteenth century. The adoption of the stationary steam engine in urban manufacturing fueled much of this expansion. High-pressure steam engines enabled power-driven industry to locate in the port cities of the Northeast. Steam power and more mechanized manufacturing also benefited the booming cities in the Great Lakes corridor of the Old Northwest. With limited access to water power, early manufacturing in the West was confined to the processing of farm goods. By turning to steam power and new machine tools, western manufacturers after 1840 enlarged their region's industrial base and created a new industry, the mass production of agricultural implements. The West was the center of the farm-machinery industry, and the region produced 20 percent of the nation's manufacturing output by the 1850s.

A greater control over natural resources, as well as new technologies, drove industrial growth. To provide their mills with a steady, reliable source of water—one that would not be affected by the whims of nature—the Boston Associates constructed a series of dams and canals that extended to the headwaters of the Merrimack River in northern New Hampshire. Inevitably, the ecology of the region under control changed. The level of the lakes was altered, the flow of rivers interrupted, the upward migration of spawning fish blocked, and the foraging terrain of wild game flooded. Farmers protested when their fields and pastures were submerged, but lawyers for the Boston Associates successful argued that water, like any other natural resource, should be treated as a commodity that could contribute to economic progress. Increasingly, the law treated nature as an economic resource to be engineered and bought and sold.

GROWING INEQUALITY AND NEW CLASSES

In the first half of the nineteenth century, the economy grew three times faster than in the eighteenth century, and per capita income doubled. Living standards for most Americans improved. Houses, for those who could afford them, became larger and better furnished and heated. There was a price to be paid, however, for the benefits of economic growth. Half of the adult white males were propertyless at mid-century. Wealth had become more concentrated, and extremes of wealth and poverty eroded the Jeffersonian ideal of a republic of independent proprietors who valued liberty because they were economically free.

The gap between the rich and the poor widened considerably in the early phases of industrialization (see Figure 12–2). In 1800, the richest 10 percent of Americans owned 40 to 50 percent of the national wealth. By the 1850s, that share was about 70 percent. The most glaring discrepancies in wealth appeared in the large cities. In all cities by the 1840s, the top 10 percent of the population owned 80 percent of urban wealth. Most of the urban rich had been born wealthy, the offspring of old-money families who had married and invested wisely. They belonged to exclusive clubs, attended lavish balls and dinners, and were waited on

FIGURE 12-2   Growth in Wealth Inequality, 1774–1860
The two benchmark years for the gathering of data on the nationwide distribution of wealth are 1774 and 1860. Specialized studies on regions and subregions indicate that wealth inequality increased most sharply from the 1820s to 1850, the period that coincides with early industrialization.

Data Source: Jeffrey G. Williamson and Peter H. Lindert, *American Inequality: A Macroeconomic History* (1980), p. 38.

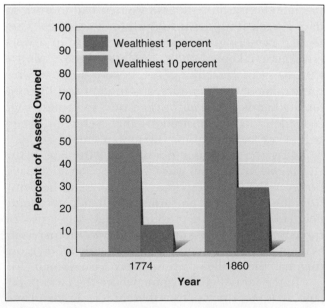

by a retinue of servants in their mansions, and generally recoiled from what they considered the "mob government" ushered in by the Jacksonian Democrats. As one of the urban elite noted, it was a society "characterized by a spirit of exclusiveness and persecution unknown in any other country. Its gradations not being regulated according to rank and titles, selfishness and conceit are its principal elements; and its arbitrary distinctions the more offensive, as they principally refer to fortune."

The new middle class.

The faster pace of economic growth that enabled the urban rich to increase their wealth also created opportunities for a rapidly expanding new middle class. This class grew as new employment opportunities opened up in nonmanual work. Most of these jobs were in northern cities and bustling market towns, where the need was greatest for office and store clerks, managerial personnel, sales agents, and independent retailers. The result by mid-century was a new middle class superimposed on the older one of independent farmers, artisans, shopkeepers, and professionals.

This scene, entitled "The Tea Room," by Henry Sargent in his 1821 painting, depicts how the wealthy elite in Boston used their social gatherings to set themselves apart as an elegantly cultured class.

The Tea Party, about 1824 Henry Sargent, American, 1770–1845 Oil on canvas 163.51 x 133.03 cm (64 3/8 x 52 3/8 in.) Museum of Fine Art, Boston Gift of Mrs. Horatio A. Lamb in memory of Mr. and Mrs. Winthrop Sargent 19.12 (c) 2003 Museum of Fine Art

The apparent separation of work and home constituted the first step in the forging of a distinctive identity for the new middle class. As the market revolution advanced, the workplace increasingly became a specialized location of production or selling. Middle-class fathers now left for work in the morning, while mothers governed households that were primarily residential units and places of material comfort, where growing quantities of consumer goods—pianos, carpets, draperies, mirrors, oil lamps, and ornate furniture—were on display. Having servants—domestic service being the single largest field of employment in the cities—became a status symbol. Shunned as degrading by most native-born white women, these low-paying jobs were filled by African-American and young immigrant (especially Irish) women. Work had not left the middle-class home; instead, it was disguised as the "domestic duties" of middle-class wives who supervised the servants.

Besides turning to etiquette books for advice on proper manners in public and in the home, the middle class also tried to shape its behavior by the tenets of evangelical religion. Revivals swept northern cities in the late 1820s. Charles G. Finney led the most dramatic and successful ones in the cities along the Erie Canal in upstate New York. Finney preached that salvation was available to those who willed it. He also stressed that both economic and moral success depended on the virtues of sobriety, self-restraint, and hard work. Aggressiveness and ambition at work were not necessarily sinful so long as businessmen reformed their own moral lives and helped others do the same. This message was immensely reassuring to employers and entrepreneurs, for it confirmed and sanctified their own pursuit of economic self-interest. It also provided them with a religious inspiration for attempting to exert moral control over their communities and employees. **Temperance**—the prohibition of alcoholic beverages—was the greatest of the evangelically inspired reforms, and abstinence from alcohol became the most telling evidence of middle-class respectability.

Women and the cult of domesticity.

In a reversal of traditional Calvinist doctrine, the evangelical ministers

This pen-and-watercolor drawing of a middle-class family in 1832 illustrates how the home, as it lost its productive functions, became idealized as a center of domestic refinement and material comfort.

of the northern middle class enshrined women as the moral superiors of men. Though considered weak and passive, women were also held to be uniquely pure and pious. Women, who easily outnumbered men at Sunday services and weeknight prayer meetings, were now responsible for converting their homes into loving, prayerful centers of domesticity, and the primary task of motherhood became the Christian nurturing of souls entrusted to a mother's care. "There is a ministry that is older and deeper and more potent than ours," wrote a liberal Presbyterian clergyman; "it is the ministry that presides over the crib and impresses the first gospel influence on the infant soul."

This sanctified notion of motherhood reflected and reinforced shifting patterns of family life. Families became smaller as the birthrate fell by 25 percent in the first half of the nineteenth century. The decline was greatest in the urban middle class after 1820. Children were no longer an economic asset as they had been on a family farm. Middle-class couples consciously limited the size of their families, and women stopped having children at an earlier age. As a result, parents were able to devote more care and financial resources to child rearing. Middle-class children lived

at home longer than children had in the past and received more schooling than working-class children.

Beginning in the 1820s, ministers and female writers elevated the family role of middle-class women into a **cult of domesticity**. This idealized conception of womanhood insisted that the biological differences of God's natural order determined separate social roles for men and women. Characterized as strong, aggressive, and ambitious, men naturally belonged to the competitive world of business and politics. Women's providential task was to preserve religion and morality in the home and family. Held to be innately weak, nurturing, and selfless, only they possessed the moral purity necessary for rearing virtuous children and preserving the home as a refuge from the outside world.

The working classes. The economic changes that produced a new middle class also fundamentally transformed the working class. In the preindustrial United States, the working class was predominately native-born and of artisan origins. By mid-century, most urban workers were immigrants or the children of immigrants and had never been artisans in a skilled craft.

Job skills, sex, race, and ethnicity, all divided workers after 1840. Master craftsmen were the most highly skilled and best-paid members of the labor force. As industrialization proceeded, the unity of the old artisan class splintered. Ambitious master craftsmen with access to capital ignored craft traditions to rise into the ranks of small businessmen and manufacturers. They expanded output and drove down the cost of production by contracting out work at piece wages and hiring the cheapest workers they could find. The result was to transform the apprentice system into a system of exploited child labor.

By the 1830s, most journeymen were becoming a class of permanent wage earners with little prospect of opening their own shops. They denounced the new industrial relations as a "system of mental and physical slavery." To protect their liberties from what they considered a new aristocracy of manufacturers, they organized workingmen's parties in the 1830s, centered in the eastern cities. At the top of these parties' list of reforms were free public education, the abolition of imprisonment for debt, and a ten-hour workday. But the depression of 1839-1843 forced mechanics to concentrate on their economic survival, and the Democrats siphoned off many of their political leaders.

Early trade unions. Journeymen also turned to trade union activity in the 1820s and 1830s to gain better wages, shorter hours, and enhanced job security. Benefiting from a strong demand for their skills, workers in the building trades organized the first unions. They were soon followed by shoemakers, printers, and weavers, workers in trades where pressure on urban journeymen was the most intense. Locals from various trades formed the National Trades Union, the first national union, in 1834. The new labor movement launched more than 150 strikes in the mid-1830s.

Although the Panic of 1837 decimated union membership, the early labor movement did achieve two notable victories. First, by the late 1830s, it had forced employers to accept the ten-hour day as the standard for most skilled workers. Second, in a landmark decision handed down in 1842, the Massachusetts Supreme Court ruled in *Commonwealth* v. *Hunt* that a trade union was not necessarily subject to laws against criminal conspiracies and that a strike could be used to force employers to hire only union members.

The unions were the defenders of artisanal rights and virtues, and they ignored workers whose jobs had never had craft status. As massive immigration merged with industrialization after 1840, this basic division between workers widened. On one side was the male, Protestant, and native-born class of skilled artisans. On the other side was the working-class majority of factory laborers and the unskilled. These workers were predominately immigrants and women who worked for a wage as domestic or factory hands. On average, they earned less than $500 a year, about half what skilled workers earned. Their financial survival rested on a family economy in which all members contributed whatever they could earn.

Increasingly fearing these workers as a threat to their job security and Protestant values, in the 1840s, American-born artisans joined **nativist** organizations that sought to curb mass immigration from Europe and limit the political rights of Catholic immigrants. Whereas the immigrants viewed temperance as business-class meddling in their lives, the nativist workers tended to embrace the evangelical, middle-class ideology of temperance and self-help. One of the few issues that brought these groups together was the nearly universal demand of white workers that black workers be confined to the most menial jobs.

Gender also divided workers. Working-class men shared the dominant ideology of female dependence. They measured their own status as husbands by their ability to keep their wives and daughters from having to work. Beginning in the 1830s, male workers argued that their wages would be higher if women were barred from the labor force. A report of the National Trades Union in 1836 insisted that a woman's "efforts to sustain herself and her family are actually the same as tying a stone around the neck of her natural protector, Man, and destroying him with the weight she has brought to his assistance."

With these views, male workers helped lock wage-earning women into the lowest-paying and most exploited jobs. "If we do not come forth in our defence, what will become of us?" asked Sarah Monroe of New York City in the midst of a strike by seamstresses in 1831. Women tried to organize as workers, but the male labor movement refused to lend much support. The men tried to channel the discontent of women workers into "proper female behavior" and generally restricted their assistance to pushing for legislation that would limit the hours worked by women and children—a stand that enhanced their male image as protectors of the family.

REFORM AND MORAL ORDER

The rapidity and extent of the social and economic changes that accompanied the market revolution were disorienting, even frightening, to many Americans. This was particularly the case with religious leaders and wealthy businessmen in the East. They saw signs of moral wickedness and disorder all around them in the more fluid, materialistic society that was emerging. In their eyes, licentiousness was rampant in the cities and the evils of drink were causing workers to forsake God and their families. Alarmed by what they perceived as a breakdown in moral authority, they sought to impose moral discipline on Americans.

These eastern elites, with the indispensable support of their wives and daughters, created a network of voluntary church-affiliated reform organizations known collectively as the **benevolent empire**. Revivals in the 1820s and 1830s then broadened the base of reform to include the newly evangelicalized middle class in northern cities and towns. From this class emerged the temperance crusade, the largest reform movement in the pre-Civil War United States.

THE BENEVOLENT EMPIRE

For the Reverend Lyman Beecher, the United States in 1814 presented "a scene of destitution and wretchedness." From his Presbyterian pulpit in Litchfield, Connecticut, and then in Boston, he became the leader of a clerical drive to restore morality to America.

The United States these ministers valued was one of respectable churchgoers whose behavior conformed to Puritan and Federalist standards of freedom as defined and ordered by an educated clergy. Evangelical businessmen in the seaboard cities backed the call to restore moral order. Worried by the increasing number of urban poor, wealthy merchants contributed vital financial support for a network of reform associations, which grew to include the American Board of Commissioners for Foreign Missions (1810), the American Bible Society (1816), the American Sunday School Union (1824), the American Tract Society (1825), and the American Home Missionary Society (1826).

The reform societies built on the Second Great Awakening's techniques of organization and communication. The Protestant reformers sent out speakers on regular schedules along prescribed routes. They developed organizations that maintained a constant pressure for reform. National and local boards of directors supervised the work of salaried managers, who inspired volunteers to combat sin among the unconverted. When steam presses and stereotype plates halved the cost of printing and dramatically increased its speed, the American Bible Society was the first organization to exploit this revolution in the print media. Between 1790 and 1830, the number of religious newspapers grew from fourteen to more than six hundred. By then, religious presses were churning out more than 1 million Bibles and 6 million tracts a year.

A host of local societies targeted individual vices. Their purpose, as summed up by a Massachusetts group, the Andover South Parish Society for the Reformation of Morals, was "to discountenance [discourage] immorality, particularly Sabbath-breaking, intemperance, and profanity, and to promote industry, order, piety, and good morals." These goals linked social and moral discipline, appealing both to churchgoers concerned about godlessness and profit-oriented businessmen eager to curb their workers' unruly behavior.

With volunteers drawn largely from the teenage daughters of evangelical businessmen, Sunday interdenominational schools combined elementary education with the teaching of the Bible and Protestant principles. The American Sunday School Union coordinated local efforts and published books and periodicals. By 1832, nearly 10 percent of all American children aged 5 to 14 were attending one of eight thousand Sunday schools.

The boldest expression of the drive to enhance Protestant Christian power was the **Sabbatarian movement**. In 1828, evangelicals led by Lyman Beecher formed the General Union for Promoting the Observance of the Christian Sabbath. Their immediate goal was the repeal of a law passed by Congress in 1810, directing post offices to deliver mail on Sunday. This law symbolized to Protestant reformers the moral degeneracy into which the republic had fallen. Their broader mission was to enforce local statutes that shut down business and leisure activities on Sundays. The Sabbatarians considered such statutes no less "necessary to the welfare of the state" than "laws against murder and polygamy."

In 1829, insisting on the separation of church and state, the Democratic Congress upheld the postal law of 1810, a crippling setback to the Sabbatarian crusade. The Sabbatarians had outraged canal operators, hotel keepers, tavern owners and other businesses threatened with the loss of their Sunday trade. Businessmen, workingmen, Southern evangelicals, and religious conservatives, all felt that the Sabbath purists had gone too far in a movement now seen as a threat to civil liberties and the rights of private property.

The General Union disbanded in 1832, but it left an important legacy for future reform movements. On the one hand, it developed techniques that converted the reform impulse into direct political action. In raising funds, training speakers, holding rallies, disseminating literature, lobbying for local Sunday regulations, and coordinating a petition to Congress, the

Sabbatarians created an organizational model for other reformers to follow in mobilizing public opinion and influencing politicians. On the other hand, the failure of the Sabbatarians revealed that a new approach was needed that encouraged individuals to reform themselves without coercive controls. It soon emerged in the temperance movement.

THE TEMPERANCE MOVEMENT

Temperance—the drive against the consumption of alcohol—had the greatest impact on the most people of any reform movement. Its success rested on what Lyman Beecher called "a new moral power." Dismayed by the popular resistance to the coercive moralism of the first wave of Protestant reform, evangelicals concluded that reform had to rest on persuasion, and it had to begin with the voluntary decision of individuals to free themselves from sin. For these evangelicals, the self-control to renounce alcohol became the key to creating a harmonious Christian society of self-regulating citizens.

In 1826, evangelicals founded the **American Temperance Society** and took control of the movement. Their goal was to bring about a radical change in American attitudes toward alcohol and its role in social life. By 1830, American consumption of alcohol reached an all-time high of 7.1 gallons of pure alcohol per year for every American aged 14 and over (about three times present-day levels). "Liquor at that time," recalled a carpenter, "was used as commonly as the food we ate." Taverns easily outnumbered churches as centers of community sociability. Alcohol was used to pay both common laborers and itinerant preachers on the early Methodist circuit. Masters and journeymen shared a drink as a customary way of taking a break from work, and no wedding, funeral, or meeting of friends was complete without alcohol.

For the temperance crusade to succeed, the reformers had to finance a massive propaganda campaign and link it to an organization that could mobilize and energize thousands of people. They built such a mass movement by merging temperance into the network of churches and lay volunteers that the benevolent empire had developed and by adopting the techniques of revivals to win new converts.

Evangelical reformers denounced intemperance as the greatest sin of the land. In the words of the Reverend Herman Humphrey, it deprived "its victims of the means of grace . . . . If there is any evil which hardens the heart faster, . . . or quickens hatred [of] God and man into a more rapid and frightful maturity, I know not what it is." Alcohol represented all that was wrong in America—crime, poverty, insanity, broken families, boisterous politicking, Sabbath-breaking.

This temperance poster depicts the evangelical virtues of faith, hope, and charity in battle against the evil temptations of drinking.

This message was thundered from the pulpit and the public lectern. Thanks to the generous financial subsidies of such wealthy benefactors as Stephen Van Rensselaer and Edward Delavan of New York, it was also broadcast in millions of tracts printed on the latest high-speed presses. As in the revivals, temperance rallies combined emotionally charged sermons with large, tearful prayer meetings to evoke guilt among sinners, who would then seek release by taking the pledge of abstinence.

Within a decade, the American Temperance Society had more than five thousand local chapters and statewide affiliates, most of them in the Northeast. A million members had pledged abstinence by 1833. Women constituted one third to over half of the members in local temperance societies. Lacking legal protections against abusive husbands who drank away the family resources, women had a compelling reason to join the crusade. As the moral protectors of the family, they pressured their husbands to take the teetotaler's pledge and stick by it, raised sons to shun alcohol, and banished liquor from their homes. By the 1840s, temperance and middle-class domesticity had become synonymous.

The first wave of temperance converts came from the upper and middle classes. Businessmen welcomed temperance as a model of self-discipline in their efforts to regiment factory work. Young, upwardly mobile professionals and petty entrepreneurs learned in temperance how to be thrifty, self-controlled, and more respectable and creditworthy. Many of them presumably agreed with *The Temperance Recorder* that "the enterprise of this country is so great, and competition so eager in every branch of business . . ., that profit can only result from . . . *temperance.*"

Temperance made its first significant inroads among the working classes during the economic depression of 1839–1843. Joining together in what they called Washington Temperance Societies, small businessmen and artisans, many of them reformed drunkards, carried temperance into working-class districts. The Washingtonians gained a considerable following by insisting that workers could survive the depression only if they stopped drinking and adopted the temperance ethic of frugality and self-help. Their wives organized auxiliary societies and pledged to enforce sobriety and economic restraint at home.

In a telling measure of the temperance movement's success, per capita consumption of alcohol had fallen to less than two gallons by 1845. In 1851, Maine passed the first statewide prohibition law. Other northern states followed suit, but antitemperance coalitions soon overturned most of these laws outside New England. Nonetheless, alcohol consumption remained at the low level set in the 1840s.

WOMEN'S ROLE IN REFORM

The first phase of women's reform activities represented an extension of the domestic ideal promoted in the Cult of Domesticity. Assumptions about their unique moral qualities permitted, and even encouraged, women to assume the role of "social mother" by organizing on behalf of the orphaned and the widowed. Founded in 1797, the Society for the Relief of Poor Widows with Small Children in New York typified these early approaches to reform. The women in the society came from socially prominent families. Motivated by religious charity and social duty, they visited poor women and children, dispensed funds, and set up work programs. However, they limited their benevolence to the "deserving poor"—socially weak but morally strong people who had suffered personal misfortune—and screened out all who were thought to be unworthy.

The revivalist call in the 1820s for moral action inspired middle-class women to join voluntary female groups. They founded maternal associations, where they prayed and fasted for the moral strength to save the souls of their children. Other associations sponsored revivals, visited the poor, established Sunday Schools, and distributed Bibles and religious tracts. These reformers widened the public role of women, but their efforts also reinforced cultural stereotypes of women as nurturing helpmates who deferred to males as the wielders of economic and political power.

A second phase in the reform efforts by women developed in the 1830s. Unlike their benevolent counterparts, the reformers now began to challenge male prerogatives and move beyond moral suasion.

The temperance crusade brought women out of their homes and into the streets to pray in front of taverns filled with drunken men.

The crusade against prostitution exemplified the new militancy. Women seized leadership of the movement in 1834 with the founding of the New York Female Moral Reform Society. In the pages of their journal, *Advocate for Moral Reform*, members identified male greed and licentiousness as the causes for the fallen state of women. Identified, too, were the male patrons of the city's brothels. The society blamed businessmen for the low wages that forced some women to resort to prostitution and denounced lustful men for engaging in "a regular crusade against [our] sex."

In 1839, this attack on the sexual double standard became a national movement with the establishment of the **American Female Moral Reform Society**. With 555 affiliates throughout the evangelical heartland of the North, female activists mounted a lobbying campaign that, unlike earlier efforts, bypassed prominent men and reached out to a mass audience for signatures. By the 1840s, such unprecedented political involvement enabled women to secure the first state laws criminalizing seduction and adultery.

Other women's groups developed a more radical critique of American society and its male leadership. The Boston Seamen's Aid Society, founded in 1833 by

Sarah Josepha Hale, a widow with five children, soon rejected the benevolent tradition of distinguishing between the "respectable" and the "unworthy" poor. Hale discovered that her efforts to guide poor women toward self-sufficiency flew in the face of the low wages and substandard housing that trapped her clients in poverty. She concluded in 1838 that "it is hardly possible for the hopeless poor to avoid being vicious." Hale attacked male employers for exploiting the poor. "Combinations of selfish men are formed to beat down the price of female labor," she wrote in her 1836 annual report, "and then they call the diminished rate the market price."

BACKLASH AGAINST BENEVOLENCE

Some of the benevolent empire's harshest critics came out of the populist revivals of the early 1800s. They considered the Protestant reformers' program a conspiracy of orthodox Calvinists from old-line denominations to impose social and moral control on behalf of a religious and economic elite. The goal of the "orthodox party," warned the Universalist *Christian Intelligencer*, was the power of "governing the nation"; the societies they formed "are but so many strings . . ., the ultimate design of which is to draw them into power."

These criticisms revealed a profound mistrust of the emerging market society. In contrast to the evangelical reformers, drawn from the well-educated business and middle classes who were benefiting from economic change, most evangelical members of the grass-roots sects and followers of the itinerant preachers were unschooled, poor, and hurt by market fluctuations that they could not control. Often they were farmers forced by debt to move west or artisans and tradesmen displaced by new forms of factory production and new commercial outlets. Socially uprooted and economically stranded, they found a sense of community in their local churches and resisted control by wealthier, better-educated outsiders. Above all, they clung to beliefs that shored up the threatened authority of the father over his household.

With the elevation of women to the status of moral guardians of the family and agents of benevolent reform outside the household, middle-class evangelicalism in the Northeast was becoming feminized. This new social role for women was especially threatening—indeed, galling—for men who were the causalities of the more competitive economy. Raised on farms where the father had been the unquestioned lawgiver and provider, these men attacked feminized evangelicalism for undermining their paternal authority. They found in Scripture an affirmation of patriarchal power for any man, no matter how poor or economically dependent.

The **Church of Jesus Christ of Latter-day Saints** (also known as the **Mormon Church**) represented the most enduring religious backlash of economically struggling men against the aggressive efforts of reforming middle-class evangelicals. Joseph Smith, who established the church in upstate New York in 1830, came from a New England farm family uprooted and impoverished by market speculations gone sour. He and his followers were alienated, not only from the new market economy but also from what they saw as the religious and social anarchy around them.

Based on Smith's divine revelations as set forth in *The Book of Mormon* (1830), their new faith offered converts to Mormonism both a sanctuary as a biblical people and a release from social and religious uncertainties. They believed that the mainstream evangelical churches had corrupted Christ's original gospel. "This generation abounds in ignorance, superstition, selfishness, and priestcraft," charged the Mormon John Whitmer; "for this generation is truly led by . . . hireling priests whose God is the substance of the world's goods."

Mormonism provided a defense of communal beliefs centered on male authority that was reassuring to rural families seeking refuge from individualism and economic dislocation. It assigned complete spiritual and secular authority to men. Unlike female-dominated evangelicalism, men led their families into Mormonism. Only through subordination and obedience to their husbands could women hope to gain salvation.

To be a Mormon was to join a large extended family that was part of a shared enterprise. Men bonded their labor in a communal economy to benefit all the faithful. A law of tithing, instituted in 1841, required Mormons to give 10 percent of their property to the church upon conversion and 10 percent of their annual income thereafter. Driven by a strong sense of social obligation, the Mormons forged the most successful alternative vision in antebellum America to the individualistic Protestant republic of the benevolent reformers. (For the Mormons' role in the westward movement, see Chapter 13.)

INSTITUTIONS AND SOCIAL IMPROVEMENT

Although evangelical Protestantism was its mainspring, antebellum reform also had its roots in the European Enlightenment. Like the evangelicals inspired by religious optimism, reformers drawing on Enlightenment doctrines of progress had unbounded faith in social improvement. They saw in America an unlimited potential to fashion a model republic of virtuous, intelligent citizens.

Studies published in the 1820s that documented increasing urban poverty, crime, and teenage delinquency created a sense of urgency for many reformers. Guided by the Enlightenment belief that environmental conditions shaped human character, reformers created a new system of public schooling in the North. They also prodded state legislatures to fund penitentiaries for criminals, asylums for the mentally ill, reformatories for the delinquent, and almshouses for the poor.

As reformers were implementing new institutions for shaping individual character after 1820, a host of utopian communities sprang up. These communities also tapped into an impulse for human betterment. They typically rejected either private property or families based on monogamous marriage and offered a communitarian life designed to help a person reach perfection. Most of these communities were short-lived because the new forms of social and economic organization they promoted were far too radical for all but a handful of Americans.

SCHOOL REFORM

"An ignorant people always has been and always will be a degraded and oppressed people—they are always at the mercy of the corrupt and designing," cautioned Philadelphia school officials in their annual report for 1836 where they warned, "if we fail by Education to awake—guide—confirm the moral energies of our people, we are lost!" Secular revivalists as much as they were institutional innovators, the school reformers embarked on a crusade to save America from ignorance and vice.

Before the 1820s, schooling in America was an informal, haphazard affair that nonetheless met the basic needs for reading, writing, and arithmetic skills of an overwhelmingly rural population. Private tutors and academies for the wealthy, a few charitable schools for the urban poor, and rural one-room schoolhouses open for a few months a year constituted formal education at the primary level.

The first political demands for free tax-supported schools originated with the **Workingmen's movement** in eastern cities in the 1820s. Decrying what the Philadelphia Working Men's Committee in 1830 described as "a monopoly of talent, which consigns the multitude to comparative ignorance, and secures the balance of knowledge on the side of the rich and the rulers," workers called for free public education. In pushing for what they called "equal republican education," they were also seeking to guarantee that all citizens, no matter how poor, could achieve meaningful liberty and equality.

Their proposals, however, met stiff resistance from wealthier property holders, who refused to be taxed to pay for the education of working-class children.

The breakthrough in public education came in New England, where the disruptive forces of industrialization and urbanization were felt the earliest. Increased economic inequality, growing numbers of impoverished Irish Catholic immigrants, and the emergence of a mass democracy based on nearly universal white male suffrage convinced reformers of the need for state-supported schools.

In 1837, the Massachusetts legislature established the nation's first state board of education. The head of the board for the next twelve years was Horace Mann, a former Whig politician and temperance advocate who now tirelessly championed educational reform. Mann demanded that the state government assume centralized control over Massachusetts schools. All schools should have the same standards of compulsory attendance, strict discipline, common textbooks, professionally trained teachers, and graded, competitive classes of age-segregated students.

Once this system was in place, Mann promised, the schools would become "the great equalizer of the conditions of men—the balance-wheel of the social machinery." Poverty would no longer threaten social disruption because the ignorant would have the knowledge to acquire property and wealth. Education, Mann stated, "does better than disarm the poor of their hostility against the rich; it prevents being poor." Trained in self-control and punctuality, youths would be able to take advantage of economic opportunities and become intelligent voters concerned with the rights of property.

Democrats in the Massachusetts legislature denounced Mann's program as "a system of centralization and of monopoly of power in a few hands, contrary in every respect, to the true spirit of our democratic institutions." The laboring poor, who depended for economic survival on the wages their children could earn, resisted compulsory-attendance laws and a longer school year. Farmers fought to maintain local control over schooling and to block the higher taxes needed for a more comprehensive and professionalized system. The Catholic Church protested the thinly veiled attempts of the reformers to indoctrinate all students in the moral strictures of middle-class Protestantism. Catholics began, at great expense, to build their own parochial schools.

Mann and his allies nonetheless prevailed in most of the industrializing states. The educational reformers received strong support from the professional and

LESSON XI.

Boys at Play.

Can you fly a kite? See how the boy flies his kite. He holds the string fast, and the wind blows it up.

Now it is high in the air, and looks like a bird. When the wind blows hard, you must hold fast, or your kite will get away.

Boys love to run and play.

But they must not be rude. Good boys do not play in a rude way, but take care not to hurt any one.

Moral Lessons such as this one for boys at play filled the pages of the McGuffey's readers.

business constituencies of the Whig party. Manufacturers hoped that the schools would turn out a more obedient and punctual labor force, and the more skilled and prosperous workers saw in public education a key to upward mobility for their children.

Most important for its political success, school reform appealed to the growing northern middle class. Opposing both the "vicious passions" of the poor and the "idle luxury" of the rich, schools would instill the moral and economic discipline that the middle class deemed essential for a progressive and ordered society. Teaching morality and national pride was central to the educational curriculum, and from the popular McGuffey Readers used as a classroom text, students learned such lessons as "God gives a great deal of money to some persons, in order that they may assist those [who] are poor."

Out of the northern middle class also came the young female teachers who increasingly staffed elementary schools. Presumed by their nature to be more nurturing than men, women now had an entry into teaching, the first profession open to them. Be-

sides, women could also be paid far less than men; school boards assumed that they would accept low wages while waiting to be married.

Just over 50 percent of the white children between 5 and 19 years of age in the United States were enrolled in school in 1850—the highest percentage in the world at the time. Working-class parents were quicker to pull their children out of school at an early age than higher-income middle-class parents. Planters continued to rely on private tutors or academies for their children, and southern farmers saw little need for public education. The slave states, especially in the Lower South, lagged behind the rest of the nation in public education.

PRISONS, WORKHOUSES, AND ASYLUMS

Up to this time, Americans had depended on voluntary efforts to cope with crime, poverty, and social deviance. Convinced that these efforts were now inadequate, reformers turned to public authorities to establish a host of new institutions—penitentiaries, workhouses, mental hospitals, orphanages, and reformatories—to deal with social problems.

All these public institutions reflected a new attitude toward conditions that had been regarded as inevitable and irreversible. For example, eighteenth-century Americans never thought of rehabilitating criminals. Prisons were simple structures whose only purpose was to hold criminals before they were fined, whipped, mutilated, or executed in a public ritual that drew large crowds of festive onlookers. But the institutional reformers of the Jacksonian era believed that criminals, as well as the poor and other deviants, could be morally redeemed.

The reformers held that people's environments shaped their character for good or evil. The Boston Children's Friend Society was devoted to the young, "whose plastic natures may be molded into images of perfect beauty, or . . . perfect repulsiveness." Samuel Gridley Howe, a prison reformer, proclaimed: "Thousands of convicts are made so in consequence of a faulty organization of society . . . . They are thrown upon society as a sacred charge; and that society is false to its trust, if it neglects any means for their reformation." In the properly ordered environment of new institutions, discipline and moral character would be instilled in criminals and other deviants who lacked the self-control to resist the corrupting vices and temptations that pervaded society.

Reformers had particularly high expectations for the penitentiary systems pioneered in Pennsylvania and New York in the 1820s. As two French observers noted in the early 1830s, "The penitentiary system . . . to them seems the remedy for all the evils of society." Unlike earlier prisons, the penitentiaries were huge, imposing structures that isolated the prisoners from each other and the outside world. Inmates in the New York system pioneered in the 1820s worked together in gangs during the day, but under the Pennsylvania plan, each prisoner was held in solitary confinement.

No longer were criminals to be brutally punished or thrown together under inhumane conditions that perpetuated a cycle of moral depravity. Now, cut off from all corrupting influences, forced to learn that hard work teaches moral discipline, and uplifted by religious literature, criminals would be guided toward becoming law-abiding, productive citizens.

Workhouses.

The same philosophy of reform provided the rationale for asylums to house the poor and the insane. The number of transient poor and the size of urban slums increased as commercial capitalism uprooted farmers from the land and undercut the security of craft trades. Believing that the poor, much like criminals, had only themselves to blame, public officials and their evangelical allies prescribed a therapeutic regimen of discipline and physical labor to cure the poor of their moral defects. The structured setting for that regiment was the workhouse.

The custodians of the workhouses banished drinking, gambling, and idleness. Under the workhouse rules in New York, officers could "rightly exercise . . . a measure of moral force upon the will of these persons, to induce them to do that which their own uncultivated understanding might oppose." Officers were to administer their duties "with strictness —severity." Their prime responsibility was to supervise the inmates in a tightly scheduled daily routine built around manual labor. Once purged of their laziness and filled with self-esteem as the result of work discipline, the poor would be released to become useful members of society.

Asylums for the Mentally Ill.

Public insane asylums offered a similar order for the mentally ill. Reformers believed that too many choices in a highly mobile, materialistic, and competitive society drove some people insane. Following the lead of New York and Massachusetts in the 1830s, twenty-eight states had established mental hospitals by 1860. These facilities set rigid rules and work assignments to teach patients how to order their lives.

In the early 1840s Dorothea Dix, a Massachusetts schoolteacher, discovered that the insane in her home state were dumped into jails and almshouses, where they suffered filthy, inhumane treatment. She found the insane "confined . . . in cages, closets, cellars,

In the concern etched in her face, this photograph captures the compassion that Dorothea Dix brought to her crusade for mental health reform.

stalls, pens! Chained, naked, beaten with rods, and lashed into obedience." Horrified, Dix lobbied state legislatures across the nation for the next twenty years to improve treatment for the mentally ill.

While the reformers did provide social deviants with cleaner and safer living conditions, their penitentiaries and asylums succeeded more in classifying and segregating their inmates than in reforming them. Submission to routine turned out not to be the best builder of character. Witnessing the rigorous control of every movement of the isolated prisoners at the Eastern State Penitentiary in Philadelphia, the English novelist Charles Dickens declared "this slow and daily tampering with the mysteries of the brain to be immeasurably worse than any torture of the body."

Penitentiaries, reformatories, and workhouses failed to eliminate or noticeably check poverty, crime, and vice. Refusing to question their basic premise that repressive institutions could promote individual responsibility, reformers abandoned their environmental explanations for deviance. By mid-century, they were defining deviants and dependents as permanent misfits with ingrained character defects. The asylums remained; but, stripped of their earlier optimism, they became little more than holding pens for the outcasts of society.

UTOPIAN ALTERNATIVES

Unlike the reformers, who aimed to improve the existing order by guiding individuals to greater self-discipline, the utopians sought perfection by withdrawing from society and its confining institutions. A radically new social order, not an improved old one, was their goal.

Though following different religious and secular philosophies of communitarian living, all the utopians wanted to fashion a more rational and personally satisfying alternative to the competitive materialism of antebellum America. Nearly all the communities sought to transform the organization and rewards of work, thus challenging the prevailing dogmas about private property.

The most successful utopian communities were religious sects whose reordering of both sexual and economic relations departed most sharply from middle-class norms. The **Shakers**, at their height in the 1830s, attracted some six thousand followers. Named for the convulsive dancing that was part of their religious ceremonies, the Shakers traced their origins to the teachings of Ann Lee ("Mother Lee"). An illiterate factory laborer in mid-eighteenth-century England, Lee had a revelation in 1770 that the Second Coming of Christ was to be fulfilled in her own womanly form, the embodiment of the female side of God. Fired by another vision in 1774, Lee led eight of her followers to America, where, after her death in 1784, her disciples established the first Shaker community in New Lebanon, New York.

Organized around doctrines of celibacy and **communism**, Shaker communities held all property in common. The sexes worked and lived apart from each other. Dancing during religious worship brought men and women together and provided an emotional release from enforced sexual denial. As an early Shaker leader explained, "There is no labor which so fully absorbs all the faculties of soul and body, as real spiritual devotion and energetic exercise in sacred worship." In worldly as well as spiritual terms, women enjoyed an equality in Shaker life that the outside world denied them. For this reason, twice as many women as men joined the Shakers.

The Shakers gradually dwindled. Their rule of celibacy meant, of course, that they could propagate themselves only be recruiting new members, and few new converts joined the movement after 1850. Viewed as eccentric outsiders by contemporaries, the Shakers today are best remembered for the beautiful simplicity of the furniture and other household objects they made in their workshops.

John Humphrey Noyes, a graduate of Dartmouth who studied for the ministry at Yale, founded another utopian community that offered women a liberating alternative to the burdens of monogamous marriage and constant child rearing. Noyes preached that marriage, the selfish "exclusive possession of one woman to one man," was the main barrier to perfection. He proposed instead "complex marriage," the mutual love for each other of all those who had been saved. His goal was a religious society in which cooperative arrangements between men and women regulated child care and the distribution of property.

After he had been drummed out of the ministry for his radical teachings, Noyes established the **Oneida Community** in upstate New York in 1847. He attracted over two hundred followers with his perfectionist vision of plural marriage, community nurseries, group discipline, and common ownership of property. Charged with adultery, Noyes fled to Canada in 1879, but the Oneida Community, reorganized in 1881 as a joint-stock company in the United States and committed thereafter to conventional sexual mores, survived into the twentieth century.

Secular utopians aspired to perfect social relations through the rational design of planned communities. Bitter critics of the social evils of industrialization, they tried to construct models for a social order free from poverty, unemployment, and inequality. They envisioned cooperative communities that balanced agricultural and industrial pursuits in a mixed economy that recycled earnings to the laborers who actually produced the wealth.

Despite their high expectations, nearly all the planned communities ran into financial difficulties and soon collapsed. The pattern was set by the first of the controversial socialist experiments, **New Harmony** in Indiana, the brainchild of the wealthy Scottish industrialist and philanthropist Robert Owen. A proponent of utopian **socialism**, Owen promised to create a new order where "the degrading and pernicious practices in which we are now well trained, of buying cheap and selling dear, will be rendered unnecessary" and "union and co-operation will supersede individual interest." But within two years of its founding in 1825, New Harmony fell victim to inadequate financing and internal bickering.

The economic misery of the depression of the 1840s revived interest in utopian ventures and helped popularize the ideas of Charles Fourier, a French utopian who proposed to restore dignity to labor and end poverty by dividing society into phalanxes, cooperative units of workers who lived communally. Scores of **Fourierist communities** were set up, but few survived into the 1850s.

About the only secular cooperative that gained lasting fame was **Brook Farm** in West Roxbury, Massa-

AMERICAN VIEWS

Appeal of a Female Abolitionist

Lydia Maria Child's Appeal, published in Boston in 1833, was a landmark in abolitionist literature for both the thoroughness of its attack on slavery and its refutation of racist ideology and discrimination. This condemnation of racial prejudice was the most radical feature of abolitionist ideology. It directly challenged the deeply held beliefs and assumptions of nearly all white Americans, in the North as well as the South. Racism and slavery, as Child shows in this excerpt from her Appeal, fed off one another in the national curse of slavery.

- How does Child argue that northern white people must bear some of the responsibility for perpetuating slavery?

- What arguments does Child make against racial discrimination in northern society?

- What did Child mean when she wrote that "the Americans are peculiarly responsible for the example they give"? Do you agree with her?

- How does Child deal with the charge that the abolitionists threatened the preservation of the Union?

While we bestow our earnest disapprobation on the system of slavery, let us not flatter ourselves that we are in reality any better than our brethren of the South. Thanks to our soil and climate, and the early exhortations of the Quakers, the form of slavery does not exist among us; but the very spirit of the hateful and mischievous thing is here in all its strength. . . . Our prejudice against colored people is even more inveterate than it is at the South. The planter is often attached to his negroes, and lavishes caresses and kind words upon them, as he would on a favorite hound: but our cold-hearted, ignoble prejudice admits of no exception—no intermission.

The Southerners have long continued habit, apparent interest and dreaded danger, to palliate the wrong they do; but we stand without excuse. . . . If the free States wished to cherish the system of slavery forever, they could not take a more direct course than they now do. Those who are kind and liberal on all other subjects, unite with the selfish and the proud in their unrelenting efforts to keep the colored

chusetts (today part of Boston). Established in 1841, Brook Farm was a showcase for the transcendentalist philosophy of Ralph Waldo Emerson. A former Unitarian minister in Boston, Emerson taught that intuition and emotion could grasp a truer ("transcendent") reality than could the senses alone. The Boston intellectuals drawn to Brook Farm in the 1840s saw it as a refuge from the pressures and coarseness of commercial society, a place where they could realize the Emersonian ideal of spontaneous creativity. Although disbanded after six years as an economic failure, Brook Farm inspired intellectuals such as Nathaniel

Hawthorne, who briefly lived there. In turn, his writings and those of other writers influenced by **transcendentalism** flowed into the great renaissance of American literature in the mid-nineteenth century, an outpouring of work that grappled with Emersonian themes of individualism and the reshaping of the American character.

In an 1837 address at Harvard titled "The American Scholar," Emerson had called for a distinctly national literature devoted to the democratic possibilities of American life. "The literature of the poor, the feelings of the child, the philosophy of the street, population in the lowest state of degradation; and the influence they unconsciously exert over children early infuses into their innocent minds the same strong feelings of contempt. . . .

The state of public feeling not only makes it difficult for the Africans to obtain information, but it prevents them from making profitable use of what knowledge they have. A colored man, however intelligent, is not allowed to pursue any business more lucrative than that of a barber, a shoe-black, or waiter. These, and all other employments, are truly respectable, whenever the duties connected with them are faithfully performed; but it is unjust that a man should, on account of his complexion, be prevented from performing more elevated uses in society. Every citizen ought to have a fair chance to try his fortune in any line of business, which he thinks he has ability to transact. Why should not colored men be employed in the manufactories of various kinds? If their ignorance is an objection, let them be enlightened, as speedily as possible. If their moral character is not sufficiently pure, remove the pressure of public scorn, and thus supply them with motives for being respectable. All this can be done. It merely requires an earnest wish to overcome a prejudice, which . . . is in fact opposed to the spirit of our religion, and contrary to the instinctive good feelings of our nature. . . . When the majority heartily desire a change, it is effected, be the difficulties what they may. The Americans are peculiarly responsible for the example they give; for in no other country does the unchecked voice of the people constitute the whole of government. . . .

The strongest and best reason that can be given for our supineness on the subject of slavery, is the fear of dissolving the Union. The Constitution of the United States demands our highest reverence. . . . But we must not forget that the Constitution provides for any change that may be required for the general good. The great machine is constructed with a safety valve, by which any rapidly increasing evil may be expelled whenever the people desire it.

If the Southern politicians are determined to make a Siamese question of this also—if they insist that the Union shall not exist without slavery—it can only be said that they join two things, which have no affinity with each other, and which cannot permanently exist together. —They chain the living and vigorous to the diseased and dying; and the former will assuredly perish in the infected neighborhood.

The universal introduction of free labor is the surest way to consolidate the Union, and enable us to live together in harmony and peace. If a history is ever written entitled "The Decay and Dissolution of the North American Republic," its author will distinctly trace our downfall to the existence of slavery among us.

Source: Lydia Maria Child, *An Appeal in Favor of That Class of Americans Called Africans* (originally published 1833), ed. Carolyn L. Karcher (University of Massachusetts Press, 1996).

---

the meaning of household life, are the topics of the time," he proclaimed. Writers soon responded to Emerson's call.

Walt Whitman, whose *Leaves of Grass* (1855) foreshadowed modern poetry in its use of free verse, shared Emerson's faith in the possibilities of individual fulfillment, and his poems celebrated the democratic variety of the American people. Henry David Thoreau, Emerson's friend and neighbor, embodied the transcendentalist fascination with nature and self-discovery by living in relative isolation for sixteen months at Walden Pond, near Concord, Massachu-

setts. His *Walden, or Life in the Woods* (1854) became an American classic. "I went to the woods," he wrote, "because I wished to . . . confront only the essential facts of life, and see if I could not learn what it had to teach, and not, when I came to die, discover that I had not lived."

Nathaniel Hawthorne and Herman Melville, the greatest novelists of the American renaissance, focused on the existence of evil and the human need for community. In *The Scarlet Letter* (1850) and *The House of the Seven Gables* (1851), Hawthorne probed themes of egoism and pride to reveal the underside of the human soul. Melville's *Moby Dick* (1851) depicted the consequences of a competitive individualism unchecked by a social conscience. In his relentless pursuit of the great white whale, Captain Ahab destroys himself and his crew.

Much of the appeal of the utopian communities flowed from the same concern about the splintering and selfishness of antebellum society that animated Hawthorne and Melville. The works of these novelists have endured, but the utopian experiments quickly collapsed. Promising economic security and social harmony to buttress a threatened sense of community, the utopians failed to lure all but a few Americans from the acquisitiveness and competitive demands of the larger society.

ABOLITIONISM AND WOMEN'S RIGHTS

Abolitionism emerged from the same religious impulse that energized reform throughout the North. Like other reformers, the abolitionists came predominately from evangelical, middle-class families, particularly those of New England stock. What distinguished the abolitionists was their insistence that slavery was *the* great national sin, mocking American ideals of liberty and Christian morality.

Under the early leadership of William Lloyd Garrison, the abolitionists uncompromisingly attacked not only slaveholders but also all others whose moral apathy helped support slavery. After provoking a storm of protest in both the North and South, the abolitionist movement split in 1840. Crucial in this division was Garrison's support of women's rights. Most abolitionists broke with him and founded their own antislavery organization. Female abolitionists took the lead in organizing a separate women's rights movement.

REJECTING COLONIZATION

In the early nineteenth century, when slavery was expanding westward, almost all white Americans regardless of class or region were convinced that emancipation would lead either to a race war or the debasement of their superior status through racial interbreeding. This paralyzing fear of general emancipation, rooted in pervasive racism, long shielded slavery from sustained attack.

In 1817, antislavery reformers from the North and the South, founded the **American Colonization Society**. Slaveholding politicians from the Upper South—notably Henry Clay, James Madison, and President James Monroe—were the leading organizers of

the society. Gradual emancipation accompanied by the removal of black people from America to Africa was the only solution that white reformers could imagine for ridding the nation of slavery and avoiding a racial bloodbath. Their goal was to make America all free *and* all white.

The American Colonization Society had no real chance of success. No form of emancipation, no matter how gradual, could appeal to slaveowners who could profit from the demand for their slaves in the Lower South. Moreover, the society could never afford to purchase the freedom of any significant number of slaves. Almost all the African Americans it transported to Liberia, the West African colony it helped found, were already free. At the height of its popularity in the 1820s, the society sent only fourteen hundred colonists to Africa. During that same decade, the American slave population increased by more than 450,000.

Free African Americans bitterly attacked the colonizers' central assumption that free black people were unfit to live as free citizens in America. Typical of the colonizers' racist thinking was the claim by Henry Clay in 1827 that the "free coloured" were the "most vicious" of all Americans. "Contaminated themselves, they extend their vices to all around them, to the slaves and to the whites." The annual report of the American Colonization Society in 1824 approvingly quoted a New England minister who said of the free African Americans: "You cannot raise him from the abyss of his degradation. You may call him free . . . but you cannot bleach him into the enjoyment of freedom."

Most free African Americans were native-born, and they considered themselves Americans with every right to enjoy the blessings of republican liberty. As a black petition in 1817 stated, banishment from America "would not only be cruel, but in direct violation of the principles, which have been the boast of this republic."

Organizing through their own churches in northern cities, free African Americans founded some fifty abolitionist societies, offered refuge to fugitive slaves, and launched the first African-American newspaper in 1827, *Freedom's Journal*. David Walker, a free black man who had moved from North Carolina to Massachusetts, published his **Appeal to the Colored Citizens of the World** in 1829. In a searing indictment of white greed and hypocrisy, he rejected colonization and insisted that "America is more our country, than it is the whites'—we have enriched it with our *blood and tears.*" He warned white America that "wo, wo, will be to you if we have to obtain our freedom by fighting."

As if in response to this call for revolutionary resistance by the enslaved, Nat Turner's Rebellion exploded in the summer of 1831(see Chapter 11). Both alarmed and inspired by the increased tempo of black militancy, a small group of antislavery white people abandoned all illusions about colonization and embarked on a radically new approach for eradicating slavery.

ABOLITIONISM

William Lloyd Garrison, a Massachusetts printer and the leading figure in early abolitionism, became coeditor of an antislavery newspaper in Baltimore in 1829. Before the year was out, Garrison was arrested and convicted of criminal libel for his editorials

The illustration on the masthead of this 1831 issue of The Liberator *condemns the relegation of slaves to the legal status of chattel, mere livestock to be bought and sold, no different from cattle or horses. Revulsion at the treatment of human beings as property was central to the abolitionist indictment of slavery.*

against a Massachusetts merchant engaged in the domestic slave trade (the foreign or African slave trade had been prohibited in 1807), and he spent seven weeks in jail before a wealthy New York City philanthropist paid his $100 fine. Recognizing that his lack of freedom in jail paled against that of the slave, Garrison emerged with an unquenchable hatred of slavery. Returning to Boston, he launched his own antislavery newspaper, *The Liberator*, in 1831. A year later, he was instrumental in founding the New England Anti-Slavery Society.

As militant as the free African Americans who comprised the bulk of the early subscribers to *The Liberator*, Garrison thundered, "If we would not see our land deluged in blood, we must instantly burst asunder the shackles of the slaves." He committed abolitionism to the twin goals of immediatism—an immediate moral commitment to end slavery—and racial equality. Only by striving toward these goals, he insisted, could white America ever hope to end slavery without massive violence.

The demand of the abolitionists for the legal equality of black people was as unsettling to public opinion as their call for immediate, uncompensated emancipation. Discriminatory laws, aptly characterized by the abolitionist Lydia Maria Child as "this legalized contempt of color," restricted the political and civil liberties of free African Americans in every state. Denied the vote outside New England, segregated in all public facilities, prohibited from moving into several western states, and excluded from most jobs save menial labor, free black people everywhere were walled off as an inferior caste, unfit for equality.

Garrison, harsh and uncompromising in denouncing slavery and advocating black rights, instilled the antislavery movement with moral urgency. But without the organizational and financial resources of a national society, the message of the early Garrisonians rarely extended beyond free black communities in the North. The success of British abolitionists in 1833, when gradual, compensated emancipation was enacted for Britain's West Indian colonies, inspired white and black abolitionists to gather at Philadelphia in December 1833 and form the **American Anti-Slavery Society**.

Arthur and Lewis Tappan, two wealthy merchants who dominated the abolitionist movement in New York City, provided financial backing for the Anti-Slavery Society. The young evangelical minister Theodore Dwight Weld, fusing abolitionism with the moral passion of religious revivalism, brought the antislavery message of the eastern radicals to the West in 1834 with the revivals he preached at Lane Theological Seminary in Cincinnati. The "Lane rebels," students gathered by Weld, fanned out as itinerant agents to seek converts for abolitionism throughout the Yankee districts of the rural North. Weld's *American Slavery as It Is: Testimony of a Thousand Witnesses*, a massively documented indictment of slavery, became a bestseller in 1839.

Revivalist exhortations were just one of the techniques the abolitionists exploited to mobilize public opinion against slavery. They spread their message through rallies, paid lecturers, children's games and toys, and the printed word. Drawing on the experience of reformers in Bible and tract societies, the

Overview

Types of Antislavery Reform

Type	Definition	Example
Gradualist	Accepts notions of black inferiority and attempts to end slavery gradually by purchasing the freedom of slaves and colonizing them in Africa	American Colonization Society
Immediatist	Calls for immediate steps to end slavery and denounces slavery and racial prejudice as moral sins	Abolitionists
Political Antislavery	Recognizes slavery in states where it exists but insists on keeping slavery out of the territories	Free-Soilers

abolitionists harnessed steam power to the cause of moral suasion. They distributed millions of antislavery tracts, and by the late 1830s, abolitionist sayings appeared on posters, emblems, song sheets, and even candy wrappers.

Women were essential in all of these activities. From the very beginning of the movement, they established their own antislavery societies as auxiliaries to the national organizations run and dominated by men. As Christian wives and mothers, they identified with the plight of the black family under slavery. Initially, their gender-segregated role was limited to raising funds, circulating petitions, and visiting homes to gain converts. Often operating out of local churches, women were grass-roots organizers of a massive petition campaign that the abolitionists launched in the mid-1830s. Women signed more than half of the antislavery memorials sent to Congress. "There would be but a few abolition petitions if the ladies . . . would let us alone," complained a Mississippi congressman.

The abolitionists focused their energies on mass propaganda because they saw their role as social agitators who had to break through white apathy and change public opinion. By 1840 they had succeeded in enlisting nearly 200,000 Northerners in two thousand local affiliates of the American Anti-Slavery Society. Most whites, however, remained unmoved, and some violently opposed the abolitionists.

Antiabolitionist mobs in the North went on a rampage in the mid-1830s (see figure 12–3). They disrupted antislavery meetings, beat and stoned speakers, destroyed printing presses, burned the homes of the wealthy benefactors of the movement, and vandalized free black neighborhoods in a wave of terror that drove many black people from several northern cities. Although Garrison and Weld, the most frequent targets of mob violence, escaped with their lives, Elijah P. Lovejoy, an abolitionist editor in Illinois, was killed by a mob in 1837. Local elites, especially those with profitable ties to the slave economy of the South, often incited the mobs, whose fury expressed the anxieties of semi-skilled and common laborers that they might lose their jobs if freed slaves move north.

In the South, the hostility to abolitionism took the form of burning and censoring antislavery literature, offering rewards for the capture of leading abolitionists to stand trial for allegedly inciting slave revolts, and tightening up slave codes and the surveillance of free black people. Meanwhile, Democrats in Congress yielded to slaveholding interests in 1836 by passing a gag rule that automatically tabled antislavery petitions with no debate, infringing Americans' constitutional right to petition their representatives for the redress of grievances.

The hostility and violence abolitionism provoked convinced Garrison and some of his followers that American institutions and values were fundamentally flawed. In 1838, Garrison helped found the New England Non-Resistant Society, dedicated to the belief that a complete moral regeneration, based on renouncing force in all human relationships, was necessary if America were ever to live up to its Christian and republican ideals. The Garrisonian nonresistants rejected all coercive authority, whether expressed in human bondage, clerical support of slavery, male dominance in the patriarchal family, the racial oppression of back people, or the police power of government. The logic of their stand as Christian **anarchists** drove them to denounce all formal political activities and even the legitimacy of the Union, based as it was on a pact with slaveholders.

FIGURE 12-3   Mob Violence and the Abolitionists
Civil disturbances resulting in attacks on individuals or property increased sharply in the 1830s. The abolitionist campaign to flood the country with antislavery literature triggered much of this surge. Nearly half of the mob activity in the 1830s was directed against the abolitionists.

Data Source: Leonard L. Richards, *"Gentlemen of Property and Standing": Anti-Abolitionist Mobs in Jacksonian America* (1970).

Garrison's opponents within the abolitionist movement accused him of alienating the public by identifying the antislavery cause with radical attacks on traditional authority. His support for the growing demand of antislavery women to be treated as equals in the movement brought the factional bickering to a head and split the American Anti-Slavery Society. In turn, the opposition of most male abolitionists to the public activities of their female counterparts provoked a militant faction of these women into founding their own movement to achieve equality in American society.

THE WOMEN'S RIGHTS MOVEMENT

Feminism grew out of abolitionism because of the parallels many women drew between the exploited lives of the slaves and their own subordinate status in northern society. Considered biologically inferior to men, women were denied the vote, deprived of property or control of any wages after marriage, and barred from most occupations and advanced education. "In striving to cut [the slave's] irons off, we found most surely that we were manacled *ourselves*," argued Abby Kelley, a Quaker abolitionist.

In 1837, Angelina and Sarah Grimké, the South Carolina born abolitionists, attracted large crowds of men and women to their antislavery lectures in New England. By publicly lecturing to a "promiscuous" (mixed) audience of men and women, they defied restrictions on women's proper role and enraged the Congregational clergy of Massachusetts. Harshly criticized for their unwomanly behavior, the Grimkés publicly responded with an indictment of the male patriarchy and the shocking assertion that "men and women are *created equal*! They are both moral and accountable beings and whatever is right for man to do is right for woman."

Now more sensitive than ever to the injustice of their assigned role as men's submissive followers, antislavery women demanded an equal voice in the abolitionist movement. Despite strong opposition from many of his fellow male abolitionists, Garrison helped Abby Kelley win a seat on the business committee of the American Anti-Slavery Society at its convention in 1840. The anti-Garrisonians walked out of the convention and formed a separate organization, the American and Foreign Anti-Slavery Society.

What was rapidly becoming known as the "woman question" also disrupted the 1840 World Anti-Slavery Convention in London. The refusal of the convention to seat the American female delegates was the final indignity that transformed the discontent of women into a self-conscious movement for women's equality. Two of the excluded delegates, Lucretia Mott and Elizabeth Cady Stanton, vowed to build an organization to "speak out for *oppressed* women."

Their work went slowly. Early feminists were dependent on the abolitionists for most of their followers, and they were unable to do more than hold local meetings and sponsor occasional speaking tours. Many women sympathetic to the feminist movement hung back lest they be shunned in their communities. A minister's wife in Portsmouth, New Hampshire, spoke for many of these women when she wrote to a feminist friend, "There are but few here who think of women as anything more than slave or plaything, and they think I am different from most women."

In 1848, Stanton and Mott were finally able to call the first national convention ever devoted to women's rights at Seneca Falls, in upstate New York. The **Seneca Falls Convention** issued the **Declaration of Sentiments**, a call for full female equality. Modeled directly on the Declaration of Independence, it identified male patriarchy as the source of women's oppression and demanded the vote for women as a sacred and inalienable right of republican citizenship. This call for suffrage raised the prospect of women's self-determination as independent citizens.

Mobs of angry men often broke up meetings organized by women to vote. Shown here is a male escort offering protection to Lucretia Mott and another suffragette at one such meeting.

The Seneca Falls agenda defined the goals of the women's movement for the rest of the century. The call for the vote met the stiffest opposition, and male legislators refused to budge. The feminists' few successes before the Civil War came in economic rights. By 1860, fourteen states had granted women greater control over their property and wages—most significantly, under New York's Married Women's Property Act of 1860. Largely the result of the intense lobbying of Susan B. Anthony, the act established women's legal right to their own wage income and to sue fathers and husbands who tried to deprive them of their wages.

Despite such successes, the feminist movement did not attract broad support. Most women found in the doctrine of separate spheres a reassuring feminine identity that they could express either at home or in benevolent and reform societies. Within the reform movement as a whole, women's rights were al-

ways of minor concern, as the abolitionists remained focused on emancipation.

POLITICAL ANTISLAVERY

Most abolitionists who had broken with Garrison in 1840 believed that emancipation could best be achieved by moving abolitionism into the mainstream of American politics. Political abolitionism had its roots in the petition campaign of the late 1830s. Congressional efforts to suppress the discussion of slavery backfired when John Quincy Adams, the former president who had become a Massachusetts congressman, resorted to an unending series of parliamentary ploys to get around the gag rule (see chapter 10). A failure as president, Adams became a hero to antislavery Northerners, a champion of the constitutional right to petition Congress for redress of grievances. White Northerners who had shown no interest in abolitionism as a moral crusade for black people now began to take a stand against slavery when the issue involved the civil liberties of whites and the dominant political power of the South. By the hundreds of thousands, they signed abolitionist petitions in 1837 and 1838 to protest the gag rule and the admission of Texas as a slave state.

In 1840, anti-Garrisonian abolitionists tried to turn this new antislavery constituency into an independent political party. They formed the **Liberty Party** and ran James G. Birney, a former slaveholder converted by Weld to abolitionism, as their candidate for the presidency. He failed to draw even 1 percent of the total popular vote, but antislavery districts dominated by evangelical New Englanders elected several antislavery congressmen.

The Liberty Party opposed any expansion of slavery in the territories, condemned racial discrimination in the North as well as slavery in the South, and won the support of most black abolitionists. "To it," recalled Samuel Ward of New York, "I devoted my political activities; with it I lived my political life." In 1843, a national African-American convention in Buffalo endorsed the Liberty party.

This political activism was part of a concerted effort by African Americans to assert leadership in an antislavery movement that rarely treated them as equals. Frederick Douglass was their most dynamic spokesman. After escaping from slavery in 1838, Douglass became a spellbinding lecturer for abolitionism and in 1845 published his classic autobiography, *Narrative of the Life of Frederick Douglass, an American Slave.* Increasingly dissatisfied with Garrison's Christian pacifism and his stand against political action, Douglass broke with Garrison in 1847 and founded a black abolitionist newspaper, *The North Star*. The break became irreparable in 1851 when Douglass publicly denied the Garrisonian position that the Constitution was a proslavery document. If properly interpreted, Douglass insisted, "the Constitution is a *glorious liberty document*," and he called for a political war against slavery.

That war had started in the 1840s with the Liberty Party. Although the party elected only one of its candidates to Congress (Gerrit Smith of New York), it kept slavery in the limelight of national politics. Led by Joshua R. Giddings, a small but vocal bloc of antislavery politicians began to popularize the frightening concept of "the Slave Power"—a vast conspiracy of planters and their northern lackeys that had seized control of the federal government and was plotting to spread slavery and subvert any free institutions that opposed it. As proof, they cited the gag rule shutting off debate on slavery and the campaign of the Tyler administration to annex slaveholding Texas. The Michigan Liberty party in 1843 claimed that slavery was "not only a monstrous legalized system of wickedness . . . but an overwhelming political monopoly . . . which has thus tyrannically subverted the constitutional liberties of more than 12,000,000 of nominal American freemen." The Liberty Party blamed the depression of 1839–1843 on the "withering and impoverishing effect of slavery on the free States." Planters, it was charged, had reneged on their debts to northern creditors and manipulated federal policies on banking and tariffs to the advantage of the South.

The specter of the Slave Power made white liberties, and not black bondage, central to northern concerns about slavery. This shift redefined the evil of slavery to appeal to the self-interests of white Northerners who had rejected the moral appeals of the Garrisonians. White people who had earlier been apathetic now began to view slavery as a threat to their rights of free speech and self-improvement through free labor untainted by the degrading competition of slave labor.

Birney again headed the Liberty Party ticket in 1844, but he ran only marginally stronger than in 1840. Nonetheless, the image of the Slave Power predisposed many Northerners to see the expansionist program of the incoming Polk administration as part of a southern plot to secure more territory for slaveholders at the expense of northern farmers. Northern fears that free labor would be shut out of the new territories won in the Mexican War provided the rallying cry for the Free-Soil Party of 1848 that foreshadowed the more powerful Republican Party of the late 1850s.

After escaping to freedom in 1838, Frederick Douglass became a commanding figure in the abolitionist movement. His speeches denouncing slavery were fiery and eloquent.

Frederick Douglass (1817?-1895). Oil on canvas, c. 1844, attr. to E. Hammond. The Granger Collection.

CONCLUSION

With surprising speed after 1815, transportation improvements, technological innovations, and expanding markets drove the economy on a path toward industrialization. Wealth inequality increased, old classes were reshaped, and new ones formed. These changes were most evident in the Northeast, where capital, labor, and growing urban markets spurred the acceleration of manufacturing. The reform impulse that both reflected and shaped these changes was also strongest in the Northeast.

The new evangelical Protestantism promised that human perfectibility was possible if individuals strove to free themselves from sin. Influenced by this promise, the northern middle class embraced reform causes that sought to improve human character. Temperance, the most widely accepted of these causes, changed American drinking habits and established sobriety as the cultural standard for respectable male behavior. Middle-class reform also emphasized institutional solutions for what were now defined as the social problems of ignorance, crime, and poverty.

FROM THEN TO NOW

Immigration: An Ambivalent Welcome

Americans have long extended an ambivalent welcome to newcomers. In the mid-nineteenth century, employment posters often read "Irish Need Not Apply," and today stepped-up border patrols seek to keep out Mexican and other Latin American immigrants. Yet America is a nation settled and built by immigrants whose founding ideals promise equality and opportunity to all. And for much of its history it has offered asylum for the world's oppressed.

In the early years of the republic, Federalists worried that immigrants from Europe might be contaminated by the radical ideas of the French revolution and sought to make it harder for them to become naturalized citizens. The nation's first naturalization law in the 1790s also barred black immigrants from citizenship. The first sustained attack against newcomers, however, emerged as a result of the surge in immigration during the 1840s and 1850s. It was directed by established immigrant groups—the descendants of settlers from Britain and northwestern Europe—at unfamiliar newcomers, particularly the Irish.

Nativist arguments of that time have found an echo in all subsequent immigration debates. The Irish, it was claimed, would take jobs away from American workers and lower their wages. Taxpayers would have to foot the bill for the strains the newcomers imposed on schools, hospitals, and other civic services. The ignorant immigrants would corrupt the political process. Nativists especially feared religious contamination, claiming that the Catholicism of the Irish was alien to the Protestant values held to be indispensable to the preservation of American liberties. So many Irish arrived so quickly that many nativists were convinced of a Papal plot to undermine American freedom. "The bloody hand of the Pope," one wrote, "has stretched itself forth to our destruction."

Eventually the Irish and Germans merged into the economic and political fabric of American life. But in the late nineteenth century a massive new immigrant surge dominated by people from Southern and Eastern Europe seeking economic opportunity and fleeing religious oppression transformed American society and renewed nativist fears. This time, race replaced religion as the basis for drawing invidious comparisons between established residents and the newcomers. Pseudo-scientific theories relegated Jews, Slavs, and Mediterranean peoples, together with Africans, to an inferior status below people of Northern European and especially Anglo-Saxon descent. The newcomers, it was claimed, were unfit for democratic government and would endanger American civilization. Strict anti-immigrant legislation in the 1920s sharply curtailed immigration from outside the Western Hemisphere, banning Asians entirely and setting quotas based on national origin for others.

Recent concerns about immigration result from the unforeseen consequences of a 1965 reform in immigration law that abolished quotas. Since then, immigration has risen sharply, and the national origin of the immigrants has diverged from previous patterns. By the 1980s, Europeans constituted but 10 percent of the newcomers. The bulk of the remainder came from Asia (40 percent) and Mexico, Central America, and the Caribbean. Once again, anti-immigrant voices worry that alien newcomers are threatening the cohesiveness of the nation's institutions and values. But, once again as well, a more inclusive vision of American identity and ideals seems likely to prevail as the newcomers establish themselves. As Abraham Lincoln expressed it, "There was no exclusively American race entitled to claim liberty by heredity. What held the nation together was an idea of equality that every newcomer could claim and defend by free choice."

The most radical of the reform movements focused on women's equality and the elimination of slavery. The women's rights movement emerged out of women's involvement in reform, especially in abolitionism. Feminism and abolitionism triggered a backlash from the more conservative majority. This backlash prevented women from gaining legal and political equality, the major demand of the feminists, and convinced most abolitionists that they had to switch from moral agitation to political persuasion. The political abolitionists soon found that the most effective approach in widening the antislavery appeal was their charge that a Slave Power conspiracy threatened the freedoms of white Northerners.

REVIEW QUESTIONS

1. Why were improvements in transportation so essential to the growth of the economy after 1815? What were the nature and scope of these improvements?

2. What is an industrial revolution? How can we explain the surge in manufacturing in the United States from 1815 to 1850?

3. What was the religious impulse behind the first wave of reform? What innovations in reaching a mass audience did the benevolent reformers pioneer?

4. What drew women into reform? Why did many of them feel a special affinity for abolitionism?

5. Why was abolitionism the most radical reform of all?

6. Why do you think so few Southern women of the plantation class followed Angelina Grimké on her journey from social privilege to social activism?

KEY TERMS

American Anti-Slavery Society (p. 379)

American Colonization Society (p. 378)

American Female Reform Society (p. 370)

American system of manufacturing (p. 364)

American Temperance Society (p. 369)

Anarchists (p. 380)

Appeal to the Colored Citizens of the World (p. 378)

Benevolent empire (p. 368)

Brook Farm (p. 375)

Charles River Bridge v. Warren Bridge (p. 356)

Church of Jesus Christ of Latter-day Saints (Mormon Church) (p. 371)

Communism (p. 375)

Cult of domesticity (p. 366)

Declaration of Sentiments (p. 381)

Fourierist communities (p. 375)

Gibbons v. Ogden (p. 356)

Liberty Party (p. 382)

Mormon Church (p. 371)

Nativist (p. 367)

New Harmony (p. 375)

Oneida Community (p. 375)

Putting-out system (p. 361)

Rhode Island system (p. 362)

Sabbatarian movement (p. 368)

Seneca Falls Convention (p. 381)

Shakers (p. 375)

Socialism (p. 375)

Temperance (p. 365)

Transcendentalism (p. 376)

Transportation revolution (p. 353)

Waltham system (p. 362)

Workingmen's movement (p. 372)

RECOMMENDED READING

Abzug, Robert H. *Cosmos Crumbling: American Reform and the Religious Imagination* (1994). Provides a fresh look at antebellum reform by using the lives of individual reformers to show how Protestant Christianity inspired a rethinking of American values in a period of rapid economic change.

Boydston, Jeanne. *Home and Work: Housework, Wages, and the Ideology of Labor in the Early Republic* (1990). Shows how issues of gender shaped the emergence of a market for labor and influenced the very notion of work itself.

Cochran, Thomas C. *Frontiers of Change: Early Industrialization in America* (1981). Argues for the importance of cultural factors in the rise and scope of manufacturing in the United States before 1850.

Davis, David Brion, ed. *Antebellum American Culture* (1979). This superb collection of source materials covers all facets of the commitment to reform and institutional change.

Larkin, Jack. *The Reshaping of Everyday Life, 1790–1840* (1988). A very readable depiction of how social and economic changes were reflected in the rhythms and customs of daily life in the first half of the nineteenth century.

Licht, Walter. *Industrializing America: The Nineteenth Century* (1995). This smoothly written survey interprets industrialization as both a product and a promoter of economic and social change.

Mintz, Steven. *Moralists and Modernizers: America's Pre-Civil War Reformers* (1995). A recent survey that demonstrates how both the fears and possibilities of change influenced the impulse of reform.

Stewart, James Brewer. *Holy Warriors: The Abolitionists and American Society* (1978). Provides the best brief overview of abolitionism and what distinguished it from the mainstream of the reform tradition.

ADDITIONAL SOURCES

Industrial Change and Urbanization

Anbinder, Tyler. *Five Points* (2001).

Blumin, Stuart M. *The Emergence of the Middle Class: Social Experience in the American City, 1760–1900* (1989).

Bushman, Richard L. *The Refinement of America: Persons, Houses, Cities* (1992).

Dublin, Thomas. *Women at Work: The Transformation of Work and Community in Lowell, Massachusetts, 1826–1860* (1979).

Fishlow, Albert. *American Railroads and the Transformation of the Ante-Bellum Economy* (1965).

Handlin, Oscar. *Boston's Immigrants: A Study of Acculturation,* rev. ed. (1959).

Horowitz, Morton J. *The Transformation of American Law, 1790–1860* (1977).

Johnson, Paul E. *A Shopkeeper's Millennium: Society and Revivals in Rochester, New York, 1815–1837* (1978).

Laurie, Bruce. *Artisans into Workers: Labor in Nineteenth-Century America* (1989).

Pessen, Edward. *Riches, Class, and Power before the Civil War* (1973).

Roediger, David. *The Wages of Whiteness: Race and the Making of the American Working Class* (1991).

Ryan, Mary. *Cradle of the Middle Class: The Family in Oneida County, New York, 1790–1865* (1981).

Shaw, Ronald E. *Canals for a Nation: The Canal Era in the United States, 1790–1860* (1990).

Stansel, Christine. *City of Women: Sex and Class in New York, 1789–1860* (1986).

Steinberg, Theodore. *Nature Incorporated: Industrialization and the Waters of New England* (1991).

Wade, Richard C. *The Urban Frontier* (1964).

Wilentz, Sean. *Chants Democratic: New York City and the Rise of the American Working Class, 1790–1865* (1984).

Reform and Moral Order

Cott, Nancy F. *The Bonds of Womanhood: "Woman's Sphere" in New England, 1780–1835* (1977).

Cross, Whitney R. *The Burned-Over District: The Social and Intellectual History of Enthusiastic Religion in Western New York, 1800–1850* (1950).

Epstein, Barbara Leslie. *The Politics of Domesticity: Women, Evangelicalism, and Temperance in Nineteenth-Century America* (1981).

Foster, Charles I. *An Errand of Mercy: The Evangelical United Front* (1960).

Ginzberg, Lori D. *Women and the Work of Benevolence: Morality, Politics, and Class in the 19th-Century United States* (1990).

Hanley, Mark Y. *Beyond a Christian Commonwealth: The Protestant Quarrel with the American Republic, 1830–1860* (1994).

Smith-Rosenberg, Carroll. *Religion and the Rise of the American City* (1971).

Rorabaugh, W. J. *The Alcoholic Republic* (1979).

Walters, Ronald A. *American Reformers, 1815–1860* (1978).

Winn, Kenneth H. *Exiles in a Land of Liberty: Mormons in America, 1830–1846* (1989).

Wosh, Peter J. *Spreading the Word: The Bible Business in Nineteenth-Century America* (1994).

Institutions and Social Improvement

Capper, Charles, and Conrad Edick Wright, eds. *Transient and Permanent: The Transcendentalist Movement and its Contexts* (1999).

Grob, Gerald N. *Mental Institutions in America: Social Policy to 1875* (1973).

Guarneri, Carl J. *The Utopian Alternative: Fourierism in Nineteenth-Century America* (1991).

Hirsh, Adam Jay. *The Rise of the Penitentiary* (1992).

Kaestle, Carl F. *Pillars of the Republic: Common Schools and American Society, 1780–1860* (1983).

Katz, Michael B. *In the Shadow of the Poorhouse: A Social History of Welfare in America* (1986).

Rothman, David. *The Discovery of the Asylum: Social Order and Disorder in the New Republic* (1971).

Stein, Stephen J. *The Shaker Experience in America* (1992).

Abolitionism and Women's Rights

Basch, Norma. *In the Eyes of the Law: Women, Marriage, and Property in Nineteenth-Century New York* (1982).

Du Bois, Ellen. *Feminism and Suffrage: The Emergence of an Independent Women's Movement, 1848–1869* (1978).

Hewitt, Nancy A. *Women's Activism and Social Change: Rochester, New York, 1822–1872* (1984).

Isenberg, Nancy. *Sex and Citizenship in Antebellum America* (1998).

Jeffrey, Julie Roy. *The Great Silent Army of Abolitionism: Ordinary Women in the Antislavery Movement* (1998).

Litwack, Leon F. *North of Slavery: The Negro in the Free States, 1790–1860* (1961).

Lumpkin, Katharine Du Pre. *The Emancipation of Angelina Grimké* (1974).

McKivigan, John R. *The War against Proslavery Religion: Abolitionism and the Northern Churches, 1830–1865* (1984).

Newman, Richard S. *The Transformation of American Abolitionism: Fighting Slavery in the Early Republic* (2002).

Rael, Patrick. *Black Identity and Black Protest in the Antebellum North* (2002).

Richards, Leonard L. *The Slave Power: The Free North and Southern Domination, 1780–1860* (2000).

Ripley, C. Peter, et al., eds. *Witness for Freedom: African-American Voices on Race, Slavery, and Emancipation* (1993).

Staudenraus, Philip J. *The African Colonization Movement, 1816–1865* (1961).

WHERE TO LEARN MORE

- **Baltimore Center for Urban Archaeology, Baltimore, Maryland.** Operated by Baltimore City Life Museum, the center has a large collection of artifacts depicting urban life in the eighteenth and nineteenth centuries and a working archaeological library.

- **Hanford Mills Museum, East Meredith, New York.** This museum preserves and interprets water-powered machinery and explains the role played by local mills in the community life of the nineteenth century. For a map and links to events, workshops, and education programs, visit www.hanfordmills.org/.

- Slater Hill Historic Site, Pawtucket, Rhode Island. The Sylvanus Brown House of 1758, the Slaren Mill of 1793, and the Wilkinson Mill of 1810 are on the site. An extensive library and holdings pro-vide insight into the social and economic world of the early industrial revolution. Information on hours, collections, and exhibits can be found at www.artcom.com/museums/vs/sz/02862-06.htm.

- **Erie Canal Museum, Syracuse, New York.** The museum houses extensive collections on the building and maintenance of the Erie Canal, and its photo holdings visually record much of the history of the canal. In addition to information on exhibits, tours, and school programs, its website, www.eriecanalmuseum.org/, includes pictures of a replica of an Erie Canal line boat.

- **Historic New Harmony, New Harmony, Indiana.** The tours and museum holdings at this preserved site offer a glimpse into the communal living that Robert Owen tried to promote in his utopian plan. For a brief history of New Harmony and links to special events and programs at the site, go to www.newharmony.org/.

- **Oberlin College Library, Oberlin, Ohio.** Oberlin was a hotbed of reform agitation, and the tracts, broadsides, photographs, and other memorabilia here are especially rich on the activities of white evangelicals and black abolitionists. For an introduction to the library and its holdings, visit www.oberlin.edu/library/.

- **Shaker Museum at South Union, Kentucky.** The exhibits, artifacts, and archives are a superb source for understanding the history and material culture of the Shakers and other radical sects. Its website, www.shakermuseum.com/, includes a brief history of the Shakers, photographs of restored buildings, and an overview of the museum's holdings.

- **Women's Rights Historical Park, Seneca Falls, New York.** The park provides an interpretive overview of the first women's rights convention and includes among its historical sites the restored home of Elizabeth Cady Stanton. Go to www.nps.gov/wori/wrnhp.htm for links to the museum's summer calendar of events and information on programs.

 Please refer to the document CD-ROM for primary sources related to this chapter.

→ As depicted in this painting by George Catlin, Native Americans were still the dominant power on the Great Plains when this Comanche war party met up with a scouting expedition of the U.S. Army in the 1830s. Within a decade, a wave of white settlement challenged the power in a series of clashes for control of the Trans-Mississippi West.

THE WAY WEST   13

CHAPTER OUTLINE

The Agricultural Frontier
The Crowded East
The Old Northwest
The Old Southwest

The Frontier of the Plains Indians
Tribal Lands
The Fur Traders
The Oregon Trail

The Mexican Borderlands
The Peoples of the Southwest
The Americanization of Texas
The Push into California and the Southwest

Politics, Expansion, and War
Manifest Destiny
The Mexican War

Conclusion

"On an occasion when I had interrogated a Sioux chief, on the upper Missouri, about their Government — their punishments and tortures of prisoners, for which I had freely condemned them for the cruelty of the practice, he took occasion, when I had got through, to ask *me* some questions relative to modes in the *civilized world*, which, with his comments upon them, were nearly as follows: and struck me, as I think they must every one, with great force.

He . . . told me he had often heard that white people hung their criminals by the neck, and choked them to death like dogs, and those their own people; to which I answered, "yes." He then told me he had learned that they shut each other up in prisons, where they keep them a great part of their lives *because they can't pay money*! I replied in the affirmative to this, which occasioned great surprise and excessive laughter, even among the women. . . . He said . . . that he had been along the Frontier, and a good deal amongst the white people, and he had seen them whip their little children — a thing that is very cruel — he had heard also, from several white *medicine-men*, that the Great Spirit of the white people was the child of a white woman, and that he was at the last put to death by the white people! This seemed to be a thing that he had not been able to comprehend, and he concluded by saying, "the Indians' Great Spirit got no mother — the Indians no kill him, he never die." He put me a chapter of other questions as to the trespasses of the white people on their lands—their continual corruption of the morals of their women—and digging open the Indians' graves to get their bones, &c. To all of which I was compelled to reply in the affirmative, and quite glad to close my note-book, and quietly to escape from the throng that had collected around me, and saying (though to myself and silently), that these and an hundred other vices belong to the civilized world, and are practiced upon (but certainly, in no instance, reciprocated by) the "cruel and relentless savage."

George Catlin

Virgil J. Vogel, ed., *A Documentary History of the American Indian* (New York: Harper and Row, 1972), pp. 138–139.

George Catlin, one of the great illustrators of the West of the American Indians, recorded these words in the 1830s when he traveled over the trans-Mississippi West painting and sketching, in his words, "the looks and customs of the vanishing races of native man in America." Unlike most whites of his generation, he approached Indian cultures with respect, and he was astute enough to realize that native peoples had a valid critique of the culture and values of white America. Born in 1796 in the Wyoming Valley of northeastern Pennsylvania, an area wracked by Indian raids during the Revolutionary War, including one in which his mother was held captive, he was raised among memories of Indians and their warfare. After attending law school in Litchfield, Connecticut, and briefly practicing law, he turned to painting and portraiture as a career in the 1820s. He was so taken with the physical grace and dignity of a group of Indians visiting Philadelphia in 1824 that he committed his life's work to a visual recording of Indian history and customs.

From his first contact with the tribes along the upper Missouri River in the early 1830s, Catlin sensed that he was witness to a way of life that was about to vanish. He worked at a feverish pace to create a pictorial record of what he saw in a collection of art he called "Catlin's Indian Gallery." The proceeds from exhibiting his work in Europe enabled him to live quite comfortably in the 1840s, but falling prey to a vice of the "civilized" world that the Sioux chief failed to mention, he suffered a severe setback in 1852 when a financial speculation went sour. He had to pledge his art collection as security to obtain a large loan, and he never did succeed in redeeming the loan. A failure as an entrepreneur, he nonetheless succeeded brilliantly as an artist in depicting the Native American peoples of the trans-Mississippi West just at the moment they were about to be engulfed by a surging tide of white settlement.

Some 300,00 Americans traveled the Oregon Trail in the 1840s and 1850s in a trek that eventually made the United States a nation that spanned the continent. These overlanders, as they came to be known, were part of a restless tide of white migration that eventually saw more than fifty thousand Americans a year migrate west of the Appalachians after the War of 1812.

After moving into the area between the Appalachian Mountains and the Mississippi River—the American West of the early nineteenth century—migrants headed beyond the Mississippi River in the 1840s. The edge of settlement pushed into the Louisiana Purchase territory and across a huge area of plains, desert, mountains, and ocean coast that had seen few American settlers before 1840.

The broad expanse of the trans-Mississippi region (stretching from the Mississippi Valley to the Pacific Coast) had become the new American West by midcentury. The West became a meeting ground of people from diverse cultures as Anglo-Americans came into contact and conflict with the Indians of the Plains and the Mexicans of the Southwest. Convinced of the superiority of their political and cultural values, Anglo-Americans asserted a God-given right to spread across the continent and impose their notions of liberty and democracy on peoples whose land they coveted. In the process, they defeated and subjugated those who stood in their way.

Manifest Destiny was the label for this presumed providential right, and it provided a justification for the aggressively expansionist Democratic administration of James K. Polk that came to power in 1845. The most dramatic result of these policies was the Mexican War of 1846–1848, which made California and the present-day Southwest part of the American continental empire.

KEY TOPICS

- Western migration spurred by economic and demographic pressures in the East after the War of 1812

- The development of free commercial agriculture tied to eastern markets and increased industrialization and urbanization of the Old Northwest

- The development of a plantation economy based on cotton and slavery in the Old Southwest

- Manifest Destiny and westward expansion, relegating Native Americans and Mexican-Americans to subjugated status

- U.S. annexation of Texas and the wresting of the Southwest and California from Mexico

THE AGRICULTURAL FRONTIER

The U.S. population ballooned from 5.3 million in 1800 to more than 23 million by 1850. The population grew about 33 percent per decade, and four-fifths of this extraordinary gain was from natural increase—the surplus of births over deaths. As the population expanded, it shifted westward. Fewer than one in ten Americans lived west of the Appalachians in 1800; by 1850, about half did (see Map 13–1).

The tremendous amount of land available for settlement accounted for both phenomena. Through purchase and conquest, the land area of the United States more than tripled in the first half of the nineteenth century. Here was space where Americans could raise the large families of a rural society in which, on average, six to eight children survived to adolescence. Millions of fertile acres lured eastern families ever westward to the next agricultural frontier.

Declining soil fertility and rising population pressure in the rural East propelled these migrations. A common desire for greater economic opportunity, however, resulted in two distinct western societies by the 1840s. North of the Ohio River, in the Old Northwest, free labor and family farms defined the social order. South of the Ohio was the Old Southwest, a society dominated by slave labor and the plantation.

THE CROWDED EAST

Looking back at his rural youth, Omar H. Morse recalled, "My Parents were in very limited circumstances financially yet blessed with a large family of children which is a poor man's capital though capital of this kind is not considered very available in case of financial Depression." Born in 1824 in the upstate New York village of Hastings, Morse was typical of the hard-pressed eastern youth who moved west after the War of 1812. With no prospect of inheriting land from his father and tired of taking orders as a farmhand for temporary wages, he moved in the 1840s to Wisconsin, where he found what he thought was "the most beautiful spot of country on God's green Earth." Even after this fresh start, bad luck and too many debts prevented Morse from ever achieving landed independence. He lost three farms and eventually settled in Minnesota, where he worked at odd jobs and built houses. Heading west did not guarantee economic success, but it was the best option open to land-starved easterners who dreamed of leaving a productive farm to their children.

By the early nineteenth century, land was scarce in the East, especially in New England. After generations of population growth and subdivisions of landholdings to male heirs, most New England communities no longer had enough arable land to satisfy all the young men who wanted their own farms. Even such recently opened areas as Vermont felt the pressure of rural overpopulation.

Land was more productive and expensive farther south, in the mid-Atlantic states. Based on the major export crop of wheat, agriculture was more commercialized than in New England, and economic inequality was thus higher. Successful farmers became wealthy by specializing in wheat and hiring the rural poor to work their fields. One-third to one-half of the young men in the commercialized agricultural districts of New Jersey and Pennsylvania were landless by the end of the eighteenth century. These men and their families, many of whom were recently arrived Scots-Irish and German immigrants, led the western migration from Pennsylvania.

The pressure to move west was greatest in the slave states along the eastern seaboard. Although population

MAP EXPLORATION To explore an interactive version of this map, go to
http://www.prenhall.com/goldfield/map13.1

Number of people per square mile

- More than 90.0
- 45.0 — 90.0
- 18.0 — 44.9
- 6.0 — 17.9
- 2.0 — 5.9
- Fewer than 2.0

MAP 13-1   The Westward Shift of the United States Population, 1790–1850
With a speed that was unimaginable in 1790, the United States quickly became a continental nation that stretched from the Atlantic to the Pacific by 1850. Particularly dramatic was the population growth in what became the Midwest.

density here was just two-thirds of that in New England, ordinary white farmers faced even more limited prospects of economic advancement. Landholdings were more concentrated and the soil more exhausted than in the Northeast. Repeated plantings of tobacco in Virginia and Maryland and of cotton farther south had depleted the soil throughout much of the region. In the Chesapeake states, established planters with extensive capital and labor resources shifted to wheat production or bought out their nonslaveholding neighbors. Tenants who wanted their own land and small farmers tired of competing against slave labor were forced west across the mountains. They were joined by the sons of planters. Despite marriages arranged to keep land within the wealthy families, there was no longer enough good land left to carve out plantations for all the younger sons.

By the early 1800s, the young and the poor in the rural East faced limited opportunities for social mobility and economic independence. They had every incentive to head west, where fertile land was abundant, accessible, and at $2 to $3 per acre, far cheaper than in the East. Land was the basis of wealth and social standing, and its ownership separated the independent from the dependent, the rooted from the rootless. According to the principles of Jeffersonian democracy, the independent farmer was the backbone of the republic, the virtuous citizen who made republican government possible. "Those who labor in the earth," Jefferson wrote in 1785, "are the chosen people of God . . . whose breasts He has made his peculiar deposit for substantial and genuine virtue."

The western settler, observed a traveler on the Missouri frontier in the 1820s, wanted "to be a freeholder, to have plenty of rich land, and to be able to settle his children around him." Government policy under the Jeffersonian Republicans and Jacksonian Democrats attempted to make it easier to reach these goals. Central to the land policy of the federal government after 1800 was the conviction that political liberties rested on the broadest possible base of land ownership. Thus public policy and private aspirations merged in the belief that access to land was the key to preserving American freedom.

When Jefferson took office in 1801, the minimum price for public land was $2 per acre, and a block of 320 acres had to be purchased at one time. By the 1830s, the price was down to $1.25 per acre, and the minimum purchase was only 80 acres. Congress also protected squatters, who had settled on public land before it was surveyed, from being outbid by speculators at land sales. The Preemption Act of 1841 guaranteed the right to purchase up to 160 acres at the minimum price of $1.25 when the public auction was held.

THE OLD NORTHWEST

The number of Americans who settled in the heartland of the Old Northwest—Ohio, Indiana, and Illinois—rose tenfold from 1810 to 1840. Ohio had already entered the Union in 1803; Indiana joined in 1816, Illinois in 1818. The end of the War of 1812 and the abandonment by the British of their former Indian allies opened up the region to a flood of migrants.

Travelers passing through the Ohio Valley just after the war were astonished by the number of Americans

Chronology

1803–1806	Lewis and Clark travel up the Missouri River in search of a water route to the Pacific.	**1837**	Smallpox epidemic hits the Plains Indians.
1816	Settlers surge into the trans-Appalachian region.	**1842**	First large parties of migrants set out on the Oregon Trail.
1821	Mexico gains its independence from Spain.	**1845**	United States annexes Texas.
	Santa Fe Trail opens.		Democrats embrace Manifest Destiny.
	Stephen F. Austin establishes the first American colony in Texas.	**1846**	Mexican War breaks out.
			United States and Britain reach an agreement in Oregon.
1824	Rocky Mountain Fur Company begins the rendezvous system.	**1847**	Mormons begin settlement of Utah.
1830	Congress creates the Indian Territory.	**1848**	Oregon Territory is organized.
1834	Protestant missions are established in Oregon.		Treaty of Guadalupe Hidalgo ends the Mexican War.
	Santa Anna seizes power in Mexico.	**1851**	Fort Laramie Treaty with the Plains Indians is signed.
1836	Texas wins its independence from Mexico.		

trekking west. Wagonloads of migrants bounced along turnpikes to disembark on the Ohio River at Pittsburgh and Wheeling, where they bought flatboats to carry them down the Ohio to the interior river valleys. Moving north across the Ohio were families from the hill country of Virginia and Kentucky. These two streams of migrants, one predominantly northern and the other southern, met in the lower Midwest and viewed each other as strangers. Lucy Maynard, a New Englander living in south-central Illinois, noted that her neighbors were "principally from Indiana and Kentucky, some from Virginia, all friendly but very different from our people in their manners and language and every other way."

A mosaic of settlements.

The Old Northwest was less a melting pot in which regional cultures merged than a mosaic of settlements in which the different values and folkways of regional cultures from throughout the East took root and expanded. Belts of migration generally ran along a line from east to west as settlers sought out soil types and ecological conditions similar to those they had left behind. Thus the same North–South cultural differences that existed along the Atlantic seaboard in 1800 were to be found half a century later in the Mississippi Valley.

A transplanted Yankee culture from New England and upstate New York spread over the upper Midwest—northern Ohio, Indiana, and Illinois, as well as Michigan and Wisconsin. These westerners were Whiggish in their politics, tended to be antislavery, and valued a communal sense of responsibility that regulated moral behavior and promoted self-improvement. The highland southerners who settled the lower Midwest—southern Ohio, Indiana, and Illinois, as well as Kentucky—were Democrats: They fiercely distrusted any centralized authority, political or moral, and considered Yankees intolerant do-gooders. Holding the balance of cultural and political power were the migrants from Pennsylvania and New Jersey, who were accustomed to ethnic diversity and the politics of competing economic groups. They settled principally in central Ohio, Indiana, and Illinois. By emphasizing economic growth and downplaying the cultural politics that pitted Yankees against Southerners, they built a consensus around community development.

Much as they had done in the East, the early settlers practiced a diversified agriculture to feed and shelter their families. The first task was to clear the land and sow a crop of corn, a hardy grain that required little care. Wild game and livestock left to forage in the woods supplemented the corn-based diet.

It took about ten years of backbreaking labor to create an 80-acre farm in heavily wooded sections. Because the Northwest Ordinance of 1787 had barred slavery north of the Ohio, settlers had to do the work themselves or hire farmhands. The work of women was essential for the success of the farm and the production of any salable surplus. Wives and daughters helped to tend the field crops, milked cows and churned butter, and they produced the homespun cloth that, along with their dairy goods, found a market in the first country stores on the frontier. Charlotte Webb Jacobs, from the Sugar Creek community on the Illinois prairie, proudly recalled, "I made everything that we wore; I even made my towels and table cloths, sheets and everything in the clothing line."

Because outside labor was scarce and expensive, communities pooled their efforts for such tasks as raising a cabin. Groups of settlers also acted as a cooperative unit at public land auctions. Local associations known as **claims clubs** enforced the extralegal right of squatters to enter noncompetitive bids on land they had settled and improved. Members of the clubs physically intimidated speculators who refused to step aside until local settlers had acquired the land they wanted.

The high cost of hauling goods to outside markets kept the early frontier economy barely above self-sufficiency. Any surplus was sold to newcomers moving into the area or bartered with local storekeepers for such essentials as salt, sugar, and metalwares. This initial economy, however, soon gave way to a more commercially oriented agriculture when steamboats, canals, and railroads opened up vast new markets (see Chapter 12). Western lands were at least twice as fertile as those in the East, and farmers could now profit from their bountiful yields.

The first large market was in the South, down the corridor of the Ohio and Mississippi Rivers, and its major staples were corn and hogs. By the 1830s, the Erie Canal and its feeder waterways in the upper Midwest began to reorient much of the western farm trade to the Northeast. Wheat, because of its ready marketability for milling into flour, became the major cash crop for the northern market.

Wheat production skyrocketed when settlers overcame their initial reluctance to farming in a treeless terrain and moved into the prairies of Indiana and Illinois in the 1840s. New plows—a cast-iron one patented by Jethro Wood in 1819 and a steel version developed by John Deere in 1837—helped break the thick prairie sod. The plows were followed in the 1840s by horse-drawn mechanical harvesters designed and manufactured by Cyrus McCormick. Traditional harvesting methods that relied on a worker using a scythe with a cradle frame were slow and relatively expensive. An experienced worker could cut no more than two acres a day. The same worker with the new machinery could harvest twelve acres a day, and the per-acre cost of labor fell dramatically. Once railroads provided direct access to eastern markets, the Midwest became the nation's breadbasket.

Although southern cotton was the raw material that fueled New England textile factories in the first stages of industrialization, the commercialization of agriculture in the West also contributed to the growth of eastern manufacturing. The productivity of western farms supplied eastern manufacturers with inexpensive raw materials for processing into finished goods. By flooding national markets with corn and wheat, western produce not only supplied eastern workers with cheap food but also forced noncompetitive eastern farmers either to move west or to work in factories in eastern cities. In turn, the West itself became an ever-growing market for eastern factory goods. For example, nearly half of the nation's iron production in the 1830s was fashioned into farm implements.

In the 1820s, the Old Northwest was just emerging from semisubsistence and depended on the southern trade. Thirty years later it had become part of a larger Midwest whose economy was increasingly integrated with that of the Northeast. Settlers continued to pour into the region, and three additional states—Michigan (1837), Iowa (1846), and Wisconsin (1848)—joined the Union.

The combination of favorable farm prices and steadily decreasing transportation costs generated a rise in disposable income that was spent on outside goods or invested in internal development. A network of canals and railroads was laid down, and manufacturing cities grew from towns favorably situated by water or rail transport. There was still room for subsistence farming, but the West north of the Ohio was now economically specialized and socially diverse.

THE OLD SOUTHWEST

"The *Alabama Feaver* rages here with great violence and has carried off vast numbers of our Citizens," wrote a North Carolina planter in 1817 about the westward migration from his state. "I am apprehensive, if it continues to spread as it has done, it will almost depopulate the country."

The planter, James Graham, had reason to be concerned. About as many people migrated from the old slave states in the East to the Old Southwest as those states gained by natural increase in the 1820s and 1830s. By 1850, more than 600,000 white settlers from Maryland, Virginia, and the Carolinas lived in slave states to the south and west, and many of them had brought their slaves with them. Indeed, from 1790 to 1860, more than 800,000 slaves were moved from the South Atlantic region into the Old Southwest.

Soaring cotton prices after the War of 1812 and the smashing of Indian confederations during the war, which opened new lands to white settlement, propelled the first surge of migration into the Old Southwest (see Map 13–1). Before cotton prices plunged in the Panic of 1819, planters flooded into western Tennessee and the Black Belt, a crescent-shaped band of rich, black loamy soil arcing westward from Georgia through central Alabama and Mississippi. Migration surged anew in the 1830s when cotton prices were again high and the Chickasaws and Choctaws had been forced out of the incredibly fertile Delta country between the Yazoo and Mississippi Rivers (see Chapter 10). The 1840s brought Texas fever to replace the Alabama fever of the 1810s, and a steady movement to the Southwest rounded out the contours of the cotton South. In less than thirty years, six new slave states—Mississippi (1817), Alabama (1819), Missouri (1821), Arkansas (1836), Florida (1845), and Texas (1845)—joined the Union (see the Overview table, "Westward Expansion and the Growth of the Union, 1815–1850").

Cyrus McCormick pioneered the development of horse-drawn mechanical reapers. Shown here demonstrating his reaper to potential customers, McCormick helped revolutionize American agriculture with labor-saving machinery that made possible far larger harvests of grain crops.

The southwestern frontier attracted both slaveholding planters and small independent farmers. The planters, though a minority, had the capital or the credit to acquire the best lands and the slave labor to make those lands productive. In abandoning the light, sandy, and overworked soils of eastern plantations for the far richer alluvial and prairie soils of the Old Southwest, these slaveholders were responding both to the need for fresh land and to the extraordinary demand for short-staple cotton. As one North Carolina planter put it, Alabama would be a "garden of plenty" compared to the "old-fields and empty corn-houses" of his native state.

Short-staple cotton could be grown anywhere with a minimum of 210 consecutive frost-free days. The crop, however, was of minor commercial importance before the 1790s, when Eli Whitney's gin eliminated the problem of removing the sticky, green seeds from cotton fiber, an essential step in preparing it to be spun and woven into cloth. Meanwhile, the mechanization of the British textile industry had created a seemingly unquenchable demand for raw cotton. No place in the world was better positioned to meet that demand than the American South. Most important, a slave labor force was available to work the land. Led by the booming output of the new plantations in the Old Southwest, the South increased its share of world cotton production from 9 percent in 1800 to 68 percent in 1850.

Thanks to cotton and slavery, aggressive, hard-driving planters loomed large in the Old Southwest. But small independent yeoman farmers, most with no slaves, were far more typical on the southern frontier. Usually settling in the valleys, on the ridges, and in the hill country, they often soon sold out to neighboring planters and headed west again. Like the yeoman farmer Gideon Linecum, they relished "the pleasure of frequent change of country."

The yeomanry moved onto the frontier in two waves. The first consisted of stockmen-hunters, a restless, transient group that spread from the pine barrens in the Carolina backcountry to the coastal plain of eastern Texas. These pioneers prized unfettered independence and measured their wealth in the livestock left to roam and fatten on the sweet grasses of uncleared forests. They were quick to move on when farmers, the second wave, started to clear the land for crops.

Like the stock herders, the yeoman farmers valued self-sufficiency and the leisure to hunt and fish. In pursuit of these goals, they practiced a diversified agriculture aimed at feeding their families. Corn and pork were the mainstays of their diet, and both could readily be produced as long as there was room for the open-range herding of swine and for patches of corn and small grains. The more ambitious farmers, usually those who owned one or two slaves, grew some cotton, but most preferred to avoid the economic risks of cotton production. The yeoman's chief source of labor was his immediate family, and to expand that labor force to produce cotton meant going into debt to purchase slaves. That debt could easily cost the yeoman his farm if the price of cotton fell.

Measured by per capita income, and as a direct result of the profits from slave-produced cotton on virgin soils, the Old Southwest was a wealthier society than the Old Northwest in 1850. In the short term, the settlement of the Old Southwest was also more significant for national economic development. Cot-

Overview

Westward Expansion and the Growth of the Union, 1815–1850

New Free States	New Slave States	Territories (1850)
Indiana, 1816	Mississippi, 1817	Minnesota
Illinois, 1818	Alabama, 1819	Oregon
Maine, 1820	Missouri, 1821	New Mexico
Michigan, 1837	Arkansas, 1836	Utah
Iowa, 1846	Florida, 1845	
Wisconsin, 1848	Texas, 1845	

ton accounted for more than half the value of all American exports after the mid-1830s. More than any other commodity, cotton paid for American imports and underpinned national credit. But southern prosperity was not accompanied by the same economic development and social change as in the Old Northwest. Compared to the slave West in 1860, the free-labor West was twice as urbanized, and far more of its workforce was engaged in nonagricultural pursuits.

The Southwest Ordinance, enacted by Congress in 1790, opened all territories south of the Ohio River to slavery. Slaves, land, and cotton were the keys to wealth on the southern frontier, and agricultural profits were continually plowed back into more land and slaves to produce more cotton. In contrast, prosperous farmers in the Old Northwest had no slaves to work additional acres. Hence they were much more likely to invest their earnings in promotional schemes designed to attract settlers whose presence would raise land values and increase business for local merchants and entrepreneurs. As early as the 1840s, rural communities in the Old Northwest were supporting bustling towns that offered jobs in trade and manufacturing on a scale far surpassing anything in the slave West. By the 1850s, the Midwest was almost as urbanized as the Northeast had been in 1830, and nearly half its labor force no longer worked on farms.

The Old Southwest remained overwhelmingly agricultural. Once the land was settled, the children of the first generation of slaveholders and yeomen moved west to the next frontier rather than compete for the good land that was left. Relatively few newcomers took their place. By the 1850s, Kentucky, Tennessee, Alabama, and Mississippi—the core states of the Old Southwest—were all losing more migrants than they were gaining.

THE FRONTIER OF THE PLAINS INDIANS

Few white Americans had ventured west of the Mississippi by 1840. What scanty knowledge there was of this huge inland expanse was the result of government-sponsored expeditions. Reports of explorations of the southern plains by Zebulon Pike in 1806 and Stephen Long in 1819 dismissed the area as the Great American Desert—an arid, treeless landscape with little agricultural potential, fit only for the Indians being removed from the East. The vast plains and plateaus climbing westward to the foothills of the Rocky Mountains in a seemingly endless ocean of grass were unfamiliar and intimidating to farmers accustomed to the wooded, well-watered, humid East.

Moreover, Americans had no legal claim to much of the trans-Mississippi West—or merely the paper title of the Louisiana Purchase, to which none of the native inhabitants had acquiesced. Beyond Texas and the boundary line drawn by the Trans-Continental Treaty of 1819 lay the northern possessions of Mexico. Horse-mounted Indian tribes dominated by the Sioux were a formidable power on the central Plains northward to the Canadian boundary.

Before the 1840s, Americans lacked the interest, numbers, and concerted military power to control this Far West, held by other peoples. Only fur trappers and traders, who worked with and not against the powerful Sioux, had pushed across the Great Plains and into the Rockies. The 1840s brought a sudden change, a large migration westward that radically altered the ecology of the Great Plains. Farm families trapped in an agricultural depression and enticed by Oregon's bounty turned the trails blazed by the fur traders into ruts on the **Oregon Trail**, the route that led to the first large settlement of Americans on the Pacific Coast.

TRIBAL LANDS

At least 350,000 Native Americans lived in the plains and mountains of the trans-Mississippi West in 1840. They were loosely organized into tribal groups, each with its own territory and way of life. Most of them inhabited the Great Plains region that lay north and west of the Indian Territory reserved for eastern tribes in the present state of Oklahoma. The point where the prairies of the Midwest gave way to the higher, drier plains marked a rough division between predominantly agricultural tribes to the east and nomadic, hunting tribes to the west. The Kansas, Osages, and Omahas in what is now Kansas and Iowa and the Arikaras, Mandans, and Hidatsas along the upper Missouri River grew corn, beans, and squash and lived in semipermanent villages, much as woodland Indians had in the East. On the open plains were hunting and raiding peoples, such as the western Sioux, Crows, Cheyennes, and Arapahos.

In the 1830s, the U.S. government set aside a broad stretch of country between the Platte River to the north and the Red River to the south (most of what is now Oklahoma and eastern Kansas) exclusively for Indians. This Indian Territory was reserved for tribes resettled from the East under the Indian Removal Act of 1830 and for village-living groups native to the area. Many government officials envisioned this territory as a permanent sanctuary that would separate Indians from white people and allow them to live in peace on allotments of land granted to individual tribes as compensation for the territory they had ceded to the federal government in earlier treaties. However, even as Congress was debating the idea of a permanent Indian reserve, the pressure on native peoples in the Mississippi Valley both from raiding parties of Plains Indians and the incessant demands of white farmers and speculators for land was rendering a stable Indian–white boundary untenable.

On the eve of Indian removal in the East, the Sauks, Foxes, Potawatomis, and other Indian peoples inhabited Iowa. The defeat of the Sauks and Foxes in what white Americans called Black Hawk's War of 1832 opened Iowa to white settlement and forced tribes to cede land. In 1838, Congress created the Territory of Iowa, which encompassed all the land between the Mississippi and Missouri Rivers north of the state of Missouri. The remaining Indians were now on the verge of being pushed completely out of the region. Throughout the upper Mississippi Valley in the 1830s, other groups suffered a similar fate, and the number of displaced Indians swelled.

The first to be displaced were farming peoples whose villages straddled the woodlands to the east and the open plains to the west. These border tribes were caught in a vise between the loss of their land to advancing white people and the seizure of their horses and agricultural provisions by Indian raiders from the plains. The Pawnees were among the hardest hit.

By the 1830s, the Pawnees were primarily an agricultural people who embarked on seasonal hunts for game in the Platte River Valley. In 1833, they signed a treaty with the U.S. government in which they agreed to withdraw from south of the Platte in return for subsidies and military protection from the hostile Indians on the plains. Once they moved north of the Platte, the Pawnees were attacked by Sioux who seized control of the prime hunting grounds. Sioux raiders seeking provisions and horses also harassed Pawnee agricultural villages. When the Pawnees in desperation filtered back south of the Platte, in violation of the treaty of 1833, they encountered constant harassment from white settlers. In vain the Pawnee leaders cited the provisions of the same treaty that promised them protection from the Sioux. Forced back north of the Platte by the U.S. government, the Pawnees were eventually driven out of their Nebraska homeland by the Sioux.

The Sioux were the dominant power on the northern and central Great Plains, more than able to hold their own against white Americans in the first half of the nineteenth century. The Tetons, Yanktons, and Yanktonais constituted the main divisions of the western Sioux. In the eighteenth century, these western Sioux had separated from their woodland kin (known as the Santee Sioux), left their homeland along the headwaters of the Mississippi River, and pushed onto the Minnesota prairies. Armed with guns they had acquired from the French, the western Sioux dominated the prairies east of the Missouri River by 1800.

The Sioux learned to use the horse from the Plains Indians. Introduced to the New World by the Spanish, horses had revolutionized the lives of native peoples on the Great Plains. As they acquired more horses through trading and raids, the Plains Indians evolved a distinctly new and nomadic culture. Horses made buffalo hunting vastly more productive, they made it easier to transport bulky possessions, and they made possible an aggressive, highly mobile form of warfare. The Sioux were the most successful of all the tribes in melding two facets of white culture, the gun and the horse, into an Indian culture of warrior-hunters.

Although the Sioux frequently fought other tribes, casualties from these encounters were light. The Sioux and other Plains Indians fought, not to kill the greatest number of the enemy, but rather to dominate hunting grounds and to win individual honor by "counting coup" (touching a live foe). When an Army officer in 1819 urged the Sioux to make peace with the Chippewas, Little Crow, a Santee Sioux, explained why war was preferable: "Why, then, should we give up such an extensive country to save the life of a man or two annually?"

When the United States acquired title to the Great Plains in the Louisiana Purchase of 1803, the western Sioux economy was based on two seasonally restricted systems of hunting. In summer, the Sioux hunted buffalo on horse on the plains. In winter, they

Shown here is a Lakota shirt, c. 1850, that was specially woven for those Sioux warriors who had distinguished themselves in battle. The blue and yellow dyes symbolize sky and earth, and the strands of human hair represent the acts of bravery performed in defense of the Lakota people.

trapped beaver. In great spring trading fairs, the western Sioux exchanged their buffalo robes and beaver pelts for goods acquired by the Santee Sioux from European traders.

As the supply of beaver dwindled and the demand for buffalo hides from American and European traders increased in the early 1800s, the Sioux extended their buffalo hunts. In a loose alliance with the Cheyennes and Arapahos, Sioux war parties pushed aside or subjugated weaker tribes to the south and west of the Missouri River basin. The Sioux gained access to new sources for buffalo and raided the village tribes for horses and provisions. Reduced to a dependent status, these tribes were forced to rely on the Sioux for meat and trading goods.

Epidemic diseases brought to the plains by white traders helped Sioux expansion. Because they lived in small wandering bands, the Sioux were less susceptible to these epidemics than the more sedentary village peoples. The Sioux were also one of the first tribes to be vaccinated against smallpox by doctors sent up the Missouri River by the Bureau of Indian Affairs in the early 1830s. Smallpox reached the plains in the 1780s, and a major epidemic in 1837 probably halved the region's Indian population. Particularly hard hit were tribes attempting to resist the Sioux advance. Sioux losses were relatively light and, unlike the other tribes, their population grew.

Some 25,000 strong by 1850, the western Sioux had increased in power and numbers since they first encountered American officials during the Lewis and Clark Expedition in 1804 and 1805. Even then,

Jefferson had cautioned Lewis to cultivate good relations with the Sioux "because of their immense power." "These are the vilest miscreants of the savage race," Lewis and Clark wrote of the Sioux, "and must ever remain the pirates of the Missouri, until such measures are pursued by our government as will make them feel a dependence on its will for their supply of merchandise."

Words were one thing, gaining power over the Sioux another. Americans could vilify the Sioux, but they could not force them into dependence in the first half of the nineteenth century. The Sioux continued to extend their influence, and they were shrewd enough to align themselves with the Americans whenever their interests dictated conciliation.

THE FUR TRADERS

"Curiosity, a love of wild adventure, and perhaps also a hope of profit—for times are hard, and my best coat has a sort of sheepish hang-dog hesitation to encounter fashionable folk—combined to make me look upon the project with an eye of favour." As best he could recollect, these were the motives that induced Warren A. Ferris, a New York civil engineer, to join the American Fur Company in 1829 at the age of 19 and go west as a fur trapper and mountain man. When Ferris joined up, the American fur trade in the trans-Mississippi West—and the spirit of adventure it stirred—was at its height. During their golden age in the 1820s and 1830s, the trappers blazed the trails that far greater numbers of white settlers would follow in the 1840s.

The western fur trade originated in the rivalry between British and American companies for profitable furs, especially beaver pelts. Until the early 1820s, the Hudson's Bay Company, a well-capitalized British concern, dominated the trans-Mississippi fur trade. A breakthrough for American interests came in 1824 when two St. Louis businessmen, William Henry Ashley and Andrew Henry of the Rocky Mountain Fur Company, developed the rendezvous system, which eliminated the need for permanent and costly posts deep in Indian territory. In keeping with Indian traditions of periodic intertribal meetings, the rendezvous system brought together trappers, Indians, and traders in a

The annual rendezvous in Wyoming of fur trappers and traders was a multinational affair in which Anglo Americans, French Canadians, Mexican Americans, and Native Americans gathered to trade, drink, and swap stories.

The Denver Public Library, Western History Department

grand annual fair at a designated site in the high mountain country of Wyoming. White trappers and Indians exchanged the animal skins they had gathered in the seasonal hunt for the guns, traps, tobacco, whiskey, textiles, and other trading goods that agents of the fur companies in St. Louis brought to the fair.

The mountain men signed up for two- or three-year stints with the fur companies. Except for the annual fairs, they lived isolated, hard lives in the wilderness. Their closest relations were with Indians, and about 40 percent of the trappers married Indian women, unions that often linked them economically and diplomatically to their bride's tribe.

Living conditions in the wilderness were primitive, even brutal. Mortality rates among trappers ran as high as 80 percent a year. Death often came suddenly from an accidental gunshot wound, an encounter with a grizzly, or an arrow from an Indian whose hunting grounds a trapper had transgressed. Survival required techniques that a "civilized" American would find repellent. Many a trapper avoided death from dehydration by sucking blood from the sliced vein of a horse or drinking the watery contents from the stomach of a buffalo carcass. "Peg-Leg" Smith became a legend for amputating his own leg after a bullet shattered it.

For all its dangers, the life of a trapper appealed to unattached young men like Warren Ferris. They

This 1845 painting depicts a trapper taking an Indian bride. It was a solemn ceremony in which the calumet, or peace pipe, was smoked and the trapper acquired his bride with goods such as guns and blankets.

Alfred Jacob Miller (American, 1810-1874), The Trapper's Bride, oil on canvas, Museum purchase. Joslyn Art Museum, Omaha, Nebraska

were fleeing the confinements, as well as the comforts, of white civilization and were as free as they could be. When on a hunt with the Indians, they were part of a spectacle unknown to other white Americans, one that was already passing into history. "Fancy to yourself," Ferris asked readers of his published journals, "three thousand horses of every variety of size and colour, with trappings almost as varied as their appearance . . . ridden by a thousand souls . . . their persons fantastically ornamented. . . . Listen to the rattle of numberless lodgepoles [trailed] by packhorses. . . . Yonder see a hundred horsemen pursuing a herd of antelopes." He was describing the color, bustle, and motion at the start of a hunt with the Salish Indians of Montana in the 1830s, played out on "a beautiful level prairie, with dark blue snow-capped mountains in the distance for the locale."

Such spectacles were increasingly rare after 1840, the year of the last mountain men's rendezvous on the Green River in Wyoming. The most exploitative phase of the fur trade in the 1830s had ravaged the fur-bearing animals and accelerated the spread of smallpox among the tribes. Whiskey, the most profitable item among the white man's trading goods, had corrupted countless Indians and undermined the vitality of tribal cultures.

The mountain men were about to pass into legend, but before they did, they explored every trail and path from the front (or eastern) range of the Rockies to the Pacific. They had gone where no white people had gone before. The main trading corridor of the fur trade—up the lower Missouri to the North Platte and across the plains to the South Pass, a wide plateau crossing the Continental Divide, and into the Wyoming basin—became the main overland route to the West that migrating farm families followed in the 1840s. The mountain men had removed the mystery of western geography, and in so doing they hastened the end of the frontier conditions that had made their unique way of life possible.

THE OREGON TRAIL

The ruts are still there. One can follow them to the horizon in the Platte River Valley of Nebraska and the dry tablelands of Wyoming, Idaho, and Nevada. They were put there by the wheels of wagons hauled by oxen on a jolting 2,000-mile journey across plains, mountains, and deserts from Missouri to Oregon, Utah, and California (see Map 13–2). Some 150,000 Americans made this overland trek in the heyday of the Oregon Trail in the 1840s and early 1850s (see Figure 13–1). Most of them walked alongside their wagons. They covered up to fifteen miles a day on a trip that lasted close to six months.

MAP 13-2   Western Overland Trails
The great overland trails to the West began at the Missouri River. The Oregon Trail crossed South Pass in Wyoming and then branched off to Oregon, California, or Utah. The Santa Fe Trail carried American goods and traders to the Mexican Southwest.

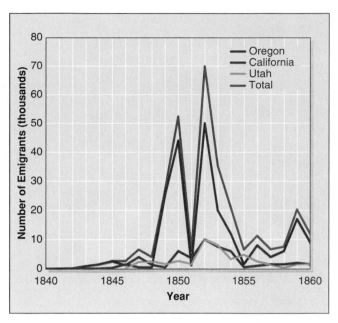

FIGURE 13-1   Overland Emigration to the West, 1840–1860
Immigration to the trans-Mississippi West steadily increased in the 1840s as farm families moved to Oregon or Utah. After the discovery of gold in California in 1849, California attracted the bulk of the emigrants, many of whom were single men hopeful of striking it rich.

Data Source: John D. Unruh, Jr., *The Plains Across: The Overland Emigrants and the Trans-Mississippi West, 1840–60* (1982), pp. 84–85.

Before the 1830s, few Americans had heard of Oregon, and practically none lived there. Under an agreement reached in 1818, the Oregon Country was still jointly administered by the United States and Great Britain. Furs—whether beaver pelts or the skins of the Pacific sea otter—had attracted a few American trappers and merchants, but the British-controlled Hudson's Bay Company dominated the region. Protestant missionaries established the first permanent white settlements in the 1830s. Under the leadership of Jason Lee, they set up their missions in the fertile Willamette Valley, south of the Columbia River. Reports of Oregon's fertility that the missionaries sent east sparked the first popular interest in the region, especially among Midwestern farmers stuck in the agricultural depression that followed the Panic of 1837.

While the missionaries were publicizing Oregon and attracting future settlers, they were failing in their efforts to convert the Indians of the region to Christianity. Unlike the trappers, the missionaries sought to change the entire structure of Indian life and beliefs. But with their numbers already thinned by the diseases brought in by the trappers, Oregon tribes such as the Cayuses refused to abandon their traditional culture based on hunting and fishing to become laborers for white farmers. During a measles epidemic in 1847, the Cayuses killed two of the most prominent missionaries, Marcus and Narcissa Whitman. In retaliation, white Americans, who now numbered more than five thousand, virtually exterminated the Cayuses.

The first large party of overlanders on the Oregon Trail left Independence, Missouri, for the Willamette Valley in 1842. Independence and St. Joseph in Missouri and, by the 1850s, Council Bluffs in Iowa were the jumping-off points for the Oregon Trail. Each town competed to capture the lucrative trade of outfitting the migrants. There was more than enough trade to go around. Merchants profited from supplying, usually at inflated prices, wagons, mules, oxen, guns, ammunition, and staples like flour, bacon, and sugar.

Most overlanders were young farm families from the Midwest, who had moved at least once before in their restless search for the perfect farm that would keep them out of debt. Indeed, Medorum Crawford said of one family that made the journey to Oregon with him in 1842 and then quickly left for California, "They had practically lived in the wagon for more than twenty years, only remaining in one locality long

This sketch reveals the sheer physical exertion demanded of the emigrants as they pushed across the Plains on the Oregon Trial.

enough to make a crop, which they had done in every State and Territory in the Mississippi Valley."

Usually the male head of a household made the decision to move. Women often regretted giving up ties with kin and friends, which provided security and assistance in their isolated, rural lives. They were well aware of the dangers of childbirth on a long, hard journey. Besides their usual work of minding the children and cooking and cleaning, they would now have to help drive wagons and tend livestock. Still, many women were also optimistic about the journey. "Ho—for California—at last we are on the way," exclaimed Helen Carpenter in 1857, "and with good luck may

In trunks such as this, women transported their fine pieces of china to the West on the Oregon Trial.

some day reach the 'promised land.'" A study of 159 women's trail diaries indicates that about one-third of the women strongly favored the move. Margaret Frink, for example, recalled that she "never had occasion to regret the prolonged hardships of the toilsome journey." By adapting to the new conditions of trail life—pitching tents, yoking oxen, cooking over open fires, and gathering buffalo chips (dried dung used for fuel)—women learned skills that would help them start a new life in the West.

The journey was long and dangerous. In the 1840s, some five thousand of the ninety thousand men, women, and children who set out on the Oregon Trail died along the way. But although the overlanders were terrified of encountering Indians—who, they assumed, would be hostile—few died from Indian attacks. As long as the wagon trains were just passing through their lands, the Plains Indians left the white people alone. At first they watched with bemused curiosity, and then, as the white migrants kept coming, they traded game for clothing and ammunition. Indians killed only 115 migrants in the 1840s, and trigger-happy white migrants provoked most clashes. Disease, especially cholera, was the great killer. Second to disease were accidents, especially drownings that resulted when drivers tried to force overloaded wagons across swollen rivers.

Cooperation between families was the key to a successful overland crossing. The men in a party often drew up a formal, written constitution at the start of a trip spelling out the assignments and work responsibilities of each wagon. Before the trail was well marked, former mountain men hired on as captains to lead wagon trains. Timing was crucial. A wagon train had to leave late enough in the spring to get good grass in Nebraska for the oxen and mules. Too early a departure, and the wagon train risked getting bogged down in spring mud; too late a departure, and it risked being trapped in the snows of the Pacific coastal ranges.

Before "Oregon fever" had run its course, the flow of white settlers across the continent radically changed the economy and ecology of the Great Plains. Pressure mounted on plants and animals, reducing the land's ability to support all the tribes accustomed to living off it. Intertribal warfare intensified as the supply of buffalo and other game dwindled. Far from being separated from white people by a permanent line of division, the Plains Indians now stood astride the main path of white migration to the Pacific.

In response, officials in the Bureau of Indian Affairs organized a great gathering of the tribes in 1851. At this conference they pushed through the Fort Laramie Treaty, the first U.S. government attempt to draw boundaries within which to contain the Plains Indians. In exchange for accepting limitations on their movement and for the loss of game, the tribes were to receive annual compensation of $50,000 a year for fifty years (later reduced by the U.S. Senate to ten years).

Most of the Indians at the Fort Laramie conference were the Sioux and their allies. The Sioux viewed the treaty as confirming their dominant power on the Great Plains. When American negotiators tried to restrict Sioux hunting to north of the Platte, the Sioux demanded and received treaty rights to lands south of the Platte as well. "These lands once belonged to the Kiowas and the Crows," argued a western Sioux, "but we whipped those nations out of them, and in this we did what the white men do when they want the lands of the Indians." This was an argument white Americans could understand, and they conceded the point.

The Fort Laramie Treaty represented a standoff between the Sioux and the U.S. government, the two great powers on the Plains. If neither yielded its claims to the region, war between them would be inevitable.

THE MEXICAN BORDERLANDS

By the mid-1840s, parties of emigrant Americans were beginning to branch off the main Oregon Trail on their way to Utah and California. These areas were then part of the northern borderlands of Mexico. Mostly a semiarid and thinly populated land of high plateaus, dry basins, and desert bisected north to south by mountain ranges, the borderlands had been part of the Spanish empire in North America. Mexico inherited this territory when it won independence from Spain in 1821. The borderlands covered roughly 1 million square miles; today, they comprise the American Southwest from Texas to California. Mexico's hold on this region was always weak. It lost Texas in 1837, and, in the next decade, the American penetration of Utah and California set the stage for the American seizure of most of the rest in the Mexican War.

THE PEOPLES OF THE SOUTHWEST

Diverse peoples lived in the Southwest. Imperial Spain had divided them into four main groupings: Indians, full-blooded Native Americans who retained their own languages and customs; mestizos, those of racially mixed ancestry, usually Spanish and Indian;

criollos, American-born whites of Spanish ancestry; and Spaniards.

By far the smallest group were the Spaniards. Compared to the English, few Spaniards emigrated to the New World, and most who did were men. Consequently, Spanish males married or lived with native women, creating a large class of mestizos. Despite their small numbers, the Spanish, along with the criollos, monopolized economic and political power. This wealthy elite controlled the labor of the *mestizos* in the predominantly ranching economy of the borderlands.

The largest single group in the borderlands were the Indians, about half the population in the 1820s. Most had not come under direct Spanish or Mexican control. Those who had were part of the mission system. This instrument of Spanish imperial policy forced Indians to live in a fixed area, to convert to Catholicism, and to work as agricultural laborers.

Spanish missions, most of them established by the Franciscan order, aimed both to Christianize and "civilize" the Indians, making them loyal imperial subjects. Mission Indians were forced to abandon their native economies and culture and settle in agricultural communities under the tight supervision of the friars (see Chapter 1). Spanish soldiers and royal officials, who lived in military garrisons known as presidios, accompanied the friars.

The largest concentration of Indians—some 300,000 when the Spanish friars arrived in the 1760s—was in California. Most of these—the Paiutes, Chumashes, Pomos, Shastas, and a host of smaller tribes—occupied their own distinct ecological zones

This painting by Alfred James Miller depicts the busy interior of Fort Laramie in 1837.

where they gathered and processed what the rivers, forests, and grasslands provided. Fish and game were abundant, and wild plants and nuts, especially acorns, provided grain and flour. The Paiutes in the Owens Valley perfected an intricate system for irrigating wild grasses, but only the Yumans along the Colorado River in southeastern California practiced full-scale agriculture. The Spanish marveled at their lush fields of wheat, maize, beans, tobacco, and melons. The Yumans also had an elaborate religion based on an oral tradition of dream songs. (Dream songs remain a distinctive feature of Native American culture.)

The paintings by George Catlin are among the best visual sources for understanding the material culture of the Plains Indians. This painting, c. 1834, shows how central was the buffalo in the life of the Comanches, the most powerful tribe on the Southern Plains.

The major farming Indians east of California were the Pueblo peoples of Arizona and New Mexico. Named after the adobe or stone community dwellings in which they lived atop mesas or on terraces carved into cliffs, the Pueblo Indians were a peaceful people closely bound to small, tightly knit communities. (*Pueblo* is Spanish for "village.") Indeed, some of their dwellings, such as those of the Hopis in Arizona or the Acomas in New Mexico, have been continuously occupied for more than 500 years. Corn and beans were the staples of their irrigation-based agriculture. Formally a part of the Spanish mission system, they had incorporated the Catholic God and Catholic rituals into their own polytheistic religion, which stressed the harmony of all living things with the forces of nature. They continued to worship in their underground sanctuaries known as *kivas*.

Once the Pueblos made their peace with the Spaniards after their great revolt in 1680 (see Chapter 3), their major enemies were the nomadic tribes that lived by hunting and raiding. These tribes outnumbered the Pueblos four to one and controlled most of the Southwest until the 1850s. The horse, which many of the tribes acquired during Spain's temporary retreat from the region during the late seventeenth century in the wake of the Pueblo Revolt, was the basis of their way of life. As the horse frontier spread, the peoples of the southern Plains gained enormous mobility and the means of ranging far and wide for the economic resources that sustained their transformation into societies of mounted warriors.

West of the pueblos around Taos was the land of the Navajos, who herded sheep, raised some crops, and raided other tribes from their mountain fastness. Spilling over onto Navajo lands, the Southern Utes ranged up and down the canyon lands of Utah. The Gila Apaches were the dominant tribe south of Albuquerque and westward into Arizona. To the east in the Pecos River Valley roamed bands of Mescalero and Jicarillo Apaches. On the broad plains rolling northward from the Texas panhandle and southward into northern Mexico were war parties of Comanches and Kiowas.

The Comanches, a branch of the mountain Shoshonis who moved to the plains when horses became available, were the most feared of the nomadic peoples. Utterly fearless, confident, and masterful horsemen, they gained a reputation of mythic proportions for their prowess as mounted warriors. For food and clothing, they relied on the immense buffalo herds of the southern plains. For guns, horses, and other trading goods, they lived off their predatory raids. When the Santa Fe Trail opened in the early 1820s, their shrewdness as traders gave them a new source of firearms that strengthened their raiding prowess.

The three focal points of white settlement in the northern borderlands of Mexico—Texas, New Mexico, and Alta California (as distinguished from Lower, or Baja, California)—were never linked by an effective network of communications or transportation. Navigable rivers were few, and travel was limited to tortuous journeys along Indian and Spanish trails that barely indented the dry and largely barren landscape. Each of these settlements was an isolated offshoot of Hispanic culture with a semiautonomous economy based on ranching and a mostly illegal trade with French, British, and American merchants that brought in a trickle of needed goods.

Neither Spain, which tried to seal off its northern outposts from economic contact with foreigners, nor Mexico, which opened up the borderlands to outsiders, had integrated this vast region into a unified economic or political whole. Indeed, Mexico's most pressing problem in the 1820s was protecting its northern states from the Comanches. To serve as a buffer against the Comanches, the Mexican government in 1821 invited Americans into Texas, opening the way to the eventual American takeover of the territory.

THE AMERICANIZATION OF TEXAS

The Mexicans faced the same problems governing Texas that the Spanish had. Mexico City was about a thousand miles from San Antonio, the center of Hispanic settlement in Texas, and communications were slow and cumbersome. The ranching elite of *Tejanos* (Spanish-speaking Mexicans born in Texas) had closer economic ties to American Louisiana than they did to Coahuila, the Mexican state to which Texas was formally attached. These large ranchers had long been smuggling horses and cattle into Louisiana in exchange for manufactured items and tobacco. Markets for farm crops were limited, and the ranchers and a scattered class of tenant farmers produced little surplus food. This low agricultural productivity, combined with the low birthrate among mission Indians, outbreaks of disease, and the generally hostile frontier environment, sharply restricted population growth. Only some five thousand Mexicans lived in Texas in the 1820s.

Sparsely populated and economically struggling, Mexican Texas shared a border with the United States along the Sabine River in Louisiana and the Red River in the Arkansas Territory (see Map 13-2). The threat that the nearby Americans posed to Mexico's security was obvious to Mexican officials. As one of them early noted with alarm: "If we do not take the present opportunity to people Texas, day by day the strength of the United States will grow until it will annex Texas, Coahuila, Saltillo, and Nuevo León like the Goths, Visigoths, and the other tribes that assailed the Roman Empire." However, attempts to promote immigration into Texas from other parts of Mexico failed. Reasoning that the Americans were going to come in any event and anxious to build up the population of Texas against Indian attacks, the Mexican government encouraged Americans to settle in Texas by offering huge grants of land in return for promises to accept Mexican citizenship, convert to Catholicism, and obey the authorities in Mexico City.

The first American *empresario*—the recipient of a large grant in return for a promise to bring in settlers—was Stephen F. Austin. He had inherited a huge Spanish grant from his father, Moses Austin, a Missourian who had had business dealings with the Spanish since 1797. After having the grant confirmed by the new Mexican government in 1821, Stephen Austin founded the first American colony in Texas. The Austin grant encompassed 18,000 square miles. Other grants were smaller but still lavish. The *empresarios* stood to grow wealthy by leasing out land, selling parcels to settlers, and organizing the rest into large-scale farms that produced cotton with slave labor in the bottomlands of the Sabine, Colorado, and Brazos Rivers. For the Americans who followed in their wake, Texas was a dream come true—the chance to acquire good land that was so cheap that it was almost free. As early as 1830, eastern and south-central Texas was becoming an extension of the plantation economy of the Gulf coastal plain. More than 25,000 white settlers, with around a thousand slaves, had poured into the region (see "American Views: A Mexican View of the Texans in 1828").

More Americans moved into Texas with slaves than the Mexicans had anticipated. Many settlers simply ignored Mexican laws, especially the Emancipation Proclamation of 1829 that forbade slavery in the Republic of Mexico. In 1830, the Mexican government attempted to assert its authority. It levied the first taxes on the Americans, prohibited the further importation of slaves, and closed the international border to additional immigration. Still, another ten thousand Americans spilled across the border in the early 1830s, and they continued to bring in slaves.

Unlike the *empresarios*, many of whom became Catholic and married into elite *Tejano* families, these newcomers lived apart from Mexicans and rejected Mexican citizenship. Cultural tensions escalated. Believing that they belonged to a superior race of liberty-loving white Anglo-Saxons, most of these new arrivals sneered at the Mexicans as a mongrelized race of black people, Indians, and Spaniards and resented having to submit to their rule. They considered Catholicism a despotic, superstitious religion and ignored legal requirements that they convert to it.

A clash became inevitable in 1835 when General Santa Anna, elected president of Mexico in 1833, overturned the liberal Mexican constitution of 1824. He established himself as a dictator in 1834, and his centralist rule ended any hope of the Americans *empresarios* and their *Tejano* allies that Texas might become an autonomous state within a federated Mexico. Skirmishing between Mexican troops and rebellious Texans began in the fall of 1835.

At first, the Anglo–*Tejano* leadership did not renounce all ties with Mexico. When these leaders drafted a constitution in November 1835, they sought to overthrow Santa Anna, restore the constitution of 1824, and win separate statehood for Texas within a liberal Mexican republic. Santa Anna, however, refused to compromise. When he raised a large army to crush the uprising, he radicalized the rebellion and pushed its leaders to declare complete independence on March 2, 1836. Four days later, a Mexican army of 4,000 annihilated the 187 defenders of the **Alamo**, an abandoned mission in San Antonio. A few weeks later at Goliad, another 300 Texans were killed after they had agreed to surrender (see Map 13–3).

"Remember the Alamo!" and "Remember Goliad!" were powerful rallying cries for the beleaguered Texans. Volunteers from the American South rushed to the aid of the main Texan army, commanded by Sam Houston. A product of the Tennessee frontier and a close friend of Andrew Jackson's, Houston did Jackson proud by catching the overconfident Santa Anna off guard in eastern Texas. Houston's victory in April 1836 at the Battle of San Jacinto established the independence of Texas. Captured while trying to flee, Santa Anna signed a treaty in May 1836, recognizing Texas as an independent republic with a boundary on the south and west at the Rio Grande. However, the Nueces River to the north of the Rio Grande had been the administrative border of Texas under Mexican rule. The Mexican Congress rejected the treaty, and the boundary remained in dispute.

Soon forgotten during the ensuing eight years of Texas independence was the support that many

MAP 13-3 Texas and Mexico after the Texas Revolt
The Battle of San Jacinto was the decisive American victory that gained the independence of Texas, but the border dispute between Texas and Mexico would not be resolved until the Mexican War a decade later.

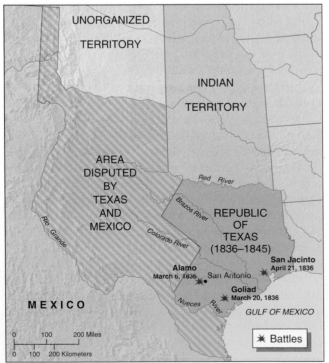

Tejanos had given to the successful revolt against Mexican rule. In part because Mexico refused to recognize the Texas Republic, Anglos feared Tejanos as a subversive element. Pressure mounted on them to leave, especially after Santa Anna launched a major counterattack in 1842, capturing San Antonio. Those who stayed lost much of their land and economic power as Anglos used their knowledge of American legal codes or just plain chicanery to reduce the *Tejanos* to second-class citizens.

More difficult to subordinate were the Comanches. While president of Texas, Houston tried to fix a permanent boundary between the Comanches and white settlers, but Texas pride and ongoing white encroachments on Indian land undercut his efforts. By the early 1840s, Texans and Comanches were in a state of nearly permanent war. Only the force of the federal army after the Civil War ended the Comanches' long reign as the effective rulers of the high, dry plains of northern and western Texas.

THE PUSH INTO CALIFORNIA AND THE SOUTHWEST

Mexican rule in California was always weak. The Sonoran desert and the resistance of the Yuman Indians in southeastern California cut off Mexico from any direct land contact with Alta California. Only irregular communications were maintained over a long sea route. For *Californios,* Californians of Spanish descent, Mexico was literally *la otra banda,* "the other shore." In trying to strengthen its hold on this remote and thinly populated region, the Mexican government relied on a program of economic development. As in Texas, however, Mexican policy had unintended consequences.

The centerpiece of the Mexican program was the secularization of the missions. This policy opened up the landholdings of the Catholic Church to private ownership and released the mission Indians from paternalistic bondage. Small allotments of land were set aside for the Indians, but most returned to their homelands. Those who remained became a source of cheap labor for the *rancheros* who carved up the mission lands into huge cattle ranches. Thus by the 1830s, California had entered what is called the *rancho* era. The main beneficiaries of this process, however, were not Mexican authorities but the American traders who responded to the economic opportunities presented by the privatization of the California economy.

New England merchants had been trading in California since the 1780s. What first attracted them were the seal fisheries off the California coast, a source of otter pelts highly prized in the China trade. After the seals had been all but exterminated by the 1820s, Yankee merchants shipped out hides and tallow, a trade fed by the immense cattle resources of the *rancheros*, to

New England for processing into shoes and candles. Ships from New England and New York sailed around Cape Horn to California ports, where they unloaded trading goods. Servicing this trade in California was a resident colony of American agents, some three hundred strong by the mid-1840s.

Whereas Yankees dominated the American colonies in coastal California, it was mostly midwestern farm families who filtered into the inner valleys of California from the Oregon Trail in the 1830s and 1840s. About one in ten of the overland parties took a cutoff on the Trail near Fort Hall on the Snake River that led them across the deserts of northern Nevada to a passage across the Sierra Nevada near Lake Tahoe. At the end of the journey, they dropped down into the fertile Sacramento River Valley. Nearly a thousand Americans had arrived by 1846.

California belonged to Mexico in name only by the early 1840s. The program of economic development had strengthened California's ties to the outside world at the expense of Mexico. American merchants and California *rancheros* ran the economy, and both groups had joined separatist movements against Mexican rule. Unlike the *Californios*, who were ambivalent about their future political allegiance, the Americans wanted to be part of the United States and assumed that California would shortly be annexed. With the outbreak of the Mexican War in 1846, their wish became reality.

Except for Utah, the American push into the interior of the Mexican Southwest followed the California pattern of trade preceding settlement. When Mexico liberalized the formerly restrictive trading policies of Spain, American merchants opened up the nine-hundred-mile-long **Santa Fe Trail** from Independence, Missouri, to Santa Fe, New Mexico. Starved for mercantile goods, the New Mexicans were a small but highly profitable market. They paid for their American imports with gold, silver, and furs.

Brent's Old Fort, an impregnable adobe structure built on the Arkansas River at the point where the Santa Fe Trail turned to the southwest and Taos, was the fulcrum for the growing economic influence of Americans over New Mexican affairs. Completed in 1832, the fort enabled the Brent brothers from Missouri to control a flourishing and almost monopolistic trade with Indians, trappers, caravans on the Santa Fe Trail, and the large landowners and merchants of New Mexico. This trade pulled New Mexico into the cultural and economic orbit of the United States and undermined what little sovereign power Mexico held in the region.

Although only a few hundred Americans were permanent residents of New Mexico in the 1840s, they had married into the Spanish-speaking landholding elite and were themselves beginning to receive large grants of land. Ties of blood and common economic interests linked this small group of American businessmen with an influential faction of the local elite. American merchants and New Mexican landlords were further united by their growing disdain for the instability of Mexican rule, Santa Anna's dictatorship, and sporadic attempts by Mexico to levy heavy taxes on the Santa Fe trade. Another bond was their concern over the aggressive efforts of the Texans to seize eastern New Mexico. After thwarting an 1841 Texan attempt to occupy Santa Fe, the leaders of New Mexico increasingly looked to the United States to protect their local autonomy. They quickly decided to cooperate with the American army of invasion when the Mexican War got under way. Over the opposition of the clergy and ranchers still loyal to Mexico, this group was instrumental in the American takeover of New Mexico.

At the extreme northern and inner reaches of the Mexican borderlands lay Utah. Dominated by an intermountain depression called the Great Basin, Utah was a starkly beautiful but dry region of alkaline flats, broken tablelands, cottonwood canyons, and mountain ranges. It was home to the Bannocks, Utes, Navajos, Hopis, and small bands of other Indians. Aside from trading ties with the Utes, Spain and Mexico had largely ignored this remote region. Its isolation and lack of white settlers, however, were precisely what made Utah so appealing to the leaders of the Mormons, the Church of Jesus Christ of Latter-day Saints. For the Mormons in the 1840s, Utah became the promised land in which to build a new Zion.

Founded by Joseph Smith in upstate New York in the 1820s, Mormonism grew rapidly within a communitarian framework that stressed hard work and economic cooperation under the leadership of patriarchal leaders. The economic success of close-knit Mormon communities, combined with the righteous zeal of their members, aroused the fears and hostility of non-Mormons. Harassed out of New York, Ohio, and Missouri, the Mormons thought they had found a permanent home by the late 1830s in Nauvoo, Illinois. But the murder of Joseph Smith and his brother by a mob in 1844 convinced the beleaguered Mormons that they had to leave the settled East for a refuge of their own in the West. In 1846 a group of Mormons migrated to the Great Basin in Utah. Under the leadership of Brigham Young, they established a new community in 1847 at the Great Salt Lake on the western slopes of the Wasatch Mountains. Ten thousand Mormons joined them.

The Mormons thrived in the arid desert. Their intense communitarianism was ideally suited to dispensing land and organizing an irrigation system that coordinated water rights with the amount of land under production. To their dismay, however, they learned in 1848 that they had not left the United

AMERICAN VIEWS

A Mexican View of the Texans in 1828

By the late 1820s, Mexico was reassessing its policy of encouraging American immigration to Texas. Concerned over the large numbers and uncertain loyalties of the American settlers, the government appointed a commission in 1827 ostensibly to survey the boundary between Louisiana and the province of Texas. The real purpose of the commission was to recommend policy changes that would strengthen Mexico's hold on Texas. The following excerpt is from a journal kept by José María Sánchez, the draftsman of the boundary commission.

- Why was the Mexican government so ineffective in maintaining control over Texas?
- What was the appeal of Texas for Americans? How did most of them enter Texas and take up land?
- Why did Sánchez have such a low opinion of the Americans in the Austin colony? What did he think of Stephen Austin?
- Why did the Mexicans fear that they would lose Texas?

The Americans from the north have taken possession of practically all the eastern part of Texas, in most cases without the permission of the authorities. They immigrate constantly, finding no one to prevent them, and take possession of the *sitio* [location] that best suits them without either asking leave or going through any formality other than that of building their homes. Thus the majority of inhabitants in the Department are North Americans, the Mexican population being reduced to only Bejar, Nacogdoches, and La Bahía del Espíritu Santo, wretched settlements that between them do not number three thousand inhabitants, and the new village of

States after all. The Union acquired Utah, along with the rest of the northern borderlands of Mexico, as a result of the Mexican War. (For more on the Mormons, see Chapter 12.)

POLITICS, EXPANSION, AND WAR

The Democrats viewed their victory in the election of 1844 (see Chapter 10) as a popular mandate for expansion. They had campaigned on a platform that boldly demanded both Texas and the "reoccupation" of Oregon up to 54°40'.

James K. Polk, the new Democratic president, fully shared the expansionist vision of his party. The greatest prize in his eyes was California. Although silent in public on California for fear of further antagonizing the Mexicans, who had never accepted the loss of Texas, Polk made the acquisition of California the cor-

nerstone of his foreign policy. When he was stymied in his efforts to purchase California and New Mexico, he tried to force concessions from the Mexican government by ordering American troops to the mouth of the Rio Grande, far within the territory claimed by Mexico. When the virtually inevitable clash of arms occurred in late April 1846, war broke out between the United States and Mexico.

Victory resulted in the **Mexican Cession of 1848**, which added a half-million square miles to the United States. Polk's administration also finalized the acquisition of Texas and reached a compromise with the British on the Oregon Territory that recognized American sovereignty in the Pacific Northwest up to the 49th parallel. The United States was now a nation that spanned a continent.

MANIFEST DESTINY

With a phrase that soon entered the nation's vocabulary, John L. O'Sullivan, editor and Democratic politi-

Guadalupe Victoria that has scarcely more than seventy settlers. The government of the state, with its seat at Saltillo, that should watch over the preservation of its most precious and interesting department, taking measures to prevent its being stolen by foreign hands, is the one that knows the least not only about actual conditions, but even about its territory. . . . Repeated and urgent appeals have been made to the Supreme Government of the Federation regarding the imminent danger in which this interesting Department is of becoming the prize of the ambitious North Americans, but never has it taken any measures that may be called conclusive. . . .

[Sánchez goes on to describe the village of Austin and the American colony founded by Stephen Austin.]

Its population is nearly two hundred persons, of which only ten are Mexicans, for the balance are all Americans from the North with an occasional European. Two wretched little stores supply the inhabitants of the colony: one sells only whiskey, rum, sugar, and coffee; the other, rice, flour, lard, and cheap cloth. . . . The Americans from the North, at least the great part of those I have seen, eat only salted meat, bread made by themselves out of corn meal, coffee, and home-made cheese. To these the greater part of those who live in the village add strong liquor, for they are in general, in my opinion, lazy people of vicious character. Some of them cultivate their small farms by planting corn; but this task they usually entrust to their negro slaves, whom they treat with considerable harshness. Beyond the village in an immense stretch of land formed by rolling hills are scattered the families brought by Stephen Austin, which today number more than two thousand persons. The diplomatic policy of this empresario, evident in all his actions, has, as one may say, lulled the authorities into a sense of security, while he works diligently for his own ends. In my judgment, the spark that will start the conflagration that will deprive us of Texas, will start from this colony. All because the government does not take vigorous measures to prevent it. Perhaps it does not realize the value of what it is about to lose.

Source: José María Sánchez, excerpted from "A Trip to Texas in 1828," trans. Carlos E. Castaneda from *Southwestern Historical Quarterly, 29* Copyright © 1926. Reprinted courtesy of Texas State Historical Association, Austin Texas. All rights reserved.

cian, proclaimed in 1845 America's "manifest destiny to overspread and to possess the whole of the continent which Providence has given us for the development of the great experiment of Liberty and federated self-government entrusted to us." Central to Manifest Destiny was the assumption that white Americans were a special people. Part of that sense of specialness was religiously inspired and dated back to the Puritans' belief that God had appointed them to establish a New Israel cleansed of the corruption of the Old World. Evangelical revivals in the early nineteenth century then added an aggressive sense of urgency to America's presumed mission to spread the benefits of Protestantism and Christian civilization. Protestant missionaries, as in Oregon, were often in the vanguard of American expansion.

What distinguished the special American mission as enunciated by Manifest Destiny was its explicitly racial component. Between 1815 and 1850, the term Anglo-Saxon, originally loosely applied to English-speaking peoples, acquired racial overtones, in keeping with the then current interest of European and American scientists in defining, classifying, and ranking human races (with themselves, of course, at the top). Caucasian Anglo-Saxon Americans, as the descendants of ancient Germanic tribes that purportedly brought the seeds of free institutions to England, were now said to be the foremost race in the world. This superior racial pedigree they claimed for themselves gave white Americans the natural right to expand westward, a chosen people carrying the blessings of democracy and progress. Only they, it was argued, had the energy, industriousness, and innate love of liberty to establish a successful free government.

Advocates of Manifest Destiny insisted that American expansion would be irresistible and peaceful. They were not warmongers calling for conquest. Still, the doctrine was undeniably a self-serving justification for what other peoples would see as territorial aggrandizement. Certainly, that was true of the Mexican-Ameri-

In this late-1872 evocation of the spirit of Manifest Destiny, Indians retreat westward as white settlers, guided by a diaphanously-clad America, spread the benefits of American civilization.

cans and Native Americans who lost land and cultural independence as they were brought under American control. Manifest Destiny and popular stereotypes lumped Indians and Mexicans together as inferior peoples. An emigrant guide of 1845 spoke of the Mexican Californians as "scarcely a visible grade in the scale of intelligence, above the barbarous tribes by whom they are surrounded." For Waddy Thompson, an American minister to Mexico in the early 1840s, the Mexicans in general were "lazy, ignorant, and, of course, vicious and dishonest." This alleged Mexican inferiority was attributed to racial intermixture with the Indians, who, it was said, were hopelessly unfit for civilization.

Manifest Destiny was closely associated with the Democratic party. For Democrats, expansionism would counterbalance the debilitating effects of industrialization and urbanization. As good Jeffersonians, they stressed the need for more land to realize the ideal of a democratic republic rooted in the virtues and rough equality of independent farmers. For their working-class Irish constituency, the Democrats touted the broad expanses of the West as the surest means to escape the misery of wage slavery. It was no coincidence that O'Sullivan was a Democrat or that he feared that the spread of factories would produce an impoverished class of workers in America as it had in England.

As a manifesto for expansion, Manifest Destiny captured the popular imagination when the country was still mired in a depression after the Panic of 1837. The way out of the depression, according to many Democrats, was to revive the export trade to soak up the agricultural surplus. Thomas Hart Benton, a De-

mocratic senator from Missouri, was the leading spokesman for the vast potential of an American trade with India and China—a trade to be secured by American possession of the harbors on the Pacific Coast.

THE MEXICAN WAR

Once in office, Polk proved far more conciliatory with the British than with the Mexicans. Despite a stridently anti-British tone in his annual message to Congress in December 1845, Polk was willing to compromise on Oregon because he dreaded the possibility of a two-front war against both the Mexicans and the British. Mexico had severed diplomatic ties with the United States over the annexation of Texas (see Chapter 10), and a war could break out at any time.

In the spring of 1846, after Polk had abrogated the agreement on the joint occupation of Oregon, the British offered a compromise that they had earlier rejected. They agreed to a boundary at the 49th parallel if they were allowed to retain Vancouver Island in Puget Sound. Polk sent the offer to the Senate, which quickly approved it in June 1846. British–American trade continued to flourish, Mexico lost a potential ally, and, most important, Polk could now concentrate on the Mexican War that had erupted a month earlier.

Unlike Oregon, where he backed off from extravagant territorial claims, Polk refused to budge on the American claim (inherited from the Texans, when the United States annexed Texas in 1845) that the Rio Grande was the border between Texas and Mexico. The Mexicans insisted that the Nueces River, a hundred miles to the north of the Rio Grande, was the border, as it had been when Texas was part of Mexico. An immense territory was at stake, for the headwaters of the Rio Grande were in northern New Mexico, and a boundary on the Rio Grande would more than double the size of Texas.

Citing rumors of a Mexican invasion, Polk sent 3,500 troops under General Zachary Taylor to the Nueces River in the summer of 1845. Polk also stepped up his efforts to acquire California. He instructed Thomas Larkin, the American consul in Monterey, California, to inform the *Californios* and Americans that the United States would support them if they revolted against Mexican rule. Polk also secretly ordered the U.S. Pacific naval squadron to seize

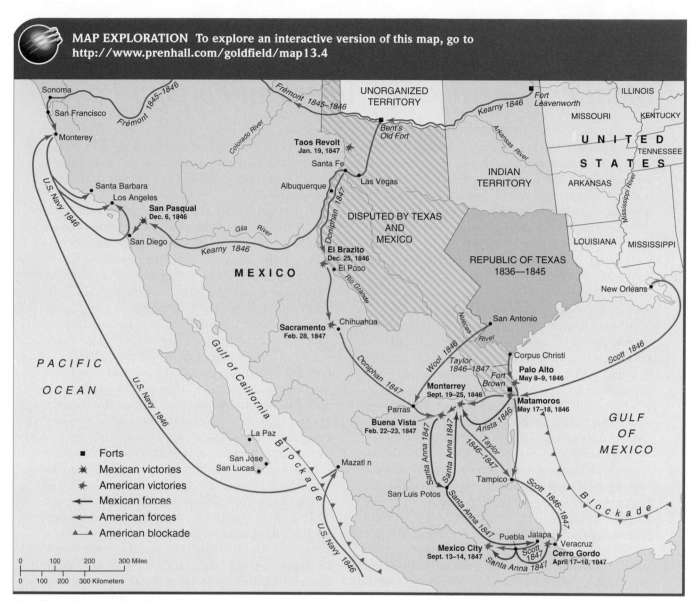

MAP EXPLORATION To explore an interactive version of this map, go to
http://www.prenhall.com/goldfield/map13.4

MAP 13-4   **The Mexican War**
Victories under General Zachary Taylor in northern Mexico secured the Rio Grande as the boundary between Texas and Mexico. Colonel Stephen Kearny's expedition won control of New Mexico, and reinforcements from Kearny assured the success of American troops landed by the Pacific Squadron in gaining Alta California for the United States. The success of General Winfield Scott's amphibious invasion at Vera Cruz and his occupation of Mexico City brought the war to an end.

California ports if war broke out with Mexico. Polk's final effort at peaceful expansion was the Slidell mission in November 1845. He sent John L. Slidell to Mexico City to offer $30 million to purchase California and New Mexico and to secure the Rio Grande boundary.

When Polk learned that the Mexican government had refused to receive Slidell, he set out to draw Mexico into a war that would result in the American acquisition of California. In early 1846, he ordered General Taylor to advance to the Rio Grande, deep in the dis-

puted border region. Taylor blockaded the mouth of the Rio Grande (an aggressive act even if the river had been an international boundary) and built a fort on the northern bank across from the Mexican town of Matamoros. The Mexicans attacked and were repulsed on April 24.

Even before the news reached Washington, Polk had decided on war, on the grounds that the Mexican government had unjustifiably refused to sell territory to the United States and had fallen behind on debt payments owed to American citizens.

FROM THEN TO NOW

Manifest Destiny and American Foreign Policy

From the birth of the nation in 1776 to the U.S. war on terrorism in the wake of the attacks on September 11, 2001, a sense of mission has often imbued American foreign policy. Manifest Destiny was one expression of that sense of mission.

Thomas Paine, in *Common Sense*, declared that America had the "power to begin the world over again." The shining force of the American republic's free government, Paine believed, would redeem those suffering under despotic monarchies. According to the lofty rhetoric of Manifest Destiny, America would fulfill this divinely ordained mission by absorbing all the people of North America—at least those deemed capable of self-government—into the republic.

Manifest Destiny helped inspire the American surge to the Pacific and justify the Mexican War. But the war also provoked a contrary fear: Was the United States guilty of an imperial conquest that threatened liberty rather than promoting it? When expansionists pushed for the acquisition of all of Mexico, opponents objected. Mexicans, they claimed, were unfit to join Anglo-Saxon Americans in assuming the responsibilities of self-rule. At the same time, to subject Mexico to colonial rule would deny it the democratic liberty that Manifest Destiny promised. Consequently, the All Mexico movement soon collapsed.

After cresting in the 1840s, Manifest Destiny lost its appeal. Expansionists in the late nineteenth century invoked Manifest Destiny to justify America's acquisition of an overseas empire following the Spanish-American War, but the new empire did not really fit that model. The advocates of Manifest Destiny had envisioned neighboring peoples in North America voluntarily joining the Republic. According to critics, the new empire, on the contrary, rested on the once-despised imperialist doctrines of Old World Europe. For former President Grover Cleveland, the annexation of the Hawaiian Islands in 1898 was "a perversion of our national mission," a signal that the nation was prepared to "abandon old landmarks and . . . follow the lights of monarchical hazards."

Cleveland and the other anti-imperialists lost the turn-of-the-century debate over whether the nation should acquire dependent possessions abroad. Still, by insisting, with Thomas Paine, that America's true mission must be to serve as the "model republic" for others to follow, they established the theme that characterized at least the public face of American diplomacy in the twentieth century. President Woodrow Wilson, for example, justified American intervention in World Was I as a moral crusade to save democracy in Europe, and he sought in vain to bring the United States into a new international body—the League of Nations—designed to curb aggressive nations and prevent future wars. Wilsonian idealism infused the foreign policy of President Franklin D. Roosevelt during World War II and inspired the formation of the United Nations. Throughout the Cold War, America identified itself as the protector of democratic freedoms from the threat of international communism. In the post–Cold War world, Presidents George Bush and Bill Clinton cited the need to uphold human rights as grounds for U.S. military intervention abroad. President George W. Bush has gone further by claiming that the United States has the right to use preemptive force against any "evil power" deemed a threat to world peace and the future security of the United States.

Critics have charged that the mantle of human rights cloaks the pursuit of less noble U.S. interests in other nations. Whether or not this critique is valid, it is clear that as the twenty-first century dawns, any interventionist foreign policy must present itself in the idealistic terms of a special American mission if it is to have public support.

Informed of the clash between Mexican and American troops in early May (it took ten days for the news to reach Washington), he sent a redrafted war message to Congress on May 9 asserting that Mexico "has invaded our territory, and shed American blood on American soil." Congress declared war on May 13, 1846.

The war was a stunning military success for the United States (see Map 13–4). The Mexicans fought bravely, but they lacked the leadership, modern artillery, and naval capacity to check the American advances. By the end of 1846, Polk had gained his objectives in the Mexican borderlands. An army sent west under Colonel Stephen W. Kearny occupied New Mexico. The conquest was relatively bloodless, because most of the local elite cooperated with the American authorities. Sporadic resistance was largely confined to poorer Mexicans and the Pueblo Indians, who feared that their land would be confiscated. The largest uprising, one that was ruthlessly suppressed, was the **Taos Revolt** in January 1847, led by Jesús Trujillo and Tomasito, a Pueblo chieftain. A sympathetic observer described the rebels as "those who defend to the last their country and their homes."

Kearny's army then moved to Tucson and eventually linked up in southern California with pro-American rebels and U.S. forces sent ashore by the Pacific squadron. As in New Mexico, the stiffest resistance came from ordinary Mexicans and the Spanish-speaking Indians.

Despite the loss of its northern provinces, Mexico refused to concede defeat. After Taylor had established a secure defensive line in northeastern Mexico with a victory at Monterrey in September 1846 and repulsed a Mexican counterattack at Buena Vista in February 1847, Polk directed General Winfield Scott to invade central Mexico. Following an amphibious assault on Vera Cruz in March 1847, Scott captured Mexico City in September.

After a frustrating delay while Mexico reorganized its government, peace talks finally got under way and concluded in the Treaty of Guadalupe Hidalgo, signed on February 2, 1848. Mexico surrendered its claim to Texas north of the Rio Grande and ceded Alta California and New Mexico (including present-day Arizona, Utah, and Nevada). The United States paid $15 million, assumed over $3 million in

claims of American citizens against Mexico, and agreed to grant U.S. citizenship to Mexicans resident in its new territories.

Polk had gained his strategic goals, but the cost was thirteen thousand American lives (most from diseases such as measles and dysentery), fifty thousand Mexican lives, and the poisoning of Mexican–American relations for generations. The war also, as will be seen in Chapter 14, heightened sectional tensions over slavery and weakened the political structure that was vital to preserving the Union.

CONCLUSION

Americans were an expansionist people. Though not necessarily proof of Manifest Destiny, their surge across the continent between 1815 and 1850 was fully in keeping with their restless desire for independence on a plot of land. Population pressure on overworked farms in the East impelled much of this westward migration, but, by the 1840s, expansion had seemingly acquired a momentum all its own, one that increasingly rejected the claims of other peoples to the land.

Far from being a process of peaceful, evolutionary, and democratic change, as was once thought, expansion involved the spread of slavery, violent confrontations, and the uprooting and displacement of native peoples. By 1850, the earlier notion of reserving the trans-Mississippi West as a permanent Indian country had been abandoned. The Sioux and Comanches were still feared by white settlers, but their final subjugation was not far off. The derogatory stereotypes of Mexican-Americans that were a staple of both popular thought and expansionist ideology showed clearly that American control after the Mexican War would relegate Spanish-speaking people to second-class status.

However misleading and false much of it was, the rhetoric of Manifest Destiny did highlight a central truth. A broad, popular base existed for expanding across the continent. As the Mexican War made clear, the United States was now unquestionably the dominant power in North America. The only serious threat to its dominance in the near future would come from inside, not outside, its continental domain.

REVIEW QUESTIONS

1. What accounted for the westward movement of Americans? How did the presence or absence of slavery affect developmental patterns in the new settlements?

2. How was the West of the Plains Indians transformed after 1830 as peoples migrated both within the region and into it from various directions? Why were the Sioux so powerful? How did they interact with other Native Americans and the U.S. government?

3. Who lived in the Mexican borderlands of the Southwest? Why was it so difficult for Mexican authorities to maintain effective control of the region? What role did trade play in the American penetration of the Southwest?

4. What did Americans mean by Manifest Destiny? Why was territorial expansion so identified with the Democratic party?

5. Who was responsible for the outbreak of the Mexican War? Were Mexicans the victims of American aggression?

6. How valid was the Sioux chief's indictment of the pretensions of white civilization as related to George Catlin?

KEY TERMS

Alamo (p. 406)

Californios (p. 406)

Claims clubs (p. 394)

Empresarios (p. 405)

Manifest Destiny (p. 390)

Mexican Cession of 1848 (p. 408)

Oregon Trail (p. 397)

Santa Fe Trail (p. 407)

Taos Revolt (p. 413)

Tejanos (p. 405)

RECOMMENDED READING

Billington, Ray Allen. *The Far Western Frontier, 1830–1860* (1956). Still a useful survey and an excellent example of an older approach to the West from the perspective of white people entering the region with their values of freedom and individualism.

Brandon, Richard. *The Last Americans: The Indian in American Culture* (1974). A beautifully written, panoramic account that looks at Indian cultures and their interactions with the spread of white settlement.

Limerick, Patricia Nelson. *The Legacy of Conquest: The Unbroken Past of the American West* (1987). A forcefully argued work that overturns many stereotypes and places the federal government and cultural antagonisms at the center of western history.

Meinig, D. W. *The Shaping of America*, Vol. 2: *Continental America, 1800–1867* (1993). A comprehensive work that offers a distinctive interpretation of continental expansion from the perspective of historical geography.

Merk, Frederick. *Manifest Destiny and Mission in American History* (1963). Valuable not only for its revisionist look at the appeal of Manifest Destiny in the 1840s but also for its insights into how a sense of mission influenced American foreign policy in the future.

Milner, Clyde A. II, Carol A. O'Connor, and Martha A. Sandweiss, eds. *The Oxford History of the American West* (1994). A comprehensive collection of essays that summarize much of the best work in the modern rethinking of the history of the American West.

Stephanson, Anders. *Manifest Destiny: American Expansionism and the Empire of Right* (1995). A tightly argued study that traces Manifest Destiny back to its roots in Puritan ideology and shows how, in revised form, it continued to influence American foreign policy well into the twentieth century.

White, Richard. *"Its Your Misfortune and None of My Own": A History of the American West* (1991). An outstanding work that draws on cultural and environmental approaches to show how complex and often unequal relationships among a host of peoples shaped the history of the West.

ADDITIONAL SOURCES

The Agricultural Frontier

Cashin, Joan E. *A Family Venture: Men and Women on the Southern Frontier* (1991).

Faragher, John Mack. *Sugar Creek: Life on the Illinois Prairie* (1986).

Gates, Paul W. *The Farmer's Age: Agriculture, 1815–1860* (1962).

Moore, John Hebron. *The Emergence of the Cotton Kingdom in the Old Southwest: Mississippi, 1770–1860* (1987).

Hudson, John C. *Making the Corn Belt: A Geographical History of Middle-Western Agriculture* (1994).

Rohrbough, Malcolm J. *The Trans-Appalachian Frontier: People, Societies, and Institutions, 1775–1850* (1978).

The Frontier of the Plains Indians

Clark, Malcolm Jr. *Eden Seekers: The Settlement of Oregon, 1810–1862* (1981).

De Voto, Bernard. *Across the Wide Missouri* (1947).

Goetzmann, William H. *Exploration and Empire: The Explorer and Scientist in the Winning of the American West* (1966).

Jeffrey, Julie R. *Frontier Women: The Trans-Mississippi West, 1840–1880* (1979).

Moore, John H., ed. *The Political Economy of the North American Indians* (1993).

Unruh, John. *The Plains Across: The Overland Emigrations and the Trans-Mississippi West, 1840–1860* (1979).

Elliott West, *The Way to the West: Essays on the Central Plains* (1995).

White, Richard. *The Roots of Dependency: Subsistence, Environment, and Social Change Among the Choctaws, Pawnees, and Navajos* (1983).

The Mexican Borderlands

Acuña, Rudolfo. *Occupied America: A History of Chicanos* (1988).

Gonzales, Manuel G. *Mexicanos: A History of Mexicans in the United States* (1999).

Lack, Paul D. *The Texas Revolutionary Experience: A Political and Social History, 1835–1836* (1992).

Lamar, Howard R. *The Far Southwest, 1846–1912* (1966).

Lecompte, Janet. *Pueblo, Hardscabble, Greenhorn: The Upper Arkansas, 1832–1856* (1978).

Phillips, George Harwood. *Indians and Intruders in Central California, 1769–1849* (1993).

Roberts, Randy, and James L. Olsen, *A Line in the Sand: The Alamo in Blood and Memory* (2001).

Tijerina, Andres. *Tejanos and Texas under the Mexican Flag, 1821–1836* (1994).

Weber, David J. *The Mexican Frontier, 1821–1846: The American Southwest under Mexico* (1982).

Politics, Expansion, and War

Griswold del Castillo, Richard. *The Treaty of Guadalupe Hidalgo: A Legacy of Conflict* (1990).

Eisenhower, John S. D. *So Far from God: The U.S. War with Mexico* (1989).

Hietala, Thomas R. *Manifest Design: American Aggrandizement in Late Jacksonian America* (1985).

Horsman, Reginald. *Race and Manifest Destiny: The Origins of American Racial Anglo-Saxonism* (1981).

Johannsen, Robert W. *To the Halls of Montezuma: The Mexican War in the American Imagination* (1985).

Sellers, Charles G. *James K. Polk: Continentalist, 1843–1846* (1966).

WHERE TO LEARN MORE

- **Indian Pueblo Cultural Center, Albuquerque, New Mexico.** This center provides an excellent orientation to the culture, crafts, and community life of the Pueblo and Southwestern Indians. It also includes much material on archaeological findings. **Visit www.indianpueblo.org/ for a calendar of events and an introduction to the history of the** nineteen pueblos.

- **Museum Association of American Frontier and Fur Trade, Chadron, Nebraska.** The library in the museum holds archives, maps, and some photographs dealing with the western fur trade. **In addition to an event calendar, its website www.stepintohistory.com/states/NE/Fur_Trade.htm provides links to other museums and preservation sites.**

- **Indian Museum of North America, Crazy Horse, South Dakota.** This is one of the best sources for learning of the culture of the Teton Sioux and other American and Canadian tribes on the Great Plains. Holdings include outstanding examples of Indian art and artifacts. **For information on exhibits, educational and cultural programs, and special collections of Native American art, go to www.crazyhorse.org/museum.shtml.**

- **Living History Farms, Des Moines, Iowa.** This site includes several working farms, operated as they were at different points in the nineteenth century, as well as a mid-twentieth-century farm. A vintage town with a general store, church, and other buildings has also been re-created. **Its website www.lhf.org/ lists events and provides a look at four farm sites.**

- **Scotts Bluff National Monument, Gering, Nebraska.** Scotts Bluff was a prominent landmark on the Oregon Trail, and the museum exhibits here have interpretive material on the trail and the western phase of expansion. Go to **www.nps.gov/scbl/** to print a park travel guide and to access a website devoted to the frontier photographer and artist William Henry Jackson.

- **Conner Prairie, Noblesville, Indiana.** The museum and historic area re-create a sense of life on the Indiana frontier during the period of the Old Northwest. **www.connerprairie.org** .

- **Fort Union National Monument, Watrous, New Mexico.** Fort Union was a nineteenth-century military post, and the holdings and exhibits in the museum relate to frontier military life and the Santa Fe Trail. **For a printable travel guide and a history of the park that includes bibliographical aides, go to www.nps.gov/foun/.**

 Please refer to the document CD-ROM for primary sources related to this chapter.

→ *Vivid illustrations accompanied the numerous editions of* Uncle Tom's Cabin *depicting the brutal realities of slavery and the unmerited suffering of the slave. These images sharpened the tragedy of Harriet Beecher Stowe's story. Here, Tom dies following a savage beating.*

THE POLITICS OF SECTIONALISM

14

1846–1861

December 16, 1852

My Dear Madam,

So you want to know what sort of woman I am! Well, if this is any object, you shall have statistics free of charge. To begin, then, I am a little bit of a woman,—somewhat more than forty, about as thin and dry as a pinch of snuff— never very much to look at in my best days and looking like a used up article now.

I was married when I was twenty-five years old to a man rich in Greek and Hebrew and Latin and Arabic, and alas, rich in nothing else . . . . But then I was abundantly furnished with wealth of another sort. I had two little curly headed twin daughters to begin with and my stock in this line has gradually increased, till I have been the mother of seven children, the most beautiful and the most loved of whom lies buried near my Cincinnati residence. It was at his dying bed and at his grave that I learned what a poor slave mother may feel when her child is torn away from her. In those depths of sorrow which seemed to me immeasurable, it was my only prayer to God that such anguish might not be suffered in vain. There were circumstances about his death of such peculiar bitterness, of what seemed almost cruel suffering that I felt that I could never be consoled for it unless this crushing of my own heart might enable me to work out some great good to others.

CHAPTER OUTLINE

Slavery in the Territories
The Wilmot Proviso
The Election of 1848
The Gold Rush
The Compromise of 1850
Response to the Fugitive Slave Act
Uncle Tom's Cabin
The Election of 1852

Political Realignment
Young America's Foreign Misadventures
Stephen Douglas's Railroad Proposal
The Kansas-Nebraska Act
"Bleeding Kansas"
Know-Nothings and Republicans: Religion and Politics
The Election of 1856
The Dred Scott Case
The Lecompton Constitution
The Lincoln–Douglas Debates

The Road to Disunion
North–South Differences
John Brown's Raid
The Election of 1860
Secession Begins
Presidential Inaction
Peace Proposals
Lincoln's Views on Secession
Fort Sumter: The Tug Comes

Conclusion

417

I allude to this here because I have often felt that much that is in that book had its root in the awful scenes and bitter sorrow of that summer. It has left now, I trust, no trace on my mind except a deep compassion for the sorrowful, especially for mothers who are separated from their children . . . .

This horror, this nightmare abomination! Can it be in my country! It lies like lead on my heart, it shadows my life with sorrow; the more so that I feel, as for my own brothers, for the South, and am pained by every horror I am obliged to write, as one who is forced by some awful oath to disclose in court some family disgrace. . . . .

Yours affectionately,

H. B. Stowe

Harriet Beecher Stowe to Eliza Cabot Follen, December 16, 1852; from Jeanne Boydston, Mary Kelley, Anne Margolis, *The Limits of Sisterhood* (Chapel Hill: University of North Carolina Press, 1988), 178–180.

Harriet Beecher Stowe, while writing to poet and fellow abolitionist, Eliza Cabot Follen, in the year that *Uncle Tom's Cabin* became an international best-seller, revealed how being a wife and a mother influenced her perception of slavery and inspired her writing. The deep piety and self-effacement expressed in the letter, as well as her transparent grief over the loss of her son, typified mid-nineteenth-century correspondence between women. Her beloved son had died of cholera in 1849; that wrenching event, coupled with the passage of the Fugitive Slave Act a year later, galvanized Stowe to pour her grief and indignation into a novel about plantation slavery.

Slavery was yet an abstract concept to most white Northerners at the time. Stowe personalized it in a way that made them see it as an institution that not just oppressed black people but destroyed families and debased well-meaning Christian masters as well. The deep piety expressed in the letter permeated the book and changed people's moral perceptions about slavery.

Stowe had grown up in a family of evangelical Protestant ministers and abolitionists. Her father, Lyman Beecher, was a prominent evangelical reformer. He had moved his large family from New England to Cincinnati in 1832 to assume the presidency of Lane Theological Seminary, where he used his office to promote the abolition of slavery. All six of his sons became ministers. Two of his three daughters, Catharine and Harriet, became accomplished writers. In Beecher's view, evangelical Christianity erased the line between public and private. Personal and societal salvation were closely con-

nected, a principle that is apparent in Harriet's letter. Stowe went on to write ten novels, became a popular children's-book author and wrote extensively on family and travel matters. She died in 1896, in Hartford, Connecticut, at the age of 85.

As slavery took on a personal and tragic meaning for Stowe, so it would move from being just another political issue to a moral crusade. Stowe's personal journey transformed into a political passion; with the millions who read her book, the political became personal. Yet, the anguish she expressed in her writing and the outrage it generated among her readers was hardly prefigured when a relatively obscure Congressman from Pennsylvania stepped forward in 1846 with a modest proposal that not only placed slavery front and center as a national political issue, a position that only strengthened over the next fifteen years, but would shake the Union to its very core.

Slavery was not, of course, a new political issue: the debate over the Missouri Compromise, the nullification controversy, and the battles in Congress over abolitionist mailings and petitions had roiled the political waters for nearly a generation prior to 1846. But after 1846, the clashes between northern and southern congressmen over issues relating to slavery became more frequent and more difficult to resolve. In the coming years, several developments—including white Southerners' growing consciousness of themselves as a minority, the mixture of political issues with religious questions, and the rise of the Republican party—would aggravate sectional antagonism. But the flash point that first brought it to the fore was the issue of slavery in the territories acquired from Mexico.

KEY TOPICS

● The controversy over slavery in the territories and the attempt to resolve it

● The causes and consequences of political realignment in the 1850s

● Why Lincoln was elected in 1860

● The secession crisis and why the political system could not fix it

SLAVERY IN THE TERRITORIES

Whatever its boundaries over the years, the West symbolized the hopes and dreams of white Americans. It was the region of fresh starts, of possibilities. To exclude slavery from the western territories was to exclude white Southerners from pursuing their vision of the American dream. Exclusion meant, an Alabamian declared, "that a free citizen of Massachusetts was a better man and entitled to more privileges than a free citizen of Alabama." Northern politicians disagreed. They argued that exclusion preserved equality—the equality of all white men and women to live and work without competition from slave labor or rule by despotic slaveholders. The issue of slavery in the territories became an issue of freedom for both sides.

From the late 1840s until 1861, northern and southern leaders attempted to fashion a solution to the problem of slavery in the territories. Four proposals dominated the debate:

● Outright exclusion

● Extension of the Missouri Compromise line to the Pacific

● Popular sovereignty—allowing the residents of a territory to decide the issue

● Protection of the property of slaveholders (meaning their right to own slaves) even if few lived in the territory

The first major debate on these proposals occurred during the early days of the Mexican War and culminated with the Compromise of 1850.

THE WILMOT PROVISO

In August 1846, David Wilmot, a Pennsylvania Democrat, offered an amendment to an appropriations bill for the Mexican War. The language of the **Wilmot Proviso** stipulated that "as an express and fundamental condition to the acquisition of any territory from the Republic of Mexico . . . neither slavery nor invol-untary servitude shall ever exist in any part of said territory." This language deliberately reflected Thomas Jefferson's Northwest Ordinance of 1787, which prohibited slavery in the Old Northwest. The proviso did not apply to Texas, which had become a state before the war began.

Wilmot explained that he wanted only to preserve the territories for "the sons of toil, of my own race and own color." By thus linking the exclusion of slavery in the territories to freedom for white people, he hoped to generate support across the North, regardless of party, and even in some areas of the Upper South.

Linking freedom for white people to the exclusion of slaves infuriated Southerners. It implied that the mere proximity of slavery was degrading and that white Southerners were therefore a degraded people, unfit to join other Americans in the territories. Georgia's Whig senator, Robert Toombs, issued a warning that reflected the feelings of many Southerners: "I do not hesitate to avow before this House and the Country, and in the presence of the living God, that if, by your legislation, you seek to drive us from the territories of California and New Mexico, purchased by the common blood and treasure of the whole people . . . , thereby attempting to fix a national degradation upon half the states of this Confederacy, I am for disunion."

Northern congressmen replied in kind. An Ohio Congressman declared, "We [the North] will establish a cordon of free states that shall surround you; and then we will light up the fires of liberty on every side until they melt your present chains and render all your people free." Now a majority in the House of Representatives (because the population of the northern states was greater than that of the southern states), northern lawmakers passed more than fifty versions of the proviso between 1846 and 1850. In the Senate, however, where each state had equal representation, the proviso was consistently rejected and never became law.

The proviso debate sowed distrust and suspicion between Northerners and Southerners. Congress had divided along sectional lines before, but seldom

Chronology

1846 Wilmot Proviso is submitted to Congress but is defeated.

1848 Gold is discovered in California.

Whig party candidate Zachary Taylor defeats Democrat Lewis Cass and Free-Soiler Martin Van Buren for the presidency.

1850 California applies for statehood.

President Taylor dies; Vice President Millard Fillmore succeeds him.

Compromise of 1850 is passed.

1851 Harriet Beecher Stowe publishes *Uncle Tom's Cabin*.

1852 Democrat Franklin Pierce is elected president in a landslide over Whig candidate Winfield Scott.

Whig party disintegrates.

1853 National Black Convention called in Rochester, New York, to demand repeal of the Fugitive Slave Act.

1854 Ostend Manifesto is issued.

Kansas-Nebraska Act repeals the Missouri Compromise.

Know-Nothing and Republican parties are formed.

1855 Civil war erupts in "Bleeding Kansas."

William Walker attempts a takeover of Nicaragua.

1856 "Sack of Lawrence" occurs in Kansas; John Brown makes a retaliatory raid at Pottawatomie Creek.

Democratic congressman Preston Brooks of South Carolina canes Massachusetts senator Charles Sumner in the U.S. Senate.

Democrat James Buchanan is elected president over Republican John C. Frémont and American (Know-Nothing) candidate Millard Fillmore.

1857 Supreme Court issues *Dred Scott* decision.

Kansas territorial legislature passes the proslavery Lecompton Constitution.

Panic of 1857 begins.

1858 Senatorial candidates Abraham Lincoln and Stephen A. Douglas hold series of debates in Illinois.

1859 John Brown's Raid fails at Harpers Ferry, Virginia.

1860 Constitutional Union party forms.

Democratic party divides into northern and southern factions.

Republican candidate Abraham Lincoln is elected president over southern Democratic candidate John C. Breckinridge, northern Democratic candidate Stephen A. Douglas, and Constitutional Unionist candidate John Bell.

South Carolina secedes from the Union.

1861 The rest of the Lower South secedes from the Union.

Crittenden Plan and Tyler's Washington peace conference fail.

Jefferson Davis assumes presidency of the Confederate States of America.

Lincoln is inaugurated.

Fort Sumter is bombarded; Civil War begins.

Several Upper South states secede.

---

had divisions become so personal. The leaders of both the Democratic and Whig parties, disturbed that the issue of slavery in the territories could so monopolize Congress and poison sectional relations, sought to defuse the issue as the presidential election of 1848 approached.

THE ELECTION OF 1848

Both Democrats and Whigs wanted to avoid identification with either side of the Wilmot Proviso controversy, and they selected their presidential candidates accordingly. The Democrats nominated Michigan senator Lewis Cass, a veteran party stalwart, whose public career stretched back to the War of 1812. Cass understood the destructive potential of the slavery issue. In 1847, he suggested that territorial residents, not Congress, should decide slavery's fate. This solution,

popular sovereignty, had a do-it-yourself charm: Keep the politicians out of it, and let the people decide. Cass was deliberately ambiguous, however, on when the people should decide. The timing was important. If residents could decide only when applying for statehood, slavery would be legal up to that point. The ambiguity aroused more fears than it allayed.

The Whigs were silent on the slavery issue. Reverting to their winning 1840 formula of nominating a war hero, they selected General Zachary Taylor of Mexican War fame. If the Whigs were looking for someone with no political record, they found him in the squat and craggy-faced Taylor. Taylor belonged to no party and had never voted. He was also inarticulate to the point of unintended humor. In one address, he intoned: "We are at peace with all of the world, and seek to maintain . . . amity with the rest of mankind." If one had to guess his views, his background provided some clues. He lived in Louisiana in the Lower South, he owned a hundred-slave plantation, and his now-deceased daughter had been married to Jefferson Davis, Mississippi's staunch proslavery senator.

Taylor's background disturbed many antislavery northern Whigs. These Conscience Whigs along with remnants of the old Liberty party and a scattering of northern Democrats bolted their parties and formed the Free-Soil party. The name reflected the party's vow to keep the territories free. Its slogan—"Free soil, free speech, free labor, free men"—was a catalog of white liberties that the South had allegedly violated over the previous decade.

The Free-Soilers' appeal centered on their opposition to slave labor in the territories. Free labor, they believed, could not compete with bonded labor. Slavery condemned the white worker to unemployment, poverty, and eventually a condition little better than slavery itself. The party nominated former president Martin Van Buren. The old New Yorker, who had remained active in state politics, had little hope of winning. But he could wield some influence if he were to prevent one of the major party candidates from winning a majority of electoral votes, thereby throwing the election into the House of Representatives.

Chalking up one out of seven northern votes, Van Buren ran strongly enough in eleven of the fifteen northern states to deny the winning candidate in those states a majority of the votes cast. But he could not overcome Taylor's strength in the South. Taylor was elected, giving the nation its first president from the Lower South.

THE GOLD RUSH

Events in distant California would leave Taylor little time to savor his victory. By the time he took office in March 1849, a gold rush was under way in that territory recently acquired from Mexico. John Sutter, a Swiss immigrant, contracted with James Marshall in late 1847 to build a sawmill on his property at the junction of the American and Sacramento Rivers in central California. In January 1848, Marshall was nearly finished with his project when something caught his eye: "I reached my hand down and picked it up; it made my heart thump, for I was certain it was gold. The piece was about half the size and shape of a pea. Then I saw another." Few believed the story at first, but Sam Brannan, a San Francisco merchant, witnessed Marshall's finds and literally ran shouting through the streets of the sparsely settled town about the new discovery. Brannan would become the wealthiest man in California, provisioning miners and staking claims.

Through 1849 and 1850, more than 100,000 hopefuls flooded into California. Anarchy and geology combined to form a volatile mixture in appropriately named settlements such as Hangtown, Gouge Eye, and Whiskeytown. One unfortunate miner wrote back east to his family in 1850: "I take this opportunity of writing these few lines to you hoping to find you in good health. Me and Charley is sentenced to be hung at five o/clock for robbery. Give my best to Frank and Sam." Though the overland or overseas treks took months, and travelers battled disease, weather, and each other, the lure of gold—easy to get at with just simple tools—was a powerful motivator.

Huge fortunes accrued, not only from the gold, but from supplying the miners. Young Levi Strauss experimented with trousers made out of canvas that miners particularly favored; two brothers, Henry Wells and William Fargo offered banking, transportation, and mail services for the newcomers. The rush also attracted migrants from around the world. California soon became a polyglot empire of Chinese, Chileans, Mexicans, Irish, Germans, and Turks. Blacks, mostly slaves brought by southern masters, also roamed the gold fields.

By 1853 gold mining operations had undergone structural and technological changes that made many miners superfluous. The new hydraulic extraction techniques also severely damaged the pristine rivers of central California.

Almost overnight, San Francisco was transformed from a modest port to a cosmopolitan metropolis. In 1847, a typical lot in the town cost $16; by 1849, that same lot sold for $45,000. During these two years, the town burned to the ground no less than six times,

Taking a break from digging and panning for gold, a group of Forty-Niners pose for the camera. Notice the African-American miner on the far left.

and six times the residents rebuilt on an ever grander scale. By the mid-1850s, a half-billion dollars in gold money had passed through the city, and a good bit of it stayed. The city by then boasted a fine theater, an opera house, and more newspapers than any other city in the world save London. The image of California, and of the West in general, as wild or golden, dates from this era. But the romance of California and the wealth it generated loomed more troubling back east as the territory filled up with people in 1849. For the western dream would soon become ensnared in the conflict over slavery.

THE COMPROMISE OF 1850

When the territory's new residents began asking for statehood and drafted a state constitution, the document contained no provision for slavery. The constitution reflected antiblack rather than antislavery sentiment. Keeping California white shielded residents against social and economic interaction with black people. In the context of territorial politics, "free" became a synonym for "whites only."

If Congress accepted the residents' request for statehood, California would enter the Union as a free state. The Union at the time consisted of fifteen free states and fifteen slave states. The admission of California would tip the balance and give free states a majority in the Senate. California, with its rapidly growing population, would also add to the sixty-one-vote majority the North enjoyed in the House of Representatives. New Mexico (which then included most of present-day New Mexico, Arizona, small parts of Nevada, and Colorado) appeared poised to follow suit and enter the Union as the seventeenth free state. Southerners saw their political power slipping away. Northern leaders saw an opportunity to stop the extension of slavery and reduce southern influence in the federal government.

When Congress confronted the issue of California statehood in December 1849, partisans on both sides began marshaling forces for what promised to be a long and bitter struggle. Because nine Free-Soil candidates had won seats in the House of Representatives, neither Whigs nor Democrats held a majority there. South Carolina senator John C. Calhoun understood that only a politically unified South could protect its interests. He urged southern congressmen to ignore party ties and unite behind a plan he proposed to gain federal protection for slavery in the territories. Most southern Whigs ignored Calhoun and waited to hear from President Taylor before abandoning him and their party.

No one, at first, knew where Taylor stood. Although a political novice, the president was not stu-

pid. Recognizing his lack of political experience, he selected Whig senator William H. Seward of New York as his adviser. Seward, a committed antislavery man, was one of the most hated politicians in the South; Taylor, a slaveholder from Louisiana, was distrusted by many northern members of his party. This odd match provided the first insight into the president's thinking on California.

He supported, it turned out, a version of popular sovereignty and favored allowing California and the other territories acquired from Mexico to decide the slavery issue for themselves. Under normal circumstances, the residents of a new territory organized a territorial government under the direction of Congress. When the territory's population approached thirty thousand or so, residents could draft a constitution and petition Congress for statehood. California already easily exceeded the population threshold. Taylor proposed bypassing the territorial stage—and congressional involvement in it—and having California and New Mexico admitted as states directly. (Before his inauguration in March 1849, he had already privately encouraged people in both territories to write state constitutions and to request admission.) The result would be to bring both into the Union as free states.

Although Seward no doubt encouraged him in it, Taylor's position was his own. The president was a nationalist and a strong believer in Manifest Destiny. He did not oppose slavery, but he abhorred the slavery issue because it threatened his vision of a continental empire. He was thus willing to forgo the extension of slavery into the territories. Southerners were certain to object strongly. But the president had a chilling message for them: "Whatever dangers may threaten [the Union] I shall stand by it and maintain it in its integrity."

Southerners resisted Taylor's plan, and Congress deadlocked on the territorial issue. Henry Clay then stepped forward with his last great compromise. To break the impasse, Clay urged that Congress should take four steps:

- Admit California as a free state, as its residents clearly preferred.
- Allow the residents of the New Mexico and Utah territories to decide the slavery issue for themselves too.
- End the slave trade in the District of Columbia.
- Pass a new fugitive slave law to enforce the constitutional provision stating that a person "held to Service or Labor in one state . . . escaping into another . . . shall be delivered upon Claim of the party to whom such Service or Labor may be due."

Clay's proposal provoked a historic Senate debate that began in February 1850, featuring America's three most prominent statesmen—Clay, Calhoun, and Daniel Webster—together for the last time. The emaciated Calhoun, who would be dead in two months, had to be carried into the Senate chamber. Too weak to read his remarks, he passed them to Virginia senator James M. Mason. Calhoun argued that the compromise did not resolve the slavery issue to the South's satisfaction, and he proposed to give Southerners in Congress the right to veto legislation in Congress as a way to safeguard their minority rights. Webster stood up to support the compromise, at deep political peril to himself. His Massachusetts constituents detested the fugitive-slave provision, which gave southern slaveholders the right to "invade" northern states to reclaim escaped slaves. Webster declared that he came to the debate "not as a Massachusetts man, nor as a Northern man, but as an American." He would swallow the fugitive slave law to save the Union.

After tumultuous deliberation that lasted into the summer of 1850, the Senate rejected the compromise. Calhoun had died at the end of March 1850, even before the debate ended. The 73-year-old Clay, exhausted, left Washington to recover his health. He would die less than two years later. Webster, estranged from fellow northern Whigs, left the Senate and went to his grave a few months after Clay.

President Taylor, who had vowed to veto any compromise, died unexpectedly of a stomach ailment after overindulging in cherries and milk in the hot sun at a July 4 celebration in Washington. Vice President Millard Fillmore, a pro-Clay New Yorker, assumed the presidency after Taylor's death. Compared with Taylor, who had stormed around the White House daring Southerners to attempt secession, Fillmore was a backroom man, quiet, at home with the cigar-and-brandy crowd, and effective with the deal. Fillmore let it be known that he favored Clay's package and would sign it if passed.

Although the Senate had rejected the compromise, Illinois senator Stephen A. Douglas kept it alive. A small man with a large head that gave him a mushroomlike appearance, Douglas epitomized the promise of American life for men of his generation. A native Vermonter, he migrated first to New York, then to Illinois as a teenager; read law; and developed a voracious appetite for politics. By the age of 28, he had already served as state legislator, chairman of the state Democratic party, and judge of the state supreme court. He envisioned an urban, industrial West linked to the East by a vast railroad network eventually extending to the Pacific. Above all, Douglas professed an unbending nationalism. To him, according to a biographer, "the Union was sacred, the symbol of all human progress." After his election to Congress in 1842, the Little Giant, as his constituents affectionately called him, developed a reputation as an astute parliamentarian and a tenacious debater.

Like Webster, Douglas feared for the Union if the compromise failed. Realizing that it would never pass as a package, he proposed to break it up into its components and hold a separate vote on each. With a handful of senators voting for all parts, and with different sectional blocs supporting one provision or another, Douglas engineered a majority for the compromise, and Fillmore signed it.

The Compromise of 1850 (see Map 14–1) was not a compromise in the sense of opposing sides consenting to certain terms desired by the other. The North gained California but would have done so in any case. Southern leaders looked to the West and saw no slave territories awaiting statehood. Their future in the Union appeared to be one of numerical and economic decline, and the survival of their institutions seemed doubtful. They gained the **Fugitive Slave Act**, which reinforced their right to seize and return to bondage slaves who had fled to free territory, but it was slight consolation. One Lower South senator termed it "useless." Because most slaves who escaped to the North did so from neighboring slave states, the law affected mainly the states of the Upper South. Few slave owners from the Lower South would bear the expense and uncertainty of chasing an escaped slave into free territory. And the North's hostile reception to the law made Southerners doubt their commitment to the compromise.

RESPONSE TO THE FUGITIVE SLAVE ACT

The Fugitive Slave Act was ready-made for abolitionist propaganda mills and heartrending stories. A few months after Congress passed it, a Kentucky slaveholder visited Madison, Indiana, and snatched a black man from his wife and children, claiming that the man had escaped nineteen years earlier. Black people living in northern communities feared capture, and some escaped across the Canadian border. Several northern cities and states vowed resistance, but except for a few publicized cases, northern authorities typically cooperated with southern slave owners to help them retrieve their runaway property. The effect of the act on public opinion, however, was to polarize North and South even further.

The strongest reaction to the act was in the black communities of the urban North. Previously, black abolitionists in the North had focused on freeing slaves in the South. The Fugitive Slave Act brought the danger of slavery much closer to home. No black per-

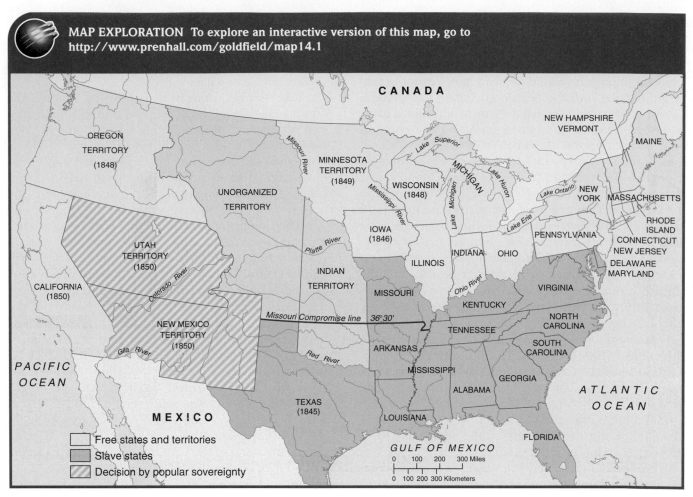

MAP EXPLORATION To explore an interactive version of this map, go to http://www.prenhall.com/goldfield/map14.1

MAP 14-1 **The Compromise of 1850**
Given the unlikely prospect that any of the western territories would opt for slavery, the compromise sealed the South's minority status in the Union.

son was safe under the new law. Mistaken identity, the support of federal courts for slaveholders' claims, and the presence of informants made reenslavement a real possibility. The lives that 400,000 black northerners had constructed, often with great difficulty, appeared suddenly uncertain.

Black Northerners formed associations to protect each other and repel—violently, if necessary—any attempt to capture and reenslave them. Boston's black leaders created the League of Freedom. Black Chicagoans organized the Liberty Association, with teams assigned to "patrol the city, spying for possible slave-hunters." Similar associations appeared in Cleveland and Cincinnati. Frederick Douglass, an escaped slave himself, explained the need for such organizations: "We must be prepared . . . to see the streets . . . running with blood . . . should this law be put into operation." Some black people left the United States. In October 1850, two hundred left Pittsburgh for Ontario, Canada, vowing that "they would die before being taken back into slavery." As many as twenty thousand African Americans may have found their way across the border during the 1850s in response to fears over capture and reenslavement. Another solution was proposed by Martin Delany, a prominent black abolitionist. He argued for the establishment of a black homeland at several potential sites in Central or South America or on the west coast of Africa. "Go we must," he wrote in 1852. "To remain here in North America and be crushed to the earth in vassalage and degradation, we never will."

During the early 1850s, black Northerners gathered in conventions to demand the repeal of the Fugitive Slave Act. Frederick Douglass convened the National Black Convention in Rochester, New York, in July 1853, at which he established a national council of black leaders to address issues of political and civil rights. Although the council was short-lived, it re-

The Fugitive Slave Act threatened the freedom of escaped slaves living in the North, and even of free black Northerners. This notice, typical of warnings posted in northern cities, urged Boston's African American population to take precautions.

flected a growing militancy. Less than a year later, for example, a black New York City woman schoolteacher defied that city's public transit segregation ordinance and succeeded in pressing state legislators to strike down the law.

On several occasions, black Northerners fought to defend their rights. In September 1851, Edward Gorsuch, a Maryland slaveholder, went to Christiana, Pennsylvania, where two of his escaped slaves were living. A fugitive slave named William Parker had organized the town's black community to defend against such an incident. Gorsuch located the two fugitives in a house occupied by Parker and a dozen other armed black men. Another fifty black people and some white people arrived and surrounded Gorsuch, his son, two other relatives, two neighbors, and a federal marshal. Gunfire erupted, wounding both Gorsuch and his son. As the elder Gorsuch lay on the ground, a group of black women "rushed from the

house with corn cutters and scythe blades [and] hacked the bleeding and lifeless body."

How much of this militancy filtered down to slaves in the South is difficult to say. Slaveholders noted an increase in black resistance during the early 1850s. A white Virginian noted in 1852 that "it is useless to disguise the fact, its truth is undeniable, that a greater degree of insubordination has been manifested by the negro population within the last few months, than at any previous period in our history as a state." Southerners often concocted tales of slave plots and unrest during times of national distress. But even if the Virginia writer exaggerated, his concern reflected genuine southern anxiety.

UNCLE TOM'S CABIN

Sectional controversy over the Fugitive Slave Act was relatively modest compared to the firestorm abolitionist writer Harriet Beecher Stowe ignited with the publication of a novel about southern slavery. *Uncle Tom's Cabin*, which first appeared in serial form in 1851, moved many northern white people from the sidelines of the sectional conflict to more active participation.

At the beginning of *Uncle Tom's Cabin*, a Kentucky slave owner is reluctantly forced by financial ruin to sell some of his slaves. Among them are the son of two mulatto slaves, George and Eliza Harris, and an older slave, Tom. Eliza escapes across the ice-choked Ohio River, clutching her son to her breast as slave catchers and their bloodhounds pursue them. Tom submits to sale to a New Orleans master. When that master dies, Tom is sold to Simon Legree, who owns a plantation on the Red River in Louisiana. Legree is vicious and sadistic—the only major slaveholding character in the book whom Stowe portrays in this manner. Tom, a devout Christian, remains loyal and obedient until Legree asks him to whip another slave. When Tom refuses, Legree beats him to death. Legree, incidentally, is from Vermont.

Stowe offered, not abstractions, but characters who seemed real. She aimed to evoke strong emotions in the reader. The broken family, the denial of freedom, and the Christian martyr were emotional themes. The presence of mulattoes in the book testified to widespread interracial and extramarital sex, which Northerners, then in the midst of a religious revival, viewed as an abhorrent sin destructive to family life. And the depiction of southern masters struggling unsuccessfully with their consciences focused public attention on how slavery subverted Christianity.

Uncle Tom's Cabin created a sensation in the United States and abroad. The book sold 10,000 copies in its first week and 300,000 within a year. By the time of the Civil War, it had sold an unprecedented 3 million copies in the United States and tens of thousands more in Europe. Stowe's book gave slavery a face; it changed people's moral perceptions about the institution in an era of deep Protestant piety; it was a Sermon on the Mount for a generation of Northerners seeking witness for their Christianity and a crusade on behalf of their faith. It transformed abolitionism, bringing a movement—whose extreme rhetoric many Northerners had previously viewed with disapproval—to the edge of respectability.

For Southerners, *Uncle Tom's Cabin* was a damnable lie, a political tract disguised as literature. One Southerner denounced the book as a "criminal prostitution of the high functions of the imagination to the pernicious intrigues of sectional animosity." Some Southerners retaliated with crude plays and books of their own. In these versions of slavery, no slave families were broken up, no slaves were killed, and all masters were models of Christian behavior. Few Northerners, however, read these southern responses. The writers penned them more to convince fellow Southerners that slavery was necessary and good than to change opinions in the North.

An advertisement for Uncle Tom's Cabin. *The book became a worldwide best-seller illuminating the tragedy of slavery in its corruption of family, human dignity, and Christianity.*

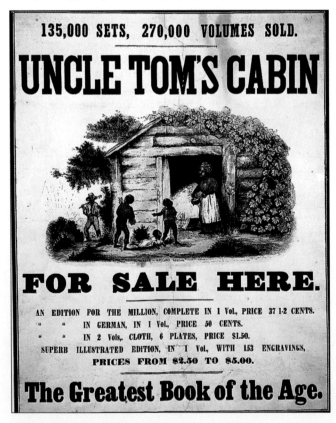

Black Northerners embraced *Uncle Tom's Cabin.* Frederick Douglass's National Black Convention resolved that the book was "a work plainly marked by the finger of God" on behalf of black people. Some black people hoped that the book's popularity would highlight the hypocrisy of white Northerners who were quick to perceive evil in the South but were often blind to discrimination against African Americans in the North. Despite reactions to Stowe's book, however, black Northerners continued to face voting restrictions, segregation, and official harassment.

THE ELECTION OF 1852

While the nation read and reacted to *Uncle Tom's Cabin*, a presidential election campaign took place. The Compromise of 1850 had divided the Whigs deeply. Northern Whigs perceived it as a capitulation to southern slaveholding interests and refused to support the renomination of President Millard Fillmore. Many southern Whigs, angered by the suspicions and insults of their erstwhile northern colleagues, abandoned the party. Although the Whigs nominated Mexican War hero and Virginian Winfield Scott for president, few southern Whigs viewed the nonslaveholding general as a friend of their region.

The Democratic Party entered the campaign more united. Despite reservations, both northern and southern wings of the party announced their support for the Compromise of 1850. Southern Democrats viewed the party's nominee, Franklin Pierce of New Hampshire, as safe on the slavery issue despite his New England heritage. Pierce satisfied Northerners as a nationalist devoted to the idea of Manifest Destiny. He belonged to Young America, a mostly Democratic group that advocated extending American influence into Central and South America and the Caribbean with an aggressive foreign policy. His service in the Mexican War and his good looks and charm won over doubters from both sections.

Given the disarray of the Whigs and the relative unity of the Democrats, the election results were predictable. Pierce won overwhelmingly with 254 electoral votes to Scott's 42. But Pierce's landslide victory could not obscure the deep fissures in the American party system. The Whigs, although they would continue to run local candidates through the rest of the 1850s, were finished as a national party. And the Democrats, despite their electoral success, emerged frayed from the election. In the Lower South, conflicts within the party between supporters and opponents of the Compromise of 1850 had overshadowed the contests between Democrats and Whigs. Southern Democrats had wielded great influence at the party's nominating convention and dominated party policy, clouding its prospects in the North. During the election, much of the party's support in the North had come from the first-time votes of mainly Catholic immigrants. But the growing political influence of Catholics alarmed evangelical Protestants of both parties, thus adding religious bigotry to the divisive issues undermining the structure of the national parties.

As Franklin Pierce took office in March 1853, it seemed that the only thing holding Democrats together was the thirst for political patronage. The low voter turnout in the 1852 election—Whig participation declined by 10 percent and Democratic participation by 17 percent, mostly in the Lower South—reflected public apathy and disgust at the prevailing party system. As the slavery issue confronted the nation with the most serious challenge it had faced since its inception, American voters were losing faith in their parties' ability to govern and in each other.

POLITICAL REALIGNMENT

Franklin Pierce, only forty-eight when he took office, was one of the youngest presidents in American history. He hoped to duck the slavery issue by focusing on Young America's dreams of empire. During the 1840s, the nationalist appeal of Manifest Destiny had helped elect Democrat James K. Polk to the presidency and had bolstered support for the Mexican War. Americans were still susceptible to nationalist fervor. For all their sectional, religious, ethnic, and racial differences, they shared a common language and political institutions. New technologies like the railroad and the telegraph were working to bind them together physically as well. The country was optimistic, and its possibilities for advancement seemed limitless. As Florida senator Stephen R. Mallory claimed, "It is no more possible for this country to pause in its career, than for the free and untrammeled eagle to cease to soar." But President Pierce's attempts to forge national sentiment around an aggressive foreign policy failed. And his administration's inept handling of a new territorial controversy in Kansas forced him to confront the slavery debate.

As Missouri senator Thomas Hart Benton, a Democrat, had realized during the debates over the Wilmot Proviso in 1848, no matter what policies a president pursued, Congress and the American people would interpret them in the light of their impact, real or potential, on slavery. The issue, said Benton, was like the plague of frogs that God had inflicted on the Egyptians to convince them to release the Hebrews from bondage. "You could not look upon the table but there were frogs, you could not sit down at the banquet but there were frogs, you could not go to the bridal couch and lift the sheets

but there were frogs!" So it was with "this black question, forever on the table, on the nuptial couch, everywhere!"

Franklin Pierce lacked the skilled leadership the times demanded. Troubled by alcoholism, worried about his chronically ill wife, and grief-stricken over the death of three young sons, including one in a train wreck, Pierce presided weakly over the nation and increasingly deferred to proslavery interests in his policies.

YOUNG AMERICA'S FOREIGN MISADVENTURES

Pierce's first missteps occurred in pursuit of Young America's foreign ambitions. The administration turned a greedy eye toward Spanish-ruled Cuba, just ninety miles off the coast of Florida. Spanish authorities were harassing American merchants exporting sugar from Cuba and the American naval vessels protecting the merchants' ships. Southerners supported an aggressive Cuba policy, seeing the island as a possible new slave state. And nationalists saw great virtue in replacing what they perceived as a despotic colonial regime with a democratic government under the guidance of the United States.

In October 1854, three American diplomats met in Ostend, Belgium, to discuss Cuba. It is not clear whether Pierce approved or even knew of their meeting, but the diplomats believed that they had the administration's blessing. One of them, the American minister to Spain, Pierre Soulé of Louisiana, was especially eager for the United States to acquire Cuba. The group composed a document on Cuba called the Ostend Manifesto that claimed that the island belonged "naturally to the great family of states of which the Union is the Providential Nursery." The implication was that Spain's control of Cuba was unnatural. The United States would offer to buy Cuba from Spain, but if Spain would not sell, the authors warned, "by every law, human and Divine, we shall be justified in wresting it from Spain."

The Ostend Manifesto caused an uproar and embarrassed the Pierce administration when it became public. In the polite world of nineteenth-century diplomacy, it was a significant breach of etiquette. Other nations quickly denounced it as a "buccaneering document" and a "highwayman's plea." It provoked a similar reaction in the United States, raising suspicions in the North that the South was willing to provoke a war with Spain to expand the number of slaveholding states.

Meanwhile, the Pierce administration's aggressive foreign policy encouraged private citizens to pursue Young America's goals in Latin America. Such was the case of self-styled "General" William Walker and his private army, "the immortals." Newspaper reporters loved the diminutive Walker, whose exploits provided excellent copy. The popular press called him "the grey-eyed man of destiny." Walker moved from Tennessee to California, and in 1853, after gathering arms and men, he invaded Mexican-owned Baja California and proclaimed a republic. Before he could establish a permanent government and legalize slavery, the Mexican authorities tossed him out. Undaunted, Walker and his followers plunged into the civil war that had erupted in Nicaragua in May 1855. He gained control of the country by the end of the year, proclaimed himself president, and invited southern slaveholders to take up residence. The Pierce administration immediately recognized Walker's government; the people of Nicaragua did not. Backed by other Central American countries, they fought to oust the little general. Congressional pressure forced the Pierce administration to cool its support for Walker, and his financial resources dried up. His foes overthrew him in 1857, and he fled Nicaragua on an American naval vessel. After two more abortive attempts at conquest in Central America, he was executed by a Honduran firing squad in 1860.

These and other setbacks frustrated Pierce's hope that foreign adventures would mute the angry debate over slavery. Instead, the proslavery overtones of the Cuban fiasco and Walker's open courting of southern support sharpened sectional conflict. As Pierce was fumbling in foreign policy, Senator Stephen A. Douglas of Illinois was developing a national project that also promised to draw the country together—the construction of a transcontinental railroad and the settling of the land it traversed. The result was worse conflict and the first outbreak of sustained sectional violence.

STEPHEN DOUGLAS'S RAILROAD PROPOSAL

Douglas, like many Westerners, wanted a transcontinental railroad. He himself had a personal stake in railroad building in that he owned some Chicago real estate and speculated in western lands. Railroads and the people and business they carried drove up property values. But beyond personal gain, Douglas, the supreme nationalist, understood that a transcontinental railroad would tie the nation together. Not only would it physically link East and West, it would also help spread American democracy. In short, a transcontinental railroad made good economic and political sense.

Douglas had in mind a transcontinental route extending westward from Chicago through the Nebraska Territory. Unfortunately for his plans, Indians already occupied this region, many of them on land the U.S. government had set aside as Indian

Territory and barred to white settlement. "How," Douglas complained, "are we to develop, cherish, and protect our immense interests and possessions on the Pacific with a vast wilderness 1,500 miles in breadth, filled with hostile savages, and cutting off all direct communication?" Removing the "Indian barrier" and establishing white government were "first steps," in the senator's view, toward a "tide of emigration and civilization."

Once again, and not for the last time, the federal government responded by reneging on earlier promises and forcing Indians to move. In 1853, President Pierce sent agents to convince the Indians in the northern part of the Indian Territory to cede land for the railroad.

With the Indian "obstacle" removed, Douglas sought congressional approval to establish a government for the Nebraska Territory. But southern senators defeated his proposal. They objected to it not only because it called for a northern rather than southern route for the transcontinental railroad but also because the new territory lay above the Missouri Compromise line and would enter the Union as yet another free state. Bowing to southern pressure, Douglas rewrote his bill and resubmitted it in January 1854. He predicted that the new bill would "raise a hell of a storm." He was right.

THE KANSAS-NEBRASKA ACT

Douglas's Kansas-Nebraska Bill split the Nebraska Territory into two territories, Kansas and Nebraska, with the implicit understanding that Kansas would become a slave state and Nebraska a free state. Consistent with Douglas's belief in popular sovereignty, it left the actual decision on slavery to the residents of the territories. But because it allowed Southerners to bring slaves into an area formerly closed to slavery, it repealed the Missouri Compromise (see Map 14–2).

Northerners of all parties were outraged. The Missouri Compromise had endured for thirty-four years as a basis for sectional accord on slavery. Now it was threatened, northern leaders charged, by the South's unquenchable desire to spread slavery and expand its political power. In defense of the bill, Douglas claimed that it was unlikely that a majority in either territory would vote for slavery. But a group of northern leaders of Douglas's own Democratic party countered vehemently that repealing the Missouri Compromise was more than a political maneuver. Using language indicative of the way religious and conspiratorial imagery had infected political debate, transforming it into a contest of good against evil, of liberty against oppression, they said it was "a gross violation of a sacred pledge," "a criminal betrayal of precious rights," and "part and parcel of

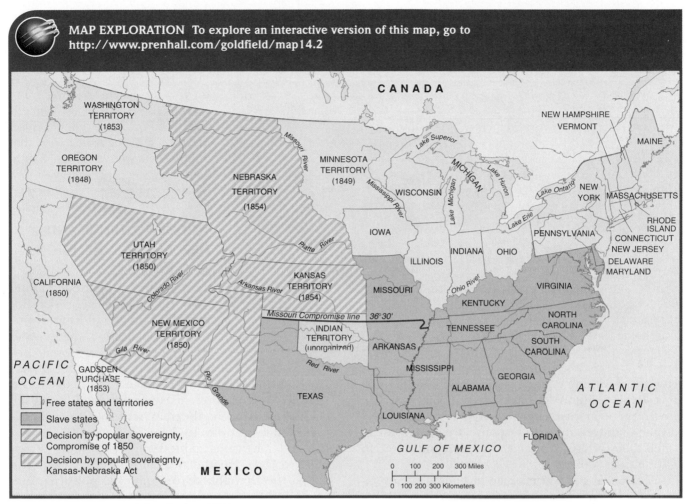

MAP EXPLORATION To explore an interactive version of this map, go to
http://www.prenhall.com/goldfield/map14.2

MAP 14-2   **The Kansas Nebraska Act, 1854.**
*The Kansas-Nebraska Act of 1854, which divided the Nebraska Territory in two and repealed
the Missouri Compromise, reopened the incendiary issue of slavery in the territories.*

an atrocious plot" to make a free territory a "dreary region of despotism, inhabited by masters and slaves." President Pierce, however, backed the bill, assuring the support of enough northern Democrats to secure it a narrow victory. The **Kansas-Nebraska Act** was law.

In August 1854, shortly after Congress adjourned, Douglas left Washington for his home in Chicago, to rest and mend political fences. He did not enjoy a pleasant journey home. "I could travel," he later recalled, ". . . by the light of my own effigy on every tree we passed." Arriving in Chicago, he addressed a large hostile crowd outside his hotel balcony. As he departed, he lost his temper and blurted, "It is now Sunday morning. I'll go to church; you can go to hell."

"BLEEDING KANSAS"

Because of its fertile soil, favorable climate, and location adjacent to the slave state of Missouri, Kansas was the most likely of the new territories to support slav-

ery. As a result, both Southerners and antislavery Northerners began an intensive drive to recruit settlers and establish a majority there. Speaking for the antislavery forces, William H. Seward said in the Senate, "We will engage in competition for the virgin soil of Kansas, and God give this victory to the side which is strong in numbers as it is in right." South Carolina editor Robert Barnwell Rhett accepted the challenge, urging fellow Southerners to "send men to Kansas, ready to cast in their lot with the proslavery part there and able to meet Abolitionism on its own issue, and with its own weapons."

As proslavery residents of Missouri poured into Kansas, antislavery organizations funded and armed their own migrants. In March 1855, proslavery forces, relying on the ineligible votes of Missouri residents, fraudulently elected a territorial legislature. This legislature promptly passed a series of harsh measures, including a law mandating the death penalty for aiding

Armed Missourians cross the border into Kansas to vote illegally for a proslavery government in 1855.

a fugitive slave and another making it a felony to question slaveholding in Kansas. For good measure, the proslavery majority expelled the few free-staters elected to the assembly. In response, free-staters established their own government in Topeka and vowed to make Kansas white.

A sporadic civil war erupted in Kansas in November 1855 and reached a climax in the spring of 1856. Journalists dubbed the conflict **"Bleeding Kansas."** On May 21, a group of proslavery officials attacked the free-state stronghold of Lawrence, subjecting it to a heavy artillery barrage. No one was killed, but the town suffered substantial damage. Eastern newspapers, exaggerating the incident, called it "the sack of Lawrence." Three days later, antislavery agitator John Brown, originally from Connecticut, went with several sympathizers to Pottawatomie Creek south of Lawrence in search of proslavery settlers. Armed with razor-sharp broadswords, they split the skulls and hacked the bodies of five men.

Kansans were not the only Americans bleeding over slavery. Five days before the **"sack of Lawrence,"** Massachusetts senator Charles Sumner delivered a long-winded diatribe, "The Crime Against Kansas," full of personal insults against several Southerners, especially elderly South Carolina senator Andrew P. Butler. Two days after Sumner's outburst, and a day after the story of the sack of Lawrence appeared in the newspapers, Butler's cousin, South Carolina congressman Preston Brooks, entered a mostly vacant Senate chamber, where Sumner sat working on a speech. Seeking to defend his cousin's honor, Brooks raised his walking cane and beat Sumner over the head. Bloody and unconscious, the senator slumped to the floor. He recovered but did not return to the Senate for over three years. His empty chair offered Northerners' mute confirmation of their growing conviction that Southerners were despotic. Southerners showered Brooks with new walking canes.

KNOW-NOTHINGS AND REPUBLICANS: RELIGION AND POLITICS

The Sumner incident, along with the Kansas-Nebraska Bill and the civil war in Kansas, further polarized North and South, widening sectional divisions within the political parties. Some northern Democrats distanced themselves from their party and looked for political alternatives; northern Whigs seized on changing public opinion to form new coalitions; and free-soil advocates gained new adherents. From 1854 to 1856, Northerners moved into new political parties that altered the national political landscape and sharpened sectional conflict.

Although the slavery issue was mainly responsible for party realignment in the North, other factors played a role as well. Nearly 3.5 million immigrants entered the United States between 1848 and 1860, the greatest influx in American history in proportion to the total population. Some of these newcomers, especially the Germans, were escaping failed democratic revolutions in Europe. They were predominantly middle-class Protestants who, along with fewer German Catholics and Jews, settled mostly in the cities, where they established shops and other businesses. More than 1 million of the immigrants, however, were poor Irish Roman Catholics, fleeing their homeland to avoid starvation.

The Irish immigrants made their homes in northern cities, at the time in the midst of Protestant revivals and reform. They also competed for jobs with native-born Protestant workers. Because the Irish would work for lower wages, the job competition bred animosity and sometimes violence. Culturally, the Irish held different views on keeping the Sabbath, and they preferred to send their children to separate sectarian schools. But it was their Roman Catholic religion that most concerned some urban Protestants. These Protestants associated Catholicism with despotism and immorality, the same evils they attributed to Southerners. For their part, the Irish made it clear that they had little use for Protestant reform, especially temperance and abolitionism. The clash of cultures would soon further disturb a political environment increasingly in flux over the slavery issue.

Democrats wooed the Irish newcomers. The champions of individual rights against intrusive government and meddling reformers, they supported the strict separation of church and state. Evangelical Protestants, especially those who were not Democrats, took a different view. They believed that the assertion of individual rights led to chaos and had to be countered by evangelically led reform. And that reform must be legislated. As a Boston minister wrote during the debate on the Wilmot Proviso, "The great problem for the Christian world now to accomplish is to effect a closer union between religion and politics . . . . We must make men to do good and be good."

Evangelicals supported government action on a wide variety of issues, from drinking to slavery to economic policy. To the reformers, every political issue had moral overtones. Those who disagreed with them were not merely political opponents but obstacles to the creation of a righteous society. These views, though, blurred the lines not only between church and state but also between the expiation of sin and the elimination of the sinner.

New parties emerged from this cauldron of religious, ethnic, and sectional strife. Anti-immigrant, anti-Catholic sentiment gave rise to the **Know-Nothing Party**, which began as a secret organization in July 1854. Its name derived from the reply that members gave when asked about the party: "I know nothing." Although strongest in the North, Know-Nothing chapters blossomed in several southern cities that had experienced some immigration since 1848, among them Richmond, Louisville, New Orleans, and Savannah. The party's members in both North and South were mostly former Whigs. In addition to their biases against Catholics and foreigners, the Know-Nothings shared a fear that the slavery issue could destroy the Union. But because attempts to solve the issue seemed only to increase sectional tensions, the Know-Nothings hoped to ignore it.

Know-Nothing candidates fared surprisingly well in local and congressional elections during the fall of 1854, carrying 63 percent of the statewide vote in Massachusetts and making strong showings in New York and Pennsylvania. In office, Know-Nothings achieved some notable reforms. In Massachusetts, where they pursued an agenda similar to that of the Whigs in earlier years, they secured administrative reforms and supported public health and public education programs.

The Know-Nothings' anti-Catholicism, however, overshadowed their reform agenda. In several states and cities, they passed legislation barring Catholics from public office and unsuccessfully sought to increase the time required for an immigrant to become a citizen from one year to twenty-one years. The Know-Nothings also fostered anti-Catholic violence such as a bloody election day riot that erupted in Louisville, Kentucky, in 1855.

Ethnic and religious bigotry were weak links to hold together a national party. Southern and northern Know-Nothings soon fell to quarreling among themselves over slavery, despite their vow to avoid it, and the party split. Many northern Know-Nothings soon found a congenial home in the new **Republican Party**.

The Republican Party formed in the summer of 1854 from a coalition of antislavery Conscience Whigs and Democrats disgusted with the Pierce administration's Kansas policy. Like the Know-Nothings, the Republicans advocated strong state and federal governments to promote economic and social reforms. But the new party did not espouse the Know-Nothings' anti-Catholic and anti-immigrant positions. The overriding bond among Republicans was their opposition to the extension of slavery in the territories.

Reflecting its opposition to slavery, the Republican party was an antisouthern sectional party. The overwhelming majority of its members were Northerners. Northern Whig merchants and entrepreneurs who joined the party were impatient with southern obstruction in Congress of federal programs for economic development, such as a transcontinental railroad, harbor and river improvements, and high tariffs to protect American industries (located mostly in the North) from foreign competition. In a bid to keep slavery out of the territories, the Republicans favored limiting homesteads in the West to 160 acres. Not incidentally, populating the territories with northern whites would ensure a western base for the new party.

Heightened sectional animosity laced with religious and ethnic prejudice fueled the emergence of new parties and the weakening of old political affiliations in the early 1850s. Accompanying the political realignment were diverging views on the proper role of government. As the nation prepared for the presidential election of 1856, the Democrats had become a party top-heavy with Southerners; the Know-Nothings splintered along sectional lines; some Whigs remained active under the old party name, mainly on the state and local levels in North and South; and the Republican party was becoming an important political force in the North and, to Southerners, the embodiment of evil.

THE ELECTION OF 1856

The presidential election of 1856 proved one of the strangest in American history. The Know-Nothings and the Republicans faced a national electorate for the first time. The Democrats were deeply divided over the Kansas issue. Rejecting both Pierce and Douglas, they turned instead to a longtime insider, James Buchanan. This Pennsylvanian's major asset was that he had been absent from the country the previous three years as ambassador to Great Britain and was thus untainted by the Kansas controversy. The members of the increasingly powerful southern wing of the party supported him because he had cooperated with them during his more than thirty years in Congress. Northerners accepted him primarily because of his clean slate on Kansas and because he hailed from a state crucial to a Democratic victory.

The Republicans passed over their most likely candidate, the New York senator and former Whig William H. Seward. Instead, they followed a tried-and-true Whig precedent and nominated a military hero, John C. Frémont, a handsome, dark-haired soldier of medium height and medium intelligence. His wife, Jessie Benton, the daughter of Missouri senator Thomas Hart Benton, was his greatest asset. In effect, she ran the campaign and wisely encouraged her husband to remain silent.

The Know-Nothings split into the "South Americans" and the "North Americans." The South Americans nominated Millard Fillmore, although he was not a Know-Nothing. The North Americans eventually and reluctantly embraced Frémont, despite the widespread but mistaken belief that he was a Roman Catholic.

Openly reviling what they called the "Black Republican party," Southerners threatened disunion if Frémont won. Virginia governor Henry A. Wise declared that Frémont's election "would be an open, overt proclamation of public war." Georgia's fire-eating Senator Robert Toombs concurred, warning that "the election of Frémont would be the end of the Union, and ought to be."

Buchanan claimed to be the only national candidate on the ballot. Writing to a colleague before the election, he stated, "I consider that all incidental questions are comparatively of little importance . . . when compared with the grand and appalling issue of Union or Disunion." Voters agreed, for Buchanan bested Frémont in the North and Fillmore in the South to win the presidency.

The overall result pleased Southerners, but the details left them uncomfortable. Buchanan won by carrying every southern state and the Lower North—Pennsylvania, New Jersey, Illinois, Indiana, and California. But Frémont, a political novice running on his party's first national ticket, carried eleven free states, and the rest he lost by scant margins to Buchanan. It was a remarkable showing for a two-year-old party. In the South and border states, Fillmore managed more than 40 percent of the vote and carried Maryland, despite bearing the standard of a fragmented party.

Buchanan, who brought more than a generation of political experience to the presidency, would need every bit and more. He had scarcely settled into office when two major crises confronted him: a Supreme Court decision that challenged the right of Congress to regulate slavery in the territories and renewed conflict over Kansas.

THE DRED SCOTT CASE

Dred Scott was a slave owned by an army surgeon based in Missouri. In the 1830s and early 1840s, he had traveled with his master to the state of Illinois and the Wisconsin Territory before returning to Missouri. In 1846, Scott sued his master's widow for freedom on the grounds that the laws of Illinois and the Wisconsin Territory barred slavery. After a series of appeals, the case reached the Supreme Court. Chief Justice Roger Taney of Maryland, joined by five other justices of the nine-member Supreme Court (five of whom came from slave states), dismissed Scott's suit two days after Buchanan's inauguration in March 1857. There is evidence that Buchanan had urged the Court to issue a sweeping ruling on slavery in the territories that would set the question to rest once and for all. Although Buchanan apparently did not suggest which way he wanted the Court to rule, such contact between the executive and the judicial branches of government concerning a pending case was inappropriate. In any case, Taney's opinion, far from settling the sectional debate over slavery, deepened it.

Taney's opinion contained two bombshells. First, using dubious logic and failing to take into account the status of African Americans in several northern states, he argued that black people were not citizens of the United States. Because Scott was not a citizen, he could not sue. In reaching this conclusion, Taney noted that the framers of the Constitution had never intended citizenship for slaves. The framers, according to Taney, respected a long-standing view that slaves were "beings of an inferior order . . . so far inferior that they had no rights which the white man was bound to respect."

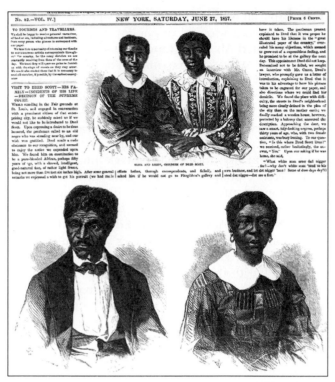

Dred Scott and his wife Harriet are portrayed here with their children as an average middle-class family, an image that fueled Northern opposition to the Supreme Court's 1857 decision that denied both Scott's freedom and his citizenship.

Second, Taney held that even if Scott had standing in court, his residence in the Wisconsin Territory did not make him a free man. This was because the Missouri Compromise, which was still in effect in the 1840s, was, in Taney's view, unconstitutional. (The Wisconsin Territory lay above the compromise line.) The compromise, the Chief Justice explained, deprived citizens of their property (slaves) without the due process of law granted by the Fifth Amendment to the U.S. Constitution. In effect, Taney ruled that Congress could not bar slavery from the territories.

Black Americans reacted bitterly to the **Dred Scott Decision**. Throughout the struggle of black abolitionists to free their compatriots in the South, they had appealed to the basic American ideals of freedom, liberty, and self-determination. Now Taney was saying that these ideals did not apply to black people. Throughout the urban North, African Americans held meetings to denounce the decision. One gathering in Philadelphia in April 1857 resolved "that the only duty the colored man owes to a constitution under which he is declared to be an inferior and degraded being . . . is to denounce and repudiate it." A statewide black convention in Ohio objected in even stronger language: "If the Dred Scott dictum be the

true . . . law of the land, then are the founders of the American Republic convicted by their descendants of base hypocrisy, and colored men absolved from all allegiance to a government which withdraws all protection." The gap between American ideals and the application of those ideals to black Americans had never been wider or more apparent.

The decision also shocked Republicans. The right of Congress to ban slavery from the territories, which Taney had apparently voided, was one of the party's central tenets. Republicans responded by ignoring the implications of the decision for the territories while promising to abide by it so far as it affected Dred Scott himself. Once in office, Republicans vowed, they would seek a reversal. This position allowed them to attack the decision without appearing to defy the law.

The Dred Scott decision boosted Republican fortunes in the North even as it seemed to undercut the party. Fears of a southern Slave Power conspiracy, which some had dismissed as fanciful and politically motivated, now seemed justified. If Congress could not ban slavery from the territories, Republicans asked, how secure was the right of states to ban slavery within their borders? A small group of slaveholders, they charged, was holding nonslaveholding white people hostage to the institution of slavery.

THE LECOMPTON CONSTITUTION

Establishing a legitimate government in Kansas was the second major issue to bedevil the Buchanan administration. The president made a good start, sending his friend and fellow Pennsylvanian Robert Walker (then a resident of Mississippi) to Kansas as territorial governor to oversee the election of a constitutional convention in June 1857. Walker, though sickly, was a man of integrity.

The violence had subsided in Kansas, and prospects had grown for a peaceful settlement. But free-staters, fearing that the slavery forces planned to stuff the ballot box with fraudulent votes, announced a boycott of the June election. As a result, proslavery forces dominated the constitutional convention, which was held in Lecompton. And Walker, although a slaveholder, let it be known that he thought Kansas would never be a slave state. He thus put himself at odds with proslavery residents from the outset.

Walker convinced the free-staters to vote in October to elect a new territorial legislature. The returns gave the proslavery forces a narrow victory, but Walker discovered irregularities. In McGee, Kansas, twenty voters somehow had cast twelve hundred votes for proslavery candidates. And in Oxford, a community of a mere six houses, 1,601 names appeared on the voting rolls, all in the same handwriting and all copied from the Cincinnati city directory. Walker threw out these returns, and the free-staters took control of the territorial legislature for the first time.

Undeterred, the proslavery forces drafted a proslavery constitution at the constitutional convention in Lecompton. Buchanan, who had promised Southerners a proslavery government in Kansas, dismissed Walker before he could rule on the Lecompton Constitution, then ignored the recommendation of Walker's successor that he reject it. He submitted the **Lecompton Constitution** to the Senate for approval even though it clearly sidestepped the popular sovereignty requirement of the Kansas-Nebraska Act.

As with the Kansas-Nebraska Act, many Northerners were outraged by the Lecompton Constitution. The proslavery Kansans behind the constitution had a record of fraud, and Buchanan's own appointee had advised him against it. Northern Democrats facing reelection refused to support a president of their own party and, though the constitution passed in the Senate, Democratic opposition killed it in the House. Among Lecompton's opponents was Stephen A. Douglas, who justified his vote with an impassioned defense of popular sovereignty, which the president and proslavery Kansans had openly defied.

Douglas knew that the Dred Scott decision and Buchanan's support of the Lecompton Constitution would help the Republicans and hurt him and his fellow northern Democrats in the 1858 congressional elections. The **Panic of 1857**, a severe economic recession that lingered into 1858, also worked to the advantage of the Republicans. The Democratic administration did nothing as unemployment rose, starvation stalked the streets of northern cities, and homeless women and children begged for food and shelter. Republicans claimed that government intervention—specifically, Republican-sponsored legislation to raise certain tariffs, give western land to homesteaders, and fund transportation projects—could have prevented the panic. The Democrats' inaction, they said, reflected the southern Slave Power's insensitivity to northern workers.

Southerners disagreed. The panic had scarcely touched them. Cotton prices were high, and few southern banks failed. Cotton seemed indeed to be king. The financial crisis in the North reinforced the southern belief that northern society was corrupt and greedy. The Republicans' proposed legislative remedies, in their view, would enrich the North and beggar the South.

Such were the issues confronting Douglas as he returned home to Illinois in the summer of 1858 to begin his reelection campaign.

THE LINCOLN–DOUGLAS DEBATES

Douglas faced a forceful opponent. The Republicans had nominated Abraham Lincoln, a 49-year-old lawyer and former Whig congressman. The Kentucky-born Lincoln had risen from modest circumstances to become a prosperous lawyer in the Illinois state capital of Springfield. His marriage to wealthy and well-connected Mary Todd helped both his law practice and his pocketbook. After one term in Congress from 1847 to 1849, he returned to his law practice but maintained his interest in politics. Strongly opposed to the extension of slavery into the territories, he considered joining the Republican Party after the passage of the Kansas-Nebraska Act. Lincoln had developed a reputation as an excellent stump speaker with a homespun sense of humor, a quick wit, and a self-deprecating style that fit well with the small-town residents and farmers who composed the majority of the Illinois electorate.

But substance counted more than style with Illinois voters. Most of them opposed the extension of slavery into the territories, although generally not out of concern for the slaves. Illinois residents, like most Northerners, wanted to keep the territories free for white people. Few voters would support dissolving the Union over the slavery issue. Douglas, who knew his constituents well, branded Lincoln a dangerous radical for warning, in a biblical paraphrase, that the United States, like "a house divided against itself," could not "endure permanently half slave and half free."

Lincoln could not allow the charge of radicalism to go unanswered. Little known beyond the Springfield area, he also had to find a way to gain greater exposure. So, in July 1858, he challenged Douglas to a series of debates across the state. Douglas was reluctant to provide exposure for his lesser-known opponent, but he could not reject Lincoln's offer outright, lest voters think he was dodging his challenger. He agreed to debates in seven of the state's nine congressional districts.

The **Lincoln–Douglas debates** were defining events in American politics. Farmers rode into such market towns as Ottawa, Galesburg, Alton, and Freeport, bringing their families and picnic baskets. They settled in their wagons or on the ground under trees to hear the two great debaters confront each other on the most troubling issue of the day. What a sight it must have been, the stubby-legged, animated, barrel-chested Little Giant engaging the gangly, deliberate former rail-splitter, Abe Lincoln.

The debates put the differences between Lincoln and Douglas, Republicans and Democrats, and North and South into sharp focus. At Freeport, Lincoln asked Douglas to reconcile popular sovereignty, which

Abraham Lincoln making a point at Coles County (Illinois) Fairgrounds, 1858. His U.S. Senate opponent, Stephen A. Douglas, sitting at Lincoln's right, waits his turn. The Lincoln-Douglas debates captivated Illinois voters who turned out in great numbers to witness the rhetorical fireworks.

Douglas had long championed, with the *Dred Scott* decision, which seemed to outlaw it by prohibiting a territorial legislature from excluding slavery before statehood. Douglas replied with what became known as the Freeport Doctrine. Slavery, he argued, could exist in a territory only if residents passed a law to protect it. Without such a law, no slaveholders would move in, and the territory would be free. Thus, if residents did nothing, there could be no slavery in the territory.

For Douglas, slavery was not a moral issue. What mattered was what white people wanted. If they wanted slavery, fine; if they did not, fine also. Lincoln and many Republicans had a very different view. For them, slavery was a moral issue. As such, it was independent of what the residents of a territory wanted. In the final Lincoln-Douglas debate, Lincoln turned to his rival and explained:

> The real issue in this controversy . . . is the sentiment on the part of one class that looks upon the institution of slavery *as a wrong*, and of another class that does not look upon it as a wrong . . . . The Republican party . . . look upon it as being a moral, social and political wrong . . . and one of the methods of treating it as a wrong is to make provision that it shall grow no

larger . . . . That is the real issue . . . . It is the eternal struggle between these two principles—right and wrong—throughout the world.

Abolitionists and evangelicals had been saying much the same thing. But Lincoln was calm and nonaccusatory, his measured words more like a conversation than a sermon. And people listened.

Lincoln tempered his moralism with practical politics. He took care to distance himself from abolitionists, asserting that he abided by the Constitution and did not seek to interfere where slavery existed. Privately, however, he prayed for its demise. Nor did he agree, publicly at least, with abolitionist calls for racial equality. Several times during the debates he noted "a physical difference between the white and black races" that would "forever forbid the two races living together on terms of social and political equality." At the Springfield debate, he echoed the wishes of most white Illinoisans when he declared, "What I would most desire would be the separation of the white and black races." Indeed, he had once advocated sending freed slaves to Africa. Slavery was immoral, but inequality was not. The Republican party was antislavery, but it did not advocate racial equality.

Illinois voters retained a narrow Democratic majority in the state legislature, which reelected Douglas to the U.S. Senate. (State legislatures elected senators until 1913, when the Seventeenth Amendment provided for direct election by the people.) But Douglas alienated southern Democrats with his strong defense of popular sovereignty and lost whatever hope he had of becoming the standard-bearer of a united Democratic party in 1860. Lincoln lost the senatorial contest but won national respect and recognition.

Despite Lincoln's defeat in Illinois, the Republicans made a strong showing in the 1858 congressional elections across the North. The increased Republican presence and the sharpening sectional divisions among Democrats portended a bitter debate over slavery in the new Congress. Americans were viewing issues and each other more than ever before in sectional terms. Northern and Southern took on meanings that expressed a great deal more than geography.

THE ROAD TO DISUNION

The unsatisfying Compromise of 1850, the various misadventures in the Caribbean and Central America, "Bleeding Kansas" and "Bleeding Sumner," and the

Dred Scott case convinced many Northerners that Southerners were conspiring with the federal government to restrict their political and economic liberties. Southerners interpreted the response to these same events as evidence of a northern conspiracy to gain increased power in the federal government and reduce the South's political and economic influence. There were no conspiracies, but with so little goodwill on either side, hostility predominated. Slavery, above all, accounted for the growing divide.

When abolitionist John Brown, who had avenged the "sack of Lawrence" in 1856, led a raid against a federal arsenal at Harpers Ferry, Virginia, in 1859 in the vain hope of sparking a slave revolt, he brought the frustrations of both sides of the sectional conflict to a head. The presidential election campaign of 1860 began before the uproar over the raid had subsided. In the course of that contest, one of the last nationally unifying institutions, the Democratic party, broke apart. The election of Abraham Lincoln, an avowedly sectional candidate, triggered a crisis that defied peaceful resolution.

Although the crisis spiraled into a civil war, this outcome did not signal the triumph of sectionalism over nationalism. Ironically, in defending their stands, both sides appealed to time-honored nationalist and democratic sentiments. Southern secessionists believed they were the true keepers of the ideals that had inspired the American Revolution. They were merely re-creating a more perfect Union. It was not

they, but the Republicans, who had sundered the old Union by subverting the Constitution's guarantee of liberty. Lincoln similarly appealed to nationalist themes, telling Northerners that the United States was "the last best hope on earth."

Northerners and Southerners both appealed to nationalism and democracy but applied different meanings to those concepts. These differences underscored how far apart the sections had grown. When Southerners and Northerners looked at each other, they no longer saw fellow Americans; they saw enemies.

NORTH–SOUTH DIFFERENCES

Behind the ideological divide that separated North and South lay real and growing social and economic differences (see the Overview table, "South and North Compared in 1860"). As the North became increasingly urban and industrial, the South remained primarily rural and agricultural. The urban population of the free states increased from 10 to 26 percent between 1820 and 1860. In the South, in the same period, it increased only from 5 to 10 percent. Likewise the proportion of the northern work force in agriculture declined from 68 percent to 40 percent between 1800 and 1860, whereas in the South it increased from 82 percent to 84 percent. Northern farmers made up for the decline in farm workers by relying on machinery instead. In 1860, the free states had twice the value of farm machinery per worker as the slave states had.

Overview

South and North Compared in 1860

	South	North
Population	Biracial; 35 percent African American	Overwhelmingly white; less than 2 percent African American
Economy	Growing though relatively undiversified; 84 percent of work force in agriculture	Developing through industrialization and urbanization; 40 percent of workforce in agriculture
Labor	Heavily dependent on slave labor, especially in Lower South	Free wage labor
Factories	15 percent of national total	85 percent of national total; concentrated in the Northeast
Railroads	Approximately ten thousand miles of track; primarily shorter lines, with fewer links to trunk lines	Approximately twenty thousand miles of track; more effectively linked in trunk lines connecting east and west
Literacy	17 percent illiteracy rate for free population	6 percent illiteracy rate

The demand for farm machinery in the North reflected growing demand for manufactured products in general. The need of city-dwellers for ready-to-wear shoes and clothing, household iron products, processed foods, homes, workplaces, and public amenities boosted industrial production in the North. In contrast, in the South, the slower rate of urbanization, the lower proportion of immigrants, and the region's labor-intensive agriculture kept industrial development modest. The proportion of manufacturing capital invested in the South declined from 31 to 16 percent between 1810 and 1860. In 1810, per capita investment in industrial enterprises was 2.5 times greater in the North than in the South; in 1860, it was 3.5 times greater.

The rate of urban and industrial growth in the North was greater than anywhere else in the world in the early nineteenth century. As a result, the South inevitably suffers by comparison. Even when compared to the West, however, the South was falling behind. The South and West had about the same levels of manufacturing investment and urban population in the 1850s, but the rate of growth was even greater in the West than in the North. What is more, a vast railroad network linked the West to the Northeast rather than the South (see Map 14–3).

More subtle distinctions between North and South became evident as well by midcentury. Southerners tended to be more violent than Northerners. The slave states had a higher homicide rate than the free states, and more Southerners carried weapons. Southern values stressed courtesy, honor, and courage. Southerners were more inclined to military service than Northerners. They had proportionately more cadets enrolled in the United States Military Academy at West Point; more than 60 percent of the volunteer soldiers for the Mexican War hailed from the South; and, excluding West Point and the Naval Academy at Annapolis,

MAP 14-3   Railroads in the United States, 1860
A vast network of railroads honeycombed the North and West by 1860. While the South made considerable progress in railroad construction during the 1850s, its lines had many different gauges, and it lacked suitable connections to the West.

seven of the nation's eight military colleges were located in the South.

The South had a high illiteracy rate, nearly three times greater than the North—eight times greater if black Southerners are included. The "ideology of literacy," as one historian called it, was not as widespread in the South as in the North. Northerners, for example, supported far more public schools and libraries than Southerners. In the South, education was barred by law to slaves and limited for most white people. Many white leaders viewed education more as a privilege for the well-to-do than a right for every citizen. A South Carolinian wrote in the 1850s that "it is better that a part should be fully and highly educated and the rest utterly ignorant."

Evangelical Protestantism attracted increasing numbers in both North and South, but its character differed in the two regions. The Methodist Church divided along sectional lines over slavery in 1844, and the Baptists split the following year. The Presbyterians splintered in 1837 over mainly doctrinal issues, but the rupture became complete in 1861. In the North, evangelical Protestants viewed social reform as a prerequisite for the Second Coming of Christ. As a result, they were in the forefront of most reform movements. Southern evangelicals generally defended slavery.

Slavery accounted for many of the differences between the North and the South. Investment in land and slaves limited investment in manufacturing. The availability of a large slave labor force reduced the need for farm machinery and limited the demand for manufactured products. Slaves were relatively immobile. They did not migrate to cities in massive numbers as did northern farmers. Nor could they quickly fill the labor demands of an expanding urban economy. Agriculture usually took precedence.

Slavery also divided northern from southern churches. And it accounted for the contrast between the inward, otherworldly emphasis of southern theology and the reformist theology of northern evangelicals. Southerners associated black slavery with white freedom; Northerners associated it with white degradation.

Slavery contributed to the South's martial tradition and its lukewarm attitude toward public education. Fully 95 percent of the nation's black population lived in the South in 1860, and 90 percent of these were slaves. As a result, the South was often a region on edge. Fearful of revolt, especially in the 1850s, when rumors of slave discontent ran rampant, white people felt compelled to maintain patrols and militias in constant readiness. The South was also determined to keep slaves as ignorant as possible. Educated slaves would be susceptible to abolitionist propaganda and more inclined to revolt.

The South's defense of slavery and the North's attack on it fostered an array of stereotypes that exaggerated the real differences between the sections. Like all stereotypes, these reduced individuals to dehumanized categories. They encouraged the people of each section to view those of the other less as fellow Americans than as aliens in their midst.

Southerners saw Northerners as crass and materialistic but themselves as generous and compassionate. Northerners saw Southerners as brutal and backward, themselves as progressive and temperate. Southerners perceived themselves as honorable and chaste and saw Northerners as corrupt and loose living. Northerners saw Southerners as perverse and lazy, themselves as righteous and hardworking. The South, according to Southerners, was the land of moonlight and magnolias (an image actually originated in the North), while the North was the region of muggings and mudslinging. Northerners saw Southerners as lords of the lash and themselves as angels of mercy.

Ironically, although slavery increasingly defined the character of the South in the 1850s, a growing majority of white Southerners did not own slaves. Slavery nonetheless implicated nonslaveholders in ways that assured their support for it. By satisfying the demand for labor on large plantations, it relieved many rural white Southerners from serving as farmhands and enabled them to work their own land. Slaveholders also recruited nonslaveholders to suppress slave violence or rebellion. It was nonslaveholders, for example, who often manned patrols and militia companies. Some nonslaveholders hoped to purchase slaves someday. Many dreamed of migrating westward to the next cotton frontier where they might find greater opportunity to own land and slaves. This dream not only bound white Southerners together on slavery but also prompted their strong support for southern access to the western territories. Finally, regardless of a white man's social or economic status, he shared an important feature with the largest slaveholder: As long as racial slavery existed, the color of his skin made him a member of a privileged class that could never be enslaved.

While white Southerners were more united on slavery than on other issues, their defense of slavery presented them with a major dilemma. It left them vulnerable to moral condemnation because, in the end, slavery was morally indefensible. By the 1850s, most western nations had condemned and abolished the institution. And because Northerners controlled the flow of information through the popular newspapers and the national network of communications, credit, and commerce, Southerners were likely to find themselves increasingly isolated. A minority in their own country and a lonely voice for a despised institution that was for them a significant source of wealth, Southerners were understandably jittery.

JOHN BROWN'S RAID

Shortly after he completed his mayhem at Pottawatomie Creek, John Brown left Kansas and approached several New England abolitionists for funds to continue his private war in the territory. By 1857, Brown had become a rustic celebrity in New England. He had dined at Ralph Waldo Emerson's home, had tea with Henry David Thoreau, and discussed theology with the abolitionist minister Theodore Dwight

Weld. Brown's frontier dress, rigid posture, reticent manner, and piercing eyes gave him the appearance of a biblical prophet. After several failed businesses, more than twenty lawsuits for nonpayment of debts, and a brush with horse rustling, he had at last found his life's calling: He had become a moderately successful fund-raiser for his own violent frontier exploits.

But when Brown returned to Kansas in late 1857, he discovered that peace had settled over that troubled territory. Residents now cared more about making money than about making war. Leaving Kansas for the last time, he went east with a new plan. He proposed to attack and capture the federal arsenal at Harpers Ferry, Virginia, a small town near the Maryland border. The assault, Brown imagined, would spark a slave uprising in the area, eventually spreading to the rest of the state. With funds from his New England friends, he equipped a few dozen men and hired an English army officer to train them.

When Brown outlined his scheme to Frederick Douglass, the noted black abolitionist warned him against it. But his white New England friends were less cautious, and a group of six prominent abolitionists (the "Secret Six") gave Brown additional funds for his project.

Brown and his "army" moved to a Maryland farmhouse in the summer of 1859 to train and complete planning for the raid. On the night of October 16, 1859, he and twenty-two followers captured the federal arsenal at Harpers Ferry and waited for the slaves to rally to his banner. Meanwhile, the townspeople alerted outside authorities. The Virginia militia and a detachment of United States Marines under the command of Colonel Robert E. Lee arrived and put a quick end to **John Brown's Raid**. They wounded Brown and killed or captured most of his force.

Brown had launched the operation without provisions and at a site from which escape was impossible. Although the primary goal of the attack had been to inspire a slave insurrection, no one had bothered to inform the local slaves. And despite the secret nature of the expedition, Brown had left behind a mountain of documents at the Maryland farmhouse. He had tried to conquer the state of Virginia with twenty-two men and an ill-conceived plan. Was he crazy? As the *Boston Post* editorialized after the raid, "John Brown may be a lunatic, [but if so] then one-fourth of the people of Massachusetts are madmen."

Although the *Post* may have exaggerated, the editorial reflected an article of faith among many abolitionists that, given the signal, slaves would immediately throw off their chains, slaughter their masters, and join a rebellion. But even those slaves in the area who knew of the raid understood the odds against Brown

JOHN BROWN AT HARPER'S FERRY.

John Brown's ill-planned raid at Harpers Ferry, Virginia, nears its desperate end as the trapped abolitionist and his supporters fall to a contingent of U.S. Marines led by Colonel Robert E. Lee, October 18, 1859.

and had the good sense not to join him. As Abraham Lincoln observed, "It was not a slave insurrection. It was an attempt by white men to get up a revolt among slaves, in which the slaves refused to participate."

The raid, though foolish and unsuccessful, played on Southerners' worst fears of slave rebellion, adding a new dimension: Here was an attack engineered not from within the South but from the North. Some southern white people may have dismissed the ability or even the desire of slaves to mount revolts on their own, but they less easily dismissed the potential impact of outside white agitators.

The state of Virginia tried Brown on the charge of treason to the state. Brown, recovering from his wounds, attended most of the trial on a stretcher. The trial was swift but fair. The jury sentenced Brown to hang. Throughout his brief imprisonment and trial, Brown maintained a quiet dignity that impressed even his jailers. The governor of Virginia spoke admiringly of him as "a man of clear head, of courage, fortitude, and simple ingenuousness." Speaking to the court after his sentencing, Brown suggested that he was God's agent in a holy war: "I believe that to have interfered as I have done . . . in behalf of [God's] despised poor, is no wrong, but right. Now, if it is deemed necessary that I should forfeit my life for the furtherance of the ends of justice, and mingle my blood further with the blood of my children and with the blood of millions in this slave country whose rights are disregarded by wicked, cruel, and unjust enactments, I say, let it be done."

Some Northerners compared Brown's execution with the death of a religious martyr. The abolitionist William Lloyd Garrison asked readers of *The Liberator* to "let the day of [Brown's] execution . . . be the occasion of such a public moral demonstration against the bloody and merciless slave system as the land has never witnessed." When the state of Virginia hanged Brown, church bells tolled across the North. Thoreau compared Brown with Jesus and called the abolitionist "an angel of light." Emerson observed that Brown would "make the gallows glorious like the cross." Writing to Margaretta Mason, wife of the Virginia senator James M. Mason, abolitionist Lydia Maria Child asserted that "in this enlightened age, all despotisms ought to come to an end by the agency of moral and rational means. But if they resist such agencies, it is in the order of Providence that they must come to an end by violence." Most Northerners, however, including many Republicans, had condemned the raid. Still, the dignity of Brown's death touched many. Condemning the deed, they nevertheless embraced the cause.

The outpouring of northern grief over Brown's death convinced white Southerners that the threat to their security was not over. The discovery of Brown's correspondence at his Maryland farmhouse further fueled southern rancor, and Southerners increasingly ceased to believe northern disclaimers about the raid. Senator Mason asserted in Congress that "John Brown's invasion was condemned [in the North] only because it failed." Several members of the Secret Six had ties to the Republican party, and Southerners targeted them for special censure. Mississippi senator Jefferson Davis remarked that the Republican party "was organized on the basis of making war" against the South.

John Brown's Raid significantly changed southern public opinion. However much they defended slavery, most Southerners were for the Union. The northern reaction to John Brown's trial and death, however, troubled them. The *Richmond Whig*, a newspaper that had reflected moderate Upper South opinion for decades, observed in early 1860 that "recent events have wrought almost a complete revolution in the sentiments, the thoughts, the hopes, of the oldest and steadiest conservatives in all the southern states. . . . There are thousands upon . . . thousands of men in our midst who, a month ago, scoffed at the idea of a dissolution of the Union as a madman's dream, but who now hold the opinion that its days are numbered, its glory perished."

It was one thing to condemn slavery in the territories but another to attack it violently where it was long established. Southerners now saw in the Republican party the embodiment of John Brown's ideals and actions. So, in their view, the election of a Republican president would be a death sentence for the South.

The impact of this shifting sentiment was immediately apparent in Congress when it reconvened three days after Virginia hanged Brown. Debate quickly turned tense and ugly. South Carolina Senator James H. Hammond captured the mood well, when he remarked of his colleagues on the Senate floor that "the only persons who do not have a revolver and a knife are those who have two revolvers." The southern and northern wings of the Democratic party were now almost totally estranged. Southern Democrats seemed concerned only to promote an extreme proslavery agenda rather than to initiate real legislation.

THE ELECTION OF 1860

An atmosphere of mutual sectional distrust and animosity characterized the campaign for the presidential election of 1860. In April, the Democratic party, the sole surviving national political organization, held its convention in Charleston, South Carolina. The location was not conducive to sectional reconciliation. The city had been a hotbed of nullification sentiment during the 1830s, and talk of disunion had surfaced periodically ever since, especially in the influential *Charleston Mercury*, edited by Robert Barnwell Rhett. At the convention, Charlestonians packed the galleries and cheered for their favorite extremists.

Northern Democrats arrived in Charleston united behind Stephen A. Douglas. Although they constituted a majority of the delegates, they could not muster the two-thirds majority vote necessary to nominate their candidate. Other issues, however, were decided on a simple majority vote, permitting northern Democrats to defeat a platform proposal for a federal slave code in the territories.

Southern extremists who favored secession hoped to disrupt the convention and divide the party. They reasoned that the Republicans would then win the presidency, providing the South with the justification to secede. The platform vote gave them the opportunity they were seeking. Accompanied by spectators' cheers, delegates from five Lower South states—South Carolina, Florida, Mississippi, Louisiana, and Texas—walked out. The Arkansas and Georgia delegations joined them the following day.

Still without a nominee, the Democrats agreed to reconvene in Baltimore in June. This time, the Upper South delegations marched out when Douglas Democrats, in a commanding majority, refused to seat the Lower South delegations that had walked out in Charleston. The remaining delegates nominated

Douglas for president. The bolters, who included almost all southern delegates plus a few Northerners loyal to President Buchanan, met in another hall and nominated John C. Breckinridge of Kentucky.

The disintegration of the national Democratic party alarmed those Southerners who understood that it would insure the election of a Republican president in November. The *Memphis Appeal* warned that "the odium of the Black-Republican party has been that it is *Sectional*." Should Southerners now allow a group of "restless and reckless or misguided men to destroy the national Democratic party?" the *Appeal* asked. Its emphatic answer was, "No!"

The *Appeal* reflected the sentiment of many former Whigs, mainly from the Upper South, who would not support Breckinridge and could not support Douglas. Together with Whig allies in the North who had not defected to the Republican party, they met in Baltimore in May 1860 to form the **Constitutional Union Party** and nominated John Bell of Tennessee for president.

Sensing victory, the Republicans convened in Chicago. If they could hold the states won by Frémont in 1856, add Minnesota (a new Republican-leaning state), and win Pennsylvania and one of three other Lower North states—Illinois, Indiana, or New Jersey—their candidate would win. These calculations dictated a platform and a candidate who could appeal to the four Lower North swing states, where antislavery sentiment was not so strong.

The issue of slavery in the territories had dominated the Republicans' 1856 platform. Now they embraced other issues as well, presenting themselves as the party of sound economy, business, and industry. Delegates enthusiastically cheered a tariff plank calling for the protection of American industry.

In selecting an appropriate presidential nominee, the Republicans faced a dilemma. Senator William H. Seward came to Chicago as the leading Republican candidate. But his immoderate condemnation of Southerners and slavery made moderate northern voters wary of him, and these were precisely the voters the party needed for victory.

Reservations about Seward benefited Abraham Lincoln. A year after his losing 1858 Senate campaign, he had embarked on a speaking tour of the East at the invitation of influential newspaper editor Horace Greeley. Lincoln's lieutenants at the convention stressed their candidate's moderation and morality, distancing him from both the abolitionists and Seward. Moreover, Chicago was Lincoln's home turf, and he had many friends working for him at the convention. When Seward faltered, Lincoln rose and won the Republican nomination.

True to their Whig heritage, the Republicans staged a colorful campaign, featuring drill teams as well as organized groups of young men called the **Wide Awakes**, outfitted in flowing black oilcloth capes. Douglas supporters countered by enrolling teams of "Little Giants." Breckinridge and Bell followed suit, and soon large groups of young men were marching all over the country in support of one candidate or another. The theme was political, but the atmosphere was an odd mix of military parade and religious revival.

The presidential campaign of 1860 actually comprised two campaigns. In the South, the contest was between Breckinridge and Bell; in the North, it was Lincoln against Douglas. Breckinridge and Bell had scattered support in the North, as did Douglas in the South, but in the main this was a sectional election. Lincoln did not even appear on the ballot in most southern states.

Lincoln's strategy was to say practically nothing. He spent the entire campaign in Springfield, Illinois. When he did speak, it was to a reporter or friends, but not in a public forum. He discounted southern threats of disunion if he were to become president. Other Republicans dismissed southern talk of secession as well. Republican leaders thought the South too fragmented to unite behind a move as drastic as disunion. "The South," Greeley wrote dismissively, "could no more unite upon a scheme of secession than a company of lunatics could conspire to break out of bedlam."

Douglas campaigned hard, trying to convince the electorate that the Union hung in the balance. Breckinridge, like Lincoln in the North, sought to assure voters that he was not the disunion candidate. And Bell ran a low-key campaign, venturing out of Tennessee infrequently. He reiterated his support of the Constitution and the Union but said little else.

In those days, states held gubernatorial elections on different days, even in different months, from the national presidential election. When, in mid-October, Republicans had swept the statehouses in two crucial states—Pennsylvania and Indiana—Douglas made an extraordinary decision, but one consistent with his ardent nationalism. He abandoned his campaign and headed south at great personal peril to urge Southerners to remain in the Union now that Lincoln's election was inevitable.

Lincoln became the nation's sixteenth president, with 40 percent of the popular vote (see Map 14–4). Bell won the three Upper South states of Virginia, Kentucky, and Tennessee. Douglas, though second

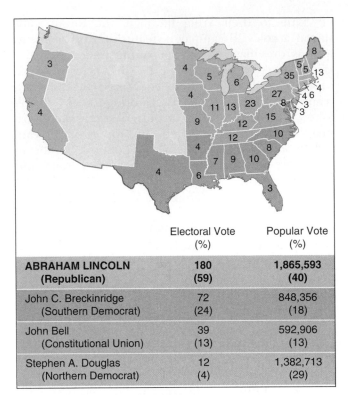

	Electoral Vote (%)	Popular Vote (%)
ABRAHAM LINCOLN (Republican)	**180 (59)**	**1,865,593 (40)**
John C. Breckinridge (Southern Democrat)	72 (24)	848,356 (18)
John Bell (Constitutional Union)	39 (13)	592,906 (13)
Stephen A. Douglas (Northern Democrat)	12 (4)	1,382,713 (29)

MAP 14-4   **The Election of 1860**
The election returns from 1860 vividly illustrate the geography of sectionalism.

after Lincoln in the popular balloting, won the undivided electoral vote of only one state, Missouri.

Lincoln took most northern states by significant margins and won all the region's electoral votes except three in New Jersey. This gave him a substantial majority of 180 electoral votes. Breckinridge won eleven southern states but received a majority of the popular vote cast in just four. In the South as a whole, his opponents, Bell and Douglas, together reaped 55 percent of the popular vote, confirming Republicans' skepticism about southern determination to secede.

The urban vote in the 1860 election is intriguing. Lincoln fared worst in the larger cities of the North, and urban voters drubbed Breckinridge in the South. City-dwellers tended to vote for the centrist candidates, Douglas and Bell. The close commercial ties of North and South, the tendency of immigrants in northern cities to vote Democratic, and the concern of affluent urban residents that disunion could bring economic uncertainty motivated their votes. The owners of large plantations in the South similarly had a strong economic interest in preserving the Union and tended to vote for the southern centrist, Bell. But the United States was still a nation mostly of farms and small towns,

and rural communities returned strong majorities for Lincoln in the North and Breckinridge in the South.

SECESSION BEGINS

The events following Lincoln's election demonstrated how wildly mistaken were those who dismissed southern threats of secession. Four days after Lincoln's victory, the South Carolina legislature called on the state's citizens to elect delegates to a convention to consider secession. Meeting on December 20, the delegates voted unanimously to leave the Union. By February 1, six other states—Mississippi, Florida, Alabama, Georgia, Louisiana, and Texas—had all held similar conventions and decided to leave the Union (see Map 14–5). Representatives from the seven seceding states met to form a separate country, the **Confederate States of America**. On February 18, Jefferson Davis was sworn in as its president.

Curiously, for a people trumpeting the virtues of democratic government, no seceding state submitted its secession ordinance for popular referendum. Further, though subsequent generations of white southerners would dwell on states' rights as the precipitating cause of secession, leaders of the new Confederate nation emphasized slavery as the state right most valued. A month after the formation of the Confederacy, Alexander H. Stephens of Georgia, vice president of the new government, praised the just-framed Confederate Constitution in the following words:

> [T]he new Constitution has put at rest forever all the agitating questions relating to our peculiar institution—African slavery as it exists amongst us—the proper status of the negro in our form of civilization. This was the immediate cause of the late rupture and present revolution . . . . Our new Government'[s] . . . foundations are laid, its cornerstone rests, upon the great truth that the negro is not equal to the white man; that slavery, subordination to the superior race, is his natural and normal condition. [Applause.] This, our new Government, is the first, in the history of the world, based upon this great physical, philosophical, and moral truth.

The swiftness of secession in the Lower South obscured divisions in most states over the issue. Secessionists barely secured a majority in the Georgia and Louisiana conventions. In Mississippi, Florida, and Alabama, the secessionist majority was more comfortable, but pro-Union candidates polled a significant minority of votes. With Lincoln headed for the White House, the greatest support for secession came from large land-

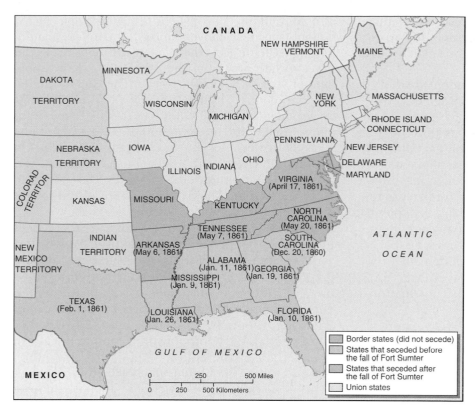

MAP 14-5   The Course of Secession
Before the firing on Fort Sumter in April 1861, the Confederacy consisted primarily of states in the Lower South. After Sumter, and after President Lincoln called upon them for troops, the Upper South states of Virginia, North Carolina, Tennessee, and Arkansas seceded.

owners in counties in which slaves comprised a majority of the population. Support for secession was weakest among small, nonslaveholding farmers.

Secessionists mounted an effective propaganda campaign, deftly using the press to convince voters to elect their delegates to the state conventions. Framing the issue as a personal challenge to every southern citizen, they argued that it would be cowardly to remain in the Union, a submission to despotism and enslavement. Southerners, they maintained, were the true heirs to the spirit of 1776. Lincoln and the Republicans were like King George III and the British—they meant to deny Southerners the right to life, liberty, and the pursuit of happiness.

Unionists, in response, could only offer voters a wait-and-see strategy. By remaining in the Union, they argued, Southerners could extract concessions from the Republicans that would protect their institutions.

PRESIDENTIAL INACTION

Because Lincoln would not take office until March 4, 1861, it was the Buchanan administration that had to cope with the secession crisis during the critical months of December and January. The president's failure to work out a solution with Congress as secession fever swept the Lower South further undermined Unionist forces in the seceding states.

When Buchanan lost the support of northern Democrats over the Lecompton Constitution, he turned to the South for support and filled his cabinet with Southerners. Now, facing the secession crisis, he proposed holding a constitutional convention to amend the Constitution in ways that would satisfy the South's demands on slavery. This outright surrender to southern demands, however, had no chance of passing in Congress.

Thereafter, Buchanan's administration quickly fell apart. As the Lower South states left the Union, their representatives and senators left Washington, and with them went Buchanan's closest advisers and key cabinet officials. Commenting on the emotionally charged atmosphere in the Senate as prominent Southerners gave their farewells and departed, one observer wrote, "There was everywhere a feeling of suspense, as if, visibly, the pillars of the temple were being withdrawn and the great Government structure was tottering."

Buchanan, a lame duck, bereft of friends and advisers, did little more than condemn secession. He was reluctant to take action that would limit the options of the incoming administration or, worse, tip the balance in the Upper South toward secession. He hoped that waiting might bring an isolated Lower South to its senses and give efforts to mediate the sectional rift a chance to succeed.

PEACE PROPOSALS

Previous sectional conflicts, dating from the Missouri Compromise of 1820, had brought forth the ingenuity and good will of political leaders to effect a compromise and draw the Union back from the brink of disintegration. Both ingenuity and good will were scarce commodities in the gray secession winter of 1860–1861. Yet, a few men believed that the opportunity, though slim, for compromise still existed. The difficulty was that the two conflicting sides had little trust of each other and the word "compromise" was viewed as more a synonym for capitulation than salvation.

Kentucky senator John J. Crittenden chaired a Senate committee that proposed a package of constitutional amendments in December 1860, designed to solve the sectional crisis. The central feature of the Crittenden Plan was the extension of the Missouri Compromise line through the territories all the way to the state of California. The plan was of marginal interest to the South, however, because it was unlikely to result in any new slave states. And Republicans opposed it because it contradicted one of their basic principles, the exclusion of slavery from the territories. Despite a flood of letters supporting the Crittenden Plan, including a petition from 38,000 citizens of New York City, Republicans successfully bottled it up in Congress and prevented action on it.

Meanwhile, ex-president John Tyler emerged from retirement to lead an effort by the border states—the Upper South and the Lower North—to forge a peace. Delegates from these states responded to Tyler's invitation and met in February 1861 at the Willard Hotel in Washington. But the plan the conference produced differed little from Crittenden's, and it, too, got nowhere in Congress.

LINCOLN'S VIEWS ON SECESSION

President-elect Lincoln monitored the secession of the Lower South states and the attempts to reach a compromise from his home in Springfield. Although he said nothing publicly, he made it known that he did not favor compromises like those proposed by Crittenden and Tyler. As he put it to a friend, "We have just carried an election on principles fairly stated to the people. Now we are told in advance, the government shall be broken up, unless we surrender to those we have beaten, before we take the offices. . . . If we surrender, it is the end of us, and of the government."

Lincoln counted on Unionist sentiment to keep the Upper South from seceding. Like Buchanan, he felt that the longer the Lower South states remained isolated, the more likely they would be to return to the fold. For a while, events seemed to bear him out. In North Carolina, the *Wilmington Herald* responded to South Carolina's secession by asking readers, "Will you suffer yourself to be spit upon in this way? Are you submissionists to the dictation of South Carolina . . . are you to be called cowards because you do not follow the crazy lead of that crazy state?"

One by one, Upper South states registered their support for the Union. North Carolinians went to the polls in February and turned down the call for a seces-

sion convention. Also in February, Virginians elected Unionists to their convention by a five-to-one margin, leading a Charleston editor to lament, "Virginia would never secede now." On the other side, a correspondent of Senator Seward rejoiced, "The Gulf Confederacy can count Virginia out of their little family arrangement—she will never join them." Tennesseans also refused to call a convention. In Missouri, not one secessionist won election to the state convention. In Kentucky, the legislature adjourned without taking any action on a convention or a statewide referendum on secession. And the Maryland legislature, already out of session, showed no inclination to reconvene.

A closer look, however, reveals that there were limits to the Upper South's Unionism. Most voters in the region went to the polls assuming that Congress would eventually reach a compromise based on the Crittenden proposals, Tyler's peace conference, or some other remedy. Leaders in the Upper South saw themselves as peacemakers. As one Virginian explained, "Without submission to the North or desertion of the South, Virginia has that moral position within the Union which will give her power to arbitrate between the sections." But what if arbitration failed? Or what if the Lower South states precipitated a crisis that forced the Upper South to choose sides? It was unlikely that the Upper South would abide the use of federal force against its southern neighbors.

Lincoln believed that the slavery issue had to come to a crisis before the nation could solve it. Although he said in public that he would never interfere with slavery in the slave states, the deep moral revulsion he felt toward the institution left him more ambivalent in private. As he confided to a colleague in 1860, "The tug has to come, and better now, than any time hereafter" (see "American Views: Lincoln on Slavery").

FORT SUMTER: THE TUG COMES

In his inaugural address on March 4, 1861, Abraham Lincoln denounced secession and vowed to uphold federal law but tempered his firmness with a conciliatory conclusion. Addressing Southerners specifically, he assured them, "We are not enemies but friends. . . . Though passion may have strained, it must not break our bonds of affection. The mystic chords of memory, stretching from every battlefield, and patriot grave, to every living heart and hearthstone, all over this broad land, will yet swell the chorus of the Union, when again touched, as surely they will be, by the better angels of our nature."

Southerners wanted concessions, not conciliation, however. The new president said nothing about slavery in the territories, nothing about constitutional

Overview

The Emerging Sectional Crisis

Event	Year	Effect
Wilmot Proviso	1846	Congressman David Wilmot's proposal to ban slavery from territories acquired from Mexico touched off a bitter sectional dispute in Congress.
Compromise of 1850	1850	Law admitted California as a free state, granted the population of Utah and New Mexico Territories the right to decide on slavery, and established a new and stronger Fugitive Slave Act, all of which "solved" the territorial issue raised by the Wilmot Proviso but satisfied neither North nor South and planted the seeds of future conflict.
Election of 1852	1852	Results confirmed demise of the Whig party, initiating a period of political realignment.
Kansas-Nebraska Act	1854	Law created the Kansas and Nebraska Territories and repealed the Missouri Compromise of 1820 by leaving the question of slavery to the territories' residents. Its passage enraged many Northerners, prompting some to form the new Republican party.
"Bleeding Kansas"	1855–1856	Sometimes violent conflict between pro- and antislavery forces in Kansas further polarized the sectional debate.
Election of 1856	1856	Presidency was won by Democrat James Buchanan of Pennsylvania, but a surprisingly strong showing by the recently formed Republican party in the North set the stage for the 1860 election.
Dred Scott Case	1857	The Supreme Court ruling that slaves were not citizens and that Congress had no authority to ban slavery from the territories boosted Republican prospects in the North.
Lecompton	1857	Proslavery document, framed by a fraudulently elected Constitution convention in Kansas and supported by President Buchanan, further convinced Northerners that the South was subverting their rights.
John Brown's Raid	1859	Unsuccessful attempt to free the South's slaves, this attack on a federal arsenal in Harpers Ferry, Virginia, increased sectional tension.
Election of 1860	1860	Republican Abraham Lincoln won a four-way race for the presidency. The last major national party, the Democrats, disintegrated. Lower South states seceded.
Fort Sumter	1861	Confederate forces attacked the fort in April 1861, Lincoln called for troops, and several Upper South states seceded. The Civil War was underway.

amendments proposed by Crittenden and Tyler, and nothing about the release of federal property in the South to the Confederacy. Even some Northerners hoping for an olive branch were disappointed. As one Ohio editor wrote, Lincoln's policies would "stain the soil and color the waters of the entire continent." But Lincoln was hoping for time—time to get the Lower South states quarreling with one another, time to allow Union sentiment to build in the Upper South,

and time to convince Northerners that the Union needed preserving. He did not get that time.

One day after Lincoln's inauguration, Major Robert Anderson (like Lincoln, a native Kentuckian), the commander of **Fort Sumter** in Charleston harbor, informed the administration that he had only four to six weeks' worth of provisions left. Sumter was one of three southern forts still under federal control. Confederate batteries had ringed the fort, and Anderson

AMERICAN VIEWS

Lincoln on Slavery

In the weeks after the 1860 election, northern and southern leaders sought out President-elect Abraham Lincoln for his views on slavery. Yet, Lincoln had spoken often on the institution in the years immediately preceding the election. His speech two years earlier, excerpted here, offered an unequivocal statement of Lincoln's moral and philosophical opposition to slavery. Implied in that speech was the fact that the contradiction between American ideals and slavery could not be brokered, compromised, or ignored.

- How do Lincoln's actions from his election in November 1860 to the firing on Fort Sumter in April 1861 reflect the principles enunciated in his Springfield address?

- The two letters, one to fellow Illinois Republican Lyman Trumbull and the other to Virginia Democrat John A. Gilmer, indicate Lincoln's firm opposition to the extension of slavery into the territories. Are they consistent with the views expressed in Springfield two years earlier?

- Despite the difference in tone, do you think the letters both say essentially the same thing?

Speech of Hon. Abraham Lincoln
  Springfield, Illinois, June 17, 1858
We are now far into the fifth year since policy was initiated with the avowed object and confident promise of putting an end to slavery agitation. Under the operation of that policy, that agitation has not only not ceased, but has constantly augmented. In my opinion, it will not cease until a crisis shall have been reached and passed. "A house divided against itself can-

---

estimated that only a force of at least twenty thousand troops could run the gauntlet and provision and defend the fort. Anderson assumed that Lincoln would understand the hopeless arithmetic and order him to evacuate Fort Sumter. The commanding general of the army, Winfield Scott, advised the president accordingly, as did many members of his cabinet. Lincoln stalled.

News of Anderson's plight changed the mood in the North. The Slave Power, some said, was holding him and his men hostage. Frustration grew over Lincoln's silence and inaction. The Confederacy's bold resolve seemed to contrast sharply with the federal government's confusion and inertia. "The bird of our country," cracked New York diarist George Templeton Strong, "is a debilitated chicken, disguised in eagle feathers . . . . We are a weak, divided, disgraced people unable to maintain our institutional existence."

By the end of March, nearly a month after Anderson had informed Lincoln of the situation at Fort Sumter, the president finally moved. By this time, northern public opinion and Lincoln's cabinet (with Secretary of State Seward a notable exception) favored an effort to provision Major Anderson.

Seward made a last, desperate attempt to avert armed conflict by drawing on the reservoir of common American nationalism. He suggested that Lincoln trump up charges of Spanish and French aggression in the Caribbean and convene Congress to declare war. Seward hoped that his absurd plan would draw seceding states back into the Union to make common cause against Spain and France. Lincoln politely rejected the advice and ordered an expedition to provision Fort Sumter.

The president still hoped to avoid a confrontation. He did not send the troops that Anderson had not stand." I believe this government cannot endure permanently half slave and half free. I do not expect the Union to be dissolved; I do not expect the house to fall; but I do expect it will cease to be divided. It will become all one thing, or the other . . . . So I say in relation to the principle that all men are created equal, let it be as nearly reached as we can. If we cannot give freedom to every creature, let us do nothing that will impose slavery upon any other creature . . . . I leave you, hoping that the lamp of liberty will burn in your bosoms until there shall no longer be a doubt that all men are created free and equal.

Springfield, Ills. Dec. 10, 1860
Hon. L. Trumbull

My dear Sir: Let there be no compromise on the question of extending slavery. If there be, all our labor is lost, and ere long, must be done again. The dangerous ground—that into which some of our friends have a hankering to run—is Pop[ular] Sov[ereignty]. Have none of it. Stand firm. The tug has to come, & better now, than any time hereafter. Yours as ever,
A. Lincoln

Springfield, Ill. Dec. 15, 1860
Hon. John A. Gilmer:

My dear Sir: . . . I have no thought of recommending the abolition of slavery in the District of Columbia, nor the slave trade among the slave states . . . and if I were to make such recommendation, it is quite clear Congress would not follow it. As to the use of patronage in the slave states, where there are few or no Republicans, I do not expect to inquire for the politics of the appointee, or whether he does or not own slaves . . . . In one word, I never have been, am not now, and probably never shall be, in a mood of harassing the people, either North or South. On the territorial question, I am inflexible . . . . On that, there is a difference between you and us; and it is the only substantial difference. You think slavery is right and ought to be extended; we think it is wrong and ought to be restricted. For this, neither has any just occasion to be angry with the other.
Your obt. Servt.
A. Lincoln

Source: John G. Nicolay and John Hay, eds., *Works of Abraham Lincoln, vol. 6* (New York, Century Co.,1905).

requested. Instead he ordered unarmed boats to proceed to the fort, deliver the provisions, and leave. Only if the Confederates fired on them were they to force their way into the fort with the help of armed reinforcements. Lincoln notified South Carolina authorities that he intended to do nothing more than "feed the hungry."

At Charleston, Confederate general P.G.T. Beauregard had standing orders to turn back any relief expedition. But President Davis wanted to take Sumter before the provisions arrived to avoid fighting Anderson and the reinforcements at the same time. He also realized that the outbreak of fighting could compel the Upper South to join the Confederacy. But his impatience to force the issue placed the Confederacy in the position of firing, unprovoked, on the American flag and at a man who had become a national hero.

On April 10, Davis ordered Beauregard to demand the immediate evacuation of Fort Sumter. Anderson refused but wondered what the hurry was, considering that his provisions would run out in a few days. The remark gave Beauregard pause and prompted additional negotiations. Anderson did not yield, and before dawn on April 12, 1861, the first Confederate shell whistled down on the fort. After more than a day of shelling, during which more than five thousand artillery rounds struck Fort Sumter, Anderson surrendered. Remarkably, neither side suffered any casualties, a deceptive beginning to an exceptionally bloody war.

When the verdict of Fort Sumter reached President Lincoln, he called on the southern states still in the Union to send troops to put down the rebellion. Refusing to make war on South Carolina, the Upper South states of Virginia, North Carolina, Tennessee,

FROM THEN TO NOW

Religion and Politics

When evangelical Protestantism first emerged in the late eighteenth century, its adherents advocated the separation of church and state. By the 1850s, however, the social landscape of America had changed. A wave of immigrants, many of them Roman Catholic, threatened Protestant dominance. Growing cities and rapid technological and economic change strained the traditional moral and social order. Alarmed by these changes, evangelicals entered the political arena. Their convictions, as we saw in Chapter 12, helped drive the antebellum reform movement.

The give and take of politics, however, posed a challenge to the evangelical belief in an absolute truth grounded in the Bible. Eventually the two great evangelical crusades of the 1850s—anti-Catholicism and abolitionism—were subsumed within the Republican Party. And after the Civil War, the Republican Party gradually lost its radical fervor.

By the twentieth century, the evangelical movement had begun to turn away from politics and revert to its traditional focus on saving souls. In 1950, Jerry Falwell, an emerging evangelical leader, declared himself "a soul-winner and a separatist," meaning he wanted little involvement with society at large, much less with politics. But then came the upheavals of the 1960s and 1970s that challenged traditional morality and authority, including the Supreme Court's decision in *Roe v. Wade* to legalize abortion. In addition, the Internal Revenue Service began questioning the tax-exempt status of various religious groups. Once again, a changing social landscape compelled evangelicals to enter the political arena, this time to defend themselves against what they perceived to be an encroaching government. Organizations emerged to mobilize evangelical voters, including Jerry Falwell's Moral Majority in the late 1970s and Pat Robertson's Christian Coalition in 1989.

In the 1850s the Northeast was the center of evangelical politics. Now evangelical political organizations speak with a mostly Southern accent. In the 1850s opposition to slavery was the focus

and Arkansas seceded, and the Confederacy expanded to eleven states.

CONCLUSION

When David Wilmot submitted his amendment to ban slavery from the territories gained from Mexico, he could not have foreseen that the debate he unleashed would end in civil war just fifteen years later. Northerners and Southerners had lived together in one nation for nearly eighty years. During that time, they had reached accommodations on slavery at the Constitutional Convention of 1787, in the Compromises of 1820 and 1850, and on numerous lesser occasions. But they could not reach agreement during the 1850s. By that time, the slavery issue had become weighted with so much moral and political freight that it defied easy resolution. Throughout the Western world, attitudes toward slavery were changing. Northern evangelical Protestants in the 1840s and 1850s branded slavery a sin and slaveholders sinners. The overwhelming popularity of *Uncle Tom's Cabin* both tapped and fed this sentiment.

Political conflict over slavery coalesced around northern efforts to curtail southern expansion and power and southern attempts to maintain their power and influence in the federal government by planting the institution in the western territories. This conflict eventually helped undo the Compromise of 1850 and turned Stephen A. Douglas's railroad bill into a battle royal over Kansas. Unable to resolve sectional differences over slavery, the Whigs disintegrated, and the Democrats divided into northern and southern factions. The Republican party formed from the political debris. Ethnic and religious conflicts further disturbed the political landscape and contributed to party realignment.

Northerners and Southerners eventually interpreted any incident or piece of legislation as an attempt of evangelical politics. Now it is opposition to abortion and other social issues that have risen to prominence with the end of the Cold War and the nation's growing prosperity. Evangelical activists have once again found a home in the Republican Party. The Democrats, they believe, are too permissive and too committed to abortion rights, just as nineteenth century Democrats had been committed to the defense of slavery.

And again, as in the 1850s, evangelical involvement has heated political discourse with the language of righteousness. In 1992, Randall Terry, founder of Operation Rescue, a militant antiabortion organization, wrote in his newsletter that "to vote for Bill Clinton is to sin against God." In a similar if more flowery declaration, a New England evangelical journal proclaimed the 1856 presidential contest a choice between "the bloodstained ticket of the Democratic party, responsible for the murder of your brothers and mine on the plains of Kansas," and a Republican ticket designated by "the God of peace and purity as the one that shall smile upon you."

Most Americans today, as in the 1850s, recoil from the overt intrusion of religion into politics, and groups like the Christian Coalition have had only limited success in electing their favored candidates. Despite these disappointments, they have been as wary of compromise as their nineteenth-century predecessors. As one evangelical leader explained in 1999: "I would rather go to bed with a clear conscience after losing."

But if evangelical political organizations cannot gain control of Congress and the presidency, it is unlikely that their social agenda—which, in addition to antiabortion legislation, includes prayer in school, the posting of the Ten Commandments in public places, and laws restricting the rights of homosexuals—will be enacted. Today, some evangelical strategists call for a "popular front" approach, allying themselves with candidates not openly associated with the evangelical agenda. Abolitionists in the 1850s faced the same quandary between ideological purity and political pragmatism. Their support of Abraham Lincoln in 1860 reflected a bow toward pragmatism, a course that ultimately proved successful for their cause, but not without a bloody civil war.

by one side to gain moral and political advantage at the other's expense. Northerners viewed the Dred Scott decision, the Lecompton Constitution, and the southern reaction to John Brown's Raid as evidence of a Slave Power conspiracy to deny white Northerners their constitutional rights. Southerners interpreted northern reaction to these same events as evidence of a conspiracy to rob them of security and equality within the Union.

By 1861, the national political parties that had muted sectional animosities were gone, and so were national church organizations and fraternal associations. The ideals that had inspired the American Revolution remained in place, especially the importance of securing individual liberty against encroachment by government. But with each side interpreting them differently, these ideals served more to divide than to unite. Southerners viewed the North in general and the Republican party in particular as threats to their individual liberties. Lincoln's victory, they believed, robbed the na-

tional government of its traditional role as "a disinterested and dispassionate umpire." Northerners believed that the South was conspiring to rob them of their individual rights as well and that only a redeemed federal government stood between their freedom and the despotism of the Slave Power. Both sides claimed for themselves the role of guardian of the Revolutionary tradition. Lincoln's election left Northerners feeling vindicated and Southerners feeling vulnerable.

Ironically, as Americans in both sections talked of freedom and self-determination, the black men and women in their midst had little of either. Lincoln went to war to preserve the Union; Davis, to defend a new nation. Slavery was the spark that ignited the conflict, but white America seemed more comfortable embracing abstract ideals than real people. Northerners and Southerners would confront this irony during the bloodiest war in American history—but they would not resolve it.

REVIEW QUESTIONS

1. How do you account for the great success of Harriet Beecher Stowe's *Uncle Tom's Cabin*?

2. If you were a Democratic representative from your state to the U.S. Congress in 1854, what would your position be on the Kansas-Nebraska Bill? What if you were a Whig?

3. Discuss the role of evangelical religion in sharpening the sectional conflict between North and South.

4. Between the time he was elected president in November and his inauguration in March, what options did Abraham Lincoln have for resolving the sectional crisis?

5. Northerners and Southerners appealed to the same American ideals in support of their respective positions. Could they both have been correct?

KEY TERMS

"Bleeding Kansas" (p. 430)

Compromise of 1850 (p. 423)

Confederate States of America (p. 442)

Constitutional Union Party (p. 441)

Dred Scott Decision (p. 433)

Fort Sumter (p. 445)

Fugitive Slave Act (p. 423)

John Brown's Raid (p. 439)

Kansas-Nebraska Act (p. 429)

Know-Nothing Party (p. 431)

Lecompton Constitution (p. 434)

Lincoln-Douglas debates (p. 434)

Panic of 1857 (p. 434)

Popular Sovereignty (p. 420)

Republican Party (p. 431)

"Sack of Lawrence" (p. 430)

Wide Awakes (p. 441)

Wilmot Proviso (p. 419)

RECOMMENDED READING

Freehling, William W. *The Road to Disunion, Vol. 1: Secessionists at Bay, 1776–1854* (1990). A detailed and lively treatment of events and personalities in the years leading up to passage of the Kansas-Nebraska Act.

Potter, David M. *The Impending Crisis, 1848–1861* (1976). Remains the most comprehensive analysis of the coming of the war; a balanced account that is especially strong on political events.

Stowe, Harriet Beecher. *Uncle Tom's Cabin* (1852; reprint edition 1982, with notes by Kathryn Kish Sklar). Reading this book is essential for understanding why and how it generated so much controversy and intensified sectional antagonisms in the early 1850s.

ADDITIONAL SOURCES

Slavery in the Territories

Berwanger, Eugene H. *The Frontier against Slavery: Western Anti-Negro Prejudice and the Slavery Extension Controversy* (1967).

Hamilton, Holman. *Prologue to Conflict: The Crisis and Compromise of 1850* (1966).

Hedrick, Joan D. *Harriet Beecher Stowe: A Life* (1993).

Johnson, Susan Lee. *Roaring Camp: The Social World of the California Gold Rush* (2000).

May, Robert E. *The Southern Dream of a Caribbean Empire, 1854–1861* (1973).

Morrison, Michael E. *Slavery and the American West: The Eclipse of Manifest Destiny and the Coming of the Civil War* (1997).

Peterson, Merrill. *The Great Triumvirate: Webster, Clay, and Calhoun* (1987).

Quarles, Benjamin. *Black Abolitionists* (1969).

Rohrbough, Malcolm J. *Days of Gold: The California Gold Rush and the American Nation* (1997).

Political Realignment

Anbinder, Tyler. *Nativism and Slavery: The Northern Know-Nothings and the Politics of the 1850s* (1992).

Carwardine, Richard J. *Evangelicals and Politics in Antebellum America* (1993).

Cooper, William J., Jr. *The South and the Politics of Slavery, 1828–1856* (1978).

Fehrenbacher, Don E. *Slavery, Law, and Politics: The Dred Scott Case in Historical Perspective* (1981).

Foner, Eric. *Free Soil, Free Labor, Free Men: The Ideology of the Republican Party before the Civil War* (1970).

Gienapp, William. *Origins of the Republican Party, 1852–1856* (1987).

Holt, Michael F. *The Political Crisis of the 1850s* (1978).

Howe, Daniel Walker. "The Evangelical Movement and Political Culture in the North during the Second Party System," *Journal of American History,* 77 (March 1991): 1216–1239.

Johannsen, Robert W. *The Frontier, the Union, and Stephen A. Douglas* (1989).

Johannsen, Robert W. ed. *The Lincoln–Douglas Debates of 1858* (1965).

Long, Kathryn Teresa. *The Revival of 1857–58: Interpreting an American Religious Awakening* (1998).

SenGupta, Ganja. *For God and Mammon: Evangelicals and Entrepreneurs, Masters and Slaves in Territorial Kansas, 1854–1860* (1996).

Rawley, James A. *Race and Politics: "Bleeding Kansas" and the Coming of the Civil War* (1969).

von Frank, Albert J. *The Trials of Anthony Burns: Freedom and Slavery in Emerson's Boston* (1998).

Wolff, Gerald W. *The Kansas-Nebraska Bill: Party, Section, and the Coming of the Civil War* (1977).

The Road to Disunion

Banks, Russell. *Cloudsplitter* (1997).

Barney, William L. *The Road to Secession: A New Perspective on the Old South* (1972).

Craven, Avery. *The Growth of Southern Nationalism, 1848–1861* (1953).

Crofts, Daniel W. *Reluctant Confederates: Upper South Unionists in the Secession Crisis* (1989).

Current, Richard N. *Lincoln and the First Shot* (1963).

Dew, Charles B. *Apostles of Disunion: Southern Secession Commissioners and the Causes of the Civil War* (2001).

Johnson, Michael P., and James L. Roark, eds. *No Chariot Let Down: Charleston's Free People of Color on the Eve of the Civil War* (1984).

McCardell, John. *The Idea of a Southern Nation: Southern Nationalists and Southern Nationalism, 1830–1860* (1979).

McPherson, James M. "Antebellum Southern Exceptionalism: A New Look at an Old Question," *Civil War History,* 29 (September 1983): 230–244.

Snay, Michael. *Gospel of Disunion: Religion and Separatism in the Antebellum South* (1993).

Stampp, Kenneth M. *America in 1857: A Nation on the Brink* (1990).

Walther, Eric H. *The Fire-Eaters* (1992).

WHERE TO LEARN MORE

- The Underground Railroad Freedom Center, Cincinnati, Ohio. The Center provides information on the Northern response to the Fugitive Slave Act. www.undergroundrailroad.org.

- Adair Cabin and John Brown Museum, John Brown Memorial Park, Osawatomie, Kansas. Maintained by the Kansas Historical Society, the cabin (which once belonged to John Brown's sister) and the museum are located on the site of the Battle of Osawatomie, one of the critical events of "Bleeding Kansas." www.kshs.org/places/adair.htm.

- Constitution Hall, Lecompton, Kansas. This site, also run by the Kansas State Historical Society, is where proslavery delegates framed the controversial Lecompton Constitution that increased sectional discord. www.kshs.org/places/constit.htm.

- Harpers Ferry National Historical Park, West Virginia. Exhibits interpret John Brown's Raid and re-create some of the atmosphere and structures of the 1850s village and the federal arsenal. www.nps.gov/hafe.

- "A House Divided," mounted by the Chicago Historical Society, Chicago. This exhibit depicts the major events of the sectional crisis during the 1850s, the election of 1860, and the coming of the Civil War. It continued until 2001. www.chicagohs.org.

- Fort Sumter National Monument, Charleston, South Carolina. This historic site interprets the bombardment of the fort and the events that immediately preceded the Civil War. www.nps.gov/fosu.

 Please refer to the document CD-ROM for primary sources related to this chapter.

→ *Awaiting combat, 1861: Union Soldiers from New York relax at camp awaiting orders to move to the front. The young men show great confidence and determination for their coming engagements, though one fellow to the left of the tent, perhaps a teenager far from home, seems to long for something as he stares beyond the camera. At this early stage of the war, a combination of romance and apprehension enveloped these hopeful recruits. Note also the young African American with a broom sitting apart from the soldiers.*

BATTLE CRIES AND FREEDOM SONGS
THE CIVIL WAR 1861–1865

15

July 14, 1861
Camp Clark, Washington, DC

My very dear Sarah:

The indications are very strong that we shall move in a few days—perhaps tomorrow. And lest I should not be able to write you again I feel impelled to write a few lines that may fall under your eye when I am no more. Our movement may be one of a few days' duration and be full of pleasure. And it may be one of severe conflict and death to me. "Not my will but thine o God be done." If it is necessary that I should fall on the battle-field for my Country I am ready. I have no misgivings about, or lack of confidence in the cause in which I am engaged, and my courage does not halt or falter. I know how American Civilization now leans upon the triumph of the government and how great a debt we owe to those who went before us through the blood and suffering of the Revolution. And I am willing—perfectly willing—to lay down all my joys in this life, to help maintain this government, and to pay that debt. But my dear wife, when I know that with my own joys I lay down nearly all of yours, and replace them in this life with cares and sorrows, when after having eaten for long years the bitter fruit of orphanage myself, I must offer it as the only sustenance to my dear little children, is it weak or dishonorable that while the banner of my purpose floats calmly and

CHAPTER OUTLINE

Mobilization, North and South
War Fever
The North's Advantage in Resources
Leaders, Governments, and Strategies

The Early War, 1861–1862
First Bull Run
The War in the West
Reassessing the War: The Human Toll
The War in the East

Turning Points, 1862–1863
The Naval War and the Diplomatic War
Antietam
Emancipation
From Fredericksburg to Gettysburg
Vicksburg, Chattanooga, and the West

The War Transforms the North
Wartime Legislation and Politics
The Northern Economy
Northern Women and the War

The Confederacy Disintegrates
Southern Politics
The Southern Economy
Southern Women and the War

The Union Prevails, 1864–1865
Grant's Plan to End the War
The Election of 1864 and Sherman's March
The Road to Appomattox and the Death of Lincoln

Conclusion

proudly in the breeze, underneath, my unbounded love for you my darling wife and children should struggle in fierce though useless contest with my love of country? . . .

Sarah, my love for you is deathless, it seems to bind me with mighty cables that nothing but omnipotence can break; and yet my love of Country comes over me like a strong wind and bears me irresistibly with all those chains to the battle-field.

The memories of the blissful moments I have enjoyed with you come crowding over me, and I feel most deeply grateful to God and you, that I have enjoyed them for so long. And how hard it is for me to give them up and burn to ashes the hopes and future years, when, God willing, we might still have lived and loved together, and see our boys grown up to honorable manhood around us. . . . If I do not [return], my dear Sarah, never forget how much I loved you, nor that when my last breath escapes me on the battle-field, it will whisper your name.

Forgive my many faults, and the many pains I have caused you. How thoughtless, how foolish I have sometimes been! . . .

But, O Sarah, if the dead can come back to this earth and flit unseen around those they love, I shall be with you, in the gladdest days and the darkest nights . . . always, always, and if there be a soft breeze upon your cheek, it shall be my breath[;] as the cool air fans your throbbing temple, it shall be my spirit passing by. Sarah do not mourn me dead; think I am gone and wait for thee, for we shall meet again . . .

Sullivan

Sullivan Ballou to Sarah Ballou, July 14, 1861. Geoffrey C. Ward, et al., *The Civil War: An Illustrated History* (New York: Alfred A. Knopf, 1990), 82–83.

Sullivan Ballou's letter to his wife on the eve of the First Battle of Bull Run typified the sentiments of the civilian armies raised by both North and South: a clear purpose of the importance of their mission, a sense of foreboding, an appeal and acknowledgment of the guiding hand of God, and, most of all, words of love for family. Such romantic expressions were common in mid-nineteenth-century American correspondence between husband and wife, lover and loved.

Yet, the Civil War lent an urgency to such expressions. Most of the soldiers had no combat experience and, aside from some perfunctory training, knew little about military life before going into battle. Just a few months earlier, Major Sullivan Ballou of the Second Regiment, Rhode Island Volunteers, was a thirty-two-year-old attorney, having risen to the bar from a childhood of poverty. He lived a quiet life in Providence with his wife, Sarah, and their two young sons, Edgar and Willie. But the events of the 1850s stoked Ballou's interest in politics and he became a dedicated Republican and devoted supporter of Abraham Lincoln. When the war came, he did not hesitate in his responsibility to the union and what it stood for. He volunteered and was sent to Washington, D.C., to await further orders. He wrote this letter from his camp. A few days later, those orders arrived and Ballou and his company marched to Manassas, Virginia, where they engaged Confederate troops on July 21 at the First Battle of Bull Run. Sullivan Ballou was killed during the battle.

Sullivan Ballou took the ultimate journey for his beliefs and his love. The Civil War preserved the Union, abolished slavery, and killed at least 620,000 soldiers—more than in all other wars the country fought, from the Revolution to the Korean conflict, combined. To come to terms with it is to try to reconcile its great accomplishments with its awful consequences. In the spring of the war, that time of sanguine expectation in April 1861, all things seemed possible on both sides as flags waved, bands played, and politicians orated. But war is a hard thing, and Union and freedom came at a dear price. We are still paying off its legacy.

When the war began, only a small minority of Northerners linked the preservation of the Union with the abolition of slavery. By 1863, Union and freedom had become inseparable Federal objectives. The Confederacy fought for independence and the preservation of slavery. The Confederate objectives dictated a defensive military strategy; the Union objectives dictated an offensive strategy. But during the war's early years, both sides faced similar problems— raising an army, financing the war effort, mobilizing the civilian population, and marshaling resources. The Confederates confronted the added burden of starting a government from scratch with relatively fewer resources than the Federals.

At the end of the war's first year, the Confederacy's strong military position east of the Appalachians belied its numerical and economic inferiority. Confederate advances resulted as much from the bungling of Union commanders as from the gallant efforts of the South's own forces. By the end of 1862, Union officers had begun to expose Southern military shortcomings, and Federal officials had expanded the North's war aims to include the abolition of slavery. Within a year, the trans-Mississippi portion of the Confederacy capitulated as dissent and despair mounted on the home front. A slim victory at Gettysburg, Sherman's destructive and demoralizing march through Georgia, and the relentless assaults of new Union commander Ulysses S. Grant overwhelmed Confederate resistance and civilian hope. The North, too, suffered social and political disruption, but the marvelous elixir of battlefield victory did wonders to allay these ills.

Black Southerners seized the initiative in the war against slavery, especially in the months after the Emancipation Proclamation, eventually joining Union forces in combat against their former masters. Soon, another war to secure the fruits of freedom would begin.

KEY TOPICS

- The comparative economic and human resources of the North and South

- Confederate and Union military strategies

- Steps leading to the Emancipation Proclamation

- The impact of the war on Northern political, economic, and social life

- How military reversals affected Confederate political and economic life and civilian morale

- The meaning of the Civil War for the nation and its citizens

MOBILIZATION, NORTH AND SOUTH

Neither side was prepared for a major war. The Confederacy lacked a national army. Each Southern state had a militia, but, by the 1850s, these companies had become more social clubs than fighting units. Aside from private boats and some captured Federal vessels, the Confederacy also lacked a navy. The Union had a regular army of only sixteen thousand men, most of whom were stationed west of the Mississippi River. Their major concern had been to intervene between white settlers and Indians.

Each government augmented these meager military reserves with thousands of new recruits and developed a bureaucracy to mount a war effort. At the same time, the administrations of Presidents Lincoln and Davis secured the loyalty of their civilian populations and devised military strategies for a war of indeterminate duration. How North and South went about these tasks reflected both the different objectives of the two sides and the distinctive personalities of their leaders, Abraham Lincoln and Jefferson Davis.

WAR FEVER

The day after Major Robert Anderson surrendered Fort Sumter, President Lincoln moved to enlarge his small, scattered army by mobilizing state militias for ninety days. Four states—Virginia, Arkansas, North Carolina, and Tennessee—refused the call and seceded from the Union. About one-third of the officer corps in the regular army, including some of the

Chronology

1861 April	Confederates fire on Fort Sumter; Civil War Begins.			New York Draft Riot occurs
July	First Battle of Bull Run.			Black Troops of the 54th Massachusetts Volunteer Infantry Regiment Assault Fort Wagner outside Charleston.
1862 February	Forts Henry and Donelson fall to Union Forces.		**September**	Battle of Chickamauga.
March	Peninsula Campaign Begins.		**November**	Battle of Chattanooga.
	Battle of Glorieta Pass, New Mexico.		**1864 May**	Battle of the Wilderness.
April	Battle of Shiloh.		**June**	Battle of Cold Harbor.
	New Orleans falls to Federal Forces.		**September**	Sherman captures Atlanta.
May	Union captures Corinth, Mississippi.		**November**	President Lincoln is reelected.
July	Seven Days' Battles end.			Sherman begins his march to the sea.
	Congress passes the Confiscation Act		**1865 January**	Congress passes Thirteenth Amendment to the Constitution, outlawing slavery (ratified December 1865).
August	Second Battle of Bull Run.		**February**	Charleston surrenders.
September	Battle of Antietam.		**March**	Confederate Congress authorizes enlistment of black soldiers.
December	Battle of Fredericksburg.		**April**	Federal troops enter Richmond.
1863 January	Emancipation Proclamation takes effect.			Lee surrenders to Grant at Appomattox Court House.
May	Battle of Chancellorsville; Stonewall Jackson is mortally wounded.			Lincoln is assassinated.
July	Battle of Gettysburg.			
	Vicksburg falls to Union Forces.			

highest-ranking officers, resigned their commissions to join the Confederacy. Still, Lincoln seemed likely to meet his target of 75,000 troops.

Lincoln's modest ninety-day call-up reflected the general belief, North and South, that the war would end quickly. The *New York Times* predicted that the "local commotion" in the South would be put down "in thirty days." Some Southerners believed that the Yankees would quit after the first battle. "Just throw three or four shells among those blue-bellied Yankees," a North Carolinian blustered, "and they'll scatter like sheep." Not everyone thought the war would be brief. William T. Sherman, who had recently headed a Louisiana military academy and would become one of the Union's few great commanders, wrote in April 1861, "I think it is to be a long war—very long—much longer than any politician thinks."

Northerners closed ranks behind the president after the Confederacy's attack on Fort Sumter. Leading Democrat Stephen A. Douglas called on the Republican Lincoln to offer his and his party's support. "There can be no neutrals in this war," Douglas said, "only patriots—or traitors." Residents of New York City, where sympathy for the South had probably been greater than anywhere else in the North, now sponsored huge public demonstrations in support of the war effort. One New Yorker exclaimed, "It seems as if we never were alive till now; never had a country till now." The city council appropriated $1 million to raise and equip Union regiments. Vigilance committees intimidated pro-Southern newspapers. And American flags flew everywhere. The *New York Daily Tribune*, an abolitionist paper, made the objective of this patriotic fervor clear: "We mean to conquer [the Southern people]—not merely to defeat, but to conquer, to SUBJUGATE them—and we shall do this the most mercifully, the more speedily we do it. But when the rebellious traitors are overwhelmed in the field, and scattered like leaves before an angry wind, it must not be to return to peaceful and contented homes. They must find poverty at their firesides, and see privation in the anxious eyes of mothers and rags of children."

Southerners were equally eager to support their new nation. A *London Times* correspondent traveling in the South witnessed large crowds with "flushed

A rousing send-off for the Union's 7th Regiment in 1861 reflects the optimism and enthusiasm of citizens at the beginning of the war.

faces, wild eyes, screaming mouths." They punctuated stirring renditions of "Dixie" with the high-pitched piercing sounds that would later be known as the "rebel yell." Enlistment rallies, wild send-offs at train stations, and auctions and balls to raise money for the troops were staged throughout the Confederacy during the war's early months. As in the North, war fever fired hatred of the enemy. A Louisiana plantation overseer wrote:

> My prayer Sincerely to God is that Every Black Republican in the Hole combined whorl Either man women o chile that is opposed to negro slavery . . . shal be trubled with pestilences & calamitys of all kinds & drag out the Balance of there existence in misry & degradation with Scarsely food & rayment enughf to keep sole & body to geather and O God I pray the to Direct a bullet or a bayonet to pirce the art of every northern Soldier that invades southern Soil.

As war fever gripped North and South, volunteers on both sides rushed to join, quickly filling the quotas of both armies. Most soldiers were motivated by patriotism, a desire to defend their homes and loved ones, and a craving for glory and adventure. A recruitment poster in one Massachusetts town promised "travel and promotion" as well as good pay. Some men succumbed to the pressure of companions and sweethearts. A young Alabamian received a package from his fiancée with a skirt, a petticoat, and a note demanding "wear these or volunteer!" The initial enthusiasm, however, wore off quickly. After four months of war, a young Confederate soldier admitted, "I have seen quite enough of a soldier's life to satisfy me that it is not what it is cracked up to be."

The South in particular faced a contradiction between its ideology and the demands of full-scale war. Southerners were loyal to their localities, counties, and states. Southern leaders had been fighting for decades to defend states' rights against national authority. Now these same leaders had to forge the states of the Confederacy into a nation. By early spring 1862, the Confederate government was compelled to order the first general draft in U.S. history. It required three years' service for men between eighteen and thirty-five (a range later expanded from seventeen to fifty). In 1864, the Confederate Congress added a compulsory reenlistment provision. At that point, the only way a recruit could get out of the army was to die or desert.

The Confederate draft law allowed several occupational exemptions. Among them was an infamous provision that allowed one white man on any plantation with more than twenty slaves to be excused from service. The reason for the exemption was to assure the security and continued productivity of large plantations, not to protect the privileged, but it led some Southerners to conclude that the struggle had become "a rich man's war but a poor man's fight."

The initial flush of enthusiasm faded in the North as well. Responding to a federal call for additional troops, some Northern states initiated a draft during the summer of 1862. In March 1863, Congress passed the Enrollment Act, a draft law that, like the Confederate draft, allowed for occupational exemptions. A provision that allowed a draftee to hire a substitute aroused resentment among working-class Northerners. Anger at the draft—as well as poor working conditions—sparked several riots during 1863. But the North was less dependent on conscription than was the South. Only 8 percent of Union forces were drafted, compared to 20 percent for the Confederacy.

The complaints of many rank-and-file soldiers may give the impression that only people of lesser or modest means fought, but in fact the armies of both sides included men from all walks of life, from common laborers to clerks to bankers. An undetermined number of women, typically disguised as men, also served in both armies. Perhaps as many as three hundred women joined the Union ranks, and about half that number enlisted in the Confederate army. They joined for the same reasons as men: adventure, patriotism, and glory

THE NORTH'S ADVANTAGE IN RESOURCES

The resources of the North—including its population, industrial and agricultural capacity, and transportation network—greatly exceeded those of the South (see

Figure 15-1). The 2.1 million men who fought for the Union represented roughly half the men of military age in the North. The 900,000 men who fought for the Confederacy, by contrast, represented fully 90 percent of its eligible population. Irish and German immigrants continued to flow into the North during the war, although at a slower rate than before 1861, and thousands of them enlisted, often as substitutes for native-born Northerners. Nearly 200,000 African Americans, most of them ex-slaves from the South, took up arms for the Union. Not until the last month of the war did the Confederacy consider arming slaves.

The Confederacy compensated somewhat for its numerical disadvantage by requiring long tours of duty, which meant that its forces tended to be more experienced than those of the Union. But the Union's greater numbers left the South vulnerable to a war of attrition. As one Confederate veteran explained to a Union veteran several years after the war, "When one of your men got killed, a dozen took his place. When one of our boys died, it was just another good man gone."

At the beginning of the war, the North controlled 90 percent of the nation's industrial capacity. It had seventeen times more cotton and woolen cloth than the South, thirty times more boots and shoes, and thirty-two times more firearms. The North had dozens of facilities for producing the tools to make war materiel; the South had no such factories and only one munitions plant, the Tredegar Iron Works in Richmond. Northern farms, more mechanized than their Southern counterparts, produced record harvests of meat, grains, and vegetables. Southern farms were also productive, but the South lacked the North's capacity to transport and distribute food efficiently. The railroad system in the North was more than twice the size of the South's.

FIGURE 15-1   A Comparison of the Union and Confederate Control of Key Resources at the Outset of the Civil War

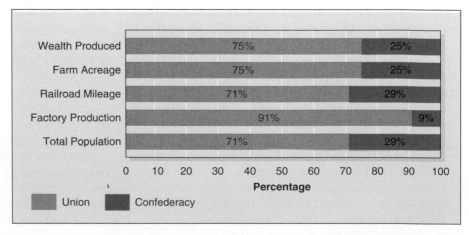

Thanks to the North's abundance of resources, no soldier in any previous army had ever been outfitted as well as the blue-uniformed Union trooper. The official color of the Confederate uniform was gray, although a dusty brown shade was more common. Most Southern soldiers, however, did not wear distinguishable uniforms, especially toward the end of the war. They also often lacked proper shoes or any footwear at all. In winter and on certain road surfaces, this shortage was a severe handicap. When the Confederate general Robert E. Lee invaded Maryland in 1862, he left behind several thousand barefoot soldiers because they could not march on gravel roads. Still, the South never lost a battle because of insufficient supplies or inadequate weaponry. New foundries opened, and manufacturing enterprises in Augusta, Georgia; Selma, Alabama; and elsewhere joined the Tredegar Iron Works in keeping the Confederate armies equipped with the weapons and other supplies they needed to keep fighting.

Unstable finances proved more of a handicap to the Confederacy than its relatively low industrial capacity. The Confederate economy—and its treasury—depended heavily on cotton exports. But a Union naval blockade and the ability of textile manufacturers in Europe to find new sources of supply restricted this crucial source of revenue. The imposition of taxes would have improved the Confederacy's finances, but Southerners resisted taxation. The government sold interest-bearing bonds to raise money, but as Confederate fortunes declined, so did bond sales. With few other options, the Confederacy financed more than 60 percent of the $1.5 billion it spent on the war with printing-press money. Inflation spiraled out of control, demoralizing civilians.

The Union had more abundant financial resources than the Confederacy, and the Federal government was more successful than the Confederate government at developing innovative ways to meet the great cost of the war. Its first recourse was to borrow money by selling long-term interest-bearing bonds and shorter-term interest-bearing treasury notes. Together these bonds accounted for 66 percent of the $4 billion that the Union raised to wage the war. Like the Confederacy, the Federal government issued paper money—bills derisively known as "greenbacks"—that was not backed by gold or silver. But the Federal government also offset its expenses with the country's first income tax, which citizens could pay in greenbacks—a move that bolstered the value and credibility of the paper currency. These financial measures eliminated the need for wage and price controls and rationing and warded off ruinous inflation in the North.

LEADERS, GOVERNMENTS, AND STRATEGIES

Leadership ability, like resources, played an important role in the war. It was up to the leaders of the two sides to determine and administer civilian and military policy, to define the war objectives of each side, and to inspire a willingness to sacrifice in both citizens and soldiers.

Confederate president Jefferson Davis had to build a government from scratch during a war. Abraham Lincoln at least had the benefit of an established governmental structure, a standing army, healthy financial resources, and established diplomatic relations with the nations of Europe.

Davis and Lincoln were both born in Kentucky within a year and 100 miles of each other. Davis, like Lincoln, was born into modest circumstances. He attended the military academy at West Point, where he was a mediocre student. He abandoned his military career after seven years of service and married the sixteen-year-old daughter of General Zachary Taylor. Davis and his bride moved to a plantation in Mississippi, where she soon died of yellow fever. Immersing himself in books and cotton farming, Davis had emerged as a gentleman planter by the 1840s and married Varina Howell in 1845. He returned to military service during the Mexican war, fought well, and used his success to become a senator from Mississippi in 1847. He served as secretary of war under President Franklin Pierce and returned to the Senate in 1857.

Although Davis's career qualified him for the prodigious task of running the Confederacy, aspects of his character compromised his effectiveness. He had a sharp intellect but related awkwardly to people and was not "one of the boys." Colleagues found him aloof. He was inclined to equate compromise with weakness and interpreted any opposition as a personal attack. His wife commented, "[I]f anyone disagrees with Mr. Davis he resents it and ascribes the difference to the perversity of his opponent." Davis was also fatalistic. According to his wife, when he heard that the Confederate Congress had selected him as president, he spoke of it "as a man might speak of a sentence of death."

Southerners viewed themselves as the genuine heirs of the American Revolution and the true defenders of the United States Constitution. If the South were to establish itself as a separate country, however, Southerners had to renounce their American identity and develop one of their own. But on what distinctive aspects of Southern life could the Confederacy build such an identity? Slavery was distinctively Southern, but most white Southerners, even if they believed that slavery served their interests, did not own slaves.

Southerners had forcefully advanced the ideology of states' rights, but, with its emphasis on the primacy of state sovereignty over central authority, states' rights, too, was a weak foundation on which to build a national consciousness.

Although Southerners fought for a variety of reasons, protecting their homes and families remained paramount. When these were threatened or destroyed, where would loyalty lie? Did Davis, or anyone else for that matter, possess the skill to hold together a new nation that was more like the nation it had renounced than anything that could replace it?

Northerners, like Southerners, needed a convincing reason to endure the prolonged sacrifice of the Civil War. For them, the struggle was a distant one, fought mostly on Southern soil, far from their homes. Lincoln and other Northern leaders secured support by convincing their compatriots of the importance of preserving the Union. Lincoln eloquently articulated this view, framing the war as more than a military conquest. In a message to Congress on July 4, 1861, he explained that the struggle to preserve the Union was "not altogether for today; it is for a vast future." The president viewed the conflict in global terms, its results affecting the hopes for democratic government around the world. He concluded that the war "embraces more than the fate of these United States. It presents to the whole family of man, the question, whether a constitutional republic . . . can or cannot maintain its territorial integrity, against its own domestic foes."

Lincoln handled disagreement better than Davis did. He defused tense situations with folksy humor, and his simple eloquence captured the imagination of ordinary people, even if it did not persuade his political enemies. Lincoln viewed himself as a man of the people. He was not aloof, like Davis. Friends and critics alike agreed that Lincoln made himself available to them. Lincoln generated the type of affection among rank-and-file soldiers that eluded Davis. The President's occasional visit to the front generated both amusement and gratitude from the troops, owing to his ungainly appearance on a horse, and his easy way of conversing with the men. They serenaded "Old Abe," as they called him affectionately with the popular tune, "We Are Coming Father Abraham." There is no record of Confederate tunesmiths composing similar ditties for their leaders. But even if Jefferson Davis had been as effective and beloved a leader as Lincoln, it is unlikely that he could have overcome the odds against him. The key to Southern independence lay less with the Confederacy's president than with its forces on the battlefield.

Lincoln's fight for the border states.

The secession of Virginia, Arkansas, North Carolina, and Tennessee left four border slave states—Maryland, Delaware, Kentucky, and Missouri—hanging in the balance. Were Maryland and Delaware to secede, the federal capital at Washington, D.C., would be surrounded by Confederate territory. The loss of Kentucky and Missouri would threaten the borders of Iowa, Illinois, Indiana, and Ohio and remove the Deep South from the threat of imminent invasion. Kentucky's manpower, livestock, and waterways were as important to hold for the Union as they were to gain for the Confederacy. The state also had special symbolic significance, as the birthplace of the rival presidents, Lincoln and Davis. Lincoln viewed Kentucky as the key to retaining the three other border states: "I think to lose Kentucky is nearly to lose the whole game. Kentucky gone, we cannot hold Missouri, nor, as I think, Maryland. . . . We would as well consent to separation at once, including the surrender of this capital."

Lincoln adopted a "soft" strategy to secure the border states, stressing the restoration of the Union as the sole objective of Federal military operations and assuring border residents that his government would not interfere with slavery. Union commanders barred fugitive slaves from their camps during the first year of the war, promising "to keep the war a lily-white crusade," as one officer put it. But, early reports from the four states were troubling. The four governors displayed polite indifference or overt hostility to the Federal government.

Maryland's strategic location north of Washington, D.C., rendered its loyalty to the Union vital. Although a majority of its citizens opposed secession, a mob attack on Union troops passing through Baltimore in April 1861 indicated strong pro-Southern sentiment. Lincoln dispatched Federal troops to monitor the fall elections in the state, placed its legislature under military surveillance, and arrested officials who opposed the Union cause, including the mayor of Baltimore. This show of force guaranteed the pro-Union candidate for governor an overwhelming victory and saved Maryland for the Union. Delaware, although nominally a slave state, remained staunchly for the Union.

Missourians settled their indecision by combat. The fighting culminated with a Union victory in March 1862 at the Battle of Pea Ridge, Arkansas. Pro-Confederate Missourians refused to concede defeat and waged an unsuccessful guerrilla war over the next two years.

Kentucky never seceded but attempted to remain neutral at the outset of the war. The legislature was pro-Union, the governor pro-Southern. Both sides ac-

Artist Winslow Homer's depiction of the place soldiers spent most of their time—camp. A soldier's life was boredom occasionally interspersed with fierce and deadly combat.

tively recruited soldiers in the state. In September 1861, when Confederate forces invaded Kentucky and Union forces moved to expel them, the state became one of the war's battlegrounds.

Although Virginia went with the Confederacy, some counties in the western part of the state opposed the state's secession and, as early as the summer of 1861, took steps to establish a pro-Union state. In June 1863, West Virginia became the nation's thirty-fifth state.

Strategies and tactics. To a great extent, the political objectives of each side determined its military strategy. Southerners wanted independence and protection of their institutions; Northerners fought to preserve the Union. The North's goal required conquest. Federal forces had to invade the South, destroy its armies, and rout its government. The Confederacy, for its part, did not need to conquer the North. Fighting a defensive battle in its own territory, the South had only to hang on until growing Northern opposition to the war or some decisive Northern military mistake convinced the Union to stop fighting.

But the South's strategy had two weaknesses. First, it demanded more patience than the South had shown in impulsively attacking Fort Sumter. Second, the South might not have sufficient resources to draw out the war long enough to swing Northern public opinion behind peace. The question was: What would break first, Northern support for the war or Southern ability to wage it?

THE EARLY WAR, 1861–1862

The North's offensive strategy dictated the course of the war for the first two years. In the West, the federal army's objectives were to hold Missouri, Kentucky, and Tennessee for the Union, to control the Mississippi River, and eventually to detach the area west of the Appalachians from the rest of the Confederacy. In the East, Union forces sought to capture Richmond, the Confederate capital. The U.S. Navy imposed a blockade along the Confederate coast and pushed into inland waterways to capture Southern ports.

The Confederates defended strategic locations throughout their territory or abandoned them when prudence required. Occasionally, taking advantage of surprise or terrain, Southern forces ventured out to engage Union armies. Between engagements, each side sniped at, bushwhacked, and trapped the other.

By the end of 1862, the result remained in the balance. Although Union forces attained some success in the West, Southern armies there remained intact. In the East, where resourceful Confederate leaders several times stopped superior Union forces, Southerners clearly had the best of it.

FIRST BULL RUN

By July 1861, when the border states appeared more secure for the Union, President Lincoln shifted his attention southward and ordered Union general Irvin McDowell to move Federal forces into Virginia to take Richmond (see Map 15-1). Confronting McDowell twenty miles southwest of Washington at Manassas, an important junction in the railway that supplied the Confederate capital, was a Confederate army under General P.G.T. Beauregard. Their armies clashed on July 21 at the First Battle of Bull Run (known to the Confederacy as the first battle of Manassas). Union troops seemed at first on the verge of winning. But Beauregard's forces, along with General Joseph E. Johnston's reinforcements, repulsed the assault, scattering not only the Union army, but also hundreds of picnickers who had come out from Washington to watch the fight. At the height of the battle, General Barnard Bee of South Carolina called out to Colonel Thomas J. Jackson for assistance. Jackson, a Virginia college professor turned officer, either did not hear Bee or chose to ignore him. In exasperation, Bee shouted, "There stands Jackson—like a damned stone wall!" The rebuke became, in the curious alchemy of battlefield gossip, a shorthand for courage and steadfastness. Jackson's men henceforth called him "Stonewall."

Bull Run dispelled some illusions and reinforced others. It boosted Southerners' confidence and seemed to confirm their boast that one Confederate could whip ten Yankees, even though the opposing armies were of relatively equal strength when the fighting began. The Union rout planted the suspicion in Northern minds that perhaps the Confederates were invincible and destroyed the widespread belief in the North that the war would be over quickly.

THE WAR IN THE WEST

While federal forces retreated in Virginia, they advanced in the west. Two Confederate forts on the Tennessee–Kentucky border, Fort Henry on the Tennessee river and Fort Donelson on the Cumberland River, guarded the strategic waterways that linked Tennessee and Kentucky to the Mississippi valley. The forts also defended Nashville, the Tennessee state capital (see Map 15-2). In February 1862, Union general Ulysses S. Grant coordinated a land and river campaign against the forts, with Flag Officer Andrew H. Foote who commanded a force of ironclad Union gunboats.

Grant, recently promoted to brigadier general, had resigned from the military in the 1850s after a mediocre career marked by bouts of excessive drink-

MAP 15-1   From First Bull Run to Antietam: The War in the East, 1861-1862
The early stages of the war demonstrated the strategies of both Confederate and Union forces. Federal troops stormed into Virginia hoping to capture Richmond and bring a quick end to the war. Through a combination of poor generalship and Confederate tenacity, they failed. Confederate troops hoped to defend their territory, prolong the war, and eventually win their independence as Northern patience evaporated. They proved successful initially, but, with the abandonment of the defensive strategy and the invasion of Maryland in the fall of 1862, the Confederates suffered a political and morale setback at Antietam.

ing. Before rejoining the army, he had worked in his family's struggling leather business in Illinois. A plain-looking man, with dark-brown hair and a beard streaked with gray, he often looked as if he had slept in his uniform. Behind the rumpled appearance lay a flexible military mind that would eventually grasp how the Civil War must be won.

Grant appreciated the strategic importance of river systems in the conquest of the western Confederacy. His combined river and land campaign caught the Southerners unprepared and outflanked. By February 16, both forts had fallen. The Union victory drove a wedge into Southern territory and closed the Confederacy's quickest path to the west from Virginia and the Carolinas. The Confederacy's only safe link across the Appalachians was now through Georgia. The Confederacy never recovered the strategic advantage in the West after the loss of Forts Henry and Donelson.

Grant next moved his main army south to Pittsburgh Landing on the Tennessee River, to prepare for an assault on the key Mississippi River port and rail center of Vicksburg. After blunting a surprise Confederate attack at Shiloh Church near Pittsburgh Landing, Grant pushed the Southerners back to Corinth, Mississippi.

Federal forces complemented their victories at Shiloh and Corinth with another important success in the western Confederacy. Admiral David G. Farragut, who remained a Unionist even though born in Tennessee, blasted the Confederate river defenses protecting New Orleans and sailed a federal fleet into the city in April 1862. The result was to open 200 miles of the Mississippi River, the nation's most vital commercial waterway, to Union traffic. With the fall of Memphis to union forces in June, Vicksburg remained the only major river town still in Confederate hands. The western losses exposed a major problem with the Confederates' defensive strategy: their military reserves were stretched too thin to defend their vast territory.

REASSESSING THE WAR: THE HUMAN TOLL

The fierce fighting at Shiloh wrought unprecedented carnage. More American soldiers were lost at Shiloh than in all of the nation's wars combined up to that

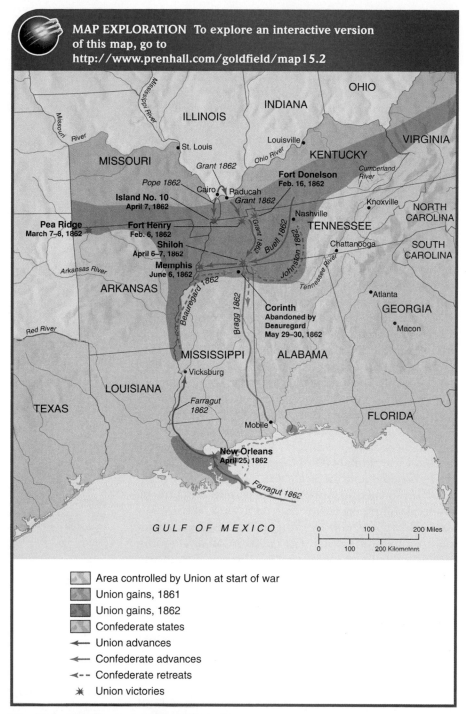

MAP 15-2   The War in the West, 1861-1862
Because of the early Union emphasis on capturing Richmond, the war in the West seemed less important to Northerners. But, from a strategic standpoint, the victories at Forts Henry and Donelson, which drove a wedge into southern territory and closed the Confederacy's quickest path to the West from Virginia and the Carolinas, and the capture of New Orleans and its Mississippi River port were crucial and set the stage for greater Federal success in the West in 1863.

time. Each side suffered more than ten thousand casualties. By the time the smoke had cleared, the soldiers' view of the war had undergone a major transformation. The initial enthusiasm and bravado were replaced by the sober realization that death or capture was a likely outcome and that heroism, courage, and piety did not guarantee survival. "Too shocking, too horrible," a Confederate survivor of Shiloh wrote. "God grant that I may never be the partaker in such scenes again . . . when released from this I shall ever be an advocate of peace." A Union soldier wrote of "the dead and dying lying in masses, some with arms, legs, and even their jaws shot off, bleeding to death, and no one to wait upon them to dress their wounds."

Landing in a hospital scarcely improved a wounded or ill soldier's chances of survival. Kate Cumming, a nurse at a Confederate hospital in Corinth, wrote of soldiers brought from the battle "mutilated in every imaginable way." The wounded lay packed together on the floor, and Cumming negotiated the rooms with great difficulty to avoid stepping on the dead and dying. Piercing the air were the screams of men undergoing amputations, often with little or no anesthetic. Some pleaded with physicians to kill them and end their misery. Others bore the pain stoically and entrusted last words and letters to nurses, dying with the word "Mother" or the name of their wife or sweetheart on their lips.

Women on both sides played a major role in caring for the wounded and sick. In the North, members of the U.S. Sanitary Commission attempted to upgrade hospital and medical care. This voluntary organization, formed in April 1861, was staffed mainly by women volunteers who collected and distributed medical supplies and clothing and advised on cleaning hospitals and camps. The commission made some headway during the first year of the war, but in the months after Shiloh and with the resumption of fighting in the east, the extent of casualties often overwhelmed the dedicated volunteers. And the bloodiest fighting lay ahead.

Even if a soldier escaped death on the battlefield and survived a hospital stay, he still faced the possibility of death from disease. Roughly twice as many men died from disease as on the battlefield during the Civil War. Heaps of garbage, contaminated food and water, and swarming mosquitoes, flies, and lice created unhealthy camp conditions. Typhoid, commonly and appropriately known as "camp fever," claimed the most lives.

Many soldiers turned to religion for consolation in response to the growing carnage. The frequency of camp prayer meetings and revivals increased after Shiloh. Many a recruit carried books with such titles as *Satan's Bait* and *A Mother's Parting Words to her Soldier Boy* in his knapsack. Soldiers often gathered with their

Several hundred women, disguised as men, made their contribution to the war effort by enlisting. Frances Clalin served with Federal forces in Missouri. Many were found out after suffering wounds or illness.

comrades to sing hymns before retiring for the night. Stories circulated of a Bible that stopped a bullet whistling toward a soldier's heart. But veterans knew that a deck of cards did just as well, and they understood that neither Bibles nor cards offered protection against artillery.

Some soldiers, responding to constant danger and fear, talked or yelled loudly. The Confederate rebel yell probably served to relieve some of the tension of battle as well as to frighten the enemy. Others shook so much that they fell down, unable to control their limbs. A few soldiers could not wake up in the morning without being doused with cold water; "they wanted to stay out, they couldn't bear to remember all this mess waiting with first light."

The harsh conditions of camp life often strained relations between officers and enlisted men. Soldiers also suffered from boredom. Battles rarely lasted more than a day or two. While in camp between engagements, a recruit faced seemingly incessant drilling (loading and firing a rifle required nine separate steps) and heavy chores such as chopping wood and hauling water. Typically, he spent what little time remained resting, writing, reading, and eating. To relieve their anxieties, soldiers talked about home and loved ones, upcoming or recent battles, and food. Soldiers also fought the boredom and harsh physical conditions of camp life by singing, playing cards, and competing in sports like footracing and makeshift forms of football and baseball.

Women camp followers cooked, did laundry, and provided sexual services for a price. The two capitals, Washington and Richmond, had notorious vice districts. A Confederate recruit lamented that "almost half of the women in the vicinity of the army, married and unmarried, are lost to all virtue." Both armies experienced soaring rates of venereal disease.

By 1862, the war's carnage and brutality had dispelled any lingering notions of war as a chivalrous enterprise. At a battle in Virginia that year, Stonewall Jackson reprimanded a Confederate general who had ordered his men not to shoot at a Union officer riding before his own men, rallying them on. "This is no ordinary war," Jackson said, "and the brave and gallant Federal officers are the very kind that must be killed. Shoot the brave officers and the cowards will run away and take the men with them." The reluctance of some commanders to pursue retreating armies or to initiate campaigns resulted in part from their recognition of how awful the war really was.

THE WAR IN THE EAST

With Grant and Farragut squeezing the Confederacy in the West, Lincoln ordered a new offensive against Richmond in the East that he believed would end the war. Following the defeat at Bull Run, he had shaken up the Union high command and appointed General George B. McClellan to lead what was now called the Army of the Potomac.

A West Point graduate, McClellan had served with distinction in the Mexican war. Called back into active duty at the outbreak of the war, he assumed command of the Army of the Potomac, which was no more than a collection of raw recruits and disgruntled veterans. McClellan succeeded in transforming it into a disciplined fighting force. He was well liked by his soldiers, who referred to him affectionately as "Little Mac." Mc-

Clellan returned their affection, perhaps too much. A superb organizer, he would prove overly cautious on the field of battle.

In March 1862, at the outset of the Peninsula Campaign, McClellan moved his 112,000-man army out of Washington and maneuvered his forces by boat down the Potomac River and Chesapeake Bay to the peninsula between the York and James Rivers southeast of the Confederate capital. Union forces took Yorktown, Williamsburg, and Norfolk. Confederate general Joseph E. Johnston, withdrew his forces up the peninsula toward Richmond, preparing for what most felt would be the decisive battle of the war. McClellan, moving ponderously up the peninsula, clashed with Johnston's army inconclusively at Seven Pines in late May 1862. Johnston was badly wounded in the clash, and president Davis replaced him with General Robert E. Lee, who renamed the forces under his command the Army of Northern Virginia.

Lee was from a prominent Virginia family long accustomed to power and command. His father, "Light-Horse Harry" Lee, had been a Revolutionary

A career army officer who resigned his commission to serve his state and new country, Confederate General Robert E. Lee's quiet courage and sense of duty inspired his men.

War hero. Lee attended West Point, served with distinction in the Mexican War, and commanded the federal force that captured John Brown at Harpers Ferry in 1859. In 1831, he married Mary Custis, the daughter of George Washington's adopted son. Their gracious home in Arlington, Virginia, had a commanding view of the Potomac and Washington, D.C. Before the war, it had seemed as if Lee would live out his days as a soldier-farmer, much like his wife's grandfather.

In 1860, the army posted Lee to Texas, where he watched the secession drama unfold. He opposed secession but was unwilling to take up arms against his native Virginia. Refusing an offer from Winfield Scott to take command of Federal forces, he resigned from the U.S. Army and went with Virginia after it left the Union.

Lee's reserved and aristocratic bearing masked a gambler's disposition. One fellow officer noted, "his name might be Audacity. He will take more chances, and take them quicker than any other general in this country." Under his daring leadership, the Confederacy's defensive strategy underwent an important shift.

Lee seized the initiative on June 25, 1862, attacking McClellan's right flank. Although inconclusive, the attack pushed the nervous McClellan into a defensive position. For a week, the armies sparred in a series of fierce engagements known collectively as the Seven Days' Battles. More than thirty thousand men were killed or wounded on both sides, the deadliest week of the war so far. Although McClellan prevailed in these contests, the carnage so shocked him that he withdrew to Harrison's Landing on the James River. An exasperated Lincoln replaced McClellan with John Pope. Although Lee had saved Richmond, his troops had suffered frightfully. He had lost one-fourth of his eighty thousand–man army, but he remained convinced of the wisdom of his offensive-defensive strategy.

Lee went to work to vindicate these tactics. A series of inconclusive skirmishes brought Union and Confederate armies together once more, near Manassas Junction. The Second Battle of Bull Run was as much a disaster for the Union as the first had been. Lee's generalship completely befuddled Pope and again saved Richmond. Lee and the Army of Northern Virginia were developing a reputation for invincibility.

TURNING POINTS, 1862–1863

The impressive Confederate victories in the East masked the delicate condition of Southern fortunes.

The longer the Confederacy held off Union offensives, the greater the likelihood of securing the South's independence. But the longer the war continued, the higher the probability that the Confederacy's shortcomings in men, finances, and materiel would erode its ability to keep fighting. Lee's offensive-defensive strategy seemed to be working, but it raised the possibility that the Confederacy could exhaust its men and resources before it sealed its independence.

The waning summer months of 1862 brought other concerns to the Davis administration in Richmond. The Union navy was choking the South's commercial link with Europe. Davis looked to the nations of Europe for diplomatic recognition as well as for trade.

But the most important arena of the war remained the battlefield. Having stymied the Union war machine, Lee contemplated a bold move—a thrust into Northern territory to bring the conflict to the North and stoke Northerners' rising hostility to the war. It was a bold plan that might end the war and secure Southern independence—or hasten an otherwise inevitable Union victory.

President Lincoln also harbored a bold plan. Gradually during the spring and summer of 1862, the president had concluded that emancipation of the Confederacy's slaves was essential for preserving the Union. Emancipation would provide Federal forces with both moral and strategic advantages over their foes. But Lincoln was reluctant to take this step before the Union's fortunes on the battlefield improved. Without a significant victory, emancipation would appear to be an act of desperation. As the fall of 1862 approached, both Union and Confederate governments prepared for the most significant conflicts of the war to date.

THE NAVAL AND THE DIPLOMATIC WAR

The Union's naval strategy was to blockade the Southern coast and capture its key seaports and river towns. The intention was to prevent arms, clothing, and food from reaching the Confederacy and keep cotton and tobacco from leaving. Destroying the South's ability to carry on trade would also prevent the Confederacy from raising money to purchase the goods it needed to wage war. This vital trade brought the Confederacy into contact with European nations, a connection they hoped to reinforce on the diplomatic front as well.

The naval war. Neither side had much of a navy at the outset of the war. With more than three thousand miles of Confederate coastline to cover, the Union blockade was weak at first. As time passed and the number of ships in the Union navy grew, the blockade tightened. The skyrocketing prices of Southern staples on world markets by 1862 attested to the effectiveness of the Union strategy.

Understandably, the Confederate naval strategy was to break the blockade and defend the South's vital rivers and seaports. The Confederacy built several warships to serve as blockade runners and as privateers to attack Union merchants ships, and, briefly, they disrupted Federal operations before Union vessels regained the advantage. Historians disagree about the effectiveness of the Union naval blockade, but with limited resources and capital, the Confederacy was heavily dependent on the flow of trade. Any restriction in that flow hurt the Southern cause.

The diplomatic front.

Southerners, remembering the crucial role that timely French assistance had played in the American Revolution, thought that the recognition of their independence by overseas governments would legitimize their cause in the eyes of the world.

Great Britain had several reasons to support the Confederate cause. After two wars and a succession of diplomatic wrangles, it had no great love of the United States. If the country divided, it would pose less of a threat to British economic and territorial ambitions. Some British textile magnates also supported the Confederacy because they feared a drastic reduction in the supply of Southern cotton.

British foreign policy, however, had been anti-slavery for a quarter century, and the slavery issue turned many Britons against the South. The Union cause had support in high ruling circles, especially from Queen Victoria, as well as from middle-class and working-class Britons. One working-class leader declared the Confederate cause "odious and . . . blasphemous" and hoped for a reunited America that would become "the hope of freedom, and a refuge for the oppressed of every race and of every clime."

Emperor Napoleon III of France, who had imperial designs on Mexico, favored the Confederacy. A restored Union, he thought, would pose a greater threat to his ambitions than a divided one. But Napoleon feared antagonizing the powerful British and would not intervene unilaterally in the Confederate cause.

He did, however, take advantage of the Civil War, by invading Mexico in June 1863 and installing Austrian archduke Maximilian as emperor. In November, however, Union forces occupied the border town of Brownsville, Texas, an unmistakable signal to the French not to expand their adventure. Following the Civil War, the United States government prevailed upon France to withdraw from Mexico. Patriot insurgents, led by Benito Juárez, who would become president of Mexico, captured and killed Maximilian, restoring Mexican rule and removing the last vestige of a foreign threat on United States borders.

The Russians were probably the staunchest supporters of the Union abroad. The odd friendship between the Western world's most autocratic country and its most democratic one resulted primarily from political expediency. The Russian tsar, Alexander II, saw the United States as a counterweight to British power. There was also some sympathy for the North's opposition to slavery in Russia, where the tsar had abolished serfdom (a form of slavery) in 1861.

Southerners were convinced that their cotton was so important to the world economy that they could use it as a diplomatic bargaining chip. "You dare not to make war on cotton. . . . cotton is king." So declared South Carolina senator James H. Hammond in a warning to the North in 1858. But King Cotton was no more successful at coercing the British—who had large cotton reserves and an alternate source of supply in Egypt—into granting recognition to the Confederacy than it was at stopping the North from going to war against the South.

The Davis administration did chalk up some minor diplomatic victories early in the war. Great Britain declared itself neutral and allowed British merchants to sell arms and supplies to both Confederate and Union forces. This policy especially benefited the Confederacy, with its limited arsenal. France followed with a similar concession.

In the end, the Confederacy's hopes for diplomatic recognition depended on its ability to show that it could secure its independence on the battlefield. After Lee's victories in Virginia in the spring of 1862 and his subsequent decision to invade the North, British intervention in the war grew more likely. The British government had more or less decided that if Lee emerged victorious from his planned invasion, it would press for mediation. William Gladstone, England's future prime minister, believed that Lee would achieve his goal. He concluded that "we may anticipate with certainty the success of the Southern states so far as regards their separation from the North."

ANTIETAM

The alarming arithmetic of the offensive-defensive strategy convinced Lee that the South could not sustain a prolonged conflict. He knew that his army must keep the pressure on Union forces and, if possible, destroy them quickly. Union success in the Mississippi valley threatened to cut the Confederacy in two and deprive it of the resources of a vast chunk of territory. Within a year, the Confederacy might cease to exist west of the Appalachians. He desperately needed a dramatic victory.

In September 1862, Lee crossed the Potomac into Maryland as his band played "Maryland, My Maryland" for the unimpressed residents. He was on his way to cut off the Pennsylvania Railroad at Harrisburg. Lee established camp at Frederick, scattering his army at various sites, convinced that McClellan and the Army of the Potomac would not attack him.

At this point, luck intervened for the North. At an abandoned Confederate encampment, a Union corporal found three wrapped cigars on the ground, evidently tossed out by a careless Confederate officer. To the corporal's amazement, the wrapping was a copy of Lee's orders for the disposition of his army. But even with this information, "Little Mac" moved so cautiously that Lee had time to gather his and Jackson's regiments and retreat to defensive positions at Sharpsburg, Maryland, along Antietam creek. There Lee's army of 39,000 men came to blows with McClellan's army of 75,000.

The Battle of Antietam saw the bloodiest single day of fighting in American history. About 2,100 Union soldiers and 2,700 Confederates died on the battlefield, and another 18,500, equally divided, were wounded. McClellan squandered his numerical superiority with uncoordinated and timid Union attacks. Although the armies had fought to a tactical draw, the battle was a strategic defeat for the Confederacy. In the battle's aftermath, Lee's troops limped back across the Potomac into Virginia and McClellan did not pursue.

 Antietam marked a major turning point in the war. It kept Lee from directly threatening Northern industry and financial institutions. It prompted Britain and France to abandon plans to grant recognition to the Confederacy. And it provided Lincoln with the victory he needed to announce the abolition of slavery.

EMANCIPATION

President Lincoln despised slavery, but he had always maintained that preserving the Union was his primary war goal. "If I could save the Union without freeing any slave I would do it," he wrote to the newspaper editor Horace Greeley in August 1862, "and if I could save it by freeing all the slaves I would do it; and if I could save it by freeing some and leaving others alone, I would also do that." An astute politician, Lincoln realized that he had to stress union and equivocate on slavery to keep the Northern public united in support of the war. But from the war's out-

set, the possibility of emancipation as a war objective was considered in the Republican Congress, within the Union army, and among citizens throughout the Northern states. Northern soldiers, as they moved South, saw slaves building trenches, earthworks, bridges, and roads for the Confederate army as well as working Southern farms. As a result, pressure grew within the Union army to declare emancipation as a way of depriving the South and the Confederate army of its labor force.

Lincoln said in his inaugural address that he had "no purpose, directly or indirectly, to interfere with the institution of slavery in the states where it exists." By March 1862, however, his moral repugnance toward slavery, and the military arguments for abolition, led him to propose a resolution, which Congress adopted, supporting the compensated emancipation of slaves. The measure died, however, when Congress failed to appropriate funds for it and slaveholders in the border states expressed no interest in the plan.

Pressure from Northern civilians, Union soldiers, and Congress for some form of emancipation mounted in the spring of 1862. In response, the Republican Congress prohibited slavery in the territories and abolished slavery in the District of Columbia. The act emancipating the district's slaves called for compensating slave owners and colonizing the freed slaves in black republics, such as Haiti and Liberia. Then, in July 1862, Congress passed the **Confiscation Act,** which ordered the seizure of land from disloyal Southerners and the emancipation of their slaves.

Although support for emancipation had grown both in the army and among civilians, Lincoln still faced political considerations that dictated against it. Emancipation was still not favored by a majority in the North, especially not in the border states. The thousands of Irish Catholic immigrants who entered the Union army and who had competed with black workers for jobs in Northern cities during the 1850s were especially opposed to emancipation, fearing a loss of economic security. They also resented the abolitionists' Protestant moralizing. The Roman Catholic Archbishop John Hughes of New York declared that "We Catholics, and a vast majority of our brave troops in the field, have not the slightest idea of carrying on a war that costs so much blood and treasure just to gratify a clique of abolitionists in the North." But other considerations favored emancipation. Freeing the slaves would appeal to the strong antislavery sentiment in Britain and gain support for the Union cause abroad. And it would weaken the Confederacy's ability to wage war by removing a crucial source of labor.

The Emancipation Proclamation.

By mid-1862, the president had resolved to act on his moral convictions and proclaim emancipation. Taking the advice of Secretary of State Seward, however, he decided to wait for a battlefield victory so that the measure would not appear an act of desperation. Antietam gave the president his opening, narrow though it was, and on September 22, 1862, he announced his intention to issue the Emancipation Proclamation, to take effect January 1, 1863, in all states still in rebellion. The proclamation exempted slaves in the border states loyal to the Union and in areas under Federal occupation.

Southerners reacted to the Emancipation Proclamation with outrage. Some viewed it as an invitation to race war and conjured up fears of freed slaves slaying white women and children while their men were at the battlefront. Jefferson Davis, taking a positive view, thought that the proclamation would invigorate the Southern war effort. Some observers abroad were skeptical. One London newspaper, noting that emancipation did not apply to all slaves, stated, "the principle is not that a human being cannot justly own another, but that he cannot own him unless he is loyal to the United States."

Northerners generally approved of the emancipation proclamation. Although abolitionists comprised a minority of the Northern population, most civilians and soldiers accepted emancipation for its military advantages. A private in the Army of the Potomac who had previously expressed serious reservations about emancipation wrote home his support for "putting away any institution if by so doing it will help put down the rebellion."

The Emancipation Proclamation represented far more than its qualified words and phrases expressed. "A mighty act," Massachusetts governor John Andrew called it. Lincoln had freed the slaves. He and the Union war effort were now tied to the cause of freedom. What began as a war to save the Union had became a holy war of deliverance. Freedom and Union entwined in the public consciousness of the North. As Lincoln noted in his December 1862 message to Congress, "[I]n giving freedom to the slave, we assure freedom to the free." Emancipation also unified the Republican party and strengthened the president's hand in conducting the war.

"Stealing" freedom.

As word of the Emancipation Proclamation raced through the slave grapevine, slaves rejoiced that their long-awaited day of jubilee had arrived. But the proclamation only continued a process that had begun when the first Union armies invaded the South. In the months before freedom came, many slaves had run away to Union camps, dug Union trenches, and scouted for Federal troops.

Southern masters fought to deter their slaves by severely punishing the families of black men who fled to the Union lines. They used the courts and slave catchers to reclaim runaways. Some Confederate masters protected their investments by removing slaves to Texas or to areas far from federal forces. And a few slave owners whipped, sold, and even killed their slaves to prevent them from joining the Union troops.

But in the end, slaveholders could not stem the tide of slaves fleeing toward the Union lines and freedom. The 1862 Confiscation Act included slaves with other Confederate property as the "contraband" of war and subject to confiscation, a term Union general Benjamin Butler had applied to escaped slaves as early as May 1861. As they helped the Union cause, contrabands also sought to help fellow slaves "steal" their freedom. When Union forces occupied part of the Georgia coast in April 1862, for example, March Haynes, a slave who had worked as a river pilot in Savannah, began smuggling slaves to the Union lines. Federal general Quincy Adams Gilmore provided a swift boat for Haynes's missions. In return, Haynes supplied Gilmore with "exact and valuable information" on the strength and location of Confederate defenses.

The former slaves who arrived at Federal camps after emancipation often encountered poor conditions but relished their freedom nonetheless. A Northern missionary in occupied Louisiana wrote in 1863 that he was surrounded by "negroes in uniform, negroes in rags, negroes in frame houses, negroes living in tents, negroes living in rail pens covered with brush, and negroes living under brush piles without any rails, negroes living on the bare ground with the sky for their covering; all hopeful . . . every one pleading to be taught, willing to do anything for learning."

The Emancipation Proclamation accelerated the slaves' flight from bondage. Personally fighting to secure their freedom and liberating those still enslaved became the objective of many, for after 1863, ex-slaves served in increasing numbers in the Union army.

Black troops in the Union Army.

More than 80 percent of the roughly 180,000 black soldiers and 20,000 black sailors who fought for the Union were slaves and free black men from the South. For the typical black Southerner who joined the army, the passage from bondage to freedom came quickly. Making his escape from his master, he perhaps "stole" his family as well. He typically experienced his first days of freedom behind Union lines, where he may have

Even before the Emancipation Proclamation, slaves throughout the South "stole" their freedom. After the Proclamation, the trickle of black slaves abandoning their masters became a flood as they sought freedom behind Union lines.

learned to read and write. Finally, he put on the Federal uniform, experiencing, as one black Southern volunteer commented, "the biggest thing that ever happened in my life."

As early as August 1862, five thousand African Americans had enrolled in the Union army in the occupied Sea Islands off South Carolina despite a widely publicized Confederate directive promising to shoot black prisoners of war. This threat was later withdrawn when Union officers declared that they would do the same with Confederate prisoners. The Confederacy, however, held fast to its refusal to parole, or send back, captured black soldiers, a policy that led to the end of prisoner exchanges in early 1863 and contributed to horrible conditions in overcrowded prisoner-of-war camps on both sides.

Initially, the enlistment of black soldiers in South Carolina encountered opposition in the North. By early 1863, however, public opinion was changing. One reason was that white Northerners realized that the enlistment of African Americans relieved them in comparable numbers from military service. President Lincoln strongly advocated enlisting former slaves. In March 1863, he wrote, with exaggerated enthusiasm, "[T]he bare sight of 50,000 armed and drilled black soldiers on the banks of the Mississippi would end the rebellion at once." On the contrary, the appearance of black Union troops infuriated the Confederates. After a battle at Milliken's Bend, Louisiana, in 1863, for example, observers found dead Confederate and black Union soldiers entangled in each other's arms and impaled on one another's bayonets.

Once orders were issued allowing the recruitment of black troops, posters like this one appeared throughout the North. The illustrations stressed the dignity and manhood of military service but also showed segregated soldiers and white officers.

the practice, noting that "their enlistment was a serious offense to popular prejudice" and the fact "that they were not to receive the same pay as white soldiers seemed a necessary concession to smooth the way to their employment at all as soldiers."

Despite discrimination, black soldiers fought valiantly at Port Hudson, Louisiana; near Charleston; and, late in the war, at the siege of Petersburg, Virginia. After hearing of African American troops fighting Confederate forces nearby, one young white Mississippian wrote in her diary, "it is said the Negro regiments fought there like mad demons." The most celebrated black encounter with Confederate troops occurred in July 1863, during a futile assault by the 54th Massachusetts Regiment on Fort Wagner outside Charleston. The Northern press, previously lukewarm toward black troops, heaped praise on the effort. "Through the cannon smoke of that dark night," intoned a writer in the *Atlantic Monthly*, "the manhood of the colored race shines before many eyes that would not see."

If only President Lincoln could find such gallantry among his generals! George McClellan had failed to follow his advantage at Antietam in September 1862, allowing Lee's army to escape to Virginia and remain a formidable fighting force. And despite Union successes in the West, the Confederate forces massed there remained largely intact.

FROM FREDERICKSBURG TO GETTYSBURG

In late 1862, after Antietam, the president replaced McClellan with General Ambrose E. Burnside. The new chief of the Army of the Potomac, an imposing physical presence, sported bushy whiskers on his cheeks that came to be known as "sideburns," a transposition of the two parts of his name. Despite his commanding stature, Burnside was shy and insecure. Claiming incompetence, he had twice refused the command. His judgment proved better than Lincoln's.

Fredericksburg. Moving swiftly against Lee's dispersed army in northern Virginia, Burnside reached

But for black volunteers, the promise of freedom and redemption outweighed the dangers of combat. Black abolitionists campaigned tirelessly for the enlistment of free black men and fugitive slaves in the Union army. Frederick Douglass, whose son Lewis distinguished himself in the all-black 54th Massachusetts Volunteer Infantry Regiment, explained in early 1863, "Once let the black man get upon his person the brass letters, 'U.S.,' let him get an eagle on his buttons and a musket on his shoulder and bullets in his pockets, and there is no power on earth which can deny that he has earned the right to citizenship in the United States." Other black abolitionists took up the refrain. Sojourner Truth, a former slave who saw many of her thirteen children sold into slavery, canvassed Northern cities to rally public opinion for the deployment of black troops.

Although black soldiers were eager to engage the enemy and fought as ably as their white comrades, they received lower pay and performed the most menial duties in camp. Abolitionists and black leaders in the North pressured President Lincoln for more equitable treatment of African American recruits. When Frederick Douglass complained to Lincoln about the lower pay that black troops received, the president defended the Rappahannock river opposite Fredericksburg in November 1862 (see Map 15-3). But the pontoon bridges to ford his 120,000 soldiers across the river arrived three weeks late, giving Lee an opportunity to gather his 78,000 men. On December 13, the Union forces launched a poorly coordinated and foolish frontal assault that the Confederates repelled, inflicting heavy federal casualties. Burnside, having performed to his own expectations, was relieved of his command, and Major General Joseph Hooker was installed in his place.

MAP 15-3 From Fredericksburg to Gettysburg: The War in the East, December 1862-July 1863

By all logic, the increasingly outgunned and outfinanced Confederacy should have been showing signs of faltering by 1863. But bungling by Union generals at Fredericksburg and Chancellorsville sustained Southern fortunes and encouraged Robert E. Lee to attempt another Northern invasion.

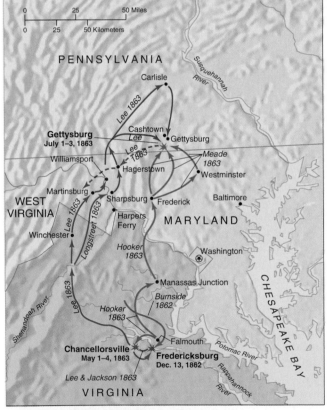

- ☐ Area controlled by Union
- ☐ Area controlled by Confederacy
- ⭠ Union advances
- ⭠ Confederate advances
- ⭠-- Confederate retreats
- ✴ Union victories
- ✴ Confederate victories

Chancellorsville.

The hard-drinking Hooker lacked Burnside's humility but not his incompetence. Resuming the offensive in the spring of 1863, Hooker hoped to outflank Lee. But the Confederate commander surprised Hooker by sending Stonewall Jackson to outflank the Union right. Between May 1 and May 4, Lee's army delivered a series of crushing attacks on Hooker's forces at Chancellorsville. Outnumbered two to one, Lee had pulled off another stunning victory—but at a high cost. Lee lost some thirteen thousand men, fewer than Hooker's seventeen thousand, but more than the Confederacy could afford.

Lee also lost Stonewall Jackson at Chancellorsville. Nervous Confederate sentries mistakenly shot and wounded him as he returned from a reconnoitering mission, and he died a few days later. Known for his lightning strikes at the enemy and his brilliant understanding of the tactics of modern warfare, Jackson had helped Lee win some of the Confederacy's most stunning victories in 1862. Lee recognized the tragedy of Jackson's loss for himself and his country. "Any victory," the Confederate commander wrote, "would be dear at such a price. I know not how to replace him."

Still, Lee appeared invincible. Chancellorsville thrust Lincoln into another bout of despair. "My God!" he exclaimed in agony, "What will the country say! What will the country say!" Meanwhile, Lee, to take advantage of the Confederacy's momentum and the Union's gloom, planned another bold move. On June 3, 1863, the 75,000-man Army of Northern Virginia broke camp and headed North once again (see "American Views: A Soldier Promotes the Union Cause").

Gettysburg.

President Lincoln sent the Union Army of the Potomac after Lee. But General Hooker dallied, requested more troops, and allowed the Confederates to march from Maryland into Pennsylvania. An infuriated Lincoln replaced Hooker with George Gordon Meade.

Lee and Meade were personal friends—they had served together during the Mexican war—and the change in command worried the Confederate general. He had counted on the bungling Hooker as his opponent. "General Meade," he commented prophetically, "will commit no blunder in my front."

Lee's Army of Northern Virginia occupied a wide swath of Pennsylvania territory from Chambersburg to Wrightsville along the Susquehanna River, across from the state capital at Harrisburg. When Lee learned of Meade's movements, he ordered his troops to consolidate in a defensive position at Cashtown, 45 miles from Harrisburg. That the greatest battle of the war erupted at nearby Gettysburg was pure chance. A

AMERICAN VIEWS

A Soldier Promotes the Union Cause

Soldiers wrote their thoughts down in diaries, in letters to their families, and, as in the case of the infantryman here, D. Beardsley, from Tompkins County, New York, to newspapers. Morale faltered in both the civilian and military ranks on both sides during the Civil War as this excerpt indicates. At the same time, Beardsley is buoyed by the elevated sense of mission in Union ranks, brought about by Abraham Lincoln's Emancipation Proclamation, which took effect one month prior to this letter.

- How to balance civil liberties with the necessity of carrying on a war is a dilemma of all armed conflicts involving democratic societies. What does this soldier think about where the balance ought to occur?

- The writer refers to "desertion" in the ranks indicating a morale problem in the Union armies. Why was this the case in February 1863?

- What impact does this soldier hope the Emancipation Proclamation will have on the war effort in the North?

I having the honor of being a volunteer from old Tompkins County, and also fighting under the same banner and for the same principles that Washington did—still holding to my priviledges [sic] as a citizen of the United States, I think it will not be out of place for me to speak a few words through your columns, to the good people of my native county. . . .

If our Government would have no rebellion, she must pluck the tares of rebellion from the heart of the nation; and if we would have this rebellion crushed, we must cease to have traitors in power. Let that class in the Northern States, who would kiss the red hand of treason for a momentary peace, remember that the hand will be no less red by the kiss, or the blow no less sure by the pause; and I would humbly beg the people of the North, in the name of a soldier for the Union, that they will, in this dark and trying hour of our country's history, give us

their undivided support, first, by stripping all power from the traitors at home, and then by their repentant prayers for our success in battles. . . . A few have deserted, and may God have mercy upon them. Let them go, their *blood* is altogether too poor to enrich the soil of worn out Virginia. We want the blood of patriots to make it bring forth the fruits of freedom. . . . We hope that in future the people and the army will become more pure, and work with a nobler purpose of heart. The first step toward this reformation has already been taken. We begin to see that all men have rights, whether white or black, and we hope that when the smoke of battle shall have cleared away, that the bright sun of peace will shine upon a truly free people.

Source: D. Beardsley, "Co. K, 137th Reg't, N.Y. Vols" that appeared in the *Ithaca Journal*, March 3, 1863; dated February 16, 1863 and written from Acquia Landing, Virginia.

Confederate brigade left Cashtown to confiscate much-needed shoes in Gettysburg. Meeting federal cavalry resistance near the town, the brigade withdrew. On July 1, 1863, a larger Confederate force advanced toward Gettysburg to disperse the cavalry and seize the shoes. What the Confederates did not realize

was that the entire Army of the Potomac was coming up behind the cavalry (see map 15-4).

During the first day of battle, July 1, the Confederates appeared to gain the upper hand, forcing Union forces back from the town to a new position on Cemetery Hill. On the second day, the entire Union army

Union positions
Confederate positions
← Union advances
← Confederate advances
◄-- Union retreats

MAP 15-4   The Battle of Gettysburg, July 1–3, 1863
*In a war that lasted four years, it is difficult to point to the deci-
sive battle. But clearly, the outcome during those hot July days
at Gettysburg set the tone for the rest of the war. The result was
unclear until the final day of battle, and, even then, it might
have gone either way. Winning by a whisker was enough to pro-
pel Union armies to a string of victories over the next year and
to throw Confederate forces back on their defenses among an increasingly despairing population. Gettysburg marked the last
major Southern invasion of the North.*

was in place, but the Confederates seized the initiative
and took several key locations along Cemetery Ridge
before federal forces pushed them back to the previous
day's positions. Although the opposing sides had suffered heavy casualties, both armies were intact; and, if
anything, Lee had the advantage. On July 3, the third

day of the battle, Lee made a fateful error. Believing
that the center of Meade's line was weak, he ordered an
all-out assault against it. The night before, Meade had
remarked to his colleague, Brigadier General John Gib-
bon, "if Lee attacks tomorrow, it will be in your front.
He has made attacks on both our flanks and failed and
if he concludes to try it again, it will be on our center."
Thus Meade was prepared for Lee's assault.

The next morning, a bright, hot summer day, the
Confederates launched an assault on Culp's Hill, only
to fall back by noon. The key battle of the day occurred at three in the afternoon at Cemetery Ridge,
preceded by a fierce artillery duel. When the Union
guns suddenly went silent, the Confederates, thinking
they had knocked them out, began a charge led by
General George Pickett. As the Confederate infantry
marched out with battle colors flying, the Union artillery opened up again and tore apart the charging
Southerners. Some managed to reach their objective,
a low stone wall at the crest of the hill, but the federals
who held the wall outnumbered them and pushed
them back. The Confederates retreated down the gen-
tle slope strewn with their fallen comrades, the hopes
of a Southern victory dashed. Half of Pickett's thirteen–thousand–man division lay dead or wounded.

After the battle, Lee explained his disastrous
frontal assault: "I believed my men were invincible."
After Pickett's charge, Lee rode among his troops and
urged them to brace for a final Union assault. The attack never came. Meade allowed Lee to withdraw into
Maryland and cross the Potomac to Virginia.

Gettysburg was the bloodiest battle of the war.
The Union suffered 23,000 casualties; the Confederacy, 28,000. The battle's outcome boosted morale in
the North and drained Lee's army of men and materiel. Yet Lincoln blasted Meade for failing to follow
up on his victory. "I do not believe you appreciate the
magnitude of the misfortune involved in Lee's escape," he wrote to his general. "He was within your
easy grasp, and to have closed upon him would, in
connection with our other late successes, have ended
the war. As it is, the war will be prolonged indefinitely.
. . . Your golden opportunity is gone, and I am dis-
tressed immeasurably because of it." Convinced by his
aides that Meade would resign when he read the letter, Lincoln never sent it.

VICKSBURG, CHATTANOOGA, AND THE WEST
As Union forces thwarted Confederate dreams in
Pennsylvania, Federal troops bore down on strategic
Rebel strongholds in the Western theater of the war.
Union military success in the West would seriously
compromise the South's ability to move goods and
men across rail lines and over waterways, and leave its

These Union and Confederate dead at Gettysburg represent the cost of the war, the price of freedom. President Lincoln transformed the battleground from a killing field to a noble symbol of sacrifice for American ideals. Gettysburg continues to occupy a special place in our nation's history and in the memory of its citizens.

Mississippi. They moved northeastward, captured the Mississippi state capital at Jackson, and turned west toward Vicksburg. On May 22, 1863, Grant settled down in front of the city, less than 600 yards from Confederate positions. Grant's tight siege and the Union navy's bombardment from the river cut the city off completely. As food stores dwindled, residents were forced to eat mules and rats to survive. Their situation hopeless, General John Pemberton and his thirty-thousand-man garrison surrendered on July 4.

Chattanooga.

As Grant was besieging Vicksburg in June 1863, Union general William S. Rosecrans, commanding the Army of the Cumberland, advanced on Confederate general Braxton Bragg, whose Army of Tennessee held Chattanooga, a "doorway" on the railroad that linked Richmond to the lower South. The capture of the city would complete the uncoupling of the West from the eastern Confederacy.

Bragg lacked confidence in his men and consistently overestimated the force and cunning of his enemy. At Rosecrans's approach, he abandoned Chattanooga and took up positions at nearby Chickamauga Creek. When the two armies clashed at Chickamauga on September 19, Bragg pushed Rosecrans back to Chattanooga. Bragg seized the railroad leading into Chattanooga and bottled up Rosecrans there, much as Grant had confined Pemberton at Vicksburg. Both sides had suffered heavily. Suddenly, the Union's careful strategy for the conquest of the western Confederacy seemed in jeopardy.

The Confederate position on the heights overlooking Chattanooga appeared impregnable. But the Confederate camp was plagued by dissension, with some officers openly questioning Bragg's ability. President Davis considered replacing him but had no one else available with Bragg's experience. Instead, Davis ordered General James Longstreet (along with one-third of Bragg's army) on a futile expedition against Union forces at Knoxville, Tennessee. Converging on Chattanooga with reinforcements, Union generals Grant, Sherman, and Hooker took advantage of the

forces vulnerable to the ultimate Western prize, the Confederate bread basket, Georgia.

Vicksburg.

When Lincoln mentioned "our other late successes" in his letter to Meade, he was referring to another crucial Union victory. On July 4, one day after Pickett's charge at Gettysburg, the city of Vicksburg, the last major Confederate stronghold on the Mississippi, surrendered to Ulysses S. Grant.

Grant had demonstrated an ability to use his forces creatively, swiftly, and with a minimum loss of life in his campaigns in the western Confederacy, but Vicksburg presented him with several strategic obstacles (see Map 15-5). In 1862, the formidable defenses on the city's western edge, which towered over the Mississippi, had thwarted a Union naval assault, and the labyrinth of swamps, creeks, and woods, protecting the city from the north, had foiled General Sherman. The only feasible approaches appeared to be from the south and east.

By March 1863, Grant, had devised a brilliant plan to take Vicksburg that called for rapid maneuvering and expert coordination. Grant had his twenty thousand Union troops ferried across the Mississippi from the Louisiana side at a point south of Vicksburg. Then he marched them quickly into the interior of

MAP 15-5   Vicksburg and Chattanooga: The War in the West, 1863

Devising a brilliant strategy, Union General Ulysses S. Grant took the last major Mississippi River stronghold from Confederate hands on July 4, 1863, dealing a significant economic and morale blow to Southern forces. Coupled with the defeat at Gettysburg a day earlier, the fall of Vicksburg portended a bitter finale to hopes for Southern independence. Grant completed his domination of the West by joining forces with several Union generals to capture Chattanooga and push Confederate forces into Georgia, setting the stage for the capture of that key southern state by the Federals in 1864.

divided Confederate army to break the siege and force Bragg's army to retreat into Georgia. The Union now dominated most of the West and faced an open road to the East.

The war in the Trans-Mississippi West.

The Confederacy's reverses at Vicksburg and Chattanooga mirrored its misfortunes farther west of the Mississippi River. Although a relatively minor theater of war, the territory west of the Mississippi provided supplies and strategic advantages for the Confederate West. Success in the Trans-Mississippi West could occupy Federal troops and relieve pressure from other parts of the Confederacy while allowing food and munitions to reach desperate Southern armies.

Native American tribes in the Trans-Mississippi West, such as the Navajos, Dakotas, and Lakotas, spent a good deal of the Civil War battling Federal troops for territory and resources, quite apart from the sectional conflict. Three regiments of Cherokee Indians, however, led by Colonel (later Brigadier General) Stand Watie, fought for the South at the Battle of Pea Ridge in 1862. The Union won the battle and, with it, control of Missouri and northern Arkansas. Most battles between pro-Union and pro-Confederate Native American forces occurred in the Indian Territory (now Oklahoma).

Texas was critical to Confederate fortunes, both as a source of supply for the East and as a base for the conquest of the Far West. President Davis envisaged a continental Confederacy that included California, with its gold fields and Pacific ports. The ports would give the Confederacy access to Asian trade and, Davis reasoned, weaken the Federal naval blockade.

Texas, however, was far from secure. It suffered from internal dissent and violence on its borders. Not all Texans supported secession. As early as 1862, areas of northern Texas, a Unionist stronghold before the war, rebelled against Confederate authorities and were brutally suppressed. Germans in the Fredericksburg-San Antonio area openly defied the Confederacy from 1862 until the war's end. And the Mexican population in southern Texas supported the Union. On the state's western border, Comanches raided homesteaders at will until late 1864. In the east and along the southern frontier in the lower Rio Grande Valley, Union gunboats and troops disrupted Confederate supply lines. For a time, Texas maintained commercial contact with the rest of the Confederacy through Matamoros Mexico. The Mexican connection was vexing to the Lincoln administration, given the presence of the French and their puppet government from 1863 on. But by 1864, with the Union in control of the

Mississippi, and Federal troops along the Mexican border, Texas had lost its strategic importance.

The Confederacy's transcontinental aspirations died early in the war. In March 1862, a Confederate army seeking to conquer the Southwest was defeated by Union forces at the Battle of Glorieta Pass in New Mexico. The Southwest, from New Mexico to California, would remain firmly in Union hands.

WAR TRANSFORMS THE NORTH

Union successes in 1863 had a profound impact on both sides. For the North, hopes of victory and reunion increased. The federal government expanded its bureaucracy to wage war efficiently, and a Republican-dominated Congress passed legislation that broadened federal power and furthered the war effort. The Lincoln administration faced opposition on these measures and on its conduct of the war from within Congress, from the Democratic party, and from state leaders. But it successfully weathered dissent, thanks to the president's political skill, the desire of the Republicans to remain in power, and the Union's improving military fortunes. Boosted by federal economic legislation and wartime demand, the Northern economy boomed. Women entered the work force in growing numbers. But labor unrest and class and racial tensions suggested that prosperity had a price.

WARTIME LEGISLATION AND POLITICS

Before the Civil War, the federal government rarely affected citizens' lives directly. But raising troops, protecting territory, and mobilizing the economy for war required a strong and active central government. With the departure of the South from the Union, Republicans dominated all branches of the federal administration. This left them in a position to test the constitutional limits of federal authority.

Suppressing dissent.

President Lincoln began almost immediately to use executive authority to suppress opposition to the war effort in the North. In one of his most controversial actions, he issued a temporary suspension of the writ of habeas corpus, the constitutional requirement that protects a defendant against illegal imprisonment. Suspending it allowed authorities to arrest suspected Confederate agents and hold them indefinitely, a procedure sanctioned by the Constitution "when in cases of rebellion or invasion the public safety may require it." Explaining his extraordinary actions in a July 4, 1861, message to Congress, Lincoln stated, "it became necessary for me to choose whether I should let the government fall into ruin, or whether . . . availing myself of the broader powers conferred by the Constitution in case of insurrection, I would make an effort to save it." The suspension became permanent in September 1862 and was used primarily in the border states to detain those suspected of trading with the enemy, defrauding the War Department, and evading the draft.

Executive sanctions fell particularly hard on the Democratic party. "Disloyalty" was difficult to define in the midst of war. Though many Democrats opposed secession and supported the Union, they challenged the president on the conduct of the war, on emancipation, and on Lincoln's coolness toward peace initiatives. A few had ties with Confederate agents. Republicans called these dissenters "**Copperheads**," after the poisonous snake.

Despite the suspension of habeas corpus, Lincoln compiled a fairly good record for upholding basic American civil liberties. Although the authorities shut down a handful of newspapers temporarily, the administration made no attempt to control the news or subvert the electoral process. Two major elections were held during the war. In the first, the off-year election in 1862, Republicans retained control of Congress but lost several seats to Democrats. In the presidential election of 1864, Lincoln won reelection in a hard-fought contest.

While fellow Republicans sometimes chastised the president for violating civil liberties, mismanaging military command assignments, or moving too slowly on emancipation, they rarely threatened to disrupt the party. But there was dissent in the Republican party, and it had an effect on national policy. **Radical Republicans** hounded Lincoln from early in his administration, establishing the Joint Committee on the Conduct of the War to examine and monitor military policy. Some of them accused Democratic generals, including McClellan, of deliberately subverting the war effort with their poor performance. They also pressed Lincoln for quicker action on emancipation, though they supported the president on most crucial matters.

Boosting the economy. Lincoln likewise supported his party on an array of initiatives in Congress. Republicans used the federal government to enhance individual opportunities, especially in the West. The **Homestead Act**, passed in May 1862, granted 160 acres free to any settler in the territories who agreed to improve the land (by cultivating it and erecting a house) within five years of the grant. The act was also a boon for railroad companies.

Other legislation to boost the nation's economy and the fortunes of individual manufacturers and farmers included the **Land Grant College Act** of 1862, a protective tariff that same year, and the National Banking Act of 1863. The Land Grant Act awarded the proceeds from the sale of public lands to the states for the establishment of colleges offering instruction in "agriculture and mechanical arts." (President Buchanan had vetoed an earlier version of this act.) The tariff legislation protected Northern industry from foreign competition while raising revenue for the Union. The National Banking Act of 1863 replaced the bank notes of individual states, which were often backed by flimsy reserves and subject to wild fluctuations in value, with a uniform national currency.

Changes in the disposition of federal lands, the protective tariff, and the establishment of a national banking system presaged the active role the federal government would henceforth play in shaping the nation's economy. These measures helped sustain the Union war effort and enjoyed widespread support. The expansion of government into other areas, however, aroused opposition in some quarters, none more than the draft laws.

Conscription and the Draft Riots. Congress passed the first national conscription law in 1863. Almost immediately, evasion, obstruction, and weak enforcement threatened to undermine it. As military authorities began arresting draft dodgers and deserters, secret societies formed to harbor draftees and instruct them on evasion.

Conflicts between citizens and federal officials over the draft sometimes erupted in violence. The worst draft riot occurred in New York City in July 1863. Opposition to what many perceived as the Republican's war ran deep in New York, and support for the Democratic party was strong. The city's merchants were hurting from their lost trade in Southern cotton, and its Irish workers feared competition for jobs from freed slaves migrating to the North.

The **New York Draft Riot** began when a mostly Irish mob, protesting conscription, burned the federal marshal's headquarters. Racial and class antagonisms quickly joined antidraft anger as the mob went on a rampage through the city's streets, fighting police, plundering houses of the wealthy, and crying, "Down with the rich!" The rioters hanged two black New Yorkers who wandered into their path and burned the Colored Orphan Asylum. City authorities and the police stood by, unable or unwilling to stem the riot, which claimed more than one hundred lives. It was finally quelled by army units fresh from Gettysburg, along with militia and naval units. The draft resumed a month later.

The lynching of a black New Yorker during the Draft Riot in July 1863. The violence against black people during the riot reflected decades of racial tensions, especially between Irish immigrants and black residents, over jobs and housing.

THE NORTHERN ECONOMY

"The North," one historian has said, "was fighting the South with one hand and getting rich with the other behind its back." After an initial downturn during the uncertain months preceding the war, the Northern economy picked up quickly. High tariffs and massive federal spending soon made up for the loss of southern markets and the closing of the Mississippi river. Profits skyrocketed for some businesses. The earnings of the Erie Railroad, for example, jumped from $5 million in 1860 to $10 million in 1863. New industries boomed, and new inventions increased manufacturing efficiency, as in the sewing machine industry, which was first commercialized in the 1850s. Technological advances there greatly increased the output of the North's garment factories. Production of petroleum, a lubricant, increased from 84,000 gallons to 128 million gallons during the war.

Despite the loss of manpower to the demands of industry and the military, the productivity of Northern agriculture grew during the war. As machines replaced men on the farm, the manufacturers of farm machinery became wealthy. Crop failures in Europe dramatically increased the demand for American grain. "Old King Cotton's dead and buried; brave young Corn is king," went a popular Northern refrain of the day.

Trade unions and strikebreakers. Working people should have benefited from wartime prosperity.

With men off to war and immigration down, labor was in short supply. Although wages increased, prices rose more. Declining real wages led to exploitation, especially of women in garment factories. The trade union movement, which suffered a serious setback in the depression of 1857, revived. Local unions of shoemakers, carpenters, and miners emerged in 1862 across the North, and so did a few national organizations. By 1865, more than 200,000 northern workers belonged to labor unions.

Employers struck back at union organizing by hiring strikebreakers, usually African Americans. Labor conflicts between striking white workers and black strikebreakers sparked riots in New York City and Cincinnati. The racial antagonism accounted in part for workers' opposition to Lincoln's Emancipation Proclamation and for the continued strength of the Democratic party in Northern cities.

Profiteers and corruption. The promise of enormous profits bred greed and corruption as well as exploitation. Illicit trade between North and South was inevitable when cotton could be bought at 20 cents a pound in New Orleans and sold for $1.90 a pound in Boston. Profiteers not only defied the government to trade with the enemy but also sometimes swindled the government outright. Some merchants reaped high profits supplying the army with shoddy (a word coined during the war denoting poor quality shoes) goods at inflated prices. A writer for *Harper's Weekly* complained that "soldiers, on the first day's march or in the earliest storm, found their clothes . . . scattering to the wind in rags."

Some Northerners viewed the spending spree uneasily. They were disturbed to see older men flaunting their wealth while young men were dying on the battlefield. "The lavish profusion in which the old Southern cotton aristocracy used to indulge," wrote an indignant reporter for the *New York World*, "is completely eclipsed by the dash, parade, and magnificence of the new Northern shoddy aristocracy. . . . [T]he individual who makes the most money—no matter how—and spends the most money—no matter for what—is considered the greatest man."

Comments like these hinted at the deep social and ethical problems that were emerging in Northern society and would become more pronounced in the decades after the Civil War. For the time being, the benefits of economic development for the Union cause outweighed its negative consequences. The thriving Northern economy fed, clothed, and armed the Union's soldiers and kept most civilians employed and well fed. Prosperity and the demands of a wartime economy also provided Northern women with unprecedented opportunities.

NORTHERN WOMEN AND THE WAR

More than 100,000 Northern women took jobs in factories, sewing rooms, and arsenals during the civil war. Stepping in for their absent husbands, fathers, and sons, they often performed tasks previously reserved for men but at lower pay. The expanding bureaucracy in Washington also offered opportunities for many women. The United States Treasury alone employed 447 women in the war years. And unlike private industry, the Federal government paid women and men equally for the same work.

Women also had the opportunity to serve the war effort directly in another profession previously dominated by men—nursing. Physicians and officers, however, although they tolerated women nurses as nurturing morale boosters, thought little of their ability to provide medical care. Women sometimes challenged this condescending view, braving dismissal to confront the medical-military establishment head-on. Clara Barton, among the most notable nurses of the war, treated soldiers on the battlefield at great peril to her safety and to the consternation of officers. One of them remarked to her, "Miss Barton, this is a rough and unseemly position for you, a woman, to occupy." She shot back, "Is it not as rough and unseemly for these pain-racked men?" The officer temporarily suspended Barton for her candor. A British journalist, impressed by Barton and the thousands of women like her, commented that no conflict in history was so much "a woman's war" as the Civil War.

If the war created opportunities for many women, it also left tens of thousands widowed and devastated. In a society that assumed that men supported women, the death of a husband could be a financial and psychological disaster. Many women were left to survive on meager pensions with few skills they could use to support themselves.

The new economic opportunities the war created for women left Northern society more open to a broader view of women's roles. One indication of this change was the admission of women to eight previously all-male state universities after the war. Like the class and racial tensions that surfaced in Northern cities, the shifting role of women during the Civil War hinted at the promises and problems of postwar life. The changing scale and nature of the American economy, the expanded role of government, and the shift in class, racial, and gender relations are all trends that signaled what historians call the "modernization" of American society. Many of these trends began before the war, but the war highlighted and accelerated them.

Nurse Ann Bell tends a fallen Union soldier. Although medical practices were primitive and many young men died from poorly treated wounds or disease, the U.S. Sanitary Commission attempted to improve care in Union hospitals during the war. The war helped open nursing as a respectable occupation for women.

THE CONFEDERACY DISINTEGRATES

Even under the best of conditions, the newly formed political and economic institutions of the Confederacy would have had difficulty maintaining control over the country's class and racial tensions. But as battlefield losses mounted, the Confederacy disintegrated.

Victory is a marvelous glue. Defeat dissolves the bonds that hold a small society, such as the Confederacy, together and exposes the large and small divisions within it. After 1863, defeat infected Confederate politics, ruined the Southern economy, and eventually invaded the hearts and minds of the Southern people. What is remarkable is that such losses did not demoralize the Confederacy sooner. In fact, desertion rates did not exceed those of the Union forces, and Lee's Army of Northern Virginia included about as many men in the spring of 1865 as it had in the spring of 1863. True, civilians battled the policies of the Richmond government, but they protested less the sacrifices that war engendered than the unequal sharing of these burdens, including taxation, the military draft, food shortages, and inflation. Disillusionment against the Confederate government did not erode support for Lee and his army. The South pinned its waning hopes on its defensive military strategy. If it could prolong the conflict a little longer, perhaps a war-weary North would replace Lincoln and the Republicans in the 1864 elections with a Democratic president and Congress inclined to make peace.

SOUTHERN POLITICS

Dissent plagued Southern politics before the end of the war's first year. Residents of western Virginia mounted a secession movement of their own, declaring themselves for the union and forming the new state of West Virginia. Several counties in northern Alabama, in German-speaking districts in Texas, and throughout the mountains of Tennessee and North Carolina contemplated similar action.

As the war turned against the Confederacy, Southerners increasingly turned against each other. Some joined the peace societies that emerged as early as 1861 in Arkansas and soon after in most other Southern states. North Carolinians opposed to the war formed the Order of the Heroes of America, whose members not only demonstrated for peace but took control of the Piedmont and mountain sections of the state as well. Other Southerners preferred quieter dissent. They refused to join the army, pay taxes, or obey laws prohibiting trade with the enemy.

States' rights, a major principle of the seceding states, proved an obstacle to the Davis administration's efforts to exert central authority. The governors of Georgia and North Carolina gave the Richmond government particular difficulty, hoarding munitions, soldiers, supplies, food, and money. Even cooperative governors refused to allow state agents to collect taxes for the Confederacy.

Unlike Abraham Lincoln, Jefferson Davis could not appeal to party loyalty to control dissent because the Confederacy had no parties. Davis's frigid personality, his insistence on attending to minute details, and his inability to accept even constructive criticism gracefully, also set him apart from Lincoln and worsened political tensions within the Confederacy.

Several parts of the South began clamoring for peace during the fateful summer of 1863. In a tour of his state that year, North Carolina political leader Jonathan Worth heard calls for the overthrow of the Davis administration and a separate peace with the North. "Every man [I] met," he concluded "was for reconstruction on the basis of the old [U.S.] constitution." By November 1864, the Confederacy suffered as much from internal disaffection as from the attacks of Union armies. Confederate authorities could not suppress civilian unrest in Virginia, North Carolina, and Tennessee, and Union spies operated openly in Mobile, Wilmington, and Richmond.

Davis and other Confederate leaders might have averted some of these political problems had they succeeded in building a strong sense of Confederate nationalism among soldiers and civilians. They tried several strategies to do so. For example, Davis tried to identify the Confederacy's fight for independence with the American Revolution of 1776. But egalitarian revolutionary ideals quickly lost their appeal in the face of poverty, starvation, and defeat. Davis also tried to cast the Confederacy as a bastion of freedom standing up to Lincoln's despotic abuse of executive authority, but he, too, eventually invoked authority similar to Lincoln's. Confederate religious leaders sought to distinguish their new nation from the North by referring to Southerners as God's "chosen people." But when Confederate military fortunes declined, religious leaders drew back from such visions of collective favor and stressed the need for individual salvation.

In a devout society convinced it was fighting a holy war, some Southerners sought some moral failing to account for their mounting losses. Some identified slavery as the culprit. A Confederate leader in South Carolina asked in 1864, "Are we not fighting against the moral sense of the world? Can we hope to succeed in such a struggle?" in a similar vein, a Louisiana woman admitted that "always I felt that moral guilt of it [slavery], felt how impossible it must be for an owner of slaves to win his way into heaven."

THE SOUTHERN ECONOMY

Defeat came to the South, according to one historian, "not because the government failed to mobilize the South's resources" but "because there was virtually nothing left to mobilize." By 1863, the Confederacy was having a difficult time feeding itself. Destruction of farms by both sides and growing Union control of waterways and rail lines restricted the distribution of food. Speculators held certain commodities off the market to drive up prices, making shortages of food, cloth, and medicines worse. Bread riots erupted in Mobile, Atlanta, and Richmond. In Mobile, a group of women marched under banners reading "Bread or Blood" and "Bread and Peace." Armed with hatchets, they looted stores for food and clothing. In a show of grim humor, people in Southern cities held "starvation parties" at which they served only water. "Deaths from starvation have absolutely occurred," a Confederate official in the state informed President Davis in 1864.

Southern soldiers had marched off to war in neat uniforms with shiny buttons, many leaving behind self-sustaining families. But in August 1863, diarist Mary Chesnut, wife of a Confederate official in Richmond, watched ten thousand men marching near Richmond and commented, "Such rags and tags as we saw now. Most garments and arms were . . . taken from the enemy." The soldiers' families were threadbare as well. The prohibitive cost of new clothing prompted a group of women in northern Georgia to raid a textile mill for calico cloth in 1863. During the winter of 1863–1864, women lined their clothes with rags and newspapers to keep warm. In the devastated areas near battle sites, civilians survived by selling fragments of dead soldiers' clothing stripped off their bodies and by collecting spent bullets and selling them for scrap.

The predations of both Union and Confederate soldiers further threatened civilians in the South. The women and children left alone on farms and plantations were vulnerable to stragglers and deserters from both armies who sometimes robbed, burned houses, raped, and murdered. Southerners also feared that slaves on isolated plantations would rise up against their masters. Most slaves, however, were more intent on escape than revenge. There was no point in murdering the master or his family when freedom was just out the door and down the road to the Union lines. Escaped slaves had children, husbands, wives, and other relatives to find and spirit away to Union camps. The business of freedom was too time-consuming to waste on white people. Leave it to God to mete out punishment for the evil of bondage.

Wartime food shortages, skyrocketing inflation, and rumors of hoarding and price-gouging drove women in several Southern cities to protest violently. Demonstrations like the 1863 food riot shown here reflected a larger rending of Southern society as Confederate losses and casualties mounted on the battlefield. Some Southern women placed survival and providing for their families ahead of boosting morale and silently supporting a war effort that had taken their men away. Their defection hurt the Confederate cause.

Some slaves felt genuine affection for the families they served and stayed on with them even after the war. Some protected white Southerners from Union soldiers and hid valuables for them. But women forced to manage plantations alone could never be sure where their slaves stood. Mary Chesnut wrote in her diary about her mother's butler, "He looks over my head—he scents freedom in the air." As slaves stopped working and abandoned plantations, the women left to run them had to work the fields themselves.

As Confederate casualties mounted, more and more Southern women and children, like their Northern counterparts, faced the pain of grief. Funeral processions became commonplace in the cities and black the color of fashion. With little food, worthless money, and a husband or father gone forever, the future looked bleak.

SOUTHERN WOMEN AND THE WAR

In the early days of the Civil War, Southern white women continued to live their lives according to antebellum conventions. Magazine articles urged them to preserve themselves as models of purity for men debased by the violence of war. The Southern woman, by her moral example, "makes the Confederate soldier a gentleman of honor, courage, virtue and truth, instead of a cut-throat and vagabond," opined one magazine. She would buttress the nation's morale through the wavering fortunes of war. On her shoulders rested "the destinies of the Southern Confederacy," the *Natchez Weekly Courier* declared.

Women flooded newspapers and periodicals with patriotic verses and songs. A major theme of these works, illustrated by the following example from the *Richmond Record* in September 1863, was the need to suppress grief and fear for the good of the men at the front:

The maid who binds her warrior's sash
And smiling, all her pain dissembles,
The mother who conceals her grief
[had] shed as sacred blood as e'er
Was poured upon the plain of battle.

A Virginia woman confided to her diary, "We must learn the lesson which so many have to endure—to struggle against our feelings."

By the time of the Civil War, such emotional concealment had become second nature to planters' wives. They had long had to endure their anguish over their husbands' nocturnal visits to the slave quarters. They were used to the condescension of men who assumed them to be intellectually inferior. And they accepted in bitter, self-sacrificing silence the contradiction between the myth of the pampered leisure they were presumed to enjoy and the hard demands their lives actually entailed. But some Southern women chafed at their supporting role and, as Confederate manpower and materiel needs became acute, took on new productive responsibilities. Initially, they did so within the domestic context: Women formed clubs to sew flags and uniforms. To raise money for the war effort, they held benefits and auctions and collected jewelry and other valuables.

Soon, however, the needs of the Confederacy drew women outside the home to fill positions vacated by men. They managed plantations. They worked in the fields alongside slaves, and, if they had worked there before, they worked harder. They worked in factories to make uniforms and munitions. They worked in government offices as clerks and secretaries. They taught school. A few, like Belle

Boyd and Rose O'Neal Greenhow, spied for the Confederacy. And many, like their Northern counterparts, served as nurses. Eventually, battlefield reverses and economic collapse undermined all these roles, leaving women and men alike struggling simply to survive.

As the war dragged on and the Southern economy and the social order deteriorated, even the patriots suffered from resentment and doubt. By 1864, many women were helping their deserting husbands or relatives elude Confederate authorities. In Randolph County, North Carolina, for example, two women torched a barn belonging to a state official in charge of rounding up deserters. Incidents like these convinced authorities that women were mainly responsible for desertion in the last years of the war. A North Carolina official explained that "desertion takes place because desertion is encouraged. . . . and though the ladies may not be willing to concede the fact, they are nevertheless responsible . . . for the desertion in the army and the dissipation in the country."

By 1864, many Southern white women had tired of the war. What had begun as a sacred cause had disintegrated into a nightmare of fear and deprivation. Uprooted from their homes, some women wandered through the war-ravaged South, exposed to violence, disease, and hunger and seeking shelter where they could find it. Those women fortunate enough to remain in their homes turned to work, others to protest, and many to religion. Some devoutly religious women concluded that it was God, not the Yankees, who had brought destruction on the South for its failure to live up to its responsibilities to women and children. Others blamed their men. After a series of reverses in the Confederate West, one woman confided to her diary that "If our soldiers continue to behave so disgracefully, we *women* had better take the field and send them home to raise chickens." Women greeted defeated troops retreating from Vicksburg with shouts of "We are disappointed in you!" However, despite hardship and privation, support for the Confederacy persisted among some women accompanied by a fierce hatred of the enemy. One woman displayed the bones of a Federal soldier in her yard and another hoped for a "Yankee skull" to use as a jewelry box.

THE UNION PREVAILS, 1864–1865

Despite the union's dominant military position after Vicksburg and Gettysburg and the Confederacy's mounting home-front problems, three obstacles to

White family "refugeeing." In advance of Union armies, tens of thousands of Southern families fled to safer locales, a bitter exodus that fulfilled the Federals' vow to bring the war to the South's civilian population.

Union victory remained. Federal troops under General William T. Sherman controlled Chattanooga and the gateway to Georgia, but the Confederate Army of Tennessee, commanded by Joseph E. Johnston, was still intact, blocking Sherman's path to Atlanta. Robert E. Lee's formidable Army of Northern Virginia still protected Richmond. And the Confederacy still controlled the rich Shenandoah Valley, which fed Lee's armies and supplied his cavalry with horses. In March 1864, President Lincoln brought General Ulysses S. Grant to Washington and appointed him commander of all Union armies. Grant set about devising a strategy to overcome these obstacles.

GRANT'S PLAN TO END THE WAR

Grant brought two innovations to the final campaign. First, he coordinated the Union war effort. Before, the Union's armies in Virginia and the West had operated independently, giving Confederate leaders the opportunity to direct troops and supplies to whichever arena most needed them. Now Grant proposed to deprive them of that option. The Union's armies in Virginia and the Lower South would attack at the same time, keeping steady pressure on all fronts. Second, Grant changed the tempo of the war. Before, long periods of rest had intervened between battles. Grant, with the advantage of superior numbers, proposed nonstop warfare. He wanted to "hammer continuously against the armed force of the enemy and his resources, until by mere attrition, if in no other way, there should be nothing left to him but an equal submission with the

loyal section of our common country to the constitution and laws of the land."

Although Grant's strategy ultimately worked, several problems and miscalculations undermined its effectiveness. With Sherman advancing in Georgia, Grant's major focus was Lee's army in Virginia. But Grant underestimated Lee. The Confederate general thwarted him for almost a year and inflicted horrendous casualties on his army. Confederate forces under Jubal Early drove off Union forces from the Shenandoah Valley in June 1864, depriving Grant of troops and allowing the Confederates to maintain their supply lines. And the incompetence of General Benjamin Butler, charged with advancing up the James River to Richmond in May 1864 to relieve Lee's pressure on Grant, further eroded Grant's plan. Finally, Grant contended with disaffection in his officer corps. Many of his officers felt enduring loyalty to General George McClellan, whom Lincoln had dismissed in 1862, and considered Grant a mediocrity who had triumphed in the West only because his opposition there had been third-rate.

Lee's only hope was to make Grant's campaign so costly and time-consuming that the Northern general would abandon it before the Southerners ran out of supplies and troops. But despite problems and setbacks, Grant kept relentless pressure on Lee. Tied down in Virginia, the Confederate general was unable to send troops to help slow Sherman's advance in Georgia.

From the Wilderness to Cold Harbor. Grant and General George Meade began their campaign against Lee in May 1864, crossing the Rapidan River near Fredericksburg, Virginia, and marching toward an area known as the Wilderness (see Map 15-6). Lee attacked the Army of the Potomac, which outnumbered his 118,000 to 60,000, in the thickets of the Wilderness on May 5 and 6 before it could reach open ground. The densely wooded terrain reduced the Union army's advantage in numbers and artillery. Much of the fighting involved fierce hand-to-hand combat. Exchanges of gunfire at close range set the dry underbrush ablaze. Wounded soldiers, trapped in the fires, begged their comrades to shoot them before they burned to death. The toll was frightful—eighteen

MAP EXPLORATION To explore an interactive version of this map, go to http://www.prenhall.com/goldfield/map15.6

PENNSYLVANIA

NEW JERSEY

MARYLAND

Baltimore

Washington

DELAWARE

WEST VIRGINIA

Winchester
Sept. 19, 1864

Cedar Creek
Oct. 19, 1864

Shenandoah River

Rappahannock River

The Wilderness
May 5–7, 1864

Chancellorsville

Fredericksburg

Waynesboro
March 2, 1865

Rapidan River

Spotsylvania Court House
May 8–21, 1864

North Anna

Grant 1864

Lee 1864

VIRGINIA

Amelia Court House

Richmond

Cold Harbor
June 3, 1864

Lee 1865

Lynchburg

Appomattox Court House
Lee surrenders to Grant
April 9, 1865

James River

Sheridan 1865

Grant 1865

Petersburg
June 1864–April 1865

Sayler's Creek
April 6, 1865

Five Forks
April 1, 1865

ATLANTIC OCEAN

CHESAPEAKE BAY

Area controlled by Union
Area controlled by Confederacy
Union advances
Confederate advances
Confederate retreats
Fortifications
Union victories
Confederate victories

MAP 15-6   **Grant and Lee in Virginia, 1864-1865**
The engagements in Virginia from May 1864 to April 1865 between the two great generals for the Union and the Confederacy proved decisive in ending the Civil War. Although General Lee fared well enough in the Wilderness, Spotsylvania, and Cold Harbor campaigns, the sheer might and relentlessness of Grant and his army wore down the Confederate forces. When Petersburg fell after a prolonged siege on April 2, 1865, Richmond, Appomattox, and dreams of Southern independence soon fell as well.

thousand casualties on the Union side, ten thousand for the Confederates. Union commanders would have pulled back and rested after such an encounter. But Grant, relentless in the pursuit of the enemy, startled Lee's army by pushing on. "Surprise and disappointment were the prevailing emotions," one Southerner wrote, "when we discovered after the contest in the Wilderness that General Grant was not going to retire." Lee's offensive in the Battle of the Wilderness

was his last. From then on, his army was on the defensive against Grant's relentless pursuit.

Marching and fighting, his casualties always higher than Lee's, Grant continued South. Attacking the entrenched Confederate army at Spotsylvania, his army suffered another eighteen thousand casualties to the Confederates' eleven thousand. Undeterred, Grant moved on toward Cold Harbor, where Lee's troops again awaited him in entrenched positions. Flinging his army against withering Confederate fire on June 3, he lost seven thousand men in eight minutes.

In less than a month of fighting, the Army of the Potomac had lost 55,000 men. The slaughter undermined Grant's support in Northern public opinion and led peace advocates to renew their quest for a cease-fire. With antiwar sentiment growing in the North as the presidential elections approached in November, Lee's defensive strategy seemed to be working.

At this point, Grant decided to change his tactics. Abandoning his march on Richmond from the north, he shifted his army south of the James River to approach the Confederate capital from the rear. Wasting no time, he crossed his army over the James and, on June 17, 1864, surprised the Confederates with an attack on Petersburg, a critical rail junction 23 miles south of Richmond. It was a brilliant maneuver, but the hesitant actions of Union corps commanders gave Lee time to reinforce the town's defenders. Both armies dug in for a lengthy siege.

Atlanta. While Grant engaged Lee in Virginia, Union forces under William T. Sherman in Georgia engaged in a deadly dance with the Army of Tennessee under the command of Joseph E. Johnston as they began the Atlanta Campaign, a scheme to take Atlanta, Georgia (see Map 15-7). Johnston had replaced the incompetent Braxton Bragg after the Confederate

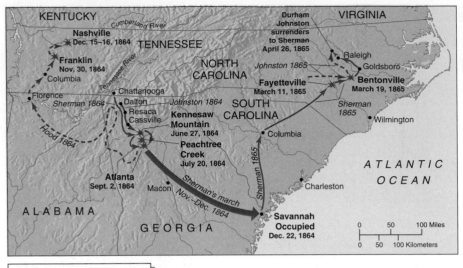

Union advances
Confederate advances
Confederate retreats
Union victories
Confederate victories

MAP 15-7   The Atlanta Campaign and Sherman's March, 1864-1865
General William T. Sherman, a brilliant tactician who generally refused to be goaded into a frontal assault, "danced" with Confederate general Joseph E. Johnston until an impatient Jefferson Davis replaced Johnston with Hood, and soon Atlanta was in Federal hands. The fall of Atlanta opened the way to the rest of Georgia, a key supply state for the Confederacy. With orders not to harm the civilian population, Sherman's men took their wrath out on property as they made their way through Georgia and South Carolina.

President Davis feared that Johnston would let Sherman take Atlanta without a fight and dance with the Union general until the sea stopped them both. Davis dismissed Johnston and installed John Bell Hood of Texas in his place. This was a grave error. Hood, in the opinion of those who fought for him, had a "lion's heart" but a "wooden head."

In late July, Hood began a series of attacks on Sherman, beginning at Peachtree Creek on July 20, and was thrown back each time with heavy losses. Sherman launched a series of flanking maneuvers around the city in late August that left Hood in danger of being surrounded. The Confederate general had no choice but to abandon Atlanta and save his army. On the night of September 1, Hood evacuated the city, burning everything of military value.

The loss of Atlanta was a severe blow to the Confederacy. Several of the South's major railroads converged at the city, and its industries helped arm and clothe the South's armies. Atlanta's fall also left Georgia's rich farmland at the mercy of Sherman's army.

Most significant, the fall of Atlanta revived the morale of the war-weary North and helped assure Lincoln's reelection in November. The last hope of the Confederacy—that a peace candidate would replace Lincoln and end the war—had faded. As the disconsolate editor of the *Richmond Examiner* explained, the "disaster at Atlanta [came] in the very nick of time" to "save the party of Lincoln from irretrievable ruin. . . . [I]t will obscure the prospect of peace, late so bright. It will also diffuse gloom over the South."

THE ELECTION OF 1864 AND SHERMAN'S MARCH

Before Sherman's victory at Atlanta, Northern dismay over Grant's enormous losses and his failure to take Richmond raised the prospect of a Democratic election victory. Nominating George B. McClellan, the former commander of the Union's armies, as their presidential candidate, the Democrats appealed to the voters as the party of peace. They also appealed to

debacle at Chattanooga in late 1863. He shared Lee's belief that the Confederacy's best hope lay in a defensive strategy. Hoping to lure Sherman into a frontal assault, Johnston settled his forces early in May at Dalton, an important railroad junction in Georgia 25 miles south of Chattanooga and seventy-five miles north of Atlanta. The wily Union general declined to attack and instead made a wide swing around the Confederates, prompting Johnston to abandon Dalton, rush south, and dig in again at Resaca to prevent Sherman from cutting the railroad. Again Sherman swung around without an assault, and again Johnston rushed south to cut him off, this time at Cassville.

This waltz continued for two months, until Johnston had retreated to a strong defensive position on Kennesaw Mountain, barely twenty miles north of Atlanta. At this point, early in July, Sherman decided to attack, with predictably disastrous consequences. The Union suffered three thousand casualties, the Confederates only six hundred. Sherman would not make such a mistake again. He resumed his maneuvering and by mid-July had forced Johnston into defensive positions on Peachtree Creek just north of Atlanta.

Union General Ulysses S. Grant had the pews from a local church moved to a grove of trees where he and his officers planned the following day's assault on Confederate troops at Cold Harbor, Virginia. Grant appears at the left of the photograph, leaning over a bench and studying a map.

the antiemancipation sentiment that was strong in some parts of the North.

The fall of Atlanta and the Union's suddenly improved military fortunes undermined Democratic prospects. Another Union victory three weeks before the elections gave Lincoln a further boost and diminished McClellan's chances. Since September, Union forces, under General Philip H. Sheridan, had been on the offensive in the Shenandoah Valley. In lightning cavalry raids on farms and supply depots, they destroyed valuable Confederate food reserves. And, in a decisive battle on October 19, they overwhelmed the valley's Confederate defenders. Lee had now been deprived of a vital source of supply.

The Republican victory. In the voting on November 8, Lincoln captured 55 percent of the popular vote, losing only New Jersey, Delaware, and Kentucky. Republicans likewise swept the congressional elections, retaining control of both the Senate and the House of Representatives.

The Republican victory reinforced the Union commitment to emancipation. A proposed constitutional amendment outlawing slavery everywhere in the United States, not just those areas still in rebellion, passed Congress and was ratified as the **Thirteenth Amendment** to the U.S. Constitution in 1865. All earlier amendments related to government powers and functions; this was the first to outlaw a domestic institution previously protected by the Constitution and state law.

Sherman's March to the Sea.

After Sherman took Atlanta, he proposed to break Confederate resistance once and for all by marching his army to the sea and destroying everything in its path. Sherman's March got under way on November 15. His force of sixty thousand men encountering little resistance, entered Savannah on December 22, 1864, and presented the city to Lincoln as a Christmas present. Just a few weeks earlier, Union forces in Tennessee had routed Hood's army at the Battle of Franklin and then crushed it entirely at the Battle of Nashville. Hood's defeat removed any threat to Sherman's rear.

Sherman's March reached a triumphant conclusion in February 1865 when black Federal troops of the 55th Massachusetts Regiment marched into battered Charleston, South Carolina. The illustration captures both the destructiveness of the total war General Sherman waged on Georgia and South Carolina and the hope among former slaves for a new birth of freedom.

Sherman resumed his march in February 1865, heading for South Carolina, the heart of the Confederacy and the state where the Civil War had begun. "The truth is," Sherman wrote a friend, "the whole army is burning with an insatiable desire to wreak vengeance on South Carolina." South Carolinians sent taunting messages promising stiff resistance, but these served only further to provoke Sherman's troops. They pushed aside the small force that assembled to oppose them, wreaked greater destruction in South Carolina than they had in Georgia, and burned the state capitol at Columbia. Sherman sent the colonel of a black regiment to receive the surrender of Charleston and ordered black troops to be the first to take possession of the city. The soldiers marched in singing "John Brown's Body" to the cheers of the city's black population.

Sherman ended his march in Goldsboro, North Carolina, in March 1865 after repelling a surprise Confederate attack at Bentonville led by the restored Joseph E. Johnston and the remnants of the Army of Tennessee. Behind the Union army lay a barren swath 425 miles long from Savannah to Goldsboro.

Arming the Confederacy's slaves.

In a move reflecting their desperation in March 1865, Confederate leaders revived a proposal that they had previously rejected to arm and free slaves. Slaves had served involuntarily in the Confederate army, and a number of free black Louisianans had volunteered for service in Southern ranks early in the war. But this proposal represented a major policy shift. President Davis hoped it would gain the Confederacy not only a military benefit but also diplomatic recognition from countries that had balked because of slavery.

The issue divided Confederate leaders. Confederate general Howell Cobb argued that "if slaves will make good soldiers, our whole theory of slavery is wrong." Others thought that it was preferable to abandon slavery than to lose independence. A Confederate congressman from Georgia wrote to a friend in October 1864 that if the South lost the war, slavery was over anyway, and "we and our children will be slaves, while our freed Negroes will lord it over us." But if the Confederacy enlisted slaves, it could "win our independence, and have liberty and homes for ourselves and our children."

Not surprisingly, slaves themselves greeted the proposal with little enthusiasm. They might have found service in the Confederate army an acceptable alternative to bondage earlier in the war, but not now, with Union victory imminent. Mary Chesnut recalled in March 1865 that early in the war, when her husband "spoke to his Negroes about it, his head men were keen to go in the army, to be free and get a bounty after the war. Now they say coolly that they don't want freedom if they have to fight for it. That means they are pretty sure of having it anyway."

Overview

Major Battles of the Civil War, 1861–1865

Battle or Campaign	Date	Outcome and Consequences
First Bull Run	July 21, 1861	Confederate victory, destroyed the widespread belief in the North that the war would end quickly, fueled Confederate sense of superiority
Forts Henry and Donelson	Feb. 6–16, 1862	Union victory, gave the North control of strategic river systems in the western Confederacy and closed an important link between the eastern and western Confederacy
Shiloh Church	Apr. 6–7, 1862	Union victory, high casualties transformed attitudes about the war on both sides
Seven Days' Battles	June 25–July 1, 1862	Standoff, halted Union General McClellan's advance on Richmond in the Peninsula Campaign
Second Bull Run	Aug. 29–30, 1862	Confederate victory, reinforced Confederate general Robert E. Lee's reputation for invincibility
Antietam	Sept. 17, 1862	Standoff, halted Lee's advance into the North, eliminated Confederacy's chance for diplomatic recognition, encouraged Lincoln to issue the Emancipation Proclamation
Fredericksburg	Dec. 13, 1862	Confederate victory, revived morale of Lee's army
Chancellorsville	May 2–6, 1863	Confederate victory, Confederate General Stonewall Jackson killed, encouraged Lee to again invade North
Gettysburg	July 1–3, 1863	Union victory, halted Confederate advance in the North, major psychological blow to Confederacy
Vicksburg	Nov. 1862–July 1863	Union victory; closed the key Confederate port on the Mississippi, also dealt a severe blow to Confederate cause
Chattanooga	Aug.–Nov. 1863	Union victory, solidified Union dominance in the West
Wilderness and Cold Harbor	May and June 1864	Both Confederate victories inflicted huge losses on Grant's army; turned public opinion against Grant but failed to force him to withdraw
Atlanta	May–September 1864	Union victory; Confederacy lost key rail depot and industrial center
Sherman's March	November 1864–March 1865	Nearly unopposed, Sherman's army cut a path of destruction through Georgia and South Carolina, breaking Southern morale
Battles of Franklin and Nashville	November and December 1864	Union victories in Tennessee; effectively destroyed Army of Tennessee
Siege of Petersburg	June 1864–April 1865	Long stalemate ended in Union victory; led to fall of Richmond and surrender of Lee's army at Appomattox Court House

On March 13, 1865, a reluctant Confederate Congress passed a bill to enlist black soldiers, but without a provision offering them freedom. President Davis and the war office bypassed the equivocal congressional legislation ten days later, issuing a general order that promised immediate freedom to slaves who enlisted. The war ended before the order could have any effect. The irony was that in the summer of 1864, a majority of Northerners probably would have accepted reunion without emancipation had the Confederacy abandoned its fight.

THE ROAD TO APPOMATTOX AND THE DEATH OF LINCOLN

With Sherman's triumph in Georgia and the Carolinas and Sheridan's rout of the Confederates in the Shenandoah Valley, Lee's army remained the last obstacle to Union victory. On April 1, Sheridan's cavalry seized a vital railway junction on Lee's right flank, forcing Lee to abandon Petersburg and the defense of Richmond. He tried a daring run westward toward Lynchburg, hoping to secure much-needed supplies and to join Johnston's Army of Tennessee in North Carolina to continue the fight.

President Davis fled Richmond with his cabinet and headed toward North Carolina. Richard Gill Forrester, a seventeen-year-old black youth, awoke to find the evacuation underway. He reached under his bed and pulled out an American flag. Maneuvering through the chaotic streets, young Forrester reached the state capitol building, climbed to the top, and affixed the banner to the flagpole. Union troops occupied the Confederate capital on April 3, and, two days later, President Lincoln walked through its streets to

This photograph of Abraham Lincoln was taken four days before John Wilkes Booth assassinated him in Ford's Theatre.

the cheers of his army and an emotional reception from thousands of black people. "I know I am free," shouted one black spectator, "for I have seen Father Abraham and felt him."

The surrender at Appomattox.   Grant's army of 60,000 outran Lee's diminishing force of 35,000 and cut off his escape at Appomattox Court House, Virginia, on April 7. Convinced that further resistance was futile, the Confederate commander met Grant on April 9, 1865, in the McLean house at Appomattox to sign the documents of surrender. The Union general offered generous terms, allowing Lee's men to go home unmolested and to take with them horses or mules "to put in a crop." Grant reported feeling "sad and depressed" at "the downfall of a foe who had fought so long and valiantly, and had suffered so much for a cause, though that cause was, I believe, one of the worst for which a people ever fought." Lee rode through the thinned ranks of his troops, who crowded around him in silent tribute, brushing the general's boots and the withers of his horse with their hats.

Though some Southerners entertained fleetingly the idea of launching a guerilla campaign against Union forces, most were sick of the war. One Confederate leader, traveling through the stricken South in April 1865, reported that soldiers and civilians alike considered any continuation of the conflict, "madness." Joseph E. Johnston surrendered to Sherman near Durham, North Carolina, on April 26. On May 10, Union cavalry captured President Davis in southern Georgia. On May 26, Texas general Kirby Smith surrendered his trans-Mississippi army, and the Civil War came to an end.

The death of Lincoln.   Washington greeted the Confederate surrender at Appomattox with predictable and raucous rejoicing—torchlight parades, cannon salutes, and crowds spontaneously bellowing "The Star-Spangled Banner." On April 11, President Lincoln addressed a large crowd from the White House balcony and spoke briefly of his plans to reconstruct the South with the help of persons loyal to the Union, including recently freed slaves. At least one listener found the speech disappointing. A sometime actor and full-time Confederate patriot, John Wilkes Booth, muttered to a friend in the throng, "That means nigger citizenship. Now, by God, I'll put him through. That is the last speech he will ever make."

On the evening of April 14, Good Friday, the president went to Ford's Theatre in Washington to view a comedy, *Our American Cousin*. During the per-

FROM THEN TO NOW

Gettysburg

Each year more than 1.8 million visitors track across Pennsylvania's rolling hills to retrace the steps of the competing armies as they fought the Battle of Gettysburg in July 1863. The fascination has become big business at the Gettysburg National Military Park, where tourists spend more than $40 million annually on items ranging from Pickett's Charge T-shirts to faked battlefield relics. For a nation not ordinarily fixated on the past, the devotion to this battle—to which a majority of Americans have no ancestral connections—is extraordinary. What accounts for it?

The Civil War was a defining event in American history, and the Battle of Gettysburg was the defining moment of the Civil War, a guidepost on the American journey. The battle has thus become a metaphor for the national ideals the war brought into focus, symbolizing them in an enduring form for subsequent generations of Americans and serving as a reminder of the work still to be done to translate those ideals into reality for all. The battle also emerged as a symbol of national reconciliation after the fratricidal conflict of the war.

For generations of white Southerners after the Civil War, Gettysburg was the place where the young men of a doomed cause displayed incomparable courage against long odds. "For every southern boy fourteen years old," William Faulkner wrote, "not once but whenever he wants it, there is the instant when it's still not yet two o'clock"—the hour before Pickett's Charge—"on that July afternoon in 1863."

But today most Americans, North and South, see Gettysburg not as a missed opportunity, but, thanks to President Lincoln's famous address dedicating the battlefield cemetery, as a place that gives meaning to the sacrifices of both sides. Consecrating the battlefield to a renewal of the nation's founding ideals, Lincoln asked his listeners to "highly resolve that these dead shall not have died in vain that this nation, under God, shall have a new birth of freedom and that government of the people, by the people, for the people, shall not perish from the earth." In the years after the war, veterans from both sides came to the battlefield seeking reconciliation, posing together for pictures and shaking hands. Tourists strike similar poses today.

African Americans, however, have not by and large shared the national fascination with Gettysburg and make up less than 3 percent of the visitors to the battlefield. "When you're black," the African American historian Allan B. Ballard explained, "the great battlefield holds mixed messages." Although the National Park Service, which oversees the site, has put up an exhibit on the role of African American troops in the Civil War, black visitors remain ambivalent about the place. Aware of the long and continuing struggle they would face to secure true equality in American society after the Civil War, they see irony in Lincoln's call for "a new birth of freedom." Yet, if, as Ballard notes, "we are still fighting our civil wars," at Gettysburg at least, it is possible for Americans today to see and learn how their freedoms were paid for in blood and to reflect, in Lincoln's words, on the "unfinished work which they who fought here have thus far so nobly advanced."

---

formance, Booth shot the president, wounding him mortally, then jumped from Lincoln's box to the stage shouting *"sic semper tyrannis"* ("Thus ever to tyrants") and fled the theater. Union troops tracked him down to a barn in northern Virginia and killed him. Investigators arrested eight accomplices, who had conspired with Booth to murder other high officials in addition to Lincoln. Four of the accomplices were hanged. Besides the president, however, the only other official attacked was Secretary of State Seward, who received serious but not fatal knife wounds.

Southerners reacted to Lincoln's assassination with surprisingly mixed emotions. Many saw in the death of the man they had regarded as their bitterest enemy for four years some slight hope of relief for the South's otherwise bleak prospects. But General Johnston and others like him understood Lincoln's influence with the radical elements in the Republican party who were pressing for harsh terms against the South. The president's death, Johnston wrote, was "the greatest possible calamity to the South."

CONCLUSION

Just before the war, William Sherman had warned a friend from Virginia, "You people of the South don't know what you are doing. This country will be drenched in blood. . . . [W]ar is a terrible thing." He was right. More than 365,000 Union soldiers died during the war, 110,000 in battle, and more than 256,000 Confederate soldiers, 94,000 of them in battle. Total casualties on both sides, including wounded, were more than 1 million.

Southern armies suffered disproportionately higher casualties than did Northern armies. One in four Confederate soldiers died or endured debilitating wounds, compared to one in ten Federal soldiers. During the first year after the war, Mississippi allocated one-fifth of its budget to artificial limbs. Compounding the suffering of the individuals behind these gruesome statistics was the incalculable suffering—in terms of grief, fatherless children, women who never married, families never made whole—of the people close to them.

The war devastated the South. The region lost one-fourth of its white male population between the ages of 20 and 40. It also lost two-fifths of its livestock and half its farm machinery. Union armies destroyed many of the South's railroads and shattered its industry. Between 1860 and 1870, the wealth of the South declined by 60 percent, and its share of the nation's total wealth dropped from more than 30 percent to 12 percent. The wealth of the North, in contrast, increased by half in the same period.

The Union victory solved the constitutional question about the right of secession and sealed the fate of slavery. The issue that dominated the prewar sectional debate had vanished. Now when politicians intoned in Independence Day orations or campaign speeches about the ideals of democracy and freedom, the glaring reality of human bondage would no longer mock their rhetoric.

For black Southerners, emancipation was the war's most significant achievement. Journalists sponsored by the federal government who recorded the testimony of ex-slaves in the 1930s during the Great Depression, seventy years after emancipation, found their memory of the jubilee as fresh as yesterday. Lincoln entered African-American folklore as a larger-than-life figure. At age 91, Fanny Burdock of Valdosta, Georgia, told a recorder a common tale of seeing Lincoln "coming all dusty and on foot" past her Georgia home.

> We run right to the fence and had the oak bucket and the dipper. When he draw up to us, he so tall, black eyes so sad. Didn't say not one word, just looked hard at all us, every one us crying. We give him nice cool water from the dipper. Then he nodded and set off and we just stood there till he get to being dust then nothing. After, didn't our owner or nobody credit it, but me and all my kin, we knowed. I still got the dipper to prove it.

The Civil War stimulated other changes that grew more significant over time. It did not make the Union an industrial nation, but it taught the effectiveness of centralized management, new financial techniques, and the coordination of production, marketing, and distribution. Entrepreneurs would apply these lessons to create the expanding corporations of the postwar American economy.

Likewise, the war did not revolutionize gender relations in American society; but, by opening new opportunities to women in fields such as nursing and teaching, it helped lay the foundation for the woman's suffrage movement of the 1870s and 1880s.

For many Americans, especially black and white Southerners, the war was the most important event in their lives. It had a devastating impact on the families and friends of those who died. But it was not responsible for every postwar change in American society, and it left many features of American life intact. The experience of pulling together in a massive war effort, for example, did not soften class antagonisms. European socialist and father of communism Karl Marx hailed Lincoln as a son of the working class and predicted that "as the American War of independence initiated a new era of ascendancy for the middle class, so the American anti-slavery war will do for the working classes." But capitalism, not labor, triumphed during the war. And it was industrialists and entrepreneurs, not working people, who most benefited from the war's bonanza. Lincoln brutally suppressed strikes at defense plants and threw labor leaders into military prisons.

The war to end slavery changed some American racial attitudes, especially in the North. When Lincoln broadened the war's objectives to include the abolition of slavery, he connected the success of the Union to freedom for the slave. At the outset of the Civil War, only a small minority of Northerners considered themselves abolitionists. After the Emancipation Proclamation, every Northern soldier became a liberator. By the end of the war, perhaps a majority of Northerners supported granting freedmen the right to vote and to equal protection under the law, even if they believed (as many did) that black people were inferior to white people. The courage of black troops and the efforts of African American leaders to link the causes of reunion and freedom were influential in bringing about this shift.

Most white Southerners did not experience a similar enlightenment. Some were relieved by the end of slavery, but most greeted it with fear, anger, and regret. For them, the freed slaves would be living reminders of the South's defeat and the end of a way of life grounded in white supremacy.

If the Civil War resolved the sectional dispute of the 1850s by ending slavery and denying the right of the Southern states to secede, it created two new equally troubling problems: how to reunite South and North and how to deal with the legacy of slavery. At his last cabinet meeting on April 14, Lincoln gave little indication of how he intended to proceed on these problems. He seemed inclined to be conciliatory, cautioning against reprisals on Confederate leaders and noting the courage of General Lee and his officers. The president said nothing about the rights of freedmen, although earlier statements indicated that he favored suffrage, but not social equality, for African Americans.

America's greatest crisis had closed. In its wake, former slaves tested their new freedom, and the nation groped for reconciliation. The struggle to preserve the Union and abolish slavery had renewed and vindicated the nation's ideals. It was time to savor the hard-fought victories before plunging into the uncertainties of Reconstruction.

In November 1863, President Lincoln was asked to say a few words at the dedication of the federal cemetery at Gettysburg. There, surrounded by a somber scene of fresh graves, Lincoln bound the cause of the Union to that of the country's founders: "Fourscore and seven years ago our fathers brought forth upon this continent a new nation, conceived in liberty and dedicated to the proposition that all men are created equal. Now we are engaged in a great civil war, testing whether that nation, or any nation so conceived and so dedicated can long endure." A Union victory, Lincoln hoped, would not only honor the past but also call forth a new nation, cleansed of its sins, to serve as an inspiration, to oppressed peoples around the world. He called on the nation to resolve "that the nation shall, under God, have a new birth of freedom; and that government of the people, by the people, for the people, shall not perish from the earth." Not only did the two-minute Gettysburg Address capture what Union supporters were fighting for, but it also connected their sacrifices to the noble causes of freedom and democratic government. That would be both the hope and the challenge of the peace that followed a hard war.

REVIEW QUESTIONS

1. How did the Union and the Confederacy compare in terms of resources, leadership, and military strategies in the period 1861–1863? What impact did these factors have on the course of the war?

2. What was the significance of the battles of Antietam and Gettysburg? In what ways were they turning points in the Civil War?

3. What effects did the Emancipation Proclamation have on both the Union and Confederate causes?

4. Compare and contrast the roles played by women, in the North and in the South, during the Civil War, and explain how their actions and activities aided or hindered the war effort of their respective nations.

5. Given the enormity of the losses in lives and property, it is not surprising that some historians have attributed major changes in American society to the Civil War. But other historians claim that the Civil War's impact has been exaggerated. Analyze and assess what the Civil War did or did not accomplish.

6. Sullivan Ballou made the ultimate sacrifice for his cause. Why did he fight?

KEY TERMS*

Confiscation Act (p. 468)

Copperheads (p. 478)

Emancipation Proclamation (p. 469)

Homestead Act (p. 478)

Land Grant College Act (p. 478)

New York Draft Riot (p. 478)

Radical Republicans (p. 478)

Thirteenth Amendment (p. 487)

* See the Overview table, on p. 489 for important battles of the Civil War.

RECOMMENDED READING

Crane, Stephen. *The Red Badge of Courage* (Originally published 1895; reprinted various dates). The Civil War did not inspire great American novels. But this is a notable exception that depicts, not only the horrors of combat, but also its impact on the soldiers who fought.

McPherson, James M. *Battle Cry of Freedom: the Civil War Era* (1982). This book is probably the best account of the war in print. The author draws a number of interesting conclusions on several controversial topics from military strategy to the home front.

ADDITIONAL SOURCES

Mobilization, North and South

Cooper, William J. *Jefferson Davis: American* (2000).

Current, Richard N. *Lincoln's Loyalists: Union Soldiers from the Confederacy* (1992).

Davis, William C. *"A Government of Our Own": the Making of the Confederacy* (1994).

Donald, David. *Lincoln* (1995).

Faust, Drew Gilpin. *The Creation of Confederate Nationalism: Ideology and Identity in the Civil War* (1988).

Marszalek, John P. *Sherman: A Soldier's Passion for Order* (1993).

Rable, George C. *The Confederate Republic: A Revolution Against Politics* (1994).

Royster, Charles. *The Destructive War: William Tecumseh Sherman, Stonewall Jackson, and the Americans* (1991).

Thomas, Emory M. *Robert E. Lee: A Biography* (1995).

The Early War, 1861–1862

Cooling, Benjamin Franklin. *Forts Henry and Donelson: The Key to the Confederate Heartland* (1988).

Daniel, Larry J. *Shiloh: The Battle That Changed the Civil War* (1997).

Fellman, Michael. *Inside War: The Guerrilla Conflict in Missouri during the Civil War* (1989).

Linderman, Gerald F. *Embattled Courage: The Experience of Combat in the American Civil War* (1989).

McPherson, James M. *What They Fought For, 1861–1865* (1994).

Robertson, James I. *Stonewall Jackson: the Man, the Soldier, the Legend* (1997).

Sears, Stephen W. *George B. McClellan: the Young Napoleon* (1988).

Turning Points, 1862–1863

Berlin, Ira, et al., eds. *Freedom: A Documentary History of Emancipation, 1861–1867*, Ser. 1, Vol. 1: *The Destruction of Slavery* (1985).

Cox, LaWanda. *Lincoln and Black Freedom: A Study in Presidential Leadership* (1981).

Foner, Eric. *Nothing but Freedom: Emancipation and its Legacy* (1983).

Josephy Jr., Alvin M. *The Civil War in the American West* (1993).

McFeely, William S. *Grant: A Biography* (1981).

Quarles, Benjamin. *The Negro in the Civil War* (1953).

Reardon, Carol. *Pickett's Charge in History and Memory* (1997).

Sears, Stephen W. *Landscape Turned Red: The Battle of Antietam* (1983).

Smith, David Paul. *Frontier Defense in the Civil War: Texas' Rangers and Rebels* (1992).

Wills, Garry. *Lincoln at Gettysburg: The Words That Remade America* (1992).

War Transforms the North

Baker, Kevin. *Paradise Alley: A Novel* (2002)

Neely, Mark E. Jr., *The Fate of Liberty: Abraham Lincoln and Civil Liberties* (1991).

Pryor, Elizabeth B. *Clara Barton: Professional Angel* (1987).

Richardson, Heather Cox. *The Greatest Nation of the Earth: Republican Economic Policies During the Civil War* (1997).

The Confederacy Disintegrates

Ash, Stephen V. *When the Yankees Came: Conflict and Chaos in the Occupied South, 1861–1865* (1995).

Campbell, Edward D. C. Jr., and Kym S. Rice, eds. *A Woman's War: Southern Women, Civil War, and the Confederate Legacy* (1996).

Clinton, Catherine, and Nina Silber, eds. *Divided Houses: Gender and the Civil War* (1992).

Durden, Robert F. *The Gray and the Black: The Confederate Debate on Emancipation* (1972).

Faust, Drew Gilpin. *Mothers of Invention: Women of the Slaveholding South in the American Civil War* (1996).

Grimsely, Mark. *The Hard Hand of War: Union Policy Toward Southern Civilians, 1861–1865* (1995).

Whites, Leeann. *The Civil War as a Crisis in Gender: Augusta, Georgia, 1860-1890* (1995).

Woodward, C. Vann, ed. *Mary Chesnut's Civil War* (1981).

The Union Prevails

Beringer, Richard E., Herman Hattaway, Archer Jones, and William N. Still, Jr. *Why the South Lost the Civil War* (1986).

Glatthaar, Joseph T. *The March to the Sea and Beyond* (1985).

Thomas, Emory. *The Confederate Nation, 1861–1865* (1979).

WHERE TO LEARN MORE

- **Museum of the Confederacy, Richmond, Virginia.** This museum has rotating exhibits on various aspects of the Confederate effort during the Civil War, both on the home front and on the battlefield. The Confederate White House, which is open to the public, is next door to the museum. [www.moc.org].

- **Gettysburg National Military Park, Gettysburg, Pennsylvania.** An excellent and balanced interpretation awaits the visitor at this national park. [www.nps.gov/gett/].

- **Antietam National Battlefield, Sharpsburg, Maryland.** Also an excellent and balanced interpretation at this battlefield site. [www.nps.gov/anti/].

- **Ford's Theatre National Historical Site, Washington, DC.** The place where John Wilkes Booth assassinated President Abraham Lincoln not only depicts those events, including artifacts from the assassination, but also presents period plays. [www.nps.gov/foth/index2.htm].

- **Appomattox Court House, Appomattox, Virginia.** What historian Bruce Catton termed "a stillness at Appomattox" can be felt at the McLean house in this south-central Virginia town. The house is much as it was when Confederate General Robert E. Lee surrendered his forces to Union General Ulysses S. Grant on April 9, 1865. An almost reverential solitude covers the house and the well-maintained grounds today. [www.nps.gov/apco/].

 Please refer to the document CD-ROM for primary sources related to this chapter.

THE "ABRAHAM LINCOLN SCHOOL" FOR FREEDMEN, NEW ORLEANS, LOUISIANA. —[PHOTOGRAPHED BY LILIENTHAL, NEW ORLEANS.]

➜ *Barred from literacy during the slavery era, freedmen devoured learning after the Civil War. Their classrooms ranged from one-room cabins to more grandiose structures such as this, the Abraham Lincoln School for Freedmen in New Orleans.*

RECONSTRUCTION 16
1865–1877

CHAPTER OUTLINE

White Southerners and the Ghosts of the Confederacy, 1865

More than Freedom: African American Aspirations in 1865

Education
"Forty Acres and a Mule"
Migration to Cities
Faith and Freedom

Federal Reconstruction, 1865–1870

Presidential Reconstruction, 1865–1867
Congressional Reconstruction, 1867–1870
Southern Republican Governments

Counter-Reconstruction, 1870–1874

The Uses of Violence
The Failure of Northern Will
Liberal Republicans and the Election of 1872

Redemption, 1874–1877

The Democrats' Violent Resurgence
The Weak Federal Response
The Election of 1876 and the Compromise of 1877
The Memory of Reconstruction

The Failed Promise of Reconstruction

Sharecropping
Modest Gains and Future Victories

Conclusion

Marianna, Florida 1866

The white academy opened about the same time the church opened the school for the Negro children. As the colored children had to pass the academy to reach the church it was easy for the white children to annoy them with taunts and jeers. The war passed from words to stones which the white children began to hurl at the colored. Several colored children were hurt and, as they had not resented the rock-throwing in kind because they were timid about going that far, the white children became more aggressive and abusive.

One morning the colored children armed themselves with stones and determined to fight their way past the academy to their school. [They] approached the academy in formation whereas in the past they had been going in pairs or small groups. When they reached hailing distance, a half dozen white boys rushed out and hurled their missiles. Instead of scampering away, the colored children not only stood their ground and hurled their missiles but maintained a solemn silence. The white children, seeing there was no backing down as they expected, came rushing out of the academy and charged the colored children.

During some fifteen minutes it was a real tug of war. In the close fighting the colored children got the advantage gradually and began to shove the white children back. As they pressed the advantage the white children broke away and ran for the academy. The colored fighters did not follow them but made it hot for the laggards until they also took to their heels. There were many bruises on both sides, but it taught the white youngsters to leave the colored ones alone thereafter.

T. Thomas Fortune, *Norfolk Journal and Guide*

T. Thomas Fortune, "Norfolk Journal and Guide," August 20, 1927, reprinted in Dorothy Sterling, ed., *The Trouble They Seen: Black People Tell the Story of Reconstruction* (Garden City, NY: Doubleday & Co., 1976): 22–24.

T. Thomas Fortune, a New York newspaper editor, recalled this battle between black and white schoolchildren sixty years earlier, at the beginning of the Reconstruction era. In the scheme of things, it did not amount to much. However, for ten-year-old Thomas, born a slave in Marianna, the incident encapsulated well the dilemma of Reconstruction. In the journey from slavery to freedom, education emerged as an important element of full citizenship for African Americans. The eagerness with which black children (and adults) flooded schools—often spaces converted in churches and staffed initially by white missionaries from the North—was matched by the hostility of the white community who resented any advance by the former bondsmen and any pretense of equality that education implied.

Reconstruction was not merely a series of white aggressions against African American aspirations, followed by black retreats. The former slaves did not shy away from asserting their rights, any more than they had waited patiently for the Emancipation Proclamation to induce them to leave their plantations. The violence and disorder that punctuated Southern society after the Civil War was due in part to the refusal of blacks to relinquish their dreams of equal citizenship, including the right to a decent education.

Young Thomas did not back down, though by 1878 he understood that the promise that characterized his schoolboy days could not be realized in the South. The journey from slavery to freedom, he felt, would always be incomplete in the South. Together with his young bride, Carrie Smiley of Jacksonville, Florida, Thomas left for New York City, where he obtained a job as a printer for the *New York Sun*. Shaped by his early years in Florida, and the difficulties involved in obtaining a decent education, Fortune used the pages of the *Sun* to promote equality of education for all races and for integrated public schools in New York State. He died there in 1928. New York's gain was the South's loss, a process repeated many times over in the decades after the Civil War as talented young black men and women left the region of their birth and their ancestors. It was a double tragedy for the South: losing people who could have rebuilt a shattered region, and missing the opportunity to create a society based on racial equality.

The position of African Americans in American society was one of the two great issues of the Reconstruction era. Americans of both sections disagreed about how much freedom to grant the former slaves, almost all of whom lived in the South. The other great issue was how and under what terms to readmit the former Confederate states. The Constitution was silent on the subject. As with the issue of black equality, opinions in both sections varied widely.

The formation of a national consensus on freedom and reunification began with the demands and hopes of three broad groups. One was the Republican party, which controlled the federal government and determined its policies. Most Republicans were unwilling to accept the seceding states back in the Union without an expression of loyalty and a commitment to protecting the rights of freedmen. A second group, the more than 4 million former slaves, demanded voting rights, access to education, and the opportunity to seek economic self-sufficiency. Few black Northerners yet enjoyed all these benefits, and few white Southerners could conceive of former slaves possessing them. The third group, white Southerners, hoped to restore their shattered lives, fortunes, and dignity. In their vision of a renewed South, black people remained subservient and the federal government stopped interfering in southern affairs.

Between 1865 and 1867, under President Andrew Johnson's Reconstruction plan, white Southerners pretty much had their way with the former slaves and with their own state governments. Congressional action between 1867 and 1870 attempted to balance black rights and home rule, with mixed results. After 1870, white Southerners gradually regained control of their states and localities, often through violence and intimidation, denying black Southerners their political gains while Republicans in Washington lost interest in policing their former enemies.

By the time the last federal troops left the South in 1877, white Southerners had prevailed. The Confederate states had returned to the Union with all of their rights and many of their leaders restored. And the freed slaves remained in mostly subservient positions with few of the rights and privileges enjoyed by other Americans.

KEY TOPICS

- African American aspirations and southern white expectations

- Federal government plans to bring the South back into the Union and secure freedom for former slaves

- Southern Republican efforts to keep the allegiance of black voters and win white support

- Why and how Reconstruction ended

WHITE SOUTHERNERS AND THE GHOSTS OF THE CONFEDERACY, 1865

Confederate soldiers—generals and troops alike—returned to devastated homes they could scarcely recognize. General Braxton Bragg returned to his "once prosperous" Alabama home to find "all, all was lost, except my debts." Bragg and his wife found temporary shelter in a slave cabin. Yeomen farmers, the backbone of the Confederacy, found uprooted fences, farm animals dead or gone, and buildings destroyed. With no income or savings to soften their plight, they and their families wandered about in a living nightmare, seeking shelter where they could. They lived in morbid fear of vengeful former slaves or the hated Yankee soldiers wreaking more damage. "The demoralization is complete," a Georgia girl noted.

Their cause lost and their society reviled, white Southerners lived through the summer and fall of 1865 surrounded by ghosts—the ghosts of lost loved ones, joyful times, bountiful harvests, self-assurance, and slavery. Defeat shook the basic tenets of their religious beliefs. A North Carolinian cried, "Oh, our God! What sins we must have been guilty of that we should be so humiliated by Thee now!" Some praised God for delivering the South from the sin of slavery. A Virginia woman expressed thanks that "we white people are no longer permitted to go on in such wickedness, heaping up more and more wrath of God upon our devoted heads."

But many other white Southerners refused to accept their defeat as a divine judgment. How could they, as a devout people, believe that God had abandoned them? Instead, they insisted, God had spared the South for a greater purpose. They came to view the war as the **Lost Cause** and interpreted it, not as a lesson in humility, but as an episode in the South's journey to salvation. Robert E. Lee became the patron saint of this cause, his poignant nobility a contrast to the crassness of the Yankee warlords. White Southerners would not allow the memory of the bloody struggle to die, transforming it into a symbol of courage against great odds and piety against sin. Eventually, they believed, redemption would come.

The Southern white view of the Civil War (and of Reconstruction) was not a deliberate attempt to falsify history, but rather a need to justify and rationalize the devastation and loss of life that accompanied the Confederate defeat. This view, in which the war became the Lost Cause, and Reconstruction became the Redemption, also served to forge a community among white Southerners at a time of great unrest. A common religion solidified that bond and sanctified it. The Lost Cause also enabled white Southerners to move on with their lives and concentrate on rebuilding their shattered region. The Lost Cause was less a backward-looking perspective than it was a historical rationalization that enabled believers to hope for a better future. The regrettable feature of elevating the Civil War to a noble, holy enterprise was that it implied a stainless Old South, a civilization worth fighting and dying for. This new history required the return of the freedmen, if not to the status of slaves, then at least to their lowly place in society. This new history also ignored the savagery of the war by romanticizing the conflict.

The Lost Cause would not merely exist as a memory, but also as a three-dimensional depiction of Southern history across the landscape, in rituals and celebrations, and as the educational foundation for future generations. The statues of the common Confederate soldier erected typically on the most important site in a town, the courthouse square; the commemorations of Confederate Memorial Day, the birthdays of prominent Confederate leaders, and the reunions of veterans, all marked with flourishing oratory, brass bands, parades, and related spectacles; and the textbooks insuring that the white history of the South was implanted into young minds and the legacy carried down through the generations—all of these insured

Chronology

1863 Lincoln proposes his Ten Percent Plan.	Republican regimes topple in North Carolina and Georgia.
1864 Congress proposes the Wade-Davis Bill.	**1871** Congress passes Ku Klux Klan Act.
1865 Sherman issues Field Order No. 15.	**1872** Freedmen's Bureau closes down.
Freedmen's Bureau is established.	Liberal Republicans emerge as a separate party.
Andrew Johnson succeeds to the presidency, unveils his Reconstruction plan.	Ulysses S. Grant is reelected.
Massachusetts desegregates all public facilities.	**1873** Severe depression begins.
Black citizens in several southern cities organize Union Leagues.	Colfax Massacre occurs.
Former Confederate states begin to pass black codes.	U.S. Supreme Court's decision in the Slaughterhouse cases weakens the intent of the Fourteenth Amendment.
1866 Congress passes Southern Homestead Act, Civil Rights Act of 1866.	Texas falls to the Democrats in the fall elections.
Ku Klux Klan is founded.	**1874** White Leaguers attempt a coup against the Republican government of New Orleans.
Fourteenth Amendment to the Constitution is passed (ratified in 1868).	Democrats win off-year elections across the South amid widespread fraud and violence.
President Johnson goes on a speaking tour.	**1875** Congress passes Civil Rights Act of 1875.
1867 Congress passes Military Reconstruction Acts, Tenure of Office Act.	**1876** Supreme Court's decision in *United States v. Cruikshank* nullifies Enforcement Act of 1870.
1868 President Johnson is impeached and tried in the Senate for defying the Tenure of Office Act.	Outcome of the presidential election between Republican Rutherford B. Hayes and Democrat Samuel J. Tilden is contested.
Republican Ulysses S. Grant is elected president.	**1877** Compromise of 1877 makes Hayes president and ends Reconstruction.
1869 Fifteenth Amendment passed (ratified 1870).	
1870 Congress passes Enforcement Act.	

that the Lost Cause would not only be an interpretation of the past, but also the basic reality of the present and the foundation for the future.

Fifteen years after the war, Mark Twain traveled the length of the East Coast. After visiting a gentlemen's club in Boston, he recalled that the conversation had covered a variety of topics, none of which included the Civil War. Northerners had relegated that conflict to history books and moved on. Such was not the case in the South. There, defeat and destruction demanded rationalization and remembrance. Thus Twain reported that, unlike in the North, gentlemen's talk in Atlanta inevitably wandered to the war and to heroism and sacrifice. "In the South," Twain wrote, "the war is what A.D. is elsewhere: they date from it." Such people would not accept the changes implied by defeat. They would fight to preserve as much of their past as the victors allowed. For the past was both their present and their future.

Most white Southerners approached the great issues of freedom and reunification with unyielding views. They saw African Americans as adversaries whose attempts at self-improvement were a direct challenge to white people's beliefs in their own racial superiority. White Southerners saw outside assistance to black Southerners as another invasion. The Yankees may have destroyed their families, their farms, and their fortunes, but they would not destroy the racial order. The war may have ended slavery, but white Southerners were determined to preserve strict racial boundaries.

MORE THAN FREEDOM: AFRICAN AMERICAN ASPIRATIONS IN 1865

Black Southerners also had a particular perspective on the Civil War and Reconstruction, the former as a great victory for freedom and the latter as a time of great possibility. But their view did not matter; it

This engraving shows Southerners decorating the graves of rebel soldiers at Hollywood Memorial Cemetery in Virginia, in 1867. Northerners and Southerners alike honored their war dead. But in the South, the practice of commemorating fallen soldiers became an important element in maintaining the myth of the Lost Cause that colored white Southerners' view of the war.

was invisible or, worse, distorted, in books, monuments, and official accounts. If, as British writer George Orwell later argued, "who controls the present controls the past, and who controls the past controls the future," then the vanishing black perspective is not surprising. The ferocity with which white Southerners attempted to take back their governments and their social structure was not only about nostalgia; it was about power and the legitimacy that power conferred.

And, of course, the black perspective was decidedly different from that of whites. As early as 1863, black Southerners carved out a very different interpretation of the Civil War which, to them, was a war of liberation, not a Lost Cause. At an emancipation parade in Norfolk that year, black women took joy in stomping on Confederate flags and burning an effigy of Jefferson Davis. Less raucous displays followed the war, especially on July 4, which, until well into the 1880s, was primarily a black holiday. And how it must have incensed white Southerners to see their former slaves celebrate their defeat and humiliation.

Yet, the response of Southern whites to black aspirations still stunned African Americans who believed, naively perhaps, that what they sought—education, land, access to employment, and equality in law and politics—were so basic to American citizenship that no one would or could deny them these modest objectives. The former slaves did not initially even dream of social equality; far less did they plot the kind of vengeful murder and mayhem white people feared. They did harbor two potentially contradictory aspirations. The first was to be left alone, free of white

supervision. Responding to the key question of the time, "What shall we do with the Negro?" the former slave and abolitionist Frederick Douglass responded, "Do nothing . . . . Give him a chance to stand on his own legs! Let him alone!" But former slaves also wanted land, voting and civil rights, and education. To secure these, they needed the intervention and support of the white power structure.

In 1865, African Americans had reason to hope that their dreams of full citizenship might be realized. They enjoyed a reservoir of support for their aspirations among some Republican leaders. The views of James A. Garfield, Union veteran, U.S. congressman, and future president, were typical of these Republicans. Commenting on the ratification of the Thirteenth Amendment, Garfield asked, "What is freedom? Is it the bare privilege of not being chained? . . . If this is all, then freedom is a bitter mockery, a cruel delusion."

The first step Congress took beyond emancipation was to establish the Bureau of Refugees, Freedmen, and Abandoned Lands in March 1865. Congress envisioned the **Freedmen's Bureau**, as it came to be called, as a multipurpose agency to provide social, educational, and economic services, advice, and protection to former slaves and destitute white Southerners. The Bureau marked the federal government's first foray into social welfare legislation. Congress also authorized the bureau to rent confiscated and abandoned farmland to freedmen in forty-acre plots, with an option to buy. This auspicious beginning belied the great disappointments that lay ahead.

EDUCATION

The greatest success of the Freedmen's Bureau was in education. The bureau coordinated more than fifty northern philanthropic and religious groups, which, in turn, established three thousand freedmen's schools in the South, serving 150,000 men, women, and children.

Initially, single young women from the Northeast comprised much of the teaching force. One of them, 26-year-old Martha Schofield, came to Aiken, South Carolina, from rural Pennsylvania in 1865. Like many of her colleagues, she had joined the abolitionist movement as a teenager and decided to make teaching her life's work. Her strong Quaker beliefs reflected the importance of Protestant Christianity in motivating the young missionaries. When her sponsoring agency, the Pennsylvania Freedmen's Relief Association, folded in 1871, her school closed. Undaunted, she opened another school on her own, and, despite chronic financial problems and the hostility of Aiken's white citizens, she and the school

The Freedmen's Bureau, Northern churches, and missionary societies established more than three thousand schools, attended by some 150,000 men, women, and children in the years after the Civil War. At first, mostly young white women from the Northeast staffed these schools.

Some black Southerners went on to one of the thirteen colleges established by the American Missionary Association and black and white churches. Between 1860 and 1880 more than one thousand black Southerners earned college degrees at institutions still serving students today, such as Howard University in Washington, D.C.; Fisk University in Nashville; Hampton Institute (now University); Tuskegee Institute; and Biddle Institute (now Johnson C. Smith University) in Charlotte.

Pursuing freedom of the mind involved challenges beyond those of learning to read and write. Many white Southerners condemned efforts at "Negro improvement." They viewed the time spent on education as wasted, forcing the former slaves to catch their lessons in bits and pieces between work, often by candlelight or on Sundays. White Southerners also harassed white female teachers, questioning their morals and threatening people who rented rooms to them. The *Atlanta Constitution*, in a vicious caricature, suggested that Harriet Beecher Stowe planned to establish a freedmen's school near Atlanta "for the benefit of mulatto children that have been born in the South since its invasion by Yankee school-marms."

After the Freedmen's Bureau folded in 1872 and many of the northern societies that supported freedmen's education collapsed or cut back their involvement, education for black Southerners became more haphazard.

endured. (Since 1953, her school has been part of the Aiken public-school system.)

By the time Schofield opened her own school in 1871, black teachers outnumbered white teachers in the "colored" schools. The financial troubles of northern missionary societies and declining interest in the freedmen's condition among white Northerners opened opportunities for black teachers. Support for them came from black churches, especially the African Methodist Episcopal (AME) Church.

The former slaves crowded into basements, shacks, and churches to attend school. "The children . . . hurry to school as soon as their work is over," wrote a teacher in Norfolk, Virginia, in 1867. "The plowmen hurry from the field at night to get their hour of study. Old men and women strain their dim sight with the book two and a half feet distant from the eye, to catch the shape of the letter. I call this heaven-inspired interest."

At the end of the Civil War, only about 10 percent of black Southerners were literate, compared with more than 70 percent of white Southerners. Within a decade, black literacy had risen above 30 percent. Joseph Wilson, a former slave, attributed the rise to "this longing of ours for freedom of the mind as well as the body."

"FORTY ACRES AND A MULE"

Although education was important to the freed slaves in their quest for civic equality, land ownership offered them the promise of economic independence. For generations, black people had worked southern farms and had received nothing for their labor. An overwhelmingly agricultural people, freedmen looked to farm ownership as a key element in their transition from slavery to freedom. "Gib us our own land and we take care of ourselves," a Charleston freedman asserted to a Northern visitor in 1865. "But without land, de ole massas can hire or starve us, as dey please."

Even before the war's end, rumors circulated through black communities in the South that the government would provide each black family with forty acres and a mule. These rumors were fueled by General William T. Sherman's **Field Order No. 15** in January 1865, which set aside a vast swath of abandoned land along the South Atlantic coast from the Charleston area to northern Florida for grants of up to forty acres. The Freedmen's Bureau likewise raised expectations when it was initially authorized to rent forty-acre plots of confiscated or abandoned land to freedmen.

By June 1865, about forty thousand former slaves had settled on "Sherman land" along the southeastern coast. In 1866, Congress passed the **Southern Homestead Act**, giving black people preferential access to public lands in five southern states. Two years later, the Republican government of South Carolina initiated a land-redistribution program financed by the sale of state bonds. The state used proceeds from the bond sales to purchase farmland, which it then resold to freedmen, who paid for it with state-funded long-term low-interest loans. By the late 1870s, more than fourteen thousand African American families had taken advantage of this program.

The highest concentration of black land ownership was in the Upper South and in areas of the Lower South with better economic conditions and less white hostility toward black people. By 1890, one out of three black farmers in the Upper South owned his land, compared to one out of five for the South as a whole. In Virginia, 43 percent of black farmers owned the land they farmed.

Land ownership did not insure financial success. Most black-owned farms were small and on marginal land. The value of these farms in 1880 was roughly half that of white-owned farms. Black farmers also had trouble obtaining credit to purchase or expand their holdings. A lifetime of field work left some freedmen without the managerial skills to operate a farm. The hostility of white neighbors and their refusal to lend tools or animals, share work, sell land, or offer advice also played a role in thwarting black aspirations. Black farmers often had the most success when groups of families settled together, as in the farm community of Promise Land in upcountry South Carolina.

Milk sampling at Hampton Institute. Hampton, which opened in Virginia in 1868, was one of the first of several schools established with the help of Northern philanthropic and missionary societies to allow freedmen to pursue a college education. Hampton stressed agricultural and vocational training. The military uniforms were typical for male students, black and white, at agricultural and mechanical schools.

The vast majority of former slaves, however, especially those in the Lower South, never fulfilled their dreams of land ownership. Rumors to the contrary, the federal government never intended to implement a land-redistribution program in the South. General Sherman viewed his field order as a temporary measure to support freedmen for the remainder of the war. President Andrew Johnson nullified the order in September 1865, returning confiscated land to its former owners. Even Republican supporters of black land ownership questioned the constitutionality of seizing privately owned real estate. Most land-redistribution programs that did emerge after the war, including government-sponsored programs, required black farmers to have capital. But in the impoverished postwar economy of the South, it was difficult for them to acquire it.

Republican party rhetoric of the 1850s extolled the virtues and dignity of free labor over the degradation of slave labor. Free labor usually meant working for a wage or under some other contractual arrangement. But unlike slaves, according to the then prevailing view, free laborers could enjoy the fruits of their work and might someday become owners or entrepreneurs themselves. It was self-help, not government assistance, that guaranteed individual success. After the war, many white Northerners envisioned former slaves assuming the status of free laborers, not necessarily of independent landowners.

For most officials of the Freedmen's Bureau, who shared these views, reviving the southern economy was a higher priority than helping former slaves acquire farms. They wanted both to get the crop in the field and start the South on the road to a free labor system. They thus encouraged freedmen to work for their former masters under contract and to postpone their quest for land. Bureau and military officials lectured former slaves on the virtues of staying home and working "faithfully" in the fields.

At first, agents of the Freedmen's Bureau supervised labor contracts between former slaves and masters. But after 1867, bureau surveillance declined. Agents assumed that both black laborers and white landowners had become accustomed to the mutual obligations of contracts. The bureau, however, underestimated the power of white landowners to coerce favorable terms or to ignore those they did not like. Contracts implied a mutuality that most planters could not accept in their relations with former slaves. As the northern journalist Whitelaw Reid noted in 1865, planters "have no sort of conception of free labor. They do not comprehend any law for controlling laborers, save the law of force."

The former slaves had their own views of their proper place in the labor hierarchy. If they could not own land in the short term, they would strive for the best labor arrangement in the meantime. As early as 1862, slaves behind Union lines abandoned the gang system of labor, which they associated with slavery and dependence. In contracts with planters (usually their former masters) after the war, freedmen in most of the South insisted on working the land independently with their families. By contrast, freedmen in the rice districts along the South Atlantic coast retained their task system of labor, which allowed them flexibility and a degree of independence.

Throughout the South in 1865 and 1866, landlords complained of a chronic labor shortage, although few freedmen had left the region. The alleged shortage was the result of former slaves' refusal to work under conditions that resembled slavery. The withdrawal of black women from field work also contributed to the impression of a labor shortage. By staying home to care for their families, black women avoided the economic and sexual exploitation of the slavery era. They also sought to place themselves on an equal social footing with white plantation women, who likewise worked in the home and not in the fields.

MIGRATION TO CITIES

While some black Southerners asserted their rights as workers on southern farms, others affirmed their freedom by moving to towns and cities. Even before the war, the city had offered slaves and free black people a measure of freedom unknown in the rural South. After the war, African Americans moved to cities to find families, seek work, escape the tedium and supervision of farm life, or simply to test their right to move about.

For these same reasons, white people disapproved of black migration to the city. It reduced the labor pool for farms. It also gave black people more opportunities to associate with white people of similar social status, to compete for jobs, and to establish schools, churches, and social organizations, fueling their hopes for racial equality. White people felt confident that they could fix the freedmen's place in southern society on the farm; the city was another matter.

Between 1860 and 1870, the African American population in every major southern city rose significantly. In Atlanta, for example, black people accounted for one in five residents in 1860 and nearly one in two by 1870. Some freedmen came to cities initially to reunite with their families. Every city newspaper after the war carried advertisements from former slaves seeking their mates and children. In 1865, the Nashville *Colored Tennessean* carried this poignant plea: "During the year 1849, Thomas Sample carried away from this city, as his slaves, our daughter, Polly, and son. . . . We will give $100 each for them to any person who will assist them . . . to get to Nashville, or get word to us of their whereabouts."

Once in the city, freedmen had to find a home and a job. They usually settled for the cheapest accommodations in low-lying areas or on the outskirts of town, where building codes did not apply. Rather than developing one large ghetto, as happened in many northern cities, black Southerners lived in several concentrations in and around cities. Sometimes armed with a letter of reference from their former masters, black people went door to door to seek employment. Many found work serving white families—as guards, laundresses, maids—for very low wages. Both skilled and unskilled laborers found work rebuilding war-torn cities such as Atlanta. Frederick Ayer, a Freedmen's Bureau agent in Atlanta, reported to a colleague in 1866 that "many of the whites are making most vigorous efforts to retrieve their broken fortunes and . . . rebuild their dwellings and shops. . . . This furnished employment to a large number of colored people as Masons, Carpenters, Teamsters, and Common Workmen."

Most rural black Southerners, however, arrived in cities untrained in the kinds of skills sought in an urban work force and so worked as unskilled laborers.

In both Atlanta and Nashville, black people comprised more than 75 percent of the unskilled workforce in 1870. Their wages were at or below subsistence level. A black laborer in Richmond admitted to a journalist in 1870 that he had difficulty making ends meet on $1.50 a day. "It's right hard," he reported. "I have to pay $15 a month rent, and only two little rooms." His family survived because his wife took in laundry, while her mother watched the children. Considering the laborer's struggle, the journalist wondered, "Were not your people better off in slavery?" The man replied, "Oh, no sir! We're a heap better off now . . . . We're men now, but when our masters had us we was only change in their pockets."

The black church was the center of African American life in the postwar urban South. Most black churches formed after the Civil War, but some, such as the first African Baptist Church in Richmond, shown here in an 1874 engraving, traced their origins to before 1861.

FAITH AND FREEDOM

Religious faith framed and inspired the efforts of African Americans to test their freedom on the farm and in the city. White Southerners used religion to transform the Lost Cause from a shattering defeat to a premonition of a greater destiny. Black Southerners, in contrast, saw emancipation in biblical terms as the beginning of an exodus from bondage to the Promised Land.

Some black churches in the postwar South originated in the slavery era, but most split from white-dominated congregations after the war. White churchgoers deplored the expressive style of black worship, and black churchgoers were uncomfortable in congregations that treated them as inferiors. A separate church also reduced white surveillance.

The First African Baptist Church in Richmond, founded before the war, originated in a white Baptist congregation. An 1846 agreement allowed black worshipers to hold separate services, but only with a white minister officiating. In 1866, the white pastor resigned, noting that black worshipers "would naturally and justly prefer a minister of their own color." The white church transferred the deed to the black congregation that year, and the Reverend James Henry Holmes, a former slave, became their first black pastor. The church flourished under Holmes, paid off its debt, and by the 1870s boasted the largest black congregation in the United States.

The church became a primary focus of African American life. It gave black people the opportunity to hone skills in self-government and administration that white-dominated society denied them. Within the supportive confines of the congregation, they could assume leadership positions, render important decisions, deal with financial matters, and engage in politics. The church also operated as an educational institution. Local governments, especially in rural areas, rarely constructed public schools for black people; churches often served that function. The desire to read the Bible inspired thousands of former slaves to attend the church school.

The church also spawned other organizations that served the black community over the next century. Burial societies, Masonic lodges, temperance groups, trade unions, and drama clubs originated in churches. By the 1870s, African Americans in Memphis had more than two hundred such organizations. They often came together to celebrate such holidays as Independence Day on July 4 and the anniversary of the Emancipation Proclamation on January 1. These commemorations antagonized white people and further divided the black and white communities.

African Americans took great pride in their churches, which became visible measures of their progress. In Charleston, the first building erected after the war was a black church. The First Colored Baptist Church in Nashville became a landmark for its imposing brick and stone façade. Black people donated a greater proportion of their earnings to their churches than did white people.

The church and the congregation were a cohesive force in black communities. They supported families under stress from discrimination and poverty. Husbands and wives joined church-affiliated societies together. Their children joined organizations such as the Young Rising Sons and Daughters of the New Testament. The church enforced family and religious values, punishing violaters guilty of such infractions as adultery. Black churchwomen—both working class and middle class—were especially prominent in the family-oriented organizations.

Most black churches looked inward to strengthen their members against the harsh realities of postwar southern society. Few ministers dared to engage in or even support protest activities. Some, especially those in the Colored Methodist Episcopal Church, counseled congregants to abide by the rules of second-class citizenship and to trust in God's will to right the wrongs of racism.

Northern-based denominations, however, notably the AME Church, were more aggressive advocates of black rights. AME ministers stressed the responsibility of individual black people to realize God's will of racial equality.

Henry McNeal Turner, probably the most influential AME minister of his day, helped expand the denomination into the South from its small primarily northern base at the end of the Civil War. The white Southern Methodist church granted the nineteen-year-old Turner a license to preach in 1853. He served as an itinerant minister for both black and white congregations during the next five years. In 1858, he joined the AME Church and moved north to lead a congregation in Baltimore. After serving as a U.S. Army chaplain, Turner moved to Georgia and evangelized former slaves who thronged to an activist church with black roots. Within five years, the AME Church had grown to 500,000 members, 80 percent of whom lived in the South. Turner entered Georgia politics in the late 1860s and held several state elective offices. His church elevated him to bishop in 1880.

Turner's career and the efforts of former slaves in the classroom, on the farm, in cities, and in the churches reflect the enthusiasm and expectations with which black Southerners greeted freedom. But the majority of white Southerners were unwilling to see those expectations fulfilled. For this reason, African Americans could not secure the fruits of their emancipation without the support and protection of the federal government. The issue of freedom was therefore inextricably linked to the other great issue of the era—the rejoining of the Confederacy to the Union, as expressed in federal Reconstruction policy.

FEDERAL RECONSTRUCTION, 1865–1870

When the Civil War ended in 1865, no acceptable blueprint existed for reconstituting the Union. President Lincoln believed that, at heart, a majority of white Southerners were Unionists and that they could and should undertake the task of reconstruction. He favored a conciliatory policy toward the South in order, as he put it in one of his last letters, "to restore the Union, so as to make it . . . a Union of hearts and hands as well as of States." He counted on the loyalists to be fair with respect to the rights of the former slaves.

The president had outlined his policy as early as 1863, when he proposed to readmit a seceding state if 10 percent of its prewar voters took an oath of loyalty to the Union and it prohibited slavery in a new state constitution. But this Ten Percent Plan did not require states to grant equal civil and political rights to former slaves, and many Republicans in Congress thought it was not stringent enough. In 1864, a group of them responded with the Wade-Davis Bill, which required a majority of a state's prewar voters to pledge their loyalty to the Union and demanded guarantees of black equality before the law. The bill was passed at the end of a congressional session, but Lincoln kept it from becoming law by refusing to sign it (an action known as a "pocket veto").

Lincoln, of course, died before he could implement a Reconstruction plan. His views on reconstructing the Union during the war did not necessarily prefigure how his views would unfold after the war. Above all, Lincoln was flexible on the issue, prepared to tailor his proposals to suit the situation. As noted of his proposed Proclamation of Amnesty, promulgated in 1863 as a way to ease the rebellious states back into the Union, "[A]s bad promises are better broken than kept, I shall treat this as a bad promise, and break it, whenever I shall be convinced that keeping it is adverse to the public interest." Given this flexibility, and given his commitment in the Gettysburg Address to promote "a new birth of freedom," it is likely that had white Southerners resisted black civil rights, Lincoln would have responded with harsher terms. But his successor, Andrew Johnson, lacked both his flexibility and his appreciation for the importance of black freedom.

The controversy over these plans introduced during the war reflected two obstacles to Reconstruction that would continue to plague the ruling Republicans after the war. First, neither the Constitution nor legal precedent offered any guidance on whether the president or Congress should take the lead on Reconstruction policy. Second, there was no agreement on what that policy should be. Proposals requiring various preconditions for readmitting a state—loyalty oaths, new constitutions with certain specific provisions, guarantees of freedmen's rights—all provoked vigorous debate.

President Andrew Johnson, some conservative Republicans, and most Democrats believed that because the Constitution made no mention of secession, the southern states had been in rebellion but had never left the Union, and that therefore there was no need for a formal process to readmit them. Moderate and radical Republicans disagreed, arguing that the defeated states had forfeited their rights. Moderates and radicals parted company, however, on the conditions necessary for readmission to the Union. The radicals wanted to treat the former Confederate states as territories—or "conquered provinces"—subject to congressional legis-

lation. Moderates wanted to grant the seceding states more autonomy and limit federal intervention in their affairs while they satisfied the conditions of readmission. No group held a majority in Congress, and legislators sometimes changed their positions (see the Overview table, "Contrasting Views of Reconstruction").

PRESIDENTIAL RECONSTRUCTION, 1865–1867

When the Civil War ended in April 1865, Congress was not in session and would not reconvene until December. Thus, the responsibility for developing a Reconstruction policy initially fell on Andrew Johnson, who succeeded to the presidency upon Lincoln's assassination. Johnson seemed well suited to the difficult task. The new president's personal and political background was promising to his Republican colleagues. Johnson was born in humble circumstances in North Carolina in 1808. He learned the tailoring trade and struck out for Tennessee as a teenager to open a tailor shop in the eastern Tennessee town of Greenville. Gaining his education informally, he

Overview

Contrasting Views of Reconstruction: President and Congress

Politician or Group	Policy on Former Slaves	Policy on Readmission of Former Confederate States
President Johnson	Opposed to black suffrage	Maintained that rebellious states were already readmitted
	Silent on protection of black civil rights	Granted pardons and restoration of property to all who swore allegiance to the United States
	Opposed to land redistribution	
Radical Republicans	Favored black suffrage	Favored treating rebellious states as territories and establishing military districts*
	Favored protection of black civil rights	Favored limiting franchise to black people and loyal white people
	Favored land redistribution	
Moderate Republicans	Favored black suffrage	Favored some restrictions on white suffrage*
	Favored protection of civil rights	Favored requiring states to meet various requirements before being readmitted*
	Opposed land redistribution	Split on military rule

*True of most but not all members of the group.

AMERICAN VIEWS

Mississippi's 1865 Black Codes

White Southerners, especially landowners and business owners, feared emancipation would produce a labor crisis; freedmen, they expected, would either refuse to work or strike hard bargains with their former masters. White Southerners also recoiled from the prospect of having to treat their former slaves as full social equals. Thus, beginning in late 1865, several southern states, including Mississippi, enacted laws designed to control black labor, mobility, and social status. Northerners responded to the codes as a provocation, a bold move to deny the result of the war and its consequences.

● How did the black codes fit into President Andrew Johnson's Reconstruction program?

● Some Northerners charged that the black codes were a backdoor attempt at reestablishing slavery. Do you agree?

● If southern states enacted black codes to stabilize labor relations, how did the provisions below effect that objective?

From An Act to Confer Civil Rights on Freedmen, and for other Purposes
   Section 1. All freedmen, free negroes and mulattoes may sue and be sued, implead and be impleaded, in all the courts of law and equity of this State, and may acquire personal property, and choose in action, by descent or purchase, and may dispose of the same in the same manner and to the same extent that white persons may: Provided, That the provisions of this section shall not be so construed as to allow any freedman, free negro or mulatto to rent or lease any lands or tenements except in incorporated cities or towns, in which places the corporate authorities shall control the same.

prospered modestly, purchased a few slaves, and began to pursue politics. He was elected alderman, mayor, state legislator, congressman, governor, and then, in 1856, U.S. senator. Johnson was the only southern senator to remain in the U.S. Senate after secession. This defiant Unionism won him acclaim in the North and credibility among Republican leaders, who welcomed him into their party. During the war, as military governor of Tennessee, he solidified his Republican credentials by advocating the abolition of slavery in Tennessee and severe punishment of Confederate leaders. His views landed him on the Republican ticket as the candidate for vice president in 1864. Indiana Republican congressman George W. Julian, who advocated harsh terms for the South and broad rights for black people, viewed Johnson's accession to the presidency in 1865 as "a godsend."

Most Northerners and many Republicans approved Johnson's Reconstruction plan when he un-

veiled it in May 1865. Johnson extended pardons and restored property rights, except in slaves, to Southerners who swore an oath of allegiance to the Union and the Constitution. Southerners who had held prominent positions in the Confederacy, however, and those with more than $20,000 in taxable property had to petition the president directly for a pardon, a reflection of Johnson's disdain for wealthy whites. The plan had nothing to say about the voting rights and civil rights of former slaves.

Northern Democrats applauded the plan's silence on these issues and its promise of a quick restoration of the southern states to the Union. They expected the southern states to favor their party and expand its political power. Republicans, although some of them would have preferred the plan to have provided for black suffrage, approved of the restoration of property rights to white Southerners. This position was consistent with their view of former slaves as

Section 7. Every civil officer shall, and every person may, arrest and carry back to his or her legal employer any freedman, free negro, or mulatto who shall have quit the service of his or her employer before the expiration of his or her term of service without good cause; and said officer and person shall be entitled to receive for arresting and carrying back every deserting employee aforesaid the sum of five dollars, and ten cents per mile from the place of arrest to the place of delivery; and the same shall be paid by the employer, and held as a set off for so much against the wages of said deserting employee: Provided, that said arrested party, after being so returned, may appeal to the justice of the peace or member of the board of police of the county, who, on notice to the alleged employer, shall try summarily whether said appellant is legally employed by the alleged employer, and has good cause to quit said employer. Either party shall have the right of appeal to the county court, pending which the alleged deserter shall be remanded to the alleged employer or otherwise disposed of, as shall be right and just; and the decision of the county court shall be final.

From An Act to Amend the Vagrant Laws of the State
Section 2. All freedmen, free negroes and mulattoes in this State, over the age of eighteen years, found on the second Monday in January, 1866, or thereafter, with no lawful employment or business, or found unlawful assembling themselves together, either in the day or night time, and all white persons assembling themselves with freedmen, Free negroes or mulattoes, or usually associating with freedmen, free negroes or mulattoes, on terms of equality, or living in adultery or fornication with a freed woman, freed negro or mulatto, shall be deemed vagrants, and on conviction thereof shall be fined in a sum not exceeding, in the case of a freedman, free negro or mulatto, fifty dollars, and a white man two hundred dollars, and imprisonment at the discretion of the court, the free negro not exceeding ten days, and the white man not exceeding six months.

Source: "Laws in Relation to Freedmen," 39 Congress, 2 Session, Senate Executive Document 6, Freedmen's Affairs, 182–86.

laborers, not property owners. Republicans also hoped that Johnson's conciliatory terms might attract some white Southerners to the Republican party.

White Southerners, however, were not so favorably impressed with Johnson's plan, and their response turned northern public opinion against the president. On the two great issues of freedom and reunion, white Southerners quickly demonstrated their eagerness to reverse the results of the Civil War. Although most states accepted President Johnson's modest requirements, several objected to one or more of them. Mississippi and Texas refused to ratify the Thirteenth Amendment, which abolished slavery. Alabama accepted only parts of the amendment. South Carolina declined to nullify its secession ordinance. No southern state authorized black voting. When Johnson ordered special congressional elections in the South in the fall of 1865, the all-white electorate returned many prominent Confederate leaders to office.

In late 1865, the newly elected southern state legislatures revised their antebellum slave codes. The updated **black codes** allowed local officials to arrest black people who could not document employment and residence or who were "disorderly" and sentence them to forced labor on farms or road crews. The codes also restricted black people to certain occupations, barred them from jury duty, and forbade them to possess firearms. Apprenticeship laws permitted judges to take black children from parents who could not, in the judges' view, adequately support them. Given the widespread poverty in the South in 1865, the law could apply to almost any freed black family. Northerners looking for contrition in the South found no sign of it. Worse, President Johnson did not seem perturbed about this turn of events.

The Republican-dominated Congress reconvened in December 1865 in a belligerent mood. A few radical Republicans pushed for swift retribution. George

W. Julian thundered that he would "indict, convict and hang Jefferson Davis in the name of God; as for Robert E. Lee, unmolested in Virginia, hang him too." His colleague, Benjamin F. Wade, suggested that "if the negroes by insurrection would contrive to slay one-half of the White Southerners, the remaining half would then hold them in respect and treat them with justice." Few in Congress took these statements seriously. Nonetheless, a consensus formed among radical Republicans, who comprised nearly half of the party's strength in Congress, that to gain readmission, a state would have to extend suffrage to black citizens, protect freedmen's civil rights, and have its white citizens officially acknowledge these rights. Some radicals also supported the redistribution of land to former slaves, but few pressed for social equality. They envisioned a new South of modest farms, some owned by former slaves, and a Republican party built on an alliance between black people and white loyalists.

Thaddeus Stevens of Pennsylvania led the radical forces in the House of Representatives, while the abolitionist veteran Charles Sumner of Massachusetts rallied radicals in the Senate. Stevens had established himself as a partisan for black political rights in the North as early as the 1840s. As a congressman during the Civil War, he pushed Lincoln to free and arm the slaves and later to extend them the right to vote. Stevens dreamed of a South populated by white and black yeoman farmers. With no large plantations and few landless farmers, the South would become an ideal republic, a boon to the rest of the nation, instead of a burden. Few shared his vision, and when he died in 1868, a reporter noted that "no man was oftener outvoted." Yet he remained the conscience of the House, a standard of idealism in an age of growing cynicism. His epitaph read in part, "The principle which I advocated through a long life, Equality of Man before his Creator."

Sumner was among the foremost abolitionist politicians before the Civil War. His combative nature won him few friends, even within his own party. As fierce as Stevens in the promotion of black civil and political rights after the war, he also believed that the Reconstruction era offered a "golden moment" to remake the South into an egalitarian region. Sumner died in 1874 as his dream was fading. The last piece of Reconstruction legislation, the Civil Rights Act of 1875, became a posthumous tribute to his uncommon ability to overcome the racial prejudices of the day with a vision of a colorblind society.

But the radicals could not unite behind a program, and it fell to their moderate colleagues to take the first step toward a congressional Reconstruction plan. The moderates shared the radicals' desire to protect the former slaves' civil and voting rights. But they would not support land redistribution schemes or punitive measures against prominent Confederates. The moderates' first measure, passed in early 1866, extended the life of the Freedmen's Bureau and provided it with authority to punish state officials who failed to extend to black citizens the civil rights enjoyed by white citizens. But President Johnson vetoed the legislation.

Undeterred, Congress passed the Civil Rights Act of 1866 in direct response to the black codes. The act specified the civil rights to which all U.S. citizens were entitled. In creating a category of national citizenship with rights that superseded state laws restricting them, the act changed federal–state relations (and in the process overturned the Dred Scott decision). President Johnson vetoed the act, but it became law when Congress mustered a two-thirds majority to override his veto—the first time in American history that Congress passed major legislation over a president's veto.

Andrew Johnson's position reflected both his view of government and his racial attitudes. The Republican president remained a Democrat in spirit. Republicans had expanded federal power during the Civil War. Johnson, however, like most Democrats, favored more of a balance between federal and state power. He also shared with many of his white southern neighbors a belief in black inferiority and a view that white plantation owners had conspired to limit the economic and political power of white yeomen like himself. Johnson supported abolition assuming that, once free, black people would emigrate to Africa. Given the president's views and his inflexible temperament, a clash between him and Congress became inevitable.

To keep freedmen's rights safe from presidential vetoes, state legislatures, and federal courts, the Republican-dominated Congress moved to incorporate some of the provisions of the 1866 Civil Rights Act into the Constitution. The **Fourteenth Amendment**, which Congress passed in June 1866, addressed the issues of civil and voting rights. It guaranteed every citizen equality before the law. The two key sections of the amendment prohibited states from violating the civil rights of their citizens, thus outlawing the black codes, and gave states the choice of enfranchising black people or losing representation in Congress. Some radical Republicans expressed disappointment that the amendment, in a reflection of northern ambivalence, failed to give the vote to black people outright.

The amendment also disappointed advocates of woman suffrage, for the first time using the word *male* in the Constitution to define who could vote. Wendell Phillips, a prominent abolitionist, counseled them, "One question at a time. This hour belongs to the Negro." Susan B. Anthony, who had campaigned for the abolition of slavery before the war and helped

"Selling a Freeman to Pay his Fine at Monticello, Florida." This 1867 engraving shows how the black codes of the early Reconstruction era reduced former slaves to virtually their pre-Civil War status. Scenes such as this convinced Northerners that the white South was unrepentant and prompted congressional Republicans to devise their own Reconstruction plans.

mount a petition drive that collected 400,000 signatures for the Thirteenth Amendment, formed the American Equal Rights Association in 1866 with her colleagues to push for woman suffrage at the state level.

The Fourteenth Amendment had little immediate impact on the South. Although enforcement of black codes diminished, white violence against black people increased. In the 1870s, several decisions by the U.S. Supreme Court would weaken the amendment's provisions. Eventually, however, it would play a major role in securing the civil rights of African Americans.

President Johnson encouraged Southern white intransigence by openly denouncing the Fourteenth Amendment. In August 1866, at the start of the congressional election campaign, he undertook an unprecedented tour of key northern states to sell his message of sectional reconciliation to the public. Although listeners appreciated Johnson's desire for peace, they questioned his claims of southern white loyalty to the Union. The president's diatribes against the Republican Congress won him followers in those northern states with a reservoir of opposition to black suffrage. But the tone and manner of his campaign offended many as undignified. In the November elections, the Democrats suffered embarrassing defeats in the North as Republicans managed better than two-thirds majorities in both the House and Senate, sufficient to override presidential vetoes. Radical Republicans, joined by moderate colleagues buoyed by the election results and revolted by the president's and the South's intransigence, seized the initiative when Congress reconvened.

CONGRESSIONAL RECONSTRUCTION, 1867–1870

The radicals' first salvo in their attempt to take control over Reconstruction occurred with the passage over President Johnson's veto of the Military Reconstruction Acts. The measures, passed in March 1867, inaugurated a period known as **Congressional Reconstruction** or Radical Reconstruction. Congress divided the ex-Confederate states (except for Tennessee, the only southern state that had ratified the Fourteenth Amendment and been readmitted to the Union) into five military districts, each headed by a general (see Map 16–1). The commanders' first order of business was to conduct voter-registration campaigns to enroll black people and bar white people who had held office before the Civil War and who had supported the Confederacy. The eligible voters would then elect delegates to a state convention to write a new constitution that guaranteed universal manhood suffrage. Once a majority of eligible voters ratified the new constitution and the Fourteenth Amendment, their state would be eligible for readmission to the Union.

MAP 16-1   Congressional Reconstruction, 1865–1877
When Congress wrested control of Reconstruction policy from President Andrew Johnson, it divided the South into the five military districts depicted here. The commanding generals for each district held the authority both to hold elections and to decide who could vote.

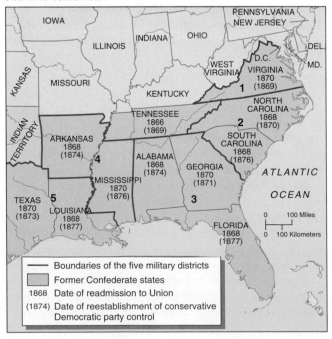

The Reconstruction Acts fulfilled the radicals' three major objectives. First, they secured the freedmen's right to vote. Second, they made it likely that southern states would be run by Republican regimes that would enforce the new constitutions, protect former slaves' rights, and maintain the Republican majority in Congress. Finally, the acts set standards for readmission that required the South to accept the consequences of defeat: the preeminence of the federal government and the end of involuntary servitude.

To limit presidential interference with their policies, Republicans passed the Tenure of Office Act, prohibiting the president from removing certain officeholders without the Senate's consent. Johnson, angered at what he believed was an unconstitutional attack on presidential authority, deliberately violated the act by firing Secretary of War Edwin M. Stanton, a leading radical, in February 1868. The House responded to this defiance by approving articles of impeachment against a president for the first time in American history. After a trial, the Senate voted 35 to 19 to convict the president, one vote short of the two-thirds necessary to remove him from office. The seven Republicans who voted against their party did so, not out of respect for the president, but because they feared that a conviction would damage the office of the presidency and violate the constitutional separation of powers. The outcome weakened the radicals and eased the way for a moderate Republican, Ulysses S. Grant, to gain the party's nomination for president in 1868.

The Republicans viewed the 1868 presidential election as a referendum on Congressional Reconstruction. They supported black suffrage in the South but equivocated on allowing African Americans to vote in the North. Black Northerners could vote in only eight of the twenty-two northern states, and, between 1865 and 1869, white Northerners had rejected equal suffrage referendums in eight of eleven states. Republicans "waved the bloody shirt," reminding voters of Democratic disloyalty, the sacrifices of war, and the peace only Republicans could redeem. Democrats denounced Congressional Reconstruction as federal tyranny and, in openly racist appeals, warned white voters that a Republican victory would mean black rule. Grant won the election, but his margin of victory was uncomfortably narrow. Reflecting growing ambivalence in the North over issues of race and federal authority, New York's Horatio Seymour, the Democratic presidential nominee, probably carried a majority of the nation's white vote. Black voters' overwhelming support for Grant probably provided him his margin of victory.

Casting a ballot. Black voters in Richmond vote on a state constitutional convention in 1867. A key objective of Congressional Reconstruction was to secure the voting rights of freedmen.

The Republicans retained a strong majority in both houses of Congress and managed to pass another major piece of Reconstruction legislation, the **Fifteenth Amendment**, in February 1869. In response to growing concerns about voter fraud and violence against freedmen, the amendment guaranteed the right of American men to vote, regardless of race. Although the amendment provided a loophole allowing states to impose restrictions on the right to vote based on literacy or property qualifications, it was nonetheless a milestone. It made the right to vote perhaps the most distinguishing characteristic of American citizenship.

The Fifteenth Amendment allowed states to keep the franchise a male prerogative, angering many in the woman-suffrage movement more than had the Fourteenth Amendment. The resulting controversy severed the ties between the movement and Republican politics. Susan B. Anthony broke with her abolitionist colleagues and opposed the amendment. A fellow abolitionist and woman suffragist, Elizabeth Cady Stanton, charged that the amendment created an "aristocracy of sex." In an appeal brimming with ethnic and racial animosity, Stanton warned that "if you do not wish the lower orders of Chinese, African, Germans and Irish, with their low ideas of womanhood to make

laws for you and your daughters . . . awake to the danger . . . and demand that woman, too, shall be represented in the government!" Such language created a major rift in the nascent women's movement. Women who supported the amendment formed the New England Woman Suffrage Association, challenging Anthony's American Equal Rights Association.

SOUTHERN REPUBLICAN GOVERNMENTS, 1867–1870

Away from Washington, the first order of business for the former Confederacy was to draft state constitutions. The documents embodied progressive principles new to the South. They mandated the election of numerous local and state offices. Self-perpetuating local elites could no longer appoint themselves or cronies to powerful positions. The constitutions committed southern states, many for the first time, to public education. Lawmakers enacted a variety of reforms, including social welfare, penal reform, legislative reapportionment, and universal manhood suffrage.

The Republican regimes that gained control in southern states promoted vigorous state government and the protection of civil and voting rights. Three diverse Republican constituencies supported these governments. One consisted of white natives, most of them yeomen farmers. Residing mainly in the upland regions of the South and long ignored by lowland planters and merchants in state government, some had supported the Union during the war. The conflict had left many of them devastated. They struggled to keep their land and hoped for an easing of credit and for debt-stay laws to help them escape foreclosure. They wanted public schools for their children and good roads to get their crops to market. Some urban merchants and large planters also called themselves Republicans. Many were Whigs before the war, and a few had been Unionists. They were attracted to the party's emphasis on economic development, especially railroad construction, and would become prominent in Republican leadership after 1867, forming a majority of party elected officials.

Collectively, opponents called these native white Southerners **scalawags**, a derogatory term for an idle or mischievous person derived from Scalloway, the name of a district on Scotland's Shetland Islands known for its scraggly livestock. The term was first applied in western New York before the Civil War to an idle person, and then to a mischievous one. Although their opponents may have perceived them as a unified group, scalawags held a variety of views. Planters and merchants opposed easy debt and credit arrangements and the use of their taxes to support programs other than railroads or port improvements. Yeomen farmers desperately needed the debt and credit legislation to retain their land. And even though they supported public schools and road building—which would require increased state revenues—they opposed higher taxes.

Northern transplants, or **carpetbaggers**, as many Southern whites called them, constituted a second group of southern Republicans. The term also had antebellum origins, referring to a suspicious stranger. Cartoonists depicted carpetbaggers as shoddily dressed and poorly groomed, their worldly possessions in a ratty cloth satchel, slinking into a town and swindling the locals before departing with their ill-gotten gains. The reality was far different from the caricature. Thousands of Northerners came south during and after the war. Many were Union soldiers who simply enjoyed the climate and perhaps married a local woman. Most were drawn by economic opportunity. Land was cheap and the price of cotton high. Although most carpetbaggers had supported the Republican party before they moved south, few became politically active until the cotton economy nosedived in 1866. Financial concerns were not all that motivated carpetbaggers to enter politics; some hoped to aid the freedmen.

Carpetbaggers never comprised more than 2 percent of any state's population. Most white Southerners viewed them as an alien presence, instruments of a hated occupying force. They provoked resentment because they seemed to prosper while most Southerners struggled in poverty. And they further estranged themselves from their neighbors by supporting and participating in the Republican state governments that most white people despised. In Alabama, local editors organized a boycott of northern-owned shops. "STARVE THEM OUT!" they wrote. "Don't put your foot in the doors of their shops, offices, and stores. Purchase from true men and patronize those of known Southern sympathies." Because many of them tended to support extending political and civil rights to black Southerners, carpetbaggers were also often at odds with their fellow white Republicans, the scalawags.

African Americans constituted the Republican party's largest southern constituency. In three states—South Carolina, Mississippi, and Louisiana—they also constituted the majority of eligible voters. They viewed the franchise as the key to civic equality and economic opportunity and demanded an active role in party and government affairs.

Black people began to take part in southern politics even before the end of the Civil War, especially in cities occupied by Union forces. In February 1865, black people in Norfolk, Virginia, gathered to demand a say in the new government that Union supporters were forming in that portion of the state. In April, they created the Colored Monitor Union club, modeled after regular Republican party organizations in north-

ern cities, called **Union Leagues**. They demanded "the right of universal suffrage" for "all loyal men, without distinction of color." Black people in other southern cities held similar meetings, seeking inclusion in the democratic process in order to protect their freedom. As a member of the Alexandria, Virginia, black Union League argued in August 1865, "The only salvation for us . . . is in the possession of the ballot. Give us this, and we will protect ourselves."

White Southerners viewed these developments with alarm but could not at first counter them. Despite white threats, black Southerners thronged to Union League meetings in 1867, even forging interracial alliances in states such as North Carolina and Alabama. Focusing on political education and recruitment, the leagues successfully mobilized black voters. In 1867, more than 90 percent of eligible black voters across the South turned out for elections. Black women, even though they could not vote, also played a role. During the 1868 presidential campaign, for example, black maids and cooks in the South wore but-

As white paramilitary organizations in the South attacked African American civil and political rights, South Carolina Congressman Robert B. Elliott rose in the House of Representatives in January 1874 to present a ringing endorsement of Charles Sumner's Civil Rights Bill. The illustration also depicts southern black aspirations for and justification of the basic rights of citizenship, the results of which Elliott embodied.

HON. ROBERT. B. ELLIOTT, of South Carolina.

AMERICAN SLAVE LABOUR IS OF THE PAST—FREE LABOUR IS OF THE PRESENT ——— WE TOIL FOR OUR OWN CHILDREN AND NOT FOR THOSE OF OTHERS.

E. Sachse and Company, "The Shackle Broken by the Genius of Freedom," Baltimore, MD: 1874.

tons touting the candidacy of the Republican presidential nominee, Ulysses S. Grant.

Black Southerners were not content just to vote; they also demanded political office. White Republican leaders in the South often took the black vote for granted. But on several occasions after 1867, black people threatened to run independent candidates, support rival Democrats, or simply stay home unless they were represented among Republican nominees. These demands brought them some success. The number of southern black congressmen in the U.S. House of Representatives increased from two in 1869 to seven in 1873, and more than six hundred African Americans, most of them former slaves from plantation counties, were elected to southern state legislatures between 1867 and 1877.

White fears that black officeholders would enact vengeful legislation proved unfounded. African Americans generally did not promote race-specific legislation. Rather, they supported measures such as debt relief and state funding for education that benefited all poor and working class people. Like all politicians, however, black officials in southern cities sought to enact measures beneficial to their constituents. In Atlanta, for example, black officeholders had a sidewalk laid in front of a prominent black church and diverted a road scheduled to cut through a black neighborhood. In Richmond, black people secured an ordinance forbidding the robbing of black graves to supply medical schools with corpses. And they succeeded in having a black police commissioner appointed in Jacksonville, Florida. Gains like these underscored the advantages of suffrage for the African American community.

During the first few years of Congressional Reconstruction, Republican governments walked a tightrope, attempting to lure moderate Democrats and unaffiliated white voters into the party without slighting the black vote. They used the lure of patronage power and the attractive salaries that accompanied public office. In 1868, for example, Louisiana's Republican governor, Henry C. Warmoth, appointed white conservatives to state and local offices, which he divided equally between ex-Confederate veterans and black people, and repealed a constitutional provision disfranchising former Confederate officials.

Republicans also gained support by expanding the role of state government to a degree unprecedented in the South. Southern Republican administrations appealed to hard-pressed upland white constituents by prohibiting foreclosure and passing stay laws that allowed farm owners additional time to repay debts. They undertook building programs that benefited both black and white citizens, erecting hospitals, schools, and orphanages. Stepping further into social policy than most northern states at the time, Republican governments in the South expanded women's property rights, enacted legislation against child abuse, and required child support from fathers of mulatto children. In South Carolina, the Republican government provided medical care for the poor; in Alabama, it provided free legal aid for needy defendants.

Despite these impressive policies, southern Republicans were unable to hold their diverse constituency together. Although the party had some success among white yeoman farmers, the liberal use of patronage to attract white conservatives failed to gain it many new adherents. At the same time, it alienated the party's core supporters, who resented seeing their former enemies rewarded with lucrative offices.

The high costs of their activist policies further undermined the Republicans by forcing them to raise state taxes. In Mississippi—where the Republican governor built a public-school system for both black and white students, founded a black university, reorganized the state judiciary, built new courthouses and two state hospitals, and pushed through legislation giving black people equal access to public facilities—the state debt soared to $1.5 million between 1869 and 1873. This was in an era in which state budgets rarely exceeded $1 million.

Unprecedented expenditures and the liberal use of patronage sometimes resulted in waste and corruption. Officials charged with selecting railroad routes, appointing lesser officials, and erecting public buildings were well positioned to benefit from their power. Their high salaries offended many in an otherwise impoverished region. Problems like these were not limited to the South. They were pervasive throughout the country in the 1860s and 1870s. The perception of dishonesty was nonetheless damaging to governments struggling to build legitimacy among a skeptical white electorate.

The excesses of some state governments, high taxes, contests over patronage, and conflicts over the relative roles of white and black party members opened rifts in Republican ranks. Patronage triggered intraparty warfare. Every office secured by a Democrat created a disappointed Republican. Class tensions erupted in the party as economic development policies, favored by former Whigs, sometimes superseded relief and social service legislation supported by small farmers. The failure of Alabama Republicans to deliver on promises of debt relief and land redistribution eroded the significant support the party had enjoyed among upcountry white voters. There were differences among black voters too. In the Lower South, divisions that had developed in the prewar era between urban, lighter-skinned free black people and darker, rural slaves persisted into the Reconstruction era. In many southern states, black clergy, because of their independence from white support and their important spiritual and educational role, became leaders. But most preached salvation in the next world rather than equality in this one, conceding more to white people than their rank-and-file constituents.

COUNTER-RECONSTRUCTION, 1870–1874

Republicans might have survived battles over patronage, differences over policy, and the resentment provoked by extravagant expenditures and high taxes. But they could not overcome racism and the violence it generated. Racism killed Republican rule in the South because it deepened divisions within the party, encouraged white violence, and eroded support in the North. Southern Democrats discovered that they could use race baiting and racial violence to create solidarity among white people that overrode their economic and class differences. Unity translated into election victories.

Northerners responded to the persistent violence in the South, not with outrage, but with a growing sense of tedium. They came to accept the arguments of white Southerners that it was folly to allow black people to vote and hold office. Racism became respectable. Noted intellectuals and journalists espoused "scientific" theories that claimed to demonstrate the natural superiority of white people over black people. These theories influenced the Liberal Republicans, followers of a new political movement that splintered the Republican Party, further weakening its will to pursue Reconstruction policy.

By 1874, Americans were concerned with an array of domestic problems that overshadowed Reconstruction. A serious economic depression left them more preoccupied with survival than racial justice. Corruption convinced many that politics was part of the nation's problems, not a solution to them. With the rest of the nation thus distracted and weary, white Southerners reclaimed control of the South.

THE USES OF VIOLENCE

Racial violence preceded Republican rule. As African Americans moved about, attempted to vote, haggled over labor contracts, and carried arms as part of occupying Union forces, they tested the patience of white Southerners. In a racial world turned upside down from the white perspective, any black assertion of equality seemed threatening.

Cities, where black and white people competed for jobs and where black political influence was most visible, became flashpoints for interracial violence. In May 1866, the collision of two wagons in Memphis, one driven by a white carter, the other by a black carter, touched off three days of white attacks on black people and black neighborhoods. Forty-six black people and two white people died in the fray, and five black women were raped. The white mob destroyed black churches, schools, and homes.

White paramilitary groups flourished in the South during the Reconstruction era and were responsible for much of the violence directed against African Americans. Probably the best known of these groups was the **Ku Klux Klan**. Founded in Tennessee by six Confederate veterans in 1866, the Klan was initially a social club. Prominent ex-Confederates such as General John B. Gordon and General Nathan Bedford Forrest, allegedly the first Grand Wizard of the Klan, saw the political potential of the new organization. Within a year, the Klan had spread throughout the South. In 1867, when black people entered politics in large numbers, the Klan unleashed a wave of terror against them. Klan night riders in ghostlike disguises intimidated black communities. The Klan directed much of its violence toward subverting the electoral process. One historian has estimated that roughly 10 percent of all black delegates to the 1867 state constitutional conventions in the South became victims of political violence during the next decade.

Not all Klan attacks had political objectives. Klansmen struck against anyone, black or white, who, they believed, had violated racial boundaries. A Georgia Klansman murdered a freedman because he could read and write. Klansmen in Florence, South Carolina, killed a black man who rented a plantation "because such a thing ought not to be." And in 1868, Klansmen murdered three southern white Republican Georgia state legislators. Membership in the Klan crossed class lines. Race became an issue on which white people, regardless of differing economic interests, could agree.

By 1868, white paramilitary organizations permeated the South. Violence was particularly severe in election years in Louisiana, which had a large and active black electorate. Before the presidential election of 1868, for example, white Louisianans killed at least seven hundred Republicans, including the black leader William R. Meadows, who was dragged from his home and shot and beheaded in front of his family. As the election neared, white mobs roamed New Orleans, attacking black people and breaking up Republican rallies. The violence cut the Republican vote in the state by 50 percent from the previous spring.

The most serious example of political violence in Louisiana, if not in the entire South, occurred in Colfax in 1873, when a white Democratic mob attempted to wrest control of local government from Republicans. For three weeks, black defenders held the town against the white onslaught. When the white mob finally broke through, they massacred the remaining black defenders, including those who had surrendered and laid down their weapons.

Racial violence and the combative reaction it provoked both among black people and Republican administrations energized white voters. Democrats regained power in North Carolina, for example, after the state's Republican governor enraged white voters by calling out the militia to counter white violence during the election of 1870. That same year, the Republican regime in Georgia fell as well.

Some Republican governments countered the violence successfully for a time. Republican Governor Edmund J. Davis of Texas, for example, organized a special force of two hundred state policemen to round up Klan night riders. Between 1870 and 1872, Davis's force arrested six thousand and broke the Klan in Texas. Arkansas Governor Powell Clayton launched an equally successful campaign against the Klan in 1869. But other governors hesitated to enforce laws directed at the Klan, fearing that to do so would further alienate white people.

The federal government responded with a variety of legislation. One example was the Fifteenth Amendment, ratified in 1869, which guaranteed the right to vote. Another was the Enforcement Act of 1870, which

The Klan directed violence at African Americans primarily for political activity. Here, a black man, John Campbell, vainly begs for mercy in Moore County, North Carolina, in August 1871.

authorized the federal government to appoint supervisors in states that failed to protect voting rights. When violence and intimidation persisted, Congress followed with a second, more sweeping measure, the Ku Klux Klan Act of 1871. This law permitted federal authorities, with military assistance, if necessary, to arrest and prosecute members of groups that denied a citizen's civil rights if state authorities failed to do so. The Klan Act was not successful in curbing racial violence, as the Colfax Massacre in 1873 made vividly clear. But with it, Congress, by claiming the right to override state authority to bring individuals to justice, established a new precedent in federal–state relations.

THE FAILURE OF NORTHERN WILL

The success of political violence after 1871 reflected less the inadequacy of congressional legislation than the failure of will on the part of northern Republicans to follow through on commitments to southern Republican administrations. The erosion of northern support for Congressional Reconstruction began as early as the presidential election of 1868. The Republican candidate Ulysses S. Grant's campaign theme that year was "Let Us Have Peace," a reference to the political turmoil in the South.

The commitment to voting rights for black Southerners, widespread among Republicans in 1865 and affirmed in the Fifteenth Amendment, faded as well. American politics in the 1870s seemed increasingly corrupt and irresponsible. Scandal abounded. The Democratic boss William M. Tweed and his associates transformed Tammany Hall, a Democratic Club, into a full-fledged political machine that robbed New York City of an astounding $100 million. Federal officials allowed private individuals to manipulate the stock market for spectacular gains. Several members of Congress and President Grant's vice president exchanged government favors for railroad stock. And the president's secretary of war was caught selling contracts to firms supplying goods to Indians.

A growing number of Americans attributed the debacle to the expansion of the right to vote. Voting was a privilege to be earned, they maintained, not a basic right of citizenship. And black people, according to some Republicans, had not earned that right.

The racist assumption behind this view found growing support among intellectuals. Racism gained an aura of scientific respectability in the late nineteenth century. Science was held in high esteem at the time, helping assure public acceptance of the putatively scientific views of the racial theorists. According to those views, some peoples are inherently inferior to others, a natural state of affairs that no government interference can change.

According to white racial theorists, it was folly to grant suffrage to African Americans, because an inferior race (black) could not hold power over a superior race (white). Black people, because of their race, could not understand the basic principles of democracy. Thus, Missouri's Republican senator Carl Schurz looked on with equanimity as white terror toppled Republican regimes in the South in 1872. He urged his colleagues to let affairs run their course and admit that southern black voters and officeholders "were ignorant and inexperienced; that the public business was an unknown world to them, and that in spite of the best intentions they were easily misled." Allowing an unfit people to vote resulted in a "more disastrous process than rebellion," intoned *The Nation*, a leading Republican journal, in 1872. The perpetual turmoil in the South, the extravagances of some Republican southern administrations, and their persistent inability to attract sufficient numbers of white voters all reinforced the view that these governments were unnatural.

Black people were not the only targets of racial theory. Immigrants were also said to derive from inferior races. Their growing numbers coincided with the flourishing of corrupt political machines in northern cities, fueling Republican reservations about an unrestricted franchise. Like black people, immigrants were held to be incapable of understanding the American electoral process. As one Republican leader observed, "What is bad among ignorant foreigners in New York will not be good among ignorant natives in South Carolina."

Concerns about the quality of the electorate reflected the rising stakes of public office in post–Civil War America. The urban industrial economy boomed in the five years after the war. Engineers flung railroads across the continent. Steam propelled factories to unprecedented levels of productivity and ships to new speed records. Discoveries of rich natural resources such as oil and iron presaged a new age of industrial might. Republicans promoted and benefited from the boom, and it influenced their priorities. Railroad, mining, and lumber lobbyists crowded Washington and state capitals begging for financial and land subsidies and favorable legislation. In an era before conflict-of-interest laws, leading Republicans sat on the boards of railroads, land development companies, and industrial corporations. While the federal government denied land to the freedman, it doled out millions of acres to corporations. Issues of fiscal responsibility, tariffs, and hard money replaced freedom and reunion, moving the Republican party, as *The Nation* explained in 1874, "out of the region of the Civil War."

Not all Republicans approved the party's promotion of economic development. Some questioned the prudence of government intervention in the "natural" operation of the economy. The emerging scandals of the Grant administration led to calls for reform. Republican governments, North and South, were condemned for their lavish spending and high taxes.

The reform movement attracted an assortment of groups concerned about the size, activism, and expense of government. Business leaders decried the ability of wealthy lobbyists to influence economic decisions. An influential group of intellectuals and opinion makers lamented the inability of politicians to understand "natural" laws. Some reformers expressed alarm at the federal government's increasing intervention in the affairs of the states since the Civil War. And some Republicans joined the reform movement out of fear that Democrats would capitalize on the turmoil in the South and the political scandals in the North to reap huge electoral victories in 1872.

LIBERAL REPUBLICANS AND THE ELECTION OF 1872

Liberal Republicans, as those reformers called themselves, put forward an array of suggestions to improve government and save the Republican party. They advocated civil service reform to reduce reliance on patronage and the abuses that accompanied office seeking. To limit government and reduce artificial economic stimuli, the reformers called for tariff reduction and an end to federal land grants to railroads. For the South, they recommended a general amnesty for white people and a return to "local self-government" by men of "property and enterprise."

When the Liberals failed to convince other Republicans to adopt their program, they broke with the party. Taking advantage of this split, the Democrats forged an alliance with the Liberals. Together, they nominated journalist Horace Greeley to challenge Ulysses S. Grant for the presidency in the election of 1872. Grant won resoundingly, helped by high turnout among black voters in the South. He carried all southern states except Georgia, Tennessee, and Texas. Elsewhere, Republicans again used the tactic of waving the bloody shirt to good effect. It was the Republicans, they declared, who had saved the Union, the Democrats who had almost destroyed it. Greeley had been a staunch Republican during the Civil War and had spent most of his career attacking Democrats. Republicans used his own words against him. Many Democratic voters stayed home.

The election suggested that the excesses of the Grant administration had not yet exceeded public tolerance and that the Republican experiment in the South retained some public support. But Greeley had helped the Republicans by running an inept campaign. Within a year, an economic depression, continued violence in the South, and the persistent corruption of the Grant administration would turn public opinion against the Republicans. With this shift, support for Reconstruction and black rights would also fade.

REDEMPTION, 1874–1877

For southern Democrats, the Republican victory in 1872 underscored the importance of turning out larger numbers of white voters and restricting the black vote. They accomplished these goals over the next four years with a surge in political violence. Southern Democrats operated in the secure knowledge that federal authorities would not intervene against them. Preoccupied with corruption and economic crisis and increasingly indifferent, if not hostile, to African American aspirations, most Americans looked the other way. The elections of 1876—on the local, state, and national levels—affirmed the triumph of white Southerners. Reconstruction did not end; it was overthrown.

In a religious metaphor that matched their view of the Civil War as a lost crusade, southern Democrats called their victory "Redemption" and depicted themselves as **Redeemers**, holy warriors who had saved the South from the hell of black Republican rule. Generations of American boys and girls would learn this interpretation of the Reconstruction era, and it would affect race relations for nearly a century.

THE DEMOCRATS' VIOLENT RESURGENCE

The violence between 1874 and 1876 differed in several respects from earlier attempts to restore white government by force. Attackers operated more openly and more closely identified themselves with the Democratic party. Mounted, gray-clad ex-Confederate soldiers flanked Democratic candidates at campaign rallies and "visited" black neighborhoods afterward to discourage black people from voting. With black people intimidated and white people already prepared to vote, election days were typically quiet.

Democrats swept to victory across the South in the 1874 elections. "A perfect reign of terror" redeemed Alabama for the Democrats. The successful appeal to white supremacy inspired a massive white turnout to unseat Republicans in Virginia, Florida (legislature only), and Arkansas. Texas had fallen to the Democrats in 1873. Only South Carolina, Missis-

sippi, and Louisiana—states with large black populations—survived the debacle. But the relentless tide of terror would soon overwhelm them as well.

In Louisiana, a group of elite Democrats in New Orleans organized a military organization, known as the White League, in 1874 to challenge the state's Republican government. In September 1874, more than eight thousand White Leaguers staged a coup to overthrow the Republican government of New Orleans. The city's police, commanded by the former Confederate general James Longstreet, and the intervention of nearby federal troops saved the government and prevented a wholesale slaughter. But the incident only inspired White Leaguers to redouble their efforts.

Few Reconstruction politicians endured greater trials than one Louisiana Republican, Marshall Harvey Twitchell. Born in Vermont, he led black troops during the Civil War and settled in Louisiana after the war. He married the daughter of a prominent plantation owner and launched a successful business career. But with the advent of Congressional Reconstruction, Twitchell entered politics and built a powerful Republican organization in Red River Parish. The hospitable reception he had until then enjoyed in his adopted state quickly evaporated. During the 1874 election campaign, White Leaguers murdered his brother and two brothers-in-law. Two years later, White Leaguers shot him six times in an assassination attempt. Although he lost both arms, he survived. He left Louisiana in 1877, never to return.

THE WEAK FEDERAL RESPONSE

Unrest such as events in Louisiana also plagued Mississippi and South Carolina. When South Carolina Governor Daniel H. Chamberlain could no longer contain the violence in his state in 1876, he asked the president for help. Grant acknowledged the gravity of Chamberlain's situation but would offer him only the lame hope that South Carolinians would exercise "better judgment and cooperation" and assist the governor in bringing offenders to justice "without aid from the federal Government."

Congress responded to the violence with the Civil Rights Act of 1875. Introduced by Charles Sumner, the bill went through several variations. Congress finally passed a watered-down version after Sumner's death. The act prohibited discrimination against black people in public accommodations such as theaters, parks, and trains and guaranteed freedmen's rights to serve on juries. It had no provision for voting rights, which Congress presumed the Fifteenth Amendment protected. The only way to enforce the law was for individuals to bring grievances related to it before federal courts in the South.

As this Thomas Nast cartoon makes clear, the paramilitary violence against black Southerners in the early 1870s threatened, not only the voting rights of freedmen, but their dreams of education, prosperity, and family life as well. In this context, the slogan, "The Union As It Was" is highly ironic.

When black people tested the law by trying to make free use of public accommodations, they were almost always turned away. Some filed suit, with disappointing results. A Texas judge fined a Galveston theater $500 for refusing to allow black people to sit wherever they wanted, but most judges either interpreted the law narrowly or declared it unconstitutional. In 1883, the U.S. Supreme Court agreed and overturned the act, declaring that only the states, not Congress, could redress "a private wrong, or a crime of the individual."

THE ELECTION OF 1876 AND THE COMPROMISE OF 1877

Reconstruction officially ended with the presidential election of 1876 in which the Democrat Samuel J. Tilden ran against the Republican Rutherford B. Hayes. Republicans again waved the bloody shirt, touting their role in preserving the Union during the Civil War, but they ignored Reconstruction. The Democrats hoped that their resurgent strength in the South and a respectable showing in the North would bring them the White House. The scandals of the Grant administration, northern weariness with southern Republican governments, and the persisting economic depression worked in the Democrats' favor.

When the ballots were counted, it appeared that Tilden, a conservative New Yorker respectable enough for northern voters and Democratic enough for white southerners, had won. But despite a majority in the popular vote, disputed returns in three southern states left him with only 184 of the 185 electoral votes needed to win (see Map 16–2). The three states—Florida, South Carolina, and Louisiana—were the last in the South still to have Republican adminstrations.

Both camps maneuvered intensively in the months following the election to claim the disputed votes. Congress appointed a fifteen-member commission to settle the issue. Because the Republicans controlled Congress, they held a one-vote majority on the commission.

Southern Democrats wanted Tilden to win, but they wanted control of their states more. They were willing to deal. As one South Carolina newspaper editorialized in February 1877, "It matters little to us who rules in Washington, if South Carolina is allowed to have [Democratic governor Wade] Hampton and Home Rule." Hayes intended to remove federal support from the remaining southern Republican governments anyway. It thus cost him nothing to promise to do so in exchange for the contested electoral votes. Republicans also made vague promises to invest in the southern economy and support a southern transcontinental railroad, but these were secondary. What the South wanted most was to be left alone, and that is what it got. The so-called Compromise of 1877 installed Hayes in the White House and gave Democrats control of all state governments in the South. Congress never carried through on the economic promises, and southern Democrats never pressed it to.

Southern Democrats emerged the major winners from the **Compromise of 1877.** President Hayes and his successors into the next century left the South alone. In practical terms, the Compromise signaled the revocation of civil rights and voting rights for black Southerners. The Fourteenth and Fifteenth Amendments would be dead letters in the South until well into the twentieth century. On the two great issues confronting the nation at the end of the Civil War, reunion and freedom, the white South had won. It reentered the Union largely on its own terms with the freedom to pursue a racial agenda consistent with its political, economic, and social interests.

THE MEMORY OF RECONSTRUCTION

Southern Democrats used the memory of Reconstruction to help maintain themselves in power. It would join the Lost Cause, as part of the glorious their white neighbors. As Republican governments and black voters succumbed to the southern white reign of terror in the early 1870s, the *Atlanta Constitution* chided black people for being so presumptuous as to want to participate in the democratic process. Politics, the Constitution intoned, "was not intended . . . for the blacks, but for the whites. . . . This government is still a white man's government, and will remain forever such. The superior intelligence of the white race . . . will for all time secure political ascendancy." The *Constitution* excused the freedman for his delusion, blaming the "infamous carpetbagger and the radical [Republican] party."

If the demise of Reconstruction elicited a sigh of relief from most white Americans, black Southerners greeted it with frustration. Their dreams of land ownership faded as a new labor system relegated them to a lowly position in southern agriculture. Redemption reversed their economic and political gains and deprived them of most of the civil rights they had enjoyed under Congressional Reconstruction. Although they continued to vote into the 1890s, they had by 1877 lost most of the voting strength and political offices they held. Rather than becoming part of southern society, they were increasingly set apart from it, valued only for their labor.

Still, the former slaves were better off in 1877 than in 1865. They were free, however limited their freedom. Some owned land; some held jobs in cities. They raised their families in relative peace and experienced the spiritual joys of a full religious life. They socialized freely with relatives and friends, and they moved about. The Reconstruction amendments to the Constitution guaranteed an array of civil and political rights and, though Southern states would evade and federal courts would eviscerate, eventually these guarantees would form the basis of the civil rights revolution after World War II. But that outcome was long, too long, in the future. By 1877, the "golden moment"—an unprecedented opportunity for the nation to live up to its ideals by extending equal rights to all its citizens, black and white alike—had passed.

SHARECROPPING

When they lost political power, black Southerners also lost economic independence. As the Freedmen's Bureau retreated from supervising farm labor contracts and opportunities for black people to possess their own land dried up, the bargaining power of black farm laborers decreased, and the power of white landlords increased. The faltering southern economy contributed to the loss of labor autonomy

as well. Cash wages were at first high enough and rental agreements between tenant farmers and landlords at first fair enough for black farmers to be able to buy their own tools and perhaps a few extra acres. But the dramatic decline of cotton prices soon after the war reduced cash surpluses in an already cash-poor region. Unable now to purchase their own animals or tools and lacking cash to buy food and other necessities at local stores, freedmen were forced to barter their crops for credit.

The upshot was that by the late 1870s, most former slaves in the rural South had been drawn into a subservient position in a new labor system called **sharecropping**. The premise of this system was relatively simple: The landlord furnished the sharecroppers with a house, a plot of land to work, seed, some farm animals, and farm implements and advanced them credit at a store the landlord typically owned. In exchange, the sharecroppers promised the landlord a share of their crop, usually one-half. The croppers kept the proceeds from the sale of the other half to pay off their debts at the store and save or spend as they and their families saw fit. In theory, a sharecropper could save enough to secure economic independence.

But white landlords perceived black independence as both contradictory and subversive. With landlords holding the accounts at the store, black sharecroppers found that the proceeds from their share of the crop never left them very far ahead. In exchange for extending credit to sharecroppers, store owners felt justified in requiring collateral, but sharecroppers had no assets other than the cotton they grew. So southern states passed crop lien laws, which gave the store owner the right to the following year's crop in exchange for the current year's credit. If the following year's harvest could not pay off the debt, the sharecropper sank deeper into dependence. Some found themselves in perpetual debt and worked as virtual slaves. They could not simply abandon their debts and go to another farm, because the new landlord would check their references. Those found to have jumped their debts could end up on a prison chain gang. Not all white landlords cheated their tenants, but given the sharecroppers' innocence regarding accounting methods and crop pricing, the temptation to do so was great. Thus weak cotton prices conspired with white chicanery to keep black people economically dependent.

MODEST GAINS AND FUTURE VICTORIES

Black Southerners experienced some advances in the decade after the Civil War, but these owed little

FROM THEN TO NOW

African American Voting Rights in the South

Right from the end of the Civil War, white Southerners resisted African American voting rights. Black people, with equal determination, used the franchise to assert their equal right to participate in the political process. Black voting rights proved so contentious that Congress sought to secure them with the Fourteenth and Fifteenth Amendments to the U.S. Constitution. But U.S. Supreme Court decisions in *United States v. Cruikshank* (1876) and in the Civil Rights Cases (1883) undermined federal authority to protect the rights of freedmen, including voting rights. A combination of violence, intimidation, and legislation effectively disfranchised black Southerners by the early twentieth century.

During the 1960s, a period some historians have referred to as the Second Reconstruction, Congress passed legislation designed to override state prohibitions and earlier court decisions limiting African American voting rights. The key measure, the 1965 Voting Rights Act, not only guaranteed black Southerners (and later, other minorities) the right to register and vote but also protected them from procedural subterfuges, many of which dated from the first Reconstruction era, that would dilute their votes. These protections proved necessary because of the extreme racial polarization of Southern elections: White people rarely voted for black candidates.

To insure African American candidates an opportunity to win elections, the federal government after 1965 insisted that states and localities establish procedures to increase the likelihood of such a result. As part of this process, the federal government also monitored state redistricting for Congressional elections, which occurs every decade in response to population shifts recorded in the national census.

By the early 1990s, states were being directed to draw districts with majority-black voting populations to insure African American representation in the U.S. Congress and in state legislatures.

The federal government cited the South's history of racial discrimination and racially polarized voting to justify these districts. But white Southerners challenged such claims, as they had more than a century earlier, and their challenges proved successful in federal court.

In 1993, the U.S. Supreme Court issued a decision in a North Carolina redistricting case, *Shaw v. Reno*, that struck down a majority-black Congressional district in that state. Subsequent decisions in other southern districts produced similar rulings. The general principle followed by the Court has been that if race is a key justification for drawing these districts, then they violate the Fourteenth Amendment, which, according to the Court majority, demands color-blind electoral procedures. But, as the late Supreme Court Justice William Brennan noted, "to read the Fourteenth Amendment to state an abstract principle of color-blindness is itself to be blind to history." The framers of the Reconstruction Amendments had the protection of the rights of the freedmen (including and especially voting rights) in mind when they wrote those measures. One voting rights expert has charged that the Court rulings have ushered in a "Second Redemption."

But it is also true that beginning in 1998 and continuing through the 2002 elections, black Congressional incumbents in Georgia and North Carolina, running in redrawn districts in which black voters were in the minority (and less than 40 percent, at that) won reelection. These results may indicate that racially polarized voting may be diminishing in the South, although they may also reflect the power of incumbency and the weak campaigns of the challengers. In any case, the issue of African American voting rights in the South and the degree to which the federal government may or may not intercede to protect those rights remains as much at issue as it was more than a century ago.

to Reconstruction. Black families functioned as economic and psychological buffers against unemployment and prejudice. Black churches played crucial roles in their communities. Self-help and labor organizations offered mutual friendship and financial assistance. All of these institutions existed in the slavery era, although on a smaller scale. And some of them, such as black labor groups, schools, and social welfare associations, endured because comparable white institutions excluded black people.

Black people also scored some modest economic successes during the Reconstruction era, mainly from their own pluck. In the Lower South, black per capita income increased 46 percent between 1857 and 1879, compared with a 35 percent decline in white per capita income. Sharecropping, oppressive as it was, represented an advance over forced and gang labor. Collectively, black people owned more than $68 million worth of property in 1870, a 240 percent increase over 1860, but the average worth of each was only $408. Those who had been free before the war sometimes fared worse after it, especially property-owning free black people in the Lower South. Black city dwellers, especially in the Upper South, fared somewhat better. The overwhelming majority of black people, however, were landless agricultural laborers eking out a meager income that merchants and landlords often snatched to cover debts.

The Fourteenth and Fifteenth Amendments to the Constitution are among the few bright spots in Reconstruction's otherwise dismal legacy. The Fourteenth Amendment guaranteed former slaves equality before the law; the Fifteenth Amendment protected their right to vote. Both amendments elevated the federal government over the states by protecting freedmen from state attempts to deny them their rights. But the benefits of these two landmark amendments did not accrue to African Americans until well into the twentieth century. White Southerners effectively nullified the Reconstruction amendments, and the U.S. Supreme Court virtually interpreted them, and other Reconstruction legislation, out of existence.

In the ***Slaughterhouse* cases** (1873), the Supreme Court contradicted the intent of the Fourteenth Amendment by decreeing that most citizenship rights remained under state, not federal, control. In ***United States v. Cruikshank*** (1876), the Court overturned the convictions of some of those responsible for the Colfax Massacre, ruling that the Enforcement Act applied only to violations of black rights by states, not individuals. Within the next two decades, the Supreme Court would uphold the legality of racial segregation and black disfranchisement, in effect declaring that the Fourteenth and Fifteenth Amendments did not apply to African Americans. The Civil War had killed secession forever, but states' rights enjoyed a remarkable revival.

As the historian John Hope Franklin accurately concluded, Reconstruction "had no significant or permanent effect on the status of the black in American life. . . . [Black people] made no meaningful steps toward economic independence or even stability."

CONCLUSION

Formerly enslaved black Southerners had entered freedom with many hopes, among the most prominent of which was to be let alone. White Southerners, after four bloody years of unwanted attention from the federal government, also longed to be left alone. But they did not include their ex-slaves as equals in their vision of solitude. Northerners, too, began to seek escape from the issues and consequences of the war, eventually abandoning their commitment to secure civil and voting rights for black Southerners.

White Southerners robbed black Southerners of their gains and sought to reduce them again to servitude and dependence, if not to slavery. But in the processs, the majority of white Southerners lost as well. Yeoman farmers missed an opportunity to break cleanly from the Old South and establish a more equitable society. Instead, they allowed the old elites to regain power and gradually ignore their needs. They preserved the social benefit of a white skin at the cost of almost everything else. Many lost their farms and sank into tenancy, leasing land from others. Fewer had a voice in state legislatures or the U.S. Congress. A new South, rid of slavery and sectional antagonism, had indeed emerged, redeemed, regenerated, and disenthralled. But the old South lingered on in the new like Spanish moss on live oaks.

As federal troops left the South to be redeployed restraining striking workers in the North and suppressing Native Americans on the Great Plains, an era of possibility for American society ended, and a new era began. "The southern question is dead," a Charleston newspaper proclaimed in 1877. "The question of labor and capital, work and wages" had moved to the forefront. The chance to redeem the sacrifice of a bloody civil war with a society that fulfilled the promise of the Declaration of Independence and the Constitution for all citizens slipped away. It would take a new generation of African Americans a long century later to revive it.

REVIEW QUESTIONS

1. Given the devastation in the South after the Civil War and the loss of property, lives, and hope among many white Southerners, do you think they should they have supported black aspirations for civil rights, land, and suffrage? How differently would things have turned out if they had?

2. Some historians have placed a great deal of the blame for Reconstruction's failures on the backs of southern Republicans. Is this fair? Explain your response.

3. Black people did achieve some notable gains during Reconstruction, despite its overall failure. What were those gains?

4. In T. Thomas Fortune's recollection of a boyhood incident, why was it important for him and his friends to fight back?

KEY TERMS

Black codes (p. 509)

Carpetbaggers (p. 514)

Compromise of 1877 (p. 520)

Congressional Reconstruction (p. 512)

Field Order No. 15 (p. 503)

Fifteenth Amendment (p. 513)

Fourteenth Amendment (p. 510)

Freedmen's Bureau (p. 501)

Ku Klux Klan (p. 516)

Lost Cause (p. 499)

Redeemers (p. 519)

Scalawags (p. 513)

Sharecropping (p. 523)

Slaughterhouse cases (p. 525)

Southern Homestead Act (p. 503)

Union Leagues (p. 514)

United States v. Cruikshank (p. 525)

RECOMMENDED READING

Du Bois, W. E. B. *Black Reconstruction in America, 1860–1880* (1935). An early and long-ignored study by the foremost black scholar of his time that refuted the contemporary historical wisdom that Reconstruction was a horror visited on the South by an overbearing federal government and ignorant, willful black people.

Foner, Eric. *Reconstruction: America's Unfinished Revolution, 1863–1877* (1988). The standard work on Reconstruction, notable for its emphasis on the experience and aspirations of black Southerners.

Foster, Gaines M. *Ghosts of the Confederacy: Defeat, the Lost Cause, and the Emergence of the New South, 1865 to 1913* (1987). A fine picture of how the memory of the Civil War affected white Southerners and their views on Reconstruction policy.

Litwack, Leon. *Been in the Storm So Long: The Aftermath of Slavery* (1979). An eloquent account of the early days of freedom from the freedmen's perspective, up to 1867.

Tourgée, Albion W. *A Fool's Errand* (1879). A novel written by an Ohioan who migrated to North Carolina in 1865 to take advantage of economic opportunities in the state and eventually became involved in politics, with his frustrations with Reconstruction and his keen analysis of racism as important themes.

ADDITIONAL SOURCES

White Southerners and the Ghosts of the Confederacy

Blight, David W. *Race and Reunion: The Civil War in American Memory* (2001).

Edwards, Laura F. *Gendered Strife and Confusion: The Political Culture of Reconstruction* (1997).

Goldfield, David, *Still Fighting the Civil War: The American South and Southern History* (2002).

Black Aspirations beyond Freedom

Berlin, Ira, et al. *Freedom: A Documentary History of Emancipation, 1861–1867. The Wartime Genesis of Free Labor: The Lower South* (1990).

Cimbala, Paul A., and Randall M. Miller, eds. *The Freedmen's Bureau and Reconstruction: A Reconsideration* (1999).

Fitzgerald, Michael W. *The Union League Movement in the Deep South: Politics and Agricultural Change during Reconstruction* (1989).

Gutman, Herbert G. *The Black Family in Slavery and Freedom, 1750–1925* (1976).

Jaynes, Gerald. *Branches Without Roots: The Genesis of the Black Working Class in the American South, 1862–1882* (1986).

Jones, Jacqueline. *Labor of Love, Labor of Sorrow: Black Women, Work, and the Family from Slavery to the Present* (1985).

Kolchin, Peter. *First Freedom: The Responses of Alabama's Blacks to Emancipation and Reconstruction* (1972).

Rabinowitz, Howard N. *Race Relations in the Urban South, 1865–1890* (1978).

Rabinowitz, Howard N., ed. *Southern Black Leaders of the Reconstruction Era* (1982).

Thornbrough, Emma Lou. ed. *Black Reconstructionists* (1972).

Williamson, Joel. *After Slavery: The Negro in South Carolina During Reconstruction, 1861–1877* (1965).

Federal Reconstruction, 1865–1870

Abbott, Richard. *The Republican Party and the South, 1855–1877* (1986).

Belz, Herman. *A New Birth of Freedom: The Republican Party and Freedmen's Rights, 1861–1866* (1976).

Benedict, Michael Les. *A Compromise of Principle: Congressional Republicans and Reconstruction, 1863–1869* (1974).

Harris, William C. *With Charity for All: Lincoln and the Restoration of the Union* (1997).

McFeely, William S. *Grant: A Biography* (1981).

Moneyhon, Carl H. *Republicanism in Reconstruction Texas* (1980).

Perman, Michael. *Reunion without Compromise: The South and Reconstruction, 1865–1868* (1973).

Rose, Willie Lee. *Rehearsal for Reconstruction: The Port Royal Experiment* (1964).

Summers, Mark W. *Railroads, Reconstruction, and the Gospel of Prosperity: Aid Under the Radical Republicans, 1865–1877* (1984).

Trefousse, Hans. *The Radical Republicans: Lincoln's Vanguard for Racial Justice* (1969).

Counter-Reconstruction, 1870–1874

Current, Richard N. *Those Terrible Carpetbaggers: A Reinterpretation* (1988).

Duncan, Russell. *Entrepreneur for Equality: Governor Rufus Bullock, Commerce, and Race in Post-Civil War Georgia* (1994).

Hyde, Samuel C., Jr. *Pistols and Politics: The Dilemma of Democracy in Louisiana's Florida Parishes, 1810–1899* (1996).

Perman, Michael. *The Road to Redemption: Southern Politics, 1869–1879* (1984).

Rable, George C. *But There Was No Peace: The Role of Violence in the Politics of Reconstruction* (1984).

Trelease, Allen W. *White Terror: The Ku Klux Klan Conspiracy and Southern Reconstruction* (1971).

Redemption, 1874–1877

Campbell, Randolph B. *Grass-Roots Reconstruction in Texas, 1865–1880* (1997).

Woodward, C. Vann. *Reunion and Reaction: The Compromise of 1877 and the End of Reconstruction* (1951).

The Failure of Reconstruction

Angell, Stephen Ward. *Bishop Henry McNeal Turner and African-American Religion in the South* (1992).

Franklin, John Hope. *Reconstruction after the Civil War* (1961).

Ransom, Roger L., and Richard Sutch. *One Kind of Freedom: The Economic Consequences of Emancipation* (1977).

Richardson, Heather Cox. *The Death of Reconstruction: Race, Labor, and Politics in the Post-Civil War North, 1865–1901* (2001).

Stampp, Kenneth M. *The Era of Reconstruction, 1865–1877* (1965).

WHERE TO LEARN MORE

- Penn Center Historic District, St. Helena Island, South Carolina. The Penn School was a sea-island experiment in the education of free black people established by northern missionaries Laura Towne and Ellen Murray in 1862 that they operated until their deaths in the early 1900s. The Penn School became Penn Community Services in 1948, serving as an educational institution, health clinic, and a social service agency. www.penncenter.com.

- Hampton University Museum, Hampton, Virginia. Hampton University was founded by the Freedmen's Bureau in 1868 to provide "practical" training in the agricultural and mechanical fields for former slaves. In addition to a history of the institution, the museum includes one of the oldest collections of African art in the United States. www.hamptonu.edu/museum.

- Beauvoir, Biloxi, Mississippi. The exhibits at Beauvoir, the home of Jefferson Davis, evoke the importance of the Lost Cause for the white survivors of the Confederacy. Especially interesting is the Jefferson Davis Soldiers Home on the premises and the Confederate Veterans Cemetery. Davis spent his retirement in Beauvoir. www.beauvoir.org.

- Levi Jordan Plantation, Brazoria County, Texas. This site provides an excellent depiction and interpretation of the lives of sharecroppers and tenants during and immediately after the Reconstruction era. The site is especially valuable for demonstrating the transition from slavery to sharecropping. www.webarchaeology.com.

 Please refer to the document CD-ROM for primary sources related to this chapter.

APPENDIX

THE DECLARATION OF INDEPENDENCE

When in the course of human events it becomes necessary for one people to dissolve the political bands which have connected them with another and to assume, among the powers of the earth, the separate and equal station to which the laws of nature and of nature's God entitle them, a decent respect to the opinions of mankind requires that they should declare the causes which impel them to the separation.

We hold these truths to be self-evident, that all men are created equal; that they are endowed by their Creator with certain unalienable rights; that among these are life, liberty, and the pursuit of happiness. That, to secure these rights, governments are instituted among men, deriving their just powers from the consent of the governed; that, whenever any form of government becomes destructive of these ends, it is the right of the people to alter or to abolish it, and to institute a new government, laying its foundation on such principles, and organizing its powers in such form, as to them shall seem most likely to effect their safety and happiness. Prudence, indeed, will dictate that governments long established should not be changed for light and transient causes; and, accordingly, all experience hath shown that mankind are more disposed to suffer, while evils are sufferable, than to right themselves by abolishing the forms to which they are accustomed. But when a long train of abuses and usurpations, pursuing invariably the same object, evinces a design to reduce them under absolute despotism, it is their right, it is their duty, to throw off such government and to provide new guards for their future security. Such has been the patient sufferance of these colonies, and such is now the necessity which constrains them to alter their former systems of government. The history of the present King of Great Britain is a history of repeated injuries and usurpations, all having, in direct object, the establishment of an absolute tyranny over these States. To prove this, let facts be submitted to a candid world:

He has refused his assent to laws the most wholesome and necessary for the public good.

He has forbidden his governors to pass laws of immediate and pressing importance, unless suspended in their operation till his assent should be obtained; and, when so suspended, he has utterly neglected to attend to them.

He has refused to pass other laws for the accommodation of large districts of people, unless those people would relinquish the right of representation in the legislature, a right inestimable to them and formidable to tyrants only.

He has called together legislative bodies at places unusual, uncomfortable, and distant from the depository of their public records, for the sole purpose of fatiguing them into compliance with his measures.

He has dissolved representative houses, repeatedly for opposing, with manly firmness, his invasions on the rights of the people.

He has refused, for a long time after such dissolutions, to cause others to be elected; whereby the legislative powers, incapable of annihilation, have returned to the people at large for their exercise; the state remaining, in the meantime, exposed to all the danger of invasion from without and convulsions within.

He has endeavored to prevent the population of these States; for that purpose, obstructing the laws for naturalization of foreigners, refusing to pass others to encourage their migration hither, and raising the conditions of new appropriations of lands.

He has obstructed the administration of justice by refusing his assent to laws for establishing judiciary powers.

He has made judges dependent on his will alone for the tenure of their offices and the amount and payment of their salaries.

He has erected a multitude of new offices and sent hither swarms of officers to harass our people and eat out their substance.

He has kept among us, in time of peace, standing armies, without the consent of our legislatures.

He has affected to render the military independent of, and superior to, the civil power.

He has combined with others to subject us to a jurisdiction foreign to our Constitution and unacknowledged by our laws, giving his assent to their acts of pretended legislation—

For quartering large bodies of armed troops among us;

For protecting them by mock trial, from punishment for any murders which they should commit on the inhabitants of these States;

For cutting off our trade with all parts of the world;

For imposing taxes on us without our consent;

For depriving us, in many cases, of the benefit of trial by jury;

For transporting us beyond seas to be tried for pretended offences;

For abolishing the free system of English laws in a neighboring province, establishing therein an arbitrary government, and enlarging its boundaries, so as to render it at once an example and fit instrument for introducing the same absolute rule into these colonies;

For taking away our charters, abolishing our most valuable laws, and altering, fundamentally, the powers of our governments.

A-1

For suspending our own legislatures and declaring themselves invested with power to legislate for us in all cases whatsoever.

He has abdicated government here by declaring us out of his protection and waging war against us.

He has plundered our seas, ravaged our coasts, burnt our towns, and destroyed the lives of our people.

He is, at this time, transporting large armies of foreign mercenaries to complete the works of death, desolation, and tyranny already begun with circumstances of cruelty and perfidy scarcely paralleled in the most barbarous ages, and totally unworthy the head of a civilized nation.

He has constrained our fellow citizens, taken captive on the high seas, to bear arms against their country, to become the executioners of their friends and brethren, or to fall themselves by their hands.

He has excited domestic insurrections amongst us and has endeavored to bring on the inhabitants of our frontiers, the merciless Indian savages, whose known rule of warfare is an undistinguished destruction of all ages, sexes, and conditions.

In every stage of these oppressions, we have petitioned for redress in the most humble terms; our repeated petitions have been answered only by repeated injury. A prince whose character is thus marked by every act which may define a tyrant is unfit to be the ruler of a free people.

Nor have we been wanting in attention to our British brethren. We have warned them, from time to time, of attempts made by their legislature to extend an unwarrantable jurisdiction over us. We have reminded them of the circumstances of our emigration and settlement here. We have appealed to their native justice and magnanimity, and we have conjured them, by the ties of our common kindred, to disavow these usurpations, which would inevitably interrupt our connections and correspondence. They, too, have been deaf to the voice of justice and consanguinity. We must, therefore, acquiesce in the necessity which denounces our separation, and hold them, as we hold the rest of mankind, enemies in war, in peace, friends.

We, therefore, the representatives of the United States of America, in general Congress assembled, appealing to the Supreme Judge of the world for the rectitude of our intentions, do, in the name and by the authority of the good people of these colonies, solemnly publish and declare, that these united colonies are, and of right ought to be, free and independent states: that they are absolved from all allegiance to the British Crown, and that all political connection between them and the state of Great Britain is, and ought to be, totally dissolved; and that, as free and independent states, they have full power to levy war, conclude peace, contract alliances, establish commerce, and to do all other acts and things which independent states may of right do. And, for the support of this declaration, with a firm reliance on the protection of Divine Providence, we mutually pledge to each other our lives, our fortunes, and our sacred honor.

THE ARTICLES OF CONFEDERATION AND PERPETUAL UNION*

Between the states of New Hampshire, Massachusetts-bay Rhode Island and Providence Plantations, Connecticut, New York, New Jersey, Pennsylvania, Delaware, Maryland, Virginia, North Carolina, South Carolina, and Georgia.

ARTICLE 1
The Stile of this Confederacy shall be "The United States of America."

ARTICLE 2
Each state retains its sovereignty, freedom, and independence, and every power, jurisdiction, and right, which is not by this Confederation expressly delegated to the United States, in Congress assembled.

ARTICLE 3
The said States hereby severally enter into a firm league of friendship with each other, for their common defense, the security of their liberties, and their mutual and general welfare, binding themselves to assist each other, against all force offered to, or attacks made upon them, or any of them, on account of religion, sovereignty, trade, or any other pretense whatever.

ARTICLE 4
The better to secure and perpetuate mutual friendship and intercourse among the people of the different States in this Union, the free inhabitants of each of these States, paupers, vagabonds, and fugitives from justice excepted, shall be entitled to all privileges and immunities of free citizens in the several States; and the people of each State shall have free ingress and regress to and from any other State, and shall enjoy therein all the privileges of trade and commerce, subject to the same duties, impositions, and restrictions as the inhabitants thereof respectively, provided that such restrictions shall not extend so far as to prevent the removal of property imported into any State, to any other State of which the owner is an inhabitant; provided also that no imposition, duties or restriction shall be laid

---

*Agreed to in Congress November 15, 1777; ratified March 1781.

by any State, on the property of the United States, or either of them.

If any person guilty of, or charged with, treason, felony, or other high misdemeanor in any State, shall flee from justice, and be found in any of the United States, he shall, upon demand of the Governor or executive power of the State from which he fled, be delivered up and removed to the State having jurisdiction of his offense.

Full faith and credit shall be given in each of these States to the records, acts, and judicial proceedings of the courts and magistrates of every other State.

ARTICLE 5

For the most convenient management of the general interests of the United States, delegates shall be annually appointed in such manner as the legislatures of each State shall direct, to meet in Congress on the first Monday in November, in every year, with a power reserved to each State to recall its delegates, or any of them, at any time within the year, and to send others in their stead for the remainder of the year.

No State shall be represented in Congress by less than two, nor by more than seven members; and no person shall be capable of being a delegate for more than three years in any term of six years; nor shall any person, being a delegate, be capable of holding any office under the United States, for which he, or another for his benefit, receives any salary, fees or emolument of any kind.

Each State shall maintain its own delegates in a meeting of the States, and while they act as members of the committee of the States.

In determining questions in the United States in Congress assembled, each State shall have one vote.

Freedom of speech and debate in Congress shall not be impeached or questioned in any court or place out of Congress, and the members of Congress shall be protected in their persons from arrests or imprisonments, during the time of their going to and from, and attendence on Congress, except for treason, felony, or breach of the peace.

ARTICLE 6

No State, without the consent of the United States in Congress assembled, shall send any embassy to, or receive any embassy from, or enter into any conference, agreement, alliance or treaty with any King, Prince or State; nor shall any person holding any office of profit or trust under the United States, or any of them, accept any present, emolument, office or title of any kind whatever from any King, Prince or foreign State; nor shall the United States in Congress assembled, or any of them, grant any title of nobility.

No two or more States shall enter into any treaty, confederation or alliance whatever between them, without the consent of the United States in Congress assembled, specifying accurately the purposes for which the same is to be entered into, and how long it shall continue.

No State shall lay any imposts or duties, which may interfere with any stipulations in treaties, entered into by the United States in Congress assembled, with any King, Prince or State, in pursuance of any treaties already proposed by Congress, to the courts of France and Spain.

No vessel of war shall be kept up in time of peace by any State, except such number only, as shall be deemed necessary by the United States in Congress assembled, for the defense of such State, or its trade; nor shall any body of forces be kept up by any State in time of peace, except such number only, as in the judgement of the United States in Congress assembled, shall be deemed requisite to garrison the forts necessary for the defense of such State; but every State shall always keep up a well-regulated and disciplined militia, sufficiently armed and accoutered, and shall provide and constantly have ready for use, in public stores, a due number of filed pieces and tents, and a proper quantity of arms, ammunition and camp equipage.

No State shall engage in any war without the consent of the United States in Congress assembled, unless such State be actually invaded by enemies, or shall have received certain advice of a resolution being formed by some nation of Indians to invade such State, and the danger is so imminent as not to admit of a delay, till the United States in Congress assembled can be consulted; nor shall any State grant commissions to any ships or vessels of war, nor letters of marque or reprisal, except it be after a declaration of war by the United States in Congress assembled, and then only against the Kingdom or State and the subjects thereof, against which war has been so declared, and under such regulations as shall be established by the United States in Congress assembled, unless such State be infested by pirates, in which case vessels of war may be fitted out for that occasion, and kept so long as the danger shall continue, or until the United States in Congress assembled shall determine otherwise.

ARTICLE 7

When land forces are raised by any State for the common defense, all officers of or under the rank of colonel, shall be appointed by the legislature of each State respectively, by whom such forces shall be raised, or in such manner as such State shall direct, and all vacancies shall be filled up by the State which first made the appointment.

ARTICLE 8

All charges of war, and all other expenses that shall be incurred for the common defense or general welfare, and allowed by the United States in Congress assembled, shall be defrayed out of a common treasury, which shall be supplied by the several States in proportion to the value of all land within each State, granted to or surveyed for any person, as such land and the buildings and improvements thereon shall be estimated according to such mode as the United States in Congress assembled, shall from time to time direct and appoint.

The taxes for paying that proportion shall be laid and levied by the authority and direction of the legislatures of the several States within the time agreed upon by the United States in Congress assembled.

ARTICLE 9

The United States in Congress assembled, shall have the sole and exclusive right and power of determining on peace and war, except in the cases mentioned in the sixth article; of sending and receiving ambassadors; entering into treaties and alliances, provided that no treaty of commerce shall be made whereby the legislative power of the respective States shall be restrained from imposing such imposts and duties on foreigners, as their own people are subjected to, or from prohibiting the exportation or importation of any species of goods or commodities whatsoever; of establishing rules for deciding in all cases, what captures on land or water shall be legal, and in what manner prizes taken by land or naval forces in the service of the United States shall be divided or appropriated; of granting letters of marque and reprisal in times of peace; appointing courts for the trial of piracies and felonies committed on the high seas and establishing courts for receiving and determining finally appeals in all cases of captures, provided that no member of Congress shall be appointed a judge of any of the said courts.

The United States in Congress assembled shall also be the last resort on appeal in all disputes and differences now subsisting or that hereafter may arise between two or more States concerning boundary, jurisdiction or any other causes whatever; which authority shall always be exercised in the manner following. Whenever the legislative or executive authority or lawful agent of any State in controversy with another shall present a petition to Congress stating the matter in question and praying for a hearing, notice thereof shall be given by order of Congress to the legislative or executive authority of the other State in controversy, and a day assigned for the appearance of the parties by their lawful agents, who shall then be directed to appoint by joint consent, commissioners or judges to constitute a court for hearing and determining the matter in question: but if they cannot agree, Congress shall name three persons out of each of the United States, and from the list of such persons each party shall alternately strike out one, the petitioners beginning, until the number shall be reduced to thirteen; and from that number not less than seven, nor more than nine names as Congress shall direct, shall in the presence of Congress be drawn out by lot, and the persons whose names shall be so drawn or any five of them, shall be commissioners or judges, to hear and finally determine the controversy, so always as a major part of the judges who shall hear the cause shall agree in the determination: and if either party shall neglect to attend at the day appointed, without showing reasons, which Congress shall judge sufficient, or being present shall refuse to strike, the Congress shall proceed to nominate three persons out of each State, and the secretary of Congress shall strike in behalf of such party absent or refusing; and the judgement and sentence of the court to be appointed, in the manner before prescribed, shall be final and conclusive; and if any of the parties shall refuse to submit to the authority of such court, or to appear or defend their claim or cause, the court shall nevertheless proceed to pronounce sentence, or judgement, which shall in like manner be final and decisive, the judgement or sentence and other proceedings being in either case transmitted to Congress, and lodged among the acts of Congress for the security of the parties concerned: provided that every commissioner, before he sits in judgement, shall take an oath to be administered by one of the judges of the supreme or superior court of the State, where the cause shall be tried, "well and truly to hear and determine the matter in question, according to the best of his judgement, without favor, affection or hope of reward:" provided also, that no State shall be deprived of territory for the benefit of the United States.

All controversies concerning the private right of soil claimed under different grants of two or more States, whose jurisdictions as they may respect such lands, and the States which passed such grants are adjusted, the said grants or either of them being at the same time claimed to have originated antecedent to such settlement of jurisdiction, shall on the petition of either party to the Congress of the United States, be finally determined as near as may be in the same manner as is before prescribed for deciding disputes respecting territorial jurisdiction between different States.

The United States in Congress assembled shall also have the sole and exclusive right and power of regulating the alloy and value of coin struck by their own authority, or by that of the respective States; fixing the standards of weights and measures throughout the United States; regulating the trade and managing all affairs with the Indians not members of any of the States; provided that the legislative right of any State within its own limits be not infringed or violated; establishing or regulating post offices from one State to another, throughout all the United States, and exacting such postage on the papers passing through the same as may be requisite to defray the expenses of the said office; appointing all officers of the land forces in the service of the United States, excepting regimental officers; appointing all the officers of the naval forces, and commissioning all officers whatever in the service of the United States; making rules for the government and regulation of the said land and naval forces, and directing their operations.

The United States in Congress assembled shall have authority to appoint a committee, to sit in the recess of Congress, to be denominated "A Committee of the States," and to consist of one delegate from each State; and to appoint such other committees and civil officers as may be necessary for managing the general affairs of the United States under their direction; to appoint one of their members to preside, provided that no person be allowed to serve in the office of president more than one year in any term of three years; to ascertain the necessary sums of money to be raised for the service of the United States, and to appropriate and apply the same for defraying the public expenses; to borrow money, or emit bills on the credit of the United States, transmitting every half year to the respective States an account of the sums of money so borrowed or emitted; to build and equip a navy; to agree upon the number of land forces, and to make requisitions from each State for its quota, in proportion to the number of white inhabitants in such State; which requisition shall be binding, and thereupon the legislature of each State shall appoint the regimental officers, raise the men and cloath, arm and equip them in a soldierlike manner, at the expense of the United States; and the officers and men so cloathed, armed and equipped shall march to the place appointed, and within the time agreed on by the United States in Congress assembled; but if the United States in Congress assembled shall, on consideration of circumstances judge proper that any State should not raise men, or should raise a smaller number of men than the quota thereof, such extra number shall be raised, officered, cloathed, armed and equipped in the same manner as the quota of each State, unless the legislature of such State shall judge that such extra number cannot be safely spared out in the same, in which case they shall raise, officer, cloath, arm and equip as many of such extra number as they judge can be safely spared. And the officers and men so cloathed, armed, and equipped, shall march to the place appointed, and within the time agreed on by the United States in Congress assembled.

The United States in Congress assembled shall never engage in a war, nor grant letters of marque or reprisal in time of peace, nor enter into any treaties or alliances, nor coin money, nor regulate the value thereof, nor ascertain the sums and expenses necessary for the defense and welfare of the United States, or any of them, nor emit bills, nor borrow money on the credit of the United States, nor appropriate money, nor agree upon the number of vessels of war, to be built or purchased, or the number of land or sea forces to be raised, nor appoint a commander in chief of the army or navy, unless nine States assent to the same: nor shall a question on any other point, except for adjourning from day to day be determined, unless by the votes of the majority of the United States in Congress assembled.

The Congress of the United States shall have power to adjourn to any time within the year, and to any place within the United States, so that no period of adjournment be for a longer duration than the space of six months, and shall publish the journal of their proceedings monthly, except such parts thereof relating to treaties, alliances or military operations, as in their judgement require secrecy; and the yeas and nays of the delegates of each State on any question shall be entered on the journal, when it is desired by any delegates of a State, or any of them, at his or their request shall be furnished with a transcript of the said journal, except such parts as are above excepted, to lay before the legislatures of the several States.

ARTICLE 10

The Committee of the States, or any nine of them, shall be authorized to execute, in the recess of Congress, such of the powers of Congress as the United States in Congress assembled, by the consent of the nine States, shall from time to time think expedient to vest them with; provided that no power be delegated to the said Committee, for the exercise of which, by the Articles of Confederation, the voice of nine States in the Congress of the United States assembled is requisite.

ARTICLE 11

Canada acceding to this confederation, and adjoining in the measures of the United States, shall be admitted into, and entitled to all the advantages of this Union; but no other colony shall be admitted into the same, unless such admission be agreed to by nine States.

ARTICLE 12

All bills of credit emitted, monies borrowed, and debts contracted by, or under the authority of Congress, before the assembling of the United States, in pursuance of the present confederation, shall be deemed and considered as a charge against the United States, for payment and satisfaction whereof the said United States, and the public faith are hereby solemnly pledged.

ARTICLE 13

Every State shall abide by the determination of the United States in Congress assembled, on all questions which by this confederation are submitted to them. And the Articles of this Confederation shall be inviolably observed by every State, and the Union shall be perpetual; nor shall any alteration at any time hereafter be made in any of them; unless such alteration be agreed to in a Congress of the United States, and be afterwards confirmed by the legislatures of every State.

These articles shall be proposed to the legislatures of all the United States, to be considered, and if approved of by them, they are advised to authorize their delegates to ratify the same in the Congress of the United States; which being done, the same shall become conclusive.

THE CONSTITUTION OF THE UNITED STATES OF AMERICA

We the people of the United States, in order to form a more perfect union, establish justice, insure domestic tranquillity, provide for the common defense, promote the general welfare, and secure the blessings of liberty to ourselves and our posterity, do ordain and establish this Constitution for the United States of America.

ARTICLE I

SECTION 1. All legislative powers herein granted shall be vested in a Congress of the United States, which shall consist of a Senate and House of Representatives.

SECTION 2. 1. The House of Representatives shall be composed of members chosen every second year by the people of the several States, and the electors in each State shall have the qualifications requisite for electors of the most numerous branch of the State legislature.

2. No person shall be a representative who shall not have attained to the age of twenty-five years, and been seven years a citizen of the United States, and who shall not, when elected, be an inhabitant of that State in which he shall be chosen.

3. Representatives and direct taxes[1] shall be apportioned among the several States which may be included within this Union, according to their respective numbers, which shall be determined by adding to the whole number of free persons, including those bound to service for a term of years, and excluding Indians not taxed, three fifths of all other persons.[2] The actual enumeration shall be made within three years after the first meeting of the Congress of the United States, and within every subsequent term of ten years, in such manner as they shall by law direct. The number of representatives shall not exceed one for every thirty thousand, but each State shall have at least one representative; and until such enumeration shall be made, the State of New Hampshire shall be entitled to choose three, Massachusetts eight, Rhode Island and Providence Plantations one, Connecticut five, New York six, New Jersey four, Pennsylvania eight, Delaware one, Maryland six, Virginia ten, North Carolina five, South Carolina five, and Georgia three.

4. When vacancies happen in the representation from any State, the executive authority thereof shall issue writs of election to fill such vacancies.

5. The House of Representatives shall choose their speaker and other officers; and shall have the sole power of impeachment.

SECTION 3. 1. The Senate of the United States shall be composed of two senators from each State, chosen by the legislature thereof,[3] for six years; and each senator shall have one vote.

2. Immediately after they shall be assembled in consequence of the first election, they shall be divided as equally as may be into three classes. The seats of the senators of the first class shall be vacated at the expiration of the second year, of the second class at the expiration of the fourth year, and of the third class at the expiration of the sixth year, so that one third may be chosen every second year; and if vacancies happen by resignation, or otherwise, during the recess of the legislature of any State, the executive thereof may make temporary appointments until the next meeting of the legislature, which shall then fill such vacancies.[4]

3. No person shall be a senator who shall not have attained to the age of thirty years, and been nine years a citizen of the United States, and who shall not, when elected, be an inhabitant of that State for which he shall be chosen.

4. The Vice President of the United States shall be President of the Senate, but shall have no vote, unless they be equally divided.

5. The Senate shall choose their other officers, and also a president pro tempore, in the absence of the Vice President, or when he shall exercise the office of the President of the United States.

6. The Senate shall have the sole power to try all impeachments. When sitting for that purpose, they shall be on oath or affirmation. When the President of the United States is tried, the chief justice shall preside: and no person shall be convicted without the concurrence of two thirds of the members present.

7. Judgment in cases of impeachment shall not extend further than to removal from office, and disqualification to hold and enjoy any office of honor, trust or profit under the United States: but the party convicted shall nevertheless be liable and subject to indictment, trial, judgment and punishment, according to law.

SECTION 4. 1. The times, places, and manner of holding elections for senators and representatives, shall be prescribed in each State by the legislature thereof; but the Congress may at any time by law make or alter such regulations, except as to the places of choosing senators.

2. The Congress shall assemble at least once in every year, and such meeting shall be on the first Monday in December, unless they shall by law appoint a different day.

SECTION 5. 1. Each House shall be the judge of the elections, returns and qualifications of its own members, and a majority of each shall constitute a quorum to do business; but a smaller number may adjourn from day to day, and

---

[1]See the Sixteenth Amendment.
[2]See the Fourteenth Amendment.

[3]See the Seventeenth Amendment.
[4]See the Seventeenth Amendment.

may be authorized to compel the attendance of absent members, in such manner, and under such penalties as each House may provide.

2. Each House may determine the rules of its proceedings, punish its members for disorderly behavior, and, with the concurrence of two thirds, expel a member.

3. Each House shall keep a journal of its proceedings, and from time to time publish the same, excepting such parts as may in their judgment require secrecy; and the yeas and nays of the members of either House on any question shall, at the desire of one fifth of those present, be entered on the journal.

4. Neither House, during the session of Congress, shall, without the consent of the other, adjourn for more than three days, nor to any other place than that in which the two Houses shall be sitting.

SECTION 6. 1. The senators and representatives shall receive a compensation for their services, to be ascertained by law, and paid out of the Treasury of the United States. They shall in all cases, except treason, felony, and breach of the peace, be privileged from arrest during their attendance at the session of their respective Houses, and in going to and returning from the same; and for any speech or debate in either House, they shall not be questioned in any other place.

2. No senator or representative shall, during the time for which he was elected, be appointed to any civil office under the authority of the United States, which shall have been created, or the emoluments whereof shall have been increased, during such time; and no person holding any office under the United States shall be a member of either House during his continuance in office.

SECTION 7. 1. All bills for raising revenue shall originate in the House of Representatives; but the Senate may propose or concur with amendments as on other bills.

2. Every bill which shall have passed the House of Representatives and the Senate, shall, before it become a law, be presented to the President of the United States; If he approves he shall sign it, but if not he shall return it, with his objections, to that House in which it shall have originated, who shall enter the objections at large on their journal, and proceed to reconsider it. If after such reconsideration two thirds of that House shall agree to pass the bill, it shall be sent, together with the objections, to the other House, by which it shall likewise be reconsidered, and if approved by two thirds of that House, it shall become a law. But in all such cases the votes of both Houses shall be determined by yeas and nays, and the names of the persons voting for and against the bill shall be entered on the journal of each House respectively. If any bill shall not be returned by the President within ten days (Sundays excepted) after it shall have been presented to him, the same shall be a law, in like manner as if he had signed it, unless the Congress by their adjournment prevent its return, in which case it shall not be a law.

3. Every order, resolution, or vote to which the concurrence of the Senate and the House of Representatives may be necessary (except on a question of adjournment)

shall be presented to the President of the United States; and before the same shall take effect, shall be approved by him, or being disapproved by him, shall be repassed by two thirds of the Senate and House of Representatives, according to the rules and limitations prescribed in the case of a bill.

SECTION 8. 1. The Congress shall have the power

1. To lay and collect taxes, duties, imposts, and excises, to pay the debts and provide for the common defense and general welfare of the United States; but all duties, imposts, and excises shall be uniform throughout the United States.

2. To borrow money on the credit of the United States;

3. To regulate commerce with foreign nations, and among the several States, and with the Indian tribes;

4. To establish a uniform rule of naturalization, and uniform laws on the subject of bankruptcies throughout the United States;

5. To coin money, regulate the value thereof, and of foreign coin, and fix the standard of weights and measures;

6. To provide for the punishment of counterfeiting the securities and current coin of the United States;

7. To establish post offices and post roads;

8. To promote the progress of science and useful arts, by securing for limited times to authors and inventors the exclusive right to their respective writings and discoveries;

9. To constitute tribunals inferior to the Supreme Court;

10. To define and punish piracies and felonies committed on the high seas, and offenses against the law of nations;

11. To declare war, grant letters of marque and reprisal, and make rules concerning captures on land and water;

12. To raise and support armies, but no appropriation of money to that use shall be for a longer term than two years;

13. To provide and maintain a navy;

14. To make rules for the government and regulation of the land and naval forces;

15. To provide for calling forth the militia to execute the laws of the Union, suppress insurrections and repel invasions;

16. To provide for organizing, arming, and disciplining the militia, and for governing such part of them as may be employed in the service of the United States, reserving to the States respectively, the appointment of the officers, and the authority of training the militia according to the discipline prescribed by Congress;

17. To exercise exclusive legislation in all cases whatsoever, over such district (not exceeding ten miles square) as may, by cession of particular States, and the acceptance of Congress, become the seat of the government of the United States, and to exercise like authority over all places purchased by the consent of the legislature of the State in which the same shall be, for the erection of forts, magazines, arsenals, dockyards, and other needful buildings; and

18. To make all laws which shall be necessary and proper for carrying into execution the foregoing powers, and all other powers vested by this Constitution in the government of the United States, or any department or officer thereof.

SECTION 9. 1. The migration or importation of such persons as any of the States now existing shall think proper to admit, shall not be prohibited by the Congress prior to the year one thousand eight hundred and eight, but a tax or duty may be imposed on such importation, not exceeding ten dollars for each person.

2. The privilege of the writ of habeas corpus shall not be suspended, unless when in cases of rebellion or invasion the public safety may require it.

3. No bill of attainder or ex post facto law shall be passed.

4. No capitation, or other direct, tax shall be laid, unless in proportion to the census or enumeration hereinbefore directed to be taken.[5]

5. No tax or duty shall be laid on articles exported from any State.

6. No preference shall be given by any regulation of commerce or revenue to the ports of one State over those of another: nor shall vessels bound to, or from, one State be obliged to enter, clear, or pay duties in another.

7. No money shall be drawn from the treasury, but in consequence of appropriations made by law; and a regular statement and account of the receipts and expenditures of all public money shall be published from time to time.

8. No title of nobility shall be granted by the United States: and no person holding any office of profit or trust under them, shall, without the consent of the Congress, accept of any present, emolument, office, or title, of any kind whatever, from any king, prince, or foreign State.

SECTION 10. 1. No State shall enter into any treaty, alliance, or confederation; grant letters of marque and reprisal; coin money; emit bills of credit; make any thing but gold and silver coin a tender in payment of debts; pass any bill of attainder, ex post facto law, or law impairing the obligation of contracts, or grant, any title of nobility.

2. No State shall, without the consent of the Congress, lay any imposts or duties on imports or exports, except what may be absolutely necessary for executing its inspection laws: and the net produce of all duties and imposts laid by any State on imports or exports, shall be for the use of the treasury of the United States; and all such laws shall be subject to the revision and control of the Congress.

3. No State shall, without the consent of the Congress, lay any duty of tonnage, keep troops, or ships of war in time of peace, enter into any agreement or compact with another State, or with a foreign power, or engage in war, unless actually invaded, or in such imminent danger as will not admit of delay.

ARTICLE II

SECTION 1. 1. The executive power shall be vested in a President of the United States of America. He shall hold his office during the term of four years, and, together with the Vice President, chosen for the same term, be elected, as follows:

2. Each State shall appoint, in such manner as the legislature thereof may direct, a number of electors, equal to the whole number of senators and representatives to which the State may be entitled in the Congress: but no senator or representative, or person holding any office of trust or profit under the United States, shall be appointed an elector.

The electors shall meet in their respective States, and vote by ballot for two persons, of whom one at least shall not be an inhabitant of the same State with themselves. And they shall make a list of all the persons voted for, and of the number of votes for each; which list they shall sign and certify, and transmit sealed to the seat of the government of the United States, directed to the president of the Senate. The president of the Senate shall, in the presence of the Senate and House of Representatives, open all the certificates, and the votes shall then be counted. The person having the greatest number of votes shall be the President, if such number be a majority of the whole number of electors appointed; and if there be more than one who have such majority, and have an equal number of votes, then the House of Representatives shall immediately choose by ballot one of them for President; and if no person have a majority, then from the five highest on the list the said House shall in like manner choose the President. But in choosing the President, the votes shall be taken by States, the representation from each State having one vote; a quorum for this purpose shall consist of a member or members from two thirds of the States, and a majority of all the States shall be necessary to a choice. In every case after the choice of the President, the person having the greatest number of votes of the electors shall be the Vice President. But if there should remain two or more who have equal votes, the Senate shall choose from them by ballot the Vice President.[6]

3. The Congress may determine the time of choosing the electors, and the day on which they shall give their votes; which day shall be the same throughout the United States.

4. No person except a natural born citizen, or a citizen of the United States, at the time of the adoption of this Constitution, shall be eligible to the office of President; neither shall any person be eligible to the office who shall not have attained to the age of thirty-five years, and been fourteen years a resident within the United States.

5. In case of the removal of the President from office, or of his death, resignation, or inability to discharge the powers and duties of the said office, the same shall devolve on the Vice President, and the congress may by law pro-

---

[5]See the Sixteenth Amendment.

[6]Superseded by the Twelfth Amendment.

vide for the case of removal, death, resignation or inability, both of the President and Vice President, declaring what officer shall then act as President, and such officer shall act accordingly until the disability be removed, or a President shall be elected.

6. The President shall, at stated times, receive for his services a compensation which shall neither be increased nor diminished during the period for which he shall have been elected, and he shall not receive within that period any other emolument from the United States, or any of them.

7. Before he enter on the execution of his office, he shall take the following oath or affirmation:—"I do solemnly swear (or affirm) that I will faithfully execute the office of President of the United States, and will to the best of my ability, preserve, protect and defend the Constitution of the United States."

SECTION 2. 1. The President shall be commander in chief of the army and navy of the United States, and of the militia of the several States, when called into the actual service of the United States; he may require the opinion in writing, of the principal officer in each of the executive departments, upon any subject relating to the duties of their respective offices, and he shall have power to grant reprieves and pardons for offenses against the United States, except in cases of impeachment.

2. He shall have power, by and with the advice and consent of the Senate, to make treaties, provided two thirds of the senators present concur; and he shall nominate, and by and with the advice and consent of the Senate, shall appoint ambassadors, other public ministers and consuls, judges of the Supreme Court, and all other officers of the United States, whose appointments are not herein otherwise provided for, and which shall be established by law; but the Congress may by law vest the appointment of such inferior officers, as they think proper, in the President alone, in the courts of laws, or in the heads of departments.

3. The President shall have power to fill up all vacancies that may happen during the recess of the Senate, by granting commissions which shall expire at the end of their next session.

SECTION 3. He shall from time to time give to the Congress information of the state of the Union, and recommend to their consideration such measures as he shall judge necessary and expedient; he may, on extraordinary occasions, convene both Houses, or either of them, and in case of disagreement between them with respect to the time of adjournment, he may adjourn them to such time as he shall think proper; he shall receive ambassadors and other public ministers; he shall take care that the laws be faithfully executed, and shall commission all the officers of the United States.

SECTION 4. The President, Vice President, and all civil officers of the United States, shall be removed from office on impeachment for, and conviction of, treason, bribery, or other high crimes and misdemeanors.

ARTICLE III
SECTION 1. The judicial power of the United States shall be vested in one Supreme Court, and in such inferior courts as the Congress may from time to time ordain and establish. The judges, both of the Supreme and inferior courts, shall hold their offices during good behavior, and shall, at stated times, receive for their services, a compensation, which shall not be diminished during their continuance in office.

SECTION 2. 1. The judicial power shall extend to all cases, in law and equity, arising under this Constitution, the laws of the United States, and treaties made, or which shall be made, under their authority;—to all cases of admiralty and maritime jurisdiction;—to controversies to which the United States shall be a party;[7]—to controversies between two or more States;—between a State and citizens of another State;—between citizens of different States;—between citizens of the same State claiming lands under grants of different States, and between a State, or the citizens thereof, and foreign States, citizens or subjects.

2. In all cases affecting ambassadors, other public ministers and consuls, and those in which a State shall be party, the Supreme Court shall have original jurisdiction. In all the other cases before mentioned, the Supreme Court shall have appellate jurisdiction, both as to law and fact, with such exceptions, and under such regulations as the Congress shall make.

3. The trial of all crimes, except in cases of impeachment, shall be by jury; and such trial shall be held in the State where the said crimes shall have been committed; but when not committed within any State, the trial shall be such place or places as the congress may by law have directed.

SECTION 3. 1. Treason against the United States shall consist only in levying war against them, or in adhering to their enemies, giving them aid and comfort. No person shall be convicted of treason unless on the testimony of two witnesses to the same overt act, or on confession in open court.

2. The Congress shall have power to declare the punishment of treason, but no attainder of treason shall work corruption of blood, or forfeiture except during the life of the person attained.

ARTICLE IV
SECTION 1. Full faith and credit shall be given in each State to the public acts, records, and judicial proceedings of every other State. And the Congress may by general laws prescribe the manner in which such acts, records and proceedings shall be proved, and the effect thereof.

SECTION 2. 1. The citizens of each State shall be entitled to all privileges and immunities of citizens in the several States.[8]

[7]See the Eleventh Amendment.
[8]See the Fourteenth Amendment, Sec. 1.

2. A person charged in any State with treason, felony, or other crime, who shall flee from justice, and be found in another State, shall on demand of the executive authority of the State from which he fled, be delivered up to be removed to the State having jurisdiction of the crime.

3. No person held to service or labor in one State under the laws thereof, escaping into another, shall, in consequence of any law or regulation therein, be discharged from such service or labor, but shall be delivered up on claim of the party to whom such service or labor may be due.[9]

SECTION 3. 1. New States may be admitted by the Congress into this Union; but no new State shall be formed or erected within the jurisdiction of any other State, nor any State be formed by the junction of two or more States, or parts of States, without the consent of the legislatures of the States concerned as well as of the Congress.

2. The Congress shall have power to dispose of and make all needful rules and regulations respecting the territory or other property belonging to the United States; and nothing in this Constitution shall be so construed as to prejudice any claims of the United States, or of any particular State.

SECTION 4. The United States shall guarantee to every State in this Union a republican form of government, and shall protect each of them against invasion; and on application of the legislature, or of the executive (when the legislature cannot be convened) against domestic violence.

ARTICLE V

The Congress, whenever two thirds of both Houses shall deem it necessary, shall propose amendments to this Constitution, or, on the application of the legislatures of two thirds of the several States, shall call a convention for proposing amendments, which in either case shall be valid to all intents and purposes, as part of this Constitution, when ratified by the legislatures of three fourths of the several States, or by conventions in three fourths thereof, as the one or the other mode of ratification may be proposed by the Congress; Provided that no amendment which may be made prior to the year one thousand eight hundred and eight shall in any manner affect the first and fourth clauses in the ninth section of the first article; and that no State, without its consent, shall be deprived of its equal suffrage in the Senate.

ARTICLE VI

1. All debts contracted and engagements entered into, before the adoption of this Constitution, shall be as valid against the United States under this Constitution, as under the Confederation.[10]

2. This Constitution, and the laws of the United States which shall be made in pursuance thereof; and all treaties made, or which shall be made, under the authority of the United States, shall be the supreme law of the land; and the judges in every State shall be bound thereby, any thing in the Constitution or laws of any State to the contrary notwithstanding.

3. The senators and representatives before mentioned, and the members of the several State legislatures, and all executive and judicial officers, both of the United States and of the several States, shall be bound by oath or affirmation to support this Constitution; but no religious test shall ever be required as a qualification to any office or public trust under the United States.

ARTICLE VII

The ratification of the conventions of nine States shall be sufficient for the establishment of this Constitution between the States so ratifying the same.

Done in Convention by the unanimous consent of the States present the seventeenth day of September in the year of our Lord one thousand seven hundred and eighty-seven, and of the independence of the United States of America the twelfth. In witness whereof we have hereunto subscribed our names.

[Signatories names' omitted]

Articles in addition to, and amendment of, the Constitution of the United States of America, proposed by Congress, and ratified by the legislatures of the several States, pursuant to the fifth article of the original Constitution.

Amendment I

[First ten amendments ratified December 15, 1791]
Congress shall make no law respecting an establishment of religion, or prohibiting the free exercise thereof; or abridging the freedom of speech, or of the press; or the right of the people peaceably to assemble, and to petition the government for a redress of grievances.

Amendment II

A well regulated militia, being necessary to the security of a free State, the right of the people to keep and bear arms, shall not be infringed.

Amendment III

No soldier shall, in time of peace be quartered in any house, without the consent of the owner, nor in time of war, but in a manner to be prescribed by law.

Amendment IV

The right of the people to be secure in their persons, houses, papers, and effects, against unreasonable searches and seizures, shall not be violated, and no warrants shall issue, but upon probable cause, supported by oath or affirmation, and particularly describing the place to be searched, and the persons or things to be seized.

---

[9]See the Thirteenth Amendment.
[10]See the Fourteenth Amendment, Sec. 4.

Amendment V

No person shall be held to answer for a capital or otherwise infamous crime, unless on a presentment or indictment of a grand jury, except in cases arising in the land or naval forces, or in the militia, when in actual service in time of war or public danger; nor shall any person be subject for the same offense to be twice put in jeopardy of life or limb; nor shall be compelled in any criminal case to be a witness against himself, nor be deprived of life, liberty, or property, without due process of law; nor shall private property be taken for public use, without just compensation.

Amendment VI

In all criminal prosecutions, the accused shall enjoy the right to a speedy and public trial, by an impartial jury of the State and district wherein the crime shall have been committed, which district shall have been previously ascertained by law, and to be informed of the nature and cause of the accusation; to be confronted with the witnesses against him; to have compulsory process for obtaining witnesses in his favor, and to have the assistance of counsel for his defense.

Amendment VII

In suits at common law, where the value in controversy shall exceed twenty dollars, the right of trial by jury shall be preserved, and no fact tried by a jury shall be otherwise reexamined in any court of the United States, than according to the rules of the common law.

Amendment VIII

Excessive bail shall not be required, nor excessive fines imposed, nor cruel and unusual punishments inflicted.

Amendment IX

The enumeration in the Constitution of certain rights shall not be construed to deny or disparage others retained by the people.

Amendment X

The powers not delegated to the United States by the Constitution, nor prohibited by it to the States, are reserved to the States respectively, or to the people.

Amendment XI [January 8, 1798]

The judicial power of the United States shall not be construed to extend to any suit in law or equity, commenced or prosecuted against one of the United States by citizens of another State, or by citizens or subjects of any foreign State.

Amendment XII [September 25, 1804]

The electors shall meet in their respective States, and vote by ballot for President and Vice President, one of whom, at least, shall not be an inhabitant of the same State with themselves; they shall name in their ballots the person voted for as President, and in distinct ballots, the person voted for as Vice President, and they shall make distinct lists of all persons voted for as President and of all persons voted for as Vice President, and of the number of votes for each, which lists they shall sign and certify, and transmit sealed to the seat of the government of the United States, directed to the President of the Senate;—The President of the Senate shall, in the presence of the Senate and House of Representatives, open all the certificates and the votes shall then be counted;—The person having the greatest number of votes for President, shall be the President, if such number be a majority of the whole number of electors appointed; and if no person have such majority, then from the persons having the highest numbers not exceeding three on the list of those voted for as President, the House of Representatives shall choose immediately, by ballot, the President. But in choosing the President, the votes shall be taken by States, the representation from each State having one vote; a quorum for this purpose shall consist of a member or members from two thirds of the States, and a majority of all the States shall be necessary to a choice. And if the House of Representatives shall not choose a President whenever the right of choice shall devolve upon them, before the fourth day of March next following, then the Vice President shall act as President, as in the case of the death or other constitutional disability of the President. The person having the greatest number of votes as Vice President shall be the Vice President, if such number be a majority of the whole number of electors appointed, and if no person have a majority, then from the two highest numbers on the list, the Senate shall choose the Vice President; a quorum for the purpose shall consist of two thirds of the whole number of Senators, and a majority of the whole number shall be necessary to a choice. But no person constitutionally ineligible to the office of President shall be eligible to that of Vice President of the United States.

Amendment XIII [December 18, 1865]

SECTION 1. Neither slavery nor involuntary servitude, except as a punishment for crime whereof the party shall have been duly convicted, shall exist within the United States, or any place subject to their jurisdiction.

SECTION 2. Congress shall have power to enforce this article by appropriate legislation.

Amendment XIV [July 28, 1868]

SECTION 1. All persons born or naturalized in the United States, and subject to the jurisdiction thereof, are citizens of the United States and of the State wherein they reside. No State shall make or enforce any law which shall abridge the privileges or immunities of citizens of the United States; nor shall any State deprive any person of life, liberty, or property, without due process of law; nor deny to any person within its jurisdiction the equal protection of the laws.

SECTION 2. Representatives shall be apportioned among the several States according to their respective numbers, counting the whole number of persons in each State, excluding Indians not taxed. But when the right to vote at any election for the choice of electors for President and Vice President of the United States, representatives in Congress, the executive and judicial officers of a State, or the members of the legislature thereof, is denied to any of the male inhabitants of such State, being twenty-one years of age, and citizens of the United States, or in any way abridged, except for participating in rebellion, or other crime, the basis of representation there shall be reduced in the proportion which the number of such male citizens shall bear to the whole number of male citizens twenty-one years of age in such State.

SECTION 3. No person shall be a senator or representative in Congress, or elector of President and Vice President, or hold any office, civil or military, under the United States, or under any State, who having previously taken an oath, as a member of Congress, or as an officer of the United States, or as a member of any State legislature, or as an executive or judicial officer of any State, to support the Constitution of the United States, shall have engaged in insurrection or rebellion against the same, or given aid or comfort to the enemies thereof. But Congress may by a vote of two thirds of each House, remove such disability.

SECTION 4. The validity of the public debt of the United States, authorized by law, including debts incurred for payment of pensions and bounties for services in suppressing insurrection or rebellion; shall not be questioned. But neither the United States nor any State shall assume or pay any debt or obligation incurred in aid of insurrection or rebellion against the United States, or any claim for the loss or emancipation of any slave; but all such debts, obligations, and claims shall be held illegal and void.

SECTION 5. The Congress shall have the power to enforce, by appropriate legislation, the provisions of this article.

Amendment XV [March 30, 1870]

SECTION 1. The right of citizens of the United States to vote shall not be denied or abridged by the United States or by any State on account of race, color, or previous condition of servitude.

SECTION 2. The Congress shall have power to enforce this article by appropriate legislation.

Amendment XVI [February 25, 1913]

The Congress shall have power to lay and collect taxes on incomes, from whatever source derived, without apportionment among the several States, and without regard to any census or enumeration.

Amendment XVII [May 31, 1913]

The Senate of the United States shall be composed of two senators from each State, elected by the people thereof, for six years; and each senator shall have one vote. The electors in each State shall have the qualifications requisite for electors of the most numerous branch of the State legislature.

When vacancies happen in the representation of any State in the Senate, the executive authority of such State shall issue writs of election to fill such vacancies: Provided, That the legislature of any State may empower the executive thereof to make temporary appointments until the people fill the vacancies by election as the legislature may direct.

This amendment shall not be so construed as to affect the election or term of any senator chosen before it becomes valid as part of the Constitution.

Amendment XVIII[11] [January 29, 1919]

After one year from the ratification of this article, the manufacture, sale, or transportation of intoxicating liquors within, the importation thereof into, or the exportation thereof from the United States and all territory subject to the jurisdiction thereof for beverage purposes is thereby prohibited.

The Congress and the several States shall have concurrent power to enforce this article by appropriate legislation.

This article shall be inoperative unless it shall have been ratified as an amendment to the Constitution by the legislatures of the several States, as provided in the constitution, within seven years from the date of the submission hereof to the States by Congress.

Amendment XIX [August 26, 1920]

The right of citizens of the United States to vote shall not be denied or abridged by the United States or by any State on account of sex.

Congress shall have the power to enforce this article by appropriate legislation.

Amendment XX [January 23, 1933]

SECTION 1. The terms of the President and Vice President shall end at noon on the 20th day of January and the terms of Senators and Representatives at noon on the 3d day of January, of the years in which such terms would have ended if this article had not been ratified; and the terms of their successors shall then begin.

SECTION 2. The Congress shall assemble at least once in every year, and such meeting shall begin at noon on the 3d day of January, unless they shall by law appoint a different day.

SECTION 3. If, at the time fixed for the beginning of the term of President, the President-elect shall have died, the Vice President-elect shall become President. If a President shall not have been chosen before the time fixed for the beginning of his term, or if the President-elect shall have failed to qualify, then the Vice President-elect shall act as President until a President shall have qualified; and the Congress may by law provide for the case wherein neither a President-elect nor a Vice President-elect shall have qualified, declaring who shall then act as President, or the manner in which one who is to act shall be selected, and such person shall act accordingly until a President or Vice President shall have qualified.

---

[11]Repealed by the Twenty-first Amendment.

SECTION 4. The Congress may by law provide for the case of the death of any of the persons from whom, the House of Representatives may choose a President whenever the right of choice shall have devolved upon them, and for the case of the death of any of the persons from whom the Senate may choose a Vice President whenever the right of choice shall have devolved upon them.

SECTION 5. Sections 1 and 2 shall take effect on the 15th day of October following the ratification of this article.

SECTION 6. This article shall be inoperative unless it shall have been ratified as an amendment to the Constitution by the legislatures of three-fourths of the several States within seven years from the date of its submission.

Amendment XXI [December 5, 1933]
SECTION 1. The Eighteenth Article of amendment to the Constitution of the United States is hereby repealed.

SECTION 2. The transportation or importation into any State, Territory, or possession of the United States for delivery or use therein of intoxicating liquors in violation of the laws thereof, is hereby prohibited.

SECTION 3. This article shall be inoperative unless it shall have been ratified as an amendment to the Constitution by conventions in the several States, as provided in the Constitution, within seven years from the date of the submission thereof to the States by the Congress.

Amendment XXII [March 1, 1951]
No person shall be elected to the office of the President more than twice, and no person who has held the office of President, or acted as President, for more than two years of a term to which some other person was elected President shall be elected to the office of the President more than once.

But this article shall not apply to any person holding the office of President when this article was proposed by the Congress, and shall not prevent any person who may be holding the office of President, or acting as President, during the term within which this article becomes operative from holding the office of President or acting as President during the remainder of such term.

This article shall be inoperative unless it shall have been ratified as an amendment to the Constitution by the legislatures of three-fourths of the several States within seven years from the date of its submission to the States by the Congress.

Amendment XXIII [March 29, 1961]
SECTION 1. The District constituting the seat of Government of the United States shall appoint in such manner as the Congress may direct.

A number of electors of President and Vice President equal to the whole number of Senators and Representatives in Congress to which the District would be entitled if it were a State, but in no event more than the least populous State; they shall be in addition to those appointed by the States, but they shall be considered, for the purposes of the elec-

tion of President and Vice President, to be electors appointed by a State; and they shall meet in the District and perform such duties as provided by the twelfth article of amendment.

SECTION 2. The Congress shall have power to enforce this article by appropriate legislation.

Amendment XXIV [January 23, 1964]
SECTION 1. The right of citizens of the United States to vote in any primary or other election for President or Vice President, for electors for President or Vice President, or for Senator or Representative in Congress, shall not be denied or abridged by the United States or any State by reason of failure to pay any poll tax or other tax.

SECTION 2. The Congress shall have power to enforce this article by appropriate legislation.

Amendment XXV [February 10, 1967]
SECTION 1. In case of the removal of the President from office or of his death or resignation, the Vice President shall become President.

SECTION 2. Whenever there is a vacancy in the office of the Vice President, the President shall nominate a Vice President who shall take office upon confirmation by a majority of both Houses of Congress.

SECTION 3. Whenever the President transmits to the President pro tempore of the Senate and the Speaker of the House of Representatives his written declaration that he is unable to discharge the powers and duties of his office, and until he transmits to them a written declaration to the contrary, such powers and duties shall be discharged by the Vice President as Acting President.

SECTION 4. Whenever the Vice President and a majority of either the principal officers of the executive departments or of such other body as Congress may by law provide, transmit to the President pro tempore of the Senate and the Speaker of the House of Representatives their written declaration that the President is unable to discharge the powers and duties of his office, the Vice President shall immediately assume the powers and duties of the office as Acting President.

Thereafter, when the President transmits to the President pro tempore of the Senate and the Speaker of the House of Representatives his written declaration that no inability exists, he shall resume the powers and duties of his office unless the Vice President and a majority of either the principal officers of the executive departments or of such other body as Congress may by law provide, transmit within four days to the President pro tempore of the Senate and the Speaker of the House of Representatives their written declaration that the President is unable to discharge the powers and duties of his office. Thereupon Congress shall decide the issue, assembling within forty-eight hours for that purpose if not in session. If the Congress, within twenty-one days after receipt of the latter written declaration, or, if Congress is not in session, within twenty-one days after Congress is required to assemble, determines by two-thirds vote of both Houses that the President is unable to discharge the powers and duties of his office, the Vice President shall continue to discharge the same as Acting President; otherwise, the President shall resume the powers and duties of his office.

Amendment XXVI [June 30, 1971]

SECTION 1. The right of citizens of the United States who are eighteen years of age or older to vote shall not be denied or abridged by the United States or by any State on account of age.

SECTION 2. The Congress shall have power to enforce this article by appropriate legislation.

Amendment XXVII[12] [May 7, 1992]

No law, varying the compensation for services of the Senators and Representatives, shall take effect until an election of Representatives shall have intervened.

---

[12]James Madison proposed this amendment in 1789 together with the ten amendments that were adopted as the Bill of Rights, but it failed to win ratification at the time. Congress, however, had set no deadline for its ratification, and over the years—particularly in the 1980s and 1990s—many states voted to add it to the Constitution. With the ratification of Michigan in 1992 it passed the threshold of 3/4ths of the states required for adoption, but because the process took more than 200 years, its validity remains in doubt.

PRESIDENTIAL ELECTIONS

Year	Number of States	Candidates	Party	Popular Vote*	Electoral Vote†	Percent-age of Popular Vote
1789	11	GEORGE WASHINGTON	No party designations		69	
		John Adams			34	
		Other Candidates			35	
1792	15	GEORGE WASHINGTON	No party designations		132	
		John Adams			77	
		George Clinton			50	
		Other Candidates			5	
1796	16	JOHN ADAMS	Federalist		71	
		Thomas Jefferson	Democratic-Republican		68	
		Thomas Pinckney	Federalist		59	
		Aaron Burr	Democratic-Republican		30	
		Other Candidates			48	
1800	16	THOMAS JEFFERSON	Democratic-Republican		73	
		Aaron Burr	Democratic-Republican		73	
		John Adams	Federalist		65	
		Charles C. Pinckney	Federalist		64	
		John Jay	Federalist		1	
1804	17	THOMAS JEFFERSON	Democratic-Republican		162	
		Charles C. Pinckney	Federalist		14	
1808	17	JAMES MADISON	Democratic-Republican		122	
		Charles C. Pinckney	Federalist		47	
		George Clinton	Democratic-Republican		6	
1812	18	JAMES MADISON	Democratic-Republican		128	
		DeWitt Clinton	Federalist		89	
1816	19	JAMES MONROE	Democratic-Republican		183	
		Rufus King	Federalist		34	
1820	24	JAMES MONROE	Democratic-Republican		231	
		John Quincy Adams	Independent-Republican		1	
1824	24	JOHN QUINCY ADAMS	Democratic-Republican	108,740	84	30.5
		Andrew Jackson	Democratic-Republican	153,544	99	43.1
		William H. Crawford	Democratic-Republican	46,618	41	13.1
		Henry Clay	Democratic-Republican	47,136	37	13.2
1828	24	ANDREW JACKSON	Democrat	647,286	178	56.0
		John Quincy Adams	National Republican	508,064	83	44.0
1832	24	ANDREW JACKSON	Democrat	687,502	219	55.0
		Henry Clay	National Republican	530,189	49	42.4
		William Wirt	Anti-Masonic	} 33,108	7	} 2.6
		John Floyd	National Republican		11	

*Percentage of popular vote given for any election year may not total 100 percent because candidates receiving less than 1 percent of the popular vote have been omitted.

† Prior to the passage of the Twelfth Amendment in 1904, the electoral college voted for two presidential candidates; the runner-up became Vice-President. Data from Historical Statistics of the United States, Colonial Times to 1957 (1961), pp. 682–683, and The World Almanac.

PRESIDENTIAL ELECTIONS (continued)

Year	Number of States	Candidates	Party	Popular Vote	Electoral Vote	Percentage of Popular Vote
1836	26	MARTIN VAN BUREN	Democrat	765,483	170	50.9
		William H. Harrison	Whig		73	
		Hugh L. White	Whig	739,795	26	
		Daniel Webster	Whig		14	49.1
		W. P. Mangum	Whig		11	
1840	26	WILLIAM H. HARRISON	Whig	1,274,624	234	53.1
		Martin Van Buren	Democrat	1,127,781	60	46.9
1844	26	JAMES K. POLK	Democrat	1,338,464	170	49.6
		Henry Clay	Whig	1,300,097	105	48.1
		James G. Birney	Liberty	62,300		2.3
1848	30	ZACHARY TAYLOR	Whig	1,360,967	163	47.4
		Lewis Cass	Democrat	1,222,342	127	42.5
		Martin Van Buren	Free Soil	291,263		10.1
1852	31	FRANKLIN PIERCE	Democrat	1,601,117	254	50.9
		Winfield Scott	Whig	1,385,453	42	44.1
		John P. Hale	Free Soil	155,825		5.0
1856	31	JAMES BUCHANAN	Democrat	1,832,955	174	45.3
		John C. Frémont	Republican	1,339,932	114	33.1
		Millard Fillmore	American ("Know Nothing")	871,731	8	21.6
1860	33	ABRAHAM LINCOLN	Republican	1,865,593	180	39.8
		Stephen A. Douglas	Democrat	1,382,713	12	29.5
		John C. Breckinridge	Democrat	848,356	72	18.1
		John Bell	Constitutional Union	592,906	39	12.6
1864	36	ABRAHAM LINCOLN	Republican	2,206,938	212	55.0
		George B. McClellan	Democrat	1,803,787	21	45.0
1868	37	ULYSSES S. GRANT	Republican	3,013,421	214	52.7
		Horatio Seymour	Democrat	2,706,829	80	47.3
1872	37	ULYSSES S. GRANT	Republican	3,596,745	286	55.6
		Horace Greeley	Democrat	2,843,446	*	43.9
1876	38	RUTHERFORD B. HAYES	Republican	4,036,572	185	48.0
		Samuel J. Tilden	Democrat	4,284,020	184	51.0
1880	38	JAMES A. GARFIELD	Republican	4,453,295	214	48.5
		Winfield S. Hancock	Democrat	4,414,082	155	48.1
		James B. Weaver	Greenback-Labor	308,578		3.4
1884	38	GROVER CLEVELAND	Democrat	4,879,507	219	48.5
		James G. Blaine	Republican	4,850,293	182	48.2
		Benjamin F. Butler	Greenback-Labor	175,370		1.8
		John P. St. John	Prohibition	150,369		1.5
1888	38	BENJAMIN HARRISON	Republican	5,447,129	233	47.9
		Grover Cleveland	Democrat	5,537,857	168	48.6
		Clinton B. Fisk	Prohibition	249,506		2.2
		Anson J. Streeter	Union Labor	146,935		1.3

* Because of the death of Greeley, Democratic electors scattered their votes.

PRESIDENTIAL ELECTIONS (continued)

Year	Number of States	Candidates	Party	Popular Vote	Electoral Vote	Percentage of Popular Vote
1892	44	GROVER CLEVELAND	Democrat	5,555,426	277	46.1
		Benjamin Harrison	Republican	5,182,690	145	43.0
		James B. Weaver	People's	1,029,846	22	8.5
		John Bidwell	Prohibition	264,133		2.2
1896	45	WILLIAM MCKINLEY	Republican	7,102,246	271	51.1
		William J. Bryan	Democrat	6,492,559	176	47.7
1900	45	WILLIAM MCKINLEY	Republican	7,218,491	292	51.7
		William J. Bryan	Democrat; Populist	6,356,734	155	45.5
		John C. Woolley	Prohibition	208,914		1.5
1904	45	THEODORE ROOSEVELT	Republican	7,628,461	336	57.4
		Alton B. Parker	Democrat	5,084,223	140	37.6
		Eugene V. Debs	Socialist	402,283		3.0
		Silas C. Swallow	Prohibition	258,536		1.9
1908	46	WILLIAM H. TAFT	Republican	7,675,320	321	51.6
		William J. Bryan	Democrat	6,412,294	162	43.1
		Eugene V. Debs	Socialist	420,793		2.8
		Eugene W. Chafin	Prohibition	253,840		1.7
1912	48	WOODROW WILSON	Democrat	6,296,547	435	41.9
		Theodore Roosevelt	Progressive	4,118,571	88	27.4
		William H. Taft	Republican	3,486,720	8	23.2
		Eugene V. Debs	Socialist	900,672		6.0
		Eugene W. Chafin	Prohibition	206,275		1.4
1916	48	WOODROW WILSON	Democrat	9,127,695	277	49.4
		Charles E. Hughes	Republican	8,533,507	254	46.2
		A. L. Benson	Socialist	585,113		3.2
		J. Frank Hanly	Prohibition	220,506		1.2
1920	48	WARREN G. HARDING	Republican	16,143,407	404	60.4
		James M. Cox	Democrat	9,130,328	127	34.2
		Eugene V. Debs	Socialist	919,799		3.4
		P. P. Christensen	Farmer-Labor	265,411		1.0
1924	48	CALVIN COOLIDGE	Republican	15,718,211	382	54.0
		John W. Davis	Democrat	8,385,283	136	28.8
		Robert M. La Follette	Progressive	4,831,289	13	16.6
1928	48	HERBERT C. HOOVER	Republican	21,391,993	444	58.2
		Alfred E. Smith	Democrat	15,016,169	87	40.9
1932	48	FRANKLIN D. ROOSEVELT	Democrat	22,809,638	472	57.4
		Herbert C. Hoover	Republican	15,758,901	59	39.7
		Norman Thomas	Socialist	881,951		2.2
1936	48	FRANKLIN D. ROOSEVELT	Democrat	27,752,869	523	60.8
		Alfred M. Landon	Republican	16,674,665	8	36.5
		William Lemke	Union	882,479		1.9
1940	48	FRANKLIN D. ROOSEVELT	Democrat	27,307,819	449	54.8
		Wendell L. Willkie	Republican	22,321,018	82	44.8

PRESIDENTIAL ELECTIONS (continued)

Year	Number of States	Candidates	Party	Popular Vote	Electoral Vote	Percent-age of Popular Vote
1944	48	FRANKLIN D. ROOSEVELT	Democrat	25,606,585	432	53.5
		Thomas E. Dewey	Republican	22,014,745	99	46.0
1948	48	HARRY S. TRUMAN	Democrat	24,105,812	303	49.5
		Thomas E. Dewey	Republican	21,970,065	189	45.1
		J. Strom Thurmond	States' Rights	1,169,063	39	2.4
		Henry A. Wallace	Progressive	1,157,172		2.4
1952	48	DWIGHT D. EISENHOWER	Republican	33,936,234	442	55.1
		Adlai E. Stevenson	Democrat	27,314,992	89	44.4
1956	48	DWIGHT D. EISENHOWER	Republican	35,590,472	457*	57.6
		Adlai E. Stevenson	Democrat	26,022,752	73	42.1
1960	50	JOHN F. KENNEDY	Democrat	34,227,096	303†	49.9
		Richard M. Nixon	Republican	34,108,546	219	49.6
1964	50	LYNDON B. JOHNSON	Democrat	42,676,220	486	61.3
		Barry M. Goldwater	Republican	26,860,314	52	38.5
1968	50	RICHARD M. NIXON	Republican	31,785,480	301	43.4
		Hubert H. Humphrey	Democrat	31,275,165	191	42.7
		George C. Wallace	American Independent	9,906,473	46	13.5
1972	50	RICHARD M. NIXON‡	Republican	47,165,234	520	60.6
		George S. McGovern	Democrat	29,168,110	17	37.5
1976	50	JIMMY CARTER	Democrat	40,828,929	297	50.1
		Gerald R. Ford	Republican	39,148,940	240	47.9
		Eugene McCarthy	Independent	739,256		
1980	50	RONALD REAGAN	Republican	43,201,220	489	50.9
		Jimmy Carter	Democrat	34,913,332	49	41.2
		John B. Anderson	Independent	5,581,379		
1984	50	RONALD REAGAN	Republican	53,428,357	525	59.0
		Walter F. Mondale	Democrat	36,930,923	13	41.0
1988	50	GEORGE BUSH	Republican	48,901,046	426	53.4
		Michael Dukakis	Democrat	41,809,030	111	45.6
1992	50	BILL CLINTON	Democrat	43,728,275	370	43.2
		George Bush	Republican	38,167,416	168	37.7
		H. Ross Perot	United We Stand, America	19,237,247		19.0
1996	50	BILL CLINTON	Democrat	45,590,703	379	49.0
		Robert Dole	Republican	37,816,307	159	41.0
		H. Ross Perot	Reform	7,866,284		8.0
2000	50	GEORGE W. BUSH	Republican	50,459,624	271	47.9
		Albert Gore, Jr.	Democrat	51,003,328	266	49.4
		Ralph Nader	Green	2,882,985		2.7

* Walter B. Jones received 1 electoral vote.

† Harry F. Byrd received 15 electoral votes.

‡ Resigned August 9, 1974: Vice President Gerald R. Ford became President.

SUPREME COURT JUSTICES

Name*	Years on Court	Appointing President
JOHN JAY	1789–1795	Washington
James Wilson	1789–1798	Washington
John Rutledge	1790–1791	Washington
William Cushing	1790–1810	Washington
John Blair	1790–1796	Washington
James Iredell	1790–1799	Washington
Thomas Jefferson	1792–1793	Washington
William Paterson	1793–1806	Washington
JOHN RUTLEDGE†	1795	Washington
Samuel Chase	1796–1811	Washington
OLIVER ELLSWORTH	1796–1800	Washington
Bushrod Washington	1799–1829	J. Adams
Alfred Moore	1800–1804	J. Adams
JOHN MARSHALL	1801–1835	J. Adams
William Johnson	1804–1834	Jefferson
Brockholst Livingston	1807–1823	Jefferson
Thomas Todd	1807–1826	Jefferson
Gabriel Duvall	1811–1835	Madison
Joseph Story	1812–1845	Madison
Smith Thompson	1823–1843	Monroe
Robert Trimble	1826–1828	J. Q. Adams
John McLean	1830–1861	Jackson
Henry Baldwin	1830–1844	Jackson
James M. Wayne	1835–1867	Jackson
ROGER B. TANEY	1836–1864	Jackson
Philip P. Barbour	1836–1841	Jackson
John Cartron	1837–1865	Van Buren
John McKinley	1838–1852	Van Buren
Peter V. Daniel	1842–1860	Van Buren
Samuel Nelson	1845–1872	Tyler
Levi Woodbury	1845–1851	Polk
Robert C. Grier	1846–1870	Polk
Benjamin R. Curtis	1851–1857	Fillmore
John A. Campbell	1853–1861	Pierce
Nathan Clifford	1858–1881	Buchanan
Noah H. Swayne	1862–1881	Lincoln
Samuel F. Miller	1862–1890	Lincoln
David Davis	1862–1877	Lincoln
Stephen J. Field	1863–1897	Lincoln
SALMON P. CHASE	1864–1873	Lincoln
William Strong	1870–1880	Grant
Joseph P. Bradley	1870–1892	Grant
Ward Hunt	1873–1882	Grant
MORRISON R. WAITE	1874–1888	Grant
John M. Harlan	1877–1911	Hayes
William B. Woods	1881–1887	Hayes
Stanley Matthews	1881–1889	Garfield
Horace Gray	1882–1902	Arthur
Samuel Blatchford	1882–1893	Arthur

SUPREME COURT JUSTICES (continued)

Name*	Years on Court	Appointing President
Lucious Q. C. Lamar	1888–1893	Cleveland
MELVILLE W. FULLER	1888–1910	Cleveland
David J. Brewer	1890–1910	B. Harrison
Henry B. Brown	1891–1906	B. Harrison
George Shiras, Jr.	1892–1903	B. Harrison
Howell E. Jackson	1893–1895	B. Harrison
Edward D. White	1894–1910	Cleveland
Rufus W. Peckham	1896–1909	Cleveland
Joseph McKenna	1898–1925	McKinley
Oliver W. Holmes	1902–1932	T. Roosevelt
William R. Day	1903–1922	T. Roosevelt
William H. Moody	1906–1910	T. Roosevelt
Horace H. Lurton	1910–1914	Taft
Charles E. Hughes	1910–1916	Taft
EDWARD D. WHITE	1910–1921	Taft
Willis Van Devanter	1911–1937	Taft
Joseph R. Lamar	1911–1916	Taft
Mahlon Pitney	1912–1922	Taft
James C. McReynolds	1914–1941	Wilson
Louis D. Brandeis	1916–1939	Wilson
John H. Clarke	1916–1922	Wilson
WILLIAM H. TAFT	1921–1930	Harding
George Sutherland	1922–1938	Harding
Pierce Butler	1923–1939	Harding
Edward T. Sanford	1923–1930	Harding
Harlan F. Stone	1925–1941	Coolidge
CHARLES E. HUGHES	1930–1941	Hoover
Owen J. Roberts	1930–1945	Hoover
Benjamin N. Cardozo	1932–1938	Hoover
Hugo L. Black	1937–1971	F. Roosevelt
Stanley F. Reed	1938–1957	F. Roosevelt
Felix Frankfurter	1939–1962	F. Roosevelt
William O. Douglas	1939–1975	F. Roosevelt
Frank Murphy	1940–1949	F. Roosevelt
HARLAN F. STONE	1941–1946	F. Roosevelt
James F. Brynes	1941–1942	F. Roosevelt
Robert H. Jackson	1941–1954	F. Roosevelt
Wiley B. Rutledge	1943–1949	F. Roosevelt
Harold H. Burton	1945–1958	Truman
FREDERICK M. VINSON	1946–1953	Truman
Tom C. Clark	1949–1967	Truman
Sherman Minton	1949–1956	Truman
EARL WARREN	1953–1969	Eisenhower
John Marshall Harlan	1955–1971	Eisenhower
William J. Brennan, Jr.	1956–1990	Eisenhower
Charles E. Whittaker	1957–1962	Eisenhower
Potter Stewart	1958–1981	Eisenhower
Byron R. White	1962–1993	Kennedy
Arthur J. Goldberg	1962–1965	Kennedy

SUPREME COURT JUSTICES (continued)

Name*	Years on Court	Appointing President
Abe Fortas	1965–1970	L. Johnson
Thurgood Marshall	1967–1991	L. Johnson
WARREN E. BURGER	1969–1986	Nixon
Harry A. Blackmun	1970–1994	Nixon
Lewis F. Powell, Jr.	1971–1987	Nixon
William H. Rehnquist	1971–1986	Nixon
John Paul Stevens	1975–	Ford
Sandra Day O'Connor	1981–	Reagan
WILLIAM H. REHNQUIJST	1986–	Reagan
Antonin Scalia	1986–	Reagan
Anthony Kennedy	1988–	Reagan
David Souter	1990–	Bush
Clarence Thomas	1991–	Bush
Ruth Bader Ginsburg	1993–	Clinton
Stephen Breyer	1994–	Clinton

* Capital letters designate Chief Justices
† Never confirmed by the Senate as Chief Justice

ADMISSION OF STATES INTO THE UNION

State	Date of Admission	State	Date of Admission
1. Delaware	December 7, 1787	26. Michigan	January 26, 1837
2. Pennsylvania	December 12, 1787	27. Florida	March 3, 1845
3. New Jersey	December 18, 1787	28. Texas	December 29, 1845
4. Georgia	January 2, 1788	29. Iowa	December 28, 1846
5. Connecticut	January 9, 1788	30. Wisconsin	May 29, 1848
6. Massachusetts	February 6, 1788	31. California	September 9, 1850
7. Maryland	April 28, 1788	32. Minnesota	May 11, 1858
8. South Carolina	May 23, 1788	33. Oregon	February 14, 1859
9. New Hampshire	June 21, 1788	34. Kansas	January 29, 1861
10. Virginia	June 25, 1788	35. West Virginia	June 20, 1863
11. New York	July 26, 1788	36. Nevada	October 31, 1864
12. North Carolina	November 21, 1789	37. Nebraska	March 1, 1867
13. Rhode Island	May 29, 1790	38. Colorado	August 1, 1876
14. Vermont	March 4, 1791	39. North Dakota	November 2, 1889
15. Kentucky	June 1, 1792	40. South Dakota	November 2, 1889
16. Tennessee	June 1, 1796	41. Montana	November 8, 1889
17. Ohio	March 1, 1803	42. Washington	November 11, 1889
18. Louisiana	April 30, 1812	43. Idaho	July 3, 1890
19. Indiana	December 11, 1816	44. Wyoming	July 10, 1890
20. Mississippi	December 10, 1817	45. Utah	January 4, 1896
21. Illinois	December 3, 1818	46. Oklahoma	November 16, 1907
22. Alabama	December 14, 1819	47. New Mexico	January 6, 1912
23. Maine	March 15, 1820	48. Arizona	February 14, 1912
24. Missouri	August 10, 1821	49. Alaska	January 3, 1959
25. Arkansas	June 15, 1836	50. Hawaii	August 21, 1959

DEMOGRAPHICS OF THE UNITED STATES

POPULATION GROWTH

Year	Population	Percent Increase
1630	4,600	
1640	26,600	478.3
1650	50,400	90.8
1660	75,100	49.0
1670	111,900	49.0
1680	151,500	35.4
1690	210,400	38.9
1700	250,900	19.2
1710	331,700	32.2
1720	466,200	40.5
1730	629,400	35.0
1740	905,600	43.9
1750	1,170,800	29.3
1760	1,593,600	36.1
1770	2,148,100	34.8
1780	2,780,400	29.4
1790	3,929,214	41.3
1800	5,308,483	35.1
1810	7,239,881	36.4
1820	9,638,453	33.1
1830	12,866,020	33.5
1840	17,069,453	32.7
1850	23,191,876	35.9
1860	31,443,321	35.6
1870	39,818,449	26.6
1880	50,155,783	26.0
1890	62,947,714	25.5
1900	75,994,575	20.7
1910	91,972,266	21.0
1920	105,710,620	14.9
1930	122,775,046	16.1
1940	131,669,275	7.2
1950	151,325,798	14.5
1960	179,323,175	18.5
1970	203,302,031	13.4
1980	226,542,199	11.4
1990	248,718,301	9.8
2000	281,421,906	13.1

Source: *Historical Statistics of the United States* (1975); *Statistical Abstract by the United States* (2001).
Note: Figures for 1630–1780 include British colonies within limits of present United States only; Native American population included only in 1930 and thereafter.

WORK FORCE

Year	Total Number Workers (1000s)	Farmers as % of Total	Women as % of Total	% Workers in Unions
1810	2,330	84	(NA)	(NA)
1840	5,660	75	(NA)	(NA)
1860	11,110	53	(NA)	(NA)
1870	12,506	53	15	(NA)
1880	17,392	52	15	(NA)
1890	23,318	43	17	(NA)
1900	29,073	40	18	3
1910	38,167	31	21	6
1920	41,614	26	21	12
1930	48,830	22	22	7
1940	53,011	17	24	27
1950	59,643	12	28	25
1960	69,877	8	32	26
1970	82,049	4	37	25
1980	106,940	3	43	23
1990	125,840	3	45	16
2000	140,863	2	47	12

Source: *Historical Statistics of the United States* (1975); *Statistical Abstract of the United States* (2001).

VITAL STATISTICS
(in thousands)

Year	Births	Deaths	Marriages	Divorces
1800	55	(NA)	(NA)	(NA)
1810	54.3	(NA)	(NA)	(NA)
1820	55.2	(NA)	(NA)	(NA)
1830	51.4	(NA)	(NA)	(NA)
1840	51.8	(NA)	(NA)	(NA)
1850	43.3	(NA)	(NA)	(NA)
1860	44.3	(NA)	(NA)	(NA)
1870	38.3	(NA)	9.6 (1867)	0.3 (1867)
1880	39.8	(NA)	9.1 (1875)	0.3 (1875)
1890	31.5	(NA)	9.0	0.5
1900	32.3	17.2	9.3	0.7
1910	30.1	14.7	10.3	0.9
1920	27.7	13.0	12.0	1.6
1930	21.3	11.3	9.2	1.6
1940	19.4	10.8	12.1	2.0
1950	24.1	9.6	11.1	2.6
1960	23.7	9.5	8.5	2.2
1970	18.4	9.5	10.6	3.5
1980	15.9	8.8	10.6	5.2
1990	16.7	8.6	9.8	4.7
1997	14.6	8.6	8.9	4.3

Source: *Historical Statistics of the United States* (1975); *Statistical Abstract of the United States* (1999).

RACIAL COMPOSITION OF THE POPULATION
(in thousands)

Year	White	Black	Indian	Hispanic	Asian/Pacific Islander
1790	3,172	757	(NA)	(NA)	(NA)
1800	4,306	1,002	(NA)	(NA)	(NA)
1820	7,867	1,772	(NA)	(NA)	(NA)
1840	14,196	2,874	(NA)	(NA)	(NA)
1860	26,923	4,442	(NA)	(NA)	(NA)
1880	43,403	6,581	(NA)	(NA)	(NA)
1900	66,809	8,834	(NA)	(NA)	(NA)
1910	81,732	9,828	(NA)	(NA)	(NA)
1920	94,821	10,463	(NA)	(NA)	(NA)
1930	110,287	11,891	(NA)	(NA)	(NA)
1940	118,215	12,866	(NA)	(NA)	(NA)
1950	134,942	15,042	(NA)	(NA)	(NA)
1960	158,832	18,872	(NA)	(NA)	(NA)
1970	178,098	22,581	(NA)	(NA)	(NA)
1980	194,713	26,683	1,420	14,609	3,729
1990	208,727	30,511	2,065	22,372	2,462
2000	211,461	34,658	2,476	35,306	10,642

Source: U.S. Bureau of the Census, U.S. *Census of Population: 1940*, vol. II, part 1, and vol. IV, part 1; *1950*, vol. II, part 1; *1960*, vol. I, part 1; *1970*, vol. I, part B; and *Current Population Reports*, P25-1095 and P25-1104; *Statistical Abstract of the United States* (2001).

THE ECONOMY AND FEDERAL SPENDING

Year	Gross National Product (GNP) (in billions)	Foreign Trade (in millions)			Federal Budget (in billions)	Federal Surplus/Deficit (in billions)	Federal Debt (in billions)
		Exports	Imports	Balance of Trade			
1790	(NA)	$ 20	$ 23	$ −3	$ 0.004	$ +0.00015	$ 0.076
1800	(NA)	71	91	−20	0.011	+0.0006	0.083
1810	(NA)	67	85	−18	0.008	+0.0012	0.053
1820	(NA)	70	74	−4	0.018	−0.0004	0.091
1830	(NA)	74	71	+3	0.015	+0.100	0.049
1840	(NA)	132	107	+25	0.024	−0.005	0.004
1850	(NA)	152	178	−26	0.040	+0.004	0.064
1860	(NA)	400	362	−38	0.063	−0.01	0.065
1870	$ 7.4	451	462	−11	0.310	+0.10	2.4
1880	11.2	853	761	+92	0.268	+0.07	2.1
1890	13.1	910	823	+87	0.318	+0.09	1.2
1900	18.7	1,499	930	+569	0.521	+0.05	1.2
1910	35.3	1,919	1,646	+273	0.694	−0.02	1.1
1920	91.5	8,664	5,784	+2,880	6.357	+0.3	24.3
1930	90.7	4,013	3,500	+513	3.320	+0.7	16.3
1940	100.0	4,030	7,433	−3,403	9.6	−2.7	43.0
1950	286.5	10,816	9,125	+1,691	43.1	−2.2	257.4
1960	506.5	19,600	15,046	+4,556	92.2	+0.3	286.3
1970	992.7	42,700	40,189	+2,511	195.6	−2.8	371.0
1980	2,631.7	220,783	244,871	+24,088	590.9	−73.8	907.7
1990	5,524.5	394,030	494,042	−101,012	1,251.8	−220.5	3,233.3
2000	9,958.7	1,068,397	1,438,086	−369,689	1,788.8	+236.4	5,629.0

Source: *U.S. Office of Management and Budget, Budget of the United States Government, annual; Statistical Abstract of the United States*, 2001.

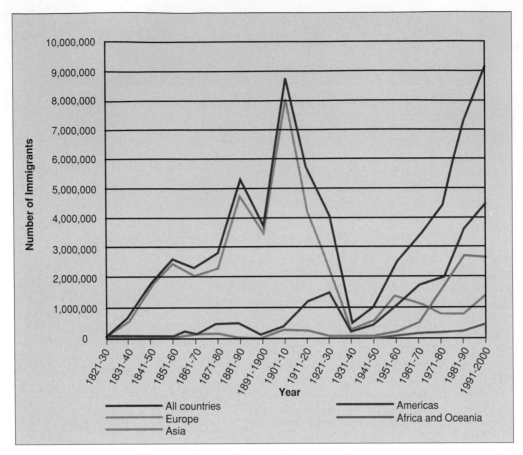

Immigration to the United States since 1820, by decade
Source: *Statistical Yearbook of the Immigration and Naturalization Service,* 2001.

GLOSSARY

Act for Religious Toleration   The first law in America to call for freedom of worship for all Christians. It was enacted in Maryland in 1649 to quell disputes between Catholics and Protestants, but it failed to bring peace.

Actual representation   The practice whereby elected representatives normally reside in their districts and are directly responsive to local interests.

Age of Enlightenment   Major intellectual movement occurring in western Europe in the late seventeenth and early eighteenth centuries. Inspired by recent scientific advances, thinkers emphasized the role of human reason in understanding the world and directing its events. Their ideas placed less emphasis on God's role in ordering worldly affairs.

Alamo   Franciscan mission at San Antonio, Texas, that was the site in 1836 of a siege and massacre of Texans by Mexican troops.

Albany Plan of Union   Plan put forward in 1754 by Massachusetts Governor William Shirley, Benjamin Franklin, and other colonial leaders, calling for an intercolonial union to manage defense and Indian affairs. The plan was rejected by participants at the Albany Congress.

Alien and Sedition Acts   Collective name given to four acts passed by Congress in 1798 that curtailed freedom of speech and the liberty of foreigners resident in the United States.

Alien Friends Act   Law passed by Congress in 1798 authorizing the president during peacetime to expel aliens suspected of subversive activities; one of the **Alien and Sedition Acts**.

American Anti-Slavery Society   The first national organization of abolitionists, founded in 1833.

American Colonization Society   Organization, founded in 1817 by antislavery reformers, that called for gradual emancipation and the removal of freed blacks to Africa.

American Female Moral Reform Society   Organization founded in 1839 by female reformers that established homes of refuge for prostitutes and petitioned for state laws that would criminalize adultery and the seduction of women.

American Revenue Act   See **Sugar Act**.

American System   The program of government subsidies favored by Henry Clay and his followers to promote American economic growth and protect domestic manufacturers from foreign competition.

American system of manufacturing   A technique of production pioneered in the United States in the first half of the nineteenth century that relied on precision manufacturing with the use of interchangeable parts.

American Temperance Society   National organization established in 1826 by evangelical Protestants that campaigned for total abstinence from alcohol and was successful in sharply lowering per capita consumption of alcohol.

Anarchist   A person who believes that all government interferes with individual liberty and should be abolished by whatever means.

Anglican   Of or belonging to the Church of England, a Protestant denomination.

Anglo–American Accords   Series of agreements reached in the British–American Convention of 1818 that fixed the western boundary between the United States and Canada at the 49th parallel, allowed for the joint occupation of the Oregon Country, and restored to Americans fishing rights off Newfoundland.

Annapolis Convention   Conference of state delegates at Annapolis, Maryland, that issued a call in September 1786 for a convention to meet at Philadelphia in May 1787 to consider fundamental changes to the **Articles of Confederation**.

Antifederalist   An opponent of the **Constitution** in the debate over its ratification.

Anti-Masons   Third party formed in 1827 in opposition to the presumed power and influence of the Masonic order.

Articles of Confederation   Written document setting up the loose confederation of states that comprised the first national government of the United States from 1781 to 1788.

Aztecs   A warrior people who dominated the Valley of Mexico from about 1100 until their conquest in 1519–21 by Spanish soldiers led by Hernán Cortés.

Bacon's Rebellion   Violent conflict in Virginia (1675–1676), beginning with settler attacks on Indians but culminating in a rebellion led by Nathaniel Bacon against Virginia's government.

Bank War   The political struggle between President Andrew Jackson and the supporters of the **Second Bank of the United States**.

Beaver Wars   Series of bloody conflicts, occurring between 1640s and 1680s, during which the Iroquois fought the French and their Indian allies for control of the fur trade in eastern North America and the Great Lakes region.

Benevolent empire   Network of reform associations affiliated with Protestant churches in the early nineteenth century dedicated to the restoration of moral order.

Bill of rights   A written summary of inalienable rights and liberties.

Black codes   Laws passed by states and municipalities denying many rights of citizenship to free blacks before the Civil War. Also, during the **Reconstruction era**, laws passed by newly elected southern state legislatures to control black labor, mobility, and employment.

Black Hawk's War   Short 1832 war in which federal troops and Illinois militia units defeated the Sauk and Fox Indians led by Black Hawk.

"Bleeding Kansas"   Violence between pro- and antislavery forces in Kansas Territory after the passage of the **Kansas-Nebraska Act** in 1854.

Boston Tea Party   Incident that occurred on December 16, 1773, in which Bostonians, disguised as Indians, destroyed £9,000 worth of tea belonging to the British East India Company in order to prevent payment of the duty on it.

British Constitution   The principles, procedures, and precedents that governed the operation of the British government. These could be found in no single written document; Parliament and the king made the Constitution by their actions.

Brook Farm   A utopian community and experimental farm established in 1841 near Boston.

Cahokia   Located near modern St. Louis, this was one of the largest urban centers created by Mississippian peoples, containing perhaps 30,000 residents in 1250.

Charles River Bridge v. Warren Bridge   Supreme Court decision of 1837 that promoted economic competition by ruling that the broader rights of the community took precedence over any presumed right of monopoly granted in a corporate charter.

Cherokee War Conflict (1759–1761) on the southern frontier between the Cherokee Indians and colonists from Virginia southward. It caused South Carolina to request the aid of British troops and resulted in the surrender of more Indian land to white colonists.

Chesapeake Incident Attack in 1807 by the British ship *Leopard* on the American ship *Chesapeake* in American territorial waters that nearly provoked an Anglo-American war.

Church of Jesus Christ of Latter-day Saints *See* **Mormon Church.**

Claims club A group of local settlers on the nineteenth-century frontier who banded together to prevent the price of their land claims from being bid up by outsiders at public land auctions.

Coercive Acts Legislation passed by Parliament in 1774; included the Boston Port Act, the Massachusetts Government Act, the Administration of Justice Act, and the **Quartering Act** of 1774.

Columbian exchange The transatlantic exchange of plants, animals, and diseases that occurred after the first European contact with the Americas.

Committees of correspondence Committees formed in Massachusetts and other colonies in the pre-Revolutionary period to keep Americans informed about British measures that would affect the colonies.

Committee of Safety Any of the extralegal committees that directed the Revolutionary movement and carried on the functions of government at the local level in the period between the breakdown of royal authority and the establishment of regular governments under the new state constitutions. Some Committees of Safety continued to function throughout the Revolutionary War.

Communism A social structure based on the common ownership of property.

Conciliatory Proposition Plan proposed by Lord North and adopted by the House of Commons in February 1775 whereby Parliament would "forbear" taxation of Americans in colonies whose assemblies imposed taxes considered satisfactory by the British government. The Continental Congress rejected this plan on July 31, 1775.

Confederate States of America Nation proclaimed in Montgomery, Alabama, in February 1861 after the seven states of the Lower South seceded from the United States.

Confiscation Act of 1862 Second confiscation law passed by Congress, ordering the seizure of land from disloyal Southerners and the emancipation of their slaves.

Congressional Reconstruction Name given to the period 1867–1870 when the Republican-dominated Congress controlled **Reconstruction Era** policy. It is sometimes known as Radical Reconstruction, after the radical faction in the **Republican party**.

Constitutional Convention Convention that met in Philadelphia in 1787 and drafted the **Constitution of the United States**.

Constitutional Union party National party formed in 1860, mainly by former **Whigs**, that emphasized allegiance to the Union and strict enforcement of all national legislation.

Constitution of the United States The written document providing for a new central government of the United States, drawn up at the **Constitutional Convention** in 1787 and ratified by the states in 1788.

Containment The policy of resisting further expansion of the Soviet bloc through diplomacy and, if necessary, military action, developed in 1947–48.

Continental Army The regular or professional army authorized by the Second Continental Congress and commanded by General George Washington during the Revolutionary War. Better training and longer service distinguished its soldiers from the state militiamen.

Continental Association Agreement, adopted by the **First Continental Congress** in 1774 in response to the **Coercive Acts**, to cut off trade with Britain until the objectionable measures were repealed. Local committees were established to enforce the provisions of the association.

Contract theory of government The belief that government is established by human beings to protect certain rights—such as life, liberty, and property—that are theirs by natural, divinely sanctioned law and that when government protects these rights, people are obligated to obey it. But when government violates its part of the bargain (or contract) between the rulers and the ruled, the people are no longer required to obey it and may establish a new government that will do a better job of protecting them. Elements of this theory date back to the ancient Greeks; John Locke used it in his *Second Treatise on Government* (1682), and Thomas Jefferson gave it memorable expression in the Declaration of Independence, where it provides the rationale for renouncing allegiance to King George III.

Copperheads A term Republicans applied to Northern war dissenters and those suspected of aiding the Confederate cause during the Civil War.

Country (Real Whig) ideology Strain of thought first appearing in England in the late seventeenth century in response to the growth of governmental power and a national debt. Main ideas stressed the threat to personal liberty posed by a standing army and high taxes and emphasized the need for property holders to retain the right to consent to taxation.

Coureur de bois French for "woods runner," an independent fur trader in New France.

Cult of domesticity The belief that women, by virtue of their sex, should stay home as the moral guardians of family life.

Currency Act Law passed by Parliament in 1764 to prevent the colonies from issuing **legal tender** paper money, which often depreciated.

Dartmouth College v. Woodward Supreme Court decision of 1819 that prohibited states from interfering with the privileges granted to a private corporation.

Declaration of Independence The document by which the Second Continental Congress announced and justified its decision (reached July 2, 1776) to renounce the colonies' allegiance to the British government. Drafted mainly by Thomas Jefferson and adopted by Congress on July 4, the declaration's indictment of the king provides a remarkably full catalog of the colonists' grievances, and Jefferson's eloquent and inspiring statement of the **contract theory of government** makes the document one of the world's great state papers.

Declaration of Rights and Grievances Resolves, adopted by the **Stamp Act Congress** at New York in 1765, asserting that the **Stamp Act** and other taxes imposed on the colonists without their consent, given through their colonial legislatures, were unconstitutional.

Declaration of Sentiments The resolutions passed at the **Seneca Falls Convention** in 1848 calling for full female equality, including the right to vote.

Declaration of the Causes and Necessity of Taking Up Arms Document, written mainly by John Dickinson of Pennsylvania and adopted on July 6, 1775, by which the Second Continental Congress justified its armed resistance against British measures.

Declaratory Act Law passed in 1766 to accompany repeal of the **Stamp Act** that stated that Parliament had the authority to legislate for the colonies "in all cases whatsoever." Whether "legislate" meant tax was not clear to Americans.

Deism Religious orientation that rejects divine revelation and holds that the workings of nature alone reveal God's design for the universe.

Democratic Party   Political party formed in the 1820s under the leadership of Andrew Jackson; favored states' rights and a limited role for the federal government, especially in economic affairs.

Denmark Vesey's Conspiracy   The most carefully devised slave revolt, named after its leader, a free black in Charleston. The rebels planned to seize control of Charleston in 1822 and escape to freedom in Haiti, a free black republic, but they were betrayed by other slaves, and seventy-five conspirators were executed.

Dominion of New England   James II's failed plan of 1686 to combine eight northern colonies into a single large province, to be governed by a royal appointee (Sir Edmund Andros) with an appointed council but no elective assembly. The plan ended with James's ouster from the English throne and rebellion in Massachusetts against Andros's rule.

***Dred Scott* decision**   Supreme Court ruling, in a lawsuit brought by Dred Scott, a slave demanding his freedom based on his residence in a free state and a free territory with his master, that slaves could not be U.S. citizens and that Congress had no jurisdiction over slavery in the territories.

Emancipation Proclamation   Decree announced by President Abraham Lincoln in September 1862 and formally issued on January 1, 1863, freeing slaves in all Confederate states still in rebellion.

Embargo Act of 1807   Act passed by Congress in 1807 prohibiting American ships from leaving for any foreign port.

Empresario   An agent who received a land grant from the Spanish or Mexican government in return for organizing settlements.

Encomienda   In the Spanish colonies, the grant to a Spanish settler of a certain number of Indian subjects, who would pay him tribute in goods and labor.

Enumerated products   Items produced in the colonies and enumerated in acts of Parliament that could be legally shipped from the colony of origin only to specified locations, usually England and other destinations within the British empire.

Era of Good Feelings   The period from 1817 to 1823 in which the disappearance of the **Federalists** enabled the **Republicans** to govern in a spirit of seemingly nonpartisan harmony.

Federalism   The sharing of powers between the national government and the states.

Federalist   A supporter of the **Constitution** who favored its ratification.

Field Order No. 15   Order by General William T. Sherman in January 1865 to set aside abandoned land along the southern Atlantic coast for forty-acre grants to freedmen; rescinded by President Andrew Johnson later that year.

First Continental Congress   Meeting of delegates from most of the colonies held in 1774 in response to the **Coercive Acts**. The Congress endorsed the **Suffolk Resolves**, adopted the **Declaration of Rights and Grievances**, and agreed to establish the **Continental Association** to put economic pressure on Britain to repeal its objectionable measures. The Congress also wrote addresses to the king, the people of Britain, and the American people.

Fletcher v. Peck   Supreme Court decision of 1810 that overturned a state law by ruling that it violated a legal contract.

Fort Sumter   Begun in the late 1820s to protect Charleston, South Carolina, it became the center of national attention in April 1861 when President Lincoln attempted to provision federal troops at the fort, triggering a hostile response from on-shore Confederate forces, opening the Civil War.

Fourierist communities   Short-live utopian communities in the 1840s based on the ideas of economic cooperation and self-sufficiency popularized by the Frenchman Charles Fourier.

Franco-American Accord of 1800   Settlement reached with France that brought an end to the **Quasi-War** and released the United States from its 1778 alliance with France.

Freedmen's Bureau   Agency established by Congress in March 1865 to provide social, educational, and economic services, advice, and protection to former slaves and destitute whites; lasted seven years.

French and Indian War   The last of the Anglo-French colonial wars (1754–1763) and the first in which fighting began in North America. The war (which merged with the European conflict known as the Seven Years' War) ended with France's defeat and loss of its North American empire.

Fugitive Slave Act   Law, part of the Compromise of 1850, that required that authorities in the North to assist southern slave catchers and return runaway slaves to their owners.

Fundamental Constitutions of Carolina   A complex plan for organizing the colony of Carolina, drafted in 1669 by Anthony Ashley Cooper and John Locke. Its provisions included a scheme for creating a hierarchy of nobles who would own vast amounts of land and wield political power; below them would be a class of freedmen and slaves. The provisions were never implemented by the Carolina colonists.

Gabriel Prosser's Rebellion   Slave revolt that failed when Gabriel Prosser, a slave preacher and blacksmith, organized a thousand slaves for an attack on Richmond, Virginia, in 1800. A thunderstorm upset the timing of the attack, and a slave informer alerted the whites. Prosser and twenty-five of his followers were executed.

Gang system   The organization and supervision of slave field hands into working teams on southern plantations.

General Union for Promoting the Observance of the Christian Sabbath   See **Sabbatarian movement**.

Ghent, Treaty of   Treaty signed in December 1814 between the United States and Britain that ended the **War of 1812**.

Gibbons v. Ogden   Supreme Court decision of 1824 involving coastal commerce that overturned a steamboat monopoly granted by the state of New York on the grounds that only Congress had the authority to regulate interstate commerce.

Glorious Revolution   Bloodless revolt that occurred in England in 1688 when parliamentary leaders invited William of Orange, a Protestant, to assume the English throne and James II fled to France. James's ouster was prompted by fears that the birth of his son would establish a Catholic dynasty in England.

Grand Settlement of 1701   Separate peace treaties negotiated by Iroquois diplomats at Montreal and Albany that marked the beginning of Iroquois neutrality in conflicts between the French and the British in North America.

Great Awakening   Tremendous religious revival in colonial America. Sparked by the tour of the English evangelical minister George Whitefield, the Awakening struck first in the Middle Colonies and New England in the 1740s and eventually spread to the southern colonies by the 1760s.

Great Compromise   Plan proposed by Roger Sherman of Connecticut at the 1787 **Constitutional Convention** for creating a national bicameral legislature in which all states would be equally represented in the Senate and proportionally represented in the House.

Greenville, Treaty of   Treaty of 1795 in which Native Americans in the Old Northwest were forced to cede most of the present state of Ohio to the United States.

Halfway Covenant   Plan adopted in 1662 by New England clergy to deal with the problem of declining church membership. It allowed adults who had been baptized because their parents were church members but who had not yet experienced conversion to have their own children baptized. Without the Halfway Covenant, these third-generation children would remain unbaptized until their parents experienced conversion.

Homestead Act Law passed by Congress in May 1862 providing homesteaders (mainly in the West) with 160 acres of free land in exchange for improving the land (as by cultivating it and erecting a house) within five years of the grant.

House of Burgesses The legislature of colonial Virginia. First organized in 1619, it was the first institution of representative government in the English colonies.

Indentured servant An individual—usually male but occasionally female—who contracted to serve a master for a period of four to seven years in return for payment of the servant's passage to America. Indentured servitude was the primary labor system in the Chesapeake colonies for most of the seventeenth century.

Independent Treasury System Fiscal arrangement first instituted by President Martin Van Buren in which the federal government kept its money in regional vaults ("pet banks") and transacted its business entirely in hard money.

Intolerable Acts American term for the **Coercive Acts** and the **Quebec Act**.

Iroquois League The union of five Indian nations (Mohawks, Oneidas, Onondagas, Cayugas, and Senecas) formed around 1450, also known as the League of Five Nations. Essentially a religious organization, its purpose was to maintain peace among the five nations and unite them to fight against other enemies. After the Tuscarora War (1713–1715), the Tuscaroras joined the league, thereafter known as the League of Six Nations.

Jacksonian Democrats *See* **Democratic Party**.

Jay's Treaty Treaty with Britain negotiated in 1794 in which the United States made major concessions to avert a war over the British seizure of American ships.

Jeffersonian Republicans See **Republican Party (Jeffersonian)**.

John Brown's Raid New England abolitionist John Brown's ill-fated attempt to free Virginia's slaves with a raid on the federal arsenal at Harpers Ferry, Virginia, in 1859.

Joint-stock company Business enterprise in which a group of stockholders pooled their money to engage in trade or to fund colonizing expeditions. Joint-stock companies participated in the founding of the Virginia, Plymouth, and Massachusetts Bay colonies.

Judicial review A power implied in the **Constitution** that gives federal courts the right to review and determine the constitutionality of acts passed by Congress and state legislatures.

Judiciary Act of 1789 Act of Congress that implemented the judiciary clause of the **Constitution** by establishing the Supreme Court and a system of lower federal courts.

Kansas-Nebraska Act Law passed in 1854 creating the Kansas and Nebraska Territories but leaving the question of slavery open to residents, thereby repealing the **Missouri Compromise**.

King George's War The third Anglo-French war in North America (1744–1748), part of the European conflict known as the War of the Austrian Succession. During the North American fighting, New Englanders captured the French fortress of Louisbourg, only to have it returned to France after the peace negotiations.

King Philip's War Conflict in New England (1675–1676) between Wampanoags, Narragansetts, and other Indian peoples against English settlers; sparked by English encroachments on native lands.

King William's War The first Anglo-French conflict in North America (1689–1697), the American phase of Europe's War of the League of Augsburg. Ended in negotiated peace that reestablished the balance of power.

Know-Nothing Party Anti-immigrant party formed from the wreckage of the **Whig Party** and some disaffected northern Democrats in 1854.

Ku Klux Klan Perhaps the most prominent of the vigilante groups that terrorized black people in the South during **Reconstruction Era**, founded by Confederate veterans in 1866.

Laissez-faire The doctrine that government should not intervene in the economy, especially through regulation.

Lancaster, Treaty of Negotiation in 1744 whereby Iroquois chiefs sold Virginia land speculators the right to trade at the Forks of the Ohio. Although the Iroquois had not intended this to include the right to settle in the Ohio Country, the Virginians assumed that it did. Ohio Valley Indians considered this treaty a great grievance against both the English and the Iroquois.

Land Grant College Act Law passed by Congress in July 1862 awarding proceeds from the sale of public lands to the states for the establishment of agricultural and mechanical (later engineering) colleges. Also known as the Morrill Act, after its sponsor, Congressman Justin Morrill of Vermont.

Land Ordinance of 1785 Act passed by Congress under the **Articles of Confederation** that created the grid system of surveys by which all subsequent public land was made available for sale.

Lecompton Constitution Proslavery draft written in 1857 by Kansas territorial delegates elected under questionable circumstances; it was rejected by two governors, supported by President Buchanan, and decisively defeated by Congress.

Legal tender An attribute of money that results from legislation declaring it to be, as in the case of modern United States currency, "legal tender for all debts public and private." Creditors must therefore accept it at face value.

Liberty Party The first antislavery political party, formed in 1840.

Lincoln-Douglas debates Series of debates in the 1858 Illinois senatorial campaign during which Democrat Stephen A. Douglas and Republican Abraham Lincoln staked out their differing opinions on the issue of slavery in the territories.

Lost Cause The phrase many white Southerners applied to their Civil War defeat. They viewed the war as a noble cause but only a temporary setback in the South's ultimate vindication.

Manifest Destiny Doctrine, first expressed in 1845, that the expansion of white Americans across the continent was inevitable and ordained by God.

Marbury v. Madison Supreme Court decision of 1803 that created the precedent of judicial review by ruling as unconstitutional part of the **Judiciary Act of 1789**.

McCulloch v. Maryland Supreme Court decision of 1819 that established the supremacy of federal over state authority by declaring that states could not tax federal institutions.

Mercantilism Economic system whereby the government intervenes in the economy for the purpose of increasing national wealth. Mercantilists advocated possession of colonies as places where the mother country could acquire raw materials not available at home.

Middle Passage The voyage between West Africa and the New World slave colonies.

Minute Men Special companies of militia formed in Massachusetts and elsewhere beginning in late 1744. These units were composed of men who were to be ready to assemble with their arms at a minute's notice.

Missouri Compromise Sectional compromise in Congress in 1820 that admitted Missouri to the Union as a slave state and Maine as a free state and prohibited slavery in the **Louisiana Purchase** territory above 36°30´ north latitude.

Mormon Church (Church of Jesus Christ of Latter-day Saints) Church founded in 1830 by Joseph Smith and based on the revelations in a sacred book he called the Book of Mormon.

Nationalists Group of leaders in the 1780s who spearheaded the drive to replace the **Articles of Confederation** with a stronger central government.

Nat Turner's Rebellion Uprising of slaves in Southampton County, Virginia, in the summer of 1831 led by Nat Turner that resulted in the death of fifty-five whites.

Natural rights Political philosophy that maintains that individuals have an inherent right, found in nature and preceding any government or written law, to life and liberty.

New Harmony Short-lived utopian community established in Indiana in 1825, based on the socialist ideas of Robert Owen, a wealthy Scottish manufacturer.

New Jersey Plan Proposal of the New Jersey delegation at the 1787 **Constitutional Convention** for a strengthened national government in which all states would have equal representation in a **unicameral legislature**.

New Lights People who experienced conversion during the revivals of the **Great Awakening**.

New Orleans, Battle of Decisive American **War of 1812** victory over British troops in January 1815 that ended any British hopes of gaining control of the lower Mississippi River Valley.

New York Draft Riot A mostly Irish-immigrant protest against conscription in New York City in July 1863 that escalated into class and racial warfare that had to be quelled by federal troops.

Nonimportation Movement A tactical means of putting economic pressure on Britain by refusing to buy its exports to the colonies. Initiated in response to the taxes imposed by the **Sugar** and **Stamp Acts**, it was used again against the **Townshend duties** and the **Coercive Acts**. The nonimportation movement popularized resistance to British measures and deepened the commitment of many ordinary people to a larger American community.

Nonintercourse Act Law passed by Congress in 1809 that prohibited American trade with Britain and France.

Northwest Ordinance of 1787 Legislation passed by Congress under the **Articles of Confederation** that prohibited slavery in the Northwest Territories and provided the model for the incorporation of future territories into the Union as coequal states.

Nullification A constitutional doctrine holding that a state has a legal right to declare a national law null and void within its borders.

Nullification crisis Sectional crisis in the early 1830s in which a **states' rights** party in South Carolina attempted to nullify federal law.

Olive Branch Petition Petition, written largely by John Dickinson and adopted by the Second Continental Congress on July 5, 1775, as a last effort of peace that avowed America's loyalty to George III and requested that he protect them from further aggressions. Congress continued military preparations, and the king never responded to the petition.

Oneida Community Utopian community established in upstate New York in 1848 by John Humphrey Noyes and his followers.

Oregon Trail Overland trail of more than two thousand miles that carried American settlers from the Midwest to new settlements in Oregon, California, and Utah.

Panic of 1857 Banking crisis that caused a credit crunch in the North; it was less severe in the South, where high cotton prices spurred a quick recovery.

Pan-Indian resistance movement Movement calling for the political and cultural unification of Indian tribes in the late eighteenth and early nineteenth centuries.

Peace of Paris Treaties signed in 1783 by Great Britain, the United States, France, Spain, and the Netherlands that ended the Revolutionary War. First in a preliminary agreement and then in the final treaty with the United States, Britain recognized the independence of the United States, agreed that the Mississippi River would be its western boundary, and permitted it to fish in some Canadian waters. Prewar debts owed by the inhabitants of one country to those of the other were to remain collectible, and Congress was to urge the states to return property confiscated from Loyalists. British troops were to evacuate United States territory without removing slaves or other property. In a separate agreement, Britain relinquished its claim to East and West Florida to Spain.

Pequot War Conflict between English settlers (who had Narragansett and Mohegan allies) and Pequot Indians over control of land and trade in eastern Connecticut. The Pequots were nearly destroyed in a set of bloody confrontations, including a deadly English attack on a Mystic River village in May 1637.

Pietists Protestants who stress a religion of the heart and the spirit of Christian living.

Pilgrims Settlers of Plymouth Colony, who viewed themselves as spiritual wanderers.

Pinckney's Treaty Treaty with Spain in 1795 in which Spain recognized the 31st parallel as the boundary between the United States and Spanish Florida and opened the Mississippi River through the port of New Orleans to American shipping.

Plattsburg, Battle of American naval victory on Lake Champlain in September 1814 in the **War of 1812** that thwarted a British invasion from Canada.

Pontiac's Rebellion Indian uprising (1763–1766) led by Pontiac of the Ottawas and Neolin of the Delawares. Fearful of their fate at the hands of the British after the French had been driven out of North America, the Indian nations of the Ohio River Valley and the Great Lakes area united to oust the British from the Ohio-Mississippi Valley. They failed and were forced to make peace in 1766.

Predestination The belief that God decided at the moment of Creation which humans would achieve salvation.

Proclamation Line Boundary, decreed as part of the **Proclamation of 1763**, that limited British settlements to the eastern side of the Appalachian Mountains, thereby threatening colonial expansionists and causing resentment. It proved unenforceable.

Proclamation of 1763 Royal proclamation setting the boundary known as the **Proclamation Line**.

Proprietary colony A colony created when the English monarch granted a huge tract of land to an individual or group of individuals, who became "lords proprietor." Many lords proprietor had distinct social visions for their colonies, but these plans were hardly ever implemented. Examples of proprietary colonies are Maryland, Carolina, New York (after it was seized from the Dutch), and Pennsylvania.

Pueblo Revolt Rebellion in 1680 of Pueblo Indians in New Mexico against their Spanish overlords, sparked by religious conflict and excessive Spanish demands for tribute.

Puritan An individual who believed that Queen Elizabeth's reforms of the Church of England had not gone far enough in improving the church, particularly in ensuring that church members were among the saved. Puritans led the settlement of Massachusetts Bay Colony.

Put-in-Bay, Battle of American naval victory on Lake Erie in September 1813 in the **War of 1812** that denied the British strategic control over the Great Lakes.

Putting-out system System of manufacturing in which merchants furnished households with raw materials for processing by family members.

Quakers Members of the Society of Friends, a radical religious group that arose in the mid-seventeenth century. Quakers rejected formal theology and an educated ministry, focusing instead on the importance of the "Inner Light," or Holy Spirit that dwelt within them. Quakers were important in the founding of Pennsylvania.

Quartering Acts Acts of Parliament requiring colonial legislatures to provide supplies and quarters for the troops stationed in America. Americans considered this taxation in disguise and objected. None of these acts passed during the pre-Revolutionary controversy required that soldiers be quartered in an occupied house without the owner's consent.

Quasi-War Undeclared naval war of 1797 to 1800 between the United States and France.

Quebec Act Law passed by Parliament in 1774 that provided an appointed government for Canada, enlarged the boundaries of Quebec southward to the Ohio River, and confirmed the privileges of the Catholic Church. Alarmed Americans termed this act and the **Coercive Acts** the **Intolerable Acts.**

Queen Anne's War American phase (1702–1713) of Europe's War of the Spanish Succession. At its conclusion, England gained Nova Scotia.

Radical Republicans A shifting group of Republican congressmen, usually a substantial minority, who favored the abolition of slavery from the beginning of the Civil War and later advocated harsh treatment of the defeated South.

Reconquista The long struggle (ending in 1492) during which Spanish Christians reconquered the Iberian peninsula from Muslim occupiers, who first invaded in the eighth century.

Redeemers Southern Democrats who wrested control of governments in the former Confederacy, often through electoral fraud and violence, from Republicans beginning in 1870.

Redemptioners Similar to **indentured servants**, except that redemptioners signed labor contracts in America rather than in Europe, as indentured servants did. Shipmasters sold redemptioners into servitude to recoup the cost of their passage if they could not pay the fare upon their arrival.

Regulators Vigilante groups active in the 1760s and 1770s in the western parts of North and South Carolina. The South Carolina Regulators attempted to rid the area of outlaws; the North Carolina Regulators sought to protect themselves against excessively high taxes and court costs. In both cases, westerners lacked sufficient representation in the legislature to obtain immediate redress of their grievances. The South Carolina government eventually made concessions; the North Carolina government suppressed its Regulator movement by force.

Repartimiento In the Spanish colonies, the assignment of Indian workers to labor on public works projects.

Republicanism A complex, changing body of ideas, values, and assumptions, closely related to **country ideology**, that influenced American political behavior during the eighteenth and nineteenth centuries. Derived from the political ideas of classical antiquity, Renaissance Europe, and early modern England, republicanism held that self-government by the citizens of a country, or their representatives, provided a more reliable foundation for the good society and individual freedom than rule by kings. The benefits of monarchy depended on the variable abilities of monarchs; the character of republican government depended on the virtue of the people. Republicanism therefore helped give the American Revolution a moral dimension. But the nature of republican virtue and the conditions favorable to it became sources of debate that influenced the writing of the state and federal constitutions as well as the development of political parties.

Republican Party Party that emerged in the 1850s in the aftermath of the bitter controversy over the **Kansas-Nebraska Act**, consisting of former **Whigs**, some northern Democrats, and many **Know-Nothings**.

Republican Party (Jeffersonian) Party headed by Thomas Jefferson that formed in opposition to the financial and diplomatic policies of the **Federalist Party**; favored limiting the powers of the national government and placing the interests of farmers and planters over those of financial and commercial groups; supported the cause of the French Revolution.

Rescate Procedure by which Spanish colonists would pay ransom to free Indians captured by rival natives. The rescued Indians then became workers in Spanish households.

Rhode Island system During the industrialization of the early nineteenth century, the recruitment of entire families for employment in a factory.

Rush–Bagot Agreement Treaty of 1817 between the United States and Britain that effectively demilitarized the Great Lakes by sharply limiting the number of ships each power could station on them.

Sabbatarian movement Reform organization founded in 1828 by Congregationalist and Presbyterian ministers that lobbied for an end to the delivery of mail on Sundays and other Sabbath violations.

"Sack of Lawrence" Vandalism and arson committed by a group of proslavery men in Lawrence, the free-state capital of Kansas Territory.

San Jacinto, Battle of Battle fought in eastern Texas on April 21, 1836, in which Texas troops under General Sam Houston overwhelmed a Mexican army and forced its commander, General Antonio López de Santa Anna, to recognize the independence of Texas.

San Lorenzo, Treaty of *See* **Pinckney's Treaty.**

Scalawags Southern whites, mainly small landowning farmers and well-off merchants and planters, who supported the southern **Republican Party** during **Reconstruction** for diverse reasons; a disparaging term.

Second Bank of the United States A national bank chartered by Congress in 1816 with extensive regulatory powers over currency and credit.

Second Continental Congress An assemblage of delegates from all the colonies that convened in May 1775 after the outbreak of fighting in Massachusetts between British and American forces. It became the national government that eventually declared independence and conducted the Revolutionary War.

Second Great Awakening Series of religious revivals in the first half of the nineteenth century characterized by great emotionalism in large public meetings.

Second party system The national two-party competition between **Democrats** and **Whigs** from the 1830s through the early 1850s.

Seneca Falls Convention The first convention for women's equality in legal rights, held in upstate New York in 1848. *See also* **Declaration of Sentiments.**

Separatist Member of an offshoot branch of Puritanism. Separatists believed that the Church of England was too corrupt to be reformed and hence were convinced that they must "separate" from it to save their souls. Separatists helped found Plymouth Colony.

Shakers The followers of Mother Ann Lee, who preached a religion of strict celibacy and communal living.

Sharecropping Labor system that evolved during and after **Reconstruction** whereby landowners furnished laborers with a house, farm animals, and tools and advanced credit in exchange for a share of the laborers' crop.

Shays's Rebellion An armed movement of debt-ridden farmers in western Massachusetts in the winter of 1786–1787. The rebellion shut down courts and created a crisis atmosphere, strengthening the case of **nationalists** that a stronger central government was needed to maintain civil order in the states.

Slaughterhouse **cases** Group of cases resulting in one sweeping decision by the U.S. Supreme Court in 1873 that contradicted the intent of the **Fourteenth Amendment** by decreeing that most citizenship rights remained under state, not federal, control.

Slave codes Sometimes known as **black codes**. A series of laws passed mainly in the southern colonies in the late seventeenth and early eighteenth centuries to define the status of slaves and codify the denial of basic civil rights to them. Also, after American independence and before the Civil War, state laws in the South defining slaves as property and specifying the legal powers of masters over slaves.

Slave Power A key concept in abolitionist and northern antislavery propaganda that depicted southern slaveholders as the driving force in a political conspiracy to promote slavery at the expense of white liberties.

Sons of Liberty Secret organizations in the colonies formed to oppose the **Stamp Act**. From 1765 until independence, they spoke, wrote, and demonstrated against British measures. Their actions often intimidated stamp distributors and British supporters in the colonies.

Southern Homestead Act Largely unsuccessful law passed in 1866 that gave black people preferential access to public lands in five southern states.

Southwest Ordinance of 1790 Legislation passed by Congress that set up a government with no prohibition on slavery in U.S. territory south of the Ohio River.

Specie Circular Proclamation issued by President Andrew Jackson in 1836 stipulating that only gold or silver could be used as payment for public land.

Spoils system The awarding of government jobs to party loyalists.

Stamp Act Law passed by Parliament in 1765 to raise revenue in America by requiring taxed, stamped paper for legal documents, publications, and playing cards. Americans opposed it as "taxation without representation" and prevented its enforcement. Parliament repealed it a year after its enactment.

Stamp Act Congress October 1765 meeting of delegates sent by nine colonies, held in New York City, that adopted the **Declaration of Rights and Grievances** and petitioned against the **Stamp Act**.

States' rights Favoring the rights of individual states over rights claimed by the national government.

Stono Rebellion Uprising in 1739 of South Carolina slaves against whites; inspired in part by Spanish officials' promise of freedom for American slaves who escaped to Florida.

Suffolk Resolves Militant resolves adopted in September 1774 in response to the **Coercive Acts** by representatives from the towns in Suffolk County, Massachusetts, including Boston. They termed the

Coercive Acts unconstitutional, advised the people to arm, and called for economic sanctions against Britain. The **First Continental Congress** endorsed these resolves.

Suffrage The right to vote in a political election.

Sugar Act Law passed in 1764 to raise revenue in the American colonies. It lowered the duty from 6 pence to 3 pence per gallon on foreign molasses imported into the colonies and increased the restrictions on colonial commerce.

Taos Revolt Uprising of Pueblo Indians in New Mexico that broke out in January 1847 over the imposition of American rule during the Mexican War; the revolt was crushed within a few weeks.

Tariff Act of 1789 Apart from a few selected industries, this first tariff passed by Congress was intended primarily to raise revenue and not protect American manufacturers from foreign competition.

Tariff Act of 1798 Law placing a duty of 5 percent on most imported goods, designed primarily to generate revenue and not to protect American goods from foreign competition.

Tea Act of 1773 Act of Parliament that permitted the East India Company to sell tea through agents in America without paying the duty customarily collected in Britain, thus reducing the retail price. Americans, who saw the act as an attempt to induce them to pay the Townshend duty still imposed in the colonies, resisted this act through the **Boston Tea Party** and other measures.

Tejano A person of Spanish or Mexican descent born in Texas.

Temperance Reform movement originating in the 1820s that sought to eliminate the consumption of alcohol.

Thirteenth Amendment Constitutional amendment ratified in 1865 that freed all slaves throughout the United States.

Tonnage Act of 1789 Duty levied on the tonnage of incoming ships to U.S. ports; tax was higher on foreign-owned ships to favor American shippers.

Tordesillas, Treaty of Treaty negotiated by the pope in 1494 to resolve the territorial claims of Spain and Portugal. It drew a north–south line approximately 1,100 miles west of the Cape Verde Islands, granting all lands west of the line to Spain and all lands east of the line to Portugal. This limited Portugal's New World empire to Brazil but confirmed its claims in Africa and Asia.

Tories A derisive term applied to **Loyalists** in America who supported the king and Parliament just before and during the American Revolution. The term derived from late-seventeenth-century English politics when the Tory party supported the Duke of York's succession to the throne as James II. Later the Tory party favored the Church of England and the crown over dissenting denominations and Parliament.

Townshend Duty Act Act of Parliament, passed in 1767, imposing duties on colonial tea, lead, paint, paper, and glass. Designed to take advantage of the supposed American distinction between internal and external taxes, the Townshend duties were to help support government in America. The act prompted a successful colonial nonimportation movement.

Trail of Tears The forced march in 1838 of the Cherokee Indians from their homelands in Georgia to the Indian Territory in the West; thousands of Cherokees died along the way.

Transcendentalism A philosophical and literary movement centered on an idealistic belief in the divinity of individuals and nature.

Trans-Continental Treaty of 1819 Treaty between the United States and Spain in which Spain ceded Florida to the United States, surrendered all claims to the Pacific Northwest, and agreed to a boundary between the Louisiana Purchase territory and the Spanish Southwest.

Transportation revolution Dramatic improvements in transportation that stimulated economic growth after 1815 by expanding the range of travel and reducing the time and cost of moving goods and people.

Underground Railroad Support system set up by antislavery groups in the Upper South and the North to assist fugitive slaves in escaping the South.

Unicameral legislature A legislative body composed of a single house.

Union League A **Republican party** organization in northern cities that became an important organizing device among freedmen in southern cities after 1865.

Valley Forge Area of Pennsylvania approximately 20 miles northwest of Philadelphia where General George Washington's continental troops were quartered from December 1777 to June 1778 while British forces occupied Philadelphia during the Revolutionary War. Approximately 2,500 men, about a quarter of those encamped there, died of hardship and disease.

Virginia Plan Proposal of the Virginia delegation at the 1787 **Constitution Convention** calling for a national legislature in which the states would be represented according to population. The national legislature would have the explicit power to veto or overrule laws passed by state legislatures.

Virtual representation The notion, current in eighteenth-century England, that parliamentary members represented the interests of the nation as a whole, not those of the particular district that elected them.

Waltham system During the industrialization of the early nineteenth century, the recruitment of unmarried young women for employment in factories.

War Hawks Members of Congress, predominantly from the South and West, who aggressively pushed for a war against Britain after their election in 1810.

War of 1812 War fought between the United States and Britain from June 1812 to January 1815 largely over British restrictions on American shipping.

Webster–Ashburton Treaty Treaty signed by the United States and Britain in 1842 that settled a boundary dispute between Maine and Canada and provided for closer cooperation in suppressing the African slave trade.

Whig party Political party, formed in the mid-1830s in opposition to the **Jacksonian Democrats**, that favored a strong role for the national government in promoting economic growth.

Whigs The name used by advocates of colonial resistance to British measures during the 1760s and 1770s. The Whig party in England unsuccessfully attempted to exclude the Catholic Duke of York from succession to the throne as James II; victorious in the **Glorious Revolution**, the Whigs later stood for religious toleration and the supremacy of Parliament over the crown.

Whiskey Rebellion Armed uprising in 1794 by farmers in western Pennsylvania who attempted to prevent the collection of the excise tax on whiskey.

Wide Awakes Group of red-shirted, black-caped young men who paraded through city streets in the North extolling the virtues of the **Republican party** during the 1860 presidential election campaign.

Women's Christian Temperance Union (WCTU) National organization formed after the Civil War dedicated to prohibiting the sale and distribution of alcohol.

World Wide Web Since 1991, the Web has expanded the use of the Internet by allowing organizations and companies to create websites that place political and commercial information only a few clicks away from wired consumers.

Writs of assistance Documents issued by a court of law that gave British officials in America the power to search for smuggled goods wherever they wished. The legality of these writs became an important cause of controversy in Massachusetts in 1761 and 1762.

XYZ Affair Diplomatic incident in 1798 in which Americans were outraged by the demand of the French for a bribe as a condition for negotiating with American diplomats.

CREDITS

Italic page references refer to illustrations.

A

Abenakis, 48
Abolitionist movement, 309, 352
  Brown's raid and, 436, 438–440, 439
  development of, 379–381
  Garrison and, 312, 378, 379–381
  political, 382–383
  violence against, 380–381, 381
  women and, 376–377, 380–381
Acoma Pueblo, 7, 24, 404
Act for Religious Toleration (1649), 47
Actual representation, 120
Adams, Abigail, 193
Adams, John, 146, 173, 254
  as American minister to London, 219
  American Revolution and, 170, 190, 191, 192
  Declaration of Independence and, 173
  election of 1796 and, 251–252
  First Continental Congress and, 157
  presidency of, 252–257
  republicanism and, 174
  as vice president, 241
Adams, John Quincy
  election of 1824 and, 287–288
  election of 1828 and, 301
  gag rule and, 382
  as secretary of state, 282–283
Adams, Samuel, 148, 148, 152, 154, 157, 168, 228
Adena-Hopewell culture, 8
Administration of Justice Act (1774), 154, 155
Aetna Insurance Co., 94
Africa
  See also West African societies
  slaves from West, 12–13, 81–82
African Americans, free
  American Revolution and, 180, 205
  before the American Revolution, 87, 109
  in Civil War, 458, 469–471, 471, 488–490
  culture, 342–344
  Dred Scott v. Sandford, 432–433, 445, 510
  employment, 343
  growth of communities following American Revolution, 205–206
  in nineteenth-century cities, 343
  religion, 343, 345
  voting and, 296–297
African Americans, free (after Reconstruction)
  black codes, 342, 508–509
  education, 501–502
  employment, 502–504
  land ownership, 502–504
  migration to cities, 504–505
  in politics, 514
  religion, 505–506
  sharecropping, 523
  voting rights, 510–513, 524
African Methodist Episcopal (AME) Church, 206, 336, 502, 506
Age of Enlightenment, 112–113
Age of Reason (Paine), 255–256
Agriculture
  See also under type of crop
  Archaic period, 4–5
  crowded conditions in the East and affects on, 391, 393
  exchange between Old and New Worlds, 25–26
  impact of transportation on, 353
  mound-building societies, 8
  Native Americans and, 4–5, 4, 403–404
  in New England, 55
  in Old Northwest, 393–395
  in Old Southwest, 395–397
  reforms in the 1840s, 329–330
  sharecropping, 523
  technological improvements, 364, 394–395
  in West African societies, 11, 12
  yeoman, 341–342
Akans, 12
Alabama
  admitted to Union, 295, 395
  Civil War, 482
  secession, 442, 443
  as a slave state, 284
Alamo, 124, 406
Albany Congress (1754), 127, 129, 144
Albany Plan of Union, 129
Albany Regency, 300
Aleuts, 5
Alexander II, 467
Algonquians, 41–42, 72
Ali, Sunni, 11
Alien and Sedition Acts (1789), 253–254
Alien Enemies Act (1789), 253
Alien Friends Act (1789), 253
Allen, Ethan, 170, 219
American and Foreign Anti-Slavery Society, 381
American Anti-Slavery Society, 379, 380, 381
American Bible Society, 368
American Board of Commissioners for Foreign Missions, 368
American Colonization Society, 378
American Equal Rights Association, 511
American Female Moral Reform Society, 370
American Fur Company, 399
American Home Missionary Society, 368
American Missionary Association, 502
American Revenue Act. See Sugar Act
American Revolution
  African Americans in, 180–181, 193–194, 205
  battles, list of, 178
  battles (1775–1776), 168–170, 169
  battles (1776–1777), 181–184
  battles (1778–1781), 184–190
  British policies and events leading to, 139–160
  casualties, 169, 171, 183, 184, 193, 196
  chronology of, 168
  Declaration of Independence and, 172–174
  early fighting (Massachusetts, Virginia, the Carolinas, and Canada), 171–172
  economic consequences, 191, 194, 196
  financing of, 211–212
  foreign support for, 175, 177, 183, 184–185
  Lexington and Concord, battles of (1775), 168–170, 169, 178
  Native Americans in, 181, 185, 194
  naval battles, 185–186
  Olive Branch Petition, 170, 172
  outbreak of, 167–168
  Peace of Paris, (1783), 190–192, 191
  professional soldiers, 175–177, 179, 179
  republicanism, 174–175, 203–210
  Second Continental Congress, 170
  societal impact of, 193–194
  women and, 180, 193, 203–205
"American Scholar, The" (Emerson), 376–377
American Slavery As It Is: Testimony of a Thousand Witnesses (Weld), 352, 379
American Sunday School Union, 368
American System
  of federal subsidies, 288
  of manufacturing, 364
American Temperance Society, 369
American Tract Society, 368
Anarchists, 380
Anasazis, 7–8, 7
Anderson, Robert, 445–446
Andover South Parish Society for the Reformation of Morals, 368
André, John, 179
Andrew, John, 469
Andros, Edmund, 117
Anglican Church (Church of England), 48, 49–50, 113–114, 117, 155, 207, 208
Anglo-American Accords (1818), 282
Annapolis Convention (1786), 221
Anthony, Susan B., 382, 510–511, 513
Antietam, battle of (1862), 467–468, 489
Antifederalists, 226–228
Antigua, 59
Anti-Masons, 313–314
Antislavery reform, types of, 380
Apaches, 77, 404
Apalachees, 23
Appalachian Mountains, 240
Appeal to the Colored Citizens of the World (Walker), 378
Appomattox Courthouse, surrender at, 490
Apprentices, 361, 362
Apthorp, Charles, 107
Arapahos, 397, 399
Archaic period
  agriculture, 4–5
  burial practices, 4
  division of labor in, 3
  hunting and gathering, 3
  trade, 3–4
Arikaras, 397
Arkansas
  admitted to Union, 395
  Civil War, 477
  secession, 448, 455, 460
Arkansas Territory, 285
Arnold, Benedict, 170, 172, 179
Art/artisans
  apprentices, 361, 362
  Archaic period, 5
  colonial, 107–108
  free blacks as, 343
  journeymen, 361–362
  Mesoamerican, 7
  in nineteenth century, 361–362, 367
  putting-out system, 361
  slaves as, 328, 333
  unions and, 367
  in West African societies, 11, 11
Articles of Confederation, 210
  Constitution compared to, 224
Asante, 11
Ashley, Henry, 399
Asylum reform, 373–374
Atahualpa, 22
Atlanta, Georgia
  Civil War, 485–486, 486, 489
  population of freed blacks in, 504
Attucks, Crispus, 152, 153
Austin, Moses, 405
Austin, Stephen F., 405
Ayer, Frederick, 504
Aztecs, 5, 6, 20–22, 26

B

Backus, Isaac, 207
Bacon, Nathaniel, 77
Bacon's Rebellion, 76, 77
Balboa, Vasco Núñez de, 20
Ballard, Allan B., 491
Ballou, Sullivan, 453–454
Baltimore
  growth of colonial, 107
  in the nineteenth century, 357
Baltimore and Ohio Railroad, 356
Banking system
  Bank of North America (first commercial bank), 211–212
  Bank of the United States, 243, 264, 278
  National Banking Act (1863), 478
  Second Bank of the United States, 280–281, 283, 284, 302, 308–309
Bank War, 301, 308–309
Bannocks, 407
Baptists, 113, 114, 115, 274, 297–299, 335, 345
Barbados, 56, 57, 59

Barré, Isaac, 145
Barton, Clara, 480
Beauregard, P. G. T., 447, 462
Beaver Wars, 71–72, 76, 78–80
Beecher, Catherine, 352, 418
Beecher, Lyman, 352, 368, 369, 418
Belknap, Jeremy, 208
Bell, Ann, *480*
Bell, John, 441, *442*
Benevolent empire, 368–369
Benin, 11, *11*
Benton, Jessie, 432
Benton, Thomas Hart, 410, 427, 432
Berkeley, William, 77, *110*
Biddle, Nicholas, 308
Biddle Institute, 502
Bill of rights, in state constitutions, 207
Bill of Rights (England) (1689), 119
Bill of Rights (U.S.) (1791), 241
Bini, 11
Birney, James G., 382, 383
Black codes, 342, 508–509
Black Death, 13
Black Hawk's War (1832), 304–305, 398
Black Legend, 24
Black Reconstruction (Du Bois), 522
Bleeding Kansas, 429–430, 445
Board of Trade, 119
Bondwoman's Narrative, The (Crafts), 324
Bon Homme Richard, 186, *186*
Book of Common Prayer, 48
Book of Mormon, The (Smith), 371
Booth, John Wilkes, 490–491
Boston
      American Revolution in, 168–170, 171
      growth of colonial, 107
      Massacre, 152, *153*
      in the nineteenth century, 357
      Port Act (1774), 154, 155
      slave population of, 107
      Tea Party, 153–154, *154*
Boston and Worcester railroad, 356, 357–358
Boston Associates, 362, 364
Boston Children's Friend Society, 373
Boston News-Letter, 111, 118
Boston Seamen's Aid Society, 370–371
Bowery, Charity, 334, 336
Bowery, Richard, 334, 336
Boyd, Belle, 483
Braddock, Edward, 130
Bradford, William, 49, *145*
Bragg, Braxton, 475, 485, 499
Brandywine Creek, battle of, 178, 184
Brannan, Sam, 421
Brant, Joseph (Thayendanegea), 181, 183
Breckinridge, John C., 441–443, *442*
Breeds Hill, battle of, 171, *172*, 178
Brennan, William, 524
Brent's Old Fort, 407
British Constitution, 146
Brocas, William, 48
Brook Farm, 375–376
Brooklyn Heights, battle of, 178, 182
Brooks, Preston, 430
Brown, Henry, 337
Brown, John
      Kansas civil war and, 430
      raid on Harpers Ferry, 436, 438–440, *439*, 445
Brown, John (Revolutionary era merchant), 153

Brown, Mather, *173*
Buchanan, James, 478
      Dred Scott v. Sandford and, 432–433
      election of 1856 and, 432
      Lecompton Constitution, 433–434
      secession and, 443
Bull Run
      first battle of (1861), 462, *462*, 489
      second battle of (1862), 466, 489
Bunker Hill, battle of, 171, *172*, 178
Bureau of Refugees, Freedmen, and Abandoned Lands, 501
Burgoyne, John, 183–184
Burnside, Ambrose E., 471–472
Burr, Aaron, 255, 257, 269
Bush, George, 256, 412
Bush, George H. W., 195, 256, 287, 412
Butler, Andrew, 430
Bulter, Benjamin F., 469, 484
Byrd, William II, 112, 122

C

Cabeza de Vaca, Álvar Núñez, 22–23
Cabinet, formation of presidential, 241
Cabot, John, 28, 30
Caddos, 124
Cahokia, 8, *9*
Cahokia, battle of, 178, 185
Calhoun, Floride, 307
Calhoun, John C., 287, 295, 313
      Compromise of 1850 and, 422–423
      economic policy of, 280, 281
      nullification crisis, 306–308
      states' rights and, 306
      Texas and, 317–318
      as vice president, 306
      as a War Hawk, 272
California
      gold rush, 421–422, *421*
      Native Americans in, 403–404
      rancho era, 406–407
      settlement of, 406–407, 422
      Spanish in, 123–125, 139, 140
Californios, 406
Calvert, Cecilius, 46, 47
Calvert, George, 46, 117
Calvert, Rosalie, 261–262
Calvin, John, 15, 48
Calvinists, 15
Camden (South Carolina), battle of, 178, 188–189
Canada
      See also New France
      American Revolution in, 172
      War of 1812, 273–280, *274*
Canals, 353 355, *356*
Canary Islands, 17
Canning, George, 283
Caribbean islands
      English in, 55–57
      history of, 9
      principal European possessions in, *54*
      slave colonies in, 19
      Spanish conquest of, 2, 17, 19–20, 55
Caribs, 9, 19, 20
Carleton, Guy, 192
Carolina
      See also North Carolina; South Carolina
      colony, overview of, 59
      settlement of, 57–60
      slavery in, 58–59, 81, 83

Carpetbaggers, 514
Carter, Landon, 89
Carter, Robert, 111
Cartier, Jacques, 27
Cass, Lewis, 420
Catawbas, 73, 181
Catherine of Aragon, 28
Catherine the Great, 185
Catholic Church, 14–15
Catholics, in Maryland, 46–47
Catlin, George, 389–390, *404*
Cato's Letters, 147
Cayugas, 71
Chamberlain, Daniel H., 519
Champlain, Samuel de, 37, *39*
Charles I, king of England, 46–47, 50
Charles II, king of England, 57, 60, 62, 116
Charles V, king of Spain, 15
Charles River Bridge v. Warren Bridge, 356–357
Charleston, South Carolina
      American Revolution in, 178, 187, *188*
      Fort Sumter, 444–448
      growth of colonial, 107
      slavery in, 90
Charleston Mercury, 440
Chase, Samuel, 266
Chattanooga, battle of (1863), 475, *476*, 477, 489
Cayuses, 401
Chancellorsville, battle of (1863), 472, *472*, 489
Cherokee, 71, 73, 181, 194, 220, 247, 477
      Indian Removal Act (1830), 303–305, *304, 305*, 306–307
      Trail of Tears, 304, *304*, 306–307
Cherokee Nation v. Georgia, 305
Cherokee War (1759–1761), 142–143, *143*
Cherry Valley, battle of, 178, 185
Chesapeake
      community life in, 47–48
      economy, 44–46, *46*
      indentured servants, 45–46
      Jamestown, 42–43
      laborers in, source of, 91
      Maryland, 46–47
      population of, *37, 77, 84*
      slavery in, 83, 239
      tobacco in, 44–46, *46*
      Virginia, 42–44
      warfare in, 43–44, 48
Chesapeake incident, 270
Chesnut, Mary, 482, 488
Cheyenne, 397, 399
Chicago, 359
Chickasaws, 181, 220
      Indian Removal Act (1830), 303–305, *304, 305*
Chief executive, office of, 223–224, 241
Child, Lydia Maria, 376–377, 379, 440
Child labor, 92, 362, 367
Children
      colonial, 53, *53*
      slave, 327, 334
      in textile mills, 362
      West African, 12
Chinooks, 5
Chippewas, 216, 398
Choctaws, 125, 181, 220
      Indian Removal Act (1830), 303–305, *304, 305*

Cholera, 333, 402
Christian Coalition, 448
Christian History, The, 115
Chumashes, 403
Church of England. *See* Anglican Church
Church of Jesus Christ of Latter-day Saints, 371, 407–408
Cincinnati, Ohio, 359
Cities and towns
      See also Communities
      growth of (1820–1860), 357–361, *358, 359*
      growth of colonial, 107–109
      impact of immigration on, 360–361
      industrial, 359–360
      inland, 358–359
      living conditions and sanitation, 358
      migration to, after the Civil War, 504–505
      port, 357–358
Civil Rights Act (1866), 510–511, 521
Civil Rights Act (1875), 510, 519–520, 521
Civil War, *452*
      African Americans in, 458, 469–471, *471*, 488–490
      Appomattox Courthouse, surrender at, 490
      arming the Confederacy's slaves, 488–490
      border states, Lincoln's fight for, 460–461
      casualties, 463–465, 466, 468, 472, 474, 484–485
      chronology, 456
      comparison of North and South (1860), 436–438, 458–459
      conscription/draft riots, 457, 458, 478
      desertions/dissenters, 477–478, 483
      diseases in, 464
      East, fighting in the, 465–466
      economy of the North, 479–480
      economy of the South, 482
      financing of, 456, 459
      leadership, 459–460
      life of a common soldier, 461, 464–465
      mobilization for, 455–461
      Native Americans in, 477
      naval fighting, 466–467
      outbreak of, 444–448
      peace movements, 481
      politics, in the South, 481
      politics/legislation, in the North, 477–478
      strategies and tactics, 461
      in trans-Mississippi West, 477
      West, fighting in the, 462–463, *463*
      women in, 458, 464, *464*, 465, 480, *480*, 482, *482*, 483
Civil War, battles
      Antietam, 467–468, 489
      Atlanta, 485–486, *486*, 489
      Bull Run, first battle of, 462, *462*, 489
      Bull Run, second battle of, 466, 489
      Chancellorsville, 472, *472*, 489
      Chattanooga, 475, *476*, 477, 489

Franklin and Nashville, 488, 489
Fredericksburg, 471–472, *472*, 489
Gettysburg, 472–474, *474, 475,* 489, 491
major battles 1861–1865, 489
Sherman's March, 488, *488,* 489
Vicksburg, 463, 475, *476,* 489
Wilderness and Cold Harbor, 484–485, *485,* 489
Claims clubs, 394
Clalin, Frances, *464*
Clark, George Rogers, 185, 206
Clark, William, 267, *267,* 286–287, 399
Clay, Henry, 308, 313, 316–317, 378
Compromise of 1850 and, 422–423
economic policy of, 280
election of 1824 and, 287–288
election of 1844 and, 318
Missouri Compromise and, 284–285
as a War Hawk, 272
Clayton, Powell, 517
Clermont, 353
Cleveland, Grover, 412
Cleveland, Ohio, 359
Clinton, Bill, 94, 412
Clinton, DeWitt, 276
Clinton, Henry, 180, 185, 186–188
Coahuila, 405
Cobb, Howell, 488
Cobb, Thomas R. R., 332
Coercive Acts, 154
Colbert, Jean-Baptiste, 38
Cold Harbor, battle of (1864), 484–485, *485, 487,* 489
Colfax Massacre (1873), 516–517
Colleges
black, 502
colonial, 115
Colonial period
See also under name of colony
art/artisans, 107–108
backcountry expansion, 121–125
diverging politics between England and, 119–121
ethnic distribution of immigrants in, 93, 95, *93, 95*
Glorious Revolution, 117, 118–119
growth of cities, 107–109
houses, 48, 110–111, *110*
importation of goods, 110
population in, 53, *84, 121, 122*
religion, 113–116
Colonial wars
See also American Revolution
French and Indian War (1756–1763), 126, 129–132
King George's War (1739–1748), 126, 127–129
King Philip's War, 76–77
King William's War (1689–1697), 126–127
Queen Anne's War (1702–1713), 126–127
Colonization, rejection of, 378–379
Colored Methodist Episcopal Church, 506
Colored Monitor Union club, 514
Columbian exchange, 25–26
Columbus, Christopher, 2, 9, 13, 17, 19, 25, 26, 27, 55
Comanches, *388,* 404, *404,* 405, 406, 477
Committee of Safety, 167

Committees of Correspondence, 153
Common Sense (Paine), 172, 412
Commonwealth v. Hunt, 367
Communism, 375
Communities
growth of free black communities following American Revolution, 205–206
Native American, *29*
slave, 89
utopian, 375–378
Company of New France, 37, 38
Compromise of 1850, 422–423, *424,* 445
Compromise of 1877, 520
Compromise Tariff of 1833, 308
Conciliatory Proposition, 168
Concord, battle of (1775), 168–170, *169,* 178
Cone, Spencer Houghton, 274
Conestogas, 143
Confederate States of America
See also Civil War
Davis as president, 442
disintegration of, 481–483
financing of, 457, 459
formation of, 442–443, *443*
Confederation Congress
Articles of Confederation, 210, 224
economic problems, 211–214
England, relations with, 218–219
France, relations with, 218
Land Ordinance (1785), 216
Native American lands and, 206
Northwest Ordinance (1787), 218
Spain, relations with, 219–221
western lands and, 216–218
Confiscation Act (1862), 468, 469
Congregationalists, 113, 207, 235
Congress
See also Confederation Congress; Continental Congress
Articles of Confederation, 210, 224
Bill of Rights and, 241
Constitutional Convention, 221–224
Congressional Reconstruction, 512–513
Connecticut
colony, overview of, 59
labor system in, 91, 92
ratification of Constitution, 227
religion in, 235
settlement of, 50–51, 59
Conquistadores, 19–20
Conscience Whigs, 421
Constantinople, 16
Constitutional Amendments
Bill of Rights, 241
Fifteenth, 513, 521, 517, 520, 524, 525
Fourteenth, 510–511, 521, 520, 524, 525
Ninth, 241
role of, 241
Second, 241
Tenth, 241, 245
Thirteenth, 487–488, 501, 509, 521
Constitutional Convention, 221–224
Constitutional Union party, 441
Constitution of the United States, 221
compared with the Articles of Confederation, 224

overview of, 224–225
ratification of, 225–228
Continental Army, 166, 170, 175–177, 179, 192
Continental Association, 157
Continental Congress
See also Confederation Congress
First, 154, 155, 157
Second, 170
Continental dollar, 170, 194, 211
Contract theory of government, 173
Cooper, Anthony Ashley, 57
Copley, John Singleton, *109, 148, 151*
Copperheads, 478
Coram, Thomas, *60*
Cornwallis, Charles, 188, 189–190, *190*
Coronado, Francisco Vásquez de, 24
Cortés, Hernán, *1,* 20–21, 26
Cotton
gin, 363–364, 396
mills, 362
prices 1825–1845, *310*
production 1800–1860, *327, 330*
slavery and, 325–326
southern expansion with, 396–397
Council of the Indies, 23
Counter-Reconstruction, 516–519
Counter-Reformation, 15
Country ideology, 127, 146–147, 174
Coureurs de bois, 38, 39, 125
Court system, formation of, 241–242
Covenant, 50
Cowpens, battle of, 178, 189
Craft, Ellen, 337
Crafts, Hannah, 323–324
Crawford, William H., 287
Creeks, 181, 220, 240, 247, 278–279, *280*
Indian Removal Act (1830), 303–305, *304, 305*
Crees, 5
Creoles, 88
Crèvecoeur, J. Hector St. John, 208–209
Criollos, 403
Crittenden, John J., 444
Crittenden Plan, 444
Croatoan Indians, 29
Cromwell, Oliver, 47
Crow, 397
CSX Corp., 94
Cuba
Ostend Manifesto, 427
Spanish exploration of, 19, 55
Cult of domesticity, 365–366
Cumming, Kate, 464
Currency
continental dollar, 170, 194, 211
establishment of national, 478
greenbacks, 459
paper money pre-American Revolution, 144
Specie Circular, 311
Currency Act (1764), 144, 156
Custis, Mary, 466

D

Dahomey, 11
Dakotas, 477
Dance, of slaves, 335
Dare, Virginia, 29
Dartmouth, 154
Dartmouth College v. Woodward, 282
Davenport, James, 115
Davenport, John, 52

Davis, Edmund J., 517
Davis, Jefferson, 440, 442, 447, 459–460, 469, 475, 477, 481, 486, 488–490
Day, Thomas, 343
Dearborn, Henry, 275
Declaration of Independence and, 172–174
Declaration of Rights and Grievances, 148
Declaration of Sentiments, 381
Declaration of the Causes and Necessity of Taking Up Arms, 170
Declaratory Act, 149
Deere, John, 394
Deism, 255, 256
Delany, Martin, 424
Delavan, Edward, 369
Delaware
labor system in, 92
ratification of Constitution, 227
secession, 460
Delawares, 61, 73, 127, 128, 129, 131, 181, 216
Democratic party
Civil War and, 478
compared with the Whigs, 313
election of 1848 and, 420
election of 1852 and, 426–427
election of 1860 and, 440–442, *442,* 445
election of 1864 and, 486–487
Jacksonian Democrats, 295, 299–301
Reconstruction, 508, 519
Democratic-Republican societies, 246–247
Denmark Vesey's Conspiracy (1822), 336
Depression, following American Revolution, 212–214
De Soto, Hernán, 23–24
Detroit, Michigan, 185, 359
Dew, Thomas R., 347
Días, Bartholomew, 17
Dickens, Charles, 358, 374
Dickinson, John, 151, 173, 210
Direct Tax of 1798, 253, 254
Discourse on Western Planting (Hakluyt), 30–31
Diseases
in American Revolution, 177
among slaves, 333
Black Death, 13
cholera, 333, 402
in the Civil War, 464
in colonies, 47
introduced in the Americas, 21
Native Americans and, 21–22, 25–26, 70–71, 399, 401
smallpox, 21, 25, 26, *26,* 399
Dix, Dorothea, 374, *374*
Djenné, 12
Dominion of New England, 117
Dominy family, 363
Doolittle, Amos, *169*
Douglas, Stephen A.
Civil War and, 456
Compromise of 1850 and, 423
debates with Lincoln, 434–435, *435*
election of 1856 and, 432
election of 1860 and, 440–442, *442*
Kansas-Nebraska Act, 428–429, *429*
Lecompton Constitution, 434

Douglass, Frederick, 382–383, *383*, 424, 439, 471, 501, 522
Douglass, Lewis, 471
Dragging Canoe, 181
Drake, Francis, 28
Drayton, William Henry, 158–159
Dream songs, 404
Dred Scott v. Sandford and, 432–433, 445, 510
Du Bois, W. E. B., 522
Dudley, Thomas, 36, 49, 50
Dunmore, Lord (John Murray), 171–172, 180
Dutch, *236*, 237
    Anglo-Dutch wars, 62
    in the Caribbean, 55, 56
    colonies, 40–41
    exploration/colonization by, 39–42
    map of colonies in North America, *42*
Dutch East India Company, 40
Dutch Reformed Church, 207, 237

E

Earl, Ralph, *169*
Early, Jubal, 484
East India Company, 153, 154
Eaton, Margaret "Peggy," 307
Eaton Affair, 306–307
Economy
    American Revolution impact on, 191, 194, 196
    Chesapeake tobacco, 44–46, *46*
    Civil War economy of the North, 479–480
    Civil War economy of the South, 482
    colonial, 101–107
    Hamilton's economic programs, 242–244, 245
    legacy of slavery, 346
    mercantilism, 101
    national debt issues, 243–244, 245
    nationalism, 280–281
    New England, 53–55, 101–107
    in the nineteenth century, 364
    Panic of 1819, 283–284
    Panic of 1837, 309–311
    Panic of 1857, 434
    problems following the American Revolution, 211–214
    slave, 326–328
Education
    for African Americans, in Reconstruction period, 501–502
    of colonial women, 111, 204–205, 235, 237, *237*
    public, 372
    reform, 372–373
    women as teachers, 373, 501–502
    of women following the Civil War, 480
Edwards, Jonathan, 115
Elections, presidential
    of 1796, 251–252
    of 1800, 255–257
    of 1804, 263
    of 1808, 270
    of 1812, 276
    of 1816, 280
    of 1820, 287
    of 1824, 287–288, *288*, 299
    of 1828, 300–301, *301*
    of 1832, 309

of 1836, 309
of 1840, 315–316, *315*
of 1844, 318
of 1848, 420–421
of 1852, 426–427, 445
of 1856, 432, 445
of 1860, 440–442, *442*, 445
of 1864, 478, 486–488
of 1868, 512
of 1872, 518–519
of 1876, 520, *522*
Eliot, John, 76
Elizabeth I, queen of England, 28, 46, 48, 49
Elliott, Robert B., *514*
Emancipation Proclamation (1829), 405
Emancipation Proclamation (1863), 468–469
Embargo Act (1807), 269–270
Emerson, Ralph Waldo, 170, 376–377, 438, 440
Employment
    See also Labor
    of children, 92, 362, 367
    for free blacks, 343
    for Irish immigrants, 363
    for women, 362–363, *363*, 365–366
    working classes, 366–367
Empresario, 405
Encomienda, 69, 77, 78
Enforcement Act (1870), 517
England
    See also American Revolution
    Anglo-Dutch wars, 62
    in the Caribbean, 55–57
    Chesapeake colonies, 42–48
    Civil War (U.S.) and, 467
    Confederation Congress and, 218–219
    diverging politics between colonies and, 119–121
    exploration/colonization by, 28–31, 42–55, 121–123
    French and Indian War (1756–1763), 126, 129–132
    Glorious Revolution, 118–119
    impressment of American sailors by, 250, 268–270
    Jay's Treaty (1794), 250–251
    King George's War (1739–1748), 126, 127–129
    King William's War (1689–1697), 126–127
    map of colonies in North America, *42*, *58*
    mercantilism, 101
    New England, 48–55
    North American territories 1750–1763, *121*
    overview of seventeenth-century colonies, 59
    proprietary colonies, 46, 57–62
    Queen Anne's War (1702–1713), 126–127
    slave trade and, 82–83
    U.S. relations with, 250–251
    War of 1812, *260*, 261–262, 273–280, *274*, *279*
Enlightenment, 112–113
Enrollment Act (1862), 458
Entertainment
    colonial, 111
    in nineteenth century, 364–365, *365*

Enumerated products, 101
Episcopalians, 207
Equiano, Olaudah, 68, 82, *83*
Era of Good Feelings, 280–283
Erie Canal, 313, 353, 355, *356*, 357, 359
Erskine, David, 271
Eskimos, 5
Essex Junto, 269
Established churches, 207–208
Ethnic groups
    in 1770s British North America, 93, 95, *93*, *95*
    in 1790s, *236*, 237
Europe
    See also Exploration and colonization; *specific countries*
    Middle Ages, 13
    patriarchal, 13
    Renaissance, 13
Evangelicalism, 298–299, 345, 365–366, 369
Exploration and colonization
    by Dutch, 39–42
    by England, 28–31, 42–55, 121–123
    expansion in 1750s, *121*
    by France, 27–28, 37–39, 125
    maps of, *18*, *20*
    by Portugal, 12–13, 16–17, 27
    by Spain, 2, 9, 12, 13–14, 16, 17, 19–25, 123–125

F

Factories. *See* Industrialization and manufacturing
Facts of Reconstruction (Lynch), 522
Fallen Timbers, battle of, 247, 248
Falwell, Jerry, 448
Family life
    in Chesapeake colonies, 47–48
    cultural perceptions and misperceptions, 26–27
    middle class, 365, *366*
    New England, 52–55
    slave, 57, 88–89, 334–336
    West African, 12
    westward expansion and, 401–402
Fargo, William, 421
Farmar, Eliza, 137–139
Farmer-Paellmann, Deandria, 94
Farming. *See* Agriculture
Farragut, David G., 463
Faulkner, William, 491
Federalism, 225, 226
Federalist, The, 228
Federalist Gazette, 246
Federalist party
    differences between Republican party and, 244
    formation of, 245
    policies of, 244, 245
Federalists, 225, 226–228
    High, 253–257
Feminism, 381–382, *382*
Ferdinand, king of Spain, 13, 14
Ferguson, Clementia, 108
Ferris, Warren A., 399, 400
Field Order No. 15, 503
Fifteenth Amendment, 513, 521, 517, 520, 524, 525
Fillmore Millard, 423, 426, 432
Finney, Charles G., 365
First African Baptist Church, 505, *505*
First Colored Baptist Church, 505

First Continental Congress, 154, 155, 157
Fishermen, 92
Fishing, 30–31
Fisk University, 502
Five Points slum area, 358
FleetBoston Financial Corp., 94
Fletcher v. Peck, 282
Florida
    admitted to Union, 395
    annexation of West, to the U.S., 268–269, 272
    British control of, following French and Indian War, 133, 140
    French exploration/colonization of, 28
    Jackson's invasion of, 283
    missionaries in, 73–74, *74*
    secession, 442, *443*
    Spanish exploration/colonization of, 20, 23, 24
Folwell, John, 108
Foote, Andrew H., 462
Force Bill (1833), 308
Forrest, Nathan Bedford, 516
Fort Dearborn, 275
Fort Donelson, 462, 463, 489
Fort Duquesne, 129, 130, 131
Fort Henry, 462, 463, 489
Fort Laramie, *403*
Fort Laramie, treaty of (1851), 403
Fort Loudoun, 143
Fort McIntosh, treaty of (1785), 216
Fort Michilimackinac, 275
Fort Necessity, 129
Fort Orange, 40
Fort Oswego, 130
Fort Stanwix, treaty of (1784), 216
Fort Sumter, 444–448
Fort Ticonderoga, 170, 178, 183
Fortune, T. Thomas, 497–498
Fort Wagner, 471
Fort Wayne, treaty of (1809), 272
Fort William Henry, 130
Forty-Niners, *421*
Fourier, Charles, 375
Fourierist communities, 375
Fourteenth Amendment, 510–511, 521, 520, 524, 525
Fox (Indians), 304, 398
Frame of Government, 61
France
    See also New France
    American Revolution and, 184–185
    in the Caribbean, 55
    Civil War (U.S.) and, 467
    Confederation Congress and, 218
    control of Native Americans, 71
    exploration/colonization by, 27–28, 37–39, 125
    French and Indian War (1756–1763), 126, 129–132
    in Louisiana, 125
    in the Mississippi Valley, 125
    North American territories 1750–1763, *121*
    War of the Austrian Succession (1739–1748), 126, 127–129
    War of the League of Augsburg (1689–1697), 126–127
    XYZ Affair, 252–253
Francis I, king of France, 27
Franciscans, 73–75, 78, 124, 403

Franco-American Accord (1800), 255
Franco-American Alliance (1778), 246
Franklin, battle of (1864), 488, 489
Franklin, Benjamin, 110, *112*, 115, 122, 143
    Albany Plan of Union, 129
    American Revolution and, 172, 184, 186, 190, *192*
    inventions, 112–113
    taxation and, 149
Franklin, Deborah, 110
Franklin, John Hope, 94, 525
Freake, Elizabeth, *34*
Fredericksburg, battle of (1862), 471–472, *472*, 489
Free blacks. *See* African Americans, free
Freedmen's Bureau, 501–502, 503, 504, 510, 521
Freedom's Journal, 378
Freemen, New England, 50
Freeport Doctrine, 435
Free-Soil party, formation of, 383, 421
Frémont, John C., 432, 441
French, Benjamin B., 293–294
French and Indian War (1756–1763), 126, 129–132
French Revolution (1789), 245–247
Fries, John, 254
Fries's Rebellion, 254
Frobisher, Martin, 28
Fugitive Slave Act (1850), 423–425
Fulton, Robert, 353
Fundamental Constitutions of Carolina, 57–58
Fundamental Orders, 51
Fur trade
    Dutch, 41
    French in, 37–38, 70, 125
    westward expansion and, 399–400, *399, 400*

G

Gabriel Prosser's Rebellion (1800), 336
Gadsden, Christopher, 148, 157
Gage, Thomas, 154, 167, 168, 171, 181
Gag rule, 312, 380, 383
Gallatin, Albert, 264, 265, 278
Galloway, Joseph, 157
Gálvez, José de, 124
Gama, Vasco da, 17
Gang system, 326
Gardoqui, Don Diego de, 220
Garfield, James A., 501
Garrison, William Lloyd, 378, 379–381, 440
    Liberator, 312, 379, *379*
Gaspee, 153
Gates, Horatio, 184
General Union for Promoting the Observance of the Christian Sabbath, 368–369
Genêt, Edmond, 246
George II, king of England, 118, 119
George III, king of England, 139, 146, 152, 170, 172, 173, 190
Georgia
    American Revolution in, 187, *188*
    Civil War, 469, 485–486, *486*, 488, 489
    Indian removal, 303–305, *304, 305*
    ratification of Constitution, 227
    secession, 442, *443*
    settlement of, 85

slavery in, 85, 239
Germans
    in colonial settlements, *236*, 237
    immigration of, in the nineteenth century, 360, 361, 430
Gerry, Elbridge, 226
Gettysburg, battle of (1863), 472–474, *474, 475*, 489, 491
Ghana, 11
Ghent, treaty of (1814), 278
Gibbons, Thomas, 356
Gibbons v. Ogden 356
Giddings, Joshua R., 383
Gilbert, Humphrey, 28–29
Gilmore, Quincy Adams, 469
Gladstone, William, 467
Glorieta Pass, battle of (1862), 477
Glorious Revolution, 117, 118–119
Gold rush, 421–422, *421*
Goliad, 406
Gordon, John B., 516
Gordon, Thomas, 147
Gorsuch, Edward, 425
Government
    contract theory of, 173
    representation, colonial, 120
Grand Banks, 30–31
Grand Settlement of 1701, 127
Grant, Ulysses S., *487*
    Civil War and, 462–463, 475, 484–486, 490
    election of 1868 and, 512
    election of 1872 and, 518–519
Great Awakening, 114–116
Great Bridge, battle at, 172, 178
Great Compromise, 222–223
Great League of Peace and Power, 71–72
Great Plains, 397–400
Greeley, Horace, 441, 468, 518–519
Green, Anne Catherine, 108
Greenbacks, 459
Greene, Nathanael, 189
Greenhow, Rose O'Neal, 483
Green Spring Mansion, *110*
Greenville, treaty of (1795), 247, *247*, 271
Gregg, William, 328
Grenville, George, 144, 145
Grimké, Angelina, 351–352, 381
Grimké, Sarah, 352, 381
Griswold, Roger, *253*
Guadalupe Hidalgo, treaty of (1848), 413
Guanahani, 19
Guanahatabeys, 9
Guilford Court House, 178, 189

H

Habeas Corpus Act (1863), 477–478
Hakluyt, Richard, 30–31
Hale, Sarah Josepha, 371
Halfway Covenant (1662), 113
Hamilton, Alexander, 269
    Annapolis Convention (1786), 221
    Constitutional Convention and, 222
    dispute with Jefferson and Madison, 245
    economic programs, 242–244, 245
    election of 1796 and, 253
    Federalist and, 228
    French Revolution and, 246
    national debt and, 256

as secretary of the Treasury and fiscal program of, 242
    Whiskey Rebellion and, 250
Hammond, James Henry, 328, 440, 467
Hampton Institute, 502, *503*
Hancock, John, *148*, 151, 167, 168, 228
Hariot, Thomas, 29
Harpers Ferry, Virginia
    federal arsenal at, 364
    John Brown's raid on, 436, 438–440, *439*, 445
Harrison, William Henry, 313, 314, 315–317
    pan-Indian resistance movement and, 271–272
    War of 1812 and, 277
Harvard College, 112, 113
Hat Act (1732), 102
Havana, Cuba, 132
Hawkins, John, 28
Hawthorne, Nathaniel, 376, 377–378
Hayes, Rutherford B., 520
Haynes, March, 469
Hays, Mary Ludwig, 180
Headright system, 43
Henry, Andrew, 399
Henry, Patrick, 144, 147, 157, 𝕸
Henry IV, king of France, 37
Henry VII, king of England, 13, 28
Henry VIII, king of England, 14, 28
Henry the Navigator, 16
Hidatsas, 397
High Federalists, 253–257
Hill, John, *356*
Hillsborough, Lord, 150
Hispaniola, 19, 24, 55
Hohokams, 8
Holmes, James Henry, 505
Holy Roman Empire, 15
Homer, Winslow, *461*
Homestead Act (1862), 478
Hood, John Bell, 486, 488
Hooker, Joseph, 472
Hooker, Thomas, 51
Hooper, William, 209
Hopi, 8, 75, 404, 407
Horses
    introduced to the Americas, 398
    Plains Indians and, 25, 398
Horseshoe Bend, battle of (1814), 278–279, *280*
House of Burgesses, 43, 44, 77, 87
House of Commons, 119, 146
House of Lords, 119
House of the Seven Gables (Hawthorne), 377
Housing
    Archaic period, 5
    backcountry log, *123*
    Chesapeake, 48
    kivas, 8, 404
    colonial, 48, 110–111, *110, 123*
    log cabins, *123, 239*
    slave, *60,* 89, 333
    slums, 358
Houston, Sam, 406
Howard University, 502
Howe, Richard, 181–183
Howe, Samuel Gridley, 373
Howe, William, 181–183, *184*
Howell, Varina, 459
Howell, William Dean, 522
Hudson, Henry, 40
Hudson's Bay Company, 399, 401
Hughes, John, 468

Hull, William, 275
Human sacrifice, 7
Hundred Years' War, 13
Hunter-gatherers, 3–5
Hurons, 26, 38, *39,* 70–72
Hutchinson, Anne, 51–52
Hutchinson, Thomas, 148, 153, 167

I

Igbos, 11, 12, 68
Illinois
    admitted to Union, 295, 393
    settlement of, 125
Immigration
    German, 360, 361
    Irish, 360–361
    in the nineteenth century, 360–361, *361,* 384
    reactions to, 384
Impeachment, 207
    of Andrew Johnson, 512
Impressment of American sailors by Britain, 250, 269–270
Incas, 22–23
In Defense of the Indians (Las Casas), 24
Indentured servants, 38, 45–46, 56, 83, 91
Independent Treasury System, 311–312
Independent Whig, 117
Indian
    See also Native Americans; *under name of tribe*
    origin of the term, 2
Indiana, admitted to Union, 295, 393
Indian Removal Act (1830), 303–305, *304, 305,* 397
Indian Territory of Oklahoma, 285, 304, *304,* 397–398, 477
Industrialization and manufacturing
    by artisans, 361–362
    children as workers, 362
    cotton mills, 362
    factory system, 362
    in Jefferson's America, 361
    household manufacturing, 361
    interchangeable machine-made parts/American system of, 364
    pollution from, 364
    putting-out system, 361
    role of technology, 362, 363–364
    sources of workers for, 362–363
    textile mills, 359–360, *360,* 361
    use of British technology, 364
    women as workers, 362–363, *363*
Intendants, 38, 139
Intolerable Acts (1774), 154–155
Iowa
    admitted to Union, 395
    settlement of, 398
Ireland, 28
Irish immigrants, 360–361, 363, 384, 430–431
Iroquois, 9, 26, 27, *39,* 41
    American Revolution and, 181, 185, 194
    Beaver Wars, 71–72, 76, 78–80
    Confederacy, 181, 206, 216
    French and Indian War (1756–1763), 126, 129–132
    Grand Settlement of 1701, 127
    King George's War (1739–1748), 126, 128–129
    King William's War (1689–1697), 126–127

Lancaster, treaty of (1744), 129
League, 71–72, 126, 127
Isabella, queen of Spain, 13, 14, 19
Islam, 12

J

Jackson, Andrew, *301*
    Bank War, 301, 308–309
    Battle of New Orleans and, 278–280
    Creeks and, 278–279, *280*
    Eaton Affair, 306–307
    election of 1824 and, 287–288
    election of 1828 and, 300–301
    inauguration of, 302, *302*
    Indian Removal Act (1830), 303–305, *304, 305*
    invasion of Florida, 283
    nullification crisis, 301, 305–308
    presidency of, 301–309
    Texas and, 317
Jackson, Stonewall, 462, 465, 472
Jacksonian Democrats, 295, 299–301
Jamaica, 19, 55, 59
James I, king of England, 42, 44, 49
James II, king of England (duke of York), 62, 116–117, 119
Jamestown, 42–43
Jay, John, 190, *192*, 219, 220–221, 228, 250
Jay's Treaty (1794), 250–251
Jefferson, Thomas, 112, *173*, 208, 239
    Alien and Sedition Acts (1789) and, 253–254
    Declaration of Independence and, 173–174
    dispute with Hamilton, 245
    election of 1796 and, 252
    election of 1800 and, 257
    election of 1804 and, 263
    Embargo Act (1807), 269–270
    Florida and western schemes, 268–269
    French Revolution and, 246
    Louisiana Purchase and, 266–268, *268*
    Ordinance of 1784 and, 216
    presidency of, 263–270
    reforms, 263–266
    slaves/slavery and, 174, 216
    states' rights and, 254
Jesuits, 38, 75, *75*, 139
Johnson, Andrew
    impeachment of, 512
    Reconstruction plan, 507–512
    Southern Homestead Act and, 503
Johnson, Anthony, 86–87
Johnson, Richard M., 295
Johnston, Joseph E., 462, 465, 484, 485–486, 488, 490, 492
Joint-stock companies, 42, 50
Jones, Charles Colcock, 345
Jones, John Paul, 186, *186*
Journeymen, 361–362, 367
Juárez, Benito, 467
Judicial nationalism, 281–282
Judicial review, 225
Judiciary Act (1789), 242, 266
Judiciary Act (1801), 265–266
Julian, George W., 508, 509–510

K

Kalb, Johann, 177
Kansas, Bleeding, 429–430, 445
Kansas Indians, 397

Kansas-Nebraska Act, 428–429, *429*, 445
Kaskaskia, battle of, 178, 185
Kearny, Stephen W., 413
Kelley, Abby, 381
Kentucky
    Civil War, 462
    secession, 460–461
    settlement of, 240
    as a slave state, 284
    statehood for, 240
Kettle Creek, battle of, 178, 187
Key, Francis Scott, 278
Kieft, Willem, 41–42
King George's War (1739–1748), 126, 127–129
King Philip's War, 76–77
Kingsley, Bathsheba, 116
Kings Mountain, battle of, 178, 189
King William's War (1689–1697), 126–127
Kiowas, 404
Kivas, 8, 404
Know-Nothings, 431, 432
Kosciuszko, Tadeusz, 175, 177
Ku Klux Klan, 516–517, *517*
Ku Klux Klan Act (1871), 517
Kwakiutls, 5

L

Labor
    See also Employment;
        Industrialization and manufacturing; Slavery; Slaves; Unions
    apprentices, 108
    child, 92, 362, 367
    in English colonies, 91–93
    immigrant, 93, 95
    indentured servants, 38, 45–46, 56, 83, 91
    redemptioner system, 91
    tenancy, 91
    unions, 367
Ladies' Association of Philadelphia, 193
Lafayette, Marquis de, 175
Lake Erie, 276–277
Lakotas, 477
Lancaster, treaty of (1744), 129
Land Grant College Act (1862), 478
Land Ordinance (1785), 216–217, *217*
Land ownership
    See also Westward expansion
    for African Americans, in Reconstruction period, 502–504
    claims clubs, 394
    contractual property rights, 282
    differences between England and colonies, 120
    European seizure of Native American land, 72–73, 123, 142
    headright system, 43
    Homestead Act (1862), 478
    Land Grant College Act (1862), 478
    problems of overcrowding (1790–1850), 391–393
    republicanism and, 203
    squatters, 240, 394
    women and, 204
Larkin, Thomas, 410
La Salle, Sieur de (Robert), 39
Las Casas, Bartolomé de, 24
Laurens, Henry, 151, 166, *192*
Laurens, John, 165–167, 180, *180*

Lawes Divine, Morall and Martiall, 43
League of Armed Neutrality, 185
League of Freedom, 424
Leaves of Grass (Whitman), 377
Lecompton Constitution, 433–434, 445
Lee, Ann (Mother Ann), 375
Lee, Jason, 401
Lee, Richard Henry, 173
Lee, Robert E., 439, 465–466, *465*, 467–468, 472–474, 484, 484–486, 487, 490, 499
Legislative action, overview of colonial, 156
Leisler, Jacob, 117
Leopard, 270
Letters from an American Farmer (Crèvecoeur), 208–209
Lewis and Clark expedition, 267, *268*, 286–287, 399
Lexington, battle of (1775), 168–170, *169*, 178
Liberal Republicans, 516, 518
Liberator, 312, 379, *379*
Liberty, 151
Liberty Association, 424
Liberty party, 382, 383
Lincoln, Abraham, 384, 439, *490*
    assassination of, 490–492
    Civil War, 455–456, 459, 460–461, 462, 465, 471, 474, 477, 484, 490
    debates with Douglas, 434–435, *435*
    election of 1860 and, 441–442, *442*
    election of 1864 and, 478, 487–488
    Emancipation Proclamation (1863), 468–469
    Fort Sumter, 446–447
    habeas corpus and, 477–478
    inauguration of, 444
    Reconstruction plan of, 506–507
    secession and, 443, 444
    on slavery, 446–447
Lincoln, Benjamin, *190*
Lincoln, Mary Todd, 434
Linn, William, 255
Literacy rates, colonial, 111
Literature
    Age of Enlightenment, 112–113
    colonial, 111–112
Little Crow, 398
Little Turtle (Mishikinakwa), 247, *247*, 248
Locke, John, 57, 59–60, 112, 146, 173
Logan, James, 73
London Company, 42
Long, Stephen, 397
Long Island, slavery on, 62
Longstreet, James, 475, 519
Lords of Trade, 117, 119
Lost Cause, 499–500
Loudoun, Lord, 130
Louis XI, king of France, 13, 14
Louis XIV, king of France, 38, 126, 246
Louisbourg, 128, 131
Louisiana
    French settlement of, 125
    naming of, 39
    secession, 442, *443*
    as a slave state, 284
Louisiana Purchase, 266–268, *268*

Lovejoy, Elijah P., 380
L'Ouverture, Touissant, 267
Lowell, Massachusetts, 359–360, *360*
Lower South, defined, 325
Loyalists/Tories, 160, 167–168
Luther, Martin, 14–15
Luther, Seth, 296
Lutheranism, 114, 207, 237
Lynch, John R., 522
Lyon, Matthew, 253, *253*
Lyon, Pat, *362*

M

Macdonough, Thomas, 278
MacIntosh, Ebenezer, 147–148
Maclay, William, 233–234
Macon, Nathaniel, 271
Macon's Bill No. 2 (1810), 271
Madison, Dolley, *266*
Madison, James, 214, 221, *228*, 268, 378
    Alien and Sedition Acts (1789) and, 253–254
    Annapolis Convention (1786) and, 221
    Bill of Rights and, 241
    Constitutional Convention and, 222, 223, 225
    dispute with Hamilton, 245
    election of 1808, 270
    election of 1812, 276
    Federalist and, 228
    Marbury v. Madison, 266
    presidency of, 270–280
    ratification of Constitution and, 228
    states' rights and, 254
    Tonnage Act of 1789 and, 242
    Virginia Plan, 222
    War of 1812, 272–280, *274, 279*
Maentel, Jacob, *237*
Maine, admitted to Union, 284, 295
Mali, 11
Mallory, Stephen R., 427
Manassas. *See* Bull Run
Mandans, 8, 397
Mandingo, 82
Manifest Destiny, 390, 408–410, 412
Manila, Philippines, 132
Mann, Horace, 372
Manufacturing. *See* Industrialization and manufacturing
Marbury, William, 266
Marbury v. Madison, 266
Marcy, Moses, *98*
Marion, Francis, 189
Marriage
    English-Indian, 43, 47
    interracial, 87, *124*
    in New England, 53, 237
    of slaves, 88, 334
Married Women's Property Act (1860), 382
Marshall, James, 421
Marshall, John, 266, 269, 281–282, *281*, 305, 356
Mary I, queen of England, 28, 117
Maryland
    Civil War, 467–468, 489
    colony, overview of, 59
    labor system in, 92
    ratification of Constitution, 228
    secession, 460
    settlement of, 46–47, 59
    slavery in, 83

Maryland Gazette, 108
Mason, David, *53*
Mason, George, 207, 226
Mason, James M., 423, 440
Mason, Margaretta, 440
Masons, 313–314
Massachusetts
    American Revolution in, 168–170, 171
    Conciliatory Proposition, 168
    Government Act (1774), 154, 155
    Lexington and Concord, battles of (1775), 168–170, *169,* 178
    labor system in, 92
    ratification of Constitution, 228
    religion in, 235
Massachusetts Bay Colony, 49–52, 59
Massachusetts Bay Company, 50
Massasoit, 49
Mather, Cotton, 112
Maximilian, 467
Mayans, 5
Mayflower, 49
Mayflower Compact, 49
Mayhew, Thomas, Jr., 76
Maysville Road Bill, 302–303
McClellan, George B., 465, 466, 468, 471, 478, 484, 486
McCormick, Cyrus, 394, *395*
McCormick reaper, 394–395
McCrea, Jane, 181
McCulloch v. Maryland, 282
McDowell, Irvin, 462
McGillivray, Alexander, 220, *221*
Meade, George Gordon, 472–474, 484, 485
Meadows, William R., 516
Melville, Herman, 377, 378
Memphis Appeal, 441
Mendes, 11
Mennonites, 114, 237
Mercantilism, 101
Mesoamerica, 5–7
Mestizos, 75, *124,* 403
Mctacom, 76–77
Methodist Episcopal Church, 345
Methodists, 205, 274, 297–299
Mexican borderlands, 403–405
Mexican Cession of 1848, 408
Mexican War, 408, 410–413, *411*
Mexico, Spanish conquest of, 24
Miamis, 181, 240, 247, *247,* 248
Miantonomo, 52
Michigan, admitted to Union, 395
Middle class, 365, *366*
Middle Passage, description of crossing the Atlantic, 82, *85*
Mifflin, Thomas and Sara Morris, *151*
Nash, Gary, 195
Nashville, battle of (1864), 488, 489
Nation, 518
National Banking Act (1863), 478
National Black Convention, 424, 426
National debt issues, 242, 256, 264
National Gazette, 251
National History Standards, 195
Nationalists, 211
National Republicans, 300, 312
National Trades Union (NTU), 367
Miller, Alfred James, *403*
Milwaukee, 359
Minuit, Peter, 40
Minutemen, 167, 169
Miranda, Francisco de, 203
Mishikinakwa (Little Turtle), 247, *247,* 248
Missionaries, Native Americans and, 73–76, 123, 401, 403
Mississippi
    admitted to Union, 295, 395
    Civil War, 463, 475, 477
    secession, 442, *443*
    as a slave state, 284
Mississippians, 8

Mississippi River, Spain and, 219–221
Mississippi Valley, French in, 125
Missouri
    admitted to Union, 295, 395
    Civil War, 477
    secession, 460
Missouri Compromise, 284–285, 428, 444
Moby Dick (Melville), 378
Moctezuma, *1,* 20, *21,* 22
Mohawks, 71, 181
Mohegans, 51
Molasses Act (1733), 102, 104
Monmouth Court House, battle of, 180, 178, 185
Monopolies, 356–357
Monroe, James, 218, 378
    presidency of, 280–283
Monroe Doctrine, 283
Montagnais, 38
Montauks, 116
Montcalm, Marquis de, 130, 131
Monticello, 265
Montreal, 37, 38
Montserrat, 59
Moore's Creek Bridge, battle of, 172, 178
Moral Majority, 448
Moral reform movement
    backlash against, 371
    benevolent empire, 368–369
    Sabbatarian movement, 368–369
    Sunday schools, 368
    temperance movement, 369–370
    women, role of, 370–371
Moravians, 76, 237
Morgan, Daniel, 189
Morgan, William, 313
Mormons, 371, 407–408
Morris, Robert, 173, 211–212
Morse, Omar H., 391
Mortality rates, trappers and, 400
Mother Bethel Church, *206*
Mott, Lucretia, 381, *382*
Mound-building societies, 8–9
Mount Vernon, 111
Mulattoes, 344
Mulberry Plantation, *60*
Murray, Judith Sargeant, 235

N

Napoleon Bonaparte, 267–268, 270, 271, 277
Napoleon III, 467
Narragansetts, 49, 51, 70, 73, 76
Narrative of the Life of Frederick Douglass, an American Slave (Douglass), 382
Nast, Thomas, *520*
Nativists, 367, 384
Nat Turner's Rebellion (1831), 306, 336, *336,* 378–379
Naturalization Act (1798), 253
Natural rights, 206
Navajos, 404, 407, 477
Navigation Acts (1651, 1660, 1696), 101, 102, 117, 119
Navy
    American Revolution and, 185–186, *186*
    Civil War and, 466–467
    formation of, 170
    Quasi-War and, 253
    War of 1812 and, 275, 276–277
Nebraska
    Kansas-Nebraska Act, 428–429, *429*
    settlement of, 428
Negro Seamen's Act, 336
Neolin, 143
Nevis, 59
New Amsterdam, 40–41
New Echota, treaty of (1835), 306
New England
    agriculture, 55
    economy, 53–55
    founding of, 48–55
    government in, 50, 54
    growth of, 53

American Revolution and, 181, 185, 194
Bacon's Rebellion, 76, 77
Beaver Wars, 71–72
before 1492, 2–9
Black Hawk's War, 304–305, 398
Cherokee War (1759–1761), 142–143, *143*
Civil War and, 477
contacts with Europeans, 68–80
cultural perceptions and misperceptions, 26–27
diseases introduced to, 21–22, 25–26, 70–71, 399, 401
European seizure of land, 72–73, 123, 142
fighting between, 71–72
French and Indian War (1756–1763), 126, 129–132
Indian Removal Act (1830), 303–305, *304, 305*
King George's War (1739–1748), 126, 127–129
King Philip's War, 76–77, 78–79
King William's War (1689–1697), 126–127
as laborers, 69–70
land cessions (1784–1800), 247, 249
missionaries and, 73–76, 123, 401, 403
origin of the term Indian, 2
pan-Indian resistance movement, 271–272
Pontiac's Rebellion (1763–1766), 143
population of, from 1600–1730, 70
Pueblo Revolt, 76, 77–78
as slaves, 77, 81
trade between Europeans and, 70–72
Trail of Tears, 304, *304,* 306–307
westward expansion and affects on, 240, 397–403
Nativists, 367, 384
Native Americans
    See also Archaic period; *under name of tribe*
    after the American Revolution, 206–207, 240
    agriculture, 4–5, *4,* 403–404

King Philip's War, 76–77
laborers in, 91–93
Massachusetts Bay Colony, 49–52
missionaries in, 75–76
Plymouth Colony, 48–49
population of, 53, *84*
Puritanism in, 48–50
in the 1790s, 235, 237
slavery in, 235
social classes in, 54
towns, 53–54
women in, 53, 235, 237, *237*
New England Anti-Slavery Society, 379
New England Non-Resistant Society, 380
New England Woman Suffrage Association, 513
Newfoundland, 29
New France
    See also Canada
    Beaver Wars, 71–72, 76, 78–80
    establishment of, 27, 37, 38–39
    French in, 37
    fur trade, 37
    map of, *38*
    missionaries in, *74,* 75
    population of, *40*
New Hampshire
    colony, overview of, 59
    labor system in, 92
    ratification of Constitution, 228
    settlement of, 52, 59
New Harmony, 375
New Haven, Connecticut, 52, 59
New Jersey
    American Revolution in, 181–183, *182*
    ethnic diversity in, 237
    labor system in, 91, 92
    overview of, 59
    ratification of Constitution, 227
    settlement of, 59, 62
    slavery in, 206, 238
    voting rights for women, 204, *204,* 296–297
New Jersey Plan, 222
New Lights, 115
New Mexico
    ceded to U.S., 413
    Civil War, 477
    missionaries in, 73–75, *74*
    Pueblo Revolt, 76, 77–78
    settlement of, 405–406, 422
    Spanish colonists in, 24, 69
New Netherland, 41, 62
New Orleans
    battle of (1815), 278–280
    Civil War, 463
    founding of, 125
New Spain, 23
Newspapers
    abolitionist, 379, *379,* 383
    colonial, 108, 111–112, 118, 251
Newton, Isaac, 112
New York City
    draft riots, 478, *479*
    Five Points slum area, 358
    in the nineteenth century, 357, *357*
New York colony
    American Revolution in, 181–184, *182*
    ethnic diversity in, 237
    growth of, 107
    labor system in, 92

overview of, 59
ratification of Constitution, 228
settlement of, 59, 62
slave revolts in, 90
slavery in, 86, 107, 205–206, 238
New York Female Moral Reform
Society, 370
New York Stock Exchange, *243*, 357
Ninth Amendment, 241
Nonimportation movement, 147,
151–152, 155, 157, 158–159
Nonintercourse Act (1809), 270, 271
North, Lord, 152, 153, 168, 190
North Carolina
American Revolution in, 172, 178,
188, 189
Civil War, 481, 488
formation of, 59
labor system in, 92
ratification of Constitution, 228
secession, 447, 455
settlement of, 59
slavery in, 83
North Star, 383
Northwest Ordinance (1787), 218,
284, 394, 425
Northwest Passage, 27, 28
Nova Scotia, 126
Noyes, John Humphrey, 375
Nullification, doctrine of, 254
Nullification crisis, 301, 305–308

O

Occom, Samson, 116
Ogden, Aaron, 356
Oglethorpe, James Edward, 85
Ohio, admitted to Union, 393
Ohio Company, 217
Ohio Indians, 240, 248
Old Northwest territories, settlement
of, 393–395
Old Republicans, 284
Old Southwest territories
peoples of, 403–405
settlement of, 395–397
Olive Branch Petition, 170, 172
Olmecs, 5
Omahas, 397
Oñate, Juan de, 24
Oneida Community, 375
Oneidas, 71, 181
Onondagas, 71
Opechancanough, 43–44, *44*, 48
Operation Rescue, 449
Order of the Heroes of America, 481
Orders in Council, 271
Ordinance of 1784, 216
Oregon, settlement of, 318, 401
Oregon Trail, 390, 397, 400–403, *402*
Orwell, George, 501
Osages, 397
Osceola, 305
Ostend Manifesto, 427
O'Sullivan, John L., 408–409
Oswald, Richard, *192*
Otis, James, Jr., 146
Ottawas, 79, 143, 216
Overland trails/overlanders, 390,
400–403, *401, 402*
Owen, Robert, 375
Oyo, 11

P

Paddock, Adino, 108
Paine, Thomas, 172, 183, 255–256, 412

Paiutes, 403, 404
Pakenham, Edward, 278
Pakenham, Richard, 317
Paleo-Indians, 3
Panic of 1819, 283–284
Panic of 1837, 309–311
Panic of 1857, 434
Pan-Indian resistance movement,
271–272
Paris, treaty of (1763), 132–133
Paris, treaty of (1783), 190–192, *192*,
218–219
Parker, William, 425
Parsons, Theophilus, 204
Parson's Cause, 144
Paterson, William, 222
Patroonships, 41
Patuxets, 49
Pawnees, 8, 81, 398
Paxton Boys, 143
Peace of Paris (1783), 190–192, *192*
Peale, Charles Willson, *129, 170, 180*
Pea Ridge, battle of (1862), 460, 477
Pemberton, John, 475
Peninsula Campaign, 465–466
Penn, William, 60, 61–62, *61*, 73
Pennsylvania
American Revolution in, *182*, 183,
185
Civil War, 472–474
colony, overview of, 59
ethnic diversity in, 237
labor system in, 91, 92
ratification of Constitution, 227
settlement of, 59, 60–62
slavery in, 86, 238
Whiskey Rebellion, 250
Pennsylvania Gazette, 127
Pennsylvania Journal, 145
Pequots, 50–51, 73
Pequot War (1637), 51, 73
Perry, Oliver Hazard, 277
Petersburg, Virginia, 471, 489, 485
Philadelphia
American Revolution in, 181, *182*
growth of colonial, 107, *108*
in the nineteenth century, 357
settlement of, 61–62
slave population of, 86, 107
Philip, King (Metacom), 76–77
Phillips, Wendell, 510
Pickens, Francis, 312
Pickering, John, 266
Pickett, George, 474
Pierce, Franklin, 426–427, 428
Pietists, 237
Pike, Zebulon, 397
Pilgrims, 48–49
Pinckney, Charles Cotesworth, 255,
270
Pinckney's Treaty (San Lorenzo
Treaty) (1795), 251
Pitcher, Molly, 180
Pitt, William, 130–131
Pittsburgh, Pennsylvania, 358–359
Pizarro, Francisco, 22
Place, Francis, *61*
Plains Indians, 8, 25–26
See also under name of
Plantation Duty Act (1673), 102
Plantations
Mulberry, *60*
rice, 58
social classes, 337–342
sugar, 55–56

wives, role of, 340
Plattsburgh, battle of (1814), 278
Plymouth colony, 48–49, 59, 117
Plymouth Company, 42, 48
Pocahontas, 43, 47
Political parties
See also under name of
development of second (two)-
party system, 312, 313
emergence of, 245
Politics
diverging, between colonies and
England, 119–121
dominion of New England and
limits of British control,
116–118
Polk, James K.
election of 1844 and, 318
Mexican War, 408, 410–413, *411*
westward expansion and, 318
Pomeiooc, *29*
Pomos, 403
Ponce de León, Juan, 20
Pontiac, 143
Pontiac's Rebellion (1763–1766), 143
Poor Richard's Almanac (Franklin), 186
Popé, 77–78, *80*
Pope, Alexander, 147
Pope, John, 466
Popular sovereignty, 420
Population
in cities (1820–1860), 357, *358,
359*
colonial, 53, *84, 121, 122*
growth of free blacks
(1750–1800), 205, *205*
Native American (1600–1730), *70*
shift of (1790–1850), 391, *392*,
393
slave, 80, *84*
in Southern states in 1850, *343*
Portugal
exploration/colonization by,
12–13, 16–17, 27
slave trade and, 55, 82
Potawatomis, 398
Potomac Company, 221
Poverty, colonial, 109
Powhatan, 43
Powhatans, 26, 30, 43–44, 48, 77
Predestination, 15, 48
Preemption Act (1841), 393
Presbyterians, 114, 207, 237, 345
Presidency
Constitutional Convention and
determining duties and elec-
tion methods for, 223–224
how to address, 241
Presidential electors, methods of
electing, 295
Prevost, George, 278
Princeton, battle of, *170,* 178, 183
Printing press, 15, *15*
Prison reform, 373–374
Proclamation Line, 141, *141*
Proclamation of 1763, 141, 144
Prophet's Town, 272
Prophet Tenkswatawa, 271–272, *272*
Proprietary colonies, 46, 57–62
Prosser, Gabriel, 336
Prostitution, 370, 465
Protective tariffs, 242, 243
Protestantism, 14–16, 76–77, 114
Pueblo Bonito, 8
Pueblo Revolt, 76, 77–78, *80,* 404

Pueblos, 7–8, 24, 25, 26, 75, 77–78,
123, 404, 413
Puerto Rico, Spanish exploration of,
19, 55
Pulaski, Kazimierz, 177
Puritans/Puritanism
in England, 46–47
in New England, 48–50, 113
relations with Indians, 76
Put-in-Bay, battle of (1813), 277
Putting-out system, 361

Q

Quakers, 60–61, 114, 207, 237
Quartering Act (1765), 141–142,
149–150
Quartering Act (1774), 154
Quasi-War, 253
Quebec, 37, 38
Act (1774), 154–155, *155*
battle of (1759), 131, *131*
Siege of (1775), 172, 178
Queen Anne's War (1702–1713),
126–127
Queenston Heights, battle of (1812),
275
Quiberon, battle of (1759), 131

R

Radical Republicans, 478, 507, 510
Railroads
in the 1830s, 355–356, 357–358
in 1860, *437*
plans for a transcontinental, 428
Raleigh, Walter, 29, 30
Rancheros, 406–407
Randolph, Edmund, 226
Ranger, 186
Real Whig ideology, 127
Reconquista, 14, 16, 17, 19, 24
Reconstruction, 521
African-American aspirations,
500–506
agriculture in, 502–504, 523
amendments/legislation, list of,
521
congressional, 512–513
counter, 516–519
education, 501–502
failure of, 522–525
government in the South, 513–516
Ku Klux Klan, 516
land redistribution programs,
502–504
Lincoln's Ten Percent Plan,
506–507
migration to cities, 504–505
presidential, 507–512
redemption period, 519–522
religion, 505–506
voting rights, 510–513, 524
Red Eagle, *280*
Redeemers, 519
Redemption period, 519–522
Redemptioner system, 91
Reformation, 15–16
Regulators, 150
Reid, Whitelaw, 504
Religion
See also under type of
for African Americans following
the Civil War, 505–506, *505*
colonial, 113–116
cultural perceptions and misperceptions, 26

decline in devotion in colonial period, 255
in the 1820s, 338–369
free blacks, 343, 345, 505–506
Great Awakening, 114–116
human sacrifice, 7
missionaries and Native Americans, 73–76, 123, 401, 403
Native American, 38, 404
politics and, 448–449
Second Great Awakening, 297–299, *298*
of slaves, 89, 335–336
state constitutions and pluralism in, 207–208
West African, 12
women and, 116, 298–299
Renaissance, 13
Repartimiento, 69
Republicanism, 174–175
Articles of Confederation, 210
defining the people, 203–207
state constitutions, 207–209
Republican party
Civil War and, 478
differences between Federalist party and, 244
in 1854, 431–432
election of 1856 and, 432
election of 1860 and, 440–442, *442*, 445
election of 1864 and, 487–488
formation of, 245, 431
Liberal, 516, 518
moderate, 507
National, 300, 312
Old Republicans, 284
policies of, 244, 245
Radical, 478, 507, 510
Reconstruction and, 507
slavery issues and, 345
in the South after Reconstruction, 513–516
Rescate, 69
Revere, Paul, 108, *109, 153,* 168
Review of the Debates in the Virginia Legislature of 1831 and 1832 (Dew), 347
Rhett, Robert Barnwell, 429, 440
Rhode Island
colony, overview of, 59
labor system in, 92
ratification of Constitution, 228
Rogue's Island, 215–216
settlement of, 51, 59
slavery in, 86
Rhode Island system, 362
Rice
exports, 105
plantations, 58
Richmond Whig, 440
Ring shout, 335
Roach, Isaac, 276
Roads, development of, 353
Roanoke Island, 29–31, 42
Robertson, Pat, 448
Roberval, Jean-François de la, 27
Rochester, New York, 358
Rockingham, Lord, 190
Rocky Mountain Fur Co., 399
Rolfe, John, 43, 44, 47
Roosevelt, Franklin D., 412
Rosecrans, William S., 475
Ross, John, 306
Rowlandson, Mary, 78–79

Royal African Company, 83
Royal Society of London, 112
Ruffin, Edmund, 329, 330–331
Rush, Benjamin, 204–205
Rush–Bagot Agreement (1817), 282
Russia, U.S. Civil War and, 467
Rutledge, Edward, 210

S

Sabbatarian movement, 368–369
Sack of Lawrence, 430
Sagadahoc, 49
St. Augustine, 24
St. Christopher, 59
St. Clair, Arthur, 247
St. Domingue (Haiti), 250, 267
St. Lawrence River, 27, 37, 39
St. Leger, Barry, 183
St. Louis, Missouri, 359
Salary Act (1816), 295
Salish Indians, 400
Samoset, 49
San Antonio, Texas
Alamo, 124, 406
founding of, 124
Sánchez, José María, 408–409
San Francisco, 421–422
San Jacinto, battle of (1836), 406
San Lorenzo (Pinckney's Treaty), treaty of (1795), 251
Santa Anna, Antonio López de, 405–406
Santa Fe Trail, 404, 407
Santee Sioux, 398
São Tomé, 17
Saratoga, battle of (1777), 178, 184
Sargent, Henry, *365*
Sauks, 304, 398
Savannah, battles of (1778, 1779), 177, 178
Scalawags, 513–514
Scarlet Letter, The (Hawthorne), 377
Schaw, Janet, 176
Schaw, Robert, 176
Schofield, Martha, 501–502
Schumacker, General, *237*
Schurz, Carl, 518
Scots-Irish, 93, *236,* 237
Scott, Dred, 432–433, *433*
Scott, Harriet, 432–433, *433*
Scott, Winfield, 413, 426, 446, 466
Scrooby separatists, 49
Secession, 442–444, *443*
Second Amendment, 241
Second Bank of the United States, 280–281, 283, 284, 302, 308–309
Second Continental Congress, 170
Second Great Awakening, 297–299, *298*
Second (two)-party system, 313
Sedition Act (1798), 253
Seminoles, 283
Indian Removal Act (1830), 303–305, *304, 305*
Seneca Falls Convention (1848), 381–382
Senecas, 71, 79, 128, 185
Separatists, 49
Sequoyah, *303*
Serapis, 186, *186*
Serra, Junípero, 124
Seven Cities of Cíbola, 24
Seven Days' Battles (1862), 465–466, 489
Seven Years' War (1756–1763), 126, 129–132

Seward, William, 314, 422, 429, 432, 441, 446, 491
Seymour, Horatio, 512
Shakers, 375
Sharecropping, 523
Shastas, 403
Shaw v. Reno, 524
Shays, Daniel, 201
Shays' Rebellion, 201–203, 215, *215*
Shelburne, Lord, 190
Shepard, William, 201–203
Sheridan, Philip H., 487, 490
Sherman, Roger, 222, 223
Sherman, William Tecumseh, 456, 484, 485, 486, 488, *488,* 503
Shiloh Church, battle of, (1862), 463, 489
Shipping/ship building
flatboats, 394
late Middle Ages, 16–17, *16*
New England, 106
steamboats, 353, 355
Shirley, William, 129
Shoshone, 5
Sioux, 389–390, 397–399, 403
Slater, Samuel, 362
Slaughterhouse cases, 525
Slave codes, 57, 87–88, 332
Slave Power, 383, 434, 446
Slaves/slavery
See also Civil War
in the American Revolution, 180–181
arguments for, 344–347
as artisans and skilled workers, 328, 333
auction, *322*
changing patterns in, 331–332, *331*
changing race relations in the colonies, 86–87
chartered generation of, 87
communities, 88–89
Constitutional Convention and issues of, 223
cotton and, 325–326
creole, 88
daily life/culture, description of, 323–324, 332–337
decline of, 331–332
destination of, *81*
economic legacy of, 346
families, 88–89, 334–336
field work of, 333
as house servants, 333
labor needs and the turn to, 80–81, 91
legacy of, 94
in the lower South, 325–326
Middle Passage, description of, 82, *85*
Missouri Compromise, 284–285
Native Americans as, 77, 81
in New Amsterdam, *41*
in the northern colonies, 85–86
origins of, 81, *82*
personal accounts, 67–68
population estimations, 80, *84*
profits of, 326–328
religion, 89, 335–336
resistance/rebellions, 89–91, 336–337, 378–379, 425
runaways, 337, 338–339
shock of enslavement, 81–82

social classes, 337–344
in the southern colonies, 83, 85
spread, *326*
three-fifths rule, 222, 279
in the upper South, 328–332
urban, 328
women, 334
Slave ship, *66*
Slave trade
Africans as slavers, 81–82
Atlantic islands and, 17
in the Caribbean islands, 19, 55–57
evolution of, 80–81
New Spain, 23
West African, 12–13, 81–82
in the West Indies, 17, 55–57
Slidell, John, 411
Smallpox, 21, 25, 26, *26,* 143, 399
Smith, Gerrit, 383
Smith, John, 43, *44*
Smith, Joseph, 371, 407
Smith, Kirby, 490
Social classes
Caribbean islanders, 9
colonial, 54, 57–58, 108–109
free blacks, 342–344
indentured servants, 38, 45–46, 56, 83, 91
Middle Ages, 13, *14*
middle class, 365, *366*
mulattoes, 344
in the nineteenth century, 364–367
the old rich, 364–365
plantation, 337–342
working classes, 366–367
yeomen, 341–342
Socialism, utopian, 375
Social reform
educational reform, 372–373
prisons, workhouses, and asylums, 373–374
utopian alternatives, 375–378
Society for the Propagation of the Gospel in Foreign Parts, 113
Society for the Relief of Poor Widows with Small Children, 370
Society of Friends. *See* Quakers
Solomon, Job ben, 82
Songhai empire, 11
Sons of Liberty, 145, *145,* 147–148, 153–154
Soulé, Pierre, 427
South Carolina
American Revolution in, 172, 178, 187–189, *188*
Civil War, 444–448, 488
formation of, 59
labor system in, 92
ratification of Constitution, 228
secession, 442, *443*
settlement of, 59
slave revolts in, 89–91
slavery in, 83, 87, *90,* 239
Stono Rebellion, 90
tariff of 1828 and nullification, 305–308
South Carolina Exposition and Protest, 306
South Carolina Gazette, 108
Southern Homestead Act (1866), 503, 521
Southern Methodist Church, 506
Southwest Ordinance (1790), 218, 284, 397

Spain
American Revolution and, 185
in California, 123–125, 139, 140
Caribbean islands, conquest by, 2, 17, 19–20, 55
Confederation Congress and, 219–221
control of Native Americans, 69–70
exploration/colonization by, 2, 9, 12, 13–14, 16, 17, 19–25, 123–125
in Florida, 20, 23, 24, 139
in Mexico, 24
North American territories 1750–1763, *121*
slave trade and, 23, 82
in Texas, 123–125
U.S. relations with, 250, 251
War of the Austrian Succession (1739–1748), 126, 127–129
War of the Spanish Succession (1702–1713), 126–127
Specie Circular, 311
Spectator, The, 111, 112
Spice Islands, 40
Spoils system, 302
Spotsylvania, battle of, 485
Squanto, 49
Squatters, 240, 394
Stamp Act (1765), 145, 147, 148, 149, *149*
Stamp Act Congress, 148
Stanton, Edwin M., 512
Stanton, Elizabeth Cady, 381, 513
Staple Act (1663), 102
"Star-Spangled Banner, The" (Key), 278
State, constitutions, 207–209
State Department, formation of, 241
States' rights, 254
Steamboats, 353, 355
Stephens, Alexander H., 442
Steuben, Baron von, 177, 184
Stevens, Thaddeus, 510
Stockton and Darlington, 356
Stono Rebellion, 90
Stowe, Harriet Beecher, 417–418, 425–426, 502
Strauss, Levi, 421
Stuyvesant, Peter, 42, 62
Suffolk Resolves, 157
Suffrage. *See* Voting
Sugar
trade, 17, 104, 105
in the West Indies, 55–56
Sugar Act (1764), 144–145, 147, 148
Sumner, Charles, 430, 510, *514*, 519
Sumter, Thomas, 189
Supreme Court
Cherokee Nation v. Georgia, 305
Constitution on, and the formation of, 225, 242
contractual property rights and, 282
Dred Scott v. Sandford and, 432–433, 510
Judiciary Act (1789), 242, 266
Judiciary Act (1801), 265–266
monopolies and, 356–357
national power over states, 281–282
Susquehannocks, 42, 77, 127
Sutter, John, 421

T

Tainos, 9, 19, *19*, 20, 26, 27
Tallmadge, James, 284

Tallmadge Amendment, 284
Tammany Hall, 517
Taney, Roger B., 309, 356–357, 432–433
Taos Revolt (1847), 413
Tappan, Arthur, 379
Tappan, Lewis, 379
Tariff Act of 1789, 242
Tariffs
Compromise Tariff of 1833, 308
of 1816, 281
of 1824 and 1828 (Abominations), 305–306
nullification crisis, 301, 305–308
protective, 242, 243
Tarleton, Banastre, 188, 189
Tatler, The, 111
Taxation, colonial
British versus American views on, 145–147
overview of, 156
protests against, 147–148
Stamp Act (1765), 145, 147, 148, 149, *149*
Sugar Act (1764), 144–145, 147, 148
Tea Act (1773), 153–154
Townshend Duty Act (1767), 150–151
whiskey, 243
Taylor, John, 284
Taylor, Zachary
Compromise of 1850 and, 422, 423
death of, 423
election of 1848 and, 420–421
Mexican War, 410–411
Tea Act (1773), 153–154
Tea Room, The (Sargent), *365*
Technology, industrialization and role of, 362, 363–364, 394
Tecumseh, 271–272, 275, 277
Tejanos, 405, 406
Tekakwitha, Kateri, 38
Temperance movement, 365, 369–370
Tenancy, 91
Tenkswatawa (Prophet), 271–272, *272*
Tennent, Gilbert, 115
Tennent, William, 114, 115
Tennessee
Civil War, 462, 463, 475–477, 485, 488
secession, 447, 455
settlement of, 240
as a slave state, 284
Tenochtitlán, 1, 2, 7
Ten Percent Plan, 506–507
Tenth Amendment, 241, 245
Tenure of Office Act (1867), 512, 521
Teotihuacán, 5
Territorial expansion, overview of, 156
Terry, Randall, 449
Tetons, 398
Texas
admitted to Union, 395
Alamo, 124, 406
Americanization of, 405–406
annexation of, 316, 317–318
Civil War, 477
independence from Mexico, 406
secession, 442, *443*
slavery in, 405
Spanish in, 123–125
Tejanos in, 405, 406
Textile mills, 359–360, *360*, 361

Thames, battle of (1814), 277
Thayendanegea (Joseph Brant), 181, 183
Thirteenth Amendment, 487–488, 501, 509, 521
Thoreau, Henry David, 377, 438, 440
Thoughts upon Female Education (Rush), 204–205
Three-fifths rule, 222, 279
Tilden, Samuel J., 520
Timbuktu, 11, 12
Timothy, Elizabeth, 108
Tippecanoe, battle of (1811), 272
Tobacco
economics and, 104–105
in Virginia, 44–46, *46*
Toltecs, 5
Tomasito, 413
Tonnage Act of 1789, 242
Tontine Coffee House, *243*
Toombs, Robert, 419, 432
Tordesillas, treaty of (1494), 27
Tories/Loyalists, 160, 167–168
Townshend, Charles, 150–151
Townshend Duty Act (1767), 150–151
Trade
See also Fur trade; Slave trade
acts, 102
Anglo-American transatlantic, 103–106, *104*
Archaic period, 3–4
between Europeans and Native Americans, 70–72
British regulation and taxation of colonial, 101–109
colonial exports, 103–106
colonial exports, value of, *105*
colonial imports, 106–107
Constitutional Convention and issues of, 223
Embargo Act (1807), 269–270
Macon's Bill No. 2 (1810), 271
Mesoamerican, 7
nullification crisis, 301, 305–308
overview of colonial, 102, 156
spice, 16
sugar, 17
Tariff Act of 1789, 242
Tariff of 1816, 281
West African, 11–13
Trail of Tears, 304, *304*, 306–307
Transcendentalism, 376–378
Trans-Continental Treaty (1819), 283, 397
Transportation
canals, 353 355, *356*
effects of, 353
flatboats, 394
funding and role of government, 356–357
impact on agriculture, 353
impact on traveling time, 309
map of 1830–1850 network, *354*
omnibuses, 357
railroads, 355–356, 357–358
roads, 353
steamboats, 353, 355
wagon trains, 402
Travis, Joseph, 336
Treasury Department
formation of, 241
Independent Treasury System, 311–312
Treaties
Fort Laramie (1851), 403

Fort McIntosh (1785), 216
Fort Stanwix (1784), 216
Fort Wayne (1809), 272
Ghent (1814), 278
Greenville (1795), 247, *247*, 271
Guadalupe Hidalgo (1848), 413
Jay's Treaty (1794), 250–251
Lancaster (1744), 121
New Echota (1835), 306
Paris (1763), 132–133
Paris (1783), 190–192, *192*, 218–219
San Lorenzo (Pinckney's Treaty) (1795), 251
Tordesillas (1494), 27
Trans-Continental (1819), 283, 397
Vincennes (1804), 271
Webster-Ashburton (1843), 317
Tredegar Iron Works, 334, 458, 459
Trenchard, John, 147
Trenton, battle of, 178, 183
Trois-Rivières, 37, 38
Trujillo, Jesús, 413
Trumbull, John, *172, 190, 221*
Truth, Sojourner, 334, 471
Tryon, William, 150
Tubman, Harriet, *337*
Turner, Henry McNeal, 506
Turner, Nat, 306, 336, *336*, 378–379
Tuscaroras, 73, 181
Tuskegee Institute, 502
Twain, Mark, 500
Tweed, William M., 517
Twitchell, Marshall Harvey, 519
Two Penny Act, 144
Tyler, John, 315, 316–317, 383, 444

U

Uncle Tom's Cabin (Stowe), 414–418, *416*, 425–426, *426*
Underground Railroad, 337
Union Leagues, 514
Unions
beginnings of trade, 367
Civil War and, 479
women in, 367
United States Sanitary Commission, 464
United States v. Cruikshank, 524, 525
Upper South, defined, 328–329
Upshur, Abel P., 317
Urban slavery, 328
Utah, settlement of, 407–408
Utes, 5, 404, 407
Utopianism, 375–378

V

Valley Forge, 184
Van Buren, Martin
Albany Regency and, 300
election of 1836 and, 309
election of 1840 and, 315–316
election of 1848 and, 421
gag rule, 312
Independent Treasury System, 311–312
presidency of, 309–312
Van Rensselaer, Stephen, 275, 369
Verger, Jean-Baptiste-Antoine de, *194*
Vermont, statehood for, 240
Verrazano, Giovanni da, 27
Vesey, Denmark, 336
Vice-admiralty courts, 145
Vicksburg, battle of (1863), 463, 475, *476*, 489

Vincennes, battle of, 178, 185
Vincennes, treaty of (1804), 271
Virginia
 American Revolution in, 171–172, 188, 189–190
 Bacon's Rebellion, 76, 77
 Civil War, 462, 465–466, 471–472, 484–485, 490
 colony, overview of, 59
 founding of, 42, 59
 Jamestown, 42–43
 labor system in, 92
 life in early, 47–48
 Parson's Cause, 144
 ratification of Constitution, 228
 Roanoke Island, 29–31, 42
 secession, 447, 455, 461, 481
 slavery in, 83, 87, 239
 as a tobacco colony, 44–46, *46,* 59
Virginia Company, 42, 44
Virginia Declaration of Rights, 207
Virginia Plan, 222
Virtual representation, 120
Voting
 African Americans following Civil War and, 510–513, 524
 after the American Revolution, 204
 Fifteenth Amendment, 513, 521, 517, 524
 free black males and, 296–297
 property requirements for, 295, 296
 universal white male, 295–297
 women and, 204, *204,* 296–297, 381–382, 513
 written ballots, use of, 295

W

Wade, Benjamin F., 510
Wade-Davis Bill, 506
Wagon trains, 402
Walden, or Life in the Woods (Thoreau), 377
Walker, David, 378
Walker, Robert, 433–434
Walker, William, 427–428
Wallace, Mary, 108
Waltham, Massachusetts, 362–363
Wampanoags, 26, 49, 76–77
Ward, Samuel, 382
War Department, formation of, 241
War for Independence. *See* American Revolution
War Hawks, 272
Warmoth, Henry C., 515
War of 1812, *260,* 261–262, 273–280, *274, 279*
War of the Austrian Succession (1739–1748), 126, 127–129
War of the League of Augsburg (1689–1697), 126–127
War of the Spanish Succession (1702–1713), 126–127
Warren, Joseph, *172*
Warren Bridge Co., 356–357
Warri, 13
Washington, D.C., British burning of, *260,* 261, 278, *279*
Washington, George, *164, 170, 190*
 American Revolution and, 171, 175, 181–182, 183, 184, 185, 192
 Annapolis Convention (1786) and, 221
 background of, 99–100

as commander of Continental Army, 170–171, 179
Constitutional Convention and, 222, *223*
farewell address, 251
foreign policy, 250–251
French and Indian War and, 129, *129,* 131
French Revolution and, 246
importation of goods by, 110
Mount Vernon, 111
presidency of, *232,* 241
Whiskey Rebellion and, 250
Washington, Martha, 184
Washington Temperance Societies, 370
Watie, Stand, 477
Watling Island, 17
Wayne, Anthony, 247, *247*
Webster, Daniel, 313, 314, 317
 Compromise of 1850 and, 423
Webster-Ashburton Treaty (1843), 317
Weed, Thurlow, 314
Weld, Theodore Dwight, 352, 379, 380, 438–439
Wells, Henry, 421
West, Benjamin, *131, 192*
West African societies, 9–13
 agriculture, 12
 artisans and merchants, 11–12
 division of labor in, 12
 family structure, 12
 map of, *10*
 religion, 12
 slavery, 12–13, 81–82
 trade, 11–13
West India Company, 40
West Indies, 17, 55–57, *84*
West Point, 179, 265
West Virginia, admitted to Union, 461
Westward expansion
 after the American Revolution, 210, *211,* 216–217, *217,* 218, 240
 agricultural frontier, 391–397
 fur traders and, 399–400, *399, 400*
 Land Ordinance (1785), 216–217, *217*
 Lewis and Clark expedition, 267, *268,* 286–287, 399
 Louisiana Purchase, 266–268, *268*
 Mexican borderlands, 403–405
 Native Americans and, 397–403
 Northwest Ordinance (1787), 218, 394
 Old Northwest, 393–395
 Old Southwest, 395–397
 overview of (1815–1850), 396
 shift of population (1790–1850), *392*
 Southwest Ordinance (1790), 218, 397
Wheat, 106, 394
Wheatley, Phillis, *205*
Wheeler, John Hill, 324
Whig party
 compared with the Democrats, 313
 Conscience, 421
 election of 1840 and, 313, 315–316
 election of 1844 and, 318
 election of 1848 and, 420–421
 election of 1852 and, 426–427
 formation of, 311

rise of, 312–318
Texas issue, 317–318
Whigs, 160, 167–168
Whiskey Rebellion, 247, 250
Whiskey tax, 243
White, Hugh Lawson, 314
White, John, 29–30
Whitefield, George, 114–115, *114*
White League, 519
White Plains, battle of, 178, 183
Whiteside, James A., *341*
Whitman, Marcus, 401
Whitman, Narcissa, 401
Whitman, Walt, 357, 377
Whitmer, John, 371
Whitney, Eli, 363–364, 396
Whitney, Jackson, 338–339
Wide Awakes, 441
Wilderness, battle of (1864), 484–485, *485,* 489
Wilkinson, Eliza, 204
Wilkinson, James, 220, 269
William of Orange, 117, 119, 126
Williams, Roger, 51, 52, 73
Wilmot, David, 419
Wilmot Proviso, 419–420, 445
Wilson, James, 158–160
Wilson, Woodrow, 412
Wingina, 29
Winslow, John, 132
Winthrop, John, 50, *50,* 51, 56
Wirt, William, 314
Wisconsin, admitted to Union, 395
Wise, Henry A., 432
Witchcraft, 117
Wolfe, James, 131, *131*
Women
 abolitionists, 376–377, 380–381
 American Revolution and, 180, 193, 203–205
 in Archaic period, 3, 4
 Civil War and, 458, 464, *464,* 465, 480, *480,* 482, *482,* 483
 colonial, 47, 53, 108, 111
 cult of domesticity, 365–366
 education of, following the Civil War, 480, 501–502
 education of colonial, 111, 204–205, 235, 237, *237*
 evangelicalism and, 298–299, 366
 in industry, 362–363, *363,* 365–366
 land ownership and, 204
 moral reform and role of, 370–371
 Native American, 26
 in New England, 53, 235, 237, *237*
 plantation mistresses, 340
 political activism and, 251
 religion and, 116, 298–299
 republicanism and, 203–205
 rights movement, 381–382, *382*
 as slaves, 334
 social reform and, 374
 as teachers, 373, 501–502
 temperance movement and, 369
 unions and, 367
 voting and, 204, *204,* 296–297, 381–382, 513
 West African, 12
 westward expansion and life for, 402
Wood, Jethro, 394
Woodlands Indians, 8–9
Woodmason, Charles, 122–123

Woolens Act (1699), 102
Worcester v. Georgia, 305
Workhouses, 373–374
Working classes, 366–367
Workingmen's movement, 372
Worth, Jonathan, 481
Writs of assistance, 146
Wyandots, 79, 181, 216
Wyoming Valley, battle of, 178, 185

X

XYZ Affair, 252–253

Y

Yale University, 113
Yamasees, 73
Yankees, use of term, 62
Yanktonais, 398
Yanktons, 398
Yaquis, 25
Yeoman, 341–342, 396
Yorktown, battle of, *170,* 178, 189–190, *190*
Yorubas, 12
Young, Brigham, 407
Young America movement, 426, 427–428
Yumans, 404, 406

Z

Zeeuw, Cornelius de, *41*
Zuni, 8, 75

SINGLE PC LICENSE AGREEMENT AND LIMITED WARRANTY

READ THIS LICENSE CAREFULLY BEFORE OPENING THIS PACKAGE. BY OPENING THIS PACKAGE, YOU ARE AGREEING TO THE TERMS AND CONDITIONS OF THIS LICENSE. IF YOU DO NOT AGREE, DO NOT OPEN THE PACKAGE. PROMPTLY RETURN THE UNOPENED PACKAGE AND ALL ACCOMPANYING ITEMS TO THE PLACE YOU OBTAINED THEM. THESE TERMS APPLY TO ALL LICENSED SOFTWARE ON THE DISK EXCEPT THAT THE TERMS FOR USE OF ANY SHAREWARE OR FREEWARE ON THE DISKETTES ARE AS SET FORTH IN THE ELECTRONIC LICENSE LOCATED ON THE DISK:

1. GRANT OF LICENSE and OWNERSHIP: The enclosed computer programs <<and data>> ("Software") are licensed, not sold, to you by Prentice-Hall, Inc. ("We" or the "Company") and in consideration of your purchase of the accompanying Company textbooks and/or other materials, and your agreement to these terms. We reserve any rights not granted to you. You own only the disk(s) but we and/or our licensors own the Software itself. This license allows you to use and display your copy of the Software on a single computer (i.e., with a single CPU) at a single location for academic use only, so long as you comply with the terms of this Agreement. You may make one copy for back up, or transfer your copy to another CPU, provided that the Software is usable on only one computer.

2. RESTRICTIONS: You may not transfer or distribute the Software or documentation to anyone else. Except for backup, you may not copy the documentation or the Software. You may not network the Software or otherwise use it on more than one computer or computer terminal at the same time. You may not reverse engineer, disassemble, decompile, modify, adapt, translate, or create derivative works based on the Software or the Documentation. You may be held legally responsible for any copying or copyright infringement which is caused by your failure to abide by the terms of these restrictions.

3. TERMINATION: This license is effective until terminated. This license will terminate automatically without notice from the Company if you fail to comply with any provisions or limitations of this license. Upon termination, you shall destroy the Documentation and all copies of the Software. All provisions of this Agreement as to limitation and disclaimer of warranties, limitation of liability, remedies or damages, and our ownership rights shall survive termination.

4. LIMITED WARRANTY AND DISCLAIMER OF WARRANTY: Company warrants that for a period of 60 days from the date you purchase this SOFTWARE (or purchase or adopt the accompanying textbook), the Software, when properly installed and used in accordance with the Documentation, will operate in substantial conformity with the description of the Software set forth in the Documentation, and that for a period of 30 days the disk(s) on which the Software is delivered shall be free from defects in materials and workmanship under normal use. The Company does not warrant that the Software will meet your requirements or that the operation of the Software will be uninterrupted or error-free. Your only remedy and the Company's only obligation under these limited warranties is, at the Company's option, return of the disk for a refund of any amounts paid for it by you or replacement of the disk. THIS LIMITED WARRANTY IS THE ONLY WARRANTY PROVIDED BY THE COMPANY AND ITS LICENSORS, AND THE COMPANY AND ITS LICENSORS DISCLAIM ALL OTHER WARRANTIES, EXPRESS OR IMPLIED, INCLUDING WITHOUT LIMITATION, THE IMPLIED WARRANTIES OF MERCHANTABILITY AND FITNESS FOR A PARTICULAR PURPOSE. THE COMPANY DOES NOT WARRANT, GUARANTEE OR MAKE ANY REPRESENTATION REGARDING THE ACCURACY, RELIABILITY, CURRENTNESS, USE, OR RESULTS OF USE, OF THE SOFTWARE.

5. LIMITATION OF REMEDIES AND DAMAGES: IN NO EVENT, SHALL THE COMPANY OR ITS EMPLOYEES, AGENTS, LICENSORS, OR CONTRACTORS BE LIABLE FOR ANY INCIDENTAL, INDIRECT, SPECIAL, OR CONSEQUENTIAL DAMAGES ARISING OUT OF OR IN CONNECTION WITH THIS LICENSE OR THE SOFTWARE, INCLUDING FOR LOSS OF USE, LOSS OF DATA, LOSS OF INCOME OR PROFIT, OR OTHER LOSSES, SUSTAINED AS A RESULT OF INJURY TO ANY PERSON, OR LOSS OF OR DAMAGE TO PROPERTY, OR CLAIMS OF THIRD PARTIES, EVEN IF THE COMPANY OR AN AUTHORIZED REPRESENTATIVE OF THE COMPANY HAS BEEN ADVISED OF THE POSSIBILITY OF SUCH DAMAGES. IN NO EVENT SHALL THE LIABILITY OF THE COMPANY FOR DAMAGES WITH RESPECT TO THE SOFTWARE EXCEED THE AMOUNTS ACTUALLY PAID BY YOU, IF ANY, FOR THE SOFTWARE OR THE ACCOMPANYING TEXTBOOK. BECAUSE SOME JURISDICTIONS DO NOT ALLOW THE LIMITATION OF LIABILITY IN CERTAIN CIRCUMSTANCES, THE ABOVE LIMITATIONS MAY NOT ALWAYS APPLY TO YOU.

6. GENERAL: THIS AGREEMENT SHALL BE CONSTRUED IN ACCORDANCE WITH THE LAWS OF THE UNITED STATES OF AMERICA AND THE STATE OF NEW YORK, APPLICABLE TO CONTRACTS MADE IN NEW YORK, AND SHALL BENEFIT THE COMPANY, ITS AFFILIATES AND ASSIGNEES. HIS AGREEMENT IS THE COMPLETE AND EXCLUSIVE STATEMENT OF THE AGREEMENT BETWEEN YOU AND THE COMPANY AND SUPERSEDES ALL PROPOSALS OR PRIOR AGREEMENTS, ORAL, OR WRITTEN, AND ANY OTHER COMMUNICATIONS BETWEEN YOU AND THE COMPANY OR ANY REPRESENTATIVE OF THE COMPANY RELATING TO THE SUBJECT MATTER OF THIS AGREEMENT. If you are a U.S. Government user, this Software is licensed with "restricted rights" as set forth in subparagraphs (a)-(d) of the Commercial Computer-Restricted Rights clause at FAR 52.227-19 or in subparagraphs (c)(1)(ii) of the Rights in Technical Data and Computer Software clause at DFARS 252.227-7013, and similar clauses, as applicable.

Should you have any questions concerning this agreement or if you wish to contact the Company for any reason, please contact in writing: Prentice Hall, One Lake Street, Upper Saddle River, NJ 07458.